HALSBURY'S
Laws of England

FOURTH EDITION
REISSUE

Volume 25

HALSBURY'S

Laws of England

FOURTH EDITION
REISSUE

LORD HAILSHAM OF ST. MARYLEBONE

Lord High Chancellor of Great Britain
1970–74 and 1979–87

Volume 25

BUTTERWORTHS

LONDON   1994

UNITED KINGDOM	Butterworth & Co (Publishers) Ltd Halsbury House, 35 Chancery Lane, **London** WC2A 1EL and 4 Hill Street, **Edinburgh** EH2 3JZ
AUSTRALIA	Butterworths Pty Ltd, **Sydney, Melbourne, Brisbane, Adelaide, Perth, Canberra** and **Hobart**
CANADA	Butterworths Canada Ltd, **Toronto** and **Vancouver**
HONG KONG	Butterworths Asia, **Hong Kong**
IRELAND	Butterworth (Ireland) Ltd, **Dublin**
MALAYSIA	Malayan Law Journal Sdn Bhd, **Kuala Lumpur**
NEW ZEALAND	Butterworths of New Zealand Ltd, **Wellington** and **Auckland**
PUERTO RICO	Butterworth of Puerto Rico, Inc, **San Juan**
SINGAPORE	Butterworth Asia, **Singapore**
SOUTH AFRICA	Butterworth Publishers (Pty) Ltd, **Durban**
USA	Butterworth Legal Publishers, **Carlsbad**, California; **Salem**, New Hampshire

---

FIRST EDITION

Published in 31 volumes between 1907 and 1917 under the Editorship of the Rt. Hon. the Earl of Halsbury, Lord High Chancellor of Great Britain, 1885–86, 1886–92 and 1895–1905

SECOND EDITION

Published in 37 volumes between 1931 and 1942 under the Editorship of the Rt. Hon. the Viscount Hailsham, Lord High Chancellor of Great Britain, 1928–29 and 1935–38

THIRD EDITION

Published in 43 volumes between 1952 and 1964 under the Editorship of the Rt. Hon. the Viscount Simonds, Lord High Chancellor of Great Britain, 1951–54

FOURTH EDITION

Published in 56 volumes between 1973 and 1987 under the Editorship of the Rt. Hon. Lord Hailsham of St. Marylebone, Lord High Chancellor of Great Britain, 1970–74 and 1979–87

ISBN   (complete set, standard binding) 0 406 03400 1
(this volume, standard binding) 0 406 02224 0

Typeset by Thomson Litho Ltd, East Kilbride, Scotland
Printed and bound in Great Britain by
Butler & Tanner, Frome

Editor in Chief

THE RIGHT HONOURABLE

LORD HAILSHAM OF ST. MARYLEBONE
LORD HIGH CHANCELLOR OF GREAT BRITAIN

1970–74 and 1979–87

Editor

DAVID HAY, M.A., LL.M.
OF THE INNER TEMPLE, BARRISTER

Managing Editor (Commissioning)

DEBORAH SAUNDERS, B.A.
OF GRAY'S INN, BARRISTER

Assistant Editor

SIMON HETHERINGTON, LL.B.

Sub-Editors

JULIANNE MULHOLLAND, LL.B.
STEPHEN PARTRIDGE, B.A., LL.B.

Administrative Manager

SARAH L. HORNSBY, Dip. Pub.

Indexer

B. BURKE, B.Sc.

Publisher

JAMES BOWMAN, LL.B.
A SOLICITOR OF THE SUPREME COURT

The titles in Volume 25 have been contributed by the following:

INSURANCE   E. R. HARDY IVAMY LL.B., Ph.D., LL.D.,
of the Middle Temple, Barrister;
Emeritus Professor of Law, University of London

INTERPLEADER   ALASTAIR BLACK C.B.E., D.L.,
a Solicitor of the Supreme Court;
former Under Sheriff of Greater London

CLAIRE SANDBROOK, LL.B.,
a Solicitor of the Supreme Court;
Deputy Sheriff of Greater London

The law stated in this volume is in general that in force on 1 April 1994.

TABLE OF CONTENTS

INTERPLEADER

REFERENCES AND
ABBREVIATIONS

ACT.	Australian Capital Territory
A-G	Attorney General
Adv-Gen	Advocate General
affd	affirmed
affg	affirming
Alta.	Alberta
App	Appendix
art	article
Aust	Australia
B.	Baron
BC	British Columbia
C.	Command Paper (of a series published before 1900)
c	chapter number of an Act
CA	Court of Appeal
CA in Ch.	Court of Appeal in Chancery
CB	Chief Baron
CCA.	Court of Criminal Appeal
CC Fees Order 1982	County Court Fees Order 1982 (SI 1982/1706) as subsequently amended (see the current County Court Practice)
CCR.	County Court Rules 1981 (SI 1981/1687) as subsequently amended (see the current County Court Practice)
CCR.	Court for Crown Cases Reserved
C-MAC.	Courts-Martial Appeal Court
CO	Crown Office
COD	Crown Office Digest
Can.	Canada
Cd.	Command Paper (of the series published 1900–18)
Cf.	compare
ch	chapter
cl.	clause
Cm	Command Paper (of the series published 1986 to date)
Cmd.	Command Paper (of the series published 1919–56)
Cmnd.	Command Paper (of the series published 1956–86)
Comr	Commissioner
Corpn.	Corporation

Court Forms (2nd Edn)......... Atkin's Encyclopaedia of Court Forms in Civil Proceedings, 2nd Edn. See note 2, p *16* post

Court Funds Rules 1987 .... Court Funds Rules 1987 (SI 1987/821) as subsequently amended (see the current Supreme Court Practice and County Court Practice)

Ct of Sess.................... Court of Session

DC......................... Divisional Court

DPP .... Director of Public Prosecutions

EAT....................... Employment Appeal Tribunal

EC .... European Communities

ECJ........................ Court of Justice of the European Communities

ECSC...................... European Coal and Steel Community

EEC....................... European Economic Community

ECt HR.................... European Court of Human Rights

Edn........................ Edition

EFTA...................... European Free Trade Association

Euratom.................... European Atomic Energy Community

Ex Ch...................... Court of Exchequer Chamber

ex p .... ex parte

FTLR...................... Financial Times Law Reports

Fed .... Federal

Forms & Precedents (5th Edn) ... Encyclopaedia of Forms and Precedents other than Court Forms, 5th Edn. See note 2, p *16* post

GLC....................... Greater London Council

HC........................ High Court

HL .... House of Lords

HLR....................... Housing Law Reports

H of C .... House of Commons

IRC........................ Inland Revenue Commissioners

Ir.......................... Ireland

J........................... Justice

JA .... Judge of Appeal

JC .... Justiciary Cases

JIBFL .... Journal of International Banking and Financial Law

Kan........................ Kansas

LA .... Lord Advocate

LC .... Lord Chancellor

LCC....................... London County Council

LCJ........................ Lord Chief Justice

LJ .... Lord Justice of Appeal

LoN .... League of Nations

MR........................ Master of the Rolls

Man .... Manitoba

n .... note

NB........................ New Brunswick

NI......................... Northern Ireland

NIRC...................... National Industrial Relations Court

NS .... Nova Scotia

NSW .... New South Wales

NZ	New Zealand
Nfld	Newfoundland
OJ	The Official Journal of the European Communities published by the Office for Official Publications of the European Communities
Ont.	Ontario
Ord.	Order
P	President
PC	Judicial Committee of the Privy Council
PEI	Prince Edward Island
PIQR	Personal Injuries and Quantum Reports
Qld.	Queensland
Que	Quebec
r	rule
RDC.	Rural District Council
RPC	Restrictive Practices Court
RSC	Rules of the Supreme Court 1965 (SI 1965/1776) as subsequently amended (see the current Supreme Court Practice)
reg	regulation
Res	Resolution
revsd.	reversed
Rly	Railway
s	section
SA.	South Africa
S Aust.	South Australia
SC.	Supreme Court
SC Fees Order 1980	Supreme Court Fees Order 1980 (SI 1980/821) as subsequently amended (see the current Supreme Court Practice)
SI	Statutory Instruments published by authority
SR & O	Statutory Rules and Orders published by authority
SR & O Rev 1904.	Revised Edition comprising all Public and General Statutory Rules and Orders in force on 31 December 1903
SR & O Rev 1948.	Revised Edition comprising all Public and General Statutory Rules and Orders and Statutory Instruments in force on 31 December 1948
SRNI	Statutory Rules of Northern Ireland
STI	Simon's Tax Intelligence
Sask	Saskatchewan
Sch	Schedule
Sess.	Session
Supp.	Halsbury's Laws Cumulative Supplement
TS.	Treaty Series
Tas	Tasmania
UDC	Urban District Council
UN.	United Nations
V-C	Vice-Chancellor
Vict.	Victoria
W Aust.	Western Australia

NOTE 1. A general list of the abbreviations of law reports and other sources used in this work can be found in vol 1(1) (Reissue) at p 15 et seq.

NOTE 2. Where references are made to other publications, the volume number precedes and the page number follows the name of the publication; eg the reference '12 Forms & Precedents (5th Edn) 44' refers to volume 12 of the Encyclopaedia of Forms and Precedents, page 44.

NOTE 3. An English statute is cited by short title or, where there is no short title, by regnal year and chapter number together with the name by which it is commonly known or a description of its subject matter and date. In the case of a foreign statute, the mode of citation generally follows the style of citation in use in the country concerned with the addition, where necessary, of the name of the country in parentheses.

NOTE 4. A statutory instrument is cited by short title, if any, followed by the year and number, or, if unnumbered, the date.

TABLE OF STATUTES

TABLE OF STATUTORY INSTRUMENTS

TABLE OF
EC LEGISLATION AND
CONVENTIONS

TABLE OF OTHER ENACTMENTS

TABLE OF CASES

43

PARA

PARA

PARA

I

J

PARA

PARA

INSURANCE

3. AVIATION INSURANCE 347

4. GENERAL PRINCIPLES OF NON-MARINE INSURANCE

5. LONG TERM INSURANCE

1. INTRODUCTION

(1) ORIGIN AND COMMON PRINCIPLES

1. Development and sources of insurance law. The concept of insurance, in England as elsewhere, arose out of the mercantile adventure of transporting goods across the sea, the adventure consisting in early times of the enormous fortune to be made if the project turned out to be successful, as contrasted with the disastrous loss, even ruin, which resulted if the project foundered amid the perils of the seas[1]. It is not surprising, therefore, that the common law of insurance developed in the first instance through decisions on marine insurance. Non-marine insurance first made its appearance in the form of life and fire insurance, but until the middle of the nineteenth century these three types of insurance comprised, in practice, substantially the whole range of insurance[2]. In life and fire policies it soon became the practice to stipulate for arbitration to decide disputes, and this was later followed in most standard forms of non-marine insurance[3]. Therefore, there are fewer court decisions bearing directly on non-marine questions than there are relating to marine insurance, and recourse must frequently be made to the basic principles as formulated in marine cases and codified in the Marine Insurance Act 1906[4]. Provided that due care is taken to differentiate features which are peculiar to marine matters and to segregate what, in relation to these matters, is a new departure introduced by the legislature, that Act and the old cases on which it is based continue to be the great depository in which the law of insurance generally is to be found.

1 For the early history of insurance law see 8 Holdsworth's History of English Law (2nd Edn) 273 et seq.

2 See 8 Holdsworth's History of English Law (2nd Edn) at 294 et seq.

3 Arbitration clauses have been criticised on the grounds that legal aid is not available in an arbitration, and that an insurer who proposes to rely on a technically valid but unmeritorious defence may, by insisting on arbitration, avoid damaging publicity which might result from proceedings in court: see the Fifth Report of the Law Reform Committee 1957 (Cmnd 62) para 11. The Association of British Insurers and Lloyd's announced an agreement by which their members generally refrain from insisting on the enforcement of an arbitration clause if the assured seeks to have a question of liability, as distinct from the amount of a claim, determined by a court in the United Kingdom; the agreement does not apply to a contract of reinsurance, a contract of marine insurance, a contract of insurance against certain aviation risks, a contract of credit insurance or where the terms of the insurance are set out in a contract or policy which is specially negotiated and in which an arbitration clause has been specifically agreed: see 107 L Jo 61; Fifth Report of the Law Reform Committee 1957 (Cmnd 62) para 13.

4 Except as provided in the Marine Insurance Act 1906 s 2 as to mixed land and sea risks (see para 37 post), nothing in the Act is to alter or affect any rule of law applicable to any contract of marine insurance as defined by that Act (see para 35 post): s 2(2).

2. Principles common to all insurances. The basic principles applicable to matters of insurance flow from the nature of an insurance contract as conceived by the law merchant and taken over by the common law. They are, therefore, common to both marine and non-marine contracts[1]. Every insurance, whatever its nature, postulates that a sum of money will be paid by the insurers on the happening of a specified event; there must be uncertainty as to the happening of the event, either as to whether it will happen or not, or, if it is bound to happen, like the death of a human being, as to the time at which it will happen[2]. There must also be an insurable interest in the assured, which is normally that the event is one which is prima facie adverse to his interest[3]. To constitute an insurable interest the same general conditions must be fulfilled in all classes of insurance[4], although there are distinctions in the way in which the topic is approached. In life insurance the assured must have an insurable interest at the commencement of the risk, but he need not retain it until the end of the life insured[5]. In fire insurance, and in marine insurance, where there is no 'lost or not lost' clause[6], the assured cannot recover unless he has an insurable interest at the time of the loss[7], but it is immaterial that he had no interest at the commencement of the insurance provided he has acquired it before the loss[8].

A contract entered into by an insurance company[9], whether established within or outside the United Kingdom[10], which carries on insurance business[11] within the United Kingdom is void if:

(1) it is a contract under which the company undertakes a liability the amount or maximum amount of which is uncertain at the time when the contract is entered into; and

(2) it is not a contract of insurance or a contract of a class or description exempted by regulations[12].

1 *Castellain v Preston* (1883) 11 QBD 380 at 386, CA, per Brett LJ.
2 *Prudential Insurance Co v IRC* [1904] 2 KB 658 at 663 per Channell J; *Department of Trade and Industry v St Christopher Motorists Association Ltd* [1974] 1 All ER 395 at 400, [1974] 1 WLR 99 at 105 per Templeman J. The right to have a claim considered by a union that conducted legal proceedings on behalf of its members, indemnified members against claims for damages and costs and gave advice on various matters, did not amount to a contract of insurance, for it was a right to a benefit other than money or money's worth: *Medical Defence Union Ltd v Department of Trade* [1980] Ch 82, [1979] 2 All ER 421 per Megarry V-C.
3 *Prudential Insurance Co v IRC* [1904] 2 KB 658 at 663 per Channell J, as explained in *Gould v Curtis* [1913] 3 KB 84, CA.
4 *Castellain v Preston* (1883) 11 QBD 380 at 397, CA, per Bowen LJ. See further paras 185–212, 535–544, 606–625, 767 post.
5 *Dalby v India and London Life Assurance Co* (1854) 15 CB 365, Ex Ch.
6 As to a 'lost or not lost' clause see para 191 post.
7 *Lynch v Dalzell* (1729) 4 Bro Parl Cas 431, HL; *Sadlers' Co v Badcock* (1743) 2 Atk 554.
8 *Williams v Baltic Insurance Association of London Ltd* [1924] 2 KB 282, applying *Rhind v Wilkinson* (1810) 2 Taunt 237.
9 For the meaning of 'insurance company' see the Insurance Companies Act 1982 s 96; and para 15 note 3 post.
10 'United Kingdom' means Great Britain and Northern Ireland: Interpretation Act 1978 s 5, Sch 1. 'Great Britain' includes England, Scotland and Wales: see the Union with Scotland Act 1706, preamble art I; the Interpretation Act 1978 s 22 (1), Sch 2 para 5 (a); and CONSTITUTIONAL LAW vol 8 para 802.
11 For the meaning of 'insurance business' see the Insurance Companies Act 1982 s 95; and para 18 post.
12 Ibid s 36.

3. The principle of indemnity. Most contracts of insurance[1] belong to the general category of contracts of indemnity[2] in the sense that the insurer's liability is limited to the actual loss which is, in fact, proved[3]. The happening of the event does not of itself entitle the assured to payment of the sum stipulated in the policy[4]; the event must, in fact, result in a pecuniary loss to the assured[5], who then becomes entitled to be indemnified subject to the limitations of his contract[6]. He cannot recover more than the sum insured, for that sum is all that he has stipulated for by his premiums and it fixes the maximum liability of the insurers[7]. Even within that limit, however, he cannot recover more than what he establishes to be the actual amount of his loss[8]. The contract being one of indemnity, and of indemnity only, he can recover the actual amount of his loss and no more[9], whatever may have been his estimate of what his loss would be likely to be, and whatever the premiums he may have paid, calculated on the basis of that estimate. However, if he wants to guard against unpredictable fluctuations in values, particularly of goods for which there may be a very variable market, and the consequent danger of paying far too much in premiums for what the goods turn out to be worth at the date of loss, he may persuade his insurers to enter into an agreement at the time of making the insurance, and from time to time afterwards, fixing the value. If recorded in or annexed to the policy, such an agreement makes it a valued or agreed value policy, and, in the absence of fraud or circumstances invalidating the agreement, the insurers will be precluded from challenging the agreed value if and when a loss occurs[10]. In all contracts of insurance, whether marine or non-marine, which are contracts of indemnity, the insurer is entitled to be subrogated[11] to the rights of the assured, and to a contribution[12] from other insurers where he has paid the whole of the loss or more than his proportionate share of it.

1 Exceptions to this principle are life insurance, personal accident and sickness insurance and some forms of contingency insurance: see paras 4, 765–767 post.
2 As to contracts of indemnity see GUARANTEE vol 20 (Reissue) paras 345–360. For distinctions between insurances and guarantees see paras 783–784 post, and GUARANTEE vol 20 (Reissue) para 110.
3 See eg *Darrell v Tibbitts* (1880) 5 QBD 560, CA; *Castellain v Preston* (1883) 11 QBD 380, CA; *Meacock v Bryant & Co* [1942] 2 All ER 661.
4 *Dane v Mortgage Insurance Corpn Ltd* [1894] 1 QB 54 at 61, CA, per Lord Esher MR; *West Wake Price & Co v Ching* [1956] 3 All ER 821 at 825, [1957] 1 WLR 45 at 49 per Devlin J.
5 *Garden v Ingram* (1852) 23 LJCh 478 at 479 per Lord St Leonards.
6 *Dalby v India and London Life Assurance Co* (1854) 15 CB 365, Ex Ch.
7 *Westminster Fire Office v Glasgow Provident Investment Society* (1888) 13 App Cas 699 at 711, HL, per Lord Selborne LC; cf *Curtis & Sons v Mathews* (1918) as reported in 35 TLR 189, CA.
8 *Chapman v Pole PO* (1870) 22 LT 306 at 307 per Cockburn CJ; *Richard Aubrey Film Productions Ltd v Graham* [1960] 2 Lloyd's Rep 101.
9 *Castellain v Preston* (1883) 11 QBD 380 at 386, CA, per Brett LJ.
10 See the Marine Insurance Act 1906 s 27; and paras 41–42 post. For instances of valued policies relating to insurance other than marine insurance see *City Tailors Ltd v Evans* (1921) 38 TLR 230, CA; *Elcock v Thomson* [1949] 2 KB 755, [1949] 2 All ER 381.
11 As to the principle of subrogation see paras 314 et seq, 505 et seq post.
12 As to the right to a contribution see paras 520–521 post.

4. Exceptions to the principle of indemnity. Contracts of life insurance, personal accident and sickness insurance and some forms of contingency insurance are not strictly contracts of indemnity[1]. In contracts of this class there is normally no necessity to prove a pecuniary loss[2]. If the assured chooses, for example, to value a leg or an eye at £50,000 or £500,000, and to pay premiums accordingly, he is entitled to recover the stipulated sum in the event of his losing the member in question. His estimate of his possible loss is, in effect, regarded as genuine and acceptable, even if not agreed, because no one is likely deliberately to inflict such damage on himself, and no one can, in fact, foresee, even at the date of loss of the member, what the full pecuniary loss is likely to be. Similarly, a proposer can value his life at any figure that he can afford, particularly as he is unlikely to be able to foresee, at the date when he takes out the policy, what at the date of his death his financial obligations to his dependants may be. Indeed, it has been said that such an insurance is really a form of investment[3]. The same principle is equally applicable whether the life insured is that of the assured himself, or of some other person in whose life he has an insurable interest[4]; the sum insured becomes payable in all cases merely by reason of the happening of the event. Similarly, in some forms of contingency insurance the contract is merely to pay a fixed sum or a sum arrived at by a stipulated calculation if the contingency matures[5].

1 See *Dalby v India and London Life Assurance Co* (1854) 15 CB 365, Ex Ch (life assurance); *Theobald v Railway Passengers Assurance Co* (1854) 10 Exch 45 at 53 per Alderson B (personal accident and sickness insurance). A policy insuring a third person against personal accident is, however, a contract of indemnity: *Blascheck v Bussell* (1916) 33 TLR 51; affd 33 TLR 74, CA; *Hebdon v West* (1863) 3 B & S 579. As to contracts of indemnity see paras 2–3 ante. As to contingency insurance see para 765 et seq post.
2 *Dalby v India and London Life Assurance Co* (1854) 15 CB 365, Ex Ch; *Law v London Indisputable Life Policy Co* (1855) 1 K & J 223; *Gould v Curtis* [1913] 3 KB 84 at 95, CA, per Buckley LJ.
3 *Gould v Curtis* [1912] 1 KB 635 at 640 per Hamilton J; affd [1913] 3 KB 84, CA.
4 See paras 535–544 post.
5 See para 766 post.

5. The principle of good faith.

5. The principle of good faith. The duty of good faith is of universal application to all classes of insurance[1], although there are various differences in detail affecting the way in which the duty is applied. In marine insurance it is not the insurers' practice to ask any questions; they rely for their protection on the common law duty of disclosure[2]. In non-marine insurance, however, there is usually a written proposal containing specific questions, indicating that information in relation to the circumstances covered by the questions is regarded by the insurers as material[3].

Hence, a fact such as a previous refusal of insurance, which is not regarded as material in marine insurance[4], is normally regarded as material in fire and burglary insurance[5]. In marine insurance every material representation made during the negotiations, even if only made as a matter of belief, must be true[6], but in life insurance it is often sufficient that a representation given on the basis of knowledge or belief is honestly made[7]. If a statement which cannot be based on the proposer's own knowledge is required to be true, an express warranty is necessary[8].

1 *Lindenau v Desborough* (1828) 8 B & C 586 at 591 per Bayley J; *London Assurance v Mansel* (1879) 11 ChD 363 at 367 per Jessel MR. As to the duty of good faith generally see para 349 et seq post.
2 As to the principle of disclosure see para 349 et seq post.
3 *Newsholme Bros v Road Transport and General Insurance Co Ltd* [1929] 2 KB 356 at 362, CA, per Scrutton LJ. See generally para 368 et seq post.
4 *Lebon & Co v Straits Insurance Co* (1894) 10 TLR 517, CA. See also para 228 text and note 1 post.
5 *Glicksman v Lancashire and General Assurance Co Ltd* [1925] 2 KB 593 at 611, CA, per Sargant J; affd [1927] AC 139, HL. As to what is included in 'burglary insurance' see paras 644–645 post.
6 As to representations see para 232 post.
7 *Wheelton v Hardisty* (1858) 8 E & B 232 at 297, Ex Ch, per Willes J; *Thomson v Weems* (1884) 9 App Cas 671 at 684, HL, per Lord Blackburn.
8 *Anderson v Fitzgerald* (1853) 4 HL Cas 484; see further paras 363–364, 374 post.

6. Principles peculiar to marine insurance.

6. Principles peculiar to marine insurance. The following distinctions exist between marine insurance and non-marine insurance:

(1) a contract of marine insurance is inadmissible in evidence unless it is embodied in a policy[1], but contracts of non-marine insurance can be made orally and are enforceable, even though no policy has been issued[2];

(2) a contract of marine insurance made by an agent may be ratified after loss[3], but a contract of fire insurance is incapable of ratification after loss[4];

(3) the amount recoverable under a contract of marine insurance is measured by the value at the commencement of the risk, and not by the value at the time of

the loss[5], whereas in non-marine insurance the basis of calculation is the value at the time of the loss[6];

(4) a policy of marine insurance is 'subject to average' as a matter of course[7], but non-marine policies are not subject to average in the absence of an express average clause[8];

(5) a voyage policy of marine insurance is liable to be avoided by a deviation from the voyage insured[9]; in non-marine insurance the effect of an alteration of the risk depends on the nature of the alteration and the terms of the contract[10];

(6) the extended right of discovery known as 'discovery of ships' papers' is confined to marine insurance; in the case of non-marine insurance the insurers are entitled to ordinary discovery only[11];

(7) it is only in marine insurance that there can be a constructive total loss[12].

1 Ie a marine policy in accordance with the Marine Insurance Act 1906, which may be executed and issued either at the time when the contract is concluded or afterwards: see s 22; and para 35 post. Apparently at common law a contract of marine insurance could be made by parol: *Davies v National Fire and Marine Insurance Co of New Zealand* [1891] AC 485 at 496, PC.

2 *Murfitt v Royal Insurance Co Ltd* (1922) 38 TLR 334.

3 Marine Insurance Act 1906 s 86: see para 213 post.

4 *Grover and Grover Ltd v Mathews* (1910) 15 Com Cas 249; but see *Waters and Steel v Monarch Fire and Life Assurance Co* (1856) 5 E & B 870, where the marine rule was apparently applied.

5 As to measuring the value see para 628 post. The rule has been called artificial: *Usher v Noble* (1810) 12 East 639 at 645 per Lord Ellenborough CJ.

6 *Re Wilson and Scottish Insurance Corpn* [1920] 2 Ch 28: see para 628 post.

7 As to average see paras 257–258 post.

8 *Joyce v Kennard* (1871) LR 7 QB 78; see para 523 post.

9 Marine Insurance Act 1906 s 46(1): see para 141 post.

10 *Shaw v Robberds* (1837) 6 Ad & El 75 at 83 per Lord Denman CJ: see para 434 et seq post.

11 *Tannenbaum & Co v Heath* [1908] 1 KB 1032, CA; *Leon v Casey* [1932] 2 KB 576, CA. As to the discovery of ships' papers see para 336 post.

12 As to constructive total loss see para 292 et seq post.

(2) CLASSIFICATION OF INSURANCE BUSINESS AND INSURERS

7. Main types of risk. For convenience the different types of insurance business may be classified as follows: (1) marine, aviation and transport insurance[1]; (2) long term insurance[2]; (3) personal accident insurance[3]; (4) property insurance[4]; (5) liability insurance[5]; (6) motor vehicle insurance[6]; (7) pecuniary loss insurance[7]; (8) war risks insurance[8]; and (9) industrial assurance[9].

The liability of an insurer either generally or under a particular contract of insurance may itself be insured against, and such insurance is known as 'reinsurance'[10].

1 As to marine, aviation and transport insurance see para 35 et seq post.

2 As to long-term insurance business see para 525 et seq post.

3 As to personal accident insurance see para 567 et seq post.

4 As to property insurance see para 591 et seq post.

5 As to liability insurance see para 660 et seq post.

6 As to motor vehicle insurance see para 706 et seq post.

7 As to pecuniary loss insurance see para 765 et seq post.

8 As to war risks insurance see para 790 et seq post.

9 See INDUSTRIAL ASSURANCE vol 24 (Reissue) para 201 et seq.

10 The principles applicable to contracts of reinsurance are the same as those applicable to contracts of insurance generally, with certain provisions particularly applicable to marine insurance: see further paras 204–210 post. Problems of conflict of laws may arise where the policies of insurance and reinsurance are governed by different proper laws: see para 204 text and note 6 post.

8. Social security and war insurance. As a matter of national policy the state undertakes the responsibility of providing on an insurance basis benefits for unemployment, sickness and invalidity, maternity, widowhood, retirement, death and industrial injuries and diseases[1].

There is statutory provision for insurance and reinsurance against war risks of ships, aircraft and cargoes, and for insurance of goods lost or damaged in transit after discharge and between the ship or aircraft and the destination of the goods[2].

1 See the Social Security Contributions and Benefits Act 1992 ss 25–30 (unemployment), ss 31, 32 (sickness), ss 33, 34 (invalidity), s 35 (maternity), ss 36–42 (widowhood), ss 43–55 (retirement), ss 94–110 (industrial injuries and diseases); and NATIONAL HEALTH AND SOCIAL SECURITY.
2 See the Marine and Aviation Insurance (War Risks) Act 1952 ss 1–3; and para 790 et seq post.

9. Classification of insurers as legal entities. At one time insurers tended to specialise in one particular kind of business such as life, fire or marine insurance, but today most insurers carry on several kinds. A classification of insurers based on the kind of business they carry on is, therefore, an unsatisfactory one, and non-etheless so because it has to some extent been adopted by the Insurance Companies Act 1982[1]. From a legal point of view insurers are best classified as follows, by having regard to the different modes in which they are constituted, privileged or governed:

(1) companies incorporated by registration in pursuance of the Companies Acts[2];

(2) companies incorporated by special Act of Parliament;

(3) companies incorporated by royal charter[3];

(4) unincorporated companies and associations on which certain privileges incident to corporations created by royal charter and certain other powers have been conferred by letters patent or by special statute[4];

(5) unincorporated and unprivileged companies which are large partnerships generally formed by deeds of settlement[5];

(6) collecting societies[6] and other friendly societies[7]; and

(7) industrial assurance companies[8].

1 See also the distinction drawn between general business and long term business in the Insurance Companies Act 1982 s 1(1): see para 18 post.
2 Ie the Companies Act 1985: see COMPANIES vol 7(1) (Reissue) para 7 et seq. For the purposes of the Companies Act 1985, a company which carries on the business of insurance in common with any other business or businesses is deemed to be an insurance company: s 720(5).
3 The charters of insurance companies have generally been granted in pursuance of some special statute: see *Elve v Boyton* [1891] 1 Ch 501, CA; and CORPORATIONS vol 9 para 1236 note 4.
4 See COMPANIES vol 7(2) (Reissue) para 2379 et seq. See also para 21 post as to Lloyd's underwriters.
5 As to the limitation on the number of members see COMPANIES vol 7(1) (Reissue) para 21, vol 7(2) (Reissue) para 2356.
6 See INDUSTRIAL AND PROVIDENT SOCIETIES.
7 See FRIENDLY SOCIETIES.
8 See INDUSTRIAL ASSURANCE.

10. Classification of insurers by offices. The following classification is rather of offices than of companies:

(1) proprietary offices, being joint stock partnerships the partners of which take all the profits;

(2) offices in which the shareholders take all the profits except the sums paid by way of bonus or rebate to policyholders who are not partners; and

(3) mutual insurance offices, where the policyholders are the only proprietors and the whole body insures each of its members for their protection and not its profit[1].

1 As to mutual insurance offices see para 25 et seq post.

(3) INSURANCE LEGISLATION AND RELATED LEGISLATION

11. Marine legislation. The law of marine insurance was codified by the Marine Insurance Act 1906[1]. The Marine Insurance (Gambling Policies) Act 1909 prohibits gambling on loss by maritime perils[2].

1 As to the Marine Insurance Act 1906 see para 35 et seq post.
2 As to the Marine Insurance (Gambling Policies) Act 1909 see para 212 post. The two Acts may be cited together as the Marine Insurance Acts 1906 and 1909: Marine Insurance (Gambling Policies) Act 1909 s 2.

12. Scope of the codification. The Marine Insurance Act 1906 codifies only those principles of the law which relate exclusively to marine insurance. It does not lay down rules which apply to contracts in general such as those relating to fraud, mistake or illegality, or those relating to special subjects which belong more properly to other departments of law such as shipping and navigation, prize and international law. It expressly provides that the rules of the common law, including the law merchant, except in so far as they are inconsistent with the express provisions of the Act, continue to apply to contracts of marine insurance[1].

1 Marine Insurance Act 1906 s 91(2).

13. Construction. The canon of construction generally applicable to a codifying statute is that the language of the statute must be given its natural meaning, regard being had to the previous state of the law only in cases of doubt or ambiguity[1]. Although this has sometimes been applied to the Marine Insurance Act 1906[2], that Act embodies only some of the legal principles and rules of marine insurance, and its language is so extremely concise and general that its full import and meaning can scarcely be understood without referring to the existing law which it was intended to express or to the decided cases from which that law was evolved[3]. Moreover, it is often left in doubt whether or not that law was intended to be altered. Where this is so, the courts will apparently hold that the Act was not intended to alter the pre-existing law[4]. For these reasons it will generally be necessary, notwithstanding the above-mentioned canon of construction, to ascertain the law as it stood at that date and to illustrate it by decided cases[5].

1 *Bank of England v Vagliano Bros* [1891] AC 107 at 144, HL; *Robinson v Canadian Pacific Rly Co* [1892] AC 481, PC; *Bristol Tramways etc Carriage Co Ltd v Fiat Motors Ltd* [1910] 2 KB 831 at 836, CA; *Compania Maritima San Basilio SA v Oceanus Mutual Underwriting Association (Bermuda) Ltd, The Eurysthenes* [1977] QB 49 at 75, [1976] 3 All ER 243 at 257, CA, per Roskill LJ; and see STATUTES.

2 See *Hall v Hayman* [1912] 2 KB 5 at 12; *Polurrian SS Co Ltd v Young* [1915] 1 KB 922 at 936, CA; *P Samuel & Co Ltd v Dumas* [1924] AC 431 at 451, HL.

3 See *Rickards v Forestal Land, Timber and Railways Co Ltd* [1942] AC 50 at 79, [1941] 3 All ER 62 at 76, HL, per Lord Wright.

4 *Sanday & Co v British and Foreign Marine Insurance Co Ltd* [1915] 2 KB 781 at 811, 831, CA; affd sub nom *British and Foreign Marine Insurance Co Ltd v Samuel Sanday & Co* [1916] 1 AC 650 at 673, HL; *Gaunt v British and Foreign Insurance Co Ltd and Standard Marine Insurance Co Ltd* [1920] 1 KB 903 at 915, CA; affd sub nom *British and Foreign Marine Insurance Co Ltd v Gaunt* [1921] 2 AC 41 at 48, 64, HL.

5 After the language has been examined without presumptions, resort may be had to the previous law for construing provisions of doubtful import or words which have previously acquired a technical meaning: *Bank of England v Vagliano Bros* [1891] AC 107 at 145, HL, per Lord Herschell.

14. Miscellaneous insurance legislation. The Life Assurance Act 1774 provides that insurance may not be effected on a person's life or any other event if the person for whose use or benefit it is effected has no interest in it, nor may it be effected by way of gaming or wagering[1]. The Policies of Assurance Act 1867 provides that, if certain conditions are fulfilled, an assignee of a life assurance policy may sue at law in his own name to recover the sum insured from the insurer concerned after due written notice of the assignment has been given[2]. The Life Insurance Companies (Payment into Court) Act 1896 provides that in the case of life assurance policies where the right to the policy money is in doubt and there are competing claims, the insurers can discharge themselves by paying the money into court[3].

Other Acts are: the Restriction of Advertisement (War Risks Insurance) Act 1939[4]; the Marine and Aviation Insurance (War Risks) Act 1952 (which entitles the Secretary of State to reinsure any war risks and to carry on insurance against war risks)[5]; the Policyholders Protection Act 1975[6]; and the Insurance Brokers (Registration) Act 1977[7].

The Reinsurance (Acts of Terrorism) Act 1993 provides that reinsurance obligations of the Secretary of State arising from acts of terrorism may be met out of money provided by Parliament[8].

1 See the Life Assurance Act 1774 s 1; and para 535 post. Such insurance is void: s 1.
2 See the Policies of Assurance Act 1867 ss 1, 3; and para 548 post.
3 See the Life Insurance Companies (Payment into Court) Act 1896 s 3 (as amended); and para 561 post.
4 See the Restriction of Advertisement (War Risks) Act 1939; and para 790 post.
5 See the Marine and Aviation Insurance (War Risks) Act 1952 s 1(1); and para 794 post.
6 See generally para 895 et seq post.
7 See generally para 869 et seq post.
8 Reinsurance (Acts of Terrorism) Act 1993 s 1; and see para 802 post.

15. Insurance companies legislation. The Insurance Companies Amendment Act 1973, in so far as it is unrepealed, validates certain group insurance policies[1].

The Insurance Companies Act 1982 places restrictions on the carrying on of insurance business[2] and provides for its regulation and conduct[3]. It also contains provisions for special classes of insurance business[4]. The responsibility for the operation of the Insurance Companies Act 1982 is that of the Secretary of State[5].

1 See the Insurance Companies Amendment Act 1973 s 50; and para 543 post.
2 See para 19 et seq post.
3 See para 803 et seq post. 'Insurance company' means a person or body of persons, whether incorporated or not, carrying on insurance business: Insurance Companies Act 1982 s 96(1). For the meaning of 'insurance business' see para 18 post.

4 As to the classes see ibid s 1; and para 18 post.
5 Ie one of Her Majesty's Principal Secretaries of State: Interpretation Act 1978 s 5, Sch 1. As to the
  office of Secretary of State see CONSTITUTIONAL LAW vol 8 para 1193. In practice the Secretary of State
  concerned with the Insurance Companies Act 1982, and also the Policyholders Protection Act 1975,
  is the Secretary of State for Trade and Industry: see the Transfer of Functions (Trade and Industry)
  Order 1983, SI 1983/1127. As to the Secretary of State's power to make regulations see the Insurance
  Companies Act 1982 s 97 (as amended); and para 864 post.

16. Related legislation. The Race Relations Act 1976 provides that it is unlawful
for any person concerned with the provision to the public or a section of the public
of facilities, including those by way of insurance, to discriminate against any
person seeking to obtain them by refusing or deliberately omitting to provide him
with facilities of the same quality in the same manner and on the same terms in and
on which he normally makes them available to other members of the public[1].

The Consumer Credit Act 1974 does not regulate a consumer credit agreement
where the creditor is of a description specified in an order made by the Secretary of
State as being an insurance company[2].

The European Communities Act 1972 empowers Her Majesty by Order in
Council and any designated minister or department to make provision for
implementing any Community obligation or enabling such obligation to be
implemented or enabling any rights to be enjoyed by the United Kingdom under
or by virtue of the treaties to be exercised[3].

Various Finance Acts relate to insurance. The provision of insurance of any
description and the making of arrangements for the provision of any insurance are
exempt from value added tax[4]. No capital gain accrues on the disposal of either the
rights of the insurer or the rights of the insured under any policy of insurance,
whether the risks relate to property or not[5]. Premiums or other payments made
under a policy of insurance against the risk of any kind of damage or injury to or
loss or depreciation of an asset are excluded from the expenditure which may be
allowed in computing the gain or loss on the disposal of an asset[6]. There are special
provisions for the taxation of underwriters[7] and for the early surrender or conversion of life policies[8]. Inheritance tax may be attracted in case of insurance[9].

The Income and Corporation Taxes Act 1988 sets out the position as to income
taxation and the basis of computation of corporation tax in so far as insurance is
concerned[10].

1 Race Relations Act 1976 s 20(1), (2)(c); see BRITISH NATIONALITY vol 4(2) (Reissue) para 171 et seq.
2 Consumer Credit Act 1974 s 16(1)(a).
3 European Communities Act 1972 s 2(2)(a). See eg the Insurance Accounts Directive (Miscellaneous
  Insurance Undertakings) Regulations 1993, SI 1993/3245, which implement EC Council Directive
  91/674 on the annual accounts and consolidated accounts of insurance undertakings. Those regulations provide for the preparation of accounts and statements by bodies which would require
  authorisation under the Insurance Companies Act 1982 s 2 (as amended) (see para 19 ante) but are not
  otherwise required by statute to prepare accounts.
4 Value Added Tax Act 1983 s 17, Sch 6 Group 2 (amended by the Value Added Tax (Insurance) Order
  1990, SI 1990/2037).
5 Taxation of Chargeable Gains Act 1992 s 204; and see CAPITAL GAINS TAXATION vol 5(1) (Reissue)
  paras 312–313.
6 Ibid ss 38(2), 205; and see CAPITAL GAINS TAXATION vol 5(1) (Reissue) paras 32, 312.
7 See the Income and Corporation Taxes Act 1988 ss 450–457 (as amended); and INCOME TAXATION vol
  23 (Reissue) para 1422 et seq.
8 Ibid s 268; and see INCOME TAXATION vol 23 (Reissue) paras 1003–1004.
9 Inheritance Tax Act 1984 ss 21, 152, 263 (ss 21, 152 as amended); and see INHERITANCE TAXATION vol
  24 (Reissue) paras 518, 410, 626 respectively.
10 Income and Corporation Taxes Act 1988 ss 266, 273, 274, Pt XIII Ch II (ss 539–554) (as amended);
  and see INCOME TAXATION vol 23 (Reissue) paras 993–998 141 et seq.

(4) AUTHORISED INSURERS

(i) Application of the Legislation

A. IN GENERAL

17. Common law. All persons competent to contract[1] may be parties to any contract of insurance subject to the restrictions imposed directly and indirectly by the Insurance Companies Act 1982[2]. Therefore a policy may be underwritten by individuals or by a company.

1 As to who is competent to contract see CONTRACT vol 9 para 225.
2 As to the restrictions see para 19 post.

18. Meaning of insurance business. For the purposes of the Insurance Companies Act 1982, 'insurance business' includes the following:
 (1) the effecting and carrying out, by a person not carrying on a banking business, of contracts for fidelity bonds, performance bonds, administration bonds, bail bonds or custom bonds or similar contracts of guarantee (effected by way of business and not incidental to some other business) in return for payment of one or more premiums[1];
 (2) the effecting and carrying out of tontines[2];
 (3) the effecting and carrying out, by a body (not being a body carrying on a banking business) which carries on business which is insurance business otherwise than under this head, of:
  (a) capital redemption contracts, and
  (b) contracts to manage the investments of pension funds, other than funds solely for the benefit of its own officers or employees and their dependants, or in the case of a company, partly for the benefit of officers or employees and their dependants of its subsidiary or holding company or a subsidiary of its holding company[3];
 (4) the effecting and carrying out of contracts to pay annuities on human life[4].
Insurance business is divided into 'long term business' and 'general business'.
 'Long term business' means any of the seven classes specified in Schedule 1 to the Insurance Companies Act 1982[5], namely: life and annuity[6]; marriage and birth[7]; linked long term[8]; permanent health[9]; tontines[10]; capital redemption[11]; and pension fund management[12].
 'General business' means any of the 18 classes specified in Part I of Schedule 2 to the Insurance Companies Act 1982[13], namely: accident[14]; sickness[15]; land vehicles[16]; railway rolling stock[17]; aircraft[18]; ships[19]; goods in transit[20]; fire and natural forces[21]; damage to property[22]; motor vehicle liability[23]; aircraft liability[24]; liability of ships[25]; general liability[26]; credit[27]; suretyship[28]; miscellaneous financial loss[29]; legal expenses[30]; and assistance[31].
 For certain purposes, the classes of general insurance are grouped as follows[32]:
Group 1: Accident and health (classes 1 and 2);
Group 2: Motor (class 1, to the extent that the relevant risks are risks of the person insured sustaining injury or dying as the result of travelling as a passenger, and classes 3, 7 and 10);
Group 3: Marine and transport (class 1, to the extent described in relation to Group 2, and classes 4, 6, 7 and 12);

Group 4: Aviation (class 1, to the extent described in relation to Group 2, and classes 5, 7 and 11);
Group 5: Fire and other damage to property (classes 8 and 9);
Group 6: Liability (classes 10, 11, 12 and 13);
Group 7: Credit and suretyship (classes 14 and 15;
Group 8: General (all classes).

1 Insurance Companies Act 1982 s 95(a). For the purposes of s 95 a European institution carrying on a listed activity which it is authorised to carry on in its home state is to be treated as if it were carrying on a banking business: Banking Coordination (Second Council Directive) Regulations 1992, SI 1992/3218, reg 66: see para 19 text and notes 6–8 post.

2 Ibid s 95(b).

3 Ibid s 95(c). 'Holding company' and 'subsidiary' must be construed in accordance with the Companies Act 1985 s 736 (substituted by the Companies Act 1989 s 144(1)): Insurance Companies Act 1982 s 96(1) (amended by the Companies Consolidation (Consequential Provisions) Act 1985 s 30, Sch 2).

4 Insurance Companies Act 1982 s 95(d). 'Annuities on human life' does not include superannuation allowances and annuities payable out of any fund applicable solely to the relief and maintenance of persons engaged or who have been engaged in any particular profession, trade or employment, or of the dependants of such persons: s 96(1).

5 Ibid s 1(1). The effecting and carrying out of a contract whose principal object is within one class of insurance business, but which contains related and subsidiary provisions within another class or classes, is taken to constitute the carrying on of insurance business of the first-mentioned class only, if the provisions of either of heads (1) or (2) below apply: s 1(2). Those provisions apply to a contract where:

(1) it is a contract the principal object of which is within any class of long term business but which contains subsidiary provisions within general business class 1 or 2 or if the insurer is authorised to carry on long term business class I (s 1(3)); or

(2) it is a contract the principal object of which is within one of the classes of general business but which contains subsidiary provisions within another of those classes other than class 14, class 15 or (except as described infra), class 17 (s 1(4) (amended by the Insurance Companies (Legal Expenses Insurance) Regulations 1990, SI 1990/1159)).

Head (2) applies to a contract whose principal object is within one of the classes of general business but contains subsidiary provisions in general business class 17 (s 1(4A) (added by the Insurance Companies (Legal Expenses Insurance) Regulations 1990) if:

(a) the principal object is the provision of assistance for persons who get into difficulties while travelling, away from home, or away from their permanent residence (Insurance Companies Act 1982 s 1(4A)(a) (as so added), or

(b) those subsidiary provisions concern disputes or risks arising out of, or in connection with, the use of sea-going vessels (s 1(4A)(b) (as so added)).

As to the classes of long term business and general business see the text and notes infra. As to authorisation to carry on long term business see ss 3, 4; para 34 post.

6 Ie effecting and carrying out contracts of insurance on human life or contracts to pay annuities on human life but excluding contracts within class III (text and note 8 infra): ibid s 1, Sch 1 class I.

7 Ie effecting and carrying out contracts of insurance to provide a sum on marriage or on the birth of a child, being contracts expressed to be in effect for a period of more than one year: ibid Sch 1 class II.

8 Ie effecting and carrying out contracts of insurance on human life or to pay annuities on human life where the benefits are wholly or partly to be determined by reference to the value of, or income from, property of any description (whether specified or not) or by reference to fluctuations in, or in an index of, the value of property of any description (whether specified or not): ibid Sch 1 class III.

9 Ie effecting and carrying out contracts of insurance providing specified benefits against risks of persons becoming incapacitated owing to injury as a result of an accident or an accident of a specified class or sickness or infirmity, being contracts that are expressed to be for not less than five years or until the normal retirement age or without time limit and either are not terminable by the insurer or are so terminable only in special circumstances mentioned in the contract: ibid Sch 1 class IV.

10 Ie effecting and carrying out tontines: ibid Sch 1 class V.

11 Ie effecting and carrying out capital redemption contracts: ibid Sch 1 class VI.

12 Ie effecting and carrying out contracts to manage the investments of pension funds, or such contracts that are combined with contracts of insurance covering either conservation of capital or a payment of a minimum interest: ibid Sch 1 class VII.

13 Insurance Companies Act 1982 s 1(1). See also note 5 supra.

14 Ie effecting and carrying out contracts of insurance providing fixed pecuniary benefits or benefits in the nature of indemnity, or a combination of both, against certain risks of the person insured (or where there is a contract is made under the Local Government Act 1972 s 140, s 140A or s 140B (as added and amended) (insurance of members and assistants of local authorities, and assistants of probation committees: see LOCAL GOVERNMENT), the person for whose benefit the contract is made): Insurance Companies Act 1982 s 1, Sch 2 Pt I class 1, which lists the following risks:

    (1) sustaining injury as the result of an accident or an accident of a specified class, or

    (2) dying as the result of an accident or an accident of a specified class, or

    (3) becoming incapacitated in consequence of disease or disease of a specified class,

inclusive of contracts relating to industrial injury and occupational disease, but exclusive of contracts of permanent health.

15 Ie effecting and carrying out contracts of insurance providing fixed pecuniary benefits or benefits in the nature of indemnity, or a combination of the two, against risks of loss to the persons insured attributable to sickness or infirmity but excluding contracts of permanent health: ibid Sch 2 Pt I class 2.

16 Ie effecting and carrying out contracts of insurance against loss of or damage to vehicles used on land, including motor vehicles but excluding railway rolling stock: ibid Sch 2 Pt I class 3.

17 Ie effecting and carrying out contracts of insurance against loss of or damage to railway rolling stock: ibid Sch 2 Pt I class 4.

18 Ie effecting and carrying out contracts of insurance upon aircraft or upon the machinery, tackle, furniture or equipment of aircraft: ibid Sch 2 Pt I class 5.

19 Ie effecting and carrying out contracts of insurance upon vessels used on the sea or on inland water, or upon the machinery, tackle, furniture or equipment of such vessels: ibid Sch 2 Pt I class 6. 'Vessels' includes hovercraft: s 96(1).

20 Ie effecting and carrying out contracts of insurance against loss of or damage to merchandise, baggage and all other goods in transit, irrespective of the form of transport: ibid Sch 2 Pt I class 7.

21 Ie effecting and carrying out contracts of insurance against loss of or damage to property, other than property to which classes 3 to 7 relate, due to fire, explosion storm, natural forces other than storm, nuclear energy or land subsidence: ibid Sch 2 Pt I class 8.

22 Ie effecting and carrying out contracts of insurance against loss of or damage to property, other than property to which classes 3 to 7 relate, due to hail or frost, or to any event such as theft, other than those mentioned under class 8: ibid Sch 2 Pt I class 9.

23 Ie effecting and carrying out contracts of insurance against damage arising out of or in connection with the use of motor vehicles on land, including third-party risks and carrier's liability: ibid Sch 2 Pt I class 10.

24 Ie effecting and carrying out contracts of insurance against damage arising out of or in connection with the use of aircraft, including third-party risks and carrier's liability: ibid Sch 2 Pt I class 11.

25 Ie effecting and carrying out contracts of insurance against damage arising out of or in connection with the use of vessels on the sea or on inland water, including third-party risks and carrier's liability: ibid Sch 2 Pt I class 12.

26 Ie effecting and carrying out contracts of insurance against risks of the persons insured incurring liabilities to third parties, the risks in question not being risks to which class 10, 11 or 12 relates: ibid Sch 2 Pt I class 13.

27 Ie effecting and carrying out contracts of insurance against risks of loss to the persons insured arising from the insolvency of debtors of theirs or from the failure, otherwise than through insolvency, of debtors of theirs to pay their debts when due: ibid Sch 2 Pt I class 14.

28 Ie effecting and carrying out the following contracts: ibid Sch 2 Pt I class 15:

    (1) contracts of insurance against risks of loss to the persons insured arising from their having to perform contracts of guarantee entered into by them;

    (2) contracts for fidelity bonds, performance bonds, bail bonds or customs bonds or similar contracts of guarantee.

29 Ie effecting and carrying out contracts of insurance against any of the following risks: ibid Sch 2 Pt I class 16 (amended by the Insurance Companies (Assistance) Regulations 1987, SI 1987/2130). Those risks are:

    (1) risks of loss to the persons insured attributable to interruptions of the carrying on of business carried on by them or to reduction in the scope of business so carried on;

    (2) risks of loss to the persons insured attributable to their incurring unforeseen expense;

    (3) risks neither falling within head (1) or (2) supra nor being of a kind such that the carrying on of the business of effecting and carrying out contracts of insurance against them constitutes

the carrying on of insurance business of some other class, other than such loss as is covered in class 18 (text and note 31 infra).

30 Ie effecting and carrying out contracts of insurance against risks of loss to the persons insured attributable to their incurring legal expenses, including costs of litigation: Insurance Companies Act 1982 Sch 2 Pt I class 17.

31 Ie effecting and carrying out contracts of insurance providing either or both of the following benefits: ibid Sch 2 Pt I class 18 (added by the Insurance Companies (Assistance) Regulations 1987). Those benefits are:
   (1) assistance, whether in cash or kind, for persons who get into difficulties while travelling, while away from home or while away from their permanent residence; or
   (2) assistance, whether in cash or kind, for persons who get into difficulties other than those mentioned in head (1) supra.

32 Insurance Companies Act 1982 s 3(3), Sch 2 Pt II; and see para 34 post.

19. Statutory restrictions on carrying on insurance business. No person may carry on any insurance business[1] in the United Kingdom unless authorised to do so[2].

A person who carries on insurance business in contravention of this provision is guilty of an offence[3] and is liable on conviction on indictment to imprisonment for a term not exceeding two years or to a fine or to both[4]. On summary conviction he is liable to a fine not exceeding £1,000 or, if it is greater, the prescribed sum[5].

However, the above provision does not prevent a European institution[6] from carrying on in the United Kingdom any listed activity[7] which it is authorised or permitted to carry on in its home state[8].

1 For the meaning of 'insurance business' see para 18 ante.
2 Insurance Companies Act 1982 s 2(1). That subsection does not apply to insurance business, other than industrial assurance business, carried on (1) by a member of Lloyd's; (2) by a body registered under the enactments relating to friendly societies (see FRIENDLY SOCIETIES); or (3) by a trade union or employers' association where the insurance business carried on by the union or association is limited to the provision for its members of provident benefits or strike benefits: s 2(2). 'Trade union' and 'employers' association' have, throughout the United Kingdom, the meanings assigned to them by the Trade Union and Labour Relations (Consolidation) Act 1992 ss 2 and 122: Insurance Companies Act 1982 s 2(2) (amended by the Trade Union and Labour Relations (Consolidation) Act 1992 s 300(2), Sch 2 para 31).
   'Trade union' means an organisation, whether temporary or permanent:
   (a) which consists wholly or mainly of workers of one or more descriptions and whose principal purposes include the regulation of relations between workers of that description or those descriptions and employers or employers' associations; or
   (b) which consists wholly or mainly of:
      (i) constituent or affiliated organisations which fulfil the conditions in head (a) supra, or themselves consist wholly or mainly of constituent or affiliated organisations which fulfil those conditions, or
      (ii) representatives of such constituent or affiliated organisations,
   and whose principal purposes include the regulation of relations between workers and employers or between workers and employers' associations, or the regulation of relations between its constituent or affiliated organisations: Trade Union and Labour Relations (Consolidation) Act 1992 s 1.
   'Employers' association' means an organisation, whether temporary or permanent:
   (a) which consists wholly or mainly of employers or individual owners of undertakings of one or more descriptions and whose principal purposes include the regulation of relations between employers of that description or those descriptions and workers or trade unions; or
   (b) which consists wholly or mainly of:
      (i) constituent or affiliated organisations which fulfil the conditions in head (a) supra, or themselves consist wholly or mainly of constituent or affiliated organisations which fulfil those conditions, or
      (ii) representatives of such constituent or affiliated organisations,

and whose principal purposes include the regulation of relations between employers and workers or between employers and trade unions, or the regulation of relations between its constituent or affiliated organisations: s 122(1). See generally TRADE AND LABOUR.

The Insurance Companies Act 1982 s 2(1) does not apply to industrial assurance business carried on by a friendly society (s 2(3)), nor to general business consisting of credit insurance suretyship insurance, miscellaneous financial loss insurance, legal expenses insurance or assistance insurance if it is carried on solely in the course of carrying on, and for the purposes of, banking business (s 2(4) (amended by the Insurance Companies (Assistance) Regulations 1987, SI 1987/2130), nor to general business consisting of the effecting and carrying out, by an insurance company that carries on no other insurance business, of contracts of such descriptions as may be prescribed, being contracts under which the benefits provided by the insurer are exclusively or primarily benefits in kind (Insurance Companies Act 1982 s 2(5)). For the contracts of benefits in kind so prescribed see the Insurance Companies Regulations 1981, SI 1981/1654, reg 23 (amended by SI 1987/2130).

3 Insurance Companies Act 1982 s 14(1).
4 Ibid s 14(3)(a).
5 Ibid s 14(3)(b). The prescribed sum is the statutory maximum within the meaning of the Magistrates' Courts Act 1980 s 32; at the date at which this volume states the law, that sum is £5,000: s 32(9) (amended by the Criminal Justice Act 1991 s 17(2)(c)).
6 'European institution' means a European authorised institution or a European subsidiary: Banking Coordination (Second Council Directive) Regulations 1992, SI 1992/3218, reg 3(1). See further reg 3(2)–(8).
7 As to the listed activities see ibid Sch 1, which sets out the Annex to the Second Council Directive (ie EC Council Directive 89/646, on the co-ordination of laws, etc relating to the taking up and pursuit of the business of credit institutions).
8 Banking Coordination (Second Council Directive) Regulations 1992 reg 5(1)(d). As to the activities which an institution may be authorised or permitted to carry on in its home state see reg 4; for the meaning of 'home state' see reg 2(1).

20. Contracts contravening statutory restrictions. An insurance contract which is entered into in contravention of the statutory restrictions[1] is unenforceable against the other party[2]; and that party is entitled to recover any money or other property paid by him under the contract, together with compensation for any loss sustained by him as a result of his having parted with it[3].

However, the court may allow the contract to be enforced or money or property paid or transferred if it is satisfied that:

(1) the insurer reasonably believed that his entering into the contract did not constitute a contravention; and

(2) it is just and equitable for the contract to be enforced or for the money or property paid or transferred under it to be retained[4].

Contravention of the statutory restrictions does not make a contract of insurance illegal or invalid to any greater extent than is provided above; nor does it affect the validity of any reinsurance contract entered into in respect of that contract[5].

1 Ie the Insurance Companies Act 1982 s 2: see para 19 ante. The provisions set out in the text and notes infra also have effect in relation to a contract of insurance entered into by a person in the course of providing insurance in contravention of s 81B or s 81G (as added: see paras 806–807 post): Insurance Companies (Amendment) Regulations 1992, SI 1992/2890, reg 10.
2 Financial Services Act 1986 s 132(1).
3 Ibid s 132(1). The compensation is to be such as the parties agree or as a court may, on the application of either party, determine: s 132(2).
4 Ibid s 132(3). Where a person elects not to perform a contract which is unenforceable against him or recovers money paid or transferred under the contract, he is not entitled to any benefits under the contract, and must repay any money and return any property received by him under the contract: s 132(4). Where any property transferred has passed to a third party, references to that property must be construed as references to its value at the time of its transfer under the contract: s 132(5).
5 Ibid s 132(6).

B. APPLICATION TO LLOYD'S

21. Lloyd's. Collective underwriting of marine risks in its modern form originated towards the end of the seventeenth century in the practice of a group of merchants and seafaring men to meet in the coffee house of Edward Lloyd in the City of London. Here any person requiring insurance could find, conveniently assembled, insurers who would each assume a part of his risk. Although the principle of individual responsibility for the part of a risk has not been altered, the early informality of Lloyd's has given way in succeeding years to an increasingly rigorous organisation and control directed by a committee. In 1871 Lloyd's was incorporated by Act of Parliament[1], and in 1911 a further Act[2] sanctioned the existing although unrecognised practice of underwriting non-marine risks. Other Acts were passed in 1925[3] and 1951[4], and a Council of Lloyd's was established in 1982[5]. Protection for the assured is ensured by the requirement of a deposit by way of security of a minimum sum where both marine and non-marine business is to be transacted, and by a stringent annual audit of each underwriter's accounts[6].

In addition to its primary function as an incorporated society of individual underwriters, Lloyd's has maintained the practice of Edward Lloyd of providing shipping intelligence by the publication of Lloyd's List and Shipping Gazette. The Society also appoints agents in all the principal ports of the world whose duty it is to forward regularly to it accounts of all departures from and arrivals at their ports as well as of losses and casualties and general information relating to shipping and insurance. These agents are appointed by the Corporation of Lloyd's and are not agents of the underwriters[7].

Where the policy is personally subscribed by individual underwriters, they sign their names at the foot of the policy, writing opposite to it the sum insured by each[8]. Unless the contrary is expressed, the effect is that each underwriter makes a separate contract with the assured for the amount set opposite his name and the assured acquires a right of action against each separately and not against all jointly[9].

It is usual for underwriters to associate themselves for business purposes into syndicates. One of the members of the syndicate takes the active part in the business and is given authority to underwrite policies in the names of the other members of the syndicate, who are known as the 'names' and who do not themselves take any active part in the business[10].

1 See the Lloyd's Act 1871.
2 Ie the Lloyd's Act 1911.
3 Lloyd's Act 1925.
4 Lloyd's Act 1951.
5 See the Lloyd's Act 1982.
6 As to the requirements to be complied with by underwriters in order to be exempt from the Insurance Companies Act 1982 see para 23 post. Lloyd's and other underwriters are subject to certain special provisions relating to income tax: see the Income and Corporation Taxes Act 1988 ss 452–457 (as amended); and INCOME TAXATION vol 23 (Reissue) para 1424 et seq. The Council of Lloyd's is required to prepare an annual account by amalgamating the accounts of syndicates in which members of Lloyd's participate: see the Insurance Accounts Directive (Miscellaneous Insurance Undertakings) Regulations 1993, SI 1993/3245.
7 *Wilson v Salamandra Assurance Co of St Petersburg* (1903) 88 LT 96.
8 Where the underwriting is effected by Lloyd's members, the policies are signed by Lloyd's Policy Signing Office on behalf of numbered syndicates, and the seal of the Signing Office is impressed. A list of the members of the syndicates is attached to the policy. See also *Society of Lloyd's v Clementson* (1994) Times, 11 January, cited in note 9 infra.
9 Marine Insurance Act 1906 s 24(2); *Tyser v Shipowners Syndicate (Reassured)* [1896] 1 QB 135; *Leo SS Co Ltd v Corderoy* (1896) 12 TLR 395, CA. See *Society of Lloyd's v Clementson* (1994) Times, 11 January, where the Society of Lloyd's was held entitled to be reimbursed by members in respect of payments made from the central fund to meet underwriting commitments of those members which they had failed to meet. See also *Touche Ross & Co v Baker* [1992] 2 Lloyd's Rep 207, HL, where it was

held that a clause giving the assured an option to renew insurance did not have to be exercised against all the underwriters or none of them, since the liability of an underwriting member was several not joint.

10 *Thompson v Adams* (1889) 23 QBD 361 at 362 per Mathew J.

22. Application of the Insurance Companies Act 1982 to members of Lloyd's. The provisions of the Insurance Companies Act 1982 which regulate insurance companies[1] do not apply to a member of Lloyd's who carries on business of any class, provided that he complies with certain requirements[2] applicable to business of that class[3].

Subject to such modifications as may be prescribed[4], and to any determination made by the Secretary of State[5] in accordance with regulations, certain provisions of the Act relating to margins of solvency[6] and the form and situation of assets[7], apply to the members of Lloyd's taken together as they apply to an insurance company[8] the head office of which is in the United Kingdom[9].

Certain powers of the Secretary of State[10] are exercisable in relation to members of Lloyd's if:

(1) there is a breach of an obligation imposed by virtue of the application of the provisions relating to margins of solvency or the form or situation of assets[11]; or

(2) there is a failure by Lloyd's to satisfy any obligation to which it is subject by virtue of any provision of any member state of the European Community giving effect to the general or long term insurance directives[12].

The provisions of the Act relating to the transfer of insurance business[13] apply in relation to a transfer to or from a member of Lloyd's if specified conditions are satisfied[14]. Those conditions are that:

(a) the transferor and the transferee are not both members of Lloyd's;

(b) the Committee of Lloyd's has by resolution authorised one person to act for the members concerned as transferor or transferee; and

(c) a copy of the resolution has been given to the Secretary of State[15].

The provisions applied have effect as if references to insurance companies or authorised persons[16] included references to members of Lloyd's, and as if anything done in connection with the transfer by the person authorised under head (b) above had been done by the members for whom he acted[17].

1 Ie the Insurance Companies Act 1982 Pt II (ss 15–71) (as amended): see para 803 et seq post. For the meaning of 'insurance company' see para 15 note 3 ante.

2 Ie the requirements of ibid s 83 (see para 23 post).

3 Ibid s 15(4). As to classes of insurance business see para 18 ante.

4 'Prescribed' means prescribed by regulations under the Insurance Companies Act 1982: s 96(1). See the Insurance (Lloyd's) Regulations 1983, SI 1983/224, reg 3.

5 As to the Secretary of State see para 15 note 5 ante.

6 Ie the Insurance Companies Act 1982 ss 32, 33: see para 857 post.

7 Ie ibid s 35: see para 857 post.

8 Ie an insurance company to which ibid Pt II applies.

9 Ibid s 84(1).

10 Ie ibid ss 38–41, 44, 45: see para 846 et seq post.

11 Ibid s 84(2).

12 Ibid s 83A (added by the Insurance Companies (Amendment) Regulations 1992, SI 1992/2890, reg 8; subsequently amended by the Insurance Companies (Amendment) Regulations 1993, SI 1993/174).

The 'first general insurance directive' is EC Council Directive 73/239 on the co-ordination of laws, etc relating to direct insurance other than life assurance; the 'second general insurance directive' is EC Council Directive 88/357 on the co-ordination of laws, etc relating to direct insurance other than life assurance, laying down provisions to facilitate the effective exercise of freedom to provide services and amending the first general insurance directive; the 'general insurance directives' means those directives as amended, and such other directives as make provision with respect to the business of direct insurance other than life assurance: Insurance Companies Act 1982 s 96A(1) (added by the Insurance Companies (Amendment) Regulations 1990, SI 1990/1333). See also the Insurance Companies Act 1982 s 96A(1A) (added by the Insurance Companies (Amendment) Regulations 1992, SI 1992/2890), which states that EC Council Directive 90/618 is included among the directives amending the first and second general insurance directives.

The 'first long term insurance directive' is EC Council Directive 79/267 on the co-ordination of laws, etc relating to the business of direct life assurance; the 'second long term insurance directive' is EC Council Directive 90/619 on the co-ordination of laws, etc relating to direct life assurance, laying down provisions to facilitate the effective exercise of freedom to provide services and amending the first long term insurance directive; the 'long term insurance directives' means those directives as amended: Insurance Companies Act 1982 s 96A(1B) (added by the Insurance Companies (Amendment) Regulations 1992; and substituted by the Insurance Companies (Amendment) Regulations 1993, SI 1993/174).

13 Ie the Insurance Companies Act 1982 ss 49–52 (as amended): see paras 825–831 post.
14 Ibid s 85(1).
15 Ibid s 85(2).
16 Ie persons authorised under ibid s 3 or s 4: see para 34 post.
17 Ibid s 85(3).

23. Requirements to be complied with by Lloyd's underwriters.

The requirements to be complied with for a member of Lloyd's carrying on business of any class to be exempt from the application of the Insurance Companies Act 1982[1] are as follows:

(1) every underwriter[2] must, in accordance with the provisions of a trust deed approved by the Secretary of State[3], carry to a trust fund all premiums received by him or on his behalf in respect of any insurance business[4];

(2) the premiums received in respect of long term business[5] must not be carried to the same trust fund as premiums received in respect of general business[6], although the trust deed may provide for carrying the premiums received in respect of all or any classes of long term business and all or any classes of general business either to a common fund or to any number of separate funds[7]; and

(3) the accounts of every underwriter must be audited annually by an accountant approved by the Committee of Lloyd's and the auditor must furnish a certificate in the prescribed form[8] to the committee or managing body and the Secretary of State[9].

The Committee of Lloyd's must deposit every year with the Secretary of State a statement in the prescribed form summarising the extent and character of the insurance done by the members of Lloyd's in the 12 months to which the statement relates[10], and the underwriter must, when required by the committee, furnish such information as the committee requires for the purpose of preparing that statement[11].

1 Insurance Companies Act 1982 s 83(1). As to the exemption see para 22 ante.
2 'Underwriter' includes any person named in a policy or other contract of insurance as liable to pay or contribute towards the payment of the sum secured by the policy or contract: ibid s 96(1). Under s 96(1) 'policy' includes:
(1) in relation to ordinary long term insurance business and industrial assurance business, an instrument evidencing a contract to pay an annuity on human life (see para 18 note 8 ante);
(2) in relation to insurance business of any other class, any policy under which there is for the time being an existing liability already accrued or under which a liability may accrue; and

(3) in relation to capital redemption business (see para 18 note 11 ante), any policy, bond, certificate, receipt or other instrument evidencing the contract with the company.
'Contract of insurance' includes any contract which constitutes the carrying on of insurance business by virtue of s 95; 'ordinary long term insurance business' means long term business which is not industrial assurance business: s 96(1). See further paras 7, 18 ante.

3 As to the Secretary of State see para 15 note 5 ante.
4 Insurance Companies Act 1982 s 83(2). For the meaning of 'insurance business' see para 18 ante.
5 'Long term business' means insurance business of any of the classes specified in ibid Sch 1: s 1(1). As to these classes see para 18 ante.
6 'General business' means insurance business of any of the classes specified in ibid Sch 2 Pt I (as amended): s 1(1). As to these classes see para 18 ante.
7 Ibid s 83(3).
8 The certificate must in particular state whether in the opinion of the auditor the value of the assets available to meet the underwriter's liabilities in respect of insurance business is correctly shown in the accounts, and whether or not that value is sufficient to meet those liabilities, calculated in the case of long term business by an actuary and in other cases by an auditor on a basis approved by the Secretary of State: ibid s 83(5). Where liabilities are calculated by an actuary, he must furnish a certificate of the amount to the Committee of Lloyd's and to the Secretary of State, and must state in it the basis on which the calculation was made; a copy of that certificate must be annexed to the auditor's certificate: s 83(6). A person performing the functions of an actuary for these purposes must be a Fellow of the Institute of Actuaries or a Fellow of the Faculty of Actuaries, and must be at least 30: Insurance (Lloyd's) Regulations 1983, SI 1983/224, reg 4(2). For the prescribed form of certificate see reg 4(1), Sch 2.
9 Insurance Companies Act 1982 s 83(4).
10 Ibid s 86(1), (2). For the prescribed form see the Insurance (Lloyd's) Regulations 1983 reg 5, Sch 3. On deposit of such a statement a fee of £97,300 is payable: Insurance (Fees) Regulations 1994, SI 1994/643, reg 9.
11 Insurance Companies Act 1982 s 83(7).

C. APPLICATION TO MARINE INSURANCE COMPANIES

24. Marine insurance companies. In 1719 the Royal Exchange Assurance Corporation and the London Assurance Corporation were incorporated with the exclusive right of making sea insurances in their corporate capacity[1], but this monopoly was taken away in 1824[2]. Soon afterwards a great number of insurance companies were formed, either by charter from the Crown or by special statutes or under the provisions of a partnership deed. Since 2 November 1862, however, no company, association or partnership consisting of more than 20 persons formed for the acquisition of gain is legal[3], and therefore no marine insurance company or mutual assurance association having more than that number of members is legal, unless registered under the Companies Acts[4] or formed in pursuance of some other Act or letters patent[5]. This restriction does not apply to persons carrying on reinsurance business under the Marine and Aviation Insurance (War Risks) Act 1952[6] with the approval of the Secretary of State[7].

1 6 Geo 1 c 18 (Royal Exchange and London Assurance Corporations) (1719) (repealed).
2 5 Geo 4 c 114 (Marine Assurance) (1824) (repealed).
3 Companies Act 1985 s 716(1); and see note 5 infra. This does not, however, prohibit the formation of certain professional partnerships, or of partnerships of a prescribed description formed for a prescribed purpose: s 716(2) (amended by the Companies Act 1989 ss 145, 212, Schs 19, 24; and the Companies Act 1989 (Eligibility for Appointment as Company Auditor) (Consequential Amendments) Regulations 1991, SI 1991/1997); see COMPANIES vol 7(1) (Reissue) paras 15, 21, 23. As to companies formed before 1862 see 7 & 8 Vict c 110 (Joint Stock Companies) (1844) (repealed), and the Companies Act 1862 ss 209, 210 (repealed); *Hambro v Hull and London Fire Insurance Co* (1858) 3 H & N 789; *Re Phoenix Life Assurance Co, Burges and Stock's Case* (1862) 2 John & H 441.

4 See COMPANIES vol 7(1) (Reissue) para 7 et seq. Companies registered under Acts prior to the Companies Act 1985 may be regulated by that Act even though they are not companies registered under it: see COMPANIES vol 7(1) (Reissue) para 11.

5 See *Hambro v Hull and London Fire Insurance Co* (1858) 3 H & N 789; *Re Phoenix Life Assurance Co, Burges and Stock's Case* (1862) 2 John & H 441; *Re Padstow Total Loss and Collision Assurance Association* (1882) 20 ChD 137, CA; *Shaw v Benson* (1883) 11 QBD 563, CA; and COMPANIES vol 7(1) paras 19–20. As to mutual assurance associations see *Re Arthur Average Association for British, Foreign and Colonial Ships, ex p Hargrove & Co* (1875) 10 Ch App 542; and para 341 et seq post. The Companies Act 1985 s 716 (and any corresponding enactment previously in force) is deemed not to have invalidated the formation of any insurance company which immediately before 3 November 1966 was carrying on in Great Britain insurance business of any class relevant for the purposes of the Insurance Companies Act 1974 Pt I (ss 1–11) (repealed), and was carrying on business of that class at 25 July 1973: Insurance Companies Act 1982 s 89(1), (2) (both amended by the Companies Consolidation (Consequential Provisions) Act 1985 s 30, Sch 2). For the meaning of 'Great Britain' see para 2 note 10 ante.

6 As to war risks see para 790 et seq post.

7 Companies Act 1985 s 716(5). As to the Secretary of State see para 15 note 5 ante.

D. APPLICATION TO MUTUAL INSURANCE COMPANIES

25. Origin of mutual insurance clubs. The monopoly created by the incorporation of the London Assurance Corporation and the Royal Exchange Assurance Corporation[1] gave rise to shipowners' mutual insurance associations or clubs for the insurance of their own vessels. In these clubs each member was both assured and insurer; he was insured as to his own property in the club by all the other members in proportion to their respective properties in it, and he was at the same time an insurer in the proportion of his own property in the club for the property of each of the others, their mutual agreements being the consideration of the contract.

Because of the monopoly of those two insurance companies it was essential to the legality of the mutual insurance clubs that their members should be liable individually only, each for his own proportion and not jointly, or one for others of them[2]. Moreover, the managers of the club had no right of action against a member for premiums[3] or for his contribution to losses paid[4].

1 See para 24 ante.

2 See the judgment of Pollock B in *Marine Mutual Insurance Association Ltd v Young* (1880) 43 LT 441; and see also *Harrison v Millar* (1796) 7 Term Rep 340n, cited in *Lees v Smith* (1797) 7 Term Rep 338; *Strong v Harvey* (1825) 3 Bing 304.

3 The premium in the case of a mutual society may consist of the liability to contribute to the losses of other members of the society: *Lion Insurance Association Ltd v Tucker* (1883) 12 QBD 176 at 187, CA; *Great Britain 100 A1 SS Insurance Association v Wyllie* (1889) 22 QBD 710 at 722, CA; *Ocean Iron SS Insurance Association Ltd v Leslie* (1887) 22 QBD 722n; and see *Re European Assurance Society, Hort's Case, Grain's Case* (1875) 1 ChD 307 at 315, 321, CA. As to social security see para 8 ante.

4 *Gray v Pearson* (1870) LR 5 CP 568; *Evans v Hooper* (1875) 1 QBD 45, CA. There was usually a rule in those clubs requiring the member whose ship or share was mortgaged to produce to the club a contract of guarantee from the mortgagee to answer for all demands that should be made on the member by the club, and this rule was generally so framed as to make the production of the guarantee a condition precedent to the recovery for a loss: *Hughes v Tindall* (1856) 18 CB 98; *Turnbull v Woolfe* (1862) 9 Jur NS 57.

26. Registration of mutual insurance associations. The monopoly granted to the London Assurance Corporation and the Royal Exchange Assurance Corporation was taken away in 1824[1], and until 1862 no restriction was placed on the formation of mutual associations or joint stock companies to carry on the business of marine insurance. However, the Companies Act 1862 produced the result that, as a marine insurance association is a company for the acquisition of gain within the meaning of that Act[2], it is, when consisting of more than 20 members, an illegal association unless registered as a company[3]. A mutual insurance association is now, therefore, always registered under the Companies Acts, usually as a company limited by shares or as a company limited by guarantee[4].

1 5 Geo 4 c 114 (Marine Assurance) (1824) (repealed). As to the monopoly see paras 24–25 ante.
2 See the Companies Act 1862 s 4 (repealed). See now the Companies Act 1985 s 716(1); and COMPANIES vol 7(1) (Reissue) paras 21–22. As to where the restriction does not apply see para 24 text to notes 6–7 ante.
3 *Re Arthur Average Association for British, Foreign and Colonial Ships, ex p Hargrove & Co* (1875) 10 Ch App 542; also *Re Padstow Total Loss and Collision Assurance Association* (1882) 20 ChD 137 at 145–149, CA. A mutual assurance association formed before 1862 did not require registration even if it consisted of more than 20 persons; such an association is not formed afresh whenever a new member joins it; see COMPANIES vol 7(1) (Reissue) para 21.
4 *Lion Assurance Association Ltd v Tucker* (1883) 12 QBD 176, CA; *Marine Mutual Insurance Association v Young* (1880) 43 LT 441. The Companies Act 1862 s 4 (repealed) only applied to associations formed after the commencement of the Act, and accordingly it was held that a mutual marine insurance association formed in 1847 and reconstituted from year to year since that date was not illegal, though not registered nor incorporated: *May v Jacobs* (1885) 1 TLR 349, CA. As to the income tax liability of mutual insurance associations see INCOME TAXATION vol 23 (Reissue) paras 1382–1383.

27. Legal character of mutual insurance associations. In general, it is a mutual insurance association itself[1] which is the insurer, and the assured's right of action is against the association and not against the other members, the consideration or premium for the insurance being his liability to contribute to the losses of the other members and the expenses of the association[2].

1 As to the origin of mutual insurance associations see paras 25–26 ante.
2 See *Lion Insurance Association Ltd v Tucker* (1883) 12 QBD 176 at 187, CA, per Brett MR; *North-Eastern 100A SS Insurance Association v Red S SS Co Ltd* (1906) 22 TLR 692, CA. Although a member of a mutual assurance association limited by guarantee may be liable to the association or its members for his proportion of losses to an amount exceeding his guarantee, he is not liable as a contributory in respect of such excess: see *Re Bangor and North Wales Mutual Marine Protection Association, Baird's Case* [1899] 2 Ch 593. In *W R Corfield & Co v Buchanan* (1913) 29 TLR 258, HL, it was held that, on the construction of the memorandum and articles, a mutual insurance company limited by guarantee had power to issue reinsurance policies to non-members, and that the policyholder in question was not a member nor liable to contribute as such in the winding up, notwithstanding that the policy provided that he 'waived any and all rights of attending or voting at the general meetings of the association'.

28. Statutory provisions concerning mutual insurance. Where two or more persons mutually agree to insure each other against marine losses, there is said to be a mutual insurance[1].

The provisions of the Marine Insurance Act 1906 relating to the premium[2] do not apply to mutual insurance, but a guarantee, or such other arrangement as may be agreed upon, may be substituted for the premium[3].

In so far as they may be modified by the agreement of the parties, the provisions of the Act may, in the case of mutual insurance, be modified by the terms of the policies issued by the association, or by the rules and regulations of the association[4]. Subject to the above exceptions, the provisions of the Act apply to a mutual insurance[5].

1 Marine Insurance Act 1906 s 85(1).

2 Ie ibid ss 52–54: see para 90 et seq post.
3 Ibid s 85(2).
4 Ibid s 85(3).
5 Ibid s 85(4).

(ii) Authorisation

29. Applications for authorisation: submission of proposals. The Secretary of State[1] must not issue an authorisation[2] unless:

(1) the applicant has submitted to him such proposals as to the manner in which it proposes to carry on business, such financial forecasts and such other information as may be required[3]; and

(2) he is satisfied on the basis of that and any other information received by him that the application ought to be granted[4].

He must decide an application for authorisation within six months of receiving the information and, if he refuses to issue the authorisation, he must inform the applicant in writing of the reasons for the refusal[5]. However, he may defer a decision on an application for such period as may be necessary for the purpose of implementing any decision of the Council or Commission of the European Communities under specified Community legislation[6].

1 As to the Secretary of State see para 15 note 5 ante.
2 Ie an authorisation under the Insurance Companies Act 1982 s 3; see para 34 post.
3 By or in accordance with regulations under the Insurance Companies Act 1982 s 5(1)(a). See the Insurance Companies Regulations 1981, SI 1981/1654, reg 29, Sch 4 (long term business), Sch 5 (general business); and the Insurance Companies (Legal Expenses Insurance) (Application for Authorisation) Regulations 1990, SI 1990/1160.
4 Insurance Companies Act 1982 s 5(1).
5 Ibid s 5(2) (amended by the Insurance Companies (Amendment) Regulations 1992, SI 1992/2890, reg 2(1)).
6 Insurance Companies Act 1982 s 5(3) (added by the Insurance Companies (Amendment) Regulations 1992 reg 2(2)).

30. Combination of long term and general business. The Secretary of State[1] must not authorise[2] a body to carry on both long term business[3] and general business[4] unless (1) the long term business is restricted to reinsurance, or (2) the body is at the time the authorisation is issued already lawfully carrying on in the United Kingdom both long term business and general business, in neither case restricted to reinsurance[5].

1 As to the Secretary of State see para 15 note 5 ante.
2 Ie under the Insurance Companies Act 1982 s 3; see para 34 post.
3 As to long term insurance business see para 18 ante.
4 As to general insurance business see para 18 ante.
5 Insurance Companies Act 1982 s 6. For the meaning of 'United Kingdom' see para 2 note 10 ante.

31. United Kingdom applicants. The Secretary of State[1] must not issue an authorisation[2] to an applicant whose head office is in the United Kingdom unless the applicant is:

(1) a company[3]; or

(2) a registered society; or

(3) a body corporate established by royal charter or Act of Parliament and already authorised to carry on business, though not to the extent proposed in the application[4].

Nor must he issue an authorisation to an applicant whose head office is in the United Kingdom if it has an issued share capital any part of which was issued after the commencement of the relevant statutory provision but is not fully paid up[5].

He must not issue an authorisation to an applicant whose head office is in the United Kingdom if it appears to him that any director[6], controller[7], manager[8] or main agent[9] of the applicant is not a fit person to hold the position held by him[10].

1 As to the Secretary of State see para 15 note 5 ante.
2 Ie an authorisation under the Insurance Companies Act 1982 s 3; see para 34 post.
3 Ie as defined in the Companies Act 1985 s 735; see COMPANIES.
4 Insurance Companies Act 1982 s 7(1) (amended by the Companies Consolidation (Consequential Provisions) Act 1985 s 30, Sch 2).
5 Insurance Companies Act 1982 s 7(2); the date of commencement of that provision was 28 January 1983.
6 'Director' includes any person occupying the position of director by whatever name called: ibid s 96(1).
7 'Controller', in relation to the applicant, is defined by ibid s 7(4) as follows:
   (1) a managing director of the applicant or of a body corporate of which the applicant is a subsidiary;
   (2) a chief executive of the applicant or of a body corporate, being an insurance company, of which the applicant is a subsidiary;
   (3) a person
       (a) in accordance with whose directions or instructions the directors of the applicant or of a body corporate of which it is a subsidiary are accustomed to act, or
       (b) who either alone or with any associate or associates is entitled to exercise, or control the exercise of, 15% or more of the voting power at any general meeting of the applicant or of a body corporate of which it is a subsidiary.
   'Chief executive', in relation to the applicant or a body corporate of which it is a subsidiary, means an employee of the applicant or that body corporate, who, either alone or jointly with others, is responsible under the immediate authority of the directors for the conduct of the whole of the insurance business of the applicant or that body corporate: s 7(7).
   'Associate', in relation to any person, means (i) the wife or husband or minor son or daughter of that person; (ii) any company of which that person is a director; (iii) any person who is an employee or partner of that person; (iv) if that person is a company (A) any director of that company; (B) any subsidiary of that company; (C) any director or employee of any such subsidiary; and for the purposes of this definition 'son' includes step-son and 'daughter' includes step-daughter: s 7(8).
8 'Manager', in relation to the applicant, means an employee of the applicant, other than a chief executive, who, under the immediate authority of a director or chief executive of the applicant (1) exercises managerial functions, or (2) is responsible for maintaining accounts or other records of the applicant, not being a person whose functions relate exclusively to business conducted from a place of business outside the United Kingdom: ibid s 7(5).
9 'Main agent', in relation to the applicant, means, subject to such exceptions as may be prescribed, a person appointed by the applicant to be its agent in respect of general business in the United Kingdom, with authority to enter into contracts on behalf of the applicant in any financial year (1) without limit on the aggregate amount of premiums; or (2) with a limit in excess of 10 per cent of the premium limit as determined in accordance with ibid Sch 3: s 7(6). The premium limit is the aggregate of gross premiums shown, in the annual accounts relating to the business of the applicant on the United Kingdom last deposited under s 22 (see para 843 post), as receivable in respect of business for the financial year to which the accounts relate: Sch 3 para 1; an adjustment is specified if that financial year was not a period of 12 months: Sch 3 para 2. If no such accounts have been deposited, reference is made to the financial forecasts submitted in accordance with regulations made under s 5(1)(a) (see para 29 note 3 ante): Sch 3 para 3. An unlimited agent is not a main agent if he was appointed before 1 April 1982 and if for the last accounts deposited before that date, and for every subsequent financial year, the value of his business has not been more than 10% of the applicant's business: Insurance Companies Regulations 1981, SI 1981/1654, reg 24.
10 Insurance Companies Act 1982 s 7(3).

32. Applicants from other member states. The Secretary of State[1] must not issue an authorisation[2] to an applicant whose head office is in a member state of the European Community other than the United Kingdom, unless the applicant has a representative fulfilling the following requirements[3]:

(1) he must be a person resident in the United Kingdom who has been designated as the applicant's representative[4];

(2) he must be authorised to act generally, and to accept service of any document, on behalf of the applicant[5];

(3) he must not be an auditor, or a partner or an employee of an auditor, of the accounts of any business carried on by the applicant[6];

(4) if the representative is not an individual, it must be a company[7] with its head office in the United Kingdom and must itself have an individual representative resident in the United Kingdom who is authorised to act generally, and to accept service of any document, on behalf of the company in its capacity as representative of the applicant[8].

The Secretary of State must not issue an authorisation to an applicant whose head office is in a member state other than the United Kingdom if it appears to him that any relevant executive[9] or main agent[10] of the applicant is not a fit and proper person to hold the position held by him[11].

Where an applicant whose head office is in a member state other than the United Kingdom seeks an authorisation restricted to reinsurance business, the Secretary of State must not issue the authorisation:

(a) unless he is satisfied that the applicant is a body corporate[12] entitled under the law of that state to carry on insurance business there[13], and

(b) if it appears to him that any specified person[14] is not fit and proper to hold the position held by him[15].

1 As to the Secretary of State see para 15 note 5 ante.
2 Ie an authorisation under the Insurance Companies Act 1982 s 3; see para 34 post.
3 Ibid ss 8(1), 10(1).
4 Ibid s 10(2). For the meaning of 'United Kingdom' see para 2 note 10 ante.
5 Ibid s 10(3).
6 Ibid s 10(4).
7 Ie as defined in the Companies Act 1985 s 735; see COMPANIES.
8 Insurance Companies Act 1982 s 10(5) (amended by the Companies Consolidation (Consequential Provisions) Act 1985 s 30, Sch 2).
9 'Relevant executive' in relation to the applicant means a person who is:
    (1) the representative referred to in the Insurance Companies Act 1982 s 8(1) or the individual representative referred to in s 10(5): s 8(4)(a);
    (2) an officer or employee of the applicant who, either alone or jointly with others, is responsible for the conduct of the whole of the insurance business carried on by the applicant in the United Kingdom, not being a person who (a) is also responsible for the conduct of insurance business carried on by the applicant elsewhere and (b) has a subordinate who is responsible for the whole of the insurance business carried on by the applicant in the United Kingdom: s 8(4)(b); or
    (3) an employee of the applicant who, under the immediate authority of a director or an officer or employee within head (2) supra, either
    (a) exercises managerial functions or
    (b) is responsible for maintaining accounts or other records of the applicant,
    not being a person whose functions relate exclusively to business conducted from a place of business outside the United Kingdom: s 8(4)(c).
10 For the meaning of 'main agent' see para 31 note 9 ante.
11 Insurance Companies Act 1982 s 8(2).
12 'Body corporate' does not include a corporation sole but does include a body incorporated outside the United Kingdom: ibid s 96(1).

13 Ibid s 8(3)(a).
14 Ie a director, controller or main agent of the applicant, or a person within ibid s 8(4)(a) or (b) (see note 9 supra): s 8(3)(b). 'Controller', 'manager' and 'main agent' have the same meanings as in s 7 (see para 31 notes 7–9 ante): s 8(4). For the meaning of 'director' see para 31 note 6 ante.
15 Ibid s 8(2), (3)(b).

33. Applicants from outside the Community. The Secretary of State[1] must not issue an authorisation[2] in respect of long term[3] or general business[4] to an applicant whose head office is not in a member state of the European Community unless he is satisfied:

(1) that the applicant is a body corporate[5] entitled under the law of the place where its head office is situated to carry on long term or, as the case may be, general business there[6];

(2) that the applicant has in the United Kingdom assets of such value as may be prescribed[7]; and

(3) that the applicant has made a deposit of such amount and with such person as may be prescribed[8].

The Secretary of State must not issue an authorisation to an applicant whose head office is not in a member state unless the applicant has a representative fulfilling certain requirements[9]. He must not issue an authorisation to an applicant whose head office is not in a member state if it appears to him that (a) the representative of the applicant or the individual representative[10], or (b) any director, controller or manager of the applicant, or (c) a main agent of the applicant, is not a fit and proper person to hold the position held by him[11].

1 As to the Secretary of State see para 15 note 5 ante.
2 Ie an authorisation under the Insurance Companies Act 1982 s 3; see para 34 post.
3 For the meaning of 'long term business' see para 18 ante.
4 For the meaning of 'general business' see para 18 ante.
5 For the meaning of 'body corporate' see para 32 note 12 ante.
6 Insurance Companies Act 1982 s 9(1)(a).
7 Ibid s 9(1)(b). The prescribed value is a value at least equal to the minimum guarantee fund appropriate to the United Kingdom margin of solvency required by s 32(2)(b) (see para 857 post): Insurance Companies Regulations 1981, SI 1981/1654, reg 30(a). For the meaning of 'United Kingdom' see para 2 note 10 ante.
8 Insurance Companies Act 1982 s 9(1)(c). As to provisions regarding deposits see s 9(7), and the Insurance Companies Regulations 1981 Pt III (regs 14–22) (as amended). Briefly, the applicant must maintain a deposit with the Accountant General at a level equal to at least one half of the minimum guarantee fund appropriate to the margin of solvency which the depositor is required to maintain under the Insurance Companies Act 1982 s 32(2)(b) or (3)(b) (see para 857 post): Insurance Companies Regulations 1981 regs 14, 15 (reg 14 amended by SI 1985/1419). The Insurance Companies Act 1982 s 9(1)(c) does not apply where the authorisation sought is one restricted to reinsurance: s 9(3).
    Where the applicant seeks to carry on insurance business in the United Kingdom and one or more other member states, the Secretary of State and the supervisory authority in the other state or states concerned may agree that the following provisions apply to the applicant: s 9(2). In that event s 9(1)(b) has effect as if the reference to the United Kingdom were a reference to the member states concerned taken together; and s 9(1)(c) has effect as if the reference to such person as may be prescribed were a reference to such person as may be agreed between the Secretary of State and the other supervisory authority or authorities concerned: s 9(2)(a), (b). In the former case the prescribed value (see text and note 7 supra) is modified accordingly: Insurance Companies Regulations 1981 reg 30(b).
9 Insurance Companies Act 1982 ss 9(4), 10(1). The requirements are those laid down by s 10(2)–(5) (as amended): see para 32 text and notes 4–8 ante.
10 Ie the representative referred to in ibid s 9(4) (see text and note 9 supra) or the individual representative referred to in s 10(5).

11 Ibid s 9(5). 'Controller', 'manager' and 'main agent' have the same meanings as in s 7 (see para 31 notes 7–9 ante) except that for the purposes of s 9 the controllers of the applicant are taken to include any officer or employee who, either alone or jointly with others, is responsible for the conduct of the whole of the insurance business carried on by the applicant in the United Kingdom, not being a person who (1) is also responsible for the conduct of the insurance business carried on by it elsewhere and (2) has a subordinate who is responsible for the whole of the insurance business carried on by the applicant in the United Kingdom: s 9(6). For the meaning of 'director' see para 31 note 6 ante.

34. Granting and revocation of authorisation. The Secretary of State[1] may authorise a body to carry on in the United Kingdom such of the classes of insurance business specified by the Insurance Companies Act 1982[2] or such parts of those classes as may be specified in the authorisation[3]. An authorisation may be restricted to industrial assurance business or to reinsurance business[4]. The authorisation may identify classes or parts of classes of general business by referring to the appropriate groups specified[5]. On the issue of any such authorisation, any previous authorisation of the body lapses[6].

The Secretary of State may at the request of the company or on various grounds[7] direct that an insurance company which has been authorised is to cease to be authorised to effect contracts of insurance or contracts of any description specified in the direction[8]. After giving a direction otherwise than at the request of the company concerned, he must inform the company in writing of his reasons for giving the direction[9].

Before giving a direction otherwise than at the request of the company he must serve on the company a written notice stating:

(1) that he is considering giving a direction and the ground on which he is considering it; and

(2) that the company may, within a period of one month from the date of the service of the notice, make written representations to an officer of the Department of Trade and Industry appointed for the purpose by him[10].

Where an insurance company ceases to carry on in the United Kingdom any insurance business, or business of any class, the Secretary of State may direct that it is to cease to be authorised to carry on insurance business, or business of that class[11].

If a body authorised to carry on insurance business has not at any time carried on business of any class, and at least 12 months have elapsed since the issue of the authorisation, the Secretary of State may direct that it is to cease to be authorised to carry on business of that class[12].

He may also direct that an insurance company is to cease to be authorised to carry on investment business[13], if it appears to him that the company has failed to satisfy an obligation to which it is subject by virtue of the Financial Services Act 1986 or, if it is a member of a recognised self-regulating organisation[14], an obligation to which it is subject by virtue of the rules of that organisation[15].

A person who, for the purpose of obtaining the issue of an authorisation, furnishes information which he knows to be false in a material particular or recklessly furnishes information which is false in a material particular, is guilty of an offence[16].

1 As to the Secretary of State see para 15 note 5 ante.
2 Ie by the Insurance Companies Act 1982 s 1(1), Sch 1 (long term business: see para 18 ante), and Sch 2 (as amended): (general business: see para 18 ante).

3 Ibid s 3(1). For the meaning of 'United Kingdom' see para 2 note 10 ante.

4 Ibid s 3(2). A body may not carry on industrial assurance business unless the authorisation expressly extends to such business: s 3(2). For the meaning of 'industrial assurance business' see the Industrial Assurance Act 1923 s 1(2) (see INDUSTRIAL ASSURANCE vol 24 (Reissue) para 201): Insurance Companies Act 1982 s 96(1).

5 Ibid s 3(3). The groups of classes are specified by Sch 2 Pt II (see para 18 ante). As to existing insurance companies (ie companies which were authorised to carry out specified business prior to the commencement of the Insurance Companies Act 1982) see s 4.

6 Ibid s 3(4).

7 The grounds are as follows:
    (1) that it appears to him that the company has failed to satisfy an obligation to which it is subject by virtue of the Insurance Companies Act 1982 or the Financial Services Act 1986 or if it is a member of a self-regulating organisation, an obligation to which it is subject by virtue of the rules thereof: Insurance Companies Act 1982 s 11(2)(a) (amended by the Financial Services Act 1986 s 129, Sch 10 para 7(1));
    (2) that it appears to him that the company has failed to satisfy an obligation by virtue of any provision of the law of another member state giving effect to the general or long term insurance directives: Insurance Companies Act 1982 s 11(2)(aa) (added by the Insurance Companies (Amendment) Regulations 1990, SI 1990/1333; and amended by the Insurance Companies (Amendment) Regulations 1993, SI 1993/174);
    (3) that there exists a ground under the Insurance Companies Act 1982 s 7, 8 or 9 (see paras 31–33 ante) on which he would be prohibited from issuing an authorisation to the company: s 11(2)(b);
    (4) that the company has ceased to be authorised to effect contracts of insurance, or contracts of a particular description, in a member state where it has its head office or where it has made a deposit under s 9(2) (see para 33 ante): s 11(2)(c).
    As to the general and long term insurance directives see para 22 note 12 ante.

8 Ibid s 11(1).

9 Ibid s 11(3). Notice of the direction must be published in the London, Edinburgh and Glasgow Gazettes, and in such other ways as appear to the Secretary of State expedient for notifying the public: s 12(8). A direction does not prevent a company from effecting a contract of insurance in pursuance of a term of a subsisting contract of insurance: s 11(4). Where a direction has been given in respect of a company which has its head office in, or has made a deposit (under s 9(2); see para 33 ante) in, a member state other than the United Kingdom, the Secretary of State may vary or revoke the direction if after consultation with the supervisory authority in that member state, he considers it appropriate to do so: s 11(5). Except in this case, a direction may not be revoked or varied, but it may cease to have effect in relation to any business if the Secretary of State subsequently issues an authorisation to the company to carry on such business: s 11(6).

10 Ibid s 12(1). A notice must give particulars of the ground on which the Secretary of State is considering giving a direction: s 12(5), (7). As to the transfer of functions see para 15 note 5 ante. Before giving a direction on the ground specified in head (3) in note 7 supra, the Secretary of State must serve a similar notice on the person whose fitness is in question: s 12(2)–(5), (7). Where representations are made in response to a notice, he must take them into account before issuing a direction: s 12(6).

11 Ibid s 13(1). A direction under s 13 is without prejudice to the subsequent issue of an authorisation to carry on business of a class to which the direction relates: s 13(3). See also the Banking Coordination (Second Council Directive) Regulations 1992, SI 1992/3218, reg 64, which provides that the Insurance Companies Act 1982 s 13 is to include provision that authorisation may be withdrawn from a European subsidiary on the application of that institution. For the meaning of 'European subsidiary' see the Banking Coordination (Second Council Directive) Regulations 1992 reg 3.

12 Insurance Companies Act 1982 s 13(2). See also note 11 supra.

13 Ie business which is insurance business within the meaning of ibid s 95(c)(ii); see para 18 ante.

14 For the meaning of 'recognised self-regulating organisation' see the Financial Services Act 1986 s 207(1).

15 Insurance Companies Act 1982 s 13(2A) (added by the Financial Services Act 1986 s 129, Sch 10 para 7(2)); the Insurance Companies Act 1982 ss 11(3), (5), (6), 12(1), (5)–(8) (see text and notes 9–10 supra) apply in such a case: s 13(2B) (as so added). See also note 11 supra.

16 Ibid s 14(2). The offence is punishable on conviction on indictment with imprisonment for up to two years, or a fine, or both; and on summary conviction, with a fine not exceeding £1,000 or, if greater, the prescribed sum: s 14(3). As to the prescribed sum see para 19 note 5 ante.

2. MARINE INSURANCE

(1) NATURE OF MARINE INSURANCE

35. Meaning of 'contract of marine insurance'. A contract of marine insurance is defined by the Marine Insurance Act 1906 as a contract whereby the insurer undertakes to indemnify the assured[1], in manner and to the extent thereby agreed, against marine losses, that is to say losses incident to marine adventure[2]. The instrument in which the contract of marine insurance is generally embodied is called a policy[3]. The insurer is usually called the underwriter, because he subscribes the policy. The thing or property insured is called the subject matter of insurance, and the assured's interest in that subject matter is called his insurable interest. The consideration for which the insurer undertakes to indemnify the assured is called the premium. That which is insured against is the loss arising from maritime perils[4] and casualties, and these are called the perils insured against, or the losses covered by the policy. When the underwriter's liability commences under the contract, the policy is said to attach; or, in other words, the risk is said to attach or to begin to run from that time.

1 The person indemnified under a contract of marine insurance is referred to throughout the Marine Insurance Act 1906, and by those engaged in or connected with the business of marine insurance, as 'the assured' and not 'the insured'. A contract of insurance is not a perfect contract of indemnity, for, as will be seen later (see paras 265, 319–321 post), the assured in some cases receives more and in others less than a complete indemnity; see also GUARANTEE vol 20 (Reissue) para 345. Where a contract which is substantially one of marine insurance contains an ancillary clause covering the assured's liability to third parties, the special rules governing the contract of marine insurance will be held applicable to this ancillary clause: *Holman & Sons Ltd v Merchants Marine Insurance Co Ltd* [1919] 1 KB 383, distinguishing *Joyce v Kennard* (1871) LR 7 QB 78, and *Cunard SS Co Ltd v Marten* [1902] 2 KB 624; affd [1903] 2 KB 511, CA.
2 Marine Insurance Act 1906 s 1. For the meaning of 'marine adventure' see para 36 post.
3 See para 39 et seq post.
4 For the meaning of 'maritime perils' see para 36 post.

36. Subject matter of the insurance. The most usual insurances are on ship or goods, freight or profits, but every lawful marine adventure may be the subject of a contract of marine insurance[1]. In particular, there is a marine adventure where any insurable property, namely any ship[2], goods or other movables[3], is exposed to maritime perils[4], or where the earning or acquisition of any freight[5], passage money, commission, profit or other pecuniary benefit, or the security for any advances, loan or disbursements, is endangered by the exposure of insurable property to maritime perils[6], or where any liability to a third party may be incurred by the owner of, or other person interested in or responsible for, insurable property by reason of maritime perils[7].

'Maritime perils' means perils consequent on, or incidental to, the navigation of the sea, that is to say perils of the seas, fire, war perils[8], pirates, rovers, thieves, captures, seizures, restraints, and detainments of princes and peoples, jettisons, barratry, and any other perils, either of the like kind or which may be designated by the policy[9].

Thus, a carrier of goods by sea, a charterer of a vessel and a company which lays down an undersea electric cable are all engaged in marine adventures[10].

1 Marine Insurance Act 1906 s 3(1). For the meaning of 'contract of marine insurance' see para 35 ante.

2 In the Marine Insurance Act 1906 'ship' includes hovercraft: Hovercraft (Application of Enactments) Order 1972, SI 1972/971, art 4, Sch 1 Pt A. See also para 113 post.
3 'Movables' means any movable tangible property, other than the ship, including money, valuable securities and other documents: Marine Insurance Act 1906 s 90.
4 Ibid s 3(2)(a). As to maritime perils see text and notes 8–9 infra.
5 'Freight' includes the profit derivable by a shipowner from the employment of his ship to carry his own goods or movables, as well as freight payable by a third party, but does not include passage money: ibid s 90. See also para 115 post.
6 Ibid s 3(2)(b).
7 Ibid s 3(2)(c).
8 War perils are usually known as 'war risks'. Those perils, in so far as they are maritime in their nature, are properly insured against under a marine policy, notwithstanding that for certain special purposes it is necessary to distinguish between 'marine' and 'war' risks. There is statutory provision for the insurance of war risks by the Secretary of State and for the reinsurance by him of those risks: see para 790 et seq post.
9 Marine Insurance Act 1906 s 3(2). The meaning of the particular perils referred to is discussed in paras 151 et seq, 905 post.
10 *Crowley v Cohen* (1832) 3 B & Ad 478 (carrier); *Paterson v Harris* (1861) 1 B & S 336 at 355; *Wilson v Jones* (1867) LR 2 Exch 139 (shareholder in cable company).

37. Land risks. A contract of marine insurance[1] may, by its express terms or by trade usage, be extended so as to protect the assured against losses on inland waters or against any land risk which may be incidental to a sea voyage, and it may also cover a ship[2] in the course of building, or the launch of a ship, or any adventure analogous to a marine adventure[3].

Generally speaking, the underwriter of a marine policy insures only against risks at sea, but where there is a usage by which the ship's furniture or stores are regularly landed at a certain stage of the voyage, they are held to be protected when thus put on shore[4].

A policy on goods often contains a 'transit' clause[5]. Frequently, also, goods are insured by the same policy for transit partly by sea and partly by land[6], or by inland navigation[7].

1 For the meaning of 'contract of marine insurance' see para 35 ante.
2 'Ship' includes hovercraft: see para 36 note 2 ante.
3 Marine Insurance Act 1906 s 2. See *Jackson v Mumford* (1904) 9 Com Cas 114 (vessel in course of construction); *James Yachts Ltd v Thames and Mersey Marine Insurance Co Ltd* [1977] 1 Lloyd's Rep 206 (BC SC) (boat builders' risk policy). For the meaning of 'marine adventure' see para 36 ante.
4 *Pelly v Royal Exchange Assurance Co* (1757) 1 Burr 341; *Brough v Whitmore* (1791) 4 Term Rep 206.
5 For the wording of this clause see para 125 post.
6 *Rodoconachi v Elliott* (1874) LR 9 CP 518, Ex Ch; *Simon, Israel & Co v Sedgwick* [1893] 1 QB 303, CA; *Hyderabad (Deccan) Co v Willoughby* [1899] 2 QB 530; *Robinson Gold Mining Co v Alliance Insurance Co* [1904] AC 359, HL; *Schloss Bros v Stevens* [1906] 2 KB 665, CA; *British and Foreign Marine Insurance Co Ltd v Gaunt* [1921] 2 AC 41, HL; *H Cousins & Co Ltd v D and C Carriers Ltd* [1971] 2 QB 230, [1971] 1 All ER 55, CA. For a clause by which goods were covered while temporarily placed on a quay see *Ide and Christie v Chalmers and White* (1900) 5 Com Cas 212.
7 *Apollinaris Co v Nord Deutsche Insurance Co* [1904] 1 KB 252; *British and Foreign Marine Insurance Co Ltd v Gaunt* [1921] 2 AC 41, HL.

38. Pollution by oil. Certain ships must be insured in respect of liability for pollution by oil[1]. A certificate that she is so insured must be in force before such a ship may enter or leave a port or terminal in the United Kingdom or, in certain cases, a foreign port or terminal[2]. Where it is alleged that the shipowner has incurred a liability as a result of any discharge or escape of oil occurring while there was in force a contract of insurance or other security to which such a certificate related, proceedings to enforce a claim in respect of the liability may be brought against the insurer[3]. In those proceedings it is a defence, in addition to any defence affecting the owner's liability, to prove that the discharge or escape was due to the wilful misconduct of the owner himself[4]. The insurer may limit his liability in respect of claims made against him by virtue of these provisions in like manner and to the same extent as the owner may limit his liability, but the insurer may do so whether or not the discharge or escape occurred without the owner's actual fault or privity[5].

1 See the Merchant Shipping (Oil Pollution) Act 1971 s 10(1) (amended as from a day to be appointed by the Merchant Shipping Act 1988 ss 34, 57(5), Schs 4, 7); and SHIPPING vol 43 para 1206.
2 See the Merchant Shipping (Oil Pollution) Act 1971 s 10(2), (3) (s 10(3) amended as from a day to be appointed by the Merchant Shipping Act 1988 Sch 4); and SHIPPING vol 43 para 1206. For the meaning of 'United Kingdom' see para 2 note 10 ante.
3 Merchant Shipping (Oil Pollution) Act 1971 s 12(1) (as prospectively amended: see note 2 supra); see SHIPPING vol 43 para 1207.
4 Ibid s 12(2) (as prospectively amended: see note 2 supra); see SHIPPING vol 43 para 1207.
5 Ibid s 12(3) (as prospectively amended: see note 2 supra). Where the owner and the insurer each apply to the court for the limitation of his liability, any sum paid into court in pursuance of either application is to be treated as paid also in pursuance of the other: s 12(4). The Third Parties (Rights against Insurers) Act 1930 (see paras 679–684 post) does not apply in relation to any contract of insurance to which a certificate under the Merchant Shipping (Oil Pollution) Act 1971 s 10 relates: s 12(5). See SHIPPING vol 43 para 1207.

(2) INSURANCE POLICIES

(i) The Policy

39. Contents and admissibility. Marine policies vary greatly in form and in the clauses they contain, but every policy must specify the name of the assured or of some person who effects the insurance on his behalf[1]. Subject to any statutory provisions, a contract of marine insurance[2] is inadmissible in evidence unless it is embodied in a marine policy in accordance with the Marine Insurance Act 1906[3].

1 Marine Insurance Act 1906 s 23(1).
2 For the meaning of 'contract of marine insurance' see para 35 ante.
3 Marine Insurance Act 1906 s 22. The policy may be executed and issued either at the time when the contract is concluded or afterwards: s 22. The contract contained in an insurance slip is therefore unenforceable: *Fisher v Liverpool Marine Insurance Co* (1874) LR 9 QB 418; see para 89 post.

40. Subscription. A marine policy must be signed by or on behalf of the insurer[1]. In the case of a corporation the corporate seal is sufficient, but the subscription of a corporation is not required to be under seal[2]; the form of execution may be infinitely varied by the statute, charter, deed or memorandum of association under which a company is constituted or the articles of association by which it is regulated[3].

1 Marine Insurance Act 1906 s 24(1).
2 Ibid s 24(1).
3 See *Reid v Allan, Cross v Allan* (1849) 4 Exch 326; *Dowdall v Allan, Dowdall v Clark* (1849) 19 LJQB 41. As to the execution of contracts by corporations see CORPORATIONS vol 9 para 1370. As to subscription by two or more individual underwriters see the Marine Insurance Act 1906 s 24(2): para 21 ante.

41. Types of policy. A marine policy may be made for a voyage, or for time, or both for a voyage and for time; in addition, it may be a floating policy[1]. Further, a policy may be valued or unvalued[2], or valued as to part of the subject matter insured and unvalued as to the remainder.

A voyage policy is one where the contract is to insure the subject matter 'at and from' or from one place to another or others; and a policy is a time policy where the contract is to insure the subject matter for a definite period of time[3].

A floating policy is one which describes the insurance in general terms, and leaves the name of the ship or ships and other particulars to be defined by subsequent declaration[4]. There are also floating policies which cover shipments of goods made on a given ship within a certain period of time fixed by the policy, as declared by the assured; but such floating policies are really insurances of goods for a series of voyages[5].

A valued policy is a policy which specifies the agreed value of the subject matter insured[6]; an unvalued policy is one which does not specify the value of the subject matter insured but, subject to the limit of the sum insured, leaves the insurable value to be subsequently ascertained[7].

1 See the text and notes infra.
2 Marine Insurance Act 1906 s 27(1).
3 Ibid s 25(1). The word 'definite' means 'specified'. The period is sufficiently specified if the policy specifies a stated period, even though that period is determinable on notice, and even though the insurance will be renewed or continued automatically at the end of the period unless determined, or will continue under a continuation clause: *Compania Maritima San Basilio SA v Oceanus Mutual Underwriting Association (Bermuda) Ltd, The Eurysthenes* [1977] QB 49, [1976] 3 All ER 243, CA. As to continuation clauses see para 121 post. A contract for both voyage and time may be included in the same policy: Marine Insurance Act 1906 s 25(1). In *Wilson v Boag* [1956] 2 Lloyd's Rep 564 (NSW SC) a policy covering a motor launch for four and a half months within a limited radius was held to be a time policy and not a mixed policy. In *M Almojil Establishment v Malayan Motor and General Underwriters (Pte) Ltd, The Al Jubail IV* [1982] 2 Lloyd's Rep 637 (Sing CA) where a vessel was insured for 12 months from and on the voyage from Singapore to the Persian Gulf and while trading within the Gulf, it was held that the policy was a 'mixed policy'.
4 Marine Insurance Act 1906 s 29(1): see further para 109 post.
5 See *Johnson & Co Ltd v Bryant* (1896) 12 TLR 368.
6 Marine Insurance Act 1906 s 27(2).
7 Ibid s 28. As to the ascertainment of the insurable value see para 255 et seq post. See also *Berger and Light Diffusers Pty Ltd v Pollock* [1973] 2 Lloyd's Rep 442. Unvalued policies are rare.

42. Attributes of valued policy. The difference in form between a valued policy and an unvalued policy[1] is that in a valued policy the blank in the valuation clause[2] is filled up with the sum at which the parties agree to value the subject matter insured, whereas in an unvalued policy it is left blank. The difference in legal effect between the two policies is that in the case of an unvalued policy the value of the subject matter insured is not admitted but has to be subsequently ascertained, whereas in the case of a valued policy, unless it is voidable on the ground of fraud or for some other reason[3], the value fixed by the policy is, as between the insurer and the assured, conclusive of the value of the subject intended to be insured whether the loss is total or partial[4]. Thus, if a ship that has been worth £800,000 is so damaged that she is not worth repairing, but, this fact being unknown to the assured, he effects an insurance upon her, whilst in that condition, by a policy for £600,000 valued at £800,000, and after the policy has attached the vessel is wholly destroyed by a storm, the valuation is binding and the assured is entitled to recover £600,000[5].

1　For the meaning of 'valued policy' and 'unvalued policy' see para 41 ante.
2　For the valuation clause contained in the statutory form of marine policy see para 905 post.
3　As to the avoidance of policies see para 215 et seq post.
4　Marine Insurance Act 1906 s 27(3). The value fixed by the policy is not, however, unless the policy otherwise provides, conclusive for determining whether there has been a constructive total loss: s 27(4); and see para 297 post.
5　*Barker v Janson* (1868) LR 3 CP 303; *Woodside v Globe Marine Insurance Co Ltd* [1896] 1 QB 105. Subject as indicated in note 4 supra, the valuation is binding generally, and not merely in cases where the question is as to the amount payable by underwriters in case of loss, for the valuation constitutes as between the parties a conclusive admission as to the value of the subject matter to which it refers: *Muirhead v Forth and North Sea Steamboat Mutual Insurance Association* [1894] AC 72 at 79, HL. It has been held, for example, to be binding on the parties to the contract with reference to questions of general average, contribution and subrogation: *Balmoral SS Co v Marten* [1902] AC 511, HL; *North of England Iron SS Insurance Association v Armstrong* (1870) LR 5 QB 244; and see also *Loders and Nucoline Ltd v Bank of New Zealand* (1929) 45 TLR 203. Where a policy on goods 'and/or advance freight valued at £26,025' contained a clause stating 'claims if any to pay at the rate of $4.15 to the £ sterling' but also contained a clause providing for payment of a total loss in sterling, it was held that the former clause had no application to a claim for total loss, but must be treated as applying only to claims for expense which might have been incurred in dollars: *Howard, Houlder & Partners v Union Marine Insurance Co Ltd* (1922) 38 TLR 515, HL.

43.　Opening of valuation. The parties are, however, only bound by the valuation as far as it goes, and it is therefore always permissible for the underwriter to show that part only of the subject matter intended to be valued in the policy was actually at risk[1]. For instance, if the insurance is on a cargo valued at £300,000 and the goods at risk amounted to only half a cargo, the underwriter in case of a total loss is liable only for £150,000. Similarly, if freight is valued at £600,000 and is intended to be freight for a full cargo, and only one-half of such a full cargo is loaded, the underwriter in case of total loss is liable only for £300,000. In this sense, and to this extent only, can the valuation be opened in the foregoing and similar cases[2]. The question as to what was intended to be valued in the valuation clause depends upon the parties' intention, and that intention is to be ascertained from the words of the clause having regard to the circumstances under which the contract of insurance was made[3].

1　Marine Insurance Act 1906 s 75(2).
2　In the following cases the valuation was opened because the whole of the subject intended to be valued was not at risk: *Forbes v Aspinall* (1811) 13 East 323 at 327 (freight); *Rickman v Carstairs* (1833) 5 B & Ad 651; *Tobin v Harford* (1864) 17 CBNS 528, Ex Ch (goods). See also note 3 infra.
3　*Williams v North China Insurance Co* (1876) 1 CPD 757, CA; *Denoon v Home and Colonial Assurance Co* (1872) LR 7 CP 341; *The Main* [1894] P 320. In club insurances on freight it is common to include a clause stating that 'in the event of the total loss of a ship, the amount insured shall be deemed the owner's interest at risk, and he shall be paid such amount whether the vessel be loaded, in ballast or under charter'. Such a clause amounts to a binding valuation of the freight covering whatsoever may be the nature of the freight lost by reason of the total loss of the ship. As to mutual insurance clubs see paras 341–346 post.

44.　Lloyd's policy. The forms of marine policy are numerous, but almost all policies effected in the United Kingdom were framed on the model of a policy called the 'Lloyd's policy'[1], which is recognised in and scheduled to the Marine Insurance Act 1906[2]. Most of the law of marine insurance is, in essence, pure interpretation of the contract contained in the common form of marine policy[3].

The language used in this policy, which in its essentials was introduced into England over three centuries ago, was both ungrammatical and obscure[4] and was not intelligible without the aid of usage and judicial decisions; but its meaning was determined by certain rules of construction, as well as by usage and statutory provisions subject to the provisions of the Marine Insurance Act 1906, and unless the context of a policy otherwise requires, the terms and expressions mentioned in the statutory rules for the construction of a policy of marine insurance in the form scheduled to the Act[5], or in other like form, have the scope and meaning assigned to them by those rules[6].

In 1982 a new form of Lloyd's Marine Policy was adopted[7]. It is used in connection with the Institute Clauses issued by the Institute of London Underwriters and revised from time to time[8].

1 The form of Lloyd's policy is set out in Appendix 1, para 905 post. The various blanks in the policy are generally filled in by written words, and in order to meet the exigencies of commerce special clauses are inserted or incorporated by way of reference; see, for instance, the York-Antwerp Rules 1974 set out in Appendix 2, para 907 post.
2 See the Marine Insurance Act 1906 s 30(1), Sch 1. See, however, text and notes 7–8 infra.
3 *Kulukundis v Norwich Union Fire Insurance Society* [1937] 1 KB 1 at 34, [1936] 2 All ER 242 at 269, CA, per Scott LJ.
4 *Marsden v Reid* (1803) 3 East 572 at 579 per Lawrence J; *Le Cheminant v Pearson* (1812) 4 Taunt 367 at 380 per Mansfield CJ; *Forestal Land, Timber and Railways Co Ltd v Rickards* [1941] KB 225 at 246–247, [1940] 4 All ER 395 at 403, CA, per MacKinnon LJ; affd sub nom *Rickards v Forestal Land, Timber and Railways Co Ltd* [1942] AC 50, [1941] 3 All ER 62, HL.
5 The form of the policy, which is known as the Lloyd's policy (see supra), and the rules governing its construction, are contained in the Marine Insurance Act 1906 Sch 1; the form is set out in Appendix 1, para 905 post, and the rules are cited in the various places in this title where the expressions concerned are considered.
6 Ibid s 30(2).
7 See Appendix 1 para 906 post. The policies issued by marine insurance companies are in a similar form.
8 The most important of these clauses are the Institute Time Clauses (Hulls), the Institute Voyage Clauses (Hulls), the Institute Time Clauses (Freight), the Institute Voyage Clauses (Freight), the Institute Cargo Clauses (A), the Institute Cargo Clauses (B), the Institute Cargo Clauses (C), the Institute War and Strikes Clauses (Hulls-Time), the Institute War and Strikes Clauses (Freight-Time), the Institute War and Strikes Clauses (Freight-Voyage), the Institute War Clauses (Cargo) and the Institute Strike Clauses (Cargo). The Institute Clauses are set out in Ivamy's Marine Insurance (4th Edn) at 516 et seq.

(ii) Construction of Marine Policies

45. General principles. A contract of marine insurance[1] is to be construed, like all other commercial instruments[2], so as to give effect to the parties' intention as expressed in the written contract[3]. The most general rule of construction is that the policy is to be construed according to its sense and meaning, as collected in the first place from the terms used in it; and these terms are to be understood in their plain, ordinary and popular sense[4], unless they have by the known usage of trade acquired a peculiar meaning distinct from the popular sense of the same words, or unless the context evidently points out that they must in the particular instance, and in order to effectuate the parties' immediate intention, be understood in some other special and peculiar sense[5].

1 For the meaning of 'contract of marine insurance' see para 35 ante.
2 The construction of written instruments in general is considered in DEEDS vol 12 para 1459 et seq.
3 *Carr v Montefiore* (1864) 5 B & S 408 at 428, Ex Ch, per Erle CJ; and see DEEDS vol 12 para 1471. On the question whether a contract made abroad should be construed by English or foreign law see CONFLICT OF LAWS vol 8 para 608; and *Royal Exchange Assurance Corpn v Sjoforsakrings Akt Vega* [1901]

2 KB 567 at 574; affd [1902] 2 KB 384 at 393, CA; *Armadora Occidental SA v Horace Mann Insurance Co* [1977] 1 All ER 347.

4 See eg *Bristol SS Corpn v London Assurance and Linard, The Delfini* [1976] 2 Lloyd's Rep 741 (Dist Ct, Southern Dist NY), where the words 'port risk' were held to mean 'a risk upon a vessel lying in port and before she has taken her departure on another voyage'; *Stolos Compania SA v Ajax Insurance Co Ltd, The Admiral C* [1981] 1 Lloyd's Rep 9, CA, where a term in the policy which stated that claims were to be 'collected' through certain brokers was held to mean 'collected in cash', and not 'brought into account between brokers and insurers in the manner customary in the market'.

5 *Robertson v French* (1803) 4 East 130 at 135 per Lord Ellenborough CJ, applied in *Hart v Standard Marine Insurance Co* (1889) 22 QBD 499 at 501, CA; *Birrell v Dryer* (1884) 9 App Cas 345, HL. See CUSTOM AND USAGE vol 12 paras 465–466; DEEDS vol 12 paras 1464, 1468.

46. Printed and written words. One of the most important of the rules of construction which have reference only to the words actually used, and not to the admission of extrinsic evidence for the purpose of explaining or adding to the contract, is that full effect must, if possible, be given to every provision, written or printed, contained in the policy, even though it may be one which the assured would have rejected had it been present to his mind at the time of his entering into the contract[1]. Greater weight is, in case of inconsistency[2], given to a written than to a printed clause, inasmuch as the written words are the immediate language and terms selected by the parties themselves for the expression of their meaning, whereas the printed words are a general formula adapted equally to their case and that of all other contracting parties upon similar occasions and subjects[3].

Printed words will, therefore, be considered as struck out if they are completely inconsistent with the written words, or if it is clear that the latter were to be in substitution for the former[4]. For a similar reason no effect will be given to a printed clause in a policy where it is inconsistent with the object and purpose of the insurance[5]. Thus, no effect will be given to the suing and labouring clause contained in a policy of reinsurance which also contains a written clause excluding liability for salvage charges[6], or in a policy indemnifying the shipowners against liability to owners of cargo for negligence[7].

1 *Pearson v Commercial Union Assurance Co* (1876) 1 App Cas 498, HL; *Haughton v Empire Marine Insurance Co* (1866) LR 1 Exch 206; *Calmar SS Corpn v Scott, The Portman* [1953] 1 Lloyd's Rep 485 at 488 (US SC) per Frankfurter J ('construing such conglomerate provisions requires a skill not unlike that called for in the decipherment of obscure palimpsest texts').

2 *Gumm v Tyrie* (1864) 4 B & S 680 at 707 per Crompton J; affd (1865) 6 B & S 298, Ex Ch.

3 *Robertson v French* (1803) 4 East 130 at 136; *Joyce v Realm Marine Insurance Co* (1872) LR 7 QB 580 at 583 per Blackburn J; *Dudgeon v Pembroke* (1877) 2 App Cas 284 at 293, HL, per Lord Penzance; cf *G H Renton & Co Ltd v Palmyra Trading Corpn of Panama* [1957] AC 149 at 168, [1956] 3 All ER 957 at 965, HL, per Lord Morton of Henryton; and *Glynn v Margetson & Co* [1893] AC 351, HL. See DEEDS vol 12 para 1503.

4 Cf *G H Renton & Co Ltd v Palmyra Trading Corpn of Panama* [1956] 1 QB 462 at 501, [1956] 1 All ER 209 at 222, CA, per Jenkins LJ (where there is not complete repugnancy between written words and the printed form the court will limit or modify the conflicting printed words); affd [1957] AC 149, [1956] 3 All ER 957, HL.

5 *Hydarnes SS Co v Indemnity Mutual Marine Assurance Co* [1895] 1 QB 500, CA (clause as to commencement of risk); and see *Dudgeon v Pembroke* (1877) 2 App Cas 284 at 293, HL; contrast *Beacon Life and Fire Assurance Co v Gibb* (1862) 1 Moo PCCNS 73 ('premises' in fire policy applied to ship); *Bensaude v Thames and Mersey Marine Insurance Co* [1897] AC 609 at 613, HL; *Marten v Vestey Bros Ltd* [1920] AC 307, HL. In the last-named case, Lords Haldane and Atkinson thought that in attempting to discover the duration of the risk in a policy on a ship, conclusions might be drawn from the printed words relating to goods. Lord Dunedin strongly dissented from this view. Printed clauses attached to the policy will probably be given greater weight in cases of inconsistency than the printed clauses in the body of the policy.

6 *Western Assurance Co of Toronto v Poole* [1903] 1 KB 376. As to the suing and labouring clause see paras 259–262 post.
7 *Cunard SS Co Ltd v Marten* [1903] 2 KB 511, CA (affg [1902] 2 KB 624 at 627 per Walton J, applied in *Western Assurance Co of Toronto v Poole* [1903] 1 KB 376).

47. Surrounding circumstances. Another general rule of construction is that, in interpreting an instrument, all the surrounding circumstances known to the parties at the time of the making of the contract must be looked at[1], and that where the words of the contract are ambiguous, the acts, conduct and course of dealing of the parties before and at the time they entered into it may and should be considered and taken into account with a view to discovering the parties' intention as expressed by them in the contract[2].

1 *Carr v Montefiore* (1864) 5 B & S 408 at 428, Ex Ch, per Erle CJ; *Lewis v Great Western Rly Co* (1877) 3 QBD 195 at 208, CA (forwarding note); *Gurney v Grimmer* (1932) 38 Com Cas 7, CA (history of reinsurance clause considered in construing current form of the clause).
2 *Houlder Bros & Co Ltd v Public Works Comr, Public Works Comr v Houlder Bros & Co Ltd* [1908] AC 276 at 285, PC (demurrage clause in contract of sale); *Bank of New Zealand v Simpson* [1900] AC 182 at 188, PC; *Montefiore v Lloyd* (1863) 15 CBNS 203; *Leathley v Spyer* (1870) LR 5 CP 595, which were actions on contracts guaranteeing that an employee would duly pay over money received, and decided entirely by reference to the surrounding circumstances; and see DEEDS vol 12 para 1490.

48. Technical words. Words used in a policy may be technical words not employed in ordinary language; in that case evidence may be given of their technical meaning as if they were words in a foreign language. Although the words used may have an ordinary meaning, evidence may nevertheless be adduced to show that they have a different and peculiar meaning in insurance business or in the export or import trade to which the particular insurance relates, and effect will be given to that secondary meaning unless it appears from the circumstances of the case or the terms of the policy that this was not the parties' intention[1]. Again, it may be shown that the word 'port' has in the business sense a more or less extensive meaning than its legal or political limits, and in that case effect will be given to its business sense[2].

1 *Mason v Skurray* (1780) 1 Park's Marine Insurances (8th Edn) 253. See also DEEDS vol 12 paras 1466, 1494.
2 *Constable v Noble* (1810) 2 Taunt 403; *Payne v Hutchinson* (1810) 2 Taunt 405n; *Cockey v Atkinson* (1819) 2 B & Ald 460; *Brown v Tayleur* (1835) 4 Ad & El 241; *Garston Sailing Ship Co v Hickie* (1885) 15 QBD 580, CA, per Brett MR; *Hunter v Northern Marine Insurance Co* (1888) 13 App Cas 717 at 733, HL, per Lord Watson.

49. Geographical terms. Where words descriptive of seas or countries have among businessmen a sense differing from their common or geographical import, evidence of their business meaning is admissible, and effect will be given to that meaning[1]. Thus, where an insurance is effected 'from London to any port in the Baltic', although according to geographers the Gulf of Finland is not included in the Baltic, on evidence showing that it is included in the Baltic in commercial parlance the court will give this extended meaning to the term 'Baltic' in the policy[2].

1 *Uhde v Walters* (1811) 3 Camp 16; *Moxon v Atkins* (1812) 3 Camp 200; *Royal Exchange Assurance Corpn v Tod* (1892) 8 TLR 669; and see CUSTOM AND USAGE vol 12 paras 488–489. In the following

cases the attempt to prove a special business meaning was unsuccessful: *Robertson v Clarke* (1824) 1 Bing 445 at 451; *Northey v Trevillion* (1902) 7 Com Cas 201; *Birrell v Dryer* (1884) 9 App Cas 345, HL; and see *Houghton v Gilbart* (1836) 7 C & P 701 (dictionary insufficient evidence).
2 *Uhde v Walters* (1811) 3 Camp 16.

50. Special rules. The following rules, of a more special and limited character, are often applied to policies of insurance. Where a particular list of causes is followed by such words as 'or other', the latter expression must in some cases be limited to matters ejusdem generis[1]. Again, there is an important rule of construction that marine insurance contracts only extend to cover losses proximately caused by the perils insured against. These two rules are discussed more fully elsewhere[2].

Moreover, where there is a latent ambiguity as to the subject matter of the policy, external evidence is admissible for the purpose of identifying it[3]. Finally, where an ambiguity cannot be removed by any other rule of construction the contra proferentem rule[4] may be applied[5], it being, however, left for determination in each case, as regards any special provision in the policy, whether the assured or the insurers are to be considered the *proferentes* within the meaning of the rule[6].

1 For a full explanation of this rule see Lord Watson's judgment in *Sun Fire Office v Hart* (1889) 14 App Cas 98 at 103, PC; and see *Bolivia Republic v Indemnity Mutual Marine Assurance Co Ltd* [1909] 1 KB 785, CA. For a general consideration of the ejusdem generis rule see DEEDS vol 12 para 1526.
2 See paras 175–176, 905 post.
3 *Macdonald v Longbottom* (1860) 1 E & E 987, Ex Ch; *Irving v Richardson* (1831) 2 B & Ad 193; *Bank of New Zealand v Simpson* [1900] AC 182, PC; cf *Birrell v Dryer* (1884) 9 App Cas 345, HL, where the court found no ambiguity. See also DEEDS vol 12 para 1501.
4 Ie the maxim *verba cartarum fortius accipiuntur contra proferentem*: the words of deeds are to be interpreted most strongly against him who uses them.
5 *Fowkes v Manchester and London Life Assurance and Loan Association* (1863) 3 B & S 917 at 929; *Thomson v Weems* (1884) 9 App Cas 671 at 687, HL; *Re Etherington and Lancashire and Yorkshire Accident Insurance Co* [1909] 1 KB 591 at 596, CA. As to this maxim see further DEEDS vol 12 paras 1472–1473; *Capital Coastal Shipping Corpn and Bulk Towing Corpn v Hartford Fire Insurance Co (United States of America, third party), The Cristie* [1975] 2 Lloyd's Rep 100 (Dist Ct, Eastern Dist Virginia) (where a warranty stated that a particular person should be the master of the vessel, the warranty was not construed contra proferentem because the evidence indicated that the assured had a clear understanding of its importance and operation and could not therefore contend that it was too vague).
6 It has been said that in dealing with the construction of policies, whether life, fire or marine, an ambiguous clause must be construed against rather than in favour of the insurer (*Re Etherington and Lancashire and Yorkshire Accident Insurance Co* [1909] 1 KB 591 at 596, CA, per Vaughan Williams LJ); but it is submitted that this proposition is inconsistent with the judgments in *Birrell v Dryer* (1884) 9 App Cas 345, HL, and with the other authorities cited in note 5 supra, at any rate as regards marine policies, which (unlike fire and life policies) are framed in accordance with the slip prepared by the assured's broker (see para 89 post). See also *Stewart & Co v Merchants Marine Insurance Co Ltd* (1885) 16 QBD 619 at 626–627, CA, per Lord Esher MR; *Bartlett & Partners Ltd v Meller* [1961] 1 Lloyd's Rep 487; and para 398 post. The last sentence of the text in an earlier edition of this work was approved by Maugham LJ in *A S Ocean v Black Sea and Baltic General Insurance Co Ltd* (1935) 51 Ll L Rep 305 at 310, CA. See also per Greer LJ at 307.

(iii) Usage

51. Evidence of usage. The language of a marine policy is so general and indeterminate that it requires, in a far greater degree than most other commercial contracts, to be supplemented by evidence of usage[1]. Such evidence is admissible not merely for the purpose of explaining ambiguous terms in the contract[2], but also for the purpose of adding incidents to it subject, however, always to the following two conditions, namely that:

(1) the usage must not be inconsistent with the express terms of the contract[3]; and

(2) it must be general and notorious in insurance business, or in the particular trade to which the contract relates, and not unreasonable[4].

Thus, looking at a policy it will be found that the voyage insured is mainly defined by naming the port of departure and the port of destination so that the course to be pursued by the vessel on the voyage between those two ports must necessarily be determined by usage. What is usually done on the insured voyage with reference to ship or cargo is understood to be implied in every policy and to make a part of it as if it were expressed in it[5]. In accordance with this principle, intermediate voyages and goods landed and stored are held to be covered by the policy if there is a general and well-known usage for ships engaged on the insured voyage to make such intermediate voyages, or for goods to be landed and stored in the course of it[6].

1 The nature of usages, their admission in evidence, and the proof required is discussed generally in CUSTOM AND USAGE vol 12 paras 426–428. As to particular marine insurance usages see CUSTOM AND USAGE vol 12 para 489 note 2.

2 As to an example of reference to usage for explaining the terms of a policy see *Otago Farmers' Co-op Association of New Zealand v Thompson* [1910] 2 KB 145.

3 Where any right, duty or liability would arise under a contract of marine insurance by implication of law, it may be negatived or varied by express agreement, or by usage, if the usage is such as to bind both parties to the contract (Marine Insurance Act 1906 s 87(1)), and this provision extends to any right, duty or liability declared by that Act which may be lawfully modified by agreement (s 87(2)); see also CUSTOM AND USAGE vol 12 para 447 note 1.

4 See further para 53 post.

5 *Pelly v Royal Exchange Assurance Co* (1757) 1 Burr 341 at 350 per Lord Mansfield.

6 *Pelly v Royal Exchange Assurance Co* (1757) 1 Burr 341; *Tierney v Etherington* (1743), cited in *Pelly v Royal Exchange Assurance Co* supra at 348 (as to storing goods). As to the effect of usages existing in the Newfoundland trade see *Noble v Kennoway* (1780) 2 Doug KB 510; *Vallance v Dewar* (1808) 1 Camp 503; *Ougier v Jennings* (1800) 1 Camp 505n per Lord Eldon CJ. As to usages in the China and East Indian trades see *Pelly v Royal Exchange Assurance Co* supra; *Brough v Whitmore* (1791) 4 Term Rep 206; *Salvador v Hopkins, Heaton v Rucker* (1765) 3 Burr 1707; *Gregory v Christie* (1784) 3 Doug KB 419; *Farquharson v Hunter* (1785) 1 Park's Marine Insurance (8th Edn) 105. Many illustrations of the same principle will be found in the section on deviation, duration and commencement of the risk (see para 121 et seq post), where it is shown that deviation may be justified by usage, and that the commencement and duration of the risk may be affected by the usages of maritime trade and business. See also *Kingston v Knibbs* (1808) 1 Camp 508n; *Moxon v Atkins* (1812) 3 Camp 200; *Brown v Carstairs* (1811) 3 Camp 161; and CUSTOM AND USAGE vol 12 paras 487–489.

52. Usage consistent with express terms. No usage will be allowed to affect a contract of insurance unless it is consistent with the express terms of the contract; in other words, evidence of usage is never admissible to contradict what is plain[1]. Thus, where the risk on goods is expressed by the policy to be 'till discharged and safely landed', evidence of usage will not be admitted to show that this clause means, in the particular trade insured, until the ship was moored 24 hours in safety, because this is inconsistent with the plain language of the policy[2].

1 *Blackett v Royal Exchange Assurance Co* (1832) 2 Cr & J 244 at 249 per Lord Lyndhurst CB; *Provincial Insurance Co of Canada v Leduc* (1874) LR 6 PC 224 at 235; *Hall v Janson* (1855) 4 E & B 500; *Crofts v Marshall* (1836) 7 C & P 597 at 607; and see CUSTOM AND USAGE vol 12 paras 463–466.

2 *Parkinson v Collier* (1797) 2 Park's Marine Insurances (8th Edn) 653. It seems probable that an established usage cannot be excluded by oral agreement: see *Fawkes v Lamb* (1862) 31 LJQB 98;

Arnould on Marine Insurance (16th Edn) s 64; and the conflicting judgments of Blackburn J and Cockburn CJ in *Burges v Wickham* (1863) 3 B & S 669 at 685, 697. It is, however, not of much practical importance, as there is no reason why the policy should not be rectified if it is drawn up so as not to express the common intention of both parties: see *Xenos v Wickham* (1863) 14 CBNS 435 at 459, Ex Ch, per Blackburn J.

53. Usage to be general and notorious. The usage, in order to be binding, must be general and notorious[1]. It need not be a usage of the whole commercial world of which the court would take judicial notice[2], but the usage merely of a particular place or a particular class of persons is not binding on other persons unless they are shown to be cognisant of it and have contracted with reference to it[3]. The usage, however, need not be followed invariably at all times and by all persons in the trade; if it is notorious and prevails generally in the trade, the assured and underwriter are presumed to have notice of it and are bound by it[4].

It is also immaterial that the trade itself is of recent origin; it is sufficient if the usage has existed in such circumstances that it may be fairly presumed to be known to persons engaged in the trade, and that contracts of insurance relating to it are made with reference to that usage[5]. In order to be binding, at any rate on persons not cognisant of it, the usage must be one which is not unreasonable[6].

The Association of Average Adjusters holds meetings from time to time at which rules of practice are established, but as these rules are always intended to be altered or modified with reference to leading decisions they are not, if inconsistent with legal principles, binding on parties to the contract of insurance, unless they are expressly incorporated in the policy[7], as is commonly the case with the York-Antwerp Rules 1974[8].

1 See CUSTOM AND USAGE vol 12 para 451.
2 *Vallance v Dewar* (1808) 1 Camp 503.
3 *Bartlett v Pentland* (1830) 10 B & C 760 at 770 per Lord Tenterden CJ; *Gabay v Lloyd* (1825) 3 B & C 793; *Scott v Irving* (1830) 1 B & Ad 605; *Sweeting v Pearce* (1861) 9 CBNS 534; *Matveieff v Crossfield* (1903) 8 Com Cas 120; *Stewart v Aberdein* (1838) 4 M & W 211, where the plaintiff's acquaintance with the usage of Lloyd's was proved; contrast *McCowin Lumber and Export Co Inc v Pacific Marine Insurance Co Ltd* (1922) 38 TLR 901; *Provincial Insurance Co Ltd v Crowder* (1927) 27 Ll L Rep 28.
4 *Vallance v Dewar* (1808) 1 Camp 503; *Russell v Provincial Insurance Co Ltd* [1959] 2 Lloyd's Rep 275 ('breasting' not same as 'towing').
5 Evidence of usage in one trade is admissible to prove that the same usage is binding on those engaged in another trade of the same kind carried on in the same way: *Noble v Kennoway* (1780) 2 Doug KB 510.
6 *Ougier v Jennings* (1800) 1 Camp 505n; *Robinson v Mollett* (1875) LR 7 HL 802 at 817–818 per Brett J; and see CUSTOM AND USAGE vol 12 paras 453–454.
7 See *Atwood v Sellar & Co* (1879) 4 QBD 342 at 363; affd (1880) 5 QBD 286 at 289, CA. These rules of practice are set out in Ivamy's Marine Insurance (4th Edn) 570 App V.
8 These rules are set out in Appendix 2, para 907 post.

(iv) Warranties

A. GENERAL NATURE

54. Nature of warranty. In the statutory provisions as to marine insurance, a warranty means a promissory warranty, that is a warranty by which the assured[1] undertakes that some particular thing is or is not to be done or that some condition is to be fulfilled, or whereby he affirms or negatives the existence of a particular state of facts[2]. Thus, a warranty may be an undertaking that the thing insured is neutral property, or that the ship insured sailed on a certain day, or that all was well at a given time, or that the ship is to sail on or before a given day, or that she will depart with convoy in time of war, etc.

A warranty may be express or implied[3]. An express warranty does not exclude an implied warranty unless inconsistent with it[4]. Thus, if a policy on cattle provides that the fittings of a ship are to be approved by a Lloyd's surveyor and they are so approved by him, the warranty of seaworthiness is not excluded by the express provision as to the approval of the fittings[5].

An express warranty must be included in, or written upon, the policy, or must be contained in some document incorporated by reference into the policy[6].

A warranty is implied if it is a condition implied by law such as, for example, a warranty in a voyage policy[7] that the ship is seaworthy at the commencement of the voyage.

1 As to the use of the term 'the assured' see para 35 note 1 ante.
2 Marine Insurance Act 1906 s 33(1). The term 'warranty' in contracts of marine insurance must be distinguished from that term as used in other contracts. A warranty in relation to a marine insurance contract is the equivalent of a condition in the general law of contract; cf CONTRACT vol 9 para 542. As used in contracts of marine insurance, a warranty is expressed to be a promissory warranty (s 33(1)), and a condition (s 33(3)).
3 Ibid s 33(2). As to express warranties see paras 57–63 post. As to implied warranties see paras 64–75 post.
4 Ibid s 35(3).
5 *Sleigh v Tyser* [1900] 2 QB 333; *Quebec Marine Insurance Co v Commercial Bank of Canada* (1870) LR 3 PC 234; cf *Greenock SS Co v Maritime Insurance Co Ltd* [1903] 1 KB 367; affd [1903] 2 KB 657, CA.
6 Marine Insurance Act 1906 s 35(2); *Blackhurst v Cockell* (1789) 3 Term Rep 360; *Pawson v Barnevelt* (1778) 1 Doug KB 12 note 4; see *Bensaude v Thames and Mersey Marine Insurance Co* [1897] AC 609 at 612, HL, per Lord Halsbury. In *Yorkshire Insurance Co Ltd v Campbell* [1917] AC 218, PC, statements in a proposal form were held to be incorporated in the policy and to amount to a warranty. In *Edwards v Aberayron Mutual Ship Insurance Society* (1876) 1 QBD 563 at 586, 588, Ex Ch, Pollock B and Brett J expressed the view that extrinsic evidence is admissible to show what documents were intended by the parties to form one contract of insurance, This is questionable, however, unless the documents are connected by reference: see CONTRACT vol 9 para 287.
7 For the meaning of 'voyage policy' see para 41 ante.

55. Non-compliance with warranty. The essential characteristic of a warranty is that it is a condition which must be exactly complied with, whether it is material to the risk or not[1]. If it is not complied with then, subject to any express provision in the policy and to the effect of waiver of the breach by the insurer[2], the insurer is discharged from liability as from the date of the breach of warranty but without prejudice to any liability incurred by him before that date[3]. Discharge from liability is automatic and is not dependent on any decision by the insurer to treat the policy as at an end[4]. Furthermore, the assured cannot avail himself of the defence that the breach has been remedied, and the warranty complied with, before loss[5].

Any inquiry into the materiality or immateriality of the risk is entirely precluded, and so are all questions whether there has or has not been a substantial compliance with the warranty; where a warranty has been broken, even though the loss may not have been in the remotest degree connected with the breach, the underwriter is none the less discharged on that account from all liability for the loss[6]. Thus, where a ship warranted to sail with convoy in fact sails without it and is lost in a storm, the underwriter is not liable for the loss[7].

Subject to the two exceptions mentioned subsequently[8], no cause, however irresistible, will excuse non-compliance with a warranty, not even the direct and unavoidable operation of a peril expressly insured against. In short, the warranty is an absolute condition precedent[9]. A breach of warranty, whether express or implied, discharges the insurer from liability as from the date of the breach, and therefore in toto if the breach takes place at the commencement of the risk[10].

1 Marine Insurance Act 1906 s 33(3).
2 A breach of warranty may be waived by the insurer (ibid s 34(3): see para 65 post), unless it is a warranty of legality (see para 83 post). See *Daneau v Laurent Gendron Ltée (Union Insurance Society of Canton Ltd, third party)* [1964] 1 Lloyd's Rep 220 (Ex Ct, Que Adm Dist) (waiver of warranty as to period during which vessel was to be laid up); *Capital Coastal Shipping Corpn and Bulk Towing Corpn v Hartford Fire Insurance Co (United States of America, third party), The Cristie* [1975] 2 Lloyd's Rep 100 (Dist Ct, Eastern Dist Virginia) (warranty that particular person should be master of vessel not waived).
3 Marine Insurance Act 1906 s 33(3). The rule applies to a reinsurer unless the policy contains special terms which preclude his questioning the settlement made by the original insurer: see *Fireman's Fund Insurance Co v Western Australian Insurance Co Ltd and Atlantic Insurance Co Ltd* (1927) 33 Com Cas 36; and see also *Australian Widows' Fund Life Assurance Society Ltd v National Mutual Life Association of Australasia Ltd* [1914] AC 634, PC (life assurance); and para 206 note 2 post; *Overseas Commodities Ltd v Style* [1958] 1 Lloyd's Rep 546 (tins to be marked with code for verification of date of manufacture; marks inaccurate or missing); *Simons (Trading as Acme Credit Services) v Gale* [1958] 2 All ER 504, [1958] 1 WLR 678, PC (warranted all arrangements made for conversion of vessel at inception of the insurance); *Daneau v Laurent Gendron Ltée (Union Insurance Society of Canton Ltd, third party)* [1964] 1 Lloyd's Rep 220 (Ex Ct, Que. Adm Dist) (warranted that the vessel is to be laid up and out of commission between 16 November and 30 April); *Capital Coastal Shipping Corpn and Bulk Towing Corpn v Hartford Fire Insurance Co (United States of America, third party), The Cristie* [1975] 2 Lloyd's Rep 100 (Dist Ct, Eastern Dist Virginia) (warranted that the master of the insured vessel should be officer named); *Pindos Shipping Corpn v Raven, The Mata Hari* [1983] 2 Lloyd's Rep 449 (warranty class maintained); *Seavision Investment SA v Evennett and Clarkson Puckle Ltd, The Tiburon* [1990] 2 Lloyd's Rep 418 (warranted that insured vessel 'German FOM', ie flag, ownership and management).
4 *Bank of Nova Scotia v Hellenic Mutual War Risks Association (Bermuda) Ltd, The Good Luck* [1992] 1 AC 233, [1991] 3 All ER 1, HL.
5 Marine Insurance Act 1906 s 34(2); *Hibbert v Pigou* (1783) 3 Doug KB 224: cf para 66 text to note 2 post.
6 *Newcastle Fire Insurance Co v Macmorran & Co* (1815) 3 Dow 255, HL, per Lord Eldon (fire policy); *De Hahn v Hartley* (1786) 1 Term Rep 343; affd (1787) 2 Term Rep 186n, Ex Ch (no reason given).
7 *Hibbert v Pigou* (1783) 3 Doug KB 224.
8 See para 56 post.
9 *Hore v Whitmore* (1778) 2 Cowp 784; *Havelock v Hancill* (1789) 3 Term Rep 277, is not, as has been sometimes supposed, any authority to the contrary: see *Cory v Burr* (1883) 8 App Cas 393 at 401, HL, per Lord Blackburn.
10 See the Marine Insurance Act 1906 s 33(3).

56. When non-compliance excused. Non-compliance with a warranty is excused when:
(1) by reason of a change of circumstances, the warranty ceases to be applicable to the circumstances of the contract[1]: thus if, during a war, a warranty to sail with convoy at a given future time is inserted in the policy, the intervention of peace before that period would excuse the necessity of compliance[2]; or
(2) when the compliance with the warranty is rendered unlawful by any subsequent law[3].

1 Marine Insurance Act 1906 s 34(1).
2 See Arnould on Marine Insurance (16th Edn) s 688.
3 Marine Insurance Act 1906 s 34(1).

B. EXPRESS WARRANTIES

57. Form of warranty. An express warranty may be in any form of words from which the intention to warrant is to be inferred[1]. The word 'warranty' or 'warranted', for instance, is unnecessary. The words 'to sail on such a day', or 'in port', or 'all well' on such a day, etc, if written on the face of the policy, amount to an express warranty as much as any formal clause[2], and even the description of the vessel insured as being of a certain nation, as a Danish brig or the Swedish ship 'Sophia', will amount to an express warranty of her nationality[3]. It is sometimes a question, however, especially in time policies[4] effected with mutual assurance associations[5], whether a clause which purports to be a warranty should be held to be an exception and not a warranty[6].

1 Marine Insurance Act 1906 s 35(1). See *F B Walker & Sons Inc v Valentine* [1970] 2 Lloyd's Rep 429 (US 5th Cir), where the court found it unnecessary to decide whether a clause had the status of a warranty under Mississippi law because, on the facts, there had been no compliance with the clause.
2 In *Union Insurance Society of Canton Ltd v George Wills & Co* [1916] 1 AC 281, PC, cited in para 109 note 2 post, the words 'Declarations of interest to be made . . . as soon as possible after sailing of vessel . . .' were held to constitute a warranty.
3 *Kenyon v Berthon* (1778) 1 Doug KB 12n; *Baring v Clagett* (1802) 3 Bos & P 201; *Baring v Christie* (1804) 5 East 398; *Lothian v Henderson* (1803) 3 Bos & P 499, HL; cf *Clapham v Cologan* (1813) 3 Camp 382; *Dent v Smith* (1869) LR 4 QB 414 (no implied warranty against change of nationality). In *Seavision Investment SA v Evennett and Clarkson Puckle Ltd, The Tiburon* [1990] 2 Lloyd's Rep 418, the vessel was expressly 'warranted German FOM' (flag, ownership, management). A strained construction must not, however, be put on a statement in the policy so as to make it a warranty: *Muller v Thompson* (1811) 2 Camp 610. Calling a vessel the 'good ship A' in a time policy is not a warranty of seaworthiness: *Small v Gibson* (1849) 16 QB 141 at 157, Ex Ch; affd sub nom *Gibson v Small* (1853) 4 HL Cas 353.
4 For the meaning of 'time policy' see para 41 ante.
5 As to mutual insurance associations see paras 341–346 post.
6 See *Colledge v Harty* (1851) 6 Exch 205 (clause held to be a warranty).

58. Interpretation. Speaking generally, the same rules of construction apply to the interpretation of a warranty as apply to any other part of the policy. Thus, in order to carry out the parties' presumed intention, a clause 'warranted no iron' has been held to cover steel, and the word 'seamen' has been held to include boys as well as adult mariners[1]. In the following paragraphs attention is drawn to the more usual and important navigation warranties[2].

1 *Hart v Standard Marine Insurance Co* (1889) 22 QBD 499, CA; *Bean v Stupart* (1778) 1 Doug KB 11. Where a marine policy on a ship contained a warranty that the amount insured on ppi terms should not exceed a certain figure, it was held that the word 'insured' included insurance against war risks: *P Samuel & Co Ltd v Dumas* [1924] AC 431, HL. As to the meaning of 'warranted uninsured' see *Roddick v Indemnity Mutual Marine Insurance Co* [1895] 2 QB 380, CA; and *General Insurance Co of Trieste (Assicurazioni Generali) v Cory* [1897] 1 QB 335; and cf *Thames and Mersey Marine Insurance Co Ltd v Gunford Ship Co Ltd, Southern Marine Mutual Insurance Association v Gunford Ship Co Ltd* [1911] AC 529, HL. See also CUSTOM AND USAGE vol 12 paras 465–466; DEEDS vol 12 para 1468. Where a ship is insured 'in any lawful trade', these words must be confined to the trade on which the ship is sent by her owners, and therefore the assured who has sent her on a lawful voyage is not precluded from recovering for a loss occasioned by her being barratrously employed in a smuggling trade: *Havelock v Hancill* (1789) 3 Term Rep 277.
2 See para 59 et seq post. Many other kinds of warranties are inserted in policies; the forms themselves and the usages affecting them change, and it is of little use to refer to cases in which clauses so variable have been interpreted.

59. Warranties as to safety and time of departure. Where the subject matter insured is warranted 'well' or 'in good safety' on a particular day, it is sufficient if it is safe at any time during that day[1]. A warranty that the ship was in port on a given day would be construed in the same way[2].

Where a ship is warranted to sail or depart before or after a given day, the warranty must be exactly complied with, and if she sails or departs, in the former case after, and in the latter case before, the prescribed day, the underwriter is discharged from liability although the loss is not in the remotest degree connected with the time of her sailing or departing. Where a ship is insured 'at and from' an island, the whole island is considered as one starting point, and the ship is not considered as having sailed on her voyage until she has cleared away from the island with the purpose of proceeding directly to the port of destination[3].

In order to satisfy a general warranty to sail on or before a given day, the ship need not on or before that day proceed any great distance on her voyage, but must have moved from her moorings on or before that day with the genuine intention of prosecuting the voyage[4] and not solely for the sake of complying with the warranty[5]. Where a warranty is not merely a general warranty but a warranty to sail or depart from a given port before a given day, it is not enough that she has sailed; she must have left the port before that day[6].

Where, however, a voyage consists of different stages such as a river and a sea voyage, and the usual course of navigation is to perform them with different crews or equipment, the general warranty to sail on or before a given date only requires the vessel to sail on the earlier stage in the condition in which that part of the voyage is usually performed[7].

1 Marine Insurance Act 1906 s 38; *Blackhurst v Cockell* (1789) 3 Term Rep 360.
2 As to when a ship is 'in port' see *Hunter v Northern Marine Insurance Co* (1888) 13 App Cas 717, HL ('port' means port in the popular or commercial sense as understood by marine traders); cf para 133 post; and as to the meaning of 'port' in relation to an arrived ship see *The Johanna Oldendorff* [1973] 3 All ER 148, [1973] 3 WLR 382, HL; and SHIPPING.
3 *Vezian v Grant* (1779) Marshall on Marine Insurances (4th Edn) 284; and *Kenyon v Berthon* (1778) 1 Doug KB 12n; *Cruickshank v Janson* (1810) 2 Taunt 301.
4 *Bond v Nutt* (1777) 2 Cowp 601; *Earle v Harris* (1780) 1 Doug KB 357; *Thellusson v Fergusson* (1780) 1 Doug KB 360; *Thellusson v Staples, Thellusson v Pigou* (1780) 1 Doug KB 366n; *Cockrane v Fisher* (1835) 1 Cr M & R 809, Ex Ch; cf *Cruickshank v Jason* (1810) 2 Taunt 301; *Sea Insurance Co v Blogg* [1898] 2 QB 398, CA; *Mersey Mutual Underwriting Association Ltd v Poland* (1910) 26 TLR 386.
5 *Ridsdale v Newnham* (1815) 3 M & S 456; *Pittegrew v Pringle* (1832) 3 B & Ad 514; *Graham v Barras* (1834) 5 B & Ad 1011.
6 *Moir v Royal Exchange Assurance Co* (1815) 3 M & S 461; *Lang v Anderdon* (1824) 3 B & C 495 at 500. On an insurance on a ship at and from New York to Quebec, during her stay there, and thence to the United Kingdom, the ship being warranted to sail from Quebec on or before 1 November, the court held that the warranty only applied to the part of the voyage between Quebec and England, and that therefore the underwriters were liable for the loss of the ship between New York and Quebec after 1 November: *Baines v Holland* (1855) 10 Exch 802.
7 *Bouillon v Lupton* (1863) 15 CBNS 113. The decisions in *Ridsdale v Newnham* (1815) 3 M & S 456, and *Pittegrew v Pringle* (1832) 3 B & Ad 514, are scarcely reconcilable with the judgment in *Bouillon v Lupton* supra. For the meaning of the warranties 'not allowed to enter the Gulf of St Lawrence before' a certain date, and 'no St Lawrence between certain dates' see *Provincial Insurance Co of Canada v Leduc* (1874) LR 6 PC 224, and *Birrell v Dryer* (1884) 9 App Cas 345, HL. See also CUSTOM AND USAGE vol 12 para 466.

60. Warranty of neutrality. There is no implied warranty as to the nationality of a ship or that her nationality is not to be changed during the risk[1], but it often happens in time of war that the assured warrants the ship or goods to be neutral.

Such a warranty is called 'a warranty of neutrality'. If the property is enemy property, or ceases to have the character of neutrality because it is employed or dealt with in such a manner as to be liable to capture, the warranty is breached[2]. For instance, if a ship violates the law of blockade or is used in carrying enemy troops or is engaged in the enemy's coasting trade or is carrying contraband goods to the enemy, the ship in the former cases, and the goods in the last case, are not of a neutral character. What is meant by the word 'enemy', whether enemy by birth or by domicile, and in what circumstances property is or becomes enemy property or forfeits its neutral character, are questions sometimes of considerable difficulty appertaining to international and prize law and not to insurance law[3].

Again, by the general law of nations, and sometimes under treaties, a ship is bound to carry certain necessary documents to establish her neutrality, and if she makes default in so doing, or if she falsifies or suppresses her papers or uses simulated papers she may render herself liable to capture. In what circumstances she may so render herself liable is also a question belonging to prize or international law[4].

1 Marine Insurance Act 1906 s 37; *Clapham v Cologan* (1813) 3 Camp 382; *Dent v Smith* (1869) LR 4 QB 414.
2 See text to notes 3–4 infra; and para 61 post.
3 See PRIZE; WAR.
4 See PRIZE.

61. Statutory provisions as to warranty of neutrality. There are two statutory provisions relating to the warranty of neutrality[1] which to a certain extent modify previous decisions. The first of these provisions provides that where insurable property[2], whether ship[3] or goods, is expressly warranted neutral, there is an implied condition that the property is to have a neutral character at the commencement of the risk, and that so far as the assured can control the matter, its neutral character is to be preserved during the risk[4]. Therefore, if the property has not a neutral character at the commencement of the risk, the insurer can avoid the policy[5]; but if the property has lost its neutral character after the commencement of the risk, the insurer's liability depends upon whether this could have been prevented by the assured or his agents. For instance, the underwriter will not be discharged from liability if after the date of the insurance a war has broken out which has made the property enemy property; nor would an insurer of goods be discharged from liability if after the commencement of the risk the ship for the same reason ceased to have a neutral character[6].

The second of these provisions provides that where a ship is expressly warranted neutral, there is also an implied condition that, so far as the assured can control the matter, she is to be properly documented, that is to say that she is to carry the necessary papers to establish her neutrality, and that she is not to falsify or suppress her papers, or use simulated papers; if any loss occurs through breach of this condition, the insurer may avoid the contract[7]. This provision is applicable only so far as the assured can control the matter, and only to the case of the ship being warranted neutral and the ship's documents not being in order. In such a case the insurer is not liable for any loss occurring through breach of the condition. It seems, however, that he remains liable for any previous loss[8].

1 See para 60 ante.
2 For the meaning of 'insurable property' see para 36 ante.

3 'Ship' includes hovercraft: see para 36 note 2 ante.
4 Marine Insurance Act 1906 s 36(1).
5 *Woolmer v Muilman* (1763) 1 Wm Bl 427.
6 *Eden v Parkison* (1781) 2 Doug KB 732. The statement in the text does not apply to an outbreak of war between the assured's country and the United Kingdom: see para 78 post.
7 Marine Insurance Act 1906 s 36(2).
8 Proper documents are those required by the general law of nations or by treaty, and do not include those which are only required by the ordinances of the belligerent power: *Price v Bell* (1801) 1 East 663; *Bell v Bromfield* (1812) 15 East 364 at 368. As to the want of proper documents where there is no warranty of neutrality see para 68 post. As the Marine Insurance Act 1906 s 36 overrides certain previous decisions, eg *Rich v Parker* (1798) 7 Term Rep 705, and as it is clear and precise, it seems useless to refer in detail to the previous cases, and it is sufficient merely to mention the following in addition to those already cited: *Baring v Clagett* (1802) 3 Bos & P 201; *Mayne v Walter* (1782) 3 Doug KB 79; *Barzillai v Lewis* (1782) 3 Doug KB 126; *Garrels v Kensington* (1799) 8 Term Rep 230; *Pollard v Bell* (1800) 8 Term Rep 434; *Bird v Appleton* (1800) 8 Term Rep 562; *Tabbs v Bendelack* (1801) 4 Esp 108; *Siffken v Lee* (1807) 2 Bos & PNR 484; *Barker v Blakes* (1808) 9 East 283; *Le Cheminant v Pearson*, *Le Cheminant v Allnutt* (1812) 4 Taunt 367 at 379.

62. Warranty against contraband. If in a policy on goods there is a warranty against contraband, and some of the goods are contraband, the policy is totally void[1].

The carriage of a belligerent's dispatches, or of military or naval personnel in his service, in circumstances which render the ship liable to condemnation is a breach of the warranty of neutrality, but the carriage of naval officers is not a breach of warranty against contraband of war, inasmuch as in legal and commercial language the word 'contraband' is not applied to persons but to goods[2].

1 *Seymour v London and Provincial Marine Insurance Co* (1872) 41 LJCP 193.
2 *Yangtsze Insurance Association v Indemnity Mutual Marine Assurance Co* [1908] 1 KB 911; affd [1908] 2 KB 504, CA. As to the warranty of neutrality see paras 60–61 ante.

63. Effect of sentence of prize court. The sentence of a competent prize court[1], either of an enemy or of a neutral country, is, in actions on a marine policy, conclusive as to the existence of the ground on which the court professes to decide. In certain cases, even where the ground on which the sentence must have been based, although not expressed, may be clearly inferred from the whole of the judgment to have been that the property was not neutral, this inference has been held conclusive in an action on the policy[2].

1 As to prize courts see ADMIRALTY vol 1(1) (Reissue) para 351; and PRIZE.
2 *Lothian v Henderson* (1803) 3 Bos & P 499, HL; *Bolton v Gladstone* (1804) 5 East 155 at 160; affd (1809) 2 Taunt 85. In this respect prize cases are exceptional: *Ballantyne v Mackinnon* [1896] 2 QB 455 at 463, CA; *Hobbs v Henning* (1865) 17 CBNS 791 at 823. See ESTOPPEL vol 16 (Reissue) para 986; PRIZE.

C. IMPLIED WARRANTIES

(A) *Seaworthiness*

64. Warranty of seaworthiness. In a voyage policy[1] there is an implied warranty that at the commencement of the voyage the ship[2] is seaworthy for the purpose of the particular adventure insured, that is to say that she is reasonably fit in all respects to encounter the ordinary perils of the seas of that adventure[3].

The implied warranty of seaworthiness also applies in the case of a 'mixed policy'[4].

1 For the meaning of 'voyage policy' see para 41 ante.
2 'Ship' includes hovercraft: see para 36 note 2 ante.
3 Marine Insurance Act 1906 s 39(1), (4). 'Seaworthiness' means the same thing with reference to a policy as it does with reference to a contract of carriage by sea: *Firemen's Fund Insurance Co v Western Australian Insurance Co Ltd and Atlantic Insurance Co Ltd* (1927) 138 LT 108, following *Becker, Gray & Co v London Assurance Corpn* [1918] AC 101 at 114, HL, per Lord Sumner. As to the meaning of 'seaworthiness' see further paras 67–68 post. For its meaning with reference to a contract of carriage see SHIPPING vol 43 para 595 et seq. As to the implied warranty of legality see para 76 post. As to the implied condition that the adventure is to be commenced within a reasonable time and must be prosecuted throughout its course with reasonable dispatch see para 140 post. As to the absence of an implied warranty of seaworthiness in a time policy see para 74 post.
4 *M Almojil Establishment v Malayan Motor and General Underwriters (Pte) Ltd, The Al-Jubail IV* [1982] 2 Lloyd's Rep 637 (Sing CA). As to mixed policies see para 41 ante.

65. Exclusion of warranty. The implied warranty of seaworthiness at the commencement of the voyage[1] may be excluded by express terms or clauses in the policy, if, but only if, these are absolutely inconsistent with that warranty[2]. Thus, where losses from rottenness, inherent defects and other unseaworthiness are excepted, the warranty of seaworthiness at the commencement of the voyage will nevertheless subsist so that if the vessel started with a defective boiler, the underwriter can avoid the policy[3].

The implied warranty will be pro tanto neutralised by the clause 'held covered in case of any breach of warranty at a premium to be hereinafter arranged'[4], and it will be excluded by the clause 'ship allowed to be seaworthy for the voyage'[5]. The implied warranty, like any other warranty[6], may be waived by the insurer[7]. Waiver is effected either by a clause in the policy to the effect that the underwriters waive any breach of the implied warranty unless the assured or their servants are privy to the unseaworthiness[8], or by an act of the underwriter such as acceptance of notice of abandonment, affirming the policy after knowledge of the breach of warranty[9].

Whether extrinsic evidence can be given to contradict or qualify the implied warranty of seaworthiness is, it is submitted, still an open question[10].

1 As to this warranty see para 64 ante.
2 Marine Insurance Act 1906 s 35(3); see text and notes infra.
3 *Quebec Marine Insurance Co v Commercial Bank of Canada* (1870) LR 3 PC 234; see also *Sleigh v Tyser* [1900] 2 QB 333.
4 *Greenock SS Co v Maritime Insurance Co Ltd* [1903] 1 KB 367, where it was held that the additional premium which the underwriters would have been entitled to charge would have at least equalled the loss sustained so that the assured recovered nothing; *Mentz, Decker & Co v Maritime Insurance Co* [1910] 1 KB 132; and see para 143 note 3 post.
5 *Parfitt v Thompson* (1844) 13 M & W 392; *Phillips v Nairne* (1847) 4 CB 343. Where, however, a reinsurance policy on a ship contained a clause to this effect, but there was no such clause in the original policy, it was held that the reinsurer was not liable for the loss because, the ship being unseaworthy, the original insurer was under no liability for the loss: *Firemen's Fund Insurance Co v Western Australian Insurance Co Ltd and Atlantic Insurance Co Ltd* (1927) 33 Com Cas 36; and see para 206 note 2 post. Such a clause may limit the duty to disclose material facts: see *Cantiere Meccanico Brindisino v Janson* [1912] 3 KB 452, CA.
6 Eg a warranty that the amount insured on ppi terms should not exceed a certain figure. See *P Samuel & Co Ltd v Dumas* [1924] AC 431, HL, where it was held (Viscount Finlay and Lord Sumner dissenting) that an underwriter who had himself participated in the excessive insurance was precluded by waiver or acquiescence from relying on the breach of warranty.
7 Marine Insurance Act 1906 s 34(3).

8 See eg Institute Cargo Clauses (A) cl 5.2, set out in Ivamy's Marine Insurance (4th Edn) at 516.
9 *Provincial Insurance Co of Canada v Leduc* (1874) LR 6 PC 224 (express warranty). In *Weir v Aberdeen* (1819) 2 B & Ald 320, as explained in *Quebec Marine Insurance Co v Commercial Bank of Canada* (1870) LR 3 PC 234 at 244, the warranty of seaworthiness was waived by a memorandum on the policy.
10 The question is discussed in Arnould on Marine Insurance (16th Edn) s 717, where English and foreign authorities on both sides are cited. The English authorities are *Fawkes v Lamb* (1862) 31 LJQB 98; *Burges v Wickham* (1863) 3 B & S 669 at 685, 697; *Clapham v Langton* (1864) 34 LJQB 46, Ex Ch.

66. Effect of breach of warranty. In the absence of waiver or of some clause affecting its operation, a breach of the implied warranty of seaworthiness[1] will discharge the underwriter from liability as from the time of that breach, even though the loss was wholly unconnected with the unseaworthiness and the unseaworthiness was remedied before the loss occurred[2].

It does not matter that the unseaworthiness was caused by the acts of third parties or by inevitable accident, or that the assured acted with perfect good faith and did not know, and had no means of knowing, of the ship's unseaworthiness[3]. If the vessel, in fact, was not seaworthy, the underwriter is not liable. In short, in a voyage policy[4] the seaworthiness of the ship at the commencement of the voyage is, unless the implied warranty is waived by the underwriter or excluded by clear and express terms in the policy, an absolute condition precedent to the underwriter's liability for any loss subsequent to the breach[5].

1 As to this warranty see para 64 ante.
2 See the Marine Insurance Act 1906 s 34(2); *Quebec Marine Insurance Co v Commercial Bank of Canada* (1870) LR 3 PC 234 at 244, following *Forshaw v Chabert* (1821) 3 Brod & Bing 158. Cf para 55 text to note 5 ante.
3 *The Glenfruin* (1885) 10 PD 103; *Quebec Marine Insurance Co v Commercial Bank of Canada* (1870) LR 3 PC 234.
4 For the meaning of 'voyage policy' see para 41 ante.
5 *Douglas v Scougall* (1816) 4 Dow 269 at 276, HL, per Lord Eldon LC. For the American law on the subject see Arnould on Marine Insurance (16th Edn) s 716.

67. Meaning of 'seaworthiness'. The vessel must be reasonably fit[1]. 'Seaworthiness' is a relative term, and may vary with the class of the ship insured. Thus, a river steamer insured for a sea voyage need not be made as fit for the voyage as an ocean-going vessel. She need only be made as seaworthy as is reasonably practicable by ordinary available means[2].

Moreover, the standard of seaworthiness varies with the nature of the voyage insured; the vessel may be seaworthy for one voyage but not for another, or for a voyage at one season of the year and not for a voyage at another season; she may be seaworthy when laden with one kind of cargo and not so when laden with another kind[3].

1 Cf the Marine Insurance Act 1906 s 39(1), (2), (4); and para 70 post.
2 *Burges v Wickham* (1863) 3 B & S 669; *Clapham v Langton* (1864) 34 LJQB 46, Ex Ch; *Harocopos v Mountain* (1934) 49 Ll L Rep 267; and *Neue Fischmehl Vertriebsgesellschaft Haselhorst mbH v Yorkshire Insurance Co Ltd* (1934) 50 Ll L Rep 151 at 154 per MacKinnon J. The underwriter may, however, be entitled to avoid the policy if the fact of the ship being only a river steamer is material to the risk and has not been disclosed to him. See also *Cantiere Meccanico Brindisino v Janson* [1912] 3 KB 452, CA, where the subject matter insured was a floating dock; and para 65 note 5 ante.
3 The ship should be in a condition to encounter whatever perils of the seas a ship of that kind and laden in that way may be fairly expected to encounter on the voyage insured: *Steel v State Line SS Co* (1877) 3 App Cas 72 at 77, HL, per Lord Cairns LC; *Daniels v Harris* (1874) LR 10 CP 1 (ship laden with deck cargo); *Stanton v Richardson, Richardson v Stanton* (1874) LR 9 CP 390, Ex Ch; affd (1875) 45 LJCP 78, HL (cargo of wet sugar).

68. Respects in which vessel must be seaworthy. The ship must be reasonably fit in all respects[1]. She must be competent in hull to encounter the ordinary perils of the seas and properly equipped with the necessary tackle, stores, supplies, provisions, medicines and other things requisite for the safety of the voyage and those on board her, and she must have her engines and boilers in sound and proper condition, and also an adequate supply of fuel for the voyage[2].

However, a temporary defect in the ship's condition, due to some negligence at the time of sailing, does not constitute a breach of the implied warranty of seaworthiness, provided that the state of the ship is such that, if the master and crew do their duty, the defect can be remedied or any danger from it averted. Thus, a ship is not unseaworthy on account of a port-hole being improperly left open at the commencement of the voyage if it can be readily closed at sea whenever necessary[3].

The vessel must also at the commencement of the voyage be properly manned with a competent master and a competent and adequate crew, and must have a pilot on board at the port of departure in cases where there is an establishment of pilots at that port and the nature of the navigation requires one[4].

A ship may be seaworthy even if not properly documented at the commencement of the voyage. Lack of proper documentation will, however, discharge an insurer from liability if the insurance is on the ship and condemnation arose on that ground[5].

1 For the meaning of this requirement see SHIPPING vol 43 para 595 et seq, where the subject is more fully discussed with reference to contracts for carriage by sea, but, as stated in para 64 note 3 ante, 'seaworthiness' means the same thing with reference to that contract as it does with reference to the contract of marine insurance.

2 A defective boiler and deficient ground tackle make the ship unseaworthy: see *Wedderburn v Bell* (1807) 1 Camp 1 (sails); *Quebec Marine Insurance Co v Commercial Bank of Canada* (1870) LR 3 PC 234 (boiler); *Wilkie v Geddes* (1815) 3 Dow 57, HL (anchors). See also *Woolf v Claggett* (1800) 3 Esp 257 (medicines, etc); *Thin v Richards & Co* [1892] 2 QB 141, CA (insufficient coal); *Greenock SS Co v Maritime Insurance Co Ltd* [1903] 1 KB 367 (coal).

3 *Steel v State Line SS Co* (1877) 3 App Cas 72, HL; *Hedley v Pinkney & Sons SS Co* [1892] 1 QB 58, CA; *Gilroy, Sons & Co v Price & Co* [1893] AC 56, HL, where the defect was not capable of easy remedy, and unseaworthiness was found.

4 *Tait v Levi* (1811) 14 East 481; *Shore v Bentall* (circa 1828) 7 B & C 798n; *Phillips v Headlam* (1831) 2 B & Ad 380 at 383 per Parke J. The master must be in reasonably good health, but there is no warranty that his state of health is perfect: *Rio Tinto Co Ltd v Seed Shipping Co* (1926) 134 LT 764. If the owners fail to tell the master of the special precautions requisite owing to the peculiar construction of the ship, the master's ignorance of this information may constitute unseaworthiness: *Standard Oil Co of New York v Clan Line Steamers Ltd* [1924] AC 100, HL. It seems clear that sailing without a pilot from a port where pilotage is compulsory, or with an uncertificated master or mate or engineer contrary to statute, cannot make the voyage illegal and the policy void on that ground. As to illegal insurance see para 77 post.

5 *Dawson v Atty* (1806) 7 East 367, as explained in *Bell v Carstairs* (1811) 14 East 374 at 393 per Lord Ellenborough CJ; *Carruthers v Gray* (1811) 3 Camp 142: *Carruthers v Gray* (1812) 15 East 35; *Hobbs v Henning* (1865) 17 CBNS 791. These decisions may be rested either on an implied condition, in case of insurance against capture, that the ship is to be properly documented, or on the principle that the want of proper documents was the proximate cause of loss: *Trinder, Anderson & Co v Thames and Mersey Marine Insurance Co* [1898] 2 QB 114 at 128, CA, per Collins LJ; and see *Price v Bell* (1801) 1 East 663 at 673 per Lawrence J. As to the warranty of neutrality see paras 60–61 ante.

69. No continuing warranty of seaworthiness. There is no warranty or condition that a ship originally seaworthy[1] for the voyage insured shall continue to be seaworthy, or that the master and crew shall do their duty during the voyage. Therefore, the negligence and misconduct of master and crew after the voyage has commenced is no defence to an action on the policy where the loss has been immediately occasioned by the perils insured against[2]. Even when the policy is on a voyage out and home, the risk being entire and indivisible, it is sufficient if the ship is seaworthy for the entire voyage when she first sails from the home port of loading[3].

1 For the meaning of 'seaworthiness' see paras 67–68 ante.
2 *Dixon v Sadler* (1839) 5 M & W 405 at 414–415 per curiam; affd sub nom *Sadler v Dixon* (1841) 8 M & W 895, Ex Ch; *Bermon v Woodbridge* (1781) 2 Doug KB 781 at 788 per Lord Mansfield CJ; *Eden v Parkison* (1781) 2 Doug KB 732 at 735; *Watson v Clark* (1813) 1 Dow 336 at 344, HL, per Lord Eldon LC; *Busk v Royal Exchange Assurance Co* (1818) 2 B & Ald 73; *Biccard v Shepherd* (1861) 14 Moo PCC 471. For cases where negligence was the remote cause of loss see also *Walker v Maitland* (1821) 5 B & Ald 171; *Bishop v Pentland* (1827) 7 B & C 219; *Holdsworth v Wise* (1828) 7 B & C 794; *Shore v Bentall* (circa 1828) 7 B & C 798n; *Phillips v Headlam* (1831) 2 B & Ad 380; *Redman v Wilson* (1845) 14 M & W 476; *Dudgeon v Pembroke* (1877) 2 App Cas 284 at 296, HL. There is no express provision in the Marine Insurance Act 1906 that the ship must be seaworthy only at the commencement of the voyage, but it is clear from the enactments it contains (see s 39(5); and para 74 post) relating to different stages of the voyage that it does not alter the law as established by the above cited cases.
3 *Bermon v Woodbridge* (1781) 2 Doug KB 781; *Redman v Wilson* (1845) 14 M & W 476.

70. Doctrine of stages. There are two exceptions to, or modifications of, the rule that the implied warranty of seaworthiness is not satisfied unless the ship is, at the beginning of the voyage, seaworthy for the whole of that voyage[1].

The first exception or modification is that, where the policy attaches while the ship is in port, there is an implied warranty that the ship is at the commencement of the risk to be reasonably fit to encounter the ordinary perils of the port[2], that is to say she must be capable of being moved from one part of the port to another for the purpose of repairs, and of being moored alongside the wharves and quays there[3]. If this warranty is satisfied, the policy is in force whilst the ship remains in port, and the insurers are liable for losses occurring during that period; but in order that the policy may continue in force so as to cover the voyage insured she must be seaworthy for that voyage[4].

The second exception, which may only be a particular instance of the first, is that, where the policy relates to a voyage which is performed in different stages, during which the ship requires different kinds of or further preparation or equipment, there is an implied warranty that at the commencement of each stage the ship is seaworthy in respect of that preparation or equipment for the purposes of that stage[5]. Thus, when a ship is insured 'at and from Lyons to Galati', and sails with a river crew and captain, and without her masts and anchors and other heavy articles, which it is impossible for her to carry on the river voyage, and afterwards takes on board her sea captain and some of her seagoing crew, and is otherwise fitted for the voyage to Galati, the ship will have satisfied the implied warranty of seaworthiness if she was river-worthy when she left Lyons and seaworthy when she sailed from Marseilles[6].

In such cases as the foregoing, the ship could not at the outset be made reasonably fit for the whole voyage, and, therefore, in order to reconcile the interests of the assured on the one hand and those of the insurers on the other, it is held that the whole voyage must be divided into two stages, and that it is necessary and sufficient for the ship to be seaworthy at the commencement of each of those stages. This principle has been applied where a ship cannot and does not at the commencement of the voyage carry enough fuel for the whole of the insured voyage, and is, therefore, obliged to take in fuel at some further port or ports. In these cases it lies on the shipowner, in order to disprove the defence of unseaworthiness, to show that he was obliged to divide, and had divided, the voyage into stages for fuelling purposes by reason of the necessities of the case, and that at the commencement of each stage the ship had on board sufficient fuel for that stage, in other words, that she was seaworthy for each stage. It further seems that it is a matter for proof as to how the necessities of the case require that voyage to be divided into stages[7].

1 As to the warranty of seaworthiness see para 64 ante.
2 Marine Insurance Act 1906 s 39(2).
3 *Parmeter v Cousins* (1809) 2 Camp 235; *Buchanan & Co v Faber* (1899) 4 Com Cas 223.
4 *Annen v Woodman* (1810) 3 Taunt 299.
5 Marine Insurance Act 1906 s 39(3), which was evidently intended to embody the law laid down in *Bouillon v Lupton* (1863) 15 CBNS 113.
6 *Bouillon v Lupton* (1863) 15 CBNS 113.
7 *The Vortigern* [1899] P 140 at 155, CA, following *Thin v Richards & Co* [1892] 2 QB 141, CA; *Greenock SS Co v Maritime Insurance Co Ltd* [1903] 1 KB 367; affd [1903] 2 KB 657, CA. These decisions do not seem inconsistent with, and are probably covered by, the Marine Insurance Act 1906 s 39(3).

71. Effect of absence of pilot. A third exception has been suggested to the general rule that an implied warranty of seaworthiness attaches to the ship only at the commencement of a voyage[1]. A policy cannot generally be avoided by the master's neglect to take on board a pilot at proper places in the course of the insured voyage, but it has been suggested that perhaps there is a breach of the warranty of seaworthiness if, in a case where the master is required by Act of Parliament to take the services of a pilot, he makes default in so doing, on the ground that the passage over the pilotage district may be considered as a distinctly intermediate voyage[2].

1 As to the warranty of seaworthiness see para 64 ante.
2 This suggestion was made by Patteson J during the argument in *Hollingworth v Brodrick* (1837) 7 Ad & El 40 at 44, explaining *Law v Hollingsworth* (1797) 7 Term Rep 160; see also *Phillips v Headlam* (1831) 2 B & Ad 380 at 382, 384; *Sadler v Dixon* (1841) 8 M & W 895 at 900, Ex Ch, per Tindal CJ; *Gibson v Small* (1853) 4 HL Cas 353 at 398 per Parke B. It is submitted, however, that the above suggestion would probably be held inconsistent with more recent cases and with the provisions of the Marine Insurance Act 1906.

72. Ship's cargoworthiness. In a voyage policy[1] on goods or other movables[2] there is an implied warranty that at the commencement of the voyage the ship is not only seaworthy as a ship, but also that she is reasonably fit to carry the goods or other movables to the destination contemplated by the policy[3]. Thus, the warranty is not satisfied in a policy on a deck cargo if in ordinary rough weather the goods must be jettisoned, although this could be done without difficulty and the ship could then perform the voyage with safety to herself[4].

Similarly, if a ship is carrying a cargo of wet sugar and the pumps are not sufficient for the drainage of the cargo and the ordinary leakage of the vessel so that she cannot safely undertake the intended voyage with that cargo on board, the implied warranty is not complied with[5].

1 For the meaning of 'voyage policy' see para 41 ante.
2 For the meaning of 'movables' see para 36 note 3 ante.
3 Marine Insurance Act 1906 s 40(2).
4 *Daniels v Harris* (1874) LR 10 CP 1; *Sleigh v Tyser* [1900] 2 QB 333 (where cattle were insured against mortality, and the ventilation was insufficient, and it was held that the implied warranty of

seaworthiness had not been complied with); and see *Biccard v Shepherd* (1861) 14 Moo PCC 471 (voyage beginning, in respect of separate parcels of goods, at separate times and warranty, therefore, attaching at different times although goods insured under one policy).
5 *Stanton v Richardson, Richardson v Stanton* (1874) LR 9 CP 390, Ex Ch; affd (1875) 45 LJCP 78, HL.

73. Seaworthiness of cargo. In a policy on goods or other movables[1] there is no implied warranty that the goods or movables are seaworthy[2]; nor does the warranty of seaworthiness which is implied as to the ship[3] extend to lighters employed to land the cargo[4].

1 For the meaning of 'movables' see para 36 note 3 ante.
2 Marine Insurance Act 1906 s 40(1). This provision is in accordance with the decision in *Koebel v Saunders* (1864) 17 CBNS 71, but, of course, the underwriter is not liable for a loss directly resulting from the inherent defect or vice of the goods. As to this see para 172 post.
3 As to the implied warranty of seaworthiness see para 64 ante.
4 *Lane v Nixon* (1866) LR 1 CP 412.

74. Time policy and seaworthiness. In a time policy[1] there is no implied warranty that the ship is to be seaworthy at any stage of the adventure[2], but where, with the privity[3] of the assured, a ship is sent to sea in an unseaworthy state, the insurer is not liable for any loss attributable to unseaworthiness[4]. Where a ship is sent to sea in a state of unseaworthiness in more than one respect, and the assured is privy to some, but not all, of the defects, the insurer will be liable unless the assured was privy to the particular defect which caused the loss[5]. Mere omission to take precautions against the ship being unseaworthy does not make the owner privy to any unseaworthiness which that precaution might have disclosed[6].

1 For the meaning of 'time policy' see para 41 ante.
2 Marine Insurance Act 1906 s 39(5). This provision is in accordance with the decisions in *Gibson v Small* (1853) 4 HL Cas 353, and *Dudgeon v Pembroke* (1877) 2 App Cas 284, HL.
3 'With the privity' means with the knowledge and consent: *Compania Maritima San Basilio SA v Oceanus Mutual Underwriting Association (Bermuda) Ltd, The Eurysthenes* [1977] QB 49, [1976] 3 All ER 243, CA.
4 Marine Insurance Act 1906 s 39(5); *Thompson v Hopper* (1858) E B & E 1038, Ex Ch; *Dudgeon v Pembroke* (1877) 2 App Cas 284; *Mountain v Whittle* [1921] 1 AC 615 at 618–619, HL, per Lord Birkenhead LC; *Frangos v Sun Insurance Office Ltd* (1934) 49 Ll L Rep 354; *Compania Naviera Vascongada v British and Foreign Marine Insurance Co Ltd* (1936) 54 Ll L Rep 35; *Ashworth v General Accident Fire and Life Assurance Corpn Ltd* [1955] IR 268; *The Pacific Queen* [1963] 2 Lloyd's Rep 201 (US 9th Cir); *Compania Maritima San Basilio SA v Oceanus Mutual Underwriting Association (Bermuda) Ltd, The Eurysthenes* [1977] QB 49, [1976] 3 All ER 243, CA. See further para 172 post. The insurer is not liable if the unseaworthiness was a proximate cause, although not the sole cause, of the loss: *M Thomas & Son Shipping Co Ltd v London and Provincial Marine and General Insurance Co Ltd* (1914) 30 TLR 595, CA. The insurer is not liable if the assured was privy to the state of things which rendered the vessel unseaworthy, even though he may not have formed the opinion that she was unseaworthy: *M Thomas & Son Shipping Co Ltd v London and Provincial Marine and General Insurance Co Ltd* supra.
5 *Thomas v Tyne and Wear SS Freight Insurance Association* [1917] 1 KB 938.
6 *Compania Naviera Vascongada v British and Foreign Marine Insurance Co Ltd* (1936) 54 Ll L Rep 35 at 58 per Branson J.

75. Burden of proof of unseaworthiness. Unseaworthiness[1] is a question of fact, the burden of proof of which is on the insurer[2]. Where, however, a ship soon after sailing founders or becomes disabled, and this cannot be ascribed to any violent storm or other adequate cause, there is a presumption of fact that it arose from unseaworthiness at the commencement of the voyage, and the burden of proof is then shifted to the assured[3].

1 For the meaning of 'seaworthiness' see generally paras 67–68 ante.
2 See eg *Pickup v Thames and Mersey Marine Insurance Co* (1878) 3 QBD 594, CA. As to the burden of proof see further EVIDENCE vol 17 paras 13–19.
3 *Parker v Potts* (1815) 3 Dow 23, HL; *Davidson v Burnand* (1868) LR 4 CP 117; *Pickup v Thames and Mersey Marine Insurance Co* (1878) 3 QBD 594, CA; *Compania Naviera Vascongada v British and Foreign Marine Insurance Co Ltd* (1936) 54 Ll L Rep 35 at 51 per Branson J; *Ajum Goolam Hossen & Co v Union Marine Insurance Co, Hajee Cassim Joosub v Ajum Goolam Hossen & Co* [1901] AC 362, PC, approving *Anderson v Morice* (1874) LR 10 CP 58 at 68; affd on this point (1875) LR 10 CP 609, Ex Ch; (1876) 1 App Cas 713, HL, without reasons given. See also *Watson v Clark* (1813) 1 Dow 336, HL; *Douglas v Scougall* (1816) 4 Dow 269, HL; *The Tatjana* [1911] AC 194; *R Silcock & Sons Ltd v Maritime Lighterage Co (J R Francis & Co) Ltd* (1937) 57 Ll L Rep 78, CA. It has been observed by Brett LJ in *Pickup v Thames and Mersey Marine Insurance Co* supra at 601, that the judgments of Lord Eldon LC, in the cases in Dow's Reports, were on appeal from Scots judgments where the courts were judges of fact as well as law, and that, therefore, the presumptions referred to in those judgments were presumptions of fact and not of law (see also at 605 per Thesiger LJ).

(B) *Legality*

76. Warranty of legality. There is an implied warranty[1] that the adventure insured is a lawful one, and that so far as the assured can control the matter, the adventure[2] is to be carried out in a lawful manner[3].

1 As to the nature of warranties in marine insurance contracts see generally para 54 ante.
2 This provision has no application to non-marine insurance in respect of goods alone: *Euro-Diam Ltd v Bathurst* [1990] 1 QB 1, [1988] 2 All ER 23, CA; and see para 494 post.
3 Marine Insurance Act 1906 s 41. See *The Pacific Queen* [1963] 2 Lloyd's Rep 201 (US 9th Cir) (where the court declined to express a view as to whether the violation of the Tanker Act (46 US Code s 391a) rendered the voyage illegal); *James Yachts Ltd v Thames and Mersey Marine Insurance Co Ltd* [1977] 1 Lloyd's Rep 206, BC SC (assured carrying on boat building business when forbidden to do so by local authority byelaws and regulations). As to contracts of insurance tainted with illegality see *Euro-Diam Ltd v Bathurst* [1990] 1 QB 1, [1988] 2 All ER 23, CA; and para 494 post.

77. Illegal insurance generally. An insurance on an illegal voyage or adventure is itself illegal for, if an original transaction is illegal, a contract intended to indemnify against loss in respect of that adventure must evidently also be illegal[1]. A contract of marine insurance[2] may be illegal by the common law or by statute, or because the insured adventure is illegal; and the adventure may be illegal either by statute, or because it is in violation of the common law or the prize law as administered in England, or in contravention of treaties made by the United Kingdom government with other countries, or of proclamations or orders made by the Queen in Council[3].

1 *Redmond v Smith* (1844) 7 Man & G 457 at 474 per Tindal CJ. See also the Marine Insurance Act 1906 s 3(1); and paras 36, 76 ante.
2 For the meaning of 'contract of marine insurance' see para 35 ante.
3 As to treaties see *The Eenrom* (1799) 2 Ch Rob 1 at 6; *Bird v Appleton* (1800) 8 Term Rep 562 at 564; and CONSTITUTIONAL LAW vol 8 paras 985–986; FOREIGN RELATIONS vol 18 para 1769 et seq; WAR; and as to statute law see *Wilson v Marryat* (1798) 8 Term Rep 31; affd sub nom *Marryat v Wilson* (1799) 1 Bos & P 430, Ex Ch. As to illegal contracts generally see CONTRACT vol 9 paras 386–388. As to proclamations see CONSTITUTIONAL LAW vol 8 para 1097.

78. Insurances by or on behalf of enemy aliens. Contracts of marine insurance, like other contracts, if entered into with a British subject by or on behalf of an enemy alien during a war with the United Kingdom are wholly void and illegal, and cannot be enforced by the assured or his agent[1].

On the other hand, insurances, if effected before the outbreak of war by persons who afterwards become enemy aliens, are valid and legal contracts, the right of action on which is only suspended during the war and revives upon its close[2]; but although those insurances are legal contracts, they are, on grounds of public policy, not allowed to cover any losses that occur during the war, and are available only as contracts of indemnity against losses which have occurred before the commencement of hostilities[3].

The fact, however, that war is expected and imminent will not free the insurer from liability for loss of property by seizure, even if it is seized by a government for the purposes of a war which it is on the point of declaring, and even though the insurance was intended to protect the property against that seizure[4].

As a general rule, whenever any property, according to prize law[5] as administered by the courts of this country, is liable to British capture, the insurance in England on that property is illegal and void. It may be liable to British capture on many various grounds, for example because it is enemy property, or contraband carried to a hostile country, or because the ship is employed in violation of a blockade by the United Kingdom government or its allies, or is engaged in carrying the enemy's troops, or in any other manner which is considered by English prize law to be illicit or illegal[6].

1 *The Hoop* (1799) 1 Ch Rob 196 at 198, 201; *Furtado v Rogers* (1802) 3 Bos & P 191 at 199–200; *Esposito v Bowden* (1857) 7 E & B 763; and see *Kellner v Le Mesurier* (1803) 4 East 396; *Gamba v Le Mesurier* (1803) 4 East 407; *Brandon v Curling* (1803) 4 East 410; *De Luneville v Phillips* (1806) 2 Bos & PNR 97; WAR. These propositions are not affected by the Hague Regulations 1907 (Cd 4175), art 23 (h), contained in the International Convention concerning the Laws and Customs of War on Land (Hague Convention IV) (The Hague, 18 October 1907; TS 9 (1910); Cd 5030): *Porter v Freudenberg* [1915] 1 KB 857, CA.

2 *Furtado v Rogers* (1802) 3 Bos & P 191 at 201; *Janson v Driefontein Consolidated Mines Ltd* [1902] AC 484, HL; *Harman v Kingston* (1811) 3 Camp 150; *Flindt v Waters* (1812) 15 East 260; and see *Boulton v Dobree* (1808) 2 Camp 163; *Shepheler v Durant* (1854) 14 CB 582. An enemy alien underwriter may be sued during the war, at any rate if the loss occurred before he became an enemy alien. He may defend the action but may not counterclaim: see WAR.

3 *Brandon v Curling* (1803) 4 East 410 at 417 per Lord Ellenborough CJ; *Gamba v Le Mesurier* (1803) 4 East 407; *Kellner v Le Mesurier* (1803) 4 East 396 (loss by British capture); *Janson v Driefontein Consolidated Mines Ltd* [1902] AC 484 at 493, 499, 508, HL. In the last case the question incidentally arose whether the action on the policy could be brought during the war where the defendant raised no objection; Vaughan Williams LJ (in the Court of Appeal: see [1901] 2 KB 419 at 433), and Lord Davey (see [1902] AC 484 at 499) stated in their opinion it could not, but in this opinion Lord Lindley (see [1902] AC 484 at 509) did not concur. The point was not expressly decided in *Porter v Freudenberg* [1915] 1 KB 857, CA, but the court appears to have taken the same view as Vaughan Williams LJ and Lord Davey. See also *Harman v Kingston* (1811) 3 Camp 150; *Flindt v Waters* (1812) 15 East 260; *Alcinous v Nigreu* (1854) 4 E & B 217; *Shepheler v Durant* (1854) 14 CB 582.

4 *Janson v Driefontein Consolidated Mines Ltd* [1902] AC 484, HL; see at 491 et seq per Lord Halsbury LC, and at 506 per Lord Lindley.

5 As to prize law see PRIZE.

6 *Janson v Driefontein Consolidated Mines Ltd* [1902] AC 484 at 499, HL, per Lord Davey. It is important to notice that a person is an enemy alien if he voluntarily resides or carries on business in an enemy country; and further that the rules relating to the transfer of property during or in contemplation of war differ materially in many respects from those which govern the rights of parties in peace (see PRIZE; WAR).

79. Policy on adventure contravening foreign law. A contract for the performance of an adventure which involves contravention of the laws of a foreign and friendly state may be unenforceable under English law[1]. However, unless the adventure is illegal under English law, an insurance on it will, it seems, be enforceable, although the fact of contravention may be a material circumstance to be disclosed to the insurer[2].

1 See *Regazzoni v K C Sethia (1944) Ltd* [1957] 3 All ER 286, HL. As to foreign laws which the English courts will not recognise, and as to the enforcement of contracts contravening the laws of foreign states, see further CONFLICT OF LAWS vol 8 paras 603–607; and consider, in the light of subsequent authority there cited, *Planché v Fletcher* (1779) 1 Doug KB 251.
2 As to non-disclosure and circumstances material to be disclosed see para 215 et seq post.

80. Insurance on neutral adventure. Neutrals, whether British subjects or foreigners, are by English law entitled to carry on their trade with a belligerent subject to the belligerent's right of capture; hence it follows that the carriage of contraband goods, and voyages in breach of blockade, are not illegal, and that insurances on those goods or voyages are valid[1].

1 *Re Grazebrook, ex p Chavasse* (1865) 34 LJBcy 17; *The Helen* (1865) LR 1 A & E 1; *Caine v Palace Steam Shipping Co* [1907] 1 KB 670 at 679, CA, per Farwell LJ. *Harratt v Wise* (1829) 9 B & C 712, and *Naylor v Taylor* (1829) 9 B & C 718, although assumed to be so in *Medeiros v Hill* (1832) 8 Bing 231 at 234, are not authorities to the contrary: see *The Helen* supra at 7; and WAR. Where, however, the rights of neutrals to trade with the enemy have been modified or abrogated by Act of Parliament or Order in Council, an insurance on an adventure disallowed by that Act or Order would doubtless be illegal; cf para 81 note 5 post. As to the power of the Crown to make Orders in Council see CONSTITUTIONAL LAW vol 8 para 1088; WAR.

81. Insurance where acts illegal by United Kingdom law are involved. A policy may be illegal because the insured adventure contravenes the law relating to revenue or navigation or any other municipal law of the United Kingdom; and whether a statute renders a voyage illegal, or is only intended to impose a penalty on the owner, master or other person violating it, is a question of construction[1].

Where the adventure which is the subject of the insurance is not in itself unlawful, the fact that in the course of the insured voyage United Kingdom law relating to revenue or navigation is contravened does not make the insurance illegal unless the insured himself was a party to the illegality or could control the matter involving the illegality[2]; and an authority from the owner to the master of the ship to do an illegal act will not be implied from the master's general powers[3]. Thus, if the master of a vessel, which has not obtained a certificate required by the statute to carry passengers, carries them without her owner's knowledge, the policy effected by the owner is not vitiated on the ground of illegality[4].

Moreover, although it was the parties' intention at the time of entering into the contract that it should be carried out in a manner which is in fact prohibited by law, if both parties were ignorant of the prohibition, and if the contract can be and is ultimately carried out without violating the law, the contract is not void[5].

1 *Atkinson v Abbott* (1809) 11 East 135 at 141 per Lord Ellenborough CJ; *Redmond v Smith* (1844) 2 Dow & L 280; and see *Smith v Mawhood* (1845) 14 M & W 452; *Cunard v Hyde* (1859) 2 E & E 1; and other cases cited in CONTRACT vol 9 para 424.
2 Cf the Marine Insurance Act 1906 s 41 (see para 76 ante); *Farmer v Legg* (1797) 7 Term Rep 186; *Cunard v Hyde* (1859) 2 E & E 1.
3 *Dudgeon v Pembroke* (1874) LR 9 QB 581; affd (1877) 2 App Cas 284, HL (but no appeal on this point); *Carstairs v Allnutt* (1813) 3 Camp 497; *Metcalfe v Parry* (1814) 4 Camp 123; *Cunard v Hyde* (1858) E B & E 670; *Hobbs v Henning* (1865) 17 CBNS 791 at 821; *Wilson v Rankin* (1865) LR 1 QB 162.

4 *Dudgeon v Pembroke* (1874) LR 9 QB 581; *Australasian Insurance Co v Jackson* (1875) 33 LT 286, PC (breach of the Pacific Islanders Protection Act 1872 (repealed)). As to these and other necessary certificates see SHIPPING.

5 *Waugh v Morris* (1873) LR 8 QB 202; contrast *Foster v Driscoll* [1929] 1 KB 470, CA. If the adventure insured was lawful by English law when the contract of insurance was effected, but subsequently becomes unlawful by reason of an 'act of state' of the United Kingdom government, and is therefore abandoned, the abandonment may give rise to a loss recoverable from the underwriter: see *Sanday & Co v British and Foreign Marine Insurance Co Ltd* [1915] 2 KB 781, CA; affd sub nom *British and Foreign Marine Insurance Co Ltd v Samuel Sanday & Co* [1916] 1 AC 650, HL; and see para 156 note 6 post. If, however, an assured persists in an adventure, and the subject matter insured is consequently seized by the United Kingdom authorities, the assured cannot recover: *Sanday & Co v British and Foreign Marine Insurance Co Ltd* supra at 788 per Bailhache J; see also the Marine Insurance Act 1906 s 41; and para 76 ante.

82. Effect of illegality of part of insured voyage. Difficult questions have arisen as to whether the illegality of part of a voyage renders the insurance of other parts illegal. The result of the cases, so far as they can be reconciled with each other, seems to be:

(1) that any illegality in the prior stages, or at the outset, of an integral voyage vitiates a policy, even though the policy is effected only to protect some later stage in which there is no illegality;

(2) that an illegality in any part of an entire risk or voyage insured vitiates the insurance as to the whole of it;

(3) that the illegality of a wholly distinct and separate voyage has no effect on the voyage insured by the policy[1].

Whether the voyage insured is to be considered a distinct and separate voyage or only part of a larger voyage is a question depending mainly on the contract of affreightment and the circumstances in which it was made[2].

1 See Arnould on Marine Insurance (16th Edn) s 753; *Wilson v Marryat* (1798) 8 Term Rep 31 at 46 per Lord Kenyon CJ; affd sub nom *Marryat v Wilson* (1799) 1 Bos & P 430, Ex Ch, but without touching this point; *Bird v Pigou* (1800), cited in 2 Selwyn's NP (13th Edn) 932; *Bird v Appleton* (1800) 8 Term Rep 562; *Sewell v Royal Exchange Assurance Co* (1813) 4 Taunt 856.

2 See the cases cited in note 1 supra. Some of those decisions are difficult to reconcile with each other (see 1 Phillips' Law of Insurance (5th edn) s 231), and some seem inconsistent with the Marine Insurance Act 1906 s 41 (see para 76 ante). It is submitted that in these circumstances the English courts are likely to follow the canon of construction which applies to a codifying statute in common with other instruments, and to give effect to the natural meaning of the enactment: see para 13 ante; and STATUTES. If this view is correct, the question whether there has been a breach of the warranty of legality will generally be determined by only two considerations, namely: (1) whether the adventure insured is a lawful one; and (2) whether, so far as the assured was in a position to control the matter, the adventure has been carried out in a lawful manner. As to non-waiver of illegality see para 83 post.

83. No waiver of implied warranty of legality. If a policy is illegal in the sense that it or the adventure insured violates a rule of public policy[1], its illegality cannot be waived by either party, nor can either party contract out of the rule, and the court is bound to declare the policy void as soon as the illegality is disclosed[2].

1 See *Equitable Life Assurance Society of the United States v Reed* [1914] AC 587 at 595, PC.

2 *North Western Salt Co Ltd v Electrolytic Alkali Co Ltd* [1914] AC 461 at 469, HL, per Lord Haldane LC; and see *Gedge v Royal Exchange Assurance Corpn* [1900] 2 QB 214 at 220 (ppi policy), cited in para 211

note 11 post. It may be worth noticing that 'warranty' in the Marine Insurance Act 1906 s 41 (see para 76 ante) seems to be used in a somewhat inaccurate manner, for although an implied warranty can be waived, the illegality of a policy cannot be waived by either party.

(v) Alteration and Rectification of Policy

84. Effect of alterations. A policy of marine insurance, like any other contract, may be altered by consent, even after it is underwritten, provided that the alteration is in writing signed or initialled by the insurer[1]. An alteration by one insurer, however, cannot bind any of the other insurers, and any material alteration of the policy, when in the possession of the assured or his agent, avoids the policy, except as to the insurers who had consented to it by signing or initialling the alteration[2]. On the other hand, an alteration, if not material, will not vitiate the policy, the only result being that if some of the insurers have consented to the alteration after the policy is executed and others refuse, those who consent make the altered instrument their own, and those who do not consent remain liable on their original contract[3].

1 *Kaines v Knightly* (1682) Skin 54; *Robinson v Tobin* (1816) 1 Stark 336.
2 *Laird v Robertson* (1791) 4 Bro Parl Cas 488; *Langhorn v Cologan* (1812) 4 Taunt 330; *Campbell v Christie* (1817) 2 Stark 64; *Fairlie v Christie* (1817) 7 Taunt 416; *Forshaw v Chabert* (1821) 3 Brod & Bing 158; *Norwich Union Fire Insurance Society v Colonial Mutual Fire Insurance Co Ltd* [1922] 2 KB 461.
3 *Sanderson v Symonds* (1819) 1 Brod & Bing 426; *Sanderson v M'Cullom* (1819) 4 Moore CP 5; *Forshaw v Chabert* (1821) 3 Brod & Bing 158 at 165.

85. What alterations are material. An alteration is material which in any degree affects the contract or any rights or remedies under it, as, for instance, where the destination of the vessel insured is altered at the time of her sailing or the subject of the insurance is altered[1], or the agreed value of the subject matter is altered[2]. An alteration or addition is not material which merely expresses what the law could otherwise imply as to the effect or construction of the instrument[3].

1 *Laird v Robertson* (1791 4 Bro Parl Cas 488; *Langhorn v Cologan* (1812) 4 Taunt 330; *Fairlie v Christie* (1817) 7 Taunt 416; *Campbell v Christie* (1817) 2 Stark 64; *Forshaw v Chabert* (1821) 3 Brod & Bing 158.
2 *Norwich Union Fire Insurance Society v Colonial Mutual Fire Insurance Co Ltd* [1922] 2 KB 461.
3 *Clapham v Cologan* (1813) 3 Camp 382; and see the cases cited in para 84 note 3 ante.

86. Rectification of policies. Where a mistake has been made in drawing up a contract, and its terms do not correctly express the real agreement between the parties, the court has jurisdiction to rectify the instrument so as to make it correspond with the parties' true intention[1]. The Marine Insurance Act 1906 provides that where there is a policy[2], reference may be made to the 'slip' or covering note in any legal proceeding[3], and the court has power to rectify a policy so as to make it correspond with the terms expressed in the 'slip' or covering note[4].

1 *Motteux v Governor & Co of London Assurance* (1739) 1 Atk 545; *Henkle v Royal Exchange Assurance Co* (1749) 1 Ves Sen 317. The remedy of rectification, and the defences available, are discussed in EQUITY vol 16 (Reissue) para 681 et seq; MISTAKE.
2 The Marine Insurance Act 1906 s 89 refers to a 'duly stamped policy', but a policy of insurance is now exempt from all stamp duties. A contract of marine insurance is inadmissible in evidence unless embodied in a policy: see para 39 ante.

3 Marine Insurance Act 1906 s 89.
4 *The Aikshaw* (1893) 9 TLR 605; *Spalding v Crocker* (1897) 2 Com Cas 189; *Allom v Property Insurance Co* (1911) Times, Finance, Commerce and Shipping section, 10 February (fire insurance); *Emanuel & Co v Andrew Weir & Co* (1914) 30 TLR 518; *Lowland SS Co v North of England Protecting and Indemnity Association* (1921) 6 Ll L Rep 230; *Gagnière & Co Ltd v Eastern Co of Warehouses Insurance and Transport of Goods with Advances Ltd* (1921) 8 Ll L Rep 365, CA; *Maignen & Co v National Benefit Assurance Co Ltd* (1922) 38 TLR 257; *Re London County Commercial Reinsurance Office Ltd* [1922] 2 Ch 67 at 83; *Wilson, Holgate & Co Ltd v Lancashire and Cheshire Insurance Corpn Ltd* (1922) 13 Ll L Rep 486; *Scottish Metropolitan Assurance Co v Stewart* (1923) 15 Ll L Rep 55; *Eagle Star and British Dominions Insurance Co Ltd v A V Reiner* (1927) 27 Ll L Rep 173; *Symington & Co v Union Insurance Society of Canton Ltd* (1928) 34 Com Cas 23; affd 34 Com Cas 233, CA; *American Employers Insurance Co v St Paul Fire and Marine Insurance Co Ltd* [1978] 1 Lloyd's Rep 417; *Pindos Shipping Corpn v Raven, The Mata Hari* [1983] 2 Lloyd's Rep 449; rectification was refused in *Mackenzie v Coulson* (1869) LR 8 Eq 368, but that case turned on its special facts and should not be regarded as authority that, in general, rectification cannot be obtained.

(3) THE COURSE OF BUSINESS OF INSURANCE

87. Insurance brokers. A marine policy is generally effected by an insurance broker, who acts as middleman between the assured and the insurers. The broker's business consists mainly in receiving instructions from the assured as to the nature of the risk and the rate of premium at which the insurance is to be effected[1], communicating these facts to the insurers and effecting the policy on the best possible terms for the assured, paying the premium to the insurers, and receiving from them whatever may be due from them under the policy in case of loss. In these matters the broker is the agent of the assured and not the agent of the insurers[2].

1 Where an insurance is effected 'at a premium to be arranged', and no arrangement is made, a reasonable premium is payable: Marine Insurance Act 1906 s 31(1). What is a reasonable premium is a question of fact: s 88.
2 *Empress Assurance Corpn Ltd v C T Bowring & Co Ltd* (1905) 11 Com Cas 107. For an application to marine insurance business of the principle of the law of agency that a dishonest agent forfeits his right to his contractual remuneration as well as being obliged to pay over to his principal any commission improperly received from a third party see *E Green & Son Ltd v G Tughan & Co* (1913) 30 TLR 64.

88. Course of business. Briefly stated, the course of the business of marine insurance as carried on in London and elsewhere in the United Kingdom is as follows. A broker on receiving orders from his principal to effect an insurance prepares what is usually known as a 'slip', containing rough notes sufficient to indicate the terms of the proposed insurance. The broker then takes the slip round to the various underwriters, who may be Lloyd's underwriters or underwriters on behalf of insurance companies. Those underwriters who are willing to accept the risk signify their willingness by initialling the slip for the amounts for which they are willing to become insurers. So far as the initials on the slip are those of Lloyd's underwriters a policy is prepared by the broker and submitted by him to Lloyd's Policy Signing Office[1]. Insurance companies, however, prepare their own policies, and in order to enable them to do so the broker sends to each company a memorandum of the engagement which the particular company has already entered into by initialling the slip[2].

1 See para 21 note 8 ante.
2 This memorandum is often called the 'long slip'. The original slip submitted by the broker to the company's underwriter is often called the 'short slip': see *Re London County Commercial Reinsurance*

Office Ltd [1922] 2 Ch 67. For a more detailed statement of this course of business see Arnould on Marine Insurance (16th Edn) s 163. As to the mode in which accounts are usually kept between the broker and underwriter, and between broker and assured see Arnould on Marine Insurance (16th Edn) ss 168–169. Sometimes insurance brokers guarantee the solvency of the underwriters. In such cases they are said to act del credere, or to be del credere agents (as to which see AGENCY vol 1(2) (Reissue) para 13), and receive therefor a commission del credere. This commission is earned by entering into the contract of guarantee, and does not at all depend upon the subsequent events: *Caruthers v Graham* (1811) 14 East 578; *Couturier v Hastie* (1852) 8 Exch 40; *Harburg India Rubber Comb Co v Martin* [1902] 1 KB 778, CA.

89. The 'slip'. In practice, and according to the understanding of those engaged in marine insurance, the insurance slip is the complete and final contract fixing the terms of the insurance and the premium, and, without the assent of the other, neither party can deviate from the terms agreed on without a breach of good faith[1]. In accordance with this practice it is provided that a contract of marine insurance[2] is deemed to be concluded when the assured's proposal is accepted by the insurer, whether the policy is then issued or not[3], and for the purpose of showing when the proposal was accepted, reference may be made to the slip or covering note or other customary memorandum of the contract[4].

By initialling a slip the insurer impliedly agrees to issue a policy in accordance with the slip, but this agreement, although binding in honour, is unenforceable in law, because a contract of marine insurance is inadmissible in evidence unless it is embodied in a marine policy[5].

1 *Ionides v Pacific Insurance Co* (1871) LR 6 QB 674 at 684; affd (1872) LR 7 QB 517, Ex Ch (where it was held that, a stamped policy being in existence, the slip might be looked at for the purpose, amongst other things, of ascertaining the parties' intention in preparing the policy); *Symington & Co v Union Insurance Society of Canton Ltd* (1928) 97 LJKB 646, CA: contrast *Re London County Commercial Reinsurance Office Ltd* [1922] 2 Ch 67, where the 'long slip' differed from the 'short slip', and it was held that the policy had been rightly made out in accordance with the 'long slip' and could not be rectified. As to the 'long slip' and the 'short slip' see para 88 note 2 ante. As to rectification see para 86 ante.

2 For the meaning of 'contract of marine insurance' see para 35 ante.

3 In practice it is not unusual for a policy to be issued after a loss has occurred.

4 Marine Insurance Act 1906 s 21 (amended by the Finance Act 1959 s 37(5), Sch 8 Pt II). This was also the previous law: *Cory v Patton* (1872) LR 7 QB 304; *Cory v Patton* (1874) LR 9 QB 577 (any fresh fact coming to the assured's knowledge after the initialling of the slip, but before the execution of the policy itself, need not be communicated to the insurers); applied in *Lishman v Northern Maritime Insurance Co* (1875) LR 10 CP 179, Ex Ch. The Marine Insurance Act 1906 s 89 provides that 'reference may be made, as heretofore, to the slip or covering note in any legal proceeding': see *Ionides v Pacific Insurance Co* (1871) LR 6 QB 674 at 678.

5 Marine Insurance Act 1906 s 22: see para 39 ante.

90. Payment of premiums. Unless otherwise agreed, the duty of the assured or his agent to pay the premium and the duty of the insurer to issue the policy to the assured or his agent are concurrent conditions, and the insurer is not bound to issue the policy until payment or tender of the premium[1].

Unless otherwise agreed, where a marine policy is effected on behalf of the assured by a broker, the broker is directly responsible to the insurer for the premium, and the insurer is directly responsible to the assured for the amount which may be payable in respect of losses or in respect of returnable premium[2].

Where a marine policy effected on behalf of the assured by a broker acknowledges the receipt of the premium, that acknowledgment is, in the absence of fraud, conclusive as between the insurer and the assured, but not as between the insurer and broker[3].

It follows from the above provisions that, as a general rule, the assured is liable to the broker for premiums as money paid on his behalf, whether or not they have been paid over by the broker to the insurerer[4].

1 Marine Insurance Act 1906 s 52. It is not easy to ascertain what effect this provision was intended to have. It seems that it cannot have any application to a policy effected at Lloyd's with individual underwriters, as, even if they can be considered as issuing a policy, it is, in fact, underwritten without any such tender or payment, nor can it apply to any insurance, whether by companies or at Lloyd's, in those cases in which the premium is paid or deemed to have been paid on or before effecting the policy.
2 Ibid s 53(1).
3 Ibid s 54. Sections 53(1), 54, embodied the law laid down in previously decided cases: see *Power v Butcher* (1829) 10 B & C 329 at 340, 347; *Dalzell v Mair* (1808) 1 Camp 532; *De Gaminde v Pigou* (1812) 4 Taunt 246; *Airy v Bland* (1774) 2 Park's Marine Insurances (8th Edn) 811; *Xenos v Wickham* (1863) 14 CBNS 435 at 456–457, Ex Ch, per Blackburn J; and on appeal (1866) LR 2 HL 296 at 319 per Lord Chelmsford LC; see also *Lamone, Nisbett & Co v Hamilton* 1907 SC 628; *Universe Insurance Co of Milan v Merchants Marine Insurance Co* [1897] 2 QB 93, CA. In the last case the policy, which was effected by a company, did not contain an acknowledgment of the receipt of the premium, and contained a promise by the assured to pay it. It is doubtful, however, whether the decision is not impliedly overruled by the Marine Insurance Act 1906 s 53(1). See also *Roberts v Security Co Ltd* [1897] 1 QB 111, CA, and the comments on this case in *Equitable Fire and Accident Office Ltd v Ching Wo Hong* [1907] AC 96, PC.
4 See also *Bain Clarkson v Owners of Sea Friends* [1991] 2 Lloyd's Rep 322, CA, where the failure to pay premiums did not entitle the brokers to arrest the ship.

91. Set-off of premiums and losses. A claim under a policy, whether the loss is total or partial, is a claim for unliquidated damages[1], so that losses and premiums could not be set off against each other under the statutes of set-off[2]; nor are they now the subject of set-off but, in an action brought by the insurer against him for premiums, the broker can counterclaim, at any rate to the extent to which he could recover on the policies for his own use and benefit[3].

Where the broker or the insurer becomes bankrupt, there can be no counterclaim in an action brought by either of them against the other, inasmuch as no action can be maintained against the trustee of a bankrupt's estate for a debt due from the bankrupt[4]. Although no counterclaim in the ordinary sense of the word can be maintained, there may, however, be a right of set-off under the mutual credit clause of the Insolvency Act 1986[5], and the rules in respect of setting off losses under that clause are as stated below.

(1) Where bankruptcy of the underwriter has intervened, and the action is brought by the trustee of the bankrupt's estate, the broker who has effected the policy in his own name and on his own account, or in his own name but on account of his principal, provided in this last case he has also a lien on the policy to the extent of his set-off[6], may set off losses allowed to him in account by the underwriter before his bankruptcy, even though unadjusted; those losses being mutual credits within the meaning of those words in the Insolvency Act 1986[7].

(2) Where, however, the broker effects the policy both in the name and on account of his principal, or where, when effected in his own name but on the principal's account, he has no lien on it, or where he effects it in his own name, but expressly on the face of the policy as agent, he has no such right of set-off. He has no such right even though he acts under a del credere commission, for such a commission, being a contract wholly between the broker and the assured, cannot affect the mutual rights and liabilities of the

broker and the underwriter, and, therefore, does not by itself entitle the broker to his right of set-off[8].

1 *Castelli v Boddington* (1852) 1 E & B 66; *Luckie v Bushby* (1853) 13 B & C 864; *Thomson v Redman* (1843) 11 M & W 487; *Pellas v Neptune Marine Insurance Co* (1879) 5 CPD 34, CA; and see *Swan and Cleland's Graving Dock and Slipway Co v Maritime Insurance Co and Croshaw* [1907] 1 KB 116 at 123; *Baker v Adam* (1910) 15 Com Cas 227. Summary judgment may be given under RSC Ord 14 in an action on a policy against default in payment of a sum of money: see *Dane v Mortgage Insurance Corpn Ltd* [1894] 1 QB 54, CA.
2 2 Geo 2 c 22 (1728); 8 Geo 2 c 24 (1734) (both repealed by the Statute Law Revision and Civil Procedure Act 1883 s 4). As to the nature of the modern right of set-off see generally SET-OFF AND COUNTERCLAIM.
3 *Young v Kitchin* (1878) 3 ExD 127; *Newfoundland Government v Newfoundland Rly Co* (1888) 13 App Cas 199, PC.
4 As to the effect of a bankruptcy order see BANKRUPTCY AND INSOLVENCY vol 3(2) (Reissue) para 186 et seq.
5 See the Insolvency Act 1986 s 323; and BANKRUPTCY AND INSOLVENCY vol 3(2) (Reissue) paras 535–547.
6 *Davies v Wilkinson* (1828) 4 Bing 573. As to lien on the policy see paras 93–94 post.
7 See the Insolvency Act 1986 s 323; and see *Grove v Dubois* (1786) 1 Term Rep 112 (as explained by Lord Ellenborough CJ in *Parker v Smith* (1812) 16 East 382 at 386); *Koster v Eason* (1813) 2 M & S 112; *Parker v Beasley* (1814) 2 M & S 423.
8 *Wilson v Creighton* (1782) 3 Doug KB 132; *Cumming v Forester* (1813) 1 M & S 494; *Koster v Eason* (1813) 2 M & S 112; *Parker v Beasley* (1814) 2 M & S 423; *Davies v Wilkinson* (1828) 4 Bing 573; *Lee v Bullen* (1858) 8 E & B 692n; *Baker v Langhorn* (1816) 4 Camp 396 (subsequent proceedings on an application for a new trial, 6 Taunt 519); *Peele v Northcote* (1817) 7 Taunt 478. These rules are the result of the cases cited in this note and notes 6–7 supra. See further Arnould on Marine Insurance (16th Edn) s 178.

92. Return of premium.

The amount of premium ultimately payable to the insurer may frequently depend on contingencies which cannot at once be ascertained, as for instance where it is agreed that the premium should be reduced if the ship should sail on or before a specified day, or in case of short interest. In these cases there is a returnable premium, and, unless otherwise agreed, where a marine policy is effected on the assured's behalf by a broker, the insurer is directly responsible to the assured in respect of returnable premium[1].

1 Marine Insurance Act 1906 s 53(1); see para 90 ante. As to the return of premiums see further paras 325–334 post. Returns of premium are dealt with as losses. The insurer is credited with the initial premium, and if a return is afterwards found to be due it is adjusted on the policy and credited to the broker, just as a loss would be adjusted or credited.

93. Insurance agent's lien on the policy.

When it is effected, the policy becomes the property of the assured, who may maintain an action for its recovery subject to any lien which the broker may have for premiums and commissions or for the general balance of his insurance account[1].

Where the policy is left by the assured in the broker's hands, unless otherwise agreed, the broker has, as against the assured, a lien on the policy for the amount of the premium and his charges in respect of effecting the policy; and, where he has dealt with the person who employs him as a principal, he has also a lien on the policy in respect of any balance on any insurance account which may be due to him from that person, unless when the debt was incurred he had reason to believe that that person was only an agent[2].

A person who, although not an insurance broker, is the agent in England of a merchant abroad has a lien on the policy, which he is authorised to effect, for the general balance due to him or becoming due on his account with his principal while the policy remains in his hands[3] or in those of an insurance broker employed by him[4].

The general lien of an insurance broker or agent is, however, confined to the balance of the insurance account, and does not extend to transactions between the broker and the assured on a distinct account having no relation to insurance, but, where bankruptcy intervenes, money becoming due under those transactions may be the subject of set-off under the mutual credit clause of the Insolvency Act 1986[5].

If an insurance broker, having a lien on a policy, is summoned as a witness to produce it under a subpoena duces tecum in an action by the assured against the insurer, he can be compelled to produce the policy, but, if the assured is successful in the action, the court will prevent the money from being paid over to him until the broker's lien is satisfied[6].

1 *Harding v Carter* (1781) 1 Park's Marine Insurances (8th Edn) 4 per Lord Mansfield CJ.
2 Marine Insurance Act 1906 s 53(2). As regards the previous law see *Fisher v Smith* (1878) 4 App Cas 1, HL. See *Fairfield Shipbuilding and Engineering Co Ltd v Gardiner, Mountain & Co Ltd* (1911) 27 TLR 281 (broker estopped as against real principal from setting up general lien; question whether lien on policies extended to proceeds collected thereunder left open). The affirmative proposition in the statutory provision cited embodies the law laid down in *Man v Shiffner* (1802) 2 East 523; *Olive v Smith* (1813) 5 Taunt 56; *Westwood v Bell* (1815) 4 Camp 349 at 353; *Mann v Forrester* (1814) 4 Camp 60; *Godin v London Assurance Co* (1758) 1 Burr 489 at 493. For the qualification in the statutory provision see *Maanss v Henderson* (1801) 1 East 335; *Man v Shiffner* supra; *Snook v Davidson* (1809) 2 Camp 218; *Lanyon v Blanchard* (1811) 2 Camp 597, as explained in *Westwood v Bell* supra; *Cahill v Dawson* (1857) 3 CBNS 106; *Maspons y Hermano v Mildred* (1882) 9 QBD 530 at 543, CA; affd sub nom *Mildred, Goyeneche & Co v Maspons* (1883) 8 App Cas 874, HL.
3 See *Godin v London Assurance Co* (1758) 1 Burr 489.
4 *Man v Shiffner* (1802) 2 East 523.
5 See the Insolvency Act 1986 s 323; and BANKRUPTCY AND INSOLVENCY vol 3(2) (Reissue) paras 535–547. See also *Olive v Smith* (1813) 5 Taunt 56; *Rose v Hart* (1818) 2 Moore CP 547; and para 91 ante.
6 *Hunter v Leathley* (1830) 10 B & C 858; 2 Duer on Marine Insurance 294, 297. As to writs of subpoena duces tecum see EVIDENCE vol 17 paras 250–252.

94. Extinction of lien. The lien of an insurance broker or agent, like the lien of every agent, is extinguished when he voluntarily delivers up the policy to his principal or his order, even by mistake, or if he parts with the policy wrongfully as by pledging it as his own, but not if it is taken from him by force or fraud[1]. If, after it has been parted with, it comes again into the broker's possession, his particular lien revives. His general lien will also revive unless at the time of regaining possession he knew or had reason to believe that the person who employed him was only an agent[2].

1 *Levy v Barnard* (1818) 8 Taunt 149 at 155. See AGENCY vol 1(2) (Reissue) para 129; LIEN.
2 *Levy v Barnard* (1818) 8 Taunt 149; *Near East Relief v King, Chasseur & Co Ltd* [1930] 2 KB 40 per Wright J, approving 2 Duer on Marine Insurance 290, 359–360; and see LIEN.

95. Settlement of losses. The assured generally leaves the policy with the broker, or hands it to him in order that he may settle the amount of loss[1] with the insurer and obtain payment from him; and it seems that in that case the broker has ostensible authority to settle the loss and receive payment of the money[2].

In the absence of an express or implied agreement to the contrary, the broker has only authority to receive payment of losses in cash, and has no authority to bind the assured by a mere settlement of the loss in account between him and the insurer[3]. In the case, however, of Lloyd's underwriters, the claims for losses fall due seven days after they have been settled, and it is customary to carry on current accounts between the broker and the underwriters, setting off losses against premium and passing cheques for the balance due at the end of each quarter; but, as this usage is not a general one and only prevails at Lloyd's, the assured, unless proved to be cognisant of it and to have assented to it, can recover the loss against the underwriter, even if the claim has, between broker and insurer, been settled and passed into account[4].

On the other hand, if the assured is proved to have been apprised of the usage and to have assented to it, he is bound by it and cannot recover from the insurer claims so settled and passed into account[5]. In this case, however, the broker, having deprived the assured of all rights remaining against the insurer, will be liable to the assured for the amount as money had and received to his use, and, in an action by the assured, will be estopped from saying that he has not that money in his hands for the plaintiff's use[6].

When the broker has been expressly instructed to effect the insurance at Lloyd's, this fact may justify the inference that the assured has consented to be bound by the usage[7].

1 As to the insurer's responsibility to the assured for the amount payable in respect of losses see the text and notes infra.

2 *Xenos v Wickham* (1863) 14 CBNS 435 at 464, Ex Ch, per Blackburn J, a minority judgment which was supported on appeal (1866) LR 2 HL 296; *Sweeting v Pearce* (1859) 7 CBNS 449; affd (1861) 9 CBNS 534, Ex Ch; *Scott v Irving* (1830) 1 B & Ad 605; *Legge v Byas, Mosley & Co* (1901) 7 Com Cas 16. As to payment by bill see *Hine Bros v Steamship Insurance Syndicate Ltd* (1895) 72 LT 79, CA.

3 *Jell v Pratt* (1817) 2 Stark 67; *Todd v Reid* (1821) 4 B & Ald 210; *Russell v Bangley* (1821) 4 B & Ald 395; *Bartlett v Pentland* (1830) 10 B & C 760, and the cases cited in note 2 supra; and see *Matveieff & Co v Crossfield* (1903) 8 Com Cas 120 (where it was held that *Sweeting v Pearce* (1859) 7 CBNS 449 (affd (1861) 9 CBNS 534, Ex Ch) was not overruled by *Robinson v Mollett* (1875) LR 7 HL 802). See also *Re Law Car and General Insurance Corpn Ltd* (1911) 55 Sol Jo 407; affd [1911] WN 101, CA (agreement for payment of premiums into joint account and deduction of losses therefrom).

4 See note 3 supra; and *McCowin Lumber and Export Co Inc v Pacific Marine Insurance Co Ltd* (1922) 38 TLR 901.

5 *Stewart v Aberdein* (1838) 4 M & W 211; see the cases cited in note 3 supra; cf *Macfarlane v Giannacopulo* (1858) 3 H & N 860 at 866; the Marine Insurance Act 1906 s 87; and as to the binding effect of usages see para 51 ante. This usage does not extend to dealings between brokers and insurance companies: *Hine Bros v Steamship Insurance Syndicate Ltd* (1895) 72 LT 79, CA.

6 *Andrew v Robinson* (1812) 3 Camp 199; *Wilkinson v Clay* (1815) 6 Taunt 110. As to estoppel by representation generally see ESTOPPEL vol 16 (Reissue) para 1038 et seq.

7 *Bartlett v Pentland* (1830) 10 B & C 760 at 770; *Stewart v Aberdein* (1838) 4 M & W 211; *Sweeting v Pearce* (1861) 9 CBNS 534 at 541, Ex Ch. See CUSTOM AND USAGE vol 12 para 467.

96. Recovery of payments for losses and premiums. Where an underwriter has, by mistake, paid a loss to the broker to which the assured is not entitled, he may recover it back from the broker if the latter has not paid it over to his principal, or settled in account with him in such manner as amounts to payment[1]. Merely passing it into account is not for this purpose equivalent to payment[2].

A premium paid in respect of an illegal insurance is not, in general, recoverable, although the insurer cannot be compelled to pay the loss[3].

It seems that an agent, to whom money has actually been paid to the use of a principal, cannot withhold it from him on the ground that the transaction out of which the payment arose was illegal. Therefore, where a loss has actually been paid over by the insurer to the broker, the broker cannot, in an action for money had and received to the use of the assured, set up as a defence the illegality of the insurance[4]. Where, however, the money has not been paid but only allowed in account, premiums on illegal insurances may be stopped by the assured while in the broker's hands, and the insurer cannot recover them from the broker[5]. Moreover, the insurance agent cannot dispute the title of his principal, and, after receiving money for him in that capacity, cannot set up that he did not so receive it, but only received it for the benefit of some other person[6].

1 *Buller v Harrison* (1777) 2 Cowp 565; *Holland v Russell* (1861) 1 B & S 424; affd (1863) 4 B & S 14. The broker cannot claim a lien for unpaid premiums due from the assured as the money is not his principal's money: see *Scottish Metropolitan Assurance Co Ltd v P Samuel & Co Ltd* [1923] 1 KB 348.
2 *Buller v Harrison* (1777) 2 Cowp 565.
3 *Lowry v Bourdieu* (1780) 2 Doug KB 468; *Allkins v Jupe* (1877) 2 CPD 375. For the full treatment of this subject see paras 325–334 post.
4 *Farmer v Russell* (1798) 1 Bos & P 296; *De Mattos v Benjamin* (1894) 63 LJQB 248; *O' Sullivan v Thomas* [1895] 1 QB 698, DC; *Burge v Ashley and Smith Ltd* [1900] 1 QB 744, CA.
5 *Edgar v Fowler* (1803) 3 East 222.
6 *Roberts v Ogilby* (1821) 9 Price 269; *Dixon v Hamond* (1819) 2 B & Ald 310. If *Bell v Jutting* (1817) 1 Moore CP 155 is inconsistent with these two cases, it must be considered to be overruled by them. See also *Dixon v Hovill* (1828) 4 Bing 665. The rules of the common law relating to principal and agent apply to the case of the assured and broker: Marine Insurance Act 1906 s 91(2). As to these rules generally see AGENCY vol 1(2) (Reissue) paras 109–110.

(4) INSURANCE AGENTS

97. Authority to insure. A person may have express or implied authority to insure on another's behalf, but, unless he has that authority, he cannot recover the premium from the other person[1].

1 *French v Backhouse* (1771) 5 Burr 2727; and see para 98 text to note 1 post. As to ratification see paras 89 note 4 ante, 213 post; and cf AGENCY vol 1(2) (Reissue) para 44 et seq.

98. Authority of particular classes of person. A partner has implied authority from other members of the firm to procure an insurance to be effected for them and himself on partnership property[1], but this rule does not apply to part owners[2] unless they are jointly interested in the particular adventure insured in such a manner as to be partners in it[3].

A consignor or commission agent to whom funds are remitted for the purpose of purchasing and shipping goods for his employer has not, merely as consignor, an implied authority to insure the goods on his principal's behalf, but that authority can be inferred from the established course of dealing between the two parties or by the usage of a particular trade[4].

As regards the consignee, he has not, merely as consignee, implied authority to insure on the consignor's behalf, and cannot, therefore, charge him with the premiums[5]; but where he has an interest exceeding that of a mere consignee, for example where he has made advances on the goods consigned to him, he acquires authority to insure them, and can effect a policy to the amount of the insurable value, and then, by alleging the interest in himself and his consignor, he can recover the whole amount from the insurers[6].

1 Partnership Act 1890 s 5. As to partnership generally see PARTNERSHIP.
2 *Bell v Humphries* (1818) 2 Stark 346; *Roberts v Ogilby* (1821) 9 Price 269 at 282.

3 *Robinson v Gleadow* (1835) 2 Bing NC 156. In such a case one co-adventurer may have a duty as well as authority to insure: see *Califatis v Olivier* (1919) 36 TLR 18; affd on a different point (1920) 36 TLR 223, CA.

4 2 Duer on Marine Insurance 101–104.

5 2 Duer on Marine Insurance 107–108.

6 Marine Insurance Act 1906 s 14(2); 2 Duer on Marine Insurance 106; *Wolff v Horncastle* (1798) 1 Bos & P 316; *Carruthers v Sheddon* (1815) 6 Taunt 14; *Craufurd v Hunter* (1798) 8 Term Rep 13 at 23; *Ebsworth v Alliance Marine Insurance Co* (1873) LR 8 CP 596. In *Cornwal v Wilson* (1750) 1 Ves Sen 509 at 511, Lord Hardwicke LC expressed an opinion that a merchant who has ordered goods from a foreign correspondent, if he justifiably refuses to receive them and elects to reship, has an implied authority to insure them on the consignor's behalf. It is submitted, however, that this opinion is probably incorrect, as the consignee in that case is not bound to reship, and need only give the consignor notice of his refusal to accept the goods: see the Sale of Goods Act 1979 s 36; and SALE OF GOODS. See further para 199 post.

99. Revocation of authority. An authority to insure may generally be revoked at any time before a binding contract of insurance has been entered into[1].

1 It seems, however, extremely doubtful whether a revocation would be effective after an insurance slip or covering note has been signed: see para 89 ante. If the authority to insure is given to enable a consignee to secure his advances, that authority may be irrevocable within the principles laid down in *Smart v Sandars* (1848) 5 CB 895 at 917–918: see AGENCY vol 1(2) (Reissue) para 183.

100. Obligation to insure. The following rules have been laid down for the determination of the question whether or not a person to whom an order to insure has been transmitted is bound to accept the order, and is liable if he does not duly comply with it.

(1) Where a merchant abroad has effects in the hands of his agent or correspondent in England, he has a right to expect that the agent will comply with an order to insure, because he is entitled to withdraw his money from the other's hands when and in what manner he pleases.

(2) Where the merchant abroad has no effects in the hands of his correspondent in England, but the course of dealing between them has been such that the one has been used to send orders for insurance and the other to execute them, the merchant has a right to expect that his orders for insurance will still be obeyed unless the correspondent gives him notice to discontinue that course of dealing.

(3) Where the merchant abroad sends bills of lading to his correspondent in England with an order to insure as the implied condition on which he is to accept the bills of lading, and the correspondent accepts the bills of lading, he must obey the order, for it is one entire transaction, and the acceptance of the bills of lading amounts to an implied agreement to perform the condition[1].

1 *Smith v Lascelles* (1788) 2 Term Rep 187 at 188–190 per Buller J; 2 Duer on Marine Insurance 124–125, 127–128. Where goods are sold for shipment, the seller is prima facie obliged to give such notice to the buyer as will enable him to insure them during the sea transit: see the Sale of Goods Act 1979 s 32(3); and SALE OF GOODS. As to carriage by sea see SHIPPING.

101. Obligation to give notice of non-compliance. Where, under the first or second of the rules previously mentioned[1], the merchant abroad has a right to expect that his order to insure will be complied with, it is the agent's duty, if he does not intend to accept the order, to give prompt notice to the merchant so that the latter may have the opportunity of effecting the insurance elsewhere, and if in consequence of his failure to give due notice no insurance is effected, the agent will be answerable for the loss arising from his default[2].

1 See para 100 ante.
2 *Smith v Lascelles* (1788) 2 Term Rep 187; *Smith v Price* (1862) 2 F & F 748 (measure of damages); cf *Prince v Clark* (1823) 1 B & C 186 at 189; see also *Callander v Oelrichs* (1838) 5 Bing NC 58, and the criticism of that case in 2 Duer on Marine Insurance 222–225.

102. Insurance broker as agent of assured. A broker who effects an insurance with an insurer is not his agent, and is under no legal liability to him to use care or skill in effecting the insurance[1].

1 *Empress Assurance Corpn v C T Bowring & Co* (1905) 11 Com Cas 107; *Glasgow Assurance Corpn Ltd v William Symondson & Co* (1911) 104 LT 254.

103. Liability of insurance agent. An insurance agent's liability to his principal is determined by the principles of the law of agency[1]. As to these, it is sufficient here to make the following general statements.

A person who, voluntarily and without any kind of consideration, promises to procure an insurance is not liable to an action for nonfeasance, because there is no consideration for his promise; but if he in fact enters upon the performance of his undertaking, he is legally bound to use due care and skill[2]. All agents, whether paid or unpaid, skilled or unskilled, are under a legal obligation to exercise due care and skill in performance of the duties which they have undertaken, a greater degree of care being required from a paid than from an unpaid, and from a skilled than from an unskilled, agent[3]. The question in all these cases is whether the act or omission complained of is inconsistent with that reasonable degree of care and skill which persons of ordinary prudence and ability might be expected to show in the agent's situation and profession[4].

Every insurance broker is assumed to be skilled in matters relating to insurance and to know the ordinary well-settled rules of insurance law[5]. He will, therefore, be held liable if he fails to communicate to the underwriter the time of the ship's sailing or any other information which may be material[6]. He is further bound to know all the details necessary to make the policy a legally valid instrument[7], and to insert in the policy the ordinary risks and such customary clauses as are proper in respect of the insured voyage[8], or the business concerned[9].

The agent is, of course, bound to obey the express orders of his principal[10], but, if those orders are so ambiguous as to be reasonably susceptible of two distinct meanings and the agent acts in good faith upon one of them, he will, according to the ordinary law of agency, be held justified in so doing and will be exempt from liability[11].

1 See AGENCY vol 1(2) (Reissue) para 88 et seq. As to liability for careless statements apart from contract see *Hedley Byrne & Co Ltd v Heller & Partners Ltd* [1964] AC 465, [1963] 2 All ER 575, HL; and AGENCY vol 1(2) (Reissue) para 147 note 14; NEGLIGENCE.
2 If a man after taking a trust on himself miscarries in the performance of his trust, an action will lie against him for that, even though nobody could have compelled him to do the things: *Coggs v Bernard* (1703) 2 Ld Raym 909 at 919 per Holt CJ. See also *Wilkinson v Coverdale* (1793) 1 Esp 74, following *Wallace v Tellfair* (1786) 2 Term Rep 188n, where the principle was applied to insurance agency.
3 See AGENCY vol 1(2) (Reissue) para 92.

4　*Chapman v Walton* (1833) 10 Bing 57 at 63 per Tindal CJ; and see *Hurrell v Bullard* (1863) 3 F & F 445; *Osman v J Ralph Moss Ltd* [1970] 1 Lloyd's Rep 313, CA (broker recommending the insured to insure with company known to be in financial difficulties); *O'Connor v B D B Kirby & Co (a firm)* [1972] 1 QB 90, [1971] 2 All ER 1415, CA (broker filling in proposal wrongly); *Everett v Hogg, Robinson and Gardner Mountain (Insurance) Ltd* [1973] 2 Lloyd's Rep 217 (misrepresentation by broker of material fact made to reinsurers); *Seavision Investment SA v Evennett and Clarkson Puckle Ltd, The Tiburon* [1990] 2 Lloyd's Rep 418 (broker's failure to make proper declaration under open cover). It is a question of construction of the terms of the contract of agency whether the agent has contracted merely to use due care and skill to procure an effective insurance or has given an absolute undertaking that he will procure an effective insurance: *Hood v West End Motor Car Packing Co* [1917] 2 KB 38, CA.

5　*Chapman v Walton* (1833) 10 Bing 57 per Tindal CJ.

6　*Maydew v Forrester* (1814) 5 Taunt 615; *Wake v Atty* (1812) 4 Taunt 493; *Claude R Ogden & Co Pty Ltd v Reliance Fire Sprinkler Co Pty Ltd* [1975] 1 Lloyd's Rep 52 (NSW SC) (failure of brokers to inform insurers of assured's bad claims record); *Warren v Henry Sutton & Co* [1976] 2 Lloyd's Rep 276, CA (failure of broker to inform insurers of assured's friend's poor driving record). See the Marine Insurance Act 1906 ss 19, 20; and paras 217, 232–241 post. It is not the broker's duty to forward a contract to the assured as soon as it is issued: *United Mills Agencies Ltd v R E Harvey, Bray & Co* [1952] 1 All ER 225n.

7　*Turpin v Bilton* (1843) 5 Man & G 455; see, however, *Wake v Atty* (1812) 4 Taunt 493.

8　*Mallough v Barber* (1815) 4 Camp 150; *Park v Hammond* (1816) 6 Taunt 495; cf *Comber v Anderson* (1808) 1 Camp 523; *Moore v Mourgite* (1776) 2 Cowp 479.

9　*Fine's Flowers Ltd v General Accident Assurance Co of Canada* (1974) 5 OR (2d) 137 (failure by agent to effect policy relating to horticultural business to give cover for damage to plants by freezing due to failure of water pump).

10　*Yuill & Co v Robson* [1908] 1 KB 270, CA; *Glaser v Cowie* (1813) 1 M & S 52; *Strong and Pearl v S Allison & Co Ltd* (1926) 25 Ll L Rep 504. The client is entitled to rely on the broker's carrying out his instructions, and if this is not done and the loss is consequently not recoverable from the insurer, the fact that the client might have discovered the broker's mistake by checking the insurance documents is no defence to an action against the broker for negligence: *Dickson & Co v Devitt* (1916) 86 LJKB 315; *General Accident, Fire and Life Assurance Corpn Ltd v J H Minet & Co Ltd* (1942) 74 Ll L Rep 1, CA.

11　*Fomin v Oswell* (1813) 3 Camp 357; *Ireland v Livingston* (1872) LR 5 HL 395; cf *Yuill & Co v Robson* [1908] 1 KB 270, CA; and see *Moore v Mourgue* (1776) 2 Cowp 479; *Comber v Anderson* (1808) 1 Camp 523; *James Vale & Co v Van Oppen & Co Ltd* (1921) 37 TLR 367. See AGENCY vol 1(2) (Reissue) para 50.

104. Evidence of requisite standard of care and skill. The question whether an insurance broker has exercised reasonable care and skill is a question of fact[1], but there are two conflicting decisions as to the admissibility of the evidence of persons engaged in the same business as to what would have been in the circumstances the conduct of a broker of reasonable care and skill[2].

1　*Hurrell v Bullard* (1863) 3 F & F 445.

2　*Campbell v Rickards* (1833) 5 B & Ad 840, where such evidence was held to be inadmissible; *Chapman v Walton* (1833) 10 Bing 57, where it was held admissible. It is submitted that such evidence is admissible. This seems to follow by analogy from the practice in admitting evidence as to what are material facts to be disclosed (see EVIDENCE vol 17 para 83 note 7), and in accordance with the principles laid down by Tindal CJ in *Chapman v Walton* (1833) 10 Bing 57.

105. Necessity for damage caused by default. In order to maintain an action against an insurance agent, the principal must not only prove that the agent was in default, but must also establish that he has sustained damage by reason of the default[1]. If the assured orders an illegal or void insurance, no action will lie against the agent for not effecting it or for failure to exercise due care and skill in effecting it[2], and, if the insurer could have successfully resisted a claim under the policy on the ground of breach of an express or implied warranty, deviation, or the like, the principal cannot recover damages from the agent for not effecting the policy, or for negligence in reference to it, unless perhaps it is clearly shown that the insurer would not have availed himself of any such defence[3].

1 *Fraser v B N Furman (Productions) Ltd (Miller Smith & Partners, third parties)* [1967] 3 All ER 57, [1967] 1 WLR 898, CA (decision turned on a condition in the policy). The measure of damages for non-insurance is that which would have been recovered from the insurers (*Smith v Price* (1862) 2 F & F 748 at 752 per Erle CJ), but, in accordance with the ordinary principles of agency, an insurance agent may be liable for the costs of a previous action which the assured has brought against the insurer if the action was brought with the agent's desire or concurrence (*Maydew v Forrester* (1814) 5 Taunt 615) or if it was reasonable to bring it having regard to the attitude assumed by the agent (*Strong and Pearl v S Allison & Co Ltd* (1926) 25 Ll L 504 at 508).

2 *Webster v De Tastet* (1797) 7 Term Rep 157; *Glaser v Cowie* (1813) 1 M & S 52; *T Cheshire & Co v Vaughan Bros & Co* [1920] 3 KB 240, CA.

3 *Delany v Stoddart* (1785) 1 Term Rep 22; 2 Duer on Marine Insurance 325; 2 Phillips' Law of Insurance (5th Edn) s 1904.

106. Duty in relation to claims. If, after being effected, the policy is left in the hands of the insurance agent, it is generally his duty to settle the loss with the insurers, and to collect the various sums due from them and pay them over to his principal, and if he does not use due care and diligence in these matters, he will be responsible to his principal for any loss the principal may sustain by reason of his default[1].

The agent may have express or implied authority, and it may become his duty, to give notice of abandonment in case of a constructive total loss, and in this case he is bound to use reasonable care and diligence, and in default of doing so will become liable to his principal for damage resulting from notice not having been given[2].

In the absence of his principal's express authority, a broker has no authority to cancel a policy, whether it is left in his hands or not[3].

1 *Bousfield v Creswell* (1810) 2 Camp 545; and see *Xenos v Wickham* (1863) 14 CBNS 435 at 464–465, Ex Ch, per Blackburn J ('Perhaps it may be put as high as to say that the broker is clothed with authority to do all that is incidentally necessary to carry out the contract in the policy left in his hands; see *Richardson v Anderson* (1805) 1 Camp 43n; *Goodson v Brooke* (1815) 4 Camp 163. I do not wish to be understood as giving a decided opinion that he has so much authority, but there are at least grounds for so contending'); and see para 95 ante.

2 *Comber v Anderson* (1808) 1 Camp 523 (sequel to *Anderson v Royal Exchange Assurance Co* (1805) 7 East 38), where a duty to give notice was not established.

3 *Xenos v Wickham* (1866) LR 2 HL 296, revsg (but not on this point) (1863) 14 CBNS 435, Ex Ch. Where, however, a broker effects a policy in England pursuant to instructions given him in a foreign country, he will have implied authority to cancel that policy if that authority is conferred upon him by the law of the foreign country: *Ruby SS Corpn Ltd v Commercial Union Assurance Co Ltd* (1933) 150 LT 30, CA.

107. Agents to subscribe policies. An agent may be appointed not only for the purpose of effecting marine policies for the assured but also for the purpose of subscribing them for the insurers[1].

The authority of the insurer's agent is generally limited by the terms and conditions contained in the agreement by which he is appointed agent; and if it is common knowledge in the place where the policy is effected that agents who subscribe for a principal have only a limited authority, that knowledge must be imputed to the assured, who cannot recover from the principal if the agent has exceeded his actual authority[2].

On the other hand, if the agent has not exceeded his actual authority, the principal is liable, even if the agent is acting fraudulently for his own benefit and not that of his principal, provided always that the assured has no knowledge of the fraud and is acting in good faith[3].

An agent who has authority to subscribe a policy has implied authority, and is also bound, to perform any subsequent act on behalf of his principal that may be rendered necessary by the relation between the principal and the assured such as the authority to sign the adjustment of a loss[4].

It has already been observed[5] that Lloyd's agents are not the agents of the underwriters, and have, therefore, no authority to make or sign any adjustment of the loss or accept an abandonment or receive notice of abandonment as the underwriters' representative[6].

1 *Neal v Erving* (1793) 1 Esp 61; *Mason v Joseph* (1804) 1 Smith KB 406; *Courteen v Touse* (1807) 1 Camp 43; *Haughton v Ewbank* (1814) 4 Camp 88; *Guthrie v Armstrong* (1822) 1 Dow & Ry KB 248; *Brockelbank v Sugrue* (1831) 5 C & P 21; *Mead v Davison* (1835) 3 Ad & El 303.
2 *Baines v Ewing* (1866) LR 1 Exch 320.
3 *Hambro v Burnand* [1904] 2 KB 10, CA; *Lloyd v Grace, Smith & Co* [1912] AC 716, HL: see AGENCY vol 1(2) (Reissue) para 134. All authority may be continued by estoppel after its expiration: see *Willis, Faber & Co Ltd v Joyce* (1911) 104 LT 576; and ESTOPPEL vol 16 (Reissue) para 1056.
4 *Richardson v Anderson* (1805) 1 Camp 43n.
5 See para 21 ante.
6 See *Drake v Marryat* (1823) 1 B & C 473 at 477 per Lord Tenterden CJ; *Vacuum Oil Co v Union Insurance Society of Canton Ltd* (1926) 32 Com Cas 53, CA, per Atkin LJ. As to abandonment and notice of abandonment see para 302 et seq post.

(5) SUBJECT MATTER INSURED AND ITS DESCRIPTION IN THE POLICY

108. Ship's name. As the subject matter must be designated in a marine policy with reasonable certainty, regard, however, being had to any usage regulating the designation[1], the name of the ship in which the insured voyage is to be performed must generally be specified in the policy[2].

As the insertion of the ship's name is only required for the purpose of identifying her, an error in the name is immaterial if it is shown that the underwriters intended the policy to cover the ship on which the loss actually occurred[3]. Accordingly, the policy usually contains the clause 'or by whatsoever other name or names the ship may be called'.

1 See the Marine Insurance Act 1906 s 26(1), (4); and para 112 post.
2 Where cover is effected by 'Cavalier and/or steamers held covered at premiums to be arranged', this means either (1) that it is open to the assured to leave the ship's name unstated until a loss has taken place or the risk has run off, or (2) that the assured is to declare the name within a reasonable time after ascertaining it: *Marine Insurance Co Ltd v Grimmer* [1944] 2 All ER 197, CA.
3 *Le Mesurier v Vaughan* (1805) 6 East 382; *Clapham v Cologan* (1813) 3 Camp 382 at 383; *Ionides v Pacific Insurance Co* (1871) LR 6 QB 674; affd (1872) LR 7 QB 517, Ex Ch. The ship's name carries no warranty of nationality: *Clapham v Cologan* supra; *Dent v Smith* (1869) LR 4 QB 414. The master's name need not be stated in the policy, and there is no implied condition that he should be correctly named, or that the same master should be in command throughout the voyage: see Arnould on Marine Insurance (16th Edn) s 292; and para 905 note 9 post.

109. Floating policies. In many cases the assured does not know on what ship or ships the insured goods have been or may be loaded, and he consequently effects what is called a floating policy[1], in which the name of the ship or ships and other particulars are left to be defined by subsequent declaration[2].

The subsequent declaration or declarations may be made by indorsement on the policy, or in other customary manner[3].

Unless the policy otherwise provides, the declarations must be made in the order of dispatch or shipment. In the case of goods they must comprise all consignments within the terms of the policy, and the value of the goods or other property must be honestly stated, but an omission or erroneous declaration may be rectified even after loss or arrival, provided the omission or declaration was made in good faith[4].

Unless the policy otherwise provides, where a declaration of value is not made until after loss or arrival the policy must be treated as an unvalued policy[5] as regards the subject matter of that declaration[6].

1 As regards the various types of marine insurance policies see generally para 41 ante.
2 See the Marine Insurance Act 1906 s 29(1). Section 29 embodies the law laid down in *Robinson v Touray* (1811) 3 Camp 158; *Harman v Kingston* (1811) 3 Camp 150; *Gledstanes v Royal Exchange Assurance* (1864) 5 B & S 797; *Stephens v Australasian Insurance Co* (1872) LR 8 CP 18; and overrules the decisions in *Kewley v Ryan* (1794) 2 Hy Bl 343; *Henchman v Offley* (1782) 2 Hy Bl 345n; and the corresponding dicta of Blackburn J in *Ionides v Pacific Insurance Co* (1875) LR 6 QB 674 at 682. A policy on specified goods 'per' a named steamer 'and/or steamers' is not a floating policy within the meaning of this section, and the assured is under no legal obligation to declare the name of the ship on which the goods are in fact shipped: *Dickson & Co Ltd v Devitt* (1916) 86 LJKB 315. Where the policy contained a clause to the effect that declarations of interest were to be made as soon as possible after the sailing of the vessel, it was held that this clause was a warranty, failure to comply with which precluded the assured from recovery for a loss, and that the provision in the Marine Insurance Act 1906 s 29(3) (see text and notes 3–4 infra) as to omissions and erroneous declarations was inapplicable: *Union Insurance Society of Canton Ltd v George Wills & Co* [1916] 1 AC 281, PC; see also *Dunlop Bros & Co v Townend* [1919] 2 KB 127.
3 Marine Insurance Act 1906 s 29(2).
4 Ibid s 29(3).
5 As to unvalued policies see para 41 ante.
6 Marine Insurance Act 1906 s 29(4).

110. Cover under a floating policy. A floating policy[1] on goods 'on board ship or ships' covers goods loaded at any port within the limits of the insured voyage[2], but a declaration under a floating policy will not make the policy attach if the declaration is made dishonestly[3], or if the floating policy was not intended to cover the interest of the assured in the property which is the subject of the declaration[4].

1 For the meaning of 'floating policy' see para 109 ante.
2 *Hunter v Leathley* (1830) 10 B & C 858.
3 *Rivaz v Gerussi* (1880) 6 QBD 222, CA.
4 *Scott v Globe Marine Insurance Co* (1896) 1 Com Cas 370. Conversely, for the purpose of declarations, the assured cannot exclude from the policy any portion of the interest which it was intended to cover: *Dunlop Bros & Co v Townend* [1919] 2 KB 127.

111. Transhipment of goods. It is an implied condition in a marine policy that the ship named in it is not to be changed after the commencement of the risk without necessity or the underwriter's consent. On the other hand, where, by a peril insured against, the voyage is interrupted at an intermediate port or place in such circumstances as, apart from any special stipulation in the contract of affreightment, to justify the master in landing and reshipping the goods or other movables[1], or in transhipping them and sending them on to their destination, the insurer's liability continues, notwithstanding the landing or transhipment[2].

1 For the meaning of 'movables' see para 36 note 3 ante.
2 Marine Insurance Act 1906 s 59. It is justly stated in Arnould on Marine Insurance (16th Edn) s 281 that the words of this provision imply that where the transhipment is made necessary by a peril not insured against, the insurer's liability does not continue; the provision seems to impose a restriction upon the right to recover on the policy for which, before the Marine Insurance Act 1906, there was no authority. As to the effect of a clause permitting transhipment see para 129 post.

112. Specification of subject matter. The subject matter insured must be designated in a marine policy with reasonable certainty[1], but the nature and extent of the assured's interest in the subject matter insured need not be specified in the policy[2].

Where the policy designates the subject matter insured in general terms, it must be construed to apply to the interest intended by the assured to be covered[3].

In the application of the above provisions, regard must be had to any usage regulating the designation of the subject matter insured[4].

1 Marine Insurance Act 1906 s 26(1).
2 Ibid s 26(2).
3 Ibid s 26(3). 'Interest' in s 26(3) means the assured's interest in the adventure insured: *Dunlop Bros & Co v Townend* [1919] 2 KB 127. When the question was which of two voyages was intended to be reinsured, Sankey J thought that this subsection was inapplicable: *Janson v Poole* (1915) 84 LJKB 1543 at 1549. See also *Reliance Marine Insurance Co v Duder* [1913] 1 KB 265, CA.
4 Marine Insurance Act 1906 s 26(4).

113. Meaning of 'ship'; hovercraft. Unless the context of the policy otherwise requires, the term 'ship' includes the hull, materials and outfit, stores and provisions for the officers and crew, and in the case of vessels engaged in a special trade, the ordinary fittings requisite for the trade, and also, in the case of a steamship, the machinery, boilers and coals and engine stores, if owned by the assured[1].

The Marine Insurance Act 1906 has effect as if any reference in it in whatever terms to ships, vessels or boats, or activities or places connected with them, included a reference to hovercraft or activities or places connected with hovercraft[2].

1 Marine Insurance Act 1906 s 30(2), Sch 1 r 15. As to the statutory rules of construction of a marine policy see generally para 44 ante. In whaling voyages 'outfit' includes the fishing stores of the ship employed, that is to say, all the instruments and apparatus necessary for taking the fish and preparing and bringing home the proceeds: *Hill v Patten* (1807) 8 East 373 at 375. Before that case, it was decided in accordance with the general custom of whaling voyages that outfits in this sense of the term were not protected by a general insurance in the ordinary form on the ship's body, tackle, apparel etc, and it would seem this would still continue to be the case (see the Marine Insurance Act 1906 s 26(4); and para 112 ante), if that custom still exists (*Hoskins v Pickersgill* (1783) 3 Doug KB 222; *The Dundee* (1823) 1 Hag Adm 109 at 123; *Gale v Laurie* (1826) 5 B & C 156 at 164). Separation cloths and dunnage mats were included in the term 'furniture' in a time policy (see para 41 ante) on a ship employed in the Black Sea grain trade: see *Hogarth v Walker* [1900] 2 QB 283, CA. It is submitted that in the absence of any custom the question raised in the cases cited above would now be determined by the application of the Marine Insurance Act 1906 Sch 1 r 15. As to whether a time policy on a ship would cover her bunker coal and stores see *Roddick v Indemnity Mutual Marine Insurance Co* [1895] 1 QB 836; affd [1895] 2 QB 380, CA. Such a policy on 'hull and machinery' does not: *Roddick v Indemnity Mutual Marine Insurance Co* supra. In *New Liverpool Eastham Ferry and Hotel Co Ltd v Ocean Accident and Guarantee Corpn Ltd* (1929) 35 Com Cas 37, CA, it was held (Russell LJ dissenting, and Scrutton LJ doubting) that the anchors and chains to which a coal hulk was moored were part of tackle and furniture, although when the hulk was temporarily moved these moorings would be left behind. In the collision clause (set out in Appendix 3, para 908 post) the words 'ship or vessel' are not

apt to include a flying boat; see *Polpen Shipping Co Ltd v Commercial Union Assurance Co Ltd* [1943] KB 161, [1943] 1 All ER 162.

2 Hovercraft (Application of Enactments) Order 1972, SI 1972/971, art 4, Sch 1 Pt A. This applies to hovercraft which are used (1) wholly or partly on or over the sea or navigable waters; or (2) on or over land to which the public have access or non-navigable waters to which the public have access; or (3) elsewhere for the carriage of passengers for reward: art 2. For the meaning of 'hovercraft' see the Hovercraft Act 1968 s 4(1); and SHIPPING vol 43 para 1221.

114. Meaning of 'goods'. Unless the context of the policy otherwise requires, the term 'goods'[1] means goods in the nature of merchandise, and does not include personal effects or provisions and stores for use on board; in the absence of any usage to the contrary deck cargo and living animals must be insured specifically and not under the general denomination of goods[2]. The term includes money, bullion or jewels if put on board as merchandise, but does not comprise jewels, ornaments, cash etc, not intended for trade and carried about or belonging to persons on board[3], and it probably does not include banknotes or bills of exchange[4].

A policy on goods will cover successive cargoes on board the same ship in the course of the insured voyage[5]. So, in whaling voyages, the term 'goods' covered the homeward-bound cargo resulting from the fishing adventure such as the oil, whalebone etc, taken in the fishery[6].

Where the goods insured are actually specified in the policy[7], it will not attach to any goods which do not answer the description given; for instance, an insurance on 'piece goods' would not cover hats[8].

1 An insurance on goods covers both loss of goods and loss of the adventure: see para 181 post.
2 Marine Insurance Act 1906 s 30(2), Sch 1 r 17. As to the statutory rules of construction of a marine policy see generally para 44 ante. The latter part of the rule, which applies even to goods usually carried on deck, simplifies and to some extent alters the law on this subject as it stood before the Act. On this subject see *Da Costa v Edmunds* (1815) 4 Camp 142; *Apollinaris Co v Nord Deutsche Insurance Co* [1904] 1 KB 252. A usage in the trade in which the goods are carried to carry them on deck is a 'usage to the contrary' within the meaning of this rule (*British and Foreign Marine Insurance Co Ltd v Gaunt* [1921] 2 AC 41, HL); but a usage of the insurance world to insure deck cargo or living animals under the general designation would also be a 'usage to the contrary' (*British and Foreign Marine Insurance Co Ltd v Gaunt* supra at 54 per Lord Finlay, and at 60 per Lord Sumner); as to usage see generally paras 51–53 ante. See also, as to insurance of deck cargo, *Hood v West End Motor Car Packing Co* [1917] 2 KB 38, CA.
3 *Brown v Stapyleton* (1827) 4 Bing 119.
4 *Palmer v Pratt* (1824) 2 Bing 185 at 191–192.
5 *Hill v Patten* (1807) 8 East 373; *Tobin v Harford* (1863) 13 CBNS 791 at 802; affd (1864) 17 CBNS 528 at 537, Ex Ch.
6 *Hill v Patten* (1807) 8 East 373.
7 See eg *De Symonds v Shedden* (1800) 2 Bos & P 153; *Brown Bros v Fleming* (1902) 7 Com Cas 245.
8 *Hunter v Prinsep* (1806) Marshall on Marine Insurance (4th Edn) 255; cf *Hart v Standard Marine Insurance Co* (1889) 22 QBD 499, CA. This statement was cited with approval in *Overseas Commodities Ltd v Style* [1958] 1 Lloyd's Rep 546 at 559.

115. Freight must be specifically insured. Certain interests must be specifically insured, and are not included in the general denomination of goods[1] or ship[2].

Freight must be specifically insured by apt wording in the policy[3]. This is generally done by inserting the words 'on freight' at the foot or in the margin of the instrument[4]. The term 'freight', when used in a policy to denote the subject matter insured, includes not only money payable to the shipowner for the carriage of goods, but also any benefit derived by him from the employment of the ship such as money paid by the charterer for the hire of the ship, or the benefit derived by the shipowner from the carriage of his own goods[5].

Passage money, namely money paid by the passenger before sailing, is not, however, covered by a policy on freight unless the terms of the particular policy necessitate a different construction[6].

1 For the meaning of 'goods' see para 114 ante.
2 For the meaning of 'ship' see para 113 ante.
3 *Gulf and Southern SS Co (Inc) v British Traders Insurance Co Ltd* [1930] 1 KB 451 at 458.
4 See eg *Griffiths v Bramley-Moore* (1878) 4 QBD 70, CA. As to the meaning of an insurance on 'freight chartered and/or as if chartered on board or not on board' see *The Bedouin* [1894] P 1 at 12, CA; *Williams & Co v Canton Insurance Office Ltd* [1901] AC 462, HL; *Scottish Shire Line Ltd v London and Provincial Marine and General Insurance Co Ltd* [1912] 3 KB 51. As to the meaning of 'anticipated freight' see *Papadimitriou v Henderson* [1939] 3 All ER 908 at 915.
5 See the Marine Insurance Act 1906 ss 30(2), 90, Sch 1 r 16, which provide that 'freight' includes the profit derivable by a shipowner from the employment of his ship to carry his own goods or movables, as well as freight payable by a third party, but does not include passage money; and see also *Winter v Haldimand* (1831) 2 B & Ad 649; *Forbes v Aspinall* (1811) 13 East 323 at 325 per Lord Ellenborough; *Flint v Flemyng* (1830) 1 B & Ad 45; *Devaux v J'Anson* (1839) 5 Bing NC 519. Where an 'open cover' or slip (see para 89 ante) provided that the policy was to cover 'invoice cost plus freight and insurance etc', it was held that 'freight' meant freight which, at the time of the loss, the assured had paid or had become liable to pay, and did not denote freight payable on delivery of the cargo at the port of destination (*Kung v Methuen* (1907) 24 TLR 145, CA); but an insurance of a shipowner's 'charges upon the cargo' will include freight in process of being earned (*Gulf and Southern SS Co (Inc) v British Traders Insurance Co Ltd* [1930] 1 KB 451). See also SHIPPING.
6 Marine Insurance Act 1906 s 90, and Sch 1 r 16; *Denoon v Home and Colonial Assurance Co* (1872) LR 7 CP 341. A policy 'on passage money' may be, on its true construction, an insurance against disbursements in respect of particular passage money, in which case the insurers would not be entitled to treat passage money subsequently earned in respect of other passengers as reducing the loss: *New Zealand Shipping Co Ltd v Duke* [1914] 2 KB 682.

116. Insurance of advance freight. The charterer may insure money advanced in part payment of freight[1] if, but only if, the advance is not repayable in case of loss[2], and he may do so by an insurance on freight, although the more usual course is to insure it specifically as advances on account of or against freight[3].

1 For the meaning of 'freight' see para 115 ante.
2 Marine Insurance Act 1906 s 12. A loan on account of freight, repayable absolutely, whether or not there is a loss of ship or goods, does not constitute an insurable interest: see *Allison v Bristol Marine Insurance Co* (1876) 1 App Cas 209, HL; and para 195 post.
3 *Hall v Janson* (1855) 4 E & B 500; *Wilson v Martin* (1856) 11 Exch 684; *Williams v North China Insurance Co* (1876) 1 CPD 757 at 761, CA; *Allison v Bristol Marine Insurance Co* (1876) 1 App Cas 209, HL; and see *Currie & Co v Bombay Native Insurance Co* (1869) LR 3 PC 72; *Thames and Mersey Marine Insurance Co Ltd v Pitts, Son and King* [1893] 1 QB 476, DC. On this point see further para 195 post.

117. Insurance of profits. Expected profits, such as the profits which a buyer of goods 'to arrive' would make if the goods arrived safely at the port of destination, are not covered by an insurance on goods, but must be insured specifically as profits[1].

Commissions to arise from the sale of goods are, like profits, an interest in the goods themselves, but such commissions are not covered by an insurance on goods. They must be specifically insured[2].

1 A policy on profits with a clause 'beginning the adventure from the loading of the goods' will cover only the profit on goods which are actually shipped (*Royal Exchange Assurance v M'Swiney* (1850) 14 QB 646, Ex Ch; *Halhead v Young* (1856) 6 E & B 312), but a policy may be so framed as to cover profits in respect of goods before they are put on board (*Royal Exchange Assurance v M'Swiney* supra at 660). See also *Wilson v Jones* (1867) LR 2 Exch 139 at 146–147 per Willes J; *Wyllie v Povah* (1907) 12 Com Cas 317.

2 *Lucena v Craufurd* (1806) 2 Bos & PNR 269 at 314–315, HL; *Anderson v Morice* (1875) LR 10 CP 609 at 624, Ex Ch; *Mackenzie v Whitworth* (1875) 1 ExD 36 at 43, CA; *Buchanan & Co v Faber* (1899) 4 Com Cas 223 (commission may be covered by a policy on disbursements). As to insurable interest in profits see para 190 post.

118. Loans on bottomry and respondentia. Loans on bottomry and respondentia[1] give rise to a maritime risk, and may be the subject of insurance by the lenders.

These interests must, however, be specifically described in the policy and cannot be insured under the general designation of ship or goods[2] unless it is shown to be the usage of any particular trade to insure them under such a general designation[3].

1 As to bottomry and respondentia see SHIPPING vol 43 para 198. See also para 201 post.
2 *Glover v Black* (1763) 3 Burr 1394.
3 *Gregory v Christie* (1784) 3 Doug KB 419; Marshall on Marine Insurance (4th Edn) 256.

119. Disbursements. A policy on disbursements will cover an advance of freight for the ship's purposes, or an expenditure on fuel, engine-room stores and port charges[1].

1 *Currie & Co v Bombay Native Insurance Co* (1869) LR 3 PC 72. As to what is covered by a policy on disbursements see further *Roddick v Indemnity Mutual Marine Insurance Co* [1895] 2 QB 380, CA; *Buchanan & Co v Faber* (1899) 4 Com Cas 223; *Lawther v Black* (1901) 6 Com Cas 5 (affd 6 Com Cas 196, CA); *Price v Maritime Insurance Co* [1901] 2 KB 412, CA (on 'advances'); *Moran, Galloway & Co v Uzielli* [1905] 2 KB 555; *New Zealand Shipping Co Ltd v Duke* [1914] 2 KB 682.

120. Specification of interest. The nature and extent of the assured's interest in the subject matter insured need not, as a general rule, be specified in the policy unless there is a usage making it necessary[1]. Thus, in a contract of reinsurance it is sufficient to designate the subject matter as being ship or goods etc, without describing the contract as one of reinsurance[2]. A policy on goods will cover the interest of carriers on goods so as to protect them against liability to the owner for the loss of the goods[3].

1 Marine Insurance Act 1906 s 26(2), (4); and see para 112 ante.
2 *Mackenzie v Whitworth* (1875) 1 ExD 36 at 42, CA; see also *Carruthers v Sheddon* (1815) 6 Taunt 14. As to reinsurance see further para 204 et seq post.
3 *Crowley v Cohen* (1832) 3 B & Ad 478. Cf *Joyce v Kennard* (1871) LR 7 QB 78; *Cunard SS Co Ltd v Marten* [1903] 2 KB 511, CA.

(6) COMMENCEMENT, DURATION AND AREA OF RISK

(i) Time Policies: Mixed Policies

121. Commencement and duration of risk. In the absence of any stipulation to the contrary, the two limits of time prescribed in a time policy[1] determine the beginning and end of the risk, or, in other words, the insured period. A time policy, however, may be effected retrospectively by the insertion of the ordinary clause 'lost or not lost'[2]; for instance if a policy is effected on 15 August to commence on the first day of the same month, it will cover any losses occurring on or after 1 August.

A time policy will cover any loss, whether total or partial, occurring[3] during the insured period, even though the extent of the loss is only ascertained after the period has expired. For instance, if there is an insurance for six months on a ship which has received fatal damage some days before, but which is kept afloat by pumping until after the expiration of the six months, the insurers would be liable for a total loss[4].

English time policies usually contain a clause, called the 'continuation clause', which continues the insurance after the expiration of the insured period until the ship arrives at her port of destination[5].

1 For the meaning of 'time policy' see para 41 ante.
2 See para 191 post.
3 It is not enough that a pre-existing injury was discovered during the period: *Hutchins Bros v Royal Exchange Assurance Corpn* (1911) 27 TLR 217; affd [1911] 2 KB 398, CA.
4 *Knight v Faith* (1850) 15 QB 649, explaining *Meretony v Dunlope* (1783), referred to by Willes J in *Lockyer v Offley* (1786) 1 Term Rep 252 at 260. Cf *Hough & Co v Head* (1885) 55 LJQB 43, CA.
5 The continuation clause may provide for the continuation of the insurance, on notice being given to the underwriters, if the vessel is at sea or in distress or in a port of call or a port of refuge: see eg Institute Time Clauses (Hulls) cl 2 (set out in Ivamy's Marine Insurance (4th Edn) at 533. It may alternatively provide simply that if the ship is at sea at the expiration of the insured period, the insurance is to continue until the ship arrives at some port: *Charlesworth v Faber* (1900) 5 Com Cas 408; *Royal Exchange Assurance Corpn v Sjoforsakrings Akt Vega* [1902] 2 KB 384, CA.

122. End of insured period. Where the insurance is expressed to be from a certain day until another day, the question whether either or both days are covered depends upon the parties' intention to be gathered from the context and the surrounding circumstances[1]. In the absence of an expressed contrary intention, in policies governed by English law time is Greenwich mean time[2] or summer time when this is in force[3]; but the enactment of summer time does not affect the use of Greenwich mean time for navigation or the construction of any document mentioning or referring to a point of time in connection with navigation[4].

1 *Scottish Metropolitan Assurance Co Ltd v Stewart* (1923) 39 TLR 407, where Rowlatt J held that the reinsurance of a risk on a ship which was expressed to run from a given date included that date. In that case the insurance was 'from 20 September 1922 inclusive', but Rowlatt J did not base his decision on the presence of this word. In *Isaacs v Royal Insurance Co Ltd* (1870) LR 5 Exch 296 (fire insurance) the point decided was that the last day was included, but Kelly CB observed that the authorities illustrated 'the principle that in general the day on which the engagement is entered into is excluded and the last day of the term is included'. In *South Staffordshire Tramways Co v Sickness and Accident Assurance Association* [1891] 1 QB 402, CA (accident policy), the Queen's Bench Division gave a similar decision which was reversed in the Court of Appeal on another point. In both these cases the insurance was expressed to be for a certain number of months from the first day, so the parties must have intended to exclude one of the two days: see *South Staffordshire Tramways Co v Sickness and Accident Assurance Association* supra at 405 per Day J. In *Johnson & Co Ltd v Bryant* (1896) 1 Com Cas 363, Mathew J decided that the last day was covered; the question whether the first day was included was not discussed.
2 See the Interpretation Act 1978 ss 9, 23(3); and TIME vol 45 para 1116.
3 Summer Time Act 1972 s 3(1). As to the period of summer time see TIME vol 45 paras 1117–1118.
4 Ibid s 3(2).

123. Risks covered by time policy. In the absence of any stipulation to the contrary, a time policy[1] covers the ship on whatever voyage or service she may be engaged during the insured period[2]. It is now, however, common for the policy to except certain geographical areas, either entirely or for certain seasons of the year, for instance, 'warranted no St Lawrence between 1 October and 1 April'[3].

1 For the meaning of 'time policy' see para 41 ante.
2 See *Dudgeon v Pembroke* (1877) 2 App Cas 284, HL, together with *Thompson v Hopper* (1856) 6 E & B 172; and *Fawcus v Sarsfield* (1856) 6 E & B 192.
3 *Birrell v Dryer* (1884) 9 App Cas 345, HL; see also *Simpson SS Co v Premier Underwriting Association Ltd* (1905) 10 Com Cas 198; and see *Mountain v Whittle* [1921] 1 AC 615, HL, where a houseboat was insured under a time policy while anchored in a certain river, 'including all risk of docking. . . as may be required during the currency of this policy'. The boat sank outside a yard which was in a different river and some seven miles from her anchorage. This yard was the nearest place for cleaning and repairs. It was held that the assured was entitled to recover by virtue of the docking clause. See also *Wilson v Boag* [1956] 2 Lloyd's Rep 564 (NSW SC) (loss occurring within the area covered by the policy recoverable although the launch was in the course of proceeding to a place outside it). As to express warranties see para 57 et seq ante; and as to mixed policies see para 124 post.

124. Mixed policies. Time policies[1] are sometimes made in which not only is the time specified for which the risk is insured, but the voyage is also described[2]; for instance the insurance may be 'at and from London to Cadiz for six months', or 'from 1 January 1994 to 1 June 1994, at and from Bristol to Marseilles etc'. These policies are called 'mixed policies'. Under them the underwriter is not liable for a loss that has not occurred within the insured period, nor is he liable for any loss unless the ship originally sailed on the voyage described in the policy and was at the time of the loss sailing on the prescribed course between the termini of the voyage[3].

1 For the meaning of 'time policy' see para 41 ante.
2 Marine Insurance Act 1906 s 25(1). As to extension of risk for a period of time beyond the voyage covered by a voyage policy see para 125 post.
3 *Way v Modigliani* (1787) 2 Term Rep 30; *Robertson v French* (1803) 4 East 130; see also *Johnson & Co Ltd v Bryant* (1896) 1 Com Cas 363; *Maritime Insurance Co Ltd v Alianza Insurance Co of Santander* [1907] 2 KB 660; *Difiori v Adams* (1884) 53 LJQB 437.

(ii) Voyage Policies

A. COMMENCEMENT AND DURATION OF RISK ON GOODS

125. Commencement of risk on goods. If goods are insured 'from the loading thereof' the risk does not attach until they are actually on board, and the insurer is not liable for a loss occurring while they are in transit from the shore to the ship[1].

The insurer's liability may, however, be extended by express words in the policy[2], and it is usual to insert in it a more extensive clause, called the 'transit clause', providing that insurance attaches from the time the goods leave the warehouse at the place named in the policy for the commencement of the transit and continues during the ordinary course of transit, until the earliest of:

(1) delivery to the final warehouse or store at the destination named in the policy;

(2) delivery to any other warehouse or store, which the assured elects to use for storage or distribution; or

(3) the expiry of 60 days after discharge of the goods from the vessel at the final port of discharge[3].

The transit clause provides for the attachment of the insurance at a named place[4], but cases decided in relation to the common clause in the Lloyd's policy[5] suggest that if there is anything in the policy to indicate that it was intended to cover goods loaded at some place other than the place of departure of the voyage, effect will be given to that intention[6], and, in particular, when it appears from the policy that the parties contemplated loading and unloading, bartering or trading with goods at any intermediate ports or places in the course of the insured voyage, the policy will attach not only on goods loaded at the port of departure, but also on those loaded at any of the ports or places where the ship is empowered to touch and trade under the terms of the policy[7].

1   Marine Insurance Act 1906 s 30(2), Sch 1 r 4. As to the effect of insurance 'from' a particular place see para 130 post. Where a reinsurance was effected on goods already afloat 'on a voyage from Spain to Antwerp', but the slip also stated that the carrying vessel had been reported from Gibraltar, the court held, after hearing evidence of usage as to the meaning of the 'slip', that the risk was limited to the voyage from Gibraltar to Antwerp: *Eagle, Star and British Dominions Insurance Co Ltd v Reiner* (1927) 43 TLR 259.
2   *Hurry v Royal Exchange Assurance Co* (1801) 2 Bos & P 430 at 435. See further the text and notes infra; and para 129 post.
3   See the Institute Cargo Clauses (A) cl 8, (B) cl 8, (C) cl 8; see Ivamy's Marine Insurance (4th Edn) at 517, 521, 524. These clauses also contain provision (1) covering the goods up to the commencement of the forwarding of the goods to a destination other than that for which they are insured, and (2) whereby the goods are held covered in the event of other transhipment or delay in excess of the time limits fixed by the clause arising from circumstances beyond the assured's control. In *Ide and Christie v Chalmers and White* (1900) 5 Com Cas 212 at 216 it was found as a fact that a transit clause was usually inserted in Lloyd's policies. The 'shipper's or manufacturer's warehouse' need not be at the port of shipment, but must be within, a reasonable distance of that port: *Symington & Co v Union Insurance Society of Canton Ltd* (1928) 34 Com Cas 23, CA; contrast *Re Traders and General Insurance Association Ltd, ex p Continental and Overseas Trading Co Ltd* [1924] 2 Ch 187. If the goods cease to be in transit, they will no longer be covered by the policy, even though not yet delivered to their final destination: *Deutsch-Australische Dampschiffs-gesellschaft v Sturge* (1913) 109 LT 905; and cf *Niger Co Ltd v Guardian Assurance Co Ltd* (1922) 13 Ll L Rep 75, HL, cited in para 142 note 8 post.
     For the meaning of 'port of discharge' see para 127 post.
4   See text and note 3 supra.
5   See Appendix 1; para 906 post. It has been held that the risk is only to attach upon goods loaded on board the ship at the place of departure of the voyage, even though it was known to the insurers that the policy was intended to protect goods loaded at some other port: *Spitta v Woodman* (1810) 2 Taunt 416; *Robertson v French* (1803) 4 East 130; *Horneyer v Lushington* (1812) 15 East 46; *Langhorn v Hardy* (1812) 4 Taunt 628; *Mellish v Allnutt* (1813) 2 M & S 106; *Rickman v Carstairs* (1833) 5 B & Ad 651; *Gladstone v Clay* (1813) 1 M & S 418 at 424. As to the limits of the port or place mentioned as the place of departure at which the goods are to be loaded see *Garston Sailing Ship Co v Hickie* (1885) 15 QBD 580, CA; *Payne v Hutchinson* (1810) 2 Taunt 405n; *Constable v Noble* (1810) 2 Taunt 403; *Moxon v Atkins* (1812) 3 Camp 200. This very strict construction, which is often not in accordance with the parties' intention, has, however, been disapproved: *Carr v Montefiore* (1864) 5 B & S 408 at 430, Ex Ch. If the goods, although originally loaded elsewhere, are wholly, or in part, first landed and then reloaded at the place of departure of the voyage, this is a sufficient loading on board the ship at that port to make the policy attach: *Carr v Montefiore* supra; *Nonnen v Reid, Nonnen v Kettlewell* (1812) 16 East 176, applied in the above case.
6   *Bell v Hobson* (1812) 16 East 240; *Joyce v Realm Marine Insurance Co* (1872) LR 7 QB 580.
7   *Gladstone v Clay* (1813) 1 M & S 418; *Violett v Allnutt* (1811) 3 Taunt 419; *Grant v Delacour* (1806) cited in 1 Taunt at 465; *Grant v Paxton* (1809) 1 Taunt 463; *Barclay v Stirling* (1816) 5 M & S 6; *Leathly v Hunter* (1831) 7 Bing 517, Ex Ch.

126. Policy from a foreign port for a homeward voyage. A policy on goods at and from a foreign port for the homeward voyage protects only the homeward cargo, and only from the time when it is wholly or partially loaded on board at the foreign port[1].

In a policy on a voyage during which goods were intended to be loaded and bartered at different places, there was commonly a clause, 'outward cargo is to be considered homeward interest 24 hours after arrival at first place of trade'. The effect of this clause is that the policy will simultaneously cover the original and the new cargoes on board, but not any goods which are on land and are not shipped goods[2].

1 *Forbes v Cowie* (1808) 1 Camp 520; *Forbes v Aspinall* (1811) 13 East 323 (homeward freight); *Rickman v Carstairs* (1833) 5 B & Ad 651. See also para 131 post.
2 *Tobin v Harford* (1864) 17 CBNS 528, Ex Ch; *Joyce v Realm Marine Insurance Co* (1872) LR 7 QB 580; cf *Harrison v Ellis* (1857) 7 E & B 465.

127. Termination of risk on goods. The transit clauses specify the termination of the risk on goods[1].

The port of discharge is either the particular port which is named in the policy for that purpose, or that which, by reason of the terms of the policy or the usage of trade, is inferred to be intended by the parties. Sometimes the place named in the policy as the place of discharge is a district containing several ports; in that case, generally speaking, the policy will protect the outward cargo until the whole of it has been or, in the usual course of trade, ought to have been safely landed[2] at that port in the district which, for the aforesaid reasons, is taken to be the ultimate port of discharge contemplated by the parties[3].

1 See para 125 text and note 3 ante.
2 As to the meaning of 'safely landed' see para 128 post.
3 *Barras v London Assurance* (1782) 1 Park's Marine Insurances (8th Edn) 74; *Leigh v Mather* (1795) 1 Esp 411; *Richardson v London Assurance Co* (1814) 4 Camp 94; cf *Oliverson v Brightman* (1846) 8 QB 781; and see *Brown v Vigne* (1810) 12 East 283 (policy on ship).

128. Time within and manner in which the goods are to be landed. For goods to be safely landed[1] they must be landed in the customary manner, and within a reasonable time after their arrival at the port of discharge[2]; if they are not so landed the risk will cease[3]. The extent of that reasonable time depends upon the nature and usages of the trade on which the ship is engaged, the object of the adventure and the circumstances existing at the port of discharge[4].

1 See para 127 ante. Note that the concept of safe landing as the point at which insurance is to cease is of limited application under the transit clauses, which anticipate the delivery of the goods to a warehouse or store, except where the insurance ceases on the expiry of 60 days after discharge of the goods; see para 125 text and note 3 ante.
2 Marine Insurance Act 1906 s 30(2), Sch 1 r 5. See *Parkinson v Collier* (1797) 2 Park's Marine Insurances (8th Edn) 653 (African barter trade); *Noble v Kennoway* (1780) 2 Doug KB 510.
3 Marine Insurance Act 1906 Sch 1 r 5.
4 See CUSTOM AND USAGE vol 12 paras 483, 487–489.

129. Transhipment. Where a policy gives express permission to tranship, the goods remain covered by the policy both in the course of transhipment and when on board the vessel into which they are transhipped[1].

Where, in the absence of such express permission, under a policy providing for 'all risk of craft until the goods are discharged and safely landed', the goods are put into lighters at the port of destination not for the purpose of being landed but for transhipment into vessels bound for another port, the loss of the goods when in these lighters is not covered by the policy, for such transhipment in fact amounts to the abandonment of the insured voyage[2].

On the other hand, even though the policy contains no such express permission to tranship, the goods will nevertheless remain covered if transhipment becomes necessary by reason of a peril insured against. Where, by a peril insured against, the voyage is interrupted at an intermediate port or place under such circumstances as, apart from any special stipulation in the contract of affreightment, to justify the master in landing and reshipping the goods or other movables[3] or in transhipping them and sending them on to their destination, the insurer's liability continues notwithstanding the landing or transhipment[4].

By the insertion of express words in a marine policy its protection may be prolonged after the landing of the goods and during their subsequent transport overland[5].

1 *Tierney v Etherington* (1743) cited in 1 Burr at 348–349 (there cited by Lord Mansfield); *Oliverson v Brightman, Bold v Rotheram* (1846) 8 QB 781 at 797; *Neale and Wilkinson v Rose* (1898) 3 Com Cas 236; *Belgian Grain and Produce Co Ltd v Cox & Co (France) Ltd* [1919] WN 308, CA; cf *Australian Agricultural Co v Saunders* (1875) LR 10 CP 668 at 676, Ex Ch.
2 *Houlder v Merchants Marine Insurance Co* (1886) 17 QBD 354, CA. It is submitted that the true ground of decision in that case is that stated in the text. See *Oliverson v Brightman, Bold v Rotheram* (1846) 8 QB 781 at 797, 808; and cf *Deutsch-Australische Dampschiffs-gesellschaft v Sturge* (1913) 109 LT 905, cited in para 125 note 3 ante.
3 For the meaning of 'movables' see para 36 note 3 ante.
4 Marine Insurance Act 1906 s 59. See also *Plantamour v Staples* (1781) 1 Term Rep 611n; *Oliverson v Brightman, Bold v Rotheram* (1846) 8 QB 781 at 797, 808; *De Cuadra v Swann* (1864) 16 CBNS 772.
5 *Rodocanachi v Elliott* (1873) LR 8 CP 649; *Simon, Israel & Co v Sedgwick* [1893] 1 QB 303, CA. In *Wingate v Foster* (1878) 3 QBD 582, CA, where a policy contained a special clause to protect certain pumps used in salvage operations, an attempt was made to apply this doctrine to their transit to a port of refuge not provided for by the policy, but it was held that this formed no part of the insured voyage; and, as will be shown later (see para 141 post), the risk is always put an end to by unexcused deviation or by abandonment of the voyage insured. As to the effect of transferring the property in the goods before the loss and without assigning the policy see *Ionides v Harford* (1859) 29 LJEx 36; *North of England Oil-Cake Co v Archangel Insurance Co* (1875) LR 10 QB 249; and para 214 post.

B. COMMENCEMENT AND DURATION OF RISK ON SHIP

130. Insurance 'from' a particular place. Where the subject matter is insured 'from' a particular place, the risk does not attach until the ship starts on the voyage insured[1]. The ship is not deemed to have started on the voyage until, being in a state of complete preparation for the insured voyage, she has quitted her moorings and broken ground[2].

1 Marine Insurance Act 1906 s 30(2), Sch 1 r 2.
2 As to what constitutes a starting or sailing on the insured voyage see *Pittegrew v Pringle* (1832) 3 B & Ad 514 (crossing the bar without full ballast not a sailing); *Cockrane v Fisher* (1835) 1 Cr M & R 809, Ex Ch (every effort made to sail); *Hunting & Son v Boulton* (1895) 1 Com Cas 120 (sailing although still within limits of port); *Sea Insurance Co v Blogg* [1898] 2 QB 398, CA (anchorage moved preparatory to sailing not a sailing); and see para 59 ante.

131. Insurance 'at and from' a particular place. Where a ship[1] is insured 'at and from'[2] a particular place, and she is at that place in good safety when the contract is concluded, the risk attaches immediately[3]. If she is not at that place when the contract is concluded, the risk attaches as soon as she arrives there in good safety, and, unless the policy otherwise provides, it is immaterial that she is covered by another policy for a specified time after arrival[4].

The ship is deemed to be in good safety, even if seriously damaged, if she is in such a condition as to enable her to lie at the port of departure in reasonable security until she is properly repaired and equipped for her insured voyage[5].

The application, however, of this rule, which determines only the prima facie meaning of the clause 'at and from', may be excluded or modified by the terms of the policy construed by the light of the surrounding circumstances[6].

1 'Ship' includes hovercraft: see para 113 ante.
2 As to insurances 'at', and 'only against harbour risks' see para 136 note 5 post.
3 Marine Insurance Act 1906 s 30(2), Sch 1 r 3(a).
4 Ibid Sch 1 r 3(b), which is in accordance with *Haughton v Empire Marine Insurance Co* (1866) LR 1 Exch 206. Where, however, the vessel is covered by successive policies with the same underwriter, it may be held that the later was intended to attach in substitution for the earlier: *Union Marine Insurance Co Ltd v Martin* (1866) 35 LJCP 181.
5 *Forbes v Wilson* (1800) 1 Park's Marine Insurances (8th Edn) 472; *Annen v Woodman* (1810) 3 Taunt 299. It seems probable from the Marine Insurance Act 1906 ss 6, 30 (see paras 44 ante, 191 post), that under a policy 'at and from' . . . 'lost or not lost', the risk attaches as from the earliest time when the ship was in the port of departure in good safety: see the discussion in Arnould on Marine Insurance (16th Edn) s 543. In *Bell v Bell* (1810) 2 Camp 475 there was a policy on ship 'at and from Riga to the United Kingdom', and immediately after the arrival of the ship at Riga her papers were seized, and both ship and cargo were later sequestrated before discharge had taken place. Lord Ellenborough CJ ruled that the policy attached because the ship was in physical safety from the perils insured against, even though not free from political danger. In order to discharge an insurer on a ship insured until 'moored twenty-four hours in good safety' she must be not only in physical safety but also in political safety (see para 135 post); and it seems somewhat doubtful whether under the Marine Insurance Act 1906 Sch 1 r 3, the policy attaches at a time when, although the ship is in physical safety, the assured is by the act of a political authority deprived of her possession or control.
6 *Hunting & Son v Boulton* (1895) 1 Com Cas 120 at 122.

132. Adventure must be commenced within a reasonable time. Where the subject matter is insured by a voyage policy 'at and from' or 'from' a particular place, it is not necessary that the ship[1] should be at that place when the contract is concluded, but there is an implied condition that the adventure must be commenced within a reasonable time, and that if the adventure is not so commenced the insurer may avoid the contract[2]. This implied condition, however, may be negatived by showing that the delay was caused by circumstances known to the insurer before the contract was concluded, or by showing that he waived the condition[3].

The question what is a reasonable time is a question of fact[4]. Before the passing of the Marine Insurance Act 1906 it had been decided that the contract was voidable if the delay in arriving at the port where the insured risk was to commence was such as materially to alter the risk, for instance to change a summer risk into a winter risk, and this although the delay was occasioned by perils of the seas or other unavoidable causes[5]. It is unclear whether the same test should be applied under the Act[6]; but, in any case, when the policy has once attached by the ship's arrival at the port where the insured risk is to commence, a detention there for a reasonable time for the purpose of the insured adventure is allowed, and whether the time is reasonable is a question of fact to be determined by the state of things existing in the port[7].

1 'Ship' includes hovercraft: see para 113 ante.
2 Marine Insurance Act 1906 s 42(1).
3 Ibid s 42(2). This provision settled one of the points left undecided in *De Wolf v Archangel Insurance Co* (1874) LR 9 QB 451.
4 Marine Insurance Act 1906 s 88.
5 *Hull v Cooper* (1811) 14 East 479; *De Wolf v Archangel Insurance Co* (1874) LR 9 QB 451; *Maritime Insurance Co v Stearns* [1901] 2 KB 912.

6 In Arnould on Marine Insurance (16th Edn) s 545, the view is expressed that the test described in text and note 5 supra is not applicable after the passing of the Marine Insurance Act 1906 s 42(2); earlier editions of that and this work have expressed the opposite.

7 *Camden v Cowley* (1763) 1 Wm Bl 417; *Cruikshank v Janson* (1810) 2 Taunt 301; *Warre v Miller* (1825) 4 B & C 538; *Brown v Tayleur* (1835) 4 Ad & El 241; *Raine v Bell* (1808) 9 East 195; *Phillips v Irving* (1844) 7 Man & G 325 at 328. It seems that delay in executing repairs at the port will not put an end to the risk unless the delay is such as to amount to an abandonment of the insured adventure: *Chitty v Selwin and Martyn* (1742) 2 Atk 359 per Lord Hardwicke LC; *Grant v King* (1802) 4 Esp 175; *Smith v Surridge* (1801) 4 Esp 25. See also *Palmer v Marshall* (1832) 8 Bing 317; and *Palmer v Fenning* (1833) 9 Bing 460 at 462 per Park J, where the delay discharged the underwriters.

133. Meaning of 'port'. Where the terminus 'at and from' which the voyage is to commence is a port named in the policy, the name is, as a general rule, presumed to mean that place which in the ordinary commercial sense is considered the port, and not to extend to all the different places it may comprise for purposes of revenue, or which may be included in the technical legal meaning of the word 'port'[1].

Where the policy is 'at and from' an island or other district containing several ports, the risk on ship commences as soon as the ship has arrived in good safety at the first port at which she touches on the island for the purpose of discharging her outward cargo. Thus, a ship insured for a homeward voyage 'at and from' any of the islands of the West Indies is protected by the word 'at' in going from port to port of the island[2].

1 *Constable v Noble* (1810) 2 Taunt 403; *Payne v Hutchinson* (1810) 2 Taunt 405n; *Brown v Tayleur* (1835) 4 Ad & El 241; *Kingston-upon-Hull Dock Co v Browne* (1831) 2 B & Ad 43; *Stockton and Darlington Rly Co v Barrett* (1844) 7 Man & G 870, HL; *Van Baggen v Baines* (1854) 9 Exch 523; *Garston Sailing Ship Co v Hickie* (1885) 15 QBD 580, CA; *Hunter v Northern Marine Insurance Co* (1888) 13 App Cas 717 at 722, 726, 733, HL: see also *Kingston v Knibbs* (1808) 1 Camp 508n; *Cockey v Atkinson* (1819) 2 B & Ald 460; *De Longuemere v Firemen Insurance Co* (1813) 10 Johns (NY) 126; *Sea Insurance Co Scotland v Gavin* (1829) 4 Bli NS 578, HL: *Maritime Insurance Co Ltd v Alianza Insurance Co of Santander* [1907] 2 KB 660; cf *Roelandts v Harrison* (1854) 9 Exch 444. As to the meaning of 'arrival at port' and 'safe port' in connection with charterparties see SHIPPING.

2 *Camden v Cowley* (1763) 1 Wm Bl 417; *Warre v Miller* (1825) 4 B & C 538; see also *Kynance Sailing Ship Co Ltd v Young* (1911) 27 TLR 306.

134. Modification of rules by usage. The general rules as to when the risk attaches, like all other rules of construction, are subject to modifications in accordance with the usage of particular trades[1].

1 Thus, in the Newfoundland trade, owing to the well-known practice of making fishing expeditions or intermediate trading voyages after the ship's first arrival off the coast of Newfoundland, the risk under policies for the homeward voyage, although expressed to be 'at and from' any port or ports in Newfoundland, was held not to attach upon the ships on their first arrival out, but only from their beginning to prepare for the homeward voyage: *Vallance v Dewar* (1808) 1 Camp 503. As to what is meant by 'preparing for the ship's voyage' in a clause describing the commencement of the risk see *Lambert v Liddard* (1814) 5 Taunt 480 at 486.

135. Termination of risk by completion of voyage. Where in a voyage policy[1] the risk on a ship is expressed to continue 'until she has moored at anchor 24 hours in good safety'[2], the ship is not deemed to have been moored for 24 hours in good safety unless she has been moored for that space of time under the three conditions described below.

(1) She must have been moored in such a state of physical safety that she can keep afloat while the cargo is being unloaded. This condition is not satisfied

when the vessel arrives as a mere wreck and is in a sinking state when she is moored, but it is satisfied if she arrives at the ordinary place of discharge, and, even though seriously damaged, is able there to keep afloat, and is kept afloat more than 24 hours after being so moored[3].

(2) The ship must have been for the 24 hours in a state of political safety. This condition is not satisfied if, for instance, she has been laid under an embargo, or if steps have been taken to seize her so that she is no longer in her owners' possession and control[4].

(3) She must have been moored for more than 24 hours in such circumstances that she has an opportunity of unloading and discharging at the place where she in fact intends to discharge. This condition is not satisfied if, for instance, she has been ordered into quarantine during the 24 hours[5].

If, however, the ship is moored in such a place and in such circumstances that she has only to wait until her turn for unloading comes without again unmooring, this is held to be a mooring in good safety[6].

1 For the meaning of 'voyage policy' see para 41 ante.
2 As to the termination of the risk by deviation, delay and abandonment of the voyage see paras 141–148 post.
3 *Shawe v Felton* (1801) 2 East 109; *Lidgett v Secretan* (1870) LR 5 CP 190 at 198–200.
4 *Minett v Anderson* (1794) Peake 277; *Horneyer v Lushington* (1812) 15 East 46 at 47; and see *Lockyer v Offley* (1786) 1 Term Rep 252. It seems clear that mere liability to seizure is not inconsistent with 'good safety'. See *Lockyer v Offley* supra at 261 per Willes J; *Lidgett v Secretan* (1870) LR 5 CP 190 at 199.
5 *Samuel v Royal Exchange Assurance Co* (1828) 8 B & C 119; *Whitwell v Harrison* (1848) 2 Exch 127; *Lindsay v Janson* (1859) 4 H & N 699; *Stone v Marine Insurance Co Ocean Ltd of Gothenburg* (1876) 1 ExD 81. If the 24 hours clause is struck out of the policy, the risk will cease as soon as the ship is at her moorings in safety: *Stone v Marine Insurance Co Ocean Ltd of Gothenburg* supra at 85; cf *Cornfoot v Royal Exchange Assurance Corpn* [1904] 1 KB 40, CA.
6 *Angerstein v Bell* (1795) 1 Park's Marine Insurances (8th Edn) 54.

136. Risk may be prolonged by express stipulation. The risk may be prolonged for a period of time beyond the termination of the insured voyage by express stipulations in the policy[1], or by usage annexing incidents to the contract[2]. In the former case effect will, in the absence of some reason to the contrary, be given to the '24 hours' clause by making the period contained in the express stipulation run from the expiration of 24 hours after the ship has moored at anchor[3].

Where the ship is insured to an island or other district comprising several ports, the risk will continue until the ship has moored 24 hours in good safety at the port at which she was intended to unload and at which the master actually breaks bulk for the purpose of unloading the whole or the greater part of her cargo[4].

A policy on ship to ports in a specified country or district may, however, be so worded that the risk does not end even at the last port of discharge; for instance, the insurance may be to any 'port or ports on the west coast of South America and for 30 days after arrival in final port however employed'. In that case the last two words will prevent the other words, 'port or ports' and 'final port', from being limited to ports of discharge[5].

1 These stipulations have been considered in *Mercantile Marine Insurance Co v Titherington* (1864) 5 B & S 765; *Gambles v Ocean Marine Insurance Co of Bombay* (1876) 1 ExD 141, CA; *Hunter v Northern Marine Insurance Co* (1887) 14 R 544, Ct of Sess; *Cornfoot v Royal Exchange Assurance Corpn* [1904] 1 KB 40, CA.

2 *Preston v Greenwood* (1784) 4 Doug KB 28; *Pelly v Royal Exchange Assurance Co* (1757) 1 Burr 341; *Brough v Whitmore* (1791) 4 Term Rep 206; and see paras 51–53 ante.

3 *Mercantile Marine Insurance Co v Titherington* (1864) 5 B & S 765. This question was left open in *Lidgett v Secretan* (1870) LR 5 CP 190 at 199, but no doubt was thrown upon the former case. The days of the extended period are reckoned as periods of 24 hours from the termination of the voyage risk: *Cornfoot v Royal Exchange Assurance Corpn* [1904] 1 KB 40, CA, where the 24 hours clause was struck out.

4 *Camden v Cowley* (1763) 1 Wm Bl 417; *Barras v London Assurance* (1782) 1 Park's Marine Insurances (8th Edn) 74; *Leigh v Mather* (1795) 1 Park's Marine Insurances (8th Edn) 74; *Inglis v Vaux* (1813) 3 Camp 437; *Moore v Taylor* (1834) 1 Ad & El 25; and see note 3 supra. Sometimes the ship is insured to her 'port of discharge' or her 'port or ports of discharge' or to her final 'port of discharge or destination'. As to the meaning which has been given to these words see *Clason v Simmonds* (1741) cited in 6 Term Rep at 533; *Moffat v Ward* (1784) 4 Doug KB 29n; *Preston v Greenwood* (1784) 4 Doug KB 28 at 33; *Moore v Taylor* supra. The words 'last port of discharge' have been held to mean the last practicable friendly port of discharge (*Brown v Vigne* (1810) 12 East 283 at 288 per Bayley J), because a hostile port could not have been in the contemplation of the parties at the time the policy was effected (*Neilson v De Lacour* (1797) 2 Esp 618).

5 *Crocker v Sturge* [1897] 1 QB 330; *Spalding v Crocker* (1897) 2 Com Cas 189; and see *Crocker v General Insurance Co Ltd of Trieste* (1897) 3 Com Cas 22, CA. Contrast *Marten v Vestey Bros Ltd* [1920] AC 307, HL, where 'final port' was held to mean the final port of discharge. Sometimes the insurance is only 'at' a place, and sometimes only against harbour risks. As to when the risk terminates in such a case see *Maritime Insurance Co Ltd v Alianza Insurance Co of Santander* [1907] 2 KB 660; *Hunting & Son v Boulton* (1895) 1 Com Cas 120; *Kynance Sailing Ship Co Ltd v Young* (1911) 27 TLR 306. Ships are also sometimes insured against fire when in dock or when in river with liberty to go into a dry dock, or sometimes in harbour while securely moored. As to when the risk in those cases terminates see —v *Westmore* (1807) 6 Esp 109; *Pearson v Commercial Union Assurance Co* (1876) 1 App Cas 498; *Grant v Aetna Insurance Co* (1862) 15 Moo PCC 516.

C. COMMENCEMENT AND DURATION OF RISK ON FREIGHT

137. Commencement of insurance on freight. In order to recover on a policy on freight[1] the assured must not only have an insurable interest[2] at the time of the loss, but the policy must be so worded as to make the risk attach before the loss. Thus, where a policy which is effected on freight 'at and from' a certain port of loading also contains a clause that the freight is to be covered 'from the time of the engagement of the goods', the assured has an insurable interest as soon as the goods are engaged, but he cannot recover for a loss of freight due to the loss of the ship if that loss occurs before she has reached the port of loading[3].

Where freight, other than chartered freight, is payable without special conditions and is insured 'at and from' a particular place, the risk attaches pro rata as the goods or merchandise are shipped, but if there is cargo in readiness which belongs to the shipowner, or which some other person has contracted with him to ship[4], the risk attaches as soon as the ship is ready to receive that cargo[5].

In order, therefore, that the policy may cover freight on goods not shipped, two conditions must be fulfilled before or at the time of the loss:

(1) the goods must belong to the shipowner or there must be a binding contract with some other person to ship them; and

(2) the goods must be in readiness to be shipped and the ship must be ready to receive them[6].

As regards the first condition, this rule is in accordance with decided cases[7].

As regards the second condition, it remains to be seen whether the English courts will interpret the rule so as to bring it into accordance with the decisions given before the passing of the Marine Insurance Act 1906 by holding that the goods are ready to be shipped and the ship is ready to receive them if the ship is at the shipper's disposal in the sense that she would load but for some preventing cause such as lack of facilities for loading[8].

1 For the meaning of 'freight' see para 115 ante.
2 As to insurable interest see para 185 et seq post.
3 *The Copernicus* [1896] P 237, CA; cf *Jones v Neptune Marine Insurance Co* (1872) LR 7 QB 702; see also *Eagle, Star and British Dominions Insurance Co Ltd v Reiner* (1927) 43 TLR 259, cited in para 125 note 1 ante.
4 Even when the insurance is on freight 'chartered or as if chartered', the risk will not attach unless there is a binding agreement to load or procure a cargo, or at any rate a binding agreement to use diligence to procure a cargo: *Scottish Shire Line Ltd v London and Provincial Marine and General Insurance Co Ltd* [1912] 3 KB 51.
5 Marine Insurance Act 1906 s 30(2), Sch 1 r 3(d).
6 See ibid Sch 1 r 3(d).
7 The principal cases on this subject are *Montgomery v Eggington* (1789) 3 Term Rep 362 (which virtually overruled the decision of Lee J in *Tonge v Watts* (1746) 2 Stra 1251); *Flint v Flemyng* (1830) 1 B & Ad 45; *Forbes v Aspinall* (1811) 13 East 323; *Patrick v Eames* (1813) 3 Camp 441.
8 These cases are *Parke v Hebson* (1820) cited in 2 Brod & Bing at 326; *Warre v Miller* (1825) 4 B & C 538; *Devaux v J'Anson* (1839) 5 Bing NC 519; *Flint v Flemyng* (1830) 1 B & Ad 45. In *Truscott v Christie* (1820) 2 Brod & Bing 320 at the time of the loss the vessel was being altered to make her able to accommodate 200 invalids; the alterations were not completed at the time of the loss, yet the court held that the assured could recover on a policy on the passage money. Again, in *Devaux v J'Anson* supra, although the ship was at the time of the loss in dry dock and not in the place where she was to receive her cargo, the assured recovered under a policy on freight. It is, on the other hand, to be observed that the rule in question is in accordance with the dictum of Lord Ellenborough CJ in *Forbes v Aspinall* (1811) 13 East 323 at 331, and with the ruling of Lord Lyndhurst CB in *Williamson v Innes* (1831) 8 Bing 81n. Lord Ellenborough's dictum, however, was not necessary for the decision of the case, and Lord Lyndhurst's ruling was only a ruling at Nisi Prius.

138. Commencement of risk on chartered freight. Whether the risk has at the time of the loss attached to the insurable interest[1] in freight[2] depends upon the terms of the policy. Where the policy is on chartered freight and the insurance is 'at and from' a particular place, and the ship is at that place in good safety when the contract is concluded, the risk attaches immediately; if she is not there when the contract is concluded, the risk attaches as soon as she arrives there in good safety[3].

An insurance on freight 'at and from' a place does not cover the freight on a voyage terminating at that place, for that freight is not at risk on the voyage described in the policy. Thus, when freight was insured at and from Riga to the United Kingdom and the ship was captured at Riga, it was held that the policy did not cover the freight on the outward voyage to Riga[4]. If suitable wording is employed, chartered freight may be at risk before the beginning of the voyage on which it is to be carried[5].

In policies on chartered freight the commencement of the risk may be made to depend on a certain event, for instance, the loading of the goods on board ship at a certain port or simply from the loading of the vessel. In these cases the risk does not attach until the happening of the specified event[6].

1 As to insurable interest see para 185 et seq post.
2 For the meaning of 'freight' see para 115 ante.
3 Marine Insurance Act 1906 s 30(2), Sch 1 r 3(c). This rule must of course be read subject to Sch 1 r 1 (see para 191 text to note 3 post, and para 131 ante), and subject also to any conditions precedent to the underwriter's liability such as the seaworthiness of the ship etc. See also *Sellar v M'Vicar* (1804) 1 Bos & PNR 23 (ship never arrived at the starting point of the insured voyage); *Hydarnes SS Co v Indemnity Mutual Marine Assurance Co* [1895] 1 QB 500, CA.
4 *Bell v Bell* (1810) 2 Camp 475.
5 *Rankin v Potter* (1873) LR 6 HL 83; *Barber v Fleming* (1869) LR 5 QB 59; and see Arnould on Marine Insurance (16th Edn) s 359.

6 *Beckett v West of England Marine Insurance Co Ltd* (1871) 25 LT 739; distinguished in *Hydarnes SS Co v Indemnity Mutual Marine Assurance Co* [1895] 1 QB 500, CA, and criticised at 509 by Rigby LJ; *Hopper v Wear Marine Insurance Co* (1882) 46 LT 107; *Jones v Neptune Marine Insurance Co* (1872) LR 7 QB 702.

139. Termination of risk on freight. Under a voyage policy[1] on freight[2], unless there is some stipulation to the contrary, the risk continues as long as the goods remain in the shipowner's custody exposed to maritime perils[3], provided there is no unjustifiable delay in discharging them[4]. In the case of a time policy[5] on freight, the rules relating to the termination of the risk are the same as those which apply to insurances on ships[6].

1 For the meaning of 'voyage policy' see para 41 ante.
2 For the meaning of 'freight' see para 115 ante.
3 For the meaning of 'maritime perils' see para 36 ante.
4 Marshall on Marine Insurance (4th Edn) 225; *Atty v Lindo* (1805) 1 Bos & PNR 236. Advance freight paid under a charterparty may continue at risk, although a stage of the adventure has been accomplished, and cargo carried in that stage delivered: *Ellis v Lafone* (1853) 8 Exch 546, Ex Ch.
5 For the meaning of 'time policy' see para 41 ante.
6 For the rules as to termination of the risk relating to insurances on ships see paras 121, 130 et seq ante.

(iii) The Voyage Insured: Change of Voyage, Deviation and Delay

140. The voyage insured. A voyage policy[1] specifies the voyage insured, that is to say the voyage intended to be covered by the policy. It is, however, only necessary that the place at which the voyage is to commence and the place at which it is to end should be stated. These places are respectively called the 'terminus a quo' and the 'terminus ad quem'. It is sufficient that these termini should be named in the policy, because, in the absence of some provision to the contrary, the ship is bound to proceed from one terminus of the voyage insured to the other with all due expedition, and without trading at any intermediate places, by the usual and customary course, or, if there is more than one such course, by one of them[2]. Thus, the proper course of the insured voyage, or, more briefly, the 'insured voyage', is determined by the termini named in the policy, the underwriter being presumed to be cognisant of the usual and customary course or courses[3].

Where the place of departure is specified by the policy, and the ship, instead of sailing from that place, sails from any other place, the risk does not attach[4], nor does it attach when the destination is specified in the policy, and the ship, instead of sailing for that destination, sails for any other destination[5].

1 For the meaning of 'voyage policy' see para 41 ante.
2 See eg *Brown v Tayleur* (1835) 4 Ad & El 241; *Redman v Lowdon* (1814) 5 Taunt 462.
3 See *The Indian City* [1939] AC 562, [1939] 3 All ER 444, HL (a charterparty case), which also decided that a customary course need not be proved with the strictness of a legal usage.
4 Marine Insurance Act 1906 s 43.
5 Ibid s 44.

141. Change of voyage and deviation. A departure from the proper course of the insured voyage[1] may arise from what is called 'a change of voyage' or from 'deviation'. It is important to note the distinction between these two modes of departure because of their very different effect on the underwriter's liability[2].

Where, after the commencement of the risk, the destination of the ship is voluntarily changed from the destination contemplated by the policy, there is said to be a change of voyage[3]. Unless the policy otherwise provides, where there is a change of voyage, the insurer is discharged from liability as from the time of the change, that is to say as from the time when the determination to change it is manifested; and it is immaterial that the ship may not in fact have left the course of voyage contemplated by the policy when the loss occurs[4].

There is a deviation from the voyage contemplated by the policy where:

(1) the course of the voyage is specifically designated by the policy, and that course is departed from; or

(2) the course of the voyage is not specifically designated by the policy, but the usual and customary course is departed from[5].

The intention to deviate is immaterial; there must be a deviation in fact to discharge the insurer from his liability under the contract[6]. Where a ship, without lawful excuse, deviates from the voyage contemplated by the policy, the insurer is discharged from liability as from the time of deviation, and it is immaterial that the ship may have regained her route before any loss occurs[7].

1 As to the insured voyage see para 140 ante.
2 See further para 142 post. As to the contractual rights and liabilities consequent on deviation as between shipowner and charterer see SHIPPING vol 43 para 431 et seq.
3 Marine Insurance Act 1906 s 45(1).
4 Ibid s 45(2).
5 Ibid s 46(2). Evidence is admissible to show what is the usual or a usual route. If the evidence is sufficient to establish a practice to follow a particular route, proceeding by that route is not a deviation: *The Indian City* [1939] AC 562, [1939] 3 All ER 444, HL (charterparty).
6 Marine Insurance Act 1906 s 46(3); *Thellusson v Fergusson* (1780) 1 Doug KB 360 at 365.
7 Marine Insurance Act 1906 s 46(1). As to what are lawful excuses see s 49; and para 147 post.

142. Change of voyage and deviation distinguished. There is a change of voyage when a purpose of abandoning the original place of destination for some other place of discharge is definitely formed[1], and as soon as that purpose is definitely formed and manifested the insurer is ipso facto discharged from liability for all subsequent losses[2]. If the resolution is formed after the commencement of the risk, the voyage is said to be changed[3].

There is deviation when, without any design of abandoning the original destination, there is an actual departure from the course of the insured voyage[4], and in that case, whether the risk is increased by the deviation or not, the insurer is discharged from liability for all losses occurring after the actual departure[5], but he remains liable for all previous losses[6].

It is a question of fact whether a departure from the proper course of the insured voyage constitutes a change of voyage or only a deviation, the question being whether or not a definite resolution was formed and manifested to abandon the terminus ad quem[7] named in the policy[8].

1 *Wooldridge v Boydell* (1778) 1 Doug KB 16; *Driscol v Passmore* (1798) 1 Bos & P 200.
2 *Wooldridge v Boydell* (1778) 1 Doug KB 16; *Way v Modigliani* (1787) 2 Term Rep 30; *Bottomley v Bovill* (1826) 5 B & C 210.
3 Marine Insurance Act 1906 s 45(1); *Tasker v Cunninghame* (1819) 1 Bli 87 at 100, 102, HL; and see para 141 ante.
4 As to the insured voyage see para 140 ante.
5 *Hamilton v Sheddon* (1837) 3 M & W 49; and see the cases cited in note 2 supra. Intention to deviate is not sufficient: *Thellusson v Fergusson* (1780) 1 Doug KB 360; *Kewley v Ryan* (1794) 2 Hy Bl 343;

Foster v Wilmer (1746) 2 Stra 1249; *Heselton v Allnutt* (1813) 1 M & S 46 at 50; *Hare v Travis* (1827) 7 B & C 14; *Kingston v Phelps* (1795) cited in 7 Term Rep at 165; and see *Simpson SS Co v Premier Underwriting Association* (1905) 10 Com Cas 198 (same principle applied to breach of warranty in time policy).

6 *Hare v Travis* (1827) 7 B & C 14; *Kingston v Phelps* (1795) cited in 7 Term Rep at 165.

7 For the meaning of 'terminus ad quem' see para 140 ante.

8 *Wooldridge v Boydell* (1778) 1 Doug KB 16. See also *Marsden v Reid* (1803) 3 East 572 (vessel insured to numerous ports; it is no change of voyage if she sails for one of them only, for a voyage to all or any of the places named is intended); and see the cases cited in notes 2, 5 supra. Where a marine policy on goods covered a land transit following a sea voyage, the Court of Appeal held that to determine whether the policy ever attached the terminus ad quem of the sea voyage only must be taken into consideration: *Simon, Israel & Co v Sedgwick* [1893] 1 QB 303, CA. The mere fact of taking in goods, and clearing for a different port from that specified in the policy as the terminus ad quem, does not by itself amount to a change of voyage: *Planché v Fletcher* (1779) 1 Doug KB 251; *Kewley v Ryan* (1794) 2 Hy Bl 343. Where goods, which were insured from the interior of Africa to any ports in Europe or the United States, were collected in the interior of Africa, taken to an ocean port, stored at that port in bulk and shipped to Europe or the United States as and when ocean steamers were available, it was held that, although it was impossible to specify the ultimate destination of the goods until they were shipped on the ocean steamer, there had been no change or abandonment of voyage because the goods were at all times destined for some port in Europe or the United States: *Niger Co Ltd v Guardian Assurance Co Ltd* (1922) 13 Ll L Rep 75, HL; cf *Hewitt v London General Insurance Co Ltd* (1925) 23 Ll L Rep 243.

143. Change of voyage and deviation: special clauses. Notice to the insurer of an intention to depart from the usual and customary course (no liberty to do so being given by the policy) will not have the effect of preventing the insurer from being discharged, although it may, with other circumstances, be evidence of his waiver of the condition not to deviate[1].

Policies of insurance now often contain a clause by which the insurer agrees to cover the assured, in case of a change of voyage or of a deviation, at an extra premium and on amended terms of cover to be arranged[2]; and where an insurance is effected on the terms that an additional premium is to be arranged in a given event, and that event happens, but no arrangement is made, then a reasonable additional premium is payable[3].

1 *Redman v Lowdon* (1814) 5 Taunt 462.

2 See Institute Voyage Clauses (Hulls) cl 2, set out in Ivamy's Marine Insurance (4th Edn) at p 541. The clause requires notice to be given to the insurer.

3 Marine Insurance Act 1906 s 31(2). The question of what is reasonable is a question of fact: s 88. 'Reasonable premium' means the premium which would have been charged for the risk by a reasonable insurer at the time of the deviation, abandonment or change of voyage had he then known of it: *Greenock SS Co v Marine Insurance Co Ltd* [1903] 1 KB 367 at 375; applied in *Mentz, Decker & Co v Marine Insurance Co Ltd* [1910] 1 KB 132. This fact renders the subject of deviation far less important than it was formerly: see *Hyderabad (Deccan) Co v Willoughby* [1899] 2 QB 530. A clause that a ship is to be held covered in case of 'deviation or change of voyage' at an extra premium has been held not to cover unreasonable delay before the commencement of the insured voyage (*Maritime Insurance Co v Stearns* [1901] 2 KB 912); nor has it any operation where the risk has never attached (*Simon, Israel & Co v Sedgwick* [1893] 1 QB 303 at 307, CA). The clause sometimes requires due notice to be given by the assured on receipt of advice, and this obligation, even if not expressed, will be implied: *Thames and Mersey Marine Insurance Co Ltd v Van Laun & Co* (1905) [1917] 2 KB 48n, HL; applied in *Hood v West End Motor Car Packing Co* [1917] 2 KB 38, CA. As to what is due notice see *Mentz, Decker & Co v Maritime Insurance Co Ltd* supra; *Hewitt v London General Insurance Co Ltd* (1925) 23 Ll L Rep 243; and para 221 note 1 post.

144. 'Touch and stay' clauses. In the absence of any further licence[1] or usage, a liberty to touch and stay 'at any port or place whatsoever' does not authorise the ship to depart from the course of her voyage from the port of departure to the port of destination[2]. This is also generally true where there is even a clause giving liberty 'to touch and stay at any place for all purposes whatever'[3].

The following are the principles[4] which may be deduced from the cases on this subject:

(1) the extent of the powers they confer on the ship is to be judged, not so much by a literal and strict interpretation of the terms employed (such as 'to call', 'to touch' or 'to touch and stay'), as by reference to the true scope and nature of the adventure contemplated by the policy[5];

(2) however extensive the language of these clauses may be, they can never confer a power of visiting ports out of that which, on a proper construction of the whole policy, appear to have been the course of the voyage insured as contemplated by the parties[6];

(3) these clauses cannot justify the ship in visiting any port, even though within the local limits of the voyage insured, for any purpose unconnected with the main object of the adventure[7]:

(4) if the ship visits an allowed port for an allowed purpose, no trading, breaking bulk, landing or loading cargo, however alien to the main object of the adventure, will make the visit a deviation if the trading, breaking bulk, landing or loading cargo is completed during the period of the ship's lawful stay in that port without additional delay or substantial variation of the risk[8];

(5) if, however, that trading gives rise to delay that would not otherwise have been incurred, it may, for the reason mentioned subsequently[9], afford a defence to the insurer[10].

Where the policy specifically describes the course which the ship is to take between the two termini, that course must be strictly followed, and if the policy names one intermediate port at which the ship may touch, this may bind her not to touch at any other intermediate port[11].

1 For a very extensive licence in a bill of lading see *Hadji Ali Akbar & Sons Ltd v Anglo-Arabian and Persian SS Co Ltd* (1906) 11 Com Cas 219.
2 Marine Insurance Act 1906 s 30(2), Sch 1 r 6.
3 *Bottomley v Bovill* (1826) 5 B & C 210.
4 See Arnould on Marine Insurance (8th Edn) s 411; cf Arnould on Marine Insurance (16th Edn) s 484–489.
5 See *Metcalfe v Parry* (1814) 4 Camp 123; *Pratt v Ashley* (1847) 1 Exch 257, Ex Ch; *Bragg v Anderson* (1812) 4 Taunt 229; *Lambert v Liddard* (1814) 5 Taunt 480; *Violett v Allnutt* (1811) 3 Taunt 419; *Barclay v Stirling* (1816) 5 M & S 6; *Rucker v Allnutt* (1812) 15 East 278; *Andrews v Mellish* (1814) 5 Taunt 496, Ex Ch; *Armet v Innes* (1820) 4 Moore CP 150; *Hunter v Leathley* (1830) 10 B & C 858; affd (1831) 7 Bing 517, Ex Ch; and see *Warre v Miller* (1825) 4 B & C 538.
6 *Lavabre v Wilson* (1779) 1 Doug KB 284 at 286; *Hogg v Horner* (1797) 2 Park's Marine Insurances (8th Edn) 626; *Ranken v Reeve* (1814) 2 Park's Marine Insurances (8th Edn) 627; *Gairdner v Senhouse* (1810) 3 Taunt 16, distinguished in *Bragg v Anderson* (1812) 4 Taunt 229; *Andrews v Mellish* (1814) 5 Taunt 496, Ex Ch; *Williams v Shee* (1813) 3 Camp 469; *Bottomley v Bovill* (1826) 5 B & C 210; *Hamilton v Sheddon* (1837) 3 M & W 49; *Kynance Sailing Ship Co v Young Ltd* (1911) 104 LT 397.
7 *Langhorn v Allnutt* (1812) 4 Taunt 511; *Hammond v Reid* (1820) 4 B & Ald 72; *Solly v Whitmore* (1821) 5 B & Ald 45; *Laing v Union Marine Insurance Co, Laing v London Assurance Corpn* (1895) 1 Com Cas 11; cf *Violett v Allnutt* (1811) 3 Taunt 419; *Leduc v Ward* (1888) 20 QBD 475 at 482, CA; *Glynn v Margetson & Co* [1893] AC 351, HL (bill of lading cases).
8 *Urquhart v Barnard* (1809) 1 Taunt 450; *Laroche v Oswin* (1810) 12 East 131; *Raine v Bell* (1808) 9 East 195; *Cormack v Gladstone* (1809) 11 East 347; *Warre v Miller* (1825) 4 B & C 538.
9 See para 146 post.
10 *Company of African Merchants v British and Foreign Marine Insurance Co* (1873) LR 8 Exch 154.
11 Ie on the principle *expressio unius est exclusio alterius*: see the Marine Insurance Act 1906 s 46(2)(a) (see para 141 text and note 5 ante); *Elliot v Wilson* (1776) 4 Bro Parl Cas 470, HL.

145. Order in which ship must proceed to ports. Where several ports of discharge are specified by the policy, the ship may proceed to all or any of them, but, in the absence of any usage or sufficient cause to the contrary, she must proceed to them, or such of them as she goes to, in the order designated by the policy. If she does not, there is a deviation[1].

Where the policy is to 'ports of discharge' within a given area, which are not named, the ship must, in the absence of any usage or sufficient cause to the contrary, proceed to them or such of them as she goes to, in their geographical order. If she does not, there is a deviation[2].

1 Marine Insurance Act 1906 s 47(1); *Beatson v Haworth* (1796) 6 Term Rep 531; *Marsden v Reid* (1803) 3 East 572 at 577. As to cases where a ship is insured 'at and from' one named port of departure, and 'other port or ports' see *Bragg v Anderson* (1812) 4 Taunt 229; *Lambert v Liddard* (1814) 5 Taunt 480; *Pratt v Ashley* (1847) 1 Exch 257, Ex Ch; cf *Brown v Tayleur* (1835) 4 Ad & El 241.
2 Marine Insurance Act 1906 s 47(2); *Clason v Simmonds* (1741) cited in 6 Term Rep at 533; *Andrews v Mellish* (1814) 5 Taunt 496 at 502, Ex Ch; distinguish *Kynance Sailing Ship Co Ltd v Young* (1911) 104 LT 397; and see para 136 ante.

146. Delay in voyage. In the case of a voyage policy[1] the adventure insured must be prosecuted throughout its course with reasonable dispatch, and if without lawful excuse it is not so prosecuted, the insurer is discharged from liability as from the time when the delay became unreasonable[2]. Whenever the delay exceeds a reasonable time either at the terminus a quo, or during the voyage, or at the terminus ad quem[3], or is incurred for purposes unconnected with the object of the voyage, the policy ceases to be in force[4].

1 For the meaning of 'voyage policy' see para 41 ante.
2 Marine Insurance Act 1906 s 48. This section does not state whether or not there may be lawful excuses other than those mentioned in s 49 (see para 147 post); it may, therefore, still be necessary to refer to decided cases.
3 For the meaning of 'terminus a quo' and 'terminus ad quem' see para 140 ante.
4 *Chitty v Selwin and Martyn* (1742) 2 Atk 359; *Hartley v Buggin* (1781) 3 Doug KB 39; *Grant v King* (1802) 4 Esp 175; *Samuel v Royal Exchange Assurance Co* (1828) 8 B & C 119; *Mount v Larkins* (1831) 8 Bing 108; *Doyle v Powell* (1832) 4 B & Ad 267; *Hamilton v Sheddon* (1837) 3 M & W 49; cf *Pearson v Commercial Union Assurance Co* (1876) 1 App Cas 498 at 504, HL. What is a reasonable time is a question of fact: see the Marine Insurance Act 1906 s 88; *Bain v Case* (1829) 3 C & P 496. *Phillips v Irving* (1844) 7 Man & G 325 lays down the principle that whether the delay at the port where the ship happens to be is reasonable or not must be determined not by any arbitrary rule but by the state of things existing at that port. The same principle was acted upon by Lord Ellenborough CJ in *Grant v King* supra; *Niger Co Ltd v Guardian Assurance Co Ltd* (1922) 13 Ll L Rep 75, HL (goods placed in store for eight months at port of shipment due to war conditions; held delay not unreasonable); *M Almojil Establishment v Malayan Motor and General Underwriters (Pte) Ltd, The Al-Jubail IV* [1982] 2 Lloyd's Rep 637 (Sing CA) (ship encountering heavy weather put into port where she was delayed for 79 days to complete non-essential repairs; held delay not unreasonable).

147. Causes excusing deviation and delay. There are certain causes which excuse a deviation or delay in prosecuting the voyage[1].

(1) Where authorised by any special term in the policy[2]; in this case the deviation or delay must not exceed what is permitted by the special terms in the policy, and the permission cannot be extended to objects not mentioned in the policy[3].

(2) Where caused by circumstances beyond the control of the master and his employer[4]; in this case only a voluntary departure from the course of the

insured voyage discharges the underwriter from further liability. Thus, if a master is obliged to go into a port of distress in order to repair his ship, or is compelled by the perils of the sea or by the violence of a mutinous crew to go out of the usual course, or where a ship is forcibly detained by a warship or is prevented by an embargo from landing, the deviation or delay is excused[5].

(3) Where reasonably necessary in order to comply with an express or implied warranty[6]; this excuse is applicable where a ship is delayed in port for repairs necessary to make her seaworthy for the voyage, or where she is delayed at an intermediate port to make her seaworthy for the next stage of the voyage[7].

(4) Where reasonably necessary for the safety of the ship or subject matter insured[8]; this excuse seems limited, except where the ship's safety is involved, to the case of a deviation or delay rendered necessary for the safety of the particular subject matter insured with the result that in the case of an insurance on cargo, freight[9] or other interest deviation for the purpose of saving the ship would be excused[10], but, in the case of an insurance on ship, deviation merely for the purpose of saving cargo or freight would not be excused. On the other hand, it is not limited to the necessity of saving the ship or the subject matter insured from some perils insured against[11].

(5) For the purpose of saving human life, or aiding a ship in distress where human life may be in danger[12].

(6) Where reasonably necessary for the purpose of obtaining medical or surgical aid for any person on board the ship[13].

(7) Where caused by the barratrous conduct of the master or crew, if barratry is one of the perils insured against[14].

1 Marine Insurance Act 1906 s 49(1). It seems doubtful whether s 49 was intended to enumerate all the causes which will excuse deviation or delay. Of course, if the ship insured under a voyage policy is unseaworthy at the time she sails because she is not sufficiently manned, equipped or furnished with supplies, the insurer will be discharged from liability whether or not there is a deviation, and the question of excuse cannot arise: see *Woolf v Claggett* (1800) 3 Esp 257; *O'Reilly v Royal Exchange Assurance* (1815) 4 Camp 246.

2 Marine Insurance Act 1906 s 49(1)(a).

3 *Doyle v Powell* (1832) 4 B & Ad 267; *Elliot v Wilson* (1776) 4 Bro Parl Cas 470, HL; *Syers v Bridge* (1780) 2 Doug KB 526; *Parr v Anderson* (1805) 6 East 202. The usual deviation clause, according to which the subject matter insured is held covered on payment of an additional premium, is, of course, a special term in the policy within the meaning of head (1) in the text.

4 Marine Insurance Act 1906 s 49(1)(b).

5 *Harrington v Halkeld* (1778) 2 Park's Marine Insurances (8th Edn) 639; *Driscol v Bovil* (1798) 1 Bos & P 313; *Woolf v Claggett* (1800) 3 Esp 257; *Grant v King* (1802) 4 Esp 175; *Scott v Thompson* (1805) 1 Bos & PNR 181; *Phelps v Auldjo* (1809) 2 Camp 350; *Schroder v Thompson* (1817) 7 Taunt 462. Where the masters of German ships in the Second World War obeyed the orders of the German government as to the disposition of their vessels, the movements of the vessels did not amount to deviations, as they were either 'caused by circumstances beyond the control of the master and his employer within the Marine Insurance Act 1906 s 49(1)(b), or 'reasonably necessary for the safety of the ship or subject matter insured' within s 49(1)(d) (see head (4) in the text): *Rickards v Forestal Land, Timber and Railways Co Ltd* [1942] AC 50, [1941] 3 All ER 62, HL.

6 Marine Insurance Act 1906 s 49(1)(c).

7 *Motteux v Governor & Co of London Assurance* (1739) 1 Atk 545 at 546; *Smith v Surridge* (1801) 4 Esp 25; *Bouillon v Lupton* (1863) 15 CBNS 113; and see *Phillips v Irving* (1844) 7 Man & G 325.

8 Marine Insurance Act 1906 s 49(1)(d).

9 For the meaning of 'freight' see para 115 ante.

10 It is also an excuse as between shipowner and cargo-owner: *The Teutonia* (1872) LR 4 PC 171; *The San Roman* (1873) LR 5 PC 301.

11 In this respect the Marine Insurance Act 1906 effected a change in the law as laid down in *O'Reilly v Royal Exchange Assurance* (1815) 4 Camp 246, but there the ship was unseaworthy when she sailed.

As to what are the elements of reasonable necessity see *James Phelps & Co v Hill* [1891] 1 QB 605 at 612, CA, per Lindley LJ (bill of lading); *The Teutonia* (1872) LR 4 PC 171; *The San Roman* (1873) LR 5 PC 301 (apprehension of capture).

12 Marine Insurance Act 1906 s 49(1)(e). This does not excuse a deviation made solely for the purpose of saving property: *Scaramanga v Stamp* (1880) 5 CPD 295, CA.

13 Marine Insurance Act 1906 s 49(1)(f).

14 Ibid s 49(1)(g). For the meaning of 'barratry' see para 161 post. Deviation is not excused by the master's ignorance or want of skill, however gross it may be: *Vallejo v Wheeler* (1774) 1 Cowp 143; *Ross v Hunter* (1790) 4 Term Rep 33.

148. Resumption of course. When the cause excusing the deviation or delay ceases to operate, the ship must resume her course, and prosecute her voyage, with reasonable dispatch[1]. This evidently does not mean that the ship must return to the actual spot where she turned aside, but that she must do her best to reach the terminus ad quem of the voyage[2].

1 Marine Insurance Act 1906 s 49(2).

2 *Harrington v Halkeld* (1778) 2 Park's Marine Insurances (8th Edn) 639; *Delany v Stoddart* (1785) 1 Term Rep 22. For the meaning of 'terminus ad quem' see para 140 ante.

(7) PERILS INSURED AGAINST

(i) Losses for which Insurer Liable

A. IN GENERAL

149. Perils insured against. The perils insured against will, of course, depend on which Institute Clauses are inserted in the policy[1].

Thus the Institute Cargo Clauses (A) cover all risks, subject to specified exceptions.

The Institute Cargo Clauses (B) cover, subject to specified exceptions, fire[2], explosion, stranding, grounding, sinking or capsizing[3], overturning or derailment of land conveyances, collision, discharge of cargo at a port of distress, earthquake, volcanic eruption or lightning, general average sacrifice[4], jettison[5] or washing overboard, entry of water, and loss or dropping of packages. The Institute Cargo Clauses (C) are in similar terms but the scope of the perils insured against is narrower.

The Institute Time Clauses (Hulls), the Institute Voyage Clauses (Hulls), the Institute Time Clauses (Freight) and the Institute Voyage Clauses (Freight) cover loss due to, inter alia, (1) perils of the seas[6]; (2) fire and explosion; (3) violent theft by persons outside the vessel; (4) jettison; (5) piracy[7]; (6) earthquake, volcanic eruption or lightning; (7) accidents in loading[8]; (8) bursting of boilers etc; (9) negligence; and (10) barratry[9].

The clauses also contain a Collision Clause[10] affording cover where a vessel collides with another vessel and causes damage to her.

The Institute War Clauses (Cargo) and the Institute Strikes Clauses (Cargo), the Institute War and Strikes Clauses (Hulls—Time), the Institute War and Strikes Clauses (Hulls—Voyage), the Institute War and Strikes Clauses (Freight—Time) and the Institute War and Strikes Clauses (Freight—Voyage) may also be attached to the policy, and cover loss by strikes[11] and war[12].

1 See generally para 44 text and note 8 ante. The Institute Clauses are set out in Ivamy's Marine Insurance (4th Edn) at p 516 et seq.
2 See para 153 post.
3 See paras 151, 168 post.
4 See para 244 et seq post.
5 See para 160 post.
6 See para 151 post.
7 See para 159 post.
8 See para 163 post.
9 See para 161 post.
10 See para 164 et seq post; and also Appendix 3, para 908 post.
11 See para 154 post.
12 See para 155 et seq post.

150. Onus of proof. The assured[1] must in every case show that the loss comes within the terms of his policy[2]; but where all risks are covered by the policy and not merely risks of a specified class or classes, he discharges the onus when he has proved that the loss was caused by some event covered by the general expression, and he is not bound to go further and prove the exact nature of the accident or casualty which, in fact, occasioned his loss[3]. Although in ordinary circumstances an insurer who wishes to rely on an exceptions clause must prove that the loss is due to an excepted peril, it is permissible for the parties to provide by contract that the assured must prove that the loss is not covered by the exception[4].

If examination of the evidence leaves the court in doubt as to the real cause of the loss, the assured has failed to prove his case[5].

1 As to the use of the term 'the assured' see para 35 note 1 ante.
2 See *Panamanian Oriental SS Corpn v Wright* [1971] 2 All ER 1028, [1971] 1 WLR 822, CA.
3 *British and Foreign Marine Insurance Co Ltd v Gaunt* [1921] 2 AC 41 at 47, HL, per Lord Birkenhead; *Theodorou v Chester* (1951) 1 Lloyd's Rep 204 at 218–219, 238–239; *F W Berk & Co Ltd v Style* [1956] 1 QB 180 at 187, [1955] 3 All ER 625 at 631; see also *C T Bowring & Co Ltd v Amsterdam Insurance Co Ltd* (1930) 36 Ll L Rep 309 at 325. For a discussion of liability under an 'all risks' policy for loss caused by inherent vice see para 173 post.
4 *Levy v Assicurazioni Generali* [1940] AC 791 at 798, [1940] 3 All ER 427 at 429–430, PC, approving *Re Hooley Hill Rubber and Chemical Co and Royal Insurance Co Ltd* [1920] 1 KB 257, CA; see further paras 409, 421 post.
5 *Rhesa Shipping Co SA v Edmunds, The Popi M* [1985] 2 All ER 712, [1985] 1 WLR 948, HL, where it was held that the judge was not bound to choose between theories advanced by the insurer and the assured, but could dismiss the assured's claim as not having been proved on the balance of probabilities.

B. PERILS OF THE SEAS

151. Meaning of 'perils of the seas'. The term 'perils of the seas', as used in a marine policy, does not include every casualty which may happen to the subject matter of the insurance[1] on the sea; it must be a peril of or due to the sea. It does not, for instance, cover fire or capture at sea, or any loss proximately caused by insects[2], or the wilful scuttling of a ship[3]. Again, unless the policy otherwise provides, it will not cover damage done by the bursting of the air-chamber of a donkey-engine, owing to a valve being closed which ought to be kept open, with the result that water is forced up into the air-chamber and causes an explosion[4].

Moreover, the purpose of a marine policy is to secure an indemnity against accidents which may happen, not against events which in the ordinary course of things must happen[5]. Therefore, in general, the term 'perils of the seas' refers only to fortuitous accidents or casualties of the seas, and does not include the ordinary action of the winds and waves[6].

However, where there is an accidental incursion of seawater into a vessel at a part of the vessel where, and in a manner in which, it is not expected to enter in the ordinary course of things, and there is consequent damage to goods insured, there is prima facie a loss by perils of the seas[7], and if the cargo has been properly stowed, the insurer will not escape liability by proving that the weather was such as might reasonably have been anticipated, for it is the damage due to the weather and not the weather itself which provides the element of the fortuitous[8]. Loss caused by an action necessarily and reasonably taken to prevent a peril of the sea from affecting the insured goods is a loss due to perils of the seas[9].

One of the most obvious cases of loss by perils of the seas is the foundering of the ship at sea, and where the ship concerned in the adventure is missing, and after the lapse of a reasonable time no news of her has been received, an actual total loss may be presumed[10]. It is also presumed that the cause of loss is foundering at sea[11].

1　As to the subject matter of the insurance see para 36 ante.
2　*Schloss Bros v Stevens* [1906] 2 KB 665 at 670, CA, per Walton J; see para 172 post.
3　*P Samuel & Co Ltd v Dumas* [1924] AC 431; and see para 174 post. The unintentional admission of seawater into a ship by which she is caused to sink is a peril of the sea: *Cohen, Sons & Co v National Benefit Assurance Co Ltd* (1924) 40 TLR 347. If the ship is scuttled by the shipowner's employees without his privity, this will be a loss by barratry: see para 161 post.
4　*Thames and Mersey Marine Insurance Co v Hamilton, Fraser & Co* (1887) 12 App Cas 484, HL (the 'Inchmaree' case); cf *Oceanic SS Co v Faber* (1907) 13 Com Cas 28, CA; see also *Yuill & Co v Robson* [1907] 1 KB 685; affd [1908] 1 KB 270, CA, but this damage will be covered by the relevant Institute Clause: see the Institute Cargo Clauses (A) cl 1, the Institute Cargo Clauses (B) cl 1, the Institute Cargo Clauses (C) cl 1, the Institute Time Clauses (Hulls) cl 6, the Institute Voyage Clauses (Hulls) cl 4, the Institute Time Clauses (Freight) cl 7, and the Institute Voyage Clauses (Freight) cl 5; para 149 ante.
5　*Wilson Sons & Co v Xantho (Cargo Owners)* (1887) 12 App Cas 503 at 509, HL, per Lord Herschell (a bill of lading case but one which has always been cited as an authority on the meaning of the words 'perils of the seas' in policies of marine insurance); see *Canada Rice Mills Ltd v Union Marine and General Insurance Co Ltd* [1941] AC 55 at 68, [1940] 4 All ER 169 at 176, PC. See also *Merchants Trading Co v Universal Marine Insurance Co* (1870) 2 Asp MLC 431n, CA; *Thames and Mersey Marine Insurance Co v Hamilton, Fraser & Co* (1887) 12 App Cas 484 at 492, 498, HL; *The Stranna* [1938] P 69, [1938] 1 All ER 458, CA; *Charles Goodfellow Lumber Sales Ltd v Verreault, Hovington and Verreault Navigation Inc* [1971] 1 Lloyd's Rep 185 (Can SC).
6　Marine Insurance Act 1906 s 30(2), Sch 1 r 7; see *Magnus v Buttemer* (1852) 11 CB 876 at 881 per Jervis CJ; *Hamilton, Fraser & Co v Pandorf & Co* (1887) 12 App Cas 518 at 524, HL, per Lord Halsbury LC; and the judgment of Walton J in *Schloss Bros v Stevens* [1906] 2 KB 665, CA. See also *E D Sassoon & Co v Western Assurance Co* [1912] AC 561, PC (where damage to goods by water percolating through a leaky hulk was held not due to perils of the seas); and *Grant, Smith & Co and McDonnell Ltd v Seattle Construction and Dry Dock Co* [1920] AC 162, PC (where the capsizing of a floating dock, owing to the unfitness of its structure for the work for which it was required, was held not to be a loss by perils of the sea). Contrast *Mountain v Whittle* [1921] 1 AC 615, HL (houseboat sank owing to entry of water through defective side seams while being towed; held loss due to perils of the sea). For a case where a loss, not proximately caused by perils of the seas, was recoverable as a loss by perils ejusdem generis to them, see *The Lapwing* [1940] P 112.
7　*Canada Rice Mills Ltd v Union Marine and General Insurance Co Ltd* [1941] AC 55 at 68, [1940] 4 All ER 169 at 176, PC.
8　*N E Neter & Co Ltd v Licenses and General Insurance Co Ltd* [1944] 1 All ER 341, DC.
9　*Canada Rice Mills Ltd v Union Marine and General Insurance Co Ltd* [1941] AC 55, [1940] 4 All ER 169, PC.
10　Marine Insurance Act 1906 s 58.
11　*Green v Brown* (1743) 2 Stra 1199; *Newby v Read* (1761) Marshall on Marine Insurances (4th Edn) 388; *Koster v Reed* (1826) 6 B & C 19.

152. Extraordinary violence of wind or waves not necessary. Having regard to certain dicta to be found in some judgments and to the wording in the Marine Insurance Act 1906[1], it is important to notice that losses by perils of the seas[2] are not confined to those occasioned by extraordinary violence of the wind or waves, but include all losses proximately occasioned by fortuitous action of the wind and waves. Thus, perils of the seas include a loss by collision with another vessel, or by the ship striking on a sudden rock or other obstruction in fair weather[3], or damage done to cargo by incursion of seawater through a hole in a pipe gnawed by rats[4], or through a valve by mistake left open[5], or through cowl ventilators[6]. The labouring of the ship in rough weather may be fortuitous even though that weather is expected[7].

1 See the Marine Insurance Act 1906 s 30(2), Sch 1 r 7; and para 151 ante.
2 For the meaning of 'perils of the seas' see para 151 ante.
3 See *William France, Fenwick & Co Ltd v North of England Protecting and Indemnity Association* [1917] 2 KB 522.
4 *Hamilton, Fraser & Co v Pandorf & Co* (1887) 12 App Cas 518, HL; *Popham v St Petersburg Insurance Co* (1904) 10 Com Cas 31 (unusual obstruction by ice).
5 *Blackburn v Liverpool, Brazil and River Plate Steam Navigation Co* [1902] 1 KB 290; cf *Ajum Goolam Hossen & Co v Union Marine Insurance Co, Hajee Cassim Joosub v Ajum Goolam Hossen & Co* [1901] AC 362, PC.
6 *Canada Rice Mills Ltd v Union Marine and General Insurance Co Ltd* [1941] AC 55 at 69, [1940] 4 All ER 169 at 176, PC; see also para 151 ante.
7 *N E Neter & Co v Licenses and General Insurance Co Ltd* [1944] 1 All ER 341, DC.

C. LOSS BY FIRE, STRIKES, WAR RISKS, PIRATES, THIEVES, JETTISON OR BARRATRY

153. Fire. Loss by fire covers fire caused by lightning, or by an enemy, or by the ship being burnt in order to prevent capture[1], or to prevent the spread of a contagious disease or the like[2]; and, where a loss of freight is due to steps taken in order to prevent a fire which, but for those steps, would have broken out and destroyed the cargo, the insurer is liable for that loss of freight[3]. Mere heating, which has not arrived at the stage of incandescence or ignition, is not within the specific word 'fire'[4]. There is no onus on the assured to show that the fire was caused otherwise than by his own act[5].

1 *Gordon v Rimmington* (1807) 1 Camp 123.
2 *Gordon v Rimmington* (1807) 1 Camp 123 at 124n.
3 *The Knight of St Michael* [1898] P 30; and see *Symington & Co v Union Insurance Society of Canton Ltd* (1928) 34 Com Cas 23, CA (insurers held liable for (1) damage to cargo by water used to prevent fire spreading, and also for (2) part of cargo thrown from quay into water for same object).
4 See *Tempus Shipping Co Ltd v Louis Dreyfus & Co Ltd* [1930] 1 KB 699 at 708; *The Knight of St Michael* [1898] P 30.
5 *Slattery v Mance* [1962] 1 QB 676, [1962] 1 All ER 525; *National Justice Compania Naviera SA v Prudential Assurance Co Ltd, The Ikarian Reefer* [1993] 2 Lloyd's Rep 68.

154. Strikes. The Institute Strikes Clauses (Cargo)[1] cover loss or damage caused by strikers, locked-out workmen, or participants in labour disturbances, riots[2] or civil commotions[3]; and terrorists or persons acting from political motives.

The Institute War and Strikes Clauses (Hulls—Time)[4], the Institute War and Strikes Clauses (Hulls—Voyage)[5], the Institute War and Strikes Clauses (Freight—

Time)[6] and the Institute War and Strikes Clauses (Freight—Voyage)[7] contain similar terms.

1 Ie the Institute Strikes Clauses (Cargo) cl 1. As to the Institute Clauses see para 149 note 1 ante.
2 For the meaning of 'riot' see para 596 post.
3 For the meaning of 'civil commotion' see para 597 post.
4 Ie the Institute War and Strikes Clauses (Hulls —Time) cl 1.4–1.5.
5 Ie the Institute War and Strikes Clauses (Hulls —Voyage) cl 1.4–1.5.
6 Ie the Institute War and Strikes Clauses (Freight —Time) cl 1.2.1–1.2.2.
7 Ie the Institute War and Strikes Clauses (Freight —Voyage) cl 1.2.1–1.2.2.

155. War risks. The Institute War Clauses (Cargo)[1] cover, subject to specified exceptions:
  (1) war, civil war, revolution, rebellion, insurrection[2], civil strife or hostile acts by or against a belligerent power;
  (2) actual or attempted capture, seizure, arrest, restraint or detainment arising from those risks, and their consequences; and
  (3) derelict mines, torpedoes, bombs or other weapons.
The Institute War and Strikes Clauses (Hulls—Time)[3], the Institute War and Strikes Clauses (Hulls—Voyage)[4], the Institute War and Strikes Clauses (Freight—Time)[5] and the Institute War and Strikes Clauses (Hulls—Voyage)[6] are in similar terms.

1 Institute War Clauses (Cargo) cl 1. As to the Institute Clauses see para 149 note 1 ante.
2 'Insurrection' means, for insurance purposes, an organised and violent internal revolt within a country, the main object of which is to overthrow the country's government: *National Oil Co of Zimbabwe (Pte) Ltd v Sturge* [1991] 2 Lloyd's Rep 281.
3 Institute War and Strikes Clauses (Hulls-Time) cl 1.1–1.3.
4 Institute War and Strikes Clauses (Hulls-Voyage) cl 1.1–1.3.
5 Institute War and Strikes Clauses (Freight-Time) cl 1.1.1–1.1.3.
6 Institute War and Strikes Clauses (Hulls-Voyage) cl 1.1.1–1.1.3.

156. Capture and seizure. Capture is a taking by an enemy as prize in time of war with intent to deprive the owner of all property in the thing taken; and if a ship is seized for the purpose of being carried into a port for adjudication, and is afterwards condemned by the prize court, the seizure constitutes an actual total loss[1]. Where the voyage is abandoned from fear of capture, the loss cannot be recovered as a loss by capture[2]. Where, however, the voyage is abandoned by a British subject because its further prosecution would be illegal owing to a declaration of war by the United Kingdom, this is a loss not by attempting to avoid a peril, but by the actual operation of the peril and may be recovered[3].
  Seizure includes takings otherwise than by capture, for instance by revenue or sanitary officers of a foreign state[4]. Seizures include deprivation of possession, whether the seizure was lawful or unlawful, and whether by enemies or pirates[5].
  If a United Kingdom ship is for any reason arrested or seized by the United Kingdom government, or if she is detained in port by embargo imposed by the government, this is a detention within the meaning of the policy[6]. The distinction between a loss by capture or restraint and a loss by fear of capture or restraint is dealt with subsequently[7].

1 *Andersen v Marten* [1908] AC 334, HL (where the ship was wrecked and became a total loss between the time of capture and condemnation); *Green v Emslie* (1794) Peake 212 (ship stranded but

undamaged and captured while stranded). A policy effected before the commencement of hostilities which insures against capture does not cover loss by British capture: *Keller v Le Mesurier* (1803) 4 East 396; *Brandon v Curling* (1803) 4 East 410. See para 78 ante.

2 *Kacianoff v China Traders Insurance Co Ltd* [1914] 3 KB 1121, CA; *Becker, Gray & Co v London Assurance Corpn* [1918] AC 101, HL; see also *Nickels & Co v London and Provincial Marine and General Insurance Co Ltd* (1900) 6 Com Cas 15.

3 *Sanday & Co v British and Foreign Marine Insurance Co Ltd* [1915] 2 KB 781, CA; affd sub nom *British and Foreign Marine Insurance Co Ltd v Samuel Sanday & Co* [1916] 1 AC 650, HL; see para 181 text to note 6 post. The loss is a 'constructive total loss', as to which see para 292 et seq post. As to the criterion of constructive total loss by capture see *Polurrian SS Co Ltd v Young* [1915] 1 KB 922, CA; *Wilson Bros, Bobbin & Co v Green* (1915) 31 TLR 605, cited in para 292 note 6 post; and *Roura and Forgas v Townend* [1919] 1 KB 189, cited in para 282 note 6 post.

4 *Cory v Burr* (1883) 8 App Cas 393, HL; *Miller v Law Accident Insurance Co* [1903] 1 KB 712, CA; *St Paul Fire and Marine Insurance Co v Morice* (1906) 11 Com Cas 153; cf *Robinson Gold Mining Co v Alliance Insurance Co* [1904] AC 359, HL (in this case, in the Court of Appeal [1902] 2 KB 489 at 500, Collins MR was of opinion that the loss would also fall within the words 'all consequences of warlike operations'). It has been held by a court in the United States that seizure requires the use or threat of force, but that there could be no seizure of a ship by her master and crew, who already had lawful possession of her: *The Hai Hsuan* [1958] 1 Lloyd's Rep 351, CA. As to barratry see para 161 post.

5 See *Goss v Withers* (1758) 2 Burr 683 at 694 per Lord Mansfield CJ; *Powell v Hyde* (1855) 5 E & B 607; *Lozano v Janson* (1859) 2 E & E 160 (unlawful seizure); *Kleinwort v Shepard* (1859) 1 E & E 447; *Dean v Hornby* (1854) 3 E & B 180 (pirates).

6 *Touteng v Hubbard* (1802) 3 Bos & P 291 at 302 per Lord Alvanley CJ; *Green v Young* (1702) 2 Ld Raym 840; *Hagedorn v Whitmore* (1816) 1 Stark 157. In *Lozano v Janson* (1859) 2 E & E 160 at 176 (see also *Aubert v Gray* (1862) 3 B & S 169 at 182, Ex Ch, it is intimated that the assured cannot recover in respect of a lawful arrest or detention by the United Kingdom government; it is submitted that this only means that if the property insured is liable to arrest or detention by the United Kingdom government on account of some illegal act of the assured, and is for that reason arrested or detained, the assured cannot recover. See also *British and Foreign Marine Insurance Co Ltd v Samuel Sanday & Co* [1916] 1 AC 650, HL, where it was held that a British merchant could recover for a constructive total loss when the further prosecution of the insured voyage had been rendered illegal by a British declaration of war, although the goods insured were undamaged and he had not been deprived of possession of them; and see para 181 post. Cf *Associated Oil Carriers Ltd v Union Insurance Society of Canton Ltd* [1917] 2 KB 184, where the assured was held entitled to recover for an actual total loss of freight on the ground that the performance of the charterparty had been rendered illegal by the outbreak of war.

7 See para 181 post. The precise imminence of peril which would make the restraint a present fact as contrasted with a future fear cannot be fixed by definition; the circumstances in each particular case must be considered: *Watts, Watts & Co Ltd v Mitsui & Co Ltd* [1917] AC 227 at 238, HL, per Lord Dunedin (restraint); and see *Atlantic Maritime Co Inc v Gibbon* [1954] 1 QB 88, [1953] 2 All ER 1086, CA. As to constructive total loss by capture see para 292 post.

157. Burden of proof in war risk cases.

Where a vessel, which is insured under a policy excepting war risks, is missing in time of war, it appears that once the assured has proved a loss there is a presumption that this was caused by perils of the seas[1]. This presumption may, however, be rebutted by the marine insurer showing that the balance of probabilities is in favour of a loss by war risks. The law on this question is far from clear. Where the policy insures against war risks only, the onus is on the assured to show that the loss was caused by those risks[2].

1 *Macbeth & Co v King* (1916) 86 LJKB 1004; *British and Burmese Steam Navigation Co Ltd v Liverpool and London War Risks Insurance Association Ltd and British Foreign Marine Insurance Co Ltd* (1917) 34 TLR 140; *General Steam Navigation Co Ltd v Commercial Union Assurance Co Ltd, General Steam Navigation Co Ltd v Janson* (1915) 31 TLR 630. See also *Munro, Brice & Co v War Risks Association* [1918] 2 KB 78 (revsd on the facts *Munro, Brice & Co v Marten* [1920] 3 KB 94, CA (brief report)); and see *Re National Benefit Assurance Co Ltd* (1933) 45 Ll L Rep 147; *Compania Maritima of Barcelona v Wishart* (1918) 87 LJKB 1027. For the meaning of 'perils of the seas' see para 151 ante.

2 *Euterpe SS Co Ltd v North of England Protecting and Indemnity Association Ltd* (1917) 33 TLR 540;
   Zachariessen v Importers and Exporters Marine Co Ltd (1924) 29 Com Cas 202, CA ('against mine risks
   only, including missing').

158. Arrests, restraints, detainments etc. The words 'arrests, restraints, and detainments' refer to political or executive acts, and do not include a loss caused by riot or by ordinary judicial process[1]. A restraint does not necessarily involve the use of actual physical force; any authoritative prohibition on the part of any governing power or the operation of any municipal law is sufficient[2]. It is doubtful whether compliance with an ultra vires order of a government department unaccompanied by a threat of force is a loss by restraint[3].

The essential distinction between capture and arrest is that capture is the forcible taking of the subject matter of insurance in time of war with a view of taking it as prize, whereas arrest is a temporary detention only, with a view of ultimately releasing it or repaying its value[4].

1 Marine Insurance Act 1906 s 30(2), Sch 1 r 10; *Finlay v Liverpool and Great Western SS Co Ltd* (1870) 23
  LT 251 (legal proceedings). As to the interpretation of an exemption clause excluding loss arising
  from arrest, restraint or detainment by reason of infringement of any customs regulations see
  Panamanian Oriental SS Corpn v Wright [1971] 2 All ER 1028, [1971] 1 WLR 882, CA. Unless a
  different intention appears, 'riot' in the Marine Insurance Act 1906 Sch 1 r 10, in the application of
  that rule to any policy of insurance taking effect on or after 1 April 1987, must be construed in
  accordance with the Public Order Act 1986 s 1: s 10(2). See CRIMINAL LAW vol 11(1) (Reissue) para
  149.
2 *Miller v Law Accident Insurance Co* [1903] 1 KB 712, CA; *British and Foreign Marine Insurance Co Ltd v
  Samuel Sanday & Co* [1916] 1 AC 650, HL; *Fooks v Smith* [1924] 2 KB 508 at 512; cf *Mansell & Co v
  Hoade* (1903) 20 TLR 150; *St Paul Fire and Marine Insurance Co v Morice* (1906) 11 Com Cas 153
  (destruction of cattle under local regulations is covered by the warranty). See also *Rickards v Forestal
  Land, Timber and Railways Co Ltd* [1942] AC 50, [1941] 2 All ER 62, HL; *Atlantic Maritime Co Inc v
  Gibbon* [1954] 1 QB 88, [1953] 2 All ER 1086, CA; *Symington & Co v Union Insurance Society of Canton
  Ltd* (1928) 34 Com Cas 23, CA.
3 In *Russian Bank for Foreign Trade v Excess Insurance Co Ltd* [1918] 2 KB 123, Bailhache J held that it
  was not a restraint; the decision was affirmed without deciding this point [1919] 1 KB 39, CA, but
  Scrutton LJ inclined to the opposite view. Restraints may excuse non-delivery of cargo under a
  contract of carriage, and yet not cause a loss of cargo recoverable under a contract of insurance: see
  Becker, Gray & Co v London Assurance Corpn [1918] AC 101 at 114, HL, per Lord Sumner. See also
  Czarnikow Ltd v Java Sea and Fire Insurance Co Ltd [1941] 3 All ER 256 at 261–262.
4 Marshall on Marine Insurance (4th Edn) 394.

159. Pirates and thieves. The term 'pirates' includes passengers who mutiny and rioters who attack the ship from the shore[1]. Revolutionaries organising and carrying out an armed expedition against the government, however, are not pirates within the meaning of that term in the policy[2].

There is no reason to limit piracy to acts outside territorial waters[3]. If a vessel is, in the ordinary meaning of the phrase, 'at sea', or if the attack can be described as a 'maritime offence', then she is in a place where piracy can be committed[4]. Theft without force or threat of force is not piracy[5]. Clandestine thieves, who use or threaten violence in order to escape after the theft has been committed, do not give rise to a loss by piracy[6].

The term 'thieves' in a policy does not cover clandestine theft or a theft committed by any of the ship's company, whether crew or passengers[7]. Robbery accompanied by violence and committed by strangers, and not by the crew, is a loss by thieves under the policy[8].

1 Marine Insurance Act 1906 s 30(2), Sch 1 r 8; *Nesbitt v Lushington* (1792) 4 Term Rep 783 at 787; *Palmer v Naylor* (1854) 10 Exch 382, Ex Ch (emigrants piratically and feloniously murdered the captain and part of the crew and carried away the ship and the rest of the crew: it was held that this was an act of piracy and covered by the policy); cf *Kleinwort v Shepard* (1859) 1 E & E 447. The Public Order Act 1986 s 10(2) (see para 158 note 1 ante) applies to the term 'rioter' in the Marine Insurance Act 1906 Sch 1 r 8.

2 *Bolivia Republic v Indemnity Mutual Marine Assurance Co Ltd* [1909] 1 KB 785, CA. Persons may be pirates according to international law if they commit acts which are otherwise piratical with a view to robbery even though the robbery itself is frustrated: *Re Piracy Jure Gentium* [1934] AC 586, PC. Although the term 'pirates' has not the same meaning as in international law, it would seem that this proposition is applicable to such a policy: *Bolivia Republic v Indemnity Mutual Marine Assurance Co Ltd* supra.

3 *Athens Maritime Enterprises Corpn v Hellenic Mutual War Risks Association (Bermuda) Ltd, The Andreas Lemos* [1983] QB 647 at 658, [1983] 1 All ER 590 at 598 per Staughton J.

4 *Athens Maritime Enterprises Corpn v Hellenic Mutual War Risks Association (Bermuda) Ltd, The Andreas Lemos* [1983] QB 647 at 658, [1983] 1 All ER 590 at 598 per Staughton J.

5 *Athens Maritime Enterprises Corpn v Hellenic Mutual War Risks Association (Bermuda) Ltd, The Andreas Lemos* [1983] QB 647 at 660, [1983] 1 All ER 590 at 599 per Staughton J.

6 *Athens Maritime Enterprises Corpn v Hellenic Mutual War Risks Association (Bermuda) Ltd, The Andreas Lemos* [1983] QB 647 at 660–661, [1983] 1 All ER 590 at 599–600 per Staughton J.

7 Marine Insurance Act 1906 Sch 1 r 9. See also *Nishina Trading Co Ltd v Chiyoda Fire & Marine Insurance Co Ltd* [1969] 2 QB 449, [1969] 2 All ER 776, CA, on the meanings of 'theft' and the rarer 'taking at sea' in a marine policy.

8 *Harford v Maynard* (1785) 1 Park's Marine Insurances (8th Edn) 36. If shipwrecked goods are plundered by wreckers on shore, this is a loss by perils of the seas (*Bondrett v Hentigg* (1816) Holt NP 149), and also, it seems, a loss by thieves. Violence in this connection is not confined to violence to a person; breaking open the doors of an unattended warehouse at night and stealing the goods will constitute theft within the meaning of a policy containing a transit clause. It may even be that where the policy contains such a clause the doctrine that only theft by violence is covered does not apply: *La Fabrique de Produits Chimiques SA v Large* [1923] 1 KB 203. As to the transit clause see para 125 ante.

160. Jettison. 'Jettison' clearly includes the general average sacrifice[1] consisting of the throwing overboard of cargo in time of peril for the common safety, but there is little authority on whether the meaning of the term is wider than this and includes any throwing overboard not amounting to such a sacrifice[2].

1 For the meaning of 'general average sacrifice' see para 244 post; and SHIPPING vol 43 para 742 et seq.
2 In *Butler v Wildman* (1820) 3 B & Ald 398, where the master of a ship which was about to be captured threw overboard the insured dollars in order to prevent their falling into the enemy's hands, it was held that this was loss by jettison.

161. Barratry. 'Barratry'[1] includes every wrongful act wilfully committed by the master or crew to the prejudice of the owner, or, as the case may be, the charterer[2], and this is so whether the master's act is induced by motive of benefit to himself, malice to the owners, or a disregard of those laws which it was his duty to obey and upon his observance of which his owners relied[3].

Sailing out of port without paying port dues or in breach of an embargo, or wilful breach of blockade, in consequence of which the ship is seized or other loss is sustained, may be barratry[4]. If the ship is fraudulently run away with by the master or by members of the crew, this is barratry on their part[5]. Deviation for a fraudulent or criminal purpose may be barratrous[6], but the commission of a crime is not an essential feature of barratry[7].

Deviation, if barratrous, does not avoid the policy, if barratry is one of the perils insured against[8].

Loss arising from the master's ignorance or incompetence, through a mistake as to the meaning of his instructions, or as to the best mode of carrying them into effect, does not amount to barratry[9].

1 Barratry, in the sense in which the term is used here, is much broader than the former criminal offence of barratry (abolished by the Criminal Law Act 1967 s 13(1)(a)), but acts which are barratrous for the purpose of the policy may amount to other criminal offences or they may be equally barratrous without any crime having been committed: see the text and notes infra. For a meaning of 'barratry' given in an American case see *The Padre Island* [1971] 2 Lloyd's Rep 431 at 432 (US Dist Ct), per Garza DJ.
2 Marine Insurance Act 1906 s 30(2), Sch 1 r 11. Thus, a wrongful refusal by the crew to discharge cargo is barratrous: *Compania Naviera Bachi v Henry Hosegood & Co Ltd* [1938] 2 All ER 189. The words in the definition 'or, as the case may be, the charterer' refer to cases in which the charterer is deemed to be owner for this purpose: see para 162 note 2 post.
3 *Earle v Rowcroft* (1806) 8 East 126 at 139; *Heyman v Parish* (1809) 2 Camp 149; but 'wilful default' within the Merchant Shipping Act 1854 s 299 (non-observance of collision regulations; see now the Merchant Shipping Act 1894 s 419(3)), is not necessarily barratry: *Grill v General Iron Screw Collier Co* (1868) LR 3 CP 476, Ex Ch.
4 *Stamma v Brown* (1742) 2 Stra 1173 at 1174 per Lee CJ; *Robertson v Ewer* (1786) 1 Term Rep 127, cited by Lord Ellenborough CJ in *Earle v Rowcroft* (1806) 8 East 126; *Goldschmidt v Whitmore* (1811) 3 Taunt 508; *Everth v Hannam* (1815) 6 Taunt 375. For further illustrations see *Moss v Byrom* (1795) 6 Term Rep 379 (cruising); *Havelock v Hancill* (1789) 3 Term Rep 277; *Pipon v Cope* (1808) 1 Camp 434 (smuggling); *Australasian Insurance Co v Jackson* (1875) 33 LT 286, PC (kidnapping).
5 *Falkner v Ritchie* (1814) 2 M & S 290; *Brown v Smith* (1813) 1 Dow 349, HL; *Dixon v Reid* (1822) 5 B & Ald 597; *Soares v Thornton* (1817) 7 Taunt 627; *Roscow v Corson* (1819) 8 Taunt 684; *Hibbert v Martin* (1808) 1 Camp 538 (barratry by master); *Toulmin v Inglis* (1808) 1 Camp 421; *Toulmin v Anderson* (1808) 1 Taunt 227; *Hucks v Thornton* (1815) Holt NP 30 (barratry of crew in conjunction with prisoners of war); *Marstrand Fishing Co Ltd v Beer* [1937] 1 All ER 158; *The Hai Hsuan* [1958] 1 Lloyd's Rep 351 (US 4th Cir).
6 *Vallejo v Wheeler* (1774) 1 Cowp 143; *Ross v Hunter* (1790) 4 Term Rep 33. If the captain is compelled by the mutiny of the crew to deviate from his course, this is barratry on the part of the mariners: *Elton v Brogden* (1747) as reported in 2 Stra 1264; and see cases cited in note 5 supra.
7 *Compania Naviera Bachi v Henry Hosegood & Co Ltd* [1938] 2 All ER 189 at 194 per Porter J.
8 See para 147 ante.
9 *Phyn v Royal Exchange Assurance Co* (1798) 7 Term Rep 505; *Todd v Ritchie* (1816) 1 Stark 240; *Bottomley v Bovill* (1826) 5 B & C 210 at 212; *Bradford v Levy* (1825) Ry & M 331.

162. Effect of consent by owners. No act can be barratrous which is sanctioned or authorised by those who are either the absolute owners of the ship[1] or may be considered her owners for the time being[2]. Unless he can be so considered, the owner of insured goods cannot recover as for a loss by barratry in respect of any act of the master which is sanctioned by the owner of the ship[3]. The shipowner cannot recover for a loss by barratry in respect of acts done by the charterer's agents where the ship is demised to the charterer, and the latter thus becomes owner of the ship for the voyage[4].

Loss by barratry seems to be an exception to the general rule of *causa proxima non remota spectatur*[5], for if there has been barratrous conduct on the part of the master and crew, and the loss happens in consequence of it, the insurers are liable as for a loss by barratry although the proximate cause of the loss is a peril of the seas or other peril insured against[6].

Once the assured has proved a casting away of the vessel by the deliberate act of the master or crew, it is for the insurers to prove that the assured consented to or connived at the casting away[7].

1 *Vallejo v Wheeler* (1774) 1 Cowp 143; *Nutt v Bourdieu* (1786) 1 Term Rep 323; cf *Stamma v Brown* (1742) 2 Stra 1173; *Pipon v Cope* (1808) 1 Camp 434; *Everth v Hannam* (1815) 6 Taunt 375; *The Michael, Piermay Shipping Co SA v Chester* [1979] 2 Lloyd's Rep 1, CA. A master who is part owner may, however, be guilty of barratry as against his innocent co-owners (*Jones v Nicholson* (1854) 10 Exch 28), or against the mortgagee of his share (*Small v United Kingdom Marine Mutual Insurance Association* [1897] 2 QB 311, CA). Where, however, the mortgagor is sole owner and is himself privy to the wrongful act which causes the loss, it seems that an innocent mortgagee, who has taken no part in the appointment of the guilty master or crew, cannot recover for a loss by barratry: see *P Samuel & Co Ltd v Dumas* [1924] AC 431 at 449, 454, HL; and see that case in the Court of Appeal [1923] 1 KB 592 at 622 per Scrutton LJ.

2 The question whether the charterer is in any particular case to be deemed for this purpose the owner of the ship depends upon the terms of the charterparty: see SHIPPING. Freighters have been so regarded for purposes of barratry in *Vallejo v Wheeler* (1774) 1 Cowp 143; *Soares v Thornton* (1817) 7 Taunt 627; *Ionides v Pender* (1872) 1 Asp MLC 432. See, however, the comments of Hilbery J at first instance in *Forestal Land, Timber and Railways Co Ltd v Rickards* [1940] 4 All ER 96 at 111–112 (revsd [1941] KB 225, [1940] 4 All ER 395, CA; affd [1942] AC 50, [1941] 3 All ER 62, HL). See also *Grauds v Dearsley* (1935) 51 Ll L Rep 203 (shipowner who allowed her husband to have possession and control of the ship could not treat his conduct as barratrous).

3 *Nutt v Bourdieu* (1786) 1 Term Rep 323; *Stamma v Brown* (1742) 2 Stra 1173; *Commercial Trading Co Inc v Hartford Fire Insurance Co* [1974] 1 Lloyd's Rep 179 (US 5th Cir).

4 *Hobbs v Hannam* (1811) 3 Camp 93.

5 As to this rule see paras 175–176 post.

6 See the judgment in *Cory v Burr* (1881) 8 QBD 313; on appeal (1882) 9 QBD 463, CA; affd (1883) 8 App Cas 393, HL, where, however, at 398 Lord Blackburn expressed a contrary opinion, and at 404 Lord Bramwell expressed a doubt on this point. It is submitted, however, that Lord Blackburn's view cannot be reconciled with *Earle v Rowcroft* (1806) 8 East 126, and *Vallejo v Wheeler* (1774) 1 Cowp 143, and other cases. There are many cases in which a loss may be recovered from the insurers, either as a loss by barratry, or a loss by perils of the seas, and some of the decided cases, involving the question whether the loss was one by barratry or one by perils of the seas have become, on account of the present system of pleading, unimportant: *Heyman v Parish* (1809) 2 Camp 149; *Arcangelo v Thompson* (1811) 2 Camp 620; *Goldschmidt v Whitmore* (1811) 3 Taunt 508; *Everth v Hannam* (1815) 6 Taunt 375; *Walker v Maitland* (1821) 5 B & Ald 171; *Blyth v Shepherd* (1842) 9 M & W 763. This note and the text are retained from the first edition of this work. In view, however, of the decision in *P Samuel & Co Ltd v Dumas* [1924] AC 431, it would seem that in the case supposed in the text the barratry must be regarded as the proximate cause of the loss, and the loss would not be recoverable as a loss by perils of the sea: see *Issaias v Marine Insurance Co Ltd* (1923) 15 Ll L Rep 186 at 193, CA, per Atkin LJ; see also *Republic of China, China Merchants Steam Navigation Co Ltd and United States of America v National Union Fire Insurance Co of Pittsburg, Pennsylvania and American International Underwriters* [1957] 1 Lloyd's Rep 428 at 443 (the appeal did not extend to the decision on proximate cause: The *Hai Hsuan* [1958] 1 Lloyd's Rep 351 (US 4th Cir)). For a discussion on proximate cause and the possibility of more than one proximate cause see para 176 post.

7 *N Michalos & Sons Maritime SA v Prudential Assurance Co Ltd, The Zinovia* [1984] 2 Lloyd's Rep 264 at 272 per Bingham J.

D. OTHER PERILS AND LOSSES

163. Accidents in loading, bursting of boilers, breakage of shafts, negligence of master, etc. It is now usual to include in policies a clause[1] expressly making the policy cover loss of or damage to the subject matter insured directly caused by accidents in loading or discharging cargo or fuel; explosions; breakdown of or accident to nuclear installations or reactors; bursting of boilers, breakage of shafts[2] or latent defects[3]; negligence of master[4], officers, crew[5], pilots or repairers; contact with aircraft, land conveyance, dock or harbour equipment or installation; earthquake, volcanic eruption or lightning; provided that such loss or damage has not resulted from want of due diligence[6] by the assured, owners or managers[7]. Masters, officers, crew or pilots are not considered part owners for this purpose if they hold shares in the vessel[8].

1 See the Institute Time Clauses (Hulls) cl 6. This part of the clause was at one time known as the 'Inchmaree' clause in consequence of the decision in *Thames and Mersey Marine Insurance Co v Hamilton, Fraser & Co* (1887) 12 App Cas 484, HL; see also the Institute Voyage Clauses (Hulls) cl 4, the Institute Time Clauses (Freight) cl 5, and the Institute Voyage Clauses (Freight) cl 5, which are in the same terms. See also para 149 note 1 ante.

2 The clause does not provide insurance against breakage of the shaft itself as this damage is not 'caused by' breakage of the shaft: *Scindia Steamships (London) Ltd v London Assurance* [1937] 1 KB 639, [1937] 3 All ER 895. See also *Jackson v Mumford* (1902) 8 Com Cas 61; affd on other grounds (1904) 9 Com Cas 114, CA; *Oceanic SS Co v Faber* (1906) 11 Com Cas 179; affd (1907) 13 Com Cas 28, CA; *Hutchins Bros v Royal Exchange Assurance Corpn* (1911) 27 TLR 217; affd [1911] 2 KB 398, CA.

3 See *The Jomie* [1973] 2 Lloyd's Rep 489 (US 5th Cir); *The Green Lion* [1974] 1 Lloyd's Rep 593 (US Dist Ct); *Robert A Parente v Bayville Marine Inc and General Insurance Co of America* [1975] 1 Lloyd's Rep 333 (US SC).

4 See *Lind v Mitchell* (1928) 98 LJKB 120, CA; *The Lapwing* [1940] P 112.

5 See *F B Walker & Sons Inc v Valentine* [1970] 2 Lloyd's Rep 429 (US 5th Cir); *The Belle of Portugal* [1970] 2 Lloyd's Rep 386 (US 9th Cir).

6 See *The Pacific Queen* [1963] 2 Lloyd's Rep 201 (US 9th Cir); *F B Walker & Sons Inc v Valentine* [1970] 2 Lloyd's Rep 429 (US 5th Cir); *The Brentwood* [1973] 2 Lloyd's Rep 232 (BC CA).

7 Institute Time Clauses (Hulls) cl 6; and see the other clauses mentioned in note 1 supra. The fact that the policy contains such a clause, which specifically covers loss caused by explosion, does not affect the burden of proof for the clause has been added only to include in the perils insured against events which have been construed not to be perils of the seas: *The Vainqueur* [1974] 2 Lloyd's Rep 398 (US 2nd Cir).

8 Institute Time Clauses (Hulls) cl 6; and see the other clauses mentioned in note 1 supra.

E. THE COLLISION CLAUSE

164. Liability for collision in the absence of collision clause. Where two vessels come into collision and it is found that both are to blame, then, according to maritime law as administered by the English admiralty courts since the passing of the Maritime Conventions Act 1911[1], the damage done to each vessel is added together and is treated as a common loss to be divided in proportion to the degree of fault attributable to each vessel. If it is not possible to establish different degrees of fault, the liability is apportioned equally between the two shipowners[2]. It has consequently become the custom for shipowners to protect themselves by a special clause in the policy called the 'collision' clause[3].

1 Claims to which the Maritime Conventions Act 1911 applies are not affected by the Law Reform (Contributory Negligence) Act 1945: see s 3(1); and SHIPPING vol 43 para 964.

2 Maritime Conventions Act 1911 s 1; and see SHIPPING vol 43 para 964 et seq. Similarly, the owners of cargo on either ship can recover such proportion of their damage as the carrying ship could recover of its damage against the owners of the other ship: *The Umona* [1914] P 141; *The Drumlanrig* [1911] AC 16, HL, applying *The Milan* (1861) Lush 388; and see SHIPPING. Before the passing of the Maritime Conventions Act 1911 the rule of English law was that where both vessels were to blame the aggregate loss must be divided equally between the two shipowners: see eg *De Vaux v Salvador* (1836) 4 Ad & El 420.

3 See the Institute Time Clauses (Hulls) cl 8; and the Institute Voyage Clauses (Hulls) cl 6. See Ivamy's *Marine Insurance* (4th Edn) at pp 534, 542. A form of this clause is set out in Appendix 3, para 908 post. As to forms of collision clause for the protection from liability of cargo or freight owners see the Institute Cargo Clauses (A) cl 3; the Institute Cargo Clauses (B) cl 3; the Institute Cargo Clauses (C) cl 3; the Institute Time Clauses (Freight) cl 9; and the Institute Voyage Clauses (Freight) cl 7. As to the Institute Clauses see para 149 note 1 ante.

165. Collision clause applies only to collision between ships. The collision clause is usually expressed to be applicable in cases of collision between the ship insured and some other vessel[1]. It therefore does not protect the shipowner against liability for his vessel running into a dock wall, breakwater or anything that is not another ship[2]; but, if there is a collision between A's tug and B, or if A strikes the anchor of B, this is a collision between two vessels within the meaning of the collision clause[3]. Moreover, where there has once been a collision within the meaning of the collision clause, the shipowner will, it seems, be protected against all damages, direct or consequential, occasioned by it which the owner of the other vessel or cargo may be entitled to recover from him[4].

1 See the Institute Time Clauses (Hulls) cl 8; and the Institute Voyage Clauses (Hulls) cl 6. See also paras 164 note 3 ante, 908 post.
2 Eg fishing nets attached to a fishing vessel which was a mile away from the nets: *Bennett SS Co Ltd v Hull Mutual Steamship Protecting Society Ltd* [1913] 3 KB 372; affd [1914] 3 KB 57, CA. This risk is, however, sometimes expressly included: *The Munroe* [1893] P 248; *Union Marine Insurance Co v Borwick* [1895] 2 QB 279; *Mancomunidad del Vapor Frumiz v Royal Exchange Assurance* [1927] 1 KB 567. A flying boat is not a 'vessel': *Polpen Shipping Co Ltd v Commercial Union Assurance Co Ltd* [1943] KB 161, [1943] 1 All ER 162. As to the meaning of 'ship' see also para 113 ante.
3 *The Niobe* [1891] AC 401, HL; *Re Margetts and Ocean Accident and Guarantee Corpn* [1901] 2 KB 792, DC; *Chandler v Blogg* [1898] 1 QB 32.
4 See *The North Britain* [1894] P 77 at 86, CA, per A L Smith LJ; *William France, Fenwick & Co Ltd v Merchants' Marine Insurance Co Ltd* [1915] 3 KB 290, CA (consecutive collisions). In *Burger v Indemnity Mutual Marine Assurance Co* [1900] 2 QB 348, CA, the insurers' liability was limited to 'payments in respect of injury to such other ship or vessel itself', and was held to exclude expenses of removing the wreck of the other vessel, paid by her owners, and recovered from the assured as damages. As to the proviso in the Institute Clauses (see note 1 supra), excluding liabilities for removal of obstructions, see *The North Britain* supra; approved in *The Engineer* [1898] AC 382, HL; *Chapman v James Fisher & Sons* (1904) 20 TLR 319.

166. Full protection policy. The collision clause does not apply to every collision nor to every class of damage occasioned by it, nor does it usually purport to insure against more than three-fourths of the damage sustained[1]. Thus, the assured is entitled to an indemnity under the clause only in respect of his liability to pay damages for acts of a tortious character[2] and cannot claim to be indemnified in respect of obligations arising from contract[3] or from special legislation[4]. In order to protect themselves against what is not covered by the clause, shipowners often insure in mutual insurance associations[5], or effect with insurers a 'full protection' policy[6].

1 See the Institute Time Clauses (Hulls) cl 8; and the Institute Voyage Clauses (Hulls) cl 6. A form of clause is set out in Appendix 3, para 908 post.
2 The act in respect of which damages are payable need not necessarily be a tort under English law: *Hall Bros SS Co Ltd v Young* [1939] 1 KB 748, [1939] 1 All ER 809, CA, explaining *Furness Withy & Co Ltd v Duder* [1936] 2 KB 461, [1936] 2 All ER 119.
3 *Furness Withy & Co Ltd v Duder* [1936] 2 KB 461, [1936] 2 All ER 119 (contract for towage by Admiralty tug providing that the shipowner should make good all damage suffered by the Admiralty).
4 *Hall Bros SS Co Ltd v Young* [1939] 1 KB 748, [1939] 1 All ER 809, CA.
5 As to mutual insurance associations see paras 341–346 post.
6 As to this see Gow's Marine Insurance (5th Edn) 261–262. For the construction of a policy indemnifying a shipowner against liability to a harbour authority in connection with the removal of a wreck see *Oceanic Steam Navigation Co Ltd v Evans* (1934) 51 TLR 67, CA.

(ii) Losses for which Insurer not Liable

167. Losses for which insurer not liable. The Marine Insurance Act 1906 provides that the insurer is not liable for any loss attributable to the wilful misconduct of the assured, but, unless the policy otherwise provides, he is liable for any loss proximately caused by a peril insured against[1], even though the loss would not have happened but for the misconduct or negligence of the master or crew[2]. Unless the policy otherwise provides, the insurer on ship[3] or goods[4] is not liable for any loss proximately caused by delay[5], even though the delay is caused by a peril insured against[6]. Again, unless the policy otherwise provides, the insurer is not liable for ordinary wear and tear[7], ordinary leakage and breakage[8], inherent vice[9] or nature of the subject matter insured, or for any loss proximately caused by rats or vermin, or for any injury to machinery not proximately caused by maritime perils[10].

In addition the Institute Clauses contain the following exceptions to liability:

(1) a General Exclusions Clause (in the case of cargo), which exempts the insurer from liability for a number of the types of loss excluded under the Marine Insurance Act 1906, such as loss by the wilful misconduct of the assured, by delay or by inherent vice[11];

(2) a War Exclusion Clause, which states that the policy does not cover loss caused by war, civil war, insurrection, etc[12];

(3) a Strikes Exclusion Clause, which states that the policy does not cover loss caused by strikes or persons taking part in riots or civil commotion, or by any terrorist[13];

(4) a Malicious Acts Exclusion Clause, which excludes libility for loss arising from the detonation of an explosive, or from any weapon, caused by any person acting maliciously or from a political motive[14]; and

(5) a Nuclear Explosion Clause, which states that the policy does not cover loss arising from any weapon employing atomic or nuclear fission[15].

1 As to the perils insured against see generally para 149 ante.
2 Marine Insurance Act 1906 s 55(2)(a).
3 'Ship' includes hovercraft: see para 113 ante.
4 For the meaning of 'goods' see para 114 ante.
5 See para 169 post.
6 Marine Insurance Act 1906 s 55(2)(b).
7 See para 170 post.
8 See para 171 post.
9 See paras 172–173 post.
10 Marine Insurance Act 1906 s 55(2)(c). For the meaning of 'maritime perils' see para 36 ante.
11 See eg the Institute Cargo Clauses (A) cl 4. As to the Institute Clauses see para 149 note 1 ante.
12 See eg the Institute Time Clauses (Hulls) cl 23. Separate clauses may cover war risks: see para 155 ante.
13 See eg the Institute Voyage Clauses (Hulls) cl 21. Separate clauses may cover risks associated with strikes, etc: see para 154 ante.
14 See eg the Institute Time Clauses (Freight) cl 19.
15 See eg the Institute Voyage Clauses (Freight) cl 17.

168. Stranding in the ordinary course of employment. The insurer is not liable for damage done by stranding in the ordinary course of the ship's employment. If the ship takes the ground in the usual course of her voyage and without the intervention of any extraordinary casualty, this is mere wear and tear[1]; to make the insurer liable there must be something fortuitous, accidental and not necessarily arising from the ordinary course of navigation[2]. Moreover, a loss by stranding can only take place when the ship, if not on the seas, is at any rate waterborne[3].

1 As to wear and tear see para 170 post.

2 *Magnus v Buttemer* (1852) 11 CB 876. The negligence of those in charge of the docking of a yacht in allowing her to sit on a dangerous bottom is a fortuitous circumstance entitling the assured to recover for a loss: *The Lapwing* [1940] P 112. A policy against liability for loss of a vessel by 'grounding or stranding' does not cover sinking to the ground in deep water: *Baker-Whiteley Coal Co v Marten* (1910) 26 TLR 314.

3 *Phillips v Barber* (1821) 5 B & Ald 161; *Thompson v Whitmore* (1810) 3 Taunt 227; *Rowcroft v Dunsmore* (1801) cited in *Thompson v Whitmore* supra at 228. These cases, however, are now of little importance, because they were decided under the old rules of pleading.

169. Loss proximately caused by delay. As previously stated[1], unless the policy otherwise provides, the insurer on ship or goods is not liable for any loss proximately caused by delay, although the delay is caused by a peril insured against[2]. From this it follows that the insurer is not liable for damage to perishable goods, even though that damage would not have arisen but for the prolongation of the voyage caused by a peril insured against. Similarly, the wages of the crew and expenses incurred and provisions consumed during detention, whether in a port of distress for repairs, or by embargo or restraint[3], are not, in the absence of a stipulation to the contrary, recoverable as such from the insurer[4], although they may be the basis of claims in respect of general average[5].

1 See para 167 ante.

2 Marine Insurance Act 1906 s 55(2)(b), which embodies the principle laid down in *Taylor v Dunbar* (1869) LR 4 CP 206, and *Pink v Fleming* (1890) 25 QBD 396, CA. The latter case is explained in *Schloss Bros v Stevens* [1906] 2 KB 665, CA, where Walton J held that an insurance against 'all risks by land and by water' covered all losses of an accidental nature of whatever kind. See further *St Margaret's Trust Ltd v Navigators & General Insurance Co Ltd* (1949) 82 Ll L Rep 752 (gradual deterioration of vessels); *Federation Insurance Co of Canada v Coret Accessories Inc and Hirsh (trading as S A Hirsh & Co)* [1968] 2 Lloyd's Rep 109 (Que Superior Ct (Dist of Montreal)) (delay in delivery of goods).

3 As to restraint see para 158 ante.

4 *Fletcher v Poole* (1769) 1 Park's Marine Insurances (8th Edn) 115; *Lateward v Curling* (1776) 1 Park's Marine Insurances (8th Edn) 288; *Eden v Poole* (1785) 1 Park's Marine Insurances (8th Edn) 117; *Robertson v Ewer* (1786) 1 Term Rep 127; cf *M'Carthy v Abel* (1804) 5 East 388; *Everth v Smith* (1814) 2 M & S 278 (policies on freight). See also *Wilson v Bank of Victoria* (1867) LR 2 QB 203 at 212.

5 As to general average see para 244 et seq post. See also the York-Antwerp Rules 1974 r XI, set out in Appendix 2, para 907 post.

170. Wear and tear. Loss by wear and tear of a ship and her appurtenances[1] differs essentially from loss by perils of the seas[2] in that it is not due to any fortuitous casualty, but is the ordinary result of navigation. Thus, the parting of a rope or cable, the splitting of a sail in ordinary weather, damage done to the vessel's copper sheathing or to the cable and anchor in a place of usual anchorage and in no extraordinary circumstances of wind and weather, or decay of or damage to masts or spars in the ordinary service of the ship, are all cases of wear and tear for which the underwriter is not liable[3].

Similarly, damage caused by the ship springing a leak is considered wear and tear, unless it is traceable to some fortuitous occurrence during the voyage[4].

1 As to liability for loss by wear and tear see the Marine Insurance Act 1906 s 55(2)(c); and also para 167 ante. See also *Wilson, Sons & Co v Xantho (Cargo Owners)* (1887) 12 App Cas 503 at 509, HL, per Lord Herschell.

2 For the meaning of 'perils of the seas' see para 151 ante.

3 In order to avoid disputes as to wear and tear, average adjusters have by the rules of their association determined the circumstances in which damage to sails, rigging, etc, is to be considered wear and

tear; see the Rules of Practice of the Association of Average Adjusters, rr D 3, D 4, set out in Ivamy's Marine Insurance (4th Edn) 570 at 576. The rules of practice are framed in accordance with what the average adjusters consider are the legal principles applicable to the subject, but if they are found at variance with legal principles, the rules of practice cannot prevail: see *Atwood v Sellar & Co* (1879) 4 QBD 342 at 363; and on appeal (1880) 5 QBD 286 at 288–289, CA. In *Harrison v Universal Marine Insurance Co* (1862) 3 F & F 190, a special jury found against the alleged custom not to pay for damage done to the hull below the water line except where the ship had taken the ground or had come into collision with some substance other than water. The finding led to the insertion of the 'metalling' clause: see McArthur's Contract of Marine Insurance (2nd Edn) 308–309.

4 See *Hamilton, Fraser & Co v Pandorf & Co* (1887) 12 App Cas 518 at 523–524, HL, per Lord Halsbury LC; *Dudgeon v Pembroke* (1874) LR 9 QB 581 at 595; affd (1877) 2 App Cas 284, HL; *Merchants Trading Co v Universal Marine Insurance Co* (1870) 2 Asp MLC 431n, CA, there cited by Blackburn J; see also *Wadsworth Lighterage and Coaling Co Ltd v Sea Insurance Co Ltd* (1929) 45 TLR 597, CA, where the insured barge sank through 'general debility', and it was held that the insurers were not liable, although the policy expressly covered 'sinking'; *Capital Coastal Shipping Corpn and Bulk Towing Corpn v Hartford Fire Insurance Co (United States of America, third party), The Cristie* [1975] 2 Lloyd's Rep 100 (Dist Ct, Eastern Dist Virginia). Contrast *Mountain v Whittle* [1921] 1 AC 615, HL, cited in para 151 note 6 ante.

171. Leakage or breakage.

As regards leakage or breakage of goods[1], the insurers are liable when it is caused by the violent pitching or labouring of the ship[2], but are not liable for ordinary leakage and breakage such as usually occurs on every voyage unless the language of the policy shows that such ordinary leakage or breakage was intended to be covered[3].

1 As to the general principle of liability for leakage or breakage see para 167 ante.
2 *Crofts v Marshall* (1836) 7 C & P 597.
3 In *Traders and General Insurance Association Ltd v Bankers and General Insurance Co Ltd* (1921) 38 TLR 94, Bailhache J expressed the opinion that the words 'to pay average, including the risks of leakage' covered leakage from any cause. See also *Phoenix Insurance Co of Hartford v De Monchy* (1929) 141 LT 439, HL.

172. Inherent vice or nature of subject matter.

As regards the inherent vice or nature of the subject matter[1], unless the policy otherwise provides[2], the insurer is not liable for loss or damage that is not the consequence of some casualty which can properly be considered a peril of the seas[3]. He is, therefore, not liable for loss or damage arising solely from decay or deterioration of the subject matter insured, as when fruit becomes rotten or flour heats, not from external causes, but from internal decomposition; nor is he liable for spontaneous combustion generated by some chemical change in the thing insured, arising from its being put on board in a wet or otherwise damaged condition[4], or for damage caused by inadequate packing of the goods[5].

Where the insurance is on live animals, the insurers are not liable for losses solely attributable to death from natural causes, for they only undertake to indemnify against losses proximately caused by the immediate agency of the perils insured against[6], and death from natural causes is not a peril insured against. Loss by mortality is, however, sometimes expressly included amongst the perils insured against[7].

The exception of inherent vice applies to damage to the ship as well as to the goods. Thus, if a ship insured under a time policy[8] starts on the voyage in an unseaworthy[9] condition, and is by reason of that unseaworthiness, and not by the perils of the seas, obliged to put into a port for repair, the expenses of doing so cannot be recovered from the insurer, although there is no warranty of seaworthiness, even if the owner was not aware of the vessel being unseaworthy[10]. On the other hand, the insurers under a time policy will be liable if the perils of the seas are the proximate cause of the ship putting into port, or of her being lost, although this would not have occurred but for the ship's unseaworthiness, provided the assured was not privy to this[11].

1 As to the general principle of liability for the inherent vice or nature of the subject matter see para 167 ante.
2 See para 173 post.
3 For the meaning of 'perils of the seas' see para 151 ante.
4 *Boyd v Dubois* (1811) 3 Camp 133; *Soya GmbH Mainz Kommanditgesellschaft v White* [1983] 1 Lloyd's Rep 122, HL; *T M Noten BV v Harding* [1990] 2 Lloyd's Rep 283, CA
5 *F W Berk & Co Ltd v Style* [1956] 1 QB 180, [1955] 3 All ER 625; *Gee and Garnham Ltd v Whittall* [1955] 2 Lloyd's Rep 562.
6 As to insurances on animals and the effect of the clause 'free of mortality and jettison' see generally *Tatham v Hodgson* (1796) 6 Term Rep 656; *Lawrence v Aberdein* (1821) 5 B & Ald 107 at 111; *Gabay v Lloyd* (1825) 3 B & C 793.
7 *Jacob v Gaviller* (1902) 7 Com Cas 116 (which see also as to the 'walking on shore' clause); *St Paul Fire and Marine Insurance Co v Morice* (1906) 11 Com Cas 153 (slaughter of bull in consequence of the existence of foot-and-mouth disease).
8 For the meaning of 'time policy' see para 41 ante.
9 For the meaning of 'seaworthiness' see para 67 ante.
10 *Fawcus v Sarsfield* (1856) 6 E & B 192 at 204; *Ballantyne v Mackinnon* [1896] 2 QB 455, CA. See also *E D Sassoon & Co v Western Assurance Co* [1912] AC 561, PC, and *Grant, Smith & Co and McDonnell Ltd v Seattle Construction and Dry Dock Co* [1920] AC 162, PC.
11 *Dudgeon v Pembroke* (1877) 2 App Cas 284 at 295, HL. If, however, with the assured's privity, the ship is sent to sea in an unseaworthy state, the underwriter is not liable for a loss attributable to unseaworthiness: see paras 74 note 4 ante, 177 post.

173. Insurance against loss due to inherent vice. It is possible by express provision in the policy to insure against a loss caused by inherent vice[1]. Whether or not the express terms of the policy do in fact render the insurer liable for such a loss is a matter of construction. The mere fact that a policy is expressed to cover 'all risks'[2] does not render the insurer liable for loss due to inherent vice[3]. Where a policy contains an Institute Clause providing that the insurance is not to cover loss or damage caused by inherent vice, an assured wishing to insure against such a peril must either use specific words to that effect, or at least have the relevant part of the Institute Clause struck out[4].

1 *E D Sassoon & Co Ltd v Yorkshire Insurance Co Ltd* (1923) 14 Ll L Rep 167; affd 16 Ll L Rep 129 at 133, CA, per Atkin LJ; *Dodwell & Co Ltd v British Dominion General Insurance Co Ltd (1918)* [1955] 2 Lloyd's Rep 391n ('risks of leaking from any cause whatsoever'); *F W Berk & Co Ltd v Style* [1956] 1 QB 180 at 186, [1955] 3 All ER 625 at 630–631; *Overseas Commodities Ltd v Style* [1958] 1 Lloyd's Rep 546; *Soya GmbH Mainz Kommanditgesellschaft v White* [1983] 1 Lloyd's Rep 122, HL.
2 As to 'all risks' policies see para 150 ante.
3 *British and Foreign Marine Insurance Co Ltd v Gaunt* [1921] 2 AC 41 at 57, HL, per Lord Sumner; *Pasquali & Co v Traders and General Insurance Association Ltd* (1921) 9 Ll L Rep 514; *Schloss Bros v Stevens* [1906] 2 KB 665 at 673, CA; see also *Wadsworth Lighterage and Coaling Co Ltd v Sea Insurance Co Ltd* (1929) 35 Com Cas 1, CA; contrast *Traders and General Insurance Association Ltd v Bankers and General Insurance Co Ltd* (1921) 38 TLR 94; *Phoenix Insurance Co of Hartford v De Monchy* (1929) 141 LT 439, HL; *London and Provincial Leather Processes Ltd v Hudson* [1939] 2 KB 724, [1939] 3 All ER 857.
4 *F W Berk & Co Ltd v Style* [1956] 1 QB 180 at 187, [1955] 3 All ER 625 at 631 (in the report of this case in [1955] 2 Lloyd's Rep 382 at 390, the word 'and' appears and not 'or' as in the other reports mentioned); see also *Biddle, Sawyer & Co Ltd v Peters* [1957] 2 Lloyd's Rep 339.

174. Scuttling. As the term 'perils of the seas'[1] refers only to fortuitous accidents or casualties, a loss by scuttling is not recoverable[2]. When, therefore, the assured alleges a loss by perils of the sea he must, in order to make out a prima facie case, adduce evidence to show that the loss was due to a cause, such as sinking or stranding[3], which, in the absence of design, would constitute a peril of the seas. If the assured makes out a prima facie case, the burden of disproving this rests on the insurer[4]. Where the court is left in doubt whether or not the vessel was scuttled, the assured must fail[5].

1 For the meaning of 'perils of the seas' see para 151 ante.
2 *P Samuel & Co Ltd v Dumas* [1924] AC 431, HL. See the comments of Lord Sumner in *Anghelatos v Northern Assurance Co Ltd* (1924) 19 Ll L Rep 255 at 262, HL.
3 As to stranding in the ordinary course of employment see para 168 ante.
4 The precise extent of the burden which rests upon the insurer is not clear. Cf *Issaias v Marine Insurance Co Ltd* (1923) 15 Ll L Rep 186, CA, and *Anghelatos v Northern Assurance Co Ltd* (1923) 16 Ll L Rep 252, CA (affd on the facts (1924) 19 Ll L Rep 255, HL) ('beyond reasonable doubt'), with *Pateras v Royal Exchange Assurance* (1934) 49 Ll L Rep 400; *Maris v London Assurance* (1935) 51 Ll L Rep 158; see also *The Tropaioforos* [1960] 2 Lloyd's Rep 469.
5 *Compañia Martiartu v Royal Exchange Assurance* [1923] 1 KB 650, CA (affd on the facts [1924] AC 850, HL); *Ansoleaga y Cia v Indemnity Mutual Marine Insurance Co Ltd* (1922) 13 Ll L Rep 231 at 248 per Scrutton LJ; *Anghelatos v Northern Assurance Co Ltd* (1923) 16 Ll L Rep 252, CA; affd (1924) 19 Ll L Rep 255, HL; *Banco de Barcelona v Union Marine Insurance Co Ltd* (1925) 30 Com Cas 316; *Grauds v Dearsley* (1935) 51 Ll L Rep 203; *Bank of Athens v Royal Exchange Assurance* (1937) 57 Ll L Rep 37; affd 59 Ll L Rep 67, CA; *The Tropaioforos* [1960] 2 Lloyd's Rep 469; *The Gold Sky* [1972] 2 Lloyd's Rep 187; *N Michalos & Sons Maritime SA v Prudential Assurance Co Ltd, The Zinovia* [1984] 2 Lloyd's Rep 264; *Rhesa Shipping Co SA v Edmunds, The Popi M* [1985] 2 All ER 712, [1985] 1 WLR 948, HL.

(iii) Proximate Cause of Loss

A. DETERMINATION OF PROXIMATE CAUSE

175. Causation. It is a fundamental principle of marine insurance that *causa proxima non remota spectatur*[1], and that the underwriter is not liable for any loss which is not proximately caused by a peril insured against[2]. This principle is embodied in the Marine Insurance Act 1906[3], but certain decisions of the House of Lords have to some extent modified the previous application of the principle[4]. Subject to the provisions of that Act, and unless the policy otherwise provides[5], the insurer is liable for any loss proximately caused by a peril insured against, but subject as aforesaid, he is not liable for any loss which is not proximately caused by a peril insured against[6]. For this purpose the word 'proximate' means proximate in efficiency, rather than proximate in time[7]. 'Proximate cause' in fact means the same thing as 'dominant' or 'effective' or 'direct' cause[8].

1 Ie the immediate, not the remote cause, is to be considered.
2 As to perils insured against see generally para 149 ante.
3 See the Marine Insurance Act 1906 s 55(1); and the text and notes infra.
4 See the observations of Scrutton LJ in *British and Foreign SS Co Ltd v R* [1918] 2 KB 879 at 886, CA, and in *P Samuel & Co Ltd v Dumas* [1923] 1 KB 592 at 629, CA. The leading case before the Act was *Ionides v Universal Marine Insurance Co* (1863) 14 CBNS 259 (followed in *Marsden v City and County Assurance Co* (1865) LR 1 CP 232 (plate glass policy)). This case turned on the effect of the 'f c and s clause'. For the modern interpretation of the doctrine of proximate cause see *Becker, Gray & Co v London Assurance Corpn* [1918] AC 101 at 112–118, HL, per Lord Sumner, and *Leyland Shipping Co Ltd v Norwich Union Fire Insurance Society Ltd* [1918] AC 350 at 363–364, HL, per Lord Dunedin.
5 In *Le Quellec et Fils v Thomson* (1916) 86 LJKB 712, where the policy was 'against war risks, including extinction of lights', it was held that as the extinction of lights could never be the proximate cause of

a loss, the policy had 'otherwise provided', within the meaning of the Marine Insurance Act 1906 s 55(1), but nevertheless the loss was not within the policy, because the master had not attempted to steer by the light, and would not have done so even if it had not been extinguished. Cf *Merchants' Marine Insurance Co Ltd v Liverpool Marine and General Insurance Co Ltd* (1928) 33 Com Cas 294, CA, where the policy provided that if the vessel was in a damaged condition at the expiration of the policy, the risk should continue for the immediate consequences of that damage, and it was held that the insurers were liable for the stranding of the vessel while on her way to a repair port after the policy had expired.

6 Marine Insurance Act 1906 s 55(1).

7 See *Leyland Shipping Co Ltd v Norwich Union Fire Insurance Society Ltd* [1918] AC 350 at 369, HL, per Lord Shaw, and at 363 per Lord Dunedin. See also *P Samuel & Co Ltd v Dumas* [1924] AC 431 at 447, HL, per Viscount Cave LC. This is contrary to the law as laid down in earlier cases; see *P Samuel & Co Ltd v Dumas* in [1923] 1 KB 592 at 619, CA, per Scrutton LJ. See also the cases cited in note 8 infra.

8 *Becker, Gray & Co v London Assurance Corpn* [1918] AC 101, HL, per Lord Sumner; *P Samuel & Co Ltd v Dumas* [1924] AC 431 at 459, HL, per Lord Finlay; *Leyland Shipping Co Ltd v Norwich Union Fire Insurance Society Ltd* [1918] AC 350, HL, per Lord Dunedin; *Canada Rice Mills Ltd v Union Marine and General Insurance Co Ltd* [1941] AC 55 at 71, [1940] 4 All ER 169 at 178, PC; *Smith, Hogg & Co Ltd v Black Sea and Baltic General Insurance Co Ltd* [1940] AC 997, [1940] 3 All ER 405, HL; *Boiler Inspection and Insurance Co of Canada v Sherwin-Williams Co of Canada Ltd* [1951] AC 319, PC. See also *Ocean SS Co v Liverpool and London War Risks Insurance Association Ltd* [1946] KB 561 at 575, [1946] 2 All ER 355 at 364, CA, per Scott LJ; *Ashworth v General Accident Fire and Life Assurance Corpn Ltd* [1955] IR 268; and for earlier observations as to causation and cases on causation in relation to insurance law see DAMAGES vol 12 para 1141 note 4.

176. Determination of proximate cause. The question whether a peril insured against was the proximate cause[1] of a loss is a question of fact 'to be determined on commonsense principles'[2], but certain rules may be deduced from the Marine Insurance Act 1906 as interpreted in the decided cases which the tribunal of fact ought to follow. It seems that there may be more than one proximate (in the sense of effective or direct) cause of a loss[3].

If one of these causes is insured against under the policy, and none of the others is expressly excluded from the policy, the assured will be entitled to recover. If, however, one of these causes is excluded from the policy by a 'warranty'[4], it becomes necessary to distinguish between the relative efficiency of the several causes, and if the most effective or dominant of the causes contributing to the loss is excluded by the warranty, the assured will not be entitled to recover. In other words, the first question in these cases is, was a peril insured against a proximate (that is, direct) cause of the loss? If it was, the next question is, was a peril excluded by the warranty also a proximate (that is, direct) cause of the loss? If this second question is answered in the affirmative, the final question arises, which of these causes was the more effective, or, in other words, the dominant cause of the loss[5]? The question whether the excluded peril was a proximate cause of the loss must be determined as if it arose under a policy insuring against the excluded peril[6].

If the subject matter insured sustains damage by a peril insured against, but is afterwards totally lost by an excepted peril before the damage is made good, the assured cannot recover either for the damage or for the total loss[7]. Once the subject matter insured is lost to the assured by an excepted peril, he cannot recover on the policy even if it is subsequently destroyed by a peril insured against[8].

Where no question arises as to an excepting warranty and the loss is proximately caused by a peril insured against, the assured is entitled to recover although the loss would not have happened but for other events, whether those events occurred before[9] or after[10] the peril insured against came into operation.

1 For the meaning of 'proximate cause' see para 175 ante.

2 *Leyland Shipping Co Ltd v Norwich Union Fire Insurance Society Ltd* [1918] AC 350, HL, per Lord Dunedin; and see at 369 per Lord Shaw; *Smith, Hogg & Co Ltd v Black Sea and Baltic General Insurance Co Ltd* [1940] AC 997 at 1003–1004, [1940] 3 All ER 405 at 409–410, HL, per Lord Wright. See also *Yorkshire Dale SS Co Ltd v Minister of War Transport* [1942] AC 691, [1942] 2 All ER 6, HL; *Boiler Inspection and Insurance Co of Canada v Sherwin-Williams Co of Canada Ltd* [1951] AC 319, PC, and Lord Sumner's warning against 'microscopic analysis of the circumstances of a casualty' in *The Clan Matheson* [1929] AC 514 at 530, HL.

3 See especially per Lindley LJ in *Reischer v Borwick* [1894] 2 QB 548 at 551–552, CA.

4 As to this use of the word 'warranty' see para 54 note 2 ante.

5 *Reischer v Borwick* [1894] 2 QB 548 at 551–552, per Lindley LJ; *Leyland Shipping Co Ltd v Norwich Union Fire Insurance Society Ltd* [1918] AC 350 at 361–362, HL, per Lord Haldane, at 363 per Lord Dunedin, and at 369–371 per Lord Shaw of Dunfermline; *William France, Fenwick & Co Ltd v North of England Protecting and Indemnity Association* [1917] 2 KB 522; *Canada Rice Mills Ltd v Union Marine and General Insurance Co Ltd* [1941] AC 55 at 71, [1940] 4 All ER 169 at 178, PC; *Athel Line Ltd v Liverpool and London War Risks Insurance Association Ltd* [1946] KB 117 at 122, [1945] 2 All ER 694 at 696–697, CA, per Lord Greene MR; *Ocean SS Co v Liverpool and London War Risks Insurance Association Ltd* [1946] KB 561 at 575, [1946] 2 All ER 355 at 364, CA (in which the text to this note, in an earlier edition of this work, was cited with approval by Scott LJ); *Boiler Inspection and Insurance Co of Canada v Sherwin-Williams Co of Canada Ltd* [1951] AC 319 at 333–334, PC; *J J Lloyd Instruments Ltd v Northern Star Insurance Co Ltd, The Miss Jay Jay* [1987] 1 Lloyd's Rep 32, CA (in which Slade J also approved the text to this note).

6 *Ionides v Universal Marine Insurance Co* (1863) 14 CBNS 259 at 285; *Leyland Shipping Co Ltd v Norwich Union Fire Insurance Society Ltd* [1918] AC 350 at 365, HL. No attempt seems to be made in the decided cases to define either the meaning of the 'substantive cause' (as distinct from the adjective 'proximate') or the standard by which the relative 'dominance' or 'effectiveness' of competing causes is to be measured. No doubt this is because 'the courts cannot act as metaphysical analysts': see *Harrisons Ltd v Shipping Controller* [1921] 1 KB 122 at 131 per McCardie J. Each tribunal of fact must therefore deal with these two matters in the light of common sense.

7 *Livie v Janson* (1810) 12 East 648.

8 *Andersen v Marten* [1908] AC 334, HL (loss by capture followed by shipwreck); contrast *Lobitos Oil Fields Ltd v Admiralty Comrs* (1918) 34 TLR 466, DC.

9 *Arcangelo v Thompson* (1811) 2 Camp 620; and see *Republic of China, China Merchants Steam Navigation Co Ltd and United States of America v National Union Fire Insurance Co of Pittsburgh, Pennsylvania and American International Underwriters Ltd* [1957] 1 Lloyd's Rep 428 at 443; affd on another point sub nom *The Hai Hsuan* [1958] 1 Lloyd's Rep 351 (US 4th Cir).

10 *Montoya v London Assurance Co* (1851) 6 Exch 451; *The Caroline* (1921) 37 TLR 617; *Lind v Mitchell* (1928) 98 LJKB 120, CA.

B. ACTS, DEFAULTS OR ELECTION OF THE ASSURED OR HIS AGENTS: FRUSTRATION

177. Wilful misconduct or negligence. The insurer is not liable for any loss attributable to wilful misconduct on the part of the assured, but unless the policy otherwise provides, he is liable for any loss proximately caused[1] by a peril insured against, and is liable even though the loss would not have happened but for the misconduct or negligence of the master or crew[2]. The same result follows when the negligence of any other person (including the assured himself)[3] contributes to the loss[4].

1 For the meaning of 'proximate cause' see para 175 ante.

2 Marine Insurance Act 1906 s 55(2)(a). It appears to follow from the language of that provision that wilful misconduct by the assured will prevent him from recovering, in all cases in which misconduct has contributed to the loss, even though it is not so closely connected with the loss as to be its proximate cause: see *Britain SS Co v R* [1921] 1 AC 99 at 132, HL, per Lord Sumner.

3 *Trinder, Anderson & Co v Thames and Mersey Marine Insurance Co* [1898] 2 QB 114, CA.

4 *Thompson v Hopper* (1858) E B & E 1038, Ex Ch; *Davidson v Burnand* (1868) LR 4 CP 117; *Trinder, Anderson & Co v Thames and Mersey Marine Insurance Co* [1898] 2 QB 114, CA; *A-G v Adelaide SS Co*

Ltd [1923] AC 292, HL; *Board of Trade v Hain SS Co Ltd* [1929] AC 534, HL. The Marine Insurance Act 1906 s 78(4), which provides that it is the duty of the assured and his agents, in all cases, to take such measures as may be reasonable for the purpose of averting or minimising a loss, only imposes a duty to sue and labour, and does not affect the assured's right to recover for a loss to which the negligence of himself or his agents has contributed: *British and Foreign Marine Insurance Co Ltd v Gaunt* [1921] 2 AC 41 at 65, HL; *Lind v Mitchell* (1928) 98 LJKB 120, CA. It does not necessarily follow that in the absence of instructions from the owners, the master of a vessel must be taken to be included within the words 'the assured and his agents' in the Marine Insurance Act 1906 s 78(4), so that a failure by the master to take such measures as are reasonable will militate against the owners' claim against the insurers; the words 'his agents' should be read as inapplicable to the master or crew unless expressly instructed by the assured as to what to do or not to do in respect of suing and labouring; a possible exception not covered is the case of a master/owner: *The Gold Sky* [1972] 2 Lloyd's Rep 187 at 221 per Mocatta J. As to suing and labouring see further paras 259–262 post.

178. Wilful misconduct: unseaworthiness. With regard to the wilful misconduct of the assured, it should be remembered that, in addition to the general provision exempting the insurer from liability for loss attributable to that misconduct[1], there is a special provision to the effect that where, with the assured's privity, a vessel insured under a time policy[2] is sent to sea in an unseaworthy[3] condition, the insurer is not liable for any loss attributable to unseaworthiness[4]. It should also be borne in mind that the defence that the loss falls within either of these provisions is available against an innocent assignee of the policy[5].

1 See para 177 ante.
2 For the meaning of 'time policy' see para 41 ante.
3 For the meaning of 'seaworthiness' see para 67 ante.
4 Marine Insurance Act 1906 s 39(5); and see paras 74, 172 ante, and the cases there cited. If the policy was a voyage policy (see para 41 ante), the assured would be precluded from recovering in all cases where the ship was unseaworthy at the commencement of the voyage. At one time it was held that in all questions arising between the subjects of different states, each is a party to the public acts of his own government, and that therefore an assured could not recover in respect of a capture, arrest or embargo by his own government: *Conway v Gray, Conway v Forbes, Maury v Sheddon* (1809) 10 East 536 at 545. The contrary has now been decided: see *Aubert v Gray* (1862) 3 B & S 169, Ex Ch. See also *Janson v Driefontein Consolidated Mines Ltd* [1902] AC 484, HL. As to British capture see para 78 ante.
5 See para 214 note 9 post.

179. Other persons' misconduct. With regard to the misconduct of persons other than the assured, the insurer is liable for a loss which would not have occurred but for the misconduct (wilful or otherwise)[1] of the master or crew (or any other person), provided the loss was proximately caused[2] by a peril insured against[3]. Where, however, the assured seeks to recover for a loss alleged to be by perils of the seas[4], and it appears that the loss was the result of wilful misconduct (as opposed to negligence), and that the misconduct is perpetrated, whether by the master or crew or any other person, with the object of bringing about the loss, the misconduct must be regarded as the proximate cause of the loss even though the means employed, for example stranding or sinking, are in themselves (that is, when they operate fortuitously) perils of the seas. In these cases the loss is not proximately caused by perils of the seas, and the insurer is only liable for the loss if the wilful act or omission in question is expressly insured against, for example, under the head of barratry, piracy etc[5].

1 *Lind v Mitchell* (1928) 98 LJKB 120, CA. An owner or master who proceeds with his contract voyage in time of war is not guilty of wilful misconduct simply because there is a risk of capture: see *Papadimitriou v Henderson* [1939] 3 All ER 908.

2 For the meaning of 'proximate cause' see para 175 ante.

3 See para 177 ante.

4 For the meaning of 'perils of the seas' see para 151 ante.

5 See *P Samuel & Co Ltd v Dumas* [1924] AC 431, HL, overruling *Small v United Kingdom Marine Mutual Insurance Association* [1897] 2 QB 311, CA. As to a mortgagee's right to recover for a loss by barratry see para 162 note 1 ante. Logically the same result appears to follow when the act or omission, although intentional, is not blameworthy. See Lord Sumner's dissenting opinion in *P Samuel & Co Ltd v Dumas* supra at 473. It may be, however, that in these cases, if the act is done for the purpose of avoiding some disaster it should not be regarded as wilful: see the cases cited in para 180 note 3 post, and para 153 notes 1–4 ante; and *British and Foreign Marine Insurance Co Ltd v Samuel Sanday & Co* [1916] 1 AC 650, HL, cited in para 156 note 6 ante. It is not clear whether the principle laid down in *P Samuel & Co Ltd v Dumas* supra would be applied in cases in which the loss was alleged to be by a peril other than a peril of the seas, eg fire.

180. Sale or hypothecation for repairs. It follows from the principle that the insurer is not liable for a loss which is not proximately caused[1] by a peril insured against, that he is not liable for a loss proximately caused by the act or election of the assured or his agents. Thus, a loss on sale of goods to defray expenses of repair in a port of distress is not a loss by perils of the seas[2], nor is a loss by hypothecation of cargo for the purposes of the ship, because in these cases the loss is proximately occasioned not by the perils insured against, but by the shipowner being in want of funds[3].

1 For the meaning of 'proximate cause' see para 175 ante.

2 *Powell v Gudgeon* (1816) 5 M & S 431; *Sarquy v Hobson* (1827) 4 Bing 131, Ex Ch. For the meaning of 'perils of the seas' see para 151 ante.

3 *Greer v Poole* (1880) 5 QBD 272.

181. Interdiction of trade or blockade. For similar reasons, neither compliance with an interdiction of commerce with the port of destination[1] nor abandonment of the adventure in consequence of the blockade of that port[2], or of an embargo imposed there[3], or of the imminent danger of capture or seizure[4], constitutes a risk for which insurers of an English policy on ship or goods are liable. Although these causes prevent the completion of the insured voyage, the loss of voyage and the expenses thereby occasioned are not considered to be caused by an 'arrest, restraint, and detainment', because they do not act directly and immediately, but only circuitously, on the subject matter insured[5]. On this point English law differs from that which prevails on the continent of Europe.

On the other hand, where an insured voyage is interrupted directly and immediately by the act or intervention of a government, so that if the insured goods are thereby prevented from being forwarded to their ultimate destination, and the detention appears likely to last for an indefinite time, the assured will be entitled to recover for a constructive total loss of the property. This is because a voyage policy on goods is regarded as an insurance not merely of the goods themselves but also of the 'contemplated adventure', that is the safe arrival of the goods at the destination named in the policy[6].

1 *Hadkinson v Robinson* (1803) 3 Bos & P 388.

2 *Lubbock v Rowcroft* (1803) 5 Esp 50.

3 *Forster v Christie* (1809) 11 East 205; *Blackenhagen v London Assurance Co* (1808) 1 Camp 454.

4 *Nickels & Co v London and Provincial Marine and General Insurance Co* (1900) 6 Com Cas 15; cf *Parkin v Tunno* (1809) 11 East 22; *Kacianoff v China Traders Insurance Co Ltd* [1914] 3 KB 1121, CA; *Becker,*

Gray & Co v London Assurance Corpn [1918] AC 101, HL. On the general principle see also *Halhead v Young* (1856) 6 E & B 312.

5 This legal principle may of course, like all rules of construction, be avoided by express stipulation in the policy. An insurance on a ship is a contract of indemnity against the loss of or damage to the ship herself, and does not indemnify against expenses proximately occasioned by reason of damage done to cargo: see the elaborate judgments in *Field SS Co v Burr* [1899] 1 QB 579, CA; applied in *Polurrian SS Co Ltd v Young* (1913) 19 Com Cas 143 at 159; affd without dealing with this point [1915] 1 KB 922, CA.

6 *Rodoconachi v Elliott* (1874) LR 9 CP 518, Ex Ch; *Miller v Law Accident Insurance Co* [1903] 1 KB 712, CA; see also *The Knight of St Michael* [1898] P 30. This rule has not been altered by the Marine Insurance Act 1906: see *British and Foreign Marine Insurance Co Ltd v Samuel Sanday & Co* [1916] 1 AC 650, HL. See, however, the frustration clause discussed in para 182 post.

182. The frustration clause. A clause, known as the frustration clause, is usually inserted in policies, providing that the policy excludes any claim based upon loss of or frustration of any insured voyage or adventure[1]. The clause protects only against claims based on loss of the insured voyage relating to the goods and does not protect against claims for loss of the goods themselves[2].

1 See eg the Institute War and Strikes Clauses (Freight—Time) cl 4.5; Institute War and Strikes Clauses (Freight—Time) cl 4.5. As to those Clauses see para 149 note 1 ante. See further *Rickards v Forestal Land, Timber and Railways Co Ltd* [1942] AC 50, [1941] 3 All ER 62, HL; *Atlantic Maritime Co Inc v Gibbon* [1954] 1 QB 88, [1953] 2 All ER 1086, CA.

2 *Rickards v Forestal Land, Timber and Railways Co Ltd* [1942] AC 50, [1941] 3 All ER 62, HL. The Law Reform (Frustrated Contracts) Act 1943 does not apply to contracts of insurance except as provided by s 1(5): see s 2(5)(b); and CONTRACT vol 9 paras 469–470.

183. Loss of freight by act or election of assured. Where the loss of freight[1] is due to the ship being abandoned by the assured to the insurer of the ship after a constructive total loss, this is deemed to be a loss occasioned by the act and election of the assured and not by a peril of the seas[2] and the loss is, therefore, not recoverable in a freight policy in the absence of a special provision[3].

Again, where there is a charterparty by which the ship is chartered on monthly hire, and there is a loss of freight owing to the exercise by the charterer of special rights under the charterparty, the loss is considered as caused by the charterer's act and not proximately by a peril of the seas, and the underwriter is not liable for it[4]. Similarly, if the charterparty is for a lump freight, payable on delivery of the cargo, in cash, the insurer will not be liable to the shipowner for loss of freight if that was really occasioned not by the perils insured against, but by reason of the master having signed bills of lading which did not reserve a general lien on each portion of the cargo for the whole lump freight[5].

This principle does not apply to a case where the charterparty provides that freight, apart from election by the charterer, is automatically to cease to be earned, for in that case the loss is considered to be proximately caused[6] by the perils insured against[7].

1 For the meaning of 'freight' see para 115 ante.

2 For the meaning of 'perils of the seas' see para 151 ante.

3 *M'Carthy v Abel* (1804) 5 East 388; *Scottish Marine Insurance Co of Glasgow v Turner* (1853) 1 Macq 334, HL; and cf *Mordy v Jones* (1825) 4 B & C 394; *Philpott v Swann* (1861) 11 CBNS 270. It is now commonly provided in freight policies that the amount insured is to be paid in full in the event of the total loss, whether actual or constructive, of the vessel: see Institute Time Clauses (Freight) cl 15.1, and Institute Voyage Clauses (Freight) cl 13.1 (and see para 149 note 1 ante). The freight policy and the hull policy are separate contracts, and the mere fact that there is a constructive total loss of the

ship does not of itself entitle the assured to recover under this clause, as there may be circumstances in which, although the assured receives no freight, the freight has not been lost, as, for instance, where it is received by the hull insurer to whom the vessel has been abandoned: *Scottish Marine Insurance Co of Glasgow v Turner* supra; and see *Carras v London and Scottish Assurance Corpn Ltd* [1936] I KB 291 at 303, CA, per Lord Wright MR. The giving of notice of abandonment of the vessel is not essential to recovery under this clause provided that the vessel is in fact a constructive total loss: *Robertson v Petros M Nomikos Ltd* [1939] AC 371, [1939] 2 All ER 723, HL.

4 *Inman SS Co v Bischoff* (1882) 7 App Cas 670, HL; *Manchester Liners v British and Foreign Marine Insurance Co Ltd* (1901) 7 Com Cas 26; cf *Mercantile SS Co Ltd v Tyser* (1881) 7 QBD 73.

5 *Williams & Co v Canton Insurance Office Ltd* [1901] AC 462, HL.

6 For the meaning of 'proximate cause' see para 175 ante.

7 *The Bedouin* [1894] P 1, CA, following and approving *The Alps* [1893] P 109. See also *Re Jamieson and Newcastle Steamship Freight Insurance Association* [1895] 2 QB 90, CA; *Jackson v Union Marine Insurance Co* (1874) LR 10 CP 125, Ex Ch. The second point in *Mercantile SS Co Ltd v Tyser* (1881) 7 QBD 73, seems overruled by *The Bedouin* supra.

(8) WHO CAN AVAIL HIMSELF OF THE INSURANCE

(i) Description of the Assured in the Policy

184. Description of the assured or his agent. A marine policy must specify the name of the assured or some person who effects the insurance on his behalf[1].

The policy may be effected in the name either of the assured, or of the broker, or of an agent of the assured whether or not he employs a broker. The broker or agent need not, however, be described in the policy as broker or agent, and the action on the policy may be brought either in the name of the assured or in that of the broker or agent[2].

1 Marine Insurance Act 1906 s 23(1).

2 *Wolff v Horncastle* (1798) 1 Bos & P 316; *Bell v Gibson* (1798) 1 Bos & P 345; *De Vignier v Swanson* (1798) 1 Bos & P 346n; *Provincial Insurance Co of Canada v Leduc* (1874) LR 6 PC 224.

(ii) Insurable Interest

A. MEANING; NATURE OF INTEREST

185. Meaning of 'insurable interest'. The Marine Insurance Act 1906 does not profess to give an exhaustive definition of insurable interest[1], but, subject to the provisions of the Act, every person has an insurable interest who is interested in a marine adventure[2]. In particular, a person is interested in a marine adventure where he stands in any legal or equitable relation to the adventure or to any insurable property at risk in it, in consequence of which he may benefit by the safety or due arrival of insurable property, or may be prejudiced by its loss, or damage to it, or by the detention of it, or may incur liability in respect of it[3].

A person may be said to be interested in an event when, if the event happens, he will gain an advantage, and, if it is frustrated, he will suffer a loss[4], and it may be stated as a general principle that to constitute an insurable interest it must be an interest such that the peril would by its proximate effect cause damage to the assured[5], that is to say cause him to lose a benefit or incur a liability[6].

1 In a celebrated judgment Lawrence J explained in the following words the nature of an insurable interest: 'A man is interested in a thing to whom advantage may arise or prejudice happen from the

circumstances which may attend it;. . . and whom it importeth that its condition as to safety or other quality should continue. Interest does not necessarily imply a right to the whole or part of the thing, nor necessarily and exclusively that which may be the subject of privation, but the having some relation to, or concerning the subject of the insurance; which relation or concern, by the happening of the perils insured against, may be so effected as to produce a damage, detriment or prejudice to the person insuring. And where a man is so circumstanced with respect to matters exposed to certain risks and dangers as to have a moral certainty of advantage or benefit but for those risks and dangers, he may be said to be interested in the safety of the thing. To be interested in the preservation of a thing is to be so circumstanced with respect to it as to have benefit from its existence, prejudice from its destruction': *Lucena v Craufurd* (1806) 2 Bos & PNR 269 at 302, HL. See also *Barclay v Cousins* (1802) 2 East 544; *Macaura v Northern Assurance Co Ltd* [1925] AC 619 at 627, HL.
2 Marine Insurance Act 1906 s 5(1). For the meaning of 'marine adventure' see para 36 ante.
3 Ibid s 5(2). The assured has an insurable interest in the charges of any insurance which he may effect: s 13.
4 *Wilson v Jones* (1867) LR 2 Exch 139 at 150–151, Ex Ch, per Blackburn J.
5 As to the use of the term 'the assured' see para 35 note 1 ante.
6 *Seagrave v Union Marine Insurance Co* (1866) LR 1 CP 305 at 320 per Willes J.

186. Interest in possession not necessary. A vested interest in possession is not necessary to constitute an insurable interest. An expectancy coupled with the present existing title to that out of which the expectancy arises is an insurable interest. Thus, freight payable either on the arrival of the goods or under a charterparty is insurable by the shipowner[1], but the expectation of benefit to arise from some subject in which the party insuring is not actually interested, but only expects to be interested, is not an insurable interest. Thus, the expectation of commission, or of profit to arise out of the sale of goods not contracted for at the time of their loss, is not an insurable interest under a policy[2].

1 See paras 193–195 post.
2 *Stockdale v Dunlop* (1840) 6 M & W 224; cf *Lucena v Craufurd* (1806) 2 Bos & PNR 269 at 323, HL; and see the judgment of Walton J in *Moran, Galloway & Co v Uzielli* [1905] 2 KB 555, where the plaintiffs had lent a sum of money to the owners of a foreign ship for disbursements. By instituting an action in rem they could, except for the loss of the ship, have acquired a lien on her, and therefore it was held that they had an insurable interest in the ship to the extent of the unsatisfied balance of their advances. This decision was explained in *Macaura v Northern Assurance Co Ltd* [1925] AC 619 at 626, HL, where it was held that an unsecured creditor of a limited company who also owned all the shares in the company, either personally or through nominees, had no insurable interest in the company's assets.

187. Partial interest. A partial interest of any nature is insurable[1]. Thus, an undivided or hotchpot interest in the subject matter insured, such as the interest of a part owner, whether a joint tenant or a tenant in common, is insurable[2]. Similarly, a portion only of the freight at risk on a particular voyage may be insured[3].

1 Marine Insurance Act 1906 s 8.
2 *Robertson v Hamilton* (1811) 14 East 522; *Inglis v Stock* (1885) 10 App Cas 263 at 274, HL.
3 *Griffiths v Bramley-Moore* (1878) 4 QBD 70, CA.

188. Defeasible interest. A defeasible interest is insurable[1]. For instance, the right of captors to their prize under the Naval Prize Act 1864 is an insurable interest before condemnation, even though defeasible by the release of the Crown or by a sentence of restoration[2].

Where a person who has contracted for the purchase of goods has insured them, he has an insurable interest notwithstanding that he might, at his election, have rejected the goods or treated them as at the seller's risk, by reason of the seller's delay in making delivery or otherwise[3].

1 Marine Insurance Act 1906 s 7(1).
2 *Stirling v Vaughan* (1809) 11 East 619, distinguishing *Lucena v Craufurd* (1806) 2 Bos & PNR 269 at 323, HL; and see the cases cited in para 200 note 1 post; and PRIZE.
3 Marine Insurance Act 1906 s 7(2); *Sparkes v Marshall* (1836) 2 Bing NC 761; *Anderson v Morice* (1876) 1 App Cas 713 at 727, 735, HL; approved in *Inglis v Stock* (1885) 10 App Cas 263 at 274, HL; explained in *Colonial Insurance Co of New Zealand v Adelaide Marine Insurance Co* (1886) 12 App Cas 128 at 136, PC.

189. Contingent interest. A contingent interest is insurable[1]. For instance, a carrier or other bailee who may become liable to the bailor for the loss of goods by the perils insured against has an insurable interest[2]. Similarly, any liability to a third party which may be incurred by the owner of property by reason of maritime perils[3] constitutes an insurable interest[4].

A shipowner who has entered into recognisances in the Admiralty Court to pay the salvors of ship and cargo has a lien on, and therefore an insurable interest in, the cargo for the contribution due to him from its owner[5].

The purchaser of a vessel abroad which is to remain at seller's risk until delivery in England probably has an insurable contingent interest in her arrival, though he has no insurable interest in the vessel herself until delivery[6].

1 Marine Insurance Act 1906 s 7(1).
2 See CARRIERS vol 5(1) (Reissue) para 446.
3 For the meaning of 'maritime perils' see para 36 ante.
4 Marine Insurance Act 1906 ss 3(2)(c), 5; *Crowley v Cohen* (1832) 3 B & Ad 478; *Joyce v Kennard* (1871) LR 7 QB 78; *Stephens v Australasian Insurance Co* (1872) LR 8 CP 18; *Hill v Scott* [1895] 2 QB 713, CA. See also *Mackenzie v Whitworth* (1875) 1 ExD 36, CA (reinsurance by underwriter); *Lucena v Craufurd* (1806) 2 Bos & PNR 269 at 323, HL, per Lord Eldon; *Moran, Galloway & Co v Uzielli* [1905] 2 KB 555 (as to which see para 186 note 2 ante). In the event of the assured becoming bankrupt or (in the case of a company) being wound up, or having a receiver or manager appointed, or possession taken of any of the property by or on behalf of debenture holders, the benefit of the insurance will be transferred to the third party by virtue of the Third Parties (Rights against Insurers) Act 1930 (as amended): see paras 678–684 post.
5 *Briggs v Merchant Traders' Ship Loan and Insurance Association* (1849) 13 QB 167.
6 *Piper v Royal Exchange Assurance* (1932) 44 Ll L Rep 103 at 116.

190. Insurable interest in profits. In order to have an insurable interest in profits, the assured must either be the owner of goods or have entered into a legally binding contract for the purchase of them[1]. Moreover, under a valued policy[2] on profits, he must prove that except for the loss he would have derived some profit[3], and, in the case of an unvalued policy[4], he cannot recover more than the amount of profit he would have made if the loss had not occurred[5].

1 *Stockdale v Dunlop* (1840) 6 M & W 224; *Sparkes v Marshall* (1836) 2 Bing NC 761. As to what profits will be covered under the phrase 'beginning of the adventure etc' see para 117 note 1 ante.
2 For the meaning of 'valued policy' see para 41 ante.
3 *Hodgson v Clover* (1805) 6 East 316.
4 For the meaning of 'unvalued policy' see para 41 ante.
5 *Eyre v Glover* (1812) 16 East 218.

191. When interest must exist. In order to recover under a policy the assured must be interested in the subject matter insured at the time of the loss, though he need not be interested when the insurance is effected, provided that where the subject matter is insured 'lost or not lost', the assured may recover although he may not have acquired his interest until after the loss[1].

It is not, therefore, a good plea to an action brought to recover a partial loss of goods on a policy 'lost or not lost' that the plaintiff first acquired an interest in the property after the loss occurred, for, where the assured purchased or acquired the goods as sound or undamaged goods, a loss has been sustained by him, and as the policy contains the clause 'lost or not lost' it covers that past loss[2]. The same considerations would evidently apply to an action brought to recover a total loss of goods on a policy 'lost or not lost' if the contract under which the assured purchased the goods makes him liable for the price, even where the goods were totally lost at the time he made the contract. The assured cannot, however, recover for a loss of which, when the contract was effected, he was aware and the insurer was not[3]; moreover, if he has no insurable interest at the time of the loss, he cannot acquire such an interest by any act or election after he is aware of the loss[4].

1 Marine Insurance Act 1906 s 6(1); *Rhind v Wilkinson* (1810) 2 Taunt 237; *Cousins v Nantes* (1811) 3 Taunt 513, Ex Ch. In *Marine Insurance Co Ltd v Grimmer* [1944] 2 All ER 197 at 201, CA, Scott LJ stated that the principle that the 'policy operates retrospectively to the loading of the insured goods' was inherent in every voyage policy in the old Lloyd's form, and that the words 'lost or not lost' are thus mere repetition of what the policy meant without them. See also Arnould on Marine Insurance (16th Edn) s 32.

2 *Sutherland v Pratt* (1843) 11 M & W 296 at 311–312; and see *Marine Insurance Co Ltd v Grimmer* [1944] 2 All ER 197 at 201, CA, per Scott LJ (reinsurance).

3 Marine Insurance Act 1906 s 6(1), Sch 1 r 1.

4 Ibid s 6(2); *Anderson v Morice* (1876) 1 App Cas 713 at 749, HL; *Stockdale v Dunlop* (1840) 6 M & W 224.

B. INTERESTS IN SHIP, FREIGHT AND ADVANCE FREIGHT

192. Interest in ship. A shipowner has an insurable interest in his ship, even when he has let her out to a charterer who has contracted to pay him her full value in case of her being lost, and he can in case of such loss recover the full value from the insurer, who is subrogated to the rights of the assured against the charterer[1].

1 *Hobbs v Hannam* (1811) 3 Camp 93; Marine Insurance Act 1906 s 14(3). As to subrogation see paras 314–318 post.

193. Interest in freight. A shipowner has an insurable interest in freight[1]. It is important, however, to observe that, as in the case of other interests, the shipowner's right to recover the insured freight depends on whether he had an insurable interest at the time of the loss[2], or in other words whether the risk had at that time attached. This question is discussed elsewhere[3].

The shipowner may insure as 'anticipated freight' not merely the amount for which the vessel is already chartered at the time of the policy but the full amount which he reasonably expects the vessel to earn during the period of the insurance[4].

The charterer, as well as the shipowner, may have an insurable interest in freight because a loss of the goods causes a loss of the bill of lading freight, but it has been suggested that as a general rule his insurable interest is not limited to the excess of the bill of lading freight over the charterparty freight. This, however, has not yet been decided. It may to some extent depend on the terms of the charterparty[5]. Such excess of the bill of lading freight may be insured as 'profit on charter'[6].

1 See the Marine Insurance Act 1906 ss 3, 5(1); and para 115 ante; see also the judgments of Brett J and Bramwell B in *Rankin v Potter* (1873) LR 6 HL 83 at 98, 133. For the meaning of 'freight' when used to describe the subject matter of the policy see para 115 ante.
2 See the Marine Insurance Act 1906 s 6; and para 191 ante.
3 As to commencement and duration of the risk see para 121 et seq ante.
4 *Papadimitriou v Henderson* [1939] 3 All ER 908; see also *Robertson v Petros M Nomikos Ltd* [1939] AC 371 at 384, [1939] 2 All ER 723 at 729, HL, per Lord Wright.
5 See the Marine Insurance Act 1906 s 16(2); and para 256 post. In *United States Shipping Co v Empress Assurance Corpn* [1907] 1 KB 259 (a case of sub-charter), the decision of Channell J was against the limitation. His judgment was affirmed, but without deciding any question of law, by the Court of Appeal: see [1908] 1 KB 115; and see Arnould on Marine Insurance (16th Edn) s 344.
6 *Asfar & Co v Blundell* [1895] 2 QB 196; affd [1896] 1 QB 123, CA.

194. Commencement of insurable interest in chartered freight. Where the interest insured is chartered freight, that is to say freight to be paid to the shipowner by the terms of a charterparty[1] for the use of his ship or part of it on a voyage described in it, there is an insurable interest in the freight at the time of the inception of the voyage so described. Thus, where by the terms of the charterparty the ship is to proceed from A to B and at B to take a cargo for delivery at C, there is an insurable interest in the freight of this cargo as soon as the ship sails from A to proceed to B[2].

In short, there is an insurable interest in chartered freight as soon as the ship commences the voyage which she must make in order to acquire an inchoate right to the chartered freight[3].

1 As to charterparties see generally SHIPPING.
2 *Thompson v Taylor* (1795) 6 Term Rep 478; *Horncastle v Suart* (1806) 7 East 400; *Atty v Lindo* (1805) 1 Bos & PNR 236; *Mackenzie v Shedden* (1810) 2 Camp 431; *Davidson v Willasey* (1813) 1 M & S 313; *Foley v United Fire, etc, Insurance Co* (1870) LR 5 CP 155, Ex Ch; *Rankin v Potter* (1873) LR 6 HL 83; and see Arnould on Marine Insurance (16th Edn) s 356.
3 See the cases cited in note 2 supra, and *Barber v Fleming* (1869) LR 5 QB 59 at 71, 73.

195. Interest in advance freight. In the case of advance freight[1], the person advancing the freight has an insurable interest in so far, but only in so far, as the freight is not repayable in case of loss[2]. Whether the money advanced is or is not repayable in case of loss depends upon the terms of the charterparty or other agreement under which the money is advanced[3]. A passenger who has paid his passage money has an insurable interest in it, but it must be designated in the policy as passage money[4].

1 As to what constitutes advance freight see SHIPPING vol 43 para 739.
2 Marine Insurance Act 1906 s 12. See also para 116 text to note 2 ante.
3 The principal cases bearing upon this question are *De Silvale v Kendall* (1815) 4 M & S 37; *Manfield v Maitland* (1821) 4 B & Ald 582 at 585; *Wilson v Martin* (1856) 11 Exch 684; *Winter v Haldimand* (1831) 2 B & Ad 649; *Hicks v Shield* (1857) 7 E & B 633; *The Karnak* (1869) LR 2 PC 505 at 514; *Allison v Bristol Marine Insurance Co* (1876) 1 App Cas 209 at 222, 229, 234, HL; *Watson & Co v Shankland* (1873) LR 2 Sc & Div 304, HL. See further SHIPPING.
4 See the Marine Insurance Act 1906 ss 3, 5(1); *Denoon v Home and Colonial Assurance Co* (1872) LR 7 CP 341; and para 116 ante.

C. PARTICULAR INTERESTS

196. Seller and buyer. As long as the seller of a ship or of goods retains any interest in the property, he can insure it to the extent of his interest. Thus, where the owner of a ship has sold her under a contract which binds him to pay the purchaser a certain sum if a loss should happen within a specified time, he has an insurable interest to the extent of that sum[1]. When, however, the property which is the subject matter of the contract of sale has completely passed from the seller to the buyer, or when it has under the contract of sale become completely at the buyer's risk, the seller ceases to have any insurable interest, and the buyer acquires one[2]. Thus, a contract for the sale of goods to be supplied on board a particular vessel may be so framed that the property in them and the risk of their loss do not pass to the buyer until a complete cargo has been loaded, in which case the buyer has no insurable interest until the complete cargo has been loaded[3]; or the contract may be so framed that the property in and the risk as to any part of the goods pass to the buyer on shipment, in which case the buyer acquires an insurable interest on any part of the goods then shipped[4].

An unpaid seller of goods has a right of stoppage in transit if the buyer has become insolvent and the goods are stopped before they get into the buyer's possession and before the buyer has transferred them to a sub-buyer by indorsement of the bill of lading; but it follows from the above principles that the seller has no insurable interest unless and until he has effectually stopped the goods in transit[5].

1 *Reed v Cole* (1764) 3 Burr 1512; cf *North of England Oil-Cake Co v Archangel Insurance Co* (1875) LR 10 QB 249, DC.
2 *Joyce v Swann* (1864) 17 CBNS 84; *Ionides v Harford* (1859) 29 LJEx 36 (termination of risk by transfer of property); *Seagrave v Union Marine Insurance Co* (1866) LR 1 CP 305; *Sparkes v Marshall* (1836) 2 Bing NC 761; *Inglis v Stock* (1885) 10 App Cas 263, HL. As to the question whether and when under a contract for the sale of goods the property passes to the buyer or is at his risk see *Fragano v Long* (1825) 4 B & C 219; *Calcutta and Burmah Steam Navigation Co v De Mattos* (1863) 32 LJQB 322 at 328; and SALE OF GOODS.
3 *Anderson v Morice* (1875) LR 10 CP 609, Ex Ch; affd (1876) 1 App Cas 713, HL (the House being equally divided); *Piper v Royal Exchange Assurance* (1932) 44 Ll L Rep 103 (vessel to be at seller's risk until delivery in England).
4 *Colonial Insurance Co of New Zealand v Adelaide Marine Insurance Co* (1886) 12 App Cas 128, PC. See also *J Aron & Co Inc v Miall* (1928) 139 LT 562, CA (c i f contract); *Yangtsze Insurance Association Ltd v Lukmanjee* [1918] AC 585, PC (sale 'ex-ship'); and see *Plata American Trading Inc and Nordhandel Gesellschaft Ruecker-Giehr & Co v Lancashire, Hamburg-Amerika Linie and Charles Martin & Co* [1957] 2 Lloyd's Rep 347 (cargo of tallow insured 'warehouse to warehouse' by buyers; cargo delivered short for transit; missing quantity never in transit and never became property of buyers, who, therefore, had no insurable interest: underwriters not liable for missing quantity).
5 *Clay v Harrison* (1829) 10 B & C 99; Arnould on Marine Insurance (16th Edn) s 369. Such an interest cannot be acquired after a loss by any election made with knowledge of it: see para 191 ante. See further SALE OF GOODS; SHIPPING.

197. Mortgagor and mortgagee. Where the subject matter insured is mortgaged, the mortgagor has an insurable interest in its full value and the mortgagee has an insurable interest in respect of any sum due or to become due under the mortgage[1]. A mortgagee, consignee or other person having an interest in the subject matter insured may insure on behalf and for the benefit of other persons interested as well as for his own benefit[2].

The mortgagor has an insurable interest in the full value of the property insured, even though it is mortgaged to its full value, because in case of loss he would not only be deprived of the property but would also remain liable for the mortgage debt[3]. Where the mortgagor has contracted to insure the mortgaged property on account of the mortgagees, he holds the proceeds of the insurance policy in trust for them[4].

The amount recoverable by a mortgagee under a policy effected by him will depend upon the intention he had in effecting it. If he intended the policy to cover the whole interest, that is his own interest and that of the mortgagor[5], he can recover the whole amount insured under trust, as to the surplus, to hold it for the mortgagor; but if he intended it only to cover his own interest as mortgagee, he can recover only to the extent of the mortgage debt[6].

1 Marine Insurance Act 1906 s 14(1).
2 Ibid s 14(2). As to the interest of persons entitled to indemnity see para 203 post. As to the onus of proving, and evidence required to prove, that the mortgagee's or other person's interest is covered see para 213 note 5 post, and the cases there cited.
3 *Alston v Campbell* (1779) 4 Bro Parl Cas 476; *Ward v Beck* (1863) 13 CBNS 668 (an instrument which is in form an absolute transfer may be shown to be a mortgage). See *Bank of Nova Scotia v Hellenic Mutual War Risks Association (Bermuda) Ltd, The Good Luck* [1992] 1 AC 233, [1991] 3 All ER 1, HL (insurers who failed to inform mortgagees that insurance had been avoided by the assured's causing vessels to enter prohibited zone, were in breach of an undertaking so to inform and liable upon that breach).
4 *Ladbroke v Lee* (1850) 4 De G & Sm 106 at 119; *Swan and Cleland's Graving Dock and Slipway Co v Maritime Insurance Co and Croshaw* [1907] 1 KB 116 at 121; cf *Levy & Co v Merchants Marine Insurance Co* (1885) 52 LT 263.
5 See the Marine Insurance Act 1906 s 14(2); and the text and notes supra.
6 *Irving v Richardson* (1831) 2 B & Ad 193; *Carruthers v Sheddon* (1815) 6 Taunt 14 at 17. Cf, however, *Denoon v Home and Colonial Assurance Co* (1872) LR 7 CP 341; some parts of the judgment in the last case are difficult to reconcile with the other cases. The amount recoverable by the mortgagee in respect of his own interest is the amount due from the mortgagor at the date of the loss; sums which became due at a later date cannot be taken into account: *Chartered Trust and Executor Co v London Scottish Assurance Corpn Ltd* (1923) 39 TLR 608.

198. Trustee. A trustee who has the legal interest in the subject matter insured may insure in respect of that interest to the full value of the subject matter, and may recover the whole amount, alleging the interest to be in himself, and he will then hold it in trust for his beneficiary[1].

1 *Lucena v Craufurd* (1806) 2 Bos & PNR 269 at 323–324, HL, per Lord Eldon; *Ebsworth v Alliance Marine Insurance Co* (1873) LR 8 CP 596 at 638 per Brett J.

199. Consignee. A consignee who at the time of the loss has a lien or charge on the property in respect of advances, and an indorsee of a bill of lading to whom a general balance is due, can effect an insurance on their own account, and can recover, averring their interest to be in themselves to the amount of their lien, charge or balance. They can also protect in the same insurance their own interest and the interest of other parties in the property, averring the interest to be in themselves and in those other parties[1]. A consignee who at the time of the loss has a mere naked right to take possession can recover on a policy effected by him, but only if he alleges the interest in the consignors, and also proves that the consignors have authorised, or subsequently adopted, the policy[2].

A consignee has an insurable interest in his commission if at the time of the loss he has a binding contract for the consignment to him of a cargo[3].

1 See the Marine Insurance Act 1906 s 14(2); and para 197 ante. This provision embodies the law as laid down in *Wolff v Horncastle* (1798) 1 Bos & P 316; *Hill v Secretan* (1798) 1 Bos & P 315; *Robertson v Hamilton* (1811) 14 East 522; *Carruthers v Sheddon* (1815) 6 Taunt 14. See also *Sutherland v Pratt* (1843) 12 M & W 16; *Hibbert v Carter* (1787) 1 Term Rep 745; *Castellain v Preston* (1883) 11 QBD 380 at 398, CA, per Bowen LJ.

2 *Lucena v Craufurd* (1806) 2 Bos & PNR 269, HL, per Lord Eldon; *Seagrave v Union Marine Insurance Co* (1866) LR 1 CP 305 at 319–320 per Willes J. Whether a consignee for sale to whom at the time of the loss the legal property in the goods has not passed, but who was beneficially interested in the whole of them, can recover the full value on an averment of interest in himself alone, or whether he must also aver the interest of the other parties, is a question on which the Court of Common Pleas was equally divided in *Ebsworth v Alliance Marine Insurance Co* (1873) LR 8 CP 596, but this question can only be material when there are peculiar circumstances, such as existed in that case, which make the plaintiff unwilling to aver the interest in himself and the consignor.

3 See *Ward & Co Ltd v Weir & Co* (1899) 4 Com Cas 216 at 223 per Mathew J (shipowner has insurable interest in commission payable by him in case of loss). Cf *Knox v Wood* (1808) 1 Camp 543; *Buchanan & Co v Faber* (1899) 4 Com Cas 223 at 226 per Bigham J.

200. Captors. Captors, prize agents and others have often effected policies on captured property. The captors generally are in possession of the property captured, and are liable to pay costs and charges if they have taken possession improperly, and are also liable to return property if it should turn out to be neutral. They therefore have an interest in the property[1].

1 *Boehm v Bell* (1799) 8 Term Rep 154 at 161; *Lucena v Craufurd* (1806) 2 Bos & PNR 269 at 323–324, HL, per Lord Eldon. Captors and prize agents will, according to the present practice, aver the interest to be in themselves and the Crown or some one or more of them, and that the insurance was effected on behalf of the person so interested, and in so far as the captors have not an insurable interest in the property the Crown can obtain the benefit of the policy. On this subject see *Le Cras v Hughes* (1782) 3 Doug KB 81, as explained in *Lucena v Crauford* supra; *Craufurd v Hunter* (1798) 8 Term Rep 13; *Stirling v Vaughan* (1809) 11 East 619; *Routh v Thompson* (1811) 13 East 274 at 284–285; *Devaux v Steele* (1840) 6 Bing NC 358 at 370. Nothing in the Naval Prize Act 1864 gives officers and crew of any of Her Majesty's ships of war or military aircraft any right in prize ships, aircraft or goods; they take only such interest, if any, as may be granted to them by the Crown: s 55(1) (amended by the Prize Act 1939 s 1(2), Schedule Pt I); see PRIZE.

201. Master and crew; bottomry and respondentia. The master or any member of the crew of a ship has an insurable interest in respect of his wages[1].

The lender of money on bottomry or respondentia[2] has an insurable interest in respect of the loan[3], because the borrower is discharged from liability if the ship or goods which are hypothecated are totally lost[4]. In order that an assured may be entitled to recover under a policy on bottomry or respondentia, the bond or instrument of hypothecation must be legally valid, creating a maritime risk; and therefore nothing can be recovered under the policy if the money is made repayable in any event and whether the property hypothecated is or is not lost on the insured voyage[5]. The borrower on bottomry or respondentia, like a mortgagor, continues to have an insurable interest in the hypothecated ship or goods, inasmuch as the debt is discharged only if the property is totally lost[6].

1 Marine Insurance Act 1906 s 11.
2 As to the nature and incidents of bottomry or respondentia see SHIPPING vol 43 para 198.
3 Marine Insurance Act 1906 s 10.
4 As to the necessity of specifically describing such interests in the policy see para 118 ante.
5 *Simonds v Hodgson* (1832) 3 B & Ad 50; *Stainbank v Fenning* (1851) 11 CB 51; *Stainbank v Shepard* (1853) 13 CB 418.
6 It seems, however, on principle, open to much doubt whether the assured in case of a total loss of the property hypothecated can recover anything more than the excess of the insurable value of the property over the amount of the debt.

202. Shareholders in companies. There may be an insurable interest in an adventure without an insurable interest in any of the property at risk. Thus, a shareholder in a company is not a part owner of the property of the company, inasmuch as the property belongs to the company, which is a legal entity independent of its shareholders[1]. But a shareholder in a company established for the laying of a submarine cable has an insurable interest in the adventure which he can protect by a properly worded policy[2].

1 *R v Arnaud* (1846) 9 QB 806; *Salomon v Salomon & Co Ltd, Salomon & Co Ltd v Salomon* [1897] AC 22, HL; see COMPANIES vol 7(1) (Reissue) para 1.
2 See the Marine Insurance Act 1906 s 5(2); *Wilson v Jones* (1867) LR 2 Exch 139, Ex Ch; cf *Paterson v Harris* (1862) 2 B & S 814, where a shareholder in a telegraph company was held, by reason of the peculiar wording of the policy, to have insured the submarine cable itself. It is to be observed, however, that in that case the assured's interest was not disputed. See these cases discussed in *Macaura v Northern Assurance Co Ltd* [1925] AC 619, HL, cited in para 186 note 2 ante.

203. Person entitled to be indemnified by another. The owner of insurable property has an insurable interest in respect of its full value, notwithstanding that some third person may have agreed, or is liable, to indemnify him in case of loss[1]. Thus, where the owner of a vessel lets her out under a charterparty to a charterer who contracts, in case of loss, to pay him her full value, he has a right to insure to the full amount, for he is not bound to trust exclusively to the charterer's credit[2]. So also the owner of goods[3] may insure them for their full value, and in case of loss recover that amount from the insurer, although the carrier may also be liable to indemnify him against their loss[4]. In these cases the insurer will be subrogated to the rights of the assured against the party liable to indemnify him[5].

1 Marine Insurance Act 1906 s 14(3). As to indemnity generally see GUARANTEE vol 20 (Reissue) para 345 et seq.
2 *Hobbs v Hannam* (1811) 3 Camp 93.
3 For the meaning of 'goods' see para 114 ante.
4 The carrier also has an insurable interest: see the Marine Insurance Act 1906 s 3(2)(c); and para 36 ante. See also para 189 ante, and the cases there cited.
5 As to subrogation see generally EQUITY vol 16 (Reissue) paras 888–893; GUARANTEE vol 20 (Reissue) para 228; and see paras 314–318 post.

D. REINSURANCE

204. Reinsurance. Inasmuch as he is liable on a policy of insurance, the insurer may insure against the risk which he has taken upon himself. This second contract of insurance is called a contract of reinsurance. The insurer under a contract of marine insurance[1] has an insurable interest in his risk, and may reinsure in respect of it[2]. A policy of reinsurance, although effected after the original policy, normally attaches from the same time as the original policy[3].

The subject matter of the reinsurance on ship, freight, goods or whatever it may be is the same as that of the original insurance, although the interest of the reassured is different from that of the original assured, and arises from the fact that the reassured is the underwriter under the original policy[4].

As it is generally unnecessary to state in the policy the nature of the assured's interest, the fact that the contract is one of reinsurance need not necessarily appear on the face of the policy[5]. In English policies it is, however, almost the universal practice to insert a clause, often called the 'reinsurance clause', to the following effect: 'Being a reinsurance, subject to the same clauses and conditions as the original policy, and to pay as may be paid thereon'[6]. The 'original policy' in this clause means the policy issued in pursuance of the slip[7] which was in force at the time the reinsurance was effected, and if this policy is varied or superseded by a fresh policy in different terms without the reinsurer's consent, a loss will not be recoverable from the reinsurer[8].

1 For the meaning of 'contract of marine insurance' see para 35 ante.
2 Marine Insurance Act 1906 s 9(1). He may then be described as the 'reassured' and his insurer as the 'reinsurer'.
3 See *Marine Insurance Co Ltd v Grimmer* [1944] 2 All ER 197 at 199, CA.
4 *Nelson v Empress Assurance Corpn Ltd* [1905] 2 KB 281 at 285, CA, per Mathew LJ; and see *British Dominions General Insurance Co Ltd v Duder* [1915] 2 KB 394, CA. The actual decision in the case of *Nelson v Empress Assurance Corpn Ltd* supra at 285 per Mathew LJ, that reinsurance was not a contract of indemnity within the then Rules of the Supreme Court governing third party procedure, is probably not applicable to the present rules (ie RSC Ord 16: see particularly Ord 16 r 1(2)(b), (c); and PRACTICE AND PROCEDURE), under which claims for contribution or indemnity are not the only proceedings in which a third party notice may be issued.
5 *Mackenzie v Whitworth* (1875) 1 ExD 36, CA.
6 Clauses which are inapplicable are not incorporated: see *Home Insurance Co of New York v Victoria-Montreal Fire Insurance Co* [1907] AC 59, PC (fire). As to the construction of particular clauses see *Insurance Co of North America v North China Insurance Co* (1898) 4 Com Cas 67, CA; *Re Law Car and General Insurance Corpn Ltd* (1911) 55 Sol Jo 407; affd [1911] WN 101, CA (reinsurance by one company with another of all its risks). See also *Forsikringsaktieselskapet Vesta v Butcher* [1989] AC 852, [1989] 1 All ER 402, HL, a non-marine case where contracts of insurance and reinsurance containing identical warranties were governed by different proper laws.
7 As to the insurance slip see para 89 ante.
8 See *Lower Rhine and Würtemberg Insurance Association v Sedgwick* [1899] 1 QB 179, CA; distinguished in *Reliance Marine Insurance Co v Duder* [1913] 1 KB 265, CA; *Scottish National Insurance Co Ltd v Poole* (1912) 107 LT 687; and in *Emanuel & Co v Andrew Weir & Co* (1914) 30 TLR 518; and applied in *Norwich Union Fire Insurance Society Ltd v Colonial Mutual Fire Insurance Co Ltd* [1922] 2 KB 461 (a case of variation of original policy). Where the reassured has underwritten more than one original policy at the time the reinsurance was effected, and he afterwards becomes liable for a loss on one of these policies, he can recover this loss from the reinsurer unless (1) the terms of the reinsurance policy show that it was not intended to cover the original policy on which the loss has occurred, or (2) the reassured intended, when he effected the reinsurance, not to cover his liability on that original policy and communicated that intention to the reinsurer: *Reliance Marine Insurance Co v Duder* supra; *Janson v Poole* (1915) 84 LJKB 1543.

205. Original assured has no interest in reinsurance. Unless the policy of reinsurance otherwise provides, the original assured has no right or interest in respect of the reinsurance[1]. The original contract of insurance and the contract of reinsurance are two distinct contracts, and the reassured remains solely liable on the original insurance and alone has any claim against the reinsurer. It therefore follows that the reinsurer is bound to pay the whole amount of the loss to the trustee of an insolvent reassured, and not merely the dividend which the original assured receives from the reassured's estate. This is true even when the reinsurance policy contains the reinsurance clause, for this clause does not prevent the reassured from recovering from the reinsurer as soon as the loss happens and before he himself has paid the original assured[2]. On the other hand, the reinsurer is entitled to the benefit of any compromise made with the original assured, even though he has refused to agree to it[3].

1 Marine Insurance Act 1906 s 9(2); see also in *Re Law Guarantee Trust and Accident Society, Godson's Claim* [1915] 1 Ch 340.
2 *Re Eddystone Marine Insurance Co, ex p Western Insurance Co* [1892] 2 Ch 423. See also *Law Guarantee Trust and Accident Society Ltd v Munich Reinsurance Co* [1912] 1 Ch 138; *Re Law Guarantee Trust and Accident Society Ltd, Liverpool Mortgage Insurance Co Ltd's Case* [1914] 2 Ch 617, CA.

3 *British Dominions General Insurance Co Ltd v Duder* [1915] 2 KB 394, CA.

206. Proof of loss. Subject to any provision to the contrary in the reinsurance policy, the reassured, in order to recover from the reinsurer, must prove the loss in the same manner as the original assured must have proved it against the reassured, and the reinsurer can raise all defences which were open to the reassured against the original assured[1]. This is true whether the reassured who is seeking to recover from his reinsurer has or has not already paid the original assured, and whether or not the reinsurance policy contains the words 'to pay as may be paid thereon'[2].

1 The reinsurers are entitled to an affidavit of ship's papers, even though they are not in the plaintiff's custody: *China Traders' Insurance Co v Royal Exchange Assurance Corpn* [1898] 2 QB 187, CA.

2 *Chippendale v Holt* (1895) 1 Com Cas 197; *Marten v SS Owners' Underwriting Association* (1902) 7 Com Cas 195; *Western Assurance Co of Toronto v Poole* [1903] 1 KB 376 at 386. Bigham J's dictum in *Western Assurance Co of Toronto v Poole* supra that the words 'to pay as may be paid thereon' preclude the reinsurer from disputing the amount paid by way of compromise provided there was a loss on the original policy, is doubted by Scrutton LJ in *Gurney v Grimmer* (1932) 38 Com Cas 7 at 12, CA; and see 1 Parsons' Marine Insurance (1st Edn) 299n; *Firemen's Fund Insurance Co v Western Australian Insurance Co Ltd* (1927) 33 Com Cas 36. See also *Australian Widows' Fund Life Assurance Society Ltd v National Mutual Life Association of Australasia Ltd* [1914] AC 634, PC (life assurance). Modern reinsurance policies against total loss only frequently contain a clause binding the reinsurer to pay in the event of a 'compromised' or 'arranged' loss. For the meaning of these terms see *Gurney v Grimmer* supra; *Oscar L Aronsen Inc v Compton, The Megara* [1973] 2 Lloyd's Rep 361 (Dist Ct, Southern Dist NY); affd [1974] 1 Lloyd's Rep 590 (US Ct of Apps (2nd Circ)). The reassured cannot recover under such a clause without proving that he was in fact liable to pay an actual or constructive total loss, or showing that the original assured had put forward a claim in good faith for a total loss, with or without an alternative claim for a partial loss: *Street v Royal Exchange Assurance* (1913) 18 Com Cas 284; affd (1914) 19 Com Cas 339, CA; *Bergens Dampskibs Assurance Forening v Sun Insurance Office Ltd* (1930) 143 LT 435. See also *Excess Insurance Co Ltd v Mathews* (1925) 31 Com Cas 43 at 52 (fire insurance).

Where a reinsurance policy under which claims were payable in a foreign currency provided that the reinsurer should 'follow the settlements' of the original insurer, Roche J held that in an action on the reinsurance policy the sum payable must be converted into sterling at the rate of exchange prevailing at the date at which the original insurers settled with their assured, on the ground that the cause of action against the reinsurer first arose on the date of the settlement: *Versicherungs und Transport A G Daugava v Henderson* (1934) 39 Com Cas 154; affd on other grounds 39 Com Cas 312, CA. See also *Chartered Trust and Executor Co v London and Scottish Insurance Corpn* (1923) 16 Ll L Rep 233. As to exchange rates for the payment of debts see generally MONEY.

207. Suing and labouring clause. The effect of the suing and labouring clause in the original policy is dealt with elsewhere[1]. When it is contained in the reinsurance policy it will be disregarded if inconsistent with written clauses in the policy[2], and where there is a chain of insurances, the reassured reinsuring his liability and the first reinsurer in turn reinsuring with a second reinsurer, it seems that, even if all the policies contain a suing and labouring clause, this will not entitle the first reinsurer to recover from the second in respect of payments which he has become liable to make to the reassured by virtue of the suing and labouring clause in the first reinsurance policy[3].

1 See para 259 post.
2 *Western Assurance Co of Toronto v Poole* [1903] 1 KB 376.
3 *Uzielli v Boston Marine Insurance Co* (1884) 15 QBD 11, CA. In *British Dominions General Insurance Co Ltd v Duder* [1915] 2 KB 394, CA, the court criticised the judgment in *Uzielli v Boston Marine Insurance Co* supra, without, however, specifically referring to the decision as to the effect of the suing and labouring clause. See, however, the observations of Bigham J in *Western Assurance Co of*

Toronto v Poole [1903] 1 KB 376 at 387. The suing and labouring clause is inapplicable to the costs incurred by the reassured in resisting a claim on the original policy, and these are not recoverable from the reinsurer in the absence of an express or implied agreement to pay them: *Scottish Metropolitan Assurance Co Ltd v Groom* (1924) 41 TLR 35, CA.

208. Incorporation of clauses from original policy. Clauses which are contained in the original insurance, if they are usual clauses, such as the 'continuation clause'[1] or the 'transit clause'[2], are considered to be incorporated in a reinsurance policy, in the usual form, if they are not inconsistent with its express terms[3].

1 As to continuation clauses see para 121 ante.
2 As to transit clauses see para 125 ante.
3 *Joyce v Realm Marine Insurance Co* (1872) LR 7 QB 580 (outward cargo considered homeward interest); *Franco-Hungarian Insurance Co v Merchants Marine Insurance Co* (1888) cited in 5 Com Cas 412; *Charlesworth v Faber* (1900) 5 Com Cas 408; *Marten v Nippon Sea and Land Insurance Co Ltd* (1898) 3 Com Cas 164 (conveyance and transhipment risks). For a clause inapplicable to reinsurance and therefore rejected see *Home Insurance Co of New York v Victoria-Montreal Fire Insurance Co* [1907] AC 59, PC (fire policy).

209. Notice of abandonment. The reassured need not give notice of abandonment in cases of a total loss[1].

1 Marine Insurance Act 1906 s 62(9); *Uzielli v Boston Marine Insurance Co* (1884) 15 QBD 11, CA. As to notice of abandonment see further paras 293, 304–309 post.

210. When reinsurer's liability arises. The reinsurer's liability to the reassured arises, and the reassured's cause of action accrues, when the reassured's liability to the original assured is ascertained, irrespective of whether the reassured has discharged that liability[1].

1 *Versicherungs und Transport A G Dauguva v Henderson* (1934) 39 Com Cas 154; affd 39 Com Cas 312, CA.

E. WAGERING POLICIES

211. Wagering and ppi policies. At common law, insurances by way of gaming or wagering were valid, but a policy which did not contain a clause expressly dispensing with proof of interest, or which did not otherwise show that the contract was not intended to be one of indemnity, was deemed to be a contract of indemnity on which the assured could not recover without proof of interest[1]. A policy expressly made 'interest or no interest' or 'without further proof of interest than the policy itself' or 'without benefit of salvage to the insurer' is usually called a 'ppi policy' (that is to say, policy proof of interest) or 'an honour or wager policy'[2].

Under the Gaming Act 1845, all contracts or agreements by way of gaming or wagering are null and void[3]. This applies to all insurances which are really wagers, whether or not they are in the form of ppi policies; but a ppi policy is not necessarily inconsistent with the assured having an insurable interest[4]; indeed, it might happen that such a policy is effected by a person who has an insurable interest but who wishes to avoid the difficulty of proving it. In that case the policy would not be a wagering contract within this particular provision of the Gaming Act 1845[5], although it will be void by virtue of the Marine Insurance Act 1906[6].

The Marine Insurance Act 1906 provides that every contract of marine insurance[7] by way of gaming or wagering is void[8]. A contract of marine insurance is deemed to be a gaming or wagering contract where the assured has no insurable interest (as defined by that Act[9]), and the contract is entered into with no expectation of acquiring such an interest[10]. Similarly, the contract is deemed to be a gaming or wagering contract where the policy is made 'interest or no interest' or 'without further proof of interest than the policy itself', or 'without benefit of salvage to the insurer', or subject to any other like term'[11], but where there is no possibility of salvage a policy may be effected without benefit of salvage to the insurer[12].

1 *Lucena v Craufurd* (1806) 2 Bos & PNR 269 at 321, HL, per Lord Eldon; *Cousins v Nantes* (1811) 3 Taunt 513, Ex Ch.
2 By the Marine Insurance Act 1745 (which, however, did not extend to Ireland (*Keith v Protection Marine Insurance Co* (1882) 10 LR Ir 51), nor to foreign ships (*Thellusson v Fletcher* (1780) 1 Doug KB 315)), such ppi policies, as well as all other policies by way of gaming and wagering, if they were insurances on British ships, or cargoes, or interests relating to the same, were, with certain unimportant exceptions, prohibited. As to this enactment (now repealed: see note 6 infra) see *Allkins v Jupe* (1877) 2 CPD 375; *Berridge v Man On Insurance Co* (1887) 18 QBD 346, CA, following *Smith v Reynolds* (1856) 1 H & N 221, and *De Mattos v North* (1868) LR 3 Exch 185.
3 Gaming Act 1845 s 18 (amended by the Statute Law Revision Act 1891). As to wagering contracts in general see BETTING, GAMING AND LOTTERIES vol 4(1) (Reissue) para 10 et seq.
4 For the meaning of 'insurable interest' see para 185 ante.
5 *Wilson v Jones* (1867) LR 2 Exch 139 at 146.
6 See text and notes 7–12 infra. The Marine Insurance Act 1906 s 92, Sch 2 (repealed), repealed the Marine Insurance Act 1745 (see note 2 supra), but not the Gaming Act 1845 s 18 (see text and note 3 supra).
7 For the meaning of 'contract of marine insurance' see para 35 ante.
8 Marine Insurance Act 1906 s 4(1).
9 See ibid s 5; and para 185 ante.
10 Ibid s 4(2)(a).
11 Ibid s 4(2)(b). A policy containing a ppi clause is void even though the assured may in fact have had an insurable interest: *T Cheshire & Co v Vaughan Bros & Co* [1920] 3 KB 240 at 254, CA. The fact that the clause is printed on a detachable slip and is expressed to be 'no part of the policy and not to be attached thereto, but is to be considered as binding in honour on the underwriters, the assured, however, having permission to remove it from the policy should they so desire,' will not prevent the policy from being void. A claim on a ppi policy cannot be enforced in a winding up, but the premiums are returnable: *Re London County Commercial Reinsurance Office Ltd* [1922] 2 Ch 67 at 85. There can be no right of subrogation under a ppi policy: *John Edwards & Co v Motor Union Insurance Co Ltd* [1922] 2 KB 249. The court will not treat such a policy as valid even if the insurer desires it to do so: *Gedge v Royal Exchange Assurance Corpn* [1900] 2 QB 214 at 220, distinguishing *Buchanan & Co v Faber* (1899) 4 Com Cas 223 at 227, where Bigham J, by consent, treated the policy as if it had contained no ppi clause. It is doubtful whether the court would adopt this course now: see *T Cheshire & Co v Vaughan Bros & Co* supra at 252 per Scrutton LJ.
12 Marine Insurance Act 1906 s 4(2) proviso.

212. Criminal offence to gamble on losses. If any person effects a contract of marine insurance[1] without having any bona fide interest, direct or indirect, either in the safe arrival of the ship in relation to which the contract is made or in the safety or preservation of the subject matter insured, or a bona fide expectation of acquiring such an interest; or if any person in the employment of the owner[2] of a ship, not being a part owner of the ship, effects a contract of marine insurance in relation to the ship, and the contract is made 'interest or no interest', or 'without further proof of interest than the policy itself', or 'without benefit of salvage to the insurer', or subject to any other like term, the contract is deemed to be a contract by way of gambling on loss by maritime perils[3]; and the person who effects it, and any broker or other person through whom, and any insurer with whom, it is effected (if these persons act knowingly) are guilty of an offence[4], and liable on summary conviction to imprisonment for a term not exceeding six months, or a fine not exceeding level 3 on the standard scale, and, in either case, forfeiture to the Crown of the proceeds of the contract[5].

1 For the meaning of 'contract of marine insurance' in the Marine Insurance Act 1906 see para 35 ante.
2 For this purpose, 'owner' includes charterer: Marine Insurance (Gambling Policies) Act 1909 s 1(8).
3 Ibid s 1(1). For the meaning of 'maritime perils' see para 36 ante.
4 Ibid s 1(1), (2). Proceedings may not be instituted without the consent of the Attorney General: s 1(3); nor, in the case of a person not in the shipowner's employment, until he has had an opportunity of showing that the contract was not a gambling contract, and information given by him for this purpose is not admissible in evidence against him in any prosecution under the Act: s 1(4). But as against such a person a contract in the terms specified above ('interest or no interest' etc) is deemed to be a gambling contract unless the contrary is proved: s 1(5). An offence is deemed to have been committed either where it was actually committed or in any place where the offender is: s 1(6). An appeal lies to the Crown Court: s 1(7) (amended by the Courts Act 1971 s 56(2), Sch 9 Pt I). As to the procedure on appeals see MAGISTRATES.
5 Marine Insurance (Gambling Policies) Act 1909 s 1(1) (amended by virtue of the Criminal Justice Act 1948 s 1(2), and the Criminal Justice Act 1982 ss 38, 46).
  The 'standard scale' means the standard scale of maximum fines for summary offences as set out in the Criminal Justice Act 1982 s 37 (2): Interpretation Act 1978 s 5, Sch 1 (amended by the Criminal Justice Act 1988 s 170 (1), Sch 15 para 58 (a)). See CRIMINAL LAW vol 11(2) (Reissue) para 808; and MAGISTRATES. At the date at which this volume states the law, the standard scale is as follows: level 1, £200; level 2, £500; level 3, £1,000; level 4, £2,500; level 5, £5,000: Criminal Justice Act 1982 s 37 (2) (substituted by the Criminal Justice Act 1991 s 17 (1)). As to the determination of the amount of the fine actually imposed, as distinct from the level on the standard scale which it may not exceed, see the Criminal Justice Act 1991 s 18 (substituted by the Criminal Justice Act 1993 s 65); and MAGISTRATES.

(iii) Ratification and Assignment

213. Ratification by the assured. Where a contract of marine insurance[1] is in good faith effected by one person on behalf of another, the person on whose behalf it is effected may ratify the contract even after he is aware of a loss[2]. Thus, where a merchant after the loss hears that a policy has been effected on his behalf although without his authority, he can at any time ratify the insurance and sue upon the policy[3]. The general rule is, however, subject to the condition that a person cannot avail himself of the policy unless it was intended in good faith to protect his interest, or at any rate to protect the interest generally of the parties who should appear ultimately to be concerned[4]. If, therefore, a policy was effected by A to protect the interest only of B, no third person would be allowed to avail himself of that policy[5].

1 For the meaning of 'contract of marine insurance' see para 35 ante.
2 Marine Insurance Act 1906 s 86.
3 *Williams v North China Insurance Co* (1876) 1 CPD 757 at 767, 770, CA; *Hagedorn v Oliverson* (1814) 2 M & S 485; *Lucena v Craufurd* (1808) 1 Taunt 325, HL; *Routh v Thompson* (1811) 13 East 274; *Barlow v Leckie* (1819) 4 Moore CP 8. Ratification after loss is peculiar to marine insurance: *Grover and Grover Ltd v Mathews* [1910] 2 KB 401 at 404.
4 2 Duer on Marine Insurance 30, 135; and see the cases cited in note 3 supra.
5 *Boston Fruit Co v British and Foreign Insurance Co Ltd* [1906] AC 336 at 339, HL; *Yangtsze Insurance Association Ltd v Lukmanjee* [1918] AC 585, PC. When a policy is effected in the name of brokers 'and/or as agents', a party interested in the subject matter insured cannot ratify the policy unless the principal upon whose instructions the insurance was effected intended to insure the interest of the party in question: *Graham Joint Stock Shipping Co Ltd v Merchants Marine Insurance Co Ltd (No 2)* [1923] 1 KB 592, CA; affd [1924] AC 294, HL. In deciding the question for whom the insurance was

effected, the intention of the principal who gave the instructions on which the insurance was effected is alone material; the intention of the brokers who effected the policy on those instructions is not material: *Boston Fruit Co v British and Foreign Marine Insurance Co Ltd* supra; *Graham Joint Stock Shipping Co Ltd v Merchants Marine Insurance Co Ltd (No 2)* supra; *P Samuel & Co Ltd v Dumas* [1923] 1 KB 592, CA; affd on another point [1924] AC 431, HL. The onus of proving that the insurance was intended to cover his interest lies on the person making this allegation: *Yangtsze Insurance Association Ltd v Lukmanjee* supra. On the subject of ratification see also *Routh v Thompson* (1811) 13 East 274, explaining at 281 *Routh v Thompson* (1809) 11 East 428; *Grant v Hill* (1812) 4 Taunt 380; *Irving v Richardson* (1831) 2 B & Ad 193; *Watson v Swann* (1862) 11 CBNS 756; *Scott v Globe Marine Insurance Co Ltd* (1896) 1 Com Cas 370; *Small v United Kingdom Marine Mutual Insurance Association* [1897] 2 QB 42; on appeal [1897] 2 QB 311, CA; *Byas v Miller* (1897) 3 Com Cas 39; and see AGENCY vol 1(2) (Reissue) paras 72–85.

214. Assignment of policy. A marine policy is not an incident to the property insured; accordingly, a transfer of the property insured does not by itself effect the transfer of the policy to the assignee[1]. Moreover, where the assured has parted with or lost his interest in the subject matter insured before the loss occurs and has not, before or at the time of so doing, expressly or impliedly agreed to assign the policy, any subsequent assignment of the policy is inoperative[2]. However, once the loss has occurred and the right to indemnity has therefore crystallised, the assured can assign his interest under the policy irrespective of whether or not he has parted with or lost his interest in the subject matter insured between loss and assignment[3].

If, therefore, the assured parts with the whole of his interest in the insured property[4] before the loss without assigning the policy of insurance and without an agreement to assign or hold it for the benefit of the transferee, the policy becomes unavailable to anyone[5]. On the other hand, if at the time of the transfer of the insured property the transferor assigned the policy, or agreed to assign it or to hold it for the transferee's benefit, the transferee was always entitled to maintain an action on the policy in the assured's name[6], and this could be done even if the assured had become a bankrupt after the assignment[7].

Where a marine policy has been assigned so as to pass the beneficial interest[8] in it, the assignee is entitled to sue on it in his own name, and the defendant is entitled to make any defence arising out of the contract which he would have been entitled to make if the action had been brought in the name of the person by or on behalf of whom the policy was effected[9].

A marine policy is assignable either before or after loss unless it contains terms expressly prohibiting assignment[10], and it may be assigned by indorsement or in any other customary manner[11].

The assignee of a policy can only avail himself of the insurance to the extent to which the assured has agreed to assign his rights to him[12].

1 Where the assured assigns or otherwise parts with his interest in the subject matter insured, he does not thereby transfer to the assignee his rights under the contract of insurance unless there is an express or implied agreement with the assignee to that effect; this provision does not, however, affect a transmission of interest by operation of law: Marine Insurance Act 1906 s 15.

2 Ibid s 51.

3 Ibid ss 50(1), 51 proviso.

4 It is otherwise if he parts only with some portion of his interest, eg where he only pledges or mortgages the insured property: *Hibbert v Carter* (1787) 1 Term Rep 745; *Alston v Campbell* (1779) 4 Bro Parl Cas 476.

5 *North of England Oil-Cake Co v Archangel Insurance Co* (1875) LR 10 QB 249.

6 *Powles v Innes* (1843) 11 M & W 10; *Sparkes v Marshall* (1836) 2 Bing NC 761 at 774; *Gibson v Winter* (1833) 5 B & Ad 96 (assignee suing in assignor's name is subject to all rights of defence that can be raised against the assignor).

7 *Castelli v Boddington* (1852) 1 E & B 66; affd sub nom *Boddington v Castelli* (1853) 1 E & B 879, Ex Ch.
8 Ie the whole beneficial interest: see *Williams v Atlantic Assurance Co Ltd* [1933] 1 KB 81, CA.
9 Marine Insurance Act 1906 s 50(2). A defence of non-disclosure by the assignor is a defence arising out of the contract within the meaning of s 50(2): *William Pickersgill & Sons Ltd v London and Provincial Marine and General Insurance Co Ltd* [1912] 3 KB 614. It is a good defence to a claim by an innocent third party (eg a mortgagee) whose title to the policy is by assignment from the assured, that the loss was attributable to the assured's wilful misconduct: *Graham Joint Stock Shipping Co Ltd v Merchants Marine Insurance Co Ltd (No 2)* [1924] AC 294, HL. It is otherwise if the third party's interest was separately insured: *P Samuel & Co Ltd v Dumas* [1924] AC 431 at 445, HL. If, however, the loss is proximately caused by and not merely attributable to the assured's wilful misconduct, the insurer will not be liable to the third party even if separately insured: *P Samuel & Co Ltd v Dumas* supra; and see para 178 ante. The claim under the policy being unliquidated, a set-off of premiums due from the assignor is not an available defence under this provision: *Pellas v Neptune Marine Insurance Co* (1879) 5 CPD 34, CA; *Castelli v Boddington* (1852) 1 E & B 66; affd sub nom *Boddington v Castelli* (1853) 1 E & B 879, Ex Ch; and see *Baker v Adam* (1910) 15 Com Cas 227.
10 Marine Insurance Act 1906 s 50(1); *Lloyd v Fleming* (1872) LR 7 QB 299; *Swan and Cleland's Graving Dock and Slipway Co v Maritime Insurance Co and Croshaw* [1907] 1 KB 116 at 123 (assignment of claim without assigning policy). For a clause prohibiting assignment see *Pyman v Marten* (1906) 24 TLR 10, CA. Unless a policy imposes such a condition, the insurer's consent is never necessary to the validity of the assignment. For a case in which the policy imposed such a condition see *Laurie v West Hartlepool SS Thirds Indemnity Association and David* (1899) 4 Com Cas 322.
11 Marine Insurance Act 1906 s 50(3). It seems that mere delivery is not a 'customary manner' (*Baker v Adam* (1910) 15 Com Cas 227 at 230 per Hamilton J); but indorsement in blank first by the brokers who effected the policy and then by the assured assigns all claims on the policy to a holder of the policy (*J Aron & Co (Inc) v Miall* (1928) 34 Com Cas 18, CA). The Institute Time Clauses (Hulls) cl 5, and the Institute Voyage Clauses (Hulls) cl 3 (and see the Institute War and Strikes Clauses (Hulls—Time) cl 2; and the Institute War and Strikes Clauses (Hulls—Voyage) cl 2) contain a special provision concerning assignment of policies; see para 149 note 1 ante.
12 *Ionides v Harford* (1859) 29 LJEx 36; *Strass v Spillers and Bakers Ltd* [1911] 2 KB 759; cf *Ralli v Universal Marine Insurance Co* (1862) 4 De G F & J 1; *Landauer v Asser* [1905] 2 KB 184, DC. As to assignment see generally CHOSES IN ACTION vol 6 (Reissue) paras 9–79.

(9) AVOIDANCE OF POLICY

(i) Fraud, Concealment or Non-disclosure

215. Effect of fraud on policy. A contract of marine insurance, like any other contract, is voidable on the ground of fraud, and any fraudulent misrepresentation (whether or not it is material within the meaning of the Marine Insurance Act 1906[1]) made in order to induce the insurer to enter into the contract entitles him to avoid the policy, unless it is proved either that he knew the true state of facts at the time of contracting or that he did not rely on the misrepresentation[2]. Independently, however, of fraud, a misrepresentation as to material facts, or a non-disclosure of material facts, may entitle the insurer to avoid the contract[3].

1 See the Marine Insurance Act 1906 s 20(2); and para 233 post. See also paras 221, 232 post.
2 *Smith v Chadwick* (1882) 20 ChD 27 at 44, CA, per Jessel MR; affd (1884) 9 App Cas 187 at 190, HL, per Lord Selborne LC; *Arnison v Smith* (1889) 41 ChD 348 at 368–369, CA, per Lord Halsbury LC. As to the effect of fraud in vitiating a contract see MISREPRESENTATION.
3 See the Marine Insurance Act 1906 ss 18, 20; and paras 217–233 post.

216. Contract of insurance is a contract uberrimae fidei. It is a fundamental principle that a contract of marine insurance[1] is a contract uberrimae fidei, that is a contract based on the utmost good faith, and, if the utmost good faith is not observed by either party, the contract may be avoided by the other party[2]. Thus, if, when the contract is concluded[3], the assured knew of the loss of the insured ship, the insurer may avoid the contract, and similarly, if at that time the insurer knew that the insured ship had safely arrived at her destination, the assured may avoid the contract and recover the premium[4].

1 For the meaning of 'contract of marine insurance' see para 35 ante.
2 Marine Insurance Act 1906 s 17. In every contract of marine insurance there is an implied condition that there is no misrepresentation or concealment: *Blackburn, Low & Co v Vigors* (1886) 17 QBD 553 at 561, CA, per Lord Esher MR (approving 1 Phillips' Law of Insurance (5th Edn) s 537); affd (1887) 12 App Cas 531, HL; see at 539 per Lord Watson; and cf GUARANTEE vol 20 (Reissue) para 110. The insurer must adduce evidence to prove that the fact was not disclosed: *Visscherij Maatschappij Nieuw Onderneming v Scottish Metropolitan Assurance Co Ltd* (1922) 27 Com Cas 198, CA; *Williams v Atlantic Assurance Co Ltd* [1933] 1 KB 81, CA. Where there is prima facie evidence of non-disclosure, the onus shifts to the assured to prove that he disclosed the fact: *Glicksman v Lancashire and General Assurance Co Ltd* [1925] 2 KB 593, CA; affd [1927] AC 139, HL (burglary insurance).
3 Ie when the assured's proposal is accepted: see para 217 note 1 post.
4 *Carter v Boehm* (1766) 3 Burr 1905 at 1909 per Lord Mansfield CJ.

217. Duty of assured to disclose material facts. Before the contract is concluded[1] the assured must disclose to the insurer every material[2] circumstance[3], subject to certain exceptions mentioned below, known to the assured; if the assured fails to make such disclosure, the insurer may avoid the contract[4]. Every circumstance is material which would influence the judgment of a prudent insurer in fixing the premium or determining whether he will take the risk[5]. An assured is deemed to know every circumstance which, in the ordinary course of business, ought to be known by him[6].

In the absence of inquiry the following circumstances[7] need not be disclosed:
(1) any circumstance which diminishes the risk[8];
(2) any circumstance which is known or presumed to be known to the insurer[9];
(3) any circumstance as to which information is waived by the insurer[10]; and
(4) any circumstance which it is superfluous to disclose by reason of any express or implied warranty[11].

Where an insurance is effected for the assured by an agent, the agent must, subject to the exceptions listed above[12], disclose to the insurer:
(a) every material circumstance which is known to himself, and an agent to insure is deemed to know every circumstance which in the ordinary course of business ought to be known by, or to have been communicated to him[13]; and
(b) every material circumstance which the assured is bound to disclose, unless it comes to his knowledge too late to communicate it to the agent[14].

1 A contract of marine insurance is deemed to be concluded when the assured's proposal is accepted by the insurer, whether the policy is then issued or not; and for the purpose of showing when the proposal was accepted, reference may be made to the slip or covering note or other customary memorandum of the contract: Marine Insurance Act 1906 s 21; see para 89 ante. See eg *Niger Co Ltd v Guardian Assurance Co Ltd* (1922) 13 Ll L Rep 75, HL; *Willmott v General Accident Fire and Life Assurance Corpn* (1935) 53 Ll L Rep 156.
2 Whether any particular circumstance which is not disclosed is or is not material is a question of fact: Marine Insurance Act 1906 s 18(4). See eg *Alluvials Mining Machinery Co v Stowe* (1922) 10 Ll L Rep 96; *Mathie v Argonaut Marine Insurance Co Ltd* (1925) 21 Ll L Rep 145, HL (deck cargo); *Piper v Royal Exchange Assurance* (1932) 44 Ll L Rep 103 (over-valued vessel); *Slattery v Mance* [1962] 1 QB 676, [1962] 1 All ER 525 (over-valued vessel); *Pacific Queen Fisheries v L Symes, The Pacific Queen* [1963] 2 Lloyd's Rep 201, US Ct of Apps (9th Circ) (vessel's gasoline carrying capacity); *Berger and Light Diffusers Pty Ltd v Pollock* [1973] 2 Lloyd's Rep 442 (condition of goods on shipment); *James Yachts Ltd v Thames and Mersey Marine Insurance Co Ltd* [1977] 1 Lloyd's Rep 206, BC SC (use of boat yard);

Liberian Insurance Agency Inc v Mosse [1977] 2 Lloyd's Rep 560 (condition of goods on shipment); *Allden v Raven, The Kylie* [1983] 2 Lloyd's Rep 444 (yacht built from kit). Further cases as to materiality, with regard to representations, are cited at para 233 note 2 post.

3   'Circumstance' includes any communication made to or information received by the assured: Marine Insurance Act 1906 s 18(5).

4   Ibid s 18(1). As regards the knowledge that the assured is deemed to have see para 219 post. The existence of an open cover does not relieve the assured from the duty to disclose material facts: *Berger and Light Diffusers Pty Ltd v Pollock* [1973] 2 Lloyd's Rep 442.

5   Marine Insurance Act 1906 s 18(2). See also *Berger and Light Diffusers Pty Ltd v Pollock* [1973] 2 Lloyd's Rep 442 at 463 per Kerr J; *Container Transport International Inc and Reliance Group Inc v Oceanus Mutual Underwriting Association (Bermuda) Ltd* [1984] 1 Lloyd's Rep 476, CA. The word 'influence' in the Act means that the disclosure is one which would have had an impact on the formation of the insurer's opinion and on his decision-making process in relation to the matters covered by the statutory provision: see per Kerr LJ at 492. The yardstick is a prudent insurer and not the particular insurer. There is no requirement that the particular insurer should have been induced to take the risk or charge a lower premium than he would otherwise have done as a result of the non-disclosure. The court cannot choose one prudent insurer rather than another. The very choice of a prudent insurer indicates that the test intended is one which can be sensibly answered in relation to prudent insurers in general: per Parker LJ at 510. See also *Pan Atlantic Insurance Co Ltd v Pine Top Insurance Co Ltd* [1993] 1 Lloyd's Rep 496, CA, where *Container Transport International Inc and Reliance Group Inc v Oceanus Mutual Underwriting Association (Bermuda) Ltd* supra is considered.

6   Marine Insurance Act 1906 s 18(1).

7   The excepted circumstances enumerated in ibid s 18(3) are taken from the judgment of Lord Mansfield in *Carter v Boehm* (1766) 3 Burr 1905 at 1910. As to these circumstances see further paras 225, 231 post.

8   Marine Insurance Act 1906 s 18(3)(a).

9   Ibid s 18(3)(b). The insurer is presumed to know matters of common notoriety or knowledge, and matters which an insurer in the ordinary course of his business as such ought to know: s 18(3)(b). As to circumstances known to the insurer see further para 225 post.

10   Ibid s 18(3)(c). As to waiver see further para 226 post.

11   Ibid s 18(3)(d). As to information covered by warranty see further para 227 post.

12   Ie in heads (1) to (4) in the text: see text and notes 7–11 supra.

13   Marine Insurance Act 1906 s 19(a); see further para 220 post.

14   Ibid s 19(b).

218. Time of the conclusion of the contract is the material time. Neither the assured's failure to disclose a fact which only became known to him after the conclusion of the contract, nor a misrepresentation made by the assured after the conclusion of the contract, entitles the insurer to avoid the contract[1]. If a statement made at the time of the policy is true, the fact that due to a change of plan on the part of the assured the statement subsequently becomes untrue does not entitle the insurer to avoid the policy, unless the change of plan is expressly prohibited by the contract[2].

1   *Cory v Patton* (1872) LR 7 QB 304; *Lishman v Northern Maritime Insurance Co* (1875) LR 10 CP 179, Ex Ch; and see *Ionides v Pacific Insurance Co* (1871) LR 6 QB 674; affd (1872) LR 7 QB 517, Ex Ch. The fact that the contract was concluded by the slip being initialled subject to ratification by the assured, and that the matter concealed came to his knowledge before the issue of the policy, makes no difference: *Cory v Patton* (1874) LR 9 QB 577, following *Hagedorn v Oliverson* (1814) 2 M & S 485. This accords with the Marine Insurance Act 1906 s 86: see para 213 ante. Where, however, a broker is instructed to effect a policy on goods and by mistake effects one on the ship, and the insurer afterwards agrees to a rectification of the policy, the broker is bound to disclose a material fact which has come to his knowledge between the execution of the policy and its rectification, for the insurer is under no obligation to make the alteration, and by doing so he is really making a new and distinct insurance: *Sawtell v Loudon* (1814) 5 Taunt 359. If on the other hand, the policy does not correspond with the slip to which the insurer has assented, so that it is his duty to correct the error, the alteration does not make a new contract, but merely declares the true meaning of that already concluded, and there is no necessity to disclose the information acquired after the making of the contract: 2 Duer on

Marine Insurance 428. It seems that if the contract is varied between the initialling of the slip and the issue of the policy, matters material to the variation, and those only, must be disclosed when the variation is made: see *Lishman v Northern Maritime Insurance Co* (1875) LR 10 CP 179 at 182, Ex Ch, per Blackburn J; and *Niger Co Ltd v Guardian Assurance Co Ltd* (1921) 6 Ll L Rep 239 at 250, CA, per Atkin LJ; on appeal (1922) 13 Ll L Rep 75 at 82, HL, per Lord Sumner. As to the insurance slip see para 89 ante.

2 *Willmott v General Accident Fire and Life Assurance Corpn Ltd* (1935) 53 Ll L Rep 156.

219. Circumstances deemed to be known by assured. The insurer is entitled to assume as the basis of the contract between him and the assured that the assured will communicate to him every material fact of which the assured has, or in the ordinary course of business ought to have, knowledge[1], and that he will take the necessary measures by the employment of competent and honest agents to obtain, through the ordinary channels of intelligence in use in the business world, all due information as to the subject matter of the insurance[2]. This condition is not complied with where, by the fraud or negligence of an agent, the party proposing the insurance is kept in ignorance of a material fact which ought to have been made known to the insurer, and through that ignorance fails to disclose it[3].

The master of a ship and the general agent of a shipowner for the transaction of his shipping business are agents whose knowledge will be imputed to the shipowner[4]; and, similarly, a factor employed to ship a cargo and forward the shipping documents, and the owner's general representative at a foreign port, are agents with whose knowledge the owner of cargo is affected[5]. Further, where the shipping agents of the assured knew that the bills of lading in respect of an insured cargo were claused, that knowledge was imputed to him[6].

1 Marine Insurance Act 1906 s 18(1): see para 217 ante. The material facts are as to the subject matter, the ship and the perils to which the ship is exposed, but the assured's name need not be disclosed unless asked for: *Glasgow Assurance Corpn Ltd v William Symondson & Co* (1911) 104 LT 254 at 257 per Scrutton J.
2 As to the subject matter of the insurance see para 36 ante.
3 *Proudfoot v Montefiore* (1867) LR 2 QB 511 at 521; *Blackburn, Low & Co v Vigors* (1887) 12 App Cas 531 at 540, 542, HL; *London General Insurance Co v General Marine Underwriters' Association* [1921] 1 KB 104.
4 *Gladstone v King* (1813) 1 M & S 35; *Blackburn, Low & Co v Vigors* (1887) 12 App Cas 531 at 537, HL, per Lord Halsbury LC, and at 540 per Lord Watson.
5 *Fitzherbert v Mather* (1785) 1 Term Rep 12; *Proudfoot v Montefiore* (1867) LR 2 QB 511. As to the knowledge of a clerk of the assured being equivalent to that of the assured see *Stewart v Dunlop* (1785) 4 Bro Parl Cas 483, HL. It has already been noted (see para 21 ante) that Lloyd's agents are not the agents of the underwriters at Lloyd's: *Wilson v Salamandra Assurance Co of St Petersburg* (1903) 8 Com Cas 129.
6 *Berger and Light Diffusers Pty Ltd v Pollock* [1973] 2 Lloyd's Rep 442. As to bills of lading and the usual clauses contained in them see SHIPPING vol 43 para 490 et seq.

220. Knowledge of agent effecting insurance. Sometimes an agent employed to effect an insurance, instead of dealing with the insurer, acts through an intermediate agent or agents, and in these cases the non-disclosure of a material fact within the knowledge of any agent through whose agency, whether indirectly or directly, the insurance has been effected, avoids the policy[1].

Where, however, a broker who is employed to obtain an insurance on a particular risk fails to do so, and it is afterwards effected by another broker, the policy is not avoided by the non-disclosure of facts which were unknown to the principal and the second broker but were within the knowledge of the first, for the knowledge of the first broker cannot be imputed to the principal[2].

1 *Blackburn, Low & Co v Haslam* (1888) 21 QBD 144; see also *Lynch v Dunsford* (1811) 14 East 494, Ex
   Ch; Marine Insurance Act 1906 s 19 (see para 217 text and notes 12–14 ante); and see *Thames and
   Mersey Marine Insurance Co Ltd v Gunford Ship Co Ltd, Southern Marine Mutual Insurance Association v
   Gunford Ship Co Ltd* [1911] AC 529, HL.

2 *Blackburn, Low & Co v Vigors* (1887) 12 App Cas 531, HL. In *Gladstone v King* (1813) 1 M & S 35, and
   Stribley v Imperial Marine Insurance Co (1876) 1 QBD 507, it was decided that when an agent whose
   duty it is to keep his principal informed omits without fraud to inform him of an occurrence causing
   an average loss, and thereby prevents the principal from disclosing the occurrence, the insurance is
   not entirely avoided, and the only consequence is that the insurer is not liable for the average loss.
   These decisions, the principle of which it is not easy to understand, were disapproved of by Lord
   Halsbury LC and Lord Watson in *Blackburn, Low & Co v Vigors* supra, and there is little doubt that
   they are overruled by the Marine Insurance Act 1906 s 18(1) (see para 217 ante). In other respects
   s 18(1) summarises the effect of the cases cited in this note, in para 219 notes 3–6 ante, and in note 1
   supra, in a single sentence.

221. What circumstances are material.

The assured is bound to disclose not
only facts which are material to the risks considered in their own nature and which
have a direct bearing on the extent of those risks, but also all circumstances which
would influence the judgment of a prudent insurer in fixing the premium or
determining whether he will take the risk[1]. Thus, the non-disclosure of the fact that
the subject matter is excessively over-valued in the policy may be a ground for
avoiding it[2].

The materiality of any particular circumstance is in no way determined or
affected by events subsequent to the conclusion of the contract, and the insurance
is therefore voidable although the information not disclosed turns out to be
altogether untrue, or the loss to have arisen from a cause wholly different from and
wholly unconnected with that referred to in the information or with any of the
matters comprised in it. The only question is whether the circumstances or
information not disclosed, whether by design or mistake, were such as would have
influenced the judgment of a prudent insurer. Thus if, in proposing an insurance on
goods on board a certain ship, the assured, having received information that the
ship has met with an accident, fails to communicate the information to the insurer,
the insurer will be discharged from liability, even if the omission is due to mere
mistake or carelessness, and the information turns out in fact to have been wholly
untrue, and even though the goods are lost by capture wholly unconnected with
the perils of the seas[3].

1 Marine Insurance Act 1906 s 18(1), (2); and see para 217 ante; and *The Spathari* 1925 SC (HL) 6
   (non-disclosure of Greek interest), and *Greenhill v Federal Insurance Co Ltd* [1927] 1 KB 65, CA
   (unusual circumstances concerning pre-carriage of cargo); *James Yachts Ltd v Thames and Mersey
   Marine Insurance Co Ltd* [1977] 1 Lloyd's Rep 206, BC SC (non-disclosure of fact that permit
   for assured to carry on boat building business at his premises was refused by local authority, and of
   fact that he was impecunious). A clause providing that the assured is to be held covered at a premium
   to be arranged in the event of any incorrect definition of the interest insured will apply to an incorrect
   description of the subject matter insured, even though the misdescription amounts to non-
   disclosure of a material fact, provided the misdescription is not fraudulent: *Hewitt Bros v Wilson*
   [1915] 2 KB 739, CA. As to the duty to give notice to the insurer under this clause see para 143 note 3
   ante.

2 *Ionides v Pender* (1874) LR 9 QB 531; *Rivaz v Gerussi Bros & Co and Gerussi* (1880) 6 QBD 222, CA;
   Herring v Janson (1895) 1 Com Cas 177; *Thames and Mersey Marine Insurance Co Ltd v Gunford Ship Co
   Ltd, Southern Marine Mutual Insurance Association v Gunford Ship Co Ltd* [1911] AC 529, HL
   (over-valuation and over-insurance: some of the policies by which over-insurance was effected were
   honour policies); *Gooding v White* (1913) 29 TLR 312; *Visscherij Maatschappij Nieuw Onderneming v
   Scottish Metropolitan Assurance Co Ltd* (1922) 27 Com Cas 198, CA; *Hoff Trading Co v Union Insurance
   Society of Canton Ltd* (1929) 45 TLR 466, CA; *Piper v Royal Exchange Assurance* (1932) 44 Ll L Rep 103

(progressive diminution in value of insured vessel); *Slattery v Mance* [1962] 1 QB 676, [1962] 1 All ER 525. It seems that over-insurance may be a material fact in the case of an unvalued policy: *Williams v Atlantic Assurance Co Ltd* [1933] 1 KB 81, CA. For the meaning of 'unvalued policy' see para 41 ante.

3 *Lynch v Hamilton* (1810) 3 Taunt 37 at 44; affd sub nom *Lynch v Dunsford* (1811) 14 East 494, Ex Ch; *De Costa v Scandret* (1723) 2 P Wms 170; *Seaman v Fonereau* (1743) 2 Stra 1183; *Nicholson v Power* (1869) 20 LT 580; *Morrison v Universal Marine Insurance Co* (1872) LR 8 Exch 40; revsd on other points (1873) LR 8 Exch 197, Ex Ch.

222. The time of ship's sailing or being last heard of. The time of the ship's sailing or her being last heard of are facts as to which the assured may be bound to disclose his knowledge or information. Such disclosure is certainly necessary where it would lead to the inference that the ship is a missing or overdue vessel, and it may also be necessary in other cases where circumstances known to the assured exist which make those times material. The question in all cases is a question of fact[1], namely whether the circumstances known to the assured, or as to which he has information, the time of a ship's sailing or when she was last heard of, would influence the judgment of a prudent insurer in fixing the premium or determining whether he would take the risk[2].

1 Marine Insurance Act 1906 s 18(4); and see para 217 ante.
2 The following are the principal cases relating to this subject, although they are of little modern use, not only because the question is one of fact depending on the particular circumstances of each case, but also because the changes in the course and mode of navigation, and the facilities of communication by way of radio or otherwise, are such as to prevent the earlier cases from being a safe guide as to inferences of fact: *Freeland v Glover* (1806) 7 East 457; *Elton v Larkins* (1832) 8 Bing 198 (subsequent proceedings 5 C & P 385); *Stribley v Imperial Marine Insurance Co* (1876) 1 QBD 507; *Ratcliffe v Shoolbred* (1780) 1 Park's Marine Insurances (8th Edn) 413; *M'Andrew v Bell* (1795) 1 Esp 373; *Webster v Foster* (1795) 1 Esp 407; *Willes v Glover* (1804) 1 Bos & PNR 14; *Mackintosh v Marshall* (1843) 11 M & W 116; *Bridges v Hunter* (1813) 1 M & S 15; *Foley v Moline* (1814) 5 Taunt 430; *Littledale v Dixon* (1805) 1 Bos & PNR 151; *Elkin v Janson* (1845) 13 M & W 655; *Rickards v Murdock* (1830) 10 B & C 527; *Westbury v Aberdein* (1837) 2 M & W 267; *Kirby v Smith* (1818) 1 B & Ald 672; *Bell v Bell* (1810) 2 Camp 475 at 479. As to cases involving the question whether when the old Convoy Acts were in force the assured was bound to disclose the fact that the ship sailed or was intended to sail without convoy see *Sawtell v Loudon* (1814) 5 Taunt 359; *Long v Duff Long v Bolton* (1800) 2 Bos & P 209; *Reid & Co v Harvey* (1816) 4 Dow 97, HL.

223. Over-valuation as ground for avoiding the policy. As long as the contract of insurance is unimpeached, any agreed variation is binding on the parties but over-valuation may be a ground for avoiding the contract. Thus, if the over-valuation is part of a scheme for defrauding the insurer, the policy will be voidable[1]. Similarly an over-valuation made in order to cover a gambling transaction will avoid the whole contract; for instance where an insurance is effected for £20,000, and it is proved that the assured's interest amounted to the value of a cable only[2]. Further, an over-valuation, whilst not fraudulent, may be so great as to constitute a material fact non-disclosure of which will entitle the insurer to avoid the policy[3].

1 *Haigh v De la Cour* (1812) 3 Camp 319; *Berger and Light Diffusers Pty Ltd v Pollock* [1973] 2 Lloyd's Rep 442; and see the Marine Insurance Act 1906 s 27(3), and para 42 ante.
2 *Lewis v Rucker* (1761) 2 Burr 1167 at 1171.
3 *Ionides v Pender* (1874) LR 9 QB 531. See also the memorandum of Willes J, cited by Mathew J in *Herring v Janson* (1895) 1 Com Cas 177 at 178. Where the valuation is speculative, being based on mere future possibilities, this fact is material and must be disclosed: *Hoff Trading Co v Union Insurance Society of Canton Ltd* (1929) 45 TLR 466, CA; *Berger and Light Diffusers Pty Ltd v Pollock* [1973] 2 Lloyd's Rep 442.

224. Materiality of special circumstances. It is important to observe that, although the policy by its express terms may cover losses by all perils of the seas[1], this does not relieve the assured from the obligation to disclose information which he has received as to the insured vessel having encountered severe weather. Similarly, if a policy is on goods on board a certain vessel 'at and from port or ports of loading in the province of Buenos Aires', and the assured learns that the ship was intended to load at a roadstead then unknown to the insurer as a place of loading, the insurer will be discharged if the assured does not communicate the place of loading[2]. If a ship is to be employed on a service of peculiar danger, or the subject matter insured is exposed to a particular and unusual risk, and this cannot be inferred from the terms of the policy, the fact ought to be communicated to the insurer[3]. Where goods are insured on 'ship or ships'[4] and the assured knows that the goods are loaded on board a vessel which was reported in Lloyd's List as having met with an accident, the insurer may avoid liability if the assured has not disclosed to him the ship's name[5]. If the assured has entered into a contract which makes the measure of ultimate loss to the insurer greater than what is usual (for instance by reason of his right of subrogation being adversely affected), and he does not disclose the fact, this may amount to non-disclosure of a material fact and the insurer may avoid the policy[6].

Moreover, if the assured has private information of any trade regulation recently introduced or of any particular danger affecting the risk insured, and which in the ordinary course of business would not be known to the insurer, the non-disclosure of that information would be a ground for avoiding the policy[7]. The assured cannot excuse his omission to communicate a material fact on the ground that it had previously come to the insurer's knowledge, unless at the time when the contract was made the fact was present to the insurer's mind[8].

1 For the meaning of 'perils of the seas' see para 151 ante.
2 *Harrower v Hutchinson* (1870) LR 5 QB 584, Ex Ch; *Laing v Union Marine Insurance Co Ltd, Laing v London Assurance Corpn* (1895) 1 Com Cas 11.
3 *T Cheshire & Co v Thompson* (1919) 24 Com Cas 114; affd 24 Com Cas 198, CA.
4 See Arnould on Marine Insurance (16th Edn) s 273; and para 109 note 2 ante.
5 *Lynch v Hamilton* (1810) 3 Taunt 37; affd sub nom *Lynch v Dunsford* (1811) 14 East 494, Ex Ch; *Leigh v Adams* (1871) 25 LT 566.
6 *Tate v Hyslop* (1885) 15 QBD 368, CA, which might also have been decided on the ground that there was a misrepresentation. In a case of insurance in freight (see para 115 ante) the fact that the assured has contracted that the vessel should be ready to load by a given date may be material: *Scottish Shire Line Ltd v London and Provincial Marine and General Insurance Co Ltd* [1912] 3 KB 51 at 70.
7 *Carter v Boehm* (1766) 3 Burr 1905 at 1915; *Greenhill v Federal Insurance Co Ltd* [1927] 1 KB 65, CA.
8 *Bates v Hewitt* (1867) LR 2 QB 595 (distinguished on the facts); *Gandy v Adelaide Insurance Co* (1871) LR 6 QB 746 at 755; *Fracis, Times & Co v Sea Insurance Co* (1898) 3 Com Cas 229 (where a trade prohibition was habitually ignored); *London General Insurance Co v General Marine Underwriters' Association* [1921] 1 KB 104.

225. Matters which need not be disclosed. There are certain circumstances which, by statute, need not be disclosed in the absence of inquiry[1]. Thus the insurer has no ground of complaint because he is not informed of a circumstance which diminishes the risk or of a circumstance which is known or presumed to be known to him[2]. Moreover, the assured is not bound to disclose any circumstance which is presumed to be known by the insurer[3]. Further, the assured need not mention general topics of speculation, or matters involving natural or political perils, such as the difficulty of the voyage, the probability of hurricanes, earthquakes, war or embargo and the like, or the established trade regulations of governments[4].

1 See the Marine Insurance Act 1906 s 18(3); and para 217 ante.
2 Ibid s 18(3)(a), (b); see para 217 ante.
3 Ibid s 18(3)(b). See also *Foley v Tabor* (1861) 2 F & F 663 at 672 per Erle CJ.
4 *Carter v Boehm* (1766) 3 Burr 1905; *Bolivia Republic v Indemnity Mutual Marine Assurance Co Ltd* (1908)
   99 LT 394; *Cantiere Meccanico Brindisino v Janson* (1912) 107 LT 281, CA; *London General Insurance Co
   Ltd v General Marine Underwriters' Association Ltd* (1920) 124 LT 67, CA; *North British Fishing Boat
   Insurance Co Ltd v Starr* (1922) 13 Ll L Rep 206; *George Cohen, Sons & Co v Standard Marine Insurance
   Co Ltd* (1925) 21 Ll L Rep 30; *Piper v Royal Exchange Assurance* (1932) 44 Ll L Rep 103; *St Margaret's
   Trust Ltd v Navigators and General Marine Insurance Co Ltd* (1949) 82 Ll L Rep 752; *Pacific Queen
   Fisheries v L Symes, The Pacific Queen* [1963] 2 Lloyd's Rep 201, US Ct of Apps (9th Circ); *Soya
   GmbH Mainz Kommanditgesellschaft v White* [1982] 1 Lloyd's Rep 136, CA; and see cases cited in paras
   226 note 2, and 227–228 post; and cf para 224 text and notes 7–8 ante.

226. Information waived by the insurer. The assured is not bound to disclose
any information which is waived by the insurer[1]. In general, where from the facts
communicated to him the insurer would naturally infer the existence of other facts
not disclosed, his omission to make inquiry is an implied waiver of a more explicit
disclosure. Thus, where an insurance is applied for in time of war on a cruiser 'from
places to places' without any limitation or description, the insurer must know from
the terms of the proposed insurance that the ship is to be employed in some warlike
expedition, and hence, if he omits to inquire, the particular nature of the service in
which she is to be employed need not be disclosed to him[2].

The omission to make inquiry is no waiver if the insurer is not put on inquiry;
waiver is not to be easily presumed[3].

1 Marine Insurance Act 1906 s 18(3)(c); see para 217 ante.
2 *Carter v Boehm* (1766) 3 Burr 1905 per Lord Mansfield CJ; *Asfar & Co v Blundell* [1896] 1 QB 123 at
   129, CA. As illustrations of the same principle see *Beckwith v Sydebotham* (1807) 1 Camp 116; *Fort v
   Lee* (1811) 3 Taunt 381; *Freeland v Glover* (1806) 7 East 457; *Cantiere Meccanico Brindisino v Janson*
   [1912] 3 KB 452, CA; *Property Insurance Co Ltd v National Protector Insurance Co Ltd* (1913) 18 Com
   Cas 119; *Mann Macneal and Steeves Ltd v Capital and Counties Insurance Co Ltd* [1921] 2 KB 300, CA
   (distinguished in *Greenhill v Federal Insurance Co Ltd* [1927] 1 KB 65, CA); *Pacific Queen Fisheries v
   L Symes, The Pacific Queen* [1963] 2 Lloyd's Rep 201, US Ct of Apps (9th Circ); *Gulfstream Cargo Ltd
   v Reliance Insurance Co, The Papoose* [1970] 1 Lloyd's Rep 178; *Allden v Raven, The Kylie* [1983] 2
   Lloyd's Rep 444; *Container Transport International Inc and Reliance Group Inc v Oceanus Mutual
   Underwriting Association (Bermuda) Ltd* [1984] 1 Lloyd's Rep 476, CA. The insurer's practice as to
   accepting risks or not making inquiries on particular points cannot affect the statutory duty or be
   received as evidence of waiver in any particular case: *Thames and Mersey Marine Insurance Co Ltd v
   Gunford Ship Co Ltd, Southern Marine Mutual Insurance Association v Gunford Ship Co Ltd* [1911] AC
   529, HL, per Lord Alverstone CJ.
3 *Greenhill v Federal Insurance Co Ltd* [1927] 1 KB 65, CA.

227. Information the subject of a warranty. In the absence of inquiry the
assured need not disclose that which it is superfluous to disclose by reason of any
express or implied warranty[1]. Thus, in the case of a voyage policy[2], the assured
need not make any disclosure of information relating to the ship's unseaworthiness
when she sailed, because if she did not start on her voyage in a seaworthy
condition, the insurer would not be liable[3]. It is, however, otherwise in the case of a
time policy[4], where there is no implied warranty of seaworthiness[5].

1 Marine Insurance Act 1906 s 18(3)(d); see para 217 ante.
2 For the meaning of 'voyage policy' see para 41 ante.
3 *Schoolbred v Nutt* (1782) 1 Park's Marine Insurances (8th Edn) 493; *Haywood v Rodgers* (1804) 4 East
   590; *Beckwith v Sydebotham* (1807) 1 Camp 116; *Gunford Ship Co Ltd v Thames and Mersey Marine
   Insurance Co Ltd* 1910 SC 1072; revsd, but not on this point, sub nom *Thames and Mersey Marine*

Insurance Co Ltd v Gunford Ship Co Ltd, Southern Marine Mutual Insurance Association v Gunford Ship Co Ltd [1911] AC 529, HL (qualification of master; it was held that neither his name nor his previous history were in ordinary circumstances, or in the circumstances of that case, material to be disclosed). In *Boyd v Dubois* (1811) 3 Camp 133 the insurers claimed to avoid the policy, which was on cargo, on the ground that the fact that the cargo had been damaged had not been disclosed to them. Lord Ellenborough CJ said that the assured was 'not bound to represent to the underwriter the state of the goods'. This observation was doubted in *Carr v Montefiore* (1864) 5 B & S 408 at 423, and cannot now be regarded as authority for the general proposition that a person insuring cargo is never bound to disclose the condition of the goods; see *Greenhill v Federal Insurance Co Ltd* [1927] 1 KB 65, CA. Probably the true view is that any unusual circumstances relating to the cargo must be disclosed, but that the assured is not bound to point out to the insurer the consequences which naturally follow from the facts which he discloses unless the insurer inquires as to those consequences: *Greenhill v Federal Insurance Co Ltd* supra, at 84 per Scrutton LJ; and see *Cantiere Meccanico Brindisino v Janson* [1912] 2 KB 112 at 115 per Scrutton J; affd [1912] 3 KB 452, CA.

4 For the meaning of 'time policy' see para 41 ante.

5 *Russell v Thornton* (1859) 4 H & N 788. As to the warranty of seaworthiness see para 64 et seq ante; and as to the absence of such a warranty in a time policy see para 74 ante.

228. Further matters which need not be disclosed. The assured is not bound to disclose the estimate formed by other insurers of the risk or the fact that they have declined it[1]. Where a fact is a matter of inference and the materials for drawing it are common to both parties, the assured is generally not bound to make any communication on the subject[2]. It must, however, be always borne in mind that the question whether any particular information which is not disclosed is or is not material, or whether the insurer has waived the disclosure, are questions of fact, and that therefore the decision in each case must depend upon its particular circumstances[3]. For instance, the payment of a very high premium may be evidence that the insurer accepted the risk and waived the disclosure of a particular matter[4].

1 *Lebon & Co v Straits Insurance Co* (1894) 10 TLR 517, CA; *Glasgow Assurance Corpn Ltd v William Symondson & Co* (1911) 16 Com Cas 109 at 119. The rule that refusals by other insurers need not be disclosed appears to be peculiar to marine insurance: see *London Assurance v Mansel* (1879) 11 ChD 363 at 370; *Re Yager and Guardian Assurance Co* (1912) 108 LT 38, DC. It was held by Lord Ellenborough CJ in *Bell v Bell* (1810) 2 Camp 475 at 479, that the assured need not communicate the apprehensions or opinions of foreign correspondents, and that it was enough for him to state the facts on which they were founded.

2 *Bates v Hewitt* (1867) LR 2 QB 595 at 605 per Cockburn CJ; *Gandy v Adelaide Insurance Co* (1871) LR 6 QB 746; *Cantiere Meccanico Brindisino v Janson* [1912] 3 KB 452, CA.

3 See para 217 ante.

4 *Court v Martineau* (1782) 3 Doug KB 161.

229. Matters contained in Lloyd's List. An underwriter who is a member of Lloyd's or a subscriber, and as such receives or has access to Lloyd's List, is not conclusively presumed to have knowledge of the contents of the List. Therefore, the insurance will be voidable if there has been a failure to disclose a material circumstance to the underwriter, even though it is recorded in the List, if in fact he is proved not to have been aware of it at the time of concluding the contract[1]. This rule applies also where there has been any false representation made to the underwriter as to the nature of the risk and he acted solely in reliance on the representation without in fact consulting Lloyd's List[2].

1 *Morrison v Universal Marine Insurance Co* (1872) LR 8 Exch 40 at 54 per Bramwell B; revsd on grounds not affecting this question (1873) LR 8 Exch 197; *Elton v Larkins* (1832) 8 Bing 198; on second trial 5

C & P 385; *Nicholson v Power* (1869) 20 LT 580 per Cockburn CJ; *Mackintosh v Marshall* (1843) 11 M & W 116. It seems that *Friere v Woodhouse* (1817) Holt NP 572, a decision contrary to what is stated in the text, can no longer be relied on as authority; see also *Lynch v Dunsford* (1811) 14 East 494, Ex Ch; *Foley v Tabor* (1861) 2 F & F 663 at 672 per Erle CJ; *Gandy v Adelaide Insurance Co* (1871) LR 6 QB 746 at 754 (where the underwriter did refer to the register, but failed to draw the correct inference); *London General Insurance Co v General Marine Underwriters' Association* [1921] 1 KB 104, applying *Bates v Hewitt* (1867) LR 2 QB 595.

2 *Mackintosh v Marshall* (1843) 11 M & W 116.

230. Evidence of insurers and brokers as to materiality. Although it was once doubtful whether the evidence of insurers and insurance brokers was admissible to prove the materiality of the representation made, or of the circumstances not disclosed[1], it has become the established practice to admit such evidence[2].

1 The evidence was held to be inadmissible in *Carter v Boehm* (1766) 3 Burr 1905, but was admitted in *Littledale v Dixon* (1805) 1 Bos & PNR 151; *Chaurand v Angerstein* (1791) Peake 43; *Campbell v Rickards* (1833) 5 B & Ad 840; *Berthon v Loughman* (1817) 2 Stark 258; *Rickards v Murdock* (1830) 10 B & C 527; and *Thames and Mersey Marine Insurance Co Ltd v Gunford Ship Co Ltd, Southern Marine Mutual Insurance Association v Gunford Ship Co Ltd* [1911] AC 529, HL; and see *Chapman v Walton* (1833) 10 Bing 57 at 65. As to the admissibility of the evidence of experts generally see EVIDENCE vol 17 paras 83–87.

2 *Ionides v Pender* (1874) LR 9 QB 531; *Herring v Janson* (1895) 1 Com Cas 177 at 179; and see *Bates v Hewitt* (1867) LR 2 QB 595 at 610; *Scottish Shire Line Ltd v London and Provincial Marine and General Insurance Co Ltd* [1912] 3 KB 51 at 70 per Hamilton J. The court may, however, take judicial notice of the materiality of the fact without evidence being given: see *Glicksman v Lancashire and General Assurance Co Ltd* [1925] 2 KB 593 at 609, CA, per Scrutton LJ; affd [1927] AC 139, HL. On the other hand, the evidence may prove that although the facts which were not disclosed increased the risk, a prudent insurer would not have appreciated the bearing of these facts on the risk. If so, the court must find that the facts in question were not material within the meaning of the Marine Insurance Act 1906 s 18(2) (see para 217 ante), and consequently that the assured was under no obligation to disclose them: *Associated Oil Carriers Ltd v Union Insurance Society of Canton Ltd* [1917] 2 KB 184. As to the onus of proof on the issue of non-disclosure see para 216 note 2 ante.

231. Insurer presumed to know the usage of the trade. The assured is entitled to assume that the insurer is acquainted with the general usage of the trade to which the insured adventure relates, and therefore need not communicate to the insurer facts as to that usage[1]. Moreover, where there is a general and notorious practice to insert a certain clause in a particular kind of commercial contract, the assured is entitled to assume that the insurer knows that the contract may contain that clause, and therefore need not inform him that it does, even if the clause may tend to increase the risk[2].

1 Marine Insurance Act 1906 s 18(3)(b) (see para 217 ante); *Vallance v Dewar* (1808) 1 Camp 503; *Ougier v Jennings* (1800) 1 Camp 505n; *Kingston v Knibbs* (1808) 1 Camp 508n; *Salvador v Hopkins* (1765) 3 Burr 1707; *Freeland v Glover* (1806) 7 East 457; *Da Costa v Edmunds* (1815) 4 Camp 142; *Stewart v Bell* (1821) 5 B & Ald 238. As to incorporation of usage in the policy see paras 51–53 ante. Cf *Tennant v Henderson* (1813) 1 Dow 324, HL, where the usage alleged was not established.

2 *Salvador v Hopkins* (1765) 3 Burr 1707; *The Bedouin* [1894] P 1, CA; *Asfar & Co v Blundell* [1896] 1 QB 123, CA; *Charlesworth v Faber* (1900) 5 Com Cas 408.

(ii) Misrepresentation

232. Representations during negotiation of contract. Every material representation[1] made by the assured or his agent to the insurer during the negotiations for the contract, and before the contract is concluded, must be true; if it is untrue, the insurer may avoid the contract[2]. A representation is an oral or written statement made by the assured or his agent before or at the time of the making of the contract, and it generally consists of oral communications made, or written instructions shown, by the broker to the insurer[3]. The main distinction in form between a representation and an express warranty is that a representation may be made either orally or in writing and need not be included in the policy, whereas an express warranty must always be included in or written on the policy, or must be contained in some document incorporated by reference into it[4].

There are two other distinctions between a warranty and a representation which it is important to notice. A breach of warranty will discharge the insurer even if it does not relate to a matter material to the risk insured against; and a warranty must be exactly complied with[5]. On the other hand, a misrepresentation which is not material will not enable the insurer to avoid the policy; nor will he be so enabled if the representation is substantially correct, that is to say if the difference between what is represented and what is actually correct would not be considered material by a prudent insurer[6].

1 As to when a representation is material see para 233 post.
2 Marine Insurance Act 1906 s 20(1).
3 Arnould on Marine Insurance (16th Edn) s 589.
4 Marine Insurance Act 1906 s 35(2). As to express warranties see paras 57–63 ante. As to misrepresentation generally see MISREPRESENTATION.
5 See para 55 ante.
6 Marine Insurance Act 1906 s 20(4): see para 233 post. See *Pawson v Watson* (1778) 2 Cowp 785 at 787 per Lord Mansfield CJ; and *Von Tungeln v Dubois* (1809) 2 Camp 151; *Nonnen v Reid, Nonnen v Kettlewell* (1812) 16 East 176 at 186. It will be observed that a 'warranty' in this branch of the law of marine insurance is equivalent to a 'condition' in the general law of contract: see para 54 note 2 ante. See also CONTRACT vol 9 paras 542–543.

233. Material representations: fact or belief: absence of fraud. A representation is material which would influence the judgment of a prudent insurer in fixing the premium or determining whether he will take the risk[1]. Whether or not the representation is material is in each case a question of fact[2].

A representation may be a representation either as to a matter of fact or as to a matter of expectation or belief[3]. If it is as to a matter of fact, it is true if it is substantially correct, that is to say if the difference between what is represented and what is actually correct would not be considered material by a prudent insurer[4]. If it is as to a matter of expectation or belief, it is true if made in good faith[5]. A representation may be withdrawn or corrected before the contract is concluded[6].

It is not necessary that a representation should be fraudulent in order to avoid the insurance; a representation, if material, even though wholly untainted with fraud, will also enable the insurer to avoid liability unless the representation is substantially correct or unless he knew the truth at the time the contract was concluded[7].

It is, however (at any rate in the absence of fraud[8]), only a material representation as already defined[9] which will entitle the insurer to avoid the contract, and all that has been said[10] concerning materiality in connection with the duty to disclose material circumstances to the insurer applies to representations made to him. Thus it is not necessary in order to avoid the policy on the ground of misrepresentation that the loss should have arisen from a cause in any way connected with the circumstances or matters represented, the only question being whether the representation was material in the sense previously mentioned[11]. As in the case of

non-disclosure, a representation may be material even if it does not relate directly
to the risks insured against[12].

1 Marine Insurance Act 1906 s 20(2).
2 Ibid s 20(7). See eg *Cantiere Maccanico Brindisino v Janson* [1912] 3 KB 452, CA; *Hamilton & Co v Eagle
   Star and British Dominions Insurance Co Ltd* (1924) 19 Ll L Rep 242; *Demetriades & Co v Northern
   Assurance Co* (1925) 21 Ll L Rep 265, HL; *Williams v Atlantic Assurance Co Ltd* [1933] 1 KB 81, CA;
   Neue Fischmehl Vertribs-Gesellschaft Haselhorst mbH v Yorkshire Insurance Co Ltd (1934) 50 Ll L Rep
   151; *Willmott v General Accident Fire and Life Assurance Corpn Ltd* (1935) 53 Ll L Rep 156; *Slattery v
   Mance* [1962] 1 QB 676, [1962] 1 All ER 525; *Liberian Insurance Agency Inc v Mosse* [1977] 2 Lloyd's
   Rep 560; *Container Transport International Inc and Reliance Group Inc v Oceanus Mutual Underwriting
   Association (Bermuda) Ltd* [1984] 1 Lloyd's Rep 476, CA
3 Marine Insurance Act 1906 s 20(3).
4 Ibid s 20(4).
5 Ibid s 20(5).
6 Ibid s 20(6). The time of conclusion of the contract is defined by s 21: see paras 89, 217 note 1 ante.
7 It is argued in Arnould on Marine Insurance (16th Edn) s 611, that, as a fraudulent representation
   will not avoid the contract if it did not influence the mind of the contracting party (see para 215 ante),
   this must a fortiori be true of an innocent misrepresentation. This contention was approved in the
   first edition of this work; but see the observations of Vaughan Willlams LJ in *Cantiere Meccanico
   Brindisino v Janson* [1912] 3 KB 452 at 460, CA, approving the view expressed by Scrutton J, which
   seems to be to the contrary effect.
8 As to fraudulent misrepresentations which are not material see para 215 ante.
9 See the Marine Insurance Act 1906 s 20(2): and text and note 1 supra.
10 See para 221 ante.
11 Marine Insurance Act 1906 s 20(1), (2); *Lynch v Dunsford* (1811) 14 East 494, Ex Ch; and see the cases
   cited in paras 221 notes 1, 3, and 222 note 2 ante.
12 *The Spathari* 1925 SC (HL) 6, where a representation that the vessel was entitled to be registered as
   British was held to be material.

234. Representations of expectation or belief. Where a representation is as to
a matter of expectation or belief, it is deemed true if it is made in good faith[1]. Where
the assured, with intention to deceive the insurer, states his belief or expectation as
to matters of which he is ignorant, the representation cannot be considered as made
in good faith and the insurance may, therefore, be avoided[2].

1 Marine Insurance Act 1906 s 20(5): see para 233 ante.
2 See *Edgington v Fitzmaurice* (1885) 29 ChD 459 at 481, CA, per Bowen LJ; *Derry v Peek* (1889) 14 App
   Cas 337 HL; *Pawson v Watson* (1778) 2 Cowp 785 at 788 per Lord Mansfield CJ.

235. Promissory representations. Before the Marine Insurance Act 1906, a
statement made before or at the time of the conclusion of the contract that a certain
fact or state of things 'shall' or 'will' thereafter exist was held to amount to a
representation which, if not substantially complied with, avoided the policy even if
the representation was made without fraud[1]. It was laid down in later decisions,
however, as a principle of the law of contract in general, that a representation of a
future fact, if binding at all, can only be binding as a contract or promise[2]. It is
submitted that this view is adopted in the provisions of the Act[3] and consequently
that promissory representations of future facts cannot be considered as representations within the meaning of the Act. If this view is correct, it follows that the
non-fulfilment of 'promissory representations' (as distinct from warranties[4]) will
not of itself entitle the insurer to avoid the contract. A promissory representation,
however, usually implies the further representation of expectation or belief that the
representation will be fulfilled. If this further representation is untrue[5], the insurer
may avoid the contract[6].

1 *Pawson v Watson* (1778) 2 Cowp 785; *Dennistoun v Lillie* (1821) 3 Bli 202, HL.
2 *Jorden v Money* (1854) 5 HL Cas 185; *Maddison v Alderson* (1883) 8 App Cas 467 at 473, HL; *Citizens' Bank of Louisiana v First National Bank of New Orleans* (1873) LR 6 HL 352 at 360; and see *Beattie v Lord Ebury* (1872) 7 Ch App 777 at 804 per Mellish LJ; and MISREPRESENTATION.
3 Ie the Marine Insurance Act 1906 s 20(4); see para 233 ante.
4 As to warranties see para 54 et seq ante.
5 As to when a representation as to a matter of expectation or belief is true see para 234 ante.
6 See paras 232–233 ante; and see also the discussion of this question in Arnould on Marine Insurance (16th Edn) ss 601–604.

236. Representation concerning information received by assured. The fact represented by the assured may be a statement that he has received certain information; if he merely submits the information to the insurer, leaving him to draw his own conclusions from it, there is no untrue representation, and the insurer cannot avoid the policy even if the information proves to be incorrect[1].

1 2 Duer on Marine Insurance 703; *Brine v Featherstone* (1813) 4 Taunt 869. Where, however, the information communicated to the insurer purports to come from an agent of the assured whose duty it is to supply him with correct intelligence in relation to the subject insured, the incorrectness of the information may enable the insurer to avoid liability: *Fitzherbert v Mather* (1785) 1 Term Rep 12.

237. Representations made in answer to inquiry. Where a representation has been made in answer to an inquiry by the insurer, the assured has had notice that the answer would influence the insurer in taking the risk, and therefore the strongest presumption exists that the matter inquired into was material to be known by the insurer, and any untrue answer will probably entitle him to avoid the policy[1].

1 See *The Bedouin* [1894] P 1 at 12, CA, per Lord Esher MR. If the answer is known by the assured to be false, the insurer can, of course, avoid the policy irrespective of the materiality of the answer: *The Bedouin* supra at 12.

238. Misrepresentation involves non-disclosure. Failure to disclose a material fact may virtually amount to a representation that the fact does not exist, and every misrepresentation clearly involves non-disclosure of the truth. It consequently follows that some cases in which it was held that the policy was avoided by misrepresentation might have been decided also on the ground that there was non-disclosure of a material fact, and vice versa[1].

1 *Fitzherbert v Mather* (1785) 1 Term Rep 12; *Tate v Hyslop* (1885) 15 QBD 368, CA.

239. Representations to one of several insurers. Where there are several insurers, a representation to the first has been considered virtually a representation to all, with the result that each subsequent insurer, when it proved to be false, might avoid the contract on this ground, as it has been presumed that the subsequent insurers subscribed the policy on the faith reposed by them in the skill and judgment of the first[1]. The correctness of this rule has, however, been strongly questioned by judges of great eminence[2]. It is submitted that the true view is that there are two questions of fact to be decided, namely, first, whether in any particular case the subsequent insurer reasonably relied on the judgment of the first insurer, and secondly, whether the first insurer was misled by the representation.

1 *Pawson v Watson* (1778) 2 Cowp 785; *Barber v Fletcher* (1779) 1 Doug KB 305; *Stackpole v Simon* (1779)
   2 Park's Marine Insurances (8th Edn) 932 (life policy); *Marsden v Reid* (1803) 3 East 572 at 573; *Feise v
   Parkinson* (1812) 4 Taunt 640.
2 *Brine v Featherstone* (1813) 4 Taunt 869; *Forrester v Pigou* (1813) 1 M & S 9 at 13, per Lord
   Ellenborough. It is not extended to representations to later insurers: *Bell v Carstairs* (1810) 2 Camp
   543; *Brine v Featherstone* supra; *Marsden v Reid* (1803) 3 East 572. See also Arnould on Marine
   Insurance (16th Edn) s 624, where the importance of the rule is considered in the light of modern
   practice.

240. Construction of representations. The construction of representations is
governed by the ordinary rules applicable to the interpretation of clauses in a
policy[1].

1 *Chaurand v Angerstein* (1791) Peake 43; *Freeland v Glover* (1806) 7 East 457 at 462; *Kirby v Smith* (1818)
   1 B & Ald 672 at 675.

241. Effect of decided cases on materiality. There are two points which must
always be borne in mind in dealing with the numerous cases that have been decided
on the subject of non-disclosure of material circumstances and material representations[1]. The first is that, as the materiality of matters not disclosed or of representations made is a question of fact[2] and not of law, each case must be decided on its
own particular facts. The second is that, in earlier times when the parties to a
contract were not allowed to give evidence, the courts were obliged in many cases
to raise presumptions of fact and to act on them, but now that the parties can be
examined and cross-examined it is in almost all cases unnecessary to have recourse
to any such presumptions[3].

1 See paras 217–240 ante.
2 Marine Insurance Act 1906 s 20(7); see para 233 ante.
3 See further Arnould on Marine Insurance (16th Edn) s 613.

(iii) Election to Avoid, and Cancellation of, Policies

242. When election to avoid the contract must be made. Where the contract
of insurance is voidable on the ground of misrepresentation[1] or non-disclosure[2] on
the assured's part, it may be important, in certain circumstances, for the assured to
know whether the insurer elects to avoid the contract, in order that he may be able
to take steps to effect another insurance. The fact that the insurer has subscribed a
policy without protest does not, however, prove that he has elected to affirm the
contract, inasmuch as he may have acted in pursuance of the usage which binds the
insurer to subscribe a policy in accordance with the slip[3].

Even when the insurer has full knowledge of the facts, he is still entitled to a
reasonable time in which to decide whether to affirm or repudiate the contract. If he
has taken no action to affirm or repudiate it and a reasonable time for making up his
mind has elapsed, he will be deemed to have affirmed the contract if either so much
time has elapsed that the necessary inference is one of affirmation or the assured has
been prejudiced by the delay in making an election or rights of third parties have
intervened[4].

1 As to avoidance on the ground of misrepresentation see para 232 et seq ante.
2 As to avoidance on the ground of non-disclosure see para 215 et seq ante.

3 As to this usage see para 89 ante.

4 *Liberian Insurance Agency Inc v Mosse* [1977] 2 Lloyd's Rep 560 at 565 per Donaldson J.

243. Cancellation of policies. Where a policy is avoided for non-disclosure or misrepresentation, it may be ordered to be given up and cancelled[1].

1 *Rivaz v Gerussi Bros & Co and Gerussi* (1880) 6 QBD 222, CA; *Brooking v Maudslay, Son and Field* (1888) 38 ChD 636. See also EQUITY; GUARANTEE; MISREPRESENTATION. As to avoidance on the ground of non-disclosure see para 215 et seq ante; as to avoidance on the ground of misrepresentation see para 232 et seq ante.

(10) GENERAL AVERAGE

(i) General Average Loss and General Average Contribution

244. General average loss and right to contribution. A general average[1] loss is a loss caused by or directly consequential on a general average act, and it includes a general average expenditure as well as a general average sacrifice[2]. There is a general average act where any extraordinary sacrifice or expenditure is voluntarily and reasonably made or incurred in time of peril[3] for the purpose of preserving the property imperilled in the common adventure[4].

Where there is a general average loss, the party on whom it falls is entitled, subject to the conditions imposed by maritime law[5], to a rateable contribution from the other parties interested, and such a contribution is called a general average contribution[6].

The question what does or does not constitute a general average loss[7] does not directly concern marine insurance law, which is more relevant to determine when and to what extent the insurer is liable in respect of a general average loss or contribution[8].

1 For a consideration of the derivation and meaning of 'average' see *Kelman v Livanos* [1955] 2 All ER 236 at 239, [1955] 1 WLR 590 at 598–599 per McNair J.

2 Marine Insurance Act 1906 s 66(1).

3 Ie at a time when a peril really exists; it is not enough that a peril is reasonably believed to exist: *Joseph Watson & Son Ltd v Firemen's Fund Insurance Co of San Francisco* [1922] 2 KB 355.

4 Marine Insurance Act 1906 s 66(2).

5 As to these conditions see para 249 post.

6 Marine Insurance Act 1906 s 66(3). These provisions mainly embody the principles laid down by Lawrence J in *Birkley v Presgrave* (1801) 1 East 220 at 228, and also in the judgments in *Svensden v Wallace* (1884) 13 QBD 69, CA; affd (1885) 10 App Cas 404, HL. The law of general average, which owes its origin to the Rhodian laws, was incorporated in the Roman law and afterwards in the common law, and it may therefore now be considered as implied in the contract of affreightment. On this point see *Burton v English* (1883) 12 QBD 218 at 223, CA; and *Wright v Marwood* (1881) 7 QBD 62, CA.

7 For a full discussion of this question see SHIPPING; and Lowndes and Rudolf's General Average and the York-Antwerp Rules (11th Edn) 65–66. It is sufficient here to notice (see para 245 post) some of the more important consequences of the statutory definitions stated in the text to notes 2–6 supra.

8 See paras 250–251 post.

245. General average expenditure. An expenditure caused by or directly consequential on a general average act is called a general average expenditure, for that expenditure may properly be considered as the cost of the general average act[1]. If at the time of peril salvors are employed at a certain remuneration to salve the whole of the property at risk[2], or if money is paid to pirates for the purpose of saving both ship and cargo, this expenditure constitutes a general average expenditure[3]. Again, where a vessel puts into a port of refuge for her own safety and that of the cargo on board her, the inward expenses, including the charges for towage, pilotage, harbour dues etc, are general average expenditure, inasmuch as they are the direct consequences of the general average act of putting into port[4]. Further, expenditure reasonably incurred in defending an action for an indemnity arising out of a general average act is directly consequential on that act[5].

1 Marine Insurance Act 1906 s 66(2): see para 244 ante.
2 *Ocean SS Co v Anderson* (1883) 13 QBD 651, CA; revsd, without affecting the principle, sub nom *Anderson v Ocean SS Co* (1884) 10 App Cas 107, HL; *Kemp v Halliday* (1866) LR 1 QB 520, Ex Ch. See further SHIPPING.
3 Marshall on Marine Insurance (4th Edn) 424.
4 See *Svensden v Wallace* (1884) 13 QBD 69, CA; affd (1885) 10 App Cas 404, HL.
5 *Australian Coastal Shipping Commission v Green* [1971] 1 QB 456, [1971] 1 All ER 353, CA (contract of towage). For the meaning of 'general average act' see para 244 ante.

246. General and particular average losses distinguished. A general average loss differs essentially from a particular average loss. A general average loss is a loss voluntarily incurred for the common safety, and therefore made good by a rateable contribution from all the parties concerned in the adventure, whereas a particular average loss is a loss fortuitously caused by a maritime peril[1], and has to be borne by the party on whom the loss originally fell[2]. In complex salvage operations the whole of the expenditure may be incurred for the common safety[3], or part may be incurred for the common safety and part for the benefit of particular interests[4], and expenditure may be of a general average nature as regards two or more interests but be particular average as regards a further interest[5]. Broadly, once an interest has reached a place of safety, expenditure incurred on it cannot be general average expenditure so far as that interest is concerned.

1 For the meaning of 'maritime perils' see para 36 ante.
2 *Nesbitt v Lushington* (1792) 4 Term Rep 783; and see SHIPPING.
3 *Moran v Jones* (1857) 7 E & B 523; *Kemp v Halliday* (1866) 6 B & S 723.
4 *Job v Langton* (1856) 6 E & B 779; *Royal Mail Steam Packet Co v English Bank of Rio de Janeiro* (1887) 19 QBD 362, DC.
5 *Royal Mail Steam Packet Co v English Bank of Rio de Janeiro* (1887) 19 QBD 362, DC.

247. Sacrifice or expenditure involved must be extraordinary. No claim for general average contribution can be sustained unless the sacrifice or expenditure out of which it arises is of an extraordinary nature, or unless the expenditure is directly occasioned by a general average act. The shipowner agrees by the contract of affreightment to give the use of his vessel, with all her appliances, as well as the services of the crew, to the shippers or charterers for the entire voyage. For what he does in performance of that obligation he has, in general, no right to claim general average contribution. On the other hand, he is not bound to expose the ship or her appliances to the risk of loss or damage by using them in a time of emergency for a purpose for which they were not intended, nor to incur an expenditure which is not only extraordinary in amount, but is incurred to procure some service which is extraordinary in its nature[1]. If, therefore, any part of the ship or her tackle is applied for the common safety to some purpose different from its ordinary use, the loss arising from that application is a general average loss[2], for instance where a ship's engines are damaged whilst being worked ahead or astern in order to get the ship off a bank[3], or spars are cut up to construct a rudder, or where, formerly, sails and cordage were used to stop a leak[4].

1 *Robinson v Price* (1877) 2 QBD 91; on appeal (1877) 2 QBD 295, CA (use of spars as fuel). See also SHIPPING.
2 *Birkley v Presgrave* (1801) 1 East 220.
3 *The Bona* [1895] P 125, CA.
4 2 Phillips' Law of Insurance (5th Edn) s 1299. See *Harrison v Bank of Australasia* (1872) LR 7 Exch 39 at 49 per Martin B; *Robinson v Price* (1877) 2 QBD 91; on appeal (1877) 2 QBD 295, CA.

248. Consequential losses. Losses which are the direct consequences of a general average act are general average losses[1]. Thus, if holes are cut in the ship in order to take goods out for the sake of lightening her, or if water is thrown down a ship's hatches to extinguish an accidental fire, and other goods are thereby damaged, the loss or damage in each case is general average[2].

1 See para 244 ante.
2 *Whitecross Wire Co Ltd v Savill* (1882) 8 QBD 653, CA; *The Birkhall, Papayanni and Jeronica v Grampian SS Co Ltd* (1896) 1 Com Cas 448. If, in order to preserve the whole adventure, the ship is taken into a port in circumstances in which she is likely to cause damage to the property of third persons and that damage in fact occurs, the compensation payable to third persons gives rise to a right to general average contribution: *Austin Friars SS Co Ltd v Spillers and Bakers Ltd* [1915] 3 KB 586, CA; see SHIPPING.

249. Conditions imposed by maritime law. The right of contribution previously referred to is expressed to be subject to the conditions imposed by maritime law[1]. One of these is that, where the peril giving rise to the claim has been occasioned by the fault[2] of the claimant or his employee, he himself is precluded from recovering a general average contribution. Thus, to a shipowner's claim for contribution, a plea that the loss was caused by the vessel's unseaworthiness may be a valid defence[3]. This rule, however, bars only the claim of the wrongdoer and not that of other innocent sufferers[4].

A further condition is that general average contribution is not recoverable in respect of the jettison of goods loaded on deck unless the loading on deck is in accordance with the usage of trade on the voyage for which the goods are shipped[5].

1 See the Marine Insurance Act 1906 s 66(3); and para 244 ante.
2 Fault in this context means fault for which the claimant is legally liable. If he is protected from legal liability for the fault in question (eg by an exception in the contract of affreightment or by statute), he will not be precluded from recovering a general average contribution: *The Carron Park* (1890) 15 PD 203 (negligence of shipowners' employees excepted); applied in *Milburn & Co v Jamaica Fruit Importing and Trading Co of London* [1900] 2 QB 540, CA (master's negligence); and see SHIPPING. Owing to the effect of the 'foreign adjustment clause' in the policy (as to which see para 253 post), it not infrequently happens that questions of general average are determined as between assured and insurer in accordance with the York-Antwerp Rules 1974, which differ in some respects from the law of England. These rules are set out in Appendix 2, para 907 post.
3 *Schloss v Heriot* (1863) 14 CBNS 59; and see *Goulandris Bros Ltd v B Goldman & Sons Ltd* [1958] 1 QB 74, [1957] 3 All ER 100 (equitable defence that shipowner could not recover for the consequence of his own wrong was not within the Carriage of Goods by Sea Act 1924 Schedule art III r 6 (repealed), which was applied by the bill of lading, and the defence was therefore not barred by lapse of time); but the plea will not be a valid defence if the shipowner is protected from liability for loss due to the unseaworthiness by the contract of affreightment or by statute (*Louis Dreyfus & Co v Tempus Shipping Co* [1931] AC 726, HL). See further SHIPPING.

4 *Strang, Steel & Co v A Scott & Co* (1889) 14 App Cas 601, PC.
5 *Wright v Marwood* (1881) 7 QBD 62, CA; *Burton v English* (1883) 12 QBD 218, CA; see also SHIPPING.

(ii) Liability of Insurer in respect of General Average

250. Insurer's liability in respect of expenditure, sacrifice and contribution.
The insurer on a marine policy is liable in respect of a general average loss to the
following extent.

Subject to any express provision in the policy, where the assured has incurred a
general average expenditure, he may recover from the insurer in respect of the
proportion of the loss which falls on him[1], and, in the case of a general average
sacrifice, he may recover from the insurer in respect of the whole loss without
having enforced his right of contribution from the other parties liable to contribute[2]. Thus, in the cases of jettison of goods or of cutting away of a mast, the owner
of the goods in the one case and the shipowner in the other can recover the full
amount of the loss from the insurer[3]. Where, however, there is a general average
expenditure, for instance that of putting into a port of refuge, the shipowner is not
entitled to recover the whole amount, but only that part which he himself has to
bear in respect of his own interest as shipowner[4].

Subject to any express provision in the policy, where the assured has paid, or is
liable to pay, a general average contribution in respect of the subject insured, he
may recover for it from the insurer[5].

In the absence of express stipulation, however, the insurer is not liable for any
general average loss or contribution where the loss was not incurred for the
purpose of avoiding, or in connection with the avoidance of, a peril insured
against[6]. Thus, in a marine policy if the peril of fire is excepted, damage done by
pouring water into the hold of the ship for the purpose of extinguishing a fire that
breaks out in her when in dock, although a general average loss, would not be one
in respect of which the insurer would be liable[7].

1 See the Marine Insurance Act 1906 s 66(4). The York-Antwerp Rules 1974 (following English
maritime law) provide that the contribution to a general average is to be made upon the actual net
values of the property at the termination of the adventure (see r XVII; and Appendix 2, para 907
post). It follows that property which has been destroyed or become valueless before the termination
of the adventure cannot be made liable to contribute in general average (*Chellew v Royal Commission
on Sugar Supply* [1922] 1 KB 12, CA) and the same principle applies between assured and insurer
(*Green Star Shipping Co Ltd v London Assurance* [1933] 1 KB 378). Consequently, if the amount of
contribution recoverable by a shipowner from a cargo owner is reduced by reason of the loss of or
damage to the cargo before the termination of the adventure, the deficiency in the cargo's contributory value represents part of the 'proportion of the loss which falls upon' the shipowner within the
meaning of the Marine Insurance Act 1906 s 66(4), and is recoverable as such from the hull
underwriters: *Green Star Shipping Co Ltd v London Assurance* supra. If no contribution is recoverable
by the shipowner either because no interest, other than the ship, has any value at the termination of
the adventure or because, in a case in which the York-Antwerp Rules 1974 do not apply, the
expenditure was necessitated by the shipowner's actionable fault, the whole expenditure may be
recoverable from the insurer.
2 Marine Insurance Act 1906 s 66(4); *Dickenson v Jardine* (1868) LR 3 CP 639, where the insurer, having
indemnified the assured, was entitled to be subrogated to the assured's rights against the owners of
other interests liable to contribute.
3 *Dickenson v Jardine* (1868) LR 3 CP 639.
4 *The Mary Thomas* [1894] P 108, CA.
5 Marine Insurance Act 1906 s 66(5). Thus, if goods are jettisoned the shipowner who has to pay a
general average contribution can recover the amount from his insurer.

6 Ibid s 66(6). As to perils insured against see generally para 149 ante. The peril must really exist; it is not enough that the person incurring the loss reasonably believed that it existed: *Joseph Watson & Son Ltd v Firemen's Fund Insurance Co of San Francisco* [1922] 2 KB 355.

7 As to the amount for which underwriters are liable in respect of general average see further para 280 post.

251. Liability where ship and cargo belong to the same person. There are certain cases in which the insurer may be liable for general average even though the different interests insured do not belong to different parties, and therefore no general average contribution is actually payable. Where ship, freight[1] and cargo, or any two of those interests, are owned by the same assured, the insurer's liability in respect of general average losses or contributions is to be determined as if those subjects were owned by different persons[2]. Therefore, if ship and cargo belong to the same person, and the thing sacrificed is part of the ship, the assured may sue the insurer on ship only for the ship's proportion of the loss, and the insurer on cargo is liable to indemnify him against so much of the loss as is properly attributable to cargo[3].

1 For the meaning of 'freight' when used to describe the subject matter of the policy see para 115 ante.
2 Marine Insurance Act 1906 s 66(7), which embodies the law laid down in *Montgomery & Co v Indemnity Mutual Marine Insurance Co* [1902] 1 KB 734, CA, where the judgment in *The Brigella* [1893] P 189 was disapproved.
3 *Montgomery & Co v Indemnity Mutual Marine Insurance Co* [1902] 1 KB 734 at 741, CA.

(iii) Place of Adjustment: Foreign Adjustment Clause

252. Place of adjustment. The proper place for the adjustment of general average is the ship's port of destination or discharge[1]. If the adventure is broken up at an intermediate port, either by necessity or by the parties' consent, that port is the proper place for adjusting the general average[2], and if the port in which the adjustment is made is a foreign port, the adjustment is called a 'foreign adjustment'[3]. The shipper of goods, inasmuch as he must be taken to assent to general average as a known maritime usage, is, by assenting to it, also deemed to have agreed to its adjustment at the usual and proper place; that adjustment is conclusive on the parties to the contract of affreightment both as to the items and as to their apportionment on the various interests, although it may be different from that which the law of the United Kingdom would have made if the adjustment had been settled in home ports[4]. There is, however, one exception to this general rule, namely where the loss declared by the adjustment to be general average does not arise from any of the perils covered by the policy[5].

1 *Simonds v White* (1824) 2 B & C 805.
2 As to what justifies the termination of the voyage at an intermediate port see *Mavro v Ocean Marine Insurance Co* (1875) LR 10 CP 414, Ex Ch; *Hill v Wilson* (1879) 4 CPD 329 (damage to ship and cargo); *Fletcher v Alexander* (1868) LR 3 CP 375 at 382; and see *Shipton v Thornton* (1838) 9 Ad & El 314; *Atwood v Sellar & Co* (1880) 5 QBD 286, CA.
3 See *Simonds v White* (1824) 2 B & C 805.
4 *Harris v Scaramanga* (1872) LR 7 CP 481; *Simonds v White* (1824) 2 B & C 805 at 813; *Dalglish v Davidson* (1824) 5 Dow & Ry KB 6; *Mavro v Ocean Marine Insurance Co* (1875) LR 10 CP 414, Ex Ch; *The Mary Thomas* [1894] P 108, CA.
5 *Harris v Scaramanga* (1872) LR 7 CP 481 at 489, 496; *Newman v Cazalet* (circa 1780) 2 Park's Marine Insurances (8th Edn) 900; *Walpole v Ewer* (1789) 2 Park's Marine Insurances (8th Edn) 898; *Power v Whitmore* (1815) 4 M & S 141. The Marine Insurance Act 1906 s 66(6) (see para 250 ante) seems to be

intended to embody the law laid down in the judgments in *Harris v Scaramanga* supra, to the effect that if a general average loss has been caused by a peril expressly excepted by the policy, the insurers would not be liable in respect of it, whatever might be the tenor of the foreign adjustment.

253. Foreign adjustment clause. It has become the regular practice to insert in policies a special clause known as the 'foreign adjustment clause', by which provision is made for the contingency of an adjustment being made abroad.

The clause in relation to cargo broadly provides for the insurance to cover general average and salvage charges, adjusted or determined according to the contract and/or the governing law and practice[1].

The clause in relation to hulls or freight broadly provides for adjustment to be either under the law and practice of the place where the adventure ends, as if the contract contains no relevant special terms, or where the contract so provides, under the York-Antwerp Rules[2].

1 See the Institute Cargo Clauses (A) cl 2; the Institute Cargo Clauses (B) cl 2; the Institute Cargo Clauses (C) cl 2; the Institute War Clauses (Cargo) cl 2; and the Institute Strikes Clauses (Cargo) cl 2. The effect of this clause is to make the insurer liable in accordance with adjustment made under the contract, or in accordance with an adjustment made under the law and practice governing the contract. As to the Institute Clauses generally see para 149 note 1 ante.

2 See the Institute Time Clauses (Hulls) cl 11.2; the Institute Voyage Clauses (Hulls) cl 9.2; the Institute War and Strikes Clauses (Hulls—Time) cl 2; the Institute War and Strikes Clauses (Hulls—Voyage) cl 2; the Institute Time Clauses (Freight) cl 11.2; and the Institute Voyage Clauses (Freight) cl 9.2; the Institute War and Strikes Clauses (Freight—Time) cl 2; the Institute War and Strikes Clauses (Freight—Voyage) cl 2. This clause has the effect of making the insurer liable either in accordance with the foreign adjustment or in accordance with an adjustment under the York-Antwerp Rules. The form of clause was framed on account of the decision in *De Hart v CA de Seguros Aurora* [1903] 2 KB 503, CA. As to the position where the contract contains no special terms as to foreign adjustment (or, under the standard clause, is deemed to contain no such terms), see *Harris v Scaramanga* (1872) LR 7 CP 481 at 495.

The Institute Time Clauses (Hulls) cl 11.3 and the Institute Voyage Clauses (Hulls) cl 9.3 (also as incorporated respectively by the Institute War and Strikes Clauses (Hulls—Time) cl 2 and the Institute War and Strikes Clauses (Hulls—Voyage) cl 2), also make special provision for the application of the York-Antwerp Rules 1974 (omitting rr XX and XXI) to ballast voyages not under charter. The York-Antwerp Rules 1974 are set out in Appendix 2, para 907 post.

254. On whom foreign adjustment is binding. The foreign adjustment, when made in accordance with the law of the foreign port, binds the assured as well as the insurer, and the assured cannot recover from the insurer, as particular average or otherwise, what the foreign statement has declared to be recoverable as general average by a contribution of the other interests. The assured is not at liberty to approbate and reprobate; he cannot take the benefit of the foreign law and claim general average in accordance with the foreign adjustment, and at the same time repudiate the foreign statement for the purpose of claiming particular average against his insurer. He is bound for all purposes by the foreign statement as to what expenses were incurred on behalf of ship and cargo[1].

1 *The Mary Thomas* [1894] P 108, CA; contrast *Green Star Shipping Co Ltd v London Assurance* [1933] 1 KB 378, where the clause was substantially in the form indicated in para 253 text to note 2 ante; it was held that the decision in *The Mary Thomas* supra was inapplicable since there was no express stipulation that payment was to be made according to the foreign adjustment. See, however, Arnould on Marine Insurance (16th Edn) s 1000, where it is suggested that the principle adopted in *De Hart v CA de Seguros Aurora* [1903] 2 KB 503, CA, that parties in effect agree to be bound by the foreign adjustment clause, should apply in the absence of reference to the York-Antwerp Rules.

(11) MEASURE OF LOSS FOR WHICH INSURERS ARE LIABLE

(i) Insurable Value

255. Insurable value. The insurable value of the subject matter insured[1] is relevant in determining the measure of indemnity in the case of an unvalued policy[2], and in the case of a valued policy[3] when the valuation is not conclusive[4] or has to be apportioned[5].

In policies on ship or goods it is generally assumed that the object of the insurance is to put the assured, in the event of loss, in the same position as he would have occupied if he had never embarked on the insured adventure; but this assumption cannot, from the nature of the case, apply to policies on profits, commissions, freight etc, nor to valued policies on ship or goods[6].

1 As to the subject matter insured see generally para 36 ante.
2 See the Marine Insurance Act 1906 ss 28, 68(2); and para 265 post. For the meaning of 'unvalued policy' see para 41 ante.
3 For the meaning of 'valued policy' see para 41 ante.
4 See the Marine Insurance Act 1906 ss 27, 29(4); and paras 41–42, 109 ante.
5 See ibid ss 71(1), 72; and para 270 post.
6 For observations on the amount recoverable under a policy on hull and machinery covering a prolongation of voyage under orders or directions of the government see *Union-Castle Mail SS Co Ltd v United Kingdom Mutual War Risks Association Ltd* [1958] 1 QB 380 at 402, [1958] 1 All ER 431 at 440 per Diplock J.

256. Rules for measuring insurable value. Subject to any express provision or valuation in the policy, the insurable value[1] of a ship is the value at the commencement of the risk[2] of the ship, including her outfit, provisions and stores for the officers and crew, money advanced for seamen's wages and other disbursements (if any) incurred to make the ship fit for the voyage or adventure contemplated by the policy, plus the charges of insurance upon the whole, and in the case of a steamship the insurable value includes also the machinery, boilers, and coals and engine stores if owned by the assured, and, in the case of a ship engaged in a special trade, the ordinary fittings requisite for that trade[3].

Subject also to any express provision or valuation in the policy:

(1) the insurable value of freight[4], whether paid in advance or otherwise, is the gross amount of the freight at the assured's risk, plus the charges of insurance[5];

(2) the insurable value of goods or merchandise is the prime cost of the property insured, plus the expenses of and incidental to shipping and the charges of insurance upon the whole[6]; and

(3) the insurable value of any other subject matter is the amount at the assured's risk when the policy attaches, plus the charges of insurance[7].

In all the rules for determining insurable value the charges of insurance are mentioned, and it is expressly provided that the assured has an insurable interest in the charges of any insurance he may effect[8].

1 The insurable value should be distinguished from the contributory value for the purposes of general average (see paras 250 note 1 ante, 280 post) and salvage (see para 280 post).
2 'At the commencement of the risk' probably means at the commencement of the risk at each stage of the voyage.

3 Marine Insurance Act 1906 s 16(1). Cf the definition of 'ship' in Sch 1 r 15 (see para 113 ante). As to what was deemed to be covered by the word 'ship' before the Act see *Roddick v Indemnity Mutual Marine Insurance Co* [1895] 2 QB 380 at 383, CA. As to outfit and ordinary fittings see also para 113 note 1 ante.

4 For the meaning of 'freight' when used to describe the subject matter of the policy see para 115 ante.

5 Marine Insurance Act 1906 s 16(2). This was the law before the Act: *Forbes v Aspinall* (1811) 13 East 323 at 326; *Palmer v Blackburn* (1822) 1 Bing 61. In *United States Shipping Co v Empress Assurance Corpn* [1907] 1 KB 259 (affd on appeal [1908] 1 KB 115, CA), Channell J held that a charterer who sublet the ship was entitled to recover the whole freight without deduction of the chartered freight which he would have had to pay to the shipowner.

6 Marine Insurance Act 1906 s 16(3); see *Berger and Light Diffusers Pty Ltd v Pollock* [1973] 2 Lloyd's Rep 442. 'Prime cost' means the prime cost to the assured at or about the time of shipment, or at any rate at some time when the prime cost can be reasonably deemed to represent the value of the goods to their owner at the date of shipment: *Williams v Atlantic Assurance Co Ltd* [1933] 1 KB 81 at 102, CA, per Greer LJ. As regards the invoice price of goods shipped from a foreign port and expressed in the currency of a foreign country see Arnould on Marine Insurance (16th Edn) s 449.

7 Marine Insurance Act 1906 s 16(4).

8 Ibid s 13. The mode in which these charges are insured is as follows: if the insurance premium, together with the insurance charges, amounts to R per cent, and if the possible loss amounts to a sum S, then the total amount required to be insured would be $\dfrac{S \times 100}{100 - R}$ (see Arnould on Marine Insurance (16th Edn) ss 445, 446).

(ii) Particular Average: Particular Charges: Salvage Charges

257. Particular average. A particular average loss is a partial loss of the subject matter insured[1], caused by a peril insured against[2], and which is not a general average loss[3]. Thus, if part of the goods is lost or if the ship is damaged by a peril insured against, that loss or damage, where not caused by a general average act so as to constitute a general average loss, is a particular average loss[4]. Expenses incurred by or on behalf of the assured for the safety or preservation of the subject matter insured, other than general average or salvage charges, are called 'particular charges', and are not included in particular average[5].

1 As to the subject matter insured see generally para 36 ante.

2 As to perils insured against see para 149 ante.

3 Marine Insurance Act 1906 s 64(1). As to general average losses see para 244 et seq ante.

4 In *Kidston v Empire Insurance Co* (1866) LR 1 CP 535 (on appeal (1867) LR 2 CP 357) it was found by a special jury that, in the business of marine insurance, particular average denotes actual damage done to or loss of part of the subject matter of the insurance, but that it does not include any expenses incurred in recovering or preserving the property insured, which were termed particular charges. Loss of a ship's earnings during detention is not a particular average loss under a policy on ship: *Polurrian SS Co Ltd v Young* (1913) 19 Com Cas 143; affd without dealing with this point [1915] 1 KB 922, CA.

5 Marine Insurance Act 1906 s 64(2). As to salvage charges and particular charges see para 258 post.

258. General average, salvage and particular charges distinguished. The distinction between general average, salvage and particular charges should be carefully noted. General average charges have already been dealt with[1]. 'Salvage charges' means the charges which are recoverable under maritime law by a salvor independently of contract[2]. The right to these is wholly dependent upon the success of the salvage operations[3]. Salvage charges do not include the expenses of services in the nature of salvage rendered by the assured or his agents, or any person employed for hire by them, for the purposes of averting a peril insured against; such expenses, where properly incurred, may be recovered as particular charges, or as a general average loss, according to the circumstances under which they were incurred[4]. Thus expenses incurred for the preservation or safety either of ship or cargo, or freight, and not of the whole property at risk, are particular charges, and are neither general average, nor particular average, nor salvage charges.

Subject to any express provision in the policy, salvage charges incurred in preventing a loss by perils insured against may be recovered as a loss by those perils[5], and are not recoverable under the suing and labouring clause[6]. Particular charges are, however, recoverable under that clause[7].

1 See para 244 et seq ante.
2 Marine Insurance Act 1906 s 65(2).
3 As to salvage see generally SHIPPING.
4 Marine Insurance Act 1906 s 65(2); *Aitchison v Lohre* (1879) 4 App Cas 755, HL. The distinction between maritime salvage which is independent of contract, and salvage services rendered under a contract, must often be one of great nicety, inasmuch as no one has a right to render salvage services to a ship against the master's will. See further Arnould on Marine Insurance (16th Edn) s 911.
5 Marine Insurance Act 1906 s 65(1); *Aitchison v Lohre* (1879) 4 App Cas 755, HL; *The Bosworth* [1962] 1 Lloyd's Rep 483 at 490. As to the conditions under which salvage remuneration is claimable, and as to the amount recoverable for it, see SHIPPING.
6 Marine Insurance Act 1906 s 78(2); see para 260 post
7 See para 260 post.

(iii) Suing and Labouring Clause

259. Suing and labouring clause. Where the policy contains a suing and labouring clause[1], the engagement thereby entered into is deemed to be supplementary to the contract of insurance, and the assured may recover from the insurer any expenses properly incurred[2] pursuant to the clause, notwithstanding that the insurer may have paid for a total loss, or that the subject matter may have been warranted free from particular average, either wholly or under a certain percentage[3].

The object of the suing and labouring clause is to encourage the assured, in case of accident, to take all necessary steps for the preservation of the property insured. For this purpose the insurers agree that any such action is to be without prejudice to the insurance or to the notice of abandonment in the case of a constructive total loss, and also to contribute to any expenditure incurred for the purpose of averting impending loss. It is because the clause is supplementary to and distinct from the contract contained in the policy that the assured can recover in respect of a total loss, not only the whole amount insured, but also in addition the expenses incurred under the clause[4].

1 The suing and labouring clause in the former Lloyd's Marine Policy was expressed in the terms set out in Appendix 1, and was followed by a waiver clause: see para 905 post.
   The suing and labouring clause is now referred to in the Institute Clauses as the 'duty of assured' clause. In relation to cargo, the waiver clause immediately follows it; in relation to hulls, the waiver clause is incorporated in the duty of assured clause. See the Institute Cargo Clauses (A) cl 16, 17; the Institute Cargo Clauses (B) cl 16, 17; the Institute Cargo Clauses (C) cl 16, 17; the Institute War Clauses (Cargo) cl 11, 12; the Institute Strikes Clauses (Cargo) cl 11, 12; the Institute Time Clauses (Hulls) cl 13; the Institute Voyage Clauses (Hulls) cl 11; the Institute War and Strikes Clauses (Hulls—Time) cl 2; the Institute War and Strikes Clauses (Hulls—Voyage) cl 2.
   As to the forms of marine policy and the Institute Clauses generally see paras 44, 149 note 1 ante.
2 Whether the expenses have been properly incurred is a matter of fact: see eg *The Pomeranian* [1895] P 349; *Wilson Bros Bobbin Co Ltd v Green* [1917] 1 KB 860; *St Margaret's Trust Ltd v Navigators and General Insurance Co Ltd* (1949) 82 Ll L Rep 752; *Integrated Container Service Inc v British Traders Insurance Co Ltd* [1984] 1 Lloyd's Rep 154, CA.

3 Marine Insurance Act 1906 s 78(1). The decision in *Emperor Goldmining Co Ltd v Switzerland General Insurance Co Ltd* [1964] 1 Lloyd's Rep 348, NSW SC, to the effect that, where there is no suing and labouring clause in the policy, particular charges incurred by the assured in preserving the subject matter insured are recoverable, would appear not to be in accordance with principle for, if it is correct, no suing and labouring clause need ever be inserted in a policy.

4 See the Marine Insurance Act 1906 s 78(1); *Lohre v Aitchison* (1878) 3 QBD 558 at 567, CA, per Brett LJ; and in the judgment in the same case in the House of Lords sub nom *Aitchison v Lohre* (1879) 4 App Cas 755 at 763, HL, per Lord Blackburn. The suing and labouring clause does not cover the costs incurred by the assured in successfully defending an action brought against him to recover a loss in respect of which the underwriters would have been liable under the 'running down clause' (now the Institute collision clauses, as to the form of which see Appendix 3, para 908 post): *Xenos v Fox* (1869) LR 4 CP 665, Ex Ch. Nor does the suing and labouring clause apply to an insurance effected by a carrier of goods, not on the cargo itself, but in order to protect himself from liabilities which he might incur as carrier: *Cunard SS Co v Marten* [1903] 2 KB 511, CA.

260. Charges covered by the suing and labouring clause. The suing and labouring clause covers particular charges[1] and not a general average loss[2], because by its very terms it is confined to expenses incurred for the safety and preservation of the particular property insured, and does not comprise expenses incurred for the purpose of averting or diminishing any loss not covered by the policy[3]. It does not cover maritime salvage charges, because maritime salvage services, as distinguished from services in the nature of salvage rendered under an agreement, are not rendered by the assured, his factors, employees and assigns[4]. Maritime salvage charges, therefore, are recoverable only under the head of a loss by a peril insured against, and cannot be recovered in addition to the sum insured[5].

1 As to particular charges see para 258 ante.
2 As to general average loss see para 244 et seq ante.
3 See the Marine Insurance Act 1906 s 78(2), (3). See eg *Weissberg v Lamb* (1950) 84 Ll L Rep 509; *F W Berk & Co Ltd v Style* [1956] 1 QB 180, [1955] 3 All ER 625.
4 This form of words is taken from the original suing and labouring clause: see para 905 post.
5 See the Marine Insurance Act 1906 s 78(2). See the judgment of Lord Blackburn in *Aitchison v Lohre* (1879) 4 App Cas 755; see also *Dixon v Whitworth, Dixon v Sea Insurance Co* (1879) 4 CPD 371, CA. As to salvage charges see para 258 ante.

261. Assured's duty to minimise loss. The provision in the original suing and labouring clause was of a permissive character[1], but it is and has long been the duty of the assured and his agents[2], in all cases, to take such measures as may be reasonable for the purpose of averting or minimising a loss[3]. Whether the assured has taken reasonable measures is a question of fact[4].

1 See para 259 text and note 1 ante.
2 'His agents' should be read as inapplicable to the master or crew unless expressly instructed by the assured in relation to what to do or not to do in respect of suing and labouring; many persons other than the master or members of the crew may be agents of the assured with the duty to act on his behalf in relation to suing and labouring. A possible exception exists in the case of a master/owner: negligent navigation by such an assured will not bar his claim under the Marine Insurance Act 1906 s 55(2)(a) (as to which see para 167 ante), but s 78(4) seems to impose the statutory duty on him: *Astrovlanis Companie Naviera SA v Linard, The Gold Sky* [1972] 2 Lloyd's Rep 187 at 221 per Mocatta J. See also note 3 infra.
3 Marine Insurance Act 1906 s 78(4). This provision is couched in substantially the same terms as the Institute Clauses relating to the duty of the assured (as to which see para 259 note 1 ante). The effect of this subsection is not clear. It seems to be taken from a dictum in the judgment in *Currie & Co v Bombay Native Insurance Co* (1869) LR 3 PC 72 at 81, 84. In *Kidston v Empire Marine Insurance Co* (1867) LR 2 CP 357 at 365, Ex Ch, Kelly CB said that although it would not be an unreasonable rule that if the owner of freight fails to earn it by his own default he should be disentitled to recover it as

against the insurer, this had never been held to be law in this country. In *Gaunt v British and Foreign Insurance Co Ltd* [1920] 1 KB 903, CA, it was contended that the effect of the Marine Insurance Act 1906 s 78(4), was that the assured could not recover for a loss which might have been prevented by due care on the part of his employees. This contention was rejected by the court, Atkin LJ saying at 917 that the Marine Insurance Act 1906 s 78(4), did not modify s 55(2)(a), and the effect of the latter subsection was that the insurers were liable for loss caused by the negligence of the assured or his employees unless the acts complained of amounted to wilful misconduct of the assured, and that the only effect of s 78(4) was to impose a duty to sue and labour — 'a very restricted duty compared with the general obligation contended for'. See also the report of that case on appeal sub nom *British and Foreign Marine Insurance Co Ltd v Gaunt* [1921] 2 AC 41 at 65, HL, per Lord Sumner, and *Lind v Mitchell* (1928) 98 LJKB 120 at 124, CA, per Scrutton LJ; and see para 179 note 5 ante. The clause does not apply where the expenses were caused by the condition of the goods at the time of shipment: *F W Berk & Co Ltd v Style* [1956] 1 QB 180, [1955] 3 All ER 625. It seems clear that the insurer cannot recover, where there is a suing and labouring clause, expenses which he has incurred in saving or protecting the property: *Crouan v Stanier* [1904] 1 KB 87. Insurers on freight are not liable under the suing and labouring clause for any part of the cost of salving a vessel where there is no prospect of preserving the insured freight by salving the vessel: *Carras v London and Scottish Insurance Corpn Ltd* (1935) 52 Ll L Rep 34; revsd on other grounds [1936] 1 KB 291, CA. Special provisions of the policy may negative the effect of a suing and labouring clause: *Berns and Koppstein Inc v Orion Insurance Co Ltd and Stone* [1960] 1 Lloyd's Rep 276, Dist Ct NY.

4 See eg *Irvine v Hine* [1950] 1 KB 555, [1949] 2 All ER 1089; *Astrovlanis Companie Naviera SA v Linard, The Gold Sky* [1972] 2 Lloyd's Rep 187; *Netherlands Insurance Co Est 1845 Ltd v Karl Ljunberg & Co AB* [1986] 3 All ER 767, [1986] 2 Lloyd's Rep 19, PC.

262. When the suing and labouring clause applies. The occasion upon which the suing and labouring clause comes into force is the happening of any loss or misfortune covered by the policy; if it is not covered by the policy, the clause has no operation. For instance, if a ship insured free of capture is in danger of being taken by an enemy, and the assured or his employees take steps to prevent the capture, this will not fall within the terms of the clause, and no charges incurred for this purpose will be recoverable. Similarly, if the policy is one against total loss only, and there is danger, not of a total loss, but only of a partial loss, the expenses incurred to prevent that partial loss are not recoverable under the clause[1]. If, however, goods are insured free of average, or free of average under a certain percentage, and there is a danger of a total loss or a loss exceeding the percentage which is averted by the action of the assured or his employees so that the resulting loss is not covered by the policy, the expenses so incurred to avert the loss may be recovered under the suing and labouring clause, even though the actual loss cannot be claimed[2].

1 *Great Indian Peninsula Rly Co v Saunders* (1862) 2 B & S 266, Ex Ch; *Booth v Gair* (1863) 15 CBNS 291. In the latter case the court proceeded, whether rightly or wrongly, on the ground that there was no risk of a total loss to the goods. Contrast *Wilson Bros Bobbin Co Ltd v Green* [1917] 1 KB 860.
2 See the Marine Insurance Act 1906 s 78(1), and para 259 ante; *Kidston v Empire Marine Insurance Co* (1866) LR 1 CP 535 at 542–544 per Willes J; affd (1867) LR 2 CP 357, Ex Ch; approved *Meyer v Ralli* (1876) 1 CPD 358.

(iv) Particular Average Warranties

263. Particular average warranties. Where the subject matter insured is warranted free from particular average[1], the assured cannot recover for a loss of part, other than a loss incurred by a general average sacrifice[2], unless the contract contained in the policy is apportionable; but, if the contract is apportionable, the assured may recover for a total loss of any apportionable part[3].

Where the subject matter is warranted free from particular average, either wholly or under a certain percentage, the insurer is nevertheless liable for salvage charges and for particular charges[4] and other expenses properly incurred pursuant to the provisions of the suing and labouring clause[5] in order to avert a loss insured against[6].

Unless the policy otherwise provides, where the subject matter insured is warranted free from particular average under a specified percentage, a general average loss may not be added to a particular average loss to make up the specified percentage[7]. For the purpose of ascertaining whether the specified percentage has been reached, regard must be had only to the actual loss suffered by the subject matter insured; particular charges and the expenses of and incidental to ascertaining and proving the loss must be excluded[8].

1 As to particular average see paras 257–258 ante. The former Lloyd's Marine Policy contained a memorandum (known as the common memorandum) to be added where the subject matter insured was one of certain types of perishable goods: see Appendix 1, para 905 post. The modern Institute Clauses do not contain this provision, so the Marine Insurance Act 1906 s 76, the provisions of which are described below, is now of little relevance. For a discussion of 'free from particular average' clauses see Arnould on Marine Insurance (16th Edn) ss 853–854.
2 As to general average sacrifice see para 244 et seq ante.
3 Marine Insurance Act 1906 s 76(1).
4 As to salvage charges and particular charges see para 258 ante.
5 As to the suing and labouring clause see paras 257, 259–262 ante.
6 Marine Insurance Act 1906 s 76(2).
7 Ibid s 76(3).
8 Ibid s 76(4); *Rohl v Parr* (1796) 1 Esp 445.

(v) Measure of Indemnity

264. Effect of under-insurance. Where the assured[1] is insured for an amount less than the insurable value, or in the case of a valued policy[2] for an amount less than the policy valuation, he is deemed to be his own insurer in respect of the uninsured balance[3]. He then bears such part of the loss as is proportional to the uninsured balance, and in case of a total loss is entitled to the same proportion of the salvage[4]. For this reason it is convenient to consider him as his own insurer, liable to pay to himself a sum proportional to the uninsured balance, for by so doing it may be laid down as a general proposition that each insurer is liable for the loss in proportion to the amount underwritten by himself[5].

1 As to the assured see para 35 note 1 ante.
2 For the meaning of 'valued policy' see para 41 ante.
3 Marine Insurance Act 1906 s 81. Where 'captain's effects' were insured under an unvalued policy against total loss of vessel only, and part of the effects were on shore at the time of the loss, it was held that this part must be included in arriving at the insurable value of the goods: *Anstey v Ocean Marine Insurance Co Ltd* (1913) 83 LJKB 218.
4 *The Welsh Girl* (1906) 22 TLR 475; affd sub nom *The Commonwealth* [1907] P 216, CA.
5 See further Arnould on Marine Insurance (16th Edn) s 1292.

265. Measure of indemnity. The sum which the assured[1] can recover in respect of a loss on a policy by which he is insured, in the case of an unvalued policy[2] to the full extent of the insurable value[3], or, in the case of a valued policy[4] to the full extent of the value fixed by the policy, is called the measure of indemnity[5]. Where there is a loss recoverable under the policy, the insurer, or each insurer if there is more than one, is liable for such proportion of the measure of indemnity as the amount of his subscription bears to the value fixed by the policy in the case of a valued policy, or to the insurable value in the case of an unvalued policy[6].

Nothing in the provisions of the Marine Insurance Act 1906 relating to the measure of indemnity[7] affects the rules relating to double insurance[8], or prohibits the insurer from disproving interest wholly or in part, or from showing that at the time of the loss the whole or any part of the subject matter insured was not at risk under the policy[9].

1 As to the assured see para 35 note 1 ante.
2 For the meaning of 'unvalued policy' see para 41 ante.
3 As to the insurable value see paras 255–266 ante.
4 For the meaning of 'valued policy' see para 41 ante.
5 Marine Insurance Act 1906 s 67(1). Sections 67 and 68 (see para 266 post) are definitive of an insurer's liability, and an assured is not entitled to any additional special or general damages: *Ventouris v Mountain, The Italia Express (No 2)* [1992] 2 Lloyd's Rep 281 at 291 per Hirst J.
6 Marine Insurance Act 1906 s 67(2). This may be illustrated as follows: if M is the measure of indemnity, ie the amount of any loss recoverable under a policy in which the assured is fully insured, S the amount subscribed by any one underwriter, and V the value fixed by the policy in the case of a valued policy, or the insurable value in the case of an unvalued policy, then the underwriter is liable for $\dfrac{S}{V} \times M$.

7 Ie in ibid ss 67–74: see paras 266–280 post.
8 As to the rules relating to double insurance see ibid s 32; para 319–321 post.
9 Ibid s 75(1).

266. Total loss. In general, where there is a total loss of the subject matter insured, in the case of a valued policy[1] the measure of indemnity[2] is the sum fixed by the policy, and in the case of an unvalued policy[3] the measure of indemnity is the insurable value[4] of the subject matter insured[5].

1 For the meaning of 'valued policy' see para 41 ante.
2 As to the measure of indemnity see para 265 ante.
3 For the meaning of 'unvalued policy' see para 41 ante.
4 As to the insurable value see paras 255–256 ante.
5 Marine Insurance Act 1906 s 68, which is expressed to be subject to the provisions of that Act and to any express provision in the policy. In *Woodside v Globe Marine Insurance Co* [1896] 1 QB 105, the rule was applied, even though, when the peril insured against occurred, the ship was already a constructive total loss. See also *Lidgett v Secretan* (1871) LR 6 CP 616; *Barker v Janson* (1868) LR 3 CP 303; *Berger and Light Diffusers Pty Ltd v Pollock* [1973] 2 Lloyd's Rep 442 (where the indemnity recovered in the case of an unvalued policy was reduced by the amount recovered under the Carriage of Goods by Sea Act 1924 (repealed) s 1, Schedule art IV para 5 (see now the Hague Rules, scheduled to the Carriage of Goods by Sea Act 1971; see further SHIPPING), from the owners of the vessel carrying the insured cargo). Sections 67 and 68 (see para 265 ante) is definitive of an insurer's liability, and an assured is not entitled to any additional special or general damages; consequently, where there is a total loss of a vessel, the assured is not entitled to claim damages for loss of income, the increase in capital value of a replacement vessel, hardship, inconvenience and mental distress: *Ventouris v Mountain, The Italia Express (No 2)* [1992] 2 Lloyd's Rep 281 at 291 per Hirst J.

267. Total loss of part of cargo. Where part of the goods, merchandise or other movables insured by a valued policy[1] is totally lost, then, subject to any express provision of the policy, the measure of indemnity[2] is such proportion of the sum fixed by the policy as the insurable value[3] of the part lost bears to the insurable value of the whole, ascertained as in the case of an unvalued policy[4]. Where, however, several different articles are insured together in the same policy and each sustains damage, the loss must be adjusted separately on each, even though the clause 'to pay average on each species if separately insured' is not inserted in the policy[5].

Where there is a total loss of part of the goods insured under an unvalued policy, the measure of indemnity, subject to any express provision of the policy, is the insurable value of the part lost, ascertained as in the case of total loss[6].

Where out of a number of packages of goods insured only a few articles or pieces in each package arrive damaged, the sound and damaged goods are frequently sold together at the same auction; but in that case the diminished value at which the sound part of the package may be sold, owing to the assortment being broken, is not a loss for which the underwriter is liable[7], nor is he liable for the cost of examining such goods as prove to be undamaged[8].

1 For the meaning of 'valued policy' see para 41 ante.
2 As to the measure of indemnity see para 265 ante.
3 As to the insurable value of goods see paras 255–256 ante.
4 Marine Insurance Act 1906 s 71(1); *Lewis v Rucker* (1761) 2 Burr 1167. For the meaning of 'unvalued policy' see para 41 ante.
5 Benecke's Principles of Indemnity in Marine Insurance 441.
6 Marine Insurance Act 1906 s 71(2).
7 *Cator v Great West Insurance Co of New York* (1873) LR 8 CP 552; *J Lysaght Ltd v Coleman* [1895] 1 QB 49, CA; *Brown Bros v Fleming* (1902) 7 Com Cas 245. As to the charges, such as brokerage and commission, incurred in the sale by auction of the damaged goods see Stevens's Essay on Average in Marine Insurance 148–150; Benecke's Principles of Indemnity in Marine Insurance 436.
8 *J Lysaght Ltd v Coleman* [1895] 1 QB 49, CA.

268. Damage to part of cargo. If the insured goods or some of them arrive damaged, then, as they can seldom be repaired and are always intended to be sold (differing in this respect from the ship)[1], the first thing to be ascertained is the extent of the depreciation caused by the damage. This is done by comparing the price for which the goods would have been sold, had they arrived sound, with the price for which they actually are sold in their damaged condition. Where the goods are sold by public auction, the gross amount they realise is called the 'damaged value', and the value they would have sold for if sound, that is to say the current price for sound articles of the same kind in the same market, is called the 'sound value'. The difference between the damaged and the sound values, calculated in the manner described, determines the depreciation of the goods caused by the damage, and is entirely independent of the rise or fall of the market value of the goods[2]. The gross value is generally the wholesale price or, if there is no such price, the estimated value, calculated (in either case) on the assumption that freight, landing charges and duty have been paid beforehand; but where the goods or merchandise are such as are customarily sold in bond, the bonded price is deemed to be the gross value[3].

The extent of depreciation, measured by the proportion which the difference between the gross sound and damaged values at the place of arrival bears to the gross sound value, may be conveniently called the percentage of loss[4]. It is this percentage of loss of the sum fixed by the policy in the case of a valued policy, or of the insurable value in the case of an unvalued policy, which is, subject to any express provision in the policy, the measure of indemnity, or, in other words, the total amount for which all the insurers, including the assured himself if he is not fully insured[5], are liable[6].

1 See *Lohre v Aitchison* (1877) 2 QBD 501 at 507 per Lush J; on appeal sub nom *Aitchison v Lohre* (1879) 4 App Cas 755 at 762, HL, per Lord Blackburn.

2 See the Marine Insurance Act 1906 s 71(3); *Lewis v Rucker* (1761) 2 Burr 1167; *Johnson v Sheddon* (1802) 2 East 581. Where damaged goods prior to sale are necessarily reconditioned, it is the value of the reconditioned goods, and not that of the goods less the cost of reconditioning, that is to be compared with the sound value in order to ascertain the proportion of loss, for the cost of reconditioning is recoverable under the suing and labouring clause: *Francis v Boulton* (1895) 65 LJQB 153. As to the suing and labouring clause see para 259 ante.

3 See the Marine Insurance Act 1906 s 71(4). 'Gross proceeds' means the actual price obtained at a sale where all charges on sale are paid by the sellers: s 71(4).

4 See ibid s 71(3).

5 As to under-insurance see para 264 ante.

6 See the Marine Insurance Act 1906 s 71(3); and para 265 ante. It may be readily shown that, whether the policy is a valued or an unvalued one, the insurer is liable to pay in respect of goods arriving in a damaged condition the same percentage of the amount actually subscribed by him. Thus, if the agreed value is V, the amount subscribed by the underwriter S, and the percentage of loss R, then the measure of indemnity is $\dfrac{R}{100} \times V$, and the underwriter is liable for $\dfrac{R}{100} V \times \dfrac{S}{V}$ or $\dfrac{R}{100} \times S$. Cf *Irvine v Hine* [1950] 1 KB 555, [1949] 2 All ER 1089, cited in para 271 note 7 post.

269. Goods sold at a port of distress.
It sometimes happens that goods are sold at a port of distress because they are found to be so damaged as not to be fit for reloading. In that case the claim is adjusted as a salvage loss, that is to say, the insurers pay the difference between the insurable or agreed value of the goods and the net proceeds of the sale[1].

1 Stevens's Essay on Average in Marine Insurance 81; Benecke's Principles of Indemnity in Marine Insurance 444.

270. Apportionment of valuation.
Where different species of property are insured under a single valuation, the valuation must be apportioned over the different species in proportion to their respective insurable values[1], as in the case of an unvalued policy[2]. The insured value of any part of a species is such proportion of the total insured value of the same as the insurable value of the part bears to the insurable value of the whole, ascertained in both cases as provided by the Marine Insurance Act 1906[3].

Where a valuation has to be apportioned, and particulars of the prime cost of each separate species, quality or description of goods cannot be ascertained, the division of the valuation may be made over the net arrived sound values of the different species, qualities or descriptions of goods[4].

1 As to insurable value see paras 255–256 ante.

2 Marine Insurance Act 1906 s 72(1). For the meaning of 'unvalued policy' see para 41 ante.

3 Ibid s 72(1).

4 Ibid s 72(2). For the meaning of 'sound value' see para 268 ante.

271. Partial loss of ship.
Where a ship[1] is damaged, but is not totally lost, the measure of indemnity[2], subject to any express provision in the policy, is as follows:

(1) where the ship has been repaired, the assured is entitled to the reasonable cost of the repairs[3], less the customary deductions[4], but not exceeding the sum insured in respect of any one casualty[5];

(2) where the ship has been only partially repaired, the assured is entitled to the reasonable cost of the repairs, computed as above, and also to be indemnified for the reasonable depreciation, if any, arising from the unrepaired damage, provided that the aggregate amount does not exceed the cost of repairing the whole damage, computed as above[6];

(3) where the ship has not been repaired, and has not been sold in her damaged state during the risk[7], the assured is entitled to be indemnified for the reasonable depreciation[8] arising from the unrepaired damage, but not exceeding the reasonable cost of repairing that damage[9], computed as above[10].

1 In the Marine Insurance Act 1906 'ship' includes hovercraft: see para 113 ante.
2 As to the measure of indemnity see para 265 ante.
3 As to the nature of the repairs which the assured is entitled to require see para 276 post. Reasonable fees for classification surveyors and other surveyors are allowable as the cost of repairs *(Agenoria SS Co Ltd v Merchants Marine Insurance Co Ltd* (1903) 8 Com Cas 212; *The Medina Princess* [1965] 1 Lloyd's Rep 361 at 523) but not crew's wages *(Robertson v Ewer* (1786) 1 Term Rep 127; *De Vaux v Salvador* (1836) 4 Ad & El 420; *The Medina Princess* supra at 523).
4 As to the customary deductions see para 273 post.
5 Marine Insurance Act 1906 s 69(1).
6 Ibid s 69(2).
7 In the case of a voyage policy (see para 41 ante) the risk terminates when the insured vessel is abandoned by the assured in circumstances and in language which make it clear that he does not intend to pursue the voyage to its destination: *Irvin v Hine* [1950] 1 KB 555 at 571, [1949] 2 All ER 1089 at 1092. In the case of a time policy (see para 41 ante) the risk terminates when the policy expires: *The Medina Princess* [1965] 1 Lloyd's Rep 361 at 516. As to the position where the ship is sold unrepaired see para 272 post.
8 The correct method of calculating depreciation for the purposes of this rule has not yet been decided. Possible tests are:
  (1) the difference between the conventional value and the true damaged value, and
  (2) the figure resulting from the application to the conventional value of the proportion of actual depreciation.
  See *Irvin v Hine* [1950] 1 KB 555, [1949] 2 All ER 1089, in which the point was left open. The second method is similar to that prescribed for the case of damaged goods (see the Marine Insurance Act 1906 s 71(3); and para 268 ante) and was applied in *The Armar* [1954] 2 Lloyd's Rep 95, NY SC. Cf *Elcock v Thomson* [1949] 2 KB 755, [1949] 2 All ER 381 (fire insurance).
9 Where it would not have been possible to repair the ship before a certain date, the cost of repairs, for the purposes of this rule, is the figure appropriate to that date: *Irvin v Hine* [1950] 1 KB 555, [1949] 2 All ER 1089.
10 Marine Insurance Act 1906 s 69(3). See also para 272 post.

272. Ship sold unrepaired. The third of the statutory rules as to the measure of indemnity in the case of the partial loss of a ship[1] deals only with the case where the ship has not been repaired and has not been sold in her damaged state during the risk. Where, after sustaining an average loss, the ship is sold by her owner unrepaired, he is entitled to recover the estimated cost of the repairs less the usual deduction[2], not exceeding the depreciation in the vessel's value[3].

1 Ie the Marine Insurance Act 1906 s 69(3): see para 271 text to notes 7–10 ante. As to the measure of indemnity see para 265 ante.
2 As to the customary deductions see para 273 post.
3 This was decided by a majority in *Pitman v Universal Marine Insurance Co* (1882) 9 QBD 192, CA (Brett LJ dissenting, being of opinion that the estimated cost of repairs was in all cases the measure of the loss). See also *Bristol Steam Navigation Co Ltd v Indemnity Mutual Marine Insurance Co* (1887) 6 Asp MLC 173, DC. See further Arnould on Marine Insurance (16th Edn) s 1131.

273. Deducting one-third new for old. It is customary to deduct one-third from the whole expense, both of labour and materials which the repairs have cost, unless the ship is a new ship. This deduction is termed 'deducting one-third new for old', and is made because the repairs will generally make the ship a better and more valuable vessel than she was before she was damaged[1]. This rule, however, is subject to certain exceptions and modifications which are sometimes expressed in clauses contained in the policy, or by reference to the York-Antwerp Rules 1974[2], and in modern policies on hulls it is excluded altogether[3].

The deduction is not made in the case of a new ship on her first voyage, but whether the vessel is or is not on her first voyage is a question of fact. If any general principle at all can be laid down, it is that she is on her first voyage at the time of the damage if the damage takes place at any part of what may be considered an integral voyage out and home at the commencement of which she was a new ship, taking into account the charterparty, the policy and all the facts of the case[4].

Again, if an old ship is newly repaired immediately before sailing on the voyage on which the loss takes place, and the loss falls exclusively on the new materials, the deduction of one-third new for old seems not to apply[5]. It is otherwise if the damage can only be proved to fall chiefly on the new part[6].

Where old materials are thrown aside in making the repairs, the practice in England is first to deduct the third, and then to deduct the value of the old materials, and this seems on principle to be the correct rule[7]. It is also the English practice to make the same deduction for any increased expenditure which may be incurred in raising funds for the repairs, such as the marine interest on a bottomry bond, but this practice seems inconsistent with principle, inasmuch as the interest has not any effect in enhancing the ship's value[8].

1 As to the operation of this rule see *Aitchison v Lohre* (1879) 4 App Cas 755 at 762, HL, per Lord Blackburn.
2 As to the York-Antwerp Rules 1974 see paras 53, 250 note 1 ante; and Appendix 2, para 907 post.
3 See the Institute Time Clauses (Hulls) cl 14; the Institute Voyage Clauses (Hulls) cl 12; the Institute War and Strikes Clauses (Hulls—Time) cl 2; and the Institute War and Strikes Clauses (Hulls—Voyage) cl 14. As to the Institute Clauses generally see para 149 note 1 ante.
4 *Fenwick v Robinson* (1828) 3 C & P 323; *Pirie v Steele* (1837) 8 C & P 200.
5 Stevens's Essay on Average in Marine Insurance 172.
6 *Poingdestre v Royal Exchange Assurance Corpn* (1826) Ry & M 378. The deduction 'one-third new for old' will not be made in certain cases where the assured by no fault of his own, by reason of the ship never coming into his possession again, never derives any benefit from the repairs: *Da Costa v Newnham* (1788) 2 Term Rep 407 (default of insurers); cf *Humphreys v Union Insurance Co* (1824) 3 Mason 429 (American) (shipowner in default).
7 Arnould on Marine Insurance (16th Edn) s 1119.
8 Arnould on Marine Insurance (16th Edn) s 1119; cf *Rosetto v Gurney* (1851) 11 CB 176.

274. Expenses of removal. It is sometimes reasonably necessary to remove a vessel from a port of distress to another port for the purpose of repairing her. In such a case the expenses incurred in and about the removal are in practice made payable by the insurers, and this practice seems right, inasmuch as these expenses being necessary in order to repair the vessel may be properly considered as part of the cost of repairs[1].

1 See the Rules of Practice of the Association of Average Adjusters, r D1; set out in Ivamy's Marine Insurance (4th Edn) 576, App V.

275. Expenses of docking for repairs. In cases where repairs of damage for which the insurers are liable and repairs the cost of which has to be borne by the owners (such as wear and tear) are executed simultaneously, the question arises whether the insurer is or is not liable for the whole of the expenses which would have been necessary for repairing the damage.

In general, the insurers are liable for all expenses incurred as a result of the operation of perils insured against and are not entitled to make any deduction on the ground that the shipowner has availed himself of the ship being in dock as a convenient opportunity for doing repairs or other work for which the insurers are not liable. Thus, where during the voyage insured a vessel is damaged by a peril insured against, and is put into dry dock for necessary repairs, and the owners, without causing delay or increased dock expenses, take advantage of her being in dry dock to have the survey made for renewing her classification, the expenses of getting her into and out of dock, as well as the necessary expenses incurred in having the use of the dock, will fall on the insurers alone, and will not be apportioned between them and the owners[1]. If, however, part of the expenditure would have been necessary in any event as a result of matters in respect of which the assured is not insured under the policy, the insurers can, it seems, make a deduction[2]. Dry docking dues are part of the reasonable cost of repairs[3].

1 *Ruabon SS Co v London Assurance* [1900] AC 6, HL. Rules of Practice of the Association of Average Adjusters, r D5; set out in Ivamy's Marine Insurance (4th Edn) 577, App V.
2 *Marine Insurance Co v China Transpacific SS Co (Vancouver Case)* (1886) 11 App Cas 573, HL; see also *Ruabon SS Co v London Assurance* [1900] AC 6 at 16, HL. See, however, *The Carslogie* [1952] AC 292, [1952] 1 All ER 20, HL (a collision action).
3 *The Medina Princess* [1965] 1 Lloyd's Rep 361 at 523.

276. Nature of repairs. As regards the repairs themselves, the assured is entitled to have his ship repaired with materials and workmanship corresponding to the original work, and if the repairs are done in such a manner that the ship is a less valuable ship than she was originally, the assured is entitled to claim, in addition to the cost of repairs, compensation for the diminution of the ship's value[1].

1 *Agenoria SS Co v Merchants Marine Insurance Co* (1903) 8 Com Cas 212 at 217. See the Marine Insurance Act 1906 s 69(2): para 271 ante.

277. Successive losses. Unless the policy otherwise provides, and subject to the provisions of the Marine Insurance Act 1906, the insurer is liable for successive losses, even though the total amount of those losses may exceed the sum insured[1]. Thus, if a ship is actually repaired during the currency of the policy and is afterwards, but before the expiration of the policy, totally lost before arriving at her port of destination on the insured voyage, the cost of the repairs may be recovered in addition to the total loss[2]. As an exception to this rule, where, under the same policy, a partial loss which has not been repaired or otherwise made good is followed by a total loss, the assured can only recover in respect of the total loss[3], the particular average loss being merged in the subsequent total loss. It follows that it is only at the moment of the expiration of the policy that the insurer's liability for a partial loss is definitely determined[4]. Thus, if a ship warranted free from capture sustains an average loss and is then captured before any repairs are done, the insurer would not be liable at all under the policy; he would not be liable for the average loss, because it is merged in the total loss, nor for the total loss by capture, because the insurance was warranted free of capture[5].

This doctrine of merger applies only to a case where the partial and total loss both occur during the currency of the same policy[6].

Claims under the suing and labouring clause[7] are not affected by the fact that the insurer has paid other claims on successive losses up to or exceeding the sum insured[8].

1 Marine Insurance Act 1906 s 77(1).
2 This rule, however, does not apply to repairs which the owner has not paid for, and for which he does not remain liable, eg when their cost has been defrayed with money raised on bottomry: *The Dora Forster* [1900] P 241.
3 Marine Insurance Act 1906 s 77(2).
4 *Knight v Faith* (1850) 15 QB 649 at 668 per Lord Campbell CJ.
5 *Livie v Janson* (1810) 12 East 648.
6 Thus, suppose a ship is insured by two policies, one 'at and from London to Calcutta and for 30 days after arrival', and the other a valued policy 'at and from Calcutta to England'. During the currency of the first policy she sustains serious damage and is kept afloat only by continual pumping until she arrives at Calcutta, where she is placed in dry dock for repairs. After part of the repairs have been carried out and after the expiration of the first policy she is totally destroyed by fire when in dry dock. In these circumstances the assured would be entitled to recover under the first policy the full amount of the partial loss repaired or unrepaired, and under the second valued policy he would be entitled to recover the full amount insured as for a total loss: *Lidgett v Secretan* (1871) LR 6 CP 616. Cf *Barker v Janson* (1868) LR 3 CP 303; *Woodside v Globe Marine Insurance Co* [1896] 1 QB 105. Contrast *British and Foreign Insurance Co Ltd v Wilson Shipping Co Ltd* [1921] 1 AC 188, HL (ship damaged by marine risks and, while unrepaired, totally lost by war risks: partial loss merged in total loss).
7 As to the suing and labouring clause see paras 259–262 ante.
8 Marine Insurance Act 1906 s 77(2) proviso.

278. Partial loss of freight. Subject to any express provision in the policy, where there is a partial loss of freight[1], the measure of indemnity[2] is such proportion of the sum fixed by the policy in the case of a valued policy[3], or of the insurable value in the case of an unvalued policy[4], as the proportion of freight lost by the assured bears to the whole freight at the assured's risk under the policy[5]. Although it is only the net freight that is really lost by the assured, the insurable value is the gross freight at risk, plus the charges of insurance[6].

Freight is generally insured in valued policies, and in such case, where only part of the full cargo to which the valuation was intended to apply was on board or contracted for at the time of the loss, the insurer is liable only to pay on such proportion of the amount insured as the part of the cargo on board, or contracted for, bears to the full intended cargo[7]. Where the policy on freight is an unvalued policy, and only part of the cargo is on board or contracted for at the time of the loss, and that part is totally lost, the insurer is liable to pay only the actual amount of freight which would have been earned by the carriage of that part, together with premiums and cost of insurance[8].

1 For the meaning of 'freight' see para 115 ante.
2 As to the measure of indemnity see para 265 ante.
3 For the meaning of 'valued policy' see para 41 ante.
4 For the meaning of 'unvalued policy' see para 41 ante.
5 Marine Insurance Act 1906 s 70.
6 Ibid s 16(2); and see para 256 ante. This rule was first established by evidence of usage: see *Palmer v Blackburn* (1822) 1 Bing 61; *United States Shipping Co v Empress Assurance Corpn* [1907] 1 KB 259; affd without deciding any question of law [1908] 1 KB 115, CA.
7 *Forbes v Aspinall* (1811) 13 East 323; *Denoon v Home and Colonial Assurance Co* (1872) LR 7 CP 341; *The Main* [1894] P 320; cf *Tobin v Harford* (1864) 17 CBNS 528, Ex Ch (policy on cargo).
8 *Forbes v Cowie* (1808) 1 Camp 520; *Forbes v Aspinall* (1811) 13 East 323 at 326 per Lord Ellenborough CJ. As to commencement of risk on freight see further paras 137–139 ante.

279. Third party liability. Where the assured has effected an insurance in express terms against any liability to a third party, the measure of indemnity[1], subject to any express provision in the policy, is the amount paid or payable by him to the third party in respect of that liability[2].

As already mentioned, a carrier of goods has, as a bailee, an insurable interest in the goods themselves, but he may also expressly insure against the liability he may incur to the owner for loss[3].

1 As to the measure of indemnity see para 265 ante.
2 Marine Insurance Act 1906 s 74.
3 See para 189 ante. As to whether an insurance by a carrier is an insurance on the goods or an insurance against liability to their owners see *Cunard SS Co Ltd v Marten* [1903] 2 KB 511, CA. As to the construction of clauses effected in policies by carriers in respect of goods carried by them see *Crowley v Cohen* (1832) 3 B & Ad 478; *Joyce v Kennard* (1871) LR 7 QB 78 (distinguished in *Holman & Sons Ltd v Merchants Marine Insurance Co Ltd* [1919] 1 KB 383, cited in para 35 note 1 ante); *Kuehne and Nagel Inc v F W Baiden* [1977] 1 Lloyd's Rep 90, NY CA.

280. Measure of indemnity for general average and salvage charges. Subject to any express provision in the policy, where the assured has paid, or is liable for, any general average contribution[1], the measure of indemnity[2] is the full amount of that contribution if the subject matter liable to contribution is insured for its full contributory value[3]. If that subject matter is not insured for that value, or if only part of it is insured, the indemnity payable by the insurer must be reduced in proportion to the under-insurance, and where there has been a particular average loss[4] which constitutes a deduction from the contributory value, and for which the insurer is liable, that amount must be deducted from the insured value in order to ascertain what the insurer is liable to contribute[5].

Where the insurer is liable for salvage charges[6], the extent of his liability must be determined on the like principle[7].

The contributory value and the insurable value may be different, inasmuch as the contributory value is generally the value at the port of adjustment, whereas the insurable value is the value at the commencement of the voyage, and the above rule provides for the case where that difference exists[8].

1 As to general average contribution see para 244 et seq ante.
2 As to the measure of indemnity see para 265 ante.
3 Marine Insurance Act 1906 s 73(1).
4 As to particular average see para 257 et seq ante.
5 Marine Insurance Act 1906 s 73(1).
6 As to salvage charges see para 258 ante.
7 Marine Insurance Act 1906 s 73(2).
8 The above principle was applied in *SS Balmoral Co v Marten* [1902] AC 511, HL; affg [1901] 2 KB 896, CA. As to the port of adjustment see para 252 ante.

281. Measure of indemnity in other cases. Where there has been a loss in respect of any subject matter not expressly provided for in the statutory provisions previously mentioned[1], the measure of indemnity is to be ascertained, as nearly as may be, in accordance with those provisions, in so far as applicable to the particular case[2].

1 Ie the Marine Insurance Act 1906 ss 67–74: paras 265–280 ante.
2 Ibid s 75(1).

(12) TOTAL LOSS

(i) Actual Total Loss

282. Distinction between actual and constructive total loss. A loss may be either total or partial; any loss other than a total loss is a partial loss[1]. A total loss may be either an actual total loss or a constructive total loss[2].

Where the subject matter insured is destroyed or so damaged as to cease to be a thing of the kind insured, or where the assured[3] is irretrievably deprived of it, there is an actual total loss[4].

Subject to any express provision in the policy, where the subject matter insured[5] is reasonably abandoned on account of its actual total loss appearing to be unavoidable, or because it could not be preserved from actual total loss without an expenditure which would exceed its value when the expenditure had been incurred, there is a constructive total loss[6].

1 Marine Insurance Act 1906 s 56(1).

2 Ibid s 56(2).

3 As to the use of the term 'the assured' see para 35 note 1 ante.

4 Marine Insurance Act 1906 s 57(1), which is evidently intended to reproduce substantially the statement in Lord Abinger's judgment in *Roux v Salvador* (1836) 3 Bing NC 266, Ex Ch, that 'there is an absolute total loss where the thing insured is wholly destroyed or annihilated by the perils insured against or is by the same perils wholly and irretrievably lost to the assured, so that it is totally out of his power or that of the underwriter to procure its arrival'.

5 In the case of insurance on goods under a voyage policy, the subject matter insured includes the adventure and is not limited to the goods themselves: *British and Foreign Marine Insurance Co Ltd v Samuel Sanday & Co* [1916] 1 AC 650, HL; approved and distinguished in *Rickards v Forestal Land, Timber and Railways Co Ltd* [1942] AC 50, [1941] 3 All ER 62, HL. Consequently, if the adventure is frustrated by an insured peril, the assured may abandon it and recover for a constructive total loss on the ground that the actual total loss of the subject matter insured appears to be unavoidable, even though the goods themselves are undamaged and in his control: *British and Foreign Marine Insurance Co Ltd v Samuel Sanday & Co* supra. In *Mitsui v Mumford* [1915] 2 KB 27 at 32, Bailhache J expressed the opinion that in considering whether there had been a loss under a policy on timber stored in warehouses in Antwerp it was 'right to take into account considerations similar to those which one would take into account in determining a question of constructive total loss under a marine policy'. In *Campbell and Phillips Ltd v Denman* (1915) 21 Com Cas 357, Bray J treated the provision in the text as applicable to a policy on goods at Antwerp. In *Moore v Evans* [1918] AC 185, HL, however, Lord Atkinson criticised the judgments in the two last-cited cases and expressed the opinion that the rules as to constructive loss under a marine policy had no application to the policy there in question, which was on jewellery 'in or upon any premises or place whatsoever or being carried or in transit by land or water in the United Kingdom or Europe, or in transit by sea from any port or place in the United Kingdom or Europe'. In *Manchester Ship Canal Co v Horlock* [1914] 2 Ch 199, CA, it was held that in deciding whether a vessel is 'constructively lost' within the meaning of the Merchant Shipping Act 1894 s 21(1) (as amended: see SHIPPING), the tests laid down in the Marine Insurance Act 1906 must be applied.

6 Marine Insurance Act 1906 s 60(1). As to the commercial considerations on which the doctrine of constructive total loss is founded see *Roux v Salvador* (1836) 3 Bing NC 266 at 286–287, Ex Ch, per Lord Abinger CJ; and see also *Goss v Withers* (1758) 2 Burr 683 per Lord Mansfield CJ; *Hamilton v Mendes* (1761) 2 Burr 1198; *Roura and Forgas v Townend* [1918] 1 KB 189 at 194. As to constructive total loss see further para 292 post. The Marine Insurance Act 1906 s 60 is a definition section which (subject to any express provision in the policy) circumscribes completely the conception of constructive total loss: *Irvin v Hine* [1950] 1 KB 555 at 568, [1949] 2 All ER 1089 at 1091 per Devlin J. If these conditions are fulfilled, there is a constructive total loss, and giving due notice of abandonment is only a condition precedent to recovery from the insurer in respect of the loss: *Robertson v Petros M Nomikos Ltd* [1939] AC 371, [1939] 2 All ER 723, HL. This distinction is important where the insurer's liability in respect of the loss of the subject matter insured (eg freight) is made to depend on the constructive total loss of another subject matter (eg the ship). Thus, where profit on charter was

insured 'against total and/or constructive total loss of steamer only', and the steamer was captured, the assured were held entitled to recover for a loss of their profit on charter, although the shipowners had given no notice of abandonment, the steamer not being insured: *Roura and Forgas v Townend* supra. Cf *Robertson v Petros M Nomikos Ltd* supra. As to notice of abandonment see paras 293, 304–309 post.

283. Need for abandonment and notice thereof. In the cases covered by the definition of an actual total loss[1], as it is impossible for the assured to treat the loss as a partial loss, he has no election to make and therefore need not give any notice of abandonment[2].

On the other hand, in the case of a constructive total loss, the assured must give notice of abandonment to the insurer before he can claim as for total loss[3].

1 See para 282 ante.
2 Marine Insurance Act 1906 s 57(2); and see para 282 note 4 ante. See also *Roura and Forgas v Townend* [1919] 1 KB 189; *Norwich Union Fire Insurance Society Ltd v Price Ltd* [1934] AC 455 at 464, PC.
3 See paras 293, 304–309 post.

284. Actual total loss of ship by destruction or damage. In accordance with the first part of the statutory definition of an actual total loss[1], if a ship is so wrecked and damaged as to lose her character as a ship completely and becomes a mere congeries of materials which could be used for rebuilding her, there is an actual total loss of the ship, even if the wreck is brought to the port of destination[2]. Again, if a ship is so damaged that she cannot sail without repairs and cannot be taken to a port at which the necessary repairs could be executed, there is an actual total loss[3]. On the other hand, although the ship is so seriously damaged as not to be worth repairing, if she can still be taken to a port and repaired there is no actual total loss unless she is so broken up as to have completely lost her character as a ship[4].

1 See the Marine Insurance Act 1906 s 57(1); and para 282 ante.
2 *Cambridge v Anderson* (1824) 2 B & C 691. For the facts of this case see the report in 1 C & P 213. The judgment, which proceeded on the assumption (whether right or wrong) that the ship had lost her character as a ship, and had become a mere congeries of planks, has been followed in *Levy & Co v Merchants Marine Insurance Co* (1885) 1 TLR 228. See also, on this point, *Allen v Sugrue* (1828) 8 B & C 561 at 564 per Lord Tenterden CJ, better reported in Dan & Ll 188 at 192; *Stewart v Greenock Marine Insurance Co* (1848) 2 HL Cas 159.
3 *Barker v Janson* (1868) LR 3 CP 303 per Willes J; *Moss v Smith* (1850) 9 CB 94 at 102 per Maule J.
4 *Barker v Janson* (1868) LR 3 CP 303 per Willes J; *Martin v Crokatt* (1811) 14 East 465 at 466; *Bell v Nixon* (1816) Holt NP 423; *Fleming v Smith* (1848) 1 HL Cas 513; *Knight v Faith* (1850) 15 QB 649. For the effect of a constructive total loss followed by a justifiable sale see para 289 post.

285. Actual total loss of goods by destruction or damage. If insured goods are so damaged by the perils insured against that in a commercial sense they have lost their original character and are not saleable under their ordinary description, or exist only in the form of a nuisance, this is an actual total loss, even if they have reached their port of destination. Thus if hides which are insured are so damaged by perils insured against that they have changed their form and can be sold only as glue, manure or ashes, there is an actual total loss of the hides whether or not they have reached their port of destination[1].

Where goods reach their destination in specie, but by reason of obliteration of marks or otherwise they are incapable of identification, the loss, if any, is partial and not total, all the owners of the goods which cannot be identified becoming tenants in common[2].

Perishable goods are generally insured 'free of average'[3], and such a clause amounts to a stipulation that the insurer is not to be liable for anything short of a total loss. Thus the question whether the insurer is liable for a total loss of the insured goods generally arises in cases where they are insured free of average. Whether the loss is to be held total or partial within the meaning of the clause depends entirely on the general principles regulating the matter, for the clause does not in the least vary the rules which determine whether a loss is partial or total, or whether notice of abandonment need be given to make the insurer liable[4].

On the other hand, no amount of damage to the insured goods will constitute an actual total loss unless their damage involves their total destruction in specie. Thus, if wheat valued at £1,000 is insured free of average from Waterford to Liverpool, and the ship is run aground to prevent her sinking and in consequence her hull is completely under water every high tide, if any portion of the wheat can be got out of the ship and can be sent on to Liverpool so as to be sold there as wheat, although at a price less than its freight, the assured cannot recover as for a total loss without giving notice of abandonment[5].

1 *Roux v Salvador* (1836) 3 Bing NC 266 at 277–278, Ex Ch; *Burnett v Kensington* (1797) 7 Term Rep 210 at 222; *Dyson v Rowcroft* (1803) 3 Bos & P 474 at 476, overruling the decision of Lord Mansfield in *Cocking v Fraser* (1785) 4 Doug KB 295; *Cologan v London Assurance Co* (1816) 5 M & S 447 at 455; *Asfar & Co v Blundell* [1895] 2 QB 196; affd [1896] 1 QB 123, CA; *Saunders v Baring* (1876) 34 LT 419; *Montreal Light, Heat and Power Co v Sedgwick* [1910] AC 598, PC (cement destroyed by barge being submerged, a total loss of the goods 'by total loss of vessel'); *Berger and Light Diffusers Pty Ltd v Pollock* [1973] 2 Lloyd's Rep 442 (steel injection moulds so badly damaged by rust as to have only scrap value; held that this was actual total loss).
2 Marine Insurance Act 1906 s 56(5); *Spence v Union Marine Insurance Co* (1868) LR 3 CP 427.
3 See further para 263, especially note 1 ante
4 *Roux v Salvador* (1836) 3 Bing NC 266 at 278, Ex Ch. As to what amounts to a total loss of disbursements under a policy on disbursements 'free from all average' see *Lawther v Black* (1901) 6 Com Cas 196, CA. As to the cases in which notice of abandonment is necessary see para 293 post.
5 *Anderson v Royal Exchange Assurance Co* (1805) 7 East 38; *Cunningham v Maritime Insurance Co* [1899] 2 IR 257; *Hedburg v Pearson* (1816) 7 Taunt 154; *Navone v Haddon* (1850) 9 CB 30; *M'Andrews v Vaughan* (1793) 1 Park's Marine Insurances (8th Edn) 252; *Mason v Skurray* (1780) 1 Park's Marine Insurances (8th Edn) 253, overruling the decision of Yorke CJ at Nisi Prius in *Boyfield v Brown* (1736) 2 Stra 1065; *Glennie v London Assurance Co* (1814) 2 M & S 371; but as to the effect of a justifiable sale see para 289 post.

286. Total loss of part of goods. In general, there is no total loss of the insured goods unless there is a total loss of all the goods[1]. The only exception to this rule is where the contract contained in the policy is severable, either by reason of express stipulation in the policy or because the goods are separately valued, or because the insured goods consist of separate articles wholly distinct in their nature so that they must be considered as separately insured[2].

1 *Ralli v Janson* (1856) 6 E & B 422, Ex Ch, overruling *Davy v Milford* (1812) 15 East 559, and the dicta in some earlier cases. The de minimis rule will be applied in calculating whether there is a total loss of all the goods: *Boon and Cheah Steel Pipes Sdn Bhd v Asia Insurance Co Ltd* [1975] 1 Lloyd's Rep 452, Malaysia HC (668 steel pipes insured, of which all except 12 fell into the sea; held, not an actual total loss because the 12 were too high a proportion to be capable of being dismissed as a matter de minimis).
2 See *Duff v Mackenzie* (1857) 3 CBNS 16; and the Marine Insurance Act 1906 s 76(1): para 263 ante. See also *Hills v London Assurance Corpn* (1839) 5 M & W 569; *Entwistle v Ellis* (1857) 2 H & N 549; *Wilkinson v Hyde* (1858) 3 CBNS 30; *Fabrique de Produits Chimiques SA v Large* [1923] 1 KB 203.

287. Actual total loss by deprivation. By the second part of the statutory definition, there is an actual total loss where the assured is irretrievably deprived of the subject matter insured[1]. Thus, if the ship founders in mid-ocean, and there is no chance of raising her or the goods on board, there is an actual total loss of the ship and goods. If, on the other hand, there is a reasonable chance of raising the ship or goods, although only at very great expense, this is not an actual, but only a constructive total loss[2]. Again, if the subject matter insured is captured, condemned and sold, there is an actual total loss[3].

1 See the Marine Insurance Act 1906 s 57(1): para 282 ante. See *Panamanian Oriental SS Corpn v Wright* [1970] 2 Lloyd's Rep 365 (vessel ordered to be confiscated by special military court was not an actual total loss as it had not been shown that the assured was irretrievably deprived of her) (revsd on other grounds [1971] 2 All ER 1028, [1971] 1 WLR 882, [1971] 1 Lloyd's Rep 487, CA).
2 *Anderson v Royal Exchange Assurance Co* (1805) 7 East 38; *Doyle v Dallas* (1831) 1 Mood & R 48; *Kemp v Halliday* (1866) LR 1 QB 520, Ex Ch; *Blairmore Co Ltd (Sailing Ship) v Macredie* [1898] AC 593, HL; *Captain J A Cates Tug and Wharfage Co Ltd v Franklin Insurance Co* [1927] AC 698, PC. As to constructive total loss see further para 292 et seq post.
3 *Stringer v English and Scottish Marine Insurance Co* (1869) LR 4 QB 676; affd (1870) LR 5 QB 599, Ex Ch. Capture, without condemnation, is not an actual total loss, although it may constitute a constructive total loss: see *Marstrand Fishing Co Ltd v Beer* [1937] 1 All ER 158 at 163 per Porter J.

288. Date of loss of missing ship. Where the ship concerned in the adventure is missing, and after the lapse of a reasonable time no news of her has been received, an actual total loss may be presumed[1]; but in order to recover on the policy the assured must prove a loss that has occurred within the period of insurance, there being no presumption that the loss took place at a particular time[2].

What is a reasonable time is a question of fact[3]. For instance, if the ship has met with some disaster or encountered a violent storm during the insured period, or if she has failed to arrive at her destination within the usual time, a loss during the insured period may be presumed[4].

1 Marine Insurance Act 1906 s 58. See further para 153 text and note 11 ante.
2 *Houstman v Thornton* (1816) Holt NP 242.
3 Marine Insurance Act 1906 s 88.
4 *Reid v Standard Marine Assurance Co Ltd* (1886) 2 TLR 807; cf *Re Rhodes v Rhodes* (1887) 36 ChD 586 at 591 (presumption of death); and EVIDENCE vol 17 para 116. As to whether in time of war this loss may be presumed to be by war or by marine risks see *Macbeth & Co v King* (1916) 86 LJKB 1004; and para 157 ante.

289. Constructive total loss followed by justifiable sale. Where there is a constructive total loss of the subject matter insured, whether ship or goods, and this is followed by a justifiable sale by the master, then, at any rate if the news of the loss and of the sale reach the assured at the same time, no notice of abandonment need be given, and therefore the loss is treated as an actual total loss[1]. It is important to observe, however, that it is not the sale alone which entitles the assured to recover for a total loss without notice of abandonment, for there is no such head in insurance law as loss by sale[2]. The true ground is that the justifiable sale has deprived the owner of his property and there is nothing to abandon, and therefore no need for notice of abandonment[3].

If perishable goods are so damaged that it is impossible to carry them to their destination, and they are left at a port of distress without being sold there, it seems that notice of abandonment should be given, as the subject matter insured is still in existence, and opportunity should be given to the insurer to deal with it as he thinks proper[4].

The Marine Insurance Act 1906 contains no express provision as to a constructive total loss being followed by a justifiable sale, but the law, as stated above, may be deduced from the provision for the case where the assured is irretrievably deprived of the subject matter insured[5], and also from the provision that notice of abandonment is unnecessary where, at the time when the assured receives information of the loss, there would be no possibility of benefit to the insurer if notice were given to him[6].

Whether the sale is justifiable or not is a question of fact[7]. If, for example, the master cannot obtain sufficient funds for repairing the ship and it appears that he will not be able to obtain them before the ship becomes an actual total loss, he will be justified in selling her, and, after the sale, the loss may be treated as an actual total loss[8]. On the other hand, even where a constructive total loss has taken place, followed by a sale, the assured may forfeit his claim to recover for a total loss by his own conduct in electing to take the proceeds of the sale instead of making his claim against the insurers, if he thereby alters the position of facts so as to affect their interests[9].

1 *Roux v Salvador* (1836) 3 Bing NC 266, Ex Ch; *Cossman v West, Cossman v British America Assurance Co* (1887) 13 App Cas 160, PC; *Cobequid Marine Insurance Co v Barteaux* (1875) LR 6 PC 319; *Navone v Haddon* (1850) 9 CB 30 at 44 per Maule J; *Farnworth v Hyde* (1866) LR 2 CP 204, Ex Ch; *Saunders v Baring* (1876) 34 LT 419; *Rankin v Potter* (1873) LR 6 HL 83 at 102, 157; *Australasian Steam Navigation Co v Morse* (1872) LR 4 PC 222; see also *Knight v Faith* (1850) 15 QB 649, and the comments on that case by Blackburn J in *Rankin v Potter* supra at 130. As to constructive total loss becoming actual by continuance of perils see *Levy & Co v Merchants Marine Insurance Co* (1885) 52 LT 263.
2 *Gardner v Salvador* (1831) 1 Mood & R 116 at 117 per Bayley B; *Navone v Haddon* (1850) 9 CB 30.
3 See the Marine Insurance Act 1906 s 62(7); and *Kaltenbach v Mackenzie* (1878) 3 CPD 467 at 480, CA, per Cotton LJ; *Norwich Union Fire Insurance Society v Price Ltd* [1934] AC 455, PC, where money paid under a mistake of fact on the footing of an actual loss was held recoverable. On this principle, where an insurer has reinsured his risk, no notice of abandonment need be given to his insurer, inasmuch as there is nothing to abandon: see the Marine Insurance Act 1906 s 62(9).
4 *Kaltenbach v Mackenzie* (1878) 3 CPD 467, CA; cf *Mansell & Co v Hoade* (1903) 20 TLR 150 (cattle slaughtered by reason of quarantine regulations preventing their being landed).
5 See the Marine Insurance Act 1906 s 57(1); and para 282 ante.
6 Ibid s 62(7). As the master has no authority to sell the ship or the goods unless the danger of a total loss is so imminent that there is no time for him to communicate with the owners, considerable caution must be used in applying the earlier cases on the subject on account of the enormous increase in the facilities for communication. It must also be noted that where the assured receives information of the loss before there has been any sale, he must, in general, at once give notice of abandonment to the insurers in order to be entitled to claim for a total loss: see *Kaltenbach v Mackenzie* (1878) 3 CPD 467, CA. As to this point see para 292 et seq post.
7 For the law as to the master's authority to sell ship or cargo in cases of necessity see *Hunter v Parker* (1840) 7 M & W 322; *Robertson v Clarke* (1824) 1 Bing 445; *Mount v Harrison* (1827) 4 Bing 388; and SHIPPING vol 43 paras 202–203, 639–643.
8 *Somes v Sugrue* (1830) 4 C & P 276 at 283 per Tindal CJ; *Morris v Robinson* (1824) 3 B & C 196; *Cannan v Meaburn* (1823) 1 Bing 243. This is provided the assured first hears of the loss and the sale at the same time: see text and note 1 supra.
9 *Mitchell v Edie* (1787) 1 Term Rep 608; and see *Roux v Salvador* (1836) 3 Bing NC 266 at 286, Ex Ch, per Lord Abinger CJ; *Allwood v Henckell* (1795) 1 Park's Marine Insurances (8th Edn) 399; *Saunders v Baring* (1876) 34 LT 419 at 421.

(ii) Total Loss of Freight

290. Instances of total loss of freight. There is a total loss of freight[1] where, by perils insured against[2], the right to freight is destroyed and the assured is irretrievably deprived of it[3]. Thus, there may be a total loss of freight where the shipowner is physically prevented from performing the contract of affreightment by a total loss of ship or cargo caused by perils insured against[4]. As the hull and the freight policies are wholly independent of one another, there may also be a total loss of freight through frustration of the charterparty by perils insured against even though there has been no total loss under the hull policies[5]. Such frustration may occur, for example, through delay[6], or through the ship suffering damage sufficiently extensive to render it commercially impracticable to incur the expense of repair[7].

In all these cases the right to freight is destroyed. For the same reason there is a total loss under a policy on commissions or profits if the goods are totally lost by perils insured against[8].

1   It is believed that there is no case which has been decided on the basis of constructive, as distinct from actual, total loss of freight, and the question of constructive total loss is therefore not dealt with separately here. It is, however, not necessarily impossible that there should be such a loss, and in *Rankin v Potter* (1873) LR 6 HL 83 at 102–103, Brett J indicated situations in which he considered that notice of abandonment should be given. For a full discussion of the concept of constructive total loss of freight see Arnould on Marine Insurance (16th Edn) s 1233 et seq. For the meaning of 'freight' when used to describe the subject matter of the policy see para 115 ante.

2   As to the perils insured against see generally para 149 ante.

3   See the Marine Insurance Act 1906 s 57(1). If, owing to the outbreak of war, it becomes illegal for the assured to earn the only freight in respect of which he has a contractual interest, and no other freight is obtainable on the insured voyage, there is an actual total loss by 'restraint of princes': *Associated Oil Carriers Ltd v Union Insurance Society of Canton Ltd* [1917] 2 KB 184.

4   *Horncastle v Suart* (1806) 7 East 400 (embargo and seizure); *Mackenzie v Shedden* (1810) 2 Camp 431 (captive); *Rankin v Potter* (1873) LR 6 HL 83 (constructive total loss of vessel before commencement of insured voyage); *Papadimitriou v Henderson* [1939] 3 All ER 908 (capture: insurance of 'anticipated freight').

5   See *Carras v London and Scottish Assurance Corpn Ltd* [1936] 1 KB 291 at 304, CA, per Lord Wright MR, and *Vrondissis v Stevens* [1940] 2 KB 90 at 96–97, [1940] 3 All ER 74 at 77–78 per Atkinson J. The question whether or not the shipowner has given notice of abandonment to hull insurers is thus irrelevant: *Robertson v Petros M Nomikos Ltd* [1939] AC 371 at 381, [1939] 2 All ER 723 at 727, HL, per Lord Wright.

6   *Jackson v Union Marine Insurance Co Ltd* (1873) LR 8 CP 572; affd (1874) LR 10 CP 125, Ex Ch; *Re Jamieson and Newcastle SS Freight Insurance Association* [1895] 2 QB 90, CA; and see SHIPPING. Such a loss will not, however, be recoverable if the policy contains a clause excepting any claim 'consequent on loss of time whether arising from a peril of the sea or otherwise' (see now eg the Institute Time Clauses (Freight) cl 14 and the Institute Voyage Clauses (Freight) cl 12; and para 149 note 1 ante): *Bensaude v Thames and Mersey Marine Insurance Co* [1897] AC 609, HL; *Turnbull, Martin & Co v Hull Underwriters' Association* [1900] 2 QB 402; *Naviera de Canarias SA v Nacional Hispanica Aseguradora SA* [1977] 1 All ER 625, [1977] 2 WLR 442, HL. In *Russian Bank for Foreign Trade v Excess Insurance Co Ltd* [1918] 2 KB 123, Bailhache J held that although the closing of the Dardanelles by Turkey during the First World War was such a restraint of princes as would, in the absence of a provision to the contrary in the policy, have given rise to a claim for constructive total loss, the assured was precluded from recovery because the policy contained a clause excluding all claims for delay. The decision was affirmed on other grounds ([1919] 1 KB 39, CA) and distinguished in *Roura and Forgas v Townend* [1919] 1 KB 189. The effect of the clause was considered (though not decided) in *Atlantic Maritime Co Inc v Gibbon* [1954] 1 QB 88, [1953] 2 All ER 1086, CA, where Evershed MR reviewed the authorities and (doubting *Russian Bank for Foreign Trade v Excess Insurance Co Ltd* supra) drew a distinction between cases in which lapse of time disposes of the bargain, in which event the clause bars a claim, and those in which the delay is relevant only to estimate correctly the extent of the peril and to ascertain the nature and quality of the accident. The question whether a claim is consequent

upon loss of time is in each case one of fact: *Robertson v Petros M Nomikos Ltd* [1939] AC 371 at 377, [1939] 2 All ER 723 at 724, HL, per Lord Atkin.

The clauses cited above are incorporated respectively by the Institute War and Strikes Clauses (Freight—Time) cl 2; and the Institute War and Strikes Clauses (Freight—Voyage) cl 2.

7 *Moss v Smith* (1850) 9 CB 94; *Carras v London and Scottish Assurance Corpn Ltd* [1936] 1 KB 291, CA; *Kulukundis v Norwich Union Fire Insurance Society* [1937] 1 KB 1, [1936] 2 All ER 242, CA; *Vrondissis v Stevens* [1940] 2 KB 90, [1940] 3 All ER 74. See also *Assicurazioni Generali v SS Bessie Morris Co Ltd and Brown* [1892] 2 QB 652, CA (a charterparty case). The only repairs to be considered when estimating the expense of repair are those necessary to enable the vessel to carry the cargo to its destination: *Kulukundis v Norwich Union Fire Insurance Society* supra per Slesser and Greene LJJ, Scott LJ contra. The provision in the Institute Voyage Clauses (Freight) cl 13, and in the Institute Time Clauses (Freight) cl 15, that in ascertaining whether the vessel is a constructive total loss the insured value in the insurances on hull and machinery is to be taken as the repaired value, only applies where the assured's claim arises under the clause which provides that in the event of the total loss of the vessel, whether absolute or constructive, the amount insured by the freight policy is to be paid in full, and is irrelevant where there has been an actual total loss of freight by perils insured against, eg by the vessel missing her cancelling date because of perils of the sea.

The clauses cited above are incorporated respectively by the Institute War and Strikes Clauses (Freight—Voyage) cl 2; and the Institute War and Strikes Clauses (Freight—Time) cl 2.

8 Partial loss of bill of lading freight may be total loss of profit on charter: *Asfar & Co v Blundell* [1896] 1 QB 123, CA.

291. Where freight is not totally lost.

A total loss of the vessel, whether actual or constructive, is not of itself, in the absence of express provision to that effect, sufficient to entitle the assured to recover for a total loss of freight, as it may be that freight is earned notwithstanding the loss of the ship. Thus if the vessel earns freight after being abandoned to hull insurers, the freight is not lost, even though the assured does not receive it[1]. Again, there is no total loss of freight if the vessel is a total loss but the cargo is recovered and delivered to its destination[2]. Similarly, there may be no total loss of freight where a ship has stranded outside the port of destination in such circumstances that the cargo can be unloaded into lighters and brought into port[3].

The insurer is not liable for loss of freight unless the loss is proximately caused by the perils insured against[4]; he is therefore not liable if the loss was proximately caused by the assured's act[5]. However, if carriage in the original ship becomes impossible owing to the operation of perils insured against, failure by the shipowner to exercise his option to tranship the cargo and carry it to its destination does not result in a loss proximately caused by an act of the assured[6].

1 *Scottish Marine Insurance Co of Glasgow v Turner* (1853) 1 Macq 334, HL; and cf *Robert S Besnard Barque Co Ltd v Murton* (1909) 101 LT 285. This hardship is excluded in practice by the introduction of an Institute Clause providing that in the event of the total loss of the vessel, whether actual or constructive, the amount insured must be paid in full, whether the vessel is fully or partly loaded, or in ballast, chartered or unchartered: *Coker v Bolton* [1912] 3 KB 315 at 320 per Hamilton J; *Robertson v Petros M Nomikos Ltd* [1939] AC 371 at 384, [1939] 2 All ER 723 at 729, HL, per Lord Wright. As to the clause now generally included see the Institute Voyage Clauses (Freight) cl 13.1; the Institute Time Clauses (Freight) cl 15.1; the Institute War and Strikes Clauses (Freight—Time) cl 2; and the Institute War and Strikes Clauses (Freight—Voyage) cl 2. As to the Institute Clauses generally see para 149 note 1 ante.

2 *Carras v London and Scottish Assurance Corpn Ltd* [1936] 1 KB 291 at 303, CA, per Lord Wright MR.

3 *Kulukundis v Norwich Union Fire Insurance Society* [1937] 1 KB 1 at 18, [1936] 2 All ER 242 at 258, CA, per Greene LJ.

4 See para 167 ante.

5 See paras 177–183 ante; and *M'Carthy v Abel* (1804) 5 East 388; *Scottish Marine Insurance Co v Turner* (1853) 1 Macq 334, HL (abandonment of vessel to hull underwriters). Contrast *The Alps* [1893] P 109; *The Bedouin* [1894] P 1, CA (ship off-hire through unseaworthiness due to perils insured against: freight recoverable under policy), with *Inman SS Co v Bischoff* (1882) 7 App Cas 670, HL

(exercise by charterer of option of abatement of freight in the event of ship becoming unseaworthy: loss of freight too remote a consequence of perils causing unseaworthiness).

6 *Kulukundis v Norwich Union Fire Insurance Society* [1937] 1 KB 1 at 36 et seq, [1936] 2 All ER 242 at 271 et seq, CA, per Scott LJ.

(iii) Constructive Total Loss

A. MEANING

292. Meaning of 'constructive total loss'. Subject to any express provision in the policy, there is a constructive total loss where the subject matter insured[1] is reasonably abandoned[2] on account of its actual total loss appearing to be unavoidable, or because it could not be preserved from actual total loss without an expenditure which would exceed its value when the expenditure had been incurred[3]. Whether these conditions as to constructive total loss are or are not satisfied is in each case a question of fact[4].

In particular[5], there is a constructive total loss:

(1) where the assured is deprived of the possession of his ship or goods by a peril insured against, and

    (a) it is unlikely[6] that he can recover the ship or goods, as the case may be, or

    (b) the cost of recovering the ship or goods, as the case may be, would exceed their value when recovered[7]; or

(2) in the case of damage to a ship, where she is so damaged by a peril insured against that the cost of repairing[8] the damage would exceed the value of the ship when repaired[9]; or

(3) in the case of damage to goods, where the cost of repairing the damage and forwarding the goods to their destination would exceed their value on arrival[10].

There are thus three main grounds on which a constructive total loss may be founded. The first is the reasonable abandonment of the ship as described above[11]. The second is that the assured may, by the perils insured against, be deprived of the possession of the insured property in circumstances which make it unlikely that he can recover it within a reasonable time[12]; thus it may be captured by the enemy, or by the assured's own government, or by pirates[13], or a ship may be deserted by the master and crew. The third ground is that, although the assured may not be forcibly dispossessed of the insured property, it may be so damaged by the perils insured against that the high cost of repairing the damage or of carrying the goods to the port of destination makes it in a commercial sense impracticable to incur that cost[14].

Modern standard Institute Clauses provide that if a vessel is the subject of capture, seizure, arrest, restraint, detainment, confiscation or expropriation and the assured has lost the free use and disposal[15] of her for 12 months, the assured is deemed to have been deprived of possession without any likelihood of recovery[16].

1 The 'subject matter' of a policy on goods includes the adventure and is not limited to the goods themselves: see para 282 note 5 ante.

2 'Abandoned' in this context means 'given up for lost', and not 'abandoned to underwriters', as it does elsewhere in the Marine Insurance Act 1906: *The Lavington Court* [1945] 2 All ER 357 per Scott LJ and Stable J, du Parcq LJ dissenting.

3 Marine Insurance Act 1906 s 60(1); see also para 282 ante. The parties are at liberty to define, and do sometimes define, in the policy what is to be considered a constructive total loss: *Re Sunderland SS Co and North of England Iron SS Insurance Association* (1894) 11 TLR 106, CA; *Rowland and Marwood's SS Co v Marine Insurance Co* (1901) 6 Com Cas 160. *Holt Hill Sailing Ship Co v United Kingdom Marine Association* [1919] 2 KB 789 distinguished *Becker, Gray & Co v London Assurance Corpn* [1918] AC 101, HL, on the ground that in the latter case the loss was not directly caused by the insured peril. In the case of a policy on freight such a frustration may give rise to an actual, not a constructive, total loss: *Associated Oil Carriers Ltd v Union Insurance Society of Canton Ltd* [1917] 2 KB 184. See further as to constructive total loss of freight para 290 note 1 ante.

4 See eg *Farnworth v Hyde* (1866) LR 2 CP 204, Ex Ch; *Rodoconachi v Elliott* (1874) LR 9 CP 518, Ex Ch; *Mullett v Shedden* (1811) 13 East 304; *Mellish v Andrews* (1812) 15 East 13; *Stringer v English and Scottish Marine Insurance Co* (1870) LR 5 QB 599, Ex Ch.

5 See the Marine Insurance Act 1906 s 60(2). The definition contained in s 60 is exhaustive, subject to express provision in the policy: *Irvin v Hine* [1950] 1 KB 555, [1949] 2 All ER 1089. Some difficulty has been experienced in the past in determining the inter-relationship of the Marine Insurance Act 1906 s 60(1) and (2). It now appears to be clear that the two subsections do not contain respectively a general rule and illustrations, but rather contain two separate and cumulative definitions, applicable to different circumstances: *Robertson v Petros M Nomikos Ltd* [1939] AC 371 at 382, [1939] 2 All ER 723 at 727, HL, per Lord Wright. The Marine Insurance Act 1906 s 60(2) gives an objective criterion which is not only more precise but is substantially different from that in s 60(1): *Rickards v Forestal Land, Timber and Railways Co Ltd* [1942] AC 50 at 84, [1941] 3 All ER 62 at 79, HL, per Lord Wright. Thus, although the Marine Insurance Act 1906 s 60(1) states that there is a constructive total loss where the subject matter is reasonably abandoned (in the sense of given up for lost), constructive total loss is not limited to cases where there has been such abandonment: *Robertson v Petros M Nomikos Ltd* supra at 392 and 734 per Lord Porter, and see also *Irvin v Hine* supra at 568 and 1091 per Devlin J.

6 Before the Marine Insurance Act 1906, it was enough to show that recovery was uncertain: *Polurrian SS Co Ltd v Young* [1915] 1 KB 922, CA; *Rickards v Forestal Land, Timber and Railways Co Ltd* [1942] AC 50 at 86–87, [1941] 3 All ER 62 at 81, HL, per Lord Wright; *Wilson Bros Bobbin Co Ltd v Green* [1917] 1 KB 860; *Czarnikow Ltd v Java Sea and Fire Insurance Co Ltd* [1941] 3 All ER 256. The likelihood of recovery must be judged in the light of the probabilities as they would have appeared to a reasonable assured at the moment when he knew of his loss and could have given notice of abandonment: *Richards v Forestal Land, Timber and Railways Co Ltd* supra at 110–111 and 97 per Lord Porter. The former rule of law that a frustration of the venture by an insured peril gives rise to a constructive total loss under a voyage policy on goods, although the goods themselves are not damaged, has not been altered: *British and Foreign Marine Insurance Co Ltd v Samuel Sanday & Co* [1916] 1 AC 650, HL; *Richards v Forestal Land, Timber and Railways Co Ltd* supra.

7 Marine Insurance Act 1906 s 60(2)(i). If the ship is obviously not worth repairing, the assured need not have a detailed examination made in order to estimate the cost of repair: see *Irvin v Hine* [1950] 1 KB 555, [1949] 2 All ER 1089 (abandonment without sale). The commercial irreparability must, however, be proved affirmatively; 'it must not be a mere measuring cost': see *Somes v Sugrue* (1830) 4 C & P 276 per Tindal CJ.

8 In estimating the cost of repairs, no deduction is to be made in respect of general average contributions to those repairs payable by other interests, but account is to be taken of the expense of future salvage operations and of any future general average contributions to which the ship would be liable if repaired: Marine Insurance Act 1906 s 60(2)(ii).

9 Ibid s 60(2)(ii).

10 Ibid s 60(2)(iii); see *Boon and Cheah Steel Pipes Sdn Bhd v Asia Insurance Co Ltd* [1975] 1 Lloyd's Rep 452 (Malaysia HC) (no proof by assured that cost of reconditioning and forwarding steel pipes would exceed their value on arrival).

11 See text and notes 1–3 supra.

12 *Polurrian SS Co Ltd v Young* (1913) 19 Com Cas 143 at 155 per Pickford J; *Roura and Forgas v Townend* [1919] 1 KB 189; *Robertson v Petros M Nomikos Ltd* [1939] AC 371 at 383, [1939] 2 All ER 723 at 728, HL, per Lord Wright; *Irvin v Hine* [1950] 1 KB 555 at 568–569, [1949] 2 All ER 1089 at 1091–1092 per Devlin J (difficulty of obtaining licence to repair); *Panamanian Oriental SS Corpn v Wright* [1970] 2 Lloyd's Rep 365 (vessel seized by customs authorities and confiscated by military court; attempts were made to obtain her release; held to be a constructive total loss because her recovery was unlikely) (revsd on other grounds [1971] 2 All ER 1028, [1971] 1 WLR 882, [1971] 1 Lloyd's Rep 487, CA); *The Bamburi* [1982] 1 Lloyd's Rep 312 (vessel detained by Iraqi authorities in war between Iraq and Iran, and forbidden to leave; held to be a constructive total loss because her recovery was unlikely); see also *Bank Line Ltd v Arthur Capel & Co* [1919] AC 435 at 454, HL (a frustration case),

where Lord Sumner said that rights ought not to be left in suspense or to hang on the chances of subsequent events, and that what happens afterwards may assist in showing what the probabilities really were, if they had been reasonably forecasted.

13 See *Goss v Withers* (1758) 2 Burr 683; *Ruys v Royal Exchange Assurance Corpn* [1897] 2 QB 135.
14 See *Moss v Smith* (1850) 9 CB 94 at 103. As to frustration of the venture as a further ground on which a claim for constructive total loss may be founded see para 282 note 5 ante.
15 As to the meaning of 'free use and disposal' see *The Bamburi* [1982] 1 Lloyd's Rep 312.
16 See the Institute War and Strikes Clauses (Hulls—Time) cl 3; Institute War and Strikes Clauses (Hulls—Voyage) cl 3. As to the Institute Clauses generally see para 149 note 1 ante.

293. Notice of abandonment. In all cases of constructive total loss, in order to recover for a total loss the assured must give notice of abandonment unless, at the time the assured hears of the loss, the insurer could derive no benefit from notice being given or unless the insurer waives notice of abandonment[1].

1 Marine Insurance Act 1906 s 62(1), (7), (8); *Hamilton v Mendes* (1761) 2 Burr 1198 at 1212; and see para 289 ante. Notice of abandonment is not an essential ingredient of a constructive total loss, but the right to claim for such a loss generally depends on due notice having been given: *Robertson v Petros M Nomikos Ltd* [1939] AC 371, [1939] 2 All ER 723, HL.

294. Distinction between insurances on ship and on goods. There is an essential distinction between an insurance on ship and an insurance on goods. An insurance on ship is a contract of indemnity against damage to, or destruction or loss of, the vessel, but not against the ship being prevented by perils insured against[1] from arriving at her point of destination; whereas an insurance on goods is a contract of indemnity not only against damage, but also against the goods being prevented by perils of the seas[2] from being carried to a port of destination. In other words, a loss of the insured voyage by reason of damage to the ship does not constitute a total loss of the ship[3].

1 As to perils insured against see generally para 149 ante.
2 For the meaning of 'perils of the seas' see para 151 ante.
3 *Pole v Fitzgerald* (1752) Willes 650n; affd (1754) 4 Bro Parl Cas 439, HL; *Parsons v Scott* (1810) 2 Taunt 363; *Falkner v Ritchie* (1814) 2 M & S 290; *Brown v Smith* (1813) 1 Dow 349, HL; *Doyle v Dallas* (1831) 1 Mood & R 48 at 55; *Naylor v Taylor* (1829) Dan & Ll 240 at 254.

B. CONSTRUCTIVE TOTAL LOSS OF SHIP

295. Ascertainment of cost of repairs. As regards the cost of repairs in the case of damage to ship, it is clear that in ascertaining whether there is a constructive total loss[1], no deduction is to be made of one-third new for old[2].

Moreover, if in order to repair the ship it is necessary to incur expenses for the purpose of obtaining possession from salvors or for the purpose of getting her off the rocks or for similar purposes, these must be taken into account either as cost of repairs, or more probably as being necessary for the preservation or recovery of the ship[3]. Similarly, if temporary repairs are to be effected at a port of refuge in order to enable the ship to be completely repaired at another port, both the temporary and the permanent repairs must be taken into account[4].

1 For the meaning of 'constructive total loss' see para 292 ante.
2 *Henderson Bros v Shankland & Co* [1896] 1 QB 525, CA. Cf the Marine Insurance Act 1906 s 60(2)(ii); and para 292 ante. As to the deduction 'one-third new for old' see para 273 ante.

3 See ibid s 60(1), (2)(i), (ii); and para 292 ante.
4 See Arnould on Marine Insurance (16th Edn) s 1208.

296. Repairs necessary to make good damage. It seems that some of the dicta in the earlier cases to the effect that there must be taken into account the cost of such repairs only as are necessary to enable the ship to sail in ballast to the port of destination, or to be navigable for any trade whatever, can no longer be considered good law[1], and that all the repairs must be estimated which are necessary to make good the damage caused by the perils insured against[2].

1 See especially the Marine Insurance Act 1906 s 60(2)(i), (ii); and para 292 ante.
2 The dicta referred to are to be found in *Doyle v Dallas* (1831) 1 Mood & R 48, and other cases. On the other hand see the direction of Erle CJ in *Phillips v Nairne* (1847) 4 CB 343, and the direction of Kennedy J in *North Atlantic SS Co v Burr* (1904) 9 Com Cas 164; and in *Agenoria SS Co v Merchants Marine Insurance Co* (1903) 8 Com Cas 212. If the repair of the damage caused by a peril of the seas makes it necessary also to repair the decayed parts of the vessel, no deduction is to be made from the cost of the first-named repairs on the ground that the decayed parts are also made good: *Phillips v Nairne* supra, where the judgment in the Louisiana case of *Hyde v Louisiana State Insurance Co* (1824) 2 Mar NS 410, was approved. In *Carras v London and Scottish Insurance Corpn Ltd* (1935) 52 Ll L Rep 34 (revsd on other grounds [1936] 1 KB 291, CA), a vessel stranded in the Magellan Straits on her way to load at Valparaiso under a charterparty. It would have been cheaper to repair her in Europe than South America. Porter J held (1) that the cost of repairs must be estimated on the footing that the vessel would be repaired in Europe, but (2) that the expense of taking the vessel to Europe and bringing her back to South America (including crew's wages and victualling and voyage insurance) could be added to the cost of repairs for the purpose of ascertaining whether she was a constructive total loss; he also held (3) that the fees of surveyors advising what repairs would be necessary might be taken into account, but (4) that the wages and maintenance of the crew during repairs and the cost of insuring the vessel during repairs must be excluded.

297. Value of wreck in determining total loss. In determining whether damage to a vessel gives rise to a claim for a constructive total loss[1], the value of the vessel in her damaged condition cannot be added to the cost of repairs unless the policy expressly authorises this addition[2].

In estimating the cost of repairs, no deduction is to be made in respect of general average contributions to those repairs payable by other interests, for those contributions, like contributions from tortfeasors, do not directly affect the amount of actual damage[3].

1 For the meaning of 'constructive total loss' see para 292 ante.
2 See *Hall v Hayman* [1912] 2 KB 5, where Bray J, applying the canon of construction appropriate to a codifying Act (see para 13 ante), held that the Marine Insurance Act 1906 s 60(2)(ii) (see para 292 ante), had altered the law as laid down in *Macbeth & Co Ltd v Maritime Insurance Co Ltd* [1908] AC 144, HL. By this latter decision which, although given after the passing of the 1906 Act, was based on the previous law, as the loss occurred before the passing of the Act, the House of Lords overruled *Angel v Merchants Marine Insurance Co* [1903] 1 KB 811, CA. In *Carras v London and Scottish Assurance Corpn Ltd* [1936] 1 KB 291 at 305 and 311, CA, respectively, Lord Wright MR and Slesser LJ suggested that the rule laid down by the 1906 Act applies only to policies on hull, and that the test established by *Macbeth & Co Ltd v Maritime Insurance Co Ltd* supra, is still to be applied when, in the case of freight policies, it is necessary to decide whether as between shipowner and charterer the prudent owner would sell or repair. The Institute Time Clauses (Hulls) cl 19.1, and the Institute Voyage Clauses (Hulls) cl 17.1 (incorporated respectively by the Institute War and Strikes Clauses (Hulls—Time) cl 2, and the the Institute War and Strikes Clauses (Hulls—Voyage) cl 2), provide that nothing in respect of the damaged or break-up value of the vessel or wreck may be taken into account. See also Arnould on Marine Insurance (16th Edn) ss 1198–1199. As to the Institute Clauses generally see para 149 note 1 ante.
3 Marine Insurance Act 1906 s 60(2)(ii): see para 292 et seq ante. On the other hand, account is to be taken of the expense of future salvage operations and any future general average contributions to

which the ship would be liable if repaired: s 60(2)(ii). In *Kemp v Halliday* (1866) LR 1 QB 520, Ex Ch, it was decided that when the ship and cargo were salved by the same operation, general average contributions due from the cargo must be deducted in estimating the cost of salving and repairing the ship. It is submitted that this decision should still be regarded as good law: see para 13 text and note 5 ante.

298. Relevance of insured value. As to the value of the ship, unless the policy contains some express provision to the contrary, no regard is to be had to the sum at which the ship may be valued in the policy. Thus, if the cost of repairs would be £1,900,000 and the ship's market value when repaired would only be £1,050,000, there could be a constructive total loss although the ship may be valued in the policy at £3,000,000[1].

1　See the Marine Insurance Act 1906 s 27(4); *Young v Turing* (1841) 2 Man & G 593; *Irving v Manning* (1847) 1 HL Cas 287. The Institute Time Clauses (Hulls) cl 19.1, and the Institute Voyage Clauses (Hulls) cl 17.1 (incorporated respectively by the Institute War and Strikes Clauses (Hulls—Time) cl 2, and the the Institute War and Strikes Clauses (Hulls—Voyage) cl 2), provide that the insured value is to be taken as the repaired value in ascertaining whether the vessel is a constructive total loss. The policies of some insurance clubs have a clause barring claims for constructive total loss unless the estimated cost of the repairs is equal to 80% of the value declared on the policy, although the cost of repairs may be greater than the value of the ship when repaired. See *Forwood v North Wales Mutual Marine Insurance Co* (1880) 9 QBD 732, CA; *North Atlantic SS Co v Burr* (1904) 9 Com Cas 164; *Irvin v Hine* [1950] 1 KB 555, [1949] 2 All ER 1089. As to the effect of the inclusion of the Institute Clause in a freight policy see *Carras v London and Scottish Insurance Corpn Ltd* [1936] 1 KB 291, CA; and paras 290–291 ante. As to the Institute Clauses generally see para 149 note 1 ante.

299. Peculiar and exceptional vessels. In general, the value of the ship with which the cost of the repairs is to be compared is her market price, but in the case of a peculiar and exceptional vessel built for her owners with a view to a particular trade the market price would not afford a true measure of her value and it is therefore necessary to ascertain what value the repaired vessel would be to her owners[1]. The market value of a vessel depends upon her general capacity to earn freight, but it is undecided whether in estimating her repaired value for the purpose of a constructive total loss, the fact that she was at the time of the loss under a peculiarly profitable charter should be taken into account[2].

1　See the judgment of Wood V-C in *African SS Co v Swanzy and Kennedy* (1856) 2 K & J 660 at 664; *The Iron-Master* (1859) Sw 441; *The Harmonides* [1903] P 1; *Grainger v Martin* (1862) 2 B & S 456; affd (1863) 4 B & S 9, Ex Ch. See Arnould on Marine Insurance (16th Edn) s 1213.
2　See Arnould on Marine Insurance (16th Edn) s 1214, where it is suggested that the value should be considered enhanced by 'beneficial engagements', but that, in view of the standard Institute Clauses, the point is of little significance.
　　Account is, however, to be taken of the expense of future salvage operations, and any future general average contributions to which the ship would be liable if repaired: Marine Insurance Act 1906 s 60(2)(ii): see para 292 note 8 ante.

C.　CONSTRUCTIVE TOTAL LOSS OF GOODS

300. Damaged goods. If it is practicable to carry to the port of destination in a marketable state any part of the insured cargo, there is no constructive total loss of goods[1]. On the other hand, any expenses which have to be incurred to enable the goods to be so carried must be taken into account[2], for instance, not only the cost of unshipping the cargo, drying, warehousing and reshipping, but also the amount of the salvage which may have to be paid in respect of the cargo salved[3].

1 *Rosetto v Gurney* (1851) 11 CB 176 at 186, 190. As to what constitutes a constructive total loss of goods see the Marine Insurance Act 1906 s 60(2)(i), (iii); and para 292 ante. The frustration of the insured adventure by a peril insured against will constitute a constructive total loss under a voyage policy on goods: see para 282 note 5 ante. If a sale of the cargo is not otherwise justifiable, it will not be rendered so by being made under a decree of a vice-admiralty court or any other similar court abroad: *Reid v Darby* (1808) 10 East 143; *The Segredo (otherwise The Eliza Cornish)* (1853) 1 Ecc & Ad 36 per Dr Lushington. As to the de minimis rule see para 286 note 1 ante.

2 Marine Insurance Act 1906 s 60(1), (2)(iii): see para 292 ante.

3 Where, however, the master hypothecates the ship and cargo to pay expenses for repairing the ship, the debt and costs paid to the holder of the bottomry bond are not to be taken into consideration in estimating the extent, whether total or partial, of the loss, inasmuch as the insurer does not insure in respect of a loss by hypothecation: *Rosetto v Gurney* (1851) 11 CB 176.

301. Whether freight may be taken into account. As regards the cost of sending on the cargo or any part of it, it was decided, before the passing of the Marine Insurance Act 1906, that it was only the increased cost of sending it on at a rate of freight higher than the original rate which could be taken into consideration[1]. The correctness of this decision was, however, impugned by eminent average adjusters, who strongly contended that the whole of the original freight, or, if the goods had to be forwarded by another ship, the whole of the freight paid to the latter ship, must be taken into consideration[2].

Considering the doubts entertained as to the decision referred to above, and the explicit language of the Act[3], it is submitted that the Act has the effect of overruling that decision; in other words that, according to the principle of construction applicable to a codifying statute[4], the 'cost of forwarding the goods' to their destination cannot be held to mean merely the excess, if any, of the substituted freight over the original freight[5].

1 See the two leading cases, *Rosetto v Gurney* (1851) 11 CB 176; and *Farnworth v Hyde* (1866) LR 2 CP 204, Ex Ch.

2 In Arnould on Marine Insurance (16th Edn) ss 1224–1231, the arguments on both sides are fully discussed, but the only question now material is whether the Marine Insurance Act 1906 s 60(2)(iii) has abrogated the rule of law which must undoubtedly be taken to have existed before the statute came into force.

3 See ibid s 60(2)(iii); and para 292 ante.

4 See para 13 ante.

5 See also Arnould on Marine Insurance (16th Edn) s 1231.

D. RIGHTS OF ASSURED: NOTICE OF ABANDONMENT

302. Right of election. Where there is a constructive total loss[1] the assured may either treat the loss as a partial loss or abandon the subject matter insured to the insurer and treat the loss as if it were an actual total loss[2].

Where the assured elects to abandon the subject matter insured to the insurer, he must (except in certain special cases) give notice of abandonment; if he fails to do so, the loss can only be treated as a partial loss[3].

If the assured elects to treat the loss as a partial loss[4], or if he fails to give due notice of abandonment, he cannot recover for a total loss in respect of the same casualty[5], unless in the event the loss becomes actually total by the operation of that casualty[6]. He is not, however, prevented from recovering for a total loss in respect of a subsequent casualty. For instance, if the insured ship is captured and the assured does not give due notice of abandonment, and the ship is afterwards recaptured and then lost by perils of the seas, the assured is not prevented from recovering for a total loss in respect of the second casualty[7]. Moreover, it seems that there may be cases where a mere prolongation of time during which the assured is deprived of his property may have the effect of reviving the right of abandonment on giving due notice of it[8].

1 For the meaning of 'constructive total loss' see para 292 ante.
2 Marine Insurance Act 1906 s 61. The right to abandon is a superimposed right of election where there is a constructive total loss, and is not an essential ingredient of such a loss: see *Robertson v Petros M Nomikos Ltd* [1939] AC 371 at 382, [1939] 2 All ER 723 at 727, HL, per Lord Wright.
3 Marine Insurance Act 1906 s 62(1); and see *Western Assurance Co of Toronto v Poole* [1903] 1 KB 376 at 383 per Bigham J. The exceptions are set out in the Marine Insurance Act 1906 s 62(7), (8), (9): see paras 209, 293 ante, 307 post.
4 See *Aitchison v Lohre* (1879) 4 App Cas 755, HL; *Pitman v Universal Marine Insurance Co* (1882) 9 QBD 192 at 208, CA, per Brett LJ; *Mellish v Andrews* (1812) 15 East 13 at 16 per Lord Ellenborough CJ.
5 *Anderson v Royal Exchange Assurance Co* (1805) 7 East 38.
6 *Mellish v Andrews* (1812) 15 East 13; *Stringer v English and Scottish Marine Insurance Co* (1870) LR 5 QB 599, Ex Ch. These cases were distinguished in *Fooks v Smith* [1924] 2 KB 508, where the voyage was frustrated by restraint of princes and the goods were landed, but the assured failed to give notice of abandonment. More than a year later, and after the expiration of the policy, they were requisitioned. The assured sought to recover on the ground that the original restraint of princes had resulted in the requisitioning and so produced an actual total loss. It was held, however, that they were not entitled to recover on the ground that the requisitioning was not the necessary or natural or direct consequence of the original restraint. As to actual total loss see para 282 ante.
7 Cf *Mellish v Andrews* (1812) 15 East 13.
8 2 Phillips' Law of Insurance (5th Edn) ss 1669, 1672, 1674; cf *Stringer v English and Scottish Marine Insurance Co* (1870) LR 5 QB 599, Ex Ch.

303. Insurance against total loss includes constructive loss. Unless a different intention appears from the terms of the policy, an insurance against total loss includes a constructive, as well as an actual, total loss[1]; and where the assured brings an action for a total loss and the evidence proves only a partial loss, he may, unless the policy otherwise provides, recover for a partial loss[2].

1 Marine Insurance Act 1906 s 56(3).
2 Ibid s 56(4).

304. Form of notice of abandonment. Notice of abandonment may be given in writing, or by word of mouth, or partly in writing and partly by word of mouth, and may be given in any terms which indicate the intention of the assured to abandon his insured interest in the subject matter insured unconditionally to the insurer[1].

In order that the abandonment to the insurer may be valid, it must be unconditional, and must also extend, unless the contract of insurance is severable, to the whole of the assured's interest in the property at risk at the time of the disaster so far as that interest is covered by the policy. The policy may, however, be so framed as to comprise several insurances: for instance £100,000 may be insured on sugar and £500,000 on wheat in the same policy, or the sugar may be valued in the policy at £100,000 and the wheat at £500,000; in such cases each interest may be separately abandoned[2].

1 Marine Insurance Act 1906 s 62(2). See *Currie & Co v Bombay Native Insurance Co* (1869) LR 3 PC 72, disapproving the judgment of Lord Ellenborough CJ in *Parmeter v Todhunter* (1808) 1 Camp 541; see *Thelluson v Fletcher* (1793) 1 Esp 73; *King v Walker* (1864) 3 H & C 209, Ex Ch; *Russian Bank for Foreign Trade v Excess Insurance Co Ltd* [1919] 1 KB 39, CA; *G Cohen, Sons & Co v Standard Marine Insurance Co Ltd* (1925) 30 Com Cas 139 at 157. The question, however, will always be whether the conditions of the Marine Insurance Act 1906 s 62(2) are fulfilled in any particular case, and this is a question of construction in which decided cases are of little assistance.

2 Marshall on Marine Insurance (4th Edn) 486. Where a vessel is insured with different insurers, each insurer who accepts the notice of abandonment acquires all interest in the subject matter insured or in its proceeds in the proportion which the amount subscribed by him bears to the full value; and the assured retains a like interest so far as he is not fully insured: see the Marine Insurance Act 1906 s 81; and para 264 ante; *The Commonwealth* [1907] P 216, CA; *Whitworth Bros v Shepherd* (1884) 12 R 204, Ct of Sess.

305. Time when notice of abandonment must be given. Notice of abandonment must be given with reasonable diligence[1] after the receipt of reliable information of the loss, but where the information is of a doubtful character the assured is entitled to a reasonable time to make inquiry[2].

If the assured receives information of a loss, such as capture or arrest, which is prima facie a constructive total loss[3], he must give notice of abandonment immediately on receipt of the information[4]. However, if the information is in itself doubtful, or if it leaves uncertain the question whether the loss or damage constitutes a prima facie constructive total loss, he may wait in order to verify the information or to ascertain the real extent of the loss[5].

The cause of action arises on the date of the casualty and not on the date of the giving of the notice of abandonment[6].

1 The question of what is reasonable diligence is a question of fact: Marine Insurance Act 1906 s 88.
2 Ibid s 62(3).
3 As to constructive total loss see para 292 ante.
4 *Hunt v Royal Exchange Assurance* (1816) 5 M & S 47; *Kaltenbach v Mackenzie* (1878) 3 CPD 467 at 480, CA; *Allwood v Henckell* (1795) 1 Park's Marine Insurances (8th Edn) 399; *Aldridge v Bell* (1816) 1 Stark 498; *Mullett v Shedden* (1811) 13 East 304; *Mellish v Andrews* (1812) 15 East 13; and see *Currie & Co v Bombay Native Insurance Co* (1869) LR 3 PC 72 at 79; *Hudson v Harrison* (1821) 3 Brod & Bing 97 at 106.
5 *Gernon v Royal Exchange Assurance* (1815) 6 Taunt 383 at 387.
6 *Bank of America National Trust and Savings Association v Chrismas, The Kyriaki* [1993] 1 Lloyd's Rep 137.

306. Loss of right to give notice. If, after receiving notice of a casualty which may give rise to a constructive total loss, the assured prosecutes the adventure, he cannot afterwards, when he has ascertained that the damage would have entitled him to treat the loss as a constructive total loss, give notice of abandonment; thus, where the owners of a ship which was damaged in a foreign port have elected to treat the loss as partial, they cannot afterwards turn it into a total loss by giving notice of abandonment merely because they find on the ship's arrival that she is not worth repairing[1]. Similarly, if, on receiving information that a casualty has occurred which amounts to a constructive total loss, the assured orders the subject matter insured to be sold, he cannot afterwards by virtue of giving notice of abandonment recover as for a total loss[2].

The assured may even lose his right to treat a loss as a constructive total loss through the master's unjustifiable delay in ascertaining whether or not the loss is total, the assured being thereby precluded from giving notice of abandonment to the insurer within a reasonable time[3].

1 *Fleming v Smith* (1848) 1 HL Cas 513; *Anderson v Royal Exchange Assurance Co* (1805) 7 East 38; *Barker v Blakes* (1808) 9 East 283.
2 *Kaltenbach v Mackenzie* (1878) 3 CPD 467.
3 *Potter v Campbell* (1867) 16 WR 399; also referred to in *Rankin v Potter* (1873) LR 6 HL 83 at 117, 119, 123.

307. Acceptance of notice of abandonment. The acceptance of a notice of abandonment may be either express or implied from the conduct of the insurer; his mere silence after notice is not an acceptance[1]. However, after receiving notice of abandonment he has no right, by salving the subject matter insured, to claim that he has reduced the total loss to a partial loss[2]. On the contrary, if, after receiving the notice, he does any act which would only be justified under a right derived from it, he will be estopped from denying that he has accepted the notice[3]. Moreover, where no notice of abandonment has been given, such conduct on his part may preclude him from denying that he has waived his right to the notice[4].

1 Marine Insurance Act 1906 s 62(5); *Smith v Robertson* (1814) 2 Dow 474, HL; *Hudson v Harrison* (1821) 3 Brod & Bing 97; *Thelluson v Fletcher* (1793) 1 Esp 73.
2 *Blairmore Co Ltd (Sailing Ship) v Macredie* [1898] AC 593, HL.
3 *Provincial Insurance Co of Canada v Leduc* (1874) LR 6 PC 224; *Shepherd v Henderson* (1881) 7 App Cas 49, HL; and see ESTOPPEL vol 16 (Reissue) para 1065. It should, however, be noted that the Marine Insurance Act 1906 s 62(5) makes no mention of estoppel, but provides that the acceptance may be either express or implied from the insurer's conduct, and it is submitted that this acceptance may be implied in some cases in which the assured may not have changed his position in reliance on the conduct in question, and, indeed, may have been ignorant of it, so that no estoppel, strictly so called, could arise. Contrast *Robertson v Royal Exchange Assurance Corpn* 1925 SC 1, with *Captain J A Cates Tug and Wharfage Co Ltd v Franklin Insurance Co* [1927] AC 698 at 701, PC.
4 See the Marine Insurance Act 1906 s 62(8); and the cases cited in note 3 supra.

308. Effect of acceptance and non-acceptance of notice of abandonment. Where notice of abandonment is accepted, the abandonment is irrevocable; the acceptance conclusively admits liability for the loss and the sufficiency of the notice[1]. However, notice of abandonment given or accepted under a mutual mistake of fact may be a nullity[2].

If the notice of abandonment is not accepted, it is defeasible either by the subsequent restoration of the insured property or by acts showing that the assured has treated the loss as partial and not total[3], but where the notice has been properly given the assured's rights are not prejudiced by the fact that the insurer refuses to accept the abandonment[4].

1 Marine Insurance Act 1906 s 62(6); *Smith v Robertson* (1814) 2 Dow 474, HL.
2 *Norwich Union Fire Insurance Society Ltd v Price Ltd* [1934] AC 455 at 466–467, PC.
3 This passage, in an earlier edition of this work, was approved by Atkinson J in *Pesquerias y Secaderos de Bacalao de Espana SA v Beer* (1946) 79 Ll L Rep 417 at 433 (revsd on the facts (1947) 80 Ll L Rep 318, CA; (1949) 82 Ll L Rep 501, HL). As to the restoration of insured property, however, see para 313 post.
4 Marine Insurance Act 1906 s 62(4). It is probable that where notice of abandonment is given but not accepted, the property does not thereby become res nullius: *Blane Steamships Ltd v Minister of Transport* [1951] 2 KB 965 at 990–991, CA, per Cohen LJ, approving *Oceanic Steam Navigation Co Ltd v Evans* (1934) 50 Ll L Rep 1 at 3, CA, per Greer LJ, and doubting the view expressed by Bailhache J in *Boston Corpn v France, Fenwick & Co Ltd* (1923) 28 Com Cas 367.

309. Master's capacity before and after notice. In general, after notice of abandonment has been given the master acts for the benefit of all concerned in dealing with the subject matter insured; however, where it clearly appears that he has been acting under the directions or for the benefit of the assured exclusively and not for the benefit of the insurers, the assured may thereby forfeit his right to insist on the notice of abandonment, or be deemed to have impliedly withdrawn it[1]. It must, however, be borne in mind that under the suing and labouring clause[2], notwithstanding the notice of abandonment, the master is authorised to take all necessary steps for the safeguard and preservation of the subject matter of the insurance, and further that he may in case of necessity sell the property and thereby turn the constructive into an actual total loss[3].

Until notice of abandonment has been given, prima facie the master acts as the assured's agent. Thus, if a captured ship is repurchased by the master in cases where no notice of abandonment is given, he acts as agent for the owner, and if he does so within the scope of his authority, the assured will be precluded from recovering for a total loss[4].

Where notice of abandonment has been given and accepted, or has become effectual, all the master's acts for the preservation of the insured property from the time of the disaster are deemed to have been done on behalf of the insurers[5].

1 *Fleming v Smith* (1848) 1 HL Cas 513; cf *Shepherd v Henderson* (1881) 7 App Cas 49, HL.
2 As to the suing and labouring clause see para 259 ante.
3 As to the conversion of a constructive into an actual total loss see para 289 ante; and see *Brown v Smith* (1813) 1 Dow 349, HL; *Allan v Sugrue* (1828) Dan & Ll 188 at 190 note (a); *Stewart v Greenock Marine Insurance Co* (1848) 2 HL Cas 159. The suing and labouring clause is now referred to in the Institute Clauses as the 'duty of assured' clause. In relation to cargo, the waiver clause immediately follows it; in relation to hulls, the waiver clause is incorporated in the duty of assured clause. The Institute Clauses provide that no act of the insurer or the assured in recovering, saving or preserving the property insured is to be considered as a waiver or acceptance of abandonment. See the Institute Cargo Clauses (A) cl 17; the Institute Cargo Clauses (B) cl 17; the Institute Cargo Clauses (C) cl 17; the Institute War Clauses (Cargo) cl 12; the Institute Strikes Clauses (Cargo) cl 12; the Institute Time Clauses (Hulls) cl 13; the Institute Voyage Clauses (Hulls) cl 11; the Institute War and Strikes Clauses (Hulls—Time) cl 2; the Institute War and Strikes Clauses (Hulls—Voyage) cl 2. See generally para 149 note 1 ante.
　　This clause will not prevent the insurers from being deemed to have accepted the notice of abandonment if they conduct salvage operations in a manner prejudicial to the property insured with a view to salving other property in which they are interested: *Robertson v Royal Exchange Assurance Corpn* 1925 SC 1.
4 *M'Masters v Shoolbred* (1794) 1 Esp 236; *Wilson v Forster* (1815) 6 Taunt 25.
5 See the American cases cited in Arnould on Marine Insurance (16th Edn), ss 1295, 1296.

E.　EFFECT OF VALID ABANDONMENT

310. Effect of valid abandonment. Where there is a valid abandonment, the insurer is entitled to take over the interest of the assured in whatever may remain of the subject matter insured, and all proprietary rights incidental to it[1].

On the abandonment of a ship, the insurer is entitled to any freight in course of being earned, and which is earned by her subsequent to the casualty causing the loss, less the expenses of earning it incurred after the casualty; and, where the ship is carrying the owner's goods, the insurer is entitled to a reasonable remuneration for the carriage of them subsequent to the casualty causing the loss[2].

If the insured ship is abandoned during the voyage, but nevertheless succeeds in completing it so far as to earn freight, that freight does not belong to the shipowner or to the insurer on freight, but, after deducting the expenses of earning it incurred after the casualty, belongs to the insurer on ship[3]. The insurer on ship, however, is entitled only to the net freight earned by the insured ship, and not to that which may be earned by a subsequent ship[4]. Nor is he entitled to receive freight paid in advance by a charterer, inasmuch as the shipowner is entitled to that freight whether the voyage is subsequently completed or not. Similarly, he is not entitled to the excess of the bill of lading freight over the chartered freight, inasmuch as that excess belongs to the charterer and not to the shipowner; moreover, from the charterparty freight receivable by the insurers there must be deducted the freight's proportion of general average and particular charges, but not expenses incurred in respect of freight earned on the voyage prior to the abandonment[5].

1 Marine Insurance Act 1906 s 63(1).
2 Ibid s 63(2). The insurer of a ship is not entitled under this clause to freight for the carriage of the goods to the place of the casualty: *Miller v Woodfall* (1857) 8 E & B 493; see note 3 infra.
3 *Case v Davidson* (1816) 5 M & S 79; affd sub nom *Davidson v Case* (1820) 2 Brod & Bing 379, Ex Ch; *Stewart v Greenock Marine Insurance Co* (1848) 2 HL Cas 159; *Sea Insurance Co v Hadden* (1884) 13 QBD 706 at 711, CA; *The Red Sea* [1896] P 20 at 24, CA. Insurers on freight may, however, be entitled to receive from the shipowner pro rata freight paid to him for carriage of the goods to the place of the casualty: *London Assurance Corpn v Williams* (1892) 9 TLR 96; affd with comment (1893) 9 TLR 257, CA.
4 *Hickie v Rodocanachi* (1859) 28 LJEx 273.
5 *The Red Sea* [1896] P 20, CA.

311. Effect of valid notice on liabilities of assured. Once a valid notice of abandonment has been given and accepted, the assured ceases to be owner and is released from all liability attaching to ownership which may have accrued since the loss[1]. On the other hand, if, on abandonment to him, the insurer takes over the interest of the assured in the insured ship, he must bear all the liabilities to which the owner would have been subject except such as accrued before the casualty took place and did not arise from perils insured against[2].

From the language of the Marine Insurance Act 1906[3] it may be argued that, although there is a valid notice of abandonment, unless the insurer at any rate actually accepts the notice, he is not bound to take over the abandoned property and may refuse to do so and thereby free himself from all such liability; but the point has not yet been decided and is one of doubt and difficulty[4].

1 *Barraclough v Brown* (1896) 65 LJQB 333, CA; affd [1897] AC 615, HL; *Arrow Shipping Co v Tyne Improvement Comrs, The Crystal* [1894] AC 508, HL, followed in *Boston Corpn v France, Fenwick & Co Ltd* (1923) 28 Com Cas 367.
2 *Sharp v Gladstone* (1805) 7 East 24; *Barclay v Stirling* (1816) 5 M & S 6; *Sea Insurance Co v Hadden* (1884) 13 QBD 706, CA. As to whether the insurer on goods to whom they are duly abandoned takes them subject to the shipowner's claim for freight see *Baillie v Moudigliani* (1785) 1 Park's Marine Insurances (8th Edn) 116, and *Mason v Marine Insurance Co* (1901) 110 Fed R 452 (Circuit CA), and compare them with 2 Phillips' Law of Insurance (5th Edn) s 1718.
3 See the Marine Insurance Act 1906 s 63(1); and para 310 ante.
4 See *Stewart v Greenock Marine Insurance Co* (1848) 2 HL Cas 159 at 183 per Lord Cottenham; and 2 Phillips' Law of Insurance (5th Edn), ss 1726–1727. In *Boston Corpn v France, Fenwick & Co Ltd* (1923) 28 Com Cas 367, Bailhache J thought that there was 'a good deal to be said' for the view that in such circumstances the wreck becomes res nullius. See, however, *Oceanic Steam Navigation Co v Evans* (1934) 50 Ll L Rep 1 at 3, CA, per Greer LJ, and *Blane Steamships Ltd v Minister of Transport* [1951] 2 KB 965 at 990–991, CA, per Cohen LJ, where a contrary view is expressed. See further Arnould on Marine Insurance (16th Edn) s 1290.

312. Apportionment of salvage on abandonment. On abandonment, if the assured is fully insured, each of the insurers is entitled to share in the proceeds of the salvage according to the proportion which the amount underwritten by him bears to the whole value of the thing insured, without regard to the date of the different subscriptions or the priority of the policies if more than one. Moreover, if the assured is not fully insured he is entitled to share in those proceeds in the proportion to which he is uninsured[1].

1 See *The Commonwealth* [1907] P 216, CA. See also *Duus, Brown & Co v Binning* (1906) 11 Com Cas 190. As to the salvage arising from a sum received from a tortfeasor, who caused the loss, see *The Welsh Girl* (1906) 22 TLR 475; affd sub nom *The Commonwealth* supra, where the owners of the insured ship, being under-insured and therefore their own insurers to a certain amount, were held entitled to share proportionately the money recovered by them against the tortfeasor who had occasioned the loss. There may, of course, be liens on the salvage which take precedence over the insurer's right, such as, for instance, the jus ad rem acquired by the holder of a bottomry bond: *Stephen v Broomfield, The Great Pacific* (1869) LR 2 PC 516; and see SHIPPING vol 43 para 1139. As to the general result of the assured not being fully insured see para 264 ante.

(iv) Ademption of Total Loss

313. Ademption of total loss. At the time of the passing of the Marine Insurance Act 1906 it was a doctrine of English insurance law that, although a constructive total loss[1] had occurred and due notice of abandonment had been given, the assured could not recover for a total loss if, before the action was brought, the subject matter insured had been restored in such circumstances that he might reasonably be expected to take possession of it[2].

A total loss was said to have been adeemed if the loss did not continue to be total at the commencement of the action[3]. Thus, where the ship or goods had been captured, then, even though due notice of abandonment was given, if the property was released so that the assured might reasonably be expected to take possession of it, he could only recover for a partial loss[4]. On the other hand the mere release or restitution of the insured property would not have this effect if the assured might eventually have to pay more for it than it was worth, and therefore could not reasonably be expected to take possession of it[5].

This doctrine is peculiar to English law. According to the law in Scotland, on the Continent and in the United States of America, a constructive total loss followed by due notice of abandonment definitely fixes the parties' rights, and the assured's right to recover for a total loss is in no way affected by subsequent events[6]. Under the provisions of the Marine Insurance Act 1906 as to the effect of constructive total loss[7], the assured's right in case of constructive total loss to abandon the subject matter insured and treat the loss as if it were an actual total loss is apparently unqualified, and although the Act enters with much detail into the law relating to constructive total loss and abandonment[8], it contains no provision that a constructive total loss is adeemed by events which take place after due notice of abandonment. Although there have been dicta on the subject since the passing of the Act, the courts have not yet decided whether the Act was intended to assimilate the law of England to that of Scotland and other countries, so that a constructive total loss followed by due notice of abandonment would definitely fix the right of the assured to recover for a total loss[9].

1 For the meaning of 'constructive total loss' see para 292 ante.
2 *Hamilton v Mendes* (1761) 2 Burr 1198; *Bainbridge v Neilson* (1808) 10 East 329; *Patterson v Ritchie* (1815) 4 M & S 393; *Brotherston v Barber* (1816) 5 M & S 418; *Naylor v Taylor* (1829) 9 B & C 718.
3 *Shepherd v Henderson* (1881) 7 App Cas 49, HL, per Lord Blackburn.

4 See the cases cited in note 2 supra.
5 *M'Iver v Henderson* (1816) 4 M & S 576; *Cologan v London Assurance Co* (1816) 5 M & S 447; *Holdsworth v Wise* (1828) 7 B & C 794; *Naylor v Taylor* (1829) 9 B & C 718; *Parry v Aberdein* (1829) 9 B & C 411; *Lozano v Janson* (1859) 2 E & E 160; *Ruys v Royal Exchange Assurance Corpn* [1897] 2 QB 135, where it was decided that the doctrine does not apply to a case where the restitution of the insured property has taken place after the commencement of the action and during the trial.
6 Lord Eldon LC expressed disapproval of the English doctrine in *Smith v Robertson* (1814) 2 Dow 474, HL; and Lord Halsbury LC in *Blairmore Co Ltd (Sailing Ship) v Macredie* [1898] AC 593, HL, suggested that it only applied to cases of capture and similar cases. As to the meaning of a clause to pay a total loss 30 days after official news of the embargo or capture, 'without waiting for condemnation' see *Fowler v English and Scottish Marine Insurance Co Ltd* (1865) 18 CBNS 818.
7 Ie the Marine Insurance Act 1906 s 61: see para 302 ante.
8 As to constructive total loss and abandonment see para 292 et seq ante.
9 In *Polurrian SS Co Ltd v Young* [1915] 1 KB 922, CA, the court, affirming the judgment of Pickford J, said 'Now it is indisputable that, according to the law of England, in deciding upon the validity of claims of this nature between the assured and the insurer, the matters must be considered as they stood on the date of the commencement of the action. That is the governing date'. See also *Rickards v Forestal Land, Timber and Railways Co Ltd* [1942] AC 50 at 85, [1941] 3 All ER 62 at 81, HL, per Lord Wright; *Roura and Forgas v Townend* [1919] 1 KB 189 at 195 per Roche J; *Captain J A Cates Tug and Wharfage Co Ltd v Franklin Insurance Co* [1927] AC 698 at 704, PC; *Marstrand Fishing Co Ltd v Beer* [1937] 1 All ER 158. Cf, however, the dicta of Atkinson J in *Pesquerias y Secoderos de Bacalao de Espana SA v Beer* (1946) 79 Ll L Rep 417 at 433 (revsd on other grounds (1947) 80 Ll L Rep 318, CA; [1949] 1 All ER 845n, HL). In order to avoid this prejudice to the assured, insurers usually agree to place the assured in the same position as if a writ had been issued on the day on which notice of abandonment was given: *Polurrian SS Co Ltd v Young* supra at 153 per Pickford J; *Panamanian Oriental SS Corpn v Wright* [1970] 2 Lloyd's Rep 365 at 383 per Mocatta J; *The Bamburi* [1982] 1 Lloyd's Rep 312 at 321 per Staughton J. It is clear, however, that if the total loss is adeemed before action brought, the assured cannot recover for a total loss, but if such ademption results from the acts of the assured, his employees or agents, the assured is entitled, under the suing and labouring clause (as to which see para 259 ante), to be recouped the expenses incurred in saving the subject matter insured: *Kidston v Empire Marine Insurance Co* (1867) LR 2 CP 357, Ex Ch. If the expenses consist of maritime salvage charges or general average expenditure, they will be recoverable, not under the suing and labouring clause, but as a loss by perils insured against: see the Marine Insurance Act 1906 s 78(2) and ss 65, 66(1), (4); and paras 244, 250, 258 and 260 ante.

(13) SUBROGATION

314. General principle of subrogation. Where the insurer pays for a total loss, either of the whole, or in the case of goods of any apportionable part, of the subject matter insured, he thereupon becomes entitled to take over[1] the interest of the assured in whatever may remain of the subject matter so paid for, and he is thereby subrogated to all the rights and remedies of the assured in and in respect of that subject matter as from the time of the casualty causing the loss[2]. Subject to these provisions, where the insurer pays for a partial loss, he acquires no title to the subject matter insured, or such part of it as may remain, but he is thereupon subrogated to all the rights and remedies of the assured in and in respect of the subject matter insured as from the time of the casualty causing the loss, in so far as the assured has been indemnified by that payment for the loss[3].

Therefore, when a loss happens, anything which reduces or diminishes it reduces or diminishes the amount the insurer is bound to pay; and if the insurer has already paid the full loss, then if anything which diminishes the loss afterwards comes into the hands of the assured, the insurer is entitled to be recouped to the extent of the benefit so received[4].

The principle of subrogation may be illustrated as follows: if two ships, A and B, come into collision and the collision is due to the negligence of those in charge of B, the owner of A, who has insured her, can recover the amount of his loss from the owner of B, and the owner of B cannot resist the claim on the ground that the owner of A was entitled to recover or even had already recovered from his insurers. If the owner of A has recovered his loss from the owner of B he will be compelled to account to the insurers for the money he has so received, and his claim against them will be pro tanto reduced or, if he has recovered a complete indemnity, extinguished[5]. The owner of A may, however, in the first instance recover his loss from the insurers, in which case they will be subrogated to his right to recover the loss from the owner of B[6].

It is immaterial whether the premium is paid by the assured or some other party; thus where shipowners were obliged by a contract to pay the premium on the insurance on cargo, this did not affect the right of the insurers of the cargo to be subrogated to the rights of the cargo-owners in order to recover damages in an action against the shipowners[7].

1 These same words appear in the Marine Insurance Act 1906 s 63(1) (see para 310 ante), and it would therefore seem that the insurer is not bound to take over the assured's interest in the subject matter insured, but has a choice whether or not to do so. See also para 311 ante.

2 Ibid s 79(1). Section 79 gives the insurer a contingent right of subrogation which attaches and vests at the moment when the policy is effected: *Boag v Standard Marine Insurance Co Ltd* [1937] 2 KB 113 at 122, [1937] 1 All ER 714 at 719, CA, per Lord Wright MR. See also *Simpson v Thomson* (1877) 3 App Cas 279 at 284, HL; and EQUITY vol 16 (Reissue) para 889; GUARANTEE vol 20 (Reissue) para 228. There can be no right of subrogation under a ppi policy, for such a policy is void: *John Edwards & Co v Motor Union Insurance Co Ltd* [1922] 2 KB 249. The fact that the assured has claimed and received payment under such a policy is immaterial: *John Edwards & Co v Motor Union Insurance Co Ltd* supra. As to ppi policies see para 211 ante.

3 Marine Insurance Act 1906 s 79(2). An insurer cannot be subrogated to the assured's rights where he has not paid the assured: *Scottish Union and National Insurance Co v Davis* [1970] 1 Lloyd's Rep 1, CA.

4 See *Burnand v Rodocanachi Sons & Co* (1882) 7 App Cas 333 at 339, HL, per Lord Blackburn; see also *Darrell v Tibbitts* (1880) 5 QBD 560, CA, and the judgments in *Castellain v Preston* (1883) 11 QBD 380, CA (where the principle of subrogation is elaborately explained); *H Cousins & Co Ltd v D and C Carriers Ltd* [1971] 2 QB 230, [1971] 1 All ER 55, CA.

5 Although he is bound to account to the insurers for the money received, he does not hold it as trustee for them: *Stearns v Village Main Reef Gold Mining Co* (1905) 10 Com Cas 89, CA, applying the principle of *Randal v Cockran* (1748) 1 Ves Sen 98.

6 For another striking illustration of the proposition that the insurer is subrogated to the assured's rights as regards his remedy for tort see *Assicurazioni Generali de Trieste v Empress Assurance Corpn Ltd* [1907] 2 KB 814; see also *The Welsh Girl* (1906) 22 TLR 475; affd on appeal sub nom *The Commonwealth* [1907] P 216, CA; *The Charlotte* [1908] P 206, CA.

7 *The Yasin* [1979] 2 Lloyd's Rep 45.

315. Extent of right. As between the insurer and the assured, the insurer is entitled to the advantage of every right of the assured, whether such right consists in contract, fulfilled or unfulfilled, or in remedy for tort capable of being insisted on or already insisted on, or in any other right, whether by way of condition or otherwise, legal or equitable, which can be or has been exercised or has accrued, and whether such right could or could not be enforced by the insurer in the name of the assured, by the exercise or acquiring of which right or condition the loss against which the assured is insured can be or has been diminished[1]. The insurer's rights cannot be affected by any contract made by the assured with another insurer or any other person except so far as the assured is supposed to reserve the right of making such another contract, and the insurer to subscribe the policy under an implied condition that the assured may avail himself of that right[2].

It follows also from the principle of subrogation that if the assured should renounce any of his rights and remedies against third persons to which, but for the renunciation, the insurers would have been subrogated, the assured will have to answer to the insurers for the full value of the rights so renounced. In short, the insurer, on payment of the loss, is entitled to the advantage of every right of the assured, whether it consists in contract or in remedy for tort, or to anything he has received or is entitled to receive in diminution of the loss[3].

The insurer is not entitled to sue a third party in the name of the assured[4] unless the assured has assigned to the insurer his right of action[5].

The right of subrogation may be waived by the insurer[6], and there may be an implied term in the policy that he will not exercise it[7].

1 *Castellain v Preston* (1882) 11 QBD 380 at 388, CA, per Brett LJ. The meaning of 'condition' in this portion of the judgment of Brett LJ seems doubtful. The word appears in the report in the Law Reports and the Law Journal, but not in that of the Law Times. An insurer who has paid the whole amount due under the policy will not be subrogated to the assured's rights against third parties if the amount paid is insufficient to give the assured a complete indemnity: *Driscoll v Driscoll* [1918] 1 IR 152 (fire insurance). If, however, the subject matter is insured for the full amount of the insured value, insurers who have paid the full amount insured as for a total loss are subrogated to sums recoverable from third parties, even though those sums are calculated on the basis of a value higher than the insured value: *Thames and Mersey Marine Insurance Co v British and Chilian SS Co* [1915] 2 KB 214; affd on this point [1916] 1 KB 30, CA. The same principle was applied to a case of partial loss in *Goole and Hull Steam Towing Co Ltd v Ocean Marine Insurance Co Ltd* [1928] 1 KB 589. In this case the cost of repairs exceeded the amount insured, but the insurers were held entitled to credit for the whole amount recovered from third parties in respect of the cost of repairs. The fact that hull and machinery were separately valued in the policy was held to be immaterial to the question of subrogation, the sole object of the separate valuation being to enable the assured to exercise the option conferred by the appropriate Institute Clause of claiming average on each valuation separately or on the whole. Where a freight policy incorporated the Institute Clause which provided that, in the event of total loss, whether absolute or constructive, of the vessel, the amount underwritten by the policy should be paid in full, and the hull policy also incorporated an Institute Clause to the effect that in the event of total or constructive total loss no claim for freight should be made by the insurers, the freight insurers were held to be subrogated to freight earned by the vessel after she had become a constructive total loss: *Coker v Bolton* [1912] 3 KB 315. See also para 317 post. Insurers are entitled by subrogation to recover interest for the period after they have paid the loss: *H Cousins & Co Ltd v D and C Carriers Ltd* [1971] 2 QB 230, [1971] 1 All ER 55, CA.

2 2 Phillips' Law of Insurance (5th Edn) s 1715, cited with approval by Lord Wright MR in *Boag v Standard Marine Insurance Co Ltd* [1937] 2 KB 113 at 125, [1937] 1 All ER 714 at 722, CA (cargo insured first under a valued policy and subsequently under an increased value policy; first insurer entitled to the whole of the recoveries in respect of the goods).

3 *West of England Fire Insurance Co v Isaacs* [1897] 1 QB 226, CA; *Compania Colombiana de Seguros v Pacific Steam Navigation Co* [1965] 1 QB 101, [1964] 1 All ER 216. The assured may give the third party a release subject to the insurer's rights of subrogation; but a release given to a third party by an assured, who has already to the knowledge of the third party received payment from his insurers, will not be effective to bar the insurers' right to be subrogated to the remedies against the third party. It was decided in *King v Victoria Insurance Co* [1896] AC 250, PC, that payment honestly made by insurers in satisfaction of a claim by the assured entitles them to the remedies available to the assured, even if the payment was not within the terms of the policy.

4 *Simpson v Thomson* (1877) 3 App Cas 279 at 293, HL; *The Charlotte* [1908] P 206, CA; *Oriental Fire and General Insurance Co Ltd v American President Lines Ltd and Cotton Trading Corpn of San Francisco* [1968] 2 Lloyd's Rep 372, HC Bombay.

5 *Compania Colombiana de Seguros v Pacific Steam Navigation Co* [1965] 1 QB 101, [1964] 1 All ER 216.

6 *The Marine Sulphur Queen* [1970] 2 Lloyd's Rep 285, Dist Ct, Southern Dist NY; *Tenneco Oil Co v Tug Tony and Coastal Towing Corpn* [1972] 1 Lloyd's Rep 514, Dist Ct, Southern Dist Texas (Houston Division).

7 *The Yasin* [1979] 2 Lloyd's Rep 45, where, however, such a term was not implied.

316. Distinction between subrogation and rights arising on abandonment.
In a case of total loss, the rights given by subrogation must be distinguished
from those resulting from abandonment. By virtue of abandonment the insurers
become entitled to the property in the thing insured and to all rights incident to the
property, whereas by subrogation they become entitled to rights and remedies
which may not depend on the ownership of the thing insured. Thus, where the
owners of an insured ship have been paid as for a total loss, the property in what
remains of the ship, and all rights incident to the property, are transferred to the
insurers as from the time of the casualty in respect of which the total loss is paid. For
instance, the right to receive payment of freight accruing due, but not earned, at the
time of the casualty is one of those rights incident to the property in the ship, and it
therefore passes to the insurers on abandonment. The right of the assured to
recover damages from a third person is not, however, one of those rights which are
incident to the property in the ship. It passes from the assured to the insurers, in
case of payment for a total loss, only on the principle of subrogation; and it is on
this principle that it passes likewise to the insurers who have satisfied a claim for a
partial loss[1].

1 *Simpson v Thomson* (1877) 3 App Cas 279 at 292, HL, per Lord Blackburn. The case of *North of
England Iron SS Insurance Association v Armstrong* (1870) LR 5 QB 244 (where the ship sank in a
collision, becoming an actual total loss, so that there was nothing to abandon; the case was,
therefore, one of subrogation and not of abandonment), has been the subject of comment, both in
Arnould on Marine Insurance (16th Edn) ss 1302–1306, and by Lord Blackburn and Lord Selborne in
Burnand v Rodocanachi Sons & Co (1882) 7 App Cas 333, HL. The decision itself presents no difficulty,
but there are certain obiter dicta in the judgments which seem to assume that by virtue of
subrogation it might be possible for the insurer to recover more than the amount of the loss he has
paid. It is submitted that, if this is the meaning of such dicta, they are erroneous, and are inconsistent
with the essential principle of subrogation as well as with the judgment in *Sea Insurance Co v Hadden*
(1884) 13 QBD 706, CA; see also *The Welsh Girl* (1906) 22 TLR 475; affd on appeal sub nom *The
Commonwealth* [1907] P 216, CA; and cf *Thames and Mersey Marine Insurance Co v British and Chilian
SS Co* [1915] 2 KB 214; affd [1916] 1 KB 30, CA, cited in para 315 note 1 ante; *Boag v Standard Marine
Insurance Co Ltd* [1937] 2 KB 113 at 122, [1937] 1 All ER 714 at 719–720, CA, per Lord Wright MR.
The judgment in *Sea Insurance Co v Hadden* supra was applied in *Glen Line Ltd v A-G* (1930) 36 Com
Cas 1, HL (hull insurers not entitled either by abandonment or by subrogation to money paid under
the Treaty of Versailles by way of compensation for loss of profits). See also *Yorkshire Insurance Co
Ltd v Nisbet Shipping Co Ltd* [1962] 2 QB 330, [1961] 2 All ER 487 (criticising *North of England Iron SS
Insurance Association v Armstrong* supra), where it was held that an insurer cannot recover more than
he has paid).

317. Conditions limiting the principle of subrogation. The principle of subrogation is limited or qualified in its application by the conditions set out below.
  (1) The insurer is entitled only to those remedies, rights or other advantages
      which are available to the assured himself. Thus, if two ships, A and B, are
      the property of the same owner, and A is sunk by the negligence of those in
      charge of B, the insurers on A, having paid as for a total loss, have no claim
      upon the owner, inasmuch as the owner cannot be answerable in damages to
      himself[1].
  (2) The insurer is subrogated only to those rights possessed by the assured in
      respect of the thing to which the contract of insurance relates. Thus, where a
      vessel is damaged by collision, and her owners recover from those by whose
      negligence it was caused damages in respect of matters which are not covered
      by a policy on the ship, for example, demurrage or freight, the insurers
      cannot, on paying for a total loss, claim from the assured the amount of those
      damages[2].

(3) It is only on payment of the whole of the loss sustained by the assured, whether total or partial, that the insurer is entitled to be subrogated to his rights of action, so that if the amount insured is less than the amount of that loss, the insurers, even though they have paid the amount insured, will not be subrogated to those rights[3]. Therefore, the assured remains the person who has control of the suit in any action brought by him against the person primarily liable, and will be entitled to compromise the action without the insurers' assent, provided always that he acts in good faith without any intention to sacrifice their interests[4].

(4) The advantages to which the insurers by subrogation succeed include any payment made in diminution of the loss in respect of which the insurers are liable, and are not confined to those which the assured has a right to demand, but they do not include benefits in the nature of a voluntary gift which he may have received from a third person if those benefits were intended to be received by him for his own use alone and not to accrue to the insurer[5].

(5) The application of the principle of subrogation may be excluded by the terms of the insurance policy or by any usage of trade to which it is subject[6].

1 *Simpson v Thomson* (1877) 3 App Cas 279 at 284, HL, per Lord Cairns LC, and at 288 per Lord Penzance.
2 *Sea Insurance Co v Hadden* (1884) 13 QBD 706 at 718, CA, per Lindley LJ. Where a vessel is partially damaged by a collision, the insurer is entitled to deduct from the cost of repairs one-third new for old (see para 273 ante), whereas the tortfeasor has no right to make any such deduction. The practice in such a case is to divide the amount recovered from the wrongdoer rateably between the owners and the insurers; thus, the owner retains all damages awarded to him in respect of demurrage, and also the money paid in respect of the thirds, the insurer retaining such portion of the damages as are attributable to the two-thirds which he has paid.
3 See para 315 note 1 ante.
4 *Commercial Union Assurance Co v Lister* (1874) 9 Ch App 483 (a fire policy, but the principle of the decision applies equally to marine insurance).
5 *Burnand v Rodocanachi Sons & Co* (1882) 7 App Cas 333, HL, explained in *Stearns v Village Main Reef Gold Mining Co* (1905) 10 Com Cas 89, CA, in a manner inconsistent with the explanation of Brett LJ in *Castellain v Preston* (1883) 11 QBD 380 at 391, CA.
6 *Tate v Hyslop* (1885) 15 QBD 368, CA.

318. Property insured by persons having different interests. It often occurs that the same property is insured by persons who have different interests in it. For example, the owner, the carrier or other bailee of goods, the mortgagor and mortgagee, may insure the same property with different insurers, and in such a case difficult questions may arise between the various insurers as to their respective rights and liabilities between themselves. The answer to these questions is to be found by the correct application of the two principles of subrogation and contribution. The cases in which one or other of those two principles are to be applied have been judicially explained in the following manner[1].

If a third person (a bailee of the goods, or, indeed, any other person) is liable in contract or tort for the loss of the goods or for damage to them, the insurer who has insured the goods for the owner is subrogated to his rights against the third person, and it follows that any insurer with whom that third person has insured his liability will be ultimately liable for the loss, and cannot recover any contribution from the first insurer[2].

Where different persons insure the same property in respect of their different rights, they may be divided into two classes. It may be that the interest of the two between them makes up the whole property, as in the case of a tenant for life and remainderman. If each insures, although they may use words apparently insuring the whole property, they would recover from their respective insurers the value of their own interests, and, of course, those values added together would make up the value of the whole property. Therefore, it would not be a case either for subrogation or contribution, because the loss would be divided between the two insurers in proportion to the interests which the respective persons assured had in the property. Then there may be cases where, although two different persons insure in respect of different rights, each of them can recover the whole, as in the case of a bailor and bailee or mortgagor and mortgagee; in such a case it will necessarily follow that one of these two has a remedy over against the other, because the same property cannot in value belong at the same time to two different persons, and, therefore, it must be that if both recover the full value of the property from their respective insurers, the insurer who has insured the person who has the remedy over is subrogated to that remedy[3].

1 *North British and Mercantile Insurance Co v London, Liverpool and Globe Insurance Co* (1877) 5 ChD 569 at 583–585, CA, per Mellish LJ (a fire policy, but the principles laid down in the judgment apply equally to marine insurance). As to fire insurance see para 591 et seq post.

2 See *North British and Mercantile Insurance Co v London, Liverpool and Globe Insurance Co* (1877) 5 ChD 569 at 584–585, CA, per Mellish LJ. As to contribution see further EQUITY vol 16 (Reissue) para 700; GUARANTEE vol 20 (Reissue) para 255 et seq.

3 See *North British and Mercantile Insurance Co v London, Liverpool and Globe Insurance Co* (1877) 5 ChD 569 at 583–584, CA, per Mellish LJ.

(14) DOUBLE INSURANCE

319. Meaning of 'double insurance'. Where two or more policies are effected by or on behalf of the assured[1] on the same adventure and interest, or any part of it, and the sums insured exceed the indemnity allowed by the Marine Insurance Act 1906[2], the assured is said to be over-insured by double insurance[3].

Where the assured is over-insured by double insurance, unless the policy otherwise provides, the assured may claim payment from the insurers in such order as he may think fit, provided he is not entitled to receive any sum in excess of the indemnity allowed by the Act[4]. Thus, if a merchant, the value of whose whole interest is £30,000, first effects a policy on this interest at Liverpool for £20,000, and then another policy on the same interest at London for £30,000, he can recover the whole amount of £30,000 on the London policy[5].

Where the policy under which the assured claims is a valued policy[6], the assured must give credit as against the valuation for any sum received by him under any other policy without regard to the actual value of the subject matter insured[7].

Where the policy is an unvalued policy[8], he must give credit, as against the full insurable value, for any sum received by him under any other policy[9].

The result is that the amount recoverable may sometimes depend on the order in which actions on different policies are instituted. Thus, if a ship is insured by policy A for £200,000 valued at £400,000, and by policy B for £200,000 valued at £300,000, and there is a total loss, the assured can recover £200,000 on policy B, and then claim £200,000 on policy A. If he first receives from the insurers on policy A £200,000, the sum insured by that policy, he can only claim on policy B the difference between £200,000 and the amount of the valuation (£300,000), that is £100,000[10].

1 As to the use of the term 'the assured' see para 35 note 1 ante.

2 As to the indemnity allowed see the Marine Insurance Act 1906 s 16 (unvalued policy) and s 27 (valued policy); and paras 41–42, 256 ante.

3 Ibid s 32(1).

4 Ibid s 32(2)(a). This provision embodies the law as laid down in *Newby v Reed* (1763) 1 Wm Bl 416; *Rogers v Davis* (1777) 2 Park's Marine Insurances (8th Edn) 601. Continental law on this subject differs from English law. It generally makes the successive policies protect the property in order of date, and United States policies usually contain a clause embodying substantially the Continental law. The policy may contain a warranty limiting the amount which the assured is permitted to insure: see para 58 note 1 ante.

5 *Rogers v Davis* (1777) 2 Park's Marine Insurances (8th Edn) 601.

6 For the meaning of 'valued policy' see para 41 ante.

7 Marine Insurance Act 1906 s 32(2)(b).

8 For the meaning of 'unvalued policy' see para 41 ante.

9 Marine Insurance Act 1906 s 32(2)(c). These provisions embody the law as laid down in *Bruce v Jones* (1863) 1 H & C 769, which virtually overruled *Bousfield v Barnes* (1815) 4 Camp 228.

10 See further Chalmers' Marine Insurance Act 1906 (10th Edn) 43, 49.

320. Right of contribution. Where the assured is over-insured by double insurance[1], each insurer is bound, as between himself and the other insurers, to contribute rateably to the loss in proportion to the amount for which he is liable under his contract[2]. If any insurer pays more than his proportion of the loss, he is entitled to maintain an action for contribution against the other insurers, and to the like remedies as a surety who has paid more than his proportion of the debt[3].

Where the assured receives any sum in excess of the indemnity allowed by the Marine Insurance Act 1906[4], he is deemed to hold that sum in trust for the insurers according to their right of contribution among themselves[5].

1 See para 319 ante.

2 Marine Insurance Act 1906 s 80(1). In general, where several persons are co-guarantors for the same debt, and one of them is called upon to pay more than his share, he is entitled to contribution from the others proportionately to the amounts for which each is a guarantor: see GUARANTEE vol 20 (Reissue) para 255 et seq; *Dering v Earl of Winchelsea* (1787) 1 Cox Eq Cas 318, and the notes thereto in 2 White & Tud LC (9th Edn) 496 et seq. How the total sum paid to the assured should be apportioned as between the different insurers is not settled by the Marine Insurance Act 1906 ss 32, 80, nor by any decided cases or established practice. An attempt to solve this problem is to be found in Arnould on Marine Insurance (16th Edn) ss 436–437.

3 Marine Insurance Act 1906 s 80(2); and see GUARANTEE vol 20 (Reissue) para 255 et seq.

4 See para 319 note 2 ante.

5 Marine Insurance Act 1906 s 32(2)(d).

321. Insurances on different interests. Double insurance[1] only arises where two or more policies are effected in the same interest. Where they are effected to cover different interests there can be no contribution among the insurers, but the principle of subrogation may then apply and limit the amount ultimately paid by all the insurers to the indemnity allowed by the Marine Insurance Act 1906[2].

1 For the meaning of 'double insurance' see para 319 ante.

2 See *North British and Mercantile Insurance Co v London, Liverpool and Globe Insurance Co* (1877) 5 ChD 569 at 576, 584, CA; *Godin v London Assurance Co* (1758) 1 Burr 489 at 495. See also the Marine Insurance Act 1906 ss 32(2)(d), 79; and paras 314, 320 ante.

(15) RECOVERY OF LOSSES AND RETURN OF PREMIUM

(i) Settlement of Losses

322. Settlement of loss. When a claim arises under a policy, the assured's broker, having ascertained the percentage of the loss, according to the usual practice indorses the percentage on the policy with the word 'settled' prefixed, and calls on the insurer to initial the indorsement. When the indorsement is initialled, the claim is said to be 'settled', or in earlier times the policy was said to be 'adjusted'[1]. This settlement amounts to an acknowledgment by the insurer of his liability and an implied promise by him to pay the indorsed percentage, but it is only an accord without satisfaction, and the only consideration is the insurer's liability for the loss. It follows, therefore, from the ordinary principles of the common law that the insurer is not precluded from disputing his liability and showing that there is no consideration for the implied promise, even though at the time of settlement he had full means of knowledge[2].

1 'Settling the claim' describes the modern practice; 'adjusting the policy' describes the older practice to which most of the cases subsequently cited refer. See Arnould on Marine Insurance (16th Edn) s 167.
2 See Lord Campbell's note to *Shepherd v Chewter* (1808) 1 Camp 274 at 276; *Steel v Lacy* (1810) 3 Taunt 285; *Reyner v Hall* (1813) 4 Taunt 725; *Luckie v Bushby* (1853) 13 B & C 864; and see *Kelly v Solari* (1841) 9 M & W 54; and CONTRACT vol 9 para 587.

323. Payment of loss after settlement. If, after settlement, the insurer pays the loss, he cannot recover it unless it was paid under a mistake of fact[1]. Moreover, where the loss is total at the time of settlement and is paid by the insurer under no mistake of fact, the money cannot be recovered by him on the ground that the constructive total loss[2] has subsequently been adeemed[3].

On the other hand, if after a loss has been paid the insurer discovers that there was fraud, misrepresentation, non-disclosure or any other matter previously unknown to him which would have afforded a good defence to the claim, he can recover the money so paid from the assured, or from the broker who has effected the policy unless that broker has actually paid over the loss to the assured[4] or accounted to him for the amount received in circumstances amounting to payment[5]. If the broker has merely placed the money received to the assured's credit in such circumstances that the account remains open, it can be recovered from the broker unless he has been induced by the insurer's conduct to alter his legal position[6]. It follows also from ordinary common law principles that if payments of losses have been made under compulsion of legal process, but under a mistake of fact, the money so paid cannot be recovered unless there has been such fraud as would enable the insurer to set aside the judgment or the process of the court[7].

Where the insurer does not resist the claim upon a policy which is void for illegality, but pays the amount of the loss to the assured's broker, the assured is entitled to recover from the broker the amount of the loss, inasmuch as he can prove that the money was paid to his use, without alleging the illegality of the policy[8].

1 *Bilbie v Lumley* (1802) 2 East 469; *Duke Cadaval v Collins* (1836) 4 Ad & El 858 at 866 per Patteson J; *Norwich Union Fire Insurance Society Ltd v Price Ltd* [1934] AC 455, PC. See *Marriot v Hampton* (1797)

7 Term Rep 269, and the notes in 2 Smith's LC (13th Edn) 387, 401, 405 et seq. As to mistake generally see MISTAKE.
2 For the meaning of 'constructive total loss' see para 292 ante.
3 *Da Costa v Firth* (1766) 4 Burr 1966; and see *Blaauwpot v Da Costa* (1758) 1 Eden 130; *Brooks v MacDonnell* (1835) 1 Y & C Ex 500; *Tunno v Edwards* (1810) 12 East 488; *Goldsmid v Gillies* (1813) 4 Taunt 803. As to ademption of loss see para 313 ante. In *Holmes v Payne* [1930] 2 KB 301, the decision in *Da Costa v Firth* supra was applied to a case of non-marine insurance where an agreement had been made by the insurer to replace the lost article instead of paying a loss: see para 659 post.
4 *Buller v Harrison* (1777) 2 Cowp 565. As to misrepresentation generally see MISREPRESENTATION.
5 *Holland v Russell* (1863) 4 B & S 14, Ex Ch. As to accounting which amounts to payment see para 95 ante. See also AGENCY vol 1(2) (Reissue) para 101; CONTRACT vol 9 para 592.
6 *Buller v Harrison* (1777) 2 Cowp 565; explained in *Holland v Russell* (1861) 1 B & S 424 at 435; affd (1863) 4 B & S 14, Ex Ch. See also AGENCY vol 1(2) (Reissue) para 174. The broker cannot retain the money in the exercise of his lien for unpaid premiums or on the ground that since he received the money he has given time to the assured for the payment of premiums: *Scottish Metropolitan Assurance Co Ltd v P Samuel & Co Ltd* [1923] 1 KB 348.
7 See *Marriot v Hampton* (1797) 7 Term Rep 269, and the notes thereto in 2 Smith's LC (13th Edn) 387. See also CONTRACT vol 9 para 662.
8 *Tenant v Elliott* (1797) 1 Bos & P 3; cf *Farmer v Russell* (1798) 1 Bos & P 296; *Bousfield v Wilson* (1846) 16 LJEx 44; and see AGENCY vol 1(2) (Reissue) para 99. As to the effect of illegality on the right to a return of premium see para 334 post.

324. Recovery of salvage by insurer. After payment of a total loss, the insurer can recover the salvage or the proceeds of its sale from the assured[1] unless he is estopped from doing so, for instance by having paid less than the whole amount of insurance in full settlement of the claim[2].

1 See the Marine Insurance Act 1906 s 79; *Roux v Salvador* (1836) 3 Bing NC 266 at 288, Ex Ch; and para 314 ante.
2 *Brooks v MacDonnell* (1835) 1 Y & C Ex 500.

(ii) Return of Premium

325. Recovery of premium. Where the premium, or a proportionate part of it, is by the Marine Insurance Act 1906 declared to be returnable[1], then if already paid, it may be recovered by the assured from the insurer, and if unpaid it may be retained by the assured or his agent[2].

1 See the Marine Insurance Act 1906 s 84(3); and para 326 post. It is open to question whether the Act, in dealing with return of premiums, did not in some particulars alter the law: see para 334 post.
2 Ibid s 82.

326. Circumstances in which a premium is returnable. Where the policy contains a stipulation for the return of the premium, or a proportionate part of it, on the happening of a certain event, and that event happens, the premium, or, as the case may be, the proportionate part, is thereupon returnable to the assured[1].

Where the consideration for the payment of the premium totally fails, and there has been no fraud or illegality on the part of the assured or his agents, the premium is thereupon returnable to the assured[2]. Where the consideration for the payment of the premium is apportionable and there is a total failure of any apportionable part of the consideration, a proportionate part of the premium is, under the like conditions, thereupon returnable to the assured[3].

In particular:

(1) where the policy is void, or is avoided by the insurer as from the commencement of the risk, the premium is returnable, provided that there has been no fraud or illegality on the part of the assured; but if the risk is not apportionable, and has once attached, the premium is not returnable[4];

(2) where the subject matter insured, or part of it, has never been imperilled, the premium, or, as the case may be, a proportionate part of it, is returnable[5], although, where the subject matter has been insured 'lost or not lost'[6] and has arrived in safety at the time when the contract is concluded, the premium is not returnable unless, at that time, the insurer knew of the safe arrival[7];

(3) where the assured has no insurable interest throughout the currency of the risk, the premium is returnable unless the policy is effected by way of gaming or wagering[8];

(4) where the assured has a defeasible interest which is terminated during the currency of the risk, the premium is not returnable[9];

(5) where the assured has over-insured under an unvalued policy[10], a proportionate part of the premium is returnable[11].

(6) subject to the above provisions, where the assured has overinsured by double insurance[12] a proportionate part of the several premiums is returnable[13]; provided, however, that if the policies are effected at different times and any earlier policy has at any time borne the entire risk, or if a claim has been paid on the policy in respect of the full sum insured by it, no premium is returnable in respect of that policy, and when the double insurance is effected knowingly by the assured no premium is returnable[14].

1 Marine Insurance Act 1906 s 83. See further para 327 post.
2 Ibid s 84(1).
3 Ibid s 84(2). As to the return of premium on failure of consideration see para 329 post.
4 Ibid s 84(3)(a). As to fraud and illegality see para 334 post.
5 Ibid s 84(3)(b).
6 For the meaning of 'lost or not lost' see para 191 ante.
7 Marine Insurance Act 1906 s 84(3)(b) proviso. Cf s 6(1), Sch 1 r 1; and para 191 ante. The proviso is founded upon the consideration that in such a case the insurer has taken on himself the risk of the property being lost before the conclusion of the contract: see *Bradford v Symondson* (1881) 7 QBD 456, CA; *Natusch v Hendewerk* (1871) 7 QBD 46on.
8 Marine Insurance Act 1906 s 84(3)(c). As to gaming and wagering policies see further paras 211–212 ante.
9 Ibid s 84(3)(d).
10 For the meaning of 'unvalued policy' see para 41 ante.
11 Marine Insurance Act 1906 s 84(3)(e).
12 As to double insurance see paras 319–320 ante. See also para 332 post.
13 Marine Insurance Act 1906 s 84(3)(f).
14 Ibid s 84(3)(f) proviso.

327. Express stipulations as to return of premium. The parties are at liberty to stipulate that the happening of any specified event should entitle the assured to a return of a certain portion of the premium[1], and the policy often contains an express clause to that effect. It is usual to insert a clause in time policies[2] stipulating for the reduction of premium in the event of the vessel not being continuously employed during the whole of the insured period[3].

1 See para 326 ante; and see *Ionides v Harford* (1859) 29 LJEx 36.
2 For the meaning of 'time policy' see para 41 ante.
3 See the Institute Time Clauses (Hulls) cl 22, and the Institute Time Clauses (Freight) cl 16; and as to those clauses generally see para 149 note 1 ante. As to the construction of such a clause see *Hunter v*

Wright (1830) 10 B & C 714. See also *Pyman v Marten* (1906) 13 Com Cas 64, CA (construction of a clause providing that if the vessel were sold or transferred to a new management the policy should become cancelled and a pro rata return of premium be made); *Gorsedd SS Co v Forbes* (1900) 5 Com Cas 413 (construction of a clause providing for the return of a portion of the premium on the condition that the vessel should not be employed in certain specified trades or within a specified area). Where the policy stipulated for a return of premium while the vessel was 'laid up in port', evidence was given as to the customary meaning of this phrase, and it was held that it did not cover a period during which the insured vessel was bunkering HM ships at Portland: *North Shipping Co Ltd v Union Marine Insurance Co Ltd* (1919) 24 Com Cas 161, CA.

328. Apportionment of premium. Where no usage is proved to the contrary, and no express stipulation to the contrary is contained in the policy, a premium paid in respect of one entire risk cannot be apportioned under the statutory provisions relating to return of premium on failure of consideration[1], unless it can be implied from the contract that the parties had two or more distinct risks in contemplation[2].

1 Ie the Marine Insurance Act 1906 s 84; see para 326 ante.
2 See *Stevenson v Snow* (1761) 1 Wm Bl 318; *Bermon v Woodbridge* (1781) 2 Doug KB 781 at 789; *Tyrie v Fletcher* (1777) 2 Cowp 666; *Gale v Machell* (1785) Marshall on Marine Insurances (4th Edn) 529; *Long v Allan* (1785) 4 Doug KB 276; better reported in Marshall on Marine Insurances (4th Edn) 529; these were very special cases in which the premium was held to be apportionable where the policy contained a warranty that the ship should depart with convoy for the voyage; they were at any rate decided to a very great extent on the evidence of usage. See also *Meyer v Gregson* (1784) 3 Doug KB 402; *Rothwell v Cooke* (1797) 1 Bos & P 172.

329. Failure of policy to attach. The consideration for the payment of the premium is the risk which the insurer takes on himself. This consideration totally fails where from any cause no risk is incurred by the insurer, as where the subject matter insured has never been imperilled or the policy has not attached[1]. This may happen by reason of a breach of an express or implied warranty, for instance where the ship is at the commencement of the risk unseaworthy[2], or where the ship does not sail on or before a certain day, or where the assured abandons the insured adventure at the outset[3], or where there is a failure to disclose a material fact or misrepresentation (even if not fraudulent) on the part of the assured, in consequence of which the insurer repudiates the contract[4]. In the same way the insurer comes under no risk where throughout the currency of the risk the assured has no insurable interest[5].

In all these cases the consideration wholly fails, and, therefore, provided there has been no fraud or illegality on the part of the assured or his agents[6], and, in the case of the assured having no insurable interest throughout the currency of the risk, provided the policy is not effected by way of gaming and wagering[7], the premium, if paid, can be recovered by the assured, and, if unpaid, is not recoverable by the insurer[8].

1 See the Marine Insurance Act 1906 s 84(1), (3)(b); and para 326 ante. See also *Henkle v Royal Exchange Assurance Co* (1749) 1 Ves Sen 317; *Long v Allan* (1785) Marshall on Marine Insurances (4th Edn) 529; *Colby v Hunter* (1827) 3 C & P 7. As to attachment of risk see the Marine Insurance Act 1906 Sch 1 rr 2–4; and para 125 et seq ante.
2 See para 64 ante.
3 See paras 59, 142 ante.
4 *Feise v Parkinson* (1812) 4 Taunt 640; *Anderson v Thornton* (1853) 8 Exch 425. See *North-Eastern 100A SS Insurance Association v Red S SS Co* (1905) 10 Com Cas 245; affd (1906) 12 Com Cas 26, CA, where the ordinary rule as to return of premium was expressly excluded by the rules of the mutual assurance association. As to the effect of misrepresentation see paras 215, 232 et seq ante.

5 After the assured on ship and freight had completed the voyage and earned freight, the court ruled that he could not recover the premium on the ground that he had no insurable interest by reason of want of title to the ship: *M'Culloch v Royal Exchange Assurance Co* (1813) 3 Camp 406.

6 As to the effect of fraud or illegality see para 334 post.

7 See the Marine Insurance Act 1906 s 84(3)(c); and para 326 ante.

8 See ibid ss 82, 84(1); and paras 325–326 ante. Where the assured himself abandons the adventure, he ought, it seems, to give notice to the insurer before he brings his action to recover the premium: *Palyart v Leckie* (1817) 6 M & S 290; cf *Gatty v Field* (1846) 9 QB 431. As has been already seen (see para 90 ante), the premium is not as a rule due to the insurer from the assured but from the broker: Marine Insurance Act 1906 s 53(1).

330. Whole subject matter at risk. If, on the true construction of the policy, the risk is entire and indivisible, then once the policy has attached there is no right to a return of premium in the absence of fraud[1]. For instance, if the insurance is 'at and from' a particular place, the premium is not returnable, even if the ship is lost before sailing on the voyage[2]. On the same principle, since a deviation, as distinguished from a change of voyage, only discharges the insurer from the time of deviation[3], the assured is not entitled to a return of the premium[4]; and the termination of a defeasible interest does not entitle him to a return of premium[5].

1 As to the effect of fraud on the insurer's part see para 334 post.

2 *Moses v Pratt* (1815) 4 Camp 297; *Annen v Woodman* (1810) 3 Taunt 299. For the meaning of 'at and from' see para 131 ante.

3 See para 142 ante.

4 *Hogg v Horner* (1797) 2 Park's Marine Insurances (8th Edn) 782n; *Tait v Levi* (1811) 14 East 481; *Tyrie v Fletcher* (1777) 2 Cowp 666; *Loraine v Thomlinson* (1781) 2 Doug KB 585; *Bermon v Woodbridge* (1781) 2 Doug KB 781.

5 Marine Insurance Act 1906 s 84(3)(d) (see para 326 ante); *Boehm v Bell* (1799) 8 Term Rep 154.

331. Part only of subject matter at risk. Where part only of the subject matter insured is at risk, a proportionate part of the premium is returnable[1]. Thus, if 100 bales of cotton are insured but only 50 are put on board, a return of half the premium must be made for short interest. Similarly, if the freight of a full cargo is insured and at the time of the loss a complete cargo is not at risk, there must be a proportionate return of premium[2].

1 See the Marine Insurance Act 1906 s 84(3)(b); and para 326 ante. As to the effect of fraud or illegality see para 334 post.

2 *Forbes v Aspinall* (1811) 13 East 323 (freight); *Rickman v Carstairs* (1833) 5 B & Ad 651; *Tobin v Harford* (1864) 34 LJCP 37, Ex Ch (cargo), afford examples of short interest, but no question of return of premium was there discussed. Cf *Eyre v Glover* (1812) 16 East 218 (profits).

332. Over-insurance. If under an unvalued policy[1] the assured has insured for £10,000 and the property at risk is only of the value of £7,500, a quarter of the premium is returnable, because the insurer could never be liable for more than three-quarters of the value of the amount insured[2]. Where the assured has over-insured by double insurance[3], a proportionate part of the several premiums is returnable[4], subject to the statutory provisions previously mentioned[5].

The principle on which the statutory provisions as to over-insurance and double insurance[6] are founded is that if the risk in consideration of which the premium is paid is not in fact incurred, or is not incurred to the full extent contemplated, there is a failure of consideration in whole or in part in respect of which the insurer must return the premium or part of it[7].

Where the over-insurance is by a single policy, all the insurers contribute rateably to the return of premium without regard to the date of their subscriptions. If there are several policies on the same subject matter and the sum insured exceeds the value of the subject matter, all the insurers on the several policies are liable to pay according to their respective subscriptions, and are therefore bound to make a return of premium for the excess of the sum insured over the value of the subject matter in proportion to their respective subscriptions[8].

These rules of law relating to double insurances do not prevail on the continent of Europe. United States policies generally contain express provisions on the subject[9].

1 For the meaning of 'unvalued policy' see para 41 ante.
2 See the Marine Insurance Act 1906 s 84(3)(e); and para 326 ante. As to the effect of fraud or illegality on the right to the return of the premium see para 334 post.
3 As to double insurance see para 319 ante.
4 Marine Insurance Act 1906 s 84(3)(f): see para 326 ante.
5 See para 326 ante.
6 Ie the Marine Insurance Act 1906 s 84(3)(e), (f): see text and notes 1–5 supra; and para 326 ante.
7 See further Arnould on Marine Insurance (16th Edn) s 1336.
8 Marshall on Marine Insurances (4th Edn) 516.
9 See Arnould on Marine Insurance (15th Edn) s 1253.

333. Effect of material alteration. Where a policy was avoided by reason of a material alteration when in the custody of the assured or his agent[1], before the passing of the Marine Insurance Act 1906 the law was that the premium was not returnable[2]. However, it has yet to be decided whether the words of the statutory provision as to return of the premium where the policy is avoided by the insurer as from the commencement of the risk[3] make the premium non-returnable in a case where the policy is so avoided before the risk has attached.

1 As to the avoidance of a policy in these circumstances see paras 84–85 ante.
2 *Langhorn v Cologan* (1812) 4 Taunt 330.
3 Ie the Marine Insurance Act 1906 s 84(3)(a): see para 326 ante.

334. Effect of fraud or illegality. Where the insurer has been induced to enter into the contract of insurance by the fraud of the assured or his agent, or where there has been illegality on the part of the assured, and the policy is avoided by the insurer, the assured cannot recover the premium[1]. On the other hand, where the assured has been induced to enter into the contract by the insurer's fraud, and consequently repudiates the contract, the premium must be returned[2].

Where the policy is effected by way of gaming or wagering, the premium is not returnable[3].

According to common law principles, if the policy was void on the ground of its illegality and the assured withdrew from the contract before the policy had attached, on giving the insurer notice of the withdrawal the assured could recover the premium[4]. He would be entitled to do so because he could prove failure of consideration without relying on or alleging the illegality of the policy[5]. It seems, however, that this rule of law, which has been strongly questioned by eminent judges, is no longer applicable to marine insurance, and that, whether or not the policy has attached, the premium is not returnable if the policy is void by reason of illegality[6].

1 Marine Insurance Act 1906 s 84(3)(a): see para 326 ante; *Rivaz v Gerussi Bros & Co and Gerussi* (1880) 6 QBD 222, CA; *Tyler v Horne* (1785) Marshall on Marine Insurances (4th Edn) 525; *Chapman v Fraser* (1793) Marshall on Marine Insurances (4th Edn) 525.

2 See paras 215–216 ante; and see *Duffell v Wilson* (1808) 1 Camp 401; *Refuge Assurance Co Ltd v Kettlewell* [1909] AC 243, HL. If an insurer insures a ship 'lost or not lost' knowing that she has arrived in safety, the premium is returnable: see the Marine Insurance Act 1906 s 84(3)(a); and para 326 ante; *Carter v Boehm* (1766) 3 Burr 1905.

3 See the Marine Insurance Act 1906 s 84(3)(a), (c); and para 326 ante. See also the Marine Insurance (Gambling Policies) Act 1909 s 1(1); and para 212 ante. Cf *Evanson v Crooks* (1911) 106 LT 264; *Elson v Crookes* (1911) 106 LT 462, DC; *Howarth v Pioneer Life Assurance Co Ltd* (1912) 107 LT 155, DC (life assurance).

4 *Palyart v Leckie* (1817) 6 M & S 290.

5 *Lowry v Bourdieu* (1780) 2 Doug KB 468 at 471 per Buller J. See also *Tappenden v Randall* (1801) 2 Bos & P 467; *Aubert v Walsh* (1810) 3 Taunt 277; *Taylor v Bowers* (1876) 1 QBD 291, CA; *Hermann v Charlesworth* [1905] 2 KB 123, CA.

6 Cf the Marine Insurance Act 1906 s 84(3)(a); and see para 326 ante. See *Morck v Abel* (1802) 3 Bos & P 35; *Lubbock v Potts* (1806) 7 East 449; *Re National Benefit Assurance Co Ltd* [1931] 1 Ch 46. Where the insurer raises the defence of illegality, the assured may recover the premium if when the policy was effected he was ignorant of the fact which rendered it illegal: *Oom v Bruce* (1810) 12 East 225; *Henry v Staniforth* (1816) 4 Camp 270; sub nom *Hentig v Staniforth* 5 M & S 122; *Siffken v Allnutt* (1813) 1 M & S 39. As to the effect of misrepresentation by the insurer or his agent as to the legality of the insurance see also *Harse v Pearl Life Assurance Co* [1904] 1 KB 558, CA; and as to the general rule in all branches of insurance see further para 447 et seq post. If the illegality is due to the fraud or negligence of the agent who effected the policy, the agent may be liable in damages to the assured: see *Connors v London and Provincial Assurance Co* (1913) 47 ILT 148 (life assurance).

(iii) Practice and Evidence

335. Pleading and practice. The principles of pleading and practice in the case of a marine insurance action are, in general, the same as in any other action, but the following special points should be noted[1]. Where the assured brings an action for a total loss and the evidence proves only a partial loss, then, unless the policy otherwise provides he may recover for a partial loss[2], but where the assured merely proves that the ship has sustained some damage without giving any evidence as to its extent, he can recover only nominal damages[3]. Where constructive total loss[4] is pleaded, particulars must be given of the general nature of the injuries to the vessel and of the heads of expense relied upon, but there is no obligation to particularise the detailed cost of repairs[5]. Where the insurers allege that the insured vessel was lost as a result of wilful misconduct on the part of the assured, the court may order that they must give further and better particulars[6].

Where there is a general averment of interest in the entire subject matter insured, the plaintiff who proves an interest in part may recover to that extent[7].

The court will prevent its process from being abused and therefore will not allow the assured to recover the full amount of his loss where he has already received the premium under a plea of payment into court[8].

A reinsurer has been held entitled to bring an action for premiums on behalf of himself and all the other reinsurers who were jointly entitled to the premium under the reinsurance contract[9].

1 The history and practice of pleading contracts of marine insurance are discussed in *Munro, Brice & Co v War Risks Association* [1918] 2 KB 78 at 82 et seq by Bailliache J. As to pleading in general see PLEADING. As to evidence generally see EVIDENCE. As to discovery, inspection and interrogatories generally see DISCOVERY.

2 Marine Insurance Act 1906 s 56(4): see para 303 ante, and *Gardiner v Crossdale* (1760) 2 Burr 904.

3 *Tanner v Bennett* (1825) Ry & M 182.

4 For the meaning of 'constructive total loss' see para 292 ante.
5 *Transport and Trading Co Ltd v Indemnity Mutual Marine Assurance Co Ltd* [1919] WN 48, CA.
6 *Palamisto General Enterprises SA v Ocean Marine Insurance Co Ltd, The Dias* [1972] 2 QB 625, [1972] 2 All ER 1112, CA, disapproving a long standing practice to the contrary; *Astrovlanis Compania Naviera SA v Linard, The Gold Sky* [1972] 2 QB 611, [1972] 2 All ER 647, CA.
7 *Rising v Burnett* (1798) Marshall on Marine Insurances (4th Edn) 570; *Page v Rogers* (1785) Marshall on Marine Insurances (4th Edn) 570.
8 *Carr v Royal Exchange Assurance Corpn v Carr v Montefiore* (1864) 34 LJQB 21. As to the person in whose name the action may be brought in the case of assignment of money due under the policy see *Swan and Cleland's Graving Dock and Slipway Co v Maritime Insurance Co and Croshaw* [1907] 1 KB 116; *Williams v Atlantic Assurance Co Ltd* [1933] 1 KB 81, CA.
9 *Janson v Property Insurance Co Ltd* (1913) 30 TLR 49.

336. Discovery of ship's papers. Since the end of the eighteenth century it has been the practice of the courts to grant discovery to a larger extent in matters arising out of policies of marine insurance than in other civil actions[1]. This more extensive discovery is granted by means of an order for the discovery of ship's papers[2]. The practice is peculiar, and strictly limited, to marine insurance[3]. The reasons for the practice are that a contract of marine insurance is one of utmost good faith, and, to a special extent during a marine transit, the knowledge and means of knowledge as to what happens to the subject of the insurance are with the assured, and these reasons govern the extent and application of the practice[4]. Moreover, until 1936 the insurer was entitled as of right to an order for ship's papers on proof that the claim in the action arose out of a policy of marine insurance, and to a stay of proceedings pending production of the papers[5]. In that year, however, the practice was changed[6], and now where in an action in the commercial list relating to a marine insurance policy an application for an order for discovery of documents[7] is made by the insurer, and the court[8] is satisfied that the circumstances of the case are such that it is necessary or expedient to do so, it may make an order for the production of such documents as are specified or described in the order[9]. The order may be made on such terms, if any, as to staying proceedings in the action or otherwise as the court thinks fit[10].

The granting of an order for ship's papers is within the court's absolute discretion[11], and the Court of Appeal will be slow to interfere with the exercise of the discretion[12]. In cases where scuttling is alleged, an order for ship's papers before service of the defence should not be made automatically[13].

1 *Goldschmidt v Marryat* (1809) 1 Camp 559; *Rayner v Ritson* (1865) 35 LJQB 59; *China SS Co v Commercial Assurance Co* (1881) 8 QBD 142, CA.
2 For an account of the historical development of the order see *Leon v Casey* [1932] 2 KB 576 at 579–582, CA, per Scrutton LJ.
3 *China Traders' Insurance Co v Royal Exchange Assurance Corpn* [1898] 2 QB 187 at 189, CA, per A L Smith LJ; *Daily Express (1908) Ltd v Mountain* (1916) 32 TLR 592, CA, in which, at 593, Swinfen Eady LJ observed that every attempt to extend the rule to other cases of insurance had failed. As regards the procedure on applications for discovery in ordinary actions generally see DISCOVERY vol 13 para 24 et seq.
4 *China SS Co v Commercial Assurance Co* (1881) 8 QBD 142 at 148, CA.
5 *Keevil and Keevil v Boag* [1940] 3 All ER 346, CA.
6 See the former RSC Ord XXXI r 12A (revoked); *Keevil and Keevil v Boag* [1940] 3 All ER 346, CA; *Probatina Shipping Co Ltd v Sun Insurance Office Ltd* [1974] QB 635 at 641–642, [1974] 2 All ER 478 at 494, CA, per Lord Denning MR, and at 646 and 498 per Roskill LJ.
7 Ie an order under RSC Ord 24 r 3: see DISCOVERY vol 13 para 10.
8 'The court' means the judge for the time being in charge of the commercial list, the district registrar of Liverpool or the district registrar of Manchester, as the case may be: RSC Ord 72 rr 2(2), 10(3).

9 RSC Ord 72 r 10(1). This is without prejudice to the court's powers under Ord 24 r 3: Ord 72 r 10(1). The order may be made either in the form given in App A, Form 94, or in such other form as the court thinks fit: Ord 72 r 10(1). As to the form of order see further para 339 note 2 post.
10 RSC Ord 72 r 10(2).
11 See RSC Ord 72 r 10(1).
12 *Keevil and Keevil v Boag* [1940] 3 All ER 346 at 348, CA, per Goddard LJ.
13 *Probatina Shipping Co Ltd v Sun Insurance Office Ltd* [1974] QB 635, [1974] 2 All ER 478 at 492, CA.

337. Extent of an affidavit of ship's papers. The papers and documents to be included in an affidavit of ship's papers are not merely those in the plaintiff's possession but also those in the possession of other persons interested in the insurance, and all material documents relating to the adventure, in whosesoever possession they may be[1].

These special rights of discovery apply to actions in respect of policies on goods shipped as well as in respect of the ship, and extend beyond the original parties to the insurance to all persons interested on the same side as the plaintiff even though they are not parties to the insurance[2], and also to an insurer when suing his reinsurer[3]. Further, they apply as against the defendants where insurers who have paid claims under a policy in excess of the amount due bring an action against the assured to recover the amount overpaid, at any rate where the insurers do not admit the claims and were led to pay them by misrepresentation, as such an action is substantially one arising out of a policy of marine insurance[4].

1 *Teneria Moderna la Franco Española v New Zealand Insurance Co* [1924] 1 KB 79, CA.
2 *West of England Bank v Canton Insurance Co* (1877) 2 ExD 472; *China SS Co v Commercial Assurance Co* (1881) 8 QBD 142 at 145, CA; *London and Provincial Marine and General Insurance Co v Chambers* (1900) 5 Com Cas 241. 'All persons interested' does not include other insurers, but only persons on the plaintiff's side (*China SS Co v Commercial Assurance Co* supra); but where mortgagees are suing it includes the mortgagor or his representative, who had sailed the ship as managing owner (*West of England Bank v Canton Insurance Co* supra). It includes a foreign owner, even if out of the jurisdiction, and also a mortgagee (*Graham Joint Stock Shipping Co Ltd v Motor Union Insurance Co Ltd* [1922] 1 KB 563, CA), and the fact that the person from whom the discovery can be obtained is out of the jurisdiction will not prevent the action being stayed until he gives discovery if he is in reality, although not in name, the plaintiff (*Willis & Co v Baddeley* [1892] 2 QB 324, CA).
3 *China Traders' Insurance Co v Royal Exchange Assurance Corpn* [1898] 2 QB 187 at 191–193, CA.
4 *Boulton v Houlder Bros & Co* [1904] 1 KB 784 at 789, CA.

338. Where policy includes transit by land. If the insurance is substantially a marine insurance, an order for discovery of ship's papers may be made notwithstanding that the policy also includes some transit by land[1]. Where the insurance is of an inland transit, part of that transit being by water, and an action is brought on the policy in respect of a loss on land, an order for ship's papers will not be made[2]. If that policy contained a clause under which risks of carriage by ships were covered, and an action was brought under that clause for a loss on an ocean transit, then different considerations would apply and an affidavit of ship's papers might be ordered[3].

1 *Harding v Bussell* [1905] 2 KB 83, CA, questioning *Henderson v Underwriting and Agency Association* [1891] 1 QB 557; *Village Main Reef Gold Mining Co v Stearns* (1900) 5 Com Cas 246; see also *Leon v Casey* [1932] 2 KB 576, CA (warehouse to warehouse clause). See generally CARRIERS.

2 *Schloss v Stevens* (1905) 10 Com Cas 224, CA.
3 *Tannenbaum & Co v Heath* [1908] 1 KB 1032 at 1037, CA, per Lord Alverstone CJ.

339. Duty imposed by order for ship's papers. The duty imposed by an order for ship's papers is not an absolute duty to produce, but to give disclosure on oath and to produce or to explain fully the inability to produce[1].

The form of order[2] requires the plaintiff (the assured) and all persons interested in the proceedings and in the insurance[3], to produce to the defendant, his solicitors or agents on oath all insurance slips, policies, letters of instruction or other orders for effecting such slips or policies, or relating to the insurance or the subject matter of the insurance on the ship or the cargo on board or the freight thereof; also all documents relating to the sailing or alleged loss of the ship, cargo or freight, and all correspondence with any person relating in any manner to the effecting of the insurance on the ship, cargo or freight, or any other insurance whatsoever effected on the ship, cargo or freight, on the voyage insured by the policy sued on or any other policy whatsoever effected on the ship, cargo or freight on the same voyage. Further, the same persons must disclose and produce all correspondence between the captain or agent of the ship and any other person with the owner or any person before the commencement of or during the voyage, and all books and documents, whether in their own custody, possession or power or that of any other person on their behalf, they may be, which in any way relate or refer to the matters in question in the action; those persons must also account for books and documents formerly but no longer in their custody, possession or power[4].

In effect, everything reasonable must be done to obtain production of documents in other persons' custody, and to give all information with respect to them[5].

The application for the order for ship's papers may be made at any time after appearance[6], and need not be supported by affidavit[7]; nor is a deposit as security for costs necessary[8].

1 See *Leon v Casey* [1932] 2 KB 576 at 581, CA, per Scrutton LJ.
2 For the form of order see RSC App A, Form 94. This form was originally prescribed in 1925 consequent upon the observations of the court in *Graham Joint Stock Shipping Co Ltd v Motor Union Insurance Co Ltd* [1922] 1 KB 563, CA; and *Teneria Moderna Franco Española v New Zealand Insurance Co* [1924] 1 KB 79, CA. Alternatively the court may make an order in such form as it thinks fit: see para 336 note 9 ante. For criticism of RSC App A, Form 94, and as to the desirability of using a modified form in appropriate cases, see *Probatina Shipping Co Ltd v Sun Insurance Office Ltd* [1974] QB 635 at 642, [1974] 2 All ER 478 at 494–495, CA, per Lord Denning MR, at 644–645 and 496 per Buckley LJ, and at 651–652 and 502 per Roskill LJ. The order may contain a direction that all further proceedings be stayed. This does not mean that all activity in preparing the case must come to an end, and a successful party who obtains an order for costs may recover costs properly incurred whilst the stay is in operation: *Pecheries Ostenddaises SA v Merchants' Marine Insurance Co* [1928] 1 KB 750, CA.
3 As to the extent of the right of discovery see para 337 ante.
4 See RSC App A, Form 94.
5 *Janson v Solarte* (1837) 2 Y & C Ex 127 at 136; *China SS Co v Commercial Assurance Co* (1881) 8 QBD 142 at 144, CA, per Jessel MR, and at 146 per Brett LJ; *West of England Bank v Canton Insurance Co* (1877) 2 ExD 472 at 474 per Kelly CB, and at 475 per Cleasby B; *China Traders' Insurance Co v Royal Exchange Assurance Corpn* [1898] 2 QB 187 at 192–193, CA, per Vaughan Williams LJ; *Boulton v Houlder Bros & Co* [1904] 1 KB 784 at 789, CA, per Collins MR, and at 791 per Romer and Mathew LJJ; *Graham Joint Stock Shipping Co Ltd v Motor Union Insurance Co Ltd* [1922] 1 KB 563, CA.
6 *Harding v Bussell* [1905] 2 KB 83, CA.
7 *China SS Co v Commercial Assurance Co* (1881) 8 QBD 142, CA. The application is usually made to the judge in charge of the commercial list on the summons for transfer.

8 *Law and Lindsay v Budd* [1883] WN 166.

340. Evidence. The rules of evidence applicable to policies of marine insurance are generally the same as those which apply to all other cases[1]. Questions as to the materiality of matters represented or not disclosed, or as to what is reasonable diligence, reasonable time or reasonable premium, are in cases of marine insurance questions of fact and not of law[2].

1 See generally EVIDENCE. As to the exceptional effect, in cases of loss by capture, given to the judgment by a foreign prize court and rendering it conclusive, not only as to the fact of condemnation, but also as to the grounds of it, see para 63 ante; and CONFLICT OF LAWS vol 8 paras 739–740; ESTOPPEL vol 16 (Reissue) paras 985–986; PRIZE.
2 Marine Insurance Act 1906 ss 18(4), 20(7), 88. See also paras 146 note 4, and 217, 233 ante.

(16) MUTUAL INSURANCE ASSOCIATIONS

341. Risks undertaken by mutual insurance associations. Where two or more persons mutually agree to insure each other against marine losses, there is said to be a mutual insurance[1].

Mutual insurance associations, called 'protection and indemnity associations', indemnify their members against certain liabilities which are not covered by the ordinary form of policy, such as liability for claims by members of the crew, for life salvage, for the loss of or damage to goods carried on their ships, for the quarter of the damages consequent on collision which is not covered by the ordinary collision clause, for wreck removal[2], or for damage to piers, jetties etc. Some associations also undertake the conduct of legal proceedings in respect of such matters as the recovery of freight, dead freight and demurrage, and claims by cargo owners[3]. Other associations give protection against war risks[4].

1 Marine Insurance Act 1906 s 85(1). As to the origin and nature of mutual insurance associations and the statutory provisions relating to them see paras 25–28 ante. See also para 344 post. For an enumeration of the kinds of risks insured against by mutual insurance and protection associations see Ivamy's Marine Insurance (4th Edn) 215–224. As to reinsurance agreements in respect of war risks between the Secretary of State and certain mutual insurance associations see para 794 post.
2 *M J Rudolph Corpn v Lumber Mutual Fire Insurance Co (Luria International, third parties), The Cape Borer* [1975] 2 Lloyd's Rep 108, Dist Ct, Eastern Dist NY.
3 See *Compania Maritima San Basilio SA v Oceanus Mutual Underwriting Association (Bermuda) Ltd, The Eurysthenes* [1977] QB 49, [1976] 3 All ER 243, CA.
4 See eg *Union-Castle Mail SS Co Ltd v United Kingdom Mutual War Risks Association Ltd* [1958] 1 QB 380, [1958] 1 All ER 431; *Atlantic Maritime Carriers SA v Hellenic Mutual War Risks Association Ltd* [1969] 1 Lloyd's Rep 359, CA.

342. Special clauses peculiar to mutual insurance. Mutual insurances are made subject to the articles of association and to the mutual insurance association's rules and regulations which are usually by express reference incorporated in the policy[1]. These generally contain some special clauses peculiar to such associations. For instance, in insurances on freight there is often a rule or clause that the interest insured is to be the amount entered in the association, which amount is to be paid in the event of the total loss of the ship entered[2].

1 *Muirhead v Forth and North Sea Steamboat Mutual Insurance Association* [1894] AC 72, HL; *Re Albert Average Association, Blythe & Co's Case* (1872) LR 13 Eq 529.

2 See *United Kingdom Mutual SS Assurance Association Ltd v Boulton* (1898) 3 Com Cas 330.

343. Liability for improper navigation of ship. A further loss against which protection associations[1] indemnify the shipowner is liability for damage to goods on board when caused by the improper navigation of the ship. Damage is caused by the improper navigation of the ship where, owing to the negligence of the ship-owner or his employees, whether before or after the commencement of the voyage, the carriage of goods is rendered unsafe and damage ensues[2], but where the cargo is damaged by putting it into the ship's hold which is not properly cleaned, this is not improper navigation, because it does not detract from the safety of the vessel for the voyage[3].

1 As to protection associations see para 341 ante.
2 *Good v London Steam-Ship Owners' Association* (1871) LR 6 CP 563; *Carmichael v Liverpool Sailing Ship Owners' Mutual Indemnity Association* (1887) 19 QBD 242, CA; *The Warkworth* (1884) 9 PD 145, CA.
3 *Canada Shipping Co v British Shipowners' Mutual Protection Association* (1889) 23 QBD 342, CA.

344. Rules of construction applicable to mutual insurance. In general, the provisions of the Marine Insurance Act 1906 apply to a mutual insurance[1]. The same rules of construction as are applicable to ordinary marine insurances apply to insurances effected in mutual insurance and protection and indemnity associations, except so far as they are modified by the terms of the policies issued by the association or by its rules and regulations[2].

1 Marine Insurance Act 1906 s 85(4). See also para 28 ante.
2 Ibid s 85(3). As to the rules of construction of marine policies see generally paras 45–50 ante. As to a rule that the insurances should be renewed from year to year unless the member or association gives notice to terminate the insurance see *Lishman v Northern Maritime Insurance Co* (1875) LR 10 CP 179, Ex Ch. As to a rule which provides that no policy issued by the association is to be dealt with so as to part with any beneficial interest in the policy without the association's consent, and as to other similar rules see *Laurie v West Hartlepool SS Thirds Indemnity Association and David* (1899) 4 Com Cas 322; *Hutchinson v Wright* (1858) 25 Beav 444; *North Eastern 100A SS Insurance Association v Red S SS Co* (1906) 12 Com Cas 26, CA.

345. Position of part owners not being members. The question sometimes arises, where mutual insurance associations are defendants or plaintiffs, whether there can be claims for losses or contributions by or against part owners of vessels insured other than members. This question depends in each case upon the particular rules of the association concerned and the form of its policies, so no general rules on the subject can be usefully laid down[1].

Similarly, the question whether a rule incorporated in a policy of mutual insurance is a warranty[2] the non-compliance with which discharges the insurers, or is only an exception from the risks insured against, is a question of construction depending on the language of that rule and the nature of the risk to which it relates[3].

1 The following are cases on this subject: *Montgomerie v United Kingdom Mutual SS Association* [1891] 1 QB 370; *United Kingdom Mutual SS Assurance Association Ltd v Nevill* (1887) 19 QBD 110, CA; *Great Britain 100 A1 SS Insurance Association v Wyllie* (1889) 22 QBD 710, CA; *Ocean Iron SS Insurance Association Ltd v Leslie* (1887) 22 QBD 722n; *British Marine Mutual Insurance Co v Jenkins* [1900] 1 QB 299.
2 As to the nature of warranties in marine insurance contracts, and as to compliance with warranties, see generally para 54 et seq ante.

3 *Stewart v Wilson* (1843) 12 M & W 11; *Dewa Gungadhur Sailing Ship Co Ltd v United Kingdom Marine Mutual Insurance Association Ltd* (1886) 2 TLR 366; *Williams v British Mutual Marine Insurance Co* (1887) 3 TLR 314, CA (affg (1886) 3 TLR 274); *Colledge v Harty* (1851) 6 Exch 205; *Harrison v Douglas* (1835) 3 Ad & El 396. Club time policies sometimes contain a rule that the policy is to be renewed on the expiration of the period for which it was originally issued, in the absence of ten days' notice to the contrary.

346. Estoppel. Even if no policy has been issued by an association, the association may, by its conduct in admitting the receipt for the plaintiff of the amount of the loss, render itself liable for the loss[1], and conversely a member of a mutual association may be estopped from denying his liability for calls on losses[2].

1 *Re Teignmouth and General Mutual Shipping Association, Martin's Claim* (1872) LR 14 Eq 148. Cf *Edwards v Aberayron Mutual Ship Insurance Society* (1876) 1 QBD 563, Ex Ch; and see ESTOPPEL vol 16 (Reissue) para 1055.
2 *Barrow Mutual Ship Insurance Co Ltd v Ashburner* (1885) 54 LJQB 377, CA. Cf *Re London Marine Insurance Association, Smith's Case* (1869) 4 Ch App 611; Buckley on the Companies Acts (14th Edn) 853–854. A policyholder need not necessarily be a member or liable to contribute as such: see *W R Corfield & Co v Buchanan* (1913) 29 TLR 258, HL, cited in para 27 note 2 ante.

3. AVIATION INSURANCE

347. Civil liabilities of air transport operators. The civil liabilities of operators of aircraft are governed mainly by statutory provisions which have modified the liabilities which would otherwise have attached to those persons at common law. The statutory liabilities imposed on operator carriers are considered generally elsewhere in this work[1]. The liabilities which may arise at common law, so far as they are not excluded by statute, in respect of the operation of aircraft are also considered generally elsewhere[2].

1 See AVIATION vol 2 (Reissue) paras 1678–1687.
2 See AVIATION vol 2 (Reissue) paras 1688–1689.

348. Insurable risks of an air transport operator. The development of air transport legislation has left an aircraft operator with several main heads of public liability to cover by insurance, namely:
(1) absolute liability to persons on land or water who have sustained personal injury or damage to their property[1];
(2) absolute liability to passengers on international carriage within certain limitations on the amount payable[2];
(3) absolute liability to passengers on non-international carriage, subject to certain limitations on the amount payable[3];
(4) absolute liability in respect of registered baggage or cargo carried, subject to certain limitations on the amount payable[4];
(5) liability based on negligence, for example to another aircraft and its passengers where there is a collision in the air[5], or to a passenger carried gratuitously by someone other than an air transport undertaking[6].
Insurance against any or all of these liabilities thus came into existence as a branch of public liability insurance. Decisions on this branch of insurance law are for the time being scanty[7].

Apart from insurance against third party liabilities, an operator may also effect insurance against loss or damage to his aircraft. The Secretary of State's powers to reinsure, and to insure, aircraft and cargoes against war risks are considered subsequently[8].

1 See the Civil Aviation Act 1949 s 76(2); and AVIATION vol 2 (Reissue) para 1685.

2 See AVIATION vol 2 (Reissue) paras 1528–1628 passim.

3 See AVIATION vol 2 (Reissue) paras 1629–1650.

4 See AVIATION vol 2 (Reissue) paras 1528–1656 passim.

5 See AVIATION vol 2 (Reissue) para 1679.

6 See AVIATION vol 2 (Reissue) para 1532.

7 For instances of decisions relating to aviation insurance see *Dunn v Campbell* (1920) 4 Ll L Rep 36, CA (where the period of insurance ran 'from the date and time of the first flight', and it was held that the policy attached from the time when the first flight began and covered an accident which happened whilst the pilot was attempting to take off but before he had left the ground); *Alliance Aeroplane Co Ltd v Union Insurance Society of Canton Ltd* (1902) 5 Ll L Rep 406 (exception against racing held to apply to a competitive flight to Australia, although not at racing speed); *Bond Air Services Ltd v Hill* [1955] 2 QB 417, [1955] 2 All ER 476 (onus of proof of breach of condition: see further para 421 post); *Obalski Chibougainau Mining Co v Aero Insurance Co* [1932] SCR 540 (denial of liability on policy insuring seaplane, on the ground that the machine was flown contrary to government regulations and was not airworthy); *Aslan v Imperial Airways Ltd* (1933) 149 LT 276 (implied warranties by carriers of bullion by air); *Arundell v Provident Mutual Life Assurance Association* (1934) 78 Sol Jo 319 (licence, in life policy, to fly on particular expedition limited to flying on that expedition); *Ilford Airways Ltd v Stevenson* (1957) 21 WWR 78 (whether aircraft was 'in flight' at time of accident); *American Airlines Inc v Hope* [1974] 2 Lloyd's Rep 301, HL (aircraft destroyed on the ground at Beirut airport by members of the armed forces of Israel); *Pan American World Airways Inc v Aetna Casualty and Surety Co* [1975] 1 Lloyd's Rep 77 (US Ct of Apps) (whether insurers of hijacked aircraft could repudiate liability on the ground that the loss fell within an exception).

8 See paras 794–799 post.

4. GENERAL PRINCIPLES OF NON-MARINE INSURANCE

(1) NON-DISCLOSURE AND MISREPRESENTATION

(i) In general

349. Requirement of the utmost good faith. In marine insurance it is provided by statute that a contract of insurance is a contract based on the utmost good faith, and if the utmost good faith is not observed by either party, the contract may be avoided by the other party[1]. This statutory provision has codified, in relation to marine insurance, a principle of universal application to all types of insurance contracts[2]. The utmost good faith requires not so much a strict interpretation of the obligations undertaken and strict preservation of the circumstances in which they are undertaken[3], as the performance of positive duties. In its practical application the principle permits either party to avoid the contract altogether if it is established against the other party either that: (1) there has been a failure by the other party to disclose a material fact; or (2) the other party has made an innocent misrepresentation of a material fact[4], since statements made in a contract must be true in fact[5].

Although an insurer's breach of the obligation to deal with the proposer with the utmost good faith does not give rise to a remedy in damages, the proposer is entitled to a return of the premium[6].

1 See the Marine Insurance Act 1906 s 17; *Carter v Boehm* (1766) 3 Burr 1905 at 1909 per Lord Mansfield; and para 215 et seq ante.

2 *Lindenau v Desborough* (1828) 8 B & C 586 at 592; *London Assurance v Mansel* (1879) 11 ChD 363 at 367; *Seaton v Heath, Seaton v Burnand* [1899] 1 QB 782 at 790, CA; revsd without affecting this point sub nom *Seaton v Burnand, Burnand v Seaton* [1900] AC 135, HL; *Re Yager and Guardian Assurance Co* (1912) 108 LT 38 at 44; see also *Moens v Heyworth* (1842) 10 M & W 147 at 157; *Dalglish v Jarvie* (1850) 2 Mac & G 231 at 243; *Brownlie v Campbell* (1850) 5 App Cas 925, HL; *Lee v British Law Insurance Co Ltd* [1972] 2 Lloyd's Rep 49, CA, per Karminski LJ; *Banque Keyser Ullman SA v Skandia (UK) Insurance Co Ltd* [1991] 2 AC 249, sub nom *Banque Financière de la Cité SA v Westgate Insurance Co Ltd* [1990] 2 All ER 947, HL.

3 These requirements are particularly applicable to contracts of guarantee: see GUARANTEE vol (Reissue) 20 paras 124, 183, 325 et seq. However, a contract of guarantee is not normally a contract of the utmost good faith: see GUARANTEE vol 20 (Reissue) para 124. Intermediaries in insurance transactions are required to state their connection with the insurers: Insurance Companies Act 1982 s 74; see para 813 post.

4 *Thomson v Weems* (1884) 9 App Cas 671; *Macdonald v Law Insurance Co* (1874) LR 9 QB 328; *Duckett v Williams* (1834) 2 Cr & M 348.

5 *Newcastle Fire Insurance Co v Macmorran & Co* (1815) 3 Dow 255, HL; *Fowkes v Manchester and London Life Assurance and Loan Association* (1863) 3 B & S 917; *Thomson v Weems* (1884) 9 App Cas 671.

6 *Banque Keyser Ullman SA v Skandia (UK) Insurance Co Ltd* [1991] 2 AC 249 at 280, sub nom *Banque Financière de la Cité SA v Westgate Insurance Co Ltd* [1990] 2 All ER 947 at 959, HL, per Lord Templeman.

350. Duty to make disclosure. The duty to disclose material facts in a contract of insurance is mutual, although the occasions for disclosure by the insurers are rare[1] since the facts material to the insurance are not, as a general rule, known to the insurers but only to the proposer for insurance[2]. Particularly, it is the duty of the proposer during the preliminary negotiations to make full disclosure of all material facts known to the proposer[3]. This duty is a positive duty to disclose and a mere negative omission constitutes a breach; it is, therefore, misleading to use the word 'concealment' in relation to the duty as it tends to suggest a positive breach of a negative duty as distinct from a negative breach of a positive duty[4]. However, it is sufficient if the facts disclosed put the insurers on inquiry, and their inquiry would in the normal course elicit such further facts as may be material[5].

The duty is a common law duty in the sense that its extent depends on the general common law principles of insurance; it is not merely a contractual duty arising from the terms of the particular contract in question[6]. In non-marine insurance it is usual to introduce into the contract special stipulations which may, expressly or by implication, define, regulate or even limit the amount of disclosure which would otherwise be necessary[7]. The introduction of such stipulations may, as a matter of interpretation of the contract, indicate a limitation of the field within which disclosure by the proposer is required, but unless it is clear from the terms of the contract that there has been a limitation of the field in this way, the full common law duty continues to be operative[8].

Questions seeking information with respect to a person's previous convictions may not be treated as relating to spent convictions[9]. The person questioned must not be subjected to any liability or otherwise be prejudiced in law by reason of any failure to acknowledge or disclose such a conviction[10].

The onus of proving that the insured has failed to perform the duty of disclosure or has broken a condition relating to disclosure lies on the insurers[11].

1 *Carter v Boehm* (1766) 3 Burr 1905; see para 362 post.

2 *London General Omnibus Co v Holloway* [1912] 2 KB 72 at 85, CA.

3 *Seaton v Burnand, Burnand v Seaton* [1900] AC 135, HL; see also *Thomson v Weems* (1884) 9 App Cas 671, HL; *Re General Provincial Life Assurance Co Ltd, ex p Daintree* (1870) 18 WR 396; *Joel v Law Union and Crown Insurance Co* [1908] 2 KB 863 at 897, CA. See para 217 ante.

4 See Chalmers' Marine Insurance Act 1906 (10th Edn) 26–32; and para 215 et seq ante.
5 *Carter v Boehm* (1766) 3 Burr 1905; *Lindenau v Desborough* (1828) 8 B & C 586; *Wheelton v Hardisty* (1858) 8 E & B 232 at 270 per Lord Campbell CJ; *Kreglinger and Fernau Ltd v Irish National Insurance Co Ltd* [1956] IR 116; *Anglo-African Merchants Ltd v Bayley* [1970] 1 QB 311, [1969] 2 All ER 421 (insurer not put on inquiry by describing goods as 'new').
6 *Joel v Law Union and Crown Insurance Co* [1908] 2 KB 863 at 886, CA; *Merchants and Manufacturers Insurance Co Ltd v Hunt and Thorne* [1941] 1 KB 295 at 313, [1941] 1 All ER 123 at 128–129, CA, per Scott LJ; *March Cabaret Club and Casino Ltd v London Assurance* [1975] 1 Lloyd's Rep 169 at 176 per May J. Nevertheless, the duty is sometimes referred to as an implied term of the contract; see eg *Moens v Heyworth* (1842) 10 M & W 147 at 157 per Parke B.
7 The proposer may, for example, be required to make express statements of fact and any statement made in answer to an explicit question will then be a representation of fact; furthermore, the strict truth of a fact thus represented, even if it is not a material fact, is often made an express condition of the contract. See para 364 post.
8 See para 351 et seq post.
9 See the Rehabilitation of Offenders Act 1974 s 4(2)(a); the Rehabilitation of Offenders Act 1974 (Exceptions) Order 1975, SI 1975/1023 (amended by SI 1986/1249; and SI 1986/2268); and CRIMINAL LAW vol 11(2) (Reissue) para 1571 et seq.
10 See the Rehabilitation of Offenders Act 1974 s 4(2)(b); the Rehabilitation of Offenders Act 1974 (Exceptions) Order 1975 (as amended: see note 9 supra); and CRIMINAL LAW vol 11(2) (Reissue) para 1571 et seq.
11 *Stebbing v Liverpool and London and Globe Insurance Co* [1917] 2 KB 433; *Babatsikos v Car Owners' Mutual Insurance Co Ltd* [1970] 2 Lloyd's Rep 314 (Vict CA) (motor insurance).

351. Material facts. Apart from any special stipulations in the contract limiting the field of disclosure[1], the rules for determining what facts are material to be disclosed have been codified in relation to marine insurance[2]. After elimination of the factors peculiarly referable to marine insurance, these rules are generally applicable to all contracts of insurance[3]. The basic test hinges on whether the mind of a prudent insurer would be affected, either in deciding whether to take the risk at all or in fixing the premium, by knowledge of a particular fact if it had been disclosed[4]. Therefore the fact must be one affecting the risk[5]. If it has no bearing on the risk it need not be disclosed[6], and if it would do no more than cause the insurers to make inquiries, delaying issue of the insurance, it is not material if the result of the inquiries would have no effect on a prudent insurer[7]. Whether a fact is material will depend on the circumstances, as proved in evidence, of the particular case[8]. It is for the court to rule as a matter of law whether a particular fact is capable of being material[9], and to give directions as to the test to be applied[10]. Rules of universal application are not therefore to be expected, but the propositions set out in the following paragraphs are well established[11].

1 See para 350 ante.
2 See the Marine Insurance Act 1906 s 18; and paras 215–231 ante.
3 *Becker v Marshall* (1922) 12 Ll L Rep 413 at 416, CA.
4 *Glicksman v Lancashire and General Assurance Co Ltd* [1927] AC 139 at 143, HL; *Zurich General Accident and Liability Insurance Co Ltd v Morrison* [1942] 2 KB 53, [1942] 1 All ER 529, CA; *Godfrey v Britannic Assurance Co Ltd* [1963] 2 Lloyd's Rep 515 at 529 per Roskill J; *Babatsikos v Car Owners' Mutual Insurance Co Ltd* [1970] 2 Lloyd's Rep 314 at 325, Vict CA, per Pape J; *Lee v British Law Insurance Co Ltd* [1972] 2 Lloyd's Rep 49, CA; *Berger and Light Diffusers Pty Ltd v Pollock* [1973] 2 Lloyd's Rep 442 at 463 per Kerr J; *March Cabaret Club and Casino Ltd v London Assurance* [1976] 1 Lloyd's Rep 169.
5 *Seaton v Burnand, Burnand v Seaton* [1900] AC 135, HL; *Dawsons Ltd v Bonnin* [1922] 2 AC 413, HL.
6 Thus, trifling details are irrelevant: see *Morrison v Muspratt* (1827) 4 Bing 60 at 63; *Perrins v Marine and General Travellers' Insurance Society* (1859) 2 E & E 317.
7 *Mutual Life Insurance Co of New York v Ontario Metal Products Co Ltd* [1925] AC 344, PC.
8 *Scottish Shire Line Ltd v London and Provincial Marine and General Insurance Co Ltd* [1912] 3 KB 51 at 70 per Hamilton J.
9 As to questions of fact see para 354 post.

10 *Seaton v Heath, Seaton v Burnand* [1899] 1 QB 782 at 791, CA, per A L Smith LJ; revsd without affecting this point sub nom *Seaton v Burnand, Burnand v Seaton* [1900] AC 135, HL.
11 See para 352 et seq post.

352. Facts affecting the physical hazard. Any fact is material which leads to the inference, in the circumstances of the particular case, that the subject matter of insurance is not an ordinary risk, but is exceptionally liable to be affected by the peril insured against[1]. This is referred to as the 'physical hazard'. It is material in fire insurance that at the time of insuring there has been a fire in adjoining premises which has just been extinguished and is likely to break out again[2], or that a large quantity of waste paper is stored in a building of the assured who had described himself as a dealer in paper board[3]. Similarly, in the case of car insurance, the date of manufacture may be material[4], as would the structure of the garage in which the car is kept where the car is insured against fire[5]. Further, in a combined hotel, catering and leisure insurance in respect of a motel the fact that a discotheque was operated on the premises should have been disclosed[6].

1 As to the duty to disclose mental illness of the assured in the case of life assurance see para 533 post.
2 *Bufe v Turner* (1815) 6 Taunt 338.
3 *A F Watkinson & Co v Hullett* (1938) 61 Ll L Rep 145
4 *Santer v Poland* (1924) 19 Ll L Rep 29.
5 *Dawsons Ltd v Bonnin* [1922] 2 AC 413, HL.
6 *Roberts v Plaisted* [1989] 2 Lloyd's Rep 341, CA.

353. Facts affecting the moral hazard. Any fact is material which leads to the inference that the particular proposer is a person, or one of a class of persons, whose proposal for insurance ought to be subjected to special consideration before it can be decided whether it should be accepted at all or accepted at the normal rate. This is usually referred to as the 'moral hazard'[1]. It is material in relation to motor vehicle insurance to know that the proposer has had convictions for motoring offences recorded against him[2], and it is irrelevant to show that in other cases policies have been issued by the same insurers even with knowledge of such convictions[3]. The age of the person who is to drive may also be material[4]. It is material under a burglary policy[5], a trader's combined insurance policy[6], an all risks insurance policy[7] or a fire policy[8] that the assured has a criminal record[9].

There is no general duty to disclose any and every sort of claim which the proposer may have made during his lifetime, in the absence of express questions directed to eliciting that information[10], but it is often material to know that, in relation to insurance comparable with that sought, there have been previous losses or claims[11]. It is also material that in relation to any class of insurance the renewal of previous policies has been refused[12] or previous proposals have been declined[13].

1 *Locker and Woolf Ltd v Western Australian Insurance Co Ltd* [1936] 1 KB 408, [1936] 54 Ll L Rep 211 at 414, CA, per Slesser LJ.
2 *Zurich General Accident and Liability Insurance Co v Leven* 1940 SC 406; *Jester-Barnes v Licenses and General Insurance Co Ltd* (1934) 49 Ll L Rep 231. See, however, para 350 text and notes 9–10 ante.
3 *Merchants' and Manufacturers' Insurance Co Ltd v Davies* [1938] 1 KB 196, [1937] 2 All ER 767, CA.
4 *Merchants' and Manufacturers' Insurance Co Ltd v Hunt* [1940] 4 All ER 205; affd on other grounds [1941] 1 KB 295, [1941] 1 All ER 123, CA.
5 *Schoolman v Hall* [1951] 1 Lloyd's Rep 139, CA; *Regina Fur Co Ltd v Bossom* [1957] 2 Lloyd's Rep 466; affd on another point [1958] 2 Lloyd's Rep 425, CA; *Roselodge Ltd (formerly Rose Diamond Products Ltd) v Castle* [1966] 2 Lloyd's Rep 105, CA. As to burglary insurance see paras 644–650 post.

6 *March Cabaret Club and Casino Ltd v London Assurance* [1975] 1 Lloyd's Rep 169 at 176 per May J.
7 *Lambert v Co-operative Insurance Society Ltd* [1975] 2 Lloyd's Rep 485, CA (assured's spouse had previous convictions for receiving stolen goods and theft). As to all risks insurance policies see paras 658–659 post.
8 *Woolcott v Excess Insurance Co Ltd and Miles, Smith, Anderson and Game Ltd (No 2)* [1979] 2 Lloyd's Rep 210 (where brokers knew of assured's criminal record, and failed to pass on information to the insurers); and see para 591 et seq post.
9 As to spent convictions see para 350 text to notes 9–10 ante.
10 *Ewer v National Employers' Mutual General Insurance Association Ltd* [1937] 2 All ER 193.
11 *Rozanes v Bowen* (1928) 32 Ll L Rep 98, CA; *Farra v Hetherington* (1931) 47 TLR 465; *Arterial Caravans Ltd v Yorkshire Insurance Co Ltd* [1973] 1 Lloyd's Rep 169; *Marene Knitting Mills Pty Ltd v Greater Pacific General Insurance Ltd* [1976] 2 Lloyd's Rep 631, PC.
12 *Taylor v Yorkshire Insurance Co* [1913] 2 IR 1; *Re Yager and Guardian Assurance Co* (1912) 108 LT 38, DC; *Claude R Ogden & Co Pty Ltd v Reliance Fire Sprinkler Co Pty* [1975] 1 Lloyd's Rep 52 (Aust SC).
13 *Glicksman v Lancashire and General Assurance Co Ltd* [1925] 2 KB 593, CA; affd [1927] AC 139, HL; *Locker and Woolf Ltd v Western Australian Insurance Co Ltd* [1936] 1 KB 408, CA; *Haase v Evans* (1934) 48 Ll L Rep 131.

354. Materiality is a question of fact. The materiality of a particular fact is determined by the circumstances of each case and is a question of fact[1]. Materiality is not a question of belief or opinion tested subjectively[2], and the proposer does not discharge his duty by a full disclosure of what he believes to be material, however honest his belief; he must go further and disclose any fact which a reasonable man would have thought material[3]. Every circumstance is material which would influence the judgment of a prudent insurer in fixing the premium or determining whether he will take the risk at all[4]. If a fact, although material, is one which the proposer did not and could not in the particular circumstances have been expected to know[5], or if its materiality would not have been apparent to a reasonable man[6], his failure to disclose it is not a breach of his duty. The proposer need not disclose matters of common notoriety which the insurer may be presumed to know[7], matters of which the insurer is well aware[8], or matters as to which he has waived information[9].

1 *Huguenin v Rayley* (1815) 6 Taunt 186; *Morrison v Muspratt* (1827) 4 Bing 60; *Lindenau v Desborough* (1828) 8 B & C 586; *Swete v Fairlie* (1833) 6 C & P 1; *Rawlins v Desborough* (1840) 2 Mood & R 328; *Seaton v Heath, Seaton v Burnand* [1899] 1 QB 782 at 791, CA, per A L Smith LJ; revsd without affecting this point sub nom *Seaton v Burnand, Burnand v Seaton* [1900] AC 135, HL.
2 *Morrison v Muspratt* (1827) 4 Bing 60; *Lindenau v Desborough* (1828) 8 B & C 586 at 592; *Anderson v Fitzgerald* (1853) 4 HL Cas 484; *Hoare v Bremridge* (1872) 8 Ch App 22, CA; *Godfrey v Britannic Assurance Co Ltd* [1963] 2 Lloyd's Rep 515 at 529 per Roskill J.
3 *Joel v Law Union and Crown Insurance Co* [1908] 2 KB 863 at 883, CA; *Horne v Poland* [1922] 2 KB 364; *Godfrey v Britannic Assurance Co Ltd* [1963] 2 Lloyd's Rep 515. The knowledge of an agent or employee may in some circumstances be imputed to the assured: see *Regina Fur Co Ltd v Bossom* [1957] 2 Lloyd's Rep 466; affd on another point [1958] 2 Lloyd's Rep 425, CA (knowledge of company chairman of his own earlier conviction for receiving imputed to company). As to the position in marine insurance see para 219 ante.
4 Marine Insurance Act 1906 s 18(2) (see para 215 et seq ante); *Godfrey v Britannic Assurance Co Ltd* [1963] 2 Lloyd's Rep 515 at 529 per Roskill J; *Zurich General Accident and Liability Insurance Co v Leven* 1940 SC 407 at 416; *March Cabaret Club and Casino Ltd v London Assurance* [1975] 1 Lloyd's Rep 169 at 176 per May J; and cf para 221 ante.
5 *Swete v Fairlie* (1833) 6 C & P 1.
6 *Fowkes v Manchester and London Assurance Association* (1862) 3 F & F 440; *Joel v Law Union and Crown Insurance Co* [1908] 2 KB 863, CA.
7 *Noble v Kennoway* (1780) 2 Doug KB 510; *Stewart v Bell* (1821) 5 B & Ald 238; *Bates v Hewitt* (1867) LR 2 QB 595; *Glasgow Assurance Corpn Ltd v William Symondson Co* (1911) 16 Com Cas 109; *Leen v Hall* (1923) 16 Ll L Rep 100; *Hales v Reliance Fire and Accident Insurance Corpn Ltd* [1960] 2 Lloyd's Rep 391.

8 *Carter v Boehm* (1766) 3 Burr 1905; *Lindenau v Desborough* (1828) 8 B & C 586; *Anglo-Californian Bank Ltd v London Provincial Marine and General Insurance Co Ltd* (1904) 10 Com Cas 1.
9 *Anglo-African Merchants Ltd and Exmouth Clothing Co Ltd v Bayley* [1970] 1 QB 311, [1969] 2 All ER 421; *Arterial Caravans Ltd v Yorkshire Insurance Co Ltd* [1973] 1 Lloyd's Rep 169; *Pan Atlantic Insurance Co Ltd v Pine Top Insurance Co Ltd* [1992] 1 Lloyd's Rep 101, CA (reinsurance).

355. Time for determining materiality. Full disclosure must be made of all relevant facts and matters which have occurred up to the time at which there is a concluded contract[1]. The non–disclosure of a material fact existing prior to the conclusion of the contract will become a ground for avoiding the concluded contract[2]. It follows from this principle that the materiality of a particular fact is determined by the circumstances existing at the time when it ought to have been disclosed, and not by the events which may subsequently transpire[3].

1 *Allis-Chalmers Co v Maryland Fidelity and Deposit Co* (1916) 114 LT 433, HL; *Wake v Atty* (1812) 4 Taunt 493.
2 For the duty of the assured to make full disclosure see para 350 ante.
3 *Seaton v Burnand, Burnand v Seaton* [1900] AC 135, HL; cf *Watson v Mainwaring* (1813) 4 Taunt 763; and para 221 ante.

356. Continuing nature of the duty. The duty to make full disclosure continues to apply throughout the negotiations for the contract, but it comes to an end when the contract is concluded; therefore, material facts which come to the proposer's knowledge subsequently need not be disclosed[1]. The proposer need not disclose the fact that, after acceptance of his proposal, another proposal made to other insurers has been declined[2]. A refusal by other insurers to renew an existing policy is material and must be disclosed[3]. If, however, any new material fact arises before acceptance of the proposal, or if an existing fact which was previously immaterial becomes material owing to a change of circumstances, it must be disclosed[4]. If, pending the acceptance of a proposal for life insurance, the proposer sustains a serious injury or contracts a serious disease, that fact too is material and must be disclosed[5]. Similarly, it may happen that a proposer for life assurance is advised by a specialist that he is in a dangerous state of health which is then for the first time diagnosed; the diagnosis must be disclosed to the insurers, even if the medical officer for the insurers has examined the proposer and passed him as fit[6].

1 As to the time of conclusion of the contract see para 218 ante.
2 *Whitwell v Autocar Fire and Accident Insurance Co* (1927) 27 Ll L Rep 418.
3 *Re Yager and Guardian Assurance Co* (1912) 108 LT 38, DC; *Uzielli v Commercial Union Insurance Co* (1865) 12 LT 399 at 401 per Mellor J.
4 *Allis-Chalmers Co v Maryland Fidelity and Deposit Co* (1916) 114 LT 433, HL; *Looker v Law Union and Rock Insurance Co* [1928] 1 KB 554; see para 373 text to note 14 post.
5 *Canning v Farquhar* (1886) 16 QBD 727, CA; cf *Harrington v Pearl Life Assurance Co Ltd* (1914) 30 TLR 613, CA.
6 *British Equitable Insurance Co v Great Western Rly Co* (1869) 38 LJCh 314; *Harrington v Pearl Life Assurance Co Ltd* (1914) 30 TLR 613.

357. Facts unknown to proposer. A proposer is under a duty to disclose to the insurer all material facts as they are within his knowledge[1]. The proposer is presumed to know all the facts and circumstances concerning the proposed insurance. Whilst the proposer can only disclose what is known to him[2] the proposer's duty of disclosure is not confined to his actual knowledge, it also extends to those material facts which, in the ordinary course of business, he ought to know[3]. However, the assured is not under a duty to disclose facts which he did not know and which he could not reasonably be expected to know at the material time[4]. If the assured fails to make reasonable inquiries which would have ascertained the material facts, he will be in breach of his duty and the policy is capable of being avoided[5].

1 *Joel v Law Union and Crown Insurance Co* [1908] 2 KB 863, CA; *London General Omnibus Co Ltd v Holloway* [1912] 2 KB 72 at 85, CA, per Kennedy LJ.
2 *Hearts of Oak Building Society v Law Union and Rock Insurance Co Ltd* [1936] 2 All ER 619 at 625 per Goddard J; see also *Wheelton v Hardisty* (1858) 8 E & B 232 at 269 per Lord Campbell CJ; *Australia and New Zealand Bank Ltd v Colonial and Eagle Wharves Ltd (Boag, third party)* [1960] 2 Lloyd's Rep 241 at 253–255 per McNair J.
3 *Proudfoot v Montefiore* (1867) LR 2 QB 511 at 519; *Blackburn, Low & Co v Vigors* (1887) 12 App Cas 531 at 537, 541, HL.
4 *Jones v Provincial Insurance Co* (1857) 3 CBNS 65; *Joel v Law Union and Crown Insurance Co* [1908] 2 KB 863 at 884, CA, per Fletcher Moulton LJ.
5 *Blackburn, Low & Co v Vigors* (1887) 12 App Cas 531, HL.

358. Representations of material facts. The second aspect of the duty of good faith arises in relation to representations made during the course of negotiations, and for this purpose all statements in relation to material facts made by the proposer during the course of negotiations for the contract[1] constitute representations and must be made in good faith[2]. Just as all material facts within his knowledge must be fully disclosed, so also any statements made about such facts must be accurate in the sense that they do not mislead[3]. A representation may be inaccurate either because it is wholly false[4] or because, although the facts actually stated are literally true, the statement is not complete and creates a misleading impression owing to the omission of other facts which ought to have been included[5]. Failure to disclose the full facts may thus render false those which are stated[6]. However, it is sufficient if the substance of the statement is accurate[7]; an unimportant misstatement which does not colour the whole picture[8] or the omission of trifling details which would not affect an insurer's mind is irrelevant[9]. A misstatement does not matter if the true position is known to the insurers, as the misstatement can have no effect in causing the contract to be concluded[10].

The onus of proving that the assured has made a misrepresentation or has broken a condition relating to misrepresentation lies on the insurers[11].

1 Statements made after the conclusion of the contract have no effect: *Roberts v Security Co* [1897] 1 QB 111, CA; *Joel v Law Union and Crown Insurance Co* [1908] 2 KB 863, CA; and cf *British Equitable Assurance Co Ltd v Bailey* [1906] AC 35.
2 As to the requirement of utmost good faith see para 349 ante.
3 *Everett v Desborough* (1829) 5 Bing 503 at 518; *Wainwright v Bland* (1836) 1 M & W 32.
4 *Re Marshall and Scottish Employers' Liability and General Insurance Co Ltd* (1901) 85 LT 757; cf *Golding v Royal London Auxiliary Insurance Co* (1914) 30 TLR 350; see para 372 post.
5 *Aaron's Reefs Ltd v Twiss* [1896] AC 273 at 281, HL, per Lord Halsbury LC; *Peek v Gurney* (1873) LR 6 HL 377 at 400, HL, per Lord Colonsay; *R v Lord Kylsant* [1932] 1 KB 442 at 444–445 per Wright J.
6 *Dimmock v Hallett* (1866) 2 Ch App 21 at 27–28 per Turner LJ; *Pulsford v Richards* (1853) 17 Beav 87 at 96 per Romilly MR; *R v Lord Kylsant* [1932] 1 KB 442 at 445 per Wright J; *London Assurance v Mansel* (1879) 11 ChD 363 (statement that negotiations were pending with other insurers omitted that some of the other insurers had already refused the proposal). See also *Cazenove v British Equitable Assurance Co* (1860) 29 LJCP 160, Ex Ch; *Re General Provincial Life Assurance Co Ltd, ex p Daintree* (1870) 18 WR 396.
7 *Fowkes v Manchester and London Assurance Association* (1863) 3 B & S 917 at 924; *Yorke v Yorkshire Insurance Co* [1918] 1 KB 662; and see para 373 post.

8 *Re Universal Non-Tariff Fire Insurance Co, Forbes & Co's Claim* (1875) LR 19 Eq 485; *Dawsons Ltd v Bonnin* [1922] 2 AC 413 at 425, HL.

9 *Morrison v Muspratt* (1827) 4 Bing 60 at 63; *Perrins v Marine etc Insurance Society* (1859) 2 E & E 317.

10 *Smith v Kay* (1859) 7 HL Cas 750 at 779 per Lord Wensleydale; *Pulsford v Richards* (1853) 17 Beav 87 at 96 per Romilly MR; see also *Bawden v London, Edinburgh and Glasgow Assurance Co* [1892] 2 QB 534, where the true position was known to the insurer's agent. As to the question when an agent's knowledge is to be imputed to the principal see para 376 post.

11 *Babatsikos v Car Owners' Mutual Insurance Co Ltd* [1970] 2 Lloyd's Rep 314, Vict CA (motor insurance); *Stebbing v Liverpool and London and Globe Insurance Co Ltd* [1917] 2 KB 433 (burglary insurance).

359. Honest misrepresentations. It is the rule in marine insurance that if any representation made which is inaccurate in a material particular, although the misstatement is innocent and the truth of the representation has not been made a matter of contract, it may be a ground for avoiding the policy even after loss[1]. This is generally accepted as being applicable in all classes of insurance[2]. However, where the proposer qualifies his representation by expressly stating that it was made to the best of his belief and is effectively a statement of honest opinion held on reasonable grounds, the innocent misrepresentation does not give grounds for avoiding the contract[3]. In life insurance it is readily assumed that statements by a proposer as to his health are asked for and given on the basis of his belief, because the ordinary man cannot be expected to know what is happening to his internal organs, or what specific symptoms may indicate[4], but the same tolerance is not afforded to a positive statement as to his habits being temperate[5]. Accordingly, in life insurance there are a number of dicta[6] and one express decision[7] to the effect that this branch of insurance is an exception to the general rule, in that fraud has to be established by insurers seeking to avoid a policy. However, it is common in this class of insurance to find inserted an express condition in the policy that the truth of any statement made in the proposal is either warranted by the proposer, is to be a condition precedent to the enforcement of the contract or is to be the basis on which the contract is made, in which case honesty of belief in the truth of the statement is not sufficient[8]. Further, where a misstatement involves a non-disclosure of a material fact, the contract may always be avoided on the latter ground[9].

1 See the Marine Insurance Act 1906 s 20; and paras 232–234 ante.

2 *Graham v Western Australian Insurance Co Ltd* (1931) 40 Ll L Rep 64 at 66 per Roche J; see also *Golding v Royal Auxiliary Insurance Co Ltd* (1914) 30 TLR 350 at 351: *Merchants' and Manufacturers' Insurance Co v Hunt and Thorne* [1941] 1 KB 295 at 318, [1941] 1 All ER 123 at 136, CA; *Zurich General Accident and Liability Insurance Co v Leven* 1940 SC 406.

3 *MacDonald v Law Union Insurance Co* (1874) LR 9 QB 328; cf *Jones v Provincial Insurance Co* (1857) 3 CBNS 65 at 86 per Cresswell J.

4 See eg *Life Association of Scotland v Forster* (1873) 11 Macph 351, Ct of Sess; *Delahaye v British Empire Mutual Life Assurance Co* (1897) 13 TLR 245, CA.

5 *Thomson v Weems* (1884) 9 App Cas 671, HL.

6 *Anderson v Fitzgerald* (1853) 4 HL Cas 484 at 504 per Lord Cranworth; *Wheelton v Hardisty* (1858) 8 E & B 232 at 299, Ex Ch, per Willes J; *Thomson v Weems* (1884) 9 App Cas 671 at 683–684, HL; *Joel v Law Union and Crown Insurance Co* [1908] 2 KB 863 at 877, CA, per Vaughan Williams LJ.

7 *Scottish Provident Institution v Boddam* (1893) 9 TLR 385.

8 See *Wheelton v Hardisty* (1858) 8 E & B 232, Ex Ch. See further para 374 post.

9 *Lindenau v Desborough* (1828) 8 B & C 586; *Dalglish v Jarvie* (1850) 2 Mac & G 231 at 243; *British Equitable Insurance Co v Great Western Rly Co* (1869) 38 LJCh 314; *London Assurance v Mansel* (1879) 11 ChD 363; *British Equitable Insurance Co v Musgrave* (1887) 3 TLR 630; *Joel v Law Union and Crown Insurance Co* [1908] 2 KB 863, CA; *Horne v Poland* [1912] 2 KB 364; *Glicksman v Lancashire and General Assurance Co* [1925] 2 KB 593, CA; affd [1927] AC 139, HL; *West v National Motor and Accident Insurance Union Ltd* [1955] 1 All ER 800, [1955] 1 WLR 343, CA. As to the extent of the duty to disclose see para 350 ante.

360. Truth at the date of the contract. Representations are the statements made by the proposer during the negotiations leading up to the conclusion of the contract, but they do not form any part of the contract[1]. The duty to make accurate representations exists up to the conclusion of that contract, and if before then statements which have been made either become or are discovered to be untrue, they must be corrected[2]. The principle is of particular importance in the case of statements of intention; these are only representations, and if honestly made, a change of intention after the contract is concluded does not affect the validity of the contract or the rights of the parties[3]. However, where the proposer changes his intention before the contract is concluded, it is his duty to correct his statement, and if he fails to do so the insurers may avoid the contract[4]. In the case of contracts for a fixed period such as a year, each renewal operates as a new contract[5] and the insurers must therefore be brought up to date on each renewal with the true state of affairs as it then exists[6].

1 *Roberts v Security Co* [1897] 1 QB 111 at 115, CA, per Lopes LJ. See para 356 ante.
2 *Canning v Farquhar* (1886) 16 QBD 727, CA.
3 *Benham v United Guarantee and Life Assurance Co* (1852) 7 Exch 744; *R v National Insurance Co* (1887) 13 VLR 914; *Grant v Aetna Insurance Co* (1862) 15 Moo PCC 516; cf *De Maurier (Jewels) Ltd v Bastion Insurance Co Ltd and Coronet Insurance Co Ltd* [1967] 2 Lloyd's Rep 550.
4 *Traill v Baring* (1864) 4 De G J & Sm 318; *Re Marshall and Scottish Employers' Liability and General Insurance Co Ltd* (1901) 85 LT 757.
5 *Pritchard v Merchant's and Tradesman's Mutual Life Assurance Society* (1858) 3 CBNS 622.
6 *Pim v Reid* (1843) 6 Man & G 1; *Re Wilson and Scottish Insurance Corpn* [1920] 2 Ch 28. A representation made in negotiations for one contract is not, however, to be regarded as carried forward in this way into new negotiations for an entirely distinct contract: *Dawson v Atty* (1806) 7 East 367.

361. Effect of non-disclosure or misrepresentation. The effect of non-dis-closure or misrepresentation, within the principles already discussed[1], is that the insurers have the right to repudiate the contract[2]. This right does not depend on any implied term in the contract itself[3], but is an inherent right derived as a matter of law from the nature of the contract. It must be distinguished from the equitable remedy of rescission which is available in the case of all contracts entered into as a result of misrepresentation[4]. The remedy is not normally available where there has been a mere non-disclosure; there must be a misrepresentation, although innocent misrepresentation will suffice[5]. Furthermore, that remedy involves in all cases the principle that the parties must be put back so far as may be into the position which they occupied before the contract was made, in particular by restoring any con-sideration which has been paid[6]. However, where the insurers answer a claim by repudiating the policy on the ground of fraud, misrepresentation or non-disclos-ure, they are not bound to offer a return of premium[7], and the court will not normally allow the proposer to set up his own fraud or misconduct in order to found a claim to such repayment[8]. Where the insurers apply to the court for relief in a case where all they can establish is a misrepresentation which is innocent and there is no clause in the policy to cover this position; the court may make it a condition of granting relief that any premiums paid are to be returned[9]. The insurers need only apply to the court for a decree where specific statutory provision has been made to that effect[10], although it is always possible to seek an order for the delivery up of the policy for cancellation[11]. The common law right is one which can only be exercised in relation to the whole contract[12]. The insurers are not entitled to treat the contract as subsisting for some purposes but not for others; if they elect to repudiate the policy, there ceases for any purpose to be a contract between the parties[13]. It is an entirely different situation, governed by different principles, where insurers seek to repudiate, not the policy, but a claim under it[14]. Like any other, the right can be waived, and insurers may find that their conduct, after acquiring full knowledge of the relevant non-disclosure or misrepresentation, is regarded either as amounting to an affirmation of the contract, or as leading the assured to suppose that it is being affirmed and to act accordingly, so as to debar the insurers afterwards from exercising the right on that ground[15]. The principles governing such a waiver are the same as in relation to a breach of condition[16].

Any person who furnishes information which he knows to be false in a material particular, or recklessly furnishes information which is false in a material particular; or causes or permits, or recklessly causes or permits, documents to be included in statements which he knows to be false in a material particular or recklessly is guilty of an offence[17].

1 See para 349 et seq ante.
2 See *Morrison v Universal Marine Insurance Co* (1873) LR 8 Exch 197; *United Shoe Machinery Co of Canada v Brunet* [1909] AC 330 at 339, PC; *Newbury International Ltd v Reliance National Insurance Co (UK) Ltd* [1994] 1 Lloyd's Rep 83; and para 359 note 9 ante. Non-disclosure does not vitiate the contract ab initio: *Mackender v Feldia AG* [1967] 2 QB 590, [1966] 3 All ER 847, CA.
3 *Merchants' and Manufacturers' Insurance Co Ltd v Hunt and Thorne* [1941] 1 KB 295 at 318, [1941] 1 All ER 123 at 136, CA; *Schoolman v Hall* [1951] 1 Lloyd's Rep 139, CA; *March Cabaret Club and Casino Ltd v London Assurance* [1975] 1 Lloyd's Rep 169 at 175 per May J.
4 See *Redgrave v Hurd* (1881) 20 ChD 1, CA; the Misrepresentation Act 1967 ss 1–5 (as amended); and MISREPRESENTATION.
5 *Kelly v Enderton* [1913] AC 191 at 194, PC; *McKeown v Bondard-Peveril Gear Co* (1896) 65 LJCh 446; affd (1896) 65 LJCh 735, CA; *Coles v White City (Manchester) Greyhound Association Ltd* (1929) 45 TLR 230, CA. See further MISREPRESENTATION.
6 *Newbigging v Adam* (1886) 34 ChD 582, CA; affd sub nom *Adam v Newbigging* (1888) 13 App Cas 308, HL; *Houldsworth v City of Glasgow Bank* (1880) 5 App Cas 317, HL; *Lagunas Nitrate Co v Lagunas Syndicate* [1899] 2 Ch 392, CA. See further MISREPRESENTATION.
7 *British Equitable Insurance Co v Musgrave* (1887) 3 TLR 630.
8 *Hambrough v Mutual Life Insurance Co of New York* (1895) 72 LT 140, CA; *Taylor v Chester* (1869) LR 4 QB 309; *Chapman v Fraser* (1793) Marshall on Marine Insurances (4th Edn) 525.
9 *Prince of Wales etc Association Co v Palmer* (1858) 25 Beav 605; *London Assurance Co v Mansel* (1879) 11 ChD 363 at 372 per Jessel MR; *Lodge v National Union Investment Co* [1907] 1 Ch 300; *Chapman v Michaelson* [1908] 2 Ch 612 at 620 per Eve J.
10 Eg by the Road Traffic Act 1988 ss 151, 152: see paras 749–750 post.
11 *Rivaz v Gerussi* (1880) 6 QBD 222, CA; *Brooking v Maudsley Son and Field* (1888) 38 ChD 636.
12 *West v National Motor and Accident Insurance Union* [1955] 1 All ER 800, [1955] 1 WLR 343, CA.
13 As to the circumstances in which a party seeking to repudiate a contract can rely on an arbitration clause contained in the contract see *Woodall v Pearl Assurance Co Ltd* [1919] 1 KB 593; para 496 post.
14 See *Woodall v Pearl Assurance Co Ltd* [1919] 1 KB 593 at 603, CA, per Bankes LJ; para 497 post.
15 *Hemmings v Sceptre Life Association Ltd* [1905] 1 Ch 365; *Holdsworth v Lancashire and Yorkshire Insurance Co* (1907) 23 TLR 521; *Ayrey v British Legal and United Provident Assurance Co* [1918] 1 KB 136.
16 See paras 422–423 post.
17 Insurance Companies Act 1982 s 71(1) (as amended): see para 812 post.

362. Insurers' duties. The duty of good faith is incumbent on insurers just as much as on the proposer[1], although the occasions for its being invoked against them are rare and the field within which it can be invoked is necessarily limited. However, examples occur where, in a prospectus or similar invitation to take out insurance, statements are made as to the nature or effect of an insurance; any such statement must be accurate[2]. A misstatement on such a point will enable the proposer in an appropriate case to obtain rectification of the policy and so enforce a claim on the basis of the insurers' statements, or will preclude the insurers from a defence to a claim which, but for the misstatement, would have been open to them[3]. When such a statement is fraudulent the proposer may elect to avoid the contract on that ground, and he can recover any premiums which have been paid[4].

1 *Carter v Boehm* (1766) 3 Burr 1905 at 1909; *Duffell v Wilson* (1808) 1 Camp 401; *Pontifex v Bignold* (1841) 3 Man & G 63; *Banque Keyser Ullman SA v Skandia (UK) Insurance Co Ltd* [1991] 2 AC 249, sub nom *Banque Financière de la Cité SA v Westgate Insurance Co Ltd* [1990] 2 All ER 947, HL.

2 *Re Bradley and Essex and Suffolk Accident Indemnity Society* [1912] 1 KB 415 at 430, CA; *Provincial Insurance Co Ltd v Morgan* [1933] AC 240 at 250, HL.

3 *Collett v Morrison* (1851) 9 Hare 162; *Wood v Dwarris* (1856) 11 Exch 493. Omitting from the policy something which has been promised is the same in effect as seeking to introduce a new term: see para 384 post.

4 *Mutual Reserve Life Insurance Co v Foster* (1904) 20 TLR 715, HL; *Cross v Mutual Reserve Life Insurance Co* (1904) 21 TLR 15; *Merino v Mutual Reserve Life Insurance Co* (1904) 21 TLR 167; and see para 449 post.

(ii) Contractual Provisions as to Non-disclosure and Misrepresentation

363. Duties laid down by the contract. A contract of non-marine insurance may comprise provisions dealing with or affecting the disclosure of information either in the policy itself or in documents which are incorporated[1]. Such provisions may either put into words what would in any case be the duty of the assured at common law or may extend[2] or restrict the scope of his duty[3]. In either case it will be a question of interpretation whether the contractual provision operates so as to supersede the common law obligations in the field which it purports to cover[4]. Where such a provision is contained in the contract the duty of disclosure is pro tanto contractual[5]; and as the provision is part of the contract between the parties, it becomes a term of the contract that disclosure is to be made in accordance with the provision; failure to make such disclosure is therefore a breach of contract, making available to the insurers such remedy as may be stipulated[6]. For the purpose of ascertaining whether the proposer has committed a breach or not, reference must be made to the precise terms or effect of the contract[7].

1 For an example of such provisions see 20 Forms & Precedents (5th Edn) 509 at 510, Form 291 cl 4.

2 *Dawsons Ltd v Bonnin* [1922] 2 AC 413, HL; and see *Australian Widows' Fund Life Assurance Society v National Mutual Life Association of Australasia Ltd* [1914] AC 634, PC.

3 *Anstey v British Natural Premium Life Association Ltd* (1908) 99 LT 16; affd 99 LT 765, CA.

4 As to the interpretation of the terms see paras 364–365 post.

5 *Anderson v Fitzgerald* (1853) 4 HL Cas 484 at 496; *Joel v Law Union and Crown Insurance Co* [1908] 2 KB 863 at 886, CA; *Stebbing v Liverpool and London and Globe Insurance Co Ltd* [1917] 2 KB 433 at 437.

6 *Anderson v Fitzgerald* (1853) 4 HL Cas 484. As to when conditions of this kind are inoperative against third parties who are subrogated by statute to the rights of the assured against his insurers see para 742 et seq post.

7 *Dawsons Ltd v Bonnin* [1922] 2 AC 413, HL (policy contained two conditions, one of which was restricted to material misstatements).

364. Express and implied terms as to disclosure. Provisions affecting the disclosure of information may be either express or implied. Expressly it may be stipulated on the part of the proposer that all matters relative to a particular topic, such as the proposer's state of health, have been disclosed and that nothing has been withheld, the stipulation being expressed in the form of a warranty or a condition precedent or a term forming the basis of the contract[1]. Similarly it may be stipulated on the part of the insurers to the effect that, apart from fraud or wilful misrepresentation, the policy is not to be avoided[2]. Such a stipulation may arise by implication from the way in which specific information is sought. Where, by questions asked in a proposal (assuming this, with the relevant answers, to be incorporated in the ultimate contract), it is plainly indicated that certain matters are regarded by the insurers as material, the questions cannot be answered merely by the letter, however correct the answers may be so far as they extend; all information which a reasonable man would recognise as being information in which the insurers are interested must be given[3]. Conversely, where the form and substance of the questions asked are such as to indicate to the proposer that the insurers' interest is confined to certain matters, the proposer need not go outside the field which has been so indicated[4].

1 As to such express stipulations see para 374 post.
2 *Wood v Dwarris* (1856) 11 Exch 493; *Fowkes v Manchester and London Assurance Association* (1863) 3 B & S 917; *Hemmings v Sceptre Life Association Ltd* [1905] 1 Ch 365; *Anstey v British Natural Premium Life Association Ltd* (1908) 99 LT 16; affd 99 LT 765, CA.
3 *Glicksman v Lancashire and General Assurance Co Ltd* [1925] 2 KB 593, CA; affd [1927] AC 139, HL (proposal by partners for insurance against burglary; proposal form contained question asking whether any company had declined proposers' burglary insurance; question answered in negative: previous proposal by one partner when trading alone had been refused; non-disclosure of material fact); *Babatsikos v Car Owners' Mutual Insurance Co Ltd* [1970] 2 Lloyd's Rep 314 at 323, Vict CA, per Pape J.
4 *Schoolman v Hall* [1951] 1 Lloyd's Rep 139 at 143, CA, per Asquith LJ; see further para 363 ante.

365. Terms as to misrepresentation.

The rules relating to representation are the same as the rules relating to disclosure of information except that, in relation to disclosure of information any special provisions in the contract are likely to be interpreted as relaxations for the benefit of the proposer, whereas in relation to representations the prime object is likely to be the protection of the insurers[1]. The most common express provision is therefore one which extends the duty of the proposer by making the validity of the contract depend upon the accuracy of all statements made by the proposer during the course of the negotiations[2]. Where there is such a provision it is unnecessary to consider whether an inaccurate statement was made fraudulently[3] or innocently[4]. If the truth of the statement has been warranted or made a condition precedent to the contract or the basis of the contract, the contract has been breached if it is in fact untrue and the stipulated consequences follow[5]. It is not necessary to consider, unless the provision is by its terms limited to material misstatements[6], whether the untrue statement was of any materiality whatsoever: it may be as to something so trivial or remote that no insurer would really be influenced one way or another. However, the contract is breached if there is in fact a breach of the stipulation that it is true[7]. In substance such a stipulation is a contractual extension of the moral hazard principle[8].

1 *Worsley v Wood* (1796) 6 Term Rep 710; *London Guarantee Co v Fearnley* (1880) 5 App Cas 911, HL; *Lancashire Insurance Co v IRC* [1899] 1 QB 353.
2 Any such condition is strictly construed against the insurers: *Anderson v Fitzgerald* (1853) 4 HL Cas 484; *Thomson v Weems* (1884) 9 App Cas 671 at 682, HL; *Joel v Law Union and Crown Insurance Co* [1908] 2 KB 863; *Anstey v British Natural Premium Life Association Ltd* (1908) 99 LT 16; affd 99 LT 765, CA.
3 *London Assurance v Mansel* (1879) 11 ChD 363; *Hambrough v Mutual Life Insurance Co of New York* (1895) 72 LT 140, CA; *Bancroft v Heath* (1901) 6 Com Cas 137, CA.
4 *Macdonald v Law Union Insurance Co* (1874) LR 9 QB 328; *Thomson v Weems* (1884) 9 App Cas 671, HL. However, there is no breach of warranty if the assured expressly qualifies his statement as being

true to the best of his belief; *Jones v Provincial Insurance Co* (1857) 3 CBNS 65; *Macdonald v Law Union Insurance Co* supra at 331 per Lush J.

5 *Newcastle Fire Insurance Co v Macmorran & Co* (1815) 3 Dow 255 at 259, H L; *Condogianis v Guardian Assurance Co Ltd* [1921] 2 AC 125, PC; *Dawsons Ltd v Bonnin* [1922] 2 AC 413, HL; *Holmes v Scottish Legal Life Assurance Society* (1932) 48 TLR 306.

6 *Re Universal Non-Tariff Fire Insurance Co, Forbes & Co's Claim* (1875) LR 19 Eq 485.

7 *Newcastle Fire Insurance Co v Macmorran & Co* (1815) 3 Dow 255, HL; *Anderson v Fitzgerald* (1853) 4 HL Cas 484; *Condogianis v Guardian Assurance Co Ltd* [1921] 2 AC 125, PC; *Dawsons Ltd v Bonnin* [1922] 2 AC 413, HL, where one of the conditions was limited to material misstatements, but the other required even immaterial statements to be true.

8 As to the moral hazard see para 353 ante.

366. Effect of fraud.

366. Effect of fraud. The foregoing rules[1] are subject to exception in the case of fraud. Whatever may be provided in the contract, either expressly or on the face of the contract by implication, if the court is satisfied that the proposer has been guilty of fraud, either in concealment or in misstatement which, as a reasonable man, he is presumed to appreciate as likely to influence the parties to the bargain in the risks they are undertaking, the insurers will not be bound by the bargain[2].

1 Ie the rules described in paras 363–365 ante.
2 *The Bedouin* [1894] P 1 at 12, CA, per Lord Esher MR; *Herring v Janson* (1895) 1 Com Cas 177 at 180 per Mathew J.

367. Remedies for breach of contractual terms.

367. Remedies for breach of contractual terms. If by the contract the observance of a stipulation as to disclosure of information or the accuracy of a representation is made the basis of the contract or a condition precedent to the validity of the contract, or the proposer has warranted that a representation is true[1], the insurers are entitled in the event of non-disclosure or the inaccuracy of the representation to repudiate all liability under the contract[2]. The insurers' right is sometimes described as a right to avoid the contract, but the description is not strictly accurate, since they are not relying upon something extrinsic to the contract as rendering it voidable, but are claiming the benefit of one of the terms of the contract itself in order to escape liability[3]. If before discovering the non-disclosure or inaccuracy the insurers have paid a claim under the contract, it seems clear that they are entitled, on discovering the true position, to recover the payment as money had and received by the payee to their use[4].

1 As to declarations of warranty see para 374 post; and as to conditions and collateral terms see para 403 post.
2 *Newcastle Fire Insurance Co v Macmorran & Co* (1815) 3 Dow 255, HL; *Condogianis v Guardian Assurance Co Ltd* [1921] 2 AC 125, PC; *Dawsons Ltd v Bonnin* [1922] 2 AC 413, HL; *Glicksman v Lancashire and General Assurance Co Ltd* [1927] AC 139, HL; *Hales v Reliance Fire and Accident Corpn Ltd* [1960] 2 Lloyd's Rep 391.
3 *Stebbing v Liverpool and London and Globe Insurance Co Ltd* [1917] 2 KB 433 at 437–438, DC. The distinction stated in the text may be important where the insurers, in addition to denying liability, are also seeking to enforce an arbitration clause in the contract: see *Stebbing v Liverpool and London and Globe Insurance Co Ltd* supra; *Woodall v Pearl Assurance Co Ltd* [1919] 1 KB 593, CA; *Golding v London and Edinburgh Insurance Co* (1932) 43 Ll L Rep 487, CA; *Stevens & Sons v Timber and General Mutual Accident Insurance Association Ltd* (1933) 102 LJKB 337, CA; *Heyman v Darwins Ltd* [1942] AC 356 at 384, 398, [1942] 1 All ER 337 at 353, 360, HL; and see para 496 post and ARBITRATION vol 2 (Reissue) para 612.
4 For examples of the right to recovery, on the ground of mistake of fact, of a payment made under a conditional contract when the condition has not been fulfilled see CONTRACT vol 9 para 669. For the right to bring an action for breach of contract in case of failure of consideration see CONTRACT vol 9 para 667. As to the recovery of money obtained by fraud see CONTRACT vol 9 para 689. As to the right of the assured to recover premiums paid see *Thomson v Weems* (1884) 9 App Cas 671 at 682, HL; and para 447 et seq post.

(iii) The Proposal and its Effect

368. Nature of a proposal. In practice it is universal in non-marine insurance, even when effected at Lloyd's[1], to require the proposer to fill up and sign a standard form of proposal. The standard form usually contains particulars of the insurance which is required, although this is often done by reference to the insurers' published leaflets as to the insurances which are on offer. It has been stated that such a statement of the particulars of the insurance should contain in clear and unambiguous language any particular events on the happening of which the insurers will escape liability[2]. The form is one prepared by the insurers, so that the contra proferentem rule applies[3]. If, therefore, the impression is created in the mind of a reasonable man that what is being asked is intended to be exhaustive, the insurer's rights in relation to non-disclosure and misrepresentation may be seriously affected[4]. In completing, signing and submitting the proposal form the proposer is providing the information on which the insurers act in deciding whether to accept the proposal at all, and if so, at what premium[5]. The actual form of the particulars given as to the insurance and of the questions which are asked is regulated in detail by the kind of insurance which is sought, but all proposal forms are framed on the same general lines, which are summarised in the following paragraphs[6].

1 For Lloyd's practice in marine insurance see paras 88–89 ante.
2 *Re Bradley and Essex and Suffolk Accident Indemnity Society* [1912] 1 KB 415 at 430, 433, CA; *Provincial Insurance Co Ltd v Morgan* [1933] AC 240 at 250, HL.
3 For this rule see para 398 post; and generally DEEDS vol 12 para 1473.
4 See paras 364 ante, 370 post.
5 *Newsholme Bros v Road Transport and General Insurance Co Ltd* [1929] 2 KB 356, CA.
6 See paras 369–372 post. For examples of the varieties of form of insurance proposal in use see generally 20 Forms & Precedents (5th Edn).

369. Proposer's status. The first matter to which the ordinary form of proposal is directed is the status of the proposer. In the case of life and personal accident insurance this is so fundamental that a considerable amount of detail is usually covered[1]. In all insurance, however, the essentials required are the name, address and occupation of the proposer. If the name given by the proposer is not his true name, the deliberate concealment may be an indication of fraud[2]. Inaccurate information given inadvertently may be disregarded if substantially true and unambiguous[3]. Similarly the full disclosure of the true address may be material[4]. Some latitude is given as regards occupation[5], but the risk may well differ according to differences in occupation. If, therefore, the proposer has several occupations in relation to which he wishes the insurance to be operative, he must state them all[6], even though a failure to do this will be immaterial (contractual provisions apart) where the premiums would not be affected[7]. In some insurances the proposer's age will be important; for example, young persons may be less experienced or considered more careless[8].

1 As to life insurance see para 525 et seq post.
2 *McCormick v National Motor and Accident Insurance Union Ltd* (1934) 50 TLR 528, CA.
3 *Dawsons Ltd v Bonnin* [1922] 2 AC 413 at 425, HL (where the statements formed the basis of the contract and were incorporated into the policy).

4 *Huguenin v Rayley* (1815) 6 Taunt 186 (proposer in gaol); see also *Grogan v London and Manchester Industrial Assurance Co* (1885) 53 LT 761.
5 *Perrins v Marine Insurance etc Insurance Society* (1859) 2 E & E 317; affd (1860) 2 E & E 324, Ex Ch; *Woodall v Pearl Assurance Co Ltd* [1919] 1 KB 593, CA.
6 *Biggar v Rock Life Assurance Co* [1902] 1 KB 516.
7 *Perrins v Marine etc Insurance Society* (1859) 2 E & E 317. For cases where knowledge of the different occupations was imputed to the insurers see *Holdsworth v Lancashire and Yorkshire Insurance Co* (1907) 23 TLR 521; *Ayrey v British Legal and United Provident Assurance Co* [1918] 1 KB 136.
8 See eg para 745 note 2 post.

370. Nature of the risk. The second matter to which the ordinary form of proposal is directed is the nature of the risk to be covered and the circumstances affecting it. Particulars given under this head constitute what is called 'the description of the risk'[1]. They define the precise nature and scope of the proposed insurance, so that particular care is required on the part of the proposer to give information as to any subsequent change in the circumstances, since this may amount to an alteration of the risk and so affect the right of recovery[2]. The questions asked under this head are necessarily detailed and varied according to the nature of the risk for which insurance is sought. In addition, there is often a general question inquiring whether there are any other circumstances material to the risk, and this is of some importance. There is the possibility that the specific questions may be interpreted as indicating that the insurers are limiting the field of their inquiries, so that no information need be disclosed which is outside the scope of the questions, however material such information would otherwise be[3]. If it is made plain, however, that the information sought by the questions is not exhaustive, this serves to remind the proposer that, notwithstanding his answers to the specific questions, there still remains the common law duty to disclose all material facts[4]. Even then immaterial matters need not be disclosed[5], but anything which a reasonable man would regard as material must be stated[6] unless the form of the question indicates that the proposer is at liberty to exercise his own judgment as to this[7].

1 *Provincial Insurance Co Ltd v Morgan* [1933] AC 240, HL; see also *Farr v Motor Traders' Mutual Insurance Society* [1920] 3 KB 669, CA; *Roberts v Anglo-Saxon Insurance Association* (1927) 96 LJKB 590, CA; *Beauchamp v National Mutual Indemnity Insurance Co Ltd* [1937] 3 All ER 19; and see para 431 note 4 post.
2 See para 435 post.
3 See *Schoolman v Hall* [1951] 1 Lloyd's Rep 139 at 143, CA, per Asquith LJ; and also *National Protector Fire Insurance Co Ltd v Nivert* [1913] AC 507, PC; *Golding v Royal London Auxiliary Insurance Co Ltd* (1914) 30 TLR 350. Cf *Joel v Law Union and Crown Insurance Co* [1908] 2 KB 863 at 876–878, CA. See also para 351 et seq ante.
4 For the principle that the common law duty is unaffected by the asking of specific questions see *Schoolman v Hall* [1951] 1 Lloyd's Rep 139, CA; and see also *Joel v Law Union and Crown Insurance Co* [1908] 2 KB 863 at 892, CA; *Yorke v Yorkshire Insurance Co Ltd* [1918] 1 KB 662 at 666; *Arthrude Press Ltd v Eagle, Star and British Dominions Insurance Co* (1924) 59 L Jo 529; *Glicksman v Lancashire and General Assurance Co Ltd* [1925] 2 KB 593, CA; affd [1927] AC 139 at 144, HL; *Bond v Commercial Assurance Co* (1930) 35 Com Cas 171, DC; *Holt's Motors Ltd v South East Lancashire Insurance Co Ltd* (1930) 35 Com Cas 281, CA; *Babatsikos v Car Owners' Mutual Insurance Co Ltd* [1970] 2 Lloyd's Rep 314 (Vict CA). Cf the duties laid down by the contract: see para 363 ante.
5 *Shilling v Accidental Death Insurance Co* (1858) 1 F & F 116.
6 *Lindenau v Desborough* (1828) 8 B & C 586 at 592.
7 *Jones v Provincial Insurance Co* (1857) 3 CBNS 65 at 86.

371. Proposer's risk experience. The third matter to which the ordinary form of proposal is directed is the previous experience of the proposer. This is common to all forms of insurance except life insurance. In the usual form the question is directed to eliciting particulars, either generally or within a specified period, of all losses sustained by the proposer in consequence of the peril to be insured against and of all claims in respect of such losses made upon insurers[1].

1 *Condogianis v Guardian Assurance Co Ltd* [1921] 2 AC 125, PC. As to the scope of the peril to be insured against see paras 664–665 post.

372. Proposer's insurance record. The fourth matter as to which information is usually sought is the proposer's insurance record. This is, of course, specifically directed to the moral hazard[1] and to the possibility of obtaining the opinion of other insurers. The proposer is accordingly asked to state whether other insurers have in the past declined proposals from him[2] or have cancelled or refused to renew insurances which he has held[3], whether he is at the time of the proposal already insured elsewhere[4] or is proposing to take out elsewhere any other insurance[5]. The questions are not always limited to the class of insurance proposed and may indeed be directed generally to all kinds of insurance, but unless it is expressly stated otherwise, questions of this nature will usually be construed as limited to the particular subject matter of the insurance sought. Thus, in a proposal for the insurance of business premises against fire, the proposer need not deal with his private record[6].

1 As to the moral hazard see para 353 ante.
2 *Anderson v Fitzgerald* (1853) 4 HL Cas 484; *Fowkes v Manchester and London Assurance Association* (1863) 3 B & S 917; *Re General Provincial Life Assurance Co Ltd, ex p Daintree* (1870) 18 WR 396; *London Assurance v Mansel* (1879) 11 ChD 363; *Scottish Provident Institution v Boddam* (1893) 9 TLR 385; *Hambrough v Mutual Life Insurance Co of New York* (1895) 72 LT 140, CA; *Taylor v Yorkshire Insurance Co* [1913] 2 IR 1.
3 *Biggar v Rock Life v Assurance Co* [1902] 1 KB 516; *Re Yager and Guardian Assurance Co* (1912) 108 LT 38, DC; *Holt's Motors v South East Lancashire Insurance Co* (1930) 35 Com Cas 281, CA; *Claude R Ogden & Co Pty Ltd v Reliance Fire Sprinkler Co Pty Ltd* [1975] 1 Lloyd's Rep 52 (NSW SC).
4 *Wainwright v Bland* (1836) 1 M & W 32; *Citizens Insurance Co of Canada v Parsons* (1881) 7 App Cas 96, PC; *Marcovitch v Liverpool Victoria Friendly Society* (1912) 28 TLR 188, CA; *National Protector Fire Insurance Co v Nivert* [1913] AC 507, PC.
5 *Re Marshall and Scottish Employers' Liability and General Insurance Co Ltd* (1901) 85 LT 757.
6 *Golding v Royal London Auxiliary Insurance Co Ltd* (1914) 30 TLR 350.

373. Rules applicable to proposal. The basic rules to be observed in making a proposal for insurance may be summarised as follows.
  (1) A fair and reasonable construction must be put upon the language of the question which is asked, and the answer given will be similarly construed[1]. This involves close attention to the language used in either case, as the question may be so framed that an unqualified answer amounts to an assertion by the proposer that he has knowledge of the facts and that the knowledge is being imparted[2]. However, provided these canons are observed, accuracy in all matters of substance will suffice and misstatements or omissions in trifling and insubstantial respects will be ignored[3].
  (2) Carelessness is no excuse, unless the error is so obvious that no one could be regarded as misled. If the proposer puts 'no' when he means 'yes' it will not avail him to say it was a slip of the pen; the answer is plainly the reverse of the truth[4].
  (3) An answer which is literally accurate, so far as it extends, will not suffice if it is misleading by reason of what is not stated[5]. It may be quite accurate for the

proposer to state that he has made a claim previously on an insurance company, but the answer is untrue if in fact he has made more than one[6].

(4) Where the space for an answer is left blank, leaving the question un-answered, the reasonable inference may be that there is nothing to enter as an answer[7]. If in fact there is something to enter as an answer, the insurers are misled in that their reasonable inference is belied. It will then be a matter of construction whether this is a mere non-disclosure, the proposer having made no positive statement at all[8], or whether in substance he is to be regarded as having asserted that there is in fact nothing to state[9].

(5) Where an answer is unsatisfactory as being on the face of it incomplete or inconsistent[10] the insurers may, as reasonable men, be regarded as put on inquiry, so that if they issue a policy without any further inquiry they are assumed to have waived any further information[11]. However, having regard to the inference mentioned in head (4) above, the mere leaving of a blank space will not normally be regarded as sufficient to put the insurers on inquiry[12].

(6) A proposer may find it convenient to bracket together two or more ques-tions and give a composite answer. There is no objection to his doing so, provided the insurers are given adequate and accurate information on all points covered by the questions[13].

(7) Any answer given, however accurate and honest at the time it was written down, must be corrected if, up to the time of acceptance of the proposal, any event or circumstance supervenes to make it inaccurate or misleading[14].

1 *Condogianis v Guardian Assurance Co Ltd* [1921] 2 AC 125, PC; *Revell v London General Insurance Co Ltd* (1934) 50 Ll L Rep 114; *Johns v Kelly* [1986] 1 Lloyd's Rep 468 (professional indemnity insurance); cf *Fidelity and Casualty Co of New York v Mitchell* [1917] AC 592, PC.

2 *Merchants' and Manufacturers' Insurance Co v Hunt and Thorne* [1941] 1 KB 295 at 311, [1941] 1 All ER 123 at 128, CA, per Scott LJ; *Zurich General Accident and Liability Insurance Co v Leven* 1940 SC 406 (proposal for motor insurance; if proposal form contains a question whether any person, who to the proposer's knowledge will drive the car, has been convicted of a motoring offence, and the proposer answers 'no', the proposer is asserting that he has knowledge which he is professing to impart of the intended driver's record and that it is clear of convictions).

3 *Huguenin v Rayley* (1815) 6 Taunt 186; see further para 358 ante. However, there may be a condition requiring accuracy even in immaterial particulars: see para 365 ante.

4 *Biggar v Rock Life Assurance Co* [1902] 1 KB 516; *Life and Health Assurance Association v Yule* (1904) 6 F 437, Ct of Sess.

5 *Re General Provincial Life Assurance Co Ltd, ex p Daintree* (1870) 18 WR 396; *London Assurance v Mansel* (1879) 11 ChD 363.

6 *Condogianis v Guardian Assurance Co Ltd* [1921] 2 AC 125, PC; see para 358 ante.

7 *Roberts v Avon Insurance Co Ltd* [1956] 2 Lloyd's Rep 240.

8 *London Assurance v Mansel* (1879) 11 ChD 363 at 369, explaining *Lindenau v Desborough* (1828) 8 B & C 586. The question whether the assured is guilty of misrepresentation or non-disclosure may be important in view of the wording of the particular condition: see *Marcovitch v Liverpool Victoria Friendly Society* (1912) 28 TLR 188, CA; cf *Perrins v Marine etc Insurance Society* (1859) 2 E & E 317 at 323.

9 *Roberts v Avon Insurance Co Ltd* [1956] 2 Lloyd's Rep 240.

10 *Keeling v Pearl Assurance Co Ltd* (1923) 129 LT 573.

11 *Thomson v Weems* (1884) 9 App Cas 671 at 694, HL; see also *Roberts v Avon Insurance Co Ltd* [1956] 2 Lloyd's Rep 240 at 249.

12 *Forbes & Co v Edinburgh Life Assurance Co* (1832) 10 Sh 451, Ct of Sess.

13 *Foster v Mentor Life Assurance Co* (1854) 3 E & B 48.

14 *Canning v Farquhar* (1886) 16 QBD 727, CA; *Re Yager and Guardian Assurance Co* (1912) 108 LT 38; *Golding v Royal London Auxiliary Insurance Co Ltd* (1914) 30 TLR 350; and see para 356 ante.

374. Declaration warranting the proposal. The proposal form concludes with a declaration, which is often required to be separately signed by the proposer so as to draw his particular attention to the importance of what he is signing, by which he warrants that the statements contained in the proposal are true, or agrees that they are to be the basis of the contract between the parties, or accepts that their truth is to be a condition precedent to the validity of the contract. All three variations of the same term may be included, and an additional clause may be inserted to the effect that no material information has been withheld[1]. The purpose of the formulae is usually to incorporate the proposal into the eventual policy. If it is incorporated the proposal becomes a contractual document by reference to which the insurers' rights to repudiate are governed[2]. If there is no incorporation the proposal provides a record, for the purpose of applying the common law rules, for establishing facts expressed and, by inference, facts withheld from the insurers[3].

1 *Taylor v Yorkshire Insurance Co* [1913] 2 IR 1.
2 *Anderson v Fitzgerald* (1853) 4 HL Cas 484; *Thomson v Weems* (1884) 9 App Cas 671, HL; *Australian Widows' Fund Life Assurance Society v National Mutual Life Association of Australasia Ltd* [1914] AC 634, PC; *Condogianis v Guardian Assurance Co Ltd* [1921] 2 AC 125, PC; *Dawsons Ltd v Bonnin* [1922] 2 AC 413, HL; *Glicksman v Lancashire and General Assurance Co Ltd* [1925] 2 KB 593, CA; affd [1927] AC 139, HL.
3 See para 349 et seq ante.

(iv) Imputation of Agent's Knowledge

375. Knowledge of the agent. The general principles of the law of agency are of particular relevance in insurance law, and govern the imputation of the agent's knowledge to the insurers[1]. Before any question of imputed knowledge can arise it is necessary to establish the capacity of the parties as agent and principal[2]. Where there are material facts disclosed to the agent the question arises how far that knowledge can be imputed to the insurer. The duty of the agent to inform the insurer of material facts as they arise exists throughout the duration of the contract[3]. Insurers may be bound by disclosures or information received by their agents but nevertheless remain unknown to themselves[4]. However, the insurers may protect themselves by adding into the policy a condition requiring the assured to make disclosures or information known to the insurers themselves and that notice to the agent will not suffice[5] until actual communication is made to them[6].

1 See generally AGENCY vol 1(2) (Reissue) para 149.
2 *Bancroft v Heath* (1901) 6 Com Cas 137, CA; *Letts v Excess Insurance Co* (1916) 32 TLR 361 at 362 per Bailhache J; *O'Keefe v London and Edinburgh Insurance Co Ltd* [1928] NI 85, CA; *Wilkinson v General Accident Fire and Life Assurance Corpn Ltd* [1967] 2 Lloyd's Rep 182.
3 *Marsden v City and County Assurance* (1866) LR 1 CP 232.
4 *Wing v Harvey* (1854) 5 De G M & G 265, distinguished by *Busteed v West of England Fire and Life Insurance Co* (1857) 5 I Ch R 553; *Gale v Lewis* (1846) 9 QB 730; *Marsden v City and County Assurance* (1866) LR 1 CP 232; *Re Solvency Mutual Guarantee Society, Hawthorne's Case* (1862) 31 LJCh 625; *Re Hennessy* (1842) IR 5 Eq 259; *Smith v Excelsior Life Assurance Co* (1912) 22 OWR 863; *Fowler v Scottish Equitable Life Insurance Society and Ritchie* (1858) 28 LJCh 225; cf *General Accident, Fire and Life Assurance Co v Robertson* [1909] AC 404 at 411, HL, per Lord Loreburn LC.
5 *Re Williams and Lancashire and Yorkshire Accident Insurance Co's Arbitration* (1902) 19 TLR 82.
6 *Shiells v Scottish Assurance Corpn Ltd* (1889) 16 R 1014, Ct of Sess.

376. Imputation to principal of agent's knowledge. Third parties dealing with the insurers' agent are entitled to assume that it is his duty in that capacity either to place at the insurers' disposal knowledge of certain matters which he in fact has, however it may have been acquired[1], or to acquire on their behalf knowledge of certain matters[2]. If the agent has actual knowledge of relevant matters, it will normally be imputed to the insurers without any question[3]. Even if the knowledge has come to the agent while acting in a distinct capacity[4], it will be imputed to the insurers if it would be a breach of the agent's duty, as an agent, to withhold it[5]. If the truth as to relevant matters ought to have been ascertained by the agent from his own inquiries in the performance of his duty, the insurers are precluded from setting up their own agent's misconduct in failing to make the necessary inquiries; they will be treated as knowing what they would have known if their agent had performed his duty[6]. In fire insurance it is often the duty of the agent to describe the premises proposed after personal inspection, and if he describes them inaccurately the insurers are treated as knowing the true position[7].

1   *Taylor v Yorkshire Insurance Co* [1913] 2 IR 1; *O'Keefe v London and Edinburgh Insurance Co* [1928] NI 85, CA; *Woolcott v Excess Insurance Co Ltd and Miles, Smith, Anderson and Game Ltd (No 2)* [1979] 2 Lloyd's Rep 210.
2   *Ayrey v British Legal and United Provident Assurance Co* [1918] 1 KB 136, as explained in *Newsholme Bros v Road Transport and General Insurance Co Ltd* [1929] 2 KB 356, CA.
3   *Blackburn, Low & Co v Vigors* (1887) 12 App Cas 531.
4   *Tate v Hyslop* (1885) 15 QBD 368, CA; cf *Re Hennessy* (1842) IR 5 Eq 259 (agent, whose knowledge of an assignment of the policy was sought to be imputed to the insurer, was himself the assignor).
5   *Bradley v Riches* (1878) 9 ChD 189.
6   *Bawden v London, Edinburgh and Glasgow Assurance Co* [1892] 2 QB 534, CA, as explained in *Newsholme Bros v Road Transport and General Insurance Co Ltd* [1929] 2 KB 356, CA.
7   *Pimm v Lewis* (1862) 2 F & F 778; *Re Universal Non-Tariff Fire Insurance Co, Forbes & Co's Claim* (1875) LR 19 Eq 485; *Blanchette v CIS Ltd* [1973] 5 WWR 547 (Can SC).

377. Scope of agent's authority. The insurers' agent is their representative for the purposes of the negotiations and so is the proper person to whom any disclosure, otherwise than on the face of the proposal, should or may be made[1]. Therefore, if full and accurate disclosure is made orally by the proposer to the agent, the duty of disclosure is discharged[2] and the insurers cannot subsequently repudiate the policy on the ground that they were not informed personally; they cannot set up against the proposer their agent's failure to transmit the information as fully and accurately as he received it[3]. The same principle applies where a correction of an inaccurate statement in a proposal is subsequently communicated to the agent[4]. Further, the agent being the only person with whom the proposer can negotiate, he is inevitably the person to whom the proposer turns for advice either as to the meaning of questions in a proposal form which is about to be completed[5], or as to the sufficiency of answers already given or proposed to be given to such questions[6], and he acts as agent on behalf of the insurers in giving advice on these topics if it is sought; accordingly, when such advice has been given the insurers cannot subsequently repudiate the policy on the ground that the answers given are inadequate[7]. The onus is on the assured to prove that he made sufficient disclosure and that any inaccuracy or misstatement made was not his responsibility at all, but that of the agent[8]. However, the position is different where there is an express warranty as to the accuracy of a particular statement; in such a case the insurers are not precluded from relying on an inaccuracy by the fact that their agent was satisfied[9]. The position is also different where the answers in a proposal form are in fact entered by the agent[10].

1   *St Margaret's Trust Ltd v Navigators and General Insurance Co Ltd* (1949) 82 Ll L Rep 752.

2 *Joel v Law Union and Crown Insurance Co* [1908] 2 KB 863, CA.
3 *Parsons v Bignold* (1846) 15 LJCh 379, as explained in *Re Universal Non-Tariff Fire Insurance Co, Forbes & Co's Claim* (1875) LR 19 Eq 485; *Ayrey v British Legal and United Provident Assurance Co* [1918] 1 KB 136; cf *Kaufman v British Surety Insurance Co Ltd* (1929) 45 TLR 399.
4 *Golding v Royal London Auxiliary Insurance Co Ltd* (1914) 30 TLR 350; *Ayrey v British Legal and United Provident Assurance Co* [1918] 1 KB 136.
5 *Joel v Law Union and Crown Insurance Co* [1908] 2 KB 863, CA.
6 *Cruikshank v Northern Accident Insurance Co Ltd* (1895) 23 R 147, Ct of Sess; cf *Hough v Guardian Fire and Life Assurance Co Ltd* (1902) 18 TLR 273; *Holdsworth v Lancashire and Yorkshire Insurance Co* (1907) 23 TLR 521.
7 See the cases cited in notes 5–6 supra.
8 *Parsons v Bignold* (1846) 15 LJCh 379.
9 *Westropp v Bruce* (1826) Batt 155.
10 See para 381 post.

378. Agent's fraud. If an agent takes part in a fraud on the insurers whether by concealing or misrepresenting a material fact in concert with the proposer or by conniving at such a concealment or misrepresentation on the part of the proposer, the agent is not regarded as acting as agent of the insurers and his knowledge of the truth is not imputed to them[1].

1 *Biggar v Rock Life Assurance Co* [1902] 1 KB 516, approved in *Newsholme Bros v Road Transport and General Insurance Co Ltd* [1929] 2 KB 356 at 375, CA, per Scrutton LJ; see also *Life and Health Assurance Association v Yule* (1904) 6 F 437, Ct of Sess; *Dunn v Ocean Accident and Guarantee Corpn Ltd* (1933) 50 TLR 32, 47 Ll L Rep 129, CA.

379. Contractual terms as to agent's authority. The rules governing the imputation of the agent's knowledge[1] apply where there is no express contractual provision to the contrary. In practice, insurers may insert in their policies a condition excluding or modifying the application of the doctrine of imputed knowledge[2]. Where there is such a condition, knowledge on the part of or disclosure to the agent, however full, does not avail the proposer[3] unless the agent has actually transmitted to the insurers what is known or has been disclosed to him in such a manner as to comply with the condition[4].

1 Ie those stated in paras 376–378 ante.
2 *Kelly v London and Staffordshire Fire Insurance Co* (1883) Cab & El 47; *Levy v Scottish Employers' Insurance Co* (1901) 17 TLR 229, DC. A common example of such a condition is one providing that the insurers are not to be affected by any knowledge on the part of, or any notice to, their agent in relation to any matter unless that matter has been communicated to the insurers and acknowledged by them in writing: see eg *M'Millan v Accident Insurance Co* 1907 SC 484.
3 *Levy v Scottish Employers' Insurance Co* (1901) 17 TLR 229, DC; *Biggar v Rock Life Assurance Co* [1902] 1 KB 516; *M'Millan v Accident Insurance Co* 1907 SC 484.
4 *Ayrey v British Legal and United Provident Assurance Co* [1918] 1 KB 136.

380. Agent acting outside scope of authority. The principles relating to the imputation of the agent's knowledge[1] derive from the agent's authority to act as the insurers' agent; they have no place where the agent is not purporting to act as their agent or acts outside the scope of his authority[2]. Except in the case of industrial assurance[3], it now appears to be settled that an agent will not generally be regarded as having authority from the insurers to write answers into a proposal form[4].

Except in the case of industrial assurance, in filling in the answers in a proposal form an insurance agent is regarded as the agent for the proposer at the proposer's request, express or implied[5]. Even if the agent knows the truth, his knowledge is not in that case imputed to the insurers[6]. If he is careless in filling up the form it is the proposer, not the insurers, who may maintain an action in negligence against him[7]. Further, where the proposer himself signs the proposal form, as is usually insisted upon by insurers, by signing he adopts whatever answers the agent has inserted and makes them his own[8]. This is clearly the case where he reads and approves the answers before signing, but the position is the same if he chooses to sign the proposal without reading them[9] or if he signs the form when it is blank, leaving it to the agent to insert the answers later[10]. It is irrelevant to inquire how the inaccuracy arose, whether the agent acted honestly[11] or dishonestly[12], whether the agent had forgotten or misunderstood the correct information he had been given[13] or whether the answers were a mere invention on the part of the agent[14]. If the result is that inaccurate or inadequate information is given on material matters or that a contractual stipulation as to accuracy or adequacy of any information given is broken, it is the proposer who has to suffer[15].

1 Ie those stated in paras 376–378 ante.

2 For the position of a principal whose agent acts outside the scope of his authority see generally AGENCY vol 1(2) (Reissue) paras 135–136.

3 It has been held in cases before the Industrial Assurance Commissioner that in industrial assurance an agent has authority from his company or society to fill in the proposal form: see eg *Long v Scottish Legal Life Assurance Society* (1926) Report of Industrial Assurance Commissioner 60; *Richmond v Royal Liver Friendly Society* (1933) Report of Industrial Assurance Commissioner 41; *White v Britannic Assurance Co Ltd* (1954) Report of Industrial Assurance Commissioner 2, following *Bawden v London, Edinburgh and Glasgow Assurance Co* [1892] 2 QB 534, CA, and distinguishing *Newsholme Bros v Road Transport and General Insurance Co Ltd* [1929] 2 KB 356, CA. For statutory provisions as to proposals filled in by agents and as to warranties or non-disclosure in the case of industrial assurance see INDUSTRIAL ASSURANCE vol 24 (Reissue) para 239.

4 *Newsholme Bros v Road Transport and General Insurance Co Ltd* [1965] 1 Lloyd's Rep 113; *Dunn v Ocean Accident and Guarantee Corpn Ltd* (1933) 50 TLR 32, CA; see also *Levy v Scottish Employers' Insurance Co* (1901) 17 TLR 229, DC; *Biggar v Rock Life Assurance Co* [1902] 1 KB 516; *Life and Health Assurance Association v Yule* (1904) 6 F 437, Ct of Sess; *M'Millan v Accident Insurance Co* 1907 SC 484; *Taylor v Yorkshire Insurance Co* [1913] 2 IR 1. There has been a conflict of judicial opinion on the point, but it appears that, in so far as it conflicts with the foregoing cases, the decision in *Bawden v London, Edinburgh and Glasgow Assurance Co* [1892] 2 QB 534, CA (with which *Brewster v National Life Insurance Society* (1892) 8 TLR 648, CA; *Thornton-Smith v Motor Union Insurance Co Ltd* (1913) 30 TLR 139; *Keeling v Pearl Assurance Co Ltd* (1923) 129 LT 573, are in accord) must be taken to apply, if at all, in special circumstances only. For criticism and explanation of that decision see *Newsholme Bros v Road Transport and General Insurance Co Ltd* supra at 368–369, 375, 381–382; and cf *Stone v Reliance Mutual Insurance Society Ltd* [1972] 1 Lloyd's Rep 469, CA (insurers held not to be entitled to avoid policy where proposal containing incorrect answers had been signed by assured's wife after being filled in by insurers' agent without asking her any questions).

5 *Life and Health Assurance Association v Yule* (1904) 6 F 437, Ct of Sess; *Taylor v Yorkshire Insurance Co* (1913) 2 IR 1; *Newsholme Bros v Road Transport and General Insurance Co Ltd* [1929] 2 KB 356, CA; *Dunn v Ocean Accident and Guarantee Corpn Ltd* (1933) 50 TLR 32, CA; cf *Stone v Reliance Mutual Insurance Society Ltd* [1972] 1 Lloyd's Rep 469 at 475, CA, per Megaw LJ.

6 See the cases cited in note 4 supra. If all that the agent does is to take down what he is told by the proposer without being aware of any inaccuracy in what he is told to write, there cannot in any case be any question of imputing to the insurers knowledge which even the agent has not got: see *Newsholme Bros v Road Transport and General Insurance Co Ltd* [1929] 2 KB 356 at 376, CA, per Scrutton LJ; see also *Davies v National Fire and Marine Insurance Co of New Zealand* [1891] AC 485, PC.

7 *Connors v London and Provincial Assurance Co* (1913) 6 BWCC 146.

8 *Rokkyer v Australian Alliance Assurance Co* (1908) 28 NZLR 305; *Newsholme Bros v Road Transport and General Insurance Co Ltd* [1929] 2 KB 356, CA; *O'Connor v B D B Kirby & Co* [1972] 1 QB 90, [1971] 2 All ER 1415, CA.

9 The presumption is that he has read them: *New York Life Insurance Co v Fletcher* (1885) 117 US 519, approved in *Biggar v Rock Life Assurance Co* [1902] 1 KB 516; *Taylor v Yorkshire Insurance Co* [1913] 2 IR 1; and in *Facer v Vehicle and General Insurance Co Ltd* [1965] 1 Lloyd's Rep 113.

10 *Parsons v Bignold* (1846) 15 LJCh 379; *Billington v Provincial Insurance Co* (1879) 3 SCR 182.

11 *Life and Health Assurance Association v Yule* (1904) 6 F 437, Ct of Sess.

12 *Biggar v Rock Life Assurance Co* [1902] 1 KB 516.

13 *Newsholme Bros v Road Transport and General Insurance Co Ltd* [1929] 2 KB 356, CA; *M'Millan v Accident Insurance Co* 1907 SC 484.

14 *Biggar v Rock Life Assurance Co* [1902] 1 KB 516, approved in *Newsholme Bros v Road Transport and General Insurance Co Ltd* [1929] 2 KB 356, CA.

15 See the cases cited in note 4 supra.

381. Insurance brokers and insurance agents. If a person wishing to obtain non-marine insurance employs an insurance broker[1], as distinct from going direct to the insurers or their agents, the broker is his agent and the ordinary law of agency governs the responsibility of the proposer for the acts and omissions of the broker. If negotiations for such insurance are conducted on behalf of the insurers by an insurance agent, the insurers' responsibility for the agent's acts and omissions is similarly governed by the general law of agency[2].

It is usual for the insurance agent, not the proposer, to fill in the proposal, although the proposer's signature is always necessary, and the completed and signed proposal is usually transmitted to the insurers by the agent[3]. The position of such an agent has therefore given rise to specific insurance problems[4].

1 As to the position of an insurance broker in relation to marine insurance see para 102 ante.

2 See *Anglo-African Merchants Ltd v Bayley* [1970] 1 QB 311, [1969] 2 All ER 421; and AGENCY. A broker who places insurance business under a cover agreement is simply the insurers' agent. His valuable connections are not his business to take elsewhere when he wishes: *Julien Praet et Cie SA v H G Poland Ltd* [1962] 1 Lloyd's Rep 566. For related proceedings see [1961] 1 Lloyd's Rep 187, CA; para 385 note 2 post.

3 *Newsholme Bros v Road Transport and General Insurance Co Ltd* [1929] 2 KB 356 at 362, CA, per Scrutton LJ.

4 Such problems arise particularly where inaccurate or inadequate information has reached the insurers while the truth, or the whole truth, has all along been known to the agent concerned: in any such case the insurers will be entitled or disentitled to exercise their common law remedy, and it may be also their contractual remedy, according to whether the agent's knowledge is, or is not, to be imputed to the insurers. As to the imputation of an agent's knowledge to the principal see para 376 ante.

(2) FORMATION OF A CONTRACT TO INSURE

382. Necessity for offer and acceptance. A contract of insurance, like any other contract, is created where there has been an unqualified acceptance by one party of an offer made by the other[1]. So long as the matter is still under negotiation there is no contract[2], although it is open to the parties, pending conclusion of the negotiations, to enter into an interim contract of a limited nature, such as the issue of a cover note[3]. An offer may be made by the insurers, as in the case of insurance by coupon, acceptance being by the assured when he purchases the coupon or the article to which it is attached[4]. Normally literature or advertising material circulated or displayed by insurers does not constitute an offer but is only an invitation to treat[5], and the formal offer comes into existence when a proposal form is completed and submitted to the insurers by the proposer[6]. In such cases there is little, if any, actual haggling as to the bargain; the proposer may wish to have specific additions to or deletions from the insurers' standard form of policy to suit his special needs or circumstances but, in general, the form sets out the only terms upon which the insurers are prepared to contract[7]. The proposer, by completing, signing and submitting the form, commits himself to those terms and undertakes to pay whatever the insurers may charge by way of premium[8]. When considering the proposal in such a case, where the insurers wish to make variations in their usual form of policy, whether by way of addition or subtraction, they must submit the variations to the proposer in the form of a counter offer[9] before they have committed themselves to an unequivocal acceptance of the proposal[10]. If the contract is created otherwise than by acceptance of a written proposal it must be shown that there has been agreement on the fundamentals of the insurance proposed, namely the subject matter of the insurance, the amount of the insurance unless this is unlimited, the nature of the risks insured against, the period for which the insurance is to last[11] and the rate of premium to be charged[12], although the exact amount may have to be calculated[13].

It is unlawful[14] for any person concerned with the provision, whether for payment or not, of insurance facilities to the public or a section of the public to discriminate[15] against a person who seeks to obtain or use those facilities by:

(1) refusing or deliberately omitting to provide him or her with them[16]; or

(2) refusing or deliberately omitting to provide him or her with facilities of the same quality, in the same manner and on the same terms as are normal in relation to other members of the public or other members of that section of the public[17].

1 *Lark v Outhwaite* [1991] 2 Lloyd's Rep 132 (reinsurance); and see generally CONTRACT vol 9 para 226 et seq.

2 *Allis-Chalmers Co v Maryland Fidelity and Deposit Co* (1916) 114 LT 433, HL; cf *Murfitt v Royal Insurance Co Ltd* (1922) 38 TLR 334 at 336.

3 *General Accident, Fire and Life Assurance Corpn v Robertson* [1909] AC 404, HL. As to cover notes see para 386 post.

4 *Carlill v Carbolic Smoke Ball Co* [1893] 1 QB 256, CA. By the terms of the coupon, the fulfilment of some condition, such as notification of acceptance or 'registration', may be necessary: *General Accident, Fire and Life Assurance Corpn v Robertson* [1909] AC 404, HL.

5 See further para 389 post, and CONTRACT vol 9 paras 227–228. As to advertisements see the Insurance Companies Act 1982 s 72 (as amended): para 810 post.

6 *Linford v Provincial Horse and Cattle Insurance Co* (1864) 34 Beav 291 at 293 per Lord Romilly; *General Accident Insurance Corpn v Cronk* (1901) 17 TLR 233; *Adie & Sons v Insurances Corpn Ltd* (1898) 14 TLR 544.

7 Frequently these terms are indicated merely by referring to the usual or standard form of policy used by the insurers in question. Where the proposal is for a policy in the ordinary form, the assured must be taken to have agreed to its terms without proof that he has approved them in detail: see para 384 post.

8 *General Accident Insurance Corpn v Cronk* (1901) 17 TLR 233; *Acme Wood Flooring Co v Marten* (1904) 9 Com Cas 157.

9 *Canning v Farquhar* (1886) 16 QBD 727, CA, followed in *Sickness and Accident Assurance Association v General Accident Assurance Corpn* (1892) 19 R 977, Ct of Sess; *Re Yager and Guardian Assurance Co* (1912) 108 LT 38, DC. But the traditional analysis of business activity into invitations to treat, offer and acceptance, or counter-offer and acceptance, presupposes an orderliness of thought which is seldom encountered in practice: *Rust v Abbey Life Assurance Co Ltd* [1978] 2 Lloyd's Rep 386 at 392; affd [1979] 2 Lloyd's Rep 334, CA.

10 *Linford v Provincial Horse and Cattle Insurance Co* (1864) 34 Beav 291.

11 Insurances are normally for one year in fire and burglary. As to fire insurance see para 591 et seq post, and as to burglary insurance see para 644 et seq post. Personal accident insurances are often for short periods such as one month; see further para 567 et seq post. The commencement date is normally indicated by the policy.

12 See eg *Allis-Chalmers Co v Maryland Fidelity and Deposit Co* (1916) 114 LT 433, HL; and see MacGillivray and Parkington on Insurance Law (8th Edn).
13 As to assessment of the premium see para 440 post.
14 As to enforcement see the Sex Discrimination Act 1975 Pt VII (ss 62–76); and DISCRIMINATION. See also the Race Relations Act 1976 Pt VIII (ss 53–69); and BRITISH NATIONALITY vol 4(2) (Reissue) para 198 et seq.
15 Ie under the Sex Discrimination Act 1975 s 1, s 2, or s 4 (see s 5 (1)(a)), or under the Race Relations Act 1976 s 1 or s 2 (see s 3(3)). As to such discrimination see DISCRIMINATION; BRITISH NATIONALITY.
16 Sex Discrimination Act 1975 s 29 (1)(a), (2)(c); Race Relations Act 1976 s 20 (1)(a), (2)(c).
17 Sex Discrimination Act 1975 s 29 (1)(b), (2)(c); Race Relations Act 1976 s 20 (1)(b), (2)(c).

383. Acceptance of the offer. Unqualified acceptance of an insurance proposal in the normal form completes the contract; the insurers are bound to issue a policy, and the proposer to accept and pay the premium[1], in accordance with the stipulations of the proposal[2]. The insurers cannot then seek to introduce variations by issuing a policy containing different terms[3], although if they do the proposer may be bound by the varied terms if, with their knowledge, he indicates by word or act his assent to the variation of the terms already agreed[4]. However, if there has not as yet been agreement on the basic terms such a variation constitutes a counter offer which requires acceptance by the proposer before there is a conclusion of the negotiations[5]. In the normal case there is conclusive acceptance of a proposal if a policy is issued in accordance with the proposal[6]; the insurers cannot then allege that there was no proposal[7], and a formal issue of the policy to the proposer is unnecessary if execution takes the form of sealing[8]. Indeed, although writing is necessary in marine insurance[9], in other forms of insurance there is no legal necessity[10]. Any positive act indicative of an intention to create a contract may be sufficient acceptance[11]. Thus there is acceptance by receipt of the premium without demur or qualification[12] or conduct precluding the insurers from disputing receipt of the premium[13]. A demand for the premium may be sufficient[14]. Where the form of prior acceptance does not preclude the imposition of a new condition, acceptance may be conditional and then performance of the condition operates as the initiation of the contract[15]. In respect of a long term policy the assured has a right to withdraw[16].

1 *General Accident Insurance Corpn v Cronk* (1901) 17 TLR 233; *Adie & Sons v Insurances Corpn Ltd* (1898) 14 TLR 544; *Star Fire and Burglary Insurance Co v Davidson* (1902) 5 F 83, Ct of Sess.
2 *Solvency Mutual Guarantee Co v Freeman* (1861) 7 H & N 17; *Adie & Sons v Insurances Corpn Ltd* (1898) 14 TLR 544.
3 *Canadian Casualty and Boiler Insurance Co v Boulter Davies & Co and Hawthorne & Co* (1907) 39 SCR 558; *General Accident Insurance Corpn v Cronk* (1901) 17 TLR 233; *Re Bradley and Essex and Suffolk Accident Indemnity Society* [1912] 1 KB 415 at 430, CA; see also *Griffiths v Fleming* [1909] 1 KB 805 at 818, CA.
4 *Ramsgate Victoria Hotel Co v Montefiore* (1866) LR 1 Exch 109; *Dunlop v Higgins* (1848) 1 HL Cas 381.
5 *Canning v Farquhar* (1886) 16 QBD 727 at 731, CA, per Lord Esher MR; *Sickness and Accident Assurance Association v General Accident Assurance Corpn* (1892) 19 R 977, Ct of Sess; *Re Yager and Guardian Assurance Co* (1912) 108 LT 38, DC.
6 *Pearl Life Assurance Co v Johnson* [1909] 2 KB 288, DC; *M'Elroy v London Assurance Corpn* (1897) 24 R 287 at 291, Ct of Sess.
7 *Pearl Life Assurance Co v Johnson* [1909] 2 KB 288, DC.
8 *Roberts v Security Co* [1897] 1 QB 111, CA.
9 See the Marine Insurance Act 1906 s 22; and para 39 ante.
10 *Murfitt v Royal Insurance Co Ltd* (1922) 38 TLR 334, followed in *Parker & Co (Sandbank) v Western Assurance Co* [1925] WC & Ins Rep 82.

11 *Rust v Abbey Life Assurance Co Ltd* [1978] 2 Lloyd's Rep 386; affd [1979] 2 Lloyd's Rep 334, CA.
12 *Canning v Farquhar* (1886) 16 QBD 727 at 731, CA; *Re Norwich Equitable Fire Assurance Society, Royal Insurance Co's Claim* (1887) 57 LT 241 at 243; cf *Solvency Mutual Guarantee Co v Froane* (1861) 7 H & N 5 at 15; *Harrington v Pearl Life Assurance Co Ltd* (1913) 30 TLR 24; affd (1914) 30 TLR 613, CA.
13 *Re Economic Fire Office* (1896) 12 TLR 142.
14 *Xenos v Wickham* (1866) LR 2 HL 296 at 308 per Pigott B.
15 *Canning v Farquhar* (1886) 16 QBD 727, CA.
16 See the Insurance Companies Act 1982 s 76 (as amended); and paras 815–816 post.

384. Contractual effect of new terms in the policy. It sometimes happens that a particular condition appears for the first time, at any rate in a precise form, in the policy itself. The question then arises whether the issue of the policy is merely part of the negotiation between the parties, in which case there is no contract unless and until there has been some acceptance of it by the proposer[1], or whether the policy as issued is, or contains the terms of, the contract. If the parties have already arrived in substance at a complete agreement a new term cannot be introduced by the insurers in issuing a policy except on the basis that it requires a new acceptance so as to amount to a variation of the prior agreement[2]. If there is no new acceptance the insurers are obliged to issue a policy which conforms with the prior agreement[3]. Once a firm contract has been entered into neither party can resile from any of the agreed terms or seek to introduce new terms which have never been agreed[4]. The proposer may decline to be bound by the new terms suggested and may take proceedings to enforce the issue of a policy on the basis of the agreed terms or to rectify a policy which does not comply with those terms[5]. Where, however, the proposer seeks to set up a prior contract he must show that the contract amounted to a full agreement as to the details of the terms of the insurance. Where he relies on the acceptance of a proposal which was a proposal for a policy containing the insurers' usual terms and conditions for such an insurance, he cannot object to the inclusion of those terms and conditions in the policy[6]. If the proposer does not intend to accept the new terms he may return the policy unless he has committed himself to taking it; if he does nothing his tacit acquiescence by itself will probably not be construed as an approval[7]; but any positive action by which he recognises or seeks to enforce the policy will amount to an affirmation of it[8], and once he has made such an affirmation he cannot seek to set it aside[9].

1 *Allis-Chalmers Co v Maryland Fidelity and Deposit Co* (1916) 114 LT 433, HL; see CONTRACT vol 9 para 256.
2 *Allis-Chalmers Co v Maryland Fidelity and Deposit Co* (1916) 114 LT 433 at 434, HL, per Lord Loreburn LC; *Sickness and Accident Assurance Association v General Accident Assurance Corpn* (1892) 19 R 977, Ct of Sess, following *Canning v Farquhar* (1886) 16 QBD 727, CA.
3 *Collett v Morrison* (1851) 9 Hare 162 at 176 per Turner V-C; *Griffiths v Fleming* [1909] 1 KB 805 at 817, CA, per Farwell LJ.
4 *McElroy v London Assurance Corpn* (1897) 24 R 287 at 290, Ct of Sess, per Lord M'Laren; *Pearl Life Assurance Co v Johnson* [1909] 2 KB 288.
5 As to rectification see para 402 post.
6 *General Accident Insurance Corpn v Cronk* (1901) 17 TLR 233 (insurance against drivers' accidents; time limit for notification of accidents); *Re Bradley and Essex and Suffolk Accident Indemnity Society* [1912] 1 KB 415 at 425, CA, per Fletcher Moulton LJ (but see also at 431 per Farwell LJ) (workmen's compensation; condition as to keeping wages' book); and see *Acme Wood Flooring Co Ltd v Marten* (1904) 90 LT 313.
7 For the need to communicate acceptance of an offer and the circumstances in which communication may be deemed to be dispensed with see CONTRACT vol 9 para 254.
8 *Baker v Yorkshire Fire and Life Assurance Co* [1892] 1 QB 144 at 145 per Lord Coleridge CJ; *Newcastle Fire Insurance Co v Macmorran & Co* (1815) 3 Dow 255 at 264, HL, per Lord Eldon.

9 *Macdonald v Law Union Insurance Co* (1874) LR 9 QB 328; *British Equitable Assurance Co Ltd v Baily* [1906] AC 35, HL; *Dawsons Ltd v Bonnin* [1922] 2 AC 413, HL. The suggestion in *Re Bradley and Essex and Suffolk Accident Indemnity Society* [1912] 1 KB 415 at 430, CA, per Farwell LJ, that the assured can affirm the policy without being bound by the new term seems to be inconsistent with these authorities.

(3) INTERIM CONTRACTS OF INSURANCE

385. Principles affecting interim insurance. Where a proposal is submitted through the insurers' agent, the agent is usually not authorised to accept the proposal himself[1], but must pass it on to the insurers for a decision to accept it or not. There then exists a lapse in time between the submission and acceptance and it has become well established commercial practice, particularly in motor vehicle insurance[2], to issue interim insurance cover pending either completion of a detailed proposal or consideration of a proposal which has been completed and submitted; alternatively a form of acceptance may be in use which itself defines the scope of interim insurance pending the issue of a formal policy. The issue of such interim insurance falls within the authority of an insurance agent[3] unless he is excluded, expressly or impliedly, by the terms of his authority, from committing his principal in that way[4]. There must, of course, be a contract for the grant of such an interim insurance, however informally[5], and being a contract of insurance, stringent attention will be paid to the duty on the proposer to make full and frank disclosure of material facts if the grant is being made without the proposer signing anything[6].

1 *Hancock v Macnamara* (1868) IR 2 Eq 486.
2 See *Julien Praet et Cie SA v H G Poland Ltd* [1960] 1 Lloyd's Rep 420 at 428 per Pearson J; on appeal sub nom *Poland v Julien Praet et Cie SA* [1961] 1 Lloyd's Rep 187, CA.
3 *Mackie v European Assurance Society* (1869) 21 LT 102; *Murfitt v Royal Insurance Co Ltd* (1922) 38 TLR 334.
4 *Levy v Scottish Employers' Insurance Co* (1901) 17 TLR 229; *Linford v Provincial Horse and Cattle Insurance Co* (1864) 34 Beav 291; *Richards v Port of Manchester Insurance Co Ltd* (1934) 152 LT 261; affd 152 LT 413, CA; cf *Rossiter v Trafalgar Life Assurance Association* (1859) 27 Beav 377.
5 *Murfitt v Royal Insurance Co Ltd* (1922) 38 TLR 334, followed in *Parker & Co (Sandbank) v Western Assurance Co* [1925] WC & Ins Rep 82.
6 *Mayne Nickless Ltd v Pegler* [1974] 1 NSWLR 228 (NSW SC), where the proposer failed to disclose a previous accident in which the life insured (subsequently deceased) was involved. As to the duty to disclose material facts see para 349 et seq ante.

386. Cover notes. The usual method in which interim insurance is granted is by a cover note which is, in practice[1], printed in common form. Normally a cover note incorporates the terms and conditions of the insurers' standard form of policy, either by express reference[2] or by reference to a signed proposal which incorporates the standard form[3]; if the proposer is to be bound by the standard terms and conditions, it must be shown that in some other way he has agreed to accept them[4]. Subject to such an incorporation of the standard terms and conditions, a cover note is a contract of insurance distinct from the contract comprised in the policy, even where a policy is issued[5]. The cover note is superseded by the subsequent issue of a policy[6], but the parties' rights and liabilities in respect of any loss which happens during the currency of the cover note normally fall to be determined by reference to the terms of the cover note, not to the terms of the subsequent policy[7].

No formal document is necessary; a verbal agreement for cover is sufficient[8].

1 Cover notes are not issued in life assurance. As to the distinction between a cover note and an insurance 'slip' see para 388 post.
2 *Citizens Insurance Co of Canada v Parsons* (1881) 7 App Cas 96, PC; *General Accident, Fire and Life Assurance Corpn Ltd v Shuttleworth* (1938) 60 Ll L Rep 301.
3 *Wyndham Rather Ltd v Eagle Star and British Dominions Insurance Co Ltd* (1925) 21 Ll L Rep 214, CA; *Neil v South-East Lancashire Insurance Co* 1932 SC 35; *Houghton v Trafalgar Insurance Co Ltd* [1953] 2 Lloyd's Rep 18; affd on another point [1954] 1 QB 247, [1953] 2 All ER 1409, [1953] 2 Lloyd's Rep 503, CA.
4 *Re Coleman's Depositories Ltd and Life and Health Assurance Association* [1907] 2 KB 798, CA; *Irving v Sun Insurance Office* [1906] ORC 24; *Golding v Royal London Auxiliary Insurance Co Ltd* (1914) 30 TLR 350.
5 *Mackie v European Assurance Society* (1869) 21 LT 102; *Citizens Insurance Co of Canada v Parsons* (1881) 7 App Cas 96, PC; *General Accident, Fire and Life Assurance Corpn Ltd v Shuttleworth* (1938) 60 Ll L Rep 301.
6 *Roberts v Security Co* [1897] 1 QB 111 at 115, CA.
7 *Re Coleman's Depositories Ltd and Life and Health Assurance Association* [1907] 2 KB 798, CA; *Parker & Co (Sandbank) v Western Assurance Co* [1925] WC & Ins Rep 82; cf *Burton and Watts v Batavia Sea and Fire Insurance Co* [1922] SASR 466; *Ellerbeck Collieries Ltd v Cornhill Insurance Co Ltd* [1932] 1 KB 401, CA.
8 *Stockton v Mason and Vehicle and General Insurance Co Ltd and Arthur Edward (Insurance) Ltd* [1978] 2 Lloyd's Rep 430, CA.

387. Duration of cover note. The acceptance of the proposal brings the cover note to an end[1]. If, within the period for which a cover note is in force[2], the insurers decide not to issue a formal policy they must give notice to the proposer terminating the cover note; otherwise they are liable for the full period of the cover note[3]. Even if they do give notice they are liable for any loss occurring before the notice has been received[4]. The cover note expires automatically on the expiration of the stipulated period of its life, and no notice of its expiration or of a subsequent declining of the proposal is necessary[5].

1 *Roberts v Security Co* [1897] 1 QB 111, CA; cf *Davies v National Fire and Marine Insurance Co of New Zealand* [1891] AC 485, PC.
2 A cover note is normally expressed to remain in force for a specified period unless cancelled by the insurers: see 20 Forms & Precedents (5th Edn) 543–544, Form 308. As to computation of time see *Cartwright v MacCormack (Trafalgar Insurance Co Ltd, third party)* [1963] 1 All ER 11, [1963] 1 WLR 18, CA.
3 *Stockton v Mason and Vehicle and General Insurance Co Ltd and Arthur Edward (Insurance) Ltd* [1978] 2 Lloyd's Rep 430, CA.
4 *Mackie v European Assurance Society* (1869) 21 LT 102.
5 *Levy v Scottish Employers' Insurance Co* (1901) 17 TLR 229, DC; *General Accident, Fire and Life Assurance Corpn v Robertson* [1909] AC 404, HL.

388. Insurance slips. When insurance is effected at Lloyd's, the cover note is replaced by a 'slip'. The slip is a document prepared by the broker containing a description of the proposer, a description of the subject matter and the amount for which it is to be insured, a statement as to what perils are to be insured against, the commencement date and the duration of the insurance[1]. The slip is used by the underwriter to assess the risk which he is invited to cover, enabling him to set the premium to be offered to the brokers; each underwriter retains the right to modify his offer to accord with the terms subsequently inserted[2]. The underwriter's acceptance of the proposal is marked by his initialling the slip and adding in the margin the amount for which he is to be liable[3].

There is a vital difference between a cover note and an insurance slip. Once a slip is initialled it operates as a final acceptance of the proposal[4] binding the insurers to issue a policy in accordance with its terms[5]. In contrast, a cover note commits the insurers to nothing; they may decline the proposal[6] without obligation to give any reasons for doing so[7].

1 See *Grover and Grover Ltd v Mathews* [1910] 2 KB 401 per Hamilton J.
2 *Jaglom v Excess Insurance Co Ltd* [1972] 2 QB 250, [1972] 1 All ER 267.
3 *Seaton v Heath, Seaton v Burnand* [1899] 1 QB 782 at 790, CA, per A L Smith LJ; rvsd without affecting this point sub nom *Seaton v Burnand, Burnand v Seaton* [1900] AC 135, HL.
4 Subject only to the contingency that the underwriter's line may fall to be written down on 'closing' to some extent if the slip turns out to have been oversubscribed: *General Reinsurance Corpn v Forsakringsaktiebolaget Fennia Patria* [1983] QB 856, [1983] 3 WLR 318, CA, per Kerr LJ.
5 *Re Yager and Guardian Assurance Co* (1912) 108 LT 38 at 43; see also *Thompson v Adams* (1889) 23 QBD 361; *Grover and Grover Ltd v Matthews* (1910) as reported in 15 Com Cas 249.
6 *Citizens Insurance Co of Canada v Parsons* (1881) 7 App Cas 96, PC; see para 89 ante.
7 *Mackie v European Assurance Society* (1869) 21 LT 102.

(4) THE POLICY

(i) Form of the Policy

389. The policy. In relation to contracts of non-marine insurance there are no statutory requirements comparable with those contained in the Marine Insurance Act 1906 prescribing the form of document to be used or the minimum particulars to be contained in it[1] although printed standard forms are normally used[2]. Therefore, any document which contains the terms of the contract may be treated as, or even called, a policy[3].

The rights of the parties are governed by the terms of the policy alone. It is possible, however, that another document such as the proposal is incorporated with the policy, in which case both documents should be read together. Whether the documents are incorporated is a matter of construction[4].

There will usually be an express term stating the duration of the policy[5], although it may be brought to an end, with the consent of the parties, before the expiration of the stated period[6].

1 See the Marine Insurance Act 1906 ss 22–24; and paras 39–40 ante.
2 However, it appears that there is no rule of law under which a parol contract of non-marine insurance would be invalid.
3 *Re Norwich Equitable Fire Insurance Society, Royal Insurance Co's Claim* (1887) 57 LT 241 at 246 per Kay J; *Re Profits and Income Insurance Co* [1929] 1 Ch 262 at 269 per Romer J; *Forsikringsakt National of Copenhagen v A-G* [1925] AC 639 at 642, HL, per Lord Cave LC.
4 *Ikerigi Compania Naviera SA v Palmer, The Wondrous* [1992] 2 Lloyd's Rep 566; *Home Insurance Co of New York v Victoria-Montreal Fire Insurance Co* [1907] AC 59, PC. For an example of a clause incorporating the proposal into the policy see 20 Forms & Precedents (5th Edn) 509, Form 291 cl 1.
5 *Allis-Chalmers Co Ltd v Maryland Fidelity and Deposit Co* (1916) 114 LT 433, HL.
6 *Bamberger v Commercial Credit Mutual Assurance Co* (1855) 15 CB 676; *Sickness and Accident Assurance v General Accident Assurance Corpn* (1892) 19 R 977, Ct of Sess.

390. Contents of policy. In form, a policy is a unilateral undertaking by the insurers[1] to pay the sum insured on the happening of the specified event[2]; unless and until rectified[3] it is the exclusive record of the contract[4]. It contains four main sections, namely:

(1) the recitals[5], which are usually inserted into a policy;
(2) the operative words[6], defining the nature and scope of the risk insured;

(3) the special particulars appropriate to the particular contract, such as the name, address and occupation of the assured, the subject matter of the insurance, the amount of the insurance, the period of the insurance, the premium and similar matters, which are usually inserted in a schedule; and

(4) the general conditions[7] to which the contract is subject, which are usually indorsed on the back and incorporated by words of reference in the operative part[8].

If there are to be any special conditions introduced to the policy, or the policy is to be subject to any variations, they must be mutually agreed[9] and in writing[10]. Alterations to the policy are usually recorded on slips called indorsements and pasted onto the back of the policy[11].

1 *Macdonald v Law Union Insurance Co* (1874) LR 9 QB 328 at 330 per Blackburn J.

2 Where an insurance company to which the Insurance Companies Act 1982 Pt II (ss 15–71 (as amended)) applies carries on capital redemption business for which the premiums in return for which a contract is effected are payable at intervals of not less than six months, the company must not give the holder of any policy issued after 2 December 1909 any advantage dependent on lot or chance: s 80: see para 818 post.

3 As to rectification see para 402 post.

4 *British Equitable Assurance Co Ltd v Bailey* [1906] AC 35 at 41, HL, per Lord Lindley.

5 As to the recitals see para 391 post.

6 As to the operative words see para 392 post.

7 As to the general conditions see para 393 post.

8 *Everett v Desborough* (1829) 5 Bing 503 at 517 per Best CJ; see also *Solvency Mutual Guarantee Co v York* (1858) 3 H & N 588; *Caledonian Insurance Co v Gilmour* [1893] AC 85 at 90, HL, per Lord Herschell; *Tootal Broadhurst Lee Co v London and Lancashire Fire Insurance Co* (1908) reported in Ivamy's Fire and Motor Insurance (4th Edn) 403. For examples of non-marine policies see 20 Forms & Precedents (5th Edn) 29 et seq, Form 2 et seq.

9 *Langham v Cologan* (1812) 4 Taunt 330; *Lishman v Northern Maritime Insurance Co* (1875) LR 10 CP 179 at 182 per Blackburn J.

10 *Robinson v Tobin* (1816) 1 Stark 336.

11 See *Royal Exchange Assurance v Hope* [1928] Ch 179, CA.

391. Recitals. The recitals are always subject to being overridden by the operative words if the latter are clear and unambiguous[1]. Recitals are of some importance in certain circumstances, namely:

(1) where the policy is under seal, in which case a recital may operate as an estoppel to preclude the insurers from disputing a fact recited[2];

(2) resolving a doubt as to ambiguity or vagueness of the operative words[3]; and

(3) where other documents or parts of documents are incorporated into the contract.

The document most commonly incorporated is the proposal[4], but a prospectus[5] or schedule[6] or another policy[7] may be incorporated as well. If the documents are not incorporated by the recital they merely record steps in the negotiations and form no part of the contract[8], and recourse can only be had to them for limited purposes[9].

1 *Blascheck v Bussell* (1916) 33 TLR 74 at 75, CA, per Swinfen Eady J; see DEEDS vol 12 paras 1509–1515.

2 *Roberts v Security Co* [1897] 1 QB 111, CA, distinguished in *Equitable Fire and Accident Office v Ching Wo Hong* [1907] AC 96, PC; *Anglo-Californian Bank v London and Provincial Marine and General Insurance Co Ltd* (1904) 10 Com Cas 1. Policies under seal are rarely used now. See also *Pearl Life Assurance Co v Johnson* [1909] 2 KB 288, DC (recital that there was a formal proposal could not be avoided by insurers).

3 *Notman v Anchor Assurance Co* (1858) 4 CBNS 476 at 480 per Cockburn CJ. As to the operative words see para 392 post.

4 If the policy and proposal are inconsistent with each other, the policy, being the later document, prevails: *Kaufmann v British Surety Insurance Co Ltd* (1929) 45 TLR 399. As to the insurer's duty to exercise good faith in a prospectus or invitation to take out insurance see para 362 ante.

5 *Routledge v Burrell* (1789) 1 Hy Bl 254, followed in *Worsley v Wood* (1796) 6 Term Rep 710.

6 *Sillem v Thornton* (1854) 3 E & B 868.

7 *Sulphite Pulp Co v Faber* (1895) 1 Com Cas 146. In facultative reinsurance, where an individual policy is reinsured, the reinsurance policy may incorporate the original policy; in this case, the necessary modifications must be made to adapt the original terms to a reinsurance (*Re Athenaeum Life Assurance Society, ex p Prince of Wales Life Assurance Society* (1859) John 633; *Excess Insurance Co v Mathews* (1925) 31 Com Cas 43), and any inconsistent terms must be rejected (*Home Insurance Co of New York v Victoria-Montreal Fire Insurance Co Ltd* [1907] AC 59, PC). Cf *Pine Top Insurance Co Ltd v Unione Italiana Anglo Saxon Reinsurance Co Ltd* [1987] 1 Lloyd's Rep 476 (arbitration clause in insurance policy not incorporated, via reinsurance contract, in retrocession contract). See further para 204 et seq ante.

8 *British Equitable Assurance Co v Baily* [1906] AC 35, HL; *Griffiths v Fleming* [1909] 1 KB 805 at 817, CA, per Farwell LJ; see, however, *Sun Life Assurance Co of Canada v Jervis* [1943] 2 All ER 425, CA, where it was held that the contract included an 'illustration' which was sent to the plaintiff by the defendant insurance company and purported to show the benefits payable under the proposed policy, without which the application for insurance was not intelligible, and the policy was ordered to be rectified so as to give effect to the contract contained in the 'illustration' and proposal form. As to rectification generally see para 402 post.

9 Eg as aids in interpreting ambiguities in the policy (see para 396 text to note 13 post) or as containing collateral bargains (*Thiselton v Commercial Union Assurance Co* [1926] Ch 888; see further para 400 text to note 7 post) or as indicating what the real contract was, where the policy is challenged as not conforming to the real contract (*Wood v Dwarris* (1856) 11 Exch 493; *Griffiths v Fleming* [1909] 1 KB 805, CA; *Collett v Morrison* (1851) 9 Hare 162). The direct way of raising the issue as to whether such documents may be referred to is to claim rectification (as to which see para 402 post), but the court, in its equitable jurisdiction, may dispense with the formality of such a prayer appearing on the pleadings (*Wood v Dwarris* supra). Consequently the judgments do not always show clearly the grounds on which letters, prospectuses, advertisements etc have been taken into consideration: see *R Smith & Son v Eagle Star and British Dominions Insurance Co Ltd* (1934) 50 TLR 208, CA; *Salvin v James* (1805) 6 East 571.

392. Operative words.

The operative words are the substance of the policy, defining the nature and extent of the risk against which the insurance is effected[1]. Where the operative words are precise, clear and unambiguous they will prevail over the recitals[2].

1 In policies of insurance against accidents to property, loss arising from war or hostilities is commonly excluded. As to statutory provision relating to war risks insurance see para 790 et seq post.

2 *Blascheck v Bussell* (1916) 33 TLR 74 at 75, CA, per Swinfen Eady LJ; *Lazard Bros & Co Ltd v Brooks* (1932) 43 Ll L Rep 372, HL; *Anglo-International Bank Ltd v General Accident Fire and Life Assurance Corpn Ltd* (1934) 48 Ll L Rep 151 at 155, HL, per Lord Russell of Killowen. As to the rules which govern the interpretation of policies see paras 394–400 post.

393. General conditions.

The general conditions cover a variety of matters, such as giving notice of any accident or other event giving rise to a claim or potential claim, furnishing evidence in support of a claim, permitting the insurers to take charge of litigation, the respective rights of the insurers and the assured to cancel the policy, furnishing information on matters relating to the insurance, submitting to medical examination and so forth. In the case of insurance companies the general conditions usually contain an arbitration clause, either in simple form or in the form which makes an arbitrator's award a condition precedent to the bringing of any action[1]. Finally, there will almost always be found among the conditions a clause providing that the due observance of the terms, provisos, conditions and indorsements in the policy, so far as they relate to anything to be done or complied with by the assured, and the truth of the statements and answers made in the proposal, are to be conditions precedent to any liability of the insurers to make any payment under the policy[2].

1 As to arbitration as a condition precedent to bringing any action see para 498 post; and ARBITRATION vol 2 (Reissue) para 635 note 1. As to the agreement reached between certain insurers to refrain from insisting on the enforcement of arbitration clauses in relation to questions of liability see para 1 text and note 3 ante. As to the interpretation of a clause in a policy by which a claim is to be paid unless a Queen's Counsel advises that it could be successfully contested by the assured see paras 695–696 post.

2 As to conditions precedent to liability under a policy see para 406 post.

(ii) Interpretation of the Policy

394. Factors governing interpretation. A policy of insurance is a document in writing; it is a contractual document and a commercial document, designed to fulfil well recognised commercial purposes and presumed to be made with due regard to well recognised commercial habits and practices. Each of these broad propositions produces a number of subsidiary rules governing its interpretation[1].

1 A policy of insurance is subject to the same general rules of interpretation as any other written contract: *Smith v Accident Insurance Co* (1870) LR 5 Exch 302 at 307 per Martin B. The principles governing the interpretation of written documents are fully discussed in DEEDS vol 12 para 1459 et seq. It is only intended in this title to summarise these principles as evidenced by insurance cases. As to the proper law of a foreign insurance policy see *Rossano v Manufacturers' Life Insurance Co Ltd* [1963] 2 QB 352, [1962] 2 All ER 214; *Forsikringsaktieselskapet Vesta v Butcher* [1989] AC 852, [1989] 1 All ER 402, HL; and CONFLICT OF LAWS vol 8 para 583 et seq. Generally, once a trial judge has made findings of fact on which his interpretation of the policy is based, an appellate court will not set them aside unless it is satisfied that he has erred: *Bohl v Great West Life Assurance Co* [1974] 1 WWR 700 (Sask CA).

395. Actual language to be construed. The fact that the document is in writing involves the application of the principle that what has to be considered is the actual language used in the policy[1] and in any documents which are contractual by virtue of being incorporated in the policy[2], this being the language which the parties themselves have chosen to express their bargain[3]. When presented with a conflict between the parties as to the meaning of the policy, the court's function is to interpret what the parties have in fact said in their contract, not to speculate as to what they may have intended when entering into the contract[4]. What the parties have in fact said is comprised in the words they have used; the problem is to ascertain what the words mean[5]. It is not the court's function, by a process of construction, to make for the parties a reasonable contract which they have not made for themselves[6]. If the words are clear, precise and unambiguous effect must be given to them, however unreasonable the result may be[7].

1 *Want v Blunt* (1810) 12 East 183 at 187 per Lord Ellenborough CJ; *Beacon Life and Fire Assurance Co v Gibb* (1862) 1 Moo PCCNS 73 at 97.

2 Eg the proposal: *South Staffordshire Tramways Co v Sickness and Accident Assurance Association* [1891] 1 QB 402, CA; *Re George and Goldsmiths and General Burglary Insurance Association Ltd* [1899] 1 QB 595, CA.

3 *Re George and Goldsmiths and General Burglary Insurance Association Ltd* [1899] 1 QB 595 at 610, CA, per Collins LJ; *Victor Melik & Co Ltd v Norwich Union Fire Insurance Society Ltd and Kemp* [1980]

1 Lloyd's Rep 523 at 530 per Woolf J; *Forsikringsaktieselskapet Vesta v Butcher* [1989] AC 852, [1989] 1 All ER 402, HL; *Hitchins (Hatfield) Ltd v Prudential Assurance Co Ltd* [1991] 2 Lloyd's Rep 580 at 586, CA, per Parker LJ.

4 *Pearson v Commercial Union Assurance Co* (1863) 15 CBNS 305 at 313 per Erle CJ; *Re George and Goldsmiths and General Burglary Insurance Association Ltd* [1899] 1 QB 595 at 609, CA, per Collins LJ.

5 As to how the meaning of the words is to be ascertained see DEEDS vol 12 para 1460.

6 *Re George and Goldsmiths and General Burglary Insurance Association Ltd* [1899] 1 QB 595 at 609, CA, per Collins LJ; *Cooke and Arkwright v Haydon* [1987] 2 Lloyd's Rep 579 at 582, CA, per Hobhouse J (liability insurance).

7 *Joel v Law Union and Crown Insurance Co* [1908] 2 KB 863 at 886, CA, per Fletcher Moulton LJ; *Re United London and Scottish Insurance Co Ltd, Brown's Claim* [1915] 2 Ch 167 at 170, CA, per Lord Cozens-Hardy MR; *Farr v Motor Traders' Mutual Insurance Society* [1920] 3 KB 669 at 673, CA, per Bankes LJ; see also *Gorman v Hand-in-Hand Insurance Co* (1877) IR 11 CL 224; *New Hampshire Insurance Co v Strabag AG* [1990] 2 Lloyd's Rep 61 (collective insurance policy).

396. Words must be given ordinary meaning. In any document the words used must prima facie be construed in their plain, ordinary, popular meaning[1] rather than their strictly precise, etymological, philosophic, or scientific meaning[2]. For this purpose the document must be looked at as a whole[3]. The meaning of a word may be controlled by its context[4]. A particular context may indicate a limited meaning for general words, as where a variety of things of a specific class are enumerated, followed by the words 'et cetera' or 'other property'; such words will be construed as referring only to things of the same genus as the detailed items[5]. A word which is used more than once in the document, in the case of doubt or ambiguity and in the absence of a context to the contrary, may be presumed to bear the same meaning throughout[6]. Unless a contrary intention appears[7], technical legal terms will be given their technical legal meaning[8] and technical words their technical meaning[9]. The grammatical construction of the words used must be followed[10], but mere considerations of grammar will not be allowed to frustrate what is plainly the effect of the document when taken as a whole[11]. Clerical errors may be disregarded[12].

The words to be considered are, in the first instance, the words in the operative part of the policy which prevails over the recitals, but if there is ambiguity in the operative part the recitals may be looked at to see if they throw any light on the difficulty[13].

1 *Platt v Young* (1843) 2 LTOS 17, 370; *Stanley v Western Insurance Co* (1868) LR 3 Exch 71 at 73 per Kelly CB (gas); *Thomson v Weems* (1884) 9 App Cas 671 at 687, HL, per Lord Watson; *Royal Insurance Co v Westminster Fire Insurance Co* (1887) Post Magazine, 22 January ('building' does not include stained glass); *Hamlyn v Crown Accidental Insurance Co Ltd* [1893] 1 QB 750 at 753, CA, per Lord Esher MR; *Re George and Goldsmiths and General Burglary Insurance Association Ltd* [1899] 1 QB 595 at 607, CA, per A L Smith LJ; *Rogers v Whittaker* [1917] 1 KB 942 (commenting on *Drinkwater v London Assurance Corpn* (1767) 2 Wils 363); *Hansford v London Express Newspaper Ltd* (1928) 44 TLR 349 (following *Harper v Associated Newspapers Ltd* (1927) 43 TLR 331 (vehicle); *Wulfson v Switzerland General Insurance Co Ltd* [1940] 3 All ER 221 (goods 'in store'); *Eisinger v General Accident Fire and Life Assurance Corpn Ltd* [1955] 2 All ER 897, [1955] 1 WLR 869 (loss); *Leo Rapp Ltd v McClure* [1955] 1 Lloyd's Rep 292 (warehouse); *Firmin and Collins Ltd v Allied Shippers Ltd (Alder, third party)* [1967] 1 Lloyd's Rep 633 (whilst in a public warehouse); *Princette Models Ltd v Reliance Fire and Accident Insurance Corpn Ltd* [1960] 1 Lloyd's Rep 49 (wherever); *Hales v Reliance Fire and Accident Insurance Corpn Ltd* [1960] 2 Lloyd's Rep 391 (inflammable); *Lewis Emanuel & Son Ltd v Hepburn* [1960] 1 Lloyd's Rep 304 (physical loss or damage or deterioration); *Sadler Bros Co v Meredith* [1963] 2 Lloyd's Rep 293 (in transit); *Mills v Smith (Sinclair, third party)* [1964] 1 QB 30, [1963] 2 All ER 1078 (caused by accident); *Clarke v Insurance Office of Australia Ltd* [1965] 1 Lloyd's Rep 308 (Vict CA) (ordinarily residing with); *Frewin v Poland* [1968] 1 Lloyd's Rep 100 (destruction or loss of manuscript); *Woolford v Liverpool County Council* [1968] 2 Lloyd's Rep 256 (policy to cover any injury); *Kumar v Life Insurance Corpn of India* [1974] 1 Lloyd's Rep 147 (operation); *Young v Sun Alliance and London*

Insurance Ltd [1976] 3 All ER 561, [1977] 1 WLR 104, CA (flood); *Oei v Foster (formerly Crawford) and Eagle Star Insurance Co Ltd* [1982] 2 Lloyd's Rep 170 ('in custody or control of'); *O'Donoghue v Harding* [1988] 2 Lloyd's Rep 281 ('left unattended'); *CTN Cash and Carry Ltd v General Accident, Fire and Life Assurance Corp plc* [1989] 1 Lloyd's Rep 299 ('attended'); *New Hampshire Insurance Co v Strabag AG* [1990] 2 Lloyd's Rep 61 ('otherwise admitted'); *Hitchens (Hatfield) Ltd v Prudential Assurance Co Ltd* [1991] 2 Lloyd's Rep 580, CA ('defective design'). A metaphorical expression is not to be taken literally: *Borradaile v Hunter* (1843) 5 Man & G 639 at 657 per Erskine J ('die by his own hands'). See generally DEEDS vol 12 para 1463.

2 *Two Hundred Cases of Tea* (1824) 9 Wheat 340 per Storey J; *Stanley v Western Insurance Co* (1868) LR 3 Exch 71; *Scragg v United Kingdom Temperance and General Provident Institution* [1976] 2 Lloyd's Rep 227 ('motor racing' means to those interested in motor sport a circuit race round a course as in a Grand Prix competition and does not include a sprint event, ie one in which competitors are timed against the clock and are started individually at intervals of ten to thirty seconds).

3 *Braunstein v Accidental Death Insurance Co* (1861) 1 B & S 782 at 799 per Blackburn J; *Cornish v Accident Insurance Co* (1889) 23 QBD 453 at 456, CA, per Lindley LJ; *Hamlyn v Crown Accidental Insurance Co Ltd* [1893] 1 QB 750 at 754, CA, per Lopes LJ; *Pennsylvania Co for Insurances on Lives and Granting Annuities v Mumford* [1920] 2 KB 537 at 543, CA, per Lord Sterndale MR; *City Tailors Ltd v Evans* (1921) 126 LT 439, CA; *Gale v Motor Union Insurance Co Ltd* [1928] 1 KB 359; *Pocock v Century Insurance Co Ltd* [1960] 2 Lloyd's Rep 150; *Simon Brooks Ltd v Hepburn* [1961] 2 Lloyd's Rep 43; *Lane v Spratt* [1970] 2 QB 480, [1970] 1 All ER 162; *Cooke and Arkwright v Haydon* [1987] 2 Lloyd's Rep 579, CA; and see DEEDS vol 12 para 1469.

4 *Re Coleman's Depositories Ltd and Life and Health Assurance Association* [1907] 2 KB 798 at 813, CA, per Buckley LJ; *Joel v Law Union and Crown Insurance Co* [1908] 2 KB 863 at 894, CA, per Buckley LJ; *Rogers v Whittaker* [1917] 1 KB 942 at 943 per Sankey J; see also *Watchorn v Langford* (1813) 3 Camp 422; *Joel v Harvey* (1857) 5 WR 488; *Fowkes v Manchester and London Assurance Association* (1863) 3 B & S 917; *Curtis & Sons v Mathews* [1918] 2 KB 825; and cf *Piddington v Co-operative Insurance Society Ltd* [1934] 2 KB 236; *Williams v Lloyd's Underwriters* [1957] 1 Lloyd's Rep 118; *Kearney v General Accident Fire and Life Assurance Corpn Ltd* [1968] 2 Lloyd's Rep 240; *Laurence v Davies (Norwich Union Fire Insurance Society Ltd, third party)* [1972] 2 Lloyd's Rep 231; *Jaglom v Excess Insurance Co Ltd* [1972] 2 QB 250, [1972] 1 All ER 267; *Young v Sun Alliance and London Insurance Ltd* [1976] 2 Lloyd's Rep 189, CA; *Rowlinson Construction Ltd v Insurance Co of North America (UK) Ltd* [1981] 1 Lloyd's Rep 322; *Petrofina (UK) Ltd v Magnaload Ltd* [1983] 2 Lloyd's Rep 91; *Commonwealth Smelting Ltd v Guardian Royal Exchange Assurance Ltd* [1984] 2 Lloyd's Rep 608; *Phillips and Stratton v Dorintal Insurance Ltd* [1987] 1 Lloyd's Rep 482; *Youell v Bland Welch & Co Ltd* [1990] 2 Lloyd's Rep 423; *Hitchens (Hatfield) Ltd v Prudential Assurance Co Ltd* [1991] 2 Lloyd's Rep 580, CA.

5 See eg *South Staffordshire Tramways Co v Sickness and Accident Assurance Association* [1891] 1 QB 402, CA; *Lake v Simmons* [1927] AC 487 at 507, HL, per Lord Sumner; *Alder v Moore* [1961] 2 QB 57, [1961] 1 All ER 1, CA; *Forney v Dominion Insurance Co Ltd* [1969] 3 All ER 831, [1969] 1 WLR 928. A difference of phrasing in different parts of the policy does not necessarily indicate a difference of meaning: *Burridge & Son v F H Haines & Sons Ltd* (1918) 118 LT 681.

6 *Lake v Simmons* [1927] AC 487 at 507, HL, per Lord Sumner; see also *Mair v Railway Passengers Assurance Co Ltd* (1877) 37 LT 356, DC; *Sangster's Trustees v General Accident Assurance Corpn Ltd* (1896) 24 R 56, Ct of Sess; *King v Travellers' Insurance Association Ltd* (1931) 48 TLR 53; cf *Ewing & Co v Sicklemore* (1918) 35 TLR 55, CA; and *Sun Fire Office v Hart* (1889) 14 App Cas 98, PC. As to the ejusdem generis rule see DEEDS vol 12 paras 1525–1526.

7 *Re George and Goldsmiths and General Burglary Insurance Association Ltd* [1899] 1 QB 595, CA (burglary and theft as hereinafter defined).

8 *Debenhams Ltd v Excess Insurance Co Ltd* (1912) 28 TLR 505 (embezzlement); *Re Calf and Sun Insurance Office* [1920] 2 KB 366, CA (entry); *London and Lancashire Fire Insurance Co Ltd v Bolands Ltd* [1924] AC 836, HL (riot); *Sturge v Hackett* [1962] 3 All ER 166, CA (legally liable); *Lim Trading Co v Haydon* [1968] 1 Lloyd's Rep 159, Sing HC (theft); *Rigby v Sun Alliance and London Insurance Co Ltd* [1980] 1 Lloyd's Rep 359 (liability as owners); *Grundy (Teddington) Ltd v Fulton* [1983] 1 Lloyd's Rep 16 (theft); *Aswan M/S Engineering Establishement Co Ltd v Iron Trades Mutual Insurance Co Ltd* [1989] 1 Lloyd's Rep 289 (liable at law to pay); *Dino Services Ltd v Prudential Assurance Co Ltd* [1989] 1 Lloyd's Rep 379, CA (forcible entry); *Dobson v General Accident Fire and Life Assurance Corp plc* [1989] 2 Lloyd's Rep 549, CA (theft); cf *Equitable Trust Co of New York v Henderson* (1930) 47 TLR 90 (forged). See generally DEEDS vol 12 para 1466.

9 *Anglo-African Merchants v Bayley* [1970] 1 QB 311, [1969] 2 All ER 421 ('new').

10 *Weir v Northern Counties of England Insurance Co* (1879) 4 LR Ir 689 at 693 per Lawson J; *Lewis Emanuel & Son Ltd v Hepburn* [1960] 1 Lloyd's Rep 304; *Balfour v Beaumont* [1984] 1 Lloyd's Rep 272, CA.

11 *Re Athenaeum Life Assurance Society, ex p Eagle Insurance Co* (1858) 4 K & J 549 at 555 per Wood V-C.

12 *Glen's Trustees v Lancashire and Yorkshire Accident Insurance Co* (1906) 8 F 915, Ct of Sess, ('not' was wrongly inserted in a condition); *Nittan (UK) Ltd v Solent Steel Fabrication Ltd (trading as Sargrove Automation) and Cornhill Insurance Co Ltd* [1981] 1 Lloyd's Rep 633, CA.

13 As to recitals see para 391 ante.

397. Intention of parties as test. The fact that the document records a contract means that the parties' intention is paramount[1]. The test is not subjective but strictly objective in that attention can normally be paid only to the language used, but where there is a general intention, as derived from the words, which is clear, this will not be allowed to be frustrated by minor inconsistencies or ambiguities; the document will be construed in such a way as to give efficacy to the transaction in accordance with the maxim *ut res magis valeat quam pereat*[2]. Where two constructions are possible, the one which tends to defeat the intention or to make it practically illusory will be rejected[3]. Similarly, where a literal construction would lead to a manifest absurdity this will be rejected in favour of a construction which is broad, liberal and reasonable[4], where both constructions are possible[5]. Words specifically chosen for the particular contract in question will receive more attention than general words; a policy is usually comprised in a form nearly all of which is printed as being required for general use[6] and written words are then inserted for its application to the particular contract. The printed portions are, of course, part of the contract and the intention evinced by them will, as far as possible, be made effective[7]. However, where there is any inconsistency or repugnancy between what is written and what is printed, the written words will prevail[8].

1 *Drinkwater v London Assurance Corpn* (1767) 2 Wils 363 at 364 per Wilmot CJ; *Tarleton v Staniforth* (1794) 5 Term Rep 695 at 699 per Lord Kenyon CJ; on appeal (1796) 1 Bos & P 471, Ex Ch; *Braunstein v Accidental Death Insurance Co* (1861) 1 B & S 782 at 799 per Blackburn J; *Lombard Australia Ltd v NRMA Insurance Ltd* [1969] 1 Lloyd's Rep 575 at 576 per Wallace A-CJ, and at 578–580 per Holmes JA (NSW CA).

2 Ie 'that the thing may rather have effect than be destroyed'; see DEEDS vol 12 para 1471.

3 *Trew v Railway Passengers' Assurance Co* (1861) 6 H & N 839 at 844, Ex Ch, per Cockburn CJ; *Cornish v Accident Insurance Co Ltd* (1889) 23 QBD 453 at 456, CA, per Lindley LJ; *Re Etherington and Lancashire and Yorkshire Accident Insurance Co* [1909] 1 KB 591 at 597, CA, per Vaughan Williams LJ; *Langford v Legal and General Assurance Society Ltd* [1986] 2 Lloyd's Rep 103; *Commercial Union Assurance Co plc v Sun Alliance Group plc* [1992] 1 Lloyd's Rep 475.

4 *Borradaile v Hunter* (1843) 5 Man & G 639; *Pim v Reid* (1843) 6 Man & G 1; *Clift v Schwabe* (1846) 3 CB 437; *Braunstein v Accidental Death Insurance Co* (1861) 1 B & S 782; *Australian Agricultural Co v Saunders* (1875) LR 10 CP 668, Ex Ch; *North British and Mercantile Insurance Co v London, Liverpool and Globe Insurance Co* (1877) 5 ChD 569, CA; *Sun Fire Office v Hart* (1889) 14 App Cas 98 at 104, PC; *Daff v Midland Colliery Owners' Mutual Indemnity Co* (1913) 82 LJKB 1340, HL; *Burridge & Son v F H Haines & Sons Ltd* (1918) 118 LT 681; *Smellie v British General Insurance Co* [1918] WC & Ins Rep 233; *Simmonds v Cockell* [1920] 1 KB 843; *John Martin of London Ltd v Russell* [1960] 1 Lloyd's Rep 554; *Lombard Australia Ltd v NRMA Insurance Ltd* [1969] 1 Lloyd's Rep 575 (NSW CA); *Jason v British Traders' Insurance Co Ltd* [1969] 1 Lloyd's Rep 281; *Gray v Barr (Prudential Assurance Co Ltd, third party)* [1971] 2 QB 554, [1971] 2 All ER 949, CA. The same principle applies to the questions in the proposal form: *Connecticut Mutual Life Insurance Co of Hertford v Moore* (1881) 6 App Cas 644 at 648, PC.

5 *Barnard v Faber* [1893] 1 QB 340 at 342, CA, per Lindley LJ; and see *Hooper v Accidental Death Insurance Co* (1860) 5 H & N 546 at 559, Ex Ch, per Wightman J; *London Guarantee Co v Fearnley* (1880) 5 App Cas 911 at 916, HL, per Lord Blackburn; *National Protector Fire Insurance Co Ltd v Nivert* [1913] AC 507 at 513, PC; *E Hulton & Co Ltd v Mountain* (1921) 37 TLR 869 at 870, CA, per Bankes LJ.

6 Phrases which have received judicial construction will normally receive the same construction in later cases *(Clift v Schwabe* (1846) 3 CB 437 at 470 per Parke B; *Glen v Lewis* (1853) 8 Exch 607; *Browning v Phoenix Assurance Co Ltd* [1960] 2 Lloyd's Rep 360 (social, domestic and pleasure purposes); *Louden v British Merchants Insurance Co Ltd* [1961] 1 All ER 705, [1961] 1 WLR 798, CA

(injury sustained whilst under the influence of drugs or intoxicating liquor); *McGoona v Motor Insurers' Bureau and Marsh* [1969] 2 Lloyd's Rep 34 (social, domestic and pleasure purposes)) even though the wording may have been altered *(Lawrence v Accidental Insurance Co Ltd* (1881) 7 QBD 216, DC; *Re Etherington and Lancashire and Yorkshire Accident Insurance Co Ltd* [1909] 1 KB 591, CA); but a decision on one form of words is no authority upon the construction of a different form *(Re Coleman's Depositories and Life and Health Assurance Association* [1907] 2 KB 798 at 812, CA, per Buckley LJ; *Re Calf and Sun Insurance Office* [1920] 2 KB 366 at 382, CA, per Atkin LJ).

7 *Foster v Mentor Life Assurance Co* (1854) 3 E & B 48 at 82 per Lord Campbell CJ.

8 *Home Insurance Co of New York v Victoria-Montreal Fire Insurance Co* [1907] AC 59, PC; *Australian Widows' Fund Life Assurance Society Ltd v National Mutual Life Association of Australasia Ltd* [1914] AC 634, PC; *City Tailors Ltd v Evans* (1921) 126 LT 439, CA; *Kaufmann v British Surety Insurance Co Ltd* (1929) 45 TLR 399; *General Accident Fire and Life Corpn Ltd v Midland Bank* [1940] 2 KB 388 ar 405, CA, per Greene MR. For the application of the rule to marine policies see para 46 ante. See generally DEEDS vol 12 para 1503.

398. Contra proferentem rule. Where there is ambiguity in the policy the court will apply the contra proferentem rule[1]. Since the printed parts of a non-marine insurance policy, and usually the written parts, are produced by the insurers, it is their business to see that precision and clarity are attained and, if they fail to do so, the ambiguity will be resolved by adopting the construction favourable to the assured[2]. Similarly, as regards language which emanates from the assured, such as the language used in answer to questions in the proposal or in a slip, a construction favourable to the insurers will prevail if the assured has created any ambiguity[3]. This rule, however, only becomes operative where the words are truly ambiguous; it is a rule for resolving ambiguity[4] and it cannot be invoked with a view to creating a doubt. Therefore, where the words used are free from ambiguity in the sense that, fairly and reasonably construed, they admit of only one meaning, the rule has no application[5].

1 Ie from the maxim *verba cartarum fortius accipiuntur contra proferentem* ('the words of deeds are to be interpreted most strongly against the party who puts them forward'). See generally DEEDS vol 12 para 1472 et seq; for the application and framing of policies in marine insurance see para 50 ante.

2 *Thomson v Weems* (1884) 9 App Cas 671 at 682, HL, per Lord Blackburn, following *Anderson v Fitzgerald* (1853) 4 HL Cas 484 at 507 per Lord St Leonards; see also *Tarleton v Staniforth* (1794) 5 Term Rep 695 at 699 per Lord Kenyon; *Braunstein v Accidental Death Insurance Co* (1861) 1 B & S 782 at 799 per Blackburn J; *Fitton v Accidental Death Insurance Co* (1864) 17 CBNS 122 at 134–135 per Willes J; *Re Etherington and Lancashire and Yorkshire Accident Insurance Co* [1909] 1 KB 591 at 596, CA, per Vaughan Williams LJ, following *Joel v Law Union and Crown Insurance Co* [1908] 2 KB 863 at 890, CA, per Fletcher Moulton LJ; *Simmonds v Cockell* [1920] 1 KB 843 at 845 per Roche J; *Lake v Simmons* [1927] AC 487 at 509, HL, per Lord Sumner; *Provincial Insurance Co Ltd v Morgan* [1933] AC 240 at 250, HL, per Lord Russell of Killlowen; *Metal Scrap and By-Products Ltd v Federated Conveyors Ltd* [1953] 1 Lloyd's Rep 221; *Houghton v Trafalgar Insurance Co Ltd* [1954] 1 QB 247, [1953] 2 All ER 1409, CA; *Hales v Reliance Fire and Accident Insurance Corpn Ltd* [1960] 2 Lloyd's Rep 391 at 396 per McNair J; *Gerhardt v Continental Insurance Companies and Firemen's Insurance Co of Newark* [1967] 1 Lloyd's Rep 380 (New Jersey SC); *Woolford v Liverpool County Council* [1968] 2 Lloyd's Rep 256; *Jason v British Traders Insurance Co Ltd* [1969] 1 Lloyd's Rep 281; *Lane v Spratt* [1970] 2 QB 480, [1970] 1 All ER 162; *Laurence v Davies (Norwich Union Fire Insurance Society Ltd, third party)* [1972] 2 Lloyd's Rep 231; *Kirkbride v Donner* [1974] 1 Lloyd's Rep 549; *Consolidated Bathurst Export Ltd v Mutual Boiler and Machinery Insurance Co* (1980) 112 DLR (3d) 49, Can SC; *McLean Enterprises Ltd v Ecclesiastical Insurance Office plc* [1986] 2 Lloyd's Rep 416; *Hitchens (Hatfield) Ltd v Prudential Assurance plc* [1991] 2 Lloyd's Rep 580.

3 *Condogianis v Guardian Assurance Co* [1921] 2 AC 125 at 130–131, PC; *Bartlett & Partners Ltd v Meller* [1961] 1 Lloyd's Rep 487; *De Maurier (Jewels) Ltd v Bastion Insurance Co Ltd and Coronet Insurance Ltd* [1967] 2 Lloyd's Rep 550; *American Airlines Inc v Hope* [1973] 1 Lloyd's Rep 233 at 250, CA, per Roskill LJ; affd [1974] 2 Lloyd's Rep 301, HL.

4 *Cornish v Accident Insurance Co* (1889) 23 QBD 453 at 456, CA, per Lindley LJ; *Cole v Accident Insurance Co Ltd* (1889) 5 TLR 736 at 737, CA, per Lindley LJ; see also *Drinkwater v London Assurance*

Corpn (1767) 2 Wils 363. Thus the rule is applied where two different meanings are equally possible and it is otherwise impossible to determine which is intended: *London and Lancashire Fire Insurance Co v Bolands Ltd* [1924] AC 836 at 848, HL, per Lord Sumner.

5 *Gamble v Accident Assurance Co* (1869) IR 4 CL 204 at 214 per Pigot CB; *Alder v Moore* [1961] 2 QB 57, [1961] 1 All ER 1, CA; *De Maurier (Jewels) Ltd v Bastion Insurance Co Ltd and Coronet Insurance Co Ltd* [1967] 2 Lloyd's Rep 550; *Stolberg v Pearl Assurance Co Ltd* [1970] 2 Lloyd's Rep 421, BC SC; *Marzouca v Atlantic and British Commercial Insurance Co Ltd* [1971] 1 Lloyd's Rep 449, PC; *Jaglom v Excess Insurance Co Ltd* [1972] 2 QB 250, [1972] 1 All ER 267; *Nittan (UK) Ltd v Solent Steel Fabrication Ltd (trading as Sargrove Automation) and Cornhill Insurance Co Ltd* [1981] 1 Lloyd's Rep 633, CA.

399. Business efficacy as test. The nature of any contract is not concluded by the name the parties give it but is determined on the substance which it contains; nonetheless, the fact that a contract is described by the parties as a policy of insurance is taken as some guidance on the question whether they intended to enter into a contract of insurance or a guarantee[1]. Similarly, where it is plain that the parties were intending to effect a contract of insurance or an insurance of a particular kind, the court will lean against a construction which would defeat this intention or make it substantially ineffective[2]. In cases of ambiguity the leaning will be in favour of the interpretation which tends to give business efficacy to the contract[3]. Regard will also be had to the known or proved customs and usages[4] and the phraseology prevalent[5], either in the insurance business or the assured's trade, these forming part of the context in which the particular words are used[6].

1 As to the nature of the contract see DEEDS vol 12 para 1462. As to the distinction between a contract of insurance and a guarantee see para 783 post.
2 As to the intention of the parties as a test see para 397 ante.
3 *Pelly v Royal Exchange Assurance Co* (1757) 1 Burr 341; *Sheridan v Phoenix Life Assurance Co* (1858) E B & E 156 at 165, Ex Ch, per Pollock CB; *Re Etherington and Lancashire and Yorkshire Accident Insurance Co* [1909] 1 KB 591 at 597, CA, per Vaughan Williams LJ.
4 *Fitton v Accidental Death Insurance Co* (1864) 17 CBNS 122; *Smith v Accident Insurance Co* (1870) LR 5 Exch 302; *Mint Security Ltd v Blair* [1982] 1 Lloyd's Rep 188; *Commercial Union Assurance Co plc v Sun Alliance Insurance Group plc* [1992] 1 Lloyd's Rep 475.
5 *Noble v Kennoway* (1780) 2 Doug KB 510; *Preston v Greenwood* (1784) 4 Doug KB 28; *Beacon Life and Fire Assurance Co v Gibb* (1862) 1 Moo PCCNS 73, PC.
6 See *Pocock v Century Co Ltd* [1960] 2 Lloyd's Rep 150; and as to the relevance of the context to the interpretation of particular words see para 396 ante.

400. Admissibility of extrinsic evidence. Since a contract of insurance is one which has been reduced into writing, then, in accordance with general principles, extrinsic evidence is not admissible to explain, contradict, add to, subtract from or otherwise vary it[1]. Evidence cannot ordinarily be given, whether orally or by producing prior drafts, to show the course the negotiations took[2]. However, where it is sought to establish the existence of a trade usage[3] or of a technical meaning in the trade of a term used[4], extrinsic evidence is admissible. Where there is an ambiguity in the language used, or where the contract is only fully intelligible in the light of the surrounding circumstances at the time when it was executed[5], extrinsic evidence directed to these circumstances is admissible[6]. Such evidence is also admissible to prove the existence and contents of a collateral oral agreement[7] or to support a claim that a written contract ought to be rectified as not truly setting out what was in fact agreed[8].

1 *Levy v Scottish Employers' Insurance Co* (1901) 17 TLR 229, DC (where the agent of the insurers varied the terms of the cover note); *Anglo-Californian Bank v London and Provincial Marine and General*

Insurance Co (1904) 10 Com Cas 1; *Horncastle v Equitable Life Assurance Society of United States* (1906) 22 TLR 735, CA; see also *Hare v Barstow* (1844) 8 Jur 928; *Platt v Young* (1843) 2 LTOS 17, 370; *Youell v Bland Welch & Co Ltd* [1992] 2 Lloyd's Rep 127 at 141, CA, per Beldam LJ. See further DEEDS vol 12 para 1478 et seq.

2 As to evidence of previous negotiations see DEEDS vol 12 para 1480. See also para 391 ante.

3 *Clift v Schwabe* (1846) 3 CB 437; *Foster v Mentor Life Assurance Co* (1854) 3 E & B 48 at 82 per Lord Campbell CJ; *Woodall v Pearl Assurance Co Ltd* [1919] 1 KB 593, CA; *Scragg v United Kingdom Temperance and General Provident Institution* [1976] 2 Lloyd's Rep 227, QBD.

4 *Watchorn v Langford* (1813) 3 Camp 422; *Beacon Life and Fire Assurance Co v Gibb* (1862) 1 Moo PCCNS 73; *Re Calf and Sun Insurance Office* [1920] 2 KB 366, CA; see also *Hooper v Accidental Death Insurance Co* (1860) 5 H & N 546, Ex Ch; and cf *Hordern Commercial Union Insurance Co* (1887) 56 LJPC 78, PC.

5 *Bank of New Zealand v Simpson* [1900] AC 182 at 188, PC, applied in *Moss v Norwich and London Insurance Association* (1922) 10 Ll L Rep 395, CA (where an employers' liability policy was intended to cover the employer's son).

6 As to the admissibility of evidence as to the surrounding circumstances see DEEDS vol 12 para 1490.

7 As to evidence of collateral oral agreements see DEEDS vol 12 para 1489.

8 See eg *Baker v Paine* (1750) 1 Ves Sen 456; *Mackenzie v Coulson* (1869) LR 8 Eq 368; and see further MISTAKE. As to the rectification of insurance policies see para 402 post.

(iii) Binding Effect of the Policy

401. The policy is the contractual document. Although a policy of insurance normally takes the form of a unilateral undertaking by the insurers to make the stipulated payment on the happening of the stipulated event, the contractual terms and conditions it contains are binding on the assured as they are on the insurers[1]. The assured cannot, therefore, enforce the insurers' promise as being contractual unless he in his turn has performed any provisions which have to be performed by him to make the contract effective[2]. The assured must pay the premium; he cannot wait to see whether the event insured against occurs or not, then tender the premium and demand fulfilment of the insurers' undertaking. The contract does not normally commence unless and until payment of the premium is made[3]. However, in the case of subsidiary provisions, such as those relating to the substantiation of a claim, it is probably sufficient if the assured is ready and willing to perform them. If the insurers wrongly repudiate on a ground going to the root of the contract, their conduct may constitute a waiver as regards the performance of these subsidiary provisions[4].

1 *Macdonald v Law Union Insurance Co* (1874) LR 9 QB 328 at 332 per Blackburn J.

2 *Routledge v Burrell* (1789) 1 Hy Bl 254; *Newcastle Fire Insurance Co v Macmorran & Co* (1815) 3 Dow 255, HL; *Equitable Fire and Accident Office Ltd v Ching Wo Hong* [1907] AC 96, PC; *Roberts v Anglo-Saxon Insurance Association* (1927) 137 LT 243, CA; *Dawsons Ltd v Bonnin* [1922] 2 AC 413, HL.

3 As to payment of premium as commencement of contract see para 460 post.

4 As to what constitutes a waiver see para 422 post.

402. Rectification. Where the policy issued does not correctly embody a contract previously agreed between the parties, either party may apply for its rectification[1]. Rectification will only be granted on the strongest evidence of mutual mistake[2]. Rectification can be claimed after loss has been suffered[3]. In order to obtain rectification it must be shown that there was a prior agreement between the parties differing from that purporting to be embodied in the policy; if the parties were never in fact in agreement the court may order the the policy to be set aside and premiums returned[4].

1 See eg *Collett v Morrison* (1851) 9 Hare 162; *Sun Life Assurance Co of Canada v Jervis* [1943] 2 All ER 425, CA (see para 391 text and note 8 ante); and see para 86 ante. As to the admission of extrinsic evidence in support of a claim for rectification see para 400 ante. As to the remedy of rectification generally see EQUITY vol 16 (Reissue) para 682; and MISTAKE.

2 *Allom v Property Insurance Co* (1911) Times, Finance, Commerce and Shipping section, 10 February; *American Airlines Inc v Hope* [1974] 2 Lloyd's Rep 301, HL; *Agip SpA v Navigazione Alta Italia SpA, The Nai Genova and Nai Superba* [1984] 1 Lloyd's Rep 353, CA; *Commercial Union Assurance Co plc v Sun Alliance Insurance Group plc* [1992] 1 Lloyd's Rep 475.

3 *Henkle v Royal Exchange Assurance Co* (1749) 1 Ves Sen 317; *Harvey v Canada Life Assurance Co* (1911) 20 OWR 54; cf *Stephens v Australasian Insurance Co* (1872) LR 8 CP 18.

4 *Fowler v Scottish Equitable Life Assurance Society and Ritchie* (1858) 28 LJCh 225; *Billington v Provincial Insurance Co* (1879) 3 SCR 182; see further MISTAKE.

(5) CONDITIONS OF THE POLICY

(i) Classification of Conditions generally

403. Distinction between conditions and collateral terms. A breach of the terms of a contract of insurance by a party to that contract will give the other party a right of action in damages for any loss sustained as a result of the breach[1]. However, a distinction exists between

(1) stipulations in such a contract which amount merely to collateral promises on the part of the assured, so that his failure to fulfil them will not entitle the insurers to repudiate liability under the contract or to resist a claim by the assured under it[2], although it may entitle them to recover damages[3]; and

(2) stipulations amounting to warranties[4] or conditions[5] the observance of which is fundamental to the existence of liability under the contract on the part of the insurers or to the enforcing of a claim under the contract by the assured[6].

1 See eg *Re Colemans Depositories Ltd and Life and Health Assurance Association* [1907] 2 KB 798 at 813, CA. As to the measure of damages in contract see DAMAGES vol 12 para 1174 et seq.

2 For stipulations which have been held to be collateral see eg *Re Bradley and Essex and Suffolk Accident Indemnity Society* [1912] 1 KB 415, CA (workmen's compensation; stipulation as to keeping wages book); *Stoneham v Ocean Railway and General, Accident Insurance Co* (1887) 19 QBD 237 (stipulation as to giving notice of accident; stipulation not expressed to be a condition precedent); *W & J Lane v Spratt* [1970] 2 QB 480, [1970] 1 All ER 162; and para 481 post.

3 But in practice this remedy affords them little or no protection: *HTV Ltd v Lintner* [1984] 2 Lloyd's Rep 125 at 128 per Neill J.

4 For the meaning of 'warranty' see para 404 post.

5 For the different classes of conditions and their effect see para 405 et seq post.

6 See *London Guarantie Co v Fearnley* (1880) 5 App Cas 911 at 915–916, HL, per Lord Blackburn. Even, however, in the case of a term which is fundamental to the contract or to the making of a claim under it, the insurers have the option of treating the contract as subsisting or the claim as validly made, as the case may be, and counterclaiming in damages: cf CONTRACT vol 9 paras 515–516. As to which terms of a contract are fundamental see paras 410–416 post.

404. Meaning of 'warranty'. In most branches of the law of contract, other than insurance law, 'warranty', as distinct from 'condition', is used to describe a provision which is subsidiary or collateral to the main purpose of the contract[1]. However, in relation to insurance 'warranty' is used where the assured undertakes that some particular thing shall or shall not be done or that a particular fact does or does not exist[2], in such circumstances that the undertaking constitutes a fundamental term of the contract so as to confer, in the event of a breach, a right on the insurers' part to repudiate the contract altogether[3]. The contrast between a condition and a warranty in insurance law, so far as any distinction exists[4], is the distinction between a term which is fundamental to the validity of the contract or the making of a claim under it[5], but which is one of the ordinary terms of the contract, and a term which, by reason of being specifically superadded to the ordinary terms, has importance as a fundamental stipulation of the contract. This use of the word is more frequently met with in marine[6] than in non-marine insurance, but the basic principle is the same. If, therefore, in a proposal a proposer signs a form of declaration by which he warrants the truth of the answers he has given, it means that, as a superadded obligation of paramount importance, he accepts that the truth of his answers is fundamental to the whole contract[7].

1 As to conditions and warranties generally see CONTRACT vol 9 paras 542–543.
2 See the Marine Insurance Act 1906 s 33 (1) (definition of 'warranty' for the purposes of marine insurance). The warranty can be express or implied: s 33(2); and para 54 ante.
3 *Pawson v Watson* (1778) 2 Cowp 785; *Barnard v Faber* [1893] 1 QB 340, CA; *Hambrough v Mutual Life Insurance Co of New York* (1895) 72 LT 140, CA.
4 See *W & J Lane v Spratt* [1970] 2 QB 480 at 486–487, [1970] 1 All ER 162 at 166–167 per Roskill J; *Provincial Insurance Co v Morgan and Foxon* [1933] AC 240 at 253–254, HL, per Lord Wright.
5 As to the different types of condition which may exist and the effect of breach in the case of each type see paras 405–409 post.
6 As to warranties in marine insurance see para 54 et seq ante.
7 As to declarations warranting the proposal see para 374 ante.

(ii) Types of Conditions

405. Conditions relating to the risk. The first type of condition in a policy, which is in practice often superadded as a warranty[1], is a condition describing, prescribing, circumscribing or otherwise defining the terms of the risk proposed or accepted for insurance. Conditions of this type are in the strictest sense conditions of the policy in that the insurers are never on risk at all unless and until the condition is question is fulfilled, and cease to be on risk if and when the condition ceases to be fulfilled[2]. However, there is an important distinction according to whether the condition is descriptive or promissory[3]. If it is merely descriptive, in the sense that the proposer states that he wants cover if and in so far as the condition is fulfilled, the insurers cannot repudiate the policy merely because, at the time when loss occurs, the condition is not fulfilled; they can merely assert that, in relation to that loss, the policy is not operative[4]. However, if the condition is promissory, in the sense that the proposer stipulates that a certain state of affairs will never be departed from, the insurers are entitled on breach to set aside the whole contract on the ground that the basic stipulation governing their acceptance of the contract has been broken[5]. Conditions of this kind are of particular importance in relation to matters affecting the delimitation of the risk[6].

1 For the meaning of 'warranty' see para 404 ante.
2 *Dawsons Ltd v Bonnin* [1922] 2 AC 413, HL.
3 *Dawsons Ltd v Bonnin* [1922] 2 AC 413, HL; *Provincial Insurance Co Ltd v Morgan* [1933] AC 240, HL; *Beauchamp v National Mutual Indemnity Insurance Co Ltd* [1937] 3 All ER 19 (as to which see para 431 note 4 post).
4 *Farr v Motor Traders' Mutual Insurance Society* [1920] 3 KB 669; *Roberts v Anglo-Saxon Insurance Association* (1927) 96 LJKB 590; *Bright v Ashfold* [1932] 2 KB 153; *Gray v Blackmore* [1934] 1 KB 95.

5 *Provincial Insurance Co Ltd v Morgan* [1933] AC 240 at 249, HL, per Lord Russell of Killowen; *Beauchamp v National Mutual Indemnity Insurance Co Ltd* [1937] 3 All ER 19.
6 As to matters affecting the risk see para 430 et seq post.

406. Conditions precedent to liability under the policy. The second type of condition is usually described as a condition precedent[1] of the policy, that is to say a term going to the root of the contract in relation to its validity in origin[2]. Whether a term is of this type may depend on the ruling given by the court as to whether, taking the contract as a whole, the term in question was fundamental to the whole contract, but the same result can be achieved if the parties have agreed that a term, otherwise less than a fundamental term, is to be deemed to be a condition precedent to the contract[3]. If the condition precedent is not fulfilled the contract will be void ab initio[4]. There is no obligation on the insurer to relate a condition to a particular aspect of the policy[5]. The language of the policy is not conclusive; it may describe as a condition precedent something which, of its very nature, is something to be done after the contract is made[6]. However, great force is given to the language which the parties themselves have chosen to adopt[7]. It is generally made a condition precedent to the validity of the policy that all statements made in the proposal or otherwise during the negotiations are to be true[8].

1 As to conditions precedent in contracts generally see CONTRACT vol 9 para 511 et seq.
2 *Barnard v Faber* [1893] 1 QBD 340 at 344, CA, per Bowen LJ.
3 *Thomson v Weems* (1884) 9 App Cas 671 at 683, HL, per Lord Blackburn; *Joel v Law Union and Crown Insurance Co* [1908] 2 KB 863 at 885–886, CA, per Fletcher Moulton LJ; see also *Newcastle Fire Insurance Co v Macmorran & Co* (1815) 3 Dow 255 at 262, HL, per Lord Eldon LC; *Barnard v Faber* [1893] 1 QB 340, CA.
4 *Thomson v Weems* (1884) 9 App Cas 671, HL; *Armstrong v Turquand* (1858) 9 ICLR 32 at 42 per Christian J; *Equitable Life Assurance Society of the United States v Reed* [1914] AC 587, PC.
5 *New India Assurance Co Ltd v Yeo Beng Chow* [1972] 3 All ER 293, [1972] 1 WLR 786, PC.
6 *Re Bradley and Essex and Suffolk Accident Indemnity Society* [1912] 1 KB 415, CA.
7 Cf the text and note 3 supra. As to the intention of the parties as a test of the meaning of the contract see *Wheelton v Hardisty* (1857) 8 E & B 232; and para 397 ante.
8 As to contractual provisions as to non-disclosure and misrepresentation see paras 363–365 ante. It is for the insurer to elect whether to avoid liability under the contract or to treat it as subsisting; cf CONTRACT vol 9 para 540. In matters relating to insurance the word 'void' is often loosely used as meaning only that the insurers are entitled to repudiate all liability under the contract; see *Equitable Life Assurance Society of the United States v Reed* [1914] AC 587 at 596, PC; see also *Doe d Pitt v Laming* (1814) 4 Camp 73 at 75; and para 367 ante.

407. Conditions subsequent affecting the policy. A condition subsequent affecting the policy is a condition relative in its essence to duties arising after the policy is in operation, which by necessary intention or express agreement affects the continued validity of the policy so that, if there is a breach, the other party may treat the policy as at an end[1]. It may be stipulated as a condition of the policy that the assured must not insure elsewhere; if he does, the insurers may avoid the policy[2]. The avoidance of the policy in such a case can only date from the breach[3]; up to that date the policy is fully effective so as to entitle the assured to recover in respect of any loss which occurred before the breach[4].

1 *Glen v Lewis* (1853) 8 Exch 607; *Farnham v Royal Insurance Co Ltd* [1976] 2 Lloyd's Rep 437.
2 *Equitable Fire and Accident Office Ltd v Ching Wo Hong* [1907] AC 96, PC. For conditions as to other insurances see para 517 post.
3 *Glen v Lewis* (1853) 8 Exch 607; *Sun and Fire Office v Hart* (1889) 14 App Cas 98, PC; *Sulphite Pulp Co v Faber* (1895) 1 Com Cas 146; *Equitable Fire and Accident Office Ltd v Ching Wo Hong* [1907] AC 96, PC; *Marcovitch v Liverpool Victoria Friendly Society* (1912) 28 TLR 188.
4 *Daff v Midland Colliery Owners' Mutual Indemnity Co* (1913) 82 LJKB 1340, HL.

408. Conditions subsequent affecting recovery. A condition subsequent affecting recovery under a policy is a condition dealing with the situation where a claim has arisen, or is alleged to have arisen, and prescribing the duties which have to be fulfilled if the claim is to be enforced[1]. A condition of this kind has to be performed before a claim can be maintained or before the enforcement of a claim in a particular manner can be obtained[2]. It may be stipulated that a claim is not enforceable unless the assured has furnished the insurers with all such proofs and information with respect to the claim as may be reasonably required; if the assured refuses to furnish such information the claim becomes unenforceable then or at any time afterwards[3]. If the true construction of the stipulation is that the claim may not be enforced until the stipulated information is given, the court would be bound to hold that pending the giving of the information the claim is premature[4]. It may be provided that it is to be a condition precedent to the enforcement of a claim in the courts that there has been a reference to, and an award by, an arbitrator; the court is then bound to rule that an action is premature if there has been no such reference or award[5]. It may be made a condition that no admission of liability be made or offer or promise of payment be made without the written consent of the insurers[6]; or it may be stated that if the insurers disclaim liability to the insured, he must institute legal proceedings against them within a specified period of the date of the disclaimer[7]. Unless there is some stipulation to the contrary[8], breach of a condition of this kind only affects the claim in question[9]; if a second claim arises during the currency of the policy the enforceability of the second claim will not be affected merely because conditions affecting the first claim have not been fulfilled, provided that the assured fulfils the conditions applicable to the second claim[10]. However, a condition may be so framed that, even though it relates to the making of a claim, failure to observe the requirement imposed by it will affect the continued validity of the policy[11].

1 *London Guarantee Co v Fearnley* (1880) 5 App Cas 911, HL.
2 *London Guarantee Co v Fearnley* (1880) 5 App Cas 911 at 915, 917, HL, per Lord Blackburn, and at 918 per Lord Watson; *Kerridge v Rush* [1952] 2 Lloyd's Rep 305; *London Crystal Window Cleaning Co Ltd v National Mutual Indemnity Insurance Co Ltd* [1952] 2 Lloyd's Rep 360; *Lickiss v Milestone Motor Policies at Lloyd's* [1966] 2 All ER 972, [1966] 1 WLR 1334, CA; *Farrell v Federated Employers Insurance Association Ltd* [1970] 3 All ER 632, [1970] 1 WLR 1400, CA (condition that all writs be notified to the insurers immediately on receipt). Thus such a condition, although subsequent to the formation of the policy, can also be considered a condition precedent to recovery.
3 *Welch v Royal Exchange Assurance* [1939] 1 KB 294 at 312, [1938] 4 All ER 289 at 295, CA, per MacKinnon LJ, and at 314–315 and 297 per Finlay LJ (information as to banking accounts used for purposes of assured's business; information refused prior to, but given during, arbitration proceedings).
4 *Welch v Royal Exchange Assurance* [1939] 1 KB 294 at 307–308, [1938] 4 All ER 289 at 292, CA, per Slesser LJ.
5 *Scott v Avery* (1856) 5 HL Cas 811; and see para 498 post. The principle stated in the text is subject to the provisions of the Arbitration Act 1950 s 25(4), as to which see para 498 text and notes 7–9 post. See also ARBITRATION vol 2 (Reissue) para 635.
6 *Terry v Trafalgar Union Insurance Co Ltd* [1970] 1 Lloyd's Rep 524.
7 *Walker v Pennine Insurance Co Ltd* [1980] 2 Lloyd's Rep 156, CA.
8 See eg *Lek v Mathews* (1927) 29 Ll L Rep 141: text and note 11 infra.
9 *Hood's Trustees v Southern Union General Insurance Co of Australasia Ltd* [1928] Ch 793 at 806, CA, per Tomlin J.
10 *Reid & Co v Employers' Accidents etc Insurance Co* (1899) 1 F 1031, Ct of Sess.
11 *Lek v Mathews* (1927) 29 Ll L Rep 141 (policy to become void in event of false or fraudulent claim). As to conditions subsequent affecting the continued validity of the policy see para 407 ante.

409. Exceptions framed as conditions. A further type of condition exists as a means to avoid overloading the operative words of a policy by the insertion of too many qualifications, riders and provisos. It is convenient when framing the policy to resort to the device of inserting among the conditions of the policy a number of common form exceptions[1]. The stipulation in question is then merely another example of the first type of condition, namely a definition of the risk[2], although it is effected by means of a limitation on the scope of the insurance[3]. If a provision is framed as an exception, it will normally be construed as being in every sense an exception; in particular, the onus of proving that a claim is within the exception, so as to be excluded from the general effect of the operative words, will be on the insurers[4]. The insurers may seek to frame the exception in such a way as to require the assured to prove that the loss does not fall within the exception[5]. As a rule, the general operative words will be treated as prevailing in the absence of concrete proof by the insurers that the provision described as an exception is applicable[6].

1 As to such common form exceptions see further paras 531, 582–583, 595–602, 647, 665 post.
2 As to conditions relating to the risk see para 405 ante.
3 *Re Hooley Hill Rubber and Chemical Co Ltd and Royal Insurance Co Ltd* [1920] 1 KB 257 at 274, CA, per Duke LJ; *Lake v Simmons* [1927] AC 487 at 507, HL, per Lord Sumner; see also *Cornish v Accident Insurance Co* (1889) 23 QBD 453, CA; *GFP Units Ltd v Monksfield* [1972] 2 Lloyd's Rep 79 (limitation to named drivers); *Kennedy v Smith and Ansvar Insurance Co Ltd* 1976 SLT 110, Ct of Sess (insured not covered when driving 'under the influence of alcohol'). An exception may be inserted to make it clear that a loss, which is not in fact covered by the policy, is excluded: *Borradaile v Hunter* (1843) 5 Man & G 639 at 658 per Erskine J.
4 *Motor Union Insurance Co Ltd v Boggan* (1923) 130 LT 588 at 590, HL, per Lord Birkenhead LC; see also *Smith v Accident Insurance Co* (1870) LR 5 Exch 302; *McSteen v McCarthy* [1952] NI 33. If the exception depends on something happening 'to the knowledge' of the assured, actual knowledge must be proved; failure to make inquiries which would have revealed the position is not sufficient: *John T Ellis Ltd v Hinds* [1947] KB 475, [1947] 1 All ER 337, DC.
5 *Re Hooley Hill Rubber and Chemical Co Ltd and Royal Insurance Co Ltd* [1920] 1 KB 257 at 272, CA, per Scrutton LJ; *Bond Air Services Ltd v Hill* [1955] 2 QB 417, [1955] 2 All ER 476.
6 *Bond Air Services Ltd v Hill* [1955] 2 QB 417, [1955] 2 All ER 476.

(iii) Identification of Fundamental Terms

410. Determination of fundamental terms. No distinction can be drawn in a contract of insurance by reference to the ordinary vocabulary of conditions and warranties used in other branches of the law of contract between a term which is fundamental[1] and a term which is not[2].

Whether a term is fundamental or not depends on the construction of the words used in the context as part of the contract as a whole[3]. It is not necessary that any particular form of words is used in this context[4] but resort must be made to the general principles of interpretation[5].

1 Ie fundamental to the existence of the contract as a contract imposing liability on the insurers or to the making of a claim under the contract. As to the distinction between conditions and collateral terms in insurance law see para 403 ante.
2 As to warranties as fundamental terms of a contract of insurance see para 404 ante.
3 *Anderson v Fitzgerald* (1853) 4 HL Cas 484 at 507 per Lord St Leonards, followed in *Thomson v Weems* (1884) 9 App Cas 671 at 682, HL, per Lord Blackburn; *Wheelton v Hardisty* (1858) 8 E & B 232, Ex Ch, following *Stokes v Cox* (1856) 1 H & N 533, Ex Ch; *Stoneham v Ocean, Railway and General Accident Insurance Co* (1887) 19 QBD 237; *Provincial Insurance Co Ltd v Morgan* [1933] AC 240 at 250, HL, per Lord Wright.
4 *Weir v Northern Counties of England Insurance Co* (1879) 4 LR Ir 689 at 692 per Lawson J.
5 As to the general principles of interpretation see paras 394–400 ante.

411. Intention of the parties. The ultimate test of what is a fundamental term in an insurance contract is whether it is the intention of the parties, as indicated by the language they have used, to make the stipulation a fundamental term. Emphasis is particularly laid on the intention of the assured[1], derived from the agreement, in the sense that it must be quite clear that from his point of view he agreed to the stipulation being a fundamental term[2]. If there is ambiguity in the language of the term in question, coming as it normally does from the pen of the insurers' draftsman[3], it will not be construed as a fundamental term[4]. If the draftsman has framed the term as an exception, the rule is stringently applied[5].

1 *Joel v Law Union and Crown Insurance Co* [1908] 2 KB 863 at 886, CA, per Fletcher Moulton LJ; *Re Bradley and Essex and Suffolk Accident Indemnity Society* [1912] 1 KB 415 at 431, CA, per Farwell LJ.
2 *Baxendale v Harvey* (1859) 4 H & N 445 at 451 per Pollock CB; *Braunstein v Accidental Death Insurance Co* (1861) 1 B & S 782 at 799 per Blackburn J; *Thomson v Weems* (1884) 9 App Cas 671, HL.
3 As to the form of the policy see para 397 text to notes 6–7 ante. As to the contra proferentem rule see para 398 ante.
4 *Cowell v Yorkshire Provident Life Assurance Co* (1901) 17 TLR 452; *Re Etherington and Lancashire and Yorkshire Accident Insurance Co* [1909] 1 KB 591, CA; *Re Bradley and Essex and Suffolk Accident Indemnity Society* [1912] 1 KB 415, CA; *Simmonds v Cockell* [1920] 1 KB 843 at 845 per Roche J.
5 *Cornish v Accident Insurance Co* (1889) 23 QBD 453 at 456, CA, per Lindley LJ. If, however, the exception is not ambiguous, full effect will be given to it: *Re United London and Scottish Insurance Co, Brown's Claim* [1915] 2 Ch 167, CA.

412. Nature of the subject matter. The nature of the subject matter of an insurance contract is significant when deciding whether a term is fundamental or not[1]. In this regard it may be apparent that a fundamental stipulation must have been intended, whatever the particular form of words which may have been adopted[2]. Thus, if the subject matter is one which obviously goes to the root of the contract[3] or affects the continuance of the policy as a valid contract[4], fundamental consequences must have been intended in the event of a breach[5]. Such stipulations are many and various: examples are stipulations in fire policies prohibiting the assured from keeping dangerous goods in the premises insured[6], stipulations in life policies against suicide[7], stipulations in any policies correlating the premium to that chargeable under other policies[8] and stipulations in any policies defining, controlling or circumscribing the risk[9].

1 *Barnard v Faber* [1893] 1 QB 340 at 344, CA, per Bowen LJ.
2 *Wheelton v Hardisty* (1858) 8 E & B 232 at 300, Ex Ch, per Bramwell B; *Worsley v Wood* (1796) 6 Term Rep 710, followed in *London Guarantie Co v Fearnley* (1880) 5 App Cas 911, HL.
3 *Barnard v Faber* [1893] 1 QB 340 at 343, CA, per Bowen LJ; *Bancroft v Heath* (1901) 6 Com Cas 137, CA; *Homes v Scottish Legal Life Assurance Society* (1932) 48 TLR 306.
4 *Barnard v Faber* [1893] 1 QB 340 at 343, CA.
5 *London Guarantie Co v Fearnley* (1880) 5 App Cas 911 at 915, HL, per Lord Blackburn; *Barnard v Faber* [1893] 1 QB 340 at 342, CA, per Lindley LJ.
6 *Dobson v Sotheby* (1827) Mood & M 90.
7 *Ellinger & Co v Mutual Life Insurance Co of New York* [1905] 1 KB 31, CA.
8 *Barnard v Faber* [1893] 1 QB 340, CA.
9 *Barnard v Faber* [1893] 1 QB 340, CA; *Ellinger & Co v Mutual Life Insurance Co of New York* [1905] 1 KB 31, CA.

413. Express words. Just as the subject matter, by necessary implication, can be decisive of the question as to what is a fundamental term in a contract of insurance, so too can the express words be vital in so far as they demonstrate the parties' express intention[1]. On its face, a stipulation may relate to something of collateral or secondary importance compared to the fundamental objects of the contract; for example, like an arbitration clause[2], it may merely regulate the manner in which rights under the contract are to be worked out[3]. However, the intention to make such a stipulation a fundamental term may be demonstrated by the use of appropriate language in the contract. The most stringent form of language for this purpose is where it is stated that performance of the term in question is the basis[4] or essence[5] of the contract, or that the stipulation is a condition precedent[6]. A less stringent form is where the term is described as a condition[7], warranty[8] or proviso[9], or where it is stipulated that a breach is to disentitle the assured from enforcing the contract[10]. If the language is adequate, on proving a breach, the insurers will be entitled to repudiate the contract as a whole, even though by itself and without express provision as to the consequences of breach the stipulation in question would not be regarded as fundamental to the contract as a whole[11].

1 *Wheelton v Hardisty* (1858) 8 E & B 232 at 297, Ex Ch, per Martin B. As to the nature of the subject matter as a test see para 412 ante.
2 As to arbitration clauses see paras 495–498 post.
3 *Lancashire Insurance Co v IRC* [1899] 1 QB 353 at 359 per Bruce J.
4 *Dawsons Ltd v Bonnin* [1922] 2 AC 413, HL; *Glicksman v Lancashire and General Assurance Co Ltd* [1925] 2 KB 593, CA; affd [1927] AC 139, HL; *Bell v Lever Bros* [1932] AC 161 at 225, HL, per Lord Atkin. See further para 374 ante.
5 *Anderson v Fitzgerald* (1853) 4 HL Cas 484 at 498 per Parke B; *Roper v Lendon* (1859) 1 E & E 825 at 829 per Lord Campbell CJ; *Elliott v Royal Exchange Assurance Co* (1867) LR 2 Exch 237 at 246 per Bramwell B; *Re Williams and Lancashire and Yorkshire Accident Insurance Co's Arbitration* (1902) 51 WR 222.
6 *Caledonian Insurance Co v Gilmour* [1893] AC 85, HL.
7 *London Guarantie Co v Fearnley* (1880) 5 App Cas 911 at 919, HL, per Lord Watson. Merely calling a stipulation a condition will not, however, make it one if, on its true interpretation, it is not a condition; *Re Bradley and Essex and Suffolk Accident Indemnity Society* [1912] 1 KB 415, CA.
8 *Newcastle Fire Insurance Co v Macmorran & Co* (1815) 3 Dow 255 at 262, HL, per Lord Eldon LC; *Anderson v Fitzgerald* (1853) 4 HL Cas 484 at 504 per Lord Cranworth; *Barnard v Faber* [1893] 1 QB 340, CA; *Palatine Insurance Co v Gregory* [1926] AC 90 at 93, PC; *Provincial Insurance Co Ltd v Morgan* [1933] AC 240, HL. But even where the word 'warranty' is used, the court may construe the term as one which merely delimits the risk: *CTN Cash and Carry Ltd v General Accident Fire and Life Assurance Corpn plc* [1989] 1 Lloyd's Rep 299 (burglary insurance).
9 *London Guarantie Co v Fearnley* (1880) 5 App Cas 911, HL; *Cassel v Lancashire and Yorkshire Accident Insurance Co Ltd* (1885) 1 TLR 495.
10 *Mason v Harvey* (1853) 8 Exch 819; *Sulphite Pulp Co v Faber* (1895) 1 Com Cas 146.
11 *Re Coleman's Depositories Ltd and Life and Health Assurance Association* [1907] 2 KB 798, CA (where in the circumstances the stipulation was held inapplicable).

414. Stipulation to be looked at as a whole. In determining whether a stipulation is fundamental to a contract the stipulation must be taken as a whole. If a substantial part of it falls within this category, the rest will belong prima facie to the same category. For example, if a stipulation requiring delivery of detailed particulars within a specified time is fundamental, the subsidiary requirement as to the time for delivery is also fundamental[1]. Conversely, if the main part of a stipulation is not in substance fundamental, other portions of it will not normally be presumed to be fundamental[2]. It may, however, be clear, as a matter of construction, that a number of entirely separate and independent stipulations are, either as a matter of drafting convenience or for other reasons, collected together so as to form in appearance a single corporate clause or provision of the policy; in such a case each stipulation ought to be looked at separately and given its value accordingly, even if the result is to make one sentence a fundamental provision, when all the others plainly are not[3].

1 *Roper v Lendon* (1859) 1 E & E 825.
2 *Re Bradley and Essex and Suffolk Accident Indemnity Society* [1912] 1 KB 415, CA.
3 *Roper v Lendon* (1859) 1 E & E 825.

415. Language not conclusive. The language of an insurance policy is by no means conclusive in determining whether a stipulation is fundamental. For example, it is not unusual to find the word 'conditions' as a general heading to a considerable number of stipulations which, although grouped together under the single heading, vary greatly in scope and importance. From their very nature, some may be quite obviously of a fundamental and primary nature, while others may equally obviously be of merely collateral and secondary importance[1]. On examination, others may well turn out to be incapable of operating as fundamental conditions, in the true sense of the term[2]. They may also vary in phrasing, the language in some cases indicating that they are designed as fundamental terms and in other cases pointing neither one way nor the other[3]. Sometimes it is provided that all stipulations grouped under a particular heading are to be regarded as fundamental, but the inclusion of a particular stipulation under that heading will not necessarily by itself be conclusive[4]. Provided that the stipulation is capable of being construed as fundamental, the test whether it should be so construed is the intention of the parties as gathered from the contract[5]. Where, however, a stipulation is one which cannot be performed until the policy itself has expired[6] or after payment has been made by the insurers under the policy because it relates solely to the insurers' subrogation rights[7], then from its very nature the stipulation cannot be fundamental[8].

1 *Re Coleman's Depositories Ltd and Life and Health Assurance Association* [1907] 2 KB 798, CA.
2 *London Guarantie Co v Fearnley* (1880) 5 App Cas 911, HL; *Re Bradley and Essex and Suffolk Accident Indemnity Society* [1912] 1 KB 415, CA.
3 *Stoneham v Ocean, Railway and General Accident Insurance Co* (1887) 19 QBD 237 at 241; *Re Coleman's Depositories Ltd and Life and Health Assurance Association* [1907] 2 KB 798 at 813, CA.
4 *London Guarantie Co v Fearnley* (1880) 5 App Cas 911 at 916–917, HL; *Re Coleman's Depositories Ltd and Life and Health Assurance Association* [1907] 2 KB 798, CA; *Re Bradley and Essex and Suffolk Accident Indemnity Society* [1912] 1 KB 415, CA.
5 *London Guarantie Co v Fearnley* (1880) 5 App Cas 911 at 917, HL.
6 *London Guarantie Co v Fearnley* (1880) 5 App Cas 911 at 919, HL (duty to assist insurers in enforcing subrogated rights).
7 *General Accident Assurance Corpn v Day* (1904) 21 TLR 88 (statement of wages paid during period of insurance for adjustment of premium); *Re Bradley and Essex and Suffolk Accident Indemnity Society* [1912] 1 KB 415, CA. As to the insurers' subrogation rights see para 505 et seq post.
8 If, however, the policy stipulates that any money paid under it is to be recoverable where there is a breach by the assured of such a stipulation it seems that a claim for recovery will lie if the breach is proved.

416. Unreasonable conditions. It has been suggested that a stipulation in a policy may be so capricious or unreasonable as to be unenforceable as a fundamental term of the contract[1]. It is difficult to reconcile this view with the basic English concept of freedom of contract[2].

However, a condition in an insurance policy which is contrary to public policy is unenforceable, for example a condition by which the insurers impliedly undertake to pay the assured's personal representatives if the assured under a life policy kills himself while not mentally disordered[3]. On the other hand a stipulation in a life policy that the assured will not voluntarily engage in military service is not contrary to public policy as being a deterrent against performing a national duty[4]. Where a stipulation is not merely unreasonable but impossible, in the sense that from the outset it never could be performed, it is a nullity which is simply disregarded[5].

1 *Doe d Pitt v Laming* (1814) 4 Camp 73 at 75 per Lord Ellenborough CJ; *London Guarantie Co v Fearnley* (1880) 5 App Cas 911 at 919, HL, per Lord Watson; *Sun Fire Office v Hart* (1889) 14 App Cas 98, PC; *Home Insurance Co of New York v Victoria-Montreal Fire Insurance Co* [1907] AC 59 at 64, PC; *Daff v Midland Colliery Owners' Mutual Indemnity Co* (1913) 6 BWCC 799 at 823, HL, per Lord Moulton.
2 *Wilkinson v Car and General Insurance Corpn Ltd* (1913) 110 LT 468 at 472 per Lord Reading CJ; *Farr v Motor Traders' Mutual Insurance Society* [1920] 3 KB 669 at 673, CA, per Bankes LJ; see also *Gamble v Accident Assurance Co* (1869) IR 4 CL 204 at 214 per Pigot CB. See generally CONTRACT.
3 *Beresford v Royal Insurance Co Ltd* [1939] AC 586, [1938] 2 All ER 602, HL.
4 *Duckworth v Scottish Widows' Fund Life Assurance Society* (1917) 33 TLR 430.
5 As to conditions which cannot be performed see para 419 post.

(iv) Performance of Conditions

417. Obligation of assured as regards performance. The fulfilment of a condition is a contractual term binding on the assured, and in the event of non-fulfilment he is the person who suffers by being unable to recover under the policy. Any person claiming through him is in the same position[1], although sometimes there is a special saving of the rights of assignees in good faith for value[2]. The condition may stipulate for performance of some act by the assured personally[3] but, unless it is so stipulated, it is immaterial how or by whom performance is effected; it may be by an agent[4], a trustee in bankruptcy[5], a personal representative[6] or a complete stranger[7].

1 *Re Carr and Sun Fire Insurance Co* (1897) 13 TLR 186, CA; *Cawley v National Employers' Accident and General Assurance Association Ltd* (1885) 1 TLR 255.
2 *Jackson v Forster* (1860) 1 E & E 470, Ex Ch; *Wigan v English and Scottish Law Life Assurance Association* [1909] 1 Ch 291; and see para 547 post.
3 *Want v Blunt* (1810) 12 East 183; *Simpson v Accidental Death Insurance Co* (1857) 2 CBNS 257; *Pritchard v Merchant's and Tradesman's Mutual Life Assurance Society* (1858) 3 CBNS 622; *Duncan Logan (Contractors) Ltd v Royal Exchange Assurance Group* 1973 SLT 192, Ct of Sess.
4 *Patton v Employers' Liability Assurance Corpn* (1887) 20 LR Ir 93.
5 *Re Carr and Sun Fire Insurance Co* (1897) 13 TLR 186, CA.
6 *Cawley v National Employers' Accident and General Assurance Association Ltd* (1885) 1 TLR 255; cf *Verelst's Administratrix v Motor Union Insurance Co Ltd* [1925] 2 KB 137.
7 *Patton v Employers' Liability Assurance Corpn* (1887) 20 LR Ir 93 at 100 per Murphy J.

418. What amounts to performance. The nature and extent of the performance required depends on the true construction of the requirement in question. If a condition is framed in general terms, performance is adequate if it covers the substance of the matter[1]; but, if the condition goes into details, performance must be strictly in accordance with the details required[2] and, however burdensome or immaterial they may appear to be, they cannot be disregarded[3]. However, it is sufficient in such a case if the precise letter of the condition is performed in the most literal sense; the insurers cannot require the assured to go beyond the precise terms of the condition or complain that a literal performance does not protect them adequately[4].

1 *Mason v Harvey* (1853) 8 Exch 819 at 821 per Pollock CB.

2 *Newcastle Fire Insurance Co v Macmorran & Co* (1815) 3 Dow 255, HL; *Provincial Insurance Co Ltd v Morgan* [1933] AC 240 at 254, HL, per Lord Wright.
3 *Want v Blunt* (1810) 12 East 183; *Roper v Lendon* (1859) 1 E & E 825.
4 *Whitehead v Price* (1835) 2 Cr M & R 447, followed in *Mayall v Mitford* (1837) 6 Ad & El 670; *Ward v Law Property Assurance and Trust Society* (1856) 4 WR 605; *National Protector Fire Insurance Co Ltd v Nivert* [1913] AC 507, PC; *Re Birkbeck Permanent Benefit Building Society, Official Receiver v Licenses Insurance Corpn* [1913] 2 Ch 34; *Fidelity and Casualty Co of New York v Mitchell* [1917] AC 592, PC.

419. Conditions which cannot be performed. If a condition, from its very nature, is such that it was never capable of being performed at all, it is a nullity and performance of it cannot be required[1]. It is different where there is no inherent impossibility in the condition itself, but events as they actually turn out produce an impossibility in fact. For example, where notice of an injury or a death has to be given within a specified time and the assured or claimant is ignorant throughout the specified time of the fact of the injury or death, he has nonetheless failed to do what the contract required him to do[2]. Similarly it is no excuse when an executor does not know that he has been appointed[3], has not perfected his title[4], does not know of the existence of the policy or cannot find it so as to apprise himself of its terms[5]. In these cases, however, the decisions have to some extent been put on the ground of the negligence of the assured in failing to keep his family or friends adequately informed about his affairs[6]. On the other hand, if the insurers have not yet issued the policy, so that no one has an opportunity of knowing about the existence or scope of such a condition, they cannot rely on it[7]. If the policy stipulates for some action on the part of a third person, such as issuing a certificate vouching for the good faith of the assured or of his claim, it is no excuse for the assured that the third person fails, neglects or refuses to do what is required[8].

1 *Worsley v Wood* (1796) 6 Term Rep 710 at 718 per Lord Kenyon CJ. It has been suggested that if the assured had no medical attention at the time he was killed, a condition requiring a report from his medical attendant is not broken by the absence of a report: *Patton v Employers' Liability Assurance Corpn* (1887) 20 LR Ir 93 at 99 per Harrison J.
2 *Cassel v Lancashire and Yorkshire Accident Insurance Co Ltd* (1885) 1 TLR 495; *Durrant v Maclaren* [1956] 2 Lloyd's Rep 70. The manifest hardship of this rule has produced both a reluctance on the part of judges to construe such a provision as a condition (*Stoneham v Ocean, Railway and General Accident Insurance Co* (1887) 19 QBD 237) and, in the United States, an inclination to imply a term as to possibility of performance: see the cases cited in MacGillivray and Parkington on Insurance Law (8th Edn) paras 1586–1587.
3 *Gamble v Accident Insurance Co* (1869) IR 4 CL 204.
4 *Patton v Employers' Liability Assurance Corpn* (1887) 20 LR Ir 93.
5 *Gamble v Accident Insurance Co* (1869) IR 4 CL 204.
6 *Gamble v Accident Insurance Co* (1869) IR 4 CL 204 at 215.
7 *Re Coleman's Depositories Ltd and Life and Health Assurance Association* [1907] 2 KB 798, CA.
8 *Oldham v Bewicke* (1786) 2 Hy Bl 577n; *Worsley v Wood* (1796) 6 Term Rep 710; but see also *Patton v Employers' Liability Assurance Corpn* (1887) 20 LR Ir 93 at 99, and note 1 supra.

420. What amounts to a breach. In relation to breach, as in relation to performance, the decisive matter is what, on the true construction, the condition requires to be done or left undone. There is no breach unless the act done or left undone comes precisely within the language used[1]. For example, if it is provided that the policy may be avoided in the event of an untrue statement being made in the proposal form, there cannot be a breach if there is, in fact, no proposal form[2]. Conversely, where there is a failure to comply with what is required it is immaterial what the reason may be for the failure; whether the conduct of the assured is deliberate[3], negligent[4] or merely inadvertent[5], the consequences are the same. Nor can ignorance, either of the existence of the condition or of its precise terms, be set up as an excuse unless the insurers' conduct can be made responsible for the ignorance, for example where they have not yet issued the policy[6].

1 *Dobson v Sotheby* (1827) Mood & M 90, followed in *Shaw v Robberds* (1837) 6 Ad & El 75; *Stokes v Cox* (1856) 1 H & N 533; *Equitable Fire and Accident Office Ltd v Ching Wo Hong* [1907] AC 96, PC; *Wilkinson v Car and General Insurance Corpn* (1913) 110 LT 468.
2 *Pearl Life Assurance Co v Johnson* [1909] 2 KB 288.
3 *Borradaile v Hunter* (1834) 5 Man & G 639.
4 *Gamble v Accident Insurance Co* (1869) IR 4 CL 204; *Joel v Law Union and Crown Insurance Co* [1908] 2 KB 863 at 884, CA, per Fletcher Moulton LJ.
5 *Cassel v Lancashire and Yorkshire Accident Insurance Co* (1885) 1 TLR 495; *Re Williams and Lancashire and Yorkshire Accident Insurance Co's Arbitration* (1902) 51 WR 222.
6 *Re Coleman's Depositories Ltd and Life and Health Assurance Association* [1907] 2 KB 798, CA.

421. Onus of proof. As a general principle, the onus is on the insurers to prove that a condition has been broken, not on the assured to prove compliance on his part with each and every stipulation[1]. It may well be that, if there is a question as to whether a contract of insurance has ever come into existence or begun to be operative, the assured has to prove the happening of any events necessary to its existence or operation[2], but where the question is as to the insurers' liability under an admittedly effective policy, the rule as to the burden of proof is axiomatic in insurance law[3]. It is open to the parties to alter this result by making an express stipulation that the onus of proof is to be on the assured[4], but very clear words are necessary to achieve such a result[5].

1 *Barrett v Jermy* (1849) 3 Exch 535 at 542 per Parke B; *Stebbing v Liverpool and London and Globe Insurance Co Ltd* [1917] 2 KB 433 at 438 per Viscount Reading CJ; *Bond Air Services Ltd v Hill* [1955] 2 QB 417 at 427, [1955] 2 All ER 476 at 479–480 per Lord Goddard CJ. The onus cannot be altered by a pleading which purports to put the assured to the proof of compliance with what has been required of him by a condition: *Bond Air Services Ltd v Hill* supra.
2 *Geach v Ingall* (1845) 14 M & W 95; *Ashby v Bates* (1846) 15 M & W 589, as explained in *Bond Air Services Ltd v Hill* [1955] 2 QB 417 at 427, [1955] 2 All ER 476 at 479–480 per Lord Goddard CJ.
3 *Bond Air Services Ltd v Hill* [1955] 2 QB 417 at 427, [1955] 2 All ER 476 at 480 per Lord Goddard CJ.
4 *Re Hooley Hill Rubber and Chemical Co Ltd and Royal Insurance Co Ltd* [1920] 1 KB 257 at 273, CA, per Scrutton LJ; *Levy v Assicurazioni Generali* [1940] AC 791, [1940] 3 All ER 427, PC; *Bond Air Services Ltd v Hill* [1955] 2 QB 417 at 428, [1955] 2 All ER 476 at 480 per Lord Goddard CJ.
5 *Bond Air Services Ltd v Hill* [1955] 2 QB 417 at 428, [1955] 2 All ER 476 at 480 per Lord Goddard CJ.

(v) Waiver in relation to Conditions

422. What constitutes a waiver. A waiver of contractual rights[1] may be express, as when the insurers indicate that performance of a particular condition will not be required[2]. The policy may indeed contain a provision dealing with waiver and, possibly, the manner in which an effective waiver can be made[3]. Such a provision is not usual because it can itself be waived by conduct and so cease to be of any operative effect[4]. More frequently waiver is implied, that is to say it arises from conduct on the part of the insurers which, whether intentionally or otherwise[5], indicates to the assured that performance is not required. For example, where payment of a premium is required to be made to the directors of a company, this obligation is waived if the company goes into liquidation[6]; again, where there is a repudiation of the policy, there is no need for the assured to perform obligations which would be incumbent on him if the policy were still subsisting[7]. If what is relied on as a waiver is conduct after a breach has occurred, the conduct must be such as to indicate an intention to treat the contract as still subsisting[8]. There can be no waiver unless the insurers have full knowledge of the material circumstances[9].

Waiver by the insurers must be expressly pleaded by the assured[10].

1 As to waiver of contractual rights generally see CONTRACT vol 9 paras 571–574.
2 Express waiver by an agent is valid if within his authority: *Wing v Harvey* (1854) 5 De G M & G 265; cf *Acey v Fernie* (1840) 7 M & W 151.
3 *M'Millan v Accident Insurance Co* 1907 SC 484.
4 *Marcovitch v Liverpool Victoria Friendly Society* (1912) 28 TLR 188, CA.
5 *Toronto Rly Co v National British and Irish Millers Insurance Co Ltd* (1914) 111 LT 555 at 563, CA, per Scrutton LJ; *Burridge & Son v F H Haines & Sons* (1918) 118 LT 681; *Lickiss v Milestone Motor Policies at Lloyd's* [1966] 2 All ER 972, [1966] 1 WLR 1334, CA; *Allan Peters (Jewellers) Ltd v Brocks Alarms Ltd* [1968] 1 Lloyd's Rep 387; *Allen v Robles (Cie Parisienne de Garantie, third party)* [1969] 3 All ER 154, [1969] 1 WLR 1193, CA; *Farrell v Federated Employers' Insurance Association Ltd* [1970] 3 All ER 632, [1970] 1 WLR 1400, CA; *Victor Melik & Co Ltd v Norwich Union Fire Insurance Society Ltd and Kemp* [1980] 1 Lloyd's Rep 523 (burglary insurance); *Mint Security Ltd v Blair* [1982] 1 Lloyd's Rep 188 (cash in transit insurance); *Hadenfayre Ltd v British National Insurance Society Ltd* [1984] 2 Lloyd's Rep 393 (contingency insurance).
6 *Re Albert Life Assurance Co, Cook's Policy* (1870) LR 9 Eq 703; and see *Burridge & Son v F H Haines & Sons* (1918) 118 LT 681 (waiver of condition that death of horse should be certified by veterinary surgeon).
7 *Re Coleman's Depositories Ltd and Life and Health Assurance Association* [1907] 2 KB 798 at 805, CA, per Vaughan Williams LJ.
8 *Hemmings v Sceptre Life Association Ltd* [1905] 1 Ch 365; *Hood's Trustees v Southern Union General Insurance Co of Australasia Ltd* [1928] Ch 793, CA; *Evans v Employers' Mutual Insurance Association Ltd* [1936] 1 KB 505, CA.
9 *M'Entire v Sun Fire Office* (1895) 29 ILT 103. The insurers are entitled to a reasonable time in which to make up their minds: *McCormick v National Motor and Accident Insurance Union Ltd* (1934) 50 TLR 528, CA. In the case of an agent, the knowledge must come to the minds of the persons whose duty it is to take action upon the knowledge: *Evans v Employers' Mutual Insurance Association Ltd* [1936] 1 KB 505, CA.
10 *Brook v Trafalgar Insurance Co Ltd* (1947) 79 Ll L Rep 365 at 367, CA, per Scott LJ (motor insurance).

423. Consideration for a waiver. Where the obligation alleged to be waived has not been broken, no consideration is required beyond the mutual agreement of the parties that performance will not be required: the promise and the reliance on the promise are sufficient to satisfy the technical requirements of the law. However, where there has already been a breach by the assured, there must be some consideration to offset the insurers' accrued rights[1]. If, after becoming aware of the breach, the insurers represent by their conduct that the policy is valid, and in reliance on that representation the assured allows them to handle claims against him which fall within the scope of the policy, this may amount to sufficient consideration on the part of the assured so as to preclude the insurers from repudiating their liability under the policy[2].

1 *Foster v Dawber* (1851) 6 Exch 839 at 851 per Parke B.
2 *Evans v Employers' Mutual Insurance Association Ltd* [1936] 1 KB 505 at 521, CA, per Roche LJ. Hence the importance in this connection of the principle of estoppel, as to which see para 424 post.

424. Estoppel distinguished from waiver. The dividing line between estoppel and waiver is so fine as to be in many cases almost indistinguishable. In theory, a waiver of a contractual right is something contractual involving agreement, express or implied, between the parties; estoppel, however, is merely a rule of evidence or law by which a party is precluded from asserting the existence of a fact including, for present purposes, a right[1]. Therefore, conduct by the insurers making performance of a condition either impossible or unnecessary can be set up as a waiver if there is the requisite assent to or consideration for it[2]. Alternatively, the same conduct can be relied on as an estoppel if it has induced the assured to believe that the condition need not be performed or that accrued rights are not going to be enforced, and to act accordingly[3]. If, however, it follows a breach of a condition, the conduct must be such as to lead the assured to suppose that the contract is being treated by the insurers as valid notwithstanding the breach, as where they accept a renewal premium[4] or do or demand something without any justification except the policy[5]. There must, moreover, be a reliance on the part of the assured on the representation as to the continued validity of the policy imparted by the insurers' conduct and a consequential alteration in his position[6]. Unless the assured is misled, there is no estoppel[7].

1 As to estoppel generally see ESTOPPEL vol 16 (Reissue) para 951 et seq.
2 As to waiver see paras 422–423 ante.
3 *Toronto Rly Co v National British and Irish Millers Insurance Co Ltd* (1914) 111 LT 555 at 563, CA; *Burridge & Son v F H Haines & Sons* (1918) 118 LT 681 at 685; *Scottish Amicable Heritable Securities Association v Northern Assurance Co* (1883) 11 R 287, Ct of Sess. As to estoppel by conduct see ESTOPPEL vol 16 (Reissue) para 1055 et seq.
4 *Wing v Harvey* (1854) 5 De G M & G 265; *Hemmings v Sceptre Life Association Ltd* [1905] 1 Ch 365; *Ayrey v British Legal and United Provident Assurance Co* [1918] 1 KB 136. A demand of premium is not apparently sufficient: *Edge v Duke* (1849) 18 LJCh 183.
5 *Yorkshire Insurance Co Ltd v Craine* [1922] 2 AC 541, PC; *Donnison v Employers' Accident and Live Stock Insurance Co* (1897) 24 R 681, Ct of Sess (where a post-mortem was demanded).
6 *Toronto Rly Co v National British and Irish Millers Insurance Co Ltd* (1914) 111 LT 555 at 563, CA.
7 *Acey v Fernie* (1840) 7 M & W 151; *Windus v Lord Tredegar* (1866) 15 LT 108, HL; *Handler v Mutual Reserve Fund Life Association* (1904) 90 LT 192, CA.

(6) THE RISK

(i) Risk in relation to the Peril Insured Against

425. Aspects of risk. There are three broad topics to be considered in relation to the risk: (1) the risk in the sense of the contractual definition of the peril insured against[1]; (2) the risk in the sense of the subject matter insured against the stipulated peril[2]; and (3) the risk in the sense of the circumstance in which the stipulated peril has to affect the assured, either in relation to a defined subject matter or in relation to his incurring a particular liability or loss[3].

1 As to the nature of the peril see para 426 post.
2 In the case of personal insurance, the person whose life or health or earning capacity is insured is in a broad sense the subject matter of the insurance; in the case of property insurance, the property insured forms the subject matter. In the cases of liability and contingency insurance, there is no basic subject matter such as a specific individual or a particular article or class of property; in these cases the activities of the assured are, in effect, the subject matter of the insurance and it is therefore usual to find explicit questions asked in the proposal, the answers being incorporated in the policy, relating to the nature of the assured's proposed activities and the means by which and the locality in which they are intended to be carried on: see 20 Forms & Precedents (5th Edn) 202–203, 207–211, Forms 135, 137–138. The subject matter of insurance must be distinguished from the subject matter of the contract of insurance, which is money and money only: *Rayner v Preston* (1881) 18 ChD 1 at 9, CA. As to the description of subject matter see para 427 post.
3 As to circumstances affecting the risk see para 430 post.

426. Nature of the peril. The nature of the peril against which the insurance is effected is a matter of interpretation of the policy in the light of the circumstances in which it is effected[1]. If a policy is effected against loss by fire, it may well be a question of interpretation whether this is operative only in the case of a fire accidentally caused, or whether the cover extends even to fires deliberately started by the assured in his own fireplace in which, unknown to him, or forgotten by him, valuable property such as currency notes have been hidden[2]. Again, if a fire policy is effected on a house, it will be a question of interpretation whether this is merely operative to indemnify the assured against the loss of the house if it is destroyed or whether it is also effective to cover the contingency of a fire spreading from the house so as to involve the assured in legal liabilities to adjoining property owners[3]. Similarly, problems may arise as to the meaning of 'loss' in a goods policy; for example, if the owner of a car intending to part with the property in it sells it and accepts a worthless cheque as a consideration for its sale, he suffers a loss, not of the car, but of the proceeds of sale[4], but if the owner merely parts with the possession of his car to a selling agent on a promise to sell it on his behalf to a particular buyer, and the agent sells it otherwise than in accordance with his promise and retains the proceeds and, after the owner has taken all reasonable steps to recover the car, recovery is still uncertain, the owner suffers a loss of the car[5]. Also, 'accident' in a liability policy in respect of a crane means an unlooked-for mishap or occurrence, such as the crane collapsing[6]. It has been held that in a policy against the cost of rewriting a lost manuscript, the cost of rewriting was not the peril insured against, but only a means of quantifying the loss[7].

1 As to the interpretation of the policy see paras 394–400 ante.
2 *Harris v Poland* [1941] 1 KB 462, [1941] 1 All ER 204.
3 *Balfour v Barty-King* [1957] 1 QB 496, [1957] 1 All ER 156, CA, although it is not an insurance case, illustrates the circumstances in which such a question may arise.
4 *Eisinger v General Accident Fire and Life Assurance Corpn Ltd* [1955] 2 All ER 897, [1955] 1 WLR 869.
5 *Webster v General Accident Fire and Life Assurance Corpn Ltd* [1953] 1 QB 520, [1953] 1 All ER 663.
6 *Canadian Indemnity Co v Walkem Machinery and Equipment Ltd* [1975] 5 WWR 510 (Can SC).
7 *Frewin v Poland* [1968] 1 Lloyd's Rep 100, where the manuscript was not, in fact, rewritten.

(ii) Risk in relation to the Subject Matter Described

427. Description of subject matter. In personal or property insurance a description of the subject matter, whether it is a human being, a chattel or a parcel of real property, is an essential element in the description of the risk because identification of the subject matter is fundamental to the policy[1]. In these classes of insurance insurers do not undertake a general liability to the assured[2]; they only assume a liability as defined in respect of a subject matter coming within the terms of the policy. The insurance is, therefore, only operative in relation to a claim if the subject matter of the claim corresponds with the description which the policy contains, whether on its face or by reference to the incorporated documents or to the surrounding circumstances admissible as aids to its interpretation[3].

1 As to the identification of terms which are fundamental see paras 410–416 ante.
2 *Collingridge v Royal Exchange Assurance Corpn* (1877) 3 QBD 173 at 176 per Lush J.
3 *Watchorn v Langford* (1813) 3 Camp 422; *Hare v Barstow* (1844) 8 Jur 928; *Sillem v Thornton* (1854) 3 E & B 868, as explained in *Stokes v Cox* (1856) 1 H & N 533, Ex Ch; *Joel v Harvey* (1857) 5 WR 488; *Roberts v Anglo-Saxon Insurance Association* (1927) 137 LT 243 at 248, CA, per Scrutton LJ; *Herman v Phoenix Assurance Co Ltd* (1924) 18 Ll L Rep 371, CA. As to the interpretation of policies see paras 394–400 ante.

428. General and specific descriptions. Descriptions of the subject matter[1] are of two kinds: (1) general descriptions designed to indicate the subject matter by way of classification under headings broadly defined; and (2) specific descriptions designed to identify individual objects which are covered. If a general description is adopted, the insurance is on the class designated by the description, and any object belonging to the class and falling within the description is covered, it being a matter of interpretation in each case what is the ambit of the class and whether the object in question falls within that ambit[2]. If a specific description is adopted, the insurance is limited to the specific object which is identified by the description[3]. The description of the property insured may be so specific as to apply only to property which was in existence at the commencement of the insurance, even though the property is of such a nature that in the ordinary course it will be, or may be, consumed or disposed of and replaced by other property of a like nature[4].

1 As to description of the subject matter see para 427 ante.
2 *Joel v Harvey* (1857) 5 WR 488 at 489 per Crompton J; *Gorman v Hand-in-Hand Insurance Co* (1877) IR 11 CL 224 at 235 per Palles CB.
3 *Hare v Barstow* (1844) 8 Jur 928; *Grover and Grover Ltd v Mathews* (1910) as reported in 15 Com Cas 249; cf *Morrison and Mason v Scottish Employers' Liability and Accident Assurance Co* (1888) 16 R 212, Ct of Sess.
4 *Gorman v Hand-in-Hand Insurance Co* (1877) IR 11 CL 224 (hayricks); *Rogerson v Scottish Automobile and General Insurance Co Ltd* (1931) 146 LT 26, HL (car).

429. Locality as part of description. The description of the subject matter often includes a description of the locality in which it is situated[1]. In the case of a building, the risk of a loss being partial or total, and very often the risk of there being a loss at all, is largely affected by the locality. Where the locality is of the essence of the description, the policy will not apply unless, at the date of the policy and of the loss, the property insured is in the locality indicated[2].

1 *Dawsons Ltd v Bonnin* [1922] 2 AC 413, HL.
2 *Grover and Grover Ltd v Mathews* (1910) as reported in 79 LJKB 1025 at 1030; *Allom v Property Insurance Co* (1911) Times, Finance, Commerce and Shipping section, 10 February. As to the adequacy of description required see para 432 post.

(iii) Risk in relation to Circumstances affecting the Subject Matter or the Incidence of the Peril

430. Circumstances affecting the risk. Frequently the description of the subject matter is framed by reference to circumstances affecting it, for example where the description hinges on the trade or business carried on by the assured[1] or the purpose for which the subject matter is used[2]. In the case of a building, for example, insurers may require details of its construction[3] or use[4] or indications of its surroundings[5] or other material circumstances[6]. Matters of this kind do not normally affect the identity of the subject matter, but they are of importance as placing on record in the policy the description of the risk as given to the insurers at the date of the insurance[7]. The insurers' acceptance of the proposal is on the basis of the description of the risk given to them, not on their own knowledge of it[8].

1 *Holdsworth v Lancashire and Yorkshire Insurance Co* (1907) 23 TLR 521; *Hales v Reliance Fire and Accident Insurance Corpn Ltd* [1960] 2 Lloyd's Rep 391.
2 *Farr v Motor Traders' Mutual Insurance Society* [1920] 3 KB 669, CA, followed in *Roberts v Anglo-Saxon Insurance Association* (1927) 137 LT 243, CA.

3 *Re Universal Non-Tariff Fire Insurance Co, Forbes & Co's Claim* (1875) LR 19 Eq 485.
4 *Whitehead v Price* (1835) 2 Cr M & R 447, followed in *Mayall v Mitford* (1837) 6 Ad & El 670; *Shaw v Robberds* (1837) 6 Ad & El 75; *Pim v Reid* (1843) 6 Man & G 1.
5 Eg in the case of insurances on timber: *J Gliksten & Son Ltd v State Assurance Co* (1922) 10 Ll L Rep 604; cf *Palatine Insurance Co v Gregory* [1926] AC 90, PC.
6 The description may be expressed in the negative: *Dobson v Sotheby* (1827) Mood & M 90; *Stokes v Cox* (1856) 1 H & N 533, Ex Ch.
7 The validity of the policy is not affected if the misdescription is due to the fault of the insurers or their agent: *Re Universal Non-Tariff Fire Insurance Co, Forbes & Co's Claim* (1875) LR 19 Eq 485, following *Parsons v Bignold* (1846) 15 LJCh 379.
8 *Sillem v Thornton* (1854) 3 E & B 868, as explained in *Thompson v Hopper* (1858) E B & E 1038, Ex Ch.

431. Nature of the assured's business. Considerations of the surrounding circumstances apply in relation to other types of insurance, such as public liability insurance[1] or pecuniary loss insurance[2]. For example, if a person carries on business as a demolition contractor, this will be recognised as a matter of general knowledge as an occupation involving substantial risks to employees and members of the public, but these risks will be greatly increased if explosives are used in the operations. If the assured takes out a policy of insurance against accidents to third parties arising out of a demolition, and in answer to a question in the proposal form, which is made the basis of the contract[3], states that he does not use explosives in his business, the risk insured is the risk arising from a demolition otherwise than by the use of explosives and, if an accident occurs of which the cause or contributing cause is the use of explosives, the insurers are not liable[4].

1 As to public liability insurance see paras 690–691 post.
2 As to pecuniary loss insurance see paras 765–789 post.
3 As to the proposal form as the basis of the contract see para 374 ante.
4 *Beauchamp v National Mutual Indemnity Co Ltd* [1937] 3 All ER 19, where it was also held that the denial of the use of explosives amounted to a warranty that they would not be used and that there had been a change in the risk. As to conditions circumscribing the risk see para 405 ante. As to alteration of the risk see paras 437–439 post.

(iv) Misdescription of the Risk

432. Adequacy of description. Any description, whether of the locality of the property insured or of the circumstances affecting the subject matter or the incidence of the peril, is, in general, sufficient if it is substantially accurate[1]. In other words a misdescription must be material if it is to affect the validity of the policy[2]. However, this is subject to the terms of any express condition contained in the policy. Such conditions are frequently limited to material misdescriptions; but if the language used is so stringent as to cover any misdescription, however immaterial, the policy will be voidable at the option of the insurers[3].

1 *Doe d Pitt v Laming* (1814) 4 Camp 73; *Dobson v Sotheby* (1827) Mood & M 90 at 92 per Lord Tenterden CJ; *Friedlander v London Assurance Co* (1832) 1 Mood & R 171; *South Australian Insurance Co v Randell* (1869) LR 3 PC 101.
2 *Re Universal Non-Tariff Fire Insurance Co, Forbes & Co's Claim* (1875) LR 19 Eq 485.
3 *Newcastle Fire Insurance Co v Macmorran & Co* (1815) 3 Dow 255, HL; *Dawsons Ltd v Bonnin* [1922] 2 AC 413, HL.

433. Descriptions and representations. Descriptive words used in a policy, whether on its face or by reference to incorporated documents such as a proposal, are operative as a description of the risk as at the date of the insurance[1]. If the words are used in relation to the future they can, of course, only operate as representations[2], and where they are accurate when made, there is no breach of duty by the assured if a subsequent change of events falsifies them in the absence of fraud[3] on his part[4]. If, however, on their true construction, the words are not merely a representation as to the future but a present definition or limitation of the risk in respect of which insurance is sought and given, no question of innocence or guilt on the part of the assured arises[5]; no liability attaches to the insurers unless the loss takes place in the circumstances[6] or in the locality[7] which by the description has been made a fundamental term of the policy. It is always a question of interpretation of the policy into which category descriptive words fall[8]. This question of interpretation is often assisted by the presence in the policy of express conditions indicating the circumstances in which, in the event of an alteration of risk, the assured is entitled to recover or the insurers are relieved of liability[9].

1 *Shaw v Robberds* (1837) 6 Ad & El 75 at 82 per Lord Denman CJ. Where a condition as to the accuracy of the description of the premises insured and the trade carried on there relates to the description at the time of the insuring, if the description was correct at that date, nothing which occurs afterwards can amount to a breach of condition: *Sillem v Thornton* (1854) 3 E & B 868, as explained in *Thompson v Hopper* (1858) E B & E 1038; *Stokes v Cox* (1856) as reported in 1 H & N 320 at 335 per Bramwell B; on appeal 1 H & N 533, Ex Ch.
2 *Benham v United Guarantee and LifeAssurance Co* (1852) 7 Exch 744; *Grant v Aetna Insurance Co* (1862) 15 Moo PCC 516.
3 As to the effect of fraud see para 366 ante.
4 *Pim v Reid* (1843) 6 Man & G 1 at 22 per Maule J; *Sweeney v Kennedy* (1948) 82 Ll L Rep 294 (Eire DC); *Hales v Reliance Fire and Accident Insurance Corpn Ltd* [1960] 2 Lloyd's Rep 391. There may, however, be a breach of a condition against alteration: see paras 438–439 post.
5 *Re Morgan and Provincial Insurance Co Ltd* [1932] 2 KB 70, CA; affd on different grounds, but without dissent from the ratio decidendi in the Court of Appeal [1933] AC 240, HL. See also para 436 post.
6 *Farr Motor Traders' Mutual Insurance Society* [1920] 3 KB 669, CA; *Roberts v Anglo-Saxon Insurance Association* (1927) 137 LT 243, CA; *Murray v Scottish Automobile and General Insurance Co* 1929 SC 49.
7 *Pearson v Commercial Union Assurance Co* (1876) 1 App Cas 498, HL; *Gorman v Hand-in-Hand Insurance Co* (1877) IR 11 CL 224; *Stoneham v Ocean, Railway and General Accident Insurance Co* (1887) 19 QBD 237; *Smellie v British General Insurance Co* [1918] WC & Ins Rep 233; *Re Calf and Sun Insurance Office* [1920] 2 KB 366 at 385, CA, per Younger LJ; cf *Lilley v Doubleday* (1881) 7 QBD 510.
8 *Benham v United Guarantee and Life Assurance Co* (1852) 7 Exch 744; *Towle v National Guardian Assurance Society* (1861) 30 LJCh 900. As to interpretation of the policy generally see paras 394–400 ante.
9 As to such conditions see para 438 post.

(v) Alteration of the Risk

434. Alteration of the subject matter. Where the policy is so framed that the peril insured against is qualified in the sense that it must affect the assured in relation to a subject matter of a defined character or in circumstances of a defined nature, the insurers' obligation is confined to the particular risk which has been so indicated. Therefore, if the risk, in this sense, is altered, their obligation ceases[1]. Such an alteration occurs whenever something is done which affects the stipulated risk, whether as regards its subject matter[2], locality[3] or circumstances[4]. The alteration must be a real alteration making the risk a different risk; there is no alteration of the risk if the alteration made is one which was within the contemplation of the parties when they entered into the contract of insurance[5].

1 *Law, Guarantee, Trust and Accident Society v Munich Re-insurance Co* [1912] 1 Ch 138 at 153–154 per Warrington J.

2　*Newcastle Fire Insurance Co v Macmorran & Co* (1815) 3 Dow 255, HL; *Sillem v Thornton* (1854) 3 E & B 868, as explained in *Thompson v Hopper* (1858) E B & E 1038 at 1049, Ex Ch; *Shaw v Royce Ltd* [1911] 1 Ch 138; *Law, Guarantee, Trust and Accident Society v Munich Re-insurance Co* [1912] 1 Ch 138 at 153–154; *Beauchamp v National Mutual Indemnity Co Ltd* [1937] 3 All ER 19; and see para 431 text and notes 3–4 ante.

3　*Pearson v Commercial Union Assurance Co* (1876) 1 App Cas 498, HL; *Gorman v Hand-in-Hand Insurance Co* (1877) IR 11 CL 224.

4　*Wembley UDC v Poor Law and Local Government Officers' Mutual Guarantee Association Ltd* (1901) 17 TLR 516; *Cosford Union v Poor Law and Local Government Officers' Mutual Guarantee Association Ltd* (1910) 103 LT 463, DC; *Hadenfayre Ltd v British National Insurance Society Ltd* [1984] 2 Lloyd's Rep 393 (contingency insurance).

5　*Re Albert Life Assurance Co, Bell's Case, Craig's Executors' Case* (1870) LR 9 Eq 706 at 719 per James V-C; *Gorman v Hand-in-Hand Insurance Co* (1877) IR 11 CL 224 at 236 per Palles CB; *Law, Guarantee, Trust and Accident Society v Munich Re-insurance Co* [1912] 1 Ch 138 at 154 per Warrington J.

435. Change of identity. Where the subject matter of the insurance is so changed as to alter its identity, there is in effect a substitution of a new subject matter to which the policy does not attach[1]. However, the subject matter of insurance may remain the same, even though temporarily the thing insured is separated into parts for repairs[2].

1　*Cosford Union v Poor Law and Local Government Officers' Mutual Guarantee Association Ltd* (1910) 103 LT 463 at 465, DC; *Shaw v Royce Ltd* [1911] 1 Ch 138; *Law, Guarantee, Trust and Accident Society v Munich Re-insurance Co* [1912] 1 Ch 138.

2　*Seaton v London General Insurance Co Ltd* (1932) 48 TLR 574 (insured lorry; engine removed for repair and taken elsewhere, but rest of lorry left in usual garage; engine destroyed by fire when at place of repair; damage held covered by insurance).

436. Change of circumstances comprised in definition. There may be an alteration of the risk not affecting the identity of the subject matter[1] which amounts to an alteration of the risk where the alteration is such that the risk no longer corresponds with that defined in the policy[2]. Where the definition of the risk includes a description of locality, or of circumstances such as the purpose for which the subject matter is used, the subject matter must, at the time of its loss, be in the locality[3] or be used for the purpose described[4]; the insurers are not responsible if its loss takes place whilst it is in a different locality[5] or is being used for a different purpose[6]. In this case, however, unless the policy expressly so provides, the alteration of the risk does not avoid the policy but merely suspends its operation during the continuance of the alteration[7]. If the subject matter is returned to the locality described[8] or is again used in accordance with the description[9], the policy reattaches.

1　As to alterations affecting the subject matter see para 434 ante.

2　*Pearson v Commercial Union Assurance Co* (1876) 1 App Cas 498 at 503, HL, per Lord Cairns LC.

3　As to locality as part of the description of the risk see para 429 ante; and see the cases cited in para 433 note 7 ante, and *Dawsons Ltd v Bonnin* [1922] 2 AC 413, HL. If removal has been authorised, the subject matter must be in the newly authorised locality: *McClure v Lancashire Insurance Co* (1860) 6 Ir Jur 63.

4　*Re Morgan and Provincial Insurance Co Ltd* [1932] 2 KB 70, CA; affd sub nom *Provincial Insurance Co Ltd v Morgan* [1933] AC 240, HL.

5　*Pearson v Commercial Union Assurance Co* (1876) 1 App Cas 498, HL; *Dawsons Ltd v Bonnin* [1922] 2 AC 413, HL.

6　*Stuart v Horse Insurance Co* (1893) 1 SLT 91; *Roberts v Anglo-Saxon Insurance Association* (1927) 137 LT 243, CA.

7　*Roberts v Anglo-Saxon Insurance Association* (1927) 137 LT 243, CA; *CTN Cash and Carry Ltd v General Accident Fire and Life Assurance Corpn plc* [1989] 1 Lloyd's Rep 299 (burglary insurance).

8 *Gorman v Hand-in-Hand Insurance Co* (1877) IR 11 CL 224.

9 *Farr v Motor Traders' Mutual Insurance Society* [1920] 3 KB 669, CA; *Provincial Insurance Co Ltd v Morgan* [1933] AC 240, HL.

437. Increase of likelihood of loss. Where insurers have issued a policy providing insurance against specified perils, their obligation to make payment in the event of the peril occurring is, in the absence of any qualifying conditions, absolute in the sense that the only question is whether the event which has occurred falls within the definition of the perils insured against[1]. It is immaterial that the assured by his conduct may have increased the likelihood of the peril occurring[2], even if it can be shown that his conduct was the direct cause of the loss[3]. Unless prohibited by the policy, such conduct does not avoid the insurance[4].

1 As to the nature of the peril insured against see para 426 ante.
2 *Baxendale v Harvey* (1859) 4 H & N 445 at 449 per Pollock CB.
3 *Shaw v Robberds* (1837) 6 Ad & El 75.
4 *Pim v Reid* (1843) 6 Man & G 1; *Thompson v Hopper* (1858) EB & E 1038 at 1049, Ex Ch, per Willes J.

438. Policy conditions dealing with alterations. A policy may contain express conditions dealing with alterations of the risk. They are usually expressed in prohibitive or restrictive terms, and may be classified as (1) conditions prohibiting or restricting an increase of the risk, (2) conditions prohibiting or restricting the removal of the subject matter from a particular locality, and (3) conditions prohibiting or restricting changes of circumstances.

To constitute a breach of a condition of the first kind, the risk must be increased by the alteration[1]. By the terms of a particular condition, an alteration, though increasing the risk, may be allowed if notice is given to the insurers[2] or their sanction is obtained[3].

Examples of the second kind occur in life or personal accident policies, travel policies[4] or fire or burglary policies, under which the removal of goods[5] may be prohibited or restricted.

Conditions of the third kind deal with a variety of circumstances, for example the trade or business carried on by the assured[6], including the methods of business[7] and the use to which the subject matter may be put[8]. Where the insurance is connected with a building, its use[9] or even the presence[10] in it of certain specified articles may be prohibited or restricted; and the building may be required always to be occupied[11].

1 *Barrett v Jermy* (1849) 3 Exch 535; *Stokes v Cox* (1856) 1 H & N 533; *Hales v Reliance Fire and Accident Insurance Corpn Ltd* [1960] 2 Lloyd's Rep 391 (fire insurance); cf *Re George and Goldsmiths and General Burglary Insurance Association Ltd* [1899] 1 QB 595 at 609, CA, per A L Smith LJ. This is a question of fact: *Baxendale v Harvey* (1859) 4 H & N 445.
2 *Glen v Lewis* (1853) 8 Exch 607.
3 A condition requiring notice to the insurers does not necessarily involve obtaining their sanction: *Re Birkbeck Permanent Benefit Building Society, Official Receiver v Licenses Insurance Corpn* [1913] 2 Ch 34.
4 *Wing v Harvey* (1854) 5 De G M & G 265; cf *Fowler v Scottish Equitable Life Insurance Society and Ritchie* (1858) 28 LJCh 225; *Notman v Anchor Assurance Co* (1858) 4 CBNS 476; *Stoneham v Ocean, Railway and General Accident Insurance Co* (1887) 19 QBD 237.
5 For an example of a policy containing such a provision see 20 Forms & Precedents (5th Edn) 29 at 30, Form 2 cl 6.
6 *Shaw v Robberds* (1837) 6 Ad & El 75; *Pim v Reid* (1843) 6 Man & G 1; see also *Hall v Star Fire Insurance Co* (1850) 14 LTOS 135, 446.
7 *Towle v National Guardian Assurance Society* (1861) 30 LJCh 900, where, however, the statement was treated not as a condition but as a representation.

8 *Whitehead v Price* (1835) 2 Cr M & R 447, followed in *Mayall v Mitford* (1837) 6 Ad & El 670; *Roberts v Anglo-Saxon Insurance Association* (1927) 137 LT 243, CA; *Provincial Insurance Co Ltd v Morgan* [1933] AC 240 at 254, HL, per Lord Wright.

9 *Barrett v Jermy* (1849) 3 Exch 535; *Glen v Lewis* (1853) 8 Exch 607; *Stokes v Cox* (1856) 1 H & N 533; *Farnham v Royal Insurance Co Ltd* [1976] 2 Lloyd's Rep 437; *Exchange Theatre Ltd v Iron Trades Mutual Insurance Co Ltd* [1984] 1 Lloyd's Rep 149, CA (fire insurance); *Linden Alimak Ltd v British Engine Insurance Ltd* [1984] 1 Lloyd's Rep 416 (extraneous damage insurance).

10 *M'Ewan v Guthridge* (1860) 13 Moo PCC 304; *Beacon Life and Fire Assurance Co v Gibb* (1862) 1 Moo PCCNS 73; *Citizens Insurance Co of Canada v Parsons* (1881) 7 App Cas 96, PC; *Thompson v Equity Fire Insurance Co* [1910] AC 592, PC.

11 *Simmonds v Cockell* [1920] 1 KB 843; *Marzouca v Atlantic and British Commercial Insurance Co Ltd* [1971] 1 Lloyd's Rep 449, PC.

439. Alterations which constitute a breach. Where there has been an alteration of the risk, the scope and ambit of the relevant condition must be examined because there can only be a breach of the condition if the alteration falls within its terms[1]. Whether the alteration must be of a permanent or habitual nature[2], or whether a temporary or casual alteration constitutes a breach, depends on the construction of the particular condition[3].

1 *Shaw v Robberds* (1837) 6 Ad & El 75 at 83 per Lord Denman CJ; *Barrett v Jermy* (1849) 3 Exch 535 at 543 per Parke B; *Stokes v Cox* (1856) 1 H & N 533 at 540 per Cockburn CJ.

2 *Dobson v Sotheby* (1827) Mood & M 90; *Shaw v Robberds* (1837) 6 Ad & El 75; *Thompson v Equity Fire Insurance Co* [1910] AC 592, PC.

3 *Glen v Lewis* (1853) 8 Exch 607.

(7) THE PREMIUM

(i) In general

440. Nature and assessment of premium. The consideration required of an assured for any form of insurance is a money payment universally referred to as a premium[1]. There may be a single lump sum premium, but more usually the premium is payable either at specified intervals, as in the case of life assurance, or as consideration for successive renewals of the policy. The amount of the premium appropriate to the risk involved is essentially a matter for the insurers, as experts in the business, to assess[2], but their assessment is not binding unless the assured prospectively or retrospectively agrees that it should be so. In making their assessment insurers normally work on the basis of an average of their previous experience of comparable risks[3], increasing or perhaps reducing the figure according to their estimate as to whether the graph of the risk is tending or likely to rise or fall. The rate of premium in fact charged may give rise to important inferences. The materiality of a representation which has been made may be inferred from a reduced rate of premium being charged[4]. Similarly, ignorance on the part of the insurers of some matter supposed to be well known may be inferred if they charge no more than the ordinary rate of premium, while an exceptionally high rate of premium may be indicative of their acceptance of the risk as hazardous without requiring disclosure of the precise facts making it so[5].

1 *Prudential Insurance Co v IRC* [1904] 2 KB 658 at 663 per Channell J; see also *Municipal Mutual Insurance Ltd v Pontefract Corpn* (1917) 116 LT 671 at 674 per Sankey J.

2 Hence, the amount charged for the premium is of assistance to show the scope of the policy: *Re George and Goldsmiths and General Burglary Insurance Association Ltd* [1899] 1 QB 595 at 611, CA, per Collins LJ.

3 *Chapman v Pole, PO* (1870) 22 LT 306 at 307 per Cockburn J; *Thomson v Weems* (1884) 9 App Cas 671 at 681, HL, per Lord Blackburn.

4 *Court v Martineau* (1782) 3 Doug KB 161; *Bridges v Hunter* (1813) 1 M & S 15; *Tate v Hyslop* (1885) 15 QBD 368, CA.

5 *Court v Martineau* (1782) 3 Doug KB 161; *Cantiere Meccanico Brindisino v Janson* [1912] 3 KB 452 at 466, CA, per Fletcher Moulton LJ; and see the United States cases discussed in Arnould on Marine Insurance (16th Edn) s 672.

441. Agreement as to premium. There cannot be a contract of insurance unless and until the premium is agreed[1]. There need not be agreement as to the exact amount, provided the rate or basis of assessment is agreed[2]. In particular, there are some classes of insurance in which the extent of the risk cannot be measured until the period of insurance has expired; a provisional premium is then paid at the commencement of the period, and a final adjustment is made at the end of the period[3]. Provision may also be made for reducing the premium where the risk turns out to be less than was anticipated. In motor insurance a deduction by way of bonus may be allowed from the premium for the following year in the event of no claim being made under the policy during the current year[4]. If the allowance of bonus is at the discretion of the insurers, their decision to allow no bonus, if made in good faith, cannot be challenged[5].

1 *Canning v Farquhar* (1886) 16 QBD 727 at 731, 734, CA; *Re Yager and Guardian Assurance Co* (1912) 108 LT 38, DC; *Murfitt v Royal Insurance Co Ltd* (1922) 38 TLR 334; *Kirby v Cosindit Societa per Azioni* [1969] 1 Lloyd's Rep 75 (builders' risk insurance); *American Airlines Inc v Hope, Banque Sabbag SAL v Hope* [1973] 1 Lloyd's Rep 233, CA (additional premium for war risks in respect of aircraft not agreed before they were destroyed); affd on different grounds [1974] 2 Lloyd's Rep 301, HL.

2 For the method of agreeing the premium payable in marine insurance see paras 89, 143 text and note 3 ante.

3 As to the calculation of the premium in liability insurance see para 666 post.

4 For examples of such a provision see 20 Forms & Precedents (5th Edn) 549 at 555, Form 311 cl 27; 561 at 566, Form 312 cl 26. As to no claims bonus clauses see further para 727 post.

5 *Want v Blunt* (1810) 12 East 183; *Manby v Gresham Life Assurance Society* (1861) 29 Beav 439.

442. Payment of premium. The premium may be paid by the assured to the insurers or to an insurance agent acting on behalf of the insurers. If the agent has authority to receive it, the payment binds the insurers[1]. The authority need not be an express authority, but may be implied by the circumstances[2]. In this case payment to the agent is binding, though he has ceased to represent the insurers, unless the assured has notice that his agency has ceased[3]. The right of the personal representatives of the assured to pay a premium on a life assurance if the assured dies after the due date for payment, but before the expiry of the days of grace, is considered subsequently[4].

1 *Acey v Fernie* (1840) 7 M & W 151. For a discussion as to the status of a collector see *Co-operative Insurance Society Ltd v Richardson* (1955) Times, 5 March.

2 *Rossiter v Trafalgar Life Assurance Association* (1859) 27 Beav 377; cf *Linford v Provincial Horse and Cattle Insurance Co* (1864) 34 Beav 291; see also *Kelly v London and Staffordshire Fire Insurance Co* (1883) Cab & El 47; cf *Towle v National Guardian Assurance Society* (1861) 30 LJCh 900 at 916, CA in Ch, per Turner LJ.

3 *Wing v Harvey* (1854) 5 De G M & G 265; *Re European Assurance Society Arbitration Acts and Wellington Reversionary Annuity and Life Assurance Society, Conquest's Case* (1875) 1 ChD 334, CA.

4 As to the effect of tendering a premium during days of grace see para 478 post.

443. Form of payment. If made to an insurance agent, payment of the premium must be made in a form in which the agent is authorised to receive it[1]. Hence, delivery of a promissory note is not binding on the insurers as payment[2], unless authorised[3]. Payment in a form which is not authorised does not bind the insurers until the agent has, in fact, received cash payment[4], and an agreement between the agent and the assured by which the assured is given credit is not effective unless the money is actually received by the insurers during the days of grace[5].

1 *Acey v Fernie* (1840) 7 M & W 151.
2 *Montreal Assurance Co v M'Gillivray* (1859) 13 Moo PCC 87.
3 *London and Lancashire Life Assurance Co v Fleming* [1897] AC 499, PC.
4 *Acey v Fernie* (1840) 7 M & W 151; *London and Lancashire Life Assurance Co v Fleming* [1897] AC 499, PC.
5 *Acey v Fernie* (1840) 7 M & W 151. As to days of grace see paras 477–478 post.

444. Agreements as to payment with insurance agent. An insurance agent may agree to advance the money for the premium and to pay it on behalf of the assured to the insurers[1], in which case the insurers are not bound until they have received payment from the agent. It is immaterial in what form they receive it, and a settlement of accounts between the agent and the insurers is, therefore, valid[2]. It is probably sufficient if the amount of the premium is debited in account, either by the agent or by the insurers[3]. If there is no agreement between the agent and the assured for the money to be advanced, the assured cannot take advantage of any debit in account between the agent and the insurers[4], nor can he take advantage of a settlement of account between them[5] or even of an actual payment by the agent to the insurers[6].

1 *Acey v Fernie* (1840) 7 M & W 151 at 155 per Lord Abinger CB; *Busteed v West of England Fire and Life Insurance Co* (1857) 5 I Ch R 553.
2 *Newcastle Fire Insurance Co v Macmorran & Co* (1815) 3 Dow 255 at 264, HL, per Lord Eldon.
3 *Prince of Wales Assurance Co v Harding* (1858) E B & E 183; *Re Law Car and General Insurance Corpn* [1911] WN 101, CA.
4 *Acey v Fernie* (1840) 7 M & W 151 at 155 per Parke B; *Busteed v West of England Fire and Life Insurance Co* (1857) 5 I Ch R 553; *London and Lancashire Life Assurance Co v Fleming* [1897] AC 499, PC; see also *Browne v Price* (1858) 4 CBNS 598.
5 *London and Lancashire Life Assurance Co v Fleming* [1897] AC 499, PC.
6 *Busteed v West of England Fire and Life Insurance Co* (1857) 5 I Ch R 553.

(ii) Prepayment of Premium

445. Assured's liability to pay premium. As soon as the contract is agreed, the assured becomes liable to pay the premium[1], but his failure to pay it does not absolve the insurers from their liability under the contract unless there is a provision in the contract to this effect, or the failure to pay the premium amounts in the circumstances to a repudiation of the contract[2]. In the event of a loss happening before payment, the insurers must pay the amount due under the contract[3] unless the contract otherwise provides.

1 *General Accident Insurance Corpn v Cronk* (1901) 17 TLR 233.
2 *Salvin v James* (1805) 6 East 571; *Edge v Duke* (1849) 18 LJCh 183.
3 *Kelly v London and Staffordshire Fire Insurance Co* (1883) Cab & El 47; *Thompson v Adams* (1889) 23 QBD 361; *Roberts v Security Co* [1897] 1 QB 111, CA; *Adie & Sons v Insurance Corpn Ltd* (1898) 14 TLR 544.

446. Prepayment as a condition precedent. In practice, payment of the premium in advance is usually made a condition precedent to liability[1], not only in the case of the first premium but also of the renewal premium[2]. The assured is then precluded from recovering for a loss which happens before the premium is paid[3] unless the circumstances are such that the insurers are estopped from denying that they have received payment[4], or have by their conduct waived the condition[5]. There may, for example, be a waiver by an agreement to give credit[6] or by the giving of an antedated receipt[7], but there is no waiver where an insurance agent accepts premiums in arrear unless he has authority from the insurers to do so[8].

1 As to conditions precedent to liability see para 406 ante.
2 See eg 20 Forms & Precedents (5th Edn) 34, Form 3; 429, Form 265 cl 1; 456, Form 275.
3 *Tarleton v Staniforth* (1796) 1 Bos & P 471, Ex Ch; *London and Lancashire Life Assurance Co v Fleming* [1897] AC 499, PC; *Equitable Fire and Accident Office Ltd v Ching Wo Hong* [1907] AC 96, PC; cf *Re Albert Life Assurance Co, Cook's Policy* (1870) LR 9 Eq 703; *Canning v Farquhar* (1886) 16 QBD 727 at 731, CA, per Lord Esher MR. As to payment during days of grace see para 478 post.
4 *Re Economic Fire Office Ltd* (1896) 12 TLR 142 (receipt given by insurers' agent who had authority to give receipts for premiums not paid). As to estoppel see para 424 ante.
5 *Cia Tirrena di Assicurazioni SpA v Grand Union Insurance Co Ltd* [1991] 2 Lloyd's Rep 143 (reinsurance). Cf *Daff v Midland Colliery Owners' Mutual Indemnity Co* (1913) 82 LJKB 1340 at 1344, HL. As to what constitutes a waiver see para 422 ante.
6 *Prince of Wales Assurance Co v Harding* (1858) EB & E 183.
7 *Howell v Kightley* (1856) 21 Beav 331 at 335 per Lord Romilly MR; affd 8 De G M & G 325, CA in Ch; cf *Pritchard v Merchant's and Tradesman's Mutual Life Assurance Society* (1858) 3 CBNS 622; *Ocean Accident and Guarantee Corpn Ltd v Cole* [1932] 2 KB 100 at 106, DC, per Avory J.
8 *British Industry Life Assurance Co v Ward* (1856) 17 CB 644.

(iii) Return of Premium

447. Return of premiums on total failure of consideration. The assured is entitled to a return of premium when there has been a total failure of the consideration for which he paid it, in the sense that the risk has never attached[1]. This does not, of course, mean that the premium is returnable if the peril has not, in fact, materialised; the test is whether the insurers have been, for however short a time, at risk, that is to say potentially liable to make a payment in the event of the peril materialising. Thus, if there never was a binding contract between the parties because the purported contract was ultra vires as regards the insurers[2], or was vitiated by a fundamental mistake[3], the insurers must repay what they have received for a risk which, in fact, they never ran. Similarly, where the policy has never begun to be operative owing to non-fulfilment of a warranty or condition precedent[4] of the policy, any premium which has been paid must be repaid unless the policy expressly provides that the premium is to be forfeited[5]. Equally, if it transpires that there never was any subject matter of the insurance, as where a person whose life is insured is found to have died before the date of the insurance[6] or where a supposed insurable interest in a life assured is found to be an illusion[7], the insurers cannot profit from an honest mistake or misunderstanding.

1 As to the failure of a policy to attach in marine insurance see para 329 ante. For the position where the risk has attached see para 450 post.
2 *Flood v Irish Provident Assurance Co Ltd* [1912] 2 Ch 597n, CA.
3 *Fowler v Scottish Equitable Life Insurance Society and Ritchie* (1858) 28 LJCh 225. As to mistake generally see CONTRACT vol 9 paras 290–295; and MISTAKE.
4 As to warranties and conditions precedent see paras 404, 406 ante.
5 *Thomson v Weems* (1884) 9 App Cas 671 at 682, HL, per Lord Blackburn.
6 *Pritchard v Merchant's and Tradesman's Mutual Life Assurance Society* (1858) 3 CBNS 622 at 645 per Byles J.

7 *Desborough v Curlewis* (1838) 3 Y & C Ex 175 at 177. As to the requirement of an insurable interest in a life policy see para 535 et seq post.

448. Return of premiums in case of illegality. The principle that the premium may be returned applies, subject to qualifications, in the case of a contract which is vitiated by illegality. Prima facie such a contract is void from the outset, and any premium which has been received by the insurers for a risk which has never commenced to run is returnable[1]. However, if the risk purporting to be insured has commenced to run, the assured can only recover the premium he has paid if he is untainted by the illegality[2]. Where both parties are equally at fault, the assured forfeits his premium as the penalty for his breach of the law[3], and the onus is on the assured to establish his innocence in this respect[4].

1 *Busk v Walsh* (1812) 4 Taunt 290, following *Aubert v Walsh* (1810) 3 Taunt 277. See also *Jaques v Golightly* (1777) 2 Wm Bl 1073. As to illegal contracts see generally CONTRACT vol 9 para 389 et seq. As to the recovery of money paid in pursuance of an illegal contract see CONTRACT vol 9 para 436.
2 *British Workman's and General Assurance Co Ltd v Cunliffe* (1902) 18 TLR 502, CA, as explained in *Harse v Pearl Life Assurance Co* [1904] 1 KB 558, CA, and in *Hughes v Liverpool Victoria Legal Friendly Society* [1916] 2 KB 482, CA. See also *London, Edinburgh and Glasgow Assurance Co Ltd v Partington* (1903) 88 LT 732, DC; *Tofts v Pearl Life Assurance Co Ltd* [1915] 1 KB 189, CA; and cf *Brewster v National Life Insurance Society* (1892) 8 TLR 648, CA.
3 *Howard v Refuge Friendly Society* (1886) 54 LT 644, followed in *Harse v Pearl Life Assurance Co* [1904] 1 KB 558, CA; *Phillips v Royal London Mutual Insurance Co Ltd* (1911) 105 LT 136; *Evanson v Crooks* (1911) 106 LT 264; *Elson v Crookes* (1911) 106 LT 462; *Goldstein v Salvation Army Assurance Society* [1917] 2 KB 291. See also *Drummond v Deey* (1794) 1 Esp 151; *Paterson v Powell* (1832) 9 Bing 320.
4 *Howarth v Pioneer Life Assurance Co Ltd* (1912) 107 LT 155, DC.

449. Return of premiums when policy voidable. Where a policy is obtained by misrepresentation or non-disclosure of material facts it is a valid and binding contract unless and until the insurers discover the true facts and, on discovering them, elect to avoid it. If, where there has been no fraud, they elect to repudiate a continuing insurance, they nullify the contract from the beginning and thereby sacrifice any premiums which they have collected[1]. However, in the case of a renewable insurance each renewal is a new contract and the premium returnable is limited to that paid for the last renewal, as the risk has, in fact, been fully borne by the insurers throughout all the earlier years. If there has been fraud on the part of the assured, there is normally no right to a return of premium, as the assured cannot make his own fraud a basis of a claim[2]. If the insurers have to apply to the court for relief, the court has power to declare the premium forfeited[3], although in its discretion it may make a condition of giving relief that premiums should be returned[4]. In the case of fraud on the part of the insurers the premiums obtained by means of the fraud are recoverable by the assured[5].

1 *Thomson v Weems* (1884) 9 App Cas 671 at 682, HL, per Lord Blackburn; *Hemmings v Sceptre Life Association Ltd* [1905] 1 Ch 365, following *Fowkes v Manchester and London Assurance Association* (1863) 3 B & S 917; see also *London Assurance v Mansel* (1879) 11 ChD 363. The Limitation Act 1980 s 5 applies to claims for return of premium (*Molloy v Mutual Reserve Life Insurance Co* (1906) 22 TLR 525, CA), but time does not run until the fraud is discovered (Limitation Act 1980 s 32(1) (amended by the Consumer Protection Act 1987 s 6(6), Sch 1 para 5); *Beer v Prudential Assurance Co* (1902) 66 JP 729): see LIMITATION OF ACTIONS.
2 *Feise v Parkinson* (1812) 4 Taunt 640 at 641 per Gibbs CJ; *Anderson v Thornton* (1853) 8 Exch 425; *Fowkes v Manchester and London Assurance Association* (1863) 3 B & S 917 at 927 per Crompton J, and at 931 per Mellor J; *Rivaz v Gerussi* (1880) 6 QBD 222 at 229, CA, per Brett LJ.
3 *British Equitable Insurance Co v Musgrave* (1887) 3 TLR 630.

4 *Barker v Walters* (1844) 8 Beav 92; *Prince of Wales etc Association Co v Palmer* (1858) 25 Beav 605; cf *Whittingham v Thornburgh* (1690) 2 Vern 206.

5 *Duffell v Wilson* (1808) 1 Camp 401; *Mutual Reserve Life Insurance Co v Foster* (1904) 20 TLR 715, HL; *Cross v Mutual Reserve Life Insurance Co* (1904) 21 TLR 15; *Merino v Mutual Reserve Life Insurance Co* (1904) 21 TLR 167; *Refuge Assurance Co v Kettlewell* [1909] AC 243, HL.

450. No return of premiums when risk has attached. The essence of the right to a return of premium is the failure of the consideration moving from the insurers[1], in other words the fact that the risk never attached. The fact that a particular event does not occur during the currency of the policy does not mean that there was never a risk, so far as the insurers were concerned, of that event occurring[2]. If a life policy contains an exception in respect of suicide and the assured commits suicide during the currency of the policy, the policy will not be enforceable; the premium is not returnable because the insurers were at all times on risk as regards death from natural, as opposed to self-induced, causes[3]. These rules are the result of applying to the law of insurance the ordinary principle of the law of contract, that a total failure of consideration on the one side is necessary to give a cause of action for repayment of consideration moving from the other side[4].

1 *Wolenberg v Royal Co-operative Collecting Society* (1915) 112 LT 1036, DC.
2 *Tyrie v Fletcher* (1777) 2 Cowp 666 at 668 per Lord Mansfield CJ.
3 *Tyrie v Fletcher* (1777) 2 Cowp 666.
4 As to total failure of consideration see CONTRACT vol 9 para 667 et seq.

451. Partial return of premiums. A modification of the ordinary principle of the law of contract exists in relation to insurance in this respect, that a partial failure of the consideration moving from the insurers may entitle the assured to a partial return of premium[1]. For example, where there is an innocent over-insurance[2], as in the case of a liability insurance where the premium is calculated on the number of persons employed in the relevant period, a pro rata return of premium may be provided for if a lower number of persons is, in fact, employed than was assumed as the basis of the calculation[3]. Similarly, if a premium is charged by the insurers for a fixed period, such as a year, any right they may have to terminate the contract before the expiration of that period, without any agreed excuse for doing so, will normally be exercisable only on the basis of making a pro rata refund of premium[4].

1 For the circumstances which may entitle the assured to a partial return of premium in connection with marine insurance see para 325 et seq ante. For the general rule as to partial failure of consideration see CONTRACT vol 9 para 670.
2 As to over-insurance by double insurance see paras 516–519 post.
3 As to the calculation of the premium in liability insurance see para 666 post.
4 In principle a pro rata refund can be claimed only if the policy contains some stipulation which leads to the policy being interpreted as divisible: see *Stevenson v Snow* (1761) 3 Burr 1237, and other marine cases discussed in para 328 note 2 ante. Normally it will be found that any condition in a policy giving any contractual right of termination is coupled with an undertaking to make a pro rata return of premium if the right is exercised.

452. Policy conditions as to return of premiums. Policies frequently contain express stipulations as to return of premiums. Such stipulations may be made on the basis of reduction of the risk insured[1] or on the basis of termination of the policy before the expiration of the contemplated period of insurance[2]. In motor insurance it is often provided that the insurance may be terminated on notice given either by the insurers[3] or by either party to the contract; and any such stipulation is usually coupled with a provision for a return to some extent of the premium paid. Any express stipulation on those lines is overriding, in the sense that the agreed terms of the stipulation are operative in preference to any result which might be deduced from the general law in the absence of express stipulation[4].

1 See *Parr's Bank v Albert Mines Syndicate* (1900) 5 Com Cas 116.
2 See *Sun Fire Office v Hart* (1889) 14 App Cas 98 at 100, PC.
3 *J H Moore & Co v Crowe* [1972] 2 Lloyd's Rep 563.
4 *Ionides v Harford* (1859) 29 LJEx 36. The general law does not allow for any return of premium merely because a portion only of the risk is run (*Loraine v Thomlinson* (1781) 2 Doug KB 585) unless the contract is divisible (*Stevenson v Snow* (1761) 3 Burr 1237). See further para 327 ante.

453. Effect of winding up of insurers. Where an insurance company to which the provisions of the Insurance Companies Act 1982 relating to the regulation of insurance companies[1] apply, goes into liquidation, the assured is entitled to prove for the value of the policy at the date of the liquidation as determined by the valuation regulations made under that Act[2]. In the case of the liquidation of any other insurance company a just estimate of the value of the policy must be made[3].

1 Ie the Insurance Companies Act 1982 Pt II (ss 15–71) (as amended): see para 803 et seq post.
2 Ie regulations made under ibid s 59 (as amended): see paras 467, 858 post.
3 *Re Northern Counties of England Fire Insurance Co* (1885) 1 TLR 629.

454. Effect of death of assured. In the case of certain types of insurance, such as property insurance, which are not inherently personal to the assured, if the assured dies, his insurable interest and his interest in the policy normally pass to his personal representatives[1]. However, where the whole policy is dependent on the continued existence of the assured, as in all types of liability insurance, it will inevitably terminate on his death[2]. In the absence of a stipulation in the policy covering that contingency, this gives no right to any return of premium if the risk has attached and there has not been a total failure of consideration[3].

1 As to the passing of the deceased's interest see para 463 text and note 1 post.
2 As to the termination of such insurances by the death of the assured see further para 463 text and note 2 post.
3 As to return of premium when the risk has attached see para 450 ante.

455. Bankruptcy of the assured. Apart from express stipulations to that effect, the bankruptcy, as opposed to the death[1], of any individual assured does not put an end to a policy of insurance[2]. If a policy by its terms terminates on bankruptcy, no question arises as to any return of premium if the risk has attached and there has not been a total failure of consideration, unless there is a provision to that effect[3].

1 As to the effect of the death of the assured see para 454 ante.
2 As to the effect on the policy of the bankruptcy of the assured see para 464 post.
3 As to return of premium when the risk has attached see para 450 ante.

456. Forfeiture of premium. Policies frequently contain conditions providing that on the occurrence of specific events any premium paid is to be forfeited. The most common conditions of this class deal with the situation where a policy is avoided by reason of some misstatement in the proposal[1] or some alteration of the risk[2]. Conditions of this kind are very near to penalties and accordingly are very strictly construed[3].

1 *Duckett v Williams* (1834) 2 Cr & M 348, approved in *Thomson v Weems* (1884) 9 App Cas 671, HL; *Howarth v Pioneer Life Assurance Co Ltd* (1912) 107 LT 155, DC. For terms as to misrepresentation see para 365 ante.

2 *Sparenborg v Edinburgh Life Assurance Co* [1912] 1 KB 195. As to alteration of the risk see paras 434–439 ante.

3 *Anderson v Fitzgerald* (1853) 4 HL Cas 484 at 507 per Lord St Leonards.

(8) DURATION OF THE POLICY

(i) Period of Insurance

457. Definite period required for insurance. Unless a perpetual insurance is plainly intended, the period for which any insurance is to run must be defined with certainty[1] but the length is entirely a matter for agreement between the parties. There is no limitation on the period for which a non-marine policy may run[2]. The period most commonly fixed is 12 months[3], but longer periods are not unusual[4], indeed the courts have had to deal with a single premium policy current for sixty-eight and a half years[5] and a perpetual insurance for a single premium has been known to be effected[6]. It is, of course, permissible to define the period by reference to the occurrence of a future event[7].

1 *Murfitt v Royal Insurance Co* (1922) 38 TLR 334 at 336 per McCardie J.

2 *M'Donnell v Carr* (1833) Hayes & Jo 256.

3 *Last v London Assurance Corpn* (1884) as reported in 12 QBD 389 at 394 per Day J.

4 *Sadlers' Co v Badcock* (1743) 2 Atk 554; *Sun Insurance Office v Clark* [1912] AC 443 at 451, HL, per Lord Loreburn; *Municipal Mutual Insurance v Pontefract Corpn* (1917) 116 LT 671.

5 *Brady v Irish Land Commission* [1921] 1 IR 56.

6 The war memorial in the House of Lords was insured under such an insurance.

7 In the normal life policy the period is defined as being the period up to death or the attainment of a certain age: see para 527 post.

458. Definition of period in policy. The policy itself frequently defines the period for which the insurance is to be current and, where it does so, normally the precise day, and sometimes the precise hour[1], at which it respectively begins and ends are specified[2]. Unless the policy expressly so provides, the day named as the day from which the insurance is to run is not included in the period for which it runs, the moment of commencement being then the earliest moment of the succeeding day[3]. If the commencement is governed by an event, the precise time will depend on the definition of the event and the interpretation of what constitutes its inception[4].

In the absence of any reference to a particular hour, a period of insurance ends at midnight at the close of the last day named[5]. Where an event is fixed as the termination of the policy, the interpretation of what constitutes the moment of happening of that event is the criterion; if the event never happens, the insurance may continue indefinitely[6].

The policy may contain an extension clause giving the assured an option to extend its duration[7].

1 As to the construction of references to a particular hour during the period of summer time see the Summer Time Act 1972 ss 2 (1), 3 (1); and TIME vol 45 paras 1117–1118.
2 See *Commercial Union Assurance plc v Sun Alliance Insurance Group plc* [1992] 1 Lloyd's Rep 475. For an example of such a provision see 20 Forms & Precedents (5th Edn) 29 at 32–33, Form 2 Schedule.
3 *South Staffordshire Tramways Co v Sickness and Accident Assurance Association* [1891] 1 QB 402, CA; *Sickness and Accident Assurance Association v General Accident Assurance Corpn* (1892) 19 R 977, Ct of Sess. See also *Isaacs v Royal Insurance Co* (1870) LR 5 Exch 296 at 300 per Kelly CB; and cf *Howard's Case* (1699) Holt KB 195.
4 *Dunn v Campbell* (1920) 4 Ll L Rep 36, CA, where an aviation policy was to commence 'from the time and date of the first flight', and it was held that it covered an accident which happened before the aircraft had actually left the ground. Whether a flight begins only when the pilot attempts to start the engine, as was suggested, may be doubtful.
5 *Isaacs v Royal Insurance Co* (1870) LR 5 Exch 296.
6 *General Accident Fire and Life Assurance Corpn v Robertson* [1909] AC 404 at 411, HL, per Lord Loreburn LC, where the insurance was to continue for 12 months after registration by the insurers of a coupon; they forgot to register and the insurance was limitless.
7 See eg *Touche Ross & Co v Baker* [1992] 2 Lloyd's Rep 207, HL, where the assured under a policy of professional indemnity insurance had the option, in the event of the insurers' refusing to renew, to extend the policy for 36 months after the date of termination in respect of acts committed before the date of termination.

459. Issue of policy as commencement. Even if a commencing date or hour is laid down in a policy, it is overridden by the rule that, unless otherwise provided, no policy is effective until it is issued, there being normally no acceptance of the proposal until the issue of the policy[1]. Therefore, if it is not issued until after the commencement of the period named it will not cover losses happening before its issue, even if it is antedated[2]. However, it is possible to frame a policy so as to manifest an intention, not merely to antedate it for the purpose of determining the commencing date from which the closing date is to be calculated, but also to make it retrospective as regards losses which have occurred since the proposal but before issue of the policy[3]. An intention that a policy is to be retrospective in this sense is plainly indicated when the policy is issued to replace a cover note[4].

1 As to the formation of a contract to insure see paras 382–384 ante.
2 *Allis-Chalmers Co v Maryland Fidelity and Deposit Co* (1916) 114 LT 433, HL.
3 *Bufe v Turner* (1815) 6 Taunt 338.
4 *Roberts v Security Co* [1897] 1 QB 111, CA. As to the right of the assured to enforce the cover note where its terms differ from those of the policy see para 386 ante.

460. Payment of premium as commencement. Whether the policy is issued before or after a date mentioned in it as the commencing date, there may none-theless be an express stipulation in it that the insurance is not to be operative until a stipulated event has occurred or a particular condition has been satisfied[1]. The event or condition most frequently made a condition precedent in this sense is payment of the premium[2].

1 *Salvin v James* (1805) 6 East 571 at 582 per Lord Ellenborough CJ; *Newcastle Fire Insurance Co v Macmorran & Co* (1815) 3 Dow 255, HL.
2 As to prepayment as a condition precedent see para 446 ante.

461. Termination of policy by payment. Even though a stipulated period may be named in the policy for the currency of its cover, the policy may none-theless terminate prior to the expiration of the named period. In the case of property insurance, once the stipulated peril occurs and the insurers have made a payment on the basis of a total loss, the insurers' liability is normally at an end[1]; and if the property is reinstated or replaced they are not on risk again unless a fresh contract relating to the property as reinstated or the replacing property is entered into between them, and the assured for a fresh consideration[2]. This does not apply to partial losses; thus if a house is insured against fire, partial damage caused by successive fires, that is when severally or cumulatively the fires do not produce a total loss, must be borne individually and successively by the insurers[3].

1 See eg *Brewster v Sewell* (1820) 3 B & Ald 296 at 299. Cf *North British and Mercantile Insurance Co v Stewart* (1871) 9 Macph 534, Ct of Sess, where a payment in full mistakenly made was held not to put an end to the policy, but entitled the insurer to repayment of the sum paid.
2 There is no direct insurance authority in England for this proposition, but an Australian decision (*Smith v Colonial Mutual Fire Insurance Co* (1880) 6 VLR 200) seems to assume its correctness; the conclusion seems to follow from the ordinary rule of contract law that a person is only required to do once what the contract requires of him (see eg *Edmundson v Longton Corpn* (1902) 19 TLR 15). As to the performance of contracts see generally CONTRACT vol 9 para 472 et seq. The policy may, of course, make express provision to the contrary effect, for example where there is a self-renewing or automatic reinstatement clause by which, after each payment of a total loss, the full sum insured is spent on reinstatement of the property and the assured, on payment usually of an additional premium, is covered in respect of the reinstated property.
3 As to valuation of partial loss see para 630 post.

462. Termination of policy by breach of a condition.

Policies frequently lay down express conditions as to matters which become operative after the commencement of the insurance. Such conditions are in the strict sense conditions subsequent of the policy; in the event of a breach, the insurers have the option to treat the policy as at an end[1].

1 As to conditions subsequent affecting the policy see para 407 ante.

463. Termination of policy by death of the assured.

Where an insurance is effected on property of the assured, or is in itself a form of investment so as to be property in itself, his death will not affect its duration in the absence of specific provision to that effect. Appropriate premiums having been paid, the value secured will normally pass as property to the personal representatives[1]. There are certain classes of insurance which are inherently personal to the assured in the sense that they insure him personally against specific losses or liabilities or the occurrence of specific contingencies, and it therefore follows that, once he personally has ceased by death to be capable of incurring such losses or liabilities or of being affected by such contingencies, the policy comes to an end[2]. This rule in principle applies where the assured is a company which ceases to exist by being dissolved[3].

1 *Mildmay v Folgham* (1797) 3 Ves 471; *Doe d Pitt v Laming* (1814) 4 Camp 73; *Durrant v Friend* (1852) 5 De G & Sm 343. See, however, *Smith v Clerical Medical Life and General Life Assurance Society* [1992] 1 FCR 262, CA, where the plaintiff, as cohabitee of the deceased, was entitled, rather than his personal representatives, to the proceeds of a joint life assurance which was charged to a mortgagee and designed to be used as the fund for repayment of the mortgage. As to the devolution of property on death see generally EXECUTORS vol 17 para 1071 et seq. As to persons entitled to payment in the case of a life policy see paras 556–560 post.
2 For the principle that where a contract is founded on personal considerations the death of a party puts an end to the relationship see CONTRACT vol 9 paras 338, 454; and EXECUTORS vol 17 para 1512. For the right of a personal representative of an assured to pay a premium on a life insurance if the assured dies after the due date for payment but before the expiry of the days of grace see para 478 post. A policy

insuring persons driving a car with the owner's consent may benefit a person driving after the owner's death: *Kelly v Cornhill Insurance Co Ltd* [1964] 1 All ER 321, [1964] 1 WLR 158, HL.

3 As to the dissolution of companies see COMPANIES.

464. Effect of bankruptcy of the assured. The adjudication of the assured as a bankrupt does not affect the currency of an insurance policy in the absence of an express condition in the policy entitling the insurers to terminate it in that event[1]. On the assured's bankruptcy his rights and interest under a policy normally vest in his trustee in bankruptcy[2]. It seems that if the risk insured against is a risk personal to the assured, as for example in the case of a personal accident policy, any right to make a claim under the policy may remain with the bankrupt[3].

1 For the principle that bankruptcy does not determine a contract see BANKRUPTCY AND INSOLVENCY vol 3(2) (Reissue) para 407.
2 See eg *Schondler v Wace* (1808) 1 Camp 487; *Marriage v Royal Exchange Assurance Co* (1849) 18 LJCh 216 (property insurance); *Manchester Fire Assurance Co v Wykes* (1875) 33 LT 142; *Leeming v Lady Murray* (1879) 13 ChD 123 (life assurance); *Re Carr and Sun Fire Insurance Co* (1897) 13 TLR 186, CA. As to the vesting of property in a trustee in bankruptcy see generally BANKRUPTCY AND INSOLVENCY vol 3(2) (Reissue) para 380 et seq. However, statutory provision is made by which, where the bankrupt is insured against liabilities to third parties and, either before or after the bankruptcy, any such liability is incurred, the rights of the bankrupt under the insurance in respect of the liability vest in the third party to whom the liability was incurred: see para 679 post.
3 For the principle that rights of action which are personal to a bankrupt and do not relate directly to his property remain with him see BANKRUPTCY AND INSOLVENCY vol 3(2) (Reissue) para 424.

465. Termination of policy by cancellation by the assured. Policies often contain a provision enabling the policy to be terminated by the assured on the giving of an appropriate notice of cancellation. It is usual in a continuous form of insurance, such as a life or endowment[1] policy, to find a provision enabling the assured, after the expiration of a stipulated period of notice, to surrender the policy and receive the surrender value, if any[2]. Other policies may contain a similar power, and in such a case there may be a provision for return of a proportionate part of the premium. If the power is exercised, the insurance comes to an end on the stipulated date, and any loss happening after the date of termination is not covered, even though the policy has not been formally cancelled or the appropriate surrender value paid[3].

An assured under an ordinary long term insurance policy has the right to cancel it if he does so within a specified time[4].

1 For an example of such a provision see 20 Forms & Precedents (5th Edn) 523 at 524, Form 298 cl 5.
2 As to surrender value see para 553 post.
3 *Ingram-Johnson v Century Insurance Co Ltd* 1909 SC 1032. As to return of the premium see paras 447–456 ante.
4 See the Insurance Companies Act 1982 s 76 (as amended): para 816 post.

466. Termination of policy by cancellation by the insurers. The express terms of a policy may give the insurers power to determine the insurance on giving a stipulated notice[1]. If such a power is exercisable at will, the insurers are not bound to give any reasons for exercising it[2]. However, the insurance will not in any case expire until after expiration of the notice and repayment of the appropriate portion of the premium, if that is provided in the condition[3].

1 As to termination of policy by cancellation by the assured see para 465 ante. For examples of terms providing for cancellation by the insurers see 20 Forms & Precedents (5th Edn) 83, Form 44. In

continuing forms of insurance such as life or endowment, it is usually inherent in the insurance that the insurers are bound to continue the insurance as long as the assured is prepared to go on paying the stipulated premium: see para 470 post.

2 *Sun Fire Office v Hart* (1889) 14 App Cas 98 at 104, PC.

3 *Bamberger v Commercial Credit Mutual Assurance Society* (1855) 15 CB 676 at 694 per Jervis CJ.

467. Termination of policy by dissolution of insurance company. Where the insurers are a company and go into liquidation the assured becomes entitled to claim in the liquidation for the value of the policy on the footing of a contingent claim[1]. The assured is not a secured creditor, even though he has brought an action on the policy and leave to defend has been granted conditionally on payment into court of the amount claimed[2]. Where an insurance company to which the provisions of the Insurance Companies Act 1982 relating to the regulation of insurance companies[3] apply goes into liquidation, the assured is entitled to prove for the value of the policy at the date of the liquidation as determined by the valuation regulations made under the Act[4].

1 See the Insolvency Act 1986 s 411, Sch 8 para 12; and COMPANIES vol 7(2) (Reissue) para 2038.

2 *Harrison v Mortgage Insurance Corpn* (1893) 10 TLR 141, DC.

3 Ie the Insurance Companies Act 1982 Pt II (ss 15–71) (as amended): see para 803 et seq post.

4 See ibid s 59 (as amended); and para 858 et seq post. As to valuation regulations see s 90; and paras 862–863 post. Under previous legislation it was held that, where the statutory provisions do not apply, the happening of a loss during the liquidation is admissible as evidence of the value of the policy and the assured may prove for the amount of his loss: see *Re Northern Counties of England Fire Insurance Co, Macfarlane's Claim* (1880) 17 ChD 337; limited by *Re Law Car and General Insurance Corpn* [1913] 2 Ch 103, CA, and *Re United Motor and General Insurance Co* (1925) 22 Ll L Rep 343. As to when the present statutory provisions apply see the Insurance Companies Act 1982 s 15 (as amended); and para 803 post.

468. Death of individual underwriter. If a policy of insurance is underwritten in whole or in part by an individual underwriter his death has no effect on the obligations that he has undertaken. The contract is not a personal contract dependent on the exercise of personal skill on his part[1], but merely a contract to pay a sum of money on a contingency, and accordingly his estate is liable to the same extent as the underwriter was in his lifetime[2]. At Lloyd's it is the normal practice on an underwriter's death for the other members of his syndicate to take over the share which he has underwritten.

1 For the principle that where a contract is founded on personal considerations the death of a party puts an end to the relationship see CONTRACT vol 9 paras 338, 454; and EXECUTORS vol 17 para 1512.

2 See *Warner Engineering Co Ltd v Brennan* (1913) 30 TLR 191, DC; *Re Worthington, ex p Pathé Frères* [1914] 2 KB 299, CA. As to termination of the contract by the death of the assured see para 463 ante.

(ii) Continuing Insurances

469. Basis of a continuing insurance. In certain classes of insurance, notably life[1] and endowment insurance[2], it is fundamental to the contract that the insurance is to be operative up to the date of its maturity on the happening of the specified event, for example the death of the assured. There may, no doubt, be an insurance with reference to a stipulated life where there is a specified period for the insurance and an obligation on the assured to renew if further insurance is required. Thus an insurance taken out to provide against the contingency of the life assured terminating prior to a specified date (there being presumably a specific interest in the continued existence of the life assured up to that date) is to be regarded rather as a contingency insurance than a strict life insurance, the contingency being that life terminates before the specified date[3]. Normally the date of death is not a fundamental consideration in a life policy; what is important is to secure that provision is made for meeting obligations which arise after death, whenever death occurs. It seems to be inherent in a policy of this type that, even though the insurance has been expressed in periodical language, the insurers are obliged to continue the policy for the stipulated period unless there is some condition entitling them to determine it at some earlier date[4].

1 As to life insurance see para 525 et seq post.
2 As to endowment insurance see para 563 et seq post.
3 As to contingency insurance, referred to as pecuniary loss insurance, see also para 765 et seq post.
4 As to the duty of insurers to accept premiums see para 470 post.

470. Insurers' duty to accept premiums. Where the consideration for life insurance is a premium payable periodically, with a provision that the policy is to be terminated on failure to pay any premium on the due date or within the days of grace[1], it seems the contract must properly be regarded as a continuing contract for the life of the assured subject to defeasance on non-payment of any premium[2], rather than as an insurance for a period with a periodic right of renewal[3]. In any case the insurers are bound to accept the payment of the periodic premiums, if proffered by the assured by the due date or within the days of grace[4], and to continue the insurance until the assured's death[5], unless there is some provision in the contract entitling them to terminate the insurance before that date[6]. If any premium is not paid by the due date or within the days of grace, the policy terminates with effect from the date when payment was due[7].

1 As to the days of grace see paras 477–478 post.
2 *Re Anchor Assurance Co* (1870) 5 Ch App 632 at 638 per Lord Hatherly LC; *Re Manchester and London Life Assurance and Loan Association* (1870) 5 Ch App 640 at 643 per Lord Hatherly LC; and see *Stuart v Freeman* [1903] 1 KB 47 at 55, CA, per Mathew LJ, where the policy was for at least a year, but was subject to defeasance on non-payment of any quarterly premium. It seems that an endowment policy is also normally a continuing insurance.
3 For instances where a policy was regarded as an annual policy see *Pritchard v Merchant's and Tradesman's Mutual Life Assurance Society* (1858) 3 CBNS 622 at 643 per Willes J, approved in *Stuart v Freeman* [1903] 1 KB 47 at 57, CA, per Collins MR; *Phoenix Life Assurance Co v Sheridan* (1860) 8 HL Cas 745 at 750 per Lord Chelmsford.
4 As to the right of the personal representatives of the assured to pay if the assured dies within the days of grace see para 478 post.
5 *Pritchard v Merchant's and Tradesman's Mutual Life Assurance Society* (1858) 3 CBNS 622 at 643 per Willes J, approved in *Stuart v Freeman* [1903] 1 KB 47 at 52, CA, per Collins MR; *Honour v Equitable Life Assurance Society of the United States* [1900] 1 Ch 852 at 855.
6 See eg *Simpson v Accidental Death Insurance Co* (1857) 2 CBNS 257, where it was provided that in every case when a new premium should become payable, the insurers should be at liberty to terminate the risk by refusing to accept the premium.
7 *Salvin v James* (1805) 6 East 571 at 582–583; *Acey v Fernie* (1840) 7 M & W 151; *Pritchard v Merchant's and Tradesman's Mutual Life Assurance Society* (1858) 3 CBNS 622; cf *McKenna v City Life Assurance Co* [1919] 2 KB 491 (power to revive policy by paying arrears of premium within 12 months from date on which last premium became due; premium became due for this purpose on specified date by which it was payable, not on last of the days of grace). If the policy money is paid in the belief that the policy has remained in effect, the money so paid can be recovered by the insurers as money paid by mistake: *Kelly v Solari* (1841) 9 M & W 54; see generally MISTAKE.

471. Effect of changes of circumstances. Where, in the case of a life insurance, the insurers are under a duty to accept premiums, the duty continues to apply even though the life assured may have become more precarious[1]. Indeed there is no obligation even to disclose to the insurers that such a change of circumstances has occurred[2]. In insurance of this kind the insurers' rights in relation to misrepresentation and non-disclosure[3] are governed by the state of affairs at the inception of the contract: if they can show that, at that stage, some material circumstance was misrepresented or not disclosed, they can repudiate even if successive premiums over years have been paid, unless, of course, they had waived their rights with full knowledge of the true facts[4]. If it is provided that a policy is to become void and the premiums are to be forfeited on breach of a condition subsequent, the provision for forfeiture applies to premiums paid after a breach has occurred but before discovery of the breach[5], unless there is a waiver of the breach[6].

1 As to the duty of the insurers to accept premiums see para 470 text and notes 4–5 ante.
2 As to the duty to make true representations before the contract is concluded see para 360 ante.
3 As to misrepresentation and non-disclosure see generally para 349 et seq ante.
4 Cf *Joel v Law Union and Grown Insurance Co* [1908] 2 KB 863, CA. As to waiver see paras 422–423 ante.
5 *Sparenborg v Edinburgh Life Assurance Co* [1912] 1 KB 195. As to conditions subsequent see paras 407–408 ante.
6 *Wing v Harvey* (1854) 5 De G M & G 265.

(iii) Renewal of Non-continuing Insurances

472. Basis of a non-continuing insurance. Many insurances are against the happening of a stipulated event, such as a fire, within a stipulated time, normally a year. Unless renewed[1], such a policy terminates on the expiration of the stipulated time, so that nothing is payable to the assured if the stipulated event does not occur within that time[2].

1 As to renewal by consent and conditions in policies as to renewal see para 476 post.
2 *Tarleton v Staniforth* (1794) 5 Term Rep 695; affd (1796) 1 Bos & P 471, Ex Ch; *Duffell v Wilson* (1808) 1 Camp 401; *Doe d Pitt v Shewin* (1811) 3 Camp 134; *Employers' Insurance Co of Great Britain v Benton* (1897) 24 R 908, Ct of Sess; *Argy Trading Development Co Ltd v Lapid Developments Ltd* [1977] 3 All ER 785, [1977] 1 WLR 444 (where the tenant was under a duty to insure against fire and the insurance policy was usually effected by the lessor, and the tenant unsuccessfully claimed against the lessor for failing to advise him that the policy had not been renewed). As to the recovery of money paid by insurers under a mistaken belief that a policy has remained in effect see para 470 note 7 ante.

473. Conditions for renewal by consent. It is inherent in any consensual renewal of an insurance policy that there has been no change in the identity of the parties: there must be the same assured[1] and insurers[2]. The subject matter must also be unaltered in its identity[3]. Subject to these conditions, the acceptance of a renewal premium without objection is normally sufficient to establish a new contract for the renewal of the old bargain[4] in the absence of any express stipulation in the policy covering renewal.

1 *Solvency Mutual Guarantee Co v Freeman* (1861) 7 H & N 17.
2 *Grover and Grover Ltd v Mathews* (1910) as reported in 79 LJKB 1025 at 1029.
3 *Law Guarantee Trust and Accident Society Ltd v Munich Re-insurance Co* (1915) 31 TLR 572.
4 *Solvency Mutual Guarantee Co v Froane* (1861) 7 H & N 5 at 15 per Bramwell B; *Solvency Mutual Guarantee Co v York* (1858) 3 H & N 588.

474. Conditions in policy as to renewal. Most non-continuing policies of insurance contain conditions providing for the renewal of the insurance, but these are normally framed on the basis of mutual consent being required[1]. A condition to this effect does not mean that the insurers are bound to accede to an application by the assured for renewal or to accept a premium tendered by the assured for renewal[2]. An offer of renewal may come from the insurers, such as where they send out a renewal notice, and then payment of the appropriate premium amounts to acceptance of their offer so as to create a binding contract and there is no room for refusing to take the premium. If the renewal notice stipulates a higher rate of premium and the assured refuses to pay it, the offer has lapsed and cannot be revived later by the assured tendering the increased premium[3]. In any case there is no obligation on the insurers to send out a renewal notice[4].

1 Cf *Jones Construction Co v Alliance Assurance Co Ltd* [1961] 1 Lloyd's Rep 121, CA (policy containing express self-extending provisions).
2 *Tarleton v Staniforth* (1794) 5 Term Rep 695; affd (1796) 1 Bos & P 471, Ex Ch, approved in *Simpson v Accidental Death Insurance Co* (1857) 2 CBNS 257; *Towle v National Guardian Assurance Society* (1861) 30 LJCh 900; *Webb and Hughes v Bracey* [1964] 1 Lloyd's Rep 465.
3 *Salvin v James* (1805) 6 East 571.
4 *Simpson v Accidental Death Insurance Co* (1857) 2 CBNS 257.

475. Conditions obliging the assured to renew. In some rather special forms of insurance it may be made an express condition of the policy that the assured, no less than the insurers, is obliged to renew[1]. In such a case there is no question of any bargaining or resiling at the renewal date; the assured is there and then legally liable to pay the premium which has then fallen due. The obligation to renew in such a case may extend over a fixed number of years[2] or it may attach indefinitely in the absence of notice to determine the insurance[3].

1 As to where the insurers may be required to renew the policy see para 474 ante.
2 *Municipal Mutual Insurance v Pontefract Corpn* (1917) 116 LT 671.
3 *Solvency Mutual Guarantee Co v York* (1858) 3 H & N 588; *Solvency Mutual Guarantee Co v Froane* (1861) 7 H & N 5; *Re Solvency Mutual Guarantee Society, Hawthorn's Case* (1862) 31 LJCh 625.

476. Renewal as a fresh contract. Where the policy is renewable only by mutual consent, each renewal constitutes a fresh contract[1]. Consequently, on each renewal the duty of disclosure reattaches[2], and the assured must disclose any facts which have become material during the preceding period of insurance[3]. In practice a fresh proposal is not used, but the original proposal is treated as if it were repeated on each renewal, and it is therefore the duty of the assured to correct any statements in the proposal which have since become inaccurate[4]. On the other hand, as on each renewal there is a fresh contract, it follows that a renewed policy is not liable to be avoided by a misstatement which would have avoided the original insurance if it has in fact become correct before the renewal[5].

1 *Stokell v Heywood* [1897] 1 Ch 459.
2 As to the duty to make disclosure see para 350 ante.
3 *Pim v Reid* (1843) 6 Man & G 1 at 25 per Cresswell J; *Law Accident Insurance Society v Boyd* 1942 SC 384. As to which facts are material see para 351 ante.
4 *Re Wilson and Scottish Insurance Corpn* [1920] 2 Ch 28; *Law Accident Insurance Society v Boyd* 1942 SC 384.
5 As to the effect of non-disclosure or misrepresentation see para 361 ante. The policy may contain an express stipulation to this effect.

(iv) Days of Grace

477. Allowance of days of grace. In the case of an insurance policy providing for avoidance in the event of non-payment of a periodical premium or of a premium for renewal, in the absence of any term in the policy relaxing the requirement, the policy lapses unless the premium is paid by the date prescribed by the policy[1]. However, it is the usual practice in many classes of insurance, either by express stipulation or by the custom of the particular insurance business, to allow a period of grace after the expiration of the period of insurance for a renewal premium to be paid. In the case of life assurance it is usually laid down by express provision in the policy, and the period is generally 30 days[2]. This operates as an offer to renew the insurance on payment of the premium within that period, and such an offer cannot be withdrawn without notice to the assured[3]. In other classes of insurance express stipulations as to days of grace are becoming more common[4].

1 See eg *Acey v Fernie* (1840) 7 M & W 151; *Phoenix Life Assurance Co v Sheridan* (1860) 8 HL Cas 745. As to the revival of policies see para 479 post.
2 See eg 20 Forms & Precedents (5th Edn) 521, Form 297 cl 3.
3 As to the duration of an offer see CONTRACT vol 9 para 238 et seq.
4 See eg *Webb and Hughes v Bracey* [1964] 1 Lloyd's Rep 465 (solicitors' indemnity policy). In the case of motor insurance the provisions of the Road Traffic Act 1988 s 143 (1) seem to exclude any period of grace, so far as compulsory insurance is concerned, unless it is added to the original period of insurance: see para 729 post.

478. Effect of tender of premium during days of grace. If, by a stipulation in the policy, days of grace are allowed for payment of a premium for the continuance or renewal of the insurance, and the event insured against occurs before payment of the premium but within the days of grace, the rights of the parties depend on the nature and terms of the policy.

In the case of a policy of non-continuing insurance which is renewable only by consent[1], such as a fire policy, if the policy stipulates that no insurance is to be effective until the premium is paid, the assured cannot recover for a loss suffered during the days of grace but before payment of the premium even if he subsequently tenders payment within the days of grace[2]. If, on the other hand, the policy incorporates a provision that the assured is to be covered during the days of grace[3], the insurers cannot after the loss and before the days of grace have expired refuse to renew the insurance, and the assured is entitled to recover in respect of the loss if he tenders the premium before the days of grace have expired[4]. However, even in this case he is not entitled to recover if, before the due date for renewal and before the loss has occurred[5], the insurers or the assured have indicated an intention not to renew the insurance[6].

In the case of a policy of continuing insurance, such as life assurance, if the insurance is expressed to be for a specific period but the premiums are payable at intervals during the period, the established principle is that payment within the days of grace is equivalent to payment on the due date. If the assured dies within the days of grace and payment is subsequently tendered by his personal representatives or the persons entitled to the benefit of the policy, the insurance is effective and the insurers are not entitled to refuse to accept the payments[7]. This principle may not be applicable if the policy contains a term giving the insurers the right to terminate the insurance and does not contain any provisions restricting the exercise of the right during the days of grace[8], or if it is clear that the policy contemplates payment of premiums only by the assured personally while alive[9].

In all classes of insurance, if a loss occurs during the period of grace the assured or his personal representatives cannot recover unless the premium is paid before the days of grace expire[10].

1 As to the renewal of policies of non-continuing insurance see paras 472–476 ante.
2 *Tarleton v Staniforth* (1794) 5 Term Rep 695; affd (1796) Bos & P 471, Ex Ch; *Simpson v Accidental Death Insurance Co* (1857) 2 CBNS 257 at 296–299. As to the effect of a renewal notice see para 477 text to note 3 ante.
3 A provision that any payment of premium made within the period of grace is to be treated as having been paid on the due date would, it is thought, have this effect.
4 *Salvin v James* (1805) 6 East 571 at 581–582; *Simpson v Accidental Death Insurance Co* (1857) 2 CBNS 257 at 296–299.
5 Possibly notice of an intention not to renew given by the insurers after the due date for renewal but before the loss occurred may be sufficient: *Salvin v James* (1805) 6 East 571 at 581–582.
6 *Salvin v James* (1805) 6 East 571.
7 See *Stuart v Freeman* [1903] 1 KB 47 at 55, CA, per Mathew LJ; *McKenna v City Life Assurance Co* [1919] 2 KB 491 at 497 per Scrutton LJ. For an example of a term expressly providing for the policy to remain effective in the event of the death of the assured during the days of grace, with the deduction of the unpaid premium from the sum insured, see 20 Forms & Precedents (5th Edn) 521, Form 297 cl 3.
8 See *Simpson v Accidental Death Insurance Co* (1857) 2 CBNS 257.
9 *Want v Blunt* (1810) 12 East 183; *Pritchard v Merchant's and Tradesman's Mutual Life Assurance Society* (1858) 3 CBNS 622 at 642–644 per Willes J. For criticism of the dicta in the latter case see *Stuart v Freeman* [1903] 1 KB 47 at 55, CA, per Mathew LJ. In *Pritchard v Merchant's and Tradesman's Mutual Life Assurance Society* supra, the effect of a payment during the days of grace was not directly in issue, since the payment was tendered after the expiration of the days of grace and the question was whether it was effective to revive the policy under a provision contained in the policy as to revival. As to the revival of policies see generally para 479 post.
10 See eg *Salvin v James* (1805) 6 East 571 at 582–583; and see para 477 ante. Under some forms of stipulation formerly in use the days of grace were added to the original period of insurance, so that a loss happening during the days of grace fell within the original policy: *Doe d Pitt v Shewin* (1811) 3 Camp 134; *McDonnell v Carr* (1833) Hayes & Jo 256.

(v) Revival of Policy

479. Revival of lapsed policy. An insurance policy may lapse for a number of reasons, but the most usual ones are the assured's failure to pay the consideration due from him in the form of premium on the due date or within the period of grace allowed[1], or his failure to renew the policy[2]. However, there may be a revival of a policy which has so lapsed, either by agreement between the parties or by conduct of the insurers such as to estop them from denying that there is a subsisting policy[3].

1 See eg *Webb and Hughes v Bracey* [1964] 1 Lloyd's Rep 465. As to days of grace see paras 477–478 ante.
2 See eg *Commercial Union Assurance plc v Sun Alliance Insurance Group plc* [1992] 1 Lloyd's Rep 475 (reinsurance).
3 *Handler v Mutual Reserve Fund Life Association* (1904) 90 LT 192 at 194, CA, per Mathew LJ; see also *Acey v Fernie* (1840) 7 M & W 151; *Edge v Duke* (1849) 18 LJCh 183; *Kirkpatrick v South Australian Insurance Co* (1886) 11 App Cas 177, PC. As to estoppel see para 424 ante.

480. Revival as new contract. A revival of an insurance policy[1] operates as a new contract, and the parties' rights and liabilities, according to ordinary principles, do not begin until the new contract has started to run. Even if the revived policy is antedated to the expiration of the period previously covered, this does not necessarily mean that a loss which has happened before the date of the revival has to be paid for by the insurers[2]; to achieve this there must be clear evidence of the parties having intended to make the revival retrospective so as to cover even interim losses[3]. There may therefore be a considerable difference in effect between a premium paid before the expiration of the period of grace, which the insurers may have to accept even if a loss has already occurred[4], and a premium paid after the expiration of that period, which will not commit the insurers to accepting a loss which has already occurred, unless it is clearly their intention, expressly or impliedly, to do so. However, they may make it plain that they are content to agree to a retrospective revival of the policy regardless of whether a loss has, in the meantime, occurred or not[5]. It is not unusual to find that fresh terms and conditions are laid down for the revival[6] and there is then no effective revival until the new terms and conditions are accepted and complied with[7].

1 As to the revival of a lapsed policy see para 479 ante.
2 *Doe d Pitt v Shewin* (1811) 3 Camp 134; *Pritchard v Merchant's and Tradesman's Mutual Life Assurance Society* (1858) 3 CBNS 622.
3 *Pritchard v Merchant's and Tradesman's Mutual Life Assurance Society* (1858) 3 CBNS 622 at 645 per Byles J.
4 As to the circumstances in which insurers are bound to accept a premium paid before the expiration of the days of grace see paras 477–478 ante.
5 It would not appear to be legitimate to infer such intent if the intervening loss was total so as to obliterate the entirety of the insurable interest: see para 2 ante.
6 Cf *Windus v Lord Tredegar* (1866) 15 LT 108, HL. The original policy may contain a condition prescribing the terms on which it may be revived: see 20 Forms & Precedents (5th Edn) 523 at 524, Form 298 cl 8.
7 *Handler v Mutual Reserve Fund Life Association* (1904) 90 LT 192, CA. However, if the original contract laid down the basis on which, in the event of revival being desired, the insurers would grant this, it is doubtful whether the insurers can add further terms and conditions if and when revival is desired.

(9) CLAIMS UNDER POLICIES

(i) Claims generally

481. Duties imposed on assured. Insurers are peculiarly exposed to unfounded or exaggerated claims, and it is therefore necessary for their protection that, whenever a claim under a policy is likely to arise, they should have the earliest opportunity of inquiring into the circumstances of the loss whilst the facts are recent and evidence can be more easily obtained[1]. Consequently, policies usually contain stipulations imposing on the assured certain specific duties, such as giving notice of his loss to the insurers[2], making a formal claim with particulars and proofs[3] and giving such information as may reasonably be required[4]. These duties are contractual, and both the performance and the consequences of non-performance are regulated by the terms of the particular stipulation employed[5].

1 *Worsley v Wood* (1796) 6 Term Rep 710 at 718 per Lord Kenyon CJ; *Mason v Harvey* (1853) 8 Exch 819 at 821 per Pollock CB; *Gamble v Accident Assurance Co* (1869) IR 4 CL 204 at 214 per Pigot CB; *Hiddle v National Fire and Marine Insurance Co of New Zealand* [1896] AC 372 at 376, PC.
2 As to notice of loss see paras 483–485 post.
3 As to particulars and proof of loss see paras 486–491 post.
4 *Welch v Royal Exchange Assurance* [1939] 1 KB 294, [1938] 4 All ER 289, CA. As to requiring further information see para 491 post.

5 *Ward v Law Property Assurance and Trust Society* (1856) 4 WR 605; *Wilkinson v Car and General Insurance Corpn Ltd* (1914) 110 LT 468; *Smellie v British General Insurance Co* [1918] WC & Ins Rep 233.

482. Failure to perform duties. Where a stipulation in an insurance policy fixes a time within which a duty is to be performed[1], the words used may not be sufficient to make a failure to perform the duty fatal to the enforcement of the claim[2]. As a general rule the stipulation is to be construed as a condition precedent to recovery[3], and no claim is maintainable unless the duty is performed in accordance with the terms of the stipulation[4]. The fact that the failure was due to circumstances beyond the claimant's control is immaterial[5]. A failure to perform the duty may be waived[6] and the assured may be relieved, either expressly or by the conduct of the insurers, from his obligation to perform it[7].

1 If no time is fixed, the duty may be performed at any time before the claim is statute-barred: *Harvey v Ocean Accident and Guarantee Corpn* [1905] 2 IR 1, CA.
2 *Stoneham v Ocean, Railway and General Accident Insurance Co* (1887) 19 QBD 237 at 239 per Mathew J. In this case, the remedy for breach is an action for damages: *Re Coleman's Depositories Ltd and Life and Health Assurance Association* [1907] 2 KB 798, CA. A stipulation which, after fixing a time for the performance of the duty, provided that no claim was to be payable until the duty was performed, has been held in Ireland not to be a condition precedent: *Weir v Northern Counties of England Insurance Co* (1879) 4 LR Ir 689 at 692; cf *Welch v Royal Exchange Assurance* [1939] 1 KB 294, [1938] 4 All ER 289, CA.
3 *Roper v Lendon* (1859) 1 E & E 825, approved in *Elliott v Royal Exchange Assurance Co* (1867) LR 2 Exch 237; *Welch v Royal Exchange Assurance* [1939] 1 KB 294, [1938] 4 All ER 289, CA. See also *Whyte v Western Assurance Co* (circa 1876) referred to in *Moore v Harris* (1876) 1 App Cas 318 at 330, PC, and reported in 22 LCJ 215, PC; and cf *Ralston v Bignold* (1853) 22 LTOS 106. As to conditions precedent to recovery see para 408 ante.
4 *Roper v Lendon* (1859) 1 E & E 825; *Cawley v National Employers' Accident and General Assurance Association Ltd* (1885) 1 TLR 255; *Re Williams and Lancashire and Yorkshire Accident Insurance Co's Arbitration* (1902) 51 WR 222.
5 *Oldman v Bewicke* (1786) 2 Hy Bl 577n; *Routledge v Burrell* (1789) 1 Hy Bl 254; *Worsley v Wood* (1796) 6 Term Rep 710; *Cassel v Lancashire and Yorkshire Accident Insurance Co Ltd* (1885) 1 TLR 495; *Gamble v Accident Assurance Co* (1869) IR 4 CL 204, followed in *Patton v Employers' Liability Assurance Corpn* (1887) 20 LR Ir 93. The position may be different where a condition is, from its very nature, impossible to perform: see para 419 ante.
6 See eg *Webster v General Accident Fire and Life Assurance Corpn Ltd* [1953] 1 QB 520, [1953] 1 All ER 663. As to waiver see generally para 422 ante.
7 *Toronto Rly Co v National British and Irish Millers Insurance Co Ltd* (1914) 111 LT 555, CA; *Yorkshire Insurance Co Ltd v Craine* [1922] 2 AC 541, PC; and see *Donnison v Employers' Accident and Live Stock Insurance Co* (1897) 24 R 681, Ct of Sess.

(ii) Notice of Loss

483. Time for giving notice of loss. The assured is usually required by a stipulation in the policy to give notice of any loss. The stipulation in ordinary use requires the notice to be given 'immediately' or 'forthwith'; the effect of this is that the notice must be given within a reasonable time[1]. However, if a stipulation excludes liability for a loss not notified within a specified time from its occurrence, as distinct from a specified time from its discovery, the assured cannot recover for losses which without his knowledge occurred earlier than the period covered by the time limit[2]. Unless required by the terms of the stipulation, the notice need not be in writing[3].

1 *Re Williams and Lancashire and Yorkshire Accident Insurance Co's Arbitration* (1902) 51 WR 222; *Verelst's Administratrix v Motor Union Insurance Co Ltd* [1925] 2 KB 137; *Webster v General Accident Fire and Life*

Assurance Corpn Ltd [1953] 1 QB 520, [1953] 1 All ER 663; *Forney v Dominion Insurance Co Ltd* [1969] 3 All ER 831, [1969] 1 WLR 928; *Farrell v Federated Employers' Insurance Association Ltd* [1970] 3 All ER 632, [1970] 1 WLR 1400, CA; *Monkfield v Vehicle and General Insurance Co Ltd* [1971] 1 Lloyd's Rep 139; *Hadenfayre Ltd v British National Insurance Society Ltd* [1984] 2 Lloyd's Rep 393.

3 *T H Adamson & Sons v Liverpool and London and Globe Insurance Co Ltd* [1953] 2 Lloyd's Rep 355.
4 *Re Solvency Mutual Guarantee Society, Hawthorn's Case* (1862) 31 LJCh 625.

484. Personal notice unnecessary. Except where the stipulation otherwise provides, the notice need not be given by the assured personally[1]; it may be given by an agent[2] or any person purporting to act on behalf of the assured[3]. Similarly, the notice need not be given to the insurers personally, but may be given to an agent having authority to receive it on their behalf; an apparent authority is sufficient[4]. Where the policy was negotiated through the insurers' agent the assured may be entitled to assume that the agent's authority to represent the insurers continues; if so, notice to the agent binds the insurers[5], even though, without the knowledge of the assured, the agent has ceased to represent them[6]. However, by the terms of the stipulation the notice may have to be given to the insurers at their head office or any branch office[7]. In this case, notice to the agent who negotiated the insurance is not in itself sufficient[8], but will be effective if it is transmitted by the agent to the office and received there within the proper time[9].

1 In the case of the death of the assured, notice need not be given by his personal representatives: *Patton v Employers' Liability Assurance Corpn* (1887) 20 LR Ir 93.
2 *Davies v National Fire and Marine Insurance Co of New Zealand* [1891] AC 485 at 489, PC.
3 *Patton v Employers' Liability Assurance Corpn* (1887) 20 LR Ir 93 at 100 per Murphy J.
4 As to apparent authority see generally AGENCY vol 1(1) (Reissue) paras 52–59, 134–136.
5 *Gale v Lewis* (1846) 9 QB 730.
6 *Marsden v City and County Assurance Co* (1865) LR 1 CP 232.
7 For an example of such a stipulation see *Brook v Trafalgar Insurance Co Ltd* (1946) 79 Ll L Rep 365, CA.
8 *Re Williams and Lancashire and Yorkshire Accident Insurance Co's Arbitration* (1902) 51 WR 222.
9 *Shiells v Scottish Assurance Corpn* (1889) 16 R 1014, Ct of Sess.

485. Notice of claims by third parties. Where the insurance is against liability to third parties, in addition to the notice of the accident giving rise to liability[1], the assured is usually required to give notice to the insurers of any claim made upon him by a third party[2].

1 There is no need to give notice of all accidents unless they are clearly ones to which the policy applies: *Smellie v British General Insurance Co* [1918] WC & Ins Rep 233. As to notice of loss see para 483 ante.
2 *Farrell v Federated Employers Insurance Association Ltd* [1970] 3 All ER 632, [1970] 1 WLR 1400, CA; *Berliner Motor Corpn v Sun Alliance and London Insurance Ltd* [1983] 1 Lloyd's Rep 320; *Pioneer Concrete (UK) Ltd v National Employers Mutual General Insurance Association* [1985] 2 All ER 395, [1985] 1 Lloyd's Rep 274; *Thorman v New Hampshire Insurance Co (UK) Ltd* [1988] 1 Lloyd's Rep 7, CA.

(iii) Particulars and Proofs of Loss

486. Form of claim. The assured is usually required by a stipulation in the policy to make a formal claim upon the insurers, containing full particulars of the loss, and to deliver proofs supporting it. In practice the claim is made on a printed form supplied by the insurers and indicating the nature of the particulars required[1]. The giving of proper particulars and proofs is usually made a condition precedent to any right of recovery for the loss[2].

1 As to fraudulent claims see paras 492–493 post.
2 *Welch v Royal Exchange Assurance* [1939] 1 KB 294, [1938] 4 All ER 289, CA; and see para 408 ante.

487. Particulars required. The particulars required necessarily vary according to the nature of the insurance. They must be furnished with such details as are reasonably practicable[1]. Whether the details given are sufficient or not is a question of degree, depending partly upon the materials available which, especially in the case of a fire, may be scanty, and partly upon the time within which they have to be furnished. In any case, the assured has not performed his duty adequately unless he has furnished the best particulars which the circumstances permit[2].

1 *Mason v Harvey* (1853) 8 Exch 819 at 820 per Pollock CB.
2 *Hiddle v National Fire and Marine Insurance Co of New Zealand* [1896] AC 372 at 375, PC.

488. Proofs of loss. Proofs of loss are necessarily documentary proofs; the loss may be proved by any satisfactory evidence[1]. In requiring proofs or in deciding as to their sufficiency, the insurers must not act capriciously; they must be satisfied with such proofs as would satisfy reasonable men[2]. In certain cases strict proof may be required[3]. The assured may be required to verify the claim by a statutory declaration[4]. The insurers may appoint a loss adjuster to assist them in dealing with the assured's claim[5].

1 A statement in the proposal as to the method of proving the loss does not preclude the assured from proving the loss by another method: *Winicofsky v Army and Navy General Assurance Association* (1919) 35 TLR 283.
2 *Braunstein v Accidental Death Insurance Co* (1861) 1 B & S 782. See also *Moore v Woolsey* (1854) 4 E & B 243; *London Guarantie Co v Fearnley* (1880) 5 App Cas 911, HL. Non-performance of a condition of this kind may be a defence available to the insurers, but it does not preclude the assured from taking proceedings to enforce the policy: *Braunstein v Accidental Death Insurance Co* supra; cf *Cowell v Yorkshire Provident Life Assurance Co* (1901) 17 TLR 452.
3 *Regina Fur Co Ltd v Bossom* [1958] 2 Lloyd's Rep 425, CA (strict proof required of burglary); *Atlantic Metal Co Ltd v Hepburn* [1960] 2 Lloyd's Rep 42 (strict proof required of loss of metal stored in warehouse).
4 *Watts v Simmons* (1924) 18 Ll L Rep 177. As to statutory declarations see the Statutory Declarations Act 1835 (as amended); and EVIDENCE vol 17 para 266.
5 As to the role of the loss adjuster see *Kitchen Design and Advice Ltd v Lea Valley Water Co* [1989] 2 Lloyd's Rep 221 at 222, where the judge set out the loss adjuster's affidavit as to his responsibilities.

489. Time prescribed. The stipulation as to particulars and proofs of loss[1] in practice prescribes a time within which the particulars and proofs are to be delivered. Generally, delivery within the prescribed time is made a condition precedent to the recovery by the assured[2], and the insurers are absolved from liability by a failure to deliver the particulars or proofs within the prescribed time[3]. The insurers may, however, extend the time; this does not set time at large, but the extension is exhausted as soon as the object for which it was granted, such as, for instance, the working out of figures, has been attained[4].

1 As to the particulars and proofs required see paras 487–488 ante.
2 As to conditions affecting recovery see para 408 ante.
3 *T H Adamson & Sons v Liverpool and London and Globe Insurance Co Ltd* [1953] 2 Lloyd's Rep 355.
4 *Re Carr and Sun Fire Insurance Co* (1897) 13 TLR 186, CA.

490. Amendment of claim. Notwithstanding the delivery of particulars and proofs[1], the assured is not precluded, in the absence of any stipulation to the contrary, from amending his claim and increasing the amount claimed in respect of his loss[2]. Unless precluded by the terms of payment, he may, even after the claim has been paid, make a fresh claim in respect of further loss[3].

1 As to delivery of particulars and proofs see para 489 ante.
2 *Mason v Harvey* (1853) 8 Exch 819 at 820 per Pollock CB; and see *Vance v Forster* (1841) IR Cir Rep 47.
3 *Prosser v Lancashire and Yorkshire Accident Insurance Co Ltd* (1890) 6 TLR 285, CA.

491. Requiring further information. Notwithstanding that proper particulars and proofs[1] have been given, the insurers may in the course of their investigations come upon other matters which they wish to examine, such as bank accounts, sales ledgers and business books generally. Therefore, there is often a condition that such further information as may reasonably be required must be given[2]. Failure to perform this condition, if it is a condition precedent to recovery, will relieve the insurers from liability for a loss, however genuine[3].

1 As to the particulars and proofs required see paras 487–488 ante.
2 *Welch v Royal Exchange Assurance* [1939] 1 KB 294, [1938] 4 All ER 289, CA.
3 *Welch v Royal Exchange Assurance* [1939] 1 KB 294, [1938] 4 All ER 289, CA; and see para 408 ante.

(iv) Fraudulent Claims

492. Effect of fraudulent claim. The making of a fraudulent claim is a breach of the duty of good faith[1] and consequently the assured forfeits all benefit under the policy, whether it contains an express condition to that effect or not[2]. Policies of non-marine insurance usually contain an express condition against fraudulent claims[3]. The insurers are not entitled to recover as damages the expenses incurred in investigating a fraudulent claim[4].

1 As to the duty of good faith see para 349 ante.
2 *Britton v Royal Insurance Co* (1866) 4 F & F 905 at 909 per Willes J. See also *Thurtell v Beaumont* (1824) 8 Moore CP 612; *Goulstone v Royal Insurance Co* (1858) 1 F & F 276 at 279 per Pollock CB.
3 Such a condition is used even in an ordinary Lloyd's policy: see *Lek v Mathews* (1927) 29 Ll L Rep 141; and, eg, 20 Forms & Precedents (5th Edn) 34 at 35, Form 3 Condition 2. Forgery of an insurance policy, an assignment of it or an indorsement on it, with intent to defraud, is an offence: see CRIMINAL LAW vol 11(1) (Reissue) paras 605–609.
4 *London Assurance v Clare* (1937) 57 Ll L Rep 254 at 270 per Goddard J.

493. What claims are fraudulent. A claim which is put forward when the assured knows that he has suffered no loss[1] or which is supported by false evidence[2] is clearly fraudulent. The position is not so clear where the claim is for an amount in excess of the real amount of the loss and the charge of fraud is based upon the suggestion that the claim has been fraudulently exaggerated. The mere fact that the assured has claimed an excessive amount is not necessarily proof of fraud; questions of amount are largely matters of opinion and the assured may have honestly over estimated the value of his property or the amount of his loss[3]. The excess may be so great as to justify the conclusion that, having regard to the circumstances, the exaggeration of the amount cannot be an honest estimate but must have been intended to deceive the insurers and to induce them to pay a larger sum than is properly payable; in this case the exaggeration is fraudulent[4]. An exaggeration of amount may also be classified as fraudulent where the assured puts forward deliberately exaggerated figures, not for the purpose of inducing the insurers to pay the full amount of the claim, but for the purpose of fixing a basis upon which to negotiate a settlement[5].

1 *Britton v Royal Insurance Co* (1866) 4 F & F 905; *Herman v Phoenix Assurance Co Ltd* (1928) 18 Ll L Rep 371, CA.
2 *R v Boynes* (1843) 1 Car & Kir 65; *Herbert v Poland* (1932) 44 Ll L Rep 139; *Shoot v Hill* (1936) 55 Ll L Rep 29.
3 *Chapman v Pole, P O* (1870) 22 LT 306; *London Assurance v Clare* (1937) 57 Ll L Rep 254.
4 *Worsley v Wood* (1796) 6 Term Rep 710 at 718; *Levy v Baillie* (1831) 7 Bing 349; *Goulstone v Royal Insurance Co* (1858) 1 F & F 276; *Chapman v Pole, P O* (1870) 22 LT 306; *Beauchamp v Faber* (1898) 3 Com Cas 308.
5 *Norton v Royal Fire and Life Assurance Co* (1885) Times, 12 August, CA, reversing (1885) 1 TLR 460.

(v) Unenforceable Claims

494. Public policy. Claims may be unenforceable on the ground that to enforce them would be against public policy. If, for example, items have been brought into the country without customs duty being paid on them and they are subsequently insured against loss, the insurers are under no liability to indemnify the assured if they are stolen[1]. However, where to avoid tax the value of items subsequently stolen is understated on an invoice but the insured party derives no benefit from the understatement, the understatement in no way contributes to the loss and the value of the items had been correctly stated to the insurer, it is not against public policy to enforce the insured party's claim[2]. Public policy precludes a claim in respect of an accident arising from threatening violence with a loaded shotgun[2].

1 *Geismar v Sun Alliance and London Insurance Ltd* [1978] QB 383, [1977] 3 All ER 570.
2 *Euro-Diam Ltd v Bathurst* [1990] 1 QB 1, [1988] 2 All ER 23, CA.
3 *Gray v Barr (Prudential Assurance Co Ltd, third party)* [1971] 2 QB 554, [1971] 2 All ER 949, CA.

(vi) Settlement of Disputed Claims

495. Arbitration clauses. A policy of non-marine insurance usually contains an arbitration clause providing for the reference to arbitration of disputes arising under the policy[1]. This constitutes a valid submission to arbitration which, even though not signed by him, is binding on the assured[2].

1 For a full treatment of arbitration law see ARBITRATION. Members of the Association of British Insurers and Lloyd's do not usually insist on the enforcement of an arbitration clause on a question of liability as distinct from mere quantum if the assured seeks to take the matter to court: see para 1 text and note 3 ante. As to ouster of the court's jurisdiction see ARBITRATION vol 2 (Reissue) paras 645–647.
2 *Baker v Yorkshire Fire and Life Assurance Co* [1892] 1 QB 144.

496. Scope of arbitration clauses. Arbitration clauses vary in their scope[1]. Such a clause may deal with questions of amount only[2] or may extend to the question of liability[3]. In the widest and most usual form of arbitration clause, all disputes which may arise under the policy are brought within its scope. Under this form the arbitrator is empowered to decide all questions of construction and all other legal questions[4] and, unless expressly excluded by the terms of the clause, the arbitrator's jurisdiction extends even to charges of fraud in relation to the claim[5]. However, the arbitrator is limited to disputes arising under the policy; he has no power to deal with disputes arising outside it. He cannot deal with a claim for a return of premium where the claim is founded upon the invalidity of the policy[6], nor enforce a compromise of a disputed claim[7]. Such an arbitration clause does not extend to a claim by the assured for a breach of a common law duty on the part of the insurers[8]. The clause does not extend to a dispute as to whether the contract was ever entered into at all or whether the apparent contract was vitiated at the outset by reason of illegality, duress or essential error[9]; in such a case the crucial question in issue is whether the contract out of which the jurisdiction of the arbitrator arises exists at all, and only the courts can normally determine such a question. Similarly, if the question in dispute is whether the contract is capable of being and has been validly avoided ab initio on the ground of fraud, misrepresentation or non-disclosure, the validity of the arbitration clause is prima facie as much in issue as any other clause[10], and the arbitrator can derive no jurisdiction from it unless it is so framed as to constitute a severable contract[11]. It is no doubt possible to frame an arbitration agreement so as to confer jurisdiction on an arbitrator to decide whether a particular contract ever came into effective existence at all[12], but this would, it is thought, have to be a separate agreement. An arbitration clause in the disputed contract could not normally constitute such an agreement, because a decision that there never was a contract would mean that the arbitration clause was never effectively agreed at all[13]. If insurers are claiming that by virtue of stipulations in the contract they are not obliged to meet a claim under it, and not that the apparent contract is a nullity, the arbitrator's jurisdiction is unimpaired[14]. An allegation that the contract has been repudiated, in the sense that fundamental terms have been broken, is within the scope of the clause[15]; so too is an allegation that further performance of the contract has been frustrated[16].

1 Arbitration clauses must be distinguished from clauses providing for a valuation: see *Sutherland v Sun Fire Office* (1852) 14 Dunl 775, Ct of Sess; *Toronto Rly Co v National British and Millers Insurance Co Ltd* (1914) 111 LT 555, CA; and cf *Hadwin v Lovelace* (1809) 1 Act 126, PC

2 *Braunstein v Accidental Death Insurance Co* (1861) 1 B & S 782; *Elliott v Royal Exchange Assurance Co* (1867) LR 2 Exch 237; *Viney v Bignold* (1887) 20 QBD 172; *Caledonian Insurance Co v Gilmour* [1893] AC 85, HL. Even though the arbitrator in such a case has no jurisdiction to determine any other questions (*O'Connor v Norwich Union Life and Fire Insurance Society* [1894] 2 IR 723), the insurers may be precluded from objecting to his jurisdiction if the other questions were raised before the insurers obtained a stay of proceedings (*South British Insurance Co v Gauci Bros & Co* [1928] AC 352, PC).

3 *Trainor v Phoenix Fire Assurance Co* (1891) 65 LT 825.

4 Eg questions of insurable interest: *Macaura v Northern Assurance Co* [1925] AC 619, HL. A stay will not be granted merely because important questions of law may arise: *Lock v Army, Navy and General Assurance Association Ltd* (1915) 31 TLR 297.

5 *Trainor v Phoenix Fire Assurance Co* (1891) 65 LT 825; *Stebbing v Liverpool and London and Globe Insurance Co Ltd* [1917] 2 KB 433, DC. This is, of course, subject to the court's discretion to refuse a stay when issues of fraud are involved: see the Arbitration Act 1950 s 24(2), (3); and ARBITRATION vol 2 (Reissue) para 616. In practice the court nearly always insists that questions of fraud should come before the court and refuses a stay on that ground.

6 *London, Edinburgh and Glasgow Assurance Co Ltd v Partington* (1903) 88 LT 732, DC.

7 *Taylor v Warden Insurance Co* (1933) 45 Ll L Rep 218, CA.

8 *Northern Publishing Office (Belfast) Ltd v Cornhill Insurance Co Ltd and Ellis* [1956] NI 157 (insurance against third party liability arising from use of lift; insurers periodically to examine and report on lift; claim by assured against insurers in respect of damage to lift alleged to arise from negligence in examination and in furnishing reports).

9 *Heyman v Darwins Ltd* [1942] AC 356 at 366, [1942] 1 All ER 337 at 343, HL, per Viscount Simon LC, and at 370–371 and 345 per Lord Macmillan; *Toller v Law Accident Insurance Co* [1936] 2 All ER 952, CA.

10 *Heyman v Darwins Ltd* [1942] AC 356 at 366, [1942] 1 All ER 337 at 343, HL, per Viscount Simon LC, at 370–371 and 345 per Lord Macmillan, and at 398 and 360 per Lord Porter.
11 *Heyman v Darwins Ltd* [1942] AC 356 at 378, [1942] 1 All ER 337 at 350, HL, per Lord Wright. Cf *MacKender v Feldia AG* [1967] 2 QB 590, [1966] 3 All ER 847, CA.
12 *Heyman v Darwins Ltd* [1942] AC 356 at 384, [1942] 1 All ER 337 at 353, HL, per Lord Wright, and at 392, 398 and 357, 360 per Lord Porter.
13 *Heyman v Darwins Ltd* [1942] AC 356 at 366, [1942] 1 All ER 337 at 343, HL, per Viscount Simon LC, and at 371 and 345 per Lord Macmillan.
14 *Woodall v Pearl Assurance Co Ltd* [1919] 1 KB 593, CA, approved in *Heyman v Darwins Ltd* [1942] AC 356 at 384, [1942] 1 All ER 337 at 353, HL, per Lord Wright; *Stebbing v Liverpool and London and Globe Insurance Co Ltd* [1917] 2 KB 433, DC; *Golding v London and Edinburgh Insurance Co* (1932) 43 Ll L Rep 487, CA; *Stevens & Sons v Timber and General Mutual Accident Insurance Association Ltd* (1933) 102 LJKB 337, CA; *Freshwater v Western Australian Assurance Co Ltd* [1933] 1 KB 515, CA. See also para 367 ante; and ARBITRATION vol 2 (Reissue) para 612.
15 *Heyman v Darwins Ltd* [1942] AC 356, [1942] 1 All ER 337, HL.
16 *Charles Mauritzen Ltd v Baltic Shipping Co* 1948 SC 646.

497. Effect of arbitration clause on right of action. An arbitration clause[1] does not necessarily preclude the assured from bringing an action to enforce his claim. The clause may be nothing more than a collateral term of the contract between the parties by which a tribunal for determining disputes is provided[2]. In this case there is a complete cause of action before the clause becomes operative[3], and if the assured brings an action the insurers are not relieved from liability, but they are entitled to apply under the clause to have the action stayed[4].

1 As to the scope of an arbitration clause see para 496 ante.
2 *Roper v Lendon* (1859) 1 E & E 825; *Stoneham v Ocean, Railway and General Accident Insurance Co* (1887) 19 QBD 237 at 240 per Mathew J.
3 *Gorman v Hand-in-Hand Insurance Co* (1877) IR 11 CL 224 at 234 per Palles CB.
4 Arbitration Act 1950 s 4(1); see generally ARBITRATION vol 2 (Reissue) para 616 et seq.

498. Arbitration as condition precedent. Arbitration clauses generally provide that an arbitrator's award is a condition precedent to actions on the policy, and that no action is to be brought except for the amount of the award[1]. The cause of action is then not complete until an arbitration has taken place in accordance with the clause and an award has been made by an arbitrator[2]. The insurers' only obligation is to pay the amount awarded[3] and unless the award is in his favour the assured can bring no action at all[4]. If in such a case the insurers apply for a stay[5], the court has no discretion and must grant it[6], except in cases falling within its power to refuse a stay where a dispute involves a question of fraud[7] or its power to order that an arbitration agreement is to cease to have effect as regards a particular dispute[8], and to order that any provision that an award is a condition precedent to the bringing of an action is to cease to have effect as regards the particular dispute[9].

1 Such a clause was considered by the House of Lords in the leading case of *Scott v Avery* (1856) 5 HL Cas 811, and is commonly known as a *Scott v Avery* clause: see para 408 text and note 5 ante; and ARBITRATION vol 2 (Reissue) para 646.
2 *Scott v Avery* (1856) 5 HL Cas 811; *Braunstein v Accidental Death Insurance Co* (1861) 1 B & S 782; *Eliott v Royal Exchange Assurance Co* (1867) LR 2 Exch 237; *Viney v Bignold* (1887) 20 QBD 172; *Scott v Mercantile Accident and Guarantee Insurance Co Ltd* (1892) 66 LT 811, CA; *Caledonian Insurance Co v Gilmour* [1893] AC 85, HL; *Spurrier v La Cloche* [1902] AC 446, PC; *Hodson v Railway Passengers' Assurance Co* [1904] 2 KB 833, CA; *King v Phoenix Assurance Co* [1910] 2 KB 666, CA; *Woodall v Pearl Assurance Co* [1919] 1 KB 593, CA; *Wales v Iron Trades Employers' Association Ltd* (1928) 21 BWCC 316, CA. This is the position even where the claim is made by a third party under the Third Parties (Rights against Insurers) Act 1930 s 1 (1) (*Freshwater v Western Australian Assurance Co Ltd* [1933] 1

KB 515, CA; *Stevens & Sons v Timber and General Mutual Accident Insurance Association* (1933) 148 LT 515, CA) except, perhaps, as regards cases falling within the Road Traffic Act 1988 ss 148(5), 151, 152 (see paras 742 et seq, 748 et seq post). As to the discretion of the court to order that a provision making an award a condition precedent is to cease to have effect where the claim is made by such a party see ARBITRATION vol 2 (Reissue) para 647.

3 *Scott v Mercantile Accident and Guarantee Insurance Co Ltd* (1892) 66 LT 811, CA; *Caledonian Insurance Co v Gilmour* [1893] AC 85, HL.
4 *Gaw v British Law Fire Insurance Co* [1908] 1 IR 245, CA.
5 They have no obligation to apply: *Viney v Bignold* (1887) 20 QBD 172.
6 *Kenworthy v Queen Insurance Co* (1892) 8 TLR 211; *Hodson v Railway Passengers' Assurance Co* [1904] 2 KB 833, CA. It is in fact to the assured's benefit that a stay should be granted; strictly, if it appears that no cause of action existed when the writ was issued, the proceedings ought to be struck out.
7 See the Arbitration Act 1950 s 24(2), (3); and ARBITRATION vol 2 (Reissue) para 636.
8 It seems that this power is exercisable only in the cases specified in ibid ss 24(2), 25(2)(b), ie where the dispute involves a question of fraud or an arbitrator is removed or his authority revoked: see ARBITRATION vol 2 (Reissue) para 636.
9 See ibid s 25(4); and ARBITRATION vol 2 (Reissue) para 647. Any application under s 24(2) for an order that an arbitration clause shall cease to have effect must be made to the Divisional Court: *Kruger Townwear Ltd v Northern Assurance Co Ltd* [1953] 2 All ER 727, [1953] 1 WLR 1049, DC.

499. Queen's Counsel clause. In the case of a policy indemnifying the assured against claims by third parties in respect of his professional negligence, it is sometimes provided that the insurers will pay any such claim which may arise without requiring the assured to dispute it, unless a Queen's Counsel advises that the claim can be successfully contested[1].

1 See *West Wake Price & Co v Ching* [1956] 3 All ER 821 at 825–828, [1957] 1 WLR 45 at 49–54. For an analysis of the nature and effect of a Queen's Counsel clause see paras 695–696 post.

(vii) Payment of Claims

500. Mode of payment of claims. Claims must generally[1] be paid in cash[2]. If a negotiable instrument taken in payment is dishonoured, in general the assured may sue the insurers either upon the instrument or upon the original consideration[3]. Where an assessor or other agent negotiates a settlement with the insurers on behalf of the assured, it is improper for the insurers to make any payment to the assessor by way of fees, costs or commission without informing the assured[4]. Any such payment made without the assured's knowledge is a bribe entitling the assured to have the settlement set aside[5]. The insurers cannot rely on the assessor's word that his principal is aware of the payment[6].

1 For the circumstances in which insurers may discharge their obligation by reinstating property see paras 632–639 post.
2 See CONTRACT vol 9 para 500 text to note 6. As to the position where the policy provides for payment in foreign currency see para 555 post. For the circumstances in which insurance money is a trade receipt for income tax purposes see INCOME TAXATION.
3 As to payment by negotiable instrument see CONTRACT vol 9 paras 482–486.
4 *Taylor v Walker* [1958] 1 Lloyd's Rep 490.
5 *Taylor v Walker* [1958] 1 Lloyd's Rep 490 at 509–513.
6 *Taylor v Walker* [1958] 1 Lloyd's Rep 490 at 513.

501. Payment must be to proper person. Payment of a claim must be made to the person entitled, that is to say to the assured[1], his personal representative[2], assignee[3] or trustee in bankruptcy[4], as the case may be. If a garnishee order is made against the insurers, payment must be made to the judgment creditor[5].

1 In the case of a joint policy, the receipt of any of the policyholders has been said to be sufficient: *Penniall v Harborne* (1848) 11 QB 368 at 376 per Lord Dennan CJ.
2 If a deceased assured was a trustee, his personal representative must account to the beneficiary for the money received: *Mildmay v Folghan* (1797) 3 Ves 471. Under some forms of personal accident insurance the insurers are empowered to exercise their discretion as to the person to whom payment is to be made: *Law v George Newnes Ltd* (1894) 21 R 1027, Ct of Sess; *Hunter v Hunter* (1904) 7 F 136, Ct of Sess; see further para 588 post. As to the persons entitled to payment in the case of life insurance see generally paras 556–560 post. As to powers of nomination conferred on members of registered friendly societies and powers to make payments on the death of a member of such a society see FRIENDLY SOCIETIES. As to the effect of a provision in the rules of an unregistered friendly society for payment of death benefit to relatives of a member see FRIENDLY SOCIETIES. As to discharge clauses permitting payment to persons other than personal representatives in the case of industrial assurance see INDUSTRIAL ASSURANCE. As to the persons entitled to give a good discharge for the policy money in the case of policies effected in favour of the assured's wife, husband or children under the Married Women's Property Act 1882 s 11 see para 558 post; and HUSBAND AND WIFE vol 22 para 980.
3 *Ottley v Gray* (1847) 16 LJCh 512; *Desborough v Harris* (1855) 5 De G M & G 439; cf *Stokell v Heywood* [1897] 1 Ch 459.
4 *Logan v Hall* (1847) 4 CB 598 at 613 per Maule J; *Hood's Trustees v Southern Union General Insurance Co of Australasia Ltd* [1928] Ch 793, CA. As to the effect of the Third Parties (Rights against Insurers) Act 1930 see para 681 post.
5 *Randall v Lithgow* (1884) 12 QBD 525, DC (where there was in fact no ascertained and attachable debt due from the insurers to the assured at the date of the garnishee order, but the insurers allowed the order to be made against them by default); cf *Israelson v Dawson* [1933] 1 KB 301, CA (liability of insurers under motor insurance policy to indemnify assured against claims by third parties held not to be a debt attachable by a third party who had recovered judgment against the assured). As to the duty of insurers to satisfy judgments obtained by third parties see para 749 post. As to garnishee proceedings generally see EXECUTION vol 17 para 507 et seq.

502. Payment in the case of conflicting claims. The insurers are entitled on payment of a claim[1] to receive a legal discharge from their liability under the policy[2]. In the case of life policies, where the right to the policy money is in doubt and conflicting claims are made, the insurers are entitled to discharge themselves from further liability by paying the money into court[3]. In other cases the insurers have no direct right to discharge their liability by making a payment into court[4]. Their only remedy is to interplead[5].

If they obtain an interpleader order, it will normally be a term of the order that the policy money is paid into court with a provision that on payment into court the insurers are to have a complete discharge[6].

1 As to the mode of payment of claims see para 500 ante; as to payment being made to the person entitled see para 501 ante.
2 *Re Haycock's Policy* (1876) 1 ChD 611.
3 Life Assurance Companies (Payment into Court) Act 1896 s 3 (as amended): see paras 561–562 post.
4 Insurers are debtors, not trustees, and therefore they cannot pay into court under the Trustee Act 1925 s 63: *Matthew v Northern Assurance Co* (1878) 9 ChD 80; and see TRUSTS.
5 *Paris v Gilham* (1813) Coop G 56; *Prudential Assurance Co v Thomas* (1867) 3 Ch App 74; cf *Sun Insurance Office v Galinsky* [1914] 2 KB 545, CA.
6 *English and Scottish Mercantile Investment Co v Brunton* [1892] 2 QB 700, CA. As to interpleader generally see INTERPLEADER.

503. Interest. The assured is not entitled to interest as a matter of course[1]. However, in proceedings for the recovery of the policy money the court may, if it thinks fit, order that there be included in the sum for which judgment is given interest at such rate as it thinks fit on the whole or part of the debt for the whole or part of the period between the date when the cause of action arose and the date of the judgment[2]. The court must exercise this power in certain circumstances in the case of damages in respect of personal injuries[3]. Interest will be awarded only if the delay in paying the policy money has been caused by the fault of the insurers[4]. If the insurers have reasonably required an opportunity of deciding whether to meet a claim, it seems that interest will be awarded only from the date by which they have enjoyed such an opportunity[5]. If, in the case of a life insurance policy, the insurers pay the money into court, interest will be awarded only up to the date of payment into court[6].

1 *Higgins v Sargent* (1823) 2 B & C 348; *Webster v British Empire Mutual Life Assurance Co* (1880) 15 ChD 169, CA.
2 Supreme Court Act 1981 s 35A (1) (added by the Administration of Justice Act 1982 s 15, Sch 1 Pt I); see further MONEY. As to the power of an arbitrator to award interest see ARBITRATION vol 2 (Reissue) para 687. The statutory power to award interest does not apply in winding up proceedings so as to enable interest to be awarded to unsecured creditors of a solvent company: *Re Fine Industrial Commodities Ltd* [1956] Ch 256, [1955] 3 All ER 707. As to the proof for interest in the winding up of a company see further COMPANIES vol 7(2) (Reissue) para 1791. As to provisions by which a judgment debt carries interest see the Judgments Act 1838 s 17 (amended by the Civil Procedure Acts Repeal Act 1879 s 2, Schedule Pt I; the Statute Law Revision Act 1888; and the Judgment Debts (Rate of Interest) Order 1985, SI 1985/437); and JUDGMENTS vol 26 para 553. An award carries interest like a judgment, unless the award otherwise directs: Arbitration Act 1950 s 20; and see ARBITRATION vol 2 (Reissue) para 687.
3 Law Reform (Miscellaneous Provisions) Act 1934 s 3 (1A) (added by the Administration of Justice Act 1969 s 22); Supreme Court Act 1981 s 35A (as added: see note 2 supra); County Courts Act 1984 s 69 (amended by the Courts and Legal Services Act 1990 s 125(3), Sch 18 para 46).
4 *Webster v British Empire Mutual Life Assurance Co* (1880) 15 ChD 169, CA, where the claimant failed to clothe himself with a legal title to the policy money and interest was held not to be payable.
5 *Mackie v European Assurance Society* (1869) 21 LT 102 (date of repudiation); *J Glicksten & Son Ltd v State Assurance Co* (1922) 10 Ll L Rep 604 (date of writ); *Burts and Harvey Ltd and Alchemy Ltd v Vulcan Boiler and General Insurance Co Ltd* [1966] 1 Lloyd's Rep 354 (date on which insurers first called on to pay); *Forney v Dominion Insurance Co Ltd* [1969] 3 All ER 831, [1969] 1 WLR 928 (date on which solicitor insured under professional indemnity policy had paid damages to the client).
6 *Re Rosier's Trusts* (1877) 37 LT 426; *Re Waterhouse's Policy* [1937] Ch 415, [1937] 2 All ER 91 (interest given at 4%); cf *French v Royal Exchange Assurance Co* (1857) 6 I Ch R 523 (conflicting claims; agreement that insurers should not bring money into court; no interest payable).

504. Ex gratia payments. To entitle the assured to receive payment under a policy, the insurers must be legally liable to make it; but it is the practice of insurers, in proper cases, to make ex gratia payments in respect of losses which are not strictly covered by the policy[1]. Ex gratia payments are made in the ordinary course of business and are therefore not ultra vires the insurers[2]. The insurers are not precluded from disputing their legal liability under a policy by the fact that they have previously made ex gratia payments under similar policies in similar circumstances[3].

1 It has been held that a trustee in bankruptcy cannot claim an ex gratia payment made to the assured after his bankruptcy (*Wills v Wells* (1818) 8 Taunt 264), but the correctness of this decision may be doubted at any rate as a general proposition; an ordinary trustee receiving an ex gratia payment must account for it to the beneficiary (*Rayner v Preston* (1881) 18 ChD 1 at 15, CA, per James LJ).
2 *Taunton v Royal Insurance Co* (1864) 2 Hem & M 135. Payment under an ultra vires policy cannot, however, be justified as an ex gratia payment: *Evanson v Crooks* (1911) 28 TLR 123 at 124 per Hamilton J.
3 *London and Manchester Plate Glass Co Ltd v Heath* [1913] 3 KB 411, CA.

(10) SUBROGATION

(i) Subrogation generally

505. Inherent right in all contracts of indemnity. The doctrine of subrogation[1] applies to all contracts of non-marine insurance which are contracts of indemnity, such as fire insurance[2], motor insurance[3] and contingency insurance covering non-payment of money[4]. It applies whether the loss is total or partial, and is a corollary of the principle of indemnity. By requiring any means of diminishing or extinguishing a loss to be taken into account, it prevents the assured from recovering more than a full indemnity[5]. The doctrine of subrogation does not apply to contracts of life insurance[6] and personal accident insurance[7].

1 As to subrogation generally see paras 314–318 ante. As to the statutory subrogation of third parties to the rights of the assured against his insurers see paras 677–684 post.
2 *Castellain v Preston* (1883) 11 QBD 380, CA. See paras 591–643 post.
3 *Horse, Carriage and General Insurance Co Ltd v Petch* (1916) 33 TLR 131; *Page v Scottish Insurance Corpn* (1929) 140 LT 571, CA. See paras 706–764 post.
4 *Meacock v Bryant & Co* [1942] 2 All ER 661. See paras 765–789 post.
5 *Castellain v Preston* (1883) 11 QBD 380 at 387–388, CA, per Brett LJ.
6 *Dalby v India and London Life Assurance Co* (1854) 15 CB 365; *Law v London Indisputable Life Policy Co* (1855) 1 K & J 223. See paras 525–566 post.
7 There is no direct authority as regards personal accident insurance; the absence of any right of subrogation seems, however, to follow from the principle that personal accident insurance is not a contract of indemnity: *Theobald v Railway Passengers Assurance Co* (1854) 10 Exch 45 at 53 per Alderson B; *Bradburn v Great Western Rly Co* (1874) LR 10 Exch 1 at 2 per Bramwell B.

506. Nature of the right. In the strict sense of the term, subrogation expresses the right of the insurers to be placed in the position of the assured so as to be entitled to the advantage of all the rights and remedies which the assured possesses against third parties in respect of the subject matter[1]. The precise nature of the third party's liability to the assured is immaterial; subrogation applies even to a statutory liability[2]. If the third parties are insured, the ultimate liability for the loss falls on their insurers[3]. The right does not arise until the insurers have admitted their liability to the assured[4], and have paid him the amount of the loss[5].

1 *Castellain v Preston* (1883) 11 QBD 380 at 388, CA, per Brett LJ, and at 404 per Bowen LJ; see also *Darrell v Tibbitts* (1880) 5 QBD 560 at 563, CA, per Brett LJ; *Meacock v Bryant & Co* [1942] 2 All ER 661 (insurance against non-receipt of money within a given time; claim paid under policy; money received after time expired; right of insurers to be subrogated); *Re Miller, Gibb & Co Ltd* [1957] 2 All ER 266, [1957] 1 WLR 703 (right of Board of Trade to subrogation in respect of payment under policy insuring exporters against loss from inability of foreign buyers to transfer currency; see further para 777 post).
2 *Ellerbeck Collieries Ltd v Cornhill Insurance Co Ltd* [1932] 1 KB 401 at 411, CA, per Scrutton LJ. Where a person who has sustained loss by riot has received, by way of insurance or otherwise, any sum to recoup him, in whole or in part, for the loss, the amount of the sum so received is deducted from the statutory compensation otherwise payable to him, and the person who has paid the sum is entitled to statutory compensation to the extent of the sum so paid; any policy of insurance given by the person who paid the sum continues in force as if he had made no payment: Riot (Damages) Act 1886 s 2(2). Where the recoupment was otherwise than by payment of a sum, the foregoing provisions apply as if the value of the recoupment were a sum paid: s 2(2); and see *Rance v Hastings Corpn* (1913) 136 LT Jo 117 (compensation payable to persons who had indemnified hotel keeper in whose hotel they had taken refuge from mob; a county court decision). As to statutory compensation in case of riot see POLICE vol 36 paras 241–245.
3 *North British and Mercantile Insurance Co v London, Liverpool and Globe Insurance Co* (1877) 5 ChD 569, CA.

4 *Midland Insurance Co v Smith* (1881) 6 QBD 561 at 564 per Watkin Williams J; *Page v Scottish Insurance Corpn Ltd* (1929) 140 LT 571, CA.

5 *Castellain v Preston* (1883) 11 QBD 380 at 389, CA, per Brett LJ; *Page v Scottish Insurance Corpn Ltd* (1929) 140 LT 571 at 575, CA, per Scrutton LJ; see also *Mason v Sainsbury* (1782) 3 Doug KB 61; *Quebec Fire Insurance Co v St Louis* (1851) 7 Moo PCC 286 at 316; *Finlay v Mexican Investment Corpn* [1897] 1 QB 517; *Scottish Union and National Insurance Co v Davis* [1970] 1 Lloyd's Rep 1, CA.

507. Rights in tort. The most obvious case of subrogation arises in tort, where the loss is attributable to some wrongful act or default of a third party. There is subrogation under a fire policy where the property insured is burned by the negligence[1] or wilful act[2] of a third party; under a motor policy there is subrogation if the insured vehicle is damaged by the third party's negligence[3], or if a third party liability has been incurred owing to negligence in the driving of the vehicle by an employee of the insured[4]. Similarly, the insurers under a fidelity policy may claim reimbursement from a dishonest employee[5]; and the insurers under a burglary policy may claim from the burglar[6].

1 *Groom v Great Western Rly Co* (1892) 8 TLR 253; *Ross Southward Tire Ltd v Pyrotech Products Ltd* (1975) 57 DLR (3d) 248 (Can SC) (where there was no right of subrogation because the tenant, who had been negligent, was responsible for the payment of the premium and the risk of loss passed to the landlord); cf *King v Victoria Insurance Co* [1896] AC 250 at 256, PC.

2 See *Midland Insurance Co v Smith* (1881) 6 QBD 561, where the wife of the assured set fire to the insured property.

3 *Horse, Carriage and General Insurance Co Ltd v Petch* (1916) 33 TLR 131. Motor insurers usually have a 'knock-for-knock' agreement under which there is no subrogation, the damage to each vehicle being borne by its owner's insurers: see eg *Morley v Moore* [1936] 2 KB 359, [1936] 2 All ER 79, CA; *Bourne v Stanbridge* [1965] 1 All ER 241, [1965] 1 WLR 189, CA; *Hobbs v Marlowe* [1978] AC 16, [1977] 2 All ER 241, HL. As to knock-for-knock agreements see paras 514 text and note 4 and 726 post.

4 *Lister v Romford Ice and Cold Storage Co Ltd* [1957] AC 555, [1957] 1 All ER 125, HL.

5 *London Guarantie Co v Fearnley* (1880) 5 App Cas 911 at 916, HL, per Lord Blackburn.

6 *Symons v Mulkern* (1882) 46 LT 763; cf *Employers' Liability Assurance Corpn v Skipper and East* (1887) 4 TLR 55.

508. Rights in contract. The doctrine of subrogation is not confined to cases of tort; the liability of the third party may arise under a contract. This is clearly the case where the contract imposes on the third party responsibility for the safety of the property. The insurers of a bailor or of a landlord may enforce their assured's rights and remedies against the bailee[1] or tenant[2]; if a debt is guaranteed, the insurers of the debt may enforce the guarantee[3]. However, it is not necessary that the contract should directly impose responsibility for the safety of the property; it is sufficient if the contract relates to the property insured, and will, if duly performed, place the assured in the same position as if the loss had not happened[4]. A possible exception to the rule that the insurers are entitled to have the contract performed exists in the case of a contract for the sale of real property, where the property has been destroyed between the date of the signing of the contract and the date of completion of the sale. In such a case, if the vendor's insurers indemnify him in respect of the destruction of the property and the circumstances are not such that the vendor holds the insurance money for the purchaser's benefit on completion[5], the insurers are entitled, if the sale is completed, to recover from the vendor out of the purchase price a sum equal to the insurance money which they have paid[6]; but if the purchaser fails to complete, it is doubtful whether the insurers can enforce specific performance of the contract[7]. The insurers of a mortgagee are entitled to enforce his rights under the mortgage against the mortgagor[8], and the insurers of a landlord may claim the benefit of a tenant's covenant to insure[9].

1 *North British and Mercantile Insurance Co v London, Liverpool and Globe Insurance Co* (1877) 5 ChD 569, CA.
2 *Darrell v Tibbitts* (1880) 5 QBD 560, CA; cf *West of England Fire Insurance Co v Isaacs* [1897] 1 QB 226, CA.
3 *Parr's Bank v Albert Mines Syndicate* (1900) 5 Com Cas 116.
4 *Castellain v Preston* (1883) 11 QBD 380 at 390, CA, per Brett LJ.
5 For statutory provisions by which, provided that certain conditions are fulfilled, the vendor holds the insurance money for the purchaser's benefit on completion and is under a duty to pay it over to him, see para 625 post. It seems that, in a case where these provisions apply, the insurers will have no right to have repayment of the insurance money out of the purchase price, since the vendor has not had the benefit of the money.
6 *Castellain v Preston* (1883) 11 QBD 380, CA; see also *Phoenix Assurance Co v Spooner* [1905] 2 KB 753 (compulsory purchase; assured agreed with acquiring authority to accept compensation reduced by amount of insurance money; insurers entitled to recover full amount of insurance money from assured).
7 *Castellain v Preston* (1883) 11 QBD 380 at 390, CA, per Brett LJ, and at 405 per Bowen LJ, who suggested that the insurers, even if unable to enforce specific performance, might be able to enforce an unpaid vendor's lien.
8 *North British and Mercantile Insurance Co v London, Liverpool and Globe Insurance Co* (1877) 5 ChD 569 at 583, CA, per Mellish LJ. There is no subrogation if the mortgagee intended to insure the mortgagor's interest as well as his own: *Nichols & Co v Scottish Union and National Insurance Co* (1885) 2 TLR 190; also reported in 14 R 1094, Ct of Sess.
9 *Enlayde Ltd v Roberts* [1917] 1 Ch 109.

509. Right to be exercised in name of assured. In the absence of a formal assignment of the right of action[1], the insurers cannot sue the third party in their own names[2]; they must bring the action in the name of the assured[3]. On receiving a proper indemnity against costs[4], it is the duty of the assured to permit his name to be used in such action[5].

1 For examples of such assignments see *Employers' Liability Assurance Corpn v Skipper and East* (1887) 4 TLR 55; *King v Victoria Insurance Co* [1896] AC 250, PC. A right of action arising under a contract or in tort is a legal chose in action: see CHOSES IN ACTION vol 6 (Reissue) paras 6, 8.
2 *London Assurance Co v Sainsbury* (1783) 3 Doug KB 245. For the principle that the assignee of a legal chose in action can sue in his own name only if there has been a legal assignment see CHOSES IN ACTION vol 6 (Reissue) paras 22, 69; and CONTRACT vol 9 paras 337–338. The insurers cannot prove in the bankruptcy of the third party in their own names: *Re Blackburne, ex p Strouts* (1892) 9 Morr 249.
3 *Mason v Sainsbury* (1782) 3 Doug KB 61; *Clark v Blything Inhabitants* (1823) 2 B & C 254. Sometimes there is an express term in the policy giving them this right: see eg *Lister v Romford Ice and Cold Storage Ltd* [1957] AC 555, [1957] 1 All ER 125, HL (motor insurance); *Kitchen Design and Advice Ltd v Lea Valley Water Co* [1989] 2 Lloyd's Rep 221 (damage and loss of profits insurance).
4 See *King v Victoria Insurance Co* [1896] AC 250, PC.
5 *Dane v Mortgage Insurance Corpn* [1894] 1 QB 54 at 61, CA, per Lord Esher MR. The doctrine of subrogation should not be used to compel employers to lend their name to an action making their employee personally liable for his negligence where the risk is covered by insurance: *Morris v Ford Motor Co Ltd* [1973] QB 792, [1973] 2 All ER 1084, CA.

510. Defences in subrogation action. In a subrogation action the third party may raise any defence which would have been available if the assured had himself brought the action[1], such as a release or compromise[2]. It is not a defence that the action is a subrogation action[3]; the third party cannot object that the assured has suffered no loss because he has been indemnified by the insurers[4], or that the payment was an ex gratia payment[5].

1 *London Assurance Co v Sainsbury* (1783) 3 Doug KB 245; *Finlay v Mexican Investment Corpn* [1897] 1 QB 517.
2 *West of England Fire Insurance Co v Isaacs* [1897] 1 QB 226, CA; *Phoenix Assurance Co v Spooner* [1905] 2 KB 753.
3 The third party cannot, therefore, insist on the insurers being made parties to the action: *Symons v Mulkern* (1882) 46 LT 763.
4 *Mason v Sainsbury* (1782) 3 Doug KB 61; *London Assurance Co v Sainsbury* (1783) 3 Doug KB 245; *Darrell v Tibbitts* (1880) 5 QBD 560, CA.
5 *Mason v Sainsbury* (1782) 3 Doug KB 61; *King v Victoria Insurance Co* [1896] AC 250, PC. As to ex gratia payments see para 504 ante.

511. Damages recoverable. The damages recoverable in a subrogation action are not limited to the amount paid by the insurers under the policy. The insurers may keep what is recovered in the action up to the amount so paid; any excess belongs to the assured, unless the policy modifies the rights of the parties or the assured has assigned his rights to the insurers[1].

1 See the cases cited in para 315 note 1 ante; and cf the distinction between subrogation and rights arising on abandonment in para 316 ante. In deciding whether interest on an award of damages is to go to the assured or to the insurers, the court must imply a term which gives business efficacy to the contract: *H Cousins & Co Ltd v D and C Carriers Ltd* [1971] 2 QB 230, [1971] 1 All ER 55, CA.

512. Assured's duties. It is the duty of the assured not to do any act which may prejudice the right of subrogation[1]. He must not, without the insurers' consent, settle the claim against the third party[2], or take proceedings himself to enforce it[3]. However, where the amount of the loss exceeds the amount paid under the policy, there is a case of partial subrogation only, and the assured is not necessarily deprived of his right to take proceedings[4]. Any proceedings which he may institute must be conducted for the benefit of the insurers as well as of himself[5]. If, after the insurers have become subrogated as regards a specific sum of money or other property, the money or property comes into the hands of the assured, he holds as trustee for the insurers; in the event of the assured having been adjudicated bankrupt or having gone into liquidation, the insurers, not the creditors generally, are entitled to the money or property[6].

1 *West of England Fire Insurance Co v Isaacs* [1897] 1 QB 226 at 229, CA, per Lord Esher MR.
2 *West of England Fire Insurance Co v Isaacs* [1897] 1 QB 226, CA; *Phoenix Assurance Co v Spooner* [1905] 2 KB 753; *Horse, Carriage and General Insurance Co Ltd v Petch* (1916) 33 TLR 131.
3 *Law Fire Assurance Co v Oakley* (1888) 4 TLR 309 per Mathew J (during the argument of counsel).
4 See *Page v Scottish Insurance Corpn* (1929) 140 LT 571 at 576, CA, per Scrutton LJ.
5 *Commercial Union Assurance Co v Lister* (1874) 9 Ch App 483. The same principle applies where, in the case of partial subrogation, the proceedings are conducted by the insurers: *Quebec Fire Insurance Co v St Louis* (1851) 7 Moo PCC 286 at 319.
6 *Re Miller, Gibb & Co Ltd* [1957] 2 All ER 266, [1957] 1 WLR 703; see also *Meacock v Bryant & Co* [1942] 2 All ER 661.

(ii) Indemnification Aliunde

513. Assured's rights. The fact that the assured may be entitled to be compensated for his loss by a third party does not in itself absolve the insurers from their obligations under the policy. Unless the policy so provides[1], the assured is not bound to exhaust his rights and remedies against third parties before having recourse to the insurers[2]; he is entitled in the first instance to claim a full indemnity under the policy, leaving the insurers to exercise their right of subrogation[3]. He is not obliged to refrain from suing a third party for damage caused by the third party's negligence merely because he has been paid in full by his own insurers, pursuant to an agreement between them and the insurers of the third party by which each insurance company pays for damage to its own assured[4]. If he sues and is successful, he must account to his insurers for any sum recovered in respect of a matter for which they have paid him[5].

1 See *London Guarantie Co v Fearnley* (1880) 5 App Cas 911, HL; and 20 Forms & Precedents (5th Edn) 29 at 31–32, Form 2 cl 11.
2 *Fifth Liverpool Starr-Bowkett Building Society v Travellers Accident Insurance Co Ltd* (1893) 9 TLR 221; cf *Collingridge v Royal Exchange Assurance Corpn* (1877) 3 QBD 173; *Darrell v Tibbitts* (1880) 5 QBD 560, CA.
3 *West of England Fire Insurance Co v Isaacs* [1897] 1 QB 226, CA. See also para 782 post.
4 *Morley v Moore* [1936] 2 KB 359, [1936] 2 All E R 79, CA. Such an agreement between insurers is known as a 'knock-for-knock' agreement; see further para 726 post.
5 *Morley v Moore* [1936] 2 KB 359 at 366, [1936] 2 All ER 79 at 83, CA.

514. Compensation before payment under policy. If, before payment is made under an insurance policy, the third party makes a payment to the assured to compensate him for the loss[1], the loss which the assured has suffered is pro tanto diminished, and he can no longer claim payment in full under the policy. The amount received from the third party must be taken into account, and the liability of the insurers, according to the amount so paid, will be diminished or entirely extinguished[2].

1 The payment is usually made in discharge of a legal liability, but the principle applies equally to voluntary payments, if made for the purpose of alleviating the loss (*Godsall v Boldero* (1807) 9 East 72, which is still applicable to contracts of indemnity); but there must be nothing in the circumstances of the payment showing an intention to exclude the insurers from benefit (*Castellain v Preston* (1883) 11 QBD 380 at 404, CA, per Bowen LJ).
2 *Darrell v Tibbitts* (1880) 5 QBD 560 at 562, CA, per Brett LJ; *Castellain v Preston* (1883) 11 QBD 380 at 393, CA, per Cotton LJ; see also *Burnand v Rodocanachi Sons & Co* (1882) 7 App Cas 333 at 389, HL, per Lord Blackburn; *Willumsen and Larwill Construction Co Ltd v Royal Insurance Co Ltd and Western Assurance Co* [1975] 5 WWR 703 (Alta App Div).

515. Compensation after payment under policy. The principle that payments made by third parties in compensation for a loss must be taken into account when paying under an insurance policy applies to payments received from third parties after payment of the loss in full under the policy[1]. As the assured has already been indemnified by the insurers, if he is allowed to retain the money paid by the third party, he will be indemnified twice over[2]. Therefore, he must account to the insurers for the money received from the third parties to the extent of the amount which they have paid him[3].

The damages recovered by the insured from a wrongdoer are subject to an equitable proprietary lien or charge in favour of the insurers[4].

1 See para 514 note 1 ante.
2 *Darrell v Tibbitts* (1880) 5 QBD 560, CA.
3 *Castellain v Preston* (1883) 11 QBD 380, CA; *Law Fire Assurance Co v Oakley* (1888) 4 TLR 309; *King v Victoria Insurance Co* [1896] AC 250, PC; *Stearns v Village Main Reef Gold Mining Co* (1905) 10 Com

Cas 89, CA; *Horse, Carriage and General Insurance Co Ltd v Petch* (1916) 33 TLR 131; *Lord Napier and Ettrick v Hunter* [1993] AC 713, [1993] 1 All ER 385, HL (stop-loss insurance).
4 *Lord Napier and Ettrick v Hunter* [1993] AC 713, [1993] 1 All ER 385, HL.

(11) CONTRIBUTION AND AVERAGE

(i) Over-insurance by Double Insurance

516. Meaning of 'double insurance'. 'Double insurance' in the strict sense exists where two or more policies are effected by or on behalf of the same assured in respect of the same interest and the total of the sums assured exceeds what is required to secure to the assured a full indemnity[1]. Generally, the existence of double insurance is important only in so far as it may affect the amount recoverable under a particular policy in the case of indemnity insurance[2]; it does not necessarily invalidate any of the policies concerned.

1 Cf the Marine Insurance Act 1906 s 32 (1); and para 319 et seq ante.
2 See para 520 post. In the case of an insurance which is not a contract of indemnity, eg an insurance on the life of the assured, the existence of other such contracts does not, in the absence of specific provision in the contract in question (see paras 517–519 post) affect either the validity of the insurance or the amount recoverable. As to insurances on the life of a third person see para 520 text and note 1 post.

517. Condition as to 'other insurances'. A proposal for non-marine insurance often contains a question requiring existing insurances to be disclosed[1]; if the truth of the answers is made the basis of the contract[2], a failure to disclose all the existing insurances will avoid the policy[3]. Occasionally the policy contains an express condition avoiding the policy unless all existing insurances are notified to the insurers and particulars are indorsed on the policy[4]. Alternatively, there may be a condition declaring the insurance not to be operative in the case of a loss covered by another insurance[5]. If the other insurance itself contains a similar condition, the two conditions are mutually destructive and each set of insurers is liable, subject to any rateable contribution clauses which there may be[6]. There must be another insurance of the same interest if such a condition is to be operative[7].

1 See eg 20 Forms & Precedents (5th Edn) 129 at 130, Form 77 para 10; 209 at 210, Form 138 para 5.
2 See para 374 ante.
3 *Wainwright v Bland* (1836) 1 M & W 32; *London Assurance v Mansel* (1879) 11 ChD 363.
4 *Citizens' Insurance Co of Canada v Parsons* (1881) 7 App Cas 96, PC; *National Protector Fire Insurance Co Ltd v Nivert* [1913] AC 507, PC; *Steadfast Insurance Co Ltd v F and B Trading Co Pty Ltd* (1971) 125 CLR 578 (Aust HC). For an example of such a condition see 20 Forms & Precedents (5th Edn) 191 at 193, Form 120 cl 7.
5 Such clauses are common in the competitive market of motor vehicle insurance and are described as 'non-contribution' clauses: see eg 20 Forms & Precedents (5th Edn) 549 at 551, Form 311 cl 9.3. Cf 'rateable contribution' clauses, which aim at providing that only a pro rata payment will be made if another insurance is operative: see eg 20 Forms & Precedents (5th Edn) 216 at 218, Form 140 cl 3; 549 at 557, Form 311 cl 32. A policy in this form will achieve its result if the other party has a rateable contribution clause or no clause dealing with contribution rate; if the other party has a non-contribution clause, its underwriters cannot be made to share because there is, ex hypothesi, another insurance on risk: see the cases cited in note 6 infra.
6 *Gale v Motor Union Insurance Co Ltd* [1928] 1 KB 359; *Weddell v Road Transport and General Insurance Co Ltd* [1932] 2 KB 563; *Monksfield v Vehicle and General Insurance Co Ltd* [1971] 1 Lloyd's Rep 139.
7 *Portavon Cinema Co Ltd v Price and Century Insurance Co Ltd* [1939] 4 All ER 601.

518. Disclosure of subsequent insurances. The duty to disclose existing insurances in answer to a question extends to insurances which come into existence after the date of the proposal, but before the issue of the policy[1]; but it has no application to insurances effected subsequently. Sometimes there is an express condition of the policy prohibiting any subsequent insurance without the insurers' consent[2]. More usually the condition merely requires any such insurances to be notified and indorsed on the policy[3].

1 *Re Marshall and Scottish Employers' Liability and General Insurance Co Ltd* (1901) 85 LT 757. See generally para 356 ante.
2 *Marcovitch v Liverpool Victoria Friendly Society* (1912) 28 TLR 188, CA (on the facts, insurers held to have consented).
3 *Sulphite Pulp Co v Faber* (1895) 1 Com Cas 146; *Equitable Fire and Accident Office Ltd v Ching Wo Hong* [1907] AC 96, PC; *National Protector Fire Insurance Co v Nivert* [1913] AC 507, PC.

519. Breach of condition against double insurance. To constitute a breach of a condition against double insurance the second policy must cover the same interest[1] against the same risk[2], and must be a valid and effective contract of insurance[3]. Further, the breach must be real; a new policy substituted for an existing policy which has been duly notified is not a breach[4].

1 As to the same interest see para 521 text to notes 3–10 post.
2 Hence there is no breach where two policies of different kinds (eg a fire policy and a marine policy) accidentally overlap, eg where property in a warehouse awaiting shipment is destroyed by fire (*Australian Agricultural Co v Saunders* (1875) LR 10 CP 668, Ex Ch); cf *Westminster Fire Office v Reliance Marine Insurance Co* (1903) 19 TLR 668, CA; see also *American Surety Co of New York v Wrightson* (1910) 16 Com Cas 37 at 51; *Gale v Motor Union Insurance Co Ltd* [1928] 1 KB 359.
3 *Equitable Fire and Accident Office Ltd v Ching Wo Hong* [1907] AC 96, PC.
4 *National Protector Fire Insurance Co v Nivert* [1913] AC 507, PC.

(ii) Contribution

520. Contribution in the case of over-insurance. Subject to any policy conditions to the contrary, the assured may effect as many policies as he pleases; but where the contract is one of indemnity[1], however numerous the policies may be, he cannot recover more than the total amount of his loss[2]. Most policies of non-marine insurance contain a contribution clause limiting the liability of the insurers to their rateable proportion of the loss[3]. In this case the assured cannot claim payment in full under any of the policies; each policy is liable for its rateable proportion only[4]. If there is no such contribution clause in the policy, the assured is entitled to claim payment in full under any of the policies, leaving the insurers under that policy to claim contribution from their co-insurers[5].

1 The same principle applies to policies of life assurance when founded upon an insurable interest in the life of a third person: *Hebdon v West* (1863) 3 B & S 579.
2 *North British and Mercantile Insurance Co v London, Liverpool and Globe Insurance Co* (1877) 5 ChD 569 at 581, CA; *Scottish Amicable Heritable Securities Association v Northern Assurance Co* (1883) 11 R 287 at 303, Ct of Sess; and see *Wolenberg v Royal Co-operative Collecting Society* (1915) 112 LT 1036, DC, followed in *Goldstein v Salvation Army Assurance Society* [1917] 2 KB 291.
3 See eg *Gale v Motor Union Insurance Co Ltd* [1928] 1 KB 359; *Commercial Union Assurance Co Ltd v Hayden* [1977] QB 804, [1977] 1 All ER 441, CA (where the independent liability and not the maximum liability basis was applied); and eg 20 Forms & Precedents (5th Edn) 29 at 31, Form 2 cl 10; 211 at 214, Form 139 cl 18.

4 *North British and Mercantile Insurance Co v London, Liverpool and Globe Insurance Co* (1877) 5 ChD 569,
   CA; *Scottish Amicable Heritable Securities Association v Northern Assurance Co* (1883) 11 R 287, Ct of
   Sess; *Nichols & Co v Scottish Union and National Insurance Co* (1885) 2 TLR 190.
5 See generally para 319 et seq ante.

521. Conditions giving rise to right of contribution. The following conditions must be satisfied before a right of contribution can arise[1].

(1) Each policy must cover the event which in fact happens, namely, the loss of
    the same property by the same peril. The policies need not be restricted to the
    same property, and they may include other perils; but there is no contri-
    bution unless there is a common loss caused by a peril common to the
    policies[2].

(2) Each policy must cover the same interest in the same property, that is to say,
    each policy must be intended to protect the same assured against the same
    loss. The policies must cover a common interest; it is not sufficient that they
    cover the same property[3]. Where separate insurances are effected on the
    same property by different persons interested in it for the purpose of protect-
    ing their separate interests only, there is no contribution[4]. There is no
    contribution where separate policies are affected by bailor and bailee[5], by
    mortgagor and mortgagee[6], or by landlord and tenant[7] for their individual
    protection. Where one of the policies is intended to enure for the benefit of
    both persons interested, as, for instance, where the bailee, mortgagor or
    tenant intends to cover the interest of his bailor, mortgagee or landlord as
    well as his own[8], a case of contribution arises between such policy and any
    policy effected by the bailor, mortgagee or landlord for his separate protec-
    tion, since both policies, in fact, cover a common interest, namely, the
    interest of the bailor, mortgagee or landlord[9]. It is for this reason that a
    tenant who, having an option to purchase, exercises it after payment for a
    loss has become due both under his own and under his landlord's policy, is
    entitled to the benefit of the payment to the landlord[10].

(3) Each policy must be in force at the time of the loss. There is no contribution
    if one of the policies has already become void[11] or the risk under it has not yet
    attached[12]; the insurer from whom contribution is claimed can repudiate
    liability under his policy on the ground that the assured has broken a
    condition[13].

(4) Each policy must be a legal contract of insurance. There is no contribution
    where one of the insurances, though expressed in the form of a policy, is not
    legally binding[14].

1 See *Sickness and Accident Assurance Association v General Accident Assurance Corpn* (1892) 19 R 977 at
   980, Ct of Sess.
2 *North British and Mercantile Insurance Co v London, Liverpool and Globe Insurance Co* (1877) 5 ChD 569
   at 581, CA, per James LJ; see also *American Surety Co of New York v Wrightson* (1910) 16 Com Cas 37.
3 *North British and Mercantile Insurance Co v London, Liverpool and Globe Insurance Co* (1877) 5 ChD 569,
   CA; applied in *Scottish Amicable Heritable Securities Association v Northern Assurance Co* (1883) 11 R
   287, Ct of Sess; and *Andrews v Patriotic Assurance Co (No 2)* (1886) 18 LR Ir 355. Cf para 519 note 2
   ante.
4 In this case there is subrogation: see para 508 ante.
5 *North British and Mercantile Insurance Co v London, Liverpool and Globe Insurance Co* (1877) 5 ChD 569,
   CA.
6 *Scottish Amicable Heritable Securities Association v Northern Assurance Co* (1883) 11 R 287, Ct of Sess.
7 *Andrews v Patriotic Assurance Co (No 2)* (1886) 18 LR Ir 355; *Portavon Cinema Co Ltd v Price and Century
   Insurance Co Ltd* [1939] 4 All ER 601.

8 As to such insurances see para 615 post.

9 *Nichols & Co v Scottish Union and National Insurance Co* (1885) 2 TLR 190, more fully reported in 14 R 1094, Ct of Sess; *Halifax Building Society v Keighley* [1931] 2 KB 248.

10 *Reynard v Arnold* (1875) 10 Ch App 386, CA; and see EQUITY vol 16 (Reissue) para 833 note 7.

11 Conversely, there is contribution if the policy is not avoided until after the loss: *Weddell v Road Transport and General Insurance Co Ltd* [1932] 2 KB 563.

12 *Sickness and Accident Assurance Association v General Accident Assurance Corpn* (1892) 19 R 977, Ct of Sess.

13 *Monksfield v Vehicle and General Insurance Co Ltd* [1971] 1 Lloyd's Rep 139; *Eagle Star Insurance Co Ltd v Provincial Insurance plc* [1994] 1 AC 130, [1993] 3 All ER 1, PC. Cf *Legal and General Assurance Society Ltd v Drake Insurance Co Ltd* [1992] QB 887, [1992] 1 All ER 283, CA.

14 *Woods v Co-operative Insurance Society* 1924 SC 692. As questions of contribution normally affect only the offices concerned and since the assured in any case receives an indemnity in respect of the loss, they are usually settled privately, and very rarely come before the court. For a full discussion of contribution see Ivamy's General Principles of Insurance Law (6th Edn) 517–536.

(iii) Under-insurance and Average

522. Under-insurance not penalised. Unlike policies of marine insurance[1], non-marine policies are not subject to average unless there is an express condition to that effect[2]. The assured is not penalised in the case of under-insurance[3]; he bears no part of the loss until the policy is exhausted[4], but, on the contrary, is entitled to recover the full amount of the loss, whether total or partial, up to the sum insured[5].

1 See para 244 ante.

2 *Joyce v Kennard* (1871) LR 7 QB 78.

3 There may, however, be a condition requiring the property to be insured for its full value, in which case an honest estimate is sufficient: *King v Traveller's Insurance Association Ltd* (1931) 48 TLR 53.

4 *Sillem v Thornton* (1854) 3 E & B 868 at 888 per Lord Campbell CJ; see also *Anglo-Californian Bank Ltd v London and Provincial Marine and General Insurance Co* (1904) 10 Com Cas 1 at 9 per Walton J.

5 *Fifth Liverpool Starr-Bowkett Building Society v Travellers Accident Insurance Co Ltd* (1893) 9 TLR 221; *Newman v Maxwell* (1899) 80 LT 681.

523. Average clauses. Policies insuring goods usually contain an average clause[1] providing that if at the time of the loss the sum insured is less than the value of the property, the assured is to be considered as his own insurer[2] for the difference and must bear a rateable proportion of the loss accordingly[3].

1 See 20 Forms & Precedents (5th Edn) 21 at 32, Form 2 cl 15. It is usually called the 'first condition of average', in contradistinction to the 'second condition of average' (see 20 Forms & Precedents (5th Edn) 34 at 35, Form 3 condition 1), which is not an average condition, but rather a contribution clause.

2 This phrase means that the assured bears the risk himself: *Grey v Ellison* (1856) 1 Giff 438 at 442 per Stuart V-C.

3 This clause is implied in a Lloyd's policy if it is stated to be 'subject to average': *Acme Wood Flooring Co Ltd v Marten* (1904) 90 LT 313. Similarly, where there is a contract between shipowner and consignee that goods arriving in ships belonging to the shipowner are to be warehoused by the shipowner and kept covered by insurance, an average clause is to be implied: *Carreras v Cunard SS Co* [1918] 1 KB 118.

524. 'First loss' and 'excess' clauses. Instead of the ordinary average clause, an insurance policy may contain a condition which throws the whole of the first loss, or a definite proportion of any loss, on the assured. Such a condition is usual in the case of reinsurances[1] and insurances on farm premises and livestock[2]. A common form of such condition, used particularly in motor insurance, requires the assured to bear the amount of any individual loss up to a specified figure, leaving the insurers with liability only for any excess over that figure[3]. A similar condition is to be found in contractors' policies[4].

1 *Traill v Baring* (1864) 4 De G J & Sm 318.
2 See 20 Forms & Precedents (5th Edn) 189, Form 119 cl 18; 199, Form 132.
3 *Re Law Guarantee Trust and Accident Society Ltd, Liverpool Mortgage Insurance Co Ltd's Case* [1914] 2 Ch 617 at 645, CA, per Scrutton J; *Beacon Insurance Co Ltd v Langdale* [1939] 4 All ER 204, CA.
4 *Trollope and Colls Ltd v Haydon* [1977] 1 Lloyd's Rep 244, CA.

5. LONG TERM INSURANCE

(1) IN GENERAL

(i) The Basis of the Contract

525. Nature of life insurance. A contract of life insurance in its strict form may be defined as a contract under which the insurers undertake, in consideration of specified premiums being continuously paid throughout the life of a particular person, to pay a specified sum of money upon the death of that person[1]. The particular person whose life forms the subject matter of the insurance need not be the person who pays the premiums; it may be a third party[2].

1 *Dalby v India and London Life Assurance Co* (1854) 15 CB 365 at 387, Ex Ch, per Parke B. As to taxation affecting life assurance see para 16 ante; and INCOME TAXATION.
2 Except where otherwise stated, the policy, for the purposes of this part of the title, is taken to be a policy upon the life of the assured. For the general principles applicable to life insurance as well as to other kinds of non-marine insurance see para 349 et seq ante.

526. Life policies for specified periods; endowment policies. It is theoretically possible for an assured to take out a life insurance policy in a strict form but limited for a period of years, that is to say upon the terms that death is to be the sole contingency upon which payment is due but the policy is only to run for a specified period, so that nothing is payable if the assured survives the period[1]. Such policies are nowadays very rare. However, policies are frequently taken out the basic feature of which is the provision of a capital sum on a given date if the assured so long survives, with or without a provision for the making of a payment, or a repayment of premiums, if he dies before that date; such policies are usually known as endowment policies[2].

1 See *Lockyer v Offley* (1786) 1 Term Rep 252 at 260.
2 See further para 563 et seq post.

527. Broad meaning of life insurance. Life insurance for many purposes has a broader meaning than the strict one given previously[1] and includes endowment insurance[2]. It has been said that the essential feature of a contract of life insurance, in this broad sense, is that it is a contract relating in any way to human life[3]. This is perhaps too wide; a public liability or employer's liability policy, in so far as it provides indemnity against death claims, could be said to relate to human life, but it could not for that reason be regarded in any real sense as a life policy[4]. However, it is provided by statute that for certain purposes any instrument under which the payment of money is assured on the happening of any contingency dependent on the duration of human life is a contract of life insurance[5]; and, apart from express statutory provision, life insurance in the broader sense comprises any contract in which one party agrees to pay a given sum upon the happening of a particular event contingent upon the duration of human life, in consideration of the immediate payment of a smaller sum or certain equivalent periodical payments by another party[6]. Thus, a contract providing for the payment of a lump sum to the assured at the expiration of a given period, but containing a stipulation for return of premiums to the assured's estate if he dies during that period, is a contract of life insurance for the purpose of a restriction on the carrying on of the business of life insurance contained in a company's memorandum of association[7]; and, for the purposes of the statutory provisions which relate to relief in respect of life insurance premiums for the purposes of income tax[8], a contract by which a sum is payable on the assured's death within a specified period and a larger sum if he is alive at the end of the period is an insurance on life[9].

A person entering a contract of long term insurance has the right to withdraw from it within a specified period[10].

1 As to the meaning of 'life insurance' see para 525 ante.
2 As to endowment insurance see para 526 ante; and notes 6, 7 infra.
3 *Joseph v Law Integrity Insurance Co Ltd* [1912] 2 Ch 581 at 594, CA, per Farwell CJ. In the Insurance Companies Act 1982 'life policy' means any instrument by which the payment of money is assured on death (except death by accident only) or the happening of any contingency dependent on human life, or any instrument evidencing a contract which is subject to payment of premiums for a term dependent on human life: s 96 (1).
4 *Lancashire Insurance Co v IRC* [1899] 1 QB 353 at 359 per Bruce J.
5 See eg the Policies of Assurance Act 1867 s 7; and para 548 note 1 post. In relation to the statutory restrictions on the carrying on of life insurance business imposed by the Insurance Companies Act 1982 see generally para 815 et seq post.
6 See *Joseph v Law Integrity Insurance Co Ltd* [1912] 2 Ch 581 at 591, CA; *Gould v Curtis* [1913] 3 KB 84 at 91, CA, per Cozens-Hardy MR (citing and approving Bunyon's Law of Life Assurance (4th Edn) 1).
7 *Joseph v Law Integrity Insurance Co Ltd* [1912] 2 Ch 581, CA; *Flood v Irish Provident Assurance Co Ltd* [1912] 2 Ch 597n, CA.
8 See INCOME TAXATION.
9 *Gould v Curtis* [1913] 3 KB 84, CA. As to reliefs in respect of contributions to approved superannuation funds and in respect of premiums paid for individuals for retirement annuities see INCOME TAXATION.
10 See para 816 post.

528. Industrial assurance. A somewhat specialised form of life insurance has developed where premiums are payable, usually in very small sums, at short intervals. Such insurances, where the premiums are received by means of collectors and are payable at intervals of less than two months, are called industrial assurance[1], and are subject to special statutory provisions[2]. The industrial assurance legislation applies to industrial assurance companies[3] and registered friendly societies which carry on industrial assurance business, and such societies are known as collecting societies[4]. Registered friendly societies are also subject generally to certain provisions of friendly society legislation affecting their power to effect life insurances[5].

1 See the Industrial Assurance Act 1923 s 1(2); and INDUSTRIAL ASSURANCE.
2 Ie those contained in the Industrial Assurance Acts 1923 to 1968: see INDUSTRIAL ASSURANCE.
3 As to industrial assurance companies see INDUSTRIAL ASSURANCE.
4 See FRIENDLY SOCIETIES and INDUSTRIAL ASSURANCE. As to the application of the industrial assurance legislation to unregistered friendly societies see FRIENDLY SOCIETIES.
5 See FRIENDLY SOCIETIES.

(ii) Event Insured Against

529. Death as stipulated contingency. Under a policy of life insurance in the strict sense the event which gives the right to payment is death during the currency of the policy[1]. Generally the cause of the death is immaterial. All cases of death, whether due to natural or accidental[2] causes, fall within the policy; even death caused by the wilful act of a third party is covered[3].

1 *Lockyer v Offley* (1786) 1 Term Rep 252.
2 Accidental death may also fall within the scope of a personal accident policy: see para 567 et seq post.
3 *Cleaver v Mutual Reserve Fund Life Association* [1892] 1 QB 147, CA. Although the fact that the assured was killed by a third party does not affect the liability of the insurers to pay the policy money, it may affect the title to the policy money since it is contrary to public policy that a man not mentally disordered who has killed another should be allowed to benefit from his crime: see *Cleaver v Mutal Reserve Fund Life Association* supra (insurance effected by husband on his life for benefit of wife under the Married Women's Property Act 1882 s 11; wife murdered husband; policy money formed part of husband's estate). The 'forfeiture rule' has been mitigated in certain circumstances, eg where the killing constitutes manslaughter, by the Forfeiture Act 1982: see further WILLS vol 50 paras 241–242. As to the position if the assured kills himself see para 530 post.

530. Death caused by criminal act of the assured or by suicide. If a policy is effected with the deliberate intention of obtaining a capital sum by procuring the maturity of the policy by a criminal act, presumably the whole policy is void ab initio on proof of the illegal object[1]; but, even if the policy was legally obtained in the first instance, public policy prohibits payment of the policy money being enforced if the death of the assured is the result of his own deliberately criminal act on the principle that no one can benefit from their own criminal act[2]. Likewise, if the assured is, after conviction on a charge of treason, sentenced to death and is subsequently executed, his insurers under a life policy are not obliged to make any payment[3].

Although suicide is no longer a criminal offence[4], if the assured kills himself whilst not mentally disordered, the insurers can avoid liability on the ground that he cannot take advantage of his own intentional act[5].

1 As to void and illegal contracts see CONTRACT vol 9 para 386 et seq.
2 *Beresford v Royal Insurance Co Ltd* [1938] AC 586, [1938] 2 All ER 602, HL. See, however, the Forfeiture Act 1982; and WILLS vol 50 paras 241–242.
3 *Amicable Society v Bolland* (1830) 4 Bli NS 194.
4 Suicide Act 1961 s 1.
5 *Beresford v Royal Insurance Co Ltd* [1938] AC 586, [1938] 2 All ER 602, HL.

531. Death due to excepted perils. The policy may, by the express terms of an exceptions clause, exclude liability on the part of the insurers if death results in particular circumstances, from exposure to specified hazards[1] or from the commission of a criminal offence[2].

In practice, the only exception which calls for consideration is the exception against suicide[3]. In the absence of some indication to the contrary, an exception against suicide covers all cases of intentional self-destruction[4]. Hence the exception applies even though the assured was unbalanced or even mentally disordered to a degree provided he knew what he was doing and was capable of appreciating the consequences[5]. On the other hand, if he was incapable of appreciating the nature of his act, his self-destruction is not intentional and the exception does not apply[6]. The policy may, however, be so worded as to cover all cases of self-destruction whether intentional or not[7]. In any of these cases the onus is as always on the insurers to establish that the conditions of the exceptions clause are fulfilled[8], and if the cause of death is left open the policy is not avoided[9].

1 Similar exceptions may be contained in personal accident policies. As to exceptions see generally para 409 ante. An exception avoiding the policy if the assured engages in military service abroad without the consent of the insurers, except under legal compulsion, is not void as contrary to public policy: *Duckworth v Scottish Widows' Fund Life Assurance Society* (1917) 33 TLR 430.

2 *Whiting v Co-operative Life Insurance Co* [1974] 4 WWR 197 (BC) (assured's death alleged to be due to driving with excess blood alcohol; no proof that it was so caused, but in any event the exception of 'criminal offence' in the exception clause did not include such an offence).

3 As to the effect of the exception upon the rights of assignees see para 547 post.

4 *Borradaile v Hunter* (1843) 5 Man & G 639; *Clift v Schwabe* (1846) 3 CB 437, Ex Ch; *Dufaur v Professional Life Assurance Co* (1858) 25 Beav 599; *Rowett, Leaky & Co v Scottish Provident Institution* [1927] 1 Ch 55, CA.

5 *Clift v Schwabe* (1846) 3 CB 437 at 464, Ex Ch, per Rolfe B.

6 *Borradaile v Hunter* (1843) 5 Man & G 639 at 654 per Maule J; *Clift v Schwabe* (1846) 3 CB 437 at 465, Ex Ch, per Patteson J; *Stormont v Waterloo Life and Casualty Assurance Co* (1858) 1 F & F 22; see also *Dormay v Borradaile* (1847) 5 CB 380.

7 *White v British Empire Mutual Life Assurance Co* (1868) LR 7 Eq 394; *Ellinger & Co v Mutual Life Insurance Co of New York* [1905] 1 KB 31, CA.

8 *Stormont v Waterloo Life and Casualty Assurance Co* (1858) 1 F & F 22; *Rowett, Leaky & Co v Scottish Provident Institution* [1927] 1 Ch 55 at 66, CA, per Lord Hanworth MR; and see further para 409 text and note 6 ante.

9 *Harvey v Ocean Accident and Guarantee Corpn* [1905] 2 IR 1, CA.

(iii) Circumstances affecting the Risk

532. What facts are material. The subject matter of a life insurance policy is a human life. Although death is bound to occur, it is an uncertain event in that it is uncertain when it will happen[1]. Since the premium is based upon the average duration of human life[2], any facts which tend to suggest that the life insured is likely to fall short of the average duration are material facts[3]. It follows that the usual personal details, which are sufficient in other branches of insurance to identify the assured and to inform the insurers as to the nature of the risk[4], will need to be amplified. In practice the details required are usually indicated by the questions and declarations contained in the proposal form[5].

1 *Prudential Insurance Co v IRC* [1904] 2 KB 658 at 663 per Channell J.

2 *Thomson v Weems* (1884) 9 App Cas 671 at 681, HL, per Lord Blackburn.

3 Similar facts are material in personal accident insurance and accordingly cases on personal accident insurance are referred to here. As to material facts see further para 351 ante.

4 As to such details see paras 368 et seq ante.

5 For forms of proposal see 20 Forms & Precedents (5th Edn) 516–521, Forms 294–296.

533. Materiality of assured's age, health, habits and history. Information is normally required by the insurers as to the assured's age[1]. However, by their conduct the insurers may be precluded from relying upon any misstatement of age[2]. If in the proposal form there is a further question as to the date of birth and the date of birth inserted is inconsistent with the age stated, the issue of the policy may be a waiver of the inaccuracy[3].

As well as a general statement that the assured is in sound health[4] at the date of the proposal[5], the insurers usually require a statement that he is not suffering from any disorder tending to shorten life[6]. Mental illness, particularly if it is such as to affect bodily health, should be disclosed[7].

Information as to the habits and pursuits of the assured is usually required, and a statement that the assured is of sober and temperate habits may be required[8]. Questions relating to hazardous sports may be asked, and there is usually a general question whether there are any circumstances in the occupation, habits or pursuits of the assured rendering him peculiarly liable to accident or disease[9].

Information respecting the assured's history is generally sought. There is usually a question inquiring whether the assured[10] has ever suffered[11] from certain specified diseases[12]; and there may be a general question requiring any illness[13] or accident[14], consultation of a medical practitioner[15] or any operation[16] during a specified period to be disclosed. Particulars of the assured's usual[17] medical attendant[18], and of any other medical practitioner consulted by him[19] within a specified period, are usually required, together with the names of persons who are acquainted with the assured, and who may be referred to for information. Those who are referred to for information, whether they are medical practitioners or not, are not the agents of the assured to give information and consequently any fraud, misrepresentation or non-disclosure on their part is not to be imputed to the assured[20].

1 Where the life insured is that of a third party, not the assured himself, the information required is normally the same. In personal accident proposals, a statement as to weight and height may also be required: *Levy v Scottish Employers' Insurance Co* (1901) 17 TLR 229.

2 *Hemmings v Sceptre Life Association Ltd* [1905] 1 Ch 365.

3 *Keeling v Pearl Assurance Co Ltd* (1923) 129 LT 573.

4 The fact that disease is latent in the system does not make the statement inaccurate: *Fidelity and Casualty Co of New York v Mitchell* [1917] AC 592, PC; cf *Ross v Bradshaw* (1761) 1 Wm Bl 312.

5 Any change in health after the date of the proposal and before its acceptance must be notified: *Morrison v Muspratt* (1827) 4 Bing 60; *British Equitable Insurance Co v Great Western Rly Co* (1869) 38 LJCh 314; *Canning v Farquhar* (1886) 16 QBD 727, CA; *Harrington v Pearl Life Assurance Co Ltd* (1914) 30 TLR 613, CA; *Looker v Law Union and Rock Insurance Co Ltd* [1928] 1 KB 554; see generally para 356 ante. The proposer is not deemed to be fully aware of the state of his internal organs: see *Life Association of Scotland v Forster* (1873) 11 Macph 351, Ct of Sess; *Delahaye v British Empire Mutual Life Assurance Co* (1897) 13 TLR 345, CA; and para 359 ante.

6 *Watson v Mainwaring* (1813) 4 Taunt 763; *Swete v Fairlie* (1833) 6 C & P 1; *Jones v Provincial Insurance Co* (1857) 3 CBNS 65; *Hutton v Waterloo Life Assurance Co* (1859) 1 F & F 735.

7 *Lindenau v Desborough* (1828) 8 B & C 586.

8 *Thomson v Weems* (1884) 9 App Cas 671, HL; see also *Southcombe v Merriman* (1842) Car & M 286; *Dennan v Scottish Widows' Fund Life Assurance Society* (1887) 3 TLR 347, CA. It has been said that the statement refers to the use or abuse of alcohol, and is inappropriate to drug habits: *Yorke v Yorkshire Insurance Co* [1918] 1 KB 662 at 666 per McCardie J.

9 For such a question see *Australian Widow's Fund Life Assurance Society Ltd v National Mutual Life Association of Australasia Ltd* [1914] AC 634 at 635, PC, and see also *Bawden v London, Edinburgh and Glasgow Assurance Co* [1892] 2 QB 534, CA.

10 The question may include relatives of the assured: *Anderson v Fitzgerald* (1853) 4 HL Cas 484; see also *Duff v Gant* (1852) 20 LTOS 71.

11 The statement does not refer to isolated symptoms not connected with disease: *Chattock v Shawe* (1835) 1 Mood & R 498; cf *Geach v Ingall* (1845) 14 M & W 95.

12 *Fowkes v Manchester and London Assurance Association* (1863) 3 B & S 917; *British Equitable Insurance Co v Musgrave* (1887) 3 TLR 630; see also *Willis v Poole* (1780) 2 Park's Marine Insurances (8th Edn) 935.

13 *Cazenove v British Equitable Assurance Co* (1860) 29 LJCP 160, Ex Ch; *Godfrey v Britannic Assurance Co Ltd* [1963] 2 Lloyd's Rep 515. A miscarriage is not an illness within the meaning of the question: *Anstey v British Natural Premium Life Association Ltd* (1908) 99 LT 765, CA.

14 A question of this kind must be read with some qualification; the assured cannot be expected to recollect and disclose every trivial disease or every trivial accident for the whole of his life: *Connecticut Mutual Life Insurance Co of Hertford v Moore* (1881) 6 App Cas 644 at 648, PC; *Joel v Law Union and Crown Insurance Co* [1908] 2 KB 863, CA; *Yorke v Yorkshire Insurance Co* [1918] 1 KB 662. Questions of this kind do not relate to members of the assured's family unless they are mentioned: *Duff v Gant* (1852) 20 LTOS 71.

15 *Kumar v Life Insurance Corpn of India* [1974] 1 Lloyd's Rep 147.

16 *Kumar v Life Insurance Corpn of India* [1974] 1 Lloyd's Rep 147, where a Caesarean incision was held to be an operation.

17 This word implies that he has attended more than once: *Huckman v Fernie* (1838) 3 M & W 505 at 520 per Lord Abinger CB. Hence, it does not apply to a medical attendant who attends the assured's family and is acquainted with the assured, if he does not attend the assured: *Everett v Desborough* (1829) 5 Bing 503; *Huckman v Fernie* (1838) 3 M & W 505; *Hutton v Waterloo Life Assurance Co* (1859) 1 F & F 735.

18 The last medical attendant ought to be named: *Morrison v Muspratt* (1827) 4 Bing 60; *Cazenove v British Equitable Assurance Co* (1860) 29 LJCP 160, Ex Ch. If the medical attendant is changed after the date of the proposal, the change ought to be communicated: *British Equitable Insurance Co v Great Western Rly Co* (1869) 38 LJCh 314.

19 A medical practitioner giving a hypodermic injection is included in this expression: *Mutual Life Insurance Co of New York v Ontario Metal Products Co Ltd* [1925] AC 344 at 349, PC.

20 *Wheelton v Hardisty* (1858) 8 E & B 232, Ex Ch, distinguishing *Maynard v Rhode* (1824) 1 C & P 360; *Everett v Desborough* (1829) 5 Bing 503; and *Rawlins v Desborough* (1840) 2 Mood & R 328. The truth of their statements may, however, be warranted: *Hambrough v Mutual Life Insurance Co of New York* (1895) 72 LT 140, CA.

534. Medical examination. The assured may be required to submit to examination by a medical practitioner nominated by the insurers. In the course of the examination questions may be put to him. These questions must be answered honestly, but unless the truth of the answers is warranted their inaccuracy does not affect the validity of the policy[1].

1 *Delahaye v British Empire Mutual Life Assurance Co* (1897) 13 TLR 245, CA; *Joel v Law Union and Crown Insurance Co* [1908] 2 KB 863, CA. No person may apply to a medical practitioner for a medical report on any individual to be supplied to him for insurance purposes unless (1) that person ('the applicant') notifies the individual that he proposes to make the application, and (2) the individual notifies the applicant that he consents to the making of the application: Access to Medical Reports Act 1988 s 3(1). As to that Act see MEDICINE vol 30 (Reissue) para 19.

(iv) Insurable Interest

A. THE LIFE ASSURANCE ACT 1774

535. Position at common law. At common law insurances by way of gaming or wagering were valid subject to certain qualifications[1]. In 1745 an Act[2] was passed to prohibit policies dispensing with proof of interest and other policies by way of gaming or wagering in relation to British ships and merchandise[3]. In 1774 a further Act was passed to prohibit insurances on lives or other events except where the persons insuring have an interest[4].

1 As to such insurances see para 211 ante.

2 Marine Insurance Act 1745 (repealed).
3 For the development of the law and the legislation at present in force in relation to marine policies unsupported by insurable interests see para 211 ante.
4 Life Assurance Act 1774. This Act, which is sometimes called the Gambling Act, remains in force; for its provisions and effect see paras 538–544 post. The provisions of the Act do not apply to such a contract as is mentioned in the Water Resources Act 1991 s 1, Sch 1 para 2(4), and the Land Drainage Act 1991 s 1, Sch 2 para 1(3): see WATER.

536. Effect of statutory provisions. No insurance is to be made on the life or lives of any person or persons, or on any other event or events whatsoever, where the person or persons for whose use or benefit, or on whose account, the policy is made has no interest, or by way of gaming or wagering; every insurance made contrary to this provision is void[1].

No policy may be made on the life or lives of any person or persons, or other event or events, without inserting the name or names of the person or persons interested or for whose use, benefit or on whose account the policy is made[2]. However, a policy for the benefit of unnamed persons from time to time falling within a specified class or description is not invalid if the class or description is stated in the policy with sufficient particularity to make it possible to establish the identity of all persons who at any given time are entitled to benefit under the policy[3].

No greater sum may be recovered from the insurers than the amount or value of the assured's interest in the life or event insured[4].

These provisions apply to documents not transactions; so unless the transaction is expressed in a document which is capable of being treated as a policy, the Act cannot apply[5].

1 Life Assurance Act 1774 s 1; see further paras 539–542 post.
2 Ibid s 2; see further para 543 post.
3 Insurance Companies Amendment Act 1973 s 50(1). This section applies to policies effected before the passing of the Act (25 July 1973) as well as to policies effected after that date: s 50(2).
4 Life Assurance Act 1774 s 3; see further para 544 post.
5 *Carlill v Carbolic Smoke Ball Co* [1892] 2 QB 484 at 493 per Hawkins J; *Cook v Field* (1850) 15 QB 460. The Marine Insurance Act 1745 (repealed) applied to contracts which were in substance insurances even if not contained in policies: *Kent v Bird* (1777) 2 Cowp 583; *Morgan v Pebrer* (1837) 3 Bing NC 457.

B. INSURANCES SUBJECT TO THE ACT

537. Application of statutory provisions. The Life Assurance Act 1774, although it refers in its long title to life insurance only, is not in its operative language so limited. Consequently, it has been held to apply also to personal accident insurance[1] and generally to insurances upon events[2]. It is not, however, of universal application. Insurances on ships, goods and merchandise are expressly excluded from its operation[3]; and this exclusion has been held to extend to policies of motor insurance[4] and to policies on money held by collectors of an insurance company[5]. There are also special statutory provisions extending the effect of the Act in the case of friendly societies and industrial assurance companies[6].

There are, therefore, many important branches of insurance which are not within the statute[7], and it is only necessary to consider its operation in detail in relation to life insurance.

1 *Shilling v Accidental Death Insurance Co* (1857) 2 H & N 42.
2 *Paterson v Powell* (1832) 9 Bing 320; *Re London County Commercial Reinsurance Office Ltd* [1922] 2 Ch 67; see also *Roebuck v Hammerton* (1778) 2 Cowp 737; *Mollison v Staples* (1778) 2 Park's Marine Insurances (7th Edn) 640n. The contract must, however, be a contract of insurance: *Cook v Field* (1850) 15 QB 460.
3 Life Assurance Act 1774 s 4.
4 *Williams v Baltic Insurance Association of London Ltd* [1924] 2 KB 282.
5 *Prudential Staff Union v Hall* [1947] KB 685. As to the application of the Life Assurance Act 1774 to fire insurance see para 607 post.
6 See FRIENDLY SOCIETIES; INDUSTRIAL ASSURANCE.
7 Ie including (in addition to motor insurance) marine insurance, fire insurance (so far as it relates to goods) and burglary insurance.

C. SCOPE OF STATUTORY REQUIREMENTS

538. Life insurances not covered by the Life Assurance Act 1774. Even in the case of life insurance, certain insurances have been held to be exempt from the operation of the Life Assurance Act 1774 as not being within its scope[1]. These insurances are insurances by the assured upon his own life[2], provided that the insurances are for his own benefit[3], and insurances by husbands and wives upon each other's lives[4].

1 As to the interpretation of statutes by reference to the mischief of the statute see STATUTES.
2 *Griffiths v Fleming* [1909] 1 KB 805 at 820–821, CA, per Farwell LJ and Kennedy LJ; see also *M'Farlane v Royal London Friendly Society* (1886) 2 TLR 755, DC.
3 *Wainwright v Bland* (1836) 1 M & W 32; *M'Farlane v Royal London Friendly Society* (1886) 2 TLR 755, DC; and see para 543 text and note 5 post.
4 *Griffiths v Fleming* [1909] 1 KB 805; CA. See also the Married Women's Property Act 1882 s 11; and HUSBAND AND WIFE vol 22 para 978.

539. Pecuniary interest required. The first requirement of the Life Assurance Act 1774 is insurable interest[1]. It must be a pecuniary interest[2], in the sense that it is reasonably capable of valuation in money[3], and its amount must be measured by the pecuniary loss which the person for whose benefit the insurance is effected is likely to sustain by reason of the death of the life insured[4].

1 See the Life Assurance Act 1774 s 1; and para 536 ante.
2 *Halford v Kymer* (1830) 10 B & C 724 at 728 per Lord Tenterden; *Macaura v Northern Assurance Co Ltd* [1925] AC 619 at 625, HL, per Lord Buckmaster.
3 *Simcock v Scottish Imperial Insurance Co Ltd* 1902 10 SLT 286.
4 *Halford v Kymer* (1830) 10 B & C 724 at 728 per Lord Tenterden CJ; *Hebden v West* (1863) 3 B & S 579.

540. Pecuniary interest of creditors. Where in the event of one party to a contract dying there will be a frustration of the contract[1] and such frustration is likely to cause pecuniary loss to the other party, the latter has a sufficient pecuniary interest in the life of the former[2]. Similarly, creditors have an insurable interest in the lives of their debtors[3] and employers and employees in the lives of each other[4].

1 As to the frustration of a contract through the death of a party see CONTRACT vol 9 paras 453–454.
2 Ie sufficient for the purposes of the Life Assurance Act 1774 (see para 539 ante): *Anderson v Edie* (1795) 2 Park's Marine Insurances (8th Edn) 914; *Lea v Hinton* (1854) 5 De G M & G 823; *Branford v Saunders* (1877) 25 WR 650. The contract, however, must be lawful: *Dwyer v Edie* (1788) 2 Park's Marine Insurances (8th Edn) 914.

3 *Anderson v Edie* (1795) 2 Park's Marine Insurances (8th Edn) 914; *Von Lindenau v Desborough* (1828) 3 C & P 353; *Dalby v India and London Life Assurance Co* (1854) 15 CB 365, Ex Ch.
4 *Hebden v West* (1863) 3 B & S 579.

541. Pecuniary interest of relatives. In the case of relatives, other than husbands and wives[1], an insurable interest may not be presumed from the mere existence of the relationship; the pecuniary interest must be proved. Parents[2] and children[3], brothers and sisters[4], or other relatives[5] have, as such, no insurable interest in each other's lives. For the purpose of establishing an interest in such cases, it is sufficient that the assured is under a legal obligation to pay the funeral expenses of the life insured but, except in the exceptional cases in which an insurance for funeral expenses is still valid under the special legislation relating to industrial assurance and to friendly societies[6], a mere moral obligation is insufficient[7]. For the purpose of the statutory provisions which prohibit insurances except by persons having insurable interests[8], a person who fosters a child privately[9] or who maintains a protected child[10] is deemed to have no interest in the life of the child[11]. Friendly societies and industrial assurance companies are only obliged to pay up to £800 on the death of a child under ten years of age, except where the money is payable to a person who has an interest in the life of the child on whose death the money is payable[12].

1 As to insurance between husbands and wives see para 538 text and note 4 ante.
2 See *Halford v Kymer* (1830) 10 B & C 724; *Worthington v Curtis* (1875) 1 ChD 419, CA.
3 See *Howard v Refuge Friendly Society* (1886) 54 LT 644; *Harse v Pearl Life Assurance Co* [1904] 1 KB 558, CA; *Elson v Crookes* (1911) 106 LT 462.
4 *Evanson v Crooks* (1911) 106 LT 264; cf *Forgan v Pearl Life Assurance Co* (1907) 51 Sol Jo 230.
5 See *Greenslade v London and Manchester Industrial Insurance Co Ltd* (1913) 48 L Jo 330.
6 See FRIENDLY SOCIETIES; and INDUSTRIAL ASSURANCE.
7 *Harse v Pearl Life Assurance Co* [1904] 1 KB 558, CA; *Tofts v Pearl Life Assurance Co Ltd* [1915] 1 KB 189, CA.
8 Ie the Life Assurance Act 1774 s 1: see para 536 ante.
9 For the meaning of 'foster a child privately' see the Children Act 1989 s 66(1), Sch 8 para 11; and CHILDREN vol 5(2) (Reissue) para 1261.
10 For the meaning of 'protected child' the Adoption Act 1976 s 32(1); and CHILDREN vol 5(2) (Reissue) para 1054.
11 Children Act 1989 s 66(5); Adoption Act 1976 s 37(2).
12 Friendly Societies Act 1992 s 99. The provision is prospectively extended to trade unions and employers' associations by the Trade Union and Labour Relations (Consolidation) Act 1992 s 19(1) (to be amended by the Friendly Societies Act 1992 s 120(1), Sch 21 Pt I para 17 as from a date to be appointed). The Trade Union and Labour Relations (Consolidation) Act 1992 s 19(1) relates to trade unions but is applied to employers' organisations by s 129(3). Section 19(1) currently applies the Industrial Assurance and Friendly Societies Act 1948 s 6(1) to trade unions and employers organisations. However, s 6(1) was repealed with effect from 1 February 1993 by the Friendly Societies Act 1992 s 120(2), Sch 22, which was brought into effect by the Friendly Societies Act 1992 (Commencement No 3 and Transitional Provisions) Order 1993, SI 1993/16, art 2, Sch 3. It would seem therefore, in the absence of any transitional provisions, that trade unions and employers' associations are under no restrictions, and benefit from no limitations on liability, in relation to insurance policies on children under the age of 10 until the Friendly Societies Act 1992 s 120(1), Sch 21 Pt I para 17 is brought into force.

542. Payment to persons without interest. The Life Assurance Act 1774[1] applies only as between the insurers and the person claiming payment under the policy; if the insurers pay over the policy money without objecting to the absence of interest, any question that may arise as to the person really entitled to the money is to be determined as if the statute did not exist[2].

1 As to the Life Assurance Act 1774 generally see paras 535–536 ante.
2 *Worthington v Curtis* (1875) 1 ChD 419, CA; *A-G v Murray* [1904] 1 KB 165, CA; cf *Re Policy No 6402 of Scottish Equitable Life Assurance Society* [1902] 1 Ch 282.

543. Name of person interested to be inserted in policy. The second requirement of the Life Assurance Act 1774[1] is that the name of the person interested must be inserted in the policy[2]. Where, therefore, the assured effects the insurance for the benefit of another, the name[3] of the person intended to benefit must appear in the policy as well as the name of the assured[4]. For this purpose it is necessary to take into account the object of the insurance and not its form. Hence, where the policy purports to be an insurance by the assured upon his own life, but its real object is to benefit another, the policy is void unless the other person is named in it[5]. On the other hand, a person such as a trustee, having an interest in the life of another, may insure it in his own name without naming the beneficiary[6].

1 As to the first requirement see para 539 ante.
2 Life Assurance Act 1774 s 2; *Mollison v Staples* (1778) 2 Park's Marine Insurances (7th Edn) 640n: *Hodson v Observer Life Assurance Society* (1857) 8 E & B 40. However, it it has been stated that this requirement was not intended to apply to indemnity insurance: *Mark Rowlands Ltd v Berni Inns Ltd* [1986] QB 211, [1985] 3 All ER 473, CA; *Siu Yin Kwan (Administratrix of the Estate of Chan Ying Lung decd) v Eastern Insurance Co Ltd* [1994] 2 WLR 370, PC (a policy taken out in the name of shipping agents which did not name employers, could nevertheless have been enforced by the employers). As to the position where unnamed persons from time to time falling within a specified class or description are included in a policy see the Insurance Companies Amendment Act 1973 s 50(1); and para 536 text and note 3 ante.
3 Ie the personal name, not a description such as 'relative or friend': *Williams v Baltic Insurance Association of London Ltd* [1924] 2 KB 282 at 290 per Roche J.
4 *Shilling v Accidental Death Insurance Co* (1857) 2 H & N 42; subsequent proceedings (1857) 27 LJEx 16, (1858) 1 F & F 116.
5 *Evans v Bignold* (1869) LR 4 QB 622; *Forgan v Pearl Life Assurance Co* (1907) 51 Sol Jo 230. See also *Shilling v Accidental Death Insurance Co* (1857) 2 H & N 42; subsequent proceedings (1857) 27 LJEx 16, (1858) 1 F & F 116; and see para 538 text and note 3 ante.
6 *Tidswell v Ankerstein* (1792) Peake 204 (insurance by executor on life of grantor of annuity forming part of the estate). In *Collett v Morrison* (1851) 9 Hare 162, both were named.

544. Date for valuing interest. The third requirement of the Life Assurance Act 1774[1] is that no more can be recovered than the value of the interest[2]. It is not, however, necessary in order to enable a person to enforce a policy of insurance upon the life of another, that his interest should continue until the death of the life insured[3]; it is sufficient that he had an interest at the commencement of the risk[4]. He need not, therefore, prove that he has sustained a loss by reason of the death, the contract not being a contract of indemnity in the strict sense[5]. Thus, in the case of a creditor whose insurable interest is founded upon the existence of a debt, the repayment of the debt by the debtor in his lifetime, though it removes the risk of pecuniary loss and puts an end to the creditor's interest, does not preclude the creditor from continuing and enforcing the policy for his own benefit[6].

1 As to the first and second requirements of the Act see paras 539, 543 ante.
2 Life Assurance Act 1774 s 3: see para 536 text to note 4 ante.
3 *Dalby v India and London Life Assurance Co* (1854) 15 CB 365, Ex Ch, overruling *Godsall v Boldero* (1807) 9 East 72; *Law v London Indisputable Life Policy Co* (1855) 1 K & J 223.
4 *Rhind v Wilkinson* (1810) 2 Taunt 237; *Williams v Baltic Insurance Association of London Ltd* [1924] 2 KB 282 at 285, 290–291 per Roche J. As to what constitutes an interest see paras 539–541 ante.
5 *Dalby v India and London Life Assurance Co* (1854) 15 CB 365, Ex Ch. As to contracts of indemnity see para 661 post.
6 *Freme v Brade* (1858) 2 De G & J 582; followed in *Bruce v Garden* (1869) 5 Ch App 32. As to the creditor's position see further para 559 post.

(2) ASSIGNMENT OF LONG TERM INSURANCE POLICIES

(i) Rights apart from Statute

545. Assignability of life policies. The transfer of a policy of life insurance from the assured to another by manual delivery is effective, if so intended, to transfer the property in the document itself; but it does not of itself transfer the right to receive payment under the policy[1]. The right to receive payment is a chose in action[2] and to entitle the transferee to payment it must be validly assigned[3]. At common law assignments of a chose in action, except to the Crown, were not recognised, but equity always took a more tolerant view and permitted the assignee to join the assignor as plaintiff or, if he refused, as defendant in an action[4]. These technical difficulties have now largely been removed by statute[5].

1 *Rummens v Hare* (1876) 1 ExD 169, CA. As to mortgages of life policies see MORTGAGE.
2 *Re Moore, ex p Ibbetson* (1878) 8 ChD 519, CA.
3 *Crossley v City of Glasgow Life Assurance Co* (1876) 4 ChD 421; cf *Neale v Molineux* (1847) 2 Car & Kir 672; *Howes v Prudential Assurance Co and Howes* (1883) 48 LT 133.
4 *Dufaur v Professional Life Assurance Co* (1858) 25 Beav 599; *Re Turcan* (1888) 40 ChD 5 at 10 per Cotton LJ; and see CHOSES IN ACTION vol 6 (Reissue) para 26 et seq.
5 As to assignment under statute see para 548 et seq post.

546. Form of equitable assignment. As between assignor and assignee, any form of assignment is sufficient to constitute an equitable assignment of a life policy[1], so long as it is clear that the object of the transaction is to transfer the benefit of the policy to the transferee[2]. Unless there is consideration for the assignment or a valid declaration of trust, the assignor must have done everything to complete the gift, since equity will not help a volunteer to complete an imperfect gift[3]. To complete the assignee's title against the insurers or third parties, notice must be given to the insurers[4]. Normally the notice need not be in writing, so that an oral notice is sufficient[5]. By giving notice, the assignee acquires priority over any previous assignees who have not given notice[6], unless he already has constructive notice of their rights[7].

1 *Fortescue v Barnett* (1834) 3 My & K 36.
2 *Watson v McLean* (1858) E B & E 75, Ex Ch; *Pearson v Amicable Assurance Office* (1859) 27 Beav 229; *Chowne v Baylis* (1862) 31 Beav 351; *Re King, Sewell v King* (1879) 14 ChD 179; *Re Williams, Williams v Ball* [1917] 1 Ch 1, CA; see further CHOSES IN ACTION vol 6 (Reissue) para 30.
3 *Pearson v Amicable Assurance Office* (1859) 27 Beav 229; *Fortescue v Barnett* (1834) 3 My & K 36.
4 *Gale v Lewis* (1846) 9 QB 730. It seems that it need not necessarily be the assignee who gives the notice: see CHOSES IN ACTION vol 6 (Reissue) para 48.
5 *North British Insurance Co v Hallett* (1861) 7 Jur NS 1263. As to the necessity for written notice in the case of an interest in trust property see CHOSES IN ACTION vol 6 (Reissue) para 47.
6 *Re Lake, ex p Cavendish* [1903] 1 KB 151.
7 *Spencer v Clarke* (1878) 9 ChD 137; *Newman v Newman* (1885) 28 ChD 674; *Re Weniger's Policy* [1910] 2 Ch 291. See CHOSES IN ACTION vol 6 (Reissue) para 44.

547. Transfer subject to equities. The effect of an equitable assignment is to transfer to the assignee the rights of the assignor[1]; any bonuses or additions to the policy money[2] therefore pass to the assignee[3]. The assignee, however, takes subject to equities[4]. If, therefore, at the time of the assignment, the policy is voidable in the hands of the assignor, it is equally voidable in the hands of the assignee[5]. Further, the rights of the assignee are liable to be defeated by any subsequent breach of condition which would have rendered the policy voidable if it had remained in the hands of the assignor[6]. The policy may, however, contain a provision saving the rights of the assignee[7]; as a general rule, this provision operates for the benefit of bona fide assignees for value only[8].

1 These include the benefit of any variations in the terms of the policy: *Royal Exchange Assurance v Hope* [1928] Ch 179, CA.
2 As to bonuses see para 552 post.
3 *Courtney v Ferrers* (1827) 1 Sim 137; *Parkes v Bott* (1838) 9 Sim 388; cf *Roberts v Edwards* (1863) 33 Beav 259.
4 See generally CHOSES IN ACTION vol 6 (Reissue) paras 61–68.
5 *Lefevre v Boyle* (1832) 3 B & Ad 877.
6 *Jackson v Forster* (1860) 1 E & E 470, Ex Ch; *Wigan v English and Scottish Law Life Assurance Association* [1909] 1 Ch 291 (cases of suicide by the assured). The assignor may enter into a covenant with the assignee not to do any act which will avoid the policy: *Vyse v Wakefield* (1840) 6 M & W 442.
7 The assured himself, even though the policy is effected upon the life of his debtor, is not entitled to the benefit of the provision: *Rowett, Leaky & Co Ltd v Scottish Provident Institution* (1926) 134 LT 660; affd [1927] 1 Ch 55, CA; cf *Royal London Mutual Insurance Society v Barrett* [1928] Ch 411 (cases of suicide by the assured).
8 *Cook v Black* (1842) 1 Hare 390; *Moore v Woolsey* (1854) 4 E & B 243; *Dufaur v Professional Life Assurance Co* (1858) 25 Beav 599; *Jones v Consolidated Investment Assurance Co* (1858) 26 Beav 256; *Solicitors' and General Life Assurance Society v Lamb* (1864) 2 De G J & Sm 251, followed in *City Bank v Sovereign Life Assurance Co* (1884) 50 LT 565; *White v British Empire Mutual Life Assurance Co* (1868) LR 7 Eq 394 (cases of suicide by the assured). It seems that an assignee for value before the suicide of the assured can enforce a policy even if the assured commits suicide while he is of sound mind if the policy contains an express promise to pay on sane suicide: *Moore v Woolsey* (1854) 4 E & B 243; *Beresford v Royal Insurance Co Ltd* [1938] AC 586 at 600, [1938] 2 All ER 602 at 607, HL, per Lord Atkin.

(ii) Rights under Statute

548. Statutory rights of assignee to sue. Under the Policies of Assurance Act 1867 any person or corporation entitled by assignment or other derivative title to a policy of life assurance[1], and possessing at the time of action the right in equity to receive and give to the assurance company[2] liable an effectual discharge for the money assured or secured under the policy, may sue at law in his or its own name to recover the money[3] after due written notice of the assignment has been given to the company concerned[4]. The Act does not affect the rights of the assignor and assignee as between themselves[5], and it is still possible to have an assignment valid in equity, though not at law because the formalities required by the Act have not been complied with[6]. The only effect of the Act, therefore, is to enable the assignee to sue the insurers in his own name[7]. The Act does not give the assignee greater rights than those of the assignor and he remains subject to equities[8].

1 'Policy of life assurance' or 'policy' means any instrument by which the payment of money by or out of the funds of an assurance company (see note 2 infra) on the happening of any contingency depending on the duration of human life is assured or secured: Policies of Assurance Act 1867 s 7. As to the exclusion of the policies issued by friendly societies see note 3 infra.
2 'Assurance company' means and includes every corporation, association, society or company carrying on the business of assuring lives or survivorships, either alone or in conjunction with any other object or objects: ibid s 7.

3 Ibid s 1. This Act is not affected by the Law of Property Act 1925 s 136(1) (see para 550 post): s 136(2). The Policies of Assurance Act 1867 does not apply to any policy of insurance granted, or to any contract for payment on death entered into, in pursuance of the Government Annuities Act 1929 Pt II (ss 41–66) (see MONEY), or the enactments replaced by that Part of that Act, or to any engagement for payment on death by any friendly society: Policies of Assurance Act 1867 s 8. As to the assignment of policies issued by friendly societies see FRIENDLY SOCIETIES.

4 As to due notice see paras 549–550 post.

5 *Newman v Newman* (1885) 28 ChD 674.

6 Cf *William Brandt's Sons & Co v Dunlop Rubber Co Ltd* [1905] AC 454, HL; and see para 546 ante.

7 Before the enactment of the Policies of Assurance Act 1867, the assignee could not sue in his own name; cf *Re Turcan* (1888) 40 ChD 5, CA; and see para 545 ante.

8 *British Equitable Insurance Co v Great Western Rly Co* (1869) 38 LJCh 314; cf the Policies of Assurance Act 1867 s 2; and see para 547 ante.

549. Statutory conditions. The rights conferred by the Policies of Assurance Act 1867[1] will be acquired if the following conditions are fulfilled:

(1) the assignment is such as would, apart from the Act, constitute a good equitable assignment[2]; and

(2) the assignment is in writing, either by indorsement upon the policy or by separate instrument[3].

Before the assignee, or his personal representatives or assigns, can sue under the Act, written notice of the date and purport of the assignment must be given to the insurers at their principal place of business or, if they have two or more, at some one of them, in England, Scotland or Northern Ireland[4]. The policy must specify the place or places at which notice of assignments may be given[5]. The insurers are bound, upon request, to give a written acknowledgment of the receipt of notice; and this acknowledgment is conclusive evidence against the insurers that notice has been given[6]. The date on which the notice is received regulates the priorities of all claims under any assignment[7]; but, notwithstanding this provision, a subsequent assignee does not by giving notice first obtain priority over a previous assignment of which he has notice[8]. A payment made in good faith by the insurers in respect of any policy before the date when notice of an assignment is received is valid as against the assignee giving such notice[9].

1 See the Policies of Assurance Act 1867 s 1; and para 548 ante.

2 Ibid s 1; *Crossley v City of Glasgow Life Assurance Co* (1876) 4 ChD 421; *Spencer v Clarke* (1878) 9 ChD 137; *Re Williams, Williams v Ball* [1917] 1 Ch 1, CA. As to equitable assignments see paras 546–547 ante.

3 Policies of Assurance Act 1867 s 5. To be valid the assignment must be in the words or to the effect of the statutory form provided: s 5. The form is 'I, A B of, etc, in consideration of, etc, do hereby assign unto C D of, etc, his executors, administrators and assigns, the [within] policy of assurance granted, etc [*here describe the policy*]. In witness, etc': s 5, Schedule.

4 Policies of Assurance Act 1867 s 3; Irish Free State (Consequential Adaptation of Enactments) Order 1923, SR & O 1923/405.

5 Policies of Assurance Act 1867 s 4.

6 Ibid s 6. A fee of not more than 25p may be charged: s 6 (amended by the Decimal Currency Act 1969 s 10(1)). As to the application of the Policies of Assurance Act 1867 s 6 see text and note 4 supra.

7 Ibid s 3. As to priority see CHOSES IN ACTION vol 6 (Reissue) para 44.

8 *Newman v Newman* (1885) 28 ChD 674.

9 Policies of Assurance Act 1867 s 3.

550. Absolute assignments. Apart from the rights under the Policies of Assurance Act 1867[1], an assignee of a life policy has the right to sue in his own name, and the other rights conferred by the general statutory provisions relating to the legal assignment of choses in action[2], provided that (1) there is an absolute assignment in writing under the hand of the assignor, not purporting to be by way of charge only; and (2) express notice in writing to the insurers has been given[3]. The effective date of the notice is the date on which it is received by or on behalf of the insurers[4]. The operation of the assignment is subject to equities having priority over the right of the assignee[5]. An assignment may be absolute notwithstanding that it is by way of mortgage subject to a right of redemption[6], or that the assignee is a trustee of the proceeds[7]. A voluntary assignment is covered equally with an assignment for value[8].

1 As to such rights see paras 548–549 ante.
2 Ie those conferred by the Law of Property Act 1925 s 136(1): see CHOSES IN ACTION vol 6 (Reissue) paras 12–25.
3 See ibid s 136(1).
4 See *Holt v Heatherfield Trust Ltd* [1942] 2 KB 1, [1942] 1 All ER 404; and CHOSES IN ACTION vol 6 (Reissue) para 20.
5 See the Law of Property Act 1925 s 136(1) proviso; *West of England Bank v Batchelor* (1882) 51 LJCh 199 at 200; and CHOSES IN ACTION vol 6 (Reissue) para 23.
6 *Tancred v Delagoa Bay and East Africa Rly Co* (1889) 23 QBD 239; *Durham Bros v Robertson* [1898] 1 QB 765, CA.
7 *Comfort v Betts* [1891] 1 QB 737, CA. See further CHOSES IN ACTION vol 6 (Reissue) para 16.
8 *Re Westerton, Public Trustee v Gray* [1919] 2 Ch 104; and see CHOSES IN ACTION vol 6 (Reissue) para 17.

551. Condition against assignment. A condition prohibiting assignment will be construed strictly. Thus, a policy which is rendered unassignable at law may still be capable of assignment in equity by declaration of trust[1].

1 *Re Turcan* (1888) 40 ChD 5, CA. See CHOSES IN ACTION vol 6 (Reissue) para 90.

(3) PAYMENT UNDER LONG TERM INSURANCE POLICIES

(i) The Amount Payable

552. Bonus and share of profits. The amount payable under the policy is not necessarily limited to the sum insured. Many policies provide for the increase of the sum insured by the addition of bonuses, which accrue after the policy has been in force for a specified period[1], or by giving the assured a share in the profits of the insurers' business[2]. Regulations have been made in relation to contracts under which the benefits are determined by reference to the value of, or the income from, property of any description or by reference to fluctuations in, or in an index of, the value of property of any description[3].

Where a policy has been effected in another country the place of payment is governed by the proper law of the contract[4].

1 *Prudential Insurance Co v IRC* [1904] 2 KB 658 at 665 per Channell J.
2 The distribution of profits is usually in the discretion of the insurers: *Baerlein v Dickson* (1909) 25 TLR 585; *British Equitable Assurance Co Ltd v Baily* [1906] AC 35, HL; *Scragg v United Kingdom Temperance and General Provident Institution* [1976] 2 Lloyd's Rep 227 (sum payable under policy limited if death caused directly or indirectly by motor racing).
3 See the Insurance Companies Regulations 1981, SI 1981/1654, reg 72 (amended by SI 1991/2511).
4 *Pick v Manufacturers Life Insurance Co* [1958] 2 Lloyd's Rep 93: see CONFLICT OF LAWS vol 8 para 585.

553. Surrender value. The value of a current policy depends upon the life expectation of the life insured, and the value, though only nominal at the commencement of the risk, usually increases according to the length of the period during which the policy has remained in force[1]. If, therefore, the policy is allowed to lapse[2], its value will be lost to the assured[3]. To obviate this, provision may be made by which the assured becomes entitled on notice[4] to surrender the policy and to be paid its surrender value[5]. In lieu of being paid the surrender value, the assured may be given the option of taking a fully paid policy for a reduced amount proportionate to the number of premiums actually paid[6].

1 This will be correct as regards the early years of the insurance, but if the assured lives beyond the average period of life upon which the premiums are based, he will have made a bad bargain: *Prudential Insurance Co Ltd v IRC* [1904] 2 KB 658 at 665 per Channell J.
2 As to lapse and revival of policies see para 479 ante.
3 For statutory provisions as to free policies and surrender values in relation to contracts of industrial assurance see INDUSTRIAL ASSURANCE.
4 Once the notice has become effective, the surrender value only will be payable, even though the assured dies before the actual surrender of the policy or the payment of the surrender value: *Ingram-Johnson v Century Insurance Co* 1909 SC 1032.
5 *Equitable Life Assurance Society of the United States v Reed* [1914] AC 587, PC.
6 As to the exercise of the option by a husband where the policy is effected for the benefit of his wife (as to which see para 538 ante) see *Re Policy of the Equitable Life Assurance Society of the United States and Mitchell* (1911) 27 TLR 213; *Re Fleetwood's Policy* [1926] Ch 48.

554. Interest. The amount payable under the policy does not carry interest as a matter of course from the time when it becomes due[1], but interest may be awarded as damages for the wrongful detention of money which ought to have been paid[2].

1 *Higgins v Sargent* (1823) 2 B & C 348.
2 As to when interest will be so awarded see para 503 ante.

555. Payment in foreign currency. Where the policy provides for payment in a foreign currency, the amount payable, for the purposes of conversion into sterling, is calculated at the rate of exchange on the day when the amount became due[1].

1 *Anderson v Equitable Life Assurance Society of the United States* (1926) 134 LT 557, CA; *Buerger v New York Life Assurance Co* (1927) 43 TLR 601, CA; and see MONEY.

(ii) Persons entitled to Payment

556. Insurance on life of assured. Where the life insured is that of the assured himself, the person entitled to payment is the owner of the legal chose in action, that is to say, the assured's personal representatives[1], legal assignee[2] or trustee in bankruptcy[3], as the case may be[4].

1 If the assured is a person domiciled abroad, the insurers may pay his representatives without a grant of representation in the United Kingdom: Revenue Act 1884 s 11 proviso (amended by the Revenue Act 1889 s 19). In relation to estate duty the insurers or representatives are entitled to retain sufficient out of the policy money to cover any duty payable: *Haas v Atlas Assurance Co Ltd* [1913] 2 KB 209. As to the replacement of estate duty by inheritance tax see INHERITANCE TAXATION vol 24 (Reissue) para 602.
2 *Ottley v Gray* (1847) 16 LJCh 512; *Desborough v Harris* (1855) 5 De G M & G 439.
3 *Jackson v Forster* (1860) 1 E & E 470 at 471, Ex Ch, per Cockburn CJ.

4 For the statutory provisions as to the persons to whom payment may be made on the death intestate of a member of a registered friendly society without having made a nomination see FRIENDLY SOCIETIES. As to the position where policy money is expressed to be payable to a third party see para 557 post.

557. Position of third party. The policy money payable on the death of the assured may be expressed to be payable to a third party and the third party is then prima facie merely the agent for the time being of the legal owner[1] and has his authority to receive the policy money and to give a good discharge; but he generally has no right to sue the insurers in his own name[2]. The question has been raised whether the third party's authority to receive the policy money is terminated by the death of the assured; it seems, however, that unless and until they are otherwise directed by the assured's personal representatives the insurers may pay the money to the third party and get a good discharge from him[3]. By taking out a policy expressed to be for the benefit of a third party, the assured does not thereby necessarily constitute himself a trustee[4]. In each case it is a question of construction of the terms of the policy or relevant deed whether or not such a trust is created[5]. There is, in any case, nothing in common law to prohibit a contract between two persons under which one party is obliged to confer a benefit on a third party not privy to the contract, and where a contract is of that type, there is no principle of equity compelling the obligor to make payment to anyone else, for example the trustee in bankruptcy of the other party to the contract[6].

1 *Re Policy No 6402 of Scottish Equitable Life Assurance Society* [1902] 1 Ch 282; cf *Re Slattery* [1917] 2 IR 278.
2 *Cleaver v Mutual Reserve Fund Life Association* [1892] 1 QB 147, CA; *Re Engelbach's Estate, Tibbetts v Engelbach* [1924] 2 Ch 348; *Re Sinclair's Life Policy* [1938] Ch 799, [1938] 3 All ER 124. For the power of a member of a registered friendly society to dispose by nomination of sums payable on his death and the right of the nominee to payment on the death of the nominator see FRIENDLY SOCIETIES. As to the effect of a provision in the rules of an unregistered friendly society for payment of death benefit to relatives of a member see FRIENDLY SOCIETIES. As to discharge clauses permitting payments to relations of the assured in the case of industrial assurance see INDUSTRIAL ASSURANCE. As to policies in favour of the wife or husband or children of the assured see para 558 post.
3 *Re Engelbach's Estate, Tibbetts v Engelbach* [1924] 2 Ch 348; *Re Sinclair's Life Policy* [1938] Ch 799, [1938] 3 All ER 124.
4 *Re Webb, Barclays Bank Ltd v Webb* [1941] Ch 225, [1941] 1 All ER 321 (see para 565 note 3 post); *Re Gordon, Lloyds Bank and Parratt v Lloyd and Gordon* [1940] Ch 851 (construction of rules of benefit society). In both these cases it was held that a trust was created. Cases in which it was held that no trust was created are *Re Engelbach's Estate, Tibbetts v Engelbach* [1924] 2 Ch 348; *Re Clay's Policy of Assurance, Clay v Earnshaw* [1937] 2 All ER 548; *Re Sinclair's Life Policy* [1938] Ch 799, [1938] 3 All ER 124; *Re Foster, Hudson v Foster* [1938] 3 All ER 357; *Re Independent Air Travel Ltd* [1961] 1 Lloyd's Rep 604; *Re Foster's Policy, Menneer v Foster* [1966] 1 All ER 432, [1966] 1 WLR 222.
5 *Cleaver v Mutual Reserve Fund Life Association* [1892] 1 QB 147 at 157, CA, per Fry LJ. Unless the right is expressly reserved, a company may not validly change the beneficial interests under a company superannuation scheme so as to confer a benefit on a third party without the consent of the employees who are parties to the scheme: *Re Alfred Herbert Ltd Pension and Life Assurance Scheme Trusts, Alfred Herbert Ltd v Hancocks* [1960] 1 All ER 618, [1960] 1 WLR 271.
6 *Re Schebsman, ex p Official Receiver, Trustee v Cargo Superintendent (London) Ltd and Schebsman* [1944] Ch 83, [1943] 2 All ER 768, CA; see also *Re Stapleton-Bretherton, Weld-Blundell v Stapleton-Bretherton* [1941] Ch 482, [1941] 3 All ER 5; *Green v Russell (McCarthy, third party)* [1959] 2 QB 226, [1959] 2 All ER 525, CA.

558. Policies in favour of spouse or children. A policy effected by a man on his life and expressed to be for the benefit of his wife or children, or by a woman on her life and expressed to be for the benefit of her husband or children, creates a trust in favour of the objects named in the policy and the money payable under the policy does not, so long as any object of the trust remains unperformed, form part of the assured's estate. Provision is made for the appointment of trustees of the money payable under such a policy; and the receipt of a trustee or trustees duly appointed, or in default of any such appointment or of notice of such appointment to the insurers the receipt of the assured's personal representatives, is a discharge to the insurers for the sum insured[1].

1 Married Women's Property Act 1882 s 11; see further HUSBAND AND WIFE vol 22 para 978. As to the application of the statutory provision to an endowment policy see para 565 post.

559. Insurance on life of third party. Where the life insured is not that of the assured, the assured is the person prima facie entitled to payment. In the absence of some agreement to that effect, the policy does not enure to the benefit of the estate of the life insured[1]. Thus, if a creditor insures the life of the debtor, payment of the debt does not in itself give any rights over the policy to the debtor; the assured effected the policy for his own protection and accordingly remains entitled to its benefit[2]. However, there may be an express agreement between the parties that the policy is to become the property of the debtor when the debt is paid; and a similar agreement is to be implied where by arrangement between the parties the creditor is to effect the policy on the life of the debtor and the debtor is to pay the premiums[3].

1 *Freme v Brade* (1858) 2 De G & J 582; *Worthington v Curtis* (1875) 1 ChD 419, CA; cf *Henson v Blackwell* (1845) 4 Hare 434; *Hatley v Liverpool Victoria Legal Friendly Society* (1918) 88 LJKB 237; *Re Engelbach's Estate, Tibbetts v Engelbach* [1924] 2 Ch 348.
2 *Freme v Brade* (1858) 2 De G & J 582; *Bruce v Garden* (1869) 5 Ch App 32; *Knox v Turner* (1870) 5 Ch App 515; *Preston v Neele* (1879) 12 ChD 760; see also *Brown v Freeman* (1851) 4 De G & Sm 444; *Lewis v King* (1875) 44 LJCh 259.
3 *Salt v Marquess of Northampton* [1892] AC 1, HL; see also *Holland v Smith* (1806) 6 Esp 11; *Lea v Hinton* (1854) 5 De G M & G 823; *Drysdale v Piggott* (1856) 8 De G M & G 546; *Courtenay v Wright* (1860) 2 Giff 337. The fact that the debtor, though charged with the premiums, has never repaid them to the creditor is immaterial: *Morland v Isaac* (1855) 20 Beav 389; cf *Triston v Hardey* (1851) 14 Beav 232.

560. Lien on policy. A voluntary payment of premiums upon a life policy does not give any lien or interest in the policy to the person making the payment[1]. However, in addition to the ordinary possessory lien[2], there are certain cases in which a lien may be acquired by payment of the premium. Instances in which such cases have arisen are the following[3]:

(1) by contract with the beneficial owner of the policy[4];
(2) by reason of the right of a trustee to an indemnity out of the trust property for money expended by him for its preservation[5];
(3) by the subrogation of some person, who at a trustee's request has advanced money for the preservation of trust property, to the right of the trustee[6];
(4) by reason of the right of a mortgagee, or other person having a charge on the policy, to add to his security any money paid by him to preserve the property charged[7];
(5) where a married woman has paid, out of her own property, the premiums on a policy effected under her marriage settlement or at her husband's request on a policy effected in their joint names[8];
(6) where an assignee, after assignment of the policy to him, has paid premiums although, in fact, a prior interest in the policy has been created[9];

(7) where the premium has been paid in the mistaken belief of all parties that the person paying them was the owner of the policy[10].

Where, however, a bankrupt pays premiums on a life policy after his bankruptcy, no lien arises in his favour against the trustee in bankruptcy[11].

1 *Burridge v Row* (1844) 13 LJCh 173; *Falcke v Scottish Imperial Insurance Co* (1886) 34 ChD 234, CA; *Re Waugh's Trusts* (1877) 46 LJCh 629; *Re Jones' Settlement, Stunt v Jones* [1915] 1 Ch 373. Payments made with the knowledge of the trustee in bankruptcy of the assured must be allowed: *Re Tyler, ex p Official Receiver* [1907] 1 KB 865, CA; cf *Tapster v Ward* (1909) 101 LT 503, CA, and see the text to note 11 infra.
2 *Head v Egerton* (1734) 3 P Wms 280; *West of England Bank v Batchelor* (1882) 51 LJCh 199.
3 The first four instances listed in the text are taken from *Re Leslie, Leslie v French* (1883) 23 ChD 552. This list is not, however, exhaustive: see *Strutt v Tippett* (1889) 62 LT 475 at 477, CA, per Lindley LJ; *Re Foster, Hudson v Foster (No 2)* [1938] 3 All ER 610.
4 *Re Leslie, Leslie v French* (1883) 23 ChD 552; and see *Richards v Platel* (1841) 1 Cr & Ph 79; *Earl Fitzwilliam v Price* (1858) 31 LTOS 389; *West of England Bank v Batchelor* (1882) 52 LJCh 199; *Re Walker, Meredith v Walker* (1893) 68 LT 517; *Re McKerrell, McKerrell v Gowans* [1912] 2 Ch 648.
5 *Re Leslie, Leslie v French* (1883) 23 ChD 552; and see *Clack v Holland* (1854) 19 Beav 262; *Re Smith's Estate, Bilham v Smith* [1937] Ch 636, [1937] 3 All ER 472; cf *Re Earl of Winchilsea's Policy Trusts* (1888) 39 ChD 168. Where, however, the relationship of parent and child or husband and wife exists between the trustee and the beneficiary, payments made by the trustee are prima facie for the advancement and benefit of the beneficiary and cannot be recovered: *Re Roberts, Public Trustee v Roberts* [1946] Ch 1.
6 *Re Leslie, Leslie v French* (1883) 23 ChD 552; and see *Clack v Holland* (1854) 19 Beav 262. A trustee of a policy who makes or obtains advances to pay the premiums under the policy cannot, however, either obtain or create a lien if he is, or in the proper performance of his trust ought to be, in possession of funds applicable for the purpose: *Clack v Holland* supra; *Re Regent's Canal Ironworks Co, ex p Grissell* (1875) 3 ChD 411, CA.
7 *Re Leslie, Leslie v French* (1883) 23 ChD 552; and see *Gill v Downing* (1874) LR 17 Eq 316; *Shaw v Scottish Widows' Fund Assurance Society* (1917) 87 LJCh 76; *Re City of Glasgow Life Assurance Co, Clare's Policy* (1914) 84 LJCh 684.
8 *Burridge v Row* (1844) 13 LJCh 173; *Re McKerrell, McKerrell v Gowans* [1912] 2 Ch 648. No lien arises, however, where the wife voluntarily pays premiums on a policy on her husband's life subject to a settlement under which she takes first life interest: *Re Jones' Settlement, Stunt v Jones* [1915] 1 Ch 373.
9 *West v Reid* (1843) 2 Hare 249; *Gill v Downing* (1874) LR 17 Eq 316.
10 *Re Foster, Hudson v Foster (No 2)* [1938] 3 All ER 610.
11 *Tapster v Ward* (1909) 101 LT 503, CA.

(iii) Payment into Court

561. Statutory right to pay into court. Subject to rules of court[1], any life assurance company[2] may pay into the Supreme Court any money payable by it under a life policy[3] in respect of which, in the opinion of the board of directors, no sufficient discharge can otherwise be obtained[4]. The receipt of the proper officer is a sufficient discharge to the company for the money so paid into court and, subject to rules of court, the money must be dealt with according to the orders of the Supreme Court[5].

1 For the rules of court relating to payment into court by life assurance companies see para 562 post.
2 'Life assurance company' means any corporation, company or society carrying on the business of life assurance, not being a society registered under the Acts relating to friendly societies: Life Assurance Companies (Payment into Court) Act 1896 s 2. For the Acts relating to friendly societies SEE FRIENDLY SOCIETIES.
3 'Life policy' includes any policy not foreign to the business of life assurance: ibid s 2.
4 Ibid s 3 (amended by the Administration of Justice Act 1965 s 17(1), Sch 1; and the Courts Act 1971 s 56(4), Sch 11 Pt II).
5 Life Assurance Companies (Payment into Court) Act 1896 s 4 (amended by the Administration of Justice Act 1965 Sch 1; and the Courts Act 1971 Sch 11 Pt II).

562. Exercise of right. A company desiring to make a payment into court under the Life Assurance Companies (Payment into Court) Act 1896[1] must file an affidavit, made by its secretary or other authorised officer, setting out:

(1) a short description of the policy in question and a statement of the persons entitled under it with their names and addresses so far as known to the company[2];

(2) a short statement of the notices received by the company claiming an interest in or title to the money assured or withdrawing any such claim with the dates of receipt of such notices and the names and addresses of the persons by whom they were given[3];

(3) a statement that, in the opinion of the board of directors of the company, no sufficient discharge can be obtained otherwise than by payment into court under the Act[4];

(4) the submission by the company to pay into court such further sum, if any, as the court may direct and to pay any costs ordered by the court to be paid by the company[5];

(5) an undertaking by the company forthwith to send to the Accountant General any notice of claim received by the company after the making of the affidavit with a letter referring to the title of the affidavit[6]; and

(6) an address where the company may be served with any summons or order, or notice of any proceeding, relating to the money paid into court[7].

The company may not deduct from the money payable by them under the policy any costs of or incidental to the payment into court[8]. No payment may be made into court under the Act where any action to which the company is a party is pending in relation to the policy or money thereby assured except with the leave of the court to be obtained by summons in the action[9]. Unless the court otherwise directs, a summons by which a claim with respect to money paid into court under the Act is made, must not, except where the summons includes an application for payment of a further sum of costs by the company which made the payment, be served on that company, but it must be served on every person who appears by the affidavit on which the payment into court was made to be entitled to, or interested in, the money in court or to have a claim upon it or who has given a notice of claim which has been sent to the Accountant General in accordance with the undertaking referred to above[10]. The company which has paid money into court must forthwith send notice of the payment to every person appearing from the affidavit on which the payment was made to be entitled to or have an interest in the money paid[11]. Where an application to the High Court for the payment or transfer to any person of any funds is made in the Chancery Division the application may be disposed of in chambers[12]. Any such application must be made by summons, and unless the application is made in a pending cause or matter or an application for the same purpose has previously been made by petition or originating summons, the summons must be an originating summons[13].

If a company acts unreasonably in paying into court, it runs the risk of paying the costs to which the person entitled is put by reason of the payment[14]. The company may have recourse to the statutory power to pay into court where the policy has been lost[15].

1 For the provisions of the Act see para 561 ante.
2 RSC Ord 92 r 1(1)(a).
3 RSC Ord 92 r 1(1)(b).
4 RSC Ord 92 r 1(1)(c).

5 RSC Ord 92 r 1(1)(d).
6 RSC Ord 92 r 1(1)(e).
7 RSC Ord 92 r 1(1)(f).
8 RSC Ord 92 r 1(2).
9 RSC Ord 92 r 1(3).
10 Ie referred to in head (5) in the text: RSC Ord 92 r 1(4).
11 RSC Ord 92 r 4.
12 RSC Ord 92 r 5(1)(a). See further PRACTICE AND PROCEDURE.
13 RSC Ord 92 r 5(2).
14 *Harrison v Alliance Assurance Co* [1903] 1 KB 184, CA.
15 *Harrison v Alliance Assurance Co* [1903] 1 KB 184, CA. Before the enactment of the Life Assurance Companies (Payment into Court) Act 1896 it had been held, in the case of conflicting claims, that if the insurers could be regarded as trustees, they could pay the policy money into court under the Trustee Relief Acts then in force (*Re Hall* (1861) 5 LT 395; *Re United Kingdom Life Assurance Co* (1865) 34 Beav 493; *Re Webb's Policy* (1866) LR 2 Eq 456; *Re Rosier's Trusts* (1877) 37 LT 426); but, if they were not in the position of trustees, they could not do so (*Re Haycock's Policy* (1876) 1 ChD 611; *Matthew v Northern Assurance Co* (1878) 9 ChD 80), and their only remedy was to interplead (*Prudential Assurance Co v Thomas* (1867) 3 Ch App 74). As to interpleader see INTERPLEADER.

(4) ENDOWMENT INSURANCE

563. Basic features of endowment insurance. The essence of a contract by way of endowment insurance is that a specified sum becomes payable, not on the death of the insured, but on the arrival of a specified date, the insured being still alive; the contingency is the duration of life up to the specified date rather than the arrival of death[1]. There may be subsidiary provisions providing that, in the event of death before the specified date, a proportion of the specified sum is payable[2] or a return of premiums will be made in whole or in part[3]. Usually there is an amalgamation of endowment and strict life insurance in the same policy, so as to make the specified sum payable either on the specified date or on death before that date[4].

1 *Prudential Assurance Co v IRC* [1904] 2 KB 658; *Joseph v Law Integrity Insurance Co Ltd* [1912] 2 Ch 581, CA; *Gould v Curtis* [1913] 3 KB 84, CA.
2 *Prudential Assurance Co v IRC* [1904] 2 KB 658; *Gould v Curtis* [1913] 3 KB 84, CA.
3 *Joseph v Law Integrity Insurance Co Ltd* [1912] 2 Ch 581, CA.
4 *Gould v Curtis* [1913] 3 KB 84 at 91, CA, per Cozens-Hardy MR, citing Bunyon's Law of Life Assurance (4th Edn) 1. As to damages for loss of pension rights suffered by reason of wrongful dismissal see *Acklam v Sentinel Insurance Co Ltd* [1959] 2 Lloyd's Rep 683; and EMPLOYMENT vol 16 (Reissue) para 307.

564. Endowment insurance as species of life insurance. Although endowment insurance is not life insurance in the strict sense[1] it is within the broad meaning of the term[2]. The general principles applicable to life insurance which have been previously set out[3] are, therefore, equally applicable to endowment insurance. In particular, endowment insurance ranks as life insurance for the purposes of the statutory restrictions on the carrying on of life insurance business[4], and a policy of combined endowment insurance and life insurance ranks as life insurance for the purpose of the provisions relating to income tax relief in respect of life insurance premiums[5].

1 For the meaning of life insurance in the strict sense see para 525 ante.
2 For the broad meaning of life insurance see para 527 ante.
3 As to these general principles see para 525 et seq ante.

4 As to such restrictions see paras 527 note 5 ante, 803 et seq post.

5 As to the extent of relief in such a case and as to relief in respect of premiums paid for retirement annuities see INCOME TAXATION vol 23 (Reissue) para 976 et seq.

565. Endowment policy for child or wife. Considerable difficulties have arisen in the case of child's endowment policies or deferred life insurance, policies taken out by a parent, because normally a person has no insurable interest in the life of his child[1], and such a policy would therefore be illegal if it were regarded as enuring for the benefit of the proposer[2]. It seems that, at any rate where the policy is in the form now commonly current, the proposer will be regarded as holding the policy in trust for the child[3]; if after attaining the age of 18[4] the child makes the appropriate payments of premium, this might well operate as a novation by which he was accepted as the assured[5].

Where a husband takes out an endowment policy expressed to be for the benefit of his wife, the statutory provisions relating to policies effected by husbands and wives for one another's benefit[6] apply[7].

1 As to insurable interests in the lives of relatives see para 541 ante.

2 As to insurances on the life of a child under ten by friendly societies and industrial insurance companies see para 541 text and note 12 ante.

3 See *Re Webb, Barclays Bank Ltd v Webb* [1941] Ch 225, [1941] 1 All ER 321 (policy taken out by father and expressed to be on behalf of and for benefit of child; sum assured to be paid to personal representatives of child on his death at or over 21; power to father to surrender, assign or charge policy before child attained 21; on twenty-first birthday of child, rights of father to cease and child to be solely interested subject to any subsisting assignment or charge; provision for partial recovery of premiums if child died under 21; if father died before child attained 21, policy to remain in force until, but not including, child's twenty-first birthday; father died while child a minor; policy held by father at his death, and thereafter by trustee of his will, in trust for child). In that case, *Re Engelbach's Estate, Tibbets v Engelbach* [1924] 2 Ch 348, and *Re Sinclair's Life Policy* [1938] Ch 799, [1938] 3 All ER 124, were distinguished. See also *Re Foster's Policy, Menneer v Foster* [1966] 1 All ER 432, [1966] 1 WLR 222; *Gee v Gee* [1973] 5 WWR 268 (Sask). As to policies expressed to be for the benefit of third parties see para 557 ante.

4 As to the reduction of the age of majority from 21 to 18 see the Family Law Reform Act 1969 ss 1(1), (2)(a); and CHILDREN vol 5(2) (Reissue) para 601.

5 Compare the position in Scots law as laid down in the House of Lords in *Carmichael v Carmichael's Executrix* 1920 SC (HL) 195.

6 As to policies effected by spouses see para 558 ante.

7 *Re Ioakimidis' Policy Trusts, Ioakimidis v Hartcup* [1925] Ch 403; and see HUSBAND AND WIFE.

566. Alienation of benefits under policy. If income tax relief is to be obtained for premiums for a contract of retirement annuity insurance, the contract must include a provision securing that no annuity payable under it will be capable in whole or in part of surrender, commutation or assignment[1]. However, it is permissible, where there is a minimum term for the annuity, for the assured to bequeath by will any sum which may become payable by reason of his death before the expiration of the minimum term, and also for the personal representatives of the assured to assign any such sum, either to give effect to a testamentary disposition, or to the rights of those entitled on intestacy, or in appropriation towards any legacy or share or interest in the estate[2].

1 Income and Corporation Taxes Act 1988 s 620(2), (3).
2 See ibid s 620(4); and INCOME TAXATION.

6. ACCIDENT AND SICKNESS INSURANCE

(1) ACCIDENT INSURANCE

(i) In general

567. Relation of accident insurance to life insurance. The object of accident insurance is to make provision for payment of a sum of money[1] in the event of the assured sustaining accidental injury[2]. It resembles life insurance[3] (and differs from other types of insurance) in that it is not a contract of indemnity[4]; it is merely a contract to pay a sum of money on the happening of a specified event[5], namely the sustaining by the assured of personal injury by such accidental means as may be defined in the policy[6]. The event may involve the death of the assured, but the insurance is not for that reason a contract of life insurance[7]. In the case of life insurance, the assured is bound to die some day, but there is uncertainty as to the date when the death will occur[8]; in the case of accident insurance it may be that no accident will ever happen; and, even if it does, there is no certainty that it will result in death or disablement to the assured[9].

1 The policy usually makes provision for the payment of different sums, varying in amount according to the nature of the injuries sustained by the assured: see para 580 post. As to the national system of insurance against industrial injuries see NATIONAL HEALTH AND SOCIAL SECURITY.
2 Accident insurance is a class of 'general insurance' under the Insurance Companies Act 1982 s 1, Sch 2 Pt I: see para 18 ante.
3 As to life insurance see para 525 et seq ante.
4 *Theobald v Railway Passengers Assurance Co* (1854) 10 Exch 45 at 53 per Alderson B. A policy insuring the assured against loss arising from any accident to a third person is, however, a contract of indemnity: *Blascheck v Bussell* (1916) 33 TLR 51; affd 33 TLR 74, CA.
5 *Bradburn v Great Western Rly Co* (1874) LR 10 Exch 1 at 2 per Bramwell B.
6 *Lloyds Bank Ltd v Eagle Star Insurance Co Ltd* [1951] 1 All ER 914 (insurance against personal injuries included personal injuries resulting in death). For examples of forms of accident policy see 20 Forms & Precedents (5th Edn) 504–512, Forms 290–292.
7 *General Accident Assurance Corpn v IRC* (1906) 8 F 477, Ct of Sess.
8 See para 525 ante.
9 *General Accident Assurance Corpn v IRC* (1906) 8 F 477, Ct of Sess; cf *Lancashire Insurance Co v IRC* [1899] 1 QB 353 at 359 per Bruce J.

568. Need for insurable interest. As in life insurance, an insurable interest is required by statute[1], the interest normally being the potential pecuniary loss of the assured as a result of the disablement, either of himself or of the third party if a third party is insured. In fact, accident insurance developed out of life insurance, but it must now be regarded as a different kind of insurance, and it is in practice generally so regarded[2].

1 See the Life Assurance Act 1774 s 1; *Shilling v Accidental Death Insurance Co* (1857) 2 H & N 42; and para 536 ante.
2 The distinction is recognised in the Insurance Companies Act 1982, where life insurance is one of the classes of 'long term business' whereas accident insurance is a class of 'general business': see s 1, Schs 1, 2; para 18 ante.

(ii) Policies Insuring against Accidental Injury

569. Meaning of 'accident'. The event insured against may be indicated in the policy solely by reference to the phrase 'injury by accident' or the equivalent phrase 'accidental injury', or it may be indicated as 'injury caused by or resulting from an accident'. The word 'accident', or its adjective 'accidental', is no doubt used with the intention of excluding the operation of natural causes such as old age, congenital or insidious disease or the natural progression of some constitutional physical or mental defect; but the ambit of what is included by the word is not entirely clear[1]. It has been said that what is postulated is the intervention of some cause which is brought into operation by chance so as to be fairly describable as fortuitous[2]. The idea of something haphazard is not necessarily inherent in the word; it covers any unlooked for mishap or an untoward event which is not expected or designed[3], or any unexpected personal injury resulting from any unlooked for mishap or occurrence[4]. The test of what is unexpected is whether the ordinary reasonable man would not have expected the occurrence, it being irrelevant that a person with expert knowledge, for example of medicine, would have regarded it as inevitable[5]. The standpoint is that of the victim, so that even wilful murder may be accidental as far as the victim is concerned[6].

1 The statement of the law contained in the text and in paras 571–575 post is founded substantially on cases which were decided under the Workmen's Compensation Acts (which are repealed), although the insurance cases are also included. In *Trim Joint District School Board of Management v Kelly* [1914] AC 667 at 675–676, HL, it was said by Lord Haldane LC that the fundamental conception of the Workmen's Compensation Act 1906 (repealed) is that of insurance in the true sense. He added, however, at 677, that 'the construction of the Act ought to be more liberal than would be the case if the Act were construed with the closeness which distinguishes the construction of words in a contract such as that of insurance'. See also *Fenton v Thorley & Co Ltd* [1903] AC 443 at 454–455, HL, per Lord Lindley, stressing the effect of the rule that the accident must be the proximate cause of the injury in insurance cases; and para 584 post. The workmen's compensation cases must be used with some caution, but it is thought that in general they afford a reliable guide to the trend of modern decisions. There was never a sufficiency of pure insurance cases to give rise to the intensive examination of the phrase 'injury by accident', in a multiplicity of different factual contexts, which became necessary in the course of the voluminous workmen's compensation litigation. Nor has there in recent years been quite such stringency as once prevailed in construing insurance policies; the trend is, if anything, to adopt a liberal interpretation in favour of the assured, so far as the ordinary and natural meaning of the words used by the insurers permits this to be done. For the principle that words must be given their ordinary and natural meaning see para 396 ante. The expression 'injury caused . . . by accident' is also used in the Social Security Contributions and Benefits Act 1992 s 94(1) (replacing earlier industrial injuries legislation): see NATIONAL HEALTH AND SOCIAL SECURITY.
2 *Sinclair v Maritime Passengers' Assurance Co* (1861) 3 E & E 478 at 485 per Cockburn CJ; *Reynolds v Accidental Insurance Co* (1870) 22 LT 820 at 821 per Willes J; *Re Scarr and General Accident Assurance Corpn* [1905] 1 KB 387 at 393 per Bray J.
3 *Fenton v Thorley & Co Ltd* [1903] AC 443 at 448, HL, per Lord Macnaghten; *Mills v Smith (Sinclair, third party)* [1964] 1 QB 30, [1963] 2 All ER 1078.
4 *Fenton v Thorley & Co Ltd* [1903] AC 443 at 451, HL, per Lord Shand, and see also at 453 per Lord Lindley; *Mills v Smith (Sinclair, third party)* [1964] 1 QB 30, [1963] 2 All ER 1078; *Marcel Beller Ltd v Hayden* [1978] QB 694, [1978] 3 All ER 111 (death of assured driving after consuming an excess of alcohol was nonetheless 'accidental', but insurers avoided liability on other grounds).
5 *Clover, Clayton & Co Ltd v Hughes* [1910] AC 242, HL.
6 See *Trim Joint District School Board of Management v Kelly* [1914] AC 667, HL; *Gray v Barr (Prudential Assurance Co Ltd, third party)* [1971] 2 QB 554, [1971] 1 All ER 949, CA; and note 1 supra.

570. Cases where there is an accident. A distinction has been drawn between the word 'accident' and the phrase 'an accident'[1]. The right to recover under a policy insuring against injury by accident is not necessarily confined to a case where injury results from circumstances which can be separately visualised and described as an accident[2]. However, where there is 'an accident', in the sense of an antecedent mishap from which injury results, the policy will plainly apply. For example, where the assured by misadventure goes in front of a train and is run over[3], falls into a stream and is drowned[4], slips on a step[5], is thrown from a horse[6], is suffocated by smoke from a burning house[7] or is drowned while bathing[8], the assured is entitled to recover under the policy, subject to any exception in the policy by which liability in respect of the particular misadventure in question is excluded[9]. Similarly, there is 'an accident' if injury or death is caused by indiscriminate stone throwing[10], by an anaesthetic administered for the purposes of a surgical operation[11], by an infection through a break in the skin[12], by the inhalation of tuberculosis germs, even though each of the many occasions could not be identified[13], or by each successive blow caused by the vibration of a machine until Raynaud's disease was set up[14].

1 *Warner v Couchman* [1912] AC 35 at 38, HL, per Lord Loreburn LC; *Mills v Smith (Sinclair, third party)* [1964] 1 QB 30, [1963] 2 All ER 1078.
2 See *Mills v Smith (Sinclair, third party)* [1964] 1 QB 30, [1963] 2 All ER 1078; and para 571 et seq post.
3 *Lawrence v Accidental Insurance Co Ltd* (1881) 7 QBD 216, DC; cf *Cornish v Accident Insurance Co* (1889) 23 QBD 453, CA.
4 *Reynolds v Accidental Insurance Co* (1870) 22 LT 820.
5 *Theobald v Railway Passengers Assurance Co* (1854) 10 Exch 45.
6 *Re Etherington and Lancashire and Yorkshire Accident Insurance Co* [1909] 1 KB 591, CA.
7 *Trew v Railway Passengers' Assurance Co* (1861) 6 H & N 839 at 844, Ex Ch, per Cockburn CJ.
8 *Trew v Railway Passengers' Assurance Co* (1861) 6 H & N 839, Ex Ch.
9 For cases where exceptions applied see *Cornish v Accident Insurance Co* (1889) 23 QBD 453, CA (exception of accidents happening by exposure to obvious risks; assured attempted to cross railway line in front of approaching train); *Re United London and Scottish Insurance Co Ltd, Brown's Claim* [1915] 2 Ch 167, CA (exception of accident caused by anything inhaled; involuntary inhalation of gas).
10 *Challis v London and South Western Rly Co* [1905] 2 KB 154, CA.
11 *Shirt v Calico Printers' Association* [1909] 2 KB 51, CA.
12 *Brintons Ltd v Turvey* [1905] AC 230, HL; *Grant v Kynoch* [1919] AC 765, HL.
13 *Pyrah v Doncaster Corpn* [1949] 1 All ER 883, CA; cf *Roberts v Dorothea Slate Quarries Co Ltd* [1948] 2 All ER 201, HL (silicosis).
14 *Fitzsimons v Ford Motor Co Ltd (Aero Engines)* [1946] 1 All ER 429, CA. See also *Gray v Barr (Prudential Assurance Co Ltd, third party)* [1971] 2 All ER 949, CA, where the assured, while in a highly emotional state, shot his wife's lover, and it was held, by the majority, for different reasons, that the death was not caused by an accident.

571. Exposure to elements. Even where there are no antecedent circumstances which can be separately visualised and described as 'an accident'[1], the results to the victim may nonetheless be accidental. Injury or death caused by lightning[2], sunstroke[3] or earthquake[4] has been held to be accidental. Similarly, where a man in the course of his work is exposed to excessive heat coming from a boiler and becomes exhausted[5] or has to stand in icy cold water and sustains pneumonia[6] or, having got overheated, is exposed to a draught resulting in pneumonia[7] or sustains sub-acute rheumatism as a result of baling out a flooded mine[8], his injuries have been held to be accidental.

1 As to the distinction between 'accident' and 'an accident' see para 570 ante.
2 *Andrew v Failsworth Industrial Society* [1904] 2 KB 32, CA.
3 *Morgan v Zenaida (Owners)* (1909) 25 TLR 446, CA; *Davies v Gillespie* (1911) 105 LT 494, CA. It is thought that *Sinclair v Maritime Passengers' Assurance Co* (1861) 3 E & E 478, which is to the contrary,

must be regarded as wrongly decided unless a valid distinction can be drawn for this purpose between 'accident' and 'an accident', or the workmen's compensation decisions are disregarded. See also *De Souza v Home and Overseas Insurance Ltd* (1990) Times, 19 September, CA, where it was considered that the term 'accidental bodily injury' had to be construed together with 'outward violent and visible means' with the result that a death from heatstroke was not covered and the insurers avoided liability.

4 *Brooker v Thomas Borthwick & Sons (Australasia) Ltd* [1933] AC 669, PC.
5 *Ismay, Imrie & Co v Williamson* [1908] AC 437, HL.
6 *Alloa Coal Co Ltd v Drylic* 1913 SC 549.
7 *Brown v John Watson Ltd* [1915] AC 1, HL.
8 *Glasgow Coal Co Ltd v Welsh* [1916] 2 AC 1, HL.

572. Excessive strain on already defective physique. Another class of case in which, although it is difficult to visualise a separate event preceding the injury which could be classified as 'an accident'[1], an injury may nonetheless fall to be regarded as accidental, is where a man with a naturally defective physique is subjected to stress, strain, exertion or shock which his system cannot stand. Where a man injures his spine by lifting a heavy weight in the ordinary course of his employment[2] or dislocates the cartilage of his knee by stooping to pick up a marble[3], or by reason of exertion sustains a hernia[4], a cerebral haemorrhage[5] or a rupture of an already diseased aorta[6], or sustains shock by witnessing an accident involving another workman[7] or an apoplectic stroke by the exertion of running and excitement[8], his injury has been held to be accidental[9]. Probably there is no distinction of substance between 'injury by accident' and 'injury caused by an accident'; if any bodily organ fails from inherent physiological processes which are merely the operation of nature the case falls within neither formula, but if something, whatever it may be, can be identified as causing a particular physiological process, be it the reception of water into the lungs leading to drowning[10] or the impact of the rays of the sun leading to sunstroke[11], that something constitutes 'an accident' if it leads to deleterious results.

1 As to the distinction between 'accident' and 'an accident' see para 570 ante.
2 *Martin v Travellers' Insurance Co* (1859) 1 F & F 505; *Horsfall v Pacific Mutual Insurance Co* (1903) 98 Am St R 846, distinguished in *Re Scarr and General Accident Assurance Corpn* [1905] 1 KB 387.
3 *Hamlyn v Crown Accidental Insurance Co Ltd* [1893] 1 QB 750, CA.
4 *Fenton v Thorley & Co Ltd* [1903] AC 443, HL.
5 *M'Innes v Dunsmuir and Jackson Ltd* 1908 SC 1021.
6 *Clover, Clayton & Co Ltd v Hughes* [1910] AC 242, HL.
7 *Yates v South Kirby Featherstone and Harmsworth Collieries Ltd* [1910] 2 KB 538, CA.
8 *Aitken v Finlayson, Bonsfield & Co Ltd* 1914 SC 770.
9 In *Re Scarr and General Accident Assurance Corpn* [1905] 1 KB 387 it was held, approving *Appel v Aetna Life Assurance Corpn* (1903) 86 App Div 83 (NY), that where a man, as a result of exertion in ejecting a drunkard, sustained a dilatation of an already diseased heart, this was not an injury sustained by accident. It is submitted that in the light of the cases cited in notes 2–8 supra this decision must be regarded as wrongly decided.
10 *Trew v Railway Passengers' Assurance Co* (1861) 6 H & N 839, Ex Ch.
11 *Morgan v Zenaida (Owners)* (1909) 25 TLR 446, CA; *Davies v Gillespie* (1911) 105 LT 494, CA.

573. Injury by disease. Where the cause of disablement or death is an idiopathic disease, that is to say a morbid condition of unknown aetiology which is dependent normally on the personal factors of the sufferer, this is not an 'injury by accident'[1]. Similarly, where an occupational disease gradually develops over a long period of exposure to certain conditions without any identifiable incident at any identifiable point of time, the resulting condition cannot be called an 'injury by accident';

examples are dermatitis due to long continued exposure to substances not necessarily irritant[2], silicosis due to prolonged inhalation of silica dust[3], anthracosis (another lung disease) due to dust[4], and enteritis due to exposure to sewer gas[5]. However, where accidental circumstances can be established as the basis of the disease, the position is different; for example, infection of a woolsorter by a stray anthrax germ[6], of a gardener by tetanus from the soil after injuring his foot at work[7], and of a man working in artificial manure consisting mainly of bone dust by a bacillus common in bone dust[8], have been held to be injury by accident.

1 *Brintons Ltd v Turvey* [1905] AC 230 at 233, HL, per Lord Halsbury LC; *Winspear v Accident Insurance Co* (1880) 6 QBD 42 at 45, CA, per Lord Coleridge CJ; see also *Isitt v Railway Passengers Assurance Co* (1889) 22 QBD 504 at 512 per Wills J. As to exceptions relating to disease see para 585 post.
2 *Petschett v Preis* (1915) 31 TLR 156, CA.
3 *Williams v Guest, Keen and Nettlefolds* [1926] 1 KB 497, CA; *Roberts v Dorothea Slate Quarries Co Ltd* [1948] 2 All ER 201, HL.
4 *Cole v London and North Eastern Rly Co* (1928) 21 BWCC 87, CA.
5 *Broderick v LCC* [1908] 2 KB 807, CA; *Eke v Hart-Dyke* [1910] 2 KB 677, CA.
6 *Brintons Ltd v Turvey* [1905] AC 230, HL.
7 *Walker v Mullins* (1908) 42 ILT 168.
8 *Grant v Kynoch* [1919] AC 765, HL.

574. Injury caused by negligence. One of the commonest causes of injury is negligence, although the injury is not by reason of the negligence rendered non-accidental[1]. Accordingly in such a case the policy applies, whether the negligence is that of a third party or of the assured himself[2]. Where the assured crosses a railway line without taking proper care and is knocked down by an approaching train[3], or takes the wrong bottle and drinks a dose of poison instead of medicine[4], his injuries are accidental within the meaning of the policy.

1 See *Marcel Beller Ltd v Hayden* [1978] QB 694, [1978] 3 All ER 111.
2 *Clidero v Scottish Accident Insurance Co* (1892) 19 R 355 at 363, Ct of Sess, per Lord M'Laren; cf para 575 post.
3 *Cornish v Accident Insurance Co* (1889) 23 QBD 453, CA.
4 *Cole v Accident Insurance Co Ltd* (1889) 5 TLR 736, CA.

575. Injury caused by a wilful act. An injury caused by the wilful or even criminal act of a third person, provided the assured is not a party or privy to it[1], is to be regarded as accidental for the purposes of the policy[2], since from the assured's point of view it is not expected or designed[3]. Injuries sustained by a gamekeeper in a criminal attack upon him by poachers[4], by a cashier who was murdered by a robber[5], and by a master at an industrial school who was murdered by the boys[6], have been held to be accidental. However, if the immediate[7] cause of the injury is the deliberate and wilful act of the assured himself, there would seem to be no accident, and no claim will lie under the policy[8], at any rate if the assured is not mentally disordered at the time of his act[9].

1 *Midland Insurance Co v Smith* (1881) 6 QBD 561.
2 *Letts v Excess Insurance Co* (1916) 32 TLR 361, where it was not suggested that the sinking of the Lusitania by a German submarine was otherwise than an accident for the purpose of the policy.
3 See *Trim Joint District School Board of Management v Kelly* [1914] AC 667, HL; and para 569 note 1 ante.
4 *Anderson v Balfour* [1910] 2 IR 497, CA.
5 *Nisbet v Rayne and Burn* [1910] 2 KB 689, CA.

6 See *Trim Joint District School Board of Management v Kelly* [1914] AC 667, HL; and para 569 note 1 ante.

7 See *Marcel Beller Ltd v Hayden* [1978] QB 694, [1978] 3 All ER 111, where the immediate cause of the injury was distinguished from the predisposing cause, following the reasoning of Salmon LJ in *Gray v Barr (Prudential Assurance Co Ltd, third party)* [1971] 2 QB 554 at 580, [1971] 2 All ER 949 at 963, CA.

8 *Beresford v Royal Insurance Co Ltd* [1938] AC 586 at 595, [1938] 2 All ER 602 at 604, HL, per Lord Atkin; *Gray v Barr (Prudential Assurance Co Ltd, third party)* [1971] 2 QB 554, [1971] 2 All ER 949, CA (person insured under public liability policy threatened another with a loaded gun and involuntarily killed him); *Marcel Beller Ltd v Hayden* [1978] QB 694, [1978] 3 All ER 111 (injury caused by driver who had consumed excess alcohol was held to be accidental, since it was his driving, not the consumption of alcohol, which was the immediate cause of injury; drinking was the predisposing cause; liability was avoided, however, by a term of the policy relating to criminal acts), and see note 7 supra. See paras 574 ante, 576 et seq post.

9 Cf *Horn v Anglo-Australian and Universal Family Life Assurance Co* (1861) 30 LJCh 511 (where in a life policy there was no exception against suicide, money was payable in the event of the assured committing suicide while insane); *Gray v Barr (Prudential Assurance Co Ltd, third party)* [1971] 2 QB 554, [1971] 2 All ER 949, CA.

(iii) Policies in More Stringent Terms

576. Injury resulting from accident caused by violent, external and visible means. A form of clause now in common use in accident insurance to indicate the kind of injury covered by the policy is 'injury resulting solely and directly from accident caused by violent external and visible means'[1]. Phrases of this kind were introduced to limit the width which might be covered by a general phrase such as 'injury by accident'. It does not seem, however, that anything of any substance has been achieved by the change of formula[2].

1 See 20 Forms & Precedents (5th Edn) 509, Form 291. The phrase 'violent, accidental, external and visible means' was adversely criticised in *Re United London and Scottish Insurance Co, Brown's Claim* [1915] 2 Ch 167, CA; but see *Hamlyn v Crown Accidental Insurance Co Ltd* [1893] 1 QB 750, CA; *Burridge & Son v F H Haines & Sons* (1918) 118 LT 681; and *Sinclair v Maritime Passengers' Assurance Co* (1861) 3 E & E 478. See *De Souza v Home and Overseas Insurance Ltd* (1990) Times, 19 September, CA, where it was considered that the term 'outward violent and visible means' had to be construed together with 'accidental bodily injury', with the result that a death from heatstroke was not covered and the insurers avoided liability.

  If the phrase 'accidental means' is used in the policy, it seems that it is synonymous with, or at any rate adds nothing to, the phrase 'by accident': see *Hamlyn v Crown Accidental Insurance Co Ltd* supra. The principles set out in paras 569–575 ante would therefore apply.

2 See note 1 supra; and paras 577–578 post.

577. Violent means. In relation to the injuries covered by a policy of accident insurance[1], 'violent' has been interpreted as connoting the antithesis to 'without any violence at all'[2]. It does not, therefore, postulate the presence of brutal strength or savage temper, as when the victim is bitten by a dog[3]. Again, an external cause of death, such as the inhalation of gas, may, it seems, be violent inasmuch as it does violence to the human frame by rendering it incapable of functioning[4]. Similarly, where the cause of injury is some extra exertion or exercise of effort on the part of the assured, as where he stoops to pick up a marble, it is violent in the sense that it does damage impairing the bodily functions, however impaired they may have been before[5].

1 See para 576 ante.

2 *Hamlyn v Crown Accidental Insurance Co Ltd* [1893] 1 QB 750 at 752, CA, per Lord Esher MR.

3 *Mardorf v Accident Insurance Co* [1903] 1 KB 584 at 588 per Wright J.

4 Cf *Re United London and Scottish Insurance Co, Brown's Claim* [1915] 2 Ch 167, CA; the actual decision was as to the application of an exception in the policy.

5 *Hamlyn v Crown Accidental Insurance Co Ltd* [1893] 1 QB 750, CA; cf *Clidero v Scottish Accident Insurance Co* (1892) 19 R 355, Ct of Sess.

578. External and visible means.

'External means' is used to point the contrast with something internal. Any cause which is not internal must be external[1], but this does not mean that the injury must be external; there may be, and often is, nothing externally visible to indicate the presence of internal injury at all[2]. The effect of the term is therefore to underline that disorders arising within the human body, without ascertainable reference at all to anything coming from outside, are not covered. Therefore, there are certain classes of injury such as hernia[3], or of disease such as pneumonia[4] or erysipelas[5], where the assured may or may not be entitled to recover, according to whether he can show that some external, as opposed to some internal, cause has operated as the effective cause[6]. Similarly, if a man falls into a river and is drowned or falls on to a railway line and is hit by a train it is immaterial that he only fell because he had an epileptic fit; if he is alive when the water gets into his lungs and leads to suffocation, or when the train cuts off his head thus stopping the motivating power to the heart, the cause of death is drowning or decapitation and not the anterior fit[7].

'Visible means' is an attempted refinement which has not succeeded in achieving any strictly rational meaning. It has been held that an external cause is necessarily a visible one[8].

1 *Hamlyn v Crown Accidental Insurance Co Ltd* [1893] 1 QB 750 at 752, CA, per Lord Esher MR.

2 *Trew v Railway Passengers' Assurance Co* (1861) 6 H & N 839 at 844, Ex Ch, per Cockburn CJ; see also *Martin v Travellers' Insurance Co* (1859) 1 F & F 505; *Hamlyn v Crown Accidental Insurance Co Ltd* [1893] 1 QB 750, CA, followed in *Burridge & Son v F H Haines & Sons* (1918) 118 LT 681.

3 *Fitton v Accidental Death Insurance Co* (1864) 17 CBNS 122.

4 *Isitt v Railway Passengers Assurance Co* (1889) 22 QBD 504; *Re Etherington and Lancashire and Yorkshire Accident Insurance Co* [1909] 1 KB 591, CA.

5 *Mardorf v Accident Insurance Co* [1903] 1 KB 584.

6 As to causation see further paras 584–586 post.

7 *Winspear v Accident Insurance Co Ltd* (1880) 6 QBD 42, CA (assured in fit fell into water); *Reynolds v Accidental Insurance Co* (1870) 22 LT 820 (assured in water seized with a fit); *Lawrence v Accidental Insurance Co Ltd* (1881) 7 QBD 216 (assured in fit fell on railway line).

8 *Hamlyn v Crown Accidental Insurance Co Ltd* [1893] 1 QB 750 at 754, CA; *Burridge & Son v F H Haines & Sons Ltd* (1918) 118 LT 681.

579. Special kinds of accident.

Sometimes the protection of the policy is limited to accidents of a particular kind, such as railway accidents[1] or accidents of transit[2]. To give rise to a claim it is not necessary, unless the policy so provides[3], that there should be an accident to the train or vehicle by which the assured is travelling; it is sufficient if the accident happens in the course of the transit and arises out of the fact of the journey[4]. The accident may happen during the actual transit, whilst the vehicle is in motion[5]; but the policy is equally applicable to an accident which happens whilst the assured is in the act of entering or leaving the vehicle at the beginning or end of his journey, as, for instance, where he slips on the step of the vehicle[6].

1 *Theobald v Railway Passengers Assurance Co* (1854) 10 Exch 45.

2 *Fidelity and Casualty Co of New York v Mitchell* [1917] AC 592, PC.
3 As to what is included in the policy see paras 580–583 post.
4 *Theobald v Railway Passengers Assurance Co* (1854) 10 Exch 45.
5 *Fidelity and Casualty Co of New York v Mitchell* [1917] AC 592, PC.
6 *Theobald v Railway Passengers Assurance Co* (1854) 10 Exch 45.

(iv) Benefits Recoverable

580. Lump sum benefits for specific injuries or death. The policy usually provides for payment of a lump sum in the event of the assured's death by accident, and of other sums, varying in amount according to the nature and extent of the injury[1], in the event of the assured sustaining certain specified injuries, such as the loss of sight in one eye or total loss of sight[2]. Where the policy provides for payment of compensation in the event of non-fatal injury, but makes no special provision for its amount, the assured is entitled to receive compensation for his pain and suffering and expenses incurred to an amount not exceeding the amount payable in case of death[3].

1 See eg 20 Forms & Precedents (5th Edn) 509, Form 291. Sometimes the policy provides for increased compensation for certain forms of accident: see *Fidelity and Casualty Co of New York v Mitchell* [1917] AC 592 at 594, PC, where double benefit was payable if the assured at the time of the accident was a passenger on a public conveyance; see also para 579 ante.
2 See eg *Bawden v London, Edinburgh and Glasgow Assurance Co* [1892] 2 QB 534, CA; *Long v Graham* [1967] NZLR 1030 (NZ SC). See also 20 Forms & Precedents (5th Edn) 509, Form 291 for an example of a policy itemising the injuries insured against.
3 *Theobald v Railway Passengers Assurance Co* (1854) 10 Exch 45.

581. Periodical payments during disablement. The injury, in addition to causing pain and suffering, may disable the assured from attending to his affairs and thus cause him pecuniary loss. This loss is in the nature of a consequential loss[1]; the injury is not its proximate, but only its remote cause, and unless the policy so provides the assured cannot claim compensation in respect of it[2]. However, in practice provision is often made for payment of compensation by means of periodical payments during the period of disablement[3]. The effect of the provision varies according to the terms in which it is expressed. The compensation may be payable in the event of the assured being wholly disabled from following his usual business or occupation[4]. In such a case the assured may be wholly disabled although he is able to attend to some details of his business. Thus a solicitor who is confined to his room by reason of a sprained ankle is wholly disabled although he is able to give directions to a clerk or dictate letters; it is sufficient that he is wholly disabled from performing the most substantial part of his business[5]. However, by the terms of the provision the assured may be disentitled to compensation if he is able to attend to any part of his business[6] or indeed to business of any kind[7].

1 As to consequential loss see paras 785–789 post.
2 *Theobald v Railway Passengers Assurance Co* (1854) 10 Exch 45.
3 There is usually a limitation of the period during which compensation for disablement is payable: see 20 Forms & Precedents (5th Edn) 509, Form 291.
4 See *Hooper v Accidental Death Insurance Co* (1860) 5 H & N 546 at 556, 558, Ex Ch. Hence the right to recover may depend upon the assured's occupation. By a sprained ankle, a teacher of dancing would be wholly disabled from following his occupation, whereas a teacher of mathematics might not be. See further *Williams v Lloyd's Underwriters* [1957] 1 Lloyd's Rep 118; *Cathay Pacific Airways Ltd v Nation Life and General Assurance Co Ltd* [1966] 2 Lloyd's Rep 179.

5 *Hooper v Accidental Death Insurance Co* (1860) 5 H & N 546, Ex Ch.
6 *Fidelity and Casualty Co of New York v Mitchell* [1917] AC 592 at 594, PC.
7 *Pocock v Century Insurance Co Ltd* [1960] 2 Lloyd's Rep 150. For an example of provisions providing for compensation on the basis of total disablement only if the assured is unable to attend to any business or occupation see 20 Forms & Precedents (5th Edn) 509 at 511, Form 291 cl 12.

(v) Exceptions

582. Exclusions of certain risks. A policy of accident insurance normally contains a number of exceptions[1], excluding from its scope either cases where the death or disablement is due to particular causes such as disease[2], war risks[3], poison[4] or inhalation[5], or to accidents happening in particular circumstances such as whilst the assured is under the influence of intoxicating liquor[6] or is travelling in a prohibited area[7] or has attained a certain age[8], or the accident results from his own criminal act[9]. Suicide also is usually excepted[10].

1 As to exceptions generally see para 409 ante.
2 For the exceptions excluding death or disablement from disease see para 585 post.
3 *Letts v Excess Insurance Co* (1916) 32 TLR 361; *Coxe v Employers' Liability Assurance Corpn Ltd* [1916] 2 KB 629. Prima facie 'war' includes civil war: *Pesquerias y Secaderos de Bacalao de Espana SA v Beer* [1949] 1 All ER 845, HL.
4 *Cole v Accident Insurance Co* (1889) 5 TLR 736, CA.
5 *Re United London and Scottish Insurance Co, Brown's Claim* [1915] 2 Ch 167, CA.
6 *Mair v Railway Passengers Assurance Co Ltd* (1877) 37 LT 356, DC; *MacRobbie v Accident Insurance Co* (1886) 23 SLR 391; *Louden v British Merchants Insurance Co Ltd* [1961] 1 All ER 705, [1961] 1 WLR 798.
7 *Stoneham v Ocean Railway and General Accident Insurance Co* (1887) 19 QBD 237 at 241.
8 *Lloyds Bank Ltd v Eagle Star Insurance Co Ltd* [1951] 1 All ER 914.
9 See *Marcel Beller Ltd v Hayden* [1978] QB 694, [1978] 3 All ER 111, where the assured was driving a car after consuming an excess amount of alcohol.
10 *Harvey v Ocean Accident and Guarantee Corpn* [1905] 2 IR 1, CA; cf paras 531, 575 ante.

583. Exposure to obvious risk, needless peril or exceptional danger. Policies of accident insurance may exclude liability for accidents caused by the assured exposing himself to the 'obvious risk of injury'. In the absence of negligence, such an exception has no application[1]; nor does it apply to all cases of negligence[2]. Its application is limited to cases where the risk of injury is obvious to the assured or would be obvious to him if he was paying reasonable attention to what he was doing[3]. Where, for example, the assured is knocked down and killed by a train whilst taking a short cut along a railway line[4] or whilst crossing the line at a place where there is no regular crossing[5], or where he goes too near the edge of a cliff whilst gathering wild flowers and falls over[6], the insurers are not liable. On the other hand, the exception does not apply to a person using the road[7] or crossing the street[8] with reasonable care or to a skilled swimmer going out for a swim even on a chilly night[9].

A more modern form of accident policy may exclude liability consequent upon the assured's deliberate exposure to 'exceptional danger' or wilfully exposing himself to 'needless peril'[10]. In the former case the word 'deliberate' imports a subjective test and the exception does not apply where he drives a car knowing that he has consumed an excessive amount of alcohol unless there is evidence that he thought about the risk he was taking and deliberately chose to ignore it[11]. In a case where injury caused by 'wilful exposure to needless peril' was excluded from cover, it was not enough to show an intentional act which caused the peril; rather there had to be a conscious act of volition (including recklessness) directed to the running of the risk[12].

1 *Cornish v Accident Insurance Co* (1889) 23 QBD 453 at 456, CA, per Lindley LJ.
2 *Cornish v Accident Insurance Co* (1889) 23 QBD 453 at 457, CA, per Lindley LJ.
3 *Cornish v Accident Insurance Co* (1889) 23 QBD 453 at 457, CA, per Lindley LJ; cf *Mair v Railway Passengers Assurance Co* (1877) 37 LT 356.
4 *Lovell v Accident Insurance Co* (1875) 39 JP 293.
5 *Cornish v Accident Insurance Co* (1889) 23 QBD 453, CA.
6 *Walker v Railway Passengers Assurance Co* (1910) 129 LT Jo 64, CA.
7 *Shilling v Accidental Death Insurance Co* (1858) 1 F & F 116.
8 *Cornish v Accident Insurance Co* (1889) 23 QBD 453 at 456, CA, per Lindley LJ.
9 *Sangster's Trustees v General Accident Assurance Corpn* (1896) 24 R 56, Ct of Sess.
10 See 20 Forms & Precedents (5th Edn) 504–512, Forms 290–291.
11 *Marcel Beller Ltd v Hayden* [1978] QB 694, [1978] 3 All ER 111.
12 *Morley and Morley v United Friendly Insurance plc* [1993] 1 Lloyd's Rep 490, CA (assured jumped on bumper of car which was then driven by fiancée, who inadvertently accelerated instead of stopping; held that although the peril was clearly unnecessary, the assured's act was a 'momentary act of stupidity', but that that did not amount to wilful exposure to the peril).

(vi) Rules of Causation

584. The doctrine of proximate cause. The doctrine of proximate cause[1] applies to accident insurance[2]. If the policy postulates the happening of something which can be called 'an accident'[3], the injury must be proximately caused by the accident and the death or disablement must be proximately caused by the injury[4]. However, the application of the doctrine may be modified or excluded by the terms of a particular policy[5]; but the intention of the parties must be clearly expressed[6]. Each case turns on the construction of the particular policy and, unless the language is identical, one case is no authority for another unless the general principle can be extracted[7].

1 As to the doctrine of proximate cause see generally paras 175–176 ante.
2 *Lawrence v Accidental Insurance Co Ltd* (1881) 7 QBD 216 at 221, DC, per Watkin Williams J; *Re Etherington and Lancashire and Yorkshire Accident Insurance Co* [1909] 1 KB 591 at 601, CA, per Kennedy LJ.
3 See *Gray v Barr (Prudential Assurance Co Ltd, third party)* [1971] 2 QB 554, [1971] 1 All ER 949, CA; and para 570 ante.
4 *Isitt v Railway Passengers Assurance Co* (1889) 22 QBD 504; *Theobald v Railway Passengers Assurance Co* (1854) 10 Exch 45; *Mardorf v Accident Insurance Co* [1903] 1 KB 584; *Smith v Cornhill Insurance Co Ltd* [1938] 3 All ER 145; *Gray v Barr (Prudential Assurance Co Ltd, third party)* [1971] 2 QB 554, [1971] 1 All ER 949, CA. Hence, if the accident renders a surgical operation necessary, and the assured dies during the operation, his death is proximately caused by the accident: *Fitton v Accidental Death Insurance Co* (1864) 17 CBNS 122; *Isitt v Railway Passengers Assurance Co* supra.
5 *Coxe v Employers' Liability Assurance Corpn* [1916] 2 KB 629.
6 *Re Etherington and Lancashire and Yorkshire Accident Insurance Co* [1909] 1 KB 591 at 602, CA, per Kennedy LJ.
7 *Smith v Cornhill Insurance Co Ltd* [1938] 3 All ER 145 at 150 per Atkinson J.

585. Disease as proximate cause of death or disablement. The policy may contain an exception relating to disease; it may be framed in general terms, or specific diseases may be excepted. Where the death or disablement is solely caused by disease there is no injury by accident and the insurers are not liable whether the policy contains such an exception or not[1]. Difficulties arise where there is some apparent connection between the disease and an accident. Much turns on the language of the exception, but generally the exception applies where the disease arises naturally and is the proximate cause of the death or disablement[2]. If the disease is only the remote cause of the death or disablement, even though the accident would not have happened but for the disease, the exception has no application. If the assured is seized with a fit and falls into a stream and is drowned or falls in front of a train and is killed the insurers are liable, notwithstanding the presence in the policy of an express exception against fits. The fit is only the remote cause of the death; the assured is drowned or killed by accident[3].

1 As to injury by disease see para 573 ante. Cf *Cawley v National Employers' Accident and General Assurance Association Ltd* (1885) Cab & El 597, where the exception excluded death by disease, although accelerated by accident.
2 *Fitton v Accidental Death Insurance Co* (1864) 17 CBNS 122, where the pleadings were amended to raise the question whether the disease arose from natural causes. As to the onus of proof in relation to exceptions see paras 409, 411 ante.
3 See *Reynolds v Accidental Insurance Co* (1870) 22 LT 820; *Winspear v Accident Insurance Co Ltd* (1880) 6 QBD 42, CA (both concerned with drowning); and *Lawrence v Accidental Insurance Co Ltd* (1881) 7 QBD 216, DC (train accident).

586. Disease as link in chain of causation. An exception relating to disease is equally inapplicable[1] where the death or disablement, though ultimately due to disease, is nevertheless proximately caused by accident, the disease being a mere link in the chain initiated dominantly and effectively by the accident[2]. Where a fall causes hernia or pneumonia, from which the assured dies, his death is caused by accident, and an express exception against hernia[3] or pneumonia[4] has no application. Even where the fall brings out tuberculosis which was latent in the assured's system, but which would not have manifested itself but for the fall, the disablement is proximately caused by the fall, and is not within an exception against disease[5]. The same principle applies to an assured who is bitten by a dog and dies of hydrophobia[6]. However, the exception may be so worded as to exclude disease, however caused, and then if the death is caused by an excepted disease the insurers will not be liable even though the disease is proximately caused by accident[7].

1 As to the exception of disease as a proximate cause of death or disablement see para 585 ante.
2 For a discussion of the principle, in relation to a policy of marine insurance, see *Leyland Shipping Co Ltd v Norwich Union Fire Insurance Society Ltd* [1918] AC 350, HL, where the death-blow was given to a ship by a torpedo (an insured peril), although the final loss of the ship was due to a storm; see paras 175–176 ante.
3 *Fitton v Accidental Death Insurance Co* (1864) 17 CBNS 122.
4 *Re Etherington and Lancashire and Yorkshire Accident Insurance Co* [1909] 1 KB 591, CA; cf *Isitt v Railway Passengers Assurance Co* (1889) 22 QBD 504; *Mardorf v Accident Insurance Co* [1903] 1 KB 584.
5 *Fidelity and Casualty Co of New York v Mitchell* [1917] AC 592, PC.
6 *Mardorf v Accident Insurance Co* [1903] 1 KB 584 at 588 per Wright J.
7 *Smith v Accident Insurance Co* (1870) LR 5 Exch 302 at 309 per Kelly CB; *Jason v British Traders Insurance Co Ltd* [1969] 1 Lloyd's Rep 281.

(vii) Accident Insurance by Coupon

587. Nature of coupon insurance. The purchase of a newspaper or other article sometimes confers upon the purchaser the right to an insurance against accident. The insurance arises by virtue of some arrangement made by the proprietors of the newspaper or article sold[1] with insurers[2], and the position of the purchaser is defined in a document or coupon which is annexed to the article or, in the case of a newspaper, printed as part of it. In some cases nothing beyond the purchase is necessary to complete the insurance[3]; in others the coupon must be filled up and it may have to be registered with the insurers[4]. The protection given by the coupon is usually in a narrow compass, being limited to accidents to vehicles in which the holder of the coupon is a passenger[5], or accidents to pedestrians[6].

1 The proprietors therefore undertake to the purchaser that such arrangements have been made: see *Law v George Newnes Ltd* (1894) 21 R 1027 at 1033, Ct of Sess.
2 The arrangement is necessary because of the requirements of the Insurance Companies Act 1982 ss 1, 2. See para 19 ante.
3 See *Carlill v Carbolic Smoke Ball Co* [1893] 1 QB 256, CA. Payment is not essential: *Shanks v Sun Life Assurance Co of India* 1896 4 SLT 65.
4 *General Accident, Fire and Life Assurance Corpn v Robertson* [1909] AC 404, HL. See para 458 note 6 ante.
5 A person riding a bicycle is not a passenger in a vehicle (*McMillan v Sun Life Insurance Co of India* 1896 4 SLT 66), but he is in charge of a vehicle for the purposes of an exception (*Harper v Associated Newspapers Ltd* (1927) 43 TLR 331; *Hansford v London Express Newspaper Ltd* (1928) 44 TLR 349).
6 A person who goes for a bicycle ride does not become a pedestrian merely because he stops for a talk or has to wheel his bicycle up a hill: *Harper v Associated Newspapers Ltd* (1927) 43 TLR 331 at 332 per Roche J.

588. Payment in case of death. In the event of a fatal accident, provision is usually made for payment of the sum insured to a specified person, such as the holder's wife[1] or next of kin. Where the coupon is issued by a newspaper power is usually reserved to make the payment to the person adjudged by the editor, or some other person, to be the holder's next of kin, in which case his decision is final[2].

1 In *Re Lambert, Public Trustee v Lambert* (1916) 84 LJCh 279, a provision that the holder's wife was to be 'entitled to the benefit' of the insurance was held to mean that she too was insured against accident and not that she was entitled to receive compensation for his death.
2 *Law v George Newnes Ltd* (1894) 21 R 1027, Ct of Sess; *Hunter v Hunter* (1904) 7 F 136, Ct of Sess; cf *Da Costa v Prudential Assurance Co* (1918) 120 LT 353, CA; *O' Reilly v Prudential Assurance Co* [1934] Ch 519, CA.

(2) SICKNESS INSURANCE

589. Nature of contract. A contract of accident insurance in the strict sense does not cover the assured against disablement or incapacity arising from disease unless the disease is directly or indirectly related to some accident or injury caused by accident. However, a contract of sickness insurance is normally drawn so as to cover the assured against incapacity arising from disease, whether or not the disease is related to an accident or injury caused by accident and whatever the nature of the disease. Accident and sickness insurance may be combined in the same policy[1].

1 As to injury by disease see para 573 ante. As to exceptions in accident policies relating to disease see para 585 ante. See 20 Forms & Precedents (5th Edn) 504–512, Forms 290–292.

590. Principles of law applicable. The law applicable to sickness insurance is basically the same as that applicable to accident insurance, although normally there is no distinction by reference to whether the sickness is due to an accident or other cause[1]. The assured is normally required to give information in the proposal form as to his previous medical history and to submit to a medical examination by a doctor nominated by the insurers[2].

  1   As to the nature of the contract see para 589 ante. Insurance against disease is included in the statutory definition of 'long-term insurance business' if it is contained in a contract expressed to be in effect for a period of not less than five years or until normal retirement age, or without limit of time, and the contract is either (1) not expressed to be terminable by the insurers, or (2) expressed to be so terminable only in the special circumstances mentioned in it: Insurance Companies Act 1982 s 1(1), Sch 1; see para 18 ante.
  2   As to questions in the proposal form as to previous medical history and medical examinations in relation to life insurance see para 534 ante; and also para 355 ante. As to the effect of non-disclosure and misrepresentation see generally para 349 et seq ante.

7. PROPERTY INSURANCE

(1) FIRE INSURANCE

(i) Peril Insured Against

591. Perils covered. A policy of fire insurance, as its name indicates, is intended to protect the assured against loss caused by fire[1]. In practice the protection normally extends to losses caused by events which are frequently the cause of fire but may occur without a fire resulting, such as lightning and certain kinds of explosion[2]. If a fire results, the policy is plainly applicable[3] unless an exception has become operative, and there is no commercial advantage in limiting the insurance by reference to such a fortuitous standard.

  1   For the general principles applicable to fire insurance as well as to other kinds of non-marine insurance see para 2 et seq ante. Fire and natural forces business is 'general business' within the Insurance Companies Act 1982 s 1, Sch 2 Pt I (as amended): see para 18 ante. For an example of a policy of fire insurance see 20 Forms & Precedents (5th Edn) 29, Form 2.
  2   As to explosions see paras 600–602 post.
  3   *Gordon v Rimmington* (1807) 1 Camp 123.

592. Ignition essential. There is no fire within the meaning of a fire insurance policy unless there is ignition, either of the property insured or of the premises where it is situated[1]; heating or fermentation unaccompanied by ignition is not sufficient. That which is ignited must be something which was not intended to be ignited[2]. Therefore, if property near to a source of heat in ordinary use is damaged by the excessive heat thrown out, but is not actually ignited, the damage is not within the policy, since there is no ignition except such ignition as was intended and nothing has been burned except what ought to have been burned[3].

It is immaterial that the fire occurs in a place, such as a grate, where fires are intended; accordingly, where an assured lit a fire forgetting that she had hidden bank notes in the kindling the loss was recoverable[4].

  1   *Everett v London Assurance* (1865) 19 CBNS 126 at 133 per Byles J. Cf the requisites of the crime of arson: see CRIMINAL LAW vol 11(1) (Reissue) para 594.
  2   *Austin v Drewe* (1816) 2 Marsh 130 at 133 per Dallas CJ.
  3   *Austin v Drewe* (1816) 2 Marsh 130; cf *Upjohn v Hitchens, Upjohn v Ford* [1918] 2 KB 48 at 51, CA, per Scrutton LJ.
  4   *Harris v Poland* [1941] 1 KB 462, [1941] 1 All ER 204.

593. Cause of fire normally immaterial. Generally, the cause of the fire may be disregarded unless it arises from an excepted peril[1] or was lit by the assured for the purpose of destroying the property insured. It is not necessary that it should be purely accidental in origin. Fires are frequently due to negligence and one of the objects of a fire policy is to protect the assured against the consequences of negligence[2]. It is immaterial whether the fire owes it origin to negligence or, though properly lit, is negligently attended[3]; and it is equally immaterial whether the negligence is that of an employee, a stranger[4] or the assured[5]. Even the fact that a fire is deliberately lit for the purpose of destroying the property insured does not disentitle the assured from recovering, unless he has lit it[6] or someone acting with his privity or consent has done so[7]. If a fire is lit in proper circumstances, for example in a fireplace, property accidentally destroyed is covered[8].

1 As to excepted perils see paras 595–602 post.
2 *Shaw v Robberds* (1837) 6 Ad & El 75 at 84 per Lord Denman CJ; *A-G v Adelaide SS Co* [1923] AC 292 at 308, HL, per Lord Wrenbury.
3 *Dixon v Sadler* (1839) 5 M & W 405 at 414 per Parke B; affd (1841) 8 M & W 895, Ex Ch.
4 *Dobson v Sotheby* (1827) Mood & M 90; *Shaw v Robberds* (1837) 6 Ad & El 75; *Mark Rowlands Ltd v Berni Inns Ltd* [1986] QB 211, [1985] 3 All ER 473, CA.
5 *Shaw v Robberds* (1837) 6 Ad & El 75; *Trinder, Anderson & Co v Thames and Mersey Marine Insurance Co* [1898] 2 QB 114 at 124, CA, per A L Smith LJ; and see *Jameson v Royal Insurance Co* (1873) IR 7 CL 126; *Herbert v Poland* (1932) 44 Ll L Rep 139; *Watkins & Davis Ltd v Legal and General Assurance Co Ltd* [1981] 1 Lloyd's Rep 674; *S & M Carpets (London) Ltd v Cornhill Insurance Co Ltd* [1982] 1 Lloyd's Rep 423, CA; *McLean Enterprises Ltd v Ecclesiastical Insurance Office plc* [1986] 2 Lloyd's Rep 416; *Broughton Park Textiles (Salford) Ltd v Commercial Union Assurance Co Ltd* [1987] 1 Lloyd's Rep 194.
6 *Upjohn v Hitchens, Upjohn v Ford* [1918] 2 KB 48 at 58, CA, per Scrutton LJ; *City Tailors Ltd v Evans* (1921) 126 LT 439 at 443, CA, per Scrutton LJ.
7 *Midland Insurance Co v Smith* (1881) 6 QBD 561.
8 *Harris v Poland* [1941] 1 KB 462, [1941] 1 All ER 204.

594. Providing information as to cause of fire. Where, in an action on a fire policy which contained an exception[1] of loss by fire occasioned by an earthquake, the insurers pleaded that the loss forming the subject of the claim was caused by earthquake and not by fire, particulars as to the cause and place of origin of the alleged fire were refused on the ground that the proper way to obtain the information required was by interrogatories[2]. However, where insurers claimed for the recovery of money paid by them under a fire policy on the ground that the fire was caused by the deliberate act of the assured they were ordered to give particulars of the deliberate act or acts alleged[3].

1 As to exceptions in fire policies see para 595 et seq post.
2 *G and W Young & Co Ltd v Scottish Union and National Insurance Co* (1907) 24 TLR 73, CA. As to the power to order particulars see generally RSC Ord 18 r 12; and PLEADING. As to interrogatories see DISCOVERY vol 13 para 100 et seq. As to the remitting of a case to an arbitrator or trial judge for the purpose of ascertaining the cause of the loss or damage see para 601 note 3 post.
3 *London Assurance v Kidson* (1935) 79 Sol Jo 641, CA.

(ii) Excepted Perils

595. Usual exceptions. Where a fire which causes a loss is itself caused by a peril expressly excluded by an exceptions clause in the policy, the assured cannot recover[1]. A fire policy in ordinary practice comprises a number of perils so excepted[2], but only a few of them call for detailed consideration. Among the most important exceptions clauses in an ordinary fire insurance policy are those relating to riot, civil commotion, war, civil war, military and usurped power and explosions[3], and those relating to natural causes, such as earthquake or subterranean fire[4].

1 A loss due to an excepted peril, where there is no fire, is not within the policy at all and therefore need not be excluded: *Re Hooley Hill Rubber and Chemical Co Ltd and Royal Insurance Co Ltd* [1920] 1 KB 257 at 273, CA, per Duke LJ.
2 See 20 Forms & Precedents (5th Edn) 29, Form 2 cl 2.1.
3 See paras 596–602 post.
4 See eg *Tootal Broadhurst Lee Co v London and Lancashire Fire Insurance Co* (1908) Ivamy's Fire and Motor Insurance (4th Edn) 403; 20 Forms & Precedents (5th Edn) 29, Form 2 cl 2.

596. Exception of riot. A claim for compensation for damage caused by a riot can be made against the police authority[1]. Having regard to this remedy, insurers as a general rule have always excluded riot from their fire policies. 'Riot' is defined by statute as involving 12 or more persons, who are present together, using or threatening unlawful violence for a common purpose, and whose conduct, taken together, is such as would cause a person of reasonable firmness present at the scene to fear for his personal safety[2]. It is immaterial whether or not the 12 or more use or threaten unlawful violence simultaneously[3]. The common purpose may be inferred from conduct[4]. No person of reasonable firmness need actually be, or be likely to be, present at the scene[5]. Riot may be committed in private as well as in public places[6].

1 Riot (Damages) Act 1886 s 2(1): see POLICE vol 36 para 241 et seq. If riot is not excluded from a policy, the insurers who pay the loss have a right to be subrogated to their assured's right to compensation: see para 506 ante. 'Riot' in the 1886 Act is to be construed in accordance with the provisions set out in the text and notes 2–6 infra: Public Order Act 1986 s 10(1).
2 Ibid s 1(1). See CRIMINAL LAW vol 11(1) (Reissue) para 149.
3 Ibid s 1(2).
4 Ibid s 1(3).
5 Ibid s 1(4).
6 Ibid s 1(5).

597. Exception of civil commotion. A civil commotion has been described as an insurrection of the people for general purposes, though not amounting to rebellion[1], but it probably cannot be precisely defined. Turbulence or tumult is essential[2]; and an organised conspiracy to commit acts where there is no tumult or disturbance until after the acts does not amount to civil commotion[3]. However, it is not necessary to show the existence of any outside organisation at whose instigation the acts were done[4]. It therefore expresses a stage intermediate between riot and civil war[5], and although technically it probably includes a riot[6], once fighting begins matters have got beyond a mere civil commotion[7].

1 *Langdale v Mason* (1780) 2 Marshall on Marine Insurances (3rd Edn) 793 at 794 per Lord Mansfield CJ. See also *Drinkwater v London Assurance Corpn* (1767) 2 Wils 363; *Mason v Sainsbury* (1782) 3 Doug KB 61; *Spinney's (1948) Ltd v Royal Insurance Co Ltd* [1980] 1 Lloyd's Rep 406.
2 *London and Manchester Plate Glass Co Ltd v Heath* [1913] 3 KB 411 at 417, CA, per Buckley LJ, approved in *Cooper v General Accident, Fire and Life Assurance Corpn Ltd* (1923) 128 LT 481, HL; *Pan American World Airways Inc v Aetna Casualty & Surety Co* [1974] 1 Lloyd's Rep 207 at 234 (NY Dist

Ct, Southern Dist) per Frankel DJ (aviation insurance); on appeal [1975] 1 Lloyd's Rep 77 (US Ct of Appeals).

3 *London and Manchester Plate Glass Co Ltd v Heath* [1913] 3 KB 411, CA; *Cooper v General Accident, Fire and Life Assurance Corpn Ltd* (1923) 128 LT 481, HL; *Craig v Eagle Star and British Dominions Insurance Co* (1922) 56 ILR 145.

4 *Levy v Assicurazioni Generali* [1940] AC 791 at 800, [1940] 3 All ER 427 at 431, PC, citing Welford and Otter-Barry's Law of Fire Insurance (3rd Edn) 64.

5 *Republic of Bolivia v Indemnity Mutual Marine Insurance Co Ltd* [1909] 1 KB 785 at 801, CA, per Farwell LJ.

6 *Motor Union Insurance Co Ltd v Boggan* (1923) 130 LT 588 at 591, HL, per Lord Birkenhead. As to riot see para 596 ante.

7 *Curtis & Sons v Mathews* [1919] 1 KB 425, CA.

598. Exception of war, civil war or rebellion. Often an exception is framed by reference to war or war risks[1]. In such a case, the actual state of affairs is taken into account, irrespective of whether there is official recognition of a state of war or a severance of diplomatic relations[2]. A rebellion may be a war[3], the rebels coming within the term 'Queen's enemies'[4]. In the absence of clear indication to the contrary the word 'war' includes a civil war[5].

A civil war is a war which has the special characteristic of being civil, that is to say internal rather than external. A decision on whether such a war exists generally involves a consideration of (1) whether it can be said that the conflict was between opposing 'sides', (2) what were the objects of the 'sides' and how did they set about pursuing them, and (3) what was the scale of the conflict and its effect on public order and on the life of its inhabitants[6].

1 As to government insurance and reinsurance against war risks see paras 794–796, 802 post.

2 *Kawasaki Kisen Kabushiki Kaisha of Kobe v Bantham SS Co Ltd* [1939] 2 KB 544, [1939] 1 All ER 819.

3 *Curtis & Sons v Mathews* [1919] 1 KB 425, CA.

4 *Secretary of State for War v Midland Great Western Rly Co of Ireland* [1923] 2 IR 102.

5 *Pesquerias y Secaderos de Bacalao de Espana SA v Beer* (1949) 82 Ll L Rep 501 at 514, HL, per Lord Morton.

6 *Spinney's (1948) Ltd v Royal Insurance Co Ltd* [1980] 1 Lloyd's Rep 406 at 430 per Mustill J.

599. Exception of military and usurped power. The exception of military and usurped power contemplates acts of warfare committed by belligerents[1] who may be either foreign enemies invading the realm[2] or subjects of the Crown engaged in internal rebellion[3]; and it covers acts done by the forces of the Crown in repelling the enemy or suppressing the rebellion[4]. However, usurped power does not include a government that has been officially recognised[5]. Military and usurped power also connotes control of territory[6]. The usurpation has been described as consisting in the arrogation to itself by the mob of a law-making and law-enforcing power which properly belongs to the sovereign[7].

1 This includes acts of incendiarism committed by private looters in the course of military operations: *American Tobacco Co Inc v Guardian Assurance Co Ltd* (1925) 69 Sol Jo 621, CA.

2 *Drinkwater v London Assurance Corpn* (1767) 2 Wils 363; *Rogers v Whittaker* [1917] 1 KB 942. The policy usually includes a separate exception of 'foreign enemy', but this is unnecessary as the exception against military power is sufficient.

3 *Drinkwater v London Assurance Corpn* (1767) 2 Wils 363; *Langdale v Mason* (1780) 2 Marshall on Marine Insurances (3rd Edn) 793. 'Rebellion' and 'insurrection' are usually specially excepted.

4 *Curtis & Sons v Mathews* [1919] 1 KB 425, CA.

5 *White, Child and Beney Ltd v Eagle, Star and British Dominions Insurance Co* (1922) 127 LT 571 at 583, CA, per Bankes LJ.

6 *Pan American World Airways Inc v Aetna Casualty and Surety Co* [1975] 1 Lloyd's Rep 77 (US Ct of Appeals) (destruction of aircraft by Popular Front for the Liberation of Palestine).
7 *Spinney's (1948) Ltd v Royal Insurance Co Ltd* [1980] 1 Lloyd's Rep 406 at 433.

600. Loss caused by explosion. Some explosions are caused by fire; others happen without its intervention, but every explosion involves the possibility of loss either by concussion[1] or by fire consequent on the explosion[2]. Apart from an exception in the policy, there is a loss by fire within the meaning of the policy whenever property is actually burned in the course of an explosion, and it is unnecessary to inquire into the connection between the explosion and the fire. The loss is equally recoverable whether the fire which caused it arose and continued independently of the explosion[3] or whether the explosion was the cause of the fire[4] or whether the explosion was the result of the fire and its effect was to make the fire burn more strongly[5]. However, if the loss is due to concussion only and there is no actual burning it becomes necessary to inquire into the cause of the explosion; there is no liability under the policy unless the explosion was caused by fire. If the explosion was not caused by fire, the policy has no application, since there is no insurance against loss by concussion[6]. Where the explosion was caused by fire, in the absence of any exception to the contrary, the position depends upon the situation of the property affected by the concussion. If it is situated on the premises where the fire is raging the loss is caused by fire, since the explosion is the direct consequence of the fire[7]. However, if the property is situated elsewhere the loss, being solely due to concussion, is not covered[8].

1 As to the exception of loss by concussion see para 602 post.
2 As to the exception of fire caused by explosion see para 601 post.
3 *Stanley v Western Insurance Co* (1868) LR 3 Exch 71 at 74 per Kelly CB.
4 *Everett v London Assurance* (1865) 19 CBNS 126 at 133 per Byles J.
5 *Stanley v Western Insurance Co* (1868) LR 3 Exch 71 at 75 per Martin B.
6 *Re Hooley Hill Rubber and Chemical Co Ltd and Royal Insurance Co Ltd* [1920] 1 KB 257 at 272, CA, per Scrutton LJ.
7 *Curtis and Harvey (Canada) Ltd v North British and Mercantile Insurance Co Ltd* [1921] 1 AC 303, PC, approving *Hobbs v Northern Assurance Co* (1886) 12 SCR 631.
8 *Everett v London Assurance* (1865) 19 CBNS 126.

601. Exception of fire caused by explosion. Explosions and their consequences are usually dealt with by a special stipulation in the policy, and the position then depends upon the interpretation of the particular stipulation employed. Under some old forms of stipulation liability may be excluded even where property is burned if the fire which burns the property is caused by explosion[1]. In such a case, where the explosion precedes and causes the fire, no difficulty arises; the policy is plainly inapplicable. However, where a fire precedes and causes the explosion it may become necessary to distinguish the consequences of the fire from the consequences of the explosion. Loss by concussion is in any case excluded; but the effect of the explosion may be to cause a further fire, and any loss due to such further fire is within the exception[2]. If the original fire still continues in operation, any loss due to it, even after the explosion, is not within the exception and remains covered by the policy[3].

1 *Re Hooley Hill Rubber and Chemical Co Ltd and Royal Insurance Co Ltd* [1920] 1 KB 257, CA; *Curtis and Harvey (Canada) Ltd v North British and Mercantile Insurance Co Ltd* [1921] 1 AC 303, PC.
2 *Stanley v Western Insurance Co* (1868) LR 3 Exch 71, approved in *Re Hooley Hill Rubber and Chemical Co Ltd and Royal Insurance Co Ltd* [1920] 1 KB 257, CA; and in *Curtis and Harvey (Canada) Ltd v North British and Mercantile Insurance Co Ltd* [1921] 1 AC 303, PC.

3 If necessary, proceedings may be remitted by the court to an arbitrator, or by an appellate court to the trial judge, for the purpose of ascertaining further facts relevant for determining the cause of the loss or damage: *Stanley v Western Insurance Co* (1868) LR 3 Exch 71; *Curtis and Harvey (Canada) Ltd v North British and Mercantile Insurance Co* [1921] 1 AC 303, PC. As to the right of the insurers to obtain information from the assured as to the cause of damage see para 594 ante. The onus of proof may, by the terms of the exception, be sought to be thrown upon the assured: *Re Hooley Hill Rubber and Chemical Co Ltd and Royal Insurance Co Ltd* [1920] 1 KB 257 at 269, CA, per Bankes LJ. See, however, paras 409, 421 ante.

602. Exception of loss by explosion.

The refinements necessitated by special stipulations[1] were found to be unnecessary and commercially undesirable. Accordingly, a simpler form of stipulation under which liability for loss by explosion is alone excluded came into general use, the insurers being ready to accept liability in all cases where the subject matter is burned even though the fire is caused by explosion[2]. However, liability is also accepted for loss by concussion where (1) the loss is due to the explosion of boilers used for domestic purposes only[3]; and (2) the loss is due to an explosion in a building not forming part of any gasworks of gas[4] used for domestic purposes or used for lighting or heating the building[5]. In these two cases there is in reality an extension of the policy.

1 As to the special stipulations see para 601 ante.
2 See 20 Forms & Precedents (5th Edn) 29, Form 2 cl 2.
3 See *Willesden Corpn v Municipal Mutual Insurance Ltd* [1945] 1 All ER 444, CA, affg [1944] 2 All ER 600.
4 *Stanley v Western Insurance Co* (1868) LR 3 Exch 71.
5 See 20 Forms & Precedents (5th Edn) 29, Form 2 cl 2.

(iii) Proximate Cause

603. Fire as proximate cause of loss.

To constitute a loss within the meaning of a fire policy, it is not necessary to show that the subject matter of the insurance has itself been burned; it is sufficient that the loss has been proximately caused by fire[1]. Losses which are the necessary consequences of a fire in the sense that, if there had been no fire, they could not have happened, are proximately caused by the fire. For example, where a fire attacks the fabric of a building and causes the roof or walls to fall upon other property in the building and destroy it, the destruction caused by the fall is proximately caused by the fire[2]. Again, losses which are the reasonable and probable consequences of fire, in that they result in the ordinary course of events from the happening of a fire, are proximately caused by the fire. For example, losses may be sustained through attempts to check the progress of a fire, property may be destroyed by the water used to extinguish the flames[3] or buildings may be blown up by the fire brigade for the purpose of preventing the fire from spreading[4]. Other losses may be sustained in attempts to save property from fire; the property may be destroyed or damaged in the course of removal[5]. In all these cases, though the property is not burned, its loss is nevertheless proximately caused by fire[6]. Losses by theft during a fire must also be regarded as proximately caused by the fire[7].

1 As to the doctrine of proximate cause generally see paras 175–176 ante.
2 *Re Hooley Hill Rubber and Chemical Co Ltd and Royal Insurance Co Ltd* [1920] 1 KB 257 at 271, CA, per Scrutton LJ; *Johnston v West of Scotland Insurance Co* (1828) 7 Sh 52, Ct of Sess. However, see *Tootal Broadhurst Lee Co v London and Lancashire Fire Insurance Co* (1908) Ivamy's Fire and Motor Insurance

(4th Edn) 403 at 406 per Bigham J, where liability was expressly excluded under the 'fallen buildings clause'. A 'fallen buildings clause' is a clause whereby the insurance ceases if the building falls through some cause other than fire: see eg Ivamy's Fire and Motor Insurance (4th Edn) 107.
3 *Ahmedbhoy Habbibhoy v Bombay Fire and Marine Insurance Co* (1912) 107 LT 668, PC; *Symington & Co v Union Insurance Society of Canton Ltd* (1928) 97 LJKB 646, CA.
4 *Stanley v Western Insurance Co* (1868) LR 3 Exch 71 at 74 per Kelly CB, approved in *Canada Rice Mills Ltd v Union Marine and General Insurance Co Ltd* [1941] AC 55 at 71, [1940] 4 All ER 169 at 179, PC. In the Metropolitan Fire Brigade Act 1865 s 12(2) (repealed), it was provided, as regards fires within the metropolitan area, that any damage occasioned by the brigade in the due execution of its duties should be deemed to be damage by fire within the meaning of any fire insurance policy. This provision appears merely to have been declaratory of the common law and, no doubt for that reason, was not re-enacted.
5 *Stanley v Western Insurance Co* (1868) LR 3 Exch 71.
6 *Stanley v Western Insurance Co* (1868) LR 3 Exch 71 at 74 per Kelly CB; *Re Etherington and Lancashire and Yorkshire Accident Insurance Co* [1909] 1 KB 591 at 599, CA, per Vaughan Williams LJ; *Marsden v City and County Assurance Co* (1865) LR 1 CP 232.
7 *The Knight of St Michael* [1898] P 30, approving the Canadian cases of *McGibbon v Queen Insurance Co* (1866) 10 LCJ 227, and *Harris v London and Lancashire Fire Insurance Co* (1866) 10 LCJ 268; cf *Levy v Baillie* (1831) 7 Bing 349.

604. Losses not proximately caused by fire. Losses which are not proximately but only remotely caused by fire are not covered by an ordinary fire policy[1]. They fall into two classes: (1) losses of which the fire is in the strict sense the remote cause; and (2) consequential losses. Where fire causes an explosion and property in other premises, situated at a distance from the fire, is destroyed by atmospheric concussion, the fire is not the proximate, but the remote cause of the loss and the loss is not covered[2]. However, where property is destroyed by fire, the direct consequence of the fire is the loss of the property itself. The loss of the property may involve the assured in further loss, according to circumstances; he may be compelled, for the purpose of continuing his business, to rent other premises to take the place of those destroyed and he may lose the profits which he would have been able to earn if his business had not been interrupted by the fire. These losses are remotely and not proximately caused by the fire; they are not its natural, but only its accidental, consequences[3].

1 As to consequential loss insurance see paras 785–789 post.
2 As to loss caused by the explosion see paras 600–602 ante.
3 *Re Wright and Pole* (1834) 1 Ad & El 621; followed in *Menzies v North British Insurance Co* (1847) 9 Dunl 694, Ct of Sess; *Westminster Fire Office v Glasgow Provident Investment Society* (1888) 13 App Cas 699, HL. See generally *Theobald v Railway Passengers Assurance Co* (1854) 10 Exch 45 at 58 per Pollock CB. A special insurance may be effected against consequential loss: see paras 785–789 post.

605. Proximate cause as basis of exceptions. The doctrine of proximate cause is applied for the purpose of determining whether a loss is caused by an excepted peril. If property is not burned at all, but is destroyed by the direct operation of an excepted peril as, for instance, by the concussion of an explosion, the explosion is the proximate cause of the loss and it is immaterial that the explosion was itself caused by fire[1]. If the subject matter is burned, but the fire which burned it derived its origin from an excepted peril, the liability of the insurers depends upon whether the excepted peril is to be regarded as the proximate cause of the loss or not. Where the fire is the natural consequence of the excepted peril, the excepted peril is the proximate cause of the loss[2]. Where a bomb dropped from a hostile aircraft in war time sets a warehouse on fire, the loss of the warehouse, though caused by fire, is the natural consequence of military operations, and is therefore proximately caused by the excepted peril of 'military or usurped' power[3]. Where there are two competing causes, the effective or dominant cause must be taken as the proximate cause even though it is more remote in point of time[4].

On the other hand, where the fire is not the natural but merely an accidental consequence of the excepted peril, the proximate cause of the loss is the fire, the excepted peril being the remote cause only, and the loss is therefore covered by the policy[5]. Where a fire which is directly caused by an excepted peril spreads solely by the operation of natural causes[6], all losses caused by the fire, however distant from the premises on which the fire originated, are proximately caused by the excepted peril[7]. However, if the spread of the fire is due not to natural causes but to the intervention of a new and independent cause, the chain of causation is broken, and the fire, being an accidental consequence only of the excepted peril, becomes a fresh fire. Therefore, the excepted peril is not the proximate cause of the subsequent losses, which are caused by the fresh fire alone, and are therefore covered by the policy; but the exception may be so framed as to exclude liability even where the excepted peril is the remote cause of the loss[8].

1 As to loss caused by the explosion see paras 600–602 ante.
2 *Langdale v Mason* (1780) 2 Marshall on Marine Insurances (3rd Edn) 793; *Stanley v Western Insurance Co* (1868) LR 3 Exch 71; *Wayne Tank and Pump Co Ltd v Employers' Liability Assurance Corpn Ltd* [1974] QB 57, [1973] 3 All ER 825, CA.
3 *Rogers v Whittaker* [1917] 1 KB 942; cf *Curtis & Sons v Mathews* [1919] 1 KB 425, CA. As to the exception of military and usurped power see para 599 ante.
4 *Wayne Tank and Pump Co Ltd v Employers' Liability Assurance Corpn Ltd* [1974] QB 57, [1973] 3 All ER 825, CA.
5 Cf *Marsden v City and County Assurance Co* (1865) LR 1 CP 232; *Winicofsky v Army and Navy General Assurance Association Ltd* (1919) 35 TLR 283.
6 A shift of the wind changing the direction of the fire is a natural cause and not the intervention of a fresh cause: *Tootal Broadhurst Lee Co v London and Lancashire Fire Insurance Co* (1908) Ivamy's Fire and Motor Insurance (4th Edn) 403 at 406 per Bigham J.
7 *Walker v London and Provincial Insurance Co* (1888) 22 LR Ir 572; *Tootal Broadhurst Lee Co v London and Lancashire Fire Insurance Co* (1908) Ivamy's Fire and Motor Insurance (4th Edn) 403 at 405 per Bigham J.
8 *Walker v London and Provincial Insurance Co* (1888) 22 LR Ir 572 at 577, per Palles C B; *Tootal Broadhurst Lee Co v London and Lancashire Fire Insurance Co* (1908) Ivamy's Fire and Motor Insurance (4th Edn) 403 at 405 per Bigham J.

(iv) Insurable Interest

A. IN GENERAL

606. Insurable interest necessary. A contract of fire insurance, like all other contracts of insurance[1], requires an insurable interest in the subject matter of the insurance to support it[2]; in the absence of an insurable interest, the assured can suffer no loss, and the contract becomes a mere wager[3].

1 The marine insurance definition of 'insurable interest' applies also to fire insurance: *Castellain v Preston* (1883) 11 QBD 380 at 397, CA, per Bowen LJ. As to insurable interest in marine insurance (and generally) see para 185 ante.
2 *Thomas v National Farmers' Union Mutual Insurance Society Ltd* [1961] 1 All ER 363, [1961] 1 WLR 386; and see *Lynch v Dalzell* (1729) 4 Bro Parl Cas 431, HL; *Sadlers' Co v Badcock* (1743) 2 Atk 554; *Castellain v Preston* (1883) 11 QBD 380, CA.
3 *Prudential Insurance Co v IRC* [1904] 2 KB 658 at 663 per Channell J.

607. Interests which are insurable. The precise nature, extent or value of the insurable interest in a contract of insurance is irrelevant[1]. An equitable or beneficial interest of any kind is as effective for this purpose as a legal interest[2]. Interest is not restricted to ownership[3]; it may arise under a contract relating to the subject matter[4] or it may be founded upon lawful possession[5]; a finder who takes the object which he finds into his possession has an insurable interest in it[6]. Similarly a defeasible or precarious interest is capable of supporting an insurance[7].

It is not clear whether the statutory provisions which require the names of persons interested to be inserted in policies[8] apply to fire insurance[9].

1 As to the requirement of an insurable interest see para 606 ante.
2 *Castellain v Preston* (1883) 11 QBD 380 at 398, CA, per Bowen LJ. Both trustees and beneficiaries have an insurable interest in the trust property: *Ex p Yallop* (1808) 15 Ves 60 at 67; *Ex p Houghton* (1810) 17 Ves 251 at 253. As to the duties and powers of trustees in respect of insurance see the Trustee Act 1925 s 19; SETTLEMENTS; and TRUSTS.
3 If a person is owner he need not be in possession: *Ward v Carttar* (1865) LR 1 Eq 29 at 31 per Romilly MR.
4 As to the interest founded on the contract see para 612 post; and see *Sellers v Continental Insurance Co* (1974) 48 DLR (3d) 369 (NS App Div) where the assured had built his house at his own expense and had a contractual right to acquire the land; he was held to be correctly described as 'owner' and to have an insurable interest in the house.
5 *Marks v Hamilton* (1852) 7 Exch 323. However, a person who merely permits the property of another to remain on his land has no insurable interest in it: *Macaura v Northern Assurance Co Ltd* [1925] AC 619 at 628, HL, per Lord Buckmaster.
6 *Marks v Hamilton* (1852) as reported in 21 LJEx 109 at 110 per Pollock CB.
7 *Goulstone v Royal Insurance Co* (1858) 1 F & F 276; *Anderson v Commercial Union Assurance Co* (1885) 55 LJQB 146, CA; see also *Marks v Hamilton* (1852) 7 Exch 323.
8 Ie the Life Assurance Act 1774 s 2 (as amended): see para 543 ante.
9 If the statute has any application to fire insurance, it can apply to insurances on buildings only, since insurances on goods are expressly excluded: ibid s 4. In practice, the statute, in so far as it requires the names of the persons interested to be inserted in the policy (see s 2 (as amended): para 543 ante), is not always observed in connection with insurances on buildings and the application of the statute to such insurances is open to question. There are many cases in which the position under fire insurances covering interests other than that of the assured has been discussed: see eg *Rayner v Preston* (1881) 18 ChD 1, CA; *Castellain v Preston* (1883) 11 QBD 380, CA; *Nichols & Co v Scottish Union and National Insurance Co* (1885) 2 TLR 190; *Matthey v Curling* [1922] 2 AC 180, CA; affd [1922] 2 AC 180 at 223, HL. In none of these cases and, it is believed, in no reported case, has any judge referred to the statute as requiring the interests to be named. As it is the duty of the judge to take the objection under the statute, if it is sound (*Griffiths v Fleming* [1909] 1 KB 805, CA, per Farwell and Kennedy LJJ), the judicial silence is not without significance. It is to be noted that the mischief which the statute was intended to remedy, ie insurances without interest, did not exist in fire insurance where an insurable interest was required even before 1774: *Sadlers' Co v Badcock* (1743) 2 Atk 554 at 556 per Lord Hardwicke LG; see also *Lynch v Dalzell* (1729) 4 Bro Parl Cas 431, HL; *Dalby v India and London Life Assurance Co* (1854) 15 CB 365 at 387, Ex Ch, per Parke B. For a full discussion of the question and for the arguments in favour of the view that the statute does not apply to fire insurance see Ivamy's *Fire and Motor Insurance* (4th Edn) 179–185.

B. INTERESTS IN PARTICULAR CASES

608. Insurable interests of vendor and purchaser. The vendor of any property retains his insurable interest as owner until the property is conveyed to the purchaser[1]. After conveyance his interest ceases unless either the purchase money is unpaid and he retains his lien as unpaid vendor[2], or he has undertaken to the purchaser to be responsible for the safety of the property[3].

The purchaser of property acquires an insurable interest by virtue of the contract of purchase[4].

1 *Collingridge v Royal Exchange Assurance Corpn* (1877) 3 QBD 173 at 177 per Lush J; *Castellain v Preston* (1883) 11 QBD 380 at 385, CA, per Brett LJ. As to the position as between vendors and purchasers see para 621 post.
2 *Castellain v Preston* (1883) 11 QBD 380 at 401, CA, per Bowen LJ.
3 *North British and Mercantile Insurance Co v Moffatt* (1871) LR 7 CP 25; cf *Martineau v Kitching* (1872) LR 7 QB 436; and see para 621 post.
4 See para 612 post.

609. Bankrupt's insurable interest. As long as he remains in possession of any of his property as apparent owner, a bankrupt retains an insurable interest in it[1] and it is immaterial that the property is being fraudulently concealed from his creditors[2].

1 *Marks v Hamilton* (1852) 7 Exch 323.
2 *Goulstone v Royal Insurance Co* (1858) 1 F & F 276.

610. Spouse's insurable interest. A husband has an insurable interest in his wife's property, so long as they are living together and sharing its use[1]. Even in the case of property which in its nature cannot be shared, for example articles of clothing or jewellery, the husband presumably has an insurable interest if he is financially responsible for replacements. It is supposed that a wife has a similar insurable interest in property of her husband which she shares and, if she is the moneyed partner, in his personal belongings[2].

1 *Goulstone v Royal Insurance Co* (1858) 1 F & F 276.
2 See *Griffiths v Fleming* [1909] 1 KB 805 at 815, CA, per Vaughan Williams LJ.

611. Interest founded on liability. A person who, by the term of some contract or through a legal relationship with the owner of property, is or may become answerable for its safety, clearly has an insurable interest in the property since he is prejudiced by its destruction[1]. A tenant who has covenanted to insure the demised premises retains an insurable interest in them, even after his tenancy has come to an end, if his liability under the covenant continues[2]. Similarly, liability under a covenant to make good fire damage confers an interest on a tenant[3]. Again, by reason of their liability under the policy, insurers under a fire insurance policy have themselves a sufficient insurable interest in the property of the assured which is the subject matter of the insurance to support a policy of reinsurance[4].

1 *Sturge v Hackett* [1962] 3 All ER 166, [1962] 1 WLR 1257, CA, where liability was restricted to claims against the assured as occupier of premises. As to the position of bailees see para 698 post; and BAILMENT vol 2 (Reissue) para 1844.
2 *Heckman v Isaac* (1862) 6 LT 383. However, when his liability comes to an end, his insurable interest ceases (*Matthey v Curling* [1922] 2 AC 180 at 219, CA, per Younger LJ; affd [1922] 2 AC 180 at 223, HL) unless his occupation continues.
3 *Andrews v Patriotic Insurance Co (No 2)* (1886) 18 LR Ir 355 at 365 per Palles CB.
4 *Forsikringsaktieselskabet National (of Copenhagen) v A-G* [1925] AC 639 at 642, HL; cf *Re Law Guarantee Trust and Accident Society Ltd, Liverpool Mortgage Insurance Co's Case* [1914] 2 Ch 617 at 631, CA, per Buckley LJ. As to the position generally of reinsurers see paras 204–210 ante.

612. Interest founded on contract. The existence of a liability to the owner of property is not essential for founding an insurable interest[1]; it is sufficient that a contract confers advantages which will be lost by the destruction of the property[2]. A purchaser of property under a contract of sale has an insurable interest in the property derived from the contract[3] and arising as soon as the contract is made[4]. Again, a bailee[5] of property, even if he is under no liability to the bailor for the loss of the property, nevertheless has an insurable interest[6] which, in this case, is founded upon his lien[7], or upon the commission[8], profit[9] or other advantages[10] which he may expect to derive from the bailment. So, too, a tenant of premises has an insurable interest founded upon the beneficial enjoyment of the premises, which he loses in the event of their destruction[11]; and any creditor whose debt is secured by legal mortgage[12] or equitable charge upon specific property has an insurable interest in that property[13]. On the other hand, an ordinary creditor whose debt is not secured by a lien or charge of some kind upon specific property has only a personal remedy against the debtor[14], and has no insurable interest in the debtor's property[15].

1 *Waters v Monarch Fire and Life Assurance Co* (1856) 5 E & B 870; *London and North Western Rly Co v Glyn* (1859) 1 E & E 652.
2 *Simpson v Scottish Union Insurance Co* (1863) 1 Hem & M 618.
3 *Collingridge v Royal Exchange Assurance Corpn* (1877) 3 QBD 173, as explained in *Phoenix Assurance Co v Spooner* [1905] 2 KB 753. Hence, the absence of a conveyance is immaterial: *Rayner v Preston* (1881) 18 ChD 1 at 13, CA, per James LJ; approved in *Ridout v Fowler* [1904] 1 Ch 658 at 661 per Farwell J; affd [1904] 2 Ch 93, CA.
4 The purchase may be on approval: *Bevington and Morris v Dale & Co Ltd* (1902) 7 Com Cas 112 at 113 per Kennedy J.
5 As to insurance by bailees see paras 698–705 post.
6 See the text to note 1 supra.
7 *Crowley v Cohen* (1832) 3 B & Ad 478.
8 *Castellain v Preston* (1883) 11 QBD 380 at 398, CA, per Bowen LJ.
9 *Dalgleish v Buchanan* (1854) 16 Dunl 332, Ct of Sess.
10 Thus a person who rents a house furnished has an insurable interest in the furniture: *Trotter v Watson* (1869) LR 4 CP 434 at 444 per Bovill CJ.
11 *Simpson v Scottish Union Insurance Co* (1863) 1 Hem & M 618 at 628 per Wood V-C; *Castellain v Preston* (1883) 11 QBD 380 at 398, CA, per Bowen LJ.
12 A legal mortgagee has an insurable interest based on legal ownership: *Dobson v Land* (1850) 8 Hare 216 at 220 per Wigram V-C; *North British and Mercantile Insurance Co v London, Liverpool and Globe Insurance Co* (1877) 5 ChD 569 at 583, CA, per Mellish LJ; *Castellain v Preston* (1883) 11 QBD 380 at 398, CA, per Bowen LJ. As to the power of a mortgagee to insure see MORTGAGE.
13 *Westminster Fire Office v Glasgow Provident Investment Society* (1888) 13 App Cas 699 at 708, HL, per Lord Halsbury LC.
14 Hence he has an insurable interest in the life of his debtor: see para 540 ante.
15 *Macaura v Northern Assurance Co Ltd* [1925] AC 619 at 626, HL, per Lord Buckmaster, approving *Moran, Galloway & Co v Uzielli* [1905] 2 KB 555 at 562.

613. Shareholder in company. A shareholder in a company, even though the company is a one-man company and he and his nominees are the only share-holders, has no insurable interest in the company's property[1]; nor has a creditor of a company any insurable interest in its property[2].

1 *Macaura v Northern Assurance Co Ltd* [1925] AC 619, HL. For the principle that a company is a legal person separate from its members see COMPANIES vol 7(1) (Reissue) para 89.
2 *Macaura v Northern Assurance Co Ltd* [1925] AC 619, HL.

C. INSURANCE OF SEPARATE INTERESTS

614. Persons interested in same property. There are many cases in which two or more persons, such as landlord and tenant[1], bailor and bailee[2], mortgagor and mortgagee[3] and tenant for life and remainderman[4], each have an interest in the same property. These interests are separate and distinct; each is capable of supporting an insurance and each of the two persons interested may insure the property for his own protection. The insurance so effected enures for the sole benefit of the person effecting it and the other persons interested in the property have no right to participate[5].

1 *Andrews v Patriotic Assurance Co (No 2)* (1886) 18 LR Ir 355.
2 *North British and Mercantile Insurance Co v London, Liverpool and Globe Insurance Co* (1877) 5 ChD 569, CA; *Hepburn v A Tomlinson (Hauliers) Ltd* [1966] AC 451, [1966] 1 All ER 418, HL. As to insurance by bailees see paras 698–705 post. As to owner and hirer under a hire purchase contract see HIRE PURCHASE AND CONSUMER CREDIT.
3 *North British and Mercantile Insurance Co v London, Liverpool and Globe Insurance Co* (1877) 5 ChD 569 at 583, CA, per Mellish LJ. The same principle applies as regards first and second mortgagees: *Westminster Fire Office v Glasgow Provident Investment Society* (1888) 13 App Cas 699, HL.
4 *North British and Mercantile Insurance Co v London, Liverpool and Globe Insurance Co* (1877) 5 ChD 569 at 577, CA, per Jessel MR.
5 *Leeds v Cheetham* (1827) 1 Sim 146, followed in *Lofft v Dennis* (1859) 1 E & E 474; *Warwicker v Bretnall* (1882) 23 ChD 188, explaining *Rook v Worth* (1750) 1 Ves Sen 460; *Gaussen v Whatman* (1905) 93 LT 101; *Re Bladon, Dando v Porter* [1911] 2 Ch 350 at 354 per Neville J; on appeal [1912] 1 Ch 45, CA.

615. Insurances for the benefit of several interests. Since it is the same property which is exposed to peril, a composite policy is sometimes taken out by two or more persons for their respective rights and interests. In such a case the policy is not a joint policy, so as to involve all participants in a fraud perpetrated by one of them; each participant has his separate rights under the policy, and these are not prejudiced by another participant's fraud[1]. Warehousemen and other bailees effect policies which will enure for the benefit of their bailors[2] and similar insurances are effected by mortgagors or mortgagees[3], tenants for life or remaindermen[4], lessors or lessees[5], and a company, its contractors and subcontractors[6], for the benefit of other persons interested in the same property. Insurances of this latter kind may be made in the performance of some contract or in the discharge of some duty[7], although this is not necessary. The person effecting the insurance need owe no duty or responsibility to the other persons interested[8]. All that is required to make the insurance effective is that at the time of insuring it is his intention to cover their interests as well as his own[9]. The intention must be that of the party to the insurance contract; the intention of the broker who places the business is irrelevant unless he has authority to act for all the interests concerned[10]. If the requisite intention is established, the insurance is a valid insurance enuring for the benefit of all persons interested[11]. The person effecting it must be regarded as effecting it as agent on their behalf. Therefore, if the insurance is unauthorised it must be ratified by the person claiming its benefit and the ratification may be given after loss[12].

1 *General Accident, Fire and Life Assurance Corpn Ltd v Midland Bank Ltd* [1940] 2 KB 388, [1940] 3 All ER 252, CA.
2 *Martineau v Kitching* (1872) LR 7 QB 436 at 458 per Blackburn J; *Hepburn v A Tomlinson (Hauliers) Ltd* [1966] AC 451, [1966] 1 All ER 418, HL; *Lombard Australia Ltd v NRMA Insurance Ltd* [1969] 1 Lloyd's Rep 575 (NSW CA); and see further para 698 post.
3 *Nichols & Co v Scottish Union and National Insurance Co* (1885) 2 TLR 190, Ct of Sess; more fully reported in 14 R 1094.

4 *Garden v Ingram* (1852) 23 LJCh 478 at 479; *Castellain v Preston* (1883) 11 QBD 380 at 399 et seq, CA, per Bowen LJ.

5 *Enlayde Ltd v Roberts* [1917] 1 Ch 109 at 117 per Sargant J; *Matthey v Curling* [1922] 2 AC 180 at 199, CA, per Atkin LJ; affd [1922] 2 AC 180 at 223.

6 *Commonwealth Construction Co Ltd v Imperial Oil Ltd and Wellman-Lord (Alberta) Ltd* (1976) 6 WWR 72 (Can SC) (subcontractor had insurable interest only in that part of project for which it was the subcontractor); *Petrofina (UK) Ltd v Magnaload Ltd* [1984] QB 127, [1983] 3 All ER 35 (contractors' all risks insurance). See also *Stone Vickers Ltd v Appledore Ferguson Shipbuilders Ltd* [1992] 2 Lloyd's Rep 578, CA.

7 *Martineau v Kitching* (1872) LR 7 QB 436; *Reynard v Arnold* (1875) 10 Ch App 386, CA; see also *Garden v Ingram* (1852) 23 LJCh 478 at 479; explained in *Lee v Whiteley* (1866) LR 2 Eq 143 at 149; and *Rayner v Preston* (1881) 18 ChD 1 at 7, CA.

8 *Waters v Monarch Fire and Life Assurance Co* (1856) 5 E & B 870; *London and North Western Rly Co v Glyn* (1859) 1 E & E 652.

9 *Castellain v Preston* (1883) 11 QBD 380 at 398, CA, per Bowen LJ; see also *Waters v Monarch Fire and Life Assurance Co* (1856) 5 E & B 870; *London and North Western Rly Co v Glyn* (1859) 1 E & E 652; *Nichols & Co v Scottish Union and National Insurance Co* (1885) 2 TLR 190; *Hepburn v A Tomlinson (Hauliers) Ltd* [1966] AC 451, [1966] 1 All ER 418, HL. As to whether the Life Assurance Act 1774 applies to such insurances in the case of buildings see para 607 note 9 ante.

10 *Graham Joint Stock Shipping Co Ltd v Merchant Marine Insurance Co Ltd (No 2)* [1924] AC 294, HL.

11 *Waters v Monarch Fire and Life Assurance Co* (1856) 5 E & B 870 at 881 per Lord Campbell CJ; *Hepburn v A Tomlinson (Hauliers) Ltd* [1966] 1 All ER 418, HL.

12 *Waters v Monarch Fire and Life Assurance Co* (1856) 5 E & B 870 at 881 per Lord Campbell CJ. In this case the rule is the same as in the case of marine insurance: see para 213 ante. As to ratification see generally AGENCY vol 1(2) (Reissue) para 72 et seq.

616. Insurances by persons without interest. A person who has himself no insurable interest in the property cannot insure it for his own benefit, but he may insure it on behalf of some person who has an insurable interest. Then if ratification is necessary, owing to the absence of any antecedent authority, it must be given before loss; ratification after loss comes too late[1].

1 *Grover and Grover Ltd v Mathews* (1910) 15 Com Cas 249; followed in *Ferguson v Aberdeen Parish Council* 1916 SC 715.

D. DESCRIPTION OF INTEREST

617. Description of interest not generally required. As a general rule, it is unnecessary for the assured to describe the nature or extent of his interest in the subject matter of insurance[1]. The description of the subject matter sufficiently covers any interest which he may have. A bailee of goods need not describe the nature of his interest or state that he is bailee; an insurance on 'goods' covers his interest as bailee even though he may be intending to cover interests other than his own[2].

1 *London and North Western Rly Co v Glyn* (1859) 1 E & E 652 at 664 per Crompton J. For the terms commonly used to describe the goods insured by a bailee's policy see paras 701–703 post.

2 See *London and North Western Rly Co v Glyn* (1859) 1 E & E 652 at 664 per Crompton J.

618. Conditions requiring description of interest. The policy may contain a condition requiring a description of the interest intended to be insured, such as a condition that goods held in trust or on commission[1] are not to be covered by the policy unless specially mentioned as insured. Such a condition has no application unless the bailee intends to cover the interest of the bailor as well as his own; a specific description is not required where the policy is intended to cover the proposer's interest only[2].

1 As to the meaning of 'goods held in trust or on commission' see paras 701–703 post.
2 *London and North Western Rly Co v Glyn* (1859) 1 E & E 652 at 664. For phrases usually used to describe the goods insured by a bailee's policy see paras 701–703 post.

E. ASSIGNMENT OF INTEREST

619. Assignment by operation of law. On the death or bankruptcy of the assured, his insurable interest in his property is assigned by operation of law to his personal representatives[1] or trustee in bankruptcy[2]. The assignment of his interest does not affect the validity of the policy which remains enforceable by, respectively, the personal representatives[3] or the trustee in bankruptcy[4].

1 As to the effect of death on the policy see paras 454, 463 ante; and EXECUTORS vol 17 para 1071 et seq.
2 As to the effect of bankruptcy on the policy see para 464 ante; and BANKRUPTCY AND INSOLVENCY vol 3(2) (Reissue) para 381.
3 *Doe d Pitt v Laming* (1814) 4 Camp 73 at 75 per Lord Ellenborough CJ. See also *Mildmay v Folgham* (1797) 3 Ves 471.
4 *Manchester Fire Insurance Co v Wykes* (1875) 33 LT 142. See also *Re Carr and Sun Fire Insurance Co* (1897) 13 TLR 186, CA; and *Marriage v Royal Exchange Assurance Co* (1849) 18 LJCh 216.

620. Voluntary assignment. Where the assignment of interest in the subject matter is effected by the voluntary act of the assured, the assured divests himself of his interest in the subject matter[1] and the policy accordingly ceases to be effective unless it is specifically and validly assigned as a policy[2].

1 *Collingridge v Royal Exchange Assurance Corpn* (1877) 3 QBD 173 at 177 per Lush J.
2 *North British and Mercantile Insurance Co v Moffatt* (1871) LR 7 CP 25; *Ecclesiastical Comrs for England v Royal Exchange Assurance Corpn* (1895) 11 TLR 476; *Rogerson v Scottish Automobile and General Insurance Co Ltd* (1931) 48 TLR 17, HL. See paras 623–624 post.

621. Assignment must be complete. To constitute an assignment of interest, the assured must have parted with all his interest in the subject matter[1]. So long as he retains any interest in the subject matter, the assignment of interest is not complete, and the policy remains effective[2]. In the case of a sale, if the property in the subject matter has passed to the purchaser and the price has been paid, the vendor's insurable interest ceases[3]. However, the mere fact that a contract of sale has been made does not divest the vendor of his interest, even though, as between him and the purchaser, the risk may have passed to the purchaser[4]. The vendor retains his insurable interest as legal owner[5], and he has a further interest in that the purchaser may refuse to complete the purchase[6]. Consequently, if a fire takes place before the purchase is completed and the price is paid, the vendor is entitled to enforce his policy and to receive payment of the insurance money[7]. Notwithstanding the execution of a conveyance and the consequent passing of the legal estate to the purchaser, the vendor may retain a lien for the unpaid price and it seems that this will be sufficient to keep the policy in force[8]. The vendor also retains an insurable interest if he undertakes to the purchaser to be responsible for the safety of the subject matter[9].

1 *Rayner v Preston* (1881) 18 ChD 1 at 7, CA, per Cotton LJ.
2 *Collingridge v Royal Exchange Assurance Corpn* (1877) 3 QBD 173.
3 *Martineau v Kitching* (1872) LR 7 QB 436; *North British and Mercantile Insurance Co v Moffatt* (1871) LR 7 CP 25.
4 *Collingridge v Royal Exchange Assurance Corpn* (1877) 3 QBD 173, as explained in *Phoenix Assurance Co v Spooner* [1905] 2 KB 753, CA.
5 As to the insurable interest of the vendor see para 608 ante.
6 See *Castellain v Preston* (1883) 11 QBD 380 at 385, CA, per Brett LJ. In such a case, if certain statutory conditions are fulfilled, the insurance money must on completion be paid over by the vendor to the purchaser: see para 625 post. In a case where the insurance money is not payable over to the purchaser, if the vendor ultimately receives the purchase price from the purchaser, the insurers are entitled to recover from the vendor a sum equal to the insurance money: see para 508 ante.
7 *Collingridge v Royal Exchange Assurance Corpn* (1877) 3 QBD 173.
8 *Castellain v Preston* (1883) 11 QBD 380 at 401, 405, CA, per Bowen LJ.
9 *Martineau v Kitching* (1872) LR 7 QB 436.

622. Change of interest. A change of interest is not equivalent to an assignment of interest; the creation of a mortgage or charge does not operate as an assignment of interest, and the policy remains effective[1]; and on a change of partnership, where the continuing partners retain their insurable interest in the partnership property, an insurance on the property is not affected[2].

1 *Garden v Ingram* (1852) 23 LJCh 478 at 479 per Lord St Leonards.
2 *Jenkins v Deane* (1933) 150 LT 314.

623. Policy must be assigned specifically. A policy of insurance is a contract personal to the assured; it is not annexed to his property, and even where it insures a building, it is not, apart from statute[1], a contract which runs with the land[2]. Consequently, on the assignment of the subject matter, the policy does not pass to the assignee by virtue of the assignment[3]; it must be specifically dealt with in accordance with certain precise rules[4].

1 For the statutory provision by which insurance money received by a vendor is payable by the vendor to the purchaser see para 625 post.
2 *Rayner v Preston* (1881) 18 ChD 1 at 11, CA, per Brett LJ; *Phoenix Assurance Co v Spooner* [1905] 2 KB 753 at 756, CA, per Bigham J.
3 *Mildmay v Folgham* (1797) 3 Ves 471 at 473 per Lord Loughborough LC; *Paine v Meller* (1801) 6 Ves 349 at 351 per Lord Eldon LC; *Poole v Adams* (1864) 33 LJCh 639; and see *Edwards v West* (1878) 7 ChD 858.
4 See *Rayner v Preston* (1881) 18 ChD 1, CA; and para 624 post.

624. Rules for assignment of fire policy. To constitute a valid assignment of a fire policy[1] there are three conditions to be fulfilled. First, the assignment of the policy must accompany the assignment of the subject matter[2]. Secondly, the consent of the insurers to the assignment must be obtained. This is necessary because the assignment is, in effect, the substitution of a new assured, and the contract is purely a personal contract between the insurers and a particular assured[3]. Thirdly, if the policy prescribes a procedure for obtaining consent, that procedure must be followed[4].

1 This must be distinguished from the assignment of the assured's right to receive the proceeds of the policy, which is the assignment not of the contract of insurance but of the debt arising under the contract, and is therefore the assignment of an ordinary chose in action: see *Randall v Lithgow* (1884)

12 QBD 525, DC; *Green v Brand* (1884) Cab & El 410; *English and Scottish Mercantile Investment Co v Brunton* [1892] 2 QB 700, CA (assignments after loss); *London Investment Co v Montefiore* (1864) 9 LT 688; *Bank of Toronto v St Lawrence Fire Insurance Co* [1903] AC 59, PC (assignments before loss); *Tallinna Laevauhisus AS v Estonian State SS Line* (1946) 80 Ll L Rep 99; *Jabbour v Custodian of Israeli Absentee Property* [1954] 1 All ER 145 at 151, [1954] 1 WLR 139 at 143. As to assignment of choses in action see CHOSES IN ACTION vol 6 (Reissue) para 9 et seq.

2 The assignment of the policy may be evidence of an assignment of interest: *Doe d Pearson v Ries and Knapp* (1832) 8 Bing 178 at 185. As to the necessity for the assignment of interest and of the policy being contemporaneous see para 214 ante.

3 *Lynch v Dalzell* (1729) 4 Bro Parl Cas 431, HL; *Sadlers' Co v Badcock* (1743) 2 Atk 554.

4 *Wilkinson v Coverdale* (1793) 1 Esp 74. This is usually by memorandum signed by or on behalf of the insurers.

625. Preservation of vendor's insurance for benefit of purchaser. At common law, if property subject to a contract for sale is damaged or destroyed in the interval between the signing of the contract and completion of the sale, the purchaser is not entitled to claim the benefit of any insurance policy effected by the vendor, unless the benefit of the policy has been duly assigned to the purchaser by the contract and the insurers have consented[1]; nor, in general, is the vendor bound to keep the policy alive or to inform the purchaser of its lapse[2]. However, it may be a term of a contract of sale that the vendor's policy is to be kept in force for the benefit of the purchaser[3].

It is provided by statute that where after the date of any contract for the sale or exchange of property, money becomes payable under any policy of insurance maintained by the vendor in respect of any damage to or destruction of property[4] included in the contract, on completion of the contract the money must be held or receivable by the vendor on behalf of the purchaser and paid by the vendor to the purchaser on completion of the sale or exchange, or as soon afterwards as the money is received by the vendor[5], subject to the fulfilment of three conditions, namely that:

(1) there is no stipulation to the contrary in the contract[6];

(2) the consent of the insurers, if required, is obtained[7]; and

(3) the purchaser pays the proportionate part of the premium from the date of the contract[8].

1 As to assignment of the policy see paras 623–624 ante. As to the vendor's right to enforce the policy see para 621 ante.

2 *Paine v Meller* (1801) 6 Ves 349; *Dowson v Solomon* (1859) 1 Drew & Sm 1 at 12. Where, however, the property is leasehold and the vendor lessee has covenanted with the lessor to insure, the omission of the vendor to keep the property insured may be a defect in his title: *Palmer v Goren* (1856) 4 WR 688; see also *Dowson v Solomon* supra (where the vendor lessee renewed the insurance so as to keep the property covered up to the contractual date for completion, but completion having been delayed, the property became uninsured, and, although the vendor subsequently renewed the insurance and obtained from the lessor a waiver of the forfeiture incurred by the lapse of the insurance, the court refused to decree specific performance against the purchaser); *Newman v Maxwell* (1899) 80 LT 681 (a case of a contract by a lessor for the purchase of the lessee's interest).

3 See *Rayner v Preston* (1881) 18 ChD 1 at 6, CA, per James LJ; *Poole v Adams* (1864) 12 WR 683 per Kindersley V-C; see also *Martineau v Kitching* (1872) LR 7 QB 436.

4 'Property' includes any thing in action and any interest in real or personal property: Law of Property Act 1925 s 205(1)(xx).

5 Ibid s 47(1).

6 Ibid s 47(2)(a).

7 Ibid s 47(2)(b).

8 Ibid s 47(2)(c). These provisions apply, with modifications, to sales or exchanges by order of the court: see s 47(3).

(v) The Amount Recoverable

626. No recovery beyond the sum insured. A fire policy always specifies the sum insured[1], which merely represents the maximum sum for which the insurers accept liability. Unless the policy is a valued policy[2], the assured does not, in the event of a loss, become entitled to be paid the sum insured as a matter of course[3]. What he is entitled to is a full indemnity within the limits of the policy[4]. He cannot recover more than the sum insured, even though the amount of the loss exceeds it, and he cannot recover even the sum insured, unless he proves a loss to that amount[5].

1 See eg 20 Forms & Precedents (5th Edn) 29 at 32, Form 2 Schedule.
2 As to the assessment of partial loss under a valued policy see *Elcock v Thomson* [1949] 2 KB 755, [1949] 2 All ER 381, CA. Valued policies are not often used in fire insurance.
3 *Chapman v Pole, PO* (1870) 22 LT 306 at 307 per Cockburn CJ; *Westminster Fire Office v Glasgow Provident Investment Society* (1888) 13 App Cas 699 at 711, HL, per Lord Selborne; see also *Vance v Forster* (1841) Ir Cir Rep 47 at 50 per Pennefather B. Hence a claim under an ordinary fire policy is a claim for an unliquidated amount and not attachable by garnishee proceedings (*Randall v Lithgow* (1884) 12 QBD 525, DC), but the claim may now be specially indorsed on a writ (RSC Ord 6 r 2).
4 *Castellain v Preston* (1883) 11 QBD 380 at 401, CA, per Bowen LJ; *Westminster Fire Office v Glasgow Provident Investment Society* (1888) 13 App Cas 699, HL; *Reynolds v Phoenix Assurance Co Ltd* [1978] 2 Lloyd's Rep 22, 440 (old maltings); *Pleasurama Ltd v Sun Alliance and London Insurance Ltd* [1979] 1 Lloyd's Rep 389 (bingo hall); *Leppard v Excess Insurance Co Ltd* [1979] 2 All ER 668, [1979] 1 WLR 512, CA (cottage); *Exchange Theatre Ltd v Iron Trades Mutual Insurance Co Ltd* [1983] 1 Lloyd's Rep 674; on appeal [1984] 1 Lloyd's Rep 149, CA (bingo hall).
5 *Vance v Forster* (1841) Ir Cir Rep 47. As to the reduction of the amount which would be otherwise payable by virtue of the operation of average and contribution clauses see paras 520, 523 ante. As to reinstatement see paras 632–633 post. As to the taxation of chargeable gains see the Taxation of Chargeable Gains Act 1992 s 205; CAPITAL GAINS TAXATION vol 5(1) (Reissue) paras 35, 312.

627. Measure of indemnity. The assured is not fully indemnified unless, so far as money can do it, he is restored to the position existing at the time of the fire. The amount recoverable must therefore be measured by the amount of his loss, that is to say, by the value which the fire has taken away from his property[1].

1 *Westminster Fire Office v Glasgow Provident Investment Society* (1888) 13 App Cas 699 at 704, HL, per Lord Selborne. High building costs mean that old buildings are often replaced by new buildings, which are built according to modern methods and to meet modern requirements, and are smaller than the buildings damaged or destroyed. The principle of indemnity may prohibit the insurance of an old property for a sum which would enable it to be replaced by a modern building; see further Ivamy's Fire and Motor Insurance (4th Edn) 170–172.

628. Valuation of total loss. In the case of a total loss, the measure of indemnity must necessarily be the value of the property destroyed[1], up to the limit of the sum insured[2]. For the purpose of ascertaining this value, the rules set out below may be applied[3].

(1) The value to be taken is the value of the physical property destroyed; no allowance is made for loss of prospective profits or other consequential loss[4].

(2) The value is the intrinsic value of the property[5] to the insured[6], its real and actual value[7]; no allowance is to be made for mere sentimental value[8].

(3) The value is the value at the time of the fire[9]. This is generally in accordance with the express undertaking of the insurers in the policy[10]. Therefore, if the value has increased during the period of insurance, and at the time of the fire

exceeds the value at the commencement of the risk, the assured is entitled to recover on the basis of the increased value[11].

(4) The value is the value at the place of the fire[12].

1 *Chapman v Pole, PO* (1870) 22 LT 306 at 307 per Cockburn CJ; see also *Hercules Insurance Co v Hunter* (1836) 14 Sh 1137 at 1142, Ct of Sess, per Lord Moncreiff.
2 As to the limit of the sum insured see para 626 text and note 5 ante.
3 The calculation of the amount recoverable may give rise to problems of considerable difficulty and complexity, on which there are only a few authorities, and even these not particularly helpful. For a full discussion of the problems raised see Ivamy's Fire and Motor Insurance (4th Edn) 167–176.
4 *Re Wright and Pole* (1834) 1 Ad & El 621; see further para 604 ante. It follows that future expenses in relation to a building which would have been incurred but for its destruction by fire, are not to be taken into consideration: *Maurice v Goldsborough, Mort & Co Ltd* [1939] AC 452, [1939] 3 All ER 63, PC.
5 *Hercules Insurance Co v Hunter* (1836) 14 Sh 1137, Ct of Sess.
6 See eg *The Harmonides* [1903] P 1.
7 *Chapman v Pole, PO* (1870) 22 LT 306.
8 *Re Earl of Egmont's Trusts, Lefroy v Earl of Egmont* [1908] 1 Ch 821 at 826 per Warrington J.
9 *Chapman v Pole, PO* (1870) 22 LT 306; *Phoenix Assurance Co v Spooner* [1905] 2 KB 753 at 756, CA, per Bigham J; see also *Re Wilson and Scottish Insurance Corpn* [1920] 2 Ch 28; *Vance v Forster* (1841) Ir Cir Rep 47; *Hercules Insurance Co v Hunter* (1836) 14 Sh 1137, Ct of Sess.
10 See 20 Forms & Precedents (5th Edn) 29, Form 2 cl 2. The rule differs from that applicable in the case of marine insurance: see para 256 ante.
11 *Re Wilson and Scottish Insurance Corpn* [1920] 2 Ch 28.
12 *Rice v Baxendale* (1861) 7 H & N 96 at 101 per Bramwell B.

629. Market value as basis. Prima facie, the value of property destroyed is measured on the basis of market value. This clearly represents an adequate indemnity where, as in the case of goods or stock-in-trade, the property destroyed is a marketable commodity, since payment of the market value will enable the assured to go into the market and, by the purchase of similar property, be restored to his original position. However, the basis of market value cannot be applied in every case; the market value does not necessarily represent the real value of the property and payment of the market value may not adequately indemnify the assured for what he has lost[1]. This is particularly the case where the property was held by the assured, not for the purpose of placing it upon the market, but for his own use or enjoyment, or for the purpose of carrying on his business[2]. The assured cannot continue the use or enjoyment or carry on his business unless the property is reinstated, and the cost of reinstatement may be considerably in excess of the market value. There are also cases in which property, such as a church, has no market value at all and where there can be no restoration to the original position unless the property is reinstated. In such cases the amount recoverable is based on the cost of reinstatement[3].

1 *Castellain v Preston* (1883) 11 QBD 380 at 400–401, CA, per Bowen LJ. See also Ivamy's Fire and Motor Insurance (4th Edn) 168–169.
2 *Grant v Aetna Insurance Co* (1862) 15 Moo PCC 516 at 518–519; *Castellain v Preston* (1883) 11 QBD 380, CA; see also *Vance v Forster* (1841) Ir Cir Rep 47.
3 *Westminster Fire Office v Glasgow Provident Investment Society* (1888) 13 App Cas 699 at 713, HL, per Lord Selborne; see also *Andrews v Patriotic Assurance Co (No 2)* (1886) 18 LR Ir 355 at 366 per Palles CB. Some allowance may have to be made for 'new for old': *Vance v Forster* (1841) Ir Cir Rep 47; *Ewer v National Employers' Mutual General Insurance Association Ltd* [1937] 2 All ER 193. But there is no certain standard such as exists in marine insurance: see para 273 ante.

630. Valuation of partial loss. Where the loss is partial only, it can usually be made good by repairing the damage to the property, and the amount recoverable is based on the cost of repairs[1]. If the policy is a valued policy the amount recoverable is such proportion of the agreed value as is represented by the depreciation in the actual value[2].

1 *Scottish Amicable Heritable Securities Association v Northern Assurance Co* (1883) 11 R 287 at 295, Ct of Sess, per Lord Craighill.
2 *Elcock v Thomson* [1949] 2 KB 755, [1949] 2 All ER 381.

631. Recovery by person with limited interest. The assured cannot usually recover more than the value of his interest in the property insured[1]. To entitle him to the full value of the property he must be interested to the full amount[2]; if he has only a limited or partial interest he can recover the value of his interest and no more[3]. The full value of the property is recoverable where the insurance was intended to enure for the benefit of all persons interested in the property[4].

1 *Castellain v Preston* (1883) 11 QBD 380 at 397, CA, per Bowen LJ.
2 A mortgagor can recover the full value, notwithstanding the existence of the mortgage: *North British and Mercantile Insurance Co v London, Liverpool and Globe Insurance Co* (1877) 5 ChD 569 at 583, CA, per Mellish LJ. As to bailees see further paras 698–705 post.
3 *Castellain v Preston* (1883) 11 QBD 380, CA. Where the different interests are separately insured, the result may be that in the aggregate the amounts paid under the different policies exceed the value of the property: *Westminster Fire Office v Glasgow Provident Investment Society* (1888) 13 App Cas 699, HL.
4 *Waters v Monarch Fire and Life Assurance Co* (1856) 5 E & B 870; see generally para 615 ante.

(vi) Reinstatement

A. REINSTATEMENT GENERALLY

632. Meaning of 'reinstatement'. 'Reinstatement' means the restoration of property affected by a fire to the condition in which it was before the fire; in the case of a total loss by rebuilding the building or replacing the goods by their equivalent, as the case may be, and in the case of a partial loss by repairing the damage[1].

1 *Anderson v Commercial Union Assurance Co* (1885) 55 LJQB 146 at 148, CA, per Lord Esher MR; cf *Sutherland v Sun Fire Office* (1852) 14 Dunl 775 at 778, Ct of Sess. See further *Beaumont v Humberts* [1990] 49 EG 46, where a valuer's reinstatement value, which was based on reconstruction in the same style and general shape, but redesigned in parts according to modern practice, was not negligent although it did not provide for an exact or nearly exact copy of the original house.

633. Rights and obligations as to reinstatement. The duty of reinstating the property is in certain cases imposed upon the insurers by statute[1]. In other cases, the policy usually gives the insurers an option to reinstate but, unless the policy so provides[2], the obligation of the insurers is to pay money only[3] and they cannot, without the consent of the assured, substitute a different method of performing their obligation and insist upon reinstating the property[4]. Similarly, on receiving the insurance money, the assured may do what he likes with it[5] and he cannot be required to expend it on reinstatement unless the obligation to do so is imposed on him by statute[6] or the terms of a contract[7].

1 As to reinstatement under statute see paras 637–639 post.

2 As to the option as to reinstatement see para 634 post.

3 *Rayner v Preston* (1881) 18 ChD 1 at 9, CA, per Brett LJ.

4 *Times Fire Assurance Co v Hawke* (1859) 28 LJEx 317 at 318 per Bramwell B; affd (1859) 28 LJEx 317.

5 *Rayner v Preston* (1881) 18 ChD 1 at 6, CA, per Cotton LJ; *Re Law Guarantee Trust and Accident Society Ltd, Liverpool Mortgage Insurance Co's Case* [1914] 2 Ch 617 at 639, CA, per Kennedy LJ.

6 See eg the Trustee Act 1925 s 20(4), and TRUSTS vol 48 para 883; the Law of Property Act 1925 s 108(3), and MORTGAGE vol 32 para 491; the Ecclesiastical Houses of Residence Act 1842 s 11 (as amended), the Repair of Benefice Buildings Measure 1972 s 12(3) (as amended), and ECCLESIASTICAL LAW vol 14 para 1182.

7 Such contracts are frequently made between lessors and lessees and between mortgagors and mortgages: see LANDLORD AND TENANT; MORTGAGE. If the money is paid to the assured by the insurers on his express promise to expend it in reinstatement, he is bound by his promise: *Queen Insurance Co v Vey* (1867) 16 LT 239.

B. REINSTATEMENT UNDER THE POLICY

634. Option as to reinstatement. By the form of policy in general use, the insurers reserve to themselves the option of reinstating the property instead of making payment in money[1]. This option is reserved for the insurers' benefit, and it is for them to elect whether to reinstate; the assured is not entitled to require them to reinstate[2]. Nor may he prevent them from reinstating if they elect to do so[3].

1 In a fire policy the option is embodied in the undertaking of the insurers: see 20 Forms & Precedents (5th Edn) 29, Form 2 cl 2.

2 *Anderson v Commercial Union Assurance Co* (1885) 55 LJQB 146 at 149, CA, per Bowen LJ.

3 *Bisset v Royal Exchange Assurance Co* (1821) 1 Sh 174, Ct of Sess.

635. Exercise of option to reinstate. An election for or against reinstatement is final once it is made, and cannot afterwards be withdrawn[1]. No formal election is necessary; an election by conduct is sufficient, provided that the conduct is clear and unequivocal. The insurers will be taken to have elected against reinstatement and in favour of a payment in money if the negotiations for a settlement have been conducted by the insurers throughout on the footing that the loss is to be made good by a payment in money[2], or if they have proceeded to arbitration for the purpose of ascertaining the amount to be paid under the policy[3]. On the other hand, they are not bound, in the absence of specific provision, to exercise the option immediately[4]; they are entitled before exercising it to investigate the loss and to ascertain what its amount is likely to be. Therefore a merely provisional assessment of the amount, even if made in conjunction with the assured, does not debar them from electing to reinstate[5].

1 *Sutherland v Sun Fire Office* (1852) 14 Dunl 775, Ct of Sess.

2 *Scottish Amicable Heritable Securities Association v Northern Assurance Co* (1883) 11 R 287, Ct of Sess.

3 *Sutherland v Sun Fire Office* (1852) 14 Dunl 775 at 777, Ct of Sess, per Lord Anderson.

4 A time may, however, be specified within which the option is to be exercised: *Bisset v Royal Exchange Assurance Co* (1821) 1 Sh 174, Ct of Sess.

5 *Sutherland v Sun Fire Office* (1852) 14 Dunl 775 at 777, Ct of Sess, per Lord Anderson.

636. Effect of election to reinstate. If the insurers do not elect to reinstate, their obligation to make good the loss by a payment in money continues[1]; but if they do elect, the obligation ceases and the contract becomes a contract to reinstate[2]. In the case of a building this contract is sufficiently performed if the building is put substantially into the same state as before the fire[3]. But the insurers are in breach of contract, for which they are liable in damages, if the reinstated building differs materially from the original building[4] or if it proves defective through bad workmanship and has to be rebuilt by the assured[5]. They are also in breach if they fail to reinstate and it is no defence that the reinstatement would cost much more to carry out than they had anticipated at the time they elected[6] or even that reinstatement had become impossible[7]. If they commit a breach of contract in either way, the damages which may be awarded against them are not necessarily limited to the amount which would have been payable under the policy if they had elected to make a payment in money[8].

1 *Rayner v Preston* (1881) 18 ChD 1, CA.
2 *Brown v Royal Insurance Co* (1859) 1 E & E 853 at 858 per Lord Campbell CJ.
3 *Times Fire Assurance Co v Hawke* (1858) as reported in 1 F & F 406 at 407 per Channell B; affd (1859) 28 LJEx 317. The policy usually contains a condition regulating the duties of the insurers as to reinstatement: see 20 Forms & Precedents (5th Edn) 29 at 31, Form 2 cl 8.
4 *Alchorne v Favill* (1825) 4 LJOS Ch 47. The insurers are not entitled to any allowance if the reinstated building is better than the original one: *Brown v Royal Insurance Co* (1859) 1 E & E 853 at 860 per Crompton J.
5 *Times Fire Assurance Co v Hawke* (1859) 28 LJEx 317; *Braithwaite v Employers' Liability Assurance Corpn Ltd (James D Day Ltd, third party)* [1964] 1 Lloyd's Rep 94.
6 *Brown v Royal Insurance Co* (1859) 1 E & E 853.
7 *Anderson v Commercial Union Assurance Co* (1885) 55 LJQB 146 at 150, CA, per Bowen LJ; see *Alchorne v Favill* (1825) 4 LJOS Ch 47; *Brown v Royal Insurance Co* (1859) 1 E & E 853. In the case of goods, if it is impossible to replace them in the locality which they occupied before the fire, they may be placed within a reasonable distance: *Anderson v Commercial Union Assurance Co* (1885) 55 LJQB 146, CA.
8 *Times Fire Assurance Co v Hawke* (1859) 28 LJEx 317; *Brown v Royal Insurance Co* (1859) 1 E & E 853.

C. REINSTATEMENT UNDER STATUTE

637. Statutory obligation as to reinstatement. The governors or directors of any insurance company in which any house or building[1] is insured against fire are required by statute[2], in case of loss or damage by fire, to reinstate it upon the request of any person interested in it or entitled to it[3].

1 This provision does not apply to trade fixtures (*Re Barker, ex p Gorely* (1864) 4 De G J & Sm 477) or to chattels (*Re Quicke's Trusts, Poltimore v Quicke* [1908] 1 Ch 887).
2 Ie the Fires Prevention (Metropolis) Act 1774, which, despite both its short and long titles, has always been treated as applicable to the whole of England and Wales (see *Re Quicke's Trusts, Poltimore v Quicke* [1908] 1 Ch 887; *Sinnott v Bowden* [1912] 2 Ch 414, following *Re Barker, ex p Gorely* (1864) 4 De G J & Sm 477), but it does not apply to Scotland (*Westminster Fire Office v Glasgow Provident Investment Society* (1888) 13 App Cas 699 at 716, HL, per Lord Watson) or Ireland (*Andrews v Patriotic Assurance Co (No 2)* (1886) 18 LR Ir 355 at 368 per Palles CB), nor to Lloyd's underwriters (*Portavon Cinema Co Ltd v Price and Century Insurance Co Ltd* [1939] 4 All ER 601).
3 Fires Prevention (Metropolis) Act 1774 s 83, which also imposes the duty of reinstatement upon the insurers where there are grounds of suspicion that the owner or occupier or other person who has insured the property is guilty of fraud or of wilfully setting fire to the property insured; but in this case the insurers would be more likely to repudiate liability.

638. Conditions of statutory obligation. No obligation to reinstate pursuant to the Fires Prevention (Metropolis) Act 1774[1] rests upon the insurers unless the assured is in a position to maintain a claim under the policy[2]; and they cannot be compelled to expend more than the sum insured[3]. The persons interested cannot do the work themselves and then call upon the insurers to pay over the insurance money to them[4]. The work must be done by the insurers[5] unless, within 60 days after the adjustment of the claim, the assured gives sufficient[6] security that he will expend the insurance money in reinstatement or the insurance money has been settled and disposed of among the contending parties[7] to the satisfaction and approbation of the insurers[8].

1 As to the obligation under the Fires Prevention (Metropolis) Act 1774 see para 637 ante.
2 *Matthey v Curling* [1922] 2 AC 180 at 219, CA, per Younger LJ; affd [1922] 2 AC 180 at 223. Hence, no claim for reinstatement can be made by a person interested if the assured is shown to have been guilty of fraud or arson: *Logan v Hall* (1847) 4 CB 598 at 623 per Maule J.
3 Fires Prevention (Metropolis) Act 1774 s 83.
4 *Simpson v Scottish Union Insurance Co* (1863) 1 Hem & M 618 at 628 per Wood V-C.
5 Whether they can be compelled by mandamus to reinstate is doubtful. In *Simpson v Scottish Union Insurance Co* (1863) 1 Hem & M 618, the court held that mandamus would lie; but in *Wimbledon Park Golf Club Ltd v Imperial Insurance Co Ltd* (1902) 18 TLR 815, a contrary view was taken. In *Sun Insurance Office v Galinsky* [1914] 2 KB 545, CA, the court, whilst doubting the accuracy of the report of *Wimbledon Park Golf Club Ltd v Imperial Insurance Co Ltd* supra, declined to decide the point.
6 The persons interested are entitled to object to the sufficiency of the security: *Wimbledon Park Golf Club Ltd v Imperial Insurance Co Ltd* (1902) 18 TLR 815.
7 This includes persons who have no interest in the insurance money, but who nevertheless, as being interested in the property, are insisting on reinstatement: *Sinnott v Bowden* [1912] 2 Ch 414 at 420 per Parker J.
8 Fires Prevention (Metropolis) Act 1774 s 83.

639. Persons entitled to reinstatement. The persons entitled to claim reinstatement under the Fires Prevention (Metropolis) Act 1774[1] include owners[2], mortgagors and mortgagees[3], tenants for life and remaindermen[4], lessors[5], lessees[6] and tenants for years[7]. There must be a distinct request for reinstatement under the statute. If not, the insurers may properly pay over the insurance money to the assured[8], but once the request has been made they are no longer justified in paying the assured, and can, if necessary, be restrained from doing so[9].

1 See paras 637–638 ante.
2 'Owner' probably includes a purchaser pending completion: *Rayner v Preston* (1881) 18 ChD 1 at 15, CA, per James LJ. Cf *Kern Corpn Ltd v Walter Reid Trading Pty Ltd* (1987) 71 ALR 417 (Aust HC) (purchaser of building requested insurers to reinstate after it was damaged by fire prior to completion of sale; insurers were not liable because original owner of building had not suffered any loss, purchaser having subsequently paid full purchase price on completion of sale after the fire).
3 *Sinnott v Bowden* [1912] 2 Ch 414, not following *Westminster Fire Office v Glasgow Provident Investment Society* (1888) 13 App Cas 699 at 714, HL, per Lord Selborne; see also *Re Barker, ex p Gorely* (1864) 4 De G J & Sm 477.
4 *Re Quicke's Trust, Poltimore v Quicke* [1908] 1 Ch 887.
5 *Vernon v Smith* (1821) 5 B & Ald 1; *Penniall v Harborne* (1848) 11 QB 368.
6 *Wimbledon Park Golf Club Ltd v Imperial Insurance Co Ltd* (1902) 18 TLR 815; *Mumford Hotels Ltd v Wheler* [1964] Ch 117, [1963] 3 All ER 250.
7 *Simpson v Scottish Union Insurance Co* (1863) 1 Hem & M 618.
8 *Simpson v Scottish Union Insurance Co* (1863) 1 Hem & M 618 at 627 per Wood V-C; *Mumford Hotels Ltd v Wheler* [1964] Ch 117, [1963] 3 All ER 250.
9 *Wimbledon Park Golf Club Ltd v Imperial Insurance Co Ltd* (1902) 18 TLR 815.

(vii) Salvage

640. Powers of insurers as to salvage. The amount for which the insurers are liable depends upon the extent to which the insured property is destroyed or damaged, so they are directly interested in the steps taken to minimise the loss[1]. Although it is the duty of the assured to minimise the loss[2], it is not a sufficient protection to the insurers to rely upon it, and therefore they are entitled to enter and remain on the premises where the fire is and to take possession of any salvage there[3]. The powers are in practice amplified and extended by the express terms of the policy[4].

1 *Ahmedbhoy Habbibhoy v Bombay Fire and Marine Insurance Co* (1912) 107 LT 668 at 670, PC.
2 *City Tailors Ltd v Evans* (1921) 126 LT 439 at 443, CA, per Scrutton LJ.
3 *Oldfield v Price* (1860) 2 F & F 80.
4 See 20 Forms & Precedents (5th Edn) 29 at 31, Form 2 cl 9.

641. Exercise of insurers' powers. The powers of the insurers must be exercised reasonably and in accordance with the terms in which they are conferred[1]. The insurers must not remain upon the premises for an unreasonable time or they will be liable in damages[2]. If they take possession of the salvage it is their duty to take proper steps to preserve it from further damage and an action lies against them if the salvage continues to deteriorate[3].

There are no rules as to notice of abandonment in fire insurance, but on payment of the loss in full the salvage is transferred to the insurers[4].

1 Where the power to take possession and keep the salvage is exercisable so long as the claim is not adjusted the exercise of the power assumes a valid claim, and by retaining possession after the claim is made the insurers are estopped from objecting that the claim is out of time and therefore invalid: *Yorkshire Insurance Co Ltd v Craine* [1922] 2 AC 541, PC.
2 *Oldfield v Price* (1860) 2 F & F 80; *Norton v Royal Fire and Life Assurance Co* (1885) 1 TLR 460 at 461; on appeal (1885) Times, 12 August, CA. Nor, it seems, may the insurers remain on the premises to the exclusion of the assured: *Oldfield v Price* supra.
3 *Ahmedbhoy Habbibhoy v Bombay Fire and Marine Insurance Co* (1912) 107 LT 668, PC.
4 *Rankin v Potter* (1873) LR 6 HL 83 at 118 per Blackburn J; see also *London Assurance Co v Sainsbury* (1783) 3 Doug KB 245 at 253; *Dane v Mortgage Insurance Corpn* [1894] 1 QB 54 at 61, CA: *Holmes v Payne* [1930] 2 KB 301. In any event, the policy may expressly exclude any entitlement of the assured to abandon the property: see eg 20 Forms & Precedents (5th Edn) 29 at 31, Form 2 cl 9.

642. Establishment of the London Salvage Corps. The London Salvage Corps was established pursuant to statutory authority by insurance companies insuring property within Greater London[1], and is charged with the duty of attending fires and saving insured property[2]. It is the duty of the London Fire Brigade[3], with the sanction of the London Fire and Civil Defence Authority[4] and subject to any regulations that may be made by that authority, to afford the necessary assistance to the London Salvage Corps in the performance of its duties and, upon the application of any officer of the London Salvage Corps, to hand over to its custody property saved from fire[5].

1 'Greater London' means the area comprising the areas of the London boroughs, the City and the Temples: London Government Act 1963 s 2 (1). References to Greater London were substituted for references to the Metropolis by virtue of s 48(3) (as amended); see generally LONDON GOVERNMENT.
2 See the Metropolitan Fire Brigade Act 1865 s 29.
3 The force of firemen established under the Metropolitan Fire Brigade Act 1865 was named the London Fire Brigade by the London County Council (General Powers) Act 1904 s 46 (repealed).
4 As to the London Fire and Civil Defence Authority see the Local Government Act 1985 s 37, Sch 11 para 2(4), by virtue of which references to the authority were substituted for references to the Metropolitan Board of Works or the Greater London Council.
5 Metropolitan Fire Brigade Act 1865 s 29. No charge may be made by the authority for the services thus rendered by the London Fire Brigade: s 29.

643. Contribution by insurers to London Fire Brigade. Every insurance company which insures against fire any property in Greater London[1] is under statutory obligation to pay to the London Fire and Civil Defence Authority[2] a contribution towards the expenses of running the London Fire Brigade[3]. The payments must be made quarterly in advance on 1 January, 1 April, 1 July and 1 October in each year, at the rate of £35 for each £1m on the gross amounts insured by it (except by way of reinsurance) in respect of property in Greater London for a year[4]. These contributions are specialty debts recoverable as such[5]. In order to enable the contributions to be calculated, each such insurance company must make to the authority an annual return of the gross amounts of its fire insurances in Greater London, vouched by a declaration made by the secretary or other officer performing the duties of secretary of the company[6]. For default in making a return there is a penalty not exceeding £5 for every day during which the company is in default[7]. In addition, power is given to any officer appointed by the authority to inspect the company's books and papers and to make extracts from them, and the secretary or officer having custody of the books and papers who does not allow this to be done is liable on summary conviction to a penalty not exceeding level 1 on the standard scale for each offence[8].

The London Fire Brigade is under a duty to send to the contributing insurance companies, in the morning of every day except Sundays, information of all fires in Greater London[9].

1 As to the meaning of 'Greater London' see para 642 note 1 ante.
2 As to the London Fire and Civil Defence Authority see para 642 note 4 ante.
3 Metropolitan Fire Brigade Act 1865 s 13 (amended by the Statute Law Revision Act 1875). As to the title of the London Fire Brigade see para 642 note 3 ante.
4 Metropolitan Fire Brigade Act 1865 s 13 (as amended: see note 3 supra). The same rate applies to any fraction of £1m and to any fractional part of a year: s 13 (as so amended).
5 Ibid s 14.
6 Ibid s 15 (as amended: see note 3 supra). The secretary or other officer must declare that he has examined the return with the books of the company, and that to the best of his knowledge, information and belief it contains a true and faithful account of the gross amount of the sums insured by the company to which he belongs in respect of property in Greater London: s 15 (as so amended). The return must be made on 1 June or on such other days as the authority may appoint, and the return made in June of one year comes into effect on 1 January of the succeeding year and is the basis of contributions for that year: s 15 (as so amended).
7 Ibid s 16. Penalties are recoverable summarily: s 24. As to the disposal of penalties see the Justices of the Peace Act 1979 s 61 (as amended); the Magistrates' Courts Act 1980 s 139, Sch 8 para 8; the Criminal Justice Act 1982 s 46 (as amended); and MAGISTRATES.
8 Metropolitan Fire Brigade Act 1865 s 17 (amended by virtue of the Criminal Law Act 1977 s 31; and consequently by the Criminal Justice Act 1982 ss 38, 46). As to the standard scale see para 212 note 5 ante.
9 Metropolitan Fire Brigade Act 1865 s 31; see also FIRE SERVICES vol 18 para 409.

(2) INSURANCE AGAINST BURGLARY, THEFT AND FRAUD

(i) Burglary Insurance: Perils Insured Against

644. Extent of protection. Movable property of all kinds is liable to attract those minded to break in and steal, and this is a risk which is capable of being covered by burglary insurance[1]. In ordinary practice the protection given by a burglary insurance policy need not refer to loss by burglary in the strict sense[2], but may refer to loss by analogous crimes such as theft[3] and robbery[4].

1 Burglary insurance falls within 'damage to property insurance', and therefore constitutes 'general business' within the meaning of the Insurance Companies Act 1982 s 1, Sch 2 Pt I Class 9; see para 18 ante.
2 For the meaning of 'burglary' see CRIMINAL LAW vol 11(1) (Reissue) para 552. As to the application of the technical meanings of criminal law terms to a policy of insurance see para 645 post.
3 For the meaning of 'theft' see CRIMINAL LAW vol 11(1) (Reissue) para 541. As to the meaning of 'theft' in marine insurance see para 159 ante.
4 For forms of burglary policy see eg 20 Forms & Precedents (5th Edn) 114, 456 et seq, 469 et seq, Forms 52, 275–276. Cover against burglary, particularly of domestic premises, is usually included in a general insurance of such premises.

645. Use of criminal law terms. Where the perils insured against are described in technical terms of the criminal law there is a presumption that they are intended to bear their technical meaning[1]. The presumption may be rebutted by the language of the policy; thus a policy insuring against loss by burglary and containing a definition of the word 'burglary' bears on the face of it an indication that the word is not intended to bear its ordinary technical meaning as used in the criminal law[2]. The act that causes the loss must fall within the definition in the policy, which may be wider or narrower than the technical meaning; accordingly it may be necessary, or alternatively it may not be sufficient, to show that a burglary has been committed according to the criminal law[3].

1 *Re Calf and Sun Insurance Office* [1920] 2 KB 366 at 380, CA, per Atkin LJ; cf *Lake v Simmons* [1927] AC 487 at 509, HL, per Lord Sumner; and see further para 396 ante.
2 *Re George and Goldsmiths and General Burglary Insurance Association Ltd* [1899] 1 QB 595 at 601, CA, per Lord Russell of Killowen CJ.
3 *Re George and Goldsmiths and General Burglary Insurance Association Ltd* [1899] 1 QB 595, CA.

646. Forcible and violent entry. The terms of a burglary insurance may exclude liability in certain circumstances unless there is forcible and violent entry into the premises[1]. If so, the entry must be obtained by the use of both force and violence or the definition is not satisfied and the policy does not apply[2]. An entry obtained by turning the handle of an outside door or by using a skeleton key, though sufficient to constitute a criminal offence[3], is not within the policy since the element of violence is absent[4]. However, an entry obtained by picking the lock or forcing back the catch by means of an instrument involves the use of violence and is therefore covered[5]. The policy may be so framed as to apply only to violent entry from the outside[6]; or the violent entry into a room within the insured premises may be sufficient[7]. In any case, the violence must be connected with the act of entry; if the entry is obtained without violence, the subsequent use of violence to effect the theft, as for instance where a show-case is broken open, does not bring the loss within the policy[8].

1 See 20 Forms & Precedents (5th Edn) 456 et seq, 469 et seq, Forms 275–276. Alternatively, the policy may refer to breaking into or out of the premises: 20 Forms & Precedents (5th Edn) 114, Form 52. See also para 644 ante.
2 *Re Calf and Sun Insurance Office* [1920] 2 KB 366, CA, explaining *Re George and Goldsmiths and General Burglary Insurance Association Ltd* [1899] 1 QB 595, CA.
3 See CRIMINAL LAW vol 11(1) (Reissue) para 552.

4   *Re George and Goldsmiths and General Burglary Insurance Association Ltd* [1899] 1 QB 595, CA; cf *Saqui and Lawrence v Stearns* [1911] 1 KB 426, CA; *Dino Services Ltd v Prudential Assurance Co Ltd* [1989] 1 All ER 422, [1989] 1 Lloyd's Rep 379, CA.
5   *Re Calf and Sun Insurance Office* [1920] 2 KB 366 at 382, CA, per Atkin LJ.
6   *Re George and Goldsmiths and General Burglary Insurance Association Ltd* [1899] 1 QB 595, CA.
7   *Re Calf and Sun Insurance Office* [1920] 2 KB 366, CA.
8   *Re George and Goldsmiths and General Burglary Insurance Association Ltd* [1899] 1 QB 595, CA.

647. Exceptions in a burglary policy. The exceptions in a burglary policy are more or less standardised[1]. There may be an exception excluding losses due to hostilities[2] and similar perils[3], and there is commonly an exception excluding losses which are capable of being covered, and which are in practice covered, by some other kind of insurance, such as fire or plate-glass policies in the usual form[4]. Therefore, if a thief breaks a plate-glass window, which is separately insured, for the purpose of obtaining entry to the premises, the breakage falls within the scope of the plate-glass policy[5]. There is usually an important exception excluding liability where the crime causing the loss is committed by, or with the connivance or assistance of, a person belonging to a specified class, such as inmates of the insured premises, members of the assured's household or business staff, tenants, lodgers and persons lawfully on the insured premises[6]. To bring such an exception into operation, it is unnecessary to prove that an excepted person was the person who actually committed the crime[7], but the onus of establishing the exception is on the insurers[8].

1   See para 644 note 4 ante.
2   Such an exception did not apply to an isolated burglary taking place during an air raid: *Winicofsky v Army and Navy General Assurance Association* (1919) 35 TLR 283.
3   See *Motor Union Insurance Co v Boggan* (1923) 130 LT 588, HL; *London and Lancashire Fire Insurance Co Ltd v Bolands Ltd* [1924] AC 836, HL; see also paras 596–599 ante.
4   In the case of fire insurance, a loss by theft in the course of fire may be a loss proximately caused by fire: see para 603 ante.
5   Cf *Marsden v City and County Assurance Co* (1865) LR 1 CP 232 (plate-glass window insured against damage except by fire or breakage during removal; damaged by mob attracted by fire in remote part of premises, and broken for purposes of plunder; mob's act was proximate cause of damage).
6   *Saqui and Lawrence v Stearns* [1911] 1 KB 426, CA; *Re Calf and Sun Insurance Office* [1920] 2 KB 366, CA; *Lake v Simmons* [1927] AC 487, HL; *Greaves v Drysdale* [1936] 2 All ER 470, CA.
7   *Saqui and Lawrence v Stearns* [1911] 1 KB 426, CA; cf *Hurst v Evans* [1917] 1 KB 352, disapproved as to onus of proof in *Munro, Brice & Co v War Risks Association* [1918] 2 KB 78.
8   *Munro, Brice & Co v War Risks Association* [1918] 2 KB 78; *Bond Air Services Ltd v Hill* [1955] 2 QB 417, [1955] 2 All ER 476. For the general principle that the onus is on the insurers to show that any exception clause of the policy applies so as to relieve them from liability see para 421 ante.

(ii) Special Features of Burglary Insurance

648. The moral hazard. The general principles relating to fire insurance[1] apply to burglary insurance[2] so far as they are appropriate. In burglary insurance the moral hazard is particularly important[3]. Consequently the nationality of origin of the assured[4], as well as his previous experience of losses[5], his previous convictions[6] and the fact that another insurer has refused to issue[7] or renew[8] a policy, have been held to be material facts which ought to be disclosed.

1   See para 591 et seq ante.
2   As to what is included in 'burglary insurance' see paras 644–645 ante.

3 As to the moral hazard see para 353 ante.
4 See *Horne v Poland* [1922] 2 KB 364.
5 See *Krantz v Allan and Faber* (1921) 9 Ll L Rep 410; *Becker v Marshall* (1922) 12 Ll L Rep 413, CA; *Rozanes v Bowen* (1928) 32 Ll L Rep 98, CA.
6 See *Schoolman v Hall* [1951] 1 Lloyd's Rep 139, CA; *Regina Fur Co Ltd v Bossom* [1957] 2 Lloyd's Rep 466; affd on another point [1958] 2 Lloyd's Rep 425, CA; *Roselodge Ltd (formerly Rose Diamond Products Ltd) v Castle* [1966] 2 Lloyd's Rep 105, 113, CA.
7 See *Glicksman v Lancashire and General Assurance Co Ltd* [1927] AC 139, HL.
8 See *Ascott v Cornhill Insurance Co Ltd* (1937) 58 Ll L Rep 41.

649. Precautions to be taken. A burglary insurance policy[1] may contain a condition imposing on the assured the duty of taking proper precautions for the safety of the insured property, such as securing all doors, windows, and other means of entrance. A failure to lock the door of an inside showcase is not a breach of such a condition[2]. This duty may be amplified by a condition which provides that the premises are always to be occupied[3] or that they are not to be left unoccupied at night[4]. Such a condition does not require the continuous presence of someone on the premises; premises do not become unoccupied for the purposes of the condition by reason of the temporary absence of all the inmates[5]. A condition may also require proper books of account to be kept[6] or a burglar alarm to be fitted[7].

1 See para 644 note 4 ante.
2 *Re George and Goldsmiths and General Burglary Insurance Association Ltd* [1899] 1 QB 595 at 609, CA, per A L Smith LJ.
3 *Simmonds v Cockell* [1920] 1 KB 843.
4 *Winicofsky v Army and Navy General Assurance Association* (1919) 88 LJKB 1111.
5 *Winicofsky v Army and Navy General Assurance Association* (1919) 88 LJKB 1111; *Simmonds v Cockell* [1920] 1 KB 843.
6 *Jacobson v Yorkshire Insurance Co Ltd* (1933) 45 Ll L Rep 281; *Shoot v Hill* (1936) 55 Ll L Rep 29; *Bennett v Yorkshire Insurance Co Ltd* [1962] 2 Lloyd's Rep 270.
7 *Shoot v Hill* (1936) 55 Ll L Rep 29; *Roberts v Eagle Star Insurance Co Ltd* [1960] 1 Lloyd's Rep 615; *Allan Peters (Jewellers) Ltd v Brocks Alarms Ltd* [1968] 1 Lloyd's Rep 387; *Victor Melik & Co Ltd v Norwich Union Fire Insurance Society Ltd* [1980] 1 Lloyd's Rep 523.

650. Limitation of risk by reference to locality. Burglary[1] is a crime associated with buildings, and burglary insurance contemplates that the property which is stolen shall have been stolen from the premises described in the policy[2]. If the premises described comprise part of a building only, the property must be stolen from that part; a theft from any other part is not covered[3]. Similarly, if theft is covered while a van is in a garage, the policy does not apply if the van is left in an unlocked yard[4].

1 For the meaning of 'burglary' see CRIMINAL LAW vol 11(1) (Reissue) para 552; and as to what is included in 'burglary insurance' see paras 644–645 ante.
2 As to the locality as part of the description see generally para 429 ante.
3 *Re Calf and Sun Insurance Office* [1920] 2 KB 366, CA.
4 *Barnett and Block v National Parcels Insurance Co Ltd* [1942] 1 All ER 221; affd [1942] 2 All ER 55n, CA; *Leo Rapp Ltd v McClure* [1955] 1 Lloyd's Rep 292 (goods insured 'whilst in warehouse'; theft of goods from lorry parked in locked compound enclosed by brick wall held not to be covered).

(iii) Bankers' and Stockbrokers' Policies

651. Necessity for special protection. Certain forms of property, such as money and securities for money, are in practice expressly excepted from the protection of an ordinary burglary policy[1]. However, bankers and stockbrokers who habitually deal with such forms of property require protection against their peculiar risks. To give them adequate protection the policy must not only cover the stealing of money and securities for money, it must extend beyond the risk of ordinary theft and cover losses occasioned by fraud. Consequently, there are special forms of insurance for protecting bankers and stockbrokers against the loss of money and securities[2].

1 See eg 20 Forms & Precedents (5th Edn) 114 at 115, Form 52 cl 4.3.
2 *Equitable Trust Co of New York v Whittaker* (1923) 17 Ll L Rep 153; *Deutsche Genossenschaftsbank v Burnhope* [1993] 2 Lloyd's Rep 518; and see *Philadelphia National Bank v Price* [1938] 2 All ER 199, CA, for a policy covering advances made by a bank on invalid documents. Cf *Equitable Trust Co of New York v Henderson* (1930) 47 TLR 90; *Lazard Bros & Co Ltd v Brooks* (1932) 38 Com Cas 46, HL. As to the information to be provided by stockbrokers as to their insurance arrangements see the International Stock Exchange Rules (as from time to time amended) rr 130, 140, 150; and see STOCK EXCHANGE.

652. Obtaining property by deception. In the case of obtaining property by deception[1], the extent of the protection in bankers' and stockbrokers' policies depends on the words used in the policy[2]. If the policy covers obtaining by fraudulent means there must be an actual fraudulent obtaining; thus a loss which results not from a fraudulent obtaining but from a fraudulent contract is not within the policy[3]. There is a fraudulent obtaining, for example, where securities are obtained from a stockbroker by a customer in exchange for a cheque which, to the customer's knowledge, will be dishonoured on presentation[4]. On the other hand, where a bank discounts for a customer bills which, to the customer's knowledge, are forgeries and places the amount of them, less discount, to the credit of his account, the subsequent withdrawal of the money from his account by means of cheques drawn by the customers upon the bank is not an obtaining by fraudulent means; the loss results from the contract between the bank and its customer[5]. However, the policy may be so worded as to cover this kind of loss[6].

1 As to obtaining property by deception see CRIMINAL LAW vol 11(1) (Reissue) para 567.
2 See *Pennsylvania Co for Insurances on Lives and Granting Annuities v Mumford* [1920] 2 KB 537, CA, where a policy covering securities 'supposed or believed to be' upon the premises of the bank at a particular date did not cover securities which were falsely represented to have been handed back to customers before that date, since the bank supposed or believed that they had been returned.
3 *Century Bank of the City of New York v Mountain* (1914) 112 LT 484, CA.
4 *Pawle & Co v Bussell* (1916) 85 LJKB 1191; *Lim Trading Co v Haydon* [1968] 1 Lloyd's Rep 159 (Sing HC).
5 *Century Bank of the City of New York v Mountain* (1914) 112 LT 484, CA.
6 *Wasserman v Blackburn* (1926) 43 TLR 95; *Lazard Bros & Co v Brooks* (1932) 38 Com Cas 46, HL.

653. Property in transit. Ordinary burglary insurance covers property stolen from particular premises only[1]. However, under bankers' and stockbrokers' policies, property may be covered in transit, in which case the loss must be sustained in the course of the transit described in the policy[2]. Transit 'between any houses or places' does not cover transit from one room to another in the same building[3].

1 As to the premises described see para 650 ante.
2 *Richardson v Roylance* (1933) 50 TLR 99.
3 *Pennsylvania Co for Insurances on Lives and Granting Annuities v Mumford* [1920] 2 KB 537, CA. As to insurance by carriers see para 705 post.

(3) MISCELLANEOUS PROPERTY INSURANCES

(i) Special Perils

654. Perils normally excepted. Any contingency which is likely to result in loss to the assured if it affects his property may be insured against if insurers can be found who are willing to bear the risk and the proposer is willing to pay what may be a heavy rate of premium[1]. In particular, insurances may be effected to cover perils which are usually excepted under a policy in the ordinary form[2]. An insurance may be effected to cover loss caused by war[3], military or usurped power[4], riot, civil commotion[5] or strikes[6]; or by the subsidence or collapse of a building[7], or by water damage[8], or by the explosion of boilers[9]. Again, flood[10], storm and tempest[11] and, in some parts of the world, earthquakes, are commonly covered. Except where special provision is made, the policy covers the actual loss of the property only[12] and not a consequential loss[13] arising from the assured's inability to deal with his property because of the intervention of the peril[14].

1 As to assessment of the premium see para 440 ante.
2 As to exceptions in fire policies see paras 595–602 ante.
3 War includes civil war: *Pesquerias y Secaderos de Bacalao de Espana SA v Beer* [1949] 1 All ER 845, HL.
4 *Curtis & Sons v Mathews* [1919] 1 KB 425, CA.
5 *London and Manchester Plate Glass Co Ltd v Heath* [1913] 3 KB 411, CA; see also *Curtis & Co v Head* (1902) 18 TLR 771, CA.
6 *Lewis Emanuel & Son Ltd v Hepburn* [1960] 1 Lloyd's Rep 304.
7 *David Allen & Sons Billposting Ltd v Drysdale* [1939] 4 All ER 113 (intentional demolition is not a collapse).
8 *Kündig v Hepburn* [1959] 1 Lloyd's Rep 183.
9 *Re Willesden Borough Council and Municipal Mutual Insurance Ltd* [1944] 2 All ER 600; affd [1945] 1 All ER 444, CA (insurance covering damage by explosion of boilers used for domestic purposes only; whether boilers used for domestic purposes depends, not on the use of the premises where the boiler is, but on the use of the boiler).
10 *Young v Sun Alliance and London Insurance Ltd* [1976] 3 All ER 561, [1976] 1 WLR 104, CA: three inches of water caused by natural seepage not a flood.
11 As to the meaning of 'storm and tempest' see *Oddy v Phoenix Assurance Co Ltd* [1966] 1 Lloyd's Rep 134. 'Storm' is something more prolonged and widespread than a gust of wind: *S and M Hotels Ltd v Legal and General Assurance Society Ltd* [1972] 1 Lloyd's Rep 157. A 'storm' includes a heavy snowfall: *Glasgow Training Group (Motor Trade) Ltd v Lombard Continental plc* 1989 SLT 375, Ct of Sess. The question whether 'storm' meant a heavy fall of rain unaccompanied by wind was left open in *Anderson v Norwich Union Fire Insurance Society Ltd* [1977] 1 Lloyd's Rep 253.
12 *Molinos De Arroz v Mumford* (1900) 16 TLR 469.
13 As to consequential loss generally see paras 785–789 post.
14 *Molinos De Arroz v Mumford* (1900) 16 TLR 469; *Mitsui v Mumford* [1915] 2 KB 27; *Campbell and Phillips Ltd v Denman* (1915) 21 Com Cas 357. Cf 'all risks insurance' in paras 658–659 post.

655. Property subject to special perils. Particular forms of property may be insured against their own special perils. Thus special forms of policy have been devised to cover plate glass in the event of breakage, whether in transit or in situ[1], or for the holder of a licence for the sale of intoxicating liquor to insure against the loss occasioned by the forfeiture of the licence or by the refusal of the licensing justices to renew it[2].

The insurance of motor vehicles is dealt with elsewhere in this title[3].

1 *Marsden v City and County Assurance Co* (1865) LR 1 CP 232; *London and Manchester Plate Glass Ltd v Heath* [1913] 3 KB 41, CA.

2 As to the construction of covenants by lessees of public houses to insure see *Williams v Lassell and Sharman Ltd* (1906) 22 TLR 443; *Wootton v Lichfield Brewery Co* [1916] 1 Ch 44, CA.
3 See para 706 et seq post.

(ii) Livestock Insurance

656. Scope of the insurance. Horses, cattle, sheep and pigs[1] may be insured by a policy of livestock insurance, which is usually on the life of the animal insured[2]. The policy may cover death by accident[3] as well as by illness or disease; death in the ordinary cause of nature from old age may be excluded[4]. Except in special cases, mere injury which does not lead to death is not covered[5]. The death is usually required to be certified by a veterinary surgeon, but this requirement can, of course, be waived[6].

Livestock policies usually contain a special condition of average, requiring the assured to bear a portion, usually a quarter, of the loss himself[7].

Livestock may also be insured against theft or unlawful removal[8].

1 Horses may also be insured under a combined policy as part of the assured's business plant: see *Gorman v Hand-in-Hand Insurance Co* (1877) IR 11 CL 224.
2 *A-G v Cleobury* (1849) 4 Exch 65.
3 *Burridge & Son v F H Haines & Sons Ltd* (1918) 87 LJKB 641.
4 See eg 20 Forms & Precedents (5th Edn) 191, Form 120.
5 See *Jacob v Gaviller* (1902) 87 LT 26.
6 *Burridge & Son v F H Haines & Sons Ltd* (1918) 118 LT 681; *Shiells v Scottish Assurance Corpn* (1889) 16 R 1014 at 1020–1022, Ct of Sess. See 20 Forms & Precedents (5th Edn) 191 at 193, Form 120 Condition 6.
7 See 20 Forms & Precedents (5th Edn) 199, Form 132. As to average see generally para 523 ante.
8 20 Forms & Precedents (5th Edn) 191, Form 120.

657. Position where animal is slaughtered. Where an animal is slaughtered the liability of the insurers depends on the terms of the policy and the circumstances in which the animal is slaughtered. The slaughter of an animal for food in the ordinary course of making use of it will clearly fall outside the policy; but where it is slaughtered for humane reasons after suffering injury in an accident, the policy applies, since the injuries are in effect fatal[1]. The policy may exclude liability even where the animal is compulsorily slaughtered under statutory powers[2].

1 *Shiells v Scottish Assurance Corpn* (1889) 16 R 1014 at 1019, Ct of Sess: the animal must, of course, be reasonably slaughtered for the purpose of saving it unnecessary suffering. The onus of proving that slaughter was necessary is on the assured: *Shiells v Scottish Assurance Corpn* supra.
   Policies usually provide that the insurers will not invoke an exclusion against slaughter where they have agreed to the slaughter or where, in prescribed circumstances, a veterinary surgeon certifies that the suffering is incurable and that immediate destruction is imperative for humane reasons: see eg 20 Forms & Precedents (5th Edn) 191–192, Form 120 Exclusion 1.
2 20 Forms & Precedents (5th Edn) 191–192, Form 120 Exclusion 1. As to the compulsory slaughter of animals see ANIMALS vol 2 (Reissue) paras 507–510.

(iii) All Risks Insurance

658. Loss however caused. Property may be insured against all risks[1]. In this case the nature of the casualty causing the loss is immaterial; the policy covers the loss however caused. The onus of proving the loss lies upon the assured[2].

1 Such insurances are frequently effected in respect of jewellery, in which case there may be an exception against theft or dishonesty by an employee, customer, broker or broker's customer: see 20 Forms & Precedents (5th Edn) 109, Form 50; *Lake v Simmons* [1927] AC 487, HL.

2 *Sofi v Prudential Assurance Co Ltd* [1993] 2 Lloyd's Rep 559, CA; *Hurst v Evans* [1917] 1 KB 352, where it was further held that the assured had to prove that the loss did not fall within an exception; but see contra *Munro, Brice & Co v War Risks Association* [1918] 2 KB 78; *Bond Air Services Ltd v Hill* [1955] 2 QB 417, [1955] 2 All ER 476.

659. What constitutes a loss. To constitute a loss under an all risks policy there must be something accidental and fortuitous which can be described as a casualty[1], but the property need not have been actually destroyed; there may be a loss though the property still exists if the assured has been deprived of it as the result of some casualty[2]. The question whether the deprivation amounts to a loss depends upon the character and extent of the deprivation. The deprivation must be more than merely temporary, but it need not be complete, amounting to a certainty that the property can never be recovered[3]. The test is uncertainty of recovery[4], and the steps to be taken to effect recovery must be such as are reasonable in all the circumstances[5]. There is a loss within the policy if it appears that the assured has at most a mere chance of recovering his property, and will in all probability never recover it[6]. However, if on the balance of probabilities there is no reason to believe that the property will not ultimately be recovered, though the time of recovery may be uncertain, then the deprivation does not constitute a loss[7]. If a pearl necklace disappears and, notwithstanding that diligent search has been made, is not found within a reasonable time, the conclusion may be that there is no reasonable prospect that it will be recovered and it is regarded as lost[8]. If pearls are consigned to a customer abroad on sale or return, the outbreak of war may render the return of them impossible until the conclusion of peace; but, in the absence of any evidence to the contrary, it cannot be assumed that they will not be returned when circumstances permit and, consequently, there is no loss[9]. Again, if a person intending to dispose of an article hands it over in return for a cheque for the agreed purchase price and the cheque turns out to be worthless, he loses his money, not the article[10]; however, if the article is entrusted to an agent for sale, and the agent converts it to his own use and fails to account for the proceeds, the article can properly be said to have been lost[11].

1 *London and Provincial Leather Processes Ltd v Hudson* [1939] 2 KB 724, [1939] 3 All ER 857.
2 *Holmes v Payne* [1930] 2 KB 301, where a pearl necklace, insured against loss at agreed value, disappeared; there was agreement between the insurers and the assured that the insurers should provide articles of equal value; articles up to part of such value were provided, but the necklace subsequently fell out of assured's cloak; it was held that the replacement agreement did not contain an implied term that if the necklace was found the agreement would be void; the assured was entitled to retain articles which she had received and to receive other articles up to the agreed value, the insurers taking the necklace as salvage; it seems that the necklace had been 'lost' within the meaning of policy.
3 *Moore v Evans* as reported in [1917] 1 KB 458 at 471, CA, per Bankes LJ; affd [1918] AC 185, HL.
4 *Holmes v Payne* [1930] 2 KB 301 at 310 per Roche J.
5 *Webster v General Accident, Fire and Life Assurance Corpn Ltd* [1953] 1 QB 520, [1953] 1 All ER 663.
6 *Moore v Evans* [1917] 1 KB 458, CA; affd [1918] AC 185, HL; *Webster v General Accident, Fire and Life Assurance Corpn Ltd* [1953] 1 QB 520, [1953] 1 All ER 663.
7 *Moore v Evans* [1917] 1 KB 458 at 473, CA, per Bankes LJ; affd [1918] AC 185, HL.
8 *Holmes v Payne* [1930] 2 KB 301 at 310: see note 2 supra.
9 *Moore v Evans* [1917] 1 KB 458 at 473, CA, per Bankes LJ; affd [1918] AC 185, HL; cf *White, Child and Beney Ltd v Eagle Star and British Dominions Insurance Co* (1922) 127 LT 571, CA.
10 *Eisinger v General Accident Fire and Life Assurance Corpn Ltd* [1955] 2 All ER 897, [1955] 1 WLR 869 (motor policy).
11 *Webster v General Accident Fire and Life Assurance Corpn Ltd* [1953] 1 QB 520, [1953] 1 All ER 663; cf *London and Provincial Leather Processes Ltd v Hudson* [1939] 2 KB 724, [1939] 3 All ER 857.

8. LIABILITY INSURANCE

(1) IN GENERAL

(i) Nature of the Insurance

660. Nature of liability insurance. In liability insurance[1] the event insured against affects the assured financially by reason of his becoming liable to pay to a third party either damages for breach of contract or tort, or some other form of compensation, restitution or reimbursement. Frequently this liability to third parties arises in connection with property, and the event which gives rise to the liability may at the same time cause loss of the property. Insurance against liability is, therefore, frequently combined with insurance against loss of the property, as in a householder's comprehensive policy, or a comprehensive policy of motor or aviation insurance[2]. However, unless special provision is made, an insurance on property does not cover a liability incidentally arising from or connected with the property, thus, for example, if a ship is insured against loss or damage, this insurance does not cover the owners' liability to pay wages, or to provide subsistence to the crew, while the ship is being repaired[3]; nor is the usual form of fire policy on a house expressed to cover the householder's legal liability if the fire spreads to adjoining property[4]. It is, of course, different where a person by contract or otherwise is responsible for the safe custody of property; his potential liability to the true owner in such a case may well be the foundation, in whole or in part, of his having an insurable interest up to the full value of the property[5].

1 For the meaning of liability insurance see para 18 ante.
2 Motor and aviation insurance are specialised branches of the law of insurance and are dealt with separately in paras 347–348 ante (aviation), 706 et seq post (motor).
3 *De Vaux v Salvador* (1836) 4 Ad & El 420.
4 For a discussion of this form of legal liability see *Balfour v Barty-King* [1957] 1 QB 496, [1957] 1 All ER 156, CA.
5 *North British and Mercantile Insurance Co v London, Liverpool and Globe Insurance Co* (1877) 5 ChD 569 at 583–584, CA, per Mellish LJ; see para 699 post. As to a carrier's insurance of goods in transit see para 705 post. Apart from such cases of potential liability to the true owner of property, third party liability is normally a peril against which specific insurance is required.

661. Indemnity as basis of contract. A contract of liability insurance is a contract of indemnity[1]. This is normally indicated by the wording of the policy which is designed to make it clear that the insurers undertake to indemnify the assured against legal liabilities incurred by him within a specified range. If a policy contains a provision by virtue of which the insurers may be bound to pay a claim even though it is legally a bad claim, the policy is, it seems, a policy of contingency insurance, rather than liability insurance[2].

1 *British Cash and Parcel Conveyors Ltd v Lamson Store Service Co Ltd* [1908] 1 KB 1006 at 1014, CA, per Fletcher Moulton LJ.
2 As to contingency or pecuniary loss insurance see para 765 et seq post. Where the loss is caused by the action of two concurrent and independent causes, one of which is the peril insured against and the other an excepted cause, and the loss is not within the policy as it may be accurately described as caused by the excepted cause, it is immaterial that it may be described in another way which would

not bring it within the exception: *Wayne Tank and Pump Co Ltd v Employers' Liability Assurance Corpn Ltd* [1974] QB 57, [1973] 3 All ER 825, CA.

662. Forms of liability insurance. Liability insurance may be in the form of a personal liability policy covering all types of liability apart from certain specified exceptions[1], or conversely it may be limited to liabilities of a particular kind. For example, policies of motor insurance and aircraft insurance are specially designed to cover liabilities arising out of the use of motor vehicles and aircraft respectively[2]. Similarly, more or less standard forms of policy have been designed to cover the risk of an employer being held liable at common law, or under some statutory provision or regulation, to his employees[3], of a professional person being held to have been negligent in carrying on practice as a solicitor, accountant, valuer, or the like[4], of a carrier or other bailee being held liable to the owner of goods in his custody which are lost, damaged or destroyed[5], or of a building, engineering or public works contractor being held liable to members of the public by reason of his operations[6]. Again, an owner and occupier of buildings, whether domestic or commercial, may incur liability to people using an adjoining highway, or liability to visitors, either generally in connection with the buildings[7], or more particularly in connection with lifts or other machinery or plant installed there. Specialised insurances may be obtained by the proprietor of a newspaper against the risk of having to pay damages for libel[8], or against other risks of liability by reason of the publication of his newspaper[9]. Even the playing of games or providing of amusements[10] may involve a third party liability, and appropriate insurances have been designed for these risks. Licensees of nuclear sites must take out special cover by insurance or some other means in respect of liability to a third party[11].

1 Normally these exclusions operate where special risks arise or where cover can be obtained under other policies. Examples are liabilities incurred to employees, or arising out of the carrying on of a trade, business or profession, or from the occupation of property or the use of a motor vehicle, aircraft or vessel.
2 As to motor insurance see para 706 et seq post. As to aviation insurance see paras 347–348 ante.
3 As to employer's liability insurances see paras 685–689 post.
4 As to professional negligence insurance see paras 692–697 post.
5 As to bailee's insurance see paras 698–705 post.
6 Such policies are generally called 'public liability policies'. As to the liability of a building or engineering contractor for injury to persons or property see generally BUILDING CONTRACTS vol 4(2) (Reissue) paras 440–443.
7 For householders, most insurers issue a 'householder's comprehensive policy' which covers the premises against fire and other damage, the contents against loss or damage over a wide range, and the occupiers against employer's liability to domestic servants and public liability to the world at large.
8 *E Hulton & Co Ltd v Mountain* (1921) 37 TLR 869, CA.
9 Cf the contract in *Daily Express (1908) Ltd v Mountain* (1916) 32 TLR 592, CA (a case relating to discovery).
10 *Captain Boyton's World's Water Show Syndicate Ltd v Employers' Liability Assurance Corpn Ltd* (1895) 11 TLR 384, CA. A marina operator may effect a liability policy in respect of operations carried out on the premises, eg alteration, repair, maintenance and storage: see *Pillgrem v Cliff Richardson Boats Ltd and Richardson (Switzerland General Insurance Co, third party)* [1977] 1 Lloyd's Rep 297 (Ont SC).
11 See the Nuclear Installations Act 1965 s 19 (amended by the Energy Act 1983 s 27(4), (5)).

(ii) Scope of the Insurance

663. Legal liability. The event upon which the obligation of the insurers to indemnify the assured depends is the happening of the liability insured against[1].

The liability must normally be a legal liability[2]; in the absence of legal liability no claim arises under a policy in the usual form[3].

1 See *Lancashire Insurance Co v IRC* [1899] 1 QB 353 at 359 per Bruce J.
2 *Haseldine v Hosken* [1933] 1 KB 822, CA. A liability which becomes effective through waiver of diplomatic privilege is a legal liability: *Dickinson v Del Solar* [1930] 1 KB 376.
3 *Scott v McIntosh* (1814) 2 Dow 322, HL (illegal ballot). A person who threatens unlawful violence to another person by means of a loaded shotgun is prohibited by public policy from obtaining an indemnity under a public liability insurance policy should injury to or the death of that other person result: *Gray v Barr (Prudential Assurance Co Ltd, third party)* [1971] 2 QB 554, [1971] 2 All ER 949, CA. A policy may contain a provision by which a claim may be payable in certain circumstances even though there is no legal liability, but such a policy is, it seems, a policy of contingency insurance: see para 767 post.

664. Description of liability. The liability must be the liability described in the policy. If the liability is described as arising out of a particular kind of accident, it must be shown that that kind of accident has happened[1]; if the liability is to arise out of accidents connected with a particular business, liability arising out of accidents not connected with that business is not covered[2]. A policy covering personal injury to any person under a contract of service with a contractor does not cover injury to a workman temporarily lent to the contractor by persons who employ the contractor[3], and a policy covering liability for a negligent act, omission or error does not cover liability for fraudulent acts[4]. Hence, the description defines the scope of the insurance, and, if expressed in terms of precision, may have the effect of considerably limiting it[5]. Thus, an insurance which is expressed to cover an employer's statutory liability to his workmen does not cover his common law liability[6]; and an insurance confined to liability for accidents happening in a particular locality has no application in the case of accidents happening elsewhere[7].

The risk is further defined in effect by the questions in the proposal form[8], which, when completed, is usually made the basis of the contract[9]. In particular, importance is attached to the occupation of the assured[10], including, in the case of a business, the nature of the business[11], the number of employees and the capacity in which they are employed[12], and to the assured's previous experience of the proposed risk[13].

1 *Captain Boyton's World's Water Show Syndicate Ltd v Employers' Liability Assurance Corpn Ltd* (1895) 11 TLR 384, CA; *Gray v Barr (Prudential Assurance Co Ltd, third party)* [1971] 2 QB 554, [1971] 2 All ER 949, CA; *Straits Towing Ltd v Walkem Machinery and Equipment Ltd* [1973] 5 WWR 212 (BC CA) (collapse of crane).
2 *Smellie v British General Insurance Co* [1918] WC & Ins Rep 233; cf *Holdsworth v Lancashire and Yorkshire Insurance Co* (1907) 23 TLR 521 at 524 per Bray J.
3 *Denham v Midland Employers' Mutual Assurance Ltd* [1955] 2 QB 437, [1955] 2 All ER 561, CA; see para 686 note 2 post.
4 See para 693 post.
5 For rules of construction see paras 394–400 ante.
6 *Morrison and Masson v Scottish Employers' Liability and Accident Assurance Co* (1888) 16 R 212, Ct of Sess.
7 *Smellie v British General Insurance Co* [1918] WC & Ins Rep 233; see further para 715 post.
8 As to the proposal generally see paras 368–374 ante.
9 *Dawsons Ltd v Bonnin* [1922] 2 AC 413, HL; see further para 374 ante.
10 *Equitable Life Assurance Society v General Accident Assurance Corpn* 1904 12 SLT 348.
11 *Holdsworth v Lancashire and Yorkshire Insurance Co* (1907) 23 TLR 521. See also para 431 ante.
12 *Smellie v British General Insurance Co* [1918] WC & Ins Rep 233.
13 *Reid & Co v Employers' Accident etc Insurance Co* (1899) 1 F 1031, Ct of Sess; *Life and Health Assurance Association v Yule* (1904) 6 F 437, Ct of Sess; *Newsholme Bros v Road Transport and General Insurance Co*

Ltd [1929] 2 KB 356 at 364, CA; see also *Dunn v Ocean Accident and Guarantee Corpn* (1933) 50 TLR 32 at 33, CA; and generally para 371 ante.

665. Use of exceptions. Where, by definition or description, the insurance afforded by a policy comes within a stipulated category, it is not usual to find in the policy the majority of the exceptions which are commonly found in other types of non-marine insurance[1]. Thus, in practice, employers' liability policies contain no exceptions, their ambit being defined by the description of the assured's business and the requirement that the liability must be to a person under a contract of service or apprenticeship with the assured[2]. Other policies may exclude such liabilities as are usually covered by a different kind of insurance. Thus, in practice, a policy insuring against public liability does not include liability to employees[3], that being a liability which can be covered by an employer's liability policy.

1 As to exceptions generally see para 409 ante.
2 See eg *Denham v Midland Employers' Mutual Assurance Ltd* [1955] 2 QB 437, [1955] 2 All ER 561, CA (discussed at para 686 note 2 post).
3 Cf *Denham v Midland Employers' Mutual Assurance Ltd* [1955] 2 QB 437, [1955] 2 All ER 561, CA; para 686 note 2 post.

(iii) Special Features

666. Calculation of premium. Where an insurance, whether against public liability or against employer's liability, is issued in relation to the carrying on of a business, the probability of accidents occurring, and also of liability consequent on those accidents arising, depends upon the size of the business[1]. The greater the number of persons employed, or the number of appliances or vehicles used, the greater is the chance of accident. In practice, therefore, a definite lump sum premium is not charged. A premium is, in the ordinary way, payable at the commencement of the insurance, but this is a provisional premium only. The premium ultimately payable is fixed by data derived from the whole of the year of insurance, such as the amount of wages paid, or the number of persons employed, or of vehicles used, and provision is made for adjustment at the end of the year. For this purpose, the assured is required to keep a proper record, such as, for instance, if the premium is based on wages, a wages book[2], and at the end of the year he must furnish the insurers with an account from which the premium properly payable can be calculated[3].

1 See *Smellie v British General Insurance Co* [1918] WC & Ins Rep 233 (where the smallness of premium indicated the limited scope of the insurance).
2 *Re Bradley and Essex and Suffolk Accident Indemnity Society* [1912] 1 KB 415, CA (where the stipulation requiring a wages book to be kept was held not to be a condition precedent to liability).
3 This obligation may arise even if the insurance has come to an end: *General Accident Assurance Corpn Ltd v Day* (1904) 21 TLR 88.

667. Duties of assured in relation to claims. Unless admitted, liability to a third party is likely to be enforced by an action brought by the third party, and upon the result of this action will depend the amount which the insurers have in their turn to pay as an indemnity to their assured. There is considerable danger that they may be prejudiced by his acts or omissions in defending any action. In practice, therefore, in addition to the usual duties imposed upon an assured making a claim under a policy[1], the policy makes it the assured's duty to give the insurers full information about any claim made against him by a third party, and requires him to forward to them any letters or documents received from the third party[2]. He is also prohibited by the terms of the policy from settling any claim by a third party[3] or making any admission of liability[4] without the insurers' consent; and they are given power, if they think fit, to take over the defence of any proceedings that may be brought against the assured[5].

1 As to claims under policies see generally para 481 et seq ante.
2 The precise effect of the requirement depends upon its form: *Wilkinson v Car and General Insurance Corpn* (1913) 110 LT 468, DC.
3 If the insurers decline to take over the defence, they cannot afterwards complain of a bona fide settlement: *Captain Boyton's World's Water Show Syndicate Ltd v Employers' Liability Assurance Corpn Ltd* (1895) 11 TLR 384, CA, per Lord Esher MR.
4 An admission of liability by an employee immediately after the accident is not within the prohibition unless the employee is authorised to make the admission: *Tustin v Arnold & Sons* (1915) 84 LJKB 2214; see also *Burr v Ware RDC* [1939] 2 All ER 688, CA.
5 As to the conduct of proceedings see paras 674–676 post.

(iv) Extent of Indemnity

668. Full or partial indemnity; partial assumption of liability by the assured. In some kinds of liability insurance, such as employer's liability insurance, the policy usually provides for a full indemnity against all liabilities falling within the scope of the policy which may be incurred by the assured during the currency of the policy[1]. In the case of motor insurance, so far as compulsorily insurable risks are concerned, it seems that a policy which contains any limitation of the amount payable (except in the case of damage to property) would not comply with the statutory requirements[2]. In other kinds of liability insurance, limitations are often imposed upon the amount recoverable so that the assured may not in fact receive a full indemnity[3]. Provisions imposing limitations of liability may take various forms and examples are given in the following paragraphs[4]. The policy may contain a provision under which part of the liability insured against is to be borne by the assured himself. The provision may be framed to apply to all accidents, and the assured may agree to bear a specified proportion of the total liability; more usually the assured is made to assume, in respect of each individual accident, all liability up to a specified amount, in which case the insurers are liable for the excess only in each case[5].

1 See eg 20 Forms & Precedents (5th Edn) 296, Form 193.
2 As to these statutory requirements see the Road Traffic Act 1988 s 145 (as amended); and para 733 et seq post. Policies containing such a limitation are not in practice issued.
3 The earlier cases as to limitation of the amount recoverable which arose out of motor insurance, although they may be no longer law in motor insurance, remain applicable to other kinds of liability insurance.
4 See para 669–671 post.
5 See para 524 ante.

669. Limitation of liability by reference to currency of policy. The policy may fix the maximum total sum payable during the currency of the policy[1]. The effect of a provision in this simple form is that, when accidents happen, the sums paid by the insurers in respect of the assured's liability are deducted from the maximum sum insured, and when that sum is exhausted the protection of the policy comes to an end[2].

1 *South Staffordshire Tramways Co v Sickness and Accident Assurance Association* [1891] 1 QB 402, CA; cf *British General Insurance Co v Mountain* (1919) 36 TLR 171 at 172, HL, where under the original policy there was a maximum liability for the year, as well as a maximum liability for each accident: 'liability not to exceed £750 for any one accident in any one year'. A policy may provide for a limitation on the maximum amount payable under each head of risk.

2 As to the cessation of the policy on payment of the total sum insured see para 461 ante. The policy may, however, contain a provision for automatic renewal.

670. Limitation by reference to any one accident. Where a policy fixes the maximum sum payable in respect of any one accident, the limitation applies to the particular accident only; if there is another accident afterwards, the assured becomes again entitled to be indemnified up to the specified maximum, and the amount paid in respect of his liability for the previous accident is not to be taken into account[1]. In considering the application of the limitation in this form, it is to be observed that the word 'accident' may be used in more than one sense. If several persons are injured by a mishap to a train, vehicle or bridge, the occurrence can in one sense be described as an accident to the train, vehicle or bridge, and there is in that sense one accident only; on the other hand, 'accident' may fall to be construed from the point of view of each individual victim[2], so as to produce, in effect, as many accidents (even in a single occurrence) as there are victims[3]. It is a question of construction in each case as to what 'accident' means; if it is construed as meaning accident to the person, the limitation of liability is to be taken to apply to the accident to each person and not to the accident to the vehicle or bridge, and the aggregate liability of the insurers is not limited to the maximum sum specified in the policy; on the contrary, they must indemnify the assured against his liability to each person injured, not exceeding in each case the specified maximum[4].

1 *South Staffordshire Tramways Co v Sickness and Accident Assurance Association* [1891] 1 QB 402, CA; see also *M'Kinlay v Life and Health Insurance Association* (1905) 13 SLT 102.

2 For the meaning of 'accident' in personal accident insurance see paras 569 et seq ante.

3 *South Staffordshire Tramways Co v Sickness and Accident Assurance Association* [1891] 1 QB 402 at 407, CA, per Bowen LJ.

4 *South Staffordshire Tramways Co v Sickness and Accident Assurance Association* [1891] 1 QB 402, CA, where the insurers were held liable to pay the total amount awarded to the various persons injured, namely £833, notwithstanding that the policy limited liability to '£250 in respect of any one accident'.

671. Limitation by reference to any one occurrence. The policy may fix the maximum sum payable in respect of any accident or accidents arising out of the same occurrence[1]. This form has been introduced to avoid the ambiguity latent in the word 'accident'[2], and it clearly shows that the limitation of liability is intended to apply to the acident to the vehicle or construction and not to the accidents to the various persons injured. In such a case, however many persons may have been injured in the same occurrence, only one maximum sum is payable[3].

1 See eg *Forney v Dominion Insurance Co Ltd* [1969] 3 All ER 831, [1969] 1 WLR 928 (professional indemnity policy).

2 As to this ambiguity see para 670 ante.

3 *Allen v London Guarantee and Accident Co Ltd* (1912) 28 TLR 254.

(v) Indemnity Against Costs

672. Need for express provision as to costs. It is open to question how far an insurance against third party liability confers liability against costs unless there is some specific reference to costs in the policy. Where the assured is held to be liable to the third party, and costs also are awarded against him, it is reasonably clear that his liability for costs is part of the legal liability to the third party, against which he is entitled to be indemnified[1]. It is difficult to see how the same can be said of costs incurred in combating the claim, as these are expenses incurred by the assured, even though he may be under a legal liability in respect of them to his solicitor[2]. If, however, the assured succeeds in his defence, and is held not to be liable to the third party, the event insured against, namely, liability to the third party, has not happened. The costs of the defence have been incurred, not as a consequence of any legal liability to the third party, but for the purpose of disproving its existence. In the absence, therefore, of some express provision in the policy, the costs of a successful defence are not covered, even though they were incurred with the consent of the insurers[3].

1 See *Xenos v Fox* (1869) LR 4 CP 665 at 668, Ex Ch, per Cockburn CJ (marine insurance). As to the inclusion in professional negligence policies of provision for the payment of costs see para 694 post. As to the duty of motor insurers to satisfy judgments, including costs, in favour of third parties see para 749 post.
2 Cf *Xenos v Fox* (1869) LR 4 CP 665 at 668, Ex Ch, per Cockburn CJ.
3 *Xenos v Fox* (1869) LR 4 CP 665, Ex Ch.

673. Provision normally made for costs. In practice, a policy of liability insurance always contains an express provision for indemnifying the assured in respect of costs of proceedings brought against the assured within the ambit of the policy. This provision covers not only any costs which may be awarded against the assured, but also any costs which he may incur in defending any claim which may be brought against him[1]. The existence of such an indemnity against costs does not preclude the assured, if he is successful in the proceedings, from recovering his costs of defence from an unsuccessful third party[2].

1 *British General Insurance Co v Mountain* (1919) 36 TLR 171 at 172, HL, per Lord Birkenhead LC. See also para 676 text to note 4 post.
2 *Cornish v Lynch* (1910) 3 BWCC 343, CA. In addition, the indemnity usually covers the costs of legal representation at any inquest or magistrates' court proceedings arising out of the accident.

(vi) Conduct of Proceedings

674. Right of insurers to intervene in own name. If an action by a third party is proceeding against the assured, the insurers are not entitled to make any application in the action in their own name[1] unless they have been made parties to the action[2]; but, if judgment in default against the assured has been obtained in such an action, and the insurers are by statute[3] liable to pay the amount of the judgment to the plaintiff, the insurers are entitled to apply[4], as persons interested, to have the judgment set aside, even though they were not parties to the action[5]. At one time, except in exceptional circumstances, the assured was not allowed to bring in his insurers as third parties[6] in an action heard before a jury, in view of the existence of a rule of practice[7] that the fact that a defendant is insured should not be disclosed to a jury[8]. It was, however, doubtful if the rule, or the consequent restriction on the bringing in of insurers as third parties, had any application if the liability alleged against the assured was one against which insurance is compulsory[9]. The restriction was not in any case applicable when the trial of the action was by a judge alone[10], and there is now no limitation on the court's power[11] to bring in a third party whenever in its discretion it thinks it right to do so; it is a question of the balance of convenience[12].

1 As to the right of insurers to conduct the defence of proceedings in the name of the assured by virtue of a term in the policy see para 675 post.
2 *Murfin v Ashbridge and Martin* [1941] 1 All ER 231, CA.
3 Eg by virtue of the Road Traffic Act 1988 ss 151, 152; see para 749 post.
4 Ie under RSC Ord 16 r 5(3), Ord 19 r 9: see JUDGMENTS.
5 *Windsor v Chalcraft* [1939] 1 KB 279, [1938] 2 All ER 751, CA.
6 As to third party procedure see RSC Ord 16; and PRACTICE AND PROCEDURE.
7 As to the rule see *Wright v Hearson* [1916] WN 216; *Askew v Grimmer* (1927) 43 TLR 354; *Grinham v Davies* [1929] 2 KB 249.
8 *Gowar v Hales* [1928] 1 KB 191, CA, distinguishing *Lothian v Epworth Press* (1926) [1928] 1 KB 199n; *Jones v Birch Bros Ltd* [1933] 2 KB 597 at 606–607, CA, per Scrutton LJ.
9 *Carpenter v Ebblewhite* [1939] 1 KB 347 at 359, [1938] 4 All ER 41 at 45, CA, per Greer LJ; *Harman v Crilly* [1943] KB 168 at 172–173, [1943] 1 All ER 140 at 143, CA.
10 *Harman v Crilly* [1943] KB 168, [1943] 1 All ER 140, CA. As to the staying of third party proceedings against insurers in the case of a policy by which arbitration is made a condition precedent to any action on the policy see *Jones v Birch Bros Ltd* [1933] 2 KB 597, CA; and see para 498 ante.
11 Ie under RSC Ord 16: see PRACTICE AND PROCEDURE.
12 *Brice v J H Wackerbarth (Australasia) Pty Ltd* [1974] 2 Lloyd's Rep 274 at 276, CA, per Lord Denning MR, and at 277 per Roskill LJ; *Walker and Knight v Donne, Mileham and Haddock (a firm)* (1976) Times, 9 November, CA, per Roskill LJ.

675. Policy conditions as to conduct of proceedings. The policy usually empowers the insurers to take over, in the name and on behalf of the assured, the conduct and control of the defence of proceedings within the ambit of the policy brought against him. This power enables the insurers to settle the proceedings without consulting the assured, and they can then recover from him any portion of the agreed damages which under the policy he has to bear[1]. The exercise of this power does not involve the insurers in any liabilities to the third party, and they do not make themselves responsible to him for payment of the amount at which the liability of the assured has been assessed[2].

1 *Beacon Insurance Co Ltd v Langdale* [1939] 4 All ER 204, CA.
2 *Nairn v South East Lancashire Insurance Co* 1930 SC 606.

676. Liability of insurers who conduct defence. It is the duty of the insurers to the assured, if they undertake the defence, to conduct it properly. If by any negligence on their part the defence is improperly conducted, and the damages awarded against the assured are accordingly increased, they are liable to make good to him the amount of the increase, and it is immaterial that it is in excess of the maximum sum insured[1]. Similarly, even if they are nominated by the insurers, solicitors acting on behalf of the assured must recognise that the assured is their client, and without clear authority in the policy, they may not put on the record in his name a defence with which he does not agree and which he may regard as a libel upon him[2]. If, on the other hand, the assured is allowed to conduct the defence himself, he may be required to obtain the insurers' consent before incurring any costs, and in such a case costs incurred without their consent will not be recoverable[3].

As regards the costs which may be awarded against the assured in the proceedings, if the insurers insist on defending the proceedings without consulting him, they must indemnify him against the whole of the costs and cannot claim the benefit of any stipulation in the policy by which their liability for costs is limited[4].

By assuming or continuing the defence of proceedings against the assured with full knowledge of the circumstances, the insurers may be precluded from disputing their liability to the assured[5].

1 *Patteson v Northern Accident Insurance Co Ltd* [1901] IR 262.
2 *Groom v Crocker* [1939] 1 KB 194, [1938] 2 All ER 394, CA.
3 *British General Insurance Co v Mountain* (1919) 36 TLR 171, HL. Consent may be implied from conduct: *E Hulton & Co v Mountain* (1921) 37 TLR 869, CA.
4 *Allen v London Guarantee and Accident Co Ltd* (1912) 28 TLR 254.
5 *Etchells, Congdon and Muir Ltd v Eagle Star and British Dominions Insurance Co Ltd* (1928) 72 Sol Jo 242; cf *McCormick v National Motor and Accident Insurance Union Ltd* (1934) 50 TLR 528, CA.

(vii) Subrogation of Injured Party

677. Injured party not subrogated at common law. At common law, where a person insured under a liability insurance policy became legally liable for injury or damage sustained by a third party, the third party, not being a party to the contract of insurance, had no right either to proceed directly against the insurers, or to attach, by garnishee proceedings or otherwise, the money payable by the insurers to the assured. Equity did not put that third party in any better position, either in relation to the insurers, if they still held the money, or in relation to the assured, if he had been paid. In the event, therefore, of the assured's insolvency, the policy money became part of his general assets and even where the policy money formed the whole of the assets the third party ranked as an ordinary creditor only[1]. Consequently, a position of great hardship was created, and this led to the progressive introduction of a limited system of statutory subrogation, by which, in the event of the insolvency of the assured, the third party was entitled to be paid the policy money and, if necessary, to enforce the policy against the insurers[2].

1 *Re Harrington Motor Co, ex p Chaplin* [1928] Ch 105, CA; *Hood's Trustees v Southern Union General Insurance Co of Australasia Ltd* [1928] Ch 793, CA; see generally *Re Law Guarantee Trust and Accident Society, Liverpool Mortgage Insurance Co's Case* [1914] 2 Ch 617, CA.
2 As to statutory subrogation see para 678 et seq post.

678. Introduction of statutory subrogation. In 1897 a statutory right of subrogation against an employer's insurers was given, in the event of the insolvency of the employer, to a workman who had a claim for compensation under the former system of workmen's compensation[1]; and a general scheme of statutory subrogation against insurers of third party risks in the case of the insolvency of the assured was established by the Third Parties (Rights against Insurers) Act 1930[2].

Specialised forms of statutory subrogation have been introduced in relation to motor insurance[3], and in favour of the assured, in case of the insolvency of the insurers, where there has been reinsurance of war risks in respect of ships, aircraft and cargoes with the Secretary of State[4].

1 Workmen's Compensation Act 1897 s 5 (repealed).
2 See paras 679–684 post.
3 See paras 748–750 post.
4 See para 795 post.

679. Application of statutory scheme of subrogation. A right of subrogation arises where, under any contract of insurance[1], the assured is insured against liabilities to third parties[2] which he may incur and one of the following events occurs:

(1) the assured becomes bankrupt or makes a composition or arrangement with his creditors[3]; or

(2) in the case of the assured being a company, a winding-up order or an administration order is made, or a resolution for a voluntary winding up is passed[4], with respect to the company, or a receiver or manager of the company's business or undertaking is duly appointed, or possession is taken, by or on behalf of the holders of any debentures secured by a floating charge, of any property comprised in or subject to the charge or of a voluntary arrangement approved under the Insolvency Act 1986[5].

If, either before or after the event in question, any liability to a third party is incurred by the assured, then, notwithstanding anything in any Act or rule of law to the contrary, his rights against the insurers under the contract in respect of the liability are transferred to and vest in the third party to whom the liability was incurred[6]. Where an order is made[7] for the administration of the estate of a deceased debtor if any debt provable in bankruptcy[8] is owing by the deceased in respect of a liability against which he was insured under a contract of insurance as being a liability to a third party, the deceased debtor's rights against the insurers under the contract in respect of that liability are, notwithstanding anything in any such order, transferred to and vest in the person to whom the debt is owing[9].

The third party has no right of action against the insurers if the insured has already been wound up and dissolved[10]. The third party must claim within the limitation period[11].

1 A contract of insurance for this purpose does not include a contract of reinsurance: see the Third Parties (Rights against Insurers) Act 1930 s 1(5), and note 2 infra. The Third Parties (Rights against Insurers) Act 1930 does not apply in the case of compulsory insurance against liability for pollution by oil: Merchant Shipping (Oil Pollution) Act 1971 s 12(5). As to this compulsory insurance see para 38 ante. Under the provisions of the former Workmen's Compensation Acts, which conferred a special statutory right of subrogation, questions arose, in certain cases where employers were members of mutual indemnity companies, as to whether what in fact existed was a contract of insurance or merely an arrangement by which in effect the indemnity company paid compensation to the workmen out of money provided by the employers: see eg *Pailin v Northern Employers' Mutual Indemnity Co* [1925] 2 KB 73, CA; *Hindmarch v Carterthorne Colliery Ltd and Durham Colliery Owners' Mutual Protection Association* (1928) 21 BWCC 44, CA; *Wooding v Monmouthshire and South Wales Mutual Indemnity Society Ltd* [1939] 4 All ER 570, HL. It is possible that a similar question might arise under the Third Parties (Rights against Insurers) Act 1930 s 1 (amended by the Insolvency Act 1985 s 235(1), Sch 8 para 7(2); and the Insolvency Act 1986 s 439(2), Sch 14).

2 For this purpose, liabilities to third parties, in relation to an insured person, do not include any liability of that person in the capacity of insurer under another contract of insurance: Third Parties (Rights against Insurers) Act 1930 s 1(5). It seems that, subject to this exception, liabilities to third parties include liabilities in contract as well as liabilities in tort, so that, eg in the case of an insurance by a bailee, if one of the events giving rise to a right of subrogation occurs, the bailor will be entitled to be subrogated to the bailee's rights against the bailee's insurers, whether the bailee's liability to the bailor arises in tort or contract; cf *North British and Mercantile Insurance Co v London, Liverpool and Globe Insurance Co* (1877) 5 ChD 569 at 584, CA, per Mellish LJ.

3 Third Parties (Rights against Insurers) Act 1930 s 1(1)(a). See eg *M/S Engineering Establishment Co Ltd v Iron Trades Mutual Insurance Co Ltd* [1989] 1 Lloyd's Rep 289. The event of the insured becoming insolvent must first occur before the Act confers on third parties any rights against insurers of third parties: *Normid Housing Association Ltd v Ralphs* [1989] 1 Lloyd's Rep 265, CA, per Slade LJ at 272–273.
4 The Third Parties (Rights against Insurers) Act 1930 does not apply where a company is wound up voluntarily merely for the purposes of reconstruction or amalgamation with another company: s 1(6)(a). As to winding up generally see COMPANIES vol 7(2) (Reissue) para 1082 et seq.
5 Ibid s 1(1)(b).
6 Ibid s 1(1). As to the effect of the transfer see para 681 post.
7 Ie under the Insolvency Act 1986 s 421: see BANKRUPTCY AND INSOLVENCY vol 3(2) (Reissue) para 809 et seq.
8 As to the debts which are provable in bankruptcy see BANKRUPTCY AND INSOLVENCY vol 3(2) (Reissue) para 478 et seq.
9 Third Parties (Rights against Insurers) Act 1930 s 1(2).
10 *Bradley v Eagle Star Insurance Co Ltd* [1988] 2 Lloyd's Rep 233.
11 *Lefevre v White* [1990] 1 Lloyd's Rep 569.

680. Invalidity of provisions terminating insurance on insolvency. Any contract of insurance made in respect of any liability of the assured to third parties is of no effect in so far as it purports, whether directly or indirectly, to avoid the contract or to alter the rights of the parties under it in the event of the assured becoming insolvent[1] or of the making of an order[2] for the administration of his estate in bankruptcy[3].

1 Ie on the happening to the assured of any of the events specified in the Third Parties (Rights against Insurers) Act 1930 s 1 (1)(a), (b): see para 679 text to notes 3–5 ante.
2 Ie under the Insolvency Act 1986 s 421: see BANKRUPTCY AND INSOLVENCY vol 3(2) (Reissue) para 809 et seq.
3 Third Parties (Rights against Insurers) Act 1930 s 1(3).

681. Extent of subrogation. The rights transferred to the third party under the Third Parties (Rights against Insurers) Act 1930 are the rights of the assured against the insurers under the contract of insurance in respect of the liability in question; rights which are not referable to that liability are not transferred[1]. In order that the statutory transfer may be effective, it is necessary, unless the claim is validly admitted, to establish the liability of the assured either by judgment of the court or by an award in an arbitration[2].

Upon a transfer of rights, the insurers are, in general, under the same liability to the third party as they would have been to the assured[3]. If, however, the liability of the insurers to the assured exceeds the liability of the assured to the third party, the assured retains his rights against the insurers in respect of the excess[4]; except where this provision applies, it seems that the effect of the statutory transfer of rights is that the insurers are not under any liability either to the trustee in bankruptcy of the assured where the assured is bankrupt[5], or to the general creditors[6] of the assured, but only to the third party[7]. In the case of compulsory motor insurance, it is expressly provided that the statutory transfer of rights against the insurers does not affect the liability of the assured to the third party[8]. In other cases, if the liability of the insurers to the assured is less than the liability of the assured to the third party, the third party retains his rights against the assured in respect of the balance[9].

1 *Murray v Legal and General Assurance Society Ltd* [1970] 2 QB 495, [1969] 3 All ER 794; *Farrell v Federated Employers Insurance Association Ltd* [1970] 2 Lloyd's Rep 170, CA. Thus where the assured,

because of failure to comply with a prior payment condition, had no rights against the insurers there could be no rights capable of transfer to the third party: *Firma C-Trade SA v Newcastle Protection and Indemnity Association* [1990] 2 All ER 705, [1990] 2 Lloyd's Rep 191, HL.

2 *Post Office v Norwich Union Fire Insurance Society Ltd* [1967] 2 QB 363 at 373–374, [1967] 1 All ER 577 at 579, CA, per Lord Denning MR, and at 377–378 and 582 per Salmon LJ, approving the statement of Devlin J in *West Wake Price & Co v Ching* [1956] 3 All ER 821 at 825, [1957] 1 WLR 45 at 49.

3 Third Parties (Rights against Insurers) Act 1930 s 1(4). As to the avoidance as against third parties of settlements made between the insurers and the assured see para 684 post. For the principle that the insurers are in general liable to the third party only if, apart from the assured's insolvency, they would have been liable to the assured see para 682 post. As to the duty of insurers in the case of compulsory motor vehicle insurance to satisfy judgments obtained by third parties, even though the insurers may be entitled to cancel or avoid the policy, see para 749 post. For the principle that the conditions of the policy are in general binding on the third party see para 682 post. As to the avoidance as against third parties of certain conditions in motor vehicle insurance see paras 742–747 post.

4 Ibid s 1(4)(a). The trustees, liquidator, receiver, manager or administrator, as the case may be, will hold the excess on behalf of the creditors of the assured.

5 See *Craig v Royal Insurance Co Ltd* (1914) 84 LJKB 333 (a decision under the former Workmen's Compensation Acts).

6 See *King v Phoenix Assurance Co* [1910] 2 KB 666 at 669–670, CA, per Cozens-Hardy MR; *Daff v Midland Colliery Owners' Indemnity Co* (1913) 82 LJKB 1340 at 1347, HL, per Lord Dunedin (decisions in relation to the subrogation provisions in the former Workmen's Compensation Acts).

7 See *Craig v Royal Insurance Co Ltd* (1914) 84 LJKB 333 (a decision under the former Workmen's Compensation Acts).

8 See the Road Traffic Act 1988 s 153; and para 747 post.

9 Third Parties (Rights against Insurers) Act 1930 s 1(4)(b).

682. Necessity that policy should have been enforceable by assured. Subject to the provisions rendering invalid against third parties certain settlements made between the insurers and the assured[1], and subject, in the case of compulsory motor insurance, to certain provisions which may impose on insurers the duty of satisfying judgments obtained in favour of third parties, even though the insurers may be entitled to avoid or cancel the policy[2], and which render invalid certain conditions in policies[3], the insurers are not liable to the third party unless they would have been liable to the assured if the statutory transfer had not taken place[4]. If the policy was obtained by material non-disclosure, misrepresentation or fraud on the part of the assured, the third party cannot recover against the insurers[5].

The fact that the insurers go into liquidation, whether before[6] or after[7] the bankruptcy of the assured, does not, it seems, prevent the statutory transfer from taking effect[8]. The conditions of the contract of insurance, other than conditions purporting to avoid or alter the contract in the event of the assured's insolvency[9] or precluding third parties from obtaining information as to the existence of the policy[10], or conditions rendered invalid against third parties in the case of motor insurance[11], are binding on the third party; he is therefore bound by an arbitration clause[12].

1 See the Third Parties (Rights against Insurers) Act 1930 s 3; and para 684 post.

2 See the Road Traffic Act 1988 ss 151, 152; and para 748 post.

3 See ibid s 148; and paras 743, 745 post.

4 *Hassett v Legal and General Assurance Society Ltd* (1939) 63 Ll L Rep 278; see also *Morris v Northern Employers' Mutual Indemnity Co* (1902) 71 LJKB 733 at 735, CA (a decision under the former Workmen's Compensation Acts); *Farrell v Federated Employers' Insurance Association Ltd* [1970] 3 All ER 632, [1970] 1 WLR 1400, CA. See also *CVG Siderurgicia del Orinoco SA v London Steamship Owners' Mutual Insurance Association Ltd* [1979] 1 Lloyd's Rep 557.

5 *McCormick v National Motor and Accident Insurance Union Ltd* (1934) 50 TLR 528, CA. The application of this decision in relation to motor insurance has been affected by statute (see the Road Traffic Act

1988 s 151, 152; and paras 751–752 post), but it is still an authority on the effect of statutory subrogation generally.

6 See *Re Renishaw Iron Co Ltd* [1917] 1 Ch 199 (a decision in relation to the subrogation provisions contained in the former Workmen's Compensation Acts). As to the invalidity against third parties of compromises between the insurers and the assured see para 684 post.

7 See *Re Pethick, Dix & Co, Burrows' Claim* [1915] 1 Ch 26 (a decision in relation to the subrogation provisions contained in the former Workmen's Compensation Acts).

8 The liability of the insurers is, it seems, ascertained at the date of their liquidation: see *Re Law Car and General Insurance Corpn Ltd* (1913) 110 LT 27 (a decision in relation to the subrogation provisions contained in the former Workmen's Compensation Acts).

9 As to the invalidity of conditions to this effect see the Third Parties (Rights against Insurers) Act 1930 s 1(3); and para 680 ante.

10 As to the invalidity of provisions purporting to avoid a contract or to alter rights on the giving of information to third parties see the Third Parties (Rights against Insurers) Act 1930 s 2(1); and para 683 post.

11 See the Road Traffic Act 1988 s 148; and paras 743, 745 post.

12 See para 498 note 2 ante.

683. Duty to give information to third parties. In the event of:
(1) a person becoming bankrupt;
(2) a person making a composition or arrangement with his creditors;
(3) an order being made for the administration of the estate of a deceased insolvent debtor[1];
(4) a winding up order or an administration order being made, or a resolution for a voluntary winding up being passed, with respect to a company;
(5) a receiver or manager of a company's business or undertaking being duly appointed; or
(6) possession being taken by or on behalf of the holders of any debentures secured by a floating charge of any property comprised in or subject to the charge,

it is the duty of such a person or company[2] to give at the request of any party claiming that that person or company is under a liability to him, such information as may reasonably be required by the party so claiming for the purpose of
(a) ascertaining whether any rights have been transferred to and vested in him by the Third Parties (Rights against Insurers) Act 1930[3] and
(b) enforcing such rights, if any[4].

In so far as any contract of insurance purports, directly or indirectly, to avoid the contract or to alter the rights of the parties under it, upon the giving of any such information in the above events, or otherwise to prohibit or prevent the giving of such information in those events, it is of no effect[5].

If the information given to any person in pursuance of the statutory requirement discloses reasonable ground for supposing that there have or may have been transferred to him under the statutory provisions rights against any particular insurer, that insurer is subject to the same duty of disclosure as is imposed on the persons previously mentioned[6]. The duty to give information includes a duty to allow all contracts of insurance, receipts for premiums and other relevant documents in the possession or power of the person on whom the duty is imposed to be inspected and copies of them to be taken[7].

1 Ie an order under the Insolvency Act 1986 s 421: see BANKRUPTCY AND INSOLVENCY vol 3(2) (Reissue) para 809 et seq.

2 Ie the bankrupt, debtor, personal representative of the deceased debtor, or the company, and, as the case may be, of the trustee in bankruptcy, trustee, liquidator, administrator, receiver or manager or person in the possession of the property. The reference to a 'trustee' includes a reference to the

supervisor of a voluntary arrangement proposed for, and approved under, the Insolvency Act 1986 Pt I (ss 1–7) or Pt VIII (ss 252–263): Third Parties (Rights against Insurers) Act 1930 s 1A (added by the Insolvency Act 1985 s 235(1), Sch 8 para 7(3)(b); amended by the Insolvency Act 1986 s 439(2), Sch 14).

3 As to the rights transferred by the Third Parties (Rights against Insurers) Act 1930 see paras 679–682 ante.

4 Ibid s 2(1) (amended by the Insolvency Act 1985 s 235(1), Sch 8 para 7(3)(a); and the Insolvency Act 1986 s 439(2), Sch 14).

5 Third Parties (Rights against Insurers) Act 1930 s 2(1) (as amended).

6 Ibid s 2(2).

7 Ibid s 2(3).

684. Settlement between insurers and assured. Where the assured has become bankrupt, or where, the assured being a company, a winding up order has been made or a resolution for a voluntary winding up has been passed, no agreement made between the insurers and the assured after liability has been incurred to a third party and after the commencement of the bankruptcy or the winding up[1], and no waiver, assignment or other disposition made by, or payment made to, the assured after the commencement of the bankruptcy or winding up, is effective to defeat or affect the rights transferred to the third party by the Third Parties (Rights against Insurers) Act 1930[2], but those rights are the same as if no such agreement, waiver, assignment, disposition or payment had been made[3].

1 As to the date when a bankruptcy is deemed to commence see BANKRUPTCY AND INSOLVENCY vol 3(2) (Reissue) para 201. As to the date of commencement of winding up see COMPANIES vol 7(2) (Reissue) para 1488.

2 As to the rights transferred by the Third Parties (Rights against Insurers) Act 1930 see paras 679–682 ante.

3 Ibid s 3 (amended by the Insolvency Act 1985 s 235(1), Sch 8 para 7(4)).

(2) EMPLOYER'S LIABILITY INSURANCE

685. Compulsory insurance. Every employer carrying on any business in Great Britain must insure and maintain insurance under one or more approved policies with an authorised insurer or insurers against liability for bodily injury or disease sustained by his employees arising out of and in the course of their employment in Great Britain in that business[1]. Provision is made by regulations for securing that certificates of insurance in the prescribed form and containing the prescribed particulars are issued by insurers to employers[2]. An employer must comply with regulations as to the display of copies of the certificate[3].

1 Employers' Liability (Compulsory Insurance) Act 1969 s 1(1). For the meaning of 'business', 'approved policy', 'authorised insurer', 'employee' and 'Great Britain' in that Act see EMPLOYMENT vol 16 (Reissue) para 36 notes 1, 4, and 5, para 38 and para 2 note 6 respectively. As to the amount for which an employer is required to insure, the employees required to be covered, the employers exempted from insurance and the penalty for failure to insure see EMPLOYMENT vol 16 (Reissue) paras 36, 38, 40.

2 See ibid s 4(1); and EMPLOYMENT vol 16 (Reissue) para 41.

3 See ibid s 4(2)(a); and EMPLOYMENT vol 16 (Reissue) paras 42–43.

686. Form of employer's liability insurance. A policy of employer's liability insurance usually provides that if any person under a contract of service or apprenticeship with the assured sustains any personal injury by accident or disease caused during the period of insurance and arising out of and in the course of his employment[1] by the assured in the business which has been specified, and if the assured becomes liable to pay damages for that injury or disease, the insurers are to indemnify the assured against all sums for which the assured is so liable[2].

1 As to the meaning of 'arising out of and in the course of his employment' see *Vandyke v Fender (Sun Insurance Office Ltd, third party)* [1970] 2 QB 292, [1970] 2 All ER 335, CA; *Stitt v Woolley* (1971) 115 Sol Jo 708, CA; *Paterson v Costain* [1979] 2 Lloyd's Rep 204; and EMPLOYMENT vol 16 (Reissue) para 36 et seq.

2 See eg the form of policy cited in *Denham v Midland Employers' Mutual Assurance Ltd* [1955] 2 QB 437 at 438, [1955] 2 All ER 561 at 563, CA. An employer's liability policy is capable of being enforced by an undisclosed principal: *Siu Yin Kwan (Administratrix of the Estate of Chan Ying Lung decd) v Eastern Insurance Co Ltd* [1994] 2 WLR 370, PC (where policy taken out in the name of shipping agents did not name employers, employers could nevertheless have enforced it). As to employers' liability for injuries suffered by employees see generally EMPLOYMENT vol 16 (Reissue) para 29 et seq. For general provisions as to the health, safety and welfare of employees see HEALTH AND SAFETY vol 20 (Reissue) para 546 et seq. Where contractors were insured under an employer's liability policy containing an express stipulation limiting the insurance to cases where there is a contract of service or apprenticeship with the assured, and also under a public liability policy covering death or injury to persons other than persons under a contract of service or apprenticeship with them, and an unskilled labourer temporarily lent to them by a firm for which they were doing work was killed as a result of their negligence, they were held to be entitled to indemnity under the public liability policy and not under the employer's liability policy, as the labourer was not under a contract of service with them but with the firm for which they were doing the work: *Denham v Midland Employers' Mutual Assurance Ltd* supra; see also *Etchells, Congdon and Muir Ltd v Eagle, Star and British Dominions Insurance Co Ltd* (1928) 72 Sol Jo 242. It seems that liability to employees of sub-contractors, or to an independent contractor who has a contract to render services, would also in such a case be regarded as falling within the ambit of public liability insurance. As to the distinction between a contract of service and a contract for services see *Simmons v Heath Laundry Co* [1910] 1 KB 543, CA; *Wardell v Kent County Council* [1938] 2 KB 768, [1938] 3 All ER 473, CA.

687. Identification of business of assured.
A proposal for insurance against employer's liability usually contains a question as to the employer's trade or occupation. If the question is not accurately answered and the proposal is made the basis of the contract, the insurers will not be on risk at all unless an agent of theirs has knowledge of the true state of affairs and this knowledge can be imputed to them[1]. If questions are asked in the proposal as to the use of explosives or other dangerous substances in the course of the employer's business, a negative answer will readily be construed as a description of the risk and may amount to a warranty that such substances will not be used[2].

1 *Holdsworth v Lancashire and Yorkshire Insurance Co* (1907) 23 TLR 521. As to imputation of an agent's knowledge see paras 376–381 ante.
2 *Beauchamp v National Mutual Indemnity Insurance Co Ltd* [1937] 3 All ER 19.

688. Calculation of premiums.
It is usual to relate the premium to the amount paid in wages by the employer to his employees during each period of insurance, and to insert a provision for adjusting the premium at the end of the period when the figures can be accurately determined. To enable this to be done there is usually an express provision compelling the assured to keep a proper wages book, but it has been held that this is not to be regarded as a condition precedent[1]. The remedy of the insurers, therefore, is limited to suing for an account[2].

1 *Re Bradley and Essex and Suffolk Accident Indemnity Society* [1912] 1 KB 415, CA.

2 *General Accident Assurance Corpn v Day* (1904) 21 TLR 88. An account was ordered to be taken in *Garthwaite v Rowland* (1948) 81 Ll L Rep 417.

689. Obligation to take reasonable precautions. It is common to find in an employer's liability policy a condition requiring the assured to take reasonable precautions to prevent accidents[1], or to secure that all reasonable safeguards are provided and used[2]. The scope of such a provision has been much discussed[3], but it seems that it cannot be construed as taking away altogether, or even as seriously undermining, the cover which would otherwise be afforded against liability at common law, a liability which in its nature assumes the possibility of negligence[4]. It is a provision which, in any case, is stringently construed; it does not extend to negligence on the part of an employee of the assured[5], and the safeguards referred to are limited to material safeguards[6]; nor, even if so described, is it necessarily regarded as a condition precedent[7].

1 See eg *Woolfall and Rimmer Ltd v Moyle* [1942] 1 KB 66, [1941] 3 All ER 304, CA; *London Crystal Window Cleaning Co Ltd v National Mutual Indemnity Insurance Co Ltd* [1952] 2 Lloyd's Rep 360; *Fraser v B N Furman (Productions) Ltd (Miller Smith & Partners, third party)* [1967] 3 All ER 57, [1967] 1 WLR 898, CA; *Lane v Spratt* [1970] 2 QB 480, [1970] 1 All ER 162.
2 See eg *Concrete Ltd v Attenborough* (1939) 65 Ll L Rep 174.
3 See the cases cited in note 1 supra.
4 See *Beauchamp v National Mutual Indemnity Insurance Co Ltd* [1937] 3 All ER 19 at 23 per Finlay J.
5 *Woolfall and Rimmer Ltd v Moyle* [1942] 1 KB 66, [1941] 3 All ER 304, CA; *T F Maltby Ltd v Pelton SS Co Ltd* [1951] 2 All ER 954.
6 *Concrete Ltd v Attenborough* (1939) 65 Ll L Rep 174.
7 *Pictorial Machinery Ltd v Nicholls* (1940) 164 LT 248.

(3) PUBLIC LIABILITY INSURANCE

690. Nature of public liability insurance. The cover afforded by a public liability policy is normally an indemnity, usually with a pecuniary maximum as regards any one accident or as regards liability during any one period of insurance, against legal liability to members of the general public, as distinct from persons in the service of the assured or as distinct from such persons as members of the assured's family or household[1]. Employer's liability and public liability may be covered in one policy, for example in a householder's comprehensive policy, but in the case of industrial concerns the two risks are usually separately insured[2]. Public liability policies usually exclude liability for bodily injury sustained by employees or arising out of the use of vehicles, ships or aircraft or arising out of food or drink poisoning, and liabilities voluntarily assumed by contract. It is usual also to exclude losses caused by radioactive contamination[3].

1 As to the scope of an employer's liability policy and the matters which fall to be covered by a public liability policy see para 686 ante.
2 Employer's liability insurance is now compulsory; see para 685 ante.
3 As to the statutory obligation to make funds available to satisfy claims in connection with nuclear installations see the Nuclear Installations Act 1969 (as amended).

691. Terms and effect of public liability policy. A public liability policy normally contains restrictions of liability by reference to the type of business carried on by the assured[1]. Where a statement by the assured as to the methods used in carrying on that business is incorporated in the policy, the insurers may not be liable if an accident occurs while methods other than those stated are being used[2]. The general principles of liability insurance which have been previously indicated[3] are applicable to public liability insurance.

1 See eg *Concrete Ltd v Attenborough* (1939) 65 Ll L Rep 174 (builders); *Pictorial Machinery Ltd v Nicolls* (1940) 67 Ll L Rep 461 (printers' engineers and suppliers); *Denham v Midland Employers' Mutual Assurance Ltd* [1955] 2 QB 437, [1955] 2 All ER 561, CA (artesian well and civil engineering contractors); *Captain Boyton's World's Water Show Syndicate Ltd v Employers' Liability Assurance Corpn Ltd* (1895) 11 TLR 384, CA (showmen); *Wayne Tank and Pump Co Ltd v Employers' Liability Assurance Corpn* [1974] QB 57, [1973] 3 All ER 825, CA (manufacturers of equipment for storage of liquids); *Pickford and Black Ltd v Canadian General Insurance Co* (1976) 64 DLR (3d) 179 (Can SC) (stevedores); *South Staffordshire Tramways Co v Sickness and Accident Assurance Association* [1891] 1 QB 402, CA (tramway company); *Allen v London Guarantee and Accident Co Ltd* (1912) 28 TLR 254 (builder and contractor).

2 See para 431 ante.

3 See para 660 et seq ante.

(4) PROFESSIONAL INDEMNITY INSURANCE

692. Form of insurance. The form of insurance which is normally obtainable from insurers against the consequences of professional negligence and breach of professional duty[1] provides in the main clause for indemnity against loss from any claim or claims which may be made against the assured in respect of any negligent act, error or omission on the part of the assured or any of his partners or employees in the conduct of the business of the assured as a professional person[2]. The limitation by reference to the business is fundamental, as there may be wide variations of risk between one profession and another[3]. It is also fundamental, so far as the main clause of the cover is concerned[4], that the policy is an indemnity policy. The assured must prove a loss and cannot recover anything, or even make a claim against the insurers, until he has been found liable and so sustained a loss[5].

1 As to liability for professional negligence see generally NEGLIGENCE.

2 See eg *West Wake Price & Co v Ching* [1956] 3 All ER 821 at 823, [1957] 1 WLR 45 at 45. In *Haseldine v Hosken* [1933] 1 KB 822, CA, the policy covered loss arising from claims 'by reason of any neglect, omission or error'. In *Goddard and Smith v Frew* [1939] 4 All ER 358, CA, the policy covered loss arising from all actions, proceedings, claims and demands by reason of 'any act, neglect, omission, mis-statement or error'. For further examples see *Whitworth v Hosken* (1939) 65 Ll L Rep 48 (accountant); *Simon Warrender Pty Ltd v Swain* [1960] 2 Lloyd's Rep 111 (NSW SC) (insurance broker); *Davies v Hosken* [1937] 3 All ER 192 (solicitor); *Forney v Dominion Insurance Co Ltd* [1969] 3 All ER 831, [1969] 1 WLR 928 (solicitor; meaning of 'occurrence' in policy with limit in respect of any claim or number of claims arising out of the same occurrence: see also para 671 ante); *Maxwell v Price* [1960] 2 Lloyd's Rep 155 (Aust HC) (solicitor; policy covering negligent act committed by a solicitor prior to his joining insured firm); *Webb and Hughes v Bracey* [1964] 1 Lloyd's Rep 465 (solicitor).

3 As to circumstances affecting the risk see generally paras 430–431 ante.

4 As to subsidiary clauses which are not indemnity clauses see para 694 post.

5 *West Wake Price & Co v Ching* [1956] 3 All ER 821 at 825, [1957] 1 WLR 45 at 49 per Devlin J. As to the effect of the presence of a Queen's Counsel clause in the policy see paras 695–696 post.

693. Extent of the main indemnity clause. The main indemnity clause operates where the proximate cause of the loss is a claim of the type specified in the policy[1]. Thus, if the proximate cause of the loss is a criminal act by an employee of the assured, such as theft[2], or obtaining property by deception[3], this cannot be regarded as a negligent act, error or omission, and the policy does not apply[4]. If it is desired to insure against losses arising from that sort of contingency, a fidelity policy is required; a liability policy cannot be made to serve the dual purpose[5].

However the case may be framed against the assured by his client, it is the court's duty to ascertain by reference to the ascertainable facts what the real essence of the case is. This can normally be done by waiting until the liability on the part of the assured is made good; the nature of the findings will then be conclusive as between the assured and his insurers, because it is the liability, as ultimately found, of the assured which is the foundation of the liability of the insurers. If, however it may be framed, the client's case is found ultimately to rest upon the dishonesty of an employee of the assured, the insurers will not be liable under a professional negligence policy[6].

1 *Goddard and Smith v Frew* [1939] 4 All ER 358 at 361, CA, per Scott LJ; see also *West Wake Price & Co v Ching* [1956] 3 All ER 821 at 825, 831, [1957] 1 WLR 45 at 49–50, 58 per Devlin J, commenting on the dictum of Lindley LJ in *Reischer v Borwick* [1894] 2 QB 548 at 551, CA, to the effect that there may be two proximate causes. See also para 176 ante.
2 As to the nature of theft see CRIMINAL LAW vol 11(1) (Reissue) para 541 et seq.
3 As to the nature of obtaining property by deception see CRIMINAL LAW vol 11(1) (Reissue) para 567.
4 *West Wake Price & Co v Ching* [1956] 3 All ER 821, [1957] 1 WLR 45. Cf *Simon Warrender Pty Ltd v Swain* [1960] 2 Lloyd's Rep 111 (NSW SC).
5 *Goddard and Smith v Frew* [1939] 4 All ER 358 at 361, CA, per Scott and Goddard LJJ. As to fidelity insurance see para 768 et seq post.
6 See *West Wake Price & Co v Ching* [1956] 3 All ER 821, [1957] 1 WLR 45, where the court's duty was considered in relation to a policy containing a Queen's Counsel clause. See further para 696 post.

694. Subsidiary cover for the cost of legal proceedings. Policies covering professional negligence always include a provision for payment of the costs of legal proceedings. It would indeed be commercially impracticable for insurers to insist on liability being established against the assured before they are prepared to accept liability, and at the same time to expect the assured to bear the cost of contesting proceedings which he might well think were incontestible. A clause of this kind has been compared to the suing and labouring clause[1] in a policy of marine insurance. It is not part of the contract of strict indemnity, and performance of it by the insurers does not involve them in any liability; if the action succeeds, a loss will be proved, but it is still open to the insurers to assert that the loss is not within the policy[2]. Part of the consideration for the contract is, however, that the insurers, if they insist on full proof, should bear the cost incurred. In other words, it is a case of a contingency insurance, the contingency being the making of the claim, and the sum to be paid in that contingency being the cost of contesting it[3]. A limit in a policy in respect of any claim or number of claims arising out of the same occurrence applies to all liability whether in respect of damages or costs[4].

1 As to the suing and labouring clause see paras 259–262 ante.
2 *West Wake Price & Co v Ching* [1956] 3 All ER 821 at 826, [1957] 1 WLR 45 at 50.
3 *West Wake Price & Co v Ching* [1956] 3 All ER 821 at 826, [1957] 1 WLR 45 at 50–51.
4 *Forney v Dominion Insurance Co Ltd* [1969] 3 All ER 831, [1969] 1 WLR 928; see also para 671 ante.

695. The effect of the Queen's Counsel clause. A professional man may object to facing litigation which, whether it is successful or not, may be damaging to his reputation[1]. The generally accepted solution of this difficulty is found in a clause in a policy against liability for professional negligence which provides that a claim will be paid without requiring the assured to contest it unless a Queen's Counsel to be mutually agreed on advises that the claim can be contested successfully[2]. In practice this means that the insurers have to pay unless the selected Queen's Counsel feels able to advise, not merely that there is a fair, or a reasonable, prospect of success, but that the balance is considerably weighted in favour of the assured's success[3]. The insurer's liability in such a case has been said to bear some similarity to the concept in marine insurance of constructive total loss[4]. The clause frequently further provides that the claim is not to be contested unless the assured consents, but that his consent is not to be unreasonably withheld[5]. The basic nature of the provision is essentially that of a contingency insurance, the contingency being the making of the claim and the circumstances making it reasonable not to contest it[6].

1 *West Wake Price & Co v Ching* [1956] 3 All ER 821 at 828, [1957] 1 WLR 45 at 53.
2 For the form of such a clause see *West Wake Price & Co v Ching* [1956] 3 All ER 821 at 823, [1957] 1 WLR 45 at 46.
3 In *West Wake Price & Co v Ching* [1956] 3 All ER 821 at 826, [1957] 1 WLR 45 at 50–51, Devlin J expressed this by saying that 'it is more likely than not that there will be a loss, the question of likelihood being determined by a Queen's Counsel'. In practice, however, a mere balance of likelihood is not regarded by Queen's Counsel who advise in this capacity as sufficient; they will not normally allow a professional man to go to court unless they feel reasonably confident in the prospects of rebutting the charges.
4 *West Wake Price & Co v Ching* [1956] 3 All ER 821 at 826, [1957] 1 WLR 45 at 50 per Devlin J. As to constructive total loss see para 292 et seq ante.
5 For the form of such a provision see *West Wake Price & Co v Ching* [1956] 3 All ER 821 at 823, [1957] 1 WLR 45 at 46.
6 *West Wake Price & Co v Ching* [1956] 3 All ER 821 at 826, [1957] 1 WLR 45 at 51 per Devlin J.

696. The Queen's Counsel clause and the mixed claim. As has been previously indicated[1], difficulties may arise wherever a claim can, so far as the client is concerned, be established without going outside the strict words of the policy as to a negligent act, error or omission, although the foundation of the claim may be dishonesty or criminality never contemplated as coming within such a policy at all[2]. These difficulties are enhanced where the scope of the Queen's Counsel clause is under consideration, as in such a case there will obviously be no record or judgment in any proceedings by the client against the assured to be studied. The court, however, is not precluded by the form in which the claim is put forward, or the cause of action which is in fact pleaded, from seeking to ascertain what the real cause of the loss is[3]. If the result of this examination indicates that the claim can properly be described as a mixed claim, with elements of negligence and fraud or dishonesty inextricably intermingled, the Queen's Counsel clause does not apply[4].

1 See para 693 ante.
2 As to the extent of the main indemnity clause see para 693 ante.
3 *West Wake Price & Co v Ching* [1956] 3 All ER 821 at 828, [1957] 1 WLR 45 at 53.
4 *West Wake Price & Co v Ching* [1956] 3 All ER 821, [1957] 1 WLR 45.

697. Criminal acts of the assured. Apart from the question whether criminality on the part of an employee is covered by a professional negligence policy[1], the general rule of public policy is that a person cannot recover an indemnity under an insurance policy in respect of deliberate conduct on his part which is against the criminal law[2]. Different considerations probably arise where a breach of the law, even of the criminal law, arises not so much from the inherent nature of something deliberately done, but from inadvertence, stupidity, ignorance or even reckless folly[3].

1 As to this question see para 693 ante.

2 See para 693 ante; and as to the illegality of contracts to commit a legal wrong see generally CONTRACT vol 9 para 389. As to the application of the rule to life insurance see para 530 ante; and as to motor insurance see para 711 post.

3 Cf *Tinline v White Cross Insurance Association* [1921] 3 KB 327; *James v British General Insurance Co* [1927] 2 KB 311.

(5) BAILEE'S INSURANCE

698. Insurable interest of a bailee. There are many different classes of commercial activity in which, from the point of view of the law, one person becomes a bailee of goods belonging to another. The commonest examples are a carrier (whether by sea, land, air, or any two or more of these means of transport), a wharfinger, a warehouseman, an artificer who does work on other people's goods, a pawnbroker and an innkeeper[1]. One feature of the position under the common law of such a bailee is that he commonly has a lien for his charges or expenses, and by virtue of this lien he is accepted as having an insurable interest in the goods bailed, not merely to the extent of his charges or expenses as at any given date, but up to the full value of the goods[2]. Furthermore, even if he has no lien, he has an insurable interest founded upon the commission[3], profit[4] or other advantages[5] which he may expect to derive from the bailment, and in that case also he is entitled to insure up to the full value provided there is evidence to indicate that his intention was to cover, on behalf of the owner, the owner's interest over and above his own limited interest[6].

1 As to bailees see generally BAILMENT. As to particular examples of bailees see eg CARRIERS; INNS; and PLEDGES AND PAWNS.

2 *Waters v Monarch Fire and Life Assurance Co* (1856) 5 E & B 870; *London and North Western Rly Co v Glyn* (1859) 1 E & E 652; *North British and Mercantile Insurance Co v Moffatt* (1871) LR 7 CP 25 at 31; *Maurice v Goldsbrough Mort & Co Ltd* [1939] AC 452 at 461–462, [1939] 3 All ER 63 at 68, PC; *Hepburn v A. Tomlinson (Hauliers) Ltd* [1966] AC 451, [1966] 1 All ER 418, HL. See also *Ebsworth v Alliance Marine Insurance Co* (1873) LR 8 CP 596 at 629 per Bovill CJ and Denman J, where the court was equally divided as to the extent of the insurable interest, and the right to recover, of a consignee who had advanced money on the security of goods; on appeal in this case, by arrangement between the parties, the court ordered the damages entered for the consignees to be reduced to a sum representing their personal pecuniary interest: see (1874) 43 LJCP 394n. As to the authority of consignees to insure see para 98 text and note 6 ante. As to the principle that it is unnecessary for a bailee to describe his interest see para 617 ante. As to the principle that anything above the bailee's accrued costs, charges and expenses must be handed over to the owners of the goods see para 702 post.

3 *Castellain v Preston* (1883) 11 QBD 380 at 398, CA, per Bowen LJ.

4 *Dalgleish v Buchanan* (1854) 16 Dunl 332, Ct of Sess.

5 *Trotter v Watson* (1869) LR 4 CP 434 at 444 per Bovill CJ (tenant of furnished house has insurable interest in the furniture).

6 *Castellain v Preston* (1883) 11 QBD 380 at 392, CA, per Bowen LJ. In *Hepburn v A Tomlinson (Hauliers) Ltd* [1966] AC 451, [1966] 1 All ER 418, HL, the court doubted the existence of a rule allowing it to look behind the words of the policy in order to discover the intention of the bailees when they took out the policy. As to insurances for the benefit of several interests see paras 615 ante, 699 post.

699. Legal liability of a bailee. Quite apart from his interest by virtue of his lien or otherwise, unless there are special terms of his contract to the contrary, a bailee may be legally liable to the owner if the subject matter of the bailment is damaged or destroyed[1]. The existence of this potential liability has equally been accepted as sufficient to provide the bailee with an insurable interest up to the full value[2]. Again, where a bailee assumes the obligation to insure goods while in his possession, he will be answerable in damages if he fails to insure, and this obligation gives him an insurable interest up to the full value[3]. It is not always easy to determine whether a bailee is intending to insure other interests as well as his own, in which case rights of contribution might arise if the other interests are collaterally insured[4], or whether he is insuring on a liability basis so as to preclude any question of contribution, at any rate so far as insurers of different interests are concerned[5]. Sometimes the policy makes it clear whether the insurance is on a title basis, so that as regards any proceeds over and above his own limited interest the bailee holds as trustee for the owner, or on a liability basis, so that the limit of the bailee's right of recovery is to the extent of his liability, if any, to the owner[6]. Often, however, this ambiguity is left unresolved so far as the form of the policy is concerned.

1 As to the degree of care demanded of particular classes of bailee, and the onus of proof in the case of loss or damage to the subject matter of the bailment, see BAILMENT vol 2 (Reissue) paras 1803, 1815, 1839, 1869 et seq. As to the liability of common carriers and innkeepers for the safety of property see CARRIERS vol 5(1) (Reissue) para 446 et seq; INNS vol 24 (Reissue) para 1125 et seq.

2 *North British and Mercantile Insurance Co v London, Liverpool and Globe Insurance Co* (1877) 5 ChD 569 at 583–584, CA, per Mellish LJ; *Castellain v Preston* (1883) 11 QBD 380 at 398, CA, per Bowen LJ.

3 *Maurice v Goldsbrough Mort & Co* [1939] AC 452 at 461, [1939] 3 All ER 63 at 68, PC.

4 As to contribution see paras 520–521 ante.

5 *North British and Mercantile Insurance Co v London, Liverpool and Globe Insurance Co* (1877) 5 ChD 569, CA.

6 *Hepburn v A Tomlinson (Hauliers) Ltd* [1966] AC 451, [1966] 1 All ER 418, HL; and see para 700 post.

700. Basis of bailee's policy. The usual form of insurance for a bailee, whatever the nature of the bailment, takes the form of indicating: (1) the perils against which the insurance is to be operative, such as fire[1], burglary, theft[2] or mere loss[3]; (2) the business carried on by the assured[4] in connection with which the loss must have occurred; and (3) the goods in respect of which the policy is to be effective. An insurance simply on 'goods' will cover the interest of the assured as a bailee[5]; but the goods covered are usually described by terms such as 'goods in trust'[6], 'goods on commission'[7] or 'goods in transit'[8], which are coupled frequently with the qualification 'for which the assured is responsible'[9].

1 As to the perils covered by fire insurance see para 591 ante.

2 As to the perils covered by burglary and theft insurance see paras 644–647 ante.

3 As to what constitutes a loss see paras 658–659 ante.

4 As to the effect of a limitation by reference to the assured's business see para 664 ante.

5 *London and North Western Rly Co v Glyn* (1859) 1 E & E 652 at 664 per Crompton J; see also para 617 ante.

6 As to 'goods in trust' see para 701 post.

7 As to 'goods on commission' see para 702 post.

8 As to 'goods in transit' see *Crows Transport Ltd v Phoenix Assurance Co Ltd* [1965] 1 All ER 596, [1965] 1 WLR 383, CA; and para 705 post.

9 As to goods 'for which the assured is responsible' see para 703 post.

701. Goods in trust. The term 'goods in trust' is not used in any technical sense as indicating that the bailee becomes in equity a trustee of the goods[1], although he will be a trustee for the owner of the goods of any money received over and above his interest[2]. The words are used in the ordinary commercial sense to indicate goods entrusted to the bailee[3], so that goods left with a seller by a buyer after the property has passed are covered[4]. Similarly, where carriers who had undertaken to carry goods for the owner as and when transport became available handed a collection order to a person pretending to be a driver employed by one of the carriers' sub-contractors, thus enabling that person to obtain delivery of a consignment of goods and steal them, the goods were held to have been entrusted to the carriers, and even though the fraudulent driver had no valid authority, as between himself and the carriers, to receive the goods, the act of giving him the collection order for presentation to the owner operated as an offer by the carriers to carry that consignment[5]. Where, however, there is no obligation to return the goods, as where a farmer sends corn to a miller with an option to receive either an equal quantity of corn of the same type and quality or the value in cash of the corn sent, the essence of the transaction is a sale and not an entrusting at all[6].

 1 *Waters v Monarch Fire and Life Insurance Co* (1856) 5 E & B 870 at 880 per Lord Campbell CJ.
 2 *Waters v Monarch Fire and Life Insurance Co* (1856) 5 E & B 870 at 881 per Lord Campbell CJ.
 3 *Waters v Monarch Fire and Life Insurance Co* (1856) 5 E & B 870; *London and North Western Rly Co v Glyn* (1859) 1 E & E 652.
 4 *North British and Mercantile Insurance Co v Moffatt* (1871) LR 7 CP 25 at 30 per Keating J.
 5 *John Rigby (Haulage) Ltd v Reliance Marine Insurance Co Ltd* [1956] 2 QB 468, [1956] 3 All ER 1, CA; *Crows Transport Ltd v Phoenix Assurance Co Ltd* [1965] 1 All ER 596, [1965] 1 WLR 383, CA.
 6 *South Australian Insurance Co v Randell* (1869) LR 3 PC 101; cf *Genn v Winkel* (1912) 107 LT 434, CA.

702. Goods on commission. The term 'goods on commission' is normally used to indicate goods entrusted to the bailee for some specific purpose, such as doing some specified work on them, or, more usually, holding them as agent for the purpose of earning a commission by selling them[1]. This does not, however, mean that the commission as such is recoverable; any commission expected to be earned is a profit, and loss of profit must always be specifically insured[2]. If goods are insured as goods held in trust or on commission, the value of the goods is normally recoverable in the event of their loss or destruction by a peril covered by the insurance[3], but anything over and above the bailee's accrued costs, charges and expenses must be handed over to the owners[4].

 1 *Waters v Monarch Fire and Life Insurance Co* (1856) 5 E & B 870 at 879 per Lord Campbell CJ; *North British and Mercantile Insurance Co v Moffatt* (1871) LR 7 CP 25.
 2 *Maurice v Goldsbrough Mort & Co Ltd* [1939] AC 452, [1939] 3 All ER 63, PC; *Lucena v Craufurd* (1806) 2 Bos & PNR 269; *Mackenzie v Whitworth* (1875) 1 ExD 36 at 43; *Stockdale v Dunlop* (1840) 6 M & W 224 at 232 per Parke B. As to insurance in respect of loss of profits see para 786 post.
 3 See the cases cited in para 698 note 2 ante.
 4 *Maurice v Goldsbrough Mort & Co Ltd* [1939] AC 452, [1939] 3 All ER 63, PC.

703. Goods for which the assured is responsible. To the general phrase 'goods in trust or on commission' there is frequently added the additional phrase 'for which the assured is responsible'. These words were derived from a suggestion[1] that if insurers wished to limit their responsibility to the responsibility of the assured they must use express words to that effect[2]. The words then came to be used and were held to achieve the desired result[3]. Where a seller holds goods after the property and the risk have passed, the goods cease to be goods for which he is responsible[4]; plainly the intention in such a case is that the buyer should effect any necessary insurance. Similarly, where a bailee is only liable for negligence and goods are lost or destroyed without any negligence on his part, there is no legal liability of the kind envisaged by these added words[5]. The addition of these words therefore has the effect of making the policy not so much an insurance on an interest but a liability insurance. The position is made quite plain if the policy indicates that the subject matter of the insurance is the legal liability of the bailee, not loss of or damage to goods[6].

1 See *London and North Western Rly Co v Glyn* (1859) 1 E & E 652 at 663 per Erle J, and at 665 per Hill J.
2 For the principle that in the absence of such a limitation the assured is entitled to recover the full value of the goods see para 699 ante.
3 *North British and Mercantile Insurance Co v Moffatt* (1871) LR 7 CP 25.
4 *North British and Mercantile Insurance Co v Moffatt* (1871) LR 7 CP 25.
5 *Engel v Lancashire and General Assurance Co Ltd* (1925) 41 TLR 408.
6 See the form in *John Rigby (Haulage) Ltd v Reliance Marine Insurance Co Ltd* [1956] 2 QB 468, [1956] 3 All ER 1, CA.

704. Floating policies. A bailee such as a warehouseman[1] may have goods constantly coming into and going out of his possession, and it is hardly practicable to effect a new insurance each time a parcel of goods comes in and to cancel it when the goods are removed. In such cases, therefore, it is common to have a floating policy covering all goods in the bailee's possession at the time of loss, usually with a named figure as the maximum covered[2]. Another variation is a 'declaration' policy under which the assured merely has to declare from time to time the goods on risk[3]. The widest form of policy is an 'open' policy covering all risks by sea, land and air, where the obligation is to declare goods as soon as the assured learns they are at his risk, which may be no sooner than he learns of their loss[4].

1 For the meaning of 'warehouse' see *Leo Rapp Ltd v McClure* [1955] 1 Lloyd's Rep 292. For the meaning of 'goods in store' see *Wulfson v Switzerland General Insurance Co Ltd* [1940] 3 All ER 221.
2 See *Crowley v Cohen* (1832) 3 B & Ad 478; *Joyce v Kennard* (1871) LR 7 QB 78; *Ewing & Co v Sicklemore* (1918) 35 TLR 55, CA.
3 See eg *Rivaz v Gerussi* (1880) 6 QBD 222.
4 *Davies v National Fire and Marine Insurance Co of New Zealand* [1891] AC 485, PC.

705. Insurance of goods by carrier. A carrier's potential liability to the owner is a peril against which insurance is normally required, and is the foundation of his having an insurable interest up to the full value of the goods[1]. The goods covered are usually described by a term such as 'goods in trust'[2].

Ordinary burglary insurance covers property stolen from particular premises only[3], but property may be covered in transit. In such a case the loss must be sustained in the course of the transit described in the policy[4]. Goods delivered to the carrier and stolen while awaiting loading are lost in the course of transit[5], and a mere delivery at the place of destination is not necessarily a termination of the transit, for the transit continues until the goods come into the possession of the consignee[6]. Where, under the terms of the policy, transit is to include loading and unloading, the goods remain on risk until the completion of the unloading[7].

Goods cease to be in transit when they are on a journey which is not in reasonable furtherance of their carriage to their ultimate destination[8]. The policy may contain a warranty that is not to apply if the vehicle carrying the goods is left 'unattended'[9].

1 See *North British and Mercantile Insurance Co v London, Liverpool and Globe Insurance Co* (1877) 5 ChD 569 at 583–584, CA, per Mellish LJ; and para 698 ante.

2 As to goods in trust see para 701 ante.
3 As to the limitation of risk by reference to locality in burglary insurance see para 650 ante.
4 *Richardson v Roylance* (1933) 50 TLR 99; *London Tobacco Co (Overseas) Ltd v DFDS Transport Ltd* [1993] 2 Lloyd's Rep 306.
5 *Crows Transport Ltd v Phoenix Assurance Co Ltd* [1965] 1 All ER 596, [1965] 1 WLR 383, CA.
6 See *Heinekey v Earle* (1857) 8 E & B 410 at 423 per Lord Campbell CJ.
7 *Hepburn v A Tomlinson (Hauliers) Ltd* [1966] AC 451, [1966] 1 All ER 418, HL.
8 *S C A (Freight) Ltd v Gibson* [1974] 2 Lloyd's Rep 533.
9 See eg *Plaistow Transport Ltd v Graham* [1966] 1 Lloyd's Rep 639; *Ingleton of Ilford Ltd v General Accident, Fire and Life Assurance Corpn Ltd* [1967] 2 Lloyd's Rep 179; *J Lowenstein & Co Ltd v Poplar Motor Transport (Lymm) Ltd (Gooda, third party)* [1968] 2 Lloyd's Rep 233; *A Cohen & Co Ltd v Plaistow Transport Ltd (Graham, third party)* [1968] 2 Lloyd's Rep 587.

9. MOTOR VEHICLE INSURANCE

(1) NATURE AND SCOPE OF INSURANCE

706. Composite nature of insurance. In any of its various forms a motor insurance policy is a composite insurance unless it is limited to the risks which are compulsorily insurable by statute[1]. It always starts by reference to a particular car[2], whether it is a specified car or a car of a specified class, or one of a fleet of cars which may be individually declared, if so required, from time to time, and is normally limited in essence to use of this car. It may, therefore, contain either the bare minimum cover without which a car cannot lawfully be used on a road at all[3] or any one or more of a number of variations in addition. Therefore, the scope of the insurance falls to be considered under the various types of insurance which a normal policy may contain.

1 As to the risks compulsorily insurable by statute see paras 733–737 post. For forms of policy see 20 Forms & Precedents (5th Edn) 549–568, Forms 311–312.
2 See *Rogerson v Scottish Automobile and General Insurance Co Ltd* (1931) 48 TLR 17, HL; *Tattersall v Drysdale* [1935] 2 KB 174. The ownership of the specified vehicle is the foundation of the insurable interest without which the policy is unenforceable even under an extension clause covering the assured while driving another vehicle: *Williams v Baltic Insurance Association of London Ltd* [1924] 2 KB 282 at 290.
3 See para 707 post.

707. Types of insurance afforded. Between the bare minimum of insurance required by statute and the most comprehensive insurance which may be obtained under a motor policy, there is a wide difference, both in the scope of cover afforded and in the premium which is required. The main heads of insurance may be summarised as follows.

(1) A Road Traffic Act policy is one which contains the bare minimum requirements of cover if a car is to be legally usable on a public road at all, namely cover against legal liability to third parties in respect of bodily injury or death or damage to property within the limited categories laid down by the Road Traffic Act 1988[1].

(2) A third party liability policy may provide cover against legal liability for bodily injury to or death of any third party, even if he is not within the limited categories laid down by the Road Traffic Act 1988, for example where liability to employees carried pursuant to a contract of employment is covered[2].

(3) Third party liability cover (limited or general) may be coupled with an insurance on the vehicle itself (including accessories) against fire and theft.

(4) Third party liability cover (limited or general) may be coupled with an insurance on the vehicle, not merely against fire and theft but also against loss or damage however caused[3]. Where unlimited third party cover is afforded, together with full cover of the vehicle against any sort of loss or damage, the policy is usually described as 'fully comprehensive'.

(5) A clause may contain provision for loss of profits during loss of use of a profit-earning vehicle (such as a bus or lorry) which is destroyed or damaged and cannot be replaced or repaired without an interval during which the profits it would have earned are lost[4].

(6) A clause may contain a degree of personal accident insurance by affording compensation for injuries or death sustained by the assured himself by reason of his use of the car[5].

(7) A common extension clause is the 'permitted driver clause' by which cover against third party liability (limited or general) is afforded to any person driving the insured car with the permission of the assured[6].

(8) Another common extension clause affords cover to the assured, within the scope of the policy, while driving any other vehicle[7].

1 As to the minimum statutory requirements see paras 733–737 post.
2 As to liability insurance see generally para 660 et seq ante.
3 As to property insurance see generally para 591 et seq ante.
4 As to insurance against loss of profits see generally para 786 post.
5 As to personal accident insurance see generally para 567 et seq ante.
6 As to the 'permitted driver clause' see paras 720–722 post.
7 See para 507 ante.

708. Indemnity as basis of contract. A contract of motor insurance is mainly a contract of indemnity[1]. This means that, so far as concerns the insurance of the car as an example of property insurance or the insurance of third party liability (whether limited or general) as an example of public liability insurance, the ordinary principles of these classes of insurance are applicable[2]. However, in so far as clauses provide for insurance cover not in the nature of an indemnity, as where provision is made for the death or disablement of the assured himself, the principles of life insurance or personal accident insurance will apply[3].

1 *British Cash and Parcel Conveyors Ltd v Lamson Store Service Co Ltd* [1908] 1 KB 1006 at 1014, CA, per Fletcher Moulton LJ; *Weld-Blundell v Stephens* [1919] 1 KB 520 at 529, CA, per Bankes LJ; affd [1920] AC 956, HL.
2 As to property insurance see generally para 591 et seq ante. As to public liability insurance see generally paras 690–691 ante. Notwithstanding anything in any enactment, a person issuing a policy of insurance under the Road Traffic Act 1988 s 145 (as amended) (see paras 731, 733–735 post), is liable to indemnify the persons or classes of persons specified in the policy in respect of any liability which the policy purports to cover in the case of those persons or classes of persons: s 148(7); see para 738 post. 'Policy of insurance' includes a covering note: s 161(1).
3 As to life insurance see generally para 525 et seq ante. As to personal accident insurance see generally para 567 et seq ante. For the principle that contracts of life insurance and personal accident insurance are not contracts of indemnity see para 4 ante.

709. Nature of public liability risk. Legal liability arising out of the use of a car on a highway is usually founded on negligence[1], either in the management and control of the car on the road or in its maintenance and upkeep as a vehicle intended to be used on the road[2]. Technically, a claim may be founded on nuisance, but there is seldom any practicable advantage to be derived from such a plea; the presence of a motor vehicle on the highway, even as an obstruction owing to a breakdown, will only be regarded as a nuisance if the obstruction continues for an unreasonable time or in unreasonable circumstances[3].

1 *Tinline v White Cross Insurance Association* [1921] 3 KB 327 at 331 per Bailhache J. Where the personal injury to a victim of a road accident is inflicted unintentionally, his only cause of action at the present day lies in negligence and not in trespass: *Letang v Cooper* [1965] 1 QB 232, [1964] 2 All ER 929, CA.
2 Conditions requiring the assured to take reasonable care to maintain the car in efficient condition are not unusual and their validity has been upheld: see para 714 post.
3 *Maitland v R T and J Raisbeck and Hewitt Ltd* [1944] KB 689, [1944] 2 All ER 272, CA; distinguishing and explaining *Ware v Garston Haulage Co Ltd* [1944] 1 KB 30, [1943] 2 All ER 558, CA; cf *Hill-Venning v Beszant* [1950] 2 All ER 1151, CA; and see generally NUISANCE.

710. Causation as the basis of public liability risk. Under a policy couched in the language normally used it is not necessary for the car itself to be directly involved in an accident involving injury to the person or property of a third party. It is usually sufficient if negligence in the control, management or maintenance of the car is a cause of the damage claimed[1]. It is, of course, essential that the injury or damage caused falls within the terms of the cover afforded by the policy[2].

1 *Captain Boyton's World's Water Show Syndicate Ltd v Employers' Liability Assurance Corpn Ltd* (1895) 11 TLR 384, CA.
2 *Tinline v White Cross Insurance Association* [1921] 3 KB 327 at 332 per Bailhache J.

711. Negligence and public policy. A motor policy is not void as being contrary to public policy because it purports to cover the driver against the consequences of his own negligence; indeed, as evidenced by the relevant legislation, public policy seems to demand that compensation should be available to the victims of the negligent use of motor vehicles[1]. Accordingly, the indemnity under the policy is valid and enforceable whether the result of the negligence is bodily injury[2] or death[3], whether the negligence established is that of an employee[4] or of the assured himself[5], and even though the negligence, where it results in the death of a third party, is so gross as to amount to manslaughter[6]. However, where injury to a third party is caused by a deliberately calculated act, the assured cannot obtain indemnity from his insurers[7]. The mere fact that a vehicle is being used illegally does not invalidate an insurance policy taken out in relation to the vehicle in so far as the policy insures the owner of the vehicle against the consequences of the vehicle being negligently driven as distinct from the consequences of illegal use[8].

1 As to compulsory motor vehicle insurance see para 729 et seq post.
2 See *Tinline v White Cross Insurance Association* [1921] 3 KB 327.
3 See *Tinline v White Cross Insurance Association* [1921] 3 KB 327; *James v British General Insurance Co* [1927] 2 KB 311.
4 *A-G v Adelaide SS Co Ltd* [1923] AC 292 at 308, HL, per Lord Wrenbury.
5 *Tinline v White Cross Insurance Association* [1921] 3 KB 327.
6 *Tinline v White Cross Insurance Association* [1921] 3 KB 327; *James v British General Insurance Co* [1927] 2 KB 311. The doubts felt about these decisions (see *Haseldine v Hosken* [1933] 1 KB 822 at 833, CA, per Scrutton LJ, and at 838 per Greer LJ) can no longer be entertained except in so far as the decision in question might tend to suggest that an assured can get indemnity against his own intentional act of illegality: see *Marles v Philip Trant & Sons Ltd* [1954] 1 QB 29 at 39, [1953] 1 All ER 651 at 659, CA, per Denning LJ, and at 44 and 662 per Hodson LJ.

7 *Tinline v White Cross Insurance Association* [1921] 3 KB 327 at 333 per Bailhache J; *Marles v Philip Trant & Sons Ltd* [1954] 1 QB 29 at 44, [1953] 1 All ER 651 at 662, CA, per Hodson LJ; see also *Beresford v Royal Insurance Co Ltd* [1938] AC 586 at 595, [1938] 2 All ER 602 at 604, HL, per Lord Atkin; *Gray v Barr (Prudential Assurance Co Ltd, third party)* [1971] 2 QB 554, [1971] 2 All ER 949, CA.

8 *Leggate v Brown* [1950] 2 All ER 564, DC. As to the effect of user not permitted by the policy see para 712 post.

(2) STIPULATIONS DEFINING THE RISK

712. Definition of risk by reference to use. A motor policy usually contains, either in express terms or by incorporation of the proposal[1], a statement or description of the purposes for which the vehicle may be used. Such a statement or description has the effect of defining the risk, so that the insurers are liable only in respect of accidents occurring while the vehicle is being used for a stipulated purpose[2]. Therefore, if the vehicle is used for a different purpose, there is a different risk which is uninsured, and, if the accident happens while the vehicle is being so used, the assured is not entitled to recover[3]. However, in the absence of a clear provision to that effect, the use of the vehicle for an unpermitted purpose does not give the insurers a right to avoid the policy altogether for all time and for all purposes; the result is merely to suspend the operation of the policy for the duration of the unpermitted use[4]. As soon, therefore, as the unpermitted use ceases and use for a permitted purpose is resumed, the policy again attaches, and the assured is not precluded from recovering in respect of an accident which occurs during a permitted use merely because, at some earlier time, he had put himself outside the scope of his insurance[5].

1 As to the incorporation of the proposal see para 374 ante.
2 *Farr v Motor Traders' Mutual Insurance Society* [1920] 3 KB 669, CA; *Roberts v Anglo-Saxon Insurance Association* (1927) 137 LT 243, CA; *Provincial Insurance Co Ltd v Morgan* [1933] AC 240, HL.
3 *Roberts v Anglo-Saxon Insurance Association* (1927) 137 LT 243, CA; *Murray v Scottish Automobile and General Insurance Co Ltd* 1929 SC 49; cf *Stuart v Horse Insurance Co* (1893) 1 SLT 108.
4 As to a change in the circumstances comprised in the definition of the risk see para 436 ante.
5 *Farr v Motor Traders' Mutual Insurance Society* [1920] 3 KB 669, CA; *Provincial Insurance Co Ltd v Morgan* [1933] AC 240, HL.

713. Prohibition by reference to type of use. A motor policy often contains a clause expressly excluding use of the vehicle for certain purposes. This is not necessary if there is an adequate statement or description of what is included, but it is not unusual to find both a description of what is included and a clause expressly excluding use for particular purposes. Thus, use for business purposes may be prohibited, either partially[1] or entirely[2], or certain types of business, such as the motor trade[3], may be specifically excluded. Again, use for hire or reward is commonly excluded[4], as also is racing or pace-making[5].

1 *Pailor v Co-operative Insurance Society* (1930) 38 Ll L Rep 237, CA (use for assured's business not extended to permitted driver); *Passmore v Vulcan Boiler and General Insurance Co Ltd* (1935) 52 TLR 193 (use in assured's business covered, but not if coupled with some other person's business); *Jones v Welsh Insurance Corpn Ltd* [1937] 4 All ER 149 (use for only one business permitted); *D H R Moody (Chemists) Ltd v Iron Trades Mutual Insurance Co Ltd* [1971] 1 Lloyd's Rep 386 (use in assured's business only covered).
2 *Piddington v Co-operative Insurance Society Ltd* [1934] 2 KB 236.
3 *Gray v Blackmore* [1934] 1 KB 95; *Browning v Phoenix Assurance Co Ltd* [1960] 2 Lloyd's Rep 360.

4 *Wyatt v Guildhall Insurance Co Ltd* [1937] 1 KB 653, [1937] 1 All ER 792; *Bonham v Zurich General Accident and Liability Insurance Co Ltd* [1945] KB 292, [1945] 1 All ER 427, CA; *Orr v Trafalgar Insurance Co Ltd* (1948) 82 Ll L Rep 1, CA. Cf *McCarthy v British Oak Insurance Co Ltd* [1938] 3 All ER 1; *East Midland Traffic Area Traffic Comrs v Tyler* [1938] 3 All ER 39, DC.

5 For the meaning of 'racing' see *Alliance Aeroplane Co Ltd v Union Insurance Society of Canton Ltd* (1920) 5 Ll L Rep 341, 406 (a case relating to an aircraft).

714. Prohibition by reference to state of vehicle. A motor policy often contains a prohibition against using the vehicle at all in a particular condition. Thus, it is usually provided that the vehicle is not to be used in a damaged or unsafe condition[1]. If the language is clear and unambiguous, the prohibition will apply even if the assured did not know of the unsafe condition[2], nor will it be limited to the condition of the car at the commencement of the journey[3]. Similarly, there may be prohibitions against towing another vehicle[4] or a trailer[5], against using a motor cycle without a sidecar attached[6] or carrying a passenger without a sidecar[7]. Again, there may be a prohibition against carrying a load in excess of that for which the vehicle is constructed[8] but, if so worded, the prohibition only applies where there is a specific weight which must not be exceeded[9]; it does not cover a case of an excessive number of passengers[10]. Sometimes there is a prohibition against carrying goods[11] or passengers[12]. All these prohibitions operate as a further description or definition of the risk[13].

1 See *Jenkins v Deane* (1933) 103 LJKB 250 (tow chain not part of insured vehicle); see also *Jones and James v Provincial Insurance Co* (1929) 46 TLR 71 (condition requiring assured to take all reasonable steps to maintain vehicle in efficient condition; condition broken by removal of foot-brake, leaving only hand-brake); *Brown v Zurich General Accident and Liability Insurance Co Ltd* [1954] 2 Lloyd's Rep 243 (similar condition; smooth front tyres a breach of the condition); *M'Innes v National Motor and Accident Insurance Union Ltd* [1963] 2 Lloyd's Rep 415; *Conn v Westminster Motor Insurance Association Ltd* [1966] 1 Lloyd's Rep 407, CA (similar condition again; condition broken by worn tyres, although state of tyres not cause of accident); *Clarke v National Insurance and Guarantee Corpn Ltd* [1964] 1 QB 199, [1963] 3 All ER 375, CA (prohibition against using four-seater car in unsafe or unroadworthy condition; prohibition applied because car carrying nine at time of accident); *A P Salmon Contractors Ltd v Monksfield* [1970] 1 Lloyd's Rep 387; *New India Assurance Co Ltd v Yeo Beng Chow (alias Yeo Beng Chong)* [1972] 3 All ER 293, [1972] 1 WLR 786, PC (condition in policy requiring assured to safeguard vehicle from loss and damage and maintain it in efficient condition still applicable after deletion of loss and damage section).

2 *Trickett v Queensland Insurance Co* [1936] AC 159, PC.

3 *Trickett v Queensland Insurance Co* [1936] AC 159, PC. The correlation of roadworthiness in a car to seaworthiness in a ship, which found favour in *Barrett v London General Insurance Co* [1935] 1 KB 238, was disapproved in *Trickett v Queensland Insurance Co* supra, but was found to be useful in *Clarke v National Insurance and Guarantee Corpn Ltd* [1964] 1 QB 199, [1963] 3 All ER 375, CA.

4 *Gray v Blackmore* [1934] 1 KB 95.

5 *Jenkins v Deane* (1933) 103 LJKB 250.

6 *Carnill v Rowland* [1953] 1 All ER 486, [1953] 1 WLR 380, DC.

7 *Bright v Ashfold* [1932] 2 KB 153.

8 *Jenkins v Deane* (1933) 103 LJKB 250.

9 *Houghton v Trafalgar Insurance Co Ltd* [1954] 1 QB 247, [1953] 2 All ER 1409, CA.

10 *Houghton v Trafalgar Insurance Co Ltd* [1954] 1 QB 247, [1953] 2 All ER 1409, CA.

11 *Piddington v Co-operative Insurance Society Ltd* [1934] 2 KB 236; *Jones v Welsh Insurance Corpn Ltd* [1937] 4 All ER 149.

12 *Roberts v Anglo-Saxon Insurance Association* (1927) 137 LT 243, CA.

13 *Bright v Ashfold* [1932] 2 KB 153; *Piddington v Co-operative Insurance Society Ltd* [1934] 2 KB 236; *Carnill v Rowland* [1953] 1 All ER 486, [1953] 1 WLR 380, DC.

715. Prohibition by reference to area. It is common to find in a motor policy a limitation of the area within which a vehicle may be used[1]. Normally the cover will only extend to the United Kingdom unless a 'foreign use' clause is specially added, but there may be limitations even within the United Kingdom[2]. A similar result is achieved where there is a stipulation as to where the vehicle is to be garaged[3]. Removal of the car from the prescribed garage or use of it outside the prescribed area does not, however, invalidate the policy altogether unless there are clear words producing this result; if the car subsequently returns to the proper garage or is used in the proper area, the policy re-attaches and recovery is, therefore, allowed in respect of an accident after it has re-attached[4]. A condition as to area only applies in relation to the use of the insured car. If a claim arises under the personal accident section of the policy and is unrelated to the use of the insured car, it will be valid even if the accident occurs abroad unless there is an appropriate limitation in the personal accident section also[5].

1 See eg *Verelst's Administratrix v Motor Union Insurance Co Ltd* [1925] 2 KB 137.
2 *Dawsons Ltd v Bonnin* [1922] 2 AC 413, HL; *Palmer v Cornhill Insurance Co Ltd* (1935) 52 Ll L Rep 78 (lorry restricted to use in Mepal, Cambridgeshire). The removal of the engine to another place is not a breach of such a stipulation if the rest of the car remains in the prescribed place: *Seaton v London General Insurance Co Ltd* (1932) 48 TLR 574.
3 *Dawsons Ltd v Bonnin* [1922] 2 AC 413, HL.
4 *Bonney v Cornhill Insurance Co* (1931) 40 Ll L Rep 39; cf *Dawsons Ltd v Bonnin* [1922] 2 AC 413, HL.
5 *Verelst's Administratrix v Motor Union Insurance Co Ltd* [1925] 2 KB 137.

716. Prohibition by reference to the driver. There is sometimes a provision limiting the driving of the vehicle to the assured himself[1]. If so, he cannot, even in an emergency, allow someone else to drive without putting his insurers off risk[2]. Frequently there is an extension clause authorising the driving of the vehicle on the assured's order or with his permission, either by a limited class of people or generally[3]. However, usually there is a provision, whether it is an 'own driver' policy or a policy with a permitted driver clause, to the effect that the driver holds, or has held and is not disqualified from holding, a driving licence[4]. For the purpose of such a provision, a person is disqualified if he has been disqualified by order of a court[5] or is not by law qualified by reason of age to hold a licence[6]. The mere fact, however, that a person is refused a licence (or has had his licence revoked) on grounds of health does not mean that he is disqualified[7].

1 A lower rate of premium is charged if the car is not to be driven by any person other than the assured.
2 *Herbert v Railway Passengers Assurance Co Ltd* [1938] 1 All ER 650; *G F P Units Ltd v Monksfield* [1972] 2 Lloyd's Rep 79.
3 As to the effect of the 'permitted driver clause' see paras 720–722 post.
4 See *Spraggon v Dominion Insurance Co Ltd* (1941) 69 Ll L Rep 1, CA; *Lester Bros (Coal Merchants) Ltd v Avon Insurance Co Ltd* (1942) 72 Ll L Rep 109; *Haworth v Dawson* (1946) 80 Ll L Rep 19.
5 *Taylor v Kenyon* [1952] 2 All ER 726, DC; cf *Edwards v Griffiths* [1953] 2 All ER 874, [1953] 1 WLR 1199, DC.
6 *Mumford v Hardy* [1956] 1 All ER 337, [1956] 1 WLR 163, DC. The holding of a provisional licence is sufficient even though the holder is unaccompanied while driving the vehicle: *Rendlesham v Dunne (Pennine Insurance Co Ltd, third party)* [1964] 1 Lloyd's Rep 192.
7 *Edwards v Griffiths* [1953] 2 All ER 874, [1953] 1 WLR 1199, DC.

(3) STANDARD FORMS OF COVER

717. Different forms of cover for different road users. The uses to which motor vehicles are put necessarily vary widely. Public service vehicles are designed to carry a large number of passengers at a time, and obviously the insurance required must be such as to cover the operator not only against the risk of injury to pedestrians and other road users but also against the risk of injury to his passengers. Special considerations also apply in the case of goods vehicles, from light vans for local delivery up to heavy long distance lorries, possibly with trailers. In both these cases the insurance may be in a special form, either a commercial transport insurance or a carrier's insurance. Most vehicles on the road, however, are private cars, and a number of provisions have become standardised for them[1].

1 As to the standard provisions see paras 718–723 post.

718. Social, domestic and pleasure purposes. The basis of most insurance policies for private cars is defined by the phrase 'use for social, domestic and pleasure purposes'. Each of the epithets is a simple, almost hackneyed, English word, but it is by no means easy to describe the precise ambit of any one of them. However, it is not difficult to recognise the sort of case which is inside or outside the phrase. Thus, if a car is used for a journey of which the object is to negotiate a business deal, the use is not for social or domestic or pleasure purposes merely because it is a more comfortable or convenient or restful method of making the journey than any other method[1].

1 *Wood v General Accident Fire and Life Assurance Corpn* (1948) 65 TLR 53; see also *Orr v Trafalgar Insurance Co Ltd* (1948) 82 Ll L Rep 1, CA; *Lee v Poole* [1954] Crim LR 942, DC; *D H R Moody (Chemists) Ltd v Iron Trades Mutual Insurance Co Ltd* [1971] 1 Lloyd's Rep 386 (local authority used car to see off visiting delegation at airport; held to be 'social use'); *Seddon v Binions (Zurich Insurance Co Ltd, third party)* [1978] 1 Lloyd's Rep 381, [1978] RTR 163, CA.

719. Use in connection with the assured's business. In addition to social, domestic and pleasure purposes there is usually cover for use in connection with the assured's business, which may be further identified by specific definition[1]. This phrase operates to circumscribe the insurance not only by reference to the particular business which is stipulated or described in the policy[2], but also by reference to its being the assured's business. If, therefore, the assured sells his business to a company[3], or uses the car jointly with another employee of the same employer for the employer's business[4], the policy will not apply; nor will use for the business of the employer of a permitted driver be covered if the use is limited to use for the assured's business[5]. If the stipulated use is for agricultural purposes, this does not cover moving household effects for a farm worker[6] or, it seems, the taking of a show pony to a show[7].

1 *Jones v Welsh Insurance Corpn Ltd* [1937] 4 All ER 149.
2 *Provincial Insurance Co Ltd v Morgan* [1933] AC 240, HL. Where a policy excludes use for hire or reward other than private hire, 'private hire' means hire for a defined journey at a defined time as distinct from plying for hire: *Lyons v Denscombe* [1949] 1 All ER 977, DC.
3 *Levinger v Licenses and General Insurance Co Ltd* (1936) 54 Ll L Rep 68.
4 *Passmore v Vulcan Boiler and General Insurance Co Ltd* (1935) 52 TLR 193.
5 *Pailor v Co-operative Insurance Society Ltd* (1930) 38 Ll L Rep 237, CA.
6 *Agnew v Robertson* 1956 SLT (Sh Ct) 90.
7 *Henderson v Robson* (1949) 113 JP 313 (a decision as to the scope of the Finance Act 1943 s 8 (repealed), relating to excise duty).

720. Scope of a permitted driver clause. A motor policy often contains a provision extending the insurance cover, usually against third party risks only, to any person driving the insured car on the order or with the permission of the assured[1], the permitted driver being treated as though he were the assured. Such a provision is required if the assured is in the habit of causing or permitting[2] his car to be driven by another person because if the assured, in the absence of such a provision, causes or permits his car to be so driven, and the other person does not himself hold an insurance policy covering him while driving the car, the assured will not only be guilty of an offence[3] but will also be responsible for injuries, within the scope of compulsory insurance, caused by the use of the car, the uninsured use being a breach of statutory duty by the assured who has caused or permitted it[4]. Sometimes the permitted driver is limited to someone who is a relative or friend of the assured[5]. However, the extension is often qualified by a provision that the permitted driver is not entitled to an indemnity under any other insurance policy[6]. There is also invariably a requirement that the permitted driver must hold[7], or must have held and must not be disqualified from holding[8], a driving licence[9] and there may be an express exclusion of certain classes of persons from the category of permitted drivers[10].

1 See eg *Smith v Ralph* [1963] 2 Lloyd's Rep 439, DC; *Kelly v Cornhill Insurance Co Ltd* [1964] 1 All ER 321, [1964] 1 WLR 158, HL (permission not terminated by death of assured). The language usually used derives from the Road Traffic Act 1988 s 156(a) (see ROAD TRAFFIC). It does not cover a purchaser who drives the car away after buying it from the assured: see *Peters v General Accident Fire and Life Assurance Corpn Ltd* [1938] 2 All ER 267, CA (assured not entitled to assign policy to third party). A policy is voidable where the assured falsely represents that another's vehicle is his own property: *Guardian Assurance Co Ltd v Sutherland* [1939] 2 All ER 246.

2 As to the meaning of 'cause or permit' (contained in the Road Traffic Act 1988 s 143(1)(b), as to which see ROAD TRAFFIC) see *Watkins v O'Shaughnessy* [1939] 1 All ER 385, CA; *Houston v Buchanan* [1940] 2 All ER 179 at 187, HL, per Lord Wright; *Goodbarne v Buck* [1940] 1 KB 771, [1940] 1 All ER 613, CA; *Lyons v May* [1948] 2 All ER 1062, DC; *Lloyd v Singleton* [1953] 1 QB 357, [1953] 1 All ER 291, DC; *Shave v Rosner* [1954] 2 QB 113, [1954] 2 All ER 280, DC; *James & Son Ltd v Smee* [1955] 1 QB 78, [1954] 3 All ER 273, DC.

3 See the Road Traffic Act 1988 s 143(1), (2); and para 729 post.

4 Failure to perform the statutory duty to insure will involve a civil liability to a person injured by the uninsured vehicle: *Monk v Warbey* [1935] 1 KB 75, CA; and see *Richards v Port of Manchester Insurance Co Ltd* (1934) 152 LT 261; affd 152 LT 413, CA; *Corfield v Groves* [1950] 1 All ER 488; cf *Daniels v Vaux* [1938] 2 KB 203, [1938] 2 All ER 271 (where the failure of the plaintiff to commence in due time an action against the negligent driver, and not the failure of the owner to insure, was the real cause of the plaintiff's loss).

5 *Williams v Baltic Insurance Association of London Ltd* [1924] 2 KB 282. The driver need not be on terms of social equality in order to qualify as 'a friend': *Pailor v Co-operative Insurance Society Ltd* (1930) 38 Ll L Rep 237, CA.

6 *Gale v Motor Union Insurance Co* [1928] 1 KB 359; *Weddell v Road Transport and General Insurance Co Ltd* [1932] 2 KB 563; *Austin v Zurich General Accident and Liability Insurance Co Ltd* [1945] KB 250, [1945] 1 All ER 316. If the permitted driver's personal insurance policy contains a similar provision, questions of contribution between the insurers will depend on whether one or other, or each, of the provisions is framed as a non-contribution clause or as a rateable contribution clause: see para 517 ante.

7 See *Mumford v Hardy* [1956] 1 All ER 337, [1956] 1 WLR 163, DC (licence obtained by false pretences by person under age; licence void by what is now the Road Traffic Act 1988 s 103(2) (substituted by the Road Traffic Act 1991 s 19); driver not covered, although insurers willing to admit liability); *Rendlesham v Dunne (Pennine Insurance Co Ltd, third party)* [1964] 1 Lloyd's Rep 192 (unaccompanied provisional licence holder covered). Cf para 732 note 2 post.

8 See *Edwards v Griffiths* [1953] 2 All ER 874, [1953] 1 WLR 1199, DC ('disqualified' means disqualified by order of court; driver who had been refused renewal of licence on ground of health was not disqualified); cf *Taylor v Kenyon* [1952] 2 All ER 726, DC.

9 See *John T Ellis Ltd v Hinds* [1947] KB 475, [1947] 1 All ER 337, DC (insurers' liability excluded while vehicle driven by person who, to the assured's knowledge, did not hold a licence; knowledge must be actual and not merely constructive); *Lester Bros (Coal Merchants) Ltd v Avon Insurance Co* (1942) 72 Ll L Rep 109 (insurer not liable if vehicle driven either by assured when assured did not

hold licence or by any person with assured's consent when that person, to assured's knowledge, did not hold licence; assured a limited company, and therefore incapable of driving except by agency of employees; vehicle driven by assured's employee held to be driven by assured, and not by a person with assured's consent within meaning of policy; insurers therefore not liable even though assured ignorant that employee did not hold licence).

10 For a list of exclusions see eg *Richards v Port of Manchester Insurance Co Ltd* (1934) 152 LT 261; affd 152 LT 415, CA.

721. Permitted drivers' rights under the policy. A permitted driver is not directly a party to the original contract of insurance, and on ordinary common law principles of contract law he cannot have any right of action against the insurers on the policy unless it is possible to show that the assured, when making the contract, intended to act as agent or trustee of the permitted driver[1]. Frequently this is not possible because the particular permitted driver was not, at that time, in contemplation at all. It is, however, laid down by statute that if insurers issue a motor policy covering compulsorily insurable risks, they are liable to indemnify any persons or classes of persons specified in the policy in respect of any liability which the policy purports to cover in the case of those persons or classes of persons[2]. The permitted driver, accordingly, has a direct right of action within the ambit of this provision against the insurers[3]. In effect he becomes a party to the contract of insurance[4], but he must take the contract as he finds it; he cannot excuse a breach of a condition by pleading that he was unaware of its terms or existence[5].

1 *Vandepitte v Preferred Accident Insurance Corpn of New York* [1933] AC 70, PC; cf *Williams v Baltic Insurance Association of London Ltd* [1924] 2 KB 282, where enforcement by the assured on behalf of the permitted driver was allowed.
2 Road Traffic Act 1988 s 148(7): see para 708 note 2 ante.
3 *Tattersall v Drysdale* [1935] 2 KB 174; *Austin v Zurich General Accident and Liability Insurance Co Ltd* [1945] KB 250, [1945] 1 All ER 316, CA. The requirement of the Life Assurance Act 1774 s 2 (as amended) (see para 543 ante), as to the insertion of the names of all persons for whose use or benefit, or on whose account, the policy is made, does not apply as the policy is a policy on goods, ie the car: *Williams v Baltic Insurance Association of London Ltd* [1924] 2 KB 282.
4 *Sutch v Burns* (1943) as reported in 60 TLR 1 at 2 per Atkinson J; revsd on appeal [1944] KB 406, [1944] 1 All ER 520n, CA, on the ground that the policy in question did not indemnify the permitted driver in the circumstances; and see *John T Ellis Ltd v Hinds* [1947] KB 475 at 485–486, [1947] 1 All ER 337 at 339, DC.
5 *Guardian Assurance Co Ltd v Sutherland* [1939] 2 All ER 246; *Austin v Zurich General Accident and Liability Insurance Co Ltd* [1945] KB 250, [1945] 1 All ER 316, CA.

722. Extent of cover afforded to a permitted driver. The formula frequently adopted to provide cover for a permitted driver states that he is to be regarded, for the purpose of having the benefits conferred by the relevant sections of the policy, as though he were the assured. The result of such wording is that, if the relevant section of the policy covers legal liability to 'any person', even the assured will rank as a person whose injuries must be paid for, if they are caused by the negligence of the permitted driver. The assured's chauffeur can thus recover from the insurers an indemnity against damages recovered from him by the assured in respect of injuries caused to the assured by the chauffeur's negligence[1]. The death of the assured does not necessarily destroy the cover afforded to a permitted driver[2]. It cannot, however, be assumed that an employer's policy, even if the driving is going to be carried out by his employees, necessarily contains a permitted driver clause or that the employer will be liable for breach of the statutory duty to insure[3] if there is no such provision covering the individual liability of each driver. The employer fulfils his statutory duty if he covers his own liabilities, even if the driving is vicariously performed; he does not, in addition, have to cover the personal liability of each driver[4]. The purpose for which the permitted driver uses the car must, in every case, be within the description of use clause as it falls to be interpreted in relation to him; if, for example, on the true construction of the policy, use for business is limited to the business of the assured, the permitted driver will not be covered if he uses the vehicle on the business of his own employer who is other than the assured[5].

1 *Digby v General Accident Fire and Life Assurance Corpn Ltd* [1943] AC 121, [1942] 2 All ER 319, HL.
2 *Kelly v Cornhill Insurance Co Ltd* [1964] 1 All ER 321, [1964] 1 WLR 158, HL.
3 As to the statutory duty see para 733 post.
4 *John T Ellis Ltd v Hinds* [1947] KB 475, [1947] 1 All ER 337, DC; *Lees v Motor Insurers' Bureau* [1952] 2 All ER 511; *Lister v Romford Ice and Cold Storage Co Ltd* [1957] AC 555, [1957] 1 All ER 125, HL; see also *Marsh v Moores* [1949] 2 KB 208, [1949] 2 All ER 27, DC. It has been held that, in a contract of service between the owner of a vehicle and a person employed to drive it, there is an implied term that compulsory insurance cover is to be maintained by the owner: see *Gregory v Ford* [1951] 1 All ER 121. This is, however, limited to compulsory insurance, and does not in any case preclude an employer from recovering from a negligent employee damages which the employer has to pay solely by reason of the employee's negligence: see *Semtex Ltd v Gladstone* [1954] 2 All ER 206, [1954] 1 WLR 945; *Lister v Romford Ice and Cold Storage Co Ltd* supra (where there was held to be no implied term in the contract of service, either that the employee should be indemnified by his employer against claims in respect of acts done in the course of his employment, or that he should receive the benefit of any contract of insurance); see further EMPLOYMENT vol 16 (Reissue) para 35.
5 *Pailor v Co-operative Insurance Society Ltd* (1930) 38 Ll L Rep 237, CA.

723. Cover for the assured driving other cars. A motor policy frequently has an extension clause covering the assured while driving any other car[1], but such a clause is only operative so long as the assured retains the insured car, because that is the basis of his insurable interest[2]. The extension clause will, therefore, cease to be operative as soon as the assured parts with his property in the insured car[3]. However, where the car is insured by a partnership, there is no change of ownership merely because a new partner joins the firm[4]. The purposes for which the other car may be used are, of course, normally correlated with the descriptions and prohibitions of use stipulated in relation to the insured car. The general principles of public liability insurance apply to such an extension clause[5].

1 *Laurence v Davies (Norwich Union Fire Insurance Society Ltd, third party)* [1972] 2 Lloyd's Rep 231 (in the absence of any clearly expressed alternative meaning, the definition of 'motor car' is that now contained in the Road Traffic Act 1988 s 185(1); the assured was, therefore, covered while driving a van). For the application of such an extension clause see *Bullock v Bellamy* (1940) 67 Ll L Rep 392.
2 *Rogerson v Scottish Automobile and General Insurance Co Ltd* (1931) 48 TLR 17, HL; see also *Williams v Baltic Insurance Association of London Ltd* [1924] 2 KB 282. If, however, the policy is limited to third party risks, an insurable interest in the vehicle is not necessary: *Boss v Kingston* [1963] 1 All ER 177, [1963] 1 WLR 99, DC.
3 *Tattersall v Drysdale* [1935] 2 KB 174; *Peters v General Accident Fire and Life Assurance Corpn Ltd* [1938] 2 All ER 267, CA.
4 *Jenkins v Deane* (1933) 150 LT 314.
5 As to public liability insurance see paras 690–691 ante.

(4) INSURANCE OF VEHICLE

724. Motor insurance as an example of property insurance. As has been indicated elsewhere, a motorist is required to be insured only against third party liabilities in the limited statutory sense[1]. The insurance operates by reference to the car proposed for insurance, but there is no obligation to insure the car itself. If, however, the proposer desires to do so, he can obtain insurance covering the car against fire or theft[2] or against any form of loss or damage. A fire insurance policy covers both a damage and a total loss risk according to the ordinary principles of fire insurance discussed elsewhere[3]. A theft insurance is usually linked with the statutory definition of 'theft'; the complications of this insurance are discussed elsewhere[4].

1 See paras 706 et seq ante, 729 et seq post.
2 *Devco Holder Ltd v Legal & General Assurance Society Ltd* [1993] 2 Lloyd's Rep 567, CA (theft of car having key in ignition).
3 As to fire insurance see para 591 et seq ante.
4 See para 644 ante. For a form of cover against fire and theft see 20 Forms & Precedents (5th Edn) 552, Form 311 cl 16.

725. Damage insurance. Frequently a motor policy provides indemnity against damage to the car insured arising from accident or other causes apart from fire or theft, the most common cause of damage being the assured's own negligence. The cost of meeting damage claims can be very heavy from the insurers' point of view[1]. The result has been the development of two common features in motor insurance, namely the knock-for-knock agreement and the excess and no claims bonus clause[2].

1 Where the insurers have authorised a garage to carry out repairs to an insured car, they may sometimes be held to have contracted as principals in the transaction and are therefore personally liable for the cost: *Cooter and Green Ltd v Tyrrell* [1962] 2 Lloyd's Rep 377, CA; *Godfrey Davis Ltd v Culling and Hecht* [1962] 2 Lloyd's Rep 349, CA; *Brown and Davis Ltd v Galbraith* [1972] 3 All ER 31, [1972] 1 WLR 997, CA. There may be a contract between the insurers and the garage to pay for the repairs and also a contract between the garage and the owner to carry out the repairs: *Charnock v Liverpool Corpn* [1968] 3 All ER 473, [1968] 1 WLR 1498, CA.
2 For forms see 20 Forms & Precedents (5th Edn) 319–327, Form 216; 549–568, Forms 311–312. See further paras 726–727 post.

726. Knock-for-knock agreements. The essence of a 'knock-for-knock' agreement is that, in the event of an accident involving more than one insured vehicle, each insurer carries the risk so far as concerns the damage to the car he has insured, whoever may be legally responsible for causing the damage. It is, however, an arrangement operative only between insurers, and there is no means of enforcing it against the individual assured. Therefore, if an assured, minded perhaps to avoid losing a 'no-claims bonus', pursues on his own a claim for damage to his car, it is no answer that he is entitled to receive or has already received indemnity for the damage from his own insurers[1]. The fact that the claimant has insurance rights against his own insurers is irrelevant so far as the tortfeasor is concerned[2].

1 *Morley v Moore* [1936] 2 KB 359, [1936] 2 All ER 79, CA; *Alexander v Lang* 1967 SLT (Sh Ct) 64 (insurers cancelled policy after bearing total loss of assured's car under 'knock-for-knock' agreement; assured's attempt to recover premium from other driver failed for remoteness); *Hobbs v Marlowe* [1978] AC 16, [1977] 2 All ER 241, HL.
2 Cf *Bradburn v Great Western Rly Co* (1874) LR 10 Exch 1; *Simpson v Thomson* (1877) 3 App Cas 279, HL.

727. Excess and no-claims bonus clauses. In order to avoid a multiplicity of claims for minor damage to the insured car two devices are usual among motor insurers. One device is to provide that the liability for damage up to a specified amount must be borne by the assured himself[1]; the result is that the assured is deterred from making claims for any trivial mishap and, even in the case of a major mishap, the insurers are entitled to call on the assured to bear the amount which he has agreed to bear himself, and to recover it from him if they have paid it[2]. Alternatively, a rebate of premium is allowed in the form of a bonus if no claim is notified. The assured cannot, however, be deprived of the benefit of his no-claims bonus merely by reason of the fact that, without his having made a claim on his insurers, they have committed themselves to paying a claim pursuant to a knock-for-knock agreement with the insurers of another car which was demonstrably at fault in producing the relevant accident[3]. Where, as a result of a third party's negligence, the assured is involved in an accident and has to bear liability for damage up to the amount specified in the excess clause and he loses his no-claims bonus, he may include these items as part of any damages he claims from the third party; but the insurers are under no duty to assist the assured in his claim[4].

1 An excess clause is also common in relation to third party claims, whether for injury or damage to property, in order to encourage greater care by a driver whose claims record is not good.
2 *Beacon Insurance Co Ltd v Langdale* [1939] 4 All ER 204, DC.
3 *Morley v Moore* [1936] 2 KB 359, [1936] 2 All ER 79, CA.
4 *Ironfield v Eastern Gas Board* [1964] 1 All ER 544n, [1964] 1 WLR 1125n.

728. Insurance against loss. In addition to cover against fire, theft or damage however caused, motor policies frequently provide cover against loss. The circumstances in which a person will be taken to have suffered a loss of his car when he has been induced to part with possession of, or property in, it by fraud have been previously considered[1].

1 As to insurance against loss see generally paras 658–659 ante.

(5) COMPULSORY INSURANCE IN RELATION TO MOTOR VEHICLES

(i) Origin and Nature of Compulsory Insurance

729. Persons requiring compulsory insurance. Subject to certain qualifications[1], it is unlawful for any person[2] to use[3], or to cause or permit[4] any other person to use[5], a motor vehicle[6] on a road[7] unless there is in force in relation to the use of the vehicle by that person or that other person[8], as the case may be, such a policy of insurance, or such a security, in respect of third party risks as complies with the statutory requirements[9].

This provision does not apply to:

(1) a vehicle owned[10], at a time when the vehicle is being driven under the owner's control, by the council of a county or county district in England or Wales, the Broads Authority[11], the Common Council of the City of London, the council of a London borough, a joint authority[12] (other than a police authority), or a joint board or joint committee in England or Wales which is so constitued as to include among its members representatives of any such council[13];

(2) a vehicle owned by a police authority or the Receiver for the Metropolitan Police District at a time when it is being driven under the owner's control, or

a vehicle at a time when it is being driven for police purposes by or under the direction of a police constable or by a person employed by a police authority or the receiver[14];

(3) a vehicle at a time when it is being driven on a journey to or from any place undertaken for salvage purposes[15];

(4) the use of a vehicle for the purpose of its being furnished in pursuance of a requisitioning order[16];

(5) a vehicle owned by a health service body[17] at a time when the vehicle is being driven under the owner's control[18];

(6) an ambulance owned by a national health service trust[19] at a time when the vehicle is being driven under the owner's control[20];

(7) a vehicle which is made available by the Secretary of State to any person, body or local authority in pursuance of the National Health Service Act 1977[21] at a time when it is being used in accordance with the terms on which it is made available[22];

(8) a vehicle owned by a person who has deposited and keeps deposited with the Accountant General of the Supreme Court the sum of £500,000 at a time when the vehicle is being driven under the owner's control[23];

(9) vehicles in the service of visiting forces[24]; or

(10) invalid carriages[25].

1 For the exemptions see the text and notes 10–25 infra.
2 'Any person' does not merely mean any owner: *Williamson v O'Keefe* [1947] 1 All ER 307, DC.
3 'To use' means to have the use of a motor vehicle on a road: see *Elliott v Grey* [1960] 1 QB 367, [1959] 3 All ER 733, DC (car laid up in road; could be moved though not driven; insurance required). If at the controls, a pupil is normally the driver of the car: *Langman v Valentine* [1952] 2 All ER 803, DC; *Evans v Walkden* [1956] 3 All ER 64, [1956] 1 WLR 1019. As to the defence to a charge of being in contravention of these provisions see para 736 note 4 post.
4 As to the meaning of 'cause or permit' see para 720 note 2 ante.
5 Failure to perform the statutory duty to insure will involve a civil liability to a person injured by the uninsured vehicle: *Richards v Port of Manchester Insurance Co Ltd* (1943) 152 LT 261; affd 152 LT 413, CA; *Monk v Warbey* [1935] 1 KB 75, CA; *Corfield v Groves* [1950] 1 All ER 488; cf *Daniels v Vaux* [1938] 2 KB 203, [1938] 2 All ER 271 (where the plaintiff's failure to commence an action in due time against the negligent driver, and not the failure of the owner to insure, was the real cause of the plaintiff's loss). The person injured is only entitled to recover against the owner for the amount of the damage which he has, in fact, suffered as a result of the owner's breach, ie the difference between the amount of damages awarded against the borrower of the vehicle and the amount which the borrower is able to pay in satisfaction: *Martin v Dean* [1971] 2 QB 208, [1971] 3 All ER 279.
6 'Motor vehicle' means, subject to the Chronically Sick and Disabled Persons Act 1970 s 20 (as amended) (special provision about invalid carriages within the meaning of that Act) a mechanically propelled vehicle intended or adapted for use on roads: Road Traffic Act 1988 s 185(1). 'Invalid carriage', for the purposes of the Chronically Sick and Disabled Persons Act 1970, means a vehicle, whether mechanically propelled or not, constructed or adapted for use for the carriage of one person, being a person suffering from some physical defect or disability: s 20(2); cf note 25 infra. For the meaning of 'road' see note 7 infra. An autocycle is included unless the motor is dismantled: *Lawrence v Howlett* [1952] 2 All ER 74; *Floyd v Bush* [1953] 1 All ER 265, [1953] 1 WLR 242, DC. An autocross racing car, although not intended to be used on the roads under its own power, is a motor vehicle: *Nichol v Leach* [1972] RTR 476, DC.
7 'Road' means any highway and any other road to which the public has access, including bridges over which a road passes: Road Traffic Act 1988 s 192 (1). A place to which the public has access is not necessarily a road (*Griffin v Squires* [1958] 3 All ER 468, [1958] 1 WLR 1106, DC), but may be (*Bugge v Taylor* [1941] 1 KB 198, DC (forecourt)); cf *Thomas v Dando* [1951] 2 KB 620, [1951] 1 All ER 1010, DC; and *Purves v Muir* 1948 JC 122; see also *Harrison v Hill* 1932 JC 13; *Knaggs v Elson* (1965) 109 Sol Jo 596, DC (both cases of private roads). A private road in a fenced-in factory or dock, which is not open to the public, is not a road: *O'Brien v Trafalgar Insurance Co Ltd* (1945) 61 TLR 225, CA; *Buchanan v Motor Insurers' Bureau* [1955] 1 All ER 607, [1955] 1 WLR 488. Even if an accident takes place on private property, it may, in certain circumstances, arise out of the use of a vehicle on a

road: *Romford Ice and Cold Storage Co Ltd v Lister* [1956] 2 QB 180 at 196, [1955] 3 All ER 460 at 469–470, CA, per Denning LJ; affd [1957] AC 555, [1957] 1 All ER 125, HL; see, however, at 204–205 and 474–475 per Birkett LJ, and at 211–212 and 479 per Romer LJ; *Randall v Motor Insurers' Bureau* [1969] 1 All ER 21, [1968] 1 WLR 1900.

8 In *Evans v Walkden* [1956] 3 All ER 64, [1956] 1 WLR 1019, a son aged 17 was at the controls, his father was in the passenger's seat, and the son was held not licensed to drive. See generally ROAD TRAFFIC.

9 Road Traffic Act 1988 s 143(1). The penalty for acting in contravention is, on summary conviction, a fine not exceeding level 5 on the standard scale: Road Traffic Offenders Act 1988 s 9, Sch 2 Pt I (amended by the Road Traffic Act 1991 s 26, Sch 2 paras 1, 26). As to the standard scale see para 212 note 5 ante. SEE also ROAD TRAFFIC.

As to the evidence which a police constable may require to be produced from a driver, and which an owner is under a duty to provide, that a motor vehicle is being driven in compliance with the Road Traffic Act 1988 s 143(1) see ss 165, 170, 171 (as amended); and ROAD TRAFFIC. In the case of a motor vehicle which is within the exceptions set out in the text to notes 10–25 infra see the Motor Vehicles (Third Party Risks) Regulations 1972, SI 1972/1217, reg 7, Schedule Pt 1 Form F (amended by SI 1973/1821; SI 1974/792; SI 1974/2187; and SI 1992/1283). The issue of a certificate of ownership of exempt vehicles has been extended to include a passenger transport executive and its subsidiaries, and the London Transport Executive (now London Regional Transport: London Regional Transport Act 1984 s 1) and its wholly owned subsidiaries: Motor Vehicles (Third Party Risks) Regulations 1972 regs 4(1), 7(3), Schedule Pt 1 Form F.

10 'Owner' in relation to a vehicle which is the subject of a hiring agreement or hire-purchase agreement means the person in possession of the vehicle under that agreement: Road Traffic Act 1988 s 192(1). The provisions of Pt VI (ss 143–162) (as amended) do not apply to vehicles and persons in the public service of the Crown: s 183(1).

11 The Broads Authority is a body corporate established under the Norfolk and Suffolk Broads Act 1988 s 1.

12 Ie a joint authority established under the Local Government Act 1985 Pt IV (ss 23–42) (as amended): see LOCAL GOVERNMENT.

13 Road Traffic Act 1988 s 144(2)(a) (amended by the Norfolk and Suffolk Broads Act 1988 s 21, Sch 6 para 9 (amended by the Road Traffic (Consequential Provisions) Act 1988 s 4, Sch 3 para 36)): see LOCAL GOVERNMENT.

14 Road Traffic Act 1988 s 144(2)(b). As to the Receiver for the Metropolitan Police District see the Metropolitan Police Act 1829 s 10 (as amended); and as to police authorities see the Police Act 1964 s 62, Sch 8 (as amended) and POLICE.

15 Ie pursuant to the Merchant Shipping Act 1894 Pt IX (ss 510–571) (as amended) (as to which see SHIPPING): Road Traffic Act 1988 s 144(2)(c). 'Salvage' means the preservation of a vessel which is wrecked, stranded or in distress, or the lives of persons belonging to, or the cargo or apparel of, such a vessel: s 161(1).

16 Ie a direction under the Army Act 1955 s 166(2)(b) or the Air Force Act 1955 s 166(2)(b) (see ROYAL FORCES vol 41 para 122): Road Traffic Act 1988 s 144(2)(d).

17 Ie as defined in the National Health Service and Community Care Act 1990 s 60(7): see NATIONAL HEALTH AND SOCIAL SECURITY.

18 Road Traffic Act 1988 s 144(2)(da) (added by the National Health Service and Community Care Act 1990 s 60, Sch 8 Pt I para 4).

19 Ie a trust established under the National Health Service and Community Care Act 1990 Pt I (ss 1–26) (as amended).

20 Road Traffic Act 1988 s 144(2)(db) (added by the National Health Service and Community Care Act 1990 Sch 8 Pt I para 4).

21 Ie under the National Health Service Act 1977 s 23 or s 26 (as amended).

22 Road Traffic Act 1988 s 144(2)(e).

23 Ibid s 144(1) (amended by the Road Traffic Act 1991 s 20): see para 757 post.

24 See the Visiting Forces and International Headquarters (Application of Law) Order 1965, SI 1965/1536, art 8; and ROYAL FORCES vol 41 para 127 et seq.

25 Road Traffic Act 1988 s 143(4). 'Invalid carriage' means a mechanically propelled vehicle the weight of which unladen does not exceed 254 kg and which is specially designed and constructed, and not merely adapted, for the use of a person suffering from some physical defect or disability and used solely by such a person: s 185(1).

730. International motor insurance cards. Visitors[1] to Great Britain[2] bringing in motor vehicles comply with the statutory requirements relating to compulsory insurance[3] if they hold a valid[4] insurance card[5].

1 'Visitor' means a person bringing a motor vehicle into Great Britain, making only a temporary stay and named in an insurance card (see note 4 infra) as the insured or user of the vehicle, and includes a hiring visitor who brings a hired motor vehicle into Great Britain but no other hiring visitor; and 'hiring visitor' means a person to whom a hired motor vehicle (see note 4 infra) is let on hire, making a temporary stay in Great Britain and named as the insured or user of the vehicle in the insurance card in which that vehicle is specified: Motor Vehicles (International Motor Insurance Card) Regulations 1971, SI 1971/792, reg 3(1).
2 For the meaning of 'Great Britain' see para 2 note 10 ante.
3 As to the statutory requirements see paras 729 ante, 731 et seq post.
4 A card is valid if: (1) the motor vehicle it specifies is brought into the United Kingdom during the specified period of validity (Motor Vehicles (International Motor Insurance Card) Regulations 1971 reg 4(1)(a)); (2) its application in Great Britain is indicated on it (reg 4(1)(b)); (3) all relevant information provided for in it is inscribed in it (reg 4(1)(c)); (4) it has been signed by the visitor, the insurer named in it and, in the case of a hired vehicle, every hiring visitor named in the card as its hirer or user (reg 4(1)(d)); and (5) in the case of a card in the form specified in Sch 2 (substituted by SI 1977/895), it bears on page 1 the name of the Foreign Bureau or the British Bureau under whose authority it was issued (reg 4(1)(e) (amended by SI 1977/895)).For the meaning of 'United Kingdom' see para 2 note 10 ante.
    'Hired motor vehicle' means a motor vehicle (a) designed for private use with seats for not more than eight persons excluding the driver; (b) specified in an insurance card; (c) last brought into Great Britain by a person making a temporary stay; and (d) owned and let for hire by a person whose business includes the letting of vehicles for hire and whose principal place of business is outside the United Kingdom: reg 3(1). 'Foreign Bureau' means a central organisation set up by motor insurers in any country outside the United Kingdom, the Isle of Man and the Channel Islands for the purpose of giving effect to international arrangements for the insurance of motorists against third-party risks when entering countries where such insurance is compulsory and with which the British Bureau has entered into such an arrangement; and 'British Bureau' means the Motor Insurers' Bureau incorporated under the Companies Act 1929 (repealed) with its registered office at 152 Silbury Boulevard, Central Milton Keynes MK9 1NB (see paras 758–764 post): Motor Vehicles (International Motor Insurance Card) Regulations 1971 reg 3(1).
5 Ibid regs 5, 6 (amended by SI 1977/895). 'Insurance card' means an international motor insurance card issued under the authority of a Foreign Bureau or of the British Bureau, which is green and (1) is in either English or a foreign language containing the particulars specified in and, and set out in two pages as shown in, Sch 1 (substituted by SI 1977/895) (reg 3(1) (amended by SI 1977/895); or (2) until 1 December 1977 was in either English or a foreign language in the form specified in Sch 2 (as so substituted) (reg 3(1) (as so amended). See also reg 4(2). As to vehicles brought from Northern Ireland see reg 10.

731. Persons able to issue valid policies. An insurance policy is not effective for the purposes of compulsory insurance unless it is issued by an authorised insurer, that is any person or body of persons carrying on motor vehicle insurance business[1] in Great Britain[2] and complying with the relevant statutory requirements[3]. The authorised insurer must be a member of the Motor Insurers' Bureau[4]. If the authorised insurer ceases to be a member of the bureau, he is still liable on any policy issued before ceasing to be a member, or on any obligation arising from any such policy[5].

1 Ie within the Insurance Companies Act 1982 s 3, Sch 2 Pt II Group 2: Road Traffic Act 1988 s 145(5).
2 For the meaning of 'Great Britain' see para 2 note 10 ante.
3 Ie the Road Traffic Act 1988 s 145 (1)–(3) (as amended).
4 Ie a company limited by guarantee and incorporated under the Companies Act 1929 (repealed) on 14 June 1946: Road Traffic Act 1988 s 145(5). See paras 758–764 post.
5 See ibid s 145(6).

732. Nature of insurance required. The conditions to be fulfilled in order to render the use of a motor vehicle lawful are that (1) there must be a policy of insurance in force[1] in relation to the use[2] of the vehicle on a road, and (2) the policy must comply with the relevant statutory requirements[3]. A cover note is a policy of insurance for this purpose[4]. The relevant statutory requirements are that the policy, apart from being issued by an authorised insurer, must provide cover against certain specified liabilities[5].

1 A policy is not invalid merely because it covers the vehicle when being unlawfully used (*Leggate v Brown* [1950] 2 All ER 564, DC: see para 711 text to note 8 ante), or is voidable, but not in fact avoided, by the insurers (*Goodbarne v Buck* [1940] 1 KB 107, [1939] 4 All ER 107; affd [1940] 1 KB 771, [1940] 1 All ER 613, CA; *Durrant v Maclaren* [1956] 2 Lloyd's Rep 70).

2 Where the construction of a policy makes it doubtful whether it was applicable to the use in question, a statement by the insurers that they would regard it as applicable is accepted: *Pilbury v Brazier* [1951] 1 KB 340, [1950] 2 All ER 835; *Carnhill v Rowland* [1953] 1 All ER 486, DC. However, if the construction of the policy is clear, the court takes account of that alone: *Carnhill v Rowland* supra; see also *Bryan v Forrow* [1950] 1 All ER 294, DC. For the position where the effectiveness of the policy depends on the holding of, or the right to hold, a driving licence see *Mumford v Hardy* [1956] 1 All ER 337, [1956] 1 WLR 163; cf *Edwards v Griffiths* [1953] 2 All ER 874, [1953] 1 WLR 1199, DC; and see para 720 text and notes 7–9 ante. A legally binding policy is essential: *Boss v Kingston* [1963] 1 All ER 177 at 180, [1963] 1 WLR 99 at 105, DC.

3 Road Traffic Act 1988 s 143 (1), (2): see para 729 ante.

4 See para 708 note 2 ante. A temporary cover note must be accepted and relied upon so that it constitutes an enforceable contract: *Taylor v Allon* [1966] 1 QB 304, [1965] 1 All ER 557, DC.

5 See the Road Traffic Act 1988 s 145 (as amended); and paras 733–737 post.

(ii) Risks required to be Insured

733. Liabilities required to be covered. In order to comply with the statutory requirements, a policy must provide insurance cover in respect of any liability which may be incurred by such persons or classes of persons as are specified in the policy in respect of the death of, or bodily injury to, any person[1], or damage to property caused by, or arising out of, the use of the vehicle on a road in Great Britain[2].

In the case of a vehicle normally based in the territory of another member state of the European Community[3], the policy must provide insurance cover in respect of any civil liability which may be incurred by the person or persons insured as a result of an event related to the use of the vehicle in Great Britain if (1) according to the law of that territory, he or they would be required to be insured in respect of a civil liability which would arise under that law as a result of that event if the place where the vehicle was used when the event occurred were in that territory; and (2) the cover required by that law would be higher than that required by the provisions mentioned[4] above[5].

In the case of a vehicle normally based in Great Britain, the policy must also provide insurance cover in respect of any liability which may be incurred by the assured in respect of the use of the vehicle[6] and of any trailer[7], whether or not coupled, in the territory, other than Great Britain and Gibraltar, of each of the member states of the European Community, according to (a) the law on compulsory insurance against civil liability in respect of the use of vehicles of the state in whose territory the event giving rise to the liability occurred; or (b) if it would give higher cover, the law which would be applicable under Part VI of the Road Traffic Act 1988 if the place where the vehicle was used when that event occurred were in Great Britain[8].

Cover must also be provided for any liability incurred in respect of emergency treatment[9].

1 For the exceptions see paras 735–737 post. 'Any person' refers to anyone injured by the insured's or permitted driver's use of the vehicle, but excluding the permitted driver himself: *Cooper v Motor Insurers' Bureau* [1985] QB 575, [1985] 1 All ER 449, CA.
2 Road Traffic Act 1988 s 145(3)(a). For the meaning of 'road' see para 729 note 7 ante. For the meaning of 'Great Britain' see para 2 note 10 ante. Liability in respect of an intentional criminal act must be covered: *Hardy v Motor Insurers' Bureau* [1964] 2 QB 745, [1964] 2 All ER 742, CA.
3 See the Interpretation Act 1978 s 5, Sch 1 (meaning of 'Communities'), applying the European Communities Act 1972 s 1, Sch 1.
4 See text to notes 1–2 supra.
5 Road Traffic Act 1988 s 145(3)(aa) (added by the Motor Vehicle (Compulsory Insurance) Regulations 1992, SI 1992/3036, reg 2(1)).
6 For the meaning of 'motor vehicle' see para 729 note 6 ante.
7 'Trailer' means a vehicle drawn by a motor vehicle: Road Traffic Act 1988 s 185(1).
8 Ibid s 145(3)(b) (amended by the Motor Vehicle (Compulsory Insurance) Regulations 1992 reg 2(2)). The Road Traffic Act 1988 Pt VI comprises ss 143–162 (as amended).
9 Ibid s 145(3)(c). 'Emergency treatment' is medical or surgical treatment or examination immediately required as a result of bodily injury (including fatal injury) to a person caused by, or arising out of, the use of a motor vehicle on a road, such treatment or examination being effected by a legally qualified medical practitioner: s 158(1). The person who was using the the vehicle at the time of the event out of which the bodily injury arose must pay to the practitioner (or, where the emergency treatment is effected by more than one practitioner, to the practitioner by whom it is first effected) (1) a fee of £18.20 in respect of each person in whose case the emergency treatment is effected by him; and (2) a sum equal to 35p for every complete mile and additional part of a mile in respect of any distance in excess of two miles which he must cover (a) to proceed from the place from which he is summoned to the place where the emergency treatment is carried out by him, and (b) to return to the place from which he is summoned: s 158(2) (amended by the Road Traffic Accidents (Payments for Treatment) Order 1991, SI 1991/2005, reg 3). For the meaning of 'legally qualified medical practitioner' see the Medical Act 1983 s 56(1), Sch 6 para 11; and MEDICINE vol 30 (Reissue) paras 3–4. As to claims in respect of emergency treatment see the Road Traffic Act 1988 s 159.

734. Liabilities not required to be covered. A policy of insurance is not required (1) to cover liability in respect of the death, arising out of and in the course of employment, of a person in the employment of a person insured by the policy or of bodily injury sustained by such a person arising out of and in the course of his employment[1]; or (2) to provide insurance of more than £250,000 for all liabilities for damage to property caused by, or arising out of, any one accident[2] involving a vehicle[3]; or (3) to cover liability for damage to a vehicle[4]; or (4) to cover liability for damage to goods carried for hire or reward in or on a vehicle or in or on a trailer[5] (whether or not coupled) drawn by the vehicle[6]; or (5) to cover any liability of a person for damage to property in his custody or control[7]; or (6) to cover any contractual liability[8].

1 Road Traffic Act 1988 s 145(4)(a). This is subject to s 145(4A) (as added). See para 735 text and note 3 post.
2 Any reference to an accident includes a reference to two or more causally related accidents: ibid s 161(3).
3 Ibid s 145(4)(b).
4 Ibid s 145(4)(c).
5 'Trailer' means a vehicle drawn by a motor vehicle: ibid s 185(1). For the meaning of 'motor vehicle' see para 729 note 6 ante.
6 Ibid s 145(4)(d).

7 Ibid s 145(4)(e).
8 Ibid s 145(4)(f).

735. Exclusion of employees. A policy is not required to cover liability in respect of the death of or bodily injury sustained by a person in the employment of a person insured by the policy where the death or injury arises out of and in the course of that employment[1]. This exclusion is framed in the language of the Workmen's Compensation Acts[2] and is presumably intended to reflect the well-established distinction in the insurance world between public liability risks and employers' liability risks. In the case of a person carried in or upon a vehicle, or entering or getting on to or alighting from a vehicle, these provisions do not apply unless cover in respect of the liability is in fact provided pursuant to a requirement of the Employers' Liability (Compulsory Insurance) Act 1969[3].

The distinctions which are involved are very finely drawn. Thus, a director of a company is not, as such, an employee of the company[4], but a managing director[5] or a working director[6] may be, in the light of the contract which he holds. Again, an accident in a public thoroughfare may arise out of and in the course of employment if, at the relevant time, the employee is performing a duty to his employers, such as responding to an emergency call to duty[7], but the mere fact that he is on call in the event of an emergency is not sufficient unless an emergency arises[8]. Similarly, if an employer provides transport to enable his employees to travel to and from work, an accident which occurs on the journey does not arise out of and in the course of the employment unless the employee is under a duty, either contractually or as a matter of necessity, to use the provided transport[9]. However, if an accident occurs on the employer's private premises, for example on a private picking up place, while the employee is attempting to enter provided or public transport, the accident is one arising out of and in the course of the employment[10].

1 Road Traffic Act 1988 s 145(4)(a).
2 As to the Workmen's Compensation Acts (repealed) see para 678 ante.
3 Road Traffic Act 1988 s 145(4A) (added by the Motor Vehicle (Compulsory Insurance) Regulations 1992, SI 1992/3036, reg 2(3)). As to the Employers' Liability (Compulsory Insurance) Act 1969 see paras 685–689 ante; and EMPLOYMENT vol 16 (Reissue) para 36 et seq.
4 *Normandy v Ind Coope & Co Ltd* [1908] 1 Ch 84; *Re Lee, Behrens & Co Ltd* [1932] 2 Ch 46; cf *Moriarty v Regent's Garage and Engineering Co Ltd* [1921] 1 KB 423 (director's remuneration held to be a salary); revsd without deciding this point [1921] 2 KB 766, CA.
5 *Trussed Steel Concrete Co Ltd v Green* [1946] Ch 115: see COMPANIES vol 7(1) (Reissue) para 618 note 4.
6 *R v Stuart* [1894] 1 QB 310; *Bloor v Liverpool Derricking and Carrying Co Ltd* [1936] 3 All ER 399, CA.
7 *Blee v London and North Eastern Rly Co* [1938] AC 126, [1937] 4 All ER 270, HL; see also *Dunn v Lockwood & Co* [1947] 1 All ER 446, CA.
8 *Alderman v Great Western Rly Co* [1937] AC 454, [1937] 2 All ER 408, HL.
9 *St Helens Colliery Co Ltd v Hewitson* [1924] AC 59, HL; applied in *Vandyke v Fender (Sun Insurance Office Ltd, third party)* [1970] 2 QB 292, [1970] 2 All ER 335. Such an accident is now, however, deemed to arise out of and in the course of employment for the purpose of national insurance against industrial injuries: see the Social Security Contributions and Benefits Act 1992 s 99; and NATIONAL HEALTH AND SOCIAL SECURITY.
10 *Weaver v Tredegar Iron and Coal Co Ltd* [1940] AC 955, [1940] 3 All ER 157, HL.

736. Exclusion is only of employee of a person insured. Normally the person insured by an insurance policy is the assured himself, and it is his needs that are in the contemplation of both himself and his insurers when the policy is issued. Complications arise, however, if the policy contains a permitted driver clause, because then the permitted driver will be a person insured by the policy[1] and the exclusion will in such a case only operate as regards a person in the employment of the permitted driver[2]. However, it does not follow from this that an offence is committed by an assured if there is no permitted driver clause in his policy, and the vehicle is sent out in the charge of an employee of the assured who holds no personal insurance[3]. Many vehicles driven on the roads belong to limited companies, and the driving of them inevitably has to be done by an employee of the company[4]. The liabilities which have to be covered, however, are the company's liabilities only; if there is no permitted driver clause in the policy, there is no breach of the statutory provisions merely because the driver's personal responsibilities, for example to a passenger who is a fellow employee of the employers but not an employee of the driver, are not covered[5].

1 Ie for the purpose of the Road Traffic Act 1988 s 145(1), (3)(a), (4)(b): see paras 731, 733 ante.
2 *Richards v Cox* [1943] 1 KB 139, [1942] 2 All ER 624, CA.
3 *Lees v Motor Insurers' Bureau* [1952] 2 All ER 511; on appeal [1953] 1 WLR 620, CA; see para 722 text and note 4 ante.
4 Cf *Lester Bros (Coal Merchants) Ltd v Avon Insurance Co Ltd* (1942) 72 Ll L Rep 109; and para 720 note 9 ante. A person charged with using a motor vehicle in contravention of the Road Traffic Act 1988 s 143(1) (see para 729 ante) cannot be convicted if he proves that (1) the vehicle did not belong to him and was not in his possession under a contract of hiring or of loan, (2) he was using the vehicle in the course of his employment, and (3) he neither knew nor had reason to believe that there was not in force in relation to the vehicle such a policy of insurance or security as complied with the statutory requirements: s 143(3).
5 As to the extent of cover afforded to a permitted driver see para 722 ante.

737. Insurance of passengers. Where a person uses a motor vehicle in circumstances requiring compulsory insurance[1], then, if any other person is carried in or upon the vehicle[2], any antecedent agreement[3] or understanding between them (whether intended to be legally binding or not) is of no effect so far as it purports, or might be held either (1) to negative or restrict the user's liability[4], or (2) to impose any conditions with respect to the enforcement of such liability[5]. The fact that a person so carried has willingly accepted the risk of negligence on the part of the user must not be treated as negativing any such liability[6].

1 Ie under the Road Traffic Act 1988 s 143 (see para 729 ante): s 149(1).
2 References to a person being carried in or upon a vehicle include references to a person entering or getting on to or alighting from the vehicle: ibid s 149(4)(a).
3 The reference to any antecedent agreement is a reference to one made at any time before liability arose: ibid s 149(4)(b).
4 Ie under ibid s 145 (as amended) (see para 733 ante): s 149(2)(a).
5 Ibid s 149(2)(b).
6 Ibid s 149(3).

(iii) Obligations of Insurers

738. Obligation to indemnify. Notwithstanding anything in any enactment[1], authorised insurers issuing a policy pursuant to the statutory requirements must indemnify the persons or classes of persons specified in the policy in respect of any liability which the policy purports to cover in the case of those persons or classes of persons[2]. From this provision there is derived the right of a permitted driver to claim directly against the insurers even though he is in no strict sense a party to the contract of insurance[3]. However, no right of action is conferred by this provision on injured third parties[4]; nor are the insurers deprived by it of their normal rights to repudiate a policy on the ground of misrepresentation or non-disclosure[5].

1 This qualification seems to have been inserted with the Life Assurance Act 1774 in mind: see *McCormick v National Motor and Accident Insurance Union Ltd* (1934) 40 Com Cas 76 at 83–85, CA, per Scrutton LJ; *Guardian Assurance Co Ltd v Sutherland* [1939] 2 All ER 246. However, that Act probably does not apply at all: *Williams v Baltic Insurance Association of London Ltd* [1924] 2 KB 282; see para 537 ante.
2 Road Traffic Act 1988 s 148(7). As to an authorised insurer see para 731 ante.
3 *Tattersall v Drysdale* [1935] 2 KB 174; *Austin v Zurich General Accident and Liability Insurance Co Ltd* [1945] KB 250, [1945] 1 All ER 316, CA; *Guardian Assurance Co Ltd v Sutherland* [1939] 2 All ER 246; and as to the rights of the permitted driver see para 721 ante.
4 *Greenlees v Port of Manchester Insurance Co* 1933 SC 383.
5 *Guardian Assurance Co Ltd v Sutherland* [1939] 2 All ER 246. As to the duty of insurers to satisfy judgments against persons insured in respect of third party risks, notwithstanding that the insurers may be entitled to repudiate the policy, see para 748 post.

739. Obligation to issue certificate of insurance. An insurance policy is of no effect, for the purposes of the statutory provisions relating to compulsory insurance[1], unless and until there is delivered to the person by whom the policy is effected[2] a certificate of insurance in the prescribed form and containing such particulars of any conditions subject to which the policy is issued, and of any other matters, as may be prescribed[3]. Separate certificates of insurance are not required for cover notes, as the prescribed particulars must be printed on the back[4]. A certificate of insurance is merely a certificate; it does not enlarge the scope of the cover which is in fact afforded by the policy[5]. It is an offence, punishable on summary conviction by a fine not exceeding level 4 on the standard scale, to issue a certificate of insurance which is known to be false in a material particular[6]. It is an offence, similarly punishable on summary conviction, to make any false statement or withhold any material information for the purpose of obtaining a certificate of insurance[7].

1 Ie the Road Traffic Act 1988 Pt VI (ss 143–162) (as amended).
2 Delivery to a finance company which is not an agent of the assured is ineffective: *Starkey v Hall* [1936] 2 All ER 18, DC.
3 Road Traffic Act 1988 s 147(1). 'Prescribed' means prescribed by regulations (made under s 160 by the Secretary of State): s 160(1). The Secretary of State concerned is the Secretary of State for Transport, as to whom see CONSTITUTIONAL LAW. Different forms and particulars may be prescribed for different circumstances: s 147(3). The relevant regulations in force are the Motor Vehicles (Third Party Risks) Regulations 1972, SI 1972/1217 (amended by SI 1973/1821; SI 1974/792; SI 1974/2187; SI 1981/1567; and SI 1992/1283). For the forms of certificate required to be used by insurance companies see reg 5, Schedule (amended by SI 1981/1567; and SI 1992/1283). As to the printing and contents of the form see Schedule Pt 2 (amended by SI 1981/1567). Every certificate of insurance must be issued not later than four days after the date on which the policy to which it relates is issued or renewed: reg 6. Where, to the knowledge of a company, a policy issued by it ceases to be effective without the consent of the person to whom it was issued, otherwise than by effluxion of time or by reason of his death, the company must forthwith notify the Secretary of State of the date on which the policy ceased to be effective: reg 11. Provision is made for the return of certificates to the insurance company when, with the consent of the person to whom it was issued, a policy is transferred or is suspended or ceases to be effective, otherwise than by effluxion of time (reg 12), and for the replacement of certificates which have become defaced or have been lost or destroyed (reg 13).
4 Ibid reg 5(3), Schedule Pt 1 Form C.
5 *Richards v Port of Manchester Insurance Co Ltd* (1934) 152 LT 261; affd 152 LT 413, CA; *McCormick v National Motor and Accident Insurance Union Ltd* (1934) 50 TLR 528, CA; *Spraggon v Dominion Insurance Co Ltd* (1941) 69 Ll L Rep 1, CA.
6 Road Traffic Act 1988 s 175 (substituted, as from a day to be appointed, by the Transport Act 1982 s 24(1) (amended by the Road Traffic (Consequential Provisions) Act 1988 s 4, Sch 2 para 13(a));

Road Traffic Offenders Act 1988 s 9, Sch 2 Pt I (amended, as from a day to be appointed, by the Transport Act 1982 s 24(3) (amended by the Road Traffic (Consequential Provisions) Act 1988 ss 3, 4, Sch 1 Pt I, Sch 2 para 13(c)). As to the standard scale see para 212 note 5 ante.
7 Road Traffic Act 1988 ss 174(5); Road Traffic Offenders Act 1988 Sch 2 Pt I.

740. Obligation to keep records. Authorised insurers[1] must keep a record of all policies, securities and certificates issued by them[2], showing (1) the full name and address of the recipient[3]; (2) in the case of a policy relating to a specified motor vehicle[4] or specified motor vehicles, the registration mark of each such vehicle[5]; (3) the dates of commencement and expiry of the policy[6]; and (4) the conditions subject to which the indemnity is afforded[7]. This record must be preserved for one year from the date of expiry of the policy[8]. Every specified body[9] must keep a record of the motor vehicles owned by it in respect of which a policy has not been obtained, and of any certificates issued by it under the regulations in respect of such motor vehicles, and of the withdrawal or destruction of any such certificates[10].

1 As to authorised insurers see para 731 ante.
2 Motor Vehicles (Third Party Risks) Regulations 1972, SI 1972/1217, reg 10(1).
3 Ibid reg 10(1)(a).
4 For the meaning of 'motor vehicle' see para 729 note 6 ante, and for excepted vehicles see para 729 text and notes 10–25 ante.
5 Motor Vehicles (Third Party Risks) Regulations 1972 reg 10(1)(b).
6 Ibid reg 10(1)(c).
7 Ibid reg 10(1)(d), (e).
8 Ibid reg 10(1).
9 'Specified body' means any authority mentioned in the Road Traffic Act 1988 s 144(2)(a) (see para 729 text and notes 10–13 ante): Motor Vehicles (Third Party Risks) Regulations 1972 reg 4(1).
10 Ibid reg 10(2). Any company, specified body or other person by whom records of documents are required by the regulations to be kept must, without charge, furnish to the Secretary of State or to any chief officer of police on request any particulars of the documents: reg 10(4). As to the Secretary of State see para 739 note 3 ante.

741. Obligation to pay for hospital treatment. Authorised insurers[1] are not merely obliged to indemnify the assured against payments he has to make in respect of emergency treatment given by medical practitioners[2], they are also made directly responsible for paying expenses reasonably incurred by hospitals which provide treatment, whether as an in-patient or as an out-patient, to a person who has sustained injury arising out of the use of the insured vehicle on a road or in a place to which the public has a right of access[3]. The conditions to be fulfilled are that: (1) a payment is made, whether with or without admission of liability, in respect of the death or bodily injury in question by the authorised insurers under or in consequence of a policy issued under the statutory provisions relating to compulsory insurance[4]; and (2) the treatment has been given to the knowledge of the authorised insurers[5].

The amount of the reasonable expenses must be calculated, in the case of an in-patient, on the basis of the average daily cost, for each in-patient, of the maintenance of the hospital and the staff and the maintenance and treatment of the in-patients[6], and, in the case of an out-patient, on the basis of reasonable expenses actually incurred[7]. However, any money actually received by the hospital in payment of a specific charge for treatment, not being money received under a contributory scheme, must be deducted[8]. The amount to be paid must not exceed £2,546 for each person treated as an in-patient or £255 for each person treated as an out-patient[9].

Payment must be made, in the case of a hospital vested in the Secretary of State for the purposes of the National Health Service Act 1977, to the district health authority or special health authority responsible for the administration of the hospital, or to the Secretary of State if no such authority is so responsible[10]. In the case of any other hospital, payment must be made to the hospital[11].

1 As to authorised insurers see para 731 ante.
2 See the Road Traffic Act 1988 ss 145(3)(c), 158 (as amended), 159; para 733 ante, and NATIONAL HEALTH AND SOCIAL SECURITY.
3 Ibid s 157(1). See *Barnet Group Hospital Management Committee v Eagle Star Insurance Co Ltd* [1960] 1 QB 107, [1959] 3 All ER 210. 'Hospital' means an institution, not being an institution carried on for profit, which provides medical or surgical treatment for in-patients: Road Traffic Act 1988 s 161(1).
4 Ie under ibid s 145 (as amended) (see paras 731, 733 ante): s 157(1)(a), (b). A party against whom hospital expenses are claimed in an action in the High Court for personal injuries may, in addition to or without any payment into court, pay the hospital the amount for which he may be liable, in which case notice of the payment must be given to the other parties within seven days: see RSC Ord 22 r 12. The payment is not deemed an admission of liability. Similar provisions apply in the county court: CCR Ord 11 r 6. As to payment into court see generally COUNTY COURTS vol 10 para 333 et seq; PRACTICE AND PROCEDURE vol 37 para 285 et seq.
5 Road Traffic Act 1988 s 157(1)(c). The insurers must have knowledge at the time when payment is made: *Barnet Group Hospital Management Committee v Eagle Star Insurance Co Ltd* [1960] 1 QB 107, [1959] 3 All ER 210.
6 Road Traffic Act 1988 s 157(3)(a).
7 Ibid s 157(3)(b).
8 Ibid s 157(1).
9 Ibid s 157(2) (amended by the Road Traffic Accidents (Payments for Treatment) Order 1991, SI 1991/2005, reg 3).
10 Road Traffic Act 1988 s 159(1)(a). As to district and special health authorities see NATIONAL HEALTH AND SOCIAL SECURITY.
11 Ibid s 159(1)(c).

(iv) Third Parties' Rights under the Policy

742. General background. At common law a person injured by reason of another person's wrongdoing has no right of action against insurers who have undertaken to indemnify the wrongdoer; his only cause of action is against the other person who has committed the wrong, whether the wrong falls to be regarded as a tort or as a breach of contract[1]. The first invasion of this principle occurred when the Third Parties (Rights against Insurers) Act 1930 was enacted. This Act enables a third party who has a claim against an assured to establish a direct right of action against the assured's insurers if the assured becomes insolvent; if this condition is fulfilled, the third party is afforded such remedies as the assured had against his insurers[2].

1 As to rights of subrogation in tort and contract see paras 507–508 ante.
2 As to the application of the Third Parties (Rights against Insurers) Act 1930 see paras 679–684 ante.

743. Benefits conferred on third parties by the Road Traffic Act 1930. It was against the background of the Third Parties (Rights against Insurers) Act 1930 that the Road Traffic Act 1930 (now replaced by the Road Traffic Act 1988), was passed. It was realised that, unless some alterations were made in the rights to which the third party was by the first-named Act subrogated, those rights would frequently be of little, if any, value. Accordingly, it was provided that certain conditions in the assured's policy were to be of no effect in relation to a claim by a person to whom an assured was under a compulsorily insurable liability[1]. The conditions to that extent avoided are any conditions providing (1) that no liability is to arise, or (2) that any liability which has arisen is to cease, in the event of some specified thing being done, or omitted to be done, after the occurrence of the event giving rise to the claim[2]. If, therefore, any admission of liability is made after an accident contrary to a condition in the policy, or if, contrary to a condition in the policy, proper notice of the accident is not given to the insurers, the injured third party is not affected so far as his claim is concerned[3].

1 See para 742 ante.
2 See the Road Traffic Act 1988 s 148(5). This provision also applies in relation to conditions in securities, as to which see para 756 post. As to the preservation of the rights of insurers against the assured see para 746 post.
3 *Revell v London General Insurance Co Ltd* (1934) 152 LT 258. For the ordinary contractual rule see *Stoneham v Ocean Railway and General Accident Insurance Co* (1887) 19 QBD 237; *Verelst's Administratrix v Motor Insurance Co Ltd* [1925] 2 KB 137. As to notice of accidents generally see paras 483–485 ante.

744. Defects in the original avoidance clause. A motor policy normally contains a large number of restrictive conditions, qualifications and provisos describing and limiting the scope of the insurance. The only conditions, however, which, as against an injured third party with a compulsorily insurable claim, were rendered void by the Road Traffic Act 1930[1] were conditions relating to something being done or omitted after the accident. In all other respects the injured third party was merely subrogated to the rights of the assured, such as they were, under the policy which he held[2]. He was, accordingly, left without remedy if, at the time of the accident, the vehicle was being used outside the scope of the description of use clause[3]. Similarly, if the policy contained an arbitration clause, the injured third party was bound by it as being a person with no better rights than the assured[4], even if the arbitration clause was in the form requiring an arbitration as a condition precedent to the bringing of any action[5]. Furthermore, it was left entirely open to the insurers to repudiate liability altogether on the basis that the policy had been obtained by misrepresentation or non-disclosure[6].

1 This Act was repealed by the Road Traffic Act 1972 (repealed) and is now replaced by the Road Traffic Act 1988: see para 743 ante.
2 *Gray v Blackmore* [1934] 1 KB 95.
3 *Bright v Ashfold* [1932] 2 KB 153; *Gray v Blackmore* [1934] 1 KB 95.
4 *Golding v London and Edinburgh Insurance Co Ltd* (1932) 43 Ll L Rep 487, CA; *Jones v Birch Bros Ltd* [1933] 2 KB 597, CA; *Freshwater v Western Australian Assurance Co Ltd* [1933] 1 KB 515; *Austin v Zurich General Accident and Liability Insurance Co Ltd* [1945] KB 250, [1945] 1 All ER 316, CA. In cases to which the Road Traffic Act 1988 s 151 (as amended) applies (see paras 748–753 post) the third party can enforce directly against the insurers any judgment obtained against the assured; the presence of an arbitration clause in the policy accordingly has no bearing.
5 *Jones v Birch Bros Ltd* [1933] 2 KB 597, CA. As to arbitration clauses see generally paras 495–499 ante.
6 *Greenlees v Port of Manchester Insurance Co* 1933 SC 383; *Cleland v London General Insurance Co Ltd* (1935) 51 Ll L Rep 156, CA.

745. Extension of conditions avoided as against third party. Further conditions usually found in motor policies have been rendered void by the Road Traffic Act 1934 (now replaced by the Road Traffic Act 1988) as against a third party with a compulsorily insurable claim, subject to the proviso that a certificate of insurance has been issued[1]. The conditions thus affected comprise any condition purporting to restrict the insurance by reference to any of the following matters: (1) the age or physical or mental condition of the person driving the vehicle[2]; (2) the condition of the vehicle[3]; (3) the number of persons that the vehicle carries[4]; (4) the weight or physical characteristics of the goods that the vehicle carrries[5]; (5) the time at which, or the areas within which, the vehicle is used[6]; (6) the horsepower or cylinder capacity or value of the vehicle[7]; (7) the carrying on the vehicle of any particular apparatus[8]; and (8) the carrying on the vehicle of any particular means of identification other than the statutory[9] identification marks[10].

In relation to compulsory insurable claims, so far as the policy restricts the insurance of persons to use of the vehicle for specified purposes (for example, social, domestic and pleasure purposes) of a non-commercial character, or excludes use for hire or reward, or business or commercial use, or use for specified purposes of a business or commercial character, use on a journey in the course of which one or more passengers are carried at separate fares is treated as falling within the restriction or not falling within the exclusion if specified conditions are satisfied[11].

1 See the Road Traffic Act 1988 s 148. This also applies in relation to securities: see para 756 post.
2 Ibid s 148(2)(a). There is sometimes a condition prohibiting the driving of the vehicle by a person under the age of 18 or over the age of 70. See also *National Farmers Union Mutual Insurance Society Ltd v Dawson* [1941] 2 KB 424.
3 Road Traffic Act 1988 s 148(2)(b); and see *Jones and James v Provincial Insurance Co Ltd* (1929) 46 TLR 71; *Brown v Zurich General Accident and Liability Insurance Co Ltd* [1954] 2 Lloyd's Rep 243.
4 Road Traffic Act 1988 s 148(2)(c); and see *Houghton v Trafalgar Insurance Co Ltd* [1953] 2 Lloyd's Rep 18; affd [1954] 1 QB 247, [1953] 2 All ER 1409, CA, where such a provision might have been useful.
5 Road Traffic Act 1988 s 148(2)(d); and see *Provincial Insurance Co Ltd v Morgan* [1933] AC 240, HL; *Jones v Welsh Insurance Corpn Ltd* [1937] 4 All ER 149; cf *Houghton v Trafalgar Insurance Co Ltd* [1954] 1 QB 247, [1953] 2 All ER 1409, CA.
6 Road Traffic Act 1988 s 148(2)(e); and see *Dawsons Ltd v Bonnin* [1922] 2 AC 413, HL.
7 Road Traffic Act 1988 s 148(2)(f).
8 Ibid s 148(2)(g); and see *Pictorial Machinery Ltd v Nicolls* (1940) 164 LT 248.
9 As to the identification marks required to be carried by mechanically propelled vehicles see the Vehicles (Excise) Act 1971 ss 19–22, Sch 7 (as amended); and ROAD TRAFFIC.
10 Road Traffic Act 1988 s 148(2)(h). As to the right of the insurers to recover payments made by virtue of these provisions see para 746 post.
11 Ibid s 150(1). This subsection also applies to securities: s 150(1). It is immaterial how the restrictions or exclusions are worded: s 150(3). The conditions are that: (1) the vehicle is not adapted to carry more than eight passengers and is not a motor cycle; (2) the fare or aggregate of the fares paid in respect of the journey does not exceed the running costs of the vehicle for the journey (including an appropriate amount in respect of depreciation and general wear); and (3) the arrangements for the payment of fares by the passenger or passengers were made before the journey began: s 150(2). The words 'fare' and 'separate fares' have the same meaning as in the Public Passenger Vehicles Act 1981 s 1(4): Road Traffic Act 1988 s 150(4); see ROAD TRAFFIC.

746. Rights of insurers who make payment outside the scope of policy. The statutory provision which renders certain conditions in policies of no effect against third parties[1] does not, however, render void any provision in a policy requiring the person insured to repay to the insurers any sums which the latter may have become liable to pay under the policy and which have been applied to the satisfaction of the claims of third parties[2]. Repayment would probably be obtainable, even in the absence of such a provision, as there can hardly be consideration for a payment which, under the terms of the contract, the insurers are not obliged to make, and the payment would, therefore, be recoverable as money paid under statutory duress to the use of the assured or for a consideration which had failed[3].

The statutory provision which extends the classes of conditions avoided as against third parties[4] does not require the insurers to pay any sum in respect of the liability of any person otherwise than in or towards the discharge of that liability[5], and any sum paid by them in or towards the discharge of any liability of any person which is covered by the policy by virtue only of that enactment is recoverable by them from that person[6].

1 Ie the Road Traffic Act 1988 s 148(5): see para 743 ante.
2 Ibid s 148(6). The provisions set out in this paragraph also apply to securities: see para 756 post.
3 See CONTRACT vol 9 para 660 et seq.
4 Ie the Road Traffic Act 1988 s 148(1): see para 745 ante.
5 Ibid s 148(3).
6 Ibid s 148(4).

747. Insolvency of the assured. Where a certificate of insurance has been delivered to the person by whom a policy has been effected[1], the happening in relation to any person insured by the policy of any such event as is mentioned in the general statutory provisions which relate to the subrogation of third parties to the rights of the assured on the insolvency of the assured[2] does not affect any such liability of that person as is required to be covered by compulsory insurance[3].

1 Ie under the Road Traffic Act 1988 s 147(1): see para 739 ante.
2 See the Third Parties (Rights against Insurers) Act 1930 s 1(1), (2) (as amended); and para 679 ante.
3 Road Traffic Act 1988 s 153(1), which applies notwithstanding anything in the Third Parties (Rights against Insurers) Act 1930, but does not affect any rights against the insurer conferred by that Act on the person to whom the liability was incurred: Road Traffic Act 1988 s 153(3). This provision also applies in relation to securities: see para 756 post. Its intention seems to be to make it clear that the assured's liability remains unaffected by his bankruptcy and the third party's consequential rights by subrogation: see Shawcross's Motor Insurance (2nd Edn) 134, 275, 314–315, and para 681 ante. However, it may be that doubt was felt as to whether the Third Parties (Rights against Insurers) Act 1930 had effectively overruled *Re Harrington Motor Co Ltd, ex p Chaplin* [1928] Ch 105, CA, and *Hood's Trustees v Southern Union General Insurance Co of Australasia* [1928] Ch 793, CA. For the effect of these conditions see para 677 ante.

(v) Third Parties' Rights outside the Policy

748. Third parties' direct rights of action against insurers. In practice, the provisions entitling an injured third party to be subrogated to the rights of the assured on the insolvency of the assured[1] were found to be insufficient to protect the interests of third parties, even in conjunction with the provisions rendering insurance compulsory against third party risks[2] and rendering certain conditions in policies ineffective against third parties[3]. A more drastic provision was accordingly enacted which imposes on insurers[4], once a certificate of insurance has been issued to the person effecting the policy[5], the obligation to pay to any person entitled to the benefit of a judgment coming within the provision[6] any sum payable under the judgment, including any amount payable in respect of costs and any sum payable in respect of interest by virtue of any enactment relating to interest on judgments[7], notwithstanding that the insurers may be entitled to avoid or cancel, or may have avoided or cancelled, the policy[8].

However, the obligation is limited by certain conditions and qualifications[9] set out subsequently[10].

1 As to these provisions see paras 679–684 ante. For the saving of the rights of third parties against the assured see para 742 ante.

2 As to compulsory insurance against third party risks see para 729 ante.
3 As to conditions avoided as against third parties see paras 743–746 ante.
4 As to the application of the Road Traffic Act 1988 ss 151, 152 (as amended) to persons who give securities see para 756 post.
5 Ie under ibid s 147 (see para 739 ante): s 151(1).
6 See ibid s 151(2)–(4).
7 As to interest on judgments see the Judgments Act 1838 s 17 (as amended); the Administration of Justice Act 1970 s 44(1); the Judgment Debts (Rate of Interest) Order 1993, SI 1993/564, which specifies the rate as 8%; and JUDGMENTS.
8 Road Traffic Act 1988 s 151(5). However, as to the right of insurers to obtain a declaration that a policy is void see s 152(2) (as amended) and para 751 post; and as to the effect of such a declaration see note 9 infra. As to the extra-statutory Motor Insurers' Bureau Agreement, by which recourse to the Road Traffic Act 1988 s 151 is in general rendered no longer necessary, see para 758 post.
9 See ibid s 151(5), by which the liability of the insurers to pay is expressed to be subject to the provisions of the section, and s 152 (as amended), which sets out exceptions; and *Croxford v Universal Insurance Co Ltd, Norman v Gresham Fire and Accident Insurance Society Ltd* [1936] 2 KB 253 at 272–274, [1936] 1 All ER 151 at 160–162, CA, per Slesser LJ, and at 280–281 and 166–167 per Scott LJ. Insurers are liable in the circumstances and under the conditions specified in the whole of the Road Traffic Act 1988 ss 151, 152 (as amended), and not merely those specified in s 151(5). Insurers may protect themselves from liability under s 151 if they obtain a declaration under s 152(2) (as amended): see para 751 post.
10 See paras 749–750 post.

749. Judgments required to be satisfied. The first condition of the obligation of the insurers to pay on a judgment[1] is that there is a judgment[2].

The second condition is that the judgment must be in respect of a liability which is required to be covered[3] by compulsory insurance[4]. In other words, the only person who can maintain a right of action direct against the insurers is a person falling within the class of third parties whose bodily injury or death or damage to whose property is required to be covered by a motor policy[5].

The third condition is that the liability is, in fact, covered by the terms of the policy, or would be covered but for the fact that the insurer is entitled to avoid or cancel, or has avoided or cancelled, the policy[6]. For this purpose, conditions declared to be invalid as against a third party[7] are ignored, but if, even after ignoring all such conditions, the relevant use of the vehicle puts it outside the scope of the policy, the insurers are left immune. The most important clause in this connection is the 'description of use' clause. The assured is criminally liable if he uses his car for purposes outside the scope of his insurance[8] and, in addition to his criminal liability, he has to bear unaided the cost of compensating third parties injured by his use if he is negligent. Subject to the statutory provision rendering certain conditions invalid against third parties[9], the insurers are not obliged to carry a wider scope of liability than they have agreed by their policy to carry.

The fourth condition is that the judgment must be against a person insured by the policy[10]. This language covers a permitted driver as well as the person by whom the policy has been effected[11].

1 Ie under the Road Traffic Act 1988 s 151: see para 748 ante.
2 Ibid s 151(1). An action for a declaration of liability against the insurers before judgment will not normally be allowed: *Carpenter v Ebblewhite* [1939] 1 KB 347, [1938] 4 All ER 41, CA.
3 Ie under the Road Traffic Act 1988 s 145: see para 733 ante.
4 Ibid s 151(2).
5 As to the persons falling within this class see paras 733–737 ante.
6 Road Traffic Act 1988 s 151(5). Any provision in the policy which restricts the insurance to the holding of a licence to drive a vehicle is to be disregarded: s 151(3). In these circumstances, the insurer has a right of recovery against the insured person: s 151(7)(a); and see *Robb v McKechnie* 1936 JC 25 (condition against use of trailer; accident while trailer used).

7 See the Road Traffic Act 1988 s 148; and paras 742–747 ante.
8 For the definition of risk by reference to use see paras 712, 717–719 ante.
9 See the Road Traffic Act 1988 s 148; and paras 742–747 ante.
10 Ibid s 151(2). An insurer is bound to satisfy a judgment even if it is obtained against a person not insured by the policy, subject to certain exceptions in the case of vehicles stolen or taken: s 151(4)(a), (5). The insurer has rights of recovery against the user or an insured person who caused or permitted the use of the vehicle: s 151(8).
11 *Tattersall v Drysdale* [1935] 2 KB 174; *Austin v Zurich General Accident and Liability Insurance Co Ltd* [1945] KB 250, [1945] 1 All ER 316, CA.

750. Qualifications of the obligation. The qualifications affecting the obligation of insurers[1] to meet a judgment in favour of a third party[2] are as described in heads (1) to (5) below.

(1) The insurers must be given notice of the bringing of the proceedings in which the judgment is obtained, either before, or within seven days after, the commencement of those proceedings[3]. Normally the issue of a High Court writ or the entry of a plaint in the county court operates as the commencement of proceedings[4], but it may happen that the relevant claim only comes on to the scene at a later stage; in such a case the initiation of the relevant claim is the material date[5]. The notice must be of sufficient formality to be understood by a reasonable man as an intimation of legal proceedings[6], although no particular formality is required[7]. There is no need to plead the giving of notice[8].

(2) No sum is payable in respect of a judgment so long as a stay of execution pending an appeal is operative[9].

(3) The insurers are not liable to pay the amount of the judgment if, before the happening of the accident causing the third party's injury or death or damage to property, the policy has been cancelled, either by mutual consent or by virtue of a provision contained in the policy and, in addition, one or other of the following conditions has been fulfilled:

    (a) before the accident there has been a surrender of the certificate of insurance, or a statutory declaration[10] by the person to whom it was delivered that it has been lost or destroyed[11];

    (b) after the accident, but before the expiration of 14 days from the taking effect of the cancellation of the policy, there has been a surrender of the certificate or such a statutory declaration as has been previously mentioned[12]; or

    (c) either before or after the accident, but within the period of 14 days from the taking effect of the cancellation of the policy, the insurers have commenced proceedings[13] in respect of the failure to surrender the certificate[14].

(4) Insurers are given protection where the policy has been obtained by misrepresentation or non-diclosure, provided they in turn fulfil certain stringent conditions[15].

(5) In the case of damage to property, if the amount of the judgment is more than £250,000, the insurer need only satisfy a proportion of the judgment[16].

1 Ie under the Road Traffic Act 1988 s 151: see para 749 ante.
2 See *Croxford v Universal Insurance Co Ltd, Norman v Gresham Fire and Accident Insurance Society Ltd* [1936] 2 KB 253, [1936] 1 All ER 151, CA; and para 748 note 9 ante.
3 Road Traffic Act 1988 s 152(1)(a).
4 See RSC Ord 5 rr 1, 2; CCR Ord 3 rr 1, 3.

5 If the relevant claim is first made by counterclaim in third party proceedings, the service or filing of the counterclaim is the commencement of the proceedings: *Cross v British Oak Insurance Co* [1938] 2 KB 167, [1938] 1 All ER 383.

6 *Herbert v Railway Passengers Assurance Co Ltd* [1938] 1 All ER 650.

7 *Harrington v Pinkey* [1989] RTR 345, [1989] 2 Lloyd's Rep 310, CA. Cf *Ceylon Motor Insurance Association Ltd v Thambugala* [1953] AC 584, [1953] 2 All ER 870, PC.

8 *Baker v Provident Accident and White Cross Insurance Co Ltd* [1939] 2 All ER 690.

9 Road Traffic Act 1988 s 152(1)(b).

10 See ibid s 147(4); Motor Vehicles (Third Party Risks) Regulations 1972, SI 1972/1217, reg 12(3), (4).

11 Road Traffic Act 1988 s 152(1)(c)(i). References to a certificate of insurance in any provision relating to the surrender, or the loss or destruction, of a certificate of insurance are, in relation to policies under which more than one certificate is issued, to be construed as references to all the certificates and, where any copy of a certificate has been issued, are to be construed as including a reference to that copy: s 161(2).

12 Ibid s 152(1)(c)(ii).

13 Ie presumably under ibid s 147(4): see para 755 post.

14 Ibid s 152(1)(c)(iii).

15 As to the rights of insurers in respect of misrepresentation and non-disclosure see para 751 post.

16 Road Traffic Act 1988 s 151(6).

(vi) Rights of the Insurers and Duties of the Assured

751. Rights in respect of misrepresentation and non-disclosure. No sum is payable by insurers[1] under the provisions relating to payment on a judgment[2] if, in an action commenced before or within three months after the commencement of the proceedings in which the judgment was given[3], they obtain a declaration that, apart from any provision contained in the policy, they are entitled to avoid the policy on the ground that it was obtained by the non-disclosure of a material[4] fact or by a representation of fact which was false in some material particular, or, if they have already avoided the policy on any such ground, a declaration that they were entitled to avoid it on that ground apart from any provision contained in it[5]. Since the right of the insurers to relief from liability is dependent upon there being non-disclosure of a material fact or misrepresentation of fact which is false in a material particular apart from any provision contained in the policy, it is irrelevant for this purpose that the insurers may have stipulated in the policy that a particular matter is to be treated as material for the purposes of the policy[6]. Any such provision has to be ignored and the statutory definition of materiality must alone be looked at. This provides that 'material' means of such a nature as to influence the judgment of a prudent insurer in determining whether he will take the risk and, if so, at what premium and on what conditions[7].

It seems that a provision in a policy that nothing contained in it is to affect the right of any person to recover against the insurers[8] does not prevent the insurers from relying on material non-disclosure or misrepresentation for the purpose of obtaining a declaration[9].

1 As to the application of the Road Traffic Act 1988 ss 151, 152 (as amended) in relation to persons who give securities see para 756 post.

2 Ie ibid s 151: see para 749 ante.

3 As to the date which is treated as the date of the commencement of proceedings see para 750 text to notes 4–5 ante.

4 See text and note 7 infra.

5 Road Traffic Act 1988 s 152(2). As to the operation of this provision see generally *Croxford v Universal Insurance Co Ltd, Norman v Gresham Fire and Accident Insurance Society Ltd* [1936] 2 KB 253, [1936] 1 All ER 151, CA, and para 748 note 9 ante; also *National Farmers Mutual Insurance Co Ltd v Tully* 1935 SLT 574 (false statements in proposal; disclosure of true facts to insurance agent not

sufficient: see further paras 376–380 ante). If the policy has been cancelled by mutual consent, no action for a declaration appears to be necessary even if the insurer's consideration for the agreement derives from allegations of misrepresentation or non-disclosure, provided the conditions laid down in s 152(1) (see para 750 text to notes 10–14 ante) as to the certificate of insurance are fulfilled; see however *Croxford v Universal Insurance Co Ltd* supra at 282 and 168 per Scott LJ.

6   For such a stipulation see *Dawsons Ltd v Bonnin* [1922] 2 AC 413, HL. As to the duties laid down by the contract see further para 363 ante.

7   Road Traffic Act 1988 s 152(2) (amended by the Road Traffic Act 1991 s 48, Sch 4 para 66). For facts found to be material see *Norman v Gresham Fire and Accident Insurance Society Ltd* (1935) 52 Ll L Rep 292 at 301; on appeal [1936] 2 KB 253, [1936] 1 All ER 151, CA (cancellation of other policies); *Cleland v London General Insurance Co Ltd* (1935) 51 Ll L Rep 156, CA (previous convictions); *Locker and Woolf Ltd v Western Australian Insurance Co Ltd* [1936] 1 KB 408, CA (a fire insurance case; non-disclosure of previous refusal of motor insurance held material); *Taylor v Eagle Star Insurance Co Ltd* (1940) 67 Ll L Rep 136 (previous convictions); see also *Merchants' and Manufacturers' Insurance Co Ltd v Davies* [1938] 1 KB 196, [1937] 2 All ER 767, CA; *Guardian Assurance Co Ltd v Sutherland* [1939] 2 All ER 246 (misrepresentation of ownership of car; declaration made against absent defendant); *Merchants and Manufacturers Insurance Co Ltd v Hunt and Thorne* [1941] 1 KB 295, [1941] 1 All ER 123, CA (age and convictions of driver of car); *Broad v Waland* (1942) 73 Ll L Rep 263 (age of proposer). For facts found not to be material see *Zurich General Accident and Liability Insurance Co Ltd v Morrison* [1942] 2 KB 53, [1942] 1 All ER 529, CA (question in proposal form as to driving experience; non-disclosure that proposer had held only provisional licence); see also *Mackay v London Insurance Co* (1935) 51 Ll L Rep 201 (proceedings by assured against insurers; statements in answer to questions in proposal that no other insurer had required from assured increased premiums or special conditions and that proposer had not been convicted; assured three years before, when aged 18, had insured motor-cycle with excess of £2 10s (£2.50) and had been fined 10s (50p) for having insufficient brakes; assured's answers not material, though insurers not liable as accuracy of assured's answer made basis of contract by stipulation therein). As to the ineffectiveness of such stipulations in relation to applications under the Road Traffic Act 1988 s 152(2) (as amended) see paras 748–750 ante.

8   Ie under ibid s 151: see paras 748–749 ante.

9   See *Zurich General Accident and Liability Insurance Co Ltd v Morrison* [1942] 1 All ER 529 at 535 per Atkinson J; affd without reference to this point [1942] 2 KB 53, [1942] 1 All ER 529, CA, disagreeing with the view expressed by Stable J in *Merchants and Manufacturers Insurance Co Ltd v Hunt* [1940] 4 All ER 205 at 211–212; affd on other grounds [1941] 1 KB 295, [1941] 1 All ER 123, CA.

752. Notice required of insurers' declaration proceedings. It would be manifestly unfair that a third party should be prejudiced by insurers obtaining a declaration of avoidance of the policy[1] without his having any opportunity to contest their claim. Accordingly, insurers are not to derive any benefit from any judgment obtained in declaration proceedings commenced after the commencement of the third party's action[2] unless, either before or within seven days after commencing their action for a declaration, they have given notice to the injured third party of their action, specifying the non-disclosure or misrepresentation on which they propose to rely[3]. Any person receiving such a notice is then given a right to be made a party to the declaration proceedings[4] so as to contest the insurers' right to repudiate, even if the assured himself does not choose to do so. If the injured third party has not commenced his proceedings before the insurers' declaration action he has at common law a right to be added as defendant to the insurers' action which might deprive him of his statutory rights[5]. The injured third party being then, if joined, a party to the action, any matters relied on must be proved by evidence admissible against him; evidence which is admissible only as against the assured will not suffice[6]. On the other hand, it is no objection to a declaration validly obtained that the assured defendant failed to appear or to defend[7]; nor are declaration proceedings necessary if the policy has been rescinded, not on the ground of misrepresentation or non-disclosure, but by the mutual consent of the insurers and assured[8].

1 Ie under the Road Traffic Act 1988 s 152(2) (as amended): see para 751 ante.
2 As to the date when proceedings are deemed to be commenced see para 750 text to notes 4–5 ante.
3 Road Traffic Act 1988 s 152(3). Insurers are bound by the terms of the notice and cannot afterwards extend them: *Contingency Insurance Co Ltd v Lyons* (1939) 65 Ll L Rep 53, CA; *Merchants and Manufacturers Insurance Co Ltd v Hunt and Thorne* [1941] 1 KB 295, [1942] 1 All ER 123, CA; *Zurich General Accident and Liability Insurance Co Ltd v Morrison* [1942] 2 KB 53, [1942] 1 All ER 529, CA; *Trafalgar Insurance Co Ltd v McGregor* [1942] 1 KB 275, CA.
4 Road Traffic Act 1988 s 152(4).
5 *Zurich General Accident and Liability Insurance Co v Livingston* 1938 SC 582.
6 *Merchants and Manufacturers Insurance Co Ltd v Hunt and Thorne* [1941] 1 KB 295, [1941] 1 All ER 123, CA. As to the scope of discovery in such an action see *Merchants' and Manufacturers' Insurance Co Ltd v Davies* [1938] 1 KB 196, [1937] 2 All ER 767, CA.
7 *Guardian Assurance Co Ltd v Sutherland* [1939] 2 All ER 246.
8 *Croxford v Universal Insurance Co Ltd, Norman v Gresham Fire and Accident Insurance Society Ltd* [1936] 2 KB 253, [1936] 1 All ER 151, CA. The requirement as to surrender of the certificate of insurance must, however, be satisfied: see para 755 post.

753. Rights of insurers against the assured. If insurers, by virtue of the provisions relating to payments on judgments[1], become liable to pay to a third party a sum in excess of what, under the policy, they would be liable to pay to their assured in respect of the relevant accident, they are entitled to recover the excess from the assured[2]. It would seem, therefore, that, where the insurers would not be liable to pay anything under their policy by reason of misrepresentation or non-disclosure giving them a right to repudiate, they are entitled to recover from the assured anything which they are compelled by the statutory provisions to pay, whether or not they seek to obtain the relief[3] which the statutory provisions afford them[4].

1 Ie the Road Traffic Act 1988 s 151: see paras 748–749 ante.
2 Ibid s 151(7).
3 As to rights of insurers in respect of misrepresentation and non-disclosure see para 751 ante.
4 See, however, Shawcross's Motor Insurance (2nd Edn) 313, where a contrary view is taken. For examples of policies providing expressly for repayment of all sums which the insurers would not have been liable to pay but for the statutory provisions see para 751 note 9 ante.

754. Duty to give information as to insurance. Any person against whom a claim is made in respect of a compulsorily insurable liability[1] must, on demand by or on behalf of the person making the claim, state whether or not he was, in fact, insured in respect of the liability by a policy having effect for the purpose of the statutory provisions relating to compulsory insurance, or would have been insured by such a policy if his insurer had not avoided or cancelled the policy[2]. If he was or, but for the avoidance or cancellation of his policy, would have been so insured, he must give such particulars of his insurance as were specified in his certificate[3] of insurance[4]. Failure to comply with these requirements without reasonable excuse, or wilfully making any false statement in reply to such a demand, is an offence[5]. Subject to the necessary adaptations, the foregoing provisions apply where a security instead of a policy has been issued[6].

1 Ie a liability under the Road Traffic Act 1988 s 145 (as amended) (see paras 731, 733 ante): s 154 (1).
2 Ibid s 154(1)(a).
3 Ie the certificate delivered pursuant to ibid s 147: see para 739 ante.
4 Ibid s 154(1)(b)(i). Where no certificate is delivered under s 147, he must give the following particulars: (1) the registration mark or other identifying particulars of the vehicle concerned; (2) the

number or other identifying particulars of the insurance policy issued in respect of the vehicle; (3) the name of the driver; and (4) the period of cover: s 154(1)(b)(ii).

5 Ibid s 154(2). The offence is punishable on summary conviction by a fine not exceeding level 4 on the standard scale: Road Traffic Offenders Act 1988 s 9, Sch 2 Pt I. As to the standard scale see para 212 note 5 ante.

6 Road Traffic Act 1988 s 154(1). As to the issue of a security as an alternative to a policy see para 756 post.

755. Duty to surrender certificate of insurance. Where a policy is cancelled by mutual consent or by virtue of any provision in the policy, the person to whom the certificate of insurance was delivered[1] must, within seven days of the cancellation taking effect, surrender the certificate to the insurers or make a statutory declaration[2] as to its having been lost or destroyed[3], if that is the case[4]. Any failure to comply with these requirements is an offence[5]. These provisions apply subject to the necessary adaptations where a security instead of a policy has been issued[6].

1 Ie under the Road Traffic Act 1988 s 147(1) (see para 739 ante): s 147(4).
2 Every statutory declaration must be delivered to the insurers in the same manner as if it were a certificate: Motor Vehicles (Third Party Risks) Regulations 1972, SI 1972/1217, reg 12(3).
3 As to where more than one certificate has been issued see para 750 note 11 ante.
4 Road Traffic Act 1988 s 147(4).
5 Ibid s 147(5). The offence is punishable on summary conviction by a fine not exceeding level 3 on the standard scale: Road Traffic Offenders Act 1988 s 9, Sch 2 Pt I. As to the standard scale see para 212 note 5 ante.
6 As to the issue of a security see para 756 post.

(vii) Statutory Alternatives to Insurance

756. Security as an alternative to a policy. The place of an insurance policy for the purposes of compulsory protection against third party risks may be taken by a security[1]. The security must be given either by an authorised insurer[2] or by some body of persons which carries on in the United Kingdom the business of giving securities of the same kind and has deposited with the Accountant General of the Supreme Court the sum of £15,000 in respect of that business[3]. The security must consist of an undertaking by the giver of the security, subject to any conditions specified in it, to make good any failure by the owner of the vehicle, or such other persons or classes of persons as may be specified in the security, duly to discharge any liability which may be incurred by him or them[4]. In the case of liabilities arising out of the use of a motor vehicle on a road in Great Britain[5], the amount secured need not exceed, in the case of a public service vehicle[6], £25,000[7], and in any other case, £5,000[8]. Any person wishing to deposit with the Accountant General the sum of £15,000 may apply to the Secretary of State[9] for a warrant, which is sufficient authority for the Accountant General to issue a direction for the payment into the Bank of England to the credit of his account by the person named in the warrant of the £15,000, which is to be credited in the books of the Accountant General to an account entitled 'ex parte the depositor'[10]. The depositor may deposit in lieu, wholly or in part, of the money deposit, an equivalent amount of securities[11]. A certificate of security corresponding with a certificate of insurance must be issued[12]. The statutory provisions relating to the duty of insurers to satisfy judgments against persons insured in respect of third party risks[13], the continuance of the liability of the assured notwithstanding the statutory subrogation of a third party on the insolvency of the assured to the assured's rights against the insurers[14], the classes of conditions which are avoided as against third parties[15], the duty of persons against whom claims are made to give information as to insurance[16] and the duty to surrender certificates on the cancellation of policies[17] apply in relation to securities having effect for purposes of compulsory protection against third party risks as they apply in relation to policies of insurance.

1 See the Road Traffic Act 1988 s 143(1); and para 729 ante.
2 As to authorised insurers see para 731 ante.
3 Road Traffic Act 1988 s 146(2). For the meaning of 'United Kingdom' see para 2 note 10 ante.
4 Ibid s 146(3). See also para 757 text to note 3 post.
5 For the meaning of 'Great Britain' see para 2 note 10 ante.
6 Ie within the meaning of the Public Passenger Vehicles Act 1981 (see s 1 (as amended); and ROAD TRAFFIC).
7 Road Traffic Act 1988 s 146(4)(a).
8 Ibid s 146(4)(b).
9 Ie the Secretary of State for Transport: Motor Vehicles (Third-Party Risks Deposits) Regulations 1992, SI 1992/1284, reg 3.
10 Ibid reg 4.
11 Ie securities in which cash under the control of, or subject to, the order of the court may for the time being be invested (their value being taken at a price as near as may be to, but not exceeding, the current market price), and in that case the Secretary of State may vary the warrant accordingly: ibid reg 4 proviso. The permitted securities in which money may be invested are those specified in the Trustee Investment Act 1961 Sch 1 Pt I, Pt II paras 1–10A, 12, and Pt III paras 2, 3, as supplemented by Pt IV (all as amended): Motor Vehicles (Third-Party Risks Deposits) Regulations 1992 regs 3, 5(1).
The issue of any warrant or any error in such warrant does not render the Secretary of State or the person signing the warrant on his behalf in any manner liable for or in respect of any money or security deposited in court, or any securities for the time being representing the same, or the interest, dividends or income accruing due on them: reg 7. As to the investment of deposits and the payment of interest on investments see reg 5. As to the payment out of court of deposits where it is just and equitable, and in particular where a person who has made a deposit otherwise complies with the provisions relating to compulsory insurance against third party risks, or, providing that subsisting liabilities have been met, where such person ceases to own or to control the use of a motor vehicle, or a person who has made a deposit ceases altogether to carry on in the United Kingdom the business of giving securities, see reg 6. Subject to these regulations, the relevant provisions of the Court Funds Rules 1987 apply to deposits made, or having effect as if made, in pursuance of the Road Traffic Act 1988 s 144(1) (as amended) or s 146(2): Motor Vehicles (Third-Party Risks Deposits) Regulations 1992 reg 8.
12 Road Traffic Act 1988 s 147(2). The certificate must be in the prescribed form and contain prescribed particulars: s 147(2). See the Motor Vehicles (Third Party Risks) Regulations 1972, SI 1972/1217, which also apply to insurance certificates; as to which see para 739 ante. Different forms and particulars may be prescribed for different circumstances: Road Traffic Act 1988 s 147(3).
13 Ie ibid ss 151, 152 (as amended): see paras 748–753 ante.
14 Ie ibid s 153: see para 747 ante.
15 Ie ibid ss 148–150: see para 745 ante.
16 Ie ibid s 154: see para 754 ante.
17 Ie ibid s 147(4), (5): see para 755 ante.

757. Deposit as alternative to policy. A special exemption from having a policy or security covering compulsorily insurable third party risks exists in the case of a person who deposits £500,000 with the Accountant General of the Supreme Court[1]. This was no doubt designed as a convenience for big operators capable of being their own insurers. The relevant rules governing such deposits apply[2]. A deposit pursuant to this exemption, like a deposit made by a person giving a security, forms a special fund which cannot be applied in discharge of any

of the depositor's other liabilities as long as any compulsorily insurable liabilities have not been discharged or otherwise provided for[3].

1 Road Traffic Act 1988 s 144(1) (amended by the Road Traffic Act 1991 s 20(1), (2)). The Secretary of State may by order made by statutory instrument substitute a greater sum for the sum for the time being specified; no order may be made unless a draft of it has been laid before and approved by a resolution of each house of Parliament: Road Traffic Act 1988 s 144(1A), (1B) (added by the Road Traffic Act 1991 s 20(3)). As to the Secretary of State see para 739 note 3 ante. As to the duty of the owner of a vehicle who has made a deposit to pay for hospital treatment to injured persons see the Road Traffic Act 1988 s 157; and para 741 ante.
2 See the Motor Vehicles (Third-Party Risks Deposits) Regulations 1992, SI 1992/1284; and para 756 ante.
3 Road Traffic Act 1988 s 155(1).

(viii) The Motor Insurers' Bureau

758. Loopholes in third parties' statutory rights. Notwithstanding the stringent provisions originally enacted in the Road Traffic Act 1930 and the Road Traffic Act 1934[1], a substantial gap remained between the theoretical legal right of a third party to be compensated for injuries negligently inflicted by a motorist and the receipt, in practice, of the appropriate compensation. The motorist might well be, and often was, impecunious, so as to make bankruptcy proceedings a barren remedy; the insurers might well be, and often were, immune because the policy had been improperly obtained[2] or the use of the vehicle was outside the scope of their cover[3]. Futher legislation would, therefore, have been inevitable if steps had not been taken to bridge the gap by an entirely novel piece of extra-statutory machinery in the form of what was called the Motor Insurers' Bureau[4]. The bureau took the form of a central organisation incorporated at the instance of insurers transacting compulsory motor insurance business in Great Britain. On 17 June 1946 it entered into an agreement with the Minister of Transport as to the provision it would make for cases of injury or death caused by uninsured motor cars. This agreement is commonly called 'the Motor Insurers' Bureau Agreement'. The funds required to fulfil these obligations were made available to the bureau pursuant to a second agreement, commonly called 'the Domestic Agreement', made between the bureau and the insurers transacting compulsory motor insurance business in Great Britain[5].

On 21 December 1988 the Secretary of State and the bureau entered into an agreement relating to the compensation of victims of uninsured drivers[6], and on 22 November 1972 an agreement relating to the compensation of victims of untraced drivers[7].

1 See paras 743, 745 ante. Both Acts are now repealed and replaced by the Road Traffic Act 1988.
2 As to the right of insurers to obtain a declaration that they are entitled to avoid a policy see para 751 ante.
3 For the principle that the liability of insurers to satisfy a judgment in favour of a third party only applies where the use of the vehicle was within the scope of the policy see para 749 ante.
4 The address of the bureau is 152 Silbury Boulevard, Central Milton Keynes MK9 1NB.
5 See further para 764 post. For the meaning of 'Great Britain' see para 2 note 10 ante.
6 See para 759 post. The text of the agreement is published by HM Stationery Office, and replaces earlier agreements. The Secretary of State who entered into this agreement was the Secretary of State for Transport.
7 See para 760 post. The text of the agreement is published by HM Stationery Office, and replaces an earlier one of 1969. The Secretary of State who entered into this agreement was the Secretary of State for the Environment; the relevant functions are now exercised by the Secretary of State for Transport.

759. Victims of uninsured drivers. The Motor Insurers' Bureau (Compensation of Victims of Uninsured Drivers) Agreement[1] provides that if judgment in respect of any relevant liability[2] is obtained against any person or persons in any court in Great Britain[3], whether or not the person is covered by a contract of insurance[4], and any such judgment is not satisfied in full within seven days from the date on which the person in whose favour the judgment was given became entitled to enforce it, the Motor Insurers' Bureau will pay[5] or satisfy, or cause to be paid or satisfied, to or to the satisfaction of the person in whose favour the judgment was given any sum payable or remaining payable in respect of the liability, including sums awarded for interest and any taxed costs or costs awarded by the court without taxation (or such proportion as is attributable to the liability), whatever may be the cause of the judgment debtor's failure to satisfy the judgment[6].

The conditions precedent to the bureau's acceptance of liability under the agreement are:

(1) notice in writing of the bringing of the proceedings[7] must be given within seven days after the commencement of the proceedings (a) to the bureau, in the case of proceedings in respect of a liability which is either not covered by a contract of insurance or covered by a contract of insurance with an insurer whose identity cannot be ascertained[8], or (b) to the insurer, in the case of proceedings in respect of a liability which is covered by a contract of insurance with an insurer whose identity can be ascertained[9];

(2) such information relating to the proceedings and to any insurance covering the damage and claims made thereunder as the bureau may reasonably require must be supplied to the bureau by the person bringing the proceedings[10];

(3) the person bringing the proceedings must have demanded from the person against whom the claim was made the statutory information as to insurance or security[11] or, if required by the bureau, have authorised the bureau to do so on his behalf[12];

(4) if so required by the bureau and subject to full indemnity by it as to costs, the person bringing the proceedings must take all reasonable steps to obtain judgment against all the persons liable in respect of the injury or death or damage to property, and, in the event of such a person being a servant or agent, against his principal[13]; and

(5) the judgment and any order for costs must be assigned to the bureau or its nominee[14].

The agreement may be determined by the Secretary of State at any time, or by the bureau on 12 months' notice, without prejudice to its continued operation in respect of accidents occurring before the date of termination[15].

Nothing in the agreement prevents insurers[16] from providing by conditions in their contracts of insurance that all sums paid by them or by the bureau in or towards the discharge of the liability of their insured are recoverable by them or by the bureau from the insured or from any other person[17].

The bureau is under no liability where:

(i) the claim arises out of the use of a vehicle owned by or in possession of the Crown[18];

(ii) the claim arises out of the use of a vehicle which is not required to be covered by a contract of insurance[19] unless the use is, in fact, covered by such a contract[20];

(iii) the claim is in respect of a judgment or any part of it which has been obtained by the exercise of a right of subrogation by any person[21];

(iv) the claim is in respect of damage to a motor vehicle or losses arising from it if at the time of the use of that vehicle giving rise to the damage there was not in force a policy of insurance, and the person or persons claiming in respect of the damage either knew or ought to have known that that was the case[22]; or

(v) at the time of the use which gave rise to the liability the person suffering death or bodily injury or damage to property was allowing himself to be carried in or on the vehicle and, either before the commencement of his journey in it or after such commencement if he could reasonably be expected to have alighted from it, he knew or ought to have known that it had been stolen or unlawfully taken, or knew or ought to have known that it was being used without there being in force in relation to its use a contract of insurance[23].

1 As to the agreement see para 758 ante.
2 'Relevant liability' means a liability in respect of which a policy of insurance must insure a person in order to comply with the Road Traffic Act 1988 Pt VI (ss 143–162) (as amended) (see para 729 et seq ante): Motor Insurers' Bureau (Compensation of Victims of Uninsured Drivers) Agreement cl 1. 'Relevant liability' does not include the liability of an owner to a permitted driver where the latter is injured while using the vehicle: *Cooper v Motor Insurers' Bureau* [1985] QB 575, [1985] 1 All ER 449, CA.
3 For the meaning of 'Great Britain' see para 2 note 10 ante.
4 'Contract of insurance' means a policy of insurance or a security: Motor Insurers' Bureau (Compensation of Victims of Uninsured Drivers) Agreement cl 1.
5 Ie subject to ibid cll 4–6 (see text and notes 8–14, 16–23 infra): cl 2.
6 Ibid cl 2(1). The bureau incurs liability in respect of any sum awarded under a judgment relating to property damage not exceeding £250,000 or the first £250,000 of any sum so awarded exceeding that amount: cl 2(2). Where a person, in whose favour a judgment in respect of a relevant liability which includes liability in respect of damage to property, has received or is entitled to receive, in consequence of a claim he has made, compensation from any source in respect of that damage, the bureau may deduct from the sum payable or remaining payable under cl 2(1) an amount equal to the amount of that compensation in addition to the deduction of £175 under cl 2(4): cl 2(3). 'Compensation' includes compensation under insurance arangements: cl 2(3). The bureau does not incur liability in respect of any amount payable or remaining payable under the judgment in respect of property damage liability where the total of amounts so payable or remaining payable is £175 or less, or, where the total of such amounts is more than £175, in respect of the first £175 of such total: cl 2(4).
7 The notice must be accompanied by a copy of the writ, summons or other document initiating the proceedings: ibid cl 5(1)(a).
8 Ibid cl 5(1)(a)(i).
9 Ibid cl 5(1)(a)(ii).
10 Ibid cl 5(1)(b). In the event of any dispute as to the reasonableness of a requirement by the bureau for the supply of information or that any particular step should be taken to obtain judgement against other persons, it may be referred to the Secretary of State, whose decision is final: cl 5(2).
11 Ie under the Road Traffic Act 1988 s 154: see para 754 ante.
12 Motor Insurers' Bureau (Compensation of Victims of Uninsured Drivers) Agreement cl 5(1)(c).
13 Ibid cl 5(1)(d). See also note 10 supra.
14 Ibid cl 5(1)(e). Where a judgment which includes an amount in respect of a liability, other than a relevant liability, has been assigned to the bureau or its nominee, the bureau must apportion any money received in pursuance of the judgment according to the proportion which the damages in respect of the relevant liability bear to the damages in respect of the other liabilities and must account to the person in whose favour the judgment was given in respect of such money received properly apportionable to the other liabilities; and where an order for costs in respect of such a judgment has been so assigned, money received pursuant to the order must be dealt with in the same manner: cl 5(3).
15 Ibid cl 3. As to the Secretary of State see para 758 note 6 ante.
16 'Insurer' includes the giver of a security (see para 756 ante): cl 1.

17 Ibid cl 4.

18 Ie except where another person has undertaken responsibility for a contract of insurance under the Road Traffic Act 1988 Pt VI (as amended) (whether or not the persons liable are covered), or where liability is, in fact, covered by a contract of insurance: Motor Insurers' Bureau (Compensation of Victims of Uninsured Drivers) Agreement cl 6(1)(a). A vehicle which has been unlawfully removed from the possession of the Crown must be taken to continue in that possession whilst it is kept so removed: cl 6(3)(a).

19 Ie under the Road Traffic Act 1988 s 144 (as amended) (see para 729 ante): Motor Insurers' Bureau (Compensation of Victims of Uninsured Drivers) Agreement cl 6(1)(b).

20 Ibid cl 6(1)(b).

21 Ibid cl 6(1)(c).

22 Ibid cl 6(1)(d).

23 Ibid cl 6(1)(e). This exception applies only where the judgment in respect of which the claim against the bureau is being made was obtained in respect of a relevant liability incurred by the owner or a person using the vehicle in which the person who suffered death or bodily injury or sustained damage to property was being carried: cl 6(2). References to a person being carried in a vehicle for the purpose of this exception include references to his being carried in or upon or getting on to or alighting from the vehicle: cl 6(3)(b). 'Owner', in relation to a vehicle which is the subject of a hiring agreement or a hire-purchase agreement, means the person in possession of the vehicle under that agreement: cl 6(3)(c).

760. Victims of untraced drivers. The Motor Insurer's Bureau (Compensation of Victims of Untraced Drivers) Agreement[1] applies where an application is made to the Motor Insurers' Bureau for a payment in respect of the death of, or bodily injury to, any person caused by or arising out of the use of a motor vehicle on a road in Great Britain if the following conditions are fulfilled[2]:

(1) the applicant must be either unable to trace any person responsible for the death or injury[3], or, where more than one person was responsible[4], unable to trace one of those persons[5];

(2) the death or injury must be caused in such circumstances that, on the balance of probabilities, the untraced person would be liable to pay damages to the applicant in respect of the death or injury[6];

(3) the liability of the untraced person to pay damages to the applicant must be one which is required to be covered by insurance or security under Part VI of the Road Traffic Act 1988[7];

(4) the death or injury must not be caused by the use of the vehicle by the untraced person as a weapon, that is to say in a deliberate attempt to run down the deceased or injured person[8];

(5) the application must be made in writing within three years from the date of the event giving rise to the death or injury[9].

The bureau is under no liability where:

(a) the claim arises out of the use of a vehicle owned by the Crown[10];

(b) at the time of the accident the person suffering death or bodily injury in respect of which the application is made was allowing himself to be carried in a vehicle[11] and either

(i) knew or had reason to believe that the vehicle had been taken without the consent of the owner[12] or other lawful authority[13]; or

(ii) being the owner of, or being a person using the vehicle, he was using or causing or permitting the vehicle to be used without there being in force a contract of insurance complying with Part VI of the Road Traffic Act 1988, knowing or having reason to believe that no such policy was in force[14].

The application may be made by the person for whose benefit the payment is to be made (known as the applicant), any solicitor acting for him, or any other person whom the bureau may be prepared to accept as acting for him[15].

Where the agreement applies, the bureau must award the applicant a payment of an amount assessed in the same manner as a court would assess the damages which the applicant would have been entitled to recover from the untraced person in respect of that death or injury if proceedings to enforce a claim for damages were successfully brought by the applicant against the untraced person[16].

The conditions precedent to the bureau's liability are:

(A) the applicant must give all such assistance as may reasonably be required by or on behalf of the bureau to enable any investigation to be carried out under the agreement, including the furnishing of statements and information either in writing or, if so required, orally at interviews between the applicant and the person acting on behalf of the bureau[17];

(B) if so required by the bureau at any time before it has communicated its decision on the application to the applicant, he must take all such steps as in the circumstances it is reasonable to require him to take to obtain judgment against any persons in respect of their liability to him as having caused or contributed to the death or injury or as being the master or principal of any person who has caused or contributed to that injury[18]; and

(C) if so required by the bureau, the applicant must assign to it or its nominee any judgment obtained by him in respect of the death or injury to which his application relates on such terms as will secure that the bureau or its nominee is accountable to the applicant for any amount by which the aggregate of all sums recovered by the bureau or its nominee under the judgment (after deducting all reasonable expenses incurred in effecting such recovery) exceeds the amount payable by the bureau to the applicant under the agreement[19].

The bureau must cause any application made to it for payment to be investigated and, unless the investigation discloses that the agreement does not apply to the application, it must cause a report to be made on it and on that basis must decide whether to make an award and what amount is to be calculated[20]. If the application is rejected on the preliminary investigation, the bureau must notify the applicant and give reasons[21]. If the application is fully investigated, the bureau must furnish the applicant with a statement setting out specified particulars[22].

On being notified by the applicant that the bureau's award is accepted[23], or after the expiration of the time allowed for lodging an appeal[24], the bureau must pay him the amount of the award[25].

The applicant may appeal to an arbitrator[26] against any decision notified to him on the ground that (I) the agreement applies and his application should be fully investigated[27]; (II) if it has been investigated, either the refusal of an award was wrong[28] or the award is insufficient[29]; or (III) a decision not to indemnify the applicant against the costs of proceedings[30] was wrong[31]. He must give the bureau notice of appeal within six weeks from the date of notice of the decision, not having previously given notification of acceptance[32]. If the only ground of appeal is that the award is insufficient, the bureau may notify the applicant that, if the appeal proceeds, it will request the arbitrator to decide whether the bureau should make an award at all, and it must send the applicant its comments on what it considers relevant to that question[33].

If the appeal is not withdrawn, the bureau must submit it to the arbitrator, sending the application, the decision and all other documents given or sent under the agreement[34]. The arbitrator must decide the appeal on the documents submitted and no further evidence may be produced to him[35]. However, he may require the bureau to make a further investigation and submit to him a report[36], which must also be sent to the applicant[37]. The applicant may submit comments to the bureau within four weeks[38], and they must also be sent to the arbitrator[39].

The arbitrator must notify his decision to the bureau which must send a copy to the applicant[40]. If the appeal is on the ground referred to in head (I) and the arbitrator decides that the agreement applies, he must remit the application to the bureau for an investigation and decision[41]. If the appeal is on the ground referred to in head (II), the arbitrator must decide whether the bureau should make an award and, if so, the amount[42]. Any award must be paid by the bureau and discharges the bureau's liability under the agreement[43]. If the appeal is on the ground referred to in head (III), the arbitrator must give his decision[44]. Each party to the appeal bears his own costs[45].

1   As to the agreement see para 758 ante. It may be determined at any time by the Secretary of State or the bureau giving the other not less than 12 months' previous notice in writing: Motor Insurers' Bureau (Compensation of Victims of Untraced Drivers) Agreement cl 24. This does not affect any case where the event giving rise to the claim occurred before the date of termination: cl 24 proviso.
2   Ibid cl 1(1). For the meaning of 'Great Britain' see para 2 note 10 ante. As to the Secretary of State see para 758 note 7 ante.
3   Ibid cl 1(1)(b)(i).
4   Ie in a case to which ibid cl 5 applies: cl 1(1)(b)(ii). Clause 5 applies where the death or injury was caused partly by an untraced person and partly by either an identified person or persons, or an untraced person whose master or principal can be identified, and so that the identified person or master or principal is liable to the applicant for the death or injury: cl 5(1). See further note 16 infra.
5   Ibid cl 1(1)(b)(ii).
6   Ibid cl 1(1)(c).
7   Ie the Road Traffic Act 1988 Pt VI (ss 143–162) (as amended) (see para 729 et seq ante): Motor Insurers' Bureau (Compensation of Victims of Untraced Drivers) Agreement cl 1(1)(d). It is assumed for these purposes that, in the absence of evidence to the contrary, the vehicle was being used in circumstances in which the user was statutorily required to be insured or secured against third party risks: cl 1(1)(d).
8   Ibid cl 1(1)(e).
9   Ibid cl 1(1)(f).
10   Ie unless some other person has undertaken responsibility for a contract of insurance under the Road Traffic Act 1988 Pt VI (as amended): Motor Insurers' Bureau (Compensation of Victims of Untraced Drivers) Agreement cl 1(2)(a). A vehicle which has been unlawfully removed from the possession of the Crown is taken to continue in that possession whilst it is kept so removed: cl 1(4)(a).
11   This includes being carried in or upon or entering or getting on to or alighting from the vehicle: ibid cl 1(4)(b).
12   'Owner', in relation to a vehicle the subject of a hiring agreement or a hire-purchase agreement, means the person in possession of the vehicle under that agreement: ibid cl 1(4)(c).
13   Ibid cl 1(2)(b)(i). This exemption does not apply in a case where either the applicant (1) believed or had reason to believe that he had legal authority to be carried or that he would have had the owner's consent if the owner had known of his being carried and the circumstances of his carriage (cl 1(2)(b)(i)(A)); or (2) had learned of the circumstances of the taking of the vehicle since the commencement of the journey and it would be unreasonable to expect him to have alighted from the vehicle (cl 1(2)(b)(i)(B)). See also note 14 infra.
14   Ibid cl 1(2)(b)(ii). The exemption in cl 1(2)(b) only applies where application is made in respect of a liability arising out of the use of the vehicle in which the person who suffered death or injury was being carried: cl 1(3).
15   Ibid cl 2 (1). Any decision, award, payment etc made under the agreement to or by the applicant or person acting for him is treated as having the same effect as if it had been done to, by or in relation to an applicant of full age and capacity: cl 2(2).

16 Ibid cl 3. As to the assessment of damages see DAMAGES vol 12 para 1138 et seq.

In the assessment of the amount to which the applicant is entitled in respect of loss of earnings, if he has received his wages or salary in full or in part from his employer, whether or not upon an undertaking given by the applicant to reimburse his employer if he recovers damages he is not, to the extent of the amount so received, to be regarded as having sustained a loss of earnings: cl 4(b). Where cl 5 applies (see note 4 supra), if the applicant has obtained judgment in respect of the relevant death or injury against an identified person or master or principal which is not satisfied in full within three months, the amount awarded is that equal to the untraced person's contribution to a full award: cl 5(2), (3)(a), (4)(a). 'Full award' means the amount that would have been awarded under cl 3 if the untraced person had been wholly responsible: cl 5(6)(a). 'Untraced person's contribution' means that proportion of a full award which on the balance of probabilities would have been apportioned by a court as the share to be borne by the untraced person in the responsibility for the event giving rise to the relevant death or injury if the applicant had brought proceedings to recover damages against the untraced person and all others with a share in the responsibility: cl 5(6)(b). If the judgment has been obtained and is satisfied in part only within the three months, the amount awarded is (1) if the unsatisfied part is less than the untraced person's contribution to a full award, an amount equal to that unsatisfied part (cl 5(4)(b)(i)); or (2) if the unsatisfied part is equal to or greater than the amount of the untraced person's contribution, an amount equal to the untraced person's contribution (cl 5(4)(b)(ii)). As to where there is an appeal from the judgment see cl 5(5). If the applicant has not obtained judgment and has not been required by the bureau to do so against the identified person or master or principal (cl 5(3)(b)(i)) and has not received any payment by way of compensation from any such person (cl 5(3)(b)(ii)), the amount awarded is that equal to the untraced person's contribution to a full award (cl 5(4)(c)). See also note 22 infra.

The bureau is under no liability in this agreement where the applicant is entitled to compensation under the agreement providing for the victims of uninsured drivers (see para 759 ante): cl 5(7).

17 Ibid cl 6(1)(a).
18 Ibid cl 6(1)(b).
19 Ibid cl 6(1)(c). As to indemnification for costs where the bureau requires the applicant to take any proceedings see cll 6(2), (3), 9(2).
20 Ibid cl 7. As to the bureau's duty under cl 7 see *Persson v London Country Buses* [1974] 1 All ER 1251, [1974] 1 WLR 569, CA. The bureau may request the applicant to furnish it with a statutory declaration setting out to the best of his knowledge, information and belief the facts and circumstances upon which his claim is based or those that may be specified by the bureau: Motor Insurers' Bureau (Compensation of Victims of Untraced Drivers) Agreement cl 8.
21 Ibid cl 9(1)(a).
22 Ibid cl 9(1)(b). The particulars are (1) the circumstances in which the death or injury occurred and the evidence bearing on it (cl 9(1)(b)(i)); (2) the circumstances relevant to the assessment and the evidence bearing on it (cl 9(1)(b)(ii)); and (3) on a refusal, the bureau's reasons (cl 9(1)(b)(iii)). Where cl 5 applies (see note 4 supra), the bureau must specify the ways in which the award was computed and its relation to the relevant provisions of cl 5: cl 9(1)(c).
23 Ibid cl 10(a).
24 Ie under ibid cl 11 (see infra): cl 10(b).
25 Ibid cl 10. The payment discharges the bureau from its liability under the agreement: cl 10. Where it appears to the bureau that there are circumstances affecting the applicant's capacity to manage his affairs and it would be in his interest for the Family Welfare Association or some other body to administer the award, it may establish a trust for the purpose, subject to appropriate provisions: cl 23.
26 The arbitrator is selected by the Secretary of State from a panel of Queen's Counsel appointed by the Lord Chancellor: ibid cl 18. As to his fees see cl 22.
27 Ibid cl 11(a).
28 Ibid cl 11(b)(i).
29 Ibid cl 11(b)(ii).
30 Ie under ibid cl 9(2) (see note 19 supra): cl 11(c).
31 Ibid cl 11(c).
32 Ibid cl 11. The notice must state the grounds of appeal and be accompanied by an undertaking to accept the arbitrator's decision (cl 12(a)) and pay his fee (cl 12(b)). The applicant may also make comments on the bureau's decision and supply the bureau with such particulars and further evidence as he considers relevant, and the bureau may investigate the evidence and report back to the applicant the result and any change in its decision. The applicant, within six weeks, may send comments on the report for the arbitrator, unless he withdraws his appeal: cl 13.

33 Ibid cl 14(1). Within six weeks the applicant may then send such comments and particulars of evidence not contained in his statement as he considers relevant, and cl 13 (see note 32 supra) applies: cl 14(2).
34 Ibid cl 15. Where an investigation is made under cl 13 or cl 14(2), or notice is given under cl 14(1), the appeal must not be submitted until after six weeks from the notification to the applicant of the result: cl 15.
35 Ibid cl 17.
36 Ibid cl 17 proviso (a).
37 Ibid cl 17 proviso (b).
38 Ibid cl 17 proviso (b).
39 Ibid cl 17 proviso (c).
40 Ibid cl 19.
41 Ibid cl 16(a).
42 Ibid cl 16(b).
43 Ibid cl 20.
44 Ibid cl 16(c).
45 Ibid cl 21.

761. Liability in respect of intentional criminal act. The Motor Insurers' Bureau is liable under the Motor Insurers' Bureau (Compensation of Victims of Uninsured Drivers) Agreement[1] to a third party injured by an uninsured driver even though that driver intentionally causes the injury[2]. The doctrine of public policy that a person is not entitled to profit from his own wrongdoing does not apply, since the satisfaction of the uninsured driver's liability to the third party is incidental to the main purpose of the agreement, which is the protection of an innocent third party[3].

1 As to the bureau see para 758 ante, and as to the agreement see para 759 ante.
2 *Hardy v Motor Insurers' Bureau* [1964] 2 QB 745, [1964] 2 All ER 742, CA (where the plaintiff, a security officer, stopped a van and questioned the driver, who drove off at speed while the plaintiff was holding on to the door; the plaintiff was held entitled to recover against the bureau); *Gardner v Moore* [1984] AC 548, [1984] 1 All ER 1100, HL.
3 *Gardner v Moore* [1984] AC 548, [1984] 1 All ER 1100, HL.

762. Effect of Motor Insurers' Bureau (Compensation of Victims of Uninsured Drivers) Agreement on the general law. The Motor Insurers' Bureau (Compensation of Victims of Uninsured Drivers) Agreement[1] applies to cases where there is no insurance in operation at all. The fact, however, that motor insurers have established this extra-statutory means of providing compensation to victims of motor accidents does not in any way relieve a person who uses, or permits to be used, a car while uninsured from his personal liability for this breach of statutory duty[2]. On questions of costs, however, it is relevant for the court to take into account that in fact the bureau is defending a case, even though the defendant on the record is the uninsured motorist and has a legal aid certificate[3]. In practice, the bureau may be sued direct in appropriate cases[4].

1 As to the agreement see para 759 ante.
2 *Corfield v Groves* [1950] 1 All ER 488.
3 *Godfrey v Smith* [1955] 2 All ER 520, [1955] 1 WLR 692.
4 *Lees v Motor Insurers' Bureau* [1952] 2 All ER 511; on appeal [1953] 1 WLR 620, CA; *Buchanan v Motor Insurers' Bureau* [1955] 1 All ER 607, [1955] 1 WLR 488; *Coward v Motor Insurers' Bureau* [1963] 1 QB 259, [1962] 1 All ER 531, CA; *Hardy v Motor Insurers' Bureau* [1964] 2 QB 745, [1964] 2 All ER 742, CA; *Randall v Motor Insurers' Bureau* [1969] 1 All ER 21, [1968] 1 WLR 1900; *Motor Insurers' Bureau v Meanen* [1971] 2 All ER 1372n, HL; *Albert v Motor Insurers' Bureau* [1972] AC 301, [1971] 2 All ER 1345, HL. The bureau would never take the point that the third party was not privy to the

agreements: *Albert v Motor Insurers' Bureau* supra at 320 and 1354 per Viscount Dilhorne. In *Hardy v Motor Insurers' Bureau* supra at 757 and 744, Lord Denning MR said he hoped the point would never be taken. The court has not raised any objection independently: *Coward v Motor Insurers' Bureau* supra.

763. Adding the Motor Insurers' Bureau as a defendant. Where a third party is injured by an uninsured driver, the Motor Insurers' Bureau[1] is entitled[2] to be added as a party to the action brought by the third party against the driver as the bureau has no power under the Motor Insurers' Bureau (Compensation of Victims of Uninsured Drivers) Agreement[3] to control the steps taken in the litigation by the third party[4].

Where the third party is injured by an untraced driver, the bureau is not entitled to be added as a party as it is not necessary to ensure that all matters in dispute in the action may be effectually and completely determined and adjudicated upon[5]. The bureau is sufficiently protected under the Motor Insurers' Bureau (Compensation of Victims of Uninsured Drivers) Agreement[6] if it requests the plaintiff to take all such steps as are necessary to obtain judgment against an identified person, for all matters would then be properly and fully investigated[7].

1 As to the bureau see para 758 ante.
2 At any stage of the proceedings in any cause or matter the court may on such terms as it thinks just, and either of its own motion or on application, order any person who ought to have been joined as a party, or whose presence before the court is necessary to ensure that all matters in dispute in the cause or matter may be effectually and completely determined and adjudicated upon, to be added as a party: see RSC Ord 15 r 6(2)(b)(i); and PRACTICE AND PROCEDURE.
3 As to the agreement see para 759 ante.
4 *Gurtner v Circuit* [1968] 2 QB 587, [1968] 1 All ER 328, CA.
5 *White v London Transport* [1971] 2 QB 721, [1971] 3 All ER 1, CA.
6 Ie under the Motor Insurers' Bureau (Compensation of Victims of Uninsured Drivers) Agreement cl 6(1)(b), (2): see para 759 text and note 23 ante.
7 *White v London Transport* [1971] 2 QB 721, [1971] 3 All ER 1, CA.

764. The Domestic Agreement. The Domestic Agreement[1] is an agreement for the efficient, expeditious and economical carrying out of certain obligations of the main Motor Insurers' Bureau (Compensation of Victims of Uninsured Drivers) Agreement[2]. Its general effect is to secure that, when a third party claim falling within the category with which the bureau has undertaken by the main agreement to deal is put forward, the insurer who is required domestically as between insurers to contest and satisfy the claim is the insurer who has, in fact, issued a policy of insurance in respect of the car in question. It is then purely a matter of financial adjustment between that insurer and other insurers who are parties to the agreement as to how the liability has to be shared out. Thus, if a car insured by an insurance company is involved in an accident involving third party liability while it is being driven by a thief who has stolen it, the insurance company must deal with and satisfy the claim in so far as it is a compulsorily insurable claim. The value of the claims so carried by the insurance company on risk in respect of cars involved in accidents not covered by insurance are then carried into the contribution account by which the Motor Insurers' Bureau is supported. How much of the bill is still left in the final accounting to the insurance company which in the first instance satisfied the claim depends on the accident and contribution ratios of all the contributing companies subscribing to the support of the bureau.

The general effect of these arrangements is that it is no longer necessary for a third party injured in a motor accident to rely on the general statutory provisions relating to subrogation on the insolvency of the assured[3], or the provisions imposing on insurers the duty of satisfying judgments in favour of third parties[4]; no advantage is to be derived from pursuing the technicalities of either statutory remedy once the same pecuniary result can be achieved by the extra-statutory Motor Insurers' Bureau Agreement, reinforced as it is by the Domestic Agreement between the insurers concerned.

1 As to the Domestic Agreement see para 758 ante.
2 See the Motor Insurers' Bureau (Compensation of Victims of Uninsured Drivers) Agreement cl 7.
3 See the Third Parties (Rights against Insurers) Act 1930 ss 1, 3 (as amended); and paras 679, 683–684 ante.
4 See the Road Traffic Act 1988 ss 151, 152 (as amended); and para 749 ante.

10. PECUNIARY LOSS INSURANCE

(1) SCOPE OF PECUNIARY LOSS INSURANCE

765. Meaning of pecuniary loss insurance. In one sense all insurances are related to a contingency; in life or endowment insurance the contingency is death or the survival of the assured to a particular date; in personal accident or sickness insurance the contingency is injury by accident or disablement by disease; in property insurance the contingency is the peril to the property which is insured against; in liability insurance the contingency is incurring the specified liability to a third party[1]. However, apart from the contingencies covered by these particular types of insurance there remains a wide field representing (1) what a person would or might have earned or acquired but for the happening of a particular event, and (2) the danger, in the sense of the possibility of a loss being incurred if a particular event happens. Therefore, pecuniary loss insurance may be defined in general terms as an insurance, not falling within any of the classes of insurance previously mentioned, which provides for the making of a payment in the event of a specified event occurring, the payment representing either the loss, or the possibility of loss, which that event entails[2].

1 For the principle that a policy which covers the assured against legal liability to a third person is a policy of liability and not of pecuniary loss insurance see para 695 text and note 6 ante.
2 For these purposes 'pecuniary loss' insurance is a class of 'general insurance': Insurance Companies 1982 s 1, Sch 2 Pt I: see para 18 ante.

766. Basis need not be indemnity. Frequently, insurances against a contingency are contracts of indemnity[1]. Although accurate ascertainment of the loss may be impossible, the policy may lay down a formula by which calculation is to be made with a view to achieving as accurate an estimate as is reasonable or practicable. In many cases the attempt to do this is not even made, the insurers being content to pay a stipulated sum, comparable with an agreed value, in the event of the contingency occurring.

1 See eg *Re Miller, Gibb & Co Ltd* [1957] 2 All ER 266, [1957] 1 WLR 703; and para 777 post. As to the principle of indemnity see para 3 ante.

767. Scope of pecuniary loss insurance and need for insurable interest. It may be said that there are very few risks which cannot be placed, either with an insurance company or at Lloyd's[1]; certainly in the field of pecuniary loss insurance the range of risks is wide and varied. Insurance can be effected against the contingency of the birth of a child who would defeat the prospects of a remainderman[2]; of bad weather interfering with an athletic meeting[3] or a cricket match[4]; of the outbreak of war or the conclusion of peace[5]; of restrictions on transferring currency operating so as to deprive an exporter of the price of goods sold to a foreign buyer[6].

A fidelity policy which insures the assured against losses which he may sustain by the default of an employee is a policy of pecuniary loss insurance[7]; but a policy which insures the assured against claims by third parties in respect of the default of the assured or his employees in the conduct of his profession is generally a policy of liability insurance and not of fidelity insurance[8]. However, if a policy of the former class contains a provision by virtue of which the insurers may be bound in certain circumstances to pay a claim even though it is legally a bad claim, it appears that the policy is one of pecuniary loss insurance[9].

A policy of pecuniary loss insurance is not valid unless the assured has an insurable interest in the sense of being likely to sustain a loss in the event of the contingency occurring[10].

1 *Seaton v Burnand, Burnand v Seaton* [1900] AC 135 at 140, HL, per Lord Halsbury.
2 *Carr v Carr* (1912) 106 LT 753.
3 *London County Cycling and Athletic Club v Beck* (1897) 3 Com Cas 49.
4 *Leon v Casey* [1932] 2 KB 576 at 581, CA, per Scrutton LJ.
5 *Kotzias v Tyser* [1920] 2 KB 69; *Lloyd v Bowring* (1920) 36 TLR 397. Such insurance is invalid unless there is an insurable interest: see note 10 infra.
6 *Re Miller, Gibb & Co Ltd* [1957] 2 All ER 266, [1957] 1 WLR 703; *L Lucas Ltd v Export Credits Guarantee Department* [1974] 2 All ER 889, [1974] 1 WLR 909, HL. See further para 777 post. As to the three main types of pecuniary loss insurance see paras 768–789 post.
7 As to fidelity policies see further paras 768–774 post.
8 See *Goddard and Smith v Frew* [1939] 4 All ER 358 at 361, CA, per Goddard LJ.
9 *West Wake Price & Co v Ching* [1956] 3 All ER 821 at 826, [1957] 1 WLR 45 at 51 per Devlin J (policy containing a Queen's Counsel clause); see para 695 ante.
10 See *Re London County Commercial Reinsurance Office Ltd* [1922] 2 Ch 67 (policies of reinsurance providing for payments in event of peace between Great Britain and Germany not being declared by specified date; policies contained ppi (policy proof of interest) clause; no proof of insurable interest by original assured; policies illegal and void under the Life Assurance Act 1774 (see paras 535–544 ante); premiums irrecoverable). As to the recovery of premiums cf *Aubert v Walsh* (1810) 3 Taunt 277; *Busk v Walsh* (1812) 4 Taunt 290 (premiums recoverable where assured indicated intention to rescind before the specified date).

(2) FIDELITY INSURANCE

(i) Scope of Fidelity Insurance

768. Breach of fidelity as an insurable contingency. A policy of fidelity insurance is intended to protect the assured against the contingency of a breach of fidelity on the part of a person in whom confidence has been placed[1]. Usually the relationship between the assured and the person whose fidelity is insured is that of employer and employee[2].

1 Protection may also be obtained in such a case by means of a fidelity guarantee. As to such guarantees see GUARANTEE vol 20 (Reissue) paras 191, 201, 240, 340.
2 See *Walker v British Guarantee Association* (1852) 18 QB 277.

769. Extent of protection. A policy of fidelity insurance normally contemplates loss by the criminal misappropriation of money or securities[1]; the insurance is not for specific subject matter but is for the pecuniary loss suffered by the employer. The perils insured against may be described as the employee's fraud or dishonesty[2] or his want of integrity, honesty or fidelity[3]. In general, the technical terms of the criminal law are used, and the policy refers specifically to losses by theft. Where this is the case, the words must be construed strictly; they bear the same meaning as in an indictment[4] and the assured cannot recover unless he proves that the particular offence described in the policy has in fact been committed[5]. The policy may be extended to cover acts which are not criminal, such as the wilful default[6] or the negligence[7] of the employee[8], but does not cover losses due to a crime in which the employee has not been guilty of any fault, for instance where he is robbed of the money belonging to the assured[9].

1 *Re Norwich Provident Insurance Society, Bath's Case* (1878) 8 ChD 334 at 341, CA, per Jessel MR. Such a policy is not, it appears, open to objection on grounds of public policy; *Goddard and Smith v Frew* [1939] 4 All ER 358 at 362, CA, per Goddard LJ.
2 *Ravenscroft v Provident Clerks' and General and Guarantee Association* (1888) 5 TLR 3.
3 *American Surety Co of New York v Wrightson* (1910) 103 LT 663.
4 As to theft see generally CRIMINAL LAW vol 11(1) (Reissue) para 541 et seq.
5 *Debenhams Ltd v Excess Insurance Co Ltd* (1912) 28 TLR 505 per Hamilton J ('embezzlement'); but see *Equitable Trust Co of New York v Henderson* (1930) 47 TLR 90 ('forged'). Prosecution for the offence is not a condition precedent to recovery unless the policy expressly so provides; see *London Guarantie Co v Fearnley* (1880) 5 App Cas 911, HL.
6 *Kenney v Employers' Liability Assurance Corpn* [1901] 1 IR 301.
7 *American Surety Co of New York v Wrightson* (1910) 103 LT 663; *Pawle & Co v Bussell* (1916) 114 TLR 805.
8 For the principle that a clause by which insurers agree to pay claims without requiring the assured to dispute them extends only to claims which are wholly within the policy see para 770 post.
9 See *Walker v British Guarantee Association* (1852) 21 LJQB 257 (robbery from treasurer of building society who had made covenant in nature of fidelity guarantee).

(ii) Special Features of Fidelity Insurance

770. Risk as described forms basis of policy. The risk of loss under a fidelity policy is governed by the opportunity to be dishonest or negligent afforded by the employee's employment; this varies according to the nature of his particular occupation and the position which he holds[1]. The proposer is usually required to provide a statement of the capacity in which the employee is employed and of the nature of his duties, and, if this statement is warranted or incorporated in the policy as part of the definition of the risk, the employee must continue to be employed in accordance with the description throughout the currency of the policy[2]. If at any time after such a policy has commenced the employee is employed in a different capacity[3] or is required to perform different duties[4], the policy does not attach whilst he is so employed or is performing those different duties[5], since there is an alteration of the risk which affects its identity[6]. An alteration in matters of routine, including the precautions against dishonesty adopted by the employer and the method of checking the employee's accounts, does not affect the identity of the risk and does not in itself preclude the employer from recovering[7] unless there is an express condition prohibiting such an alteration[8].

1 *Hay v Employers' Liability Assurance Corporation* (1905) 6 OWR 459, followed in *Elgin Loan and Savings Co v London Guarantee and Accident Co* (1906) 11 OLR 330.
2 *Towle v National Guardian Assurance Society* (1861) 30 LJCh 900; *Haworth & Co v Sickness and Accident Assurance Society* 1891 28 SLR 394; cf *Hearts of Oak Building Society v Law Union and Rock Insurance Co Ltd* [1936] 2 All ER 619 (statements in a proposal as to an employee's duties were no more than statements of present fact); and *Benham v United Guarantee and Life Assurance Co* (1852) 7 Exch 744. As to the effect of variation in the principal debtor's office or duties in the case of a fidelity guarantee see GUARANTEE vol 20 (Reissue) paras 191, 204.
3 See *Cosford Union v Poor Law etc Officers' Mutual Guarantee Association* (1910) 103 LT 463.
4 *Wembley UDC v Poor Law and Local Government Officers' Mutual Guarantee Association Ltd* (1901) 17 TLR 516.
5 See *Cosford Union v Poor Law etc Officers' Mutual Guarantee Association* (1910) 103 LT 463.
6 As to alteration of risk see para 437 et seq ante.
7 *Benham v United Guarantee and Life Assurance Co* (1852) 7 Exch 744.
8 *Towle v National Guardian Assurance Society* (1861) 30 LJCh 900.

771. Payment of premium by employee. A fidelity policy may provide for payment of the premium by the employee and in such a case power is reserved to the employer to pay it if the employee fails to do so[1].

1 Ie if a receipt for premium is given to the employee to be shown to the employer, the insurers cannot repudiate liability on the ground that the premium was not in fact paid: *Re Economic Fire Office* (1896) 12 TLR 142.

772. Time and notice of loss. The loss under a fidelity policy takes place when the employer's property is misappropriated, not when the misappropriation is discovered[1]. The policy may, in express terms, cover losses discovered during its currency[2]; the discovery of the loss is not sufficient and the act of misappropriation must have been committed after the policy came into force[3]. In the absence of some prescribed time limit[4] the fact that the loss is not discovered until after the policy has expired does not preclude the assured from recovery if the act of misappropriation was committed during its currency[5].

The duty of giving notice of the loss[6] to the insurers does not arise until the employer has satisfied himself of his employee's dishonesty; the employer is under no duty to notify mere suspicion[7]. However, if the policy fixes a time from the date of loss for giving notice to the insurers, the assured will be unable to recover if the time has expired before he becomes aware of the loss[8].

1 *New Zealand University v Standard Fire and Marine Insurance Co* [1916] NZLR 509 (NZ CA).
2 *Pennsylvania Co for Insurances on Lives and Granting Annuities v Mumford* [1920] 2 KB 537, CA.
3 *Banque Nationale v Lesperance* (1881) 4 LN 147; *Allis-Chalmers Co v Maryland Fidelity and Deposit Co* (1916) 114 LT 433, HL; *London Guarantee and Accident Co v Cornish* (1905) 17 Man LR 148.
4 *Fanning v London Guarantee and Accident Co* [1884] 10 VLR (L) 8; *Commercial Mutual Building Society v London Guarantee and Accident Co* (1891) MLR 7 QB 307.
5 *Ward v Law Property Assurance and Trust Society* (1856) 4 WR 605.
6 As to notice of loss see generally paras 483–485 ante.
7 *Ward v Law Property Assurance and Trust Society* (1856) 4 WR 605.
8 *T H Adamson & Sons v Liverpool and London and Globe Insurance Co Ltd* [1953] 2 Lloyd's Rep 355.

773. Prosecution of employee. A fidelity policy may contain a condition requiring the employer to prosecute the defaulting employee upon the request and at the expense of the insurers[1], and a failure to comply with the condition may preclude the assured from enforcing the policy[2]. If, as a result of a successful prosecution, the employer recovers any portion of the misappropriated property, the insurers are entitled to deduct their costs from the amount recovered[3].

1 *London Guarantie Co v Fearnley* (1880) 5 App Cas 911, HL.
2 *London Guarantie Co v Fearnley* (1880) 5 App Cas 911, HL; *Canada Life Assurances Co v London Guarantee Co* (1900) 9 Que QB 183.
3 See *Hatch, Mansfield and Co Ltd v Weingott* (1906) 22 TLR 366, followed in *Crown Bank v London Guarantee and Accident Co* (1908) 17 OLR 95.

774. Deductions from amount of loss. In calculating the amount payable under a fidelity policy, the insurers are entitled to be credited with any commission or salary which would have been payable to the employee if he had not been dishonest, and with any money belonging to the employee in the employer's hands. The amounts owing to the employee must be deducted from the amount of the loss and the insurers are liable for the balance up to the sum insured[1]. Where the amount of the loss is greater than the amount insured the deductions are made from the whole amount of the loss and the insurers remain liable for the balance up to the full amount insured[2]. They are also entitled to the benefit of all other policies of insurance, securities or guarantees available in the hands of the employer towards the recoupment of the loss; such benefit is enforceable by contribution[3] or subrogation[4], as the case may be.

1 *Fifth Liverpool Starr-Bowkett Building Society v Travellers Accident Insurance Co Ltd* (1893) 9 TLR 221.
2 *Fifth Liverpool Starr-Bowkett Building Society v Travellers Accident Insurance Co Ltd* (1893) 9 TLR 221; cf *Board of Trade v Guarantee Society* [1910] 1 KB 408n.
3 *American Surety Co of New York v Wrightson* (1910) 103 LT 663. As to contribution see paras 520–521 ante.
4 *Employers' Liability Assurance Corpn v Skipper and East* (1887) 4 TLR 55. As to subrogation see paras 505–512 ante.

(3) DEBT INSURANCE

(i) Scope of Debt Insurance

775. Non-payment of debts as an insurable contingency. Wherever a debt exists the creditor is exposed to the risk of loss by reason of the debtor's failure to make repayment[1]. This is a risk against which the creditor can protect himself by insurance[2], which may be effected before the debt is actually incurred[3]. The insurance may cover the general balance of indebtedness from a particular person or class or persons[4], and a specific debt is capable of being insured. The debt may be unsecured, as in the case of an ordinary loan[5] or deposit at a bank[6], or it may be secured by mortgage[7] or debenture[8]. In either case the debtor whose default is insured against need not be the principal debtor; if a debt is already secured by means of a guarantee or policy of insurance a policy may be effected to cover the default of the sureties[9] or of the other insurers[10].

1 As to the distinction between insurance and guarantee see paras 783–784 post.
2 The insurance may cover the costs incurred in taking proceedings to enforce payment by the debtor, but special provision must be made: *Re Law Guarantee Trust and Accident Society* (1913) 108 LT 830.
3 *Seaton v Burnand, Burnand v Seaton* [1900] AC 135 at 141, HL; *Anglo-Californian Bank Ltd v London and Provincial Marine and General Insurance Co Ltd* (1904) 10 Com Cas 1. Cf *Re Miller, Gibb & Co Ltd* [1957] 2 All ER 266, [1957] 1 WLR 703 (insurance covering loss to an exporter caused by currency

restrictions interfering with his receipt of the price of goods exported; see further paras 767 ante, 777 post).
4 *Solvency Mutual Guarantee Co v York* (1858) 3 H & N 588; *Solvency Mutual Guarantee Co v Froane* (1861) 7 H & N 5.
5 *Parr's Bank v Albert Mines Syndicate* (1900) 5 Com Cas 116; *Anglo-Californian Bank Ltd v London and Provincial Marine and General Insurance Co Ltd* (1904) 10 Com Cas 1.
6 *Dane v Mortgage Insurance Corpn* [1894] 1 QB 54, CA; *Murdock v Heath* (1899) 80 LT 50.
7 *Re Birkbeck Permanent Benefit Building Society, Official Receiver v Licenses Insurance Corpn* [1913] 2 Ch 34; *Re Law Guarantee Trust and Accident Society* (1913) 108 LT 830.
8 *Shaw v Royce Ltd* [1911] 1 Ch 138; *Finlay v Mexican Investment Corpn* [1897] 1 QB 517; *Re Law Guarantee Trust and Accident Society Ltd, Liverpool Mortgage Insurance Co's Case* [1914] 2 Ch 617, CA.
9 *Seaton v Burnand, Burnand v Seaton* [1900] AC 135 at 141, HL.
10 *Macvicar v Poland* (1894) 10 TLR 566; *Anglo-Californian Bank Ltd v London and Provincial Marine and General Insurance Co Ltd* (1904) 10 Com Cas 1.

776. Nature of default insured against. The nature of the default which gives rise to a claim under a policy of debt insurance varies according to the terms of the policy[1]. Non-payment of the debt on the due date[2] or within a specified time afterwards[3] may be sufficient. In such a case it is immaterial to consider the cause of the default[4]. In other circumstances the policy covers non-payment by reason only of the debtor's insolvency[5], and by the terms of the policy the cover may be restricted to insolvency from a particular cause[6].

1 Ie *Sturge & Co v Excess Insurance Co Ltd* [1938] 4 All ER 424 (terms of the policy were not effective to incorporate a gold clause in a bond, the case being limited to guaranteeing redemption of the bond at par).
2 *Shaw v Royce Ltd* [1911] 1 Ch 138; *Young v Assets and Investment Insurance Co's Trustee* (1893) 21 R 222, Ct of Sess.
3 *Finlay v Mexican Investment Corpn* [1897] 1 QB 517; and see *Laird v Securities Insurance Co Ltd* (1895) 22 R 452, Ct of Sess.
4 *Mortgage Insurance Corpn v IRC* (1887) 57 LJQB 174 at 181 per Hawkins J; *Laird v Securities Insurance Co* (1895) 22 R 452 at 459, Ct of Sess, per Lord Maclaren.
5 *Hambro v Burnand* [1904] 2 KB 10 at 19, CA, per Collins MR; see also *Murdock v Heath* (1899) 80 LT 50. If the debtor is insolvent, a refusal to pay on other grounds is immaterial: *Macvicar v Poland* (1894) 10 TLR 566.
6 *Waterkeyn v Eagle, Star and British Dominions Insurance Co* (1920) 5 Ll L Rep 42.

777. Export credit guarantee insurance. An exporter of goods to a foreign country is peculiarly vulnerable as regards receiving payment for his goods, and from time to time new devices have to be created in order to facilitate and stimulate international trade[1]. One such device takes the form of an insurance against the loss an exporter incurs when:

(1) the buyer fails to pay for goods he has received; or
(2) without any breach of condition or warranty on the part of the exporter, the buyer declines to accept goods; or
(3) without the buyer being in default, governmental difficulties arise in connection with the transfer of currency representing the purchase price.

The Export Credits Guarantee Department of the Department of Trade issues to exporters policies covering them up to specified percentages against non-commercial risk[2]. These policies are contracts of indemnity[3] and, if payment has been made under a policy by the Department of Trade in respect of a loss due to restrictions on the export of currency, and the currency is ultimately released and the purchase price paid, the Department of Trade, by subrogation, is entitled to receive the purchase price to the extent of its payment, even against the liquidator of the exporters where the exporters are in liquidation[4].

1 An example in the field of banking may be found in commercial letters of credit; see BANKING vol 3(1) (Reissue) para 252 et seq.
2 See the Export and Investment Guarantees Act 1991 s 2; and TRADE AND LABOUR.
3 *Re Miller, Gibb & Co Ltd* [1957] 2 All ER 266, [1957] 1 WLR 703; *L Lucas Ltd v Export Credits Guarantee Department* [1974] 2 All ER 889, [1974] 1 WLR 909, HL.
4 *Re Miller, Gibb & Co Ltd* [1957] 2 All ER 266, [1957] 1 WLR 703. As to subrogation see generally para 505 et seq ante.

(ii) Special Features of Debt Insurance

778. Duration of insurance. Where a policy is effected to cover a creditor against the risk of a debtor's default, it may be that the policy is a species of continuing insurance[1] so that, where by agreement[2] annual premiums are payable, the policy does not necessarily lapse on the non-payment of a particular premium[3]. This is the case where, by arrangement between the parties, the annual premium is payable by the debtor; his failure to pay it does not prevent the creditor from recovering under the policy in the event of the non-payment of the debt[4]. Payment of the annual premium within the days of grace[5] may, however, be expressly made a condition precedent to the insurers' liability[6], and performance of the condition is not excused by reason of the fact that the risk of non-payment has already become a certainty[7].

1 *Stuart v Freeman* [1903] 1 KB 47, CA, distinguishing *Pritchard v Merchant's and Tradesman's Life Assurance Society* (1858) 3 CBNS 622.
2 Agreement may be inferred by the conduct of the parties: *Whitehorn v Canadian Guardian Life Insurance Co* (1909) 19 OLR 535.
3 *Phoenix Life Assurance Co v Sheridan* (1860) 8 HL Cas 745; *Stuart v Freeman* [1903] 1 KB 47, CA; cf *McKenna v City Life Assurance Co* [1919] 2 KB 491.
4 *Shaw v Royce Ltd* [1911] 1 Ch 138 at 148 per Warrington J.
5 As to days of grace see paras 477–478 ante.
6 *Re Law Guarantee Trust and Accident Society Ltd, Liverpool Mortgage Insurance Co's Case* [1914] 2 Ch 617, CA.
7 *Employers' Insurance Co of Great Britain v Benton* (1897) 24 R 908, Ct of Sess; cf *Simpson v Mortgage Insurance Corpn Ltd* (1893) 38 Sol Jo 99, DC.

779. Duty to disclose financial position of debtor. The risk of loss under a policy of debt insurance depends upon the debtor's financial position, and it is a breach of the duty of good faith for a creditor to seek insurance for a debt when he knows or suspects that the debtor will be unable to pay it[1]. Unless the insurers are themselves acquainted with the debtor's position[2] or are put on inquiry, the creditor must disclose any knowledge or suspicion which he may have of the circumstances[3]. If the insurance is in respect of a surety's liability, the financial position both of the surety[4] and of the principal debtor[5] may be material, but the rate of interest and the circumstances of the original loan need not be disclosed[6].

1 As to non-disclosure and misrepresentation see para 349 et seq ante.
2 *Anglo-Californian Bank v London and Provincial Marine and General Insurance Co Ltd* (1904) 20 TLR 665 at 666.
3 *Seaton v Burnand, Burnand v Seaton* [1900] AC 135 at 147, HL, per Lord Shand.
4 *Seaton v Burnand, Burnand v Seaton* [1900] AC 135, HL.
5 *Anglo-Californian Bank v London and Provincial Marine and General Insurance Co Ltd* (1904) 20 TLR 665.
6 *Seaton v Burnand, Burnand v Seaton* [1900] AC 135, HL; cf *Anglo-Californian Bank v London and Provincial Marine and General Insurance Co Ltd* (1904) 20 TLR 665.

780. Alteration of risk. A policy of debt insurance usually has an express condition to prohibit giving time to the debtor or making any alteration in the terms of the loan modifying the creditor's rights and remedies without the insurers' consent[1]. However, such a condition has no application to an alteration which was within the contemplation of the parties at the time when the contract of insurance was made[2]. In the case of an insurance of debentures, if power is reserved to the debenture holders to sanction any modification or compromise of their rights against the debtor company or its property, and the date of payment is accordingly postponed, the risk that payment may be postponed is within the contemplation of the parties[3]. Where the creditor does not himself consent to the postponement he is entitled to claim payment under the policy when the original date of payment under his debenture arrives, leaving the insurers to enforce by subrogation his rights as modified against the company[4]. The same principle applies to a scheme of arrangement made binding upon the creditors by statute[5]. On the other hand, if the debenture holders agree to release the company from its liability under the insured debentures and to accept fresh debentures in their place the creditor is bound whether he consents or not; any default in payment is a default under the fresh debentures, which are not insured, and consequently the insurers are not liable[6].

    1 *Finlay v Mexican Investment Corpn* [1897] 1 QB 517. In the case of a mortgage the mortgagee may be prohibited from selling the property for less than the sum insured without the insurers' consent; *Re Law Guarantee Trust and Accident Society Ltd* (1913) 108 LT 830 at 832 per Neville J.
    2 *Law Guarantee Trust and Accident Society v Munich Re-insurance Co* [1912] 1 Ch 138. As to such an alteration see further para 434 ante.
    3 *Laird v Securities Insurance Co Ltd* (1895) 22 R 452, Ct of Sess.
    4 *Finlay v Mexican Investment Corpn* [1897] 1 QB 517 at 522 per Charles J.
    5 *Dane v Mortgage Insurance Corpn* [1894] 1 QB 54, CA; *Laird v Securities Insurance Co Ltd* (1895) 22 R 452, Ct of Sess.
    6 *Shaw v Royce Ltd* [1911] 1 Ch 138.

781. Proceedings by assured against debtor. Except where the policy of debt insurance so provides, the creditor is not bound to sue the debtor or to enforce his security first. On the occurance of a default within the meaning of the policy, he may claim payment from the insurers[1]. However, the policy may be limited to cover only the deficiency which remains after the creditor has exhausted his remedies against the debtor or his sureties[2].

    1 *Dane v Mortgage Insurance Corpn* [1894] 1 QB 54 at 61, CA, per Lord Esher MR; and see paras 513–515 ante.
    2 *Murdock v Heath* (1899) 80 LT 50; *Re Law Guarantee Trust and Accident Society Ltd, Liverpool Mortgage Insurance Co's Case* [1914] 2 Ch 617, CA. Where insurers of a debt have reinsured their liability, the creditor is not entitled to the benefit of the reinsurance policy as against the general creditors of the insurers: *Re Law Guarantee Trust and Accident Society, Godson's Claim* [1915] 1 Ch 340.

782. Insurers' rights of subrogation and contribution. On payment, the insurers are subrogated to the creditor's rights and remedies against the debtor and his securities[1]. By a special term in the policy the insurers may be empowered, upon a claim being made, to call upon the creditor to transfer to them his rights in respect of the debt and securities[2]. In this case it is sufficient if he transfers such rights as he has[3]. In the case of securities, the doctrine of subrogation applies only where the other securities are intended to be primarily liable for the debt; if the other securities are intended to operate as co-securities with the policy, a case of contribution arises[4].

1 *Laird v Securities Insurance Co Ltd* (1895) 22 R 452, Ct of Sess; *Dane v Mortgage Insurance Corpn* [1894] 1 QB 54, CA; *Parr's Bank v Albert Mines Syndicate* (1900) 5 Com Cas 116. As to subrogation generally see paras 505–512 ante.
2 *Dane v Mortgage Insurance Corpn* [1894] 1 QB 54 at 61, CA, per Lord Esher MR; *Re Law Guarantee Trust and Accident Society Ltd* (1913) 108 LT 830 at 831–832; *Murdock v Heath* (1899) 80 LT 50 at 51 per Bingham J.
3 *Laird v Securities Insurance Co Ltd* (1895) 22 R 452, Ct of Sess.
4 *Anglo-Californian Bank Ltd v London and Provincial Marine and General Insurance Co Ltd* (1904) 10 Com Cas 1. As to contribution see generally paras 520–521 ante.

(iii) Distinction between Insurance and Guarantee

783. Intention of the parties as the basis of distinction. A contract under which insurers undertake to make good losses caused by the default of an employee or a debtor bears a close resemblance to a contract of guarantee[1]. However, there is a broad distinction which exists between an insurance and a guarantee[2]. The distinction depends upon the intention of the parties[3], and may be summarised as described below[4].

(1) Insurance is purely a business contract, and liability is accepted in consideration of a premium based upon an estimate of the risk[5]. In a guarantee, liability is usually accepted on personal grounds and without payment[6].

(2) The insurers have no personal knowledge of the risk, and rely entirely upon the information they receive. Consequently, as in the case of other contracts of insurance, they are entitled to a full disclosure of all material facts[7]. In a guarantee the duty of disclosure is less extensive[8].

(3) The insurers are not sureties; they undertake to pay not the original debt[9], but a new debt arising under a contract of indemnity; this may differ from the original debt both in amount and as regards the date of payment[10].

(4) The insurers have no independent rights against the debtor, but are merely subrogated to the remedies of the assured[11], whereas a surety has a direct claim against the debtor[12].

1 As to contracts of guarantee see GUARANTEE.
2 See *Dane v Mortgage Insurance Corpn* [1894] 1 QB 54 at 60, CA, per Lord Esher, MR; *American Surety Co of New York v Wrightson* (1910) 103 LT 663 at 665 per Hamilton LJ; *Shaw v Royce Ltd* [1911] 1 Ch 138 at 147 per Warrington J; and see further GUARANTEE vol 20 (Reissue) para 107.
3 *Dane v Mortgage Insurance Corpn* [1894] 1 QB 54, CA; and see *Trade Indemnity Co Ltd v Workington Harbour and Dock Board* [1937] AC 1 at 16–17, [1936] 1 All ER 454 at 458–459, HL; *Kreglinger and Fernau Ltd v Irish National Insurance Co Ltd* [1956] IR 116.
4 For a full discussion of the distinction see *Seaton v Heath, Seaton v Burnand* [1899] 1 QB 782 at 792–793, CA, per Romer LJ, which, notwithstanding the reversal of the decision of the Court of Appeal in *Seaton v Burnand, Burnand v Seaton* [1900] AC 135, HL, remains unaffected as a statement of the law; *Re Denton's Estate, Licenses Insurance Corpn and Guarantee Fund Ltd v Denton* [1904] 2 Ch 178 at 188, CA, per Vaughan Williams LJ.
5 *Seaton v Heath, Seaton v Burnand* [1899] 1 QB 782 at 793, CA, per Romer LJ (and see note 4 supra).
6 *Lee v Jones* (1864) 17 CBNS 482 at 503, Ex Ch, per Blackburn J.
7 *Seaton v Heath, Seaton v Burnand* [1899] 1 QB 782 at 793, CA, per Romer LJ (and see note 4 supra). As to non-disclosure and misrepresentation see generally para 349 et seq ante.
8 *North British Insurance Co v Lloyd* (1854) 10 Exch 523; approved in *Lee v Jones* (1864) 17 CBNS 482, Ex Ch; *Re Denton's Licenses Insurance Corpn and Guarantee Fund Ltd v Denton* [1904] 2 Ch 178. See further GUARANTEE vol 20 (Reissue) para 240.
9 *Dane v Mortgage Insurance Corpn* [1894] 1 QB 54 at 60, CA, per Lord Esher MR.
10 *Dane v Mortgage Insurance Corpn* [1894] 1 QB 54, CA; *Finlay v Mexican Investment Corpn* [1897] 1 QB 517 at 522 per Charles J; *Re Law Guarantee Trust and Accident Society Ltd, Liverpool Mortgage Insurance Co's Case* [1914] 2 Ch 617 at 630, CA, per Buckley LJ.

11 As to subrogation see paras 505–512 ante.
12 See GUARANTEE vol 20 (Reissue) para 237. In insurance the insurers are not able to control the occurrence of the event insured against, whereas a guarantor is supposed to undertake that the principal debtor will meet his obligation and is under a duty to see that he does: *Wright v Simpson* (1802) 6 Ves 714 at 734; *Re Lockey* (1845) 1 Ph 509 at 511.

784. Evidence of intention. The fact that a contract is framed in the form of a policy is some evidence of the parties' intention that it should be a contract of insurance, rather than a contract of guarantee[1]. However, the form of contract is not conclusive[2]. A contract which is in form a guarantee may in effect be a contract of insurance, and a contract expressed in the form of a policy may nevertheless be a guarantee[3]. It is possible that many contracts may with equal propriety be called either contracts of insurance or guarantees[4], and in many cases it is immaterial to which of the two classes the particular contract belongs[5].

1 *Dane v Mortgage Insurance Corpn* [1894] 1 QB 54, CA.
2 See *Trade Indemnity Co Ltd v Workington Harbour and Dock Board* [1937] AC 1 at 16–17, [1936] 1 All ER 454 at 458–459, HL.
3 *Re Denton's Estate, Licenses Insurance Corpn and Guarantee Fund Ltd v Denton* [1904] 2 Ch 178; *Re Law Guarantee Trust and Accident Society Ltd, Liverpool Mortgage Insurance Co's Case* [1914] 2 Ch 617 at 631, CA, per Buckley LJ. See also GUARANTEE vol 20 (Reissue) para 160.
4 *Seaton v Heath, Seaton v Burnand* [1899] 1 QB 782 at 792, CA, per Romer LJ; revsd, without affecting this point, sub nom *Seaton v Burnand, Burnand v Seaton* [1900] AC 135, HL.
5 *Dane v Mortgage Insurance Corpn* [1894] 1 QB 54 at 62, CA, per Kay J, followed in *Re Law Guarantee Trust and Accident Society Ltd, Liverpool Mortgage Insurance Co's Case* [1914] 2 Ch 617 at 636, CA, per Kennedy LJ; *Seaton v Burnand, Burnand v Seaton* [1900] AC 135 at 148, HL, per Lord Robertson; cf *Shaw v Royce Ltd* [1911] 1 Ch 138 at 147 per Warrington J.

(4) CONSEQUENTIAL LOSS INSURANCE

785. Purpose of consequential loss insurance. Consequential loss insurance was devised for the purpose of giving protection to the assured against losses which, although consequent upon the loss of his property by a peril insured against, such as fire, are not recoverable under an ordinary form of policy[1]. Usually, the losses contemplated are the losses which flow from the interruption of the assured's business by reason of a fire which destroys or damages the premises on which the business is carried on. In such a case, therefore, a claim under a consequential loss policy necessarily assumes that the premises have been so destroyed or damaged[2].

1 *Re Wright and Pole* (1834) 1 Ad & El 621. For forms of consequential loss policy see 20 Forms & Precedents (5th Edn) 131–133 Form 78.
2 *Waterkeyn v Eagle, Star and British Dominions Insurance Co* (1920) 5 Ll L Rep 42; cf *R v British Columbia Fir and Cedar Lumber Co Ltd* [1932] AC 441 at 447, PC. This form of insurance has, however, been extended to profit-earning goods, such as lorries, which can be effectively put out of commission by many causes other than fire, and to goods and merchandise which may be destroyed elsewhere than on the assured's premises.

786. Insurance in respect of loss of profits. Profits are insured only if they are specifically described as such[1] and are usually net profits[2]. Insurance on goods merely covers the value of the goods[3] and insurance on a building covers no more than the fabric of the building[4]. If profits are insured, a valued policy may be used[5];

the policy normally contains provisions prescribing the standard for measuring the loss of profits and the method of ascertaining the amount to be paid[6]. If, during negotiations for insurance against an overall loss of profit, a proposer is carrying on business at a loss, this may be a material fact to be disclosed to the insurers[7].

1 *Maurice v Goldsborough Mort & Co Ltd* [1939] AC 452 at 461, [1939] 3 All ER 63 at 67, PC, per Lord Wright, citing *Lucena v Craufurd* (1806) 2 Bos & PNR 269, HL; *Mackenzie v Whitworth* (1875) 1 ExD 36 at 43; see also *Stockdale v Dunlop* (1840) 6 M & W 224 at 232–233 per Parke B; *Lewis Emanuel & Son Ltd v Hepburn* [1960] 1 Lloyd's Rep 304 (the words 'physical loss or damage or deterioration caused by strikes' did not cover loss of market); *De Meza and Stuart v Apple Van Straten, Shena and Stone* [1975] 1 Lloyd's Rep 498, CA.
2 The policy moneys are, therefore, liable to income tax: *R v British Columbia Fir and Cedar Lumber Co Ltd* [1932] AC 441, PC, following *J Glicksten & Son Ltd v Green* [1929] AC 381.
3 *Maurice v Goldsborough Mort & Co Ltd* [1939] AC 452, [1939] 3 All ER 63, PC (a loss in value of goods carried by the loss of other goods in the same consignment is not covered); *Cator v Great Western Insurance Co of New York* (1873) LR 8 CP 552.
4 *Re Wright and Pole* (1834) 1 Ad & El 621.
5 See eg *City Tailors Ltd v Evans* (1921) 126 LT 439, CA; cf *Beauchamp v Faber* (1898) 3 Com Cas 308. As to valued policies see para 4 ante.
6 See *Recher & Co v North British and Mercantile Insurance Co* [1915] 3 KB 277, DC; *Brunton v Marshall* (1922) 10 Ll L Rep 689; *Plummer Hat Co Ltd v British Trading Insurance Co Ltd* [1932] NZLR 576.
7 *Stavers v Mountain* (1912) Times, 27 July, CA (the question of materiality ought to have been left to the jury). *Polikoff Ltd v North British and Mercantile Insurance Co Ltd* (1936) 55 Ll L Rep 279; *Plummer Hat Co Ltd v British Trading Insurance Co Ltd* [1932] NZLR 576. It does not follow that a general overall loss must be disclosed if the proposer, in an insurance on property such as an individual factory building, seeks to insure its income-bearing capacity.

787. Insurance in respect of standing charges. In every business there are certain items of expenditure such as rent, rates and taxes, salaries and debenture interest which are payable in the ordinary course out of the earnings of the business, but which continue to be payable notwithstanding the peril insured against occurring interrupting the business and the consequent cessation or diminution of its earning capacity[1]. Where standing charges are intended to be covered they must be specified in the policy, and they are covered to the extent only to which they would have been earned if the peril insured against had not occurred[2]. Generally, such charges are constant in amount, but provision is made for credit to be given if they cease to be payable or are reduced[3].

1 *Mount Royal Assurance Co v Cameron Lumber Co Ltd* [1934] AC 313, PC, (jury was held entitled, in estimating the probable earnings, to adopt an arbitrary method of valuation widely recognised in the industry).
2 *Plummer Hat Co Ltd v British Trading Insurance Co Ltd* [1932] NZLR 576; *Mount Royal Assurance Co v Cameron Lumber Co Ltd* [1934] AC 313, PC.
3 *City Tailors Ltd v Evans* (1921) 126 LT 439, CA; *Brunton v Marshall* (1922) 10 Ll L Rep 689.

788. Insurance in respect of loss of rent. An ordinary policy on buildings may contain a rent clause[1] protecting the assured from the pecuniary loss which he may sustain, (1) if he is a tenant, by reason of his continuing liability to pay rent after the destruction of, or damage to the buildings[2], or (2) if he is a landlord, by reason of the suspension of rent, pending reinstatement, where the tenancy agreement so provides. Under the normal rent clause no liability attaches to the insurers unless the premises become unoccupied, and the extent of their liability is governed by the length of the period for which they continue to be unoccupied[3].

1 See 20 Forms & Precedents (5th Edn) 136, Form 81.
2 See eg *Matthey v Curling* [1922] 2 AC 180, HL; and see also LANDLORD AND TENANT vol 27(1) (Reissue) para 242.
3 *Buchanan v Liverpool and London and Globe Insurance Co* (1884) 11 R 1032, Ct of Sess.

789. Insurance in respect of increased cost of working. Insurance may be effected to cover any additional expenditure incurred for the purpose of keeping the business going during the period required for reinstatement, such as the extra cost of labour or materials[1]. Other forms of policy may be effected to cover the increased cost of reinstatement where, owing to a rise in prices or the expense of new materials, the cost of reinstatement exceeds the value of the subject matter at the time of the loss.

1 This includes the cost of partly manufactured goods if bought for the purpose of keeping the business going; *Henry Booth & Sons v Commercial Union Assurance Co* (1922) 14 Ll L Rep 114.

11. WAR RISKS AND ACTS OF TERRORISM

(1) WAR RISKS

(i) Restriction of Advertisements

790. Circulars and advertisements controlled. It is an offence[1]:
  (1) to distribute or cause to be distributed any circulars inviting persons to insure any property[2] in the United Kingdom in which they are interested against war risks[3], or containing information calculated to lead the recipient to insure such property against war risks[4];
  (2) to be in possession for the purpose of distribution of any circulars of such a nature as to show that the object or principal object of distribution would be to communicate such an invitation or such information[5]; or
  (3) to cause or permit the appearance of any advertisement containing such an invitation or such information[6];
unless permission for the distribution of the circular, or the appearance of the advertisement, has been granted by the Secretary of State[7], and any conditions imposed by him in relation to the circular or advertisement have been complied with[8]. For this purpose documents are not deemed to be other than circulars by reason only of the fact that they are in the form of a newspaper, journal, magazine or other periodical publication[9].

1 As to penalties and proceedings see para 793 post.
2 A reference to the insuring of any property by any person includes a reference to the making of a contract or arrangement (not being a contract of sale or bailment of that property), under which, in the event of damage to the property, he is entitled or eligible, absolutely or conditionally, to or for any form of indemnification, total or partial, and whether by way of a money payment or not, in respect of that damage: Restriction of Advertisement (War Risks Insurance) Act 1939 s 6(1)(b).
3 Ibid s 1(1)(a)(i). 'War risks' means risks arising from action taken by an enemy or from action taken in combating an enemy or repelling an imagined attack by an enemy: s 6(1)(a).
4 Ibid s 1(1)(a)(ii).
5 Ibid s 1(1)(b).
6 Ibid s 1(1)(c).

7 Every application for permission to issue a circular or advertisement must be referred by the Secretary of State to an advisory committee appointed by him, consisting of such persons as he thinks fit: ibid s 3(1), (2); the Secretary of State may not grant permission except (1) on the recommendation of the committee, or (2) where the committee recommends the granting of permission subject to requirements or conditions, without imposing such conditions or requirements: s 3(2)(a), (b). However, this provision does not limit the discretion of the Secretary of State to refuse altogether to grant the permission or to impose further conditions or requirements: s 3(2). The committee may not recommend the granting of permission unless, having regard to all relevant circumstances and particularly the nature and situation of the property proposed to be eligible for insurance and the classes of persons to be invited to insure, it is satisfied that such grant, subject to any conditions or requirements included in the committee's recommendations, would not be contrary to public interest: s 3(3). As to the Secretary of State see para 15 note 5 ante.

8 Ibid s 1(1).

9 Ibid s 6(2). A person is not to be taken to contravene the Act merely by distributing or causing to be distributed to purchasers, or having in his possession for the purpose of distribution to purchasers, copies of any newspaper, journal, magazine or other periodical publication of which he is not the publisher: s 6(2).

791. Savings. The restriction on the distribution of circulars and the issue of advertisements relating to war risks[1] does not render unlawful:

(1) anything done with a view to inducing persons to enter into a contract of insurance if the Secretary of State could lawfully reinsure the person liable under that contract[2]; or

(2) anything done with a view to inducing persons to enter into any contract of insurance:

    (a) of goods consigned for carriage by sea or air from a place outside the United Kingdom[3] to a place in the United Kingdom, while the goods are in transit between the ship or aircraft and their destination[4]; or

    (b) of goods consigned for carriage by sea or air from a place in the United Kingdom to a place outside the United Kingdom, while the goods are in transit between the premises from which they are consigned and the ship or aircraft[5].

1 As to this restriction, and for the meaning of 'war risks', see para 790 ante.

2 Ie under the Marine and Aviation Insurance (War Risks) Act 1952 s 1 (see para 791 post): Restriction of Advertisement (War Risks Insurance) Act 1939 s 1(2)(b) (amended by the Marine and Aviation Insurance (War Risks) Act 1952 s 8; the Transfer of Functions (Sea Transport, etc) Order 1968, SI 1968/2038, art 4(1)(a). As to the Secretary of State see para 15 note 5 ante.

3 For the meaning of 'United Kingdom' see para 2 note 10 ante.

4 Restriction of Advertisement (War Risks Insurance) Act 1939 s 1(2)(c)(i).

5 Ibid s 1(2)(c)(ii).

792. Imposition of requirements. Where permission is granted for the distribution of any circulars, or the appearance of any advertisement, inviting insurance against war risks[1], the Secretary of State[2] may, in addition to imposing conditions as to such distribution or appearance[3], by order specify requirements[4] designed to secure that any representation in the circular or advertisement is complied with[5]. If the persons to whom the permission is granted avail themselves of it, such requirements must be complied with by every person concerned in carrying on the business in connection with which the circulars are to be distributed or the advertisement is to appear[6].

If the Secretary of State thinks fit, the requirements which may be imposed include requirements as to:

(1) the total or partial separation of the funds respectively available for the payment of claims and the payment of expenses[7];

(2) the proportion of premiums or similar payments which is to be allocated to the payments of claims[8];

(3) the manner in which any fund available for the payment of claims is to be maintained and dealt with[9]; and

(4) the keeping, drawing up, auditing and publication of accounts[10].

1 As to circulars and advertisements which are controlled, and for the meaning of 'war risks', see para 790 ante.
2 As to the Secretary of State see para 15 note 5 ante.
3 See para 790 ante.
4 The Secretary of State must impose any requirements recommended by his advisory committee: see para 790 note 7 ante.
5 Restriction of Advertisement (War Risks Insurance) Act 1939 s 2(1).
6 Ibid s 2(1), (2). Except in so far as the Secretary of State dispenses with compliance with any requirement, non-compliance by any person concerned in carrying on the business is an offence: s 2(2). For penalties for offences see para 793 post.
7 Ibid s 2(1)(a).
8 Ibid s 2(1)(b).
9 Ibid s 2(1)(c).
10 Ibid s 2(1)(d).

793. Penalties and proceedings. A person who commits an offence under the Restriction of Advertisement (War Risks Insurance) Act 1939[1] is liable on summary conviction to a fine not exceeding the prescribed sum or to imprisonment for a period not exceeding three months, or both[2], and on conviction on indictment to a fine or to imprisonment for a period not exceeding two years, or both[3]. Where an offence under the Act committed by a body corporate is proved to have been committed with the consent or connivance of any director, manager, secretary or other officer of the body corporate, he, as well as the body corporate, is deemed to be guilty of the offence and is liable to be proceeded against and punished accordingly[4].

No prosecution in respect of an offence under the Act may be instituted otherwise than with the consent of the Secretary of State[5].

1 See paras 790, 792 note 6 ante.
2 Restriction of Advertisement (War Risks Insurance) Act 1939 s 4(1)(a) (amended by virtue of the Magistrates' Courts Act 1980 s 32(2)). As to the prescribed sum see para 19 note 5 ante.
3 Restriction of Advertisement (War Risks Insurance) Act 1939 s 4(1)(b).
4 Ibid s 4(2).
5 Ibid s 4(3). As to the Secretary of State see para 15 note 5 ante.

(ii) Insurance of Ships, Aircraft and Cargoes

A. REINSURANCE BY THE SECRETARY OF STATE

794. Power to enter into reinsurance agreements. The Secretary of State[1] may with the approval of the Treasury make agreements with any authorities or persons whereby he undertakes the liability of reinsuring any war risks[2] against which a ship or aircraft[3], or the cargo carried in a ship or aircraft, is for the time being insured[4]. However, he may not enter into an agreement for the reinsurance

of any war risks against which a ship or aircraft which is not a British ship[5] or
British aircraft[6] is for the time being insured, except in so far as they arise during the
continuance of any war or other hostilities in which Her Majesty is engaged, or
arise after such war or hostilities in consequence of things done or omitted during
the continuance of such war or hostilities[7]. A copy of every agreement for reinsurance made by the Secretary of State must be laid before both Houses of Parliament
as soon as may be after it is made, and if either House, within the period of 14 days[8]
beginning with the day on which a copy is laid before it, resolves that the
agreement be annulled, it then becomes void except in so far as it confers rights or
imposes obligations in respect of things previously done or omitted, but without
prejudice to the making of a new agreement[9].

In pursuance of the powers described above, agreements[10] were entered into
with certain shipowners' mutual insurance associations[11] for the reinsurance of
British ships insured against war risks by the associations in so far as such risks arise
from hostilities involving the United Kingdom. No premiums are payable under
the agreements in respect of risks assumed by the Secretary of State, unless and
until circumstances arise in which British ships are or may be exposed to hostile
action[12]. Disputes between the Secretary of State and an association as to the
entered value of a ship fixed under any insurance policy reinsured under the
agreements are to be decided by a sole arbitrator, experienced in the valuation of
ships, appointed by the Chairman of the Corporation of Lloyd's[13].

Agreements have also been entered into for the reinsurance of Norwegian ships
insured against war risks by the Norwegian Shipowners' Mutual War Risk
Insurance Association and for the reinsurance of Danish ships insured against war
risks by the Institute for the War Risk Insurance of Danish Ships, during war or
other hostilities in which the United Kingdom and Norway or Denmark respectively may be involved against a common enemy[14].

1 As to the Secretary of State see para 15 note 5 ante.
2 'War risks' means risks arising from hostilities, rebellion, revolution and civil war, civil strife
  consequent on the happening of any of those events, or action taken (whether before or after the
  outbreak of any hostilities, rebellion, revolution or civil war) for repelling an imagined attack or
  preventing or hindering the carrying out of any attack, and includes piracy: Marine and Aviation
  Insurance (War Risks) Act 1952 s 10(1). As to pirates see para 159 ante.
3 A reference to a ship or aircraft is for this purpose construed as including any machinery, tackle,
  furniture or equipment of the ship or aircraft and any goods on board the ship or aircraft other than
  cargo carried in it: ibid s 1(3). 'Goods' includes currency and bearer securities, not being bills of
  exchange or promissory notes: s 10(1).
4 Ibid s 1(1)(a), (b).
5 As to the ships which may be included in the central register of British ships see now the Merchant
  Shipping (Registration, etc) Act 1993; and SHIPPING. The provisions of the Marine and Aviation
  Insurance (War Risks) Act 1952 relating to British ships apply also to ships of India and ships of the
  Republic of Ireland, and references in the Act to British ships must be construed accordingly: s 10(2).
6 'British aircraft' means aircraft registered in Her Majesty's dominions: ibid s 10(1). The provisions
  of the Act also apply to aircraft registered in India, the Republic of Ireland, the Federation of Malaya,
  a protectorate, a protected state, a trust territory or a mandated territory, and references in the Act to
  British aircraft must be construed accordingly: s 10(3), which further provides that the references to
  a protectorate, a protected state, a trust territory and a mandated territory are to be construed as if
  they were contained in the British Nationality Act 1948 (repealed). These terms are now obsolete:
  see generally COMMONWEALTH.
7 Marine and Aviation Insurance (War Risks) Act 1952 s 1(1) proviso. Under s 7 (as amended)
  agreements made under s 1 are exempt from the operation of the Marine Insurance Act 1906: see para
  797 post.

8 In reckoning the period of 14 days no account is taken of any period during which Parliament is dissolved or prorogued or both Houses are adjourned for more than 4 days: Marine and Aviation Insurance (War Risks) Act 1952 s 1(2).
9 Ibid s 1(2).
10 The Agreements are dated 18 February 1954. Treasury approval to the making of the Agreements was given on 17 February 1954. The text of the Agreements, which are all in the same form, is published by HM Stationery Office.
11 The associations in question are: (1) the Britannia Steam Ship Insurance Association Ltd, (2) the British Marine Mutual Insurance Association Ltd, (3) the Coasting Vessels Mutual War Risks Association Ltd, (4) the Liverpool and London War Risks Insurance Association Ltd, (5) the Newcastle War Risks Indemnity Association Ltd, (6) the North of England Protecting and Indemnity Association Ltd, (7) the Standard Steamship Owners' Mutual War Risks Association Ltd, (8) the Sunderland Steamship Mutual War Risks Association Ltd, (9) the United Kingdom Mutual War Risks Association Ltd, and (10) the West of England Mutual War Risks Association Ltd. As to mutual insurance associations see generally paras 341–346 ante.
12 See the Agreements dated 18 February 1954, cll 1–2, in conjunction with the forms of policies of insurance and reinsurance set out in Schs 1–4 to the Agreements.
13 See the Agreements dated 18 February 1954, cl 3(1)(c).
14 See the Agreement dated 18 May 1954 made between Norske Krigsforsikring for S K I B (the Norwegian Shipowners' Mutual War Risks Insurance Association) and the Minister of Transport and Civil Aviation; and the Agreement dated 11 March 1957 made between Krigsforsikringen for Danske Skibe (the Institute for the War Risks Insurance of Danish Ships) and the Minister of Transport and Civil Aviation. Treasury approval to the making of the Agreements was given on 18 May 1954 and 6 March 1957 respectvely. The Agreements are published by HM Stationery Office.

795. Liabilities of reinsurance on insolvency of insurer. Where, in respect of any loss or damage arising from a war risk[1] against which an assured has been insured, either originally or by way of reinsurance, a sum has become payable to the insurer either:

(1) by the Secretary of State by virtue of a reinsurance agreement made under the Marine and Aviation Insurance (War Risks) Act 1952[2], or

(2) under a contract of insurance by some intermediate insurer who has reinsured the risk with the Secretary of State under such an agreement[3];

then if before payment of the sum is made by the Secretary of State or the intermediate insurer the insurer becomes insolvent[4], the sum ceases to be payable to the insurer and becomes payable by the Secretary of State or the intermediate insurer, as the case may be, to the assured, and the right of the assured to receive payment from the insurer in respect of the loss or damage is extinguished to the extent that the risk was reinsured by the Secretary of State[5].

1 For the meaning of 'war risk' see para 794 note 2 ante.
2 Ie the Marine and Aviation Insurance (War Risks) Act 1952 s 1 (see para 794 ante): s 4(a). As to the Secretary of State see para 15 note 5 ante.
3 Ibid s 4(b).
4 Ie if the insurer becomes bankrupt or, where the insurer is a company, the company commences to be wound up or a receiver is appointed on behalf of the holders of any debentures of the company secured by a floating charge or possession is taken by or on behalf of the holders of such debentures of any property comprised in or subject to the charge: ibid s 4. As to floating charge see COMPANIES vol 7(2) (Reissue) para 1098 et seq.
5 Ibid s 4. In the case of other reinsurances of marine risks the assured has no right or interest in respect of the reinsurance unless the policy so provides: see the Marine Insurance Act 1906 s 9(2); and para 205 ante.

B. INSURANCE BY THE SECRETARY OF STATE

796. Power to carry on insurance business. If at any time it appears to the Secretary of State[1] that reasonable and adequate facilities are not available for the insurance of British ships or British aircraft[2], or for the insurance of cargoes carried in ships or aircraft, against war risks[3] or any description of such risks, he may with the approval of the Treasury carry on the business of insuring such ships, aircraft or cargoes against war risks or, as the case may be, the description of war risks in question[4].

During the continuance of any war or other hostilities in which Her Majesty may be engaged the Secretary of State may with the approval of the Treasury carry on business as an insurer against all risks, of:

(1) ships and aircraft (whether British or not)[5], or

(2) cargoes carried in ships and aircraft[6], or

(3) goods[7] consigned for carriage by sea or air while the goods are in transit between the premises from which they are consigned and the ship or aircraft, or between the ship or aircraft[8] and their destination[9];

or may carry on business simultaneously as such as an insurer in all three categories[10]. However, the Secretary of State must not, by virtue of any of these three categories, undertake the insurance of a ship, aircraft or cargo against risks other than war risks unless he is satisfied that, in the interests of the defence of the realm or the efficient prosecution of any war or hostilities in which Her Majesty is engaged, it is necessary or expedient to do so[11].

1 As to the Secretary of State see para 15 note 5 ante. The words 'when it appears' make the Secretary of State the sole judge of whether the facilities available are reasonable and adequate: see *Point of Ayr Collieries Ltd v Lloyd-George* [1943] 2 All ER 546, CA.

2 For the purposes of the Marine and Aviation Insurance (War Risks) Act 1952 s 2 (1)(a) and (b) and s 2(1) proviso, references to ships and aircraft of any description are construed as including references to any machinery, tackle, furniture or equipment of ships and aircraft of those respective descriptions and to any goods on board ships and aircraft of those respective descriptions not being cargo carried in them: s 2(2). For the meaning of 'goods' see para 794 note 3 ante. For the meaning of 'British ships' and 'British aircraft' see para 794 notes 5–6 ante.

3 For the meaning of 'war risks' see para 794 note 2 ante.

4 Marine and Aviation Insurance (War Risks) Act 1952 s 2(1)(a), (c). The Secretary of State may carry on business under all or any of the categories described in these provisions: s 2(1). Under s 7 (as amended) agreements made under s 1 are exempt from the operation of the Marine Insurance Act 1906: see para 797 post.

5 Marine and Aviation Insurance (War Risks) Act 1952 s 2(1)(b); and see text and note 11 infra.

6 Ibid s 2(1)(d); and see text and note 11 infra.

7 For transitional provisions as to compensation for goods lost or damaged in transit see paras 798–799 post.

8 'Ship or aircraft' here does not include a vessel from which the goods are discharged for the purpose of being carried by sea or air or into which they are discharged for the purpose of being landed: Marine and Aviation Insurance (War Risks) Act 1952 s 2(3).

9 Ibid s 2(1)(e); and see text and note 11 infra.

10 Ibid s 2(1).

11 Ibid s 2(1) proviso.

C. EXEMPTIONS AS TO FORM OF INSTRUMENTS

797. Saving of instruments from being inadmissible in evidence. The fact that certain instruments are not embodied in marine policies in accordance with the general statutory requirement[1] does not of itself make the instruments inadmissible in evidence[2]. The instruments are:

(1) an agreement for reinsurance of war risks made between the Secretary of State and any other authority or person[3], and a policy of reinsurance issued by the Secretary of State in pursuance of such an agreement[4];

(2) an agreement entered into by a body of persons approved by the Secretary of State[5] for the reinsurance of a war risk insured by another person which may be reinsured by the Secretary of State, and a policy issued in pursuance of such an agreement, being a policy only for the reinsurance of such a risk[6]; or

(3) a contract of insurance entered into by the Secretary of State pursuant to his power to insure, whether against war risks or generally[7], and a policy and certificate of insurance issued by him in connection with any such contract[8].

1 As to the general statutory requirement see the Marine Insurance Act 1906 s 22; and para 39 et seq ante.
2 Marine and Aviation Insurance (War Risks) Act 1952 s 7(1) (amended by the Finance Act 1959 s 37, Sch 8 Pt II).
3 Ie made under the Marine and Aviation Insurance (War Risks) Act 1952 s 1 (see para 794 ante): s 7(1)(a). As to the Secretary of State see para 15 note 5 ante. For the meaning of 'war risks' see para 794 note 2 ante.
4 Ibid s 7(1)(a).
5 Ie a body of persons for the time being approved by the Secretary of State for the purpose of the Marine and Aviation Insurance (War Risks) Act 1952, being a body the objects of which are or include the carrying on of business by way of the reinsurance against war risks of cargoes carried in ships and aircraft: s 7(4), applying s 1(1)(b) (see para 794 text to notes 1–4 ante).
6 Ibid s 7(1)(b).
7 As to this power see para 796 ante.
8 Marine and Aviation Insurance (War Risks) Act 1952 s 7(1)(c).

D. PROVISION FOR TRANSITIONAL COMPENSATION FOR GOODS IN TRANSIT

798. Power to pay compensation. The Secretary of State's power to carry on, during the continuance of any war or hostilities in which Her Majesty is engaged, the business of insurance on goods in transit[1], postulates that difficulty may well have existed, even before the Secretary of State decides to exercise his power, in obtaining insurance particularly against the impending war risks. Accordingly, special transitional provisions were enacted[2] to provide compensation when goods in transit were lost or damaged by a war risk during an interim period when commercial insurance was not obtainable and the state insurance was not available. In order to obtain such transitional compensation a person must satisfy the Secretary of State that the requisite conditions are fulfilled with respect to any goods[3]; If he does so, the Secretary of State must pay him compensation for loss or damage to the goods[4].

The requisite conditions are:

(1) in the case of goods which have been consigned for carriage by sea or air from a place outside the United Kingdom, the Isle of Man or any of the

Channel Islands[5] to a place in one of those countries (ie goods in process of import), that the goods were:

(a) discharged in that country from the ship or aircraft[6] before the expiration of the period of seven days beginning with such day as the Secretary of State may declare to be the day from which he will, during the continuance of any war or hostilities in which Her Majesty is engaged, carry on the business of insurance of goods in transit[7];

(b) after the beginning of that day and before the expiration of the appropriate period[8], lost or damaged in consequence of a war risk, being one which the Secretary of State was on that day prepared to insure under his general power of insuring goods in transit during such war or hostilities[9];

(c) lost or damaged while in transit between the ship or aircraft and their destination[10];

(2) in the case of goods which have been consigned for carriage by sea or air from a place in any one of the countries mentioned above to a place outside that country (ie goods in process of export), that before the expiration of that period of seven days, after the beginning of the declared day, the goods were lost or damaged in consequence of such a war risk while in transit between the premises from which they were consigned and the ship or aircraft[11].

The further requisite conditions, applicable both to goods in process of import and to goods in process of export, are that:

(i) the goods were not insured against the war risk in consequence of which they were lost or damaged[12];

(ii) the claimant and his agents exercised all due diligence for securing that no delay occurred while the goods were in transit[13]; and

(iii) the property in the goods was vested in the claimant when the loss or damage occurred[14].

1 As to the power of the Secretary of State to carry on such business see para 827 ante. As to the Secretary of State see para 15 note 5 ante.
2 See the Marine and Aviation Insurance (War Risks) Act 1952 s 3.
3 For the meaning of 'goods' see para 794 note 3 ante.
4 See the Marine and Aviation Insurance (War Risks) Act 1952 s 3(1). As to the amount of transitional compensation see para 799 post.
5 Ibid s 3(1)(a), (4). For the meaning of 'United Kingdom' see para 2 note 10 ante.
6 'Ship or aircraft' does not include a vessel into which the goods are discharged at a port or place in the country in question for the purpose of being landed at that port or place, or from which the goods are discharged for the purpose of being carried by sea or air from the country in question: s 3(5)(a).
7 Ibid s 3(1)(a)(i). For the Secretary of State's power during the continuance of war or hostilities to carry on the business of insuring goods consigned for carriage by sea or air while the goods are in transit to or from the ship or aircraft see para 796 text to note 7 ante.
8 'The appropriate period' means, in a case where the destination of the goods is within the port or place at which they were discharged from the ship or aircraft, the period of 15 days beginning with the day on which they were so discharged, or, in a case where the destination of the goods is outside that port or place, the period of 30 days beginning with the day on which they were so discharged: ibid s 3(5)(b).
9 Ibid s 3(1)(a)(ii).
10 Ibid s 3(1)(a)(iii).
11 Ibid s 3(1)(a).
12 Ibid s 3(1)(b).
13 Ibid s 3(1)(c).
14 Ibid s 3(1)(d).

799. Amount of transitional compensation. The amount of the compensation payable by the Secretary of State under the Marine and Aviation Insurance (War Risks) Act 1952[1] is:

(1) in the case of lost goods, their insurable value[2];

(2) in the case of damaged goods which have been delivered at their destination, an amount equal to such proportion of their insurable value as the difference between the gross sound and damaged values at the place of arrival bears to the gross sound value[3];

(3) in the case of damaged goods which have not been so delivered, an amount equal to such proportion of their insurable value as the difference between the gross sound and damaged values at the place from which they were consigned bears to the gross sound value[4].

Where, at the time of the loss or damage for which compensation in respect of any goods has become payable under the provisions for transitional compensation, the goods were subject to a mortgage, charge or other similar obligation, the amount of the compensation is deemed to be comprised in the mortgage, charge or obligation[5].

1 As to the power of the Secretary of State to award transitional compensation under the Marine and Aviation Insurance (War Risks) Act 1952 see s 3; and para 789 ante. As to the Secretary of State see para 15 note 5 ante.

2 Ibid s 3(2)(a). 'Insurable value' means the prime cost of the goods plus the expenses of and incidental to the carriage of the goods by sea or air and the charges of insurance on the whole: s 3(5)(c).

3 Ibid s 3(2)(b)(i). The gross value of goods for this purpose is their wholesale price, or, if there is none, their estimated value, plus, in either case, the expenses of and incidental to the carriage of the goods: s 3(5).

4 Ibid s 3(2)(b)(ii); and see note 3 supra.

5 Ibid s 3(3).

E. MARINE AND AVIATION (WAR RISKS) FUND

800. Payments in and out. All sums received by the Secretary of State[1] under the Marine and Aviation Insurance (War Risks) Act 1952 are payable into a fund under his control called the Marine and Aviation Insurance (War Risks) Fund[2]. All sums required by him for the fulfilment of any of his obligations under that Act must be paid out of that fund[3]. At any time when a payment falls to be made out of the fund, if the sum standing to the credit of the fund is less than the sum required for making that payment, an amount equal to the deficiency must be paid into the fund out of money provided by Parliament, but if and in so far as that amount is not paid out of such money it is to be charged on and issued out of the Consolidated Fund[4].

Any amount standing to the credit of the fund at any time, which is in excess of what, in the opinion of the Secretary of State and the Treasury, is likely to be required to meet payments out of the fund, must be paid into the Exchequer[5].

1 As to the Secretary of State see para 15 note 5 ante.

2 Marine and Aviation Insurance (War Risks) Act 1952 s 5(1)(a) (amended by the Statute Law (Repeals) Act 1981).

3 Marine and Aviation Insurance (War Risks) Act 1952 s 5(1)(b) (as amended: see note 2 supra). Any expenses incurred by the Secretary of State for the purposes of the Act which are not required to be defrayed out of the fund must be defrayed out of money provided by Parliament: s 9.

4 Ibid s 5(2) (amended by the Statute Law Revision Act 1963). As to payments out of the Consolidated Fund see CONSTITUTIONAL LAW vol 8 para 1381.

5 Marine and Aviation Insurance (War Risks) Act 1952 s 5(3) (amended by the National Loans Act 1968 s 24(2), Sch 6 Pt I).

801. Accounts and audit. An account of the sums paid into and out of the Marine and Aviation Insurance (War Risks) Fund[1] in each financial year must be prepared by the Secretary of State[2] in such form and manner as the Treasury may direct, and must be transmitted by the Secretary of State to the Comptroller and Auditor General on or before 30 November in each year[3]. The Comptroller and Auditor General must examine and certify the account and lay copies of the account and of his report on it before both Houses of Parliament[4], unless the Treasury certifies that, in the interests of the defence of the realm or the efficient prosecution of any war or hostilities in which Her Majesty is engaged, it is inexpedient that copies of the account for any year, and of the report on it, should be laid before Parliament; in such a case, a copy of the certificate must be laid before both Houses of Parliament and, so long as the certificate remains in force, the copies of the account and of the report on it must not be so laid[5].

1 As to the Marine and Aviation Insurance (War Risks) Fund see para 800 ante.
2 As to the Secretary of State see para 15 note 5 ante.
3 Marine and Aviation Insurance (War Risks) Act 1952 s 5(4). As to the Comptroller and Auditor General see CONSTITUTIONAL LAW vol 8 para 1372.
4 Ibid s 5(4). As to the audit of public accounts generally see CONSTITUTIONAL LAW vol 8 para 1371.
5 Ibid s 5(4) proviso.

(2) ACTS OF TERRORISM

802. Reinsurance by Secretary of State against acts of terrorism. There must be paid out of money provided by Parliament sums necessary to meet the obligations of the Secretary of State[1] under:
(1) any reinsurance agreement entered into with the consent of the Treasury, pursuant to certain arrangments[2]; or
(2) any guarantee entered into with such consent pursuant to any such agreement[3].
This applies to arrangements under which the Secretary of State, with the consent of the Treasury, undertakes to any extent the liability of reinsuring risks against:
(a) loss of or damage to property in Great Britain resulting from or consequential on acts of terrorism[4]; and
(b) any loss which is consequential on such loss or damage[5].
Any sums received by the Secretary of State pursuant to any such arrangements must be paid into the Consolidated Fund[6].
As soon as practicable after entering into an agreement or guarantee the Secretary of State must lay a copy of it before each House of Parliament[7].

1 The Secretary of State here concerned is the Secretary of State for Trade and Industry.
2 As to the arrangements in question see text and note 4 infra.
3 Reinsurance (Acts of Terrorism) Act 1993 s 1(1).
4 'Acts of terrorism' means acts of persons acting on behalf of or in connection with any organisation which carries out activities directed towards the overthrowing or influencing, by force or violence, of Her Majesty's government in the United Kingdom or any government de jure or de facto: ibid s 2(2). 'Organisation' includes any association or combination of persons: s 2(3).

5 Ibid s 2(1). To the extent that the arrangements relate to events occurring before as well as after an agreement of reinsurance comes into being, the reference in s 1(1) (text and notes 1–3 supra) to the obligations of the Secretary of State are to be construed accordingly: s 2(1).
6 Ibid s 1(3).
7 Ibid s 1(2), which also imposed the same duties on the Secretary of State with regard to agreements or guarantees already existing, to be carried out as soon as practicable after the commencement of the Act (ie 27 May 1993).

12. REGULATION OF INSURANCE COMPANIES

(1) SCOPE OF LEGISLATION

803. In general. The Insurance Companies Act 1982 Part II, which relates to the regulation of insurance companies, applies in general to all insurance companies, whether established within or outside the United Kingdom, which carry on insurance business within the United Kingdom[1]. Part II of the Act does not apply to:

(1) any insurance company which is registered under the enactments[2] relating to friendly societies[3];

(2) a trade union or an employers' association[4] carrying on insurance business, if the insurance business is limited to the provision for its members of provident benefits or strike benefits[5];

(3) a member of Lloyd's[6] who carries on insurance business of any class, provided that he complies with the statutory requirements[7] applicable to business of that class[8];

(4) a person by reason only that he carries on credit insurance, suretyship insurance, miscellaneous financial loss insurance, legal expenses insurance and assistance insurance business in the course of carrying on, and for the purposes of, banking business[9];

(5) an insurance company whose insurance business is restricted to general business consisting in the effecting and carrying out of contracts of such descriptions as may be prescribed, being contracts under which the benefits provided by the insurer are exclusively or primarily benefits in kind[10]; and

(6) a European institution[11] by reason only that it carries on in the United Kingdom certain listed activities[12] which it is authorised or permitted to carry on in its home state[13].

On the application or with the consent of an insurance company to which Part II of the Act applies, the Secretary of State[14] may by order direct that all or any of certain specified provisions of the Act[15] and certain regulations[16] made under it are not to apply to the company, or are to apply to it with such modifications as may be specified in the order[17]. Such an order may be subject to conditions[18], and may be revoked by the Secretary of State at any time or varied by him at any time on the application or with the consent of the company to which it applies[19].

Part III of the Insurance Companies Act 1982 governs the conduct of insurance business with regard to permitted forms of advertisement and the protection afforded to persons entering into a contract of insurance[20].

1 Insurance Companies Act 1982 s 15(1). Part II comprises ss 15–71 (as amended). For the meaning of 'insurance business' see para 18 ante. For the meaning of 'United Kingdom' see para 2 note 10 ante.
2 These include Acts of the Parliament of Northern Ireland and Measures of the Northern Ireland Assembly: ibid s 96(1).

3 Ibid s 15(2). As to registered friendly societies see FRIENDLY SOCIETIES.
4 'Trade union' and 'employers' association' have (throughout the United Kingdom) the same meanings as they have assigned to them by the Trade Union and Labour Relations (Consolidation) Act 1992 ss 1, 122(2) (see TRADE AND LABOUR): Insurance Companies Act 1982 s 15(3) (amended by the Trade Union and Labur Relations (Consolidation) Act 1992 s 300(2), Sch 2 para 31).
5 Insurance Companies Act 1982 s 15(3) (as amended).
6 As to Lloyd's underwriters see generally para 21 ante.
7 Ie the requirements set out in the Insurance Companies Act 1982 s 83: see para 23 ante.
8 Ibid s 15(4).
9 Ibid s 15(5), Sch 2 (amended by the Insurance Companies (Assistance) Regulations 1987, SI 1987/2130, reg 2(a), (b)).
10 Insurance Companies Act 1982 s 15(6). For the contracts for benefits in kind prescribed for this purpose see the Insurance Companies Regulations 1981, SI 1981/1654, reg 23 (amended by SI 1987/2130).
11 For the meaning of 'European institution' see the Banking Coordination (Second Council Directive) Regulations 1992, SI 1992/3218, regs 2(1), 3, Sch 2.
12 Ie those activities listed in the annex to the Second Council Directive (EC) 89/646 on the coordination of laws, regulations and administrative provisions relating to the taking up and pursuit of the business of credit institutions, reproduced in the Banking Coordination (Second Council Directive) Regulations 1992 Sch 1.
13 Ibid reg 65.
14 As to the Secretary of State see para 15 note 5 ante.
15 Ie the Insurance Companies Act 1982 ss 16–22, 23(1), 25–36 (as amended): s 68(4).
16 Ie regulations made for the purposes of any of the sections mentioned in note 13 supra, and the provisions of any valuation regulations: ibid s 68(4). 'Valuation regulations' means regulations made under s 90: s 96(1); see para 863 post.
17 Ibid s 68(1). In relation to s 31 (as amended) (restricted transactions: see para 821 post) s 68(1) has effect as if the reference to an insurance company to which Pt II of the Act applies included a reference to any subordinate company within the meaning of s 31 (as amended) of any such insurance company: s 68(5).
18 Ibid s 68(2).
19 Ibid s 68(3).
20 See ibid ss 72–81 (as amended); and paras 810–818 post.

804. Financial Services Act 1986: application of investment business provisions to insurance companies. The Financial Services Act 1986 confers automatic authorisation to carry on investment business on insurance companies authorised to carry on insurance business under the Insurance Companies Act 1982[1].

The investment business provisions of the Financial Services Act 1986[2] are adapted for regulated insurance companies[3]. Regulated insurance companies are required to comply with the conduct of business rules made under the Financial Services Act 1986[4] in relation to the marketing and promotion of policies, the management of the investments of pension funds and the marketing and promotion of contracts for the management of such investments, and incidental matters[5]. The indemnification and compensation rules[6] do not apply to loss arising as a result of a regulated insurance company being unable to meet its liabilities under a contract of insurance[7]. The restrictions on the employment of prohibited persons[8] apply only to the operations mentioned above, or carried on in connection with or for the purposes of those operations[9]. Limitations are imposed on the application of statutory intervention powers[10].

The grounds on which insurance business authorisation can be withdrawn under the 1982 Act are amended[11]. Provision is made for consultation between the Secretary of State[12] and designated agencies[13].

1 Financial Services Act 1986 s 22. Such authorisation extends to (1) any insurance business which is investment business, and (2) investment business which may be carried on without contravention of the Insurance Companies Act 1982 s 16: Financial Services Act 1986 s 22(a), (b). For the meaning of 'insurance business' see para 18 ante. For the meaning of 'investment business' see s 1(2), Sch 1 Pts II, III (as amended). Accordingly, insurance companies authorised by s 22 do not need to obtain authorisation to carry on investment business by way of membership of a self-regulating organis-ation (SRO) or directly from the Securities and Investments Board (SIB). An insurance company authorised by s 22 cannot be authorised by any other route (s 129, Sch 10 para 2(1)) although it may join an SRO for its regulation. Specific provision is made for the recognition of an SRO whose members include regulated insurance companies: Sch 10 para 3.
2 Ibid Pt I (ss 1–128C) (as amended).
3 Ibid s 129, Sch 10 (amended by the Companies Act 1989 s 206(1), Sch 23 para 25. 'Regulated insurance companies' means insurance companies (1) to which the Insurance Companies Act 1982 Pt II (ss 15–71) (as amended) applies, and (2) authorised in another member state of the European Community under the Financial Services Act 1986 s 31, to carry on investment business: s 129(a), (b).
4 Ie ibid s 48 (as amended).
5 Ibid Sch 10 para 4(1)–(2A) (subs (2A) added by the Companies Act 1989 Sch 23 para 25).
6 Ie the Financial Services Act 1986 ss 53, 54.
7 Ibid Sch 10 para 4(4). Protection is provided in this respect by the solvency requirements of the Insurance Companies Act 1982 and the provisions for indemnifying policyholders under the Policyholders Protection Act 1975: see para 895 et seq post.
8 Ie the Financial Services Act 1986 s 59.
9 Ibid Sch 10 para 4(5).
10 Ibid Sch 10 para 6, which relates to the limitation of powers conferred by Pt I Ch VI (ss 64–74) (as amended).
11 Ibid Sch 10 para 7 (amended by the Companies Act 1989 Sch 23 para 25).
12 By the Transfer of Functions (Financial Services) Order 1992, SI 1992/1315, the functions of the Secretary of State generally for Trade and Industry under the Financial Services Act 1986 Sch 10 are transferred to the Treasury, except the Secretary of State's functions under Sch 10 para 3(2), 4(6), 6, 10. As to the Secretary of State generally see para 15 note 5 ante.
13 Ibid Sch 10 para 10.

805. Restriction of business to insurance. An insurance company[1] must not carry on any activities, in the United Kingdom or elsewhere, otherwise than in connection with or for the purposes of its insurance business[2].

1 Ie an insurance company to which the Insurance Companies Act 1982 Pt II (ss 15–71) (as amended) applies: see para 803 ante.
2 Ibid s 16(1). For the meaning of 'insurance business' see para 18 ante. Any activities of an insurance company that are excluded from the definition of insurance business by s 95(c)(ii) (see para 18 ante) are to be treated as carried on or in connection with its insurance business: s 16(2). A person is not guilty of an offence under the Act by reason of default in complying with s 16: s 71(7).

806. Provision of insurance in the United Kingdom from another member state. An insurance company[1] which intends to provide insurance[2] in the United Kingdom[3] must send to the Secretary of State[4]:
(1) a certificate issued by the competent authorities of the member state of the European Community in which the company's head office is situated attest-ing that the company possesses for its activities as a whole the minimum solvency margin[5] and that the company's authorisation[6] enables it to operate outside its member state of establishment[7];
(2) a certificate, issued by the competent authorities of the member state of the establishment through which the company intends to provide insurance in the United Kingdom:
(a) indicating the classes of insurance business which the company has been authorised to undertake through that establishment[8];

    (b) stating that the authorities do not object to the company providing insurance in the United Kingdom[9]; and

    (c) where the company intends to provide long term insurance in the United Kingdom, confirming that all the commitments[10] which the company intends to cover fall within the classes of insurance business which the company has been authorised to undertake through that establishment[11];

(3) a statement by the company of the nature of the risks or commitments which it proposes to cover in the United Kingdom[12];

(4) a notice stating the address of the company for the purpose of the service of documents[13]; and

(5) in the case of an insurance company which intends to provide cover for relevant motor vehicle risks[14]:

    (a) a notice stating the name and address of the claims representative[15]; and

    (b) a declaration that the insurance company has become a member of the Motor Insurers' Bureau[16].

The company must not provide insurance in the United Kingdom before the date certified as that on which such documents were received by the Secretary of State[17].

The insurance company must notify the Secretary of State in writing of any change of address for service of documents and, where it intends to provide cover for relevant motor vehicle risks, of any change of name or address of the claims representative, within one month of the change[18].

Where an insurance company wishes to provide insurance in the United Kingdom in respect of risks or commitments other than those mentioned in the statement referred to in head (3) above, it must give written notice to the Secretary of State amending the statement, and must not provide that insurance before the date certified as that on which written notice of the amendment was received by the Secretary of State[19].

Before entering into a contract for the provision of insurance in the United Kingdom, other than a contract for the coverage of large risks[20] only, the insurance company must inform the policyholder[21] of the member state in which the establishment is situated through which the risk or commitment is to be covered[22]. An insurance company must not provide insurance in the United Kingdom to cover relevant motor vehicle risks unless it is a member of the Motor Insurers' Bureau and has appointed a claims representative who satisfies the relevant requirements[23].

The Secretary of State may require an insurance company providing insurance in the United Kingdom which fails to comply with the requirements of the Insurance Companies Act 1982 to take specified steps to comply with any such provisions[24]. Where the Secretary of State is notified by the competent authorities of the member state of establishment or of the head office of an insurance company that the company's authorisation has been withdrawn[25], the Secretary of State may direct it to cease providing insurance, or insurance of any specified description, in the United Kingdom through all, or any specified establishments[26].

1 Ie a company authorised in accordance with the first general insurance directive or the first long term insurance directive: Insurance Companies Act 1982 s 81A(3)(a) (added by the Insurance Companies (Amendment) Regulations 1990, SI 1990/1333; amended by the Insurance Companies (Amendment) Regulations 1993, SI 1993/174). As to those directives see para 22 note 12 ante. See EUROPEAN COMMUNITIES vol 52 para 16.83 et seq.

2 References in the Insurance Companies Act 1982 Pt IIIA (ss 81A–81J) (added by the Insurance Companies (Amendment) Regulations 1990 reg 10 and subsequently amended) to the 'provision of insurance' in a member state are to either or both of (1) the covering of a risk there through an establishment in another member state (referred to as the provision of general insurance), and (2) the covering of a commitment there through an establishment in another state (referred to as the provision of long term insurance): Insurance Companies Act 1982 s 81A(1) (added by the Insurance Companies (Amendment) Regulations 1990; amended by the Insurance Companies (Amendment) Regulations 1993). In the Insurance Companies Act 1982 Pt IIIA 'the covering of a risk' means the covering, otherwise than by way of reinsurance, of a risk to which Pt IIIA applies and 'the covering of a commitment' means the covering, otherwise than by way of reinsurance, of a commitment to which Pt IIIA applies: s 81A(3)(b), (c) (added by the Insurance Companies (Amendment) Regulations 1990 and the Insurance Companies (Amendment) Regulations 1993 respectively). The Insurance Companies Act 1982 Pt IIIA applies to (a) risks falling within Sch 2 (see para 18 ante) other than: (i) class 1, so far as it relates to accidents at work, (ii) class 13, so far as it relates to nuclear civil liability and pharmaceutical product liability, (iii) classes 9 and 13, so far as they relate to the compulsory insurance of building works; and (b) commitments falling with Sch 1 (see para 18 ante) other than class VII: s 81A(4) (added by the Insurance Companies (Amendment) Regulations 1990; subsequently substituted by the Insurance Companies (Amendment) Regulations 1993). For the meaning of 'commitment' see note 10 infra.

3 For the meaning of 'United Kingdom' see para 2 note 10 ante. For the purposes of the Insurance Companies Act 1982 Pts II (ss 15–71) and III (ss 72–81) (as amended) a company is not regarded as carrying on insurance business in the United Kingdom by reason only of the fact that it provides insurance in the United Kingdom: s 81A(5) (as added: see note 2 supra).

4 As to the Secretary of State see para 15 note 5 ante.

5 Insurance Companies Act 1982 s 81B(1)(a)(i) (as added: see note 2 supra; amended by the Insurance Companies (Amendment) Regulations 1993). The minimum solvency margin must be calculated in accordance with arts 16–17 of the first general insurance directive or arts 18–20 of the first long term insurance directive: Insurance Companies Act 1982 s 81B(1)(a), (1B) (as so added and amended). See also EUROPEAN COMMUNITIES vol 52 paras 16.88, 16.95. For the interpretation of expressions derived from general insurance directives see the Insurance Companies Act 1982 s 96A(1B) (added by the Insurance Companies (Amendment) Regulations 1990 and by the Insurance Companies (Amendment) Regulations 1993).

6 As to the meaning of 'authorisation' see note 1 supra.

7 Insurance Companies Act 1982 s 81B(1)(a)(iii) (as added and amended: see note 5 supra). 'Member state of establishment' means the member state in which the establishment is situated: Insurance Companies Act 1982 s 81A(2) (as added: see note 2 supra). 'Establishment' means the head office or a branch or agency of the company and references to a company being established in a particular member state mean that the company has its head office or a branch or agency there. Any permanent presence of a company in a member state must be regarded as a branch or agency, even if that presence consists merely of an office managed by the company's own staff or by a person who is independent but has permanent authority to act for the company in the same way as a agent: Insurance Companies Act 1982 s 96A(2) (added by the Insurance Companies (Amendment) Regulations 1990; amended by the Insurance Companies (Amendment) Regulations 1993).

8 Insurance Companies Act 1982 s 81B(1)(b)(i) (as added: see note 2 supra).

9 Ibid s 81B(1)(b)(ii) (as added: see note 2 supra).

10 'Commitment' means a commitment represented by insurance business of any of the classes specified in ibid Sch 1 (as amended) (see para 18 ante): s 96(1) (amended by the Insurance Companies (Amendment) Regulations 1993 reg 6(1), (2)(a)).

11 Insurance Companies Act 1982 s 81B(1)(b)(iii) (added by the Insurance Companies (Amendment) Regulations 1993).

12 Insurance Companies Act 1982 s 81B(1)(c) (as added and amended: see note 5 supra).

13 Ibid s 81B(1)(d) (as added: see note 2 supra).

14 References in ibid Pt IIIA to relevant motor vehicle risks are to risks, other than carrier's liability, falling within Sch 2 class 10 (see para 18 ante): s 81A(1A) (added by the Insurance Companies (Cancellation) Regulations 1993, SI 1993/1327).

15 As to claims representatives see text and note 23 infra.

16 Insurance Companies Act 1982 s 81B(1)(e) (added by the Insurance Companies (Amendment) Regulations 1992, SI 1992/2890). As to the Motor Insurers' Bureau see para 758 et seq ante.

17 Insurance Companies Act 1982 s 81B(1) (as added: see note 2 supra).

18 Ibid s 81B(1A) (added by the Insurance Companies (Amendment) Regulations 1992).

19 Insurance Companies Act 1982 s 81B(2) (as added: see note 2 supra; amended by the Insurance Companies (Amendment) Regulations 1993).

20 Under the Insurance Companies Act 1982 s 96B(1), (2) (added by the Insurance Companies (Amendment) Regulations 1990) 'large risks' means:

 (1) risks falling within the Insurance Companies Act 1982 Sch 2 Pt I classes 4–7, 11–12 (see para 18 ante);

 (2) risks falling within Sch 2 Pt I classes 14–15 (see para 18 ante) which relate to a business carried on by the policyholder; and

 (3) risks falling within Sch 2 Pt I classes 3, 8–9, 13, 16 (see para 18 ante) in respect of which the following condition has been met, namely that at least two of the three following criteria were exceeded in the most recent financial year for which information is available. The criteria are:

 (a) a balance sheet total of 6.2 million ECU;

 (b) a net turnover of 24 million ECU; and

 (c) a number of employees of 250.

As to the meaning of 'ECU' see EC Council Regulation 3180/78; Insurance Companies Act 1982 s 96A(4) (added by the Insurance Companies (Amendment) Regulations 1990). For this purpose 'business' includes a trade or profession, and (for the purpose of head (3) supra) any activity of a professional association, joint venture or temporary grouping: Insurance Companies Act 1982 s 96B(6) (as so added).

Where the policyholder is a member of a group for which consolidated accounts are drawn up, the question whether the condition referred to in head (3) above has been met is determined by reference to those accounts; where the policyholder is a professional association, joint venture or temporary grouping, that question is determined by reference to the aggregate of the relevant figures for all the members of the association, joint venture or temporary grouping: s 96B(4), (5) (as so added). For the meaning of 'policyholder' see note 21 infra.

21 'Policyholder' means the person who for the time being is the legal holder of the policy for securing the contract with the insurance company or, in relation to capital redemption business, the person who for the time being is the legal holder of the policy, bond, certificate, receipt or other instrument evidencing the contract with the company, and (1) in relation to such ordinary long term insurance business or industrial assurance business as consists in the granting of annuities upon human life, includes an annuitant; and (2) in relation to insurance business of any kind other than such as is mentioned under head (1), or capital redemption business, includes a person to whom, under a policy, a sum is due or a periodic payment is payable: Insurance Companies Act 1982 s 96(1). For the meaning of 'capital redemption business' and 'ordinary long term insurance business' see paras 818 note 2 post, 23 note 2 ante respectively. As to industrial assurance see para 528 ante.

22 Ibid s 81C(1) (added by the Insurance Companies (Amendment) Regulations 1990; amended by the Insurance Companies (Amendment) Regulations 1993). Any document issued to a policyholder by the company must also contain that information: Insurance Companies Act 1982 s 81C(1) (as so added and amended). Further specified information, whether the contract is for the coverage of large risks or other risks, must be included in the insurance policy and any other document under the terms of which insurance is granted, and on the proposal form if statements in the proposal bind the proposer; that information is: the address of the establishment through which the risk is to be covered, the address of the company's head office and, where the insurance relates to relevant motor vehicle risks, the name and address of the claims representative: Insurance Companies Act 1982 s 81C(2) (as so added; amended by the Insurance Companies (Amendment) Regulations 1992, SI 1992/2890).

23 Insurance Companies Act 1982 s 81CC(1) (added by the Insurance Companies (Amendment) Regulations 1992). The requirements referred to are as follows:

 (1) the claims representative must have been designated as the insurance company's claims representative for the purposes of the Insurance Companies Act 1982 s 81CC (s 81CC(2) (as so added));

 (2) the claims representative must be authorised to:

 (a) act on behalf of the insurance company and to represent, or to instruct others to represent, the insurance company in relation to any matters giving rise to relevant claims;

 (b) to pay sums in settlement of relevant claims; and

 (c) to accept service on behalf of the insurance company of proceedings in respect of relevant claims;

 but the authority must not extend to the settlement of claims (s 81CC(3) (as so added));

 (3) the claims representative must be authorised to represent the company in any proceedings or inquiry to establish the existence or validity of a policy issued by the insurance company which covers or purports to cover relevant motor vehicle risks (s 81CC(4) (as so added));

(4) without prejudice to head (2) supra, the claims representative must not act on behalf of the insurance company in the carrying on of its general business in the United Kingdom other than its reinsurance business, if any (s 81CC(5) (as so added); and

(5) the claims representative must, (a) in the case of an individual, be resident in the United Kingdom, or (b) in the case of a corporation, have a place of business in the United Kingdom (s 81CC(6) (as so added)).

'Relevant claim' means any claim which may be made against a policy issued by the insurance company to the extent that it covers relevant motor vehicle risks, whether or not submitted by the company and whether by a policyholder or by a third party having rights of action against the company or the policyholder or both: Insurance Companies Act 1982 s 81CC(7) (as so added). As to rights of third parties against insurers see para 677 et seq ante.

24 Insurance Companies Act 1982 s 81D(1) (as added: see note 2 supra). If the company fails to comply with a requirement made by the Secretary of State he must notify the competent authority of the member state of establishment: s 81D(2) (as so added). If such a company persists in such contravention, the Secretary of State may, after informing the competent authorities of the member state of establishment, direct the company to cease to provide insurance, or insurance of any specified description, in the United Kingdom: s 81D(3) (as so added). After giving such a direction, the Secretary of State must by notice in writing inform the company of his reasons for doing so: s 81D(4) (as so added). Such a direction does not prevent the company from effecting a contract of insurance in pursuance of a term of a subsisting contract of insurance: s 81D(5) (as so added). A requirement or direction under this section may be varied or revoked by the Secretary of State: s 81D(6) (added by the Insurance Companies (Amendment) Regulations 1990). For the purposes of the Insurance Companies Act 1982 s 81D, the Secretary of State may require insurance companies to furnish him with information about such matters as he may specify, being, if he so requires, verified in a prescribed manner: s 81E (as added: see note 2 supra).

25 Ie under art 22 of the first general insurance directive or art 26 of the first long term insurance directive.

26 Insurance Companies Act 1982 s 81F(1) (as added: see note 2 supra; amended by the Insurance Companies (Amendment) Regulations 1993). After giving such a direction, the Secretary of State must by notice in writing inform the company of his reasons for doing so: Insurance Companies Act 1982 s 81F(2) (as so added). Such a direction does not prevent the company from effecting a contract of insurance in pursuance of a term of a subsisting contract of insurance: s 81F(3) (as so added).

807. Provision of insurance in a member state other than the United Kingdom. Where an insurance company[1] intends to provide insurance[2] in a member state of the European Community other than the United Kingdom[3] and its head office is situated in the United Kingdom or the insurance is to be provided through an establishment[4] in the United Kingdom, it must before doing so notify the Secretary of State of its intention[5]. Such notification must indicate (1) the member state in which the insurance is to be provided; (2) the nature of the risks or commitments which the company proposes to cover[6]; and (3) where the company's head office is situated in the United Kingdom, the member state in which the establishment through which the risks or commitments will be covered is situated[7].

An insurance company whose head office is situated in the United Kingdom and which intends to provide insurance in another member state may apply to the Secretary of State for a certificate attesting that the company possesses for its activities as a whole a minimum solvency margin[8] and that its authorisation[9] to carry on business in the United Kingdom enables it to operate outside the member state of establishment[10]. An insurance company which intends to provide insurance in another member state through an establishment in the United Kingdom may apply to the Secretary of State for a certificate indicating the classes of insurance business which the company has been authorised to carry on in the United Kingdom and stating that the Secretary of State does not object to the company providing the insurance[11]. If it appears to the Secretary of State that a certificate ought to be issued, he must issue it accordingly[12]; if he refuses to issue a certificate, he must inform the company in writing of his decision and of the reasons for it[13].

Before the Secretary of State approves[14] a transfer to another company in the United Kingdom of general business policies written by way of provision of insurance in another member state, he must be satisfied that the transferee fulfils certain conditions[15] in the member state where the risk is situated and that the supervisory authorities of that member state agree to the transfer[16]. Subject to being satisfied as to specified matters[17], the Secretary of State may approve[18] a transfer to an insurance company established in another member state of policies written by way of the provision of insurance in another member state[19]. An instrument giving effect to such a transfer will not bind a policyholder[20] whose policy is included in the instrument unless notice of the execution of the instrument is published, in a manner directed by the Secretary of State, in the member state in which the risk is situated[21].

1 Ie a company authorised in accordance with art 6 of the first general insurance directive or art 6 of the first long term insurance directive (as to which see para 22 note 12 ante): Insurance Companies Act 1982 s 81A(3)(a) (added by the Insurance Companies (Amendment) Regulations 1990, SI 1990/1333, reg 10; amended by the Insurance Companies (Amendment) Regulations 1993, SI 1993/174, reg 4(1), (3)(a)).
2 As to providing insurance in a member state see para 806 note 2 ante.
3 For the meaning of 'United Kingdom' see para 2 note 10 ante.
4 For the meaning of 'establishment' see para 806 note 7 ante.
5 Insurance Companies Act 1982 s 81G(1) (added by the Insurance Companies (Amendment) Regulations 1990 reg 10). As to the Secretary of State see para 15 note 5 ante.
6 As to the covering of risks or commitments see para 806 note 2 ante. For the meaning of 'commitment' see para 806 note 10 ante.
7 Insurance Companies Act 1982 s 81G(2) (as added: see note 4 supra; amended by the Insurance Companies (Amendment) Regulations 1993 reg 4(10)). Where the company intends to provide insurance in more than one member state, the specified information may be contained in a single notification but must be set out separately in relation to each member state: Insurance Companies Act 1982 s 81G(3) (as so added). Where a company has duly notified the Secretary of State of its intention to provide insurance in another member state where administrative authorisation is required for the provision of insurance, then, if the original notification related only to risks or commitments in respect of which such authorisation is required, or only to risks or commitments in respect of which such authorisation is not required, and the company subsequently intends to extend its activities to risks or commitments falling within the other category, it must before doing so comply with the provisions set out above in relation to those risks or commitments: s 81G(4) (as so added and amended).
8 Ie calculated in accordance with the relevant provisions: ibid s 81H(1)(a) (added by the Insurance Companies (Amendment) Regulations 1990 reg 10; amended by the Insurance Companies (Amendment) Regulations 1993 reg 4(11)). 'The relevant provisions' means, if the company intends to cover risks, arts 16, 17 of the first general insurance directive; and if the company intends to cover commitments, arts 18–20 of the first long term insurance directive: Insurance Companies Act 1982 s 81H(1A) (added by the Insurance Companies (Amendment) Regulations 1993 reg 4(12)). As to the minimum solvency margin see para 857 post.
9 Ie in accordance with art 7(1) of the relevant directive: Insurance Companies Act 1982 s 81H(1)(b) (as added and amended: see note 8 supra). 'The relevant directive' means, if the company intends to cover risks, the first general insurance directive; and if the company intends to cover commitments, the first long term insurance directive: Insurance Companies Act 1982 s 81H(1A) (as added: see note 8 supra).
10 Ibid s 81H(1) (as added and amended: see note 8 supra).
11 Ibid s 81H(2) (as added: see note 8 supra).
12 Ibid s 81H(3) (as added: see note 8 supra).
13 Ibid s 81H(4) (as added: see note 8 supra).
14 Ie under ibid s 51 (as amended): see para 828 post.
15 Ie the conditions in arts 13–16 of the second general insurance directive.

16 Insurance Companies Act 1982 s 81I(1) (added by the Insurance Companies (Amendment) Regulations 1990 reg 10).

17 Ie that (1) the transfer relates to policies covering risks situated in another member state; (2) the transferee is an insurance company established in another member state the supervisory authorities of which agree to the transfer; and (3) where the risk is not situated in the transferee's member state of establishment, (a) the transferee fulfils the conditions in arts 13–16 of the second general insurance directive in the member state where the risk is situated, (b) the law of that member state provides for the possibility of such a transfer, and (c) the supervisory authorities of that member state agree to the transfer: Insurance Companies Act 1982 s 81I(2)(a)–(c) (as added: see note 16 supra).

18 Notwithstanding ibid s 51(4)(a)(ii), (b): see para 828 post.

19 Ibid s 81I(2) (as added: see note 16 supra).

20 For the meaning of 'policyholder' see para 806 note 21 ante.

21 Insurance Companies Act 1982 s 81I(3) (as added: see note 16 supra).

808. Offences relating to the provision of insurance from or in another member state. An insurance company[1] commits an offence if it provides insurance[2] in the United Kingdom[3] before furnishing the Secretary of State[4] with the appropriate documents[5], or if it makes default in complying with, or with a requirement imposed under, the specified statutory provisions[6].

A person commits an offence if (1) in purported compliance with a requirement of the Secretary of State[7], he furnishes information which he knows to be false in a material particular or recklessly furnishes information which is false in a material particular[8]; or (2) he causes or permits to be included in (a) a document required[9] to be sent to the Secretary of State, or (b) a notification[10] sent to the Secretary of State, a statement which he knows to be false in a material particular or recklessly causes or permits to be so included a statement which is false in a material particular[11].

A person committing an offence under these provisions is liable on summary conviction to a fine not exceeding level 5 on the standard scale[12].

1 Ie a company authorised in accordance with art 6 of the first general insurance directive or art 6 of the first long term insurance directive (as to which see para 22 note 12 ante): Insurance Companies Act 1982 s 81A(3)(a) (added by the Insurance Companies (Amendment) Regulations 1990, SI 1990/1333, reg 10; amended by the Insurance Companies (Amendment) Regulations 1993, SI 1993/174, reg 4(1), (3)(a)).

2 As to the meaning of 'provides insurance' see para 806 note 2 ante.

3 For the meaning of 'United Kingdom' see para 2 note 10 ante.

4 As to the Secretary of State see para 15 note 5 ante.

5 Ie in contravention of the Insurance Companies Act 1982 s 81B (as added and amended): see para 806 ante: s 81J(1)(a) (added by the Insurance Companies (Amendment) Regulations 1990 reg 10).

6 Ie the provisions of the Insurance Companies Act 1982 Pt IIIA (ss 81A–81J) (as added and amended): s 81J(1)(b) (as added: see note 5 supra).

7 Ie under ibid s 81E (as added): see para 806 ante.

8 Ibid s 81J(2)(a) (as added: see note 5 supra).

9 Ie by ibid s 81B (as added and amended): see para 806 ante.

10 Ibid s 81G (as added and amended): see para 806 ante.

11 Ibid s 81J(2)(b) (as added: see note 5 supra).

12 Ibid s 81J(3) (as added: see note 5 supra). As to the standard scale see para 212 note 5 ante.

809. Unregistered companies. Every insurance company to which Part II of the Insurance Companies Act 1982 applies[1] and which is not registered[2] must (1) if it has not incorporated in its deed of settlement[3] the appropriate provision of the Companies Clauses Consolidation Act 1845[4], keep a shareholders' address book in accordance with that provision and, on the application of any shareholder or policyholder[5] of the company, furnish to him a copy of the book on payment of a sum not exceeding 2½p for every 100 words required to be copied; and (2) cause a sufficient number of copies of its deed of settlement to be printed and, on the application of any shareholder or policyholder of the company, furnish to him one of those copies on payment of a sum not exceeding 5p[6].

1 As to the insurance companies to which the Insurance Companies Act 1982 Pt II (ss 15–71) (as amended) applies: see para 803 ante.
2 Ie under the Companies Act 1985 or under the former Companies Acts: see generally COMPANIES vol 7(1) (Reissue) para 7 et seq.
3 'Deed of settlement' includes any instrument constituting the company: Insurance Companies Act 1982 s 96(1).
4 Ie the Companies Clauses Consolidation Act 1845 s 10, which provides for the keeping of a shareholders' address book: see COMPANIES vol 7(2) (Reissue) para 2231.
5 For the meaning of 'policyholder' see para 806 note 21 ante.
6 Insurance Companies Act 1982 s 88(1). Any insurance company which makes default in complying with this provision is liable, on summary conviction, to a fine not exceeding level 5 on the standard scale: s 88(2). As to the standard scale see para 212 note 5 ante.

(2) REGULATION OF CONDUCT OF INSURANCE BUSINESS

(i) Advertisements, Inducements and Intermediaries

810. Insurance advertisements. Regulations may be made as to the form and contents of insurance advertisements[1]. The regulations may make different provision in relation to advertisements of different classes or descriptions[2].

Where an insurer is not named or otherwise referred to[3] in an insurance advertisement[4] and is not an authorised[5] or permitted[6] insurer, the advertisement is required to include a warning that the insurer is not authorised in the United Kingdom and is not supervised by a United Kingdom government department and that there is no protection for policyholders under the Policyholders Protection Act 1975[7]. In addition the advertisement must state, if that be the case, that it is also about securities or other investments[8]. Where the insurer to which an advertisement relates is authorised or permitted but is not named in the advertisement, the advertisement is required only to state whether it is about insurance alone or about securities or other investments[9]. These provisions do not apply where the insurer concerned is authorised or permitted to carry on long term business in the United Kingdom and is named in the advertisement[10].

Where an insurer is not authorised or permitted but is named or otherwise referred to in an advertisement and is permitted to carry on business in another member state of the European Community, the advertisement need contain only the insurer's full name, the country where he is registered and, if different, his principal office, together with a warning that the Policyholders Protection Act 1975 does not apply[11]. In all other cases the advertisement must contain: (1) the insurer's full name[12], country of registration and principal office, if different; (2) the full name of any trustee of property of any description maintained by the insurer in respect of contracts of insurance to which the advertisement relates; (3) an indication whether the investment of such property is managed by the insurer or another person and, in the latter case, the full name of the investment manager; (4) the registered office of any such trustee or investment manager, and of his principal office if different; (5) where the insurer employs an agent in relation to any contracts of insurance, the full name and registered or principal office in the United Kingdom of that agent; and (6) a warning that the insurer is not authorised by a United Kingdom government department and that there is no protection for policyholders under the Policyholders Protection Act 1975[13].

The matters required to be included in an advertisement must be shown prominently, clearly and legibly[14]. Any advertisement containing the name of an insurance company[15] having a share capital, and which states the amount of its authorised capital, must also state the amount of that capital which has been subscribed[16].

Any person who issues an insurance advertisement which contravenes these regulations is guilty of an offence[17] and is liable, on conviction on indictment, to imprisonment for a term not exceeding two years or to a fine, or to both, and on summary conviction, to a fine not exceeding the prescribed sum[18]. For this purpose, an advertisement issued by any person on behalf of or to the order of another person must be treated as an advertisement issued by that other person, and, for the purposes of any proceedings, an advertisement inviting persons to enter into or to offer to enter into contracts with a person specified in the advertisement is presumed, unless the contrary is proved, to have been issued by that person[19]. A person who in the ordinary course of his business issues an advertisement to the order of another person, being an advertisement the issue of which by that other person constitutes an offence, is not himself guilty of an offence if he proves that the matters contained in the advertisement were not, wholly or in part, devised or selected by him or by any person under his direction or control[20].

1 Insurance Companies Act 1982 s 72(1). 'Insurance advertisement' means an advertisement inviting persons to enter into or to offer to enter into contracts of insurance, and an advertisement which contains information calculated to lead directly or indirectly to persons entering into or offering to enter into such contracts must be treated as an advertisement inviting them to do so: s 72(5). 'Advertisement' includes every form of advertising, whether in a publication or by the display of notices or by means of circulars or other documents or by an exhibition of photographs or cinematograph films or by way of sound broadcasting or television or by inclusion in any programme service (within the meaning of the Broadcasting Act 1990) other than a sound or television broadcasting service, and references to the issue of an advertisement must be construed accordingly: s 72(6) (amended by the Broadcasting Act 1990 s 203(1), Sch 20 para 34).

2 Insurance Companies Act 1982 s 72(2).

3 An insurance advertisement (as to which see note 4 infra) is taken to refer to an insurer if (1) the insurer is named in the advertisement; (2) the insurer is identifiable from information contained in the advertisement; or (3) particulars of any of the terms on which the insurer may be prepared to effect contracts of insurance or of any of the benefits which may accrue to the insured under a contract of insurance are contained in the advertisement: Insurance Companies Regulations 1981, SI 1981/1654, reg 65(2) (substituted by SI 1983/396).

4 'Insurance advertisement', for the purposes of ibid regs 65A–65C (as added), means an insurance advertisement (see note 1 supra) which invites any person to enter into or to offer to enter into, or which contains information calculated to lead directly or indirectly to any person entering or offering to enter into, any contract of insurance (other than a contract of reinsurance) the effecting of which would constitute the carrying on of ordinary long term insurance business: reg 65(1)(b) (as substituted: see note 3 supra). For the meaning of 'ordinary long term insurance business' see para 23 note 2 ante.

5 'Authorised', in relation to an insurer, means authorised to carry on long term business in the United Kingdom by or under the Insurance Companies Act 1982 s 3 or s 4 (see para 34 ante): Insurance Companies Regulations 1981 reg 65(1)(a) (as substituted: see note 3 supra). For the meaning of 'United Kingdom' see para 2 note 10 ante.

6 'Permitted', in relation to an insurer, means permitted to carry on long term business in the United Kingdom otherwise than by virtue of the Insurance Companies Act 1982 s 3 or s 4: Insurance Companies Regulations 1981 reg 65(1)(c) (as substituted: see note 3 supra).

7 Ibid reg 65A(2) (added by SI 1983/396). As to the Policyholders Protection Act 1975 see para 895 et seq post.
8 Insurance Companies Regulations 1981 reg 65A(2)(b).
9 Ibid reg 65A(3) (added by SI 1983/396).
10 Ibid reg 65A(1) (added by SI 1983/396).
11 Ibid reg 65B(1), (2), (4) (added by SI 1983/396).
12 'Full name' means (1) in the case of a body corporate, its corporate name; and (2) in the case of an individual or an unincorporated body, the name under which the individual or body lawfully carries on business: ibid reg 65C(5) (added by SI 1983/396).
13 Ibid reg 65B(2), (3) (added by SI 1983/396).
14 Ibid reg 65C(1) (added by SI 1983/396). For further requirements as to the manner of statement see reg 65C(2)–(4) (as so added).
15 Ie an insurance company to which the Insurance Companies Act 1982 Pt II (ss 15–71) (as amended) applies. For the meaning of 'insurance company' see para 15 note 3 ante.
16 Insurance Companies Regulations 1981 reg 66.
17 Insurance Companies Act 1982 s 72(3).
18 Ibid s 81(1) (amended by the Fines and Penalties (Northern Ireland) Order 1984, SI 1984/703). As to the prescribed sum see para 19 note 5 ante. The provision reads '. . . to a fine not exceeding £1,000 or, if it is greater, the prescribed sum . . . '. The prescribed sum is currently greater than £1,000.
19 Insurance Companies Act 1982 s 72(7).
20 Ibid s 72(4).

811. Restrictions on promotion of contracts of insurance. Subject to the exceptions below it is prohibited:

(1) to issue an advertisement in the United Kingdom[1] which invites persons to enter, or offer to enter, into a contract of insurance which constitutes an investment for the purposes of the Financial Services Act 1986[2], or which contains information calculated to lead to persons doing so; or
(2) in the course of business, advise or procure any person in the United Kingdom to enter into such a contract[3].

Contravention of this restriction is an offence[4], subject to two defences, namely:

(a) a person who in the ordinary course of business other than investment business issues an advertisement to the order of another person does not commit an offence if he proves that the matters contained in the advertisement were not devised or selected by him or a person under his control, and that he believed on reasonable grounds after due inquiry that the person to whose order the advertisement was issued was an authorised person[5]; and
(b) a person other than an insurance company with which the contract is to be made does not commit an offence if he proves that he believed on reasonable grounds after due inquiry that one of two following exceptions to the offence applied[6].

The above restriction does not apply where the contract is to be with (i) a United Kingdom authorised insurer; (ii) a registered friendly society; (iii) an insurance company whose head office or a branch or agency of which is in a member state of the European Community other than the United Kingdom and which is entitled to carry on there insurance business of the relevant class[7]. Nor does the restriction apply where the contract of insurance is to be with an insurance company authorised to effect or carry out such contracts of insurance in a designated country or territory so long as any conditions imposed by the designating order have been satisfied[8].

Contracts of insurance made in contravention of the above restriction are unenforceable by the insurance company, and the other party is entitled to recover any money or other property paid or transferred by him under the contract, and also to compensation for any consequential loss sustained[9].

The court may allow the contract to be enforced and money or property to be retained if it is satisfied:

(A) if the contravention was by the insurance company, that the person against whom enforcement is sought or who is seeking recovery was not influenced, or not influenced materially, by the advertisement or advice in deciding to enter the contract, or that the advertisement was not misleading as to the nature of the company or the terms of the risk and fairly stated the risks[10]; or

(B) if the contravention was some other person, that at the time the contract was made the company had no reason to believe that any contravention had taken place[11].

1 For the meaning of 'United Kingdom' see para 2 note 10 ante.
2 As to the meaning of 'investment' under the Financial Services Act 1986 see MONEY vol 32 para 327.
3 Financial Services Act 1986 s 130(1)(a), (b). As to powers of entry, search and seizure in relation to an offence under s 130 see s 199.
4 Ibid s 130(6). The maximum penalty on conviction on indictment is imprisonment for up to two years, or an unlimited fine, or both; on summary conviction, imprisonment for up to six months, or a fine not exceeding the statutory maximum (ie the prescribed sum), or both: s 130(6). As to the prescribed sum see para 19 note 5 ante. A contravention is actionable at the suit of any person who suffers loss as a result; the court has power to grant injunction and restitution orders: s 131(7), (8).
5 Ibid s 130(7).
6 Ibid s 130(8).
7 Ibid s 130(2). 'Relevant class' means the class of insurance business specified in the Insurance Companies Act 1982 Sch 1 or 2 into which the effecting and carrying out of the contract in question falls: Financial Services Act 1986 s 130(2).
8 Ibid s 130(2). Before the Secretary of State makes an order designating any country or territory for these purposes, he must be satisfied that the law under which insurance companies are authorised and supervised there affords adequate protection to policyholders and potential policyholders against the risk that the companies may be unable to meet their liabilities; the order may be revoked where it appears that this is no longer the case: s 130(4), (5). Guernsey and the Isle of Man were designated by the Financial Services (Designated Countries and Territories) (Overseas Insurance Companies) Order 1988, SI 1988/439; the Commonwealth of Pennsylvania was designated by the Financial Services (Designated Countries and Territories) (Overseas Insurance Companies) Order 1989, SI 1989/2380; and the State of Iowa by the Financial Services (Designated Countries and Territories) (Overseas Insurance Companies) Order 1993, SI 1993/1237. As to the Secretary of State see para 15 note 5 ante.
9 Financial Services Act 1986 s 131(4). Compensation is such as is agreed by the parties or, on the application of either party, determined by the court: s 131(2). As to consequential provisions relating to the repayment of money etc where a person elects not to perform a contract which is unenforceable under s 131(1) see s 131(5), (6).
10 Ibid s 131(3).
11 Ibid s 131(4).

812. Misleading statements as to insurance contracts. Any person who:

(1) makes a statement, promise or forecast which he knows to be misleading, false or deceptive or dishonestly conceals any material facts; or

(2) recklessly makes, dishonestly or otherwise, a statement, promise or forecast which is misleading, false or deceptive;

is guilty of an offence if he makes the statement, promise or forecast or conceals the facts for the purpose of inducing, or is reckless as to whether it may induce, another person (whether or not that person is the one to whom the statement, promise or forecast is made or from whom the facts are concealed) to enter into or offer to enter into, or to refrain from entering or offering to enter into, a contract of insurance with an insurance company (not being an investment agreement) or to exercise, or refrain from exercising, any rights conferred by such a contract[1]. A person guilty of an offence is liable:

    (a) on conviction on indictment, to imprisonment for a term not exceeding seven years or to a fine or to both; or

    (b) on summary conviction, to imprisonment for a term not exceeding six months or to a fine not exceeding the statutory maximum or to both[2].

1 Financial Services Act 1986 s 133(1). This subsection does not apply unless (1) the statement, promise or forecast is made in or from, or the facts are concealed in or from, the United Kingdom; (2) the person on whom the inducement is intended to, or may have, an effect is in the United Kingdom; or (3) the contract is or would be entered into, or the rights are or would be exercisable, in the United Kingdom: s 133(2).

2 Ibid s 133(3). As to fines on indictment see CRIMINAL LAW vol 11(2) (Reissue) para 1232. As to the statutory maximum (ie the prescribed sum) see para 19 note 5 ante.

813. Intermediaries in insurance transactions. Except in certain cases[1], any person who invites another person who is ordinarily resident[2] in the United Kingdom[3] to make an offer or proposal or to take any other step with a view to entering into a contract of insurance[4] with an insurance company must, if he is connected with[5] that company at the time the invitation is issued, provide the person to whom the invitation is issued, in the specified manner[6], with information indicating the circumstances of his connection with that company[7]. Further, except in certain cases[8], any person who, in the course of carrying on any business or profession, invites another person who is ordinarily resident in the United Kingdom to make an offer or proposal or to take any other step with a view to entering into a contract of insurance[9] with an insurance company which is not an authorised insurer[10] must provide the person to whom the invitation is issued, in the prescribed manner[11], with information indicating that the insurance company to which the invitation relates is not an authorised insurer in respect of the contract in question[12].

The information required under these provisions must be provided, where the invitation is issued in writing and is sent or delivered, by sending or (as the case may be) by delivering with the invitation a written statement containing that information[13] or, where the invitation is issued orally, by supplying that person with the information orally and (1) if the person is present when the invitation is issued, by delivering to him immediately thereafter a written statement containing that information[14]; or (2) if the person is not so present, by sending by post or causing to be delivered to him as soon as reasonably practicable, at the address supplied by him for the purpose or at his last known address, a written statement containing that information[15].

A person who contravenes any of these provisions is guilty of an offence[16] and is liable, on summary conviction, to a fine not exceeding the prescribed sum[17].

The above provisions do not apply in respect of an invitation issued by, or by an appointed representative of, an authorised person in relation to a contract of insurance the rights under which constitute an investment for the purposes of the Financial Services Act 1986[18].

1 For the excepted cases see para 814 post. See also note 4 infra.
2 As to the meaning of 'ordinarily resident' see generally CONFLICT OF LAWS vol 8 para 445.
3 For the meaning of 'United Kingdom' see para 2 note 10 ante.
4 For this purpose 'contract of insurance' does not include a contract of reinsurance or a contract of insurance the effecting and carrying out of which constitutes the carrying on of industrial assurance

business or insurance business of groups 3 and 4 as specified in the Insurance Companies Act 1982 Sch 2 Pt II as to which see para 18 ante: Insurance Companies Regulations 1981, SI 1981/1654, reg 68(5).

5 For this purpose a person is connected with an insurance company if:

(1) that person, or any partner, director, controller or manager of that person, is a partner, director, controller or manager of the insurance company or of any controller thereof (ibid reg 67(1)(a));

(2) the insurance company, or any partner, director, controller or manager of the insurance company, is a partner, director, controller or manager of that person or of any controller thereof (reg 67(1)(b));

(3) that person or any controller thereof has a significant interest (see infra) in shares of the insurance company or of any controller of it (reg 67(1)(c));

(4) the insurance company or any controller of it has a significant interest (see infra) in shares of that person or of any controller thereof (reg 67(1)(d));

(5) that person, under any contract, not being a contract of employment, or under any other arrangement (whether legally enforceable or not) with the insurance company or with any associated company, undertakes not to perform any services relating to any class of insurance business (or any category of it) for any insurance company other than the insurance company and, where the undertaking also relates to any associated company, the associated company (reg 67(1)(e)). However, an individual who gives such an undertaking to any registered society is not, by virtue of the undertaking, a person connected with the society or with any company which is, within the meaning of the Companies Act 1985 s 736 (as amended by the Companies Act 1989 s 144(1)) (see COMPANIES vol 7(1) (Reissue) para 813), a wholly owned subsidiary of the society: Insurance Companies Regulations 1981 reg 67(1)(e) proviso.

In the above provisions, 'associated company' in relation to a body corporate means a subsidiary or holding company or subsidiary of the holding company of that body; 'controller' in relation to a body corporate which is not an insurance company means a person who is or would, if he were a company, be a holding company of that body; and 'manager' in relation to such a body means a person who directly or indirectly takes part in or is concerned in the management of the affairs of that body: reg 67(4).' Subsidiary' and 'holding company' are to be construed in accordance with the Companies Act 1985 s 736 (as amended), see COMPANIES vol 7(1) (Reissue) para 813. For the purposes of the Insurance Companies Regulations 1981 reg 67(1)(c), (d), a person is treated as having an interest in shares of a company if, by virtue of the Companies Act 1985 Sch 13 Pt I (other than Sch 13 Pt I para 4(b)), he would be so treated for the purposes of s 324: Insurance Companies Regulations 1981 reg 67(2); and see COMPANIES vol 7(1) (Reissue) para 598. Regulation 67(2) also states that an interest in shares of a company is treated as significant if it is such that notification of it would be required under the Companies Act 1967 s 33. That section, which dealt with the disclosure of substantial interest in share capital carrying unrestricted voting rights, was repealed by the Companies Act 1981 which has now been consolidated in the Companies Act 1985. The corresponding provisions of the Companies Act 1985 are contained in ss 198–210 but are sufficiently different from the previous provision for it to be unclear whether the unamended reference in the Insurance Companies Regulations 1981 reg 67(2) to the Companies Act 1967 s 33 can be taken as referring to the new provisions.

A person who issues an invitation as is mentioned in reg 68(1) in respect of a contract of insurance which will be underwritten at Lloyd's is, in respect of such contract of insurance, connected with the insurance company to which the contract relates if that person or any partner, director, controller or manager of that person will take a share in the contract as a member of Lloyd's: reg 67(3). As to Lloyd's see generally para 21 ante.

6 See infra.

7 Insurance Companies Regulations 1981 reg 68 made pursuant to what is now the Insurance Companies Act 1982 s 74(1). As to the making of regulations under that Act see generally para 864 post.

8 For the excepted cases see para 814 post.

9 See note 3 supra.

10 For this purpose, in relation to a contract of any description, 'authorised insurer' means a person entitled to carry on in the United Kingdom insurance business of a class comprising the effecting of contracts of that description: Insurance Companies Act 1982 s 74(2).

11 See infra.

12 Insurance Companies Regulations 1981 reg 68(2) made pusuant to what is now the Insurance Companies Act 1982 s 74(2).

13 Insurance Companies Regulations 1981 reg 68(3)(a). As to the written statement see note 15 infra.

14 Ibid reg 68(3)(b)(i).

15 Ibid reg 68(3)(b)(ii). The requirement of the written statement is deemed to have been complied with where the invitation issued by the intermediary under reg 68(1) (see the text to notes 1–6, supra) is issued on stationery having printed upon it, in prominent positions, on the side on which the invitation is contained, the name of the intermediary, the name of the insurance company and a clear statement of the relationship between them and which contains in the body of the invitation a clear indication of the name of the insurance company to which the invitation relates, expressed in the same style as in the printed statement: reg 68(4). Where, however, the intermediary is a Lloyd's broker or a member of Lloyd's and it is clearly indicated in the invitation that the contract will be underwritten at Lloyd's, there may be inserted, in place of this statement of relationship, the expression 'Lloyd's Brokers' or (as the case may be) 'Mr — is a member of Lloyd's' without a reference to the names of the underwriters concerned: reg 68(4) proviso.
16 Insurance Companies Act 1982 s 74(3).
17 Ibid s 81(1). As to the prescribed sum see para 19 note 5 ante. The section reads '... to a fine not exceeding £1,000 or, if it is greater, the prescribed sum ...'. The prescribed sum is currently greater than £1,000.
18 Financial Services Act 1986 s 129, Sch 10 para 5.

814. Excepted cases. The regulations as to the information to be provided by certain intermediaries in insurance transactions[1] do not apply to:

(1) an invitation for the renewal or amendment of the terms of any contract of insurance[2] effected before 11 October 1976[3];

(2) an invitation for the renewal or amendment of the terms of a contract of insurance effected as a result of an invitation issued by an intermediary[4] in accordance with those regulations where there has been no significant change in the circumstances relevant to the information provided when the contract was first effected[5];

(3) an amendment of an invitation issued by an intermediary in accordance with those regulations where there has been no significant change in the circumstances relevant to the information provided when the invitation was first issued[6];

(4) an invitation for the effecting of a contract of insurance in respect of general business where (a) the contract relates to motor insurance business or to fire and other damage to property insurance business and the initial premium to be paid exceeds £5,000; or where the person to whom the invitation is made has, through the intermediary, prior to that invitation entered into other contracts of insurance of the class to which the contract relates and has paid premiums in respect of them which in the aggregate either exceed £5,000 in the previous calendar year or exceed that figure in the calendar year during which the invitation in question is made[7]; or (b) the contract relates to any other class of insurance business and the initial premium to be paid exceeds £1,000; or where the person to whom the invitation is made has, through the intermediary, prior to that invitation entered into contracts of insurance of the class to which the contract relates and has paid premiums in respect of them which in the aggregate either exceed £1,000 in the previous calendar year or exceed that figure in the calendar year during which the invitation is made[8];

(5) an invitation for the effecting of a contract of insurance with a body registered under the Acts relating to friendly societies[9] or a trade union or employers' association[10] where the insurance business carried on by the union or association is limited to the provision for its members of provident benefits or strike benefits[11].

In addition, the regulation requiring an intermediary to give information as to his connection with the insurance company[12] does not apply to an invitation for the effecting of a contract of insurance the carrying out of which is to be shared between two or more insurance companies where the share to be taken by any company, or the share in the aggregate to be taken by two or more companies, with which the intermediary is connected, does not exceed one-quarter of the total[13]. Similarly, the regulation requiring an intermediary to disclose that the insurance company is not an authorised insurer[14] does not apply to an invitation for the effecting of a contract of insurance the carrying out of which is to be shared between two or more insurance companies where the share to be taken by any company which is not an authorised insurer, or the share in the aggregate to be taken by two or more companies which are not authorised insurers, does not exceed one-quarter of the total[15].

1 Ie the Insurance Companies Regulations 1981, SI 1981/1654, reg 68: see para 813 ante.
2 Certain contracts of insurance are excluded altogether from the effect of the Insurance Companies Regulations 1981: see para 813 note 4 ante.
3 Ibid reg 69(1)(a).
4 'Intermediary' means a person to whom the requirements of ibid reg 68(1) or (2) apply in respect of an invitation issued by him: reg 68(4); see para 813 ante.
5 Ibid reg 69(1)(b).
6 Ibid reg 69(1)(c).
7 Ibid reg 69(1)(d)(i).
8 Ibid reg 69(1)(d)(ii).
9 As to registered friendly societies see FRIENDLY SOCIETIES.
10 Ie within the meaning of the Trade Union and Labour Relations (Consolidation) Act 1992 ss 1, 122(1): see TRADE AND LABOUR.
11 Insurance Companies Regulations 1981 reg 69(1)(e). As to the right of friendly societies, trade unions and employers' associations to carry on insurance business see para 19 ante.
12 Ie ibid reg 68: see para 813 ante.
13 Ibid reg 69(2).
14 Ie ibid reg 68(2): see para 813 ante.
15 Ibid reg 69(3).

(ii) Long Term Insurance Business

A. RESTRICTIONS ON AND WITHDRAWAL FROM LONG TERM CONTRACTS

815. Statutory notice by insurer. Except in specified circumstances, no insurance company[1] and no member of Lloyd's[2] may enter into a contract, the effecting of which constitutes the carrying on of long term insurance business[3], and no company which has been authorised in accordance with the first long term insurance directive[4] may enter a contract the effecting of which constitutes the provision in the United Kingdom[5] of long term insurance[6], unless that company or member ('the insurer') has sent by post to the other party to the contract, at or before the time it is entered into, a statutory notice in relation to that contractor, in the case of an EC contract[7], a representative of the insurer gives such a notice to the party at that time[8].

A statutory notice is a notice which: (1) contains such matters, and no others, and is in such form as may be prescribed[9] for the purpose and complies with prescribed requirements for securing that the notice is easily legible[10]; and (2) has annexed to it a form of notice of cancellation of the prescribed description[11].

These provisions do not apply: (a) to a contract if the party other than the insurer is habitually resident in a member state other than the United Kingdom[12]; or (b) to any non-EC contract the effecting of which by the insurer constitutes the carrying on of industrial assurance business[13].

Any insurer who contravenes these provisions is guilty of an offence and liable on summary conviction to a fine not exceeding level 5 on the standard scale[14], but no contract is to be invalidated by reason of the fact that the insurer has contravened these provisions in relation to it[15].

The above provisions do not apply to insurance companies[16] in respect of a contract of insurance the rights under which constitute an investment for the purposes of the Financial Services Act 1986[17].

1 Ie no insurance company to which the Insurance Companies Act 1982 Pt II (ss 15–71) (as amended) applies: see para 803 ante.
2 As to Lloyd's underwriters see generally para 21 ante
3 As to what constitutes 'long term insurance business' see para 18 ante.
4 Ie under art 6 of that directive. For the meaning of 'the first long term insurance directive' see para 22 note 12 ante.
5 For the meaning of 'United Kingdom' see para 2 note 10 ante.
6 Ie long term insurance within the meaning of the Insurance Companies Act 1982 Pt IIIA (ss 81A–81J) (added by the Insurance Companies (Amendment) Regulations 1990, SI 1990/1333; and as amended): see para 806 et seq ante.
7 'EC contract' means a contract to which the Insurance Companies Act 1982 s 75(1) (as substituted) applies and which fulfils the following conditions, namely (1) the insurer is a company whose head office in a member state or a member of Lloyd's, and (2) the other party is habitually resident in the United Kingdom: s 75(5B) (added by the Insurance Companies (Cancellation) Regulations 1993, SI 1993/1327). 'Non-EC contract' means a contract to which the Insurance Companies Act 1982 s 75(1) (as substituted) applies which is not an EC contract: s 75(5B) (as so added).
8 Ibid s 75(1), (1A) (substituted by the Insurance Companies (Cancellation) Regulations 1993, SI 1993/1327).
9 Ie prescribed by regulations under the Insurance Companies Act 1982: s 97(1). See note 10 infra.
10 Ibid s 75(2)(a). The prescribed regulations may be as to type, size, colour or disposition of the lettering, quality and colour of paper or otherwise: s 75(2)(a). See the Insurance Companies Regulations 1981, SI 1981/1654, regs 70–71, Schs 10–12. The Secretary of State may, on the application of any insurer, alter the requirements of any regulations made for the purpose of the Insurance Companies Act 1982 s 75(2)(a) so as to adapt those requirements to the circumstances of that insurer or to any particular kind of contract proposed to be entered into by him: s 75(3). As to the Secretary of State see para 15 note 5 ante.
11 Ibid s 75(2)(b). As to regulations for this purpose see note 10 supra. As to the use of the notice of cancellation see para 816 post.
12 Ibid s 75(5) (amended by the Insurance Companies (Cancellation) Regulations 1993).
13 Insurance Companies Act 1982 s 75(5A) (added by the Insurance Companies (Cancellation) Regulations 1993).
14 Insurance Companies Act 1982 ss 75(4), 81(2). As to the standard scale see para 212 note 5 ante.
15 Ibid s 75(4).
16 Ie to which ibid Pt II (as amended) applies: see para 803 ante.
17 Financial Services Act 1986 s 129, Sch 10 para 5.

816. Right to withdraw from transaction. A person who has received a statutory notice[1] in relation an EC contract[2] may, before the expiration of the fourteenth day after that on which he is informed in writing that the contract has become binding, serve[3] a notice of cancellation on the insurer[4]. A person who has received a statutory notice in relation to a non-EC contract[5] may, before the expiration of the tenth day after that on which he received the notice or the earliest day on which he knows both that the contract has been entered into and that the first or only premium has been paid, whichever is the later, serve a notice of cancellation on the insurer[6]. A person to whom an insurer ought to have, but has not, sent a statutory notice may serve a notice of cancellation on the insurer[7].

A notice of cancellation may, but need not, be in the form annexed to the statutory notice and has effect if, however expressed, it indicates the intention of the person serving it to withdraw from the transaction in relation to which the statutory notice was or ought to have been sent[8].

Where a person serves a notice of cancellation, then, if at the time when the notice is served the contract has been entered into, the notice operates so as to rescind the contract[9]; in any other case the service of the notice operates as a withdrawal of any offer to enter into the contract which is contained in, or implied by, any proposal made to the insurer by the person serving the notice of cancellation and as notice to the insurer that any such offer is withdrawn[10]. Where a notice of cancellation operates to rescind a contract or as the withdrawal of an offer to enter into a contract, any sum which the person serving the notice has paid in connection with the contract[11] is recoverable from the insurer by the person serving the notice[12], and any sum which the insurer has paid under the contract is recoverable by him from the person serving the notice[13]. Any sum so recoverable is recoverable as a simple contract debt in any court of competent jurisdiction[14].

1 For the meaning of 'statutory notice' see para 815 text and notes 9–11 ante.
2 For the meaning of 'EC contract' see para 815 note 7 ante.
3 A notice of cancellation is deemed to be served on the insurer if it is sent by post addressed to any person specified in the statutory notice as a person to whom a notice of cancellation may be sent, and is addressed to that person at an address so specified; and in these circumstances the notice is deemed to be served on the insurer at the time when it is posted: Insurance Companies Act 1982 s 77(1). This is without prejudice to the service of a notice of cancellation (whether by post or otherwise) in any other way in which the notice could be served, whether the notice is served on the insurer or on a person who is his agent for the purpose of receiving such a notice: s 77(2). A notice of cancellation which is sent by post to a person at his proper address, otherwise than in accordance with s 77(1), is deemed to be served on him at the time when it is posted: s 77(3). So much of the Interpretation Act 1978 s 7 (see EVIDENCE vol 17 para 211 note 6) as relates to the time when service is deemed to have been effected does not apply to a notice of cancellation: Insurance Companies Act 1982 s 77(4).
4 Ibid s 76(1) (substituted by the Insurance Companies (Cancellation) Regulations 1993, SI 1993/1327).
5 For the meaning of 'non-EC contract' see para 815 note 7 ante.
6 Insurance Companies Act 1982 s 76(1A) (added by the Insurance Companies (Cancellation) Regulations 1993).
7 Insurance Companies Act 1982 s 76(2) (amended by the Insurance Companies (Cancellation) Regulations 1993). If that person is sent a statutory notice before he has served the notice of cancellation, then his right to serve the notice under the Insurance Companies Act 1982 s 76(2) ceases, but not his right under s 76(1), (1A) (see text and notes 1–6 supra): s 76(2) (as so amended).
8 Ibid s 76(3).
9 Ibid s 76(4)(a).
10 Ibid s 76(4)(b).
11 Ie whether by way of premium or otherwise and whether to the insurer or to a person who is the agent of the insurer for the purpose of receiving that sum: ibid s 76(5)(a).
12 Ibid s 76(5)(a).
13 Ibid s 76(5)(b).
14 Ibid s 76(6).

817. Linked long term policies. Regulations may be made, as respects specified matters[1], in relation to contracts the effecting of which constitutes the carrying on of ordinary long term business[2] which are entered into by insurance companies[3] or by members of Lloyd's, and are contracts under which the benefits payable to the policyholder[4] are wholly or partly to be determined by reference to the value of, or the income from, property of any description (whether or not specified in the contract) or by reference to fluctuations in, or in an index of, the value of property of any description (whether or not so specified)[5]. The regulations may make provision for:

(1) restricting the descriptions of property or the indices of the value of property by reference to which benefits under the contracts may be determined[6];

(2) restricting the proportion of those benefits which may be determined by reference to a property of a specified description or a specified index[7];

(3) regulating the manner in which and the frequency with which property of any description is to be valued for the purpose of determining those benefits and the times at which reference is to be made for that purpose to any index of the value of property[8];

(4) requiring insurers under the contracts to appoint valuers for carrying out valuations of property for the purpose of determining those benefits (being valuers who comply with the prescribed requirements as to qualifications and independence from the insurer) and to furnish the Secretary of State with the prescribed information in relation to such appointments[9];

(5) requiring insurers under the contracts to furnish such information relating to the value of benefits under the contracts as may be prescribed[10];

(6) requiring insurers under the contracts to furnish to the Secretary of State such information certified in such manner as may be prescribed with respect to so much of their business as is concerned with the contracts or with any class or description of the contracts, and enabling the Secretary of State to publish that information in such ways as he thinks appropriate[11].

1 See the text to notes 7–12 infra.
2 For the meaning of 'ordinary long term business' see para 23 note 2 ante.
3 Ie an insurance companies to which the Insurance Companies Act 1982 Pt II (ss 15–71) (as amended) applies: see para 803 ante.
4 For the meaning of 'policyholder' see para 806 note 21 ante.
5 Insurance Companies Act 1982 s 78(1). The Secretary of State, on the application of any insurer, may alter the requirements of any regulations so as to adapt those requirements to the circumstances of that insurer or to any particular kind of contract entered into or proposed to be entered into by that insurer: s 78(4). The regulations may, to such extent as may be specified in them, apply in relation to contracts entered into before the coming into operation of the regulations, including contracts entered into before 28 January 1983 (ie the date on which the Act was passed): s 78(5). For regulations made under these provisions see note 6 infra. As to the making of regulations see generally para 864 post.
6 Ibid s 78(2)(a). See the Insurance Companies Regulations 1981, SI 1981/1654, which restrict the descriptions of property and the indices of the value of property to which benefits may be linked under ordinary long term insurance business contracts, and state in what circumstances those provisions do not apply (reg 72, Sch 13 (amended by SI 1991/2511)).
7 Insurance Companies Act 1982 s 78(2)(aa) (added by the Financial Services Act 1986 s 137).
8 Insurance Companies Act 1982 s 78(2)(b).
9 Ibid s 78(2)(c).
10 Ibid s 78(2)(d). The information may be required to be furnished in such manner and at such times or intervals as may be prescribed, whether by sending notices to policyholders, depositing statements with the Secretary of State or the registrar of companies, publication in the press or otherwise: s 78(2)(d). In relation to notices required to be sent to policyholders, requirements may be imposed (whether as to type, size, colour or disposition of lettering, quality or colour of paper, or otherwise) for securing that the notices are easily legible: s 78(3).
11 Ibid s 78(2)(e).

818. Capital redemption business. Where an insurance company[1] carries on capital redemption business[2] in the case of which the premiums in return for which

6 Ie served under ibid s 30(3)(a): see infra.
7 Ibid s 30(1). Failure to comply with s 30 is an offence: s 71(1)(a); see para 866 post. As to the Secretary of State's power to exclude or modify the application of these provisions in the case of a particular insurance company see para 803 ante.
8 Ibid s 30(7).
9 Ibid s 30(2), which specifies that the relevant minimum is the amount represented by the formula:

$$\frac{b \times c}{a} - \frac{c}{200}$$

   where:
       a is the last previously established surplus in respect of which an amount was allocated to policyholders of the category in question;
       b is the amount so allocated; and
       c is the surplus referred to in s 30(1)(a).
10 Ibid s 25(3)(a).
11 Ie in the London, Edinburgh and Belfast Gazettes and in such other ways as the Secretary of State may have directed: ibid s 30(3)(b).
12 Ibid s 30(3)(b).
13 Ibid s 30(3).

C. RESTRICTIONS ON TRANSACTIONS WITH CONNECTED PERSONS

821. Restricted transactions. Neither an insurance company[1] which carries on long term business[2] nor a subordinate company[3] of any such insurance company may enter into certain transactions with connected persons[4]:

(1) at a time when the aggregate value of the assets[5] and the amount of the liabilities[6] attributable to such transactions already entered into by the insurance company and its subordinate companies exceeds the prescribed percentage[7] of the total amount standing to the credit of the insurance company's long term funds[8]; or

(2) at any other time when the aggregate of the value of those assets and the amount of those liabilities would exceed that percentage if the transaction were entered into[9].

These restrictions apply to any transaction entered into by an insurance company carrying on long term business (whether or not itself a subordinate company of another company), being a transaction under which:

(a) a person connected with the insurance company[10] will owe it money[11]; or

(b) the insurance company acquires shares in a company which is a person connected with it[12]; or

(c) the insurance company undertakes a liability to meet an obligation of a person connected with it or to help such a person to meet an obligation[13],

if the right to receive the money would constitute a long term asset of the insurance company, the acquisition is made out of its long term funds or the liability would fall to be discharged out of those funds, as the case may be[14].

The restrictions also apply to any transaction entered into by a subordinate company of any insurance company carrying on long term business, being a transaction under which:

(i) the insurance company or person connected with it will owe money to the subordinate company (not being money owed by the insurance company which can be properly paid out of its long term funds)[15]; or

(ii) the subordinate company acquires shares in the insurance company or in a company which is a person connected with the insurance company[16]; or

(iii) the subordinate company undertakes a liability to meet an obligation of the insurance company or of a person connected with that company or to help the insurance company or such a person to meet an obligation[17].

The above provisions are not to be construed as making any transaction unenforceable as between the parties to it or as otherwise making unenforceable any rights or liabilities in respect of property[18].

1 Ie an insurance company to which the Insurance Companies Act 1982 Pt II (ss 15–71) (as amended) applies: see para 803 ante.

2 For the meaning of 'long term business' see para 18 ante, and as to the Secretary of State's power to direct that for the purposes of the application of ibid s 31 (see infra) to any particular insurance company certain business is to be treated as, or as not being, ordinary long term insurance business, see para 803 ante.

3 For this purpose 'subordinate company' means (1) a company having equity share capital some or all of which is held by the insurance company as part of its long term assets where the share capital so held by the insurance company amounts to more than half in nominal value of that share capital, and confers on the insurance company the power to appoint or remove the holders of all or a majority of the directorships of the company whose share capital is held and more than one half of the voting power at any general meeting of that company (ibid s 31(4)(a)); or (2) a company having equity share capital some of all of which is held by another company which is itself a subordinate company of the insurance company where the share capital held by that other company amounts to more than half in nominal value of that share capital, and confers on that other company power to appoint or remove the holders of all or a majority of the directorships of the company whose share capital is held and more than one-half of the voting power at any general meeting of that company (s 31(4)(b)). Share capital held for any person by a nominee is (except where that person is concerned only in a fiduciary capacity) treated as held by that person, and share capital held by a person in a fiduciary capacity or by way of security is treated as not held by that person: s 31(4). 'Company' (except in the expression 'insurance company') includes a body corporate: s 31(7). 'Equity share capital' means, in relation to a company, its issued share capital excluding any part which, neither as respects dividends nor as respects capital, carries any right to participate beyond a specified amount in a distribution: s 31(7). 'Share' has the same meaning as in the Companies Act 1985: Insurance Companies Act 1982 s 31(7). See further COMPANIES vol 7(1) (Reissue) paras 420, 211 note 1.

4 As to these transactions see text and notes 10–18 infra.

5 The Insurance Companies Regulations 1981, SI 1981/1654 (as amended), apply with respect to the determination of the value of insurance companies' assets and the amount of their liabilities for this purpose: Insurance Companies Act 1982 s 31(6).

6 'Liability' includes a contingent liability: ibid s 31(7). As to the determination of the amount of liabilities see note 5 supra.

7 See the Insurance Companies Regulations 1981 Pt V (regs 37–49) (as amended).

8 Insurance Companies Act 1982 s 31(1)(a). 'Long term assets' and 'long term funds', in relation to an insurance company, mean respectively assets representing the fund or funds maintained by the company in respect of its long term business and that fund or those funds: s 31(7).

9 Ibid s 31(1)(b). Failure to comply with s 31 is an offence: s 71(3); see para 866 post. As to the Secretary of State's power to exclude or modify the application of these provisions in the case of a particular insurance company or subordinate company see para 803 ante.

10 A person is connected with an insurance company if that person is not a subordinate company of the insurance company but controls, or is a partner of a person who controls, the insurance company, or, being a company, is controlled by the insurance company or by another person who also controls the insurance company, or is a director of the insurance company or the wife or husband or a minor son or daughter of such a director: ibid s 31(5). A person controls a company if he is a controller of it within the meaning of s 7(4)(c) (see para 31 note 7 ante): s 31(5). 'Son' includes step-son and adopted son, and 'daughter' includes step-daughter and adopted daughter: s 31(7).

11 Ibid s 31(2)(a).

12 Ibid s 31(2)(b).

13 Ibid s 31(2)(c).

14 Ibid s 31(2).

15 Ibid s 31(3)(a).

16 Ibid s 31(3)(b).

17 Ibid s 31(3)(c). Where the subordinate company is itself an insurance company carrying on long term business, s 31 does not by virtue of s 31(3) apply to any transaction if the right to receive the money

would consitute a long term asset of the subordinate company, the acquisition is made out of its long term funds, or the liability would fall to be discharged out of those funds, as the case may be: s 31(3).
18 Ibid s 31(8).

D. ACTUARIAL INVESTIGATION

822. Appointment of actuary. Within one month of beginning to carry on long term business[1], every insurance company[2] must appoint an actuary[3] as actuary to the company, and whenever such an appointment comes to an end the company must make a fresh appointment as soon as practicable[4]. A company making an appointment must within 14 days serve on the Secretary of State[5] a written notice stating that fact and the name and qualifications of the person appointed, and if an appointment comes to an end the company must within 14 days serve on the Secretary of State a written notice stating that fact and the name of the person concerned[6].

1 For the meaning of 'long term business' see para 18 ante, and as to the Secretary of State's power to direct that for the purposes of the application of the Insurance Companies Act 1982 s 19 (see infra) to any particular insurance company certain business is to be treated as, or as not being, ordinary long term insurance business, see para 803 ante.
2 Ie an insurance company to which ibid Pt II (ss 15–71) (as amended) applies: see para 803 ante.
3 'Actuary' means actuary possessing the prescribed qualifications (ibid s 96(1)), ie a person who is either a Fellow of the Institute of Actuaries or of the Faculty of Actuaries: Insurance Companies (Accounts and Statements) Regulations 1983, SI 1983/1811, reg 28(1). He must have attained the age of 30 years: reg 28(1). A company must annex to the balance sheet, the profit and loss account and the revenue account certain information relating to the person appointed as actuary: reg 29.
4 Insurance Companies Act 1982 s 19(1). Failure to comply with s 19 is an offence: s 71(3)(a); see para 866 post. As to the Secretary of State's power to exclude or modify the application of s 19 in the case of a particular insurance company see para 803 ante.
5 As to the Secretary of State see para 15 note 5 ante.
6 Insurance Companies Act 1982 s 19(2). It is an offence to include a false statement in such a notice: s 71(1)(c)(ii); see para 866 post. See also note 4 supra.

823. Periodic actuarial investigation. Every insurance company[1] which carries on long term business must, once in every period of 12 months:
   (1) cause an investigation to be made into its financial condition in respect of that business by the person who for the time being is its actuary[2]; and
   (2) when such an investigation has been made, or when at any other time an investigation into the financial condition of the company in respect of its long term business has been made with a view to the distribution of profits, or the results of which are made public, cause an abstract of the actuary's report of the investigation to be made[3].
An investigation must include:
   (a) a valuation of the liabilities of the company attributable to its long term business; and
   (b) a determination of any excess over those liabilities of the assets representing the fund or funds maintained by the company in respect of that business and, where any rights of any long term policyholders to participate in profits relate to particular parts of such a fund, a determination of any excess of assets over liabilities in respect of each of those parts[4].
At least once in every period of five years an insurance company must prepare a statement of its long term business at the date to which the accounts of the company are made up for the purposes of an investigation[5].

1 Ie every insurance company to which the Insurance Companies Act 1982 Pt II (ss 15–71) (as amended) applies.
2 Under ibid s 19: see para 822 ante.
3 Ibid s 18(1).
4 Ibid s 18(2). For the purposes of any investigation, the value of any assets and the amount of any liabilities must be determined in accordance with any applicable valuation regulations: s 18(4). The form and contents of any abstract or statement under this section must be such as may be prescribed: s 18(5). For the meaning of 'valuation regulations' see para 803 note 15 ante. See the Insurance Companies (Accounts and Statements) Regulations 1983, SI 1983/1811, reg 24, Schs 4, 5.
5 Insurance Companies Act 1982 s 18(3).

824. Investigation required by Secretary of State. The Secretary of State[1] may require a company which carries on long term business[2] (1) to cause the company's actuary[3] to make an investigation into its financial condition in respect of that business, or any specified part of that business, as at a specified date[4]; (2) to cause an abstract of the actuary's report of the investigation to be made[5]; and (3) to prepare a statement of its long term business, or the specified part of its business, as at that date[6]. Five copies of any abstract or statement made in pursuance of the requirement must be deposited by the company with the Secretary of State on or before such date as he may specify, and one of those copies must be signed by certain persons[7].

1 As to the Secretary of State see para 15 note 5 ante.
2 For the meaning of 'long term business' see para 18 ante, and as to the Secretary of State's power to direct that for the purposes of the application of the Insurance Companies Act 1982 s 42 (see infra) to any particular insurance company certain business is to be treated as, or as not being, ordinary long term insurance business, see para 803 ante.
3 As to the appointment of actuaries see para 822 ante.
4 Insurance Companies Act 1982 s 42(1)(a). For the purposes of the investigation, the value of any assets and the amount of any liabilities are to be determined in accordance with any applicable valuation regulations: s 42(2). For the meaning of 'valuation regulations' see para 803 note 15 ante. The regulations at present applicable are the Insurance Companies Regulations 1981, SI 1981/1654, Pt V (regs 37–49) (as amended): see reg 38.
5 Insurance Companies Act 1982 s 42(1)(b). The form and contents of any abstract or statement made in pursuance of a requirement under s 42 are the same as for an abstract or statement made under s 18 (as to which see para 823 note 4 ante): s 42(3).
6 Ibid s 42(1)(c). As to the form of statement see note 5 supra. Failure to comply with s 42 is an offence: s 71(3)(a); see para 866 post.
7 Insurance Companies Act 1982 s 42(4). The signatories are those specified in ss 22(3), 96(1); Insurance Companies (Accounts and Statements) Regulations 1983, SI 1983/1811, regs 2, 25 (see para 843 post): Insurance Companies Act 1982 s 42(4). The inclusion of a false statement in any document deposited under s 42(4) is an offence: s 71(1)(c)(iii), (4); see para 866 post.

(iii) Transfer of Business

825. Transfer of long term business: sanction of court. Where it is proposed to carry out a scheme under which the whole or part of the long term business[1] carried on by an insurance company[2] is to be transferred to another body, whether incorporated or not, the transferor company or the transferee company may apply to the court[3], by petition, for an order sanctioning the scheme[4]. On any petition the Secretary of State[5] and any person, including any employee of the transferor company or the transferee company, who alleges that he would be adversely affected by the carrying out of the scheme is entitled to be heard[6].

A transfer of long term business is not to be carried out unless the scheme relating to it has been sanctioned by the court, and no court order[7] is to be made under the

Companies Act 1985 sanctioning a compromise or arrangement[8] in respect of so much of any compromise or arrangement as involves any such transfer[9].

1 For the meaning of 'long term business' see para 18 ante.
2 Ie an insurance company to which the Insurance Companies Act 1982 Pt II (ss 15–71) (as amended) applies: see para 803 ante.
3 'The court' means the High Court of Justice in England except that it means:
   (1) the Court of Session if the transferor company and the transferee company are registered or have their head offices in Scotland;
   (2) either the High Court or the Court of Session if one only of those companies is registered or has its head office in Scotland;
   (3) the High Court of Justice in Northern Ireland if both companies are registered or have their head offices in Northern Ireland;
   (4) the High Court of Justice in England or the High Court of Justice of Northern Ireland if either company is registered or has its head office in Northern Ireland; and
   (5) either the Court of Session or the High Court of Justice in Northern Ireland if one company is registered or has its head office in Scotland and the other is registered or has its head office in Northern Ireland: ibid s 49(8).
4 Ibid s 49(1). This is subject to s 49A (as added) in the case of transfer of long term business to an authorised friendly society: s 49(1) (amended by the Friendly Societies Act 1992 s 120(1), Sch 21 Pt I para 6(1)): see note 5 infra and paras 826–827 post.
5 As to the Secretary of State see para 15 note 5 ante. In the case of transfer of business to an authorised friendly society, the Friendly Societies Commission is also entitled to be heard: Insurance Companies Act 1982 s 59(5)(a), modified by s 49A(1), (3) (added by the Friendly Societies Act 1992 Sch 21 Pt I para 6(2)). A society is authorised under the Friendly Societies Act 1992 Pt IV (ss 31–43). As to friendly societies and the Friendly Societies Commission see generally FRIENDLY SOCIETIES.
6 Insurance Companies Act 1982 s 49(5).
7 Except in the case of any such scheme as is mentioned in ibid s 49(1A) (as added): see note 8 infra.
8 Ie under the Companies Act 1985 ss 425–427 (as amended), which provide for the sanctioning of compromises and arrangements between a company and its creditors or members: see COMPANIES vol 7(2) (Reissue) para 2135 et seq. If any scheme under the Insurance Companies Act 1982 involves a compromise or arrangement within the meaning of the Companies Act 1985 s 427A (added by the Companies (Mergers and Divisions) Regulations 1987, SI 1987/1991; amended by the Companies Act 1989 s 114(2)) (application of provisions about compromises and arrangements to mergers and divisions of public companies) the Companies Act 1985 ss 425–427 (as amended) have effect, as regards that compromise or arrangement, as provided by s 427A(1) (as so added and amended), but without prejudice to the operation of the Insurance Companies Act 1982 s 49: s 49(1A) (added by the Insurance Companies (Mergers and Divisions) Regulations 1987, SI 1987/2118).
9 Insurance Companies Act 1982 s 49(7) (amended by the Insurance Companies (Mergers and Divisions) Regulations 1987).

826. Preliminaries to application for sanction. The court[1] must not entertain an application[2] for the sanction of a scheme of transfer of long term business[3] of an insurance company[4] to another body unless the petition is accompanied by a report on the terms of the scheme by an independent actuary[5] and the court is satisfied that the following requirements have been complied with[6]:

   (1) that a notice has been published in the London, Edinburgh and Belfast Gazettes and, except where the court has otherwise directed, in two national newspapers stating that the application is to be made and giving the address of the offices at which, and the period for which, copies of the relevant documents[7] will be available for inspection[8];

   (2) except where the court has otherwise directed, that a statement setting out the terms of the scheme and containing a summary of the actuary's report sufficient to indicate his opinion on the likely effects of the scheme on the long term policyholders[9] of the companies concerned has been sent to each of the policyholders and to every member of those companies[10];

(3) that a copy of the petition, of the actuary's report and of any statement sent out to policyholders[11] has been served on the Secretary of State and that a period of not less than 21 days has elapsed since the date of service[12];

(4) that copies of the petition and of the actuary's report have been open to inspection at offices in the United Kingdom[13] of the companies concerned for a period of not less than 21 days beginning with the date on which the notice of application was published[14]; and

(5) in the case of a scheme involving a compromise or arrangement[15], that copies of certain documents[16] had been served on the Secretary of State by the beginning of a specified[17] period[18].

Each of the companies concerned must, on payment of such fee as may be prescribed by rules of court[19], furnish a copy of the petition and of the actuary's report to any person who asks for one at any time before an order sanctioning the scheme is made on the petition[20].

1 For the meaning of 'the court' see para 825 note 3 ante.
2 See para 825 ante.
3 For the meaning of 'long term business' see para 18 ante.
4 Ie an insurance company to which the Insurance Companies Act 1982 Pt II (ss 15–71) (as amended) applies: see para 803 ante.
5 For the meaning of 'actuary' see para 822 note 3 ante.
6 Insurance Companies Act 1982 s 49(2).
7 Ie the documents mentioned in ibid s 49(3)(d): see head (4) in the text.
8 Ibid s 49(3)(a).
9 For the meaning of 'long term policyholder' see para 820 note 3 ante.
10 Insurance Companies Act 1982 s 49(3)(b). The inclusion of a false statement in the statement sent out under this provision is an offence: see s 71(1)(c)(iv); and para 866 post.
11 Ie any statement sent out under ibid s 49(3)(b).
12 Ibid s 49(3)(c). As to the Secretary of State see para 15 note 5 ante. In the case of transfer of business to an authorised friendly society, copies must also be served on the Friendly Societies Commission: s 49(3)(a), modified by s 49A(1), (2) (added by the Friendly Societies Act 1992 s 120(1), Sch 21 Pt I para 6(2)). A society is authorised under the Friendly Societies Act 1992 Pt IV (ss 31–43). As to friendly societies and the Friendly Societies Commission see generally FRIENDLY SOCIETIES.
13 For the meaning of 'United Kingdom' see para 2 note 10 ante.
14 Insurance Companies Act 1982 s 49(3)(d).
15 Ie under ibid s 49(1A) (added by the Insurance Companies (Mergers and Divisions) Regulations 1987, SI 1987/2118): see para 825 note 8 ante.
16 Ie those listed in the Companies Act 1985 Sch 15B para 6(1) (added by the Companies (Mergers and Divisions) Regulations 1987, SI 1987/1991; renumbered by the Companies Act 1989 s 114(2); amended by the Companies Act 1989 s 23, Sch 10 Pt I para 22).
17 Ie specified by the Companies Act 1985 Sch 15B para 3(e) (as added and renumbered: see note 16 supra).
18 Insurance Companies Act 1982 s 49(3)(e) (added by the Insurance Companies (Mergers and Divisions) Regulations 1987; amended by the Insurance Companies (Transfer of Long Term Business) Regulations 1990, SI 1990/1207).
19 No rules of court had been made for this purpose at the date at which this volume states the law and none had effect by virtue of the Interpretation Act 1978 s 17(2)(b).
20 Insurance Companies Act 1982 s 49(4). Failure to comply with this provision is an offence: s 71(3); see para 866 post.

827. Order for sanction of scheme. The court must not make an order sanctioning a scheme of transfer of long term business[1] unless it is satisfied that the transferee company is, or immediately after the making of the order will be, authorised[2] to carry on long term business of the class or classes to be transferred under the scheme[3].

Where the court makes an order sanctioning a scheme it may, either by that order or by any subsequent order, make provision for:

(1) the transfer to the transferee company of the whole or any part of the undertaking and of the property[4] or liabilities[5] of the transferor company[6];

(2) the allotting or appropriation by the transferee company of any shares[7], debentures[8], policies or other like interests in that company which under the scheme are to be allotted or appropriated by that company to or for any person[9];

(3) the continuation by or against the transferee company of any legal proceedings pending by or against the transferor company[10];

(4) the dissolution, without winding up, of the transferor company[11]; and

(5) such incidental, consequential and supplementary matters as are necessary to secure that the scheme is fully and effectively carried out[12].

Where an order provides for the transfer of property or liabilities, by virtue of the order that property is transferred to and vests in, and those liabilities are transferred to and become the liabilities of, the transferee company, and in the case of any property, if the order so directs, freed from any mortgage or charge which is by virtue of the scheme to cease to have effect[13]. For the purposes of any provision requiring the delivery of an instrument of transfer as a condition for the registration of a transfer of any property[14], an order which by virtue of these provisions operates to transfer any property is treated as an instrument of transfer[15].

Within ten days from the date on which an order sanctioning a scheme is made or such longer period as the Secretary of State may allow, the transferee company must deposit two office copies of the order with the Secretary of State[16].

1 See para 825 ante. For the meaning of 'long term business' see para 18 ante.

2 Ie authorised under the Insurance Companies Act 1982 s 3 or s 4 (see para 34 ante) or, in the case of transfer of business to an incorporated or registered friendly society, authorised under the Friendly Societies Act 1992 Pt IV (ss 31–43). As to friendly societies see generally FRIENDLY SOCIETIES.

3 Insurance Companies Act 1982 s 49(6), modified in relation to transfer to an authorised friendly society by s 49A(4) (added by the Friendly Societies Act 1992 s 120(1), Sch 21 Pt I para 6(2)). Where the head office of the transferee company is situated in a member state of the European Community other than the United Kingdom, the court must not sanction the scheme unless (1) the supervisory authorities of that member state certify that the transferee company possesses the necessary margin of solvency after taking the proposed transfer into account, or (2) every policy included in the proposed transfer evidences a contract of reinsurance: s 49(6A) (added by the Insurance Companies (Amendment) Regulations 1993, SI 1993/174, reg 3(1), (2)). Where the establishment of the transferee company to which the policies are to be transferred is situated in a member state other than the United Kingdom the court must sanction the scheme if it is satisfied that (a) the transfer relates to commitments situated in the United Kingdom, (b) the transferee company is entitled in accordance with the Insurance Companies Act 1982 s 81B (added by the Insurance Companies (Amendment) Regulations 1990, SI 1990/1333; amended by the Insurance Companies (Amendment) Regulations 1992, SI 1992/2890, and the Insurance Companies (Amendment) Regulations 1993 (see para 806 ante) to provide insurance in the United Kingdom through that establishment, and (c) the supervisory authorities of that member state agree to the transfer: Insurance Companies Act 1982 s 49(6B) (added by the Insurance Companies (Amendment) Regulations 1993 reg 3(2)). For the meaning of 'commitments' see para 806 note 10 ante. For the meaning of 'margin of solvency' see para 857 note 3 post.

4 'Property' includes property, rights and powers of every description: Insurance Companies Act 1982 s 50(5).

5 'Liabilities' includes duties: ibid s 50(5).

6 Ibid s 50(1)(a).

7 'Shares' has the same meaning as in the Companies Act 1985 (see s 744; and COMPANIES vol 7(1) (Reissue) para 415 note 1): Insurance Companies Act 1982 s 50(5) (amended by the Companies Consolidation (Consequential Provisions) Act 1985 s 30, Sch 2).

8 'Debentures' has the same meaning as in the Companies Act 1985 (see s 744; and COMPANIES vol 7(1) (Reissue) para 1087 note 3): Insurance Companies Act 1982 s 50(5) (as amended: see note 7 supra).
9 Ibid s 50(1)(b).
10 Ibid s 50(1)(c).
11 Ibid s 50(1)(d).
12 Ibid s 50(1)(e).
13 Ibid s 50(2).
14 This includes in particular the Companies Act 1985 s 183(1) (see COMPANIES vol 7(1) (Reissue) para 479) and the Finance Act 1946 s 56(4) (see STAMP DUTIES vol 44 para 704): Insurance Companies Act 1982 s 50(3).
15 Ibid s 50(3) (amended by the Companies Consolidation (Consequential Provisions) Act 1985 Sch 2).
16 Insurance Companies Act 1982 s 50(4). Failure to comply with this provision is an offence: s 71(3): see para 866 post.

828. Transfer of general business: approval of transfer. Where it is proposed to execute an instrument by which an insurance company[1] (the transferor) is to transfer to another body (the transferee) all its rights and obligations under such general policies[2], or general policies of such descriptions, as may be specified in the instrument, the transferor may apply to the Secretary of State[3] for his approval of the transfer[4].

The Secretary of State may not determine an application for approval unless he is satisfied that:

(1) a notice[5] approved by him has been published in the London, Edinburgh and Belfast Gazettes and, if he thinks fit, in two national newspapers which have been so approved;

(2) except in so far as he has otherwise directed, a copy of the notice has been sent to every affected policyholder[6] and every other person who claims an interest in a policy included in the transfer and has given written notice of his claim to the transferor; and

(3) copies of a statement setting out particulars of the transfer and approved by him have been available for inspection at one or more places in the United Kingdom for a period of not less than 30 days beginning with the date of the first publication of the notice[7].

The Secretary of State must not approve a transfer unless he is satisfied that:

(a) every policy included in the transfer evidences a contract which:

   (i) was entered into before the date of the application; and

   (ii) imposes on the insurer obligations the performance of which will constitute the carrying on of insurance business in the United Kingdom; and

(b) the transferee is, or immediately after the approval will be, authorised[8] to carry on in the United Kingdom insurance business of the appropriate class or classes,

and unless in his opinion the transferee's financial resources and the other circumstances of the case justify the giving of his approval[9].

The Secretary of State must not approve a transfer to a company whose head office is in another member state of the European Community unless the supervisory authorities of that state certify that the company possesses the necessary margin of solvency after taking the proposed transfer into account, or every policy included in the proposed transfer evidences a contract of reinsurance[10].

On determining an application for approval of a transfer, the Secretary of State must (A) publish a notice of his decision in the London, Edinburgh and Belfast Gazettes and in such other manner as he may think fit, and (B) send a copy of that notice to the transferor, the transferee and every person who made representations following the publication of the notice of application[11]. If he refuses the application he must inform the transferor and the transferee in writing of the reasons for the refusal[12].

1 Ie an insurance company to which the Insurance Companies Act 1982 Pt II (ss 15–71) (as amended) applies: see para 803 ante.
2 'General policy' means a policy evidencing a contract the effecting of which constituted the carrying on of general business: ibid s 51(7). As to general business see para 18 ante
3 As to the Secretary of State see para 15 note 5 ante.
4 Insurance Companies Act 1982 s 51(1).
5 The notice must include a statement that written representations concerning the transfer may be sent to the Secretary of State before a specified day, which must not be earlier than 60 days after the day of first publication of the notice under ibid s 51(2)(a): s 51(3). He must not determine the application until after considering any representations made to him before the specified day: s 51(3).
6 A policyholder is an affected policyholder in relation to a proposed transfer if (a) his policy is included in the transfer or (b) his policy is with the transferor and the Secretary of State has certified, after consulting the transferor, that in his opinion the policyholder's rights and obligations under the policy will or may be materially affected by the transfer: ibid s 51(7).
7 Ibid s 51(2)(a)–(c).
8 Ie under ibid s 3 or s 4: see para 34 ante.
9 Ibid s 51(4).
10 Ibid s 51(4A) (added by the Insurance Companies (Amendment) Regulations 1990, SI 1990/1333; amended by the Insurance Companies (Amendment) Regulations 1992, SI 1992/2890). Notwithstanding the provisions of the Insurance Companies Act 1982 s 51(4)(a)(ii), (b), the Secretary of State may approve a transfer to an insurance company established in another member state where he is satisfied that (1) the transfer relates to policies covering risks situated in the United Kingdom, (2) the transferee is entitled in accordance with s 81B (as added) (see para 806 ante) to provide insurance in the United Kingdom in respect of those risks through that establishment, and (3) the supervisory authorities of the member state of that establishment agree to the transfer: s 51(4B) (added by the Insurance Companies (Amendment) Regulations 1990).
11 Insurance Companies Act 1982 s 51(5)(a), (b). See note 4 supra. Any notice or other document authorised or required to be given or served under s 51 or s 52 may be served by post, without prejudice to any other method of service: s 51(6). A letter containing the notice or other document is deemed to be properly addressed if it is addressed to that person at his last known residence or last known place of business in the United Kingdom: s 51(6).
12 Ibid s 51(5).

829. Transfer of general business: effect of approval. An instrument giving effect to a transfer approved[1] by the Secretary of State[2] is effectual in law (1) to transfer to the transferee all the transferor's rights and obligations under the policies included in the instrument, and (2) if the instrument so provides, to secure the continuation by or against the transferee of any legal proceedings by or against the transferor which relate to those rights or obligations, notwithstanding the absence of any agreements or consents which would otherwise be necessary for it to be effectual in law for those purposes[3]. However, except in so far as the Secretary of State may otherwise direct, a policyholder whose policy is included in such an instrument is not bound by it unless he has been given written notice of its execution by the transferor or the transferee[4].

Where it is proposed to execute an instrument by which an insurance company established in another member state of the European Community is to transfer to an insurance company whose head office is situated in the United Kingdom[5] all its rights and obligations under such general policies[6], or general policies of such descriptions as may be specified in the instrument, the Secretary of State may, if he is satisfied that the latter insurance company possesses the necessary margin of solvency after taking the proposed transfer into account, issue a certificate to that effect[7].

1 Insurance Companies Act 1982 s 51.
2 As to the Secretary of State see para 15 note 5 ante.
3 Insurance Companies Act 1982 s 52(1).
4 Ibid s 52(2). For the meaning of 'policyholder' see para 806 note 21 ante.
5 For the meaning of 'United Kingdom' see para 2 note 10 ante.
6 'General policy' means a policy evidencing a contract the effecting of which constituted the carrying on of general business other than reinsurance, and 'long term policy' means a policy evidencing a contract the effecting of which constitutes the carrying on of long term business, other than reinsurance: Insurance Companies Act 1982 s 52A(2) (amended by the Insurance Companies (Amendment) Regulations 1993, SI 1993/174).
7 Ibid s 52A(1) (amended by the Insurance Companies (Amendment) Regulations 1993).

830. Transfer of business: Lloyd's underwriters. The provisions[1] relating to the transfer of long term and general business apply to transfers to and from members of Lloyd's[2] if the following conditions are satisfied[3]: (1) the transfer is not one where both the transferor and the transferee are members of Lloyd's; (2) the Committee of Lloyd's[4] has by resolution authorised one person to act in connection with the transfer for the members concerned as transferor or transferee; (3) a copy of the resolution has been given to the Secretary of State[5].

1 Ie the Insurance Companies Act 1982 ss 49–52 (as amended).
2 As to Lloyd's generally see para 19 ante.
3 Insurance Companies Act 1982 s 85(1).
4 As to the Committee of Lloyd's see para 19 ante.
5 Insurance Companies Act 1982 s 85(2)(a)–(c). Where ss 49, 50 (as amended) (see paras 825–826 ante) or ss 51, 52 (see paras 828–829 ante) apply to a transfer to or from members of Lloyd's, they apply as if (1) references to insurance companies to which Pt II (ss 15–71) (as amended) applies, or to persons authorised under s 3 or s 4 (see para 34 ante), included references to members of Lloyd's, and (2) anything done in connection with the transfer by the person authorised under s 85(2)(b) had been done by the members for whom he acted: s 85(3). As to the Secretary of State see para 15 note 5 ante.

831. Transfer of long term business to company elsewhere in European Community. Special provisions apply where (1) it is proposed to carry out a scheme under which the whole or part of any long term business[1] (other than reinsurance) carried on in the United Kingdom[2] by an insurance company[3] is to be transferred to another insurance company; (2) all of the policies comprised in the business proposed to be transferred were written in the course of the provision of services in a member state of the European Community other than the United Kingdom; and (3) the head office of the transferee company is situated in a member state[4].

The requirements as to applying by petition to obtain the sanction of the court are the same as for other proposed transfers of long term business[5], as are those, in general, relating to preliminaries to the application[6]. The requirements as to notice, however, are as follows. The court must be satisfied before determining an application[7]:

(a) that a notice has been published in two national newspapers in the United Kingdom and in such publications or in such manner in the member state of the commitment[8] as the court has directed, stating that the application is to be made and giving the address of the offices at which, and the period for which, copies of the relevant documents[9] will be available for inspection[10];
(b) except where the court has otherwise directed, that a statement setting out the terms of the scheme and containing a summary of the actuary's report

sufficient to indicate his opinion on the likely effects of the scheme on the long term policyholders[11] of the companies concerned has been sent to each of the policyholders and to every member of those companies[12];

(c) that a copy of the petition, of the actuary's report and of any statement sent out to policyholders[13] has been served on the Secretary of State and that a period of not less than 21 days has elapsed since the date of service[14];

(d) that copies of the petition and of the actuary's report have been open to inspection at offices in the United Kingdom of the transferor company and at such place in the member state of the commitment as the court has directed for a period of not less than 21 days beginning with the date on which the notice of application was published[15]; and

(e) in the case of a scheme involving a compromise or arrangement[16], that copies of certain documents[17] had been served on the Secretary of State by the beginning of a specified[18] period[19].

Where the establishment of the transferee company to which the policies are to be transferred is situated in the United Kingdom, the court must not make an order sanctioning the scheme unless it is satisfied that (i) the transferee company fulfils specified conditions of the second long term insurance directive[20] in the member state of the commitment; (ii) the supervisory authorities of that member state agree to the transfer; and (iii) the transferee company is, or immediately after the making of the order will be, authorised to carry on long term business of the class or classes to be transferred under the scheme[21]. Where the establishment of the transferee company to which the policies are to be transferred is situated in a member state other than the United Kingdom, the court must not make an order sanctioning the scheme unless (A) it is satisfied that the supervisory authorities of the member state where the establishment of the transferee company to which the policies are to be transferred is situated agree to the transfer; and (B) where the member state of the commitment is not the member state in which the establishment is situated, it is also satisfied that (I) the establishment fulfils specified conditions of the second long term insurance directive[22] in the member state of the commitment, (II) the law of that member state provides for the possibility of such a transfer, and (III) the supervisory authorities of that member state agree to the transfer[23]. Where the head office of the transferee company is situated in a member state other than the United Kingdom, the court must not make an order sanctioning the scheme unless the supervisory authorities of that member state certify that the transferee company possesses the necessary margin of solvency after taking the proposed transfer into account[24].

Where the court makes an order sanctioning a scheme it must direct that notice of the making of any order, or the execution of any instrument, giving effect to the transfer be published in the member state of the commitment, and the notice must specify a period during which any policyholder affected may cancel the policy[25]. Such an instrument or order will not bind such a policyholder if either such a notice is not so published or the policyholder cancels the policy during the period so specified[26].

1 For the meaning of 'long term business' see para 18 ante.

2 For the meaning of 'United Kingdom' see para 2 note 10 ante.

3 Ie an insurance company to which the Insurance Companies Act 1982 Pt II (ss 15–71) (as amended) applies: see para 803 ante.

4 Ibid s 49B(1) (added by the Insurance Companies (Amendment) Regulations 1993, SI 1993/174, reg 3(1), (3); renumbered by the Insurance Companies (Cancellation) Regulations 1993, SI 1993/1327, reg 3(1)).
5 See para 825 ante. For the meaning of 'the court' see para 825 note 3 ante.
6 See para 826 ante.
7 Insurance Companies Act 1982 s 49(2).
8 For the meaning of 'commitment' see para 806 note 10 ante.
9 Ie the documents mentioned in the Insurance Companies Act 1982 s 49(3)(d): see head (d) in the text.
10 Ibid s 49(3)(a), modified by s 49B(2)(a) (as added and renumbered: see note 4 supra).
11 For the meaning of 'long term policyholder' see para 820 note 3 ante.
12 Insurance Companies Act 1982 s 49(3)(b). The inclusion of a false statement in the statement sent out under this provision is an offence: see s 71(1)(c)(iv); and para 866 post.
13 Ie any statement sent out under ibid s 49(3)(b).
14 Ibid s 49(3)(c). As to the Secretary of State see para 15 note 5 ante.
15 Insurance Companies Act 1982 s 49(3)(d), modified by s 49B(2)(b) (as added and renumbered: see note 4 supra).
16 Ie under ibid s 49(1A) (added by the Insurance Companies (Mergers and Divisions) Regulations 1987, SI 1987/2118): see para 825 note 8 ante.
17 Ie those listed in the Companies Act 1985 Sch 15B para 6(1) (added by the Companies (Mergers and Divisions) Regulations 1987, SI 1987/1991; renumbered by the Companies Act 1989 s 114(2); amended by the Companies Act 1989 s 23, Sch 10 Pt I para 22).
18 Ie specified by the Companies Act 1985 Sch 15B para 3(e) (as added and renumbered: see note 17 supra).
19 Insurance Companies Act 1982 s 49(3)(e) (amended by the Insurance Companies (Transfer of Long Term Business) Regulations 1990, SI 1990/1207).
20 Ie in arts 11, 12, 14, 16 of the second long term insurance directive, as to which see para 22 note 12 ante.
21 Insurance Companies Act 1982 s 49B(3) (as added and renumbered: see note 4 supra).
22 Ie in arts 11, 12, 14, 16 of the second long term insurance directive, as to which see para 22 note 12 ante.
23 Insurance Companies Act 1982 s 49B(4) (as added and renumbered: see note 4 supra)
24 Ibid s 49B(5) (as added and renumbered: see note 4 supra).
25 Ibid s 49B(6)(a), (b) (as added and renumbered: see note 4 supra).
26 Ibid s 49B(6) (as added and renumbered: see note 4 supra).

(iv) Changes in Management

832. Approval of proposed managing director or chief executive. No insurance company[1] may appoint a person as managing director or chief executive[2] of the company unless the company has served[3] on the Secretary of State[4] a written notice stating that it proposes to appoint that person to that position and containing prescribed particulars[5], and either the Secretary of State, before the expiration of the period of three months beginning with the date of service of that notice, has notified the company in writing that there is no objection to that person being appointed to that position or that period has elapsed without the Secretary of State having served on the company a written notice of objection[6].

The Secretary of State may serve a notice of objection on the ground that it appears to him that the person proposed to be appointed is not a fit and proper person to be appointed to the position in question[7]. Before serving such a notice, the Secretary of State must serve on the company and that person a preliminary written notice stating that he is considering the service of a notice of objection on that ground[7], and that within one month from the date of service of the preliminary notice the company and that person may make written representations to the Secretary of State and, if the company or that person so requests, oral representations to an officer of the Department of Trade and Industry appointed for the purpose by the Secretary of State[9]. Where representations are made, the Secretary of State must take them into consideration before serving the notice of objection[10].

1 Ie no insurance company to which the Insurance Companies Act 1982 Pt II (ss 15–71) (as amended) applies: see para 803 ante.
2 For the meaning of 'chief executive' see para 31 note 7 ante.
3 As to the Secretary of State see para 15 note 5 ante.
4 As to service of notices see generally para 865 post.
5 Insurance Companies Act 1982 s 60(1)(a). The particulars are prescribed by the Insurance Companies Regulations 1981, SI 1981/1654, reg 31, Sch 6 Forms A, C. The notice must also contain a statement signed by the person proposed to be appointed that it is served with his knowledge and consent: Insurance Companies Act 1982 s 60(2). In relation to an insurance company whose head office is in a member state of the European Community other than the United Kingdom, excluding a company whose business is restricted to reinsurance, s 60 has effect as if the references to a managing director or chief executive were to a principal United Kingdom executive: s 63(1)(a). In relation to any other insurance company whose head office is outside the United Kingdom, s 60 has effect as if the references to a chief executive included references to a principal United Kingdom executive: s 63(2)(a). 'Principal United kingdom executive' means an officer or employee within s 8(4)(b) or s 9(6): s 63(3). As to the prescribed particulars of a proposed principal United Kingdom executive see the Insurance Companies Regulations 1981 reg 31, Sch 6 Forms A, C.
6 Insurance Companies Act 1982 s 60(1)(b). Failure to comply with these provisions is an offence: s 71(3)(a); see para 866 post.
7 Ibid s 60(3).
8 Ibid s 60(3)(a). The Secretary of State is not obliged to disclose to the company or the proposed appointee any particulars of the ground on which he is considering the service on the company of a notice of objection: s 60(4).
9 Ibid s 60(3)(b).
10 Ibid s 60(5).

833. Approval of proposed controller. No person may become a controller[1] of an insurance company[2], otherwise than by virtue of an appointment as managing director or chief executive[3], unless he has served[4] on the Secretary of State[5] a written notice stating that he intends to become a controller of that company and containing prescribed particulars[6], and either the Secretary of State, before the expiration of the period of three months beginning with the date of service of that notice, has notified him in writing that there is no objection to his becoming a controller of the company or that period has elapsed without the Secretary of State having served on him a written notice of objection[7].

The Secretary of State may serve a notice of objection on the ground that it appears to him that the person concerned is not a fit and proper person to be a controller of the company[8]. Before serving such a notice, the Secretary of State must serve on that person a preliminary written notice stating that the Secretary of State is considering the service of a notice of objection on that ground[9], and that within a period of one month from the date of service of the preliminary notice that person may make written representations to the Secretary of State and, if that person so requests, oral representations to an officer of the Department of Trade and Industry[10] appointed for the purpose by the Secretary of State[11]. Where representations are made, the Secretary of State must take them into consideration before serving the notice of objection[12].

1 For the meaning of 'controller' see para 31 note 7 ante.
2 Ie an insurance company to which the Insurance Companies Act 1982 Pt II (ss 15–71) (as amended) applies: see para 803 ante.
3 Ie an appointment in relation to which ibid s 60 has effect: see para 832 ante.
4 As to service of notices see generally para 865 post.

5 As to the Secretary of State see para 15 note 5 ante.
6 Insurance Companies Act 1982 s 61(1)(a). Section 61 does not apply in relation to an insurance company whose head office is in a member state of the European Community other than the United Kingdom, excluding a company whose business in the United Kingdom is restricted to reinsurance: s 63(1). The particulars are prescribed by the Insurance Companies Regulations 1981, SI 1981/1654, reg 32, Sch 6 Forms B, C (amended by SI 1985/1419).
7 Insurance Companies Act 1982 s 61(1)(b). Failure to comply with these provisions is an offence: s 71(3); see para 866 post. A person is not guilty of such an offence, however, if he proves that he did not know that the acts or circumstances by virtue of which he became a controller of the body in question were such as to have that effect: s 71(5).
8 Ibid s 61(2). He may also serve a notice of objection under s 61(1) for the purposes of implementing any decision of the Council or Commission of the European Communities under art 29b(4) of the first general insurance directive or art 32b(4) of the first long term insurance directive: Insurance Companies Act 1982 s 61(2A) (added by the Insurance Companies (Amendment) Regulations 1992, SI 1992/2890). For the meaning of 'first general insurance directive' and 'first long term insurance directive' see para 22 note 12 ante.
9 Insurance Companies Act 1982 s 61(2)(a). The Secretary of State is not obliged to disclose to any person any particulars of the ground on which he is considering the service on him of a notice of objection: s 61(3).
10 As to the Department of Trade and Industry see para 15 note 5 ante.
11 Insurance Companies Act 1982 s 61(2)(b).
12 Ibid s 61(4).

834. Duty to notify change of director, controller or manager. A person who becomes or ceases to be a controller[1] of an insurance company[2] must, before the expiration of the period of seven days beginning with the day next following that on which he does so, notify the insurance company in writing of that fact and of such other matters as may be prescribed[3]. A person who becomes a director[4] or manager[5] of an insurance company[6] must, before the expiration of the period of seven days beginning with the day next following that on which he does so, notify the insurance company in writing of such matters as may be prescribed[7].

An insurance company[8] must give written notice to the Secretary of State[9] of the fact that any person has become or ceased to be a director, controller or manager of the company and of any matter of which any such person is required[10] to notify the company[11]. The notice must be given before the expiration of 14 days beginning with the day next following that on which that fact or matter comes to the company's knowledge[12].

A person resident or having its head office in a country or territory other than a member state of the European Community who becomes the parent undertaking of an insurance company[13] which has its head office in the United Kingdom must before the expiration of the period of 14 days beginning with the day next following that on which he becomes the parent undertaking notify the Secretary of State in writing of that fact[14].

1 For the meaning of 'controller' see para 31 note 7 ante.
2 Ie an insurance company to which the Insurance Companies Act 1982 Pt II (ss 15–71) (as amended) applies: see para 803 ante.
3 Ibid s 62(1). The other matters are prescribed by the Insurance Companies Regulations 1981, SI 1981/1654, reg 33, Sch 6 Form D. Failure to comply with this provision is an offence: Insurance Companies Act 1982 s 71(1)(a); see para 866 post. A person is not guilty of such an offence, however, if he proves that he did not know that the acts or circumstances by virtue of which he became or ceased to be a controller of the body in question were such as to have that effect: s 71(5). In relation to an insurance company whose head office is in a member state other than the United Kingdom, excluding a company whose business in the United Kingdom is restricted to reinsurance, s 62 has effect as if references to a director or manager were references to a principal United Kingdom executive, an employee with s 8(4)(c) or an authorised United Kingdom representative: s 63(1)(c). In

relation to any other insurance company whose head office is outside the United Kingdom, s 62 has effect as if the reference to a director includes references to a principal United Kingdom executive and to an authorised United Kingdom representative: s 63(2)(b). 'Authorised United Kingdom representative' means a representative fulfilling the requirements of s 10(5) (as amended) (see para 32 ante): s 63(3). As to the prescribed particulars for the purpose of s 62 when s 63 applies see the Insurance Companies Regulations 1981, SI 1981/1654, regs 34–36, Sch 6 Forms B–D (amended by SI 1985/1419).

4 'Director' includes any person occupying the position of director by whatever name called: Insurance Compnaies Act 1982 s 96(1).

5 For the meaning of 'manager' see para 31 note 8 ante.

6 See note 2 supra.

7 Insurance Companies Act 1982 s 62(1). The matters are prescribed by the Insurance Companies Regulations 1981 reg 35, Sch 6 Forms B–C (amended by SI 1985/1419) (person becoming director), and reg 36, Sch 6 Forms B–C (as so amended) (person becoming manager). Failure to comply with this provision is an offence: Insurance Companies Act 1982 s 71(1)(a); see para 866 post.

8 See note 2 supra.

9 As to the Secretary of State see para 15 note 5 ante.

10 Ie required under the Insurance Companies Act 1982 s 62(1): see supra.

11 Ibid s 62(2). Failure to comply with this provision is an offence: s 71(3)(a); see para 866 post.

12 Ibid s 62(2).

13 Ie an insurance company to which ibid Pt II (ss 15–71) (as amended) applies: see para 803 ante.

14 Ibid s 63A(1) (added by the Insurance Companies (Amendment) Regulations 1992, SI 1992/2890). This provision does not apply if the insurance company concerned is required to give notice to the Secretary of State in accordance with the Insurance Companies Act 1982 s 62(2) or is not authorised to carry on in any member state any insurance business other than reinsurance business: s 63A(2) (as so added).

835. Duty to notify change of main agent. An insurance company[1] must give written notice to the Secretary of State[2] of the fact that any person has become or ceased to be a main agent[3] of the company and, if a main agent is a body corporate or a firm, of the fact that any person has become or ceased to be a director of the body or partner of the firm[4]. Such notice must be given before the expiration of the period of 14 days beginning with the day next following that on which the change comes to the knowledge of the insurance company[5].

1 Ie an insurance company to which the Insurance Companies Act 1982 Pt II (ss 15–71) (as amended) applies: see para 803 ante.

2 As to the Secretary of State see para 15 note 5 ante.

3 For the meaning of 'main agent' see ibid s 7; and para 31 note 9 ante.

4 Ibid s 64(1).

5 Ibid s 64(2).

(3) ACCOUNTS AND STATEMENTS

(i) Accounts and Audit

836. Annual accounts and balance sheets. Every insurance company[1] must, with respect to each financial year[2] of the company, prepare a revenue account for the year, a balance sheet as at the end of the year and a profit and loss account for the year or, in the case of a company not trading for profit, an income and expenditure account of the year[3]. The contents of these documents must be such as may be prescribed[4], but regulations may provide for enabling information required to be given by the documents to be given instead in a note on them or statement or report annexed to them, or may require there to be given in such a note, statement or report such information in addition to that given in the documents as may be prescribed[5]. As respects such matters stated in the documents or in statements or reports annexed to them as may be prescribed, regulations may require certificates to be given by prescribed persons and to be annexed to the documents[6]. If a form is prescribed for any document or for the giving of information in a statement or report annexed to a document or for the annexing of a certificate, that form must be used[7].

An insurance company whose head office is not in a member state of the European Community must keep in the United Kingdom proper accounts and records in respect of insurance business[8] carried on in the United Kingdom[9].

1 Ie an insurance company to which the Insurance Companies Act 1982 Pt II (ss 15–71) (as amended) applies: see para 803 ante.
2 'Financial year' in general means each period of 12 months at the end of which the balance of the accounts of the insurance company is struck or, if no such balance is struck, the calendar year (ibid s 96(1)), but for the purposes of Pt II the Secretary of State may extend or shorten the duration of a company's financial year (s 69). As to the Secretary of State see para 15 note 5 ante.
3 Ibid s 17(1). Failure to comply with s 17, or with a requirement imposed under s 17, is an offence: see s 71(3)(a); and para 866 post. As to the Secretary of State's power to exclude or modify the application of s 17 in the case of a particular insurance company see para 803 ante.
4 Ibid s 17(2). 'Prescribed' means prescribed by regulations under that Act: s 96(1). See the Insurance Companies (Accounts and Statements) Regulations 1983, SI 1983/1811, regs 2, 4–22 (amended by SI 1990/1333; SI 1991/2736; and SI 1992/2890), 26, Schs 1, 2 (amended by SI 1990/1181; and SI 1991/2736), Sch 6 Pts I, II (amended by SI 1989/1962; and SI 1993/946).
5 Insurance Companies Act 1982 s 17(2).
6 Ibid s 17(3).
7 Ibid s 17(4).
8 For the meaning of 'insurance business' see para 18 ante.
9 Insurance Companies Act 1982 s 27. For the meaning of 'United Kingdom' see para 2 note 10 ante.

837. Audit of accounts. The accounts and balance sheets[1] of every insurance company[2] must be audited in the prescribed manner by a person of the prescribed description[3]. Regulations made for this purpose may apply the provisions relating to the audit of the accounts of companies under the Companies Acts[4], subject to such adaptations and modifications as may appear necessary or expedient[5].

1 This includes any statement or report annexed to those documents giving information authorised or required by virtue of the Insurance Companies Act 1982 s 17(2) (see para 836 ante): s 21(2).
2 Ie an insurance company to which ibid Pt II (ss 15–71) (as amended) applies: see para 803 ante.
3 Ibid s 21(1). As to the Secretary of State's power to exclude or modify the application of s 21 in the case of a particular insurance company see para 803 ante. For the meaning of 'prescribed' see para 836 note 4 ante. See the Insurance Companies (Accounts and Statements) Regulations 1983, SI 1983/1811, reg 27 (audit and auditor's report), reg 30 (qualifications of auditor).
4 As to these provisions see COMPANIES vol 7(1) (Reissue) para 894 et seq.
5 Insurance Companies Act 1982 s 21(1) (amended by the Companies Consolidation (Consequential Provisions) Act 1985 s 30, Sch 2; and the Companies Act 1989 (Eligibility for Appointment as Company Auditor) (Consequential Amendments) Regulations 1991, SI 1991/1997, reg 2, Schedule para 47). See the Insurance Companies (Accounts and Statements) Regulations 1983 (as amended).

838. Communication by auditor with Secretary of State. No duty to which an auditor of an insurance company[1] may be subject is to be regarded as contravened by reason of his communicating in good faith to the Secretary of State[2], whether or not in response to a request from him, any information or opinion on a matter of which the auditor has become aware in his capacity as auditor of that company and which is relevant to any functions of the Secretary of State under the Insurance Companies Act 1982[3].

If it appears to the Secretary of State that any auditor or class of auditor is not subject to satisfactory rules made or guidance issued by a professional body specifying circumstances in which matters are to be communicated to the Secretary of State, he may make regulations applying to that auditor or class of auditors and specifying such circumstances[4]. It is the duty of an auditor to whom the regulations apply to communicate a matter to the Secretary of State in the specified circumstances[5].

The matters to be communicated to the Secretary of State in accordance with any such rules or guidance or regulations may include matters relating to persons other than the company[6].

If it appears to the Secretary of State that an auditor has failed to comply with the above duty, he may disqualify him from being the auditor of an insurance company or any class of insurance company to which the Insurance Companies Act 1982 applies[7]. The Secretary of State may, however, remove any disqualification if he is satisfied that the person in question will in future comply with that duty[8].

An insurance company must not appoint as auditor a person disqualified under the above provisions[9].

1 Ie an insurance company to which the Insurance Companies Act 1982 Pt II (ss 15–71) (as amended) applies: see para 803 ante.
2 As to the Secretary of State see para 15 note 5 ante.
3 Insurance Companies Act 1982 s 21A(1) (added by the Financial Services Act 1986 s 135(1)).
4 Ibid s 21A(2) (as added: see note 3 supra). No regulations must be made unless a draft of them has been laid before and approved by a resolution of each House of Parliament: ibid s 21A(4) (as so added). For regulations so made see note 5 infra.
5 Ibid s 21A(2) (as added: see note 3 supra). See the Auditors (Insurance Companies Act 1982) Regulations 1994, SI 1994/449: matters are to be communicated to the Secretary of State where they are such as to give an auditor reasonable cause to believe that they are or may be of material significance for determining whether any of the powers of intervention conferred on the Secretary of State by the Insurance Companies Act 1982 ss 38–45 (as amended) (see paras 824 ante, 846 et seq post) should be exercised.
6 Ibid s 21A(3) (as added: see note 3 supra).
7 Ibid s 21A(5) (as added: see note 3 supra).
8 Ibid s 21A(5) (as added: see note 3 supra).
9 Ibid s 21A(6) (as added: see note 3 supra).

839. Separation of assets and liabilities attributable to long term business. Where an insurance company[1] carries on ordinary long term business or industrial assurance business or both of those kinds of insurance business[2], the company must maintain an account in respect of that business or, as the case may be, each of those kinds of business[3], and the receipts of that business or, as the case may be, each of those kinds of business must be entered in the account maintained for that business and must be carried to and form a separate insurance fund with an appropriate name[4]. The company must also maintain such accounting and other records as are necessary for identifying the assets representing the separate insurance fund or funds[5] maintained by the company[6] and the liabilities attributable to that business or, as the case may be, each of those kinds of business[7].

1 Ie an insurance company to which the Insurance Companies Act 1982 Pt II (ss 15–71) (as amended) applies: see para 803 ante.

2 As to ordinary long term insurance business and industrial assurance business see para 18 ante. As to the Secretary of State's power to direct that, for the purposes of the application of ibid s 28 (see infra) to any particular insurance company, certain business is to be treated as, or as not being, ordinary long term insurance business, see para 803 ante.

3 Ibid s 28(1)(a). Failure to comply with s 28 is an offence: see s 71(1)(a); and para 866 post. As to the Secretary of State's power to exclude or modify the application of s 28 in the case of a particular insurance company see para 803 ante.

4 Ibid s 28(1)(b). An insurance company which carries on long term business in the United Kingdom must secure that adequate arrangements are in force for securing that transactions affecting assets of the company (other than transactions outside its control) do not operate unfairly between the s 28 fund or funds and the other assets of the company or, in a case where the company has one or more than one identified fund, between those funds: s 31A (added by the Financial Services Act 1986 s 136(1)). For the meaning of 'United Kingdom' see para 2 note 10 ante.

5 If there is more than one fund, the record need not necessarily distinguish between them: Insurance Companies Act 1982 s 28(2)(a).

6 Ibid s 28(2)(a). See text and note 3 supra.

7 Ibid s 28(2)(b).

(ii) Annual, Periodic and Prescribed Statements

840. Annual statement. Every insurance company[1] which carries on business of a prescribed class[2] must prepare annually the prescribed statement of business of that class, being, if a form is prescribed for the statement, a statement in the prescribed form[3].

1 Ie an insurance company to which the Insurance Companies Act 1982 Pt II (ss 15–71) (as amended) applies: see para 803 ante.

2 Classes of insurance business may be prescribed for this purpose: ibid s 20. For the meaning of 'prescribed' see para 836 note 4 ante. See the Insurance Companies (Accounts and Statements) Regulations 1983, SI 1983/1811, reg 23. As to the Secretary of State's power to direct that for the purposes of the application of the Insurance Companies Act 1982 s 20 to any particular insurance company certain business is to be treated as, or as not being, ordinary long term insurance business, see para 803 ante.

3 Ibid s 20. Failure to comply with s 20, or with a requirement imposed under s 20, is an offence: see s 71(3)(a); and para 866 post. As to the Secretary of State's power to exclude or modify the application of s 20 in the case of a particular insurance company see para 803 ante. As to the statements to be prepared and the forms prescribed for those statements see the Insurance Companies (Accounts and Statements) Regulations 1983 regs 8–14 (amended by SI 1990/1333), Sch 3.

841. Periodic statement. Every insurance company[1] which carries on business of a prescribed[2] class or description must prepare, at such intervals and for such periods as may be prescribed[2], a statement of its business of that class or description[3]. Regulations may require certificates relating to prescribed[4] matters in the statement to be given by prescribed[4] persons and to be annexed to the statement[5]. Five copies[6] of the statement with any certificate annexed must be deposited by the company with the Secretary of State within the prescribed period[7].

1 Ie an insurance company to which the Insurance Companies Act 1982 Pt II (ss 15–71) (as amended) applies: see para 803 ante.

2 For the meaning of 'prescribed' see para 836 note 4 ante. At the date at which this volume states the law no regulations had been made for this purpose.

3 Insurance Companies Act 1982 s 25(1). The form and contents of the statement are such as may be prescribed: s 25(2); and see note 2 supra. Failure to comply with s 25 or with a requirement imposed under s 25 is an offence: see s 71(3)(a); and para 866 post. As to the Secretary of State's power to exclude or modify the application of s 25 in the case of a particular insurance company see para 803 ante.

4 See note 2 supra.
5 Insurance Companies Act 1982 s 25(3).
6 One of the copies must be a copy signed by the persons required to sign copies of statements under ibid s 20 (see para 840 ante): s 25(4).
7 Ibid s 25(4). As to the Secretary of State see para 15 note 5 ante. The Secretary of State may require a statement to be deposited with him before the end of the prescribed period: s 43(2). As to the publication of the statement by the Secretary of State see para 845 post. The inclusion of a false statement in any document deposited under s 25(4) is an offence: see s 71(1)(c)(iii), (4)(a); and para 866 post.

842. Statement as to undesirable agreement or arrangement. Classes or descriptions of agreements or arrangements appearing to the Secretary of State as likely to be undesirable in the interests of policyholders[1] may be prescribed[2]. Every insurance company[3] or subordinate company[4] of any such company which enters into an agreement or arrangement of a class or description so prescribed must, within such period as may be prescribed[5], furnish the Secretary of State with a statement containing such particulars of that agreement or arrangement as may be prescribed[6].

1 For the meaning of 'policyholder' see para 806 note 21 ante.
2 Insurance Companies Act 1982 s 26(1). Different classes or descriptions of agreements or arrangements may be prescribed in relation to companies of different classes or descriptions: s 26(2). As to the Secretary of State see para 15 note 5 ante. For the meaning of 'prescribed' see para 836 note 4 ante. At the date at which this volume states the law no regulations had been made for the purposes of s 26.
3 Ie an insurance company to which ibid Pt II (ss 15–71) (as amended) applies: see para 803 ante.
4 Ie a subordinate company within the meaning of ibid s 31: see s 26(1); and para 821 note 3 ante.
5 See note 2 supra.
6 Insurance Companies Act 1982 s 26(1). As to the Secretary of State's power to exclude or modify the application of s 26 in the case of a particular insurance company see para 803 ante. As to the publication of the statement by the Secretary of State see para 845 post. Failure to comply with s 26 is an offence, as is the inclusion of a false statement in any statement furnished under s 26(1): see s 71(1)(c)(ii), (3)(b); and para 866 post.

(iii) Deposit of Accounts: Copies and Publication

843. Deposit of accounts with Secretary of State. Every account[1], balance sheet[2], abstract or statement required[3] to be prepared by an insurance company and any report of the company's auditor[4] must be printed, and five copies must be deposited with the Secretary of State[5] within six months after the close of the period to which the account, balance sheet, abstract, statement or report relates[6], together with five printed copies of a statement of the names and connection with the company of any persons who, during the period to which the documents relate: (1) were authorised by the company to issue, or to the knowledge of the company have issued, an invitation to another person to make an offer or proposal or to take any other step with a view to entering into a contract of insurance with the company[7]; and (2) were connected with[8] the company[9]. There must also be deposited with every revenue account and balance sheet of a company any report on the company's affairs submitted to the company's shareholders or policyholders[10] in respect of the financial year[11] to which the account and balance sheet relate[12].

One of the copies of any document deposited under these provisions, except an auditor's report, must be signed by such persons as may be prescribed[13]. In the case of an auditor's report, one of the copies must be signed by the auditor[14].

The Secretary of State must consider the documents which have been deposited, and if any document appears to him to be inaccurate or incomplete in any respect he must communicate with the company with a view to the correction of any inaccuracies and the supply of deficiencies[15].

1 This includes any statement or report annexed to an account giving information authorised or required by virtue of the Insurance Companies Act 1982 s 17(2) (see para 836 ante) to be so given and any certificate so annexed by virtue of s 17(3) (see para 836 ante): s 22(7).

2 This includes any statement or report annexed to a balance sheet giving information authorised or required by virtue of ibid s 17(2) (see para 836 ante) to be so given and any certificate so annexed by virtue of s 17(3) (see para 836 ante): s 22(7).

3 Ie required by ibid ss 17 (see para 836 ante), 18 (see para 823 ante), 20 (see para 840 ante).

4 Ie a report made in pursuance of ibid s 21 (as amended) (see para 837 ante).

5 As to the Secretary of State see para 15 note 5 ante.

6 Insurance Companies Act 1982 s 22(1). If in any case it is made to appear to the Secretary of State that the circumstances are such that a longer period than six months should be allowed, he may extend that period by such period not exceeding three months as he thinks fit: s 22(1). The Secretary of State may require any documents which under s 22 are required to be deposited by a company within a specified period to be deposited with him on or before a specified date before the end of that period, being a date not earlier than three months before the end of that period and not earlier than one month after the date on which the requirement is imposed: s 43(1). As to the Secretary of State's power to exclude or modify the application of s 22 in the case of a particular insurance company see para 803 ante.

   Failure to comply with s 22 is an offence, as is the inclusion of a false statement in any document required to be deposited: see s 71(1)(c)(i), (3)(a), (4)(a); and para 866 post.

7 Ibid s 22(2)(a). As to the statutory requirements in connection with such an invitation see s 74; and para 813 ante.

8 Ie connected with the company as provided by regulations under ibid s 74: see para 813 ante.

9 Ibid s 22(2)(b). For further requirements as to the deposit of accounts etc by a registered industrial and provident society see s 24; and INDUSTRIAL AND PROVIDENT SOCIETIES vol 24 (Reissue) para 13 note 2.

10 For the meaning of 'policyholder' see para 806 note 21 ante.

11 For the meaning of 'financial year' see para 836 note 2 ante.

12 Insurance Companies Act 1982 s 22(6).

13 Ibid s 22(3). For the meaning of 'prescribed' see para 836 note 4 ante. As to the persons prescribed see the Insurance Companies (Accounts and Statements) Regulations 1983, SI 1983/1811, regs 2, 25.

14 Insurance Companies Act 1982 s 22(4).

15 Ibid s 22(5). As to the deposit with the registrar of companies of any document deposited under s 22, and the right of any person to inspect the document, see s 65; and para 845 post.

844. Right of shareholders and policyholders to copies. An insurance company[1] must forward by post or otherwise to any shareholder or policyholder[2] who applies for one: (1) a printed copy of any of the documents last deposited with the Secretary of State[3]; (2) a copy of any document supplied to the Secretary of State with a view to the correction of any inaccuracies or the supply of any deficiencies in the documents originally deposited[4]; and (3) a copy of any report on the company's affairs for the financial year deposited with a revenue account and balance sheet[5].

If, in the opinion of the Secretary of State, the disclosure of information contained in a statement or report annexed to the accounts and balance sheets[6], or in the annual statement relating to the company's classes of business[7], would be harmful to the company's business, he may dispense the company from complying with the obligation to forward a copy of the document containing the information to a shareholder or policyholder who applies for it[8].

1 For the meaning of 'insurance company' see para 15 note 3 ante.

2 For the meaning of 'policyholder' see para 806 note 21 ante.
3 Insurance Companies Act 1982 s 23(1)(a). As to the Secretary of State see para 15 note 5 ante. As to the documents to be deposited with the Secretary of State see para 843 ante.
4 Ibid s 23(1)(b). As to the correction of deposited documents see para 843 ante.
5 Ibid s 23(1)(c). As to the deposit of this report see para 843 ante. Failure to comply with s 23(1) is an offence: see s 71(3)(a); and para 866 post. As to the Secretary of State's power to exclude or modify the application of s 23(1) in the case of a particular insurance company see para 803 ante.
6 Ie annexed to a document prepared in pursuance of ibid s 17(1): see para 836 ante.
7 Ie a statement prepared in pursuance of ibid s 20: see para 840 ante.
8 Ibid s 23(2).

845. Deposit of documents with registrar of companies; publication and inspection.

The Secretary of State[1] must deposit with the registrar of companies[2] one copy of: (1) any account, balance sheet, abstract of actuarial investigation, statement of business or auditor's report which is deposited[3] with the Secretary of State[4]; (2) any abstract of actuarial investigation or statement of business made and deposited[5] with the Secretary of State in pursuance of a requirement by him[6]; and (3) any court order sanctioning a scheme of transfer of long term business which is deposited[7] with him[8].

The Secretary of State may deposit with the registrar of companies and publish in such ways as he thinks appropriate (a) the whole or any part of any periodic statement made by a company with respect to its business of a prescribed class or description[9], and any certificate annexed to that statement[10], which has been deposited with him[11], and (b) the whole or any part of any statement with respect to undesirable transactions[12] which has been furnished to him[13].

Unless a dispensation has been granted in respect of it[14], any document deposited under the above provisions with the registrar of companies is to be open to inspection and copies of it may be procured by any person on payment of such fees as the Secretary of State may direct[15].

1 As to the Secretary of State see para 15 note 5 ante.
2 'Registrar of companies' has the meaning given in the Companies Act 1985 s 744 (see COMPANIES vol 7(1) (Reissue) para 60 note 2): Insurance Companies Act 1982 s 96(1).
3 Ie deposited under ibid s 22: see para 843 ante.
4 Ibid s 65(1)(a). This includes any document obtained with a view to the correction of inaccuracies (ie under s 22(5): see para 843 ante): s 65(1)(a).
5 Ie deposited under ibid s 42(4): see para 824 ante.
6 Ibid s 65(1)(b).
7 Ie deposited under ibid s 50(4): see para 827 ante.
8 Ibid s 65(1)(b).
9 As to the deposit of such a statement see para 843 ante.
10 As to the deposit of such a certificate see para 843 ante.
11 Insurance Companies Act 1982 s 25(5).
12 As to the making of such statements see para 842 ante.
13 Insurance Companies Act 1982 s 26(3).
14 Ie a dispensation granted under ibid s 23(2), where the disclosure of information may harm the company's business: s 65(3). See para 844 ante.
15 Ibid s 65(2). Every document deposited with the Secretary of State under Pt II (ss 15–71) (as amended) and certified by the registrar of companies to be a document so deposited is deemed to be a document so deposited, and every document purporting to be certified by the registrar of companies to be a copy of a document so deposited is deemed to be a copy of that document and is to be received in evidence as if it were the original document unless some variation between it and the original is proved: s 65(4).

(4) INTERVENTION BY SECRETARY OF STATE

(i) In general

846. Secretary of State's powers. The Secretary of State[1] has extensive powers to intervene in certain circumstances in the affairs of an insurance company[2] to which Part II of the Insurance Companies Act 1982[3] applies[4]. On specified grounds he may require an insurance company to make or realise certain investments[5], limit premium income[6], maintain assets in the United Kingdom[7] and place them in the custody of a trustee[8], carry out actuarial investigations[9], supply information and produce documents[10], and accelerate the supply of information required by the accounting provisions of the Act[11]. He may take action for the protection of policyholders[12], and bring civil proceedings on behalf of an insurance company[13].

1 As to the Secretary of State see para 15 note 5 ante.
2 For the meaning of 'insurance company' see para 15 note 3 ante.
3 Ie the Insurance Companies Act 1982 ss 15–71 (as amended): see para 803 ante.
4 See ibid ss 37–48 (as amended). Any requirement imposed under ss 29–37 (as amended) may be rescinded by the Secretary of State if it appears to him that it is no longer necessary for it to remain in force and may be from time to time varied (s 47(1)), but no requirement imposed under s 37(5) (see para 848 text to note 24 post) may be varied after the expiration of the period of five years except in a manner which relaxes that requirement (s 47(2)).
5 See ibid s 38; and para 850 post.
6 See ibid s 41; and para 852 post.
7 See ibid s 39; and para 853 post. For the meaning of 'United Kingdom' see para 2 note 10 ante.
8 See ibid s 40; and para 853 post.
9 See ibid s 42; and para 824 ante.
10 See ibid s 44 (as amended); and para 854 post.
11 See ibid s 43; and paras 841 note 7, 843 note 6 ante.
12 See ibid s 45; and para 847 post.
13 See ibid s 48 (as amended); and para 864 post.

847. Residual power to impose requirements for protection of policyholders. The Secretary of State[1] may require a company to take such action as appears to him to be appropriate for the purpose of protecting policyholders[2] or potential policyholders of the company against the risk that the company may be unable to meet its liabilities or, in the case of long term business[3], to fulfil the reasonable expectations of policyholders or potential policyholders[4].

1 As to the Secretary of State see para 15 note 5 ante.
2 For the meaning of 'policyholder' see para 806 note 21 ante.
3 For the meaning of 'long term business' see para 18 ante.
4 Insurance Companies Act 1982 s 45(1). Except in defined circumstances (see s 45(2)(a)–(c)), this power must not be exercised in such a way as to restrict the company's freedom to dispose of its assets: s 45(2). Any insurance company and any other person who makes default in complying with, or with a requirement imposed under, s 45 is guilty of an offence: see s 71(3); and para 866 post.

848. Grounds on which powers of intervention are exercisable. Any statutory power of the Secretary of State[1] is exercisable in relation to any insurance company[2] to which Part II of the Insurance Companies Act 1982[3] applies on any of the following grounds:
   (1) that the Secretary of State considers the exercise of the power to be desirable for protecting policyholders[4] or potential policyholders of the company

against the risk that the company may be unable to meet its liabilities or, in the case of long term business[5], to fulfil the reasonable expectations of policyholders[6];

(2) that it appears to him:

 (a) that the company has failed to satisfy statutory obligations[7];

 (b) that it has failed to satisfy an obligation to which it is subject by virtue of any provision of the law of another member state of the European Community giving effect to the general or long term insurance directives[8]; or

 (c) that a company of which it is a subsidiary has failed to satisfy an obligation with respect to the declaration of dividends[9]; or

 (d) that a subordinate company[10] of the company has failed to satisfy an obligation with respect to restrictions on transactions with connected persons[11] or the furnishing of statements with respect to undesirable transactions[12];

(3) that it appears to him that the company has furnished misleading or inaccurate information to him[13];

(4) that he is not satisfied that adequate arrangements are in force or will be made for the reinsurance of risks against which persons are insured by the company in the course of carrying on business, being risks of a class in the case of which he considers that such arrangements are required[14];

(5) that there exists a ground on which he would be prohibited, by the provisions with respect to companies under the control of unfit persons[15], from issuing an authorisation with respect to the company if it were applied for[16];

(6) that it appears to him that there has been a substantial departure from any proposal or forecast submitted to him by the company[17];

(7) that the company has ceased to be authorised to effect contracts of insurance, or contracts of a particular description, in a member state where it has its head office or has made a deposit[18].

The Secretary of State's power to require any insurance company to produce documents[19] is also exercisable on the ground that he considers the exercise of that power to be in the general interests of persons who are or may become policyholders of insurance companies[20].

Any power of the Secretary of State, other than a power to require an insurance company to deposit documents or statements earlier than would otherwise be required, or to produce documents[21], is also exercisable, whether or not any of the above grounds exist, in relation to any body authorised by the Secretary of State to carry on insurance business[22] and any insurance company in the case of which a person has become a controller[23]. This power must, however, be exercised before the expiration of five years beginning with the date on which the authorisation was issued, or that person became a controller, and no requirement imposed continues in force after the expiration of ten years beginning with that date[24].

When exercising any power, the Secretary of State must state the ground on which he is exercising it or, if he is exercising it by virtue of the last-mentioned provision[25], that he is so exercising it[26].

The powers conferred on the Secretary of State relating to the maintenance of assets in the United Kingdom[27] and the custody of assets[28] are not exercisable in relation to an insurance company:

 (i) where he has given (and not revoked) a direction[29] concerning the withdrawal of authorisation in respect of new business[30]; or

(ii) on the ground that it appears to him that the company has failed to satisfy obligations relating to the maintenance of the margin of solvency[31], the security of the assets supervised in other member states[32] or the form and situation[33] of assets[34]; or

(iii) on the ground that a submission by the company to him of an account or statement specifies, as the amount of any liabilities of the company, an amount appearing to him to have been determined otherwise than in accordance with valuation regulations[35] or, where no such regulations are applicable, generally accepted accounting concepts, bases and policies or other generally accepted methods appropriate for insurance companies[36].

1 Ie a power conferred by the Insurance Companies Act 1982 ss 38–45 (as amended) (see paras 824, 846–847 ante, 850, 852–855 post): s 37(1). As to the Secretary of State see para 15 note 5 ante.
2 For the meaning of 'insurance company' see para 15 note 3 ante.
3 Ie the Insurance Companies Act 1982 ss 15–71 (as amended): see para 803 ante.
4 For the meaning of 'policyholder' see para 806 note 21 ante.
5 For the meaning of 'long term business' see para 18 ante.
6 Insurance Companies Act 1982 s 37(2)(a).
7 Ie any obligation to which the company is subject under the Insurance Companies Act 1982 or any enactment repealed by it: s 37(2)(b)(i). The grounds specified in s 37(2)(b)–(g) (as amended) are without prejudice to that in s 37(2)(a) or (4): s 37(8).
8 Ibid s 37(2)(b)(ia) (added by the Insurance Companies (Amendment) Regulations 1990, SI 1990/1333, reg 8(2); amended by the Insurance Companies (Amendment) Regulations 1993, SI 1993/174, reg 2). As to the general and long term insurance directives see the Insurance Companies Act 1982 s 96A(1), (1A), (1B) (as added and amended); and para 22 note 12 ante.
9 Ie under ibid s 29(7) or the Insurance Companies Act 1974 s 24(6) (repealed) or the Insurance Companies Amendment Act 1973 s 8(6) (repealed): Insurance Companies Act 1982 s 37(2)(b)(ii).
10 Ie a subordinate company within the meaning of ibid s 31: see para 821 note 3 ante.
11 Ie an obligation under ibid s 31 or s 26 (see para 821 ante) or under the Insurance Companies Act 1974 s 22 or s 26 (repealed) or the Insurance Companies Amendment Act 1973 s 6 or s 10 (repealed).
12 Insurance Companies Act 1982 s 37(2)(b)(iii). As to statements with respect to undesirable transactions see s 26; and para 842 ante.
13 Ibid s 37(2)(c).
14 Ibid s 37(2)(d).
15 Ie by ibid s 7 (as amended), s 8 or s 9: see paras 31–33 ante.
16 Ibid s 37(2)(e).
17 Ibid s 37(2)(f).
18 Ibid s 37(2)(g).
19 Ie ibid s 44(2)–(4) (as amended) (see para 854 post): s 37(4).
20 Ibid s 37(4).
21 Ie any power under ibid ss 38, 41, 42, 44(1) or 45: s 37(5).
22 Ie authorised under ibid s 3 (see para 342 ante): s 37(5)(a).
23 Ie within the meaning of ibid s 7(4)(c) (see para 31 ante): s 37(5)(b).
24 Ibid s 37(5). See further para 846 note 4 ante.
25 Ie by virtue of ibid s 37(5): see text to notes 21–24 supra.
26 Ibid s 37(7). This does not apply when notice has been given under s 46 (see para 849 post): s 37(7).
27 Ie required by ibid s 39: see para 853 post.
28 Ie required by ibid s 40: see para 853 post.
29 Ie under ibid s 11 or the Insurance Companies Act 1981 s 11 (repealed): see para 34 ante.
30 Insurance Companies Act 1982 s 37(3)(a).
31 Ie required by ibid s 33 or the Insurance Companies Act 1974 s 26B (repealed): see para 857 post.
32 Ie required by the Insurance Companies Act 1982 s 34 or the Insurance Companies Act 1974 s 26C (repealed): see para 857 post.
33 Ie required by the Insurance Companies Act 1982 s 35 or the Insurance Companies Act 1974 s 26D (repealed): see para 857 post.
34 Insurance Companies Act 1982 s 37(3)(b).
35 For the meaning of 'valuation regulations' see para 863 post.
36 Insurance Companies Act 1982 s 37(3)(c).

849. Notice of proposed exercise of powers on grounds of unfitness. Before exercising with respect to a company any power conferred by certain provisions[1] on the ground that he would be prohibited from issuing an authorisation to the company because of the unfitness of a person for the position (not being that of controller[2] of the company), the Secretary of State[3] must serve on that person a written notice[4]. The notice must state (1) that the Secretary of State is considering exercising a power and the ground on which he is considering exercising the power[5], and (2) that the person served may, within one month, make written representations to the Secretary of State and, if that person so requests, oral representations to an officer of the Department of Trade and Industry appointed for the purpose by the Secretary of State[6]. After considering any representations, unless the Secretary of State decides not to exercise the power, he must, before exercising it, serve on the company a written notice containing similar particulars to those required for the notice to the person whose fitness is in question[7] and specifying the power which the Secretary of State proposes to exercise, and, if the power is the residual power[8], specifying the manner in which he proposes to exercise it[9]. A requirement imposed on a company may be framed so as to come into effect after the expiration of a specified period, or such longer period as the Secretary of State may allow, unless before the expiration of that period the person whose fitness is in question has ceased to hold the position concerned[10].

Where representations are made, the Secretary of State must take them into consideration before exercising the power in question[11].

1 Ie the Insurance Companies Act 1982 ss 38–45 (as amended). See paras 824, 846–847 ante, 850, 852–855 post).
2 For the meaning of 'controller' see para 31 note 7 ante.
3 As to the Secretary of State see para 15 note 5 ante.
4 Insurance Companies Act 1982 s 46(1).
5 Ibid s 46(1)(a). Particulars of the ground must be given: s 46(3).
6 Ibid s 46(1)(b).
7 Ibid s 46(2)(a).
8 Ie under ibid s 45 (see para 847 ante): s 46(2)(b).
9 Ibid s 46(2)(b).
10 Ibid s 46(5).
11 Ibid s 46(4).

(ii) Investments: Contracts: Premium Income

850. Requirements as to investments. The Secretary of State[1] may require a company (1) not to make investments of a specified class or description[2], and (2) to realise, before the expiration of a specified period (or such longer period as he may allow), the whole or a specified proportion of investments of a specified class or description held by the company when the requirement is imposed[3].

1 As to the Secretary of State see para 15 note 5 ante.
2 Insurance Companies Act 1982 s 38(1)(a).
3 Ibid s 38(1)(b). A requirement under s 38 may be framed so as to apply only to investments which are (or, if made, would be) assets representing a fund or funds maintained by the company in respect of its long term business or so as to apply only to other investments: s 38(2). A requirement does not apply to the assets of a company so far as their value exceeds: (1) in the case of a company whose head office is in a member state of the European Community other than the United Kingdom, or which has made a deposit in accordance with s 9(2) (see para 33 ante), the amount of the liabilities of the business of the company carried on in the United Kingdom; (2) in any other case, the amount of the company's liabilities, that value and amount being determined in accordance with any applicable

valuation regulations: s 38(3). As to valuation regulations see para 863 post. For the meaning of 'United Kingdom' see para 2 note 10 ante.

Any insurance company and any other person who makes default in complying with or with a requirement under s 38 is guilty of an offence: see s 71(3); and para 866 post.

851. Avoidance of contracts for unlimited amounts. A contract entered into after the coming into force of the relevant statutory provisions[1] by an insurance company[2] is void if (1) it is a contract under which the company undertakes a liability the amount, or maximum amount, of which is uncertain at the time when the contract is entered into[3], and (2) it is not a contract of insurance[4] or a contract of a class or description exempted by regulations[5].

1 Ie after the coming into force of the Insurance Companies Act 1982 s 36. Section 36 is not to take effect until the first regulations under it (see text to note 5 infra) come into operation: s 99(1), Sch 4 para 6 (amended by the Statute Law (Repeals) Act 1993 s 1(1), Sch 1 Pt V). At the date at which this volume states the law, no such regulations had been made.
2 Ie an insurance company to which the Insurance Companies Act 1982 Pt II (ss 15–71) (as amended) applies: see para 803 ante.
3 Ibid s 36(a).
4 'Contract of insurance' includes a contract to pay an annuity on human life: ibid ss 96(1), 95(d).
5 Ibid s 36(b). As to the regulations see note 1 supra.

852. Premium income. The Secretary of State[1] may require a company to take all such steps as are requisite to secure that the aggregate of the premiums to be received by the company (1) in consideration of the undertaking by it during a specified period of liabilities in the course of carrying on general business[2] or any specified part of such business[3], or (2) in a specified period in consideration of the undertaking by the company during that period of liabilities in the course of carrying on long term business[4] or any specified part of such business, must not exceed a specified amount[5].

1 As to the Secretary of State see para 15 note 5 ante.
2 For the meaning of 'general business' see para 18 ante.
3 Insurance Companies Act 1982 s 41(1)(a).
4 For the meaning of 'long term business' see para 18 ante.
5 Insurance Companies Act 1982 s 41(1)(b). The power conferred on the Secretary of State by s 41 is exercisable in relation to the members of Lloyd's if there is a breach of an obligation imposed under s 84(1) (see para 22 ante): s 84(2). A requirement under s 41 may apply either to the aggregate premiums to be received or the aggregate of those premiums after deducting reinsurance premiums: s 41(2). Any insurance company and any other person who makes default in complying with, or with a requirement under, s 41 is guilty of an offence: see s 71(3); and para 866 post.

(iii) Assets

853. Maintenance of assets in the United Kingdom; custody of assets. The Secretary of State[1] may require that assets of a company of a value which at any time is equal to the whole or a specified proportion of the amount of its domestic liabilities[2] must be maintained in the United Kingdom[3]. Where such a requirement has been imposed, the Secretary of State may require that the whole or a specified proportion of the assets to be maintained in the United Kingdom must be held by a person approved by him as trustee for the company[4]. Assets so held by a trustee may not be released except with the consent of the Secretary of State[5]. A mortgage or charge created by the company conferring a security on any assets so held by a trustee, to the extent that it confers such a security, is void against the liquidator and any creditor of the company[6].

1 As to the Secretary of State see para 15 note 5 ante.
2 'Domestic liability' is a reference to a liability of the business carried on by the company in the United Kingdom: Insurance Companies Act 1982 s 39(5). For the meaning of 'United Kingdom' see para 2 note 10 ante. The Secretary of State may direct that the domestic liabilities of a company, or such liabilities of any class or description, are to be taken to be the net liabilities after deducting any part of them which is reinsured: s 39(3).
3 Ibid s 39(1). The powers conferred on the Secretary of State by s 39 are exercisable in relation to the members of Lloyd's if there is a breach of an obligation imposed by s 84(1) (see para 22 ante): s 84(2). The Secretary of State may direct that assets of a specified class or description are or are not to be treated as assets maintained in the United Kingdom: s 39(2). A requirement may be framed so as to come into effect immediately after the day on which it is imposed or so as to come into effect after the expiration of a specified period (or such longer period as the Secretary of State may allow): s 39(4).
   Subject to s 39(7), in computing the amount of any liabilities all contingent and prospective liabilities must be taken into account, but not liabilities in respect of share capital: s 39(6). The value of any assets and the amount of any liabilities must be determined in accordance with any applicable valuation regulations (see para 863 post); and s 39(6) has effect subject to any such regulations made under s 90(2) (see para 863 post): s 39(7). See the Insurance Companies Regulations 1981, SI 1981/1645, Pt V (regs 37–49) (amended by SI 1985/1419; SI 1988/673; and SI 1992/445). Any insurance company and any other person who makes default in complying with, or with a requirement under, the Insurance Companies Act 1982 s 39 is guilty of an offence: see s 71(3); and para 866 post. Where a requirement under s 40 (see text and notes 4–6 infra) is imposed, rescinded or varied under s 47(1), the Secretary of State must serve:
   (1) if the requirement is imposed on a registered society (other than one registered in Northern Ireland) (ie a society registered or deemed to be registered under the Industrial and Provident Societies Act 1965 (see INDUSTRIAL AND PROVIDENT SOCIETIES vol 24 (Reissue) para 16 et seq): Insurance Companies Act 1982 s 96(1)), on the appropriate registrar (as defined in the Industrial and Provident Societies Act 1965 s 73(1): see INDUSTRIAL AND PROVIDENT SOCIETIES vol 24 (Reissue) para 16); or
   (2) in any other case, on the registrar of companies,
   a written notice stating that fact and, where a requirement is imposed, setting out its terms, where it is rescinded, identifying the requirement or, where it is varied, identifying the requirement and setting out the terms of the variation: Insurance Companies Act 1982 s 47(3). The notice must be open to inspection and a copy may be procured by any person on payment of such fee as the Secretary of State may direct: s 47(4). Every document purporting to be certified by the registrar of companies to be such a copy is deemed to be such a copy and must be received in evidence as if it were the original unless some variation between it and the original is proved: s 47(4).
4 Ibid s 40(1). The powers conferred on the Secretary of State by s 40 are exercisable in relation to the members of Lloyd's if there is a breach of an obligation imposed by s 84(1) (see para 22 ante): s 84(2). A requirement may be framed so as to come into effect immediately after the day on which it is imposed or so as to come into effect after the expiration of a specified period (or such longer period as the Secretary of State may allow): ss 39(4), 40(2). Any insurance company and any other person who makes default in complying with, or with a requirement under, s 40 is guilty of an offence: see s 71(3); and para 866 post. Assets of a company held by a person as trustee for a company are to be taken to be held by him in compliance with a requirement imposed under s 40 if, and only if, they are assets in whose case the company has given him written notice that they are to be held by him in compliance with such a requirement or they are assets into which assets in whose case the company has given him such written notice have, by any transaction or series of transactions, been transposed by him on the instructions of the company: s 40(3).
5 Ibid s 40(4).
6 Ibid s 40(5).

(iv) Information and Production of Documents

854. Secretary of State's powers. The Secretary of State[1] may require a company to furnish him, at specified times or intervals, with information about specified matters being, if he so requires, information verified in a specified manner[2].

He may also require a company[3] to produce, at such time and place as he may specify, such documents[4] as he may specify[5], or authorise any person, on producing (if required so to do) evidence of his authority, to require a company to produce to him forthwith any documents which that person may specify[6]. The Secretary of State, or any person authorised by him, has the like power to require production of those documents from any person who appears to be in possession of them[7]. The power includes power, if the documents are produced, to take copies and extracts[8] and require certain persons[9] to provide an explanation of any of them[10], and, if the books or papers are not produced, to require the person who was required to produce them to state, to the best of his knowledge and belief, where they are[11].

A warrant for the entry and search of premises may be issued where the above provisions are not complied with[12]. A requirement under these provisions may not compel the production by any person of a document which he would in an action in the High Court be entitled to refuse to produce on grounds of legal professional privilege or authorise the taking of possession of any such document which is in his possession[13].

The powers conferred on the Secretary of State are also exercisable in relation to the members of Lloyd's[14].

1 As to the Secretary of State see para 15 note 5 ante.
2 Insurance Companies Act 1982 s 44(1). Any person who, in purported compliance with a requirement imposed under s 44, furnishes information which he knows to be false in a material particular or recklessly furnishes information which is false in a material particular, is guilty of an offence: see s 71(1)(b); and para 866 post. Any insurance company and any other person who makes default in complying with, or with a requirement under, s 44 is guilty of an offence: see s 71(3); and para 866 post. Where a person is charged with an offence in respect of his default in complying with a requirement imposed under s 44(2) or (3) (as amended) (see infra) to produce any documents, it is a defence to prove that they were not in his possession or control and that it was not reasonably practicable for him to comply with the requirement: s 71(6).
3 References in ibid s 44(2)–(4) (as amended) to a company include references to any body (whether incorporated or not) which appears to the Secretary of State to be an insurance company to which Pt II (ss 15–71) (as amended) applies: s 37(4).
4 'Document' includes information recorded in any form; and, in relation to information recorded otherwise than in legible form, the power to require its production includes power to require the production of a copy of the information in legible form: s 44(6) (substituted by the Companies Act 1989 s 77(1), (2)).
5 Insurance Companies Act 1982 s 44(2)(a) (amended by the Companies Act 1989 s 77(2)). As to offences see note 2 supra.
6 Insurance Companies Act 1982 s 44(2)(b) (as amended: see note 5 supra). No information relating to the business or other affairs of any person which has been obtained under s 44(2)–(4) (as amended) must be disclosed without the consent of the person from whom the information was obtained and, if different, the person to whom it relates: s 47A(1) (added by the Companies Consolidation (Consequential Provisions) Act 1985 s 25; substituted by the Financial Services Act 1986 s 182, Sch 13 para 6). This does not preclude the disclosure of information to any person who is a competent authority for the purposes of the Companies Act 1985 s 449 (as amended) (see COMPANIES vol 7(2) (Reissue) para 1215): Insurance Companies Act 1982 s 47A(2) (as so added and substituted). Nor does it preclude the disclosure of information (1) as mentioned in the Financial Services Act 1986 s 180(1), (3) or (4) (as amended) except s 180(1)(m); or (2) as mentioned in s 180(5) by any person who is by virtue of s 180 (as amended) not precluded by s 179 (as amended) from disclosing it (see MONEY); or (3) as mentioned in the Companies Act 1985 s 449(1) (as amended): Insurance Companies Act 1982 s 47A(2A), (2B) (added by the Financial Services Act 1986 Sch 13 para 6). Contravention of the Insurance Companies Act 1982 s 47A (as so added) is an offence: s 71(4A) (added by the Companies Consolidation (Consequential Provisions) Act 1985 s 30, Sch 2); see para 866 post.

7 Insurance Companies Act 1982 s 44(3) (as amended: see note 5 supra). Where any person from whom such production is required claims a lien on documents produced by him, the production must be without prejudice to the lien: s 44(3) (as so amended). As to offences see note 2 supra.

8 Ibid s 44(4)(a)(i) (as amended: see note 5 supra).

9 Ie the person producing them, or any present or past director, controller, auditor or employee of the company in question: ibid s 44(4)(a)(ii).

10 Ibid s 44(4)(a)(ii) (as amended: see note 5 supra).

11 Ibid s 44(4)(b) (as amended: see note 5 supra). A statement made by a person may be used in evidence against him: s 44(5).

12 Ibid s 44A (added by the Companies Act 1989 s 77(3)). See para 855 post.

13 Insurance Companies Act 1982 s 47B(1) (added by the Companies Consolidation (Consequential Provisions) Act 1985 s 25).

14 Insurance Companies Act 1982 s 84(2). See also s 83A (added by the Insurance Companies (Amendment) Regulations 1992, SI 1992/2890, reg 8; amended by the Insurance Companies (Amendment) Regulations 1993, SI 1993/174, reg 2); and para 22 ante.

855. Entry and search of premises. A justice of the peace may issue a warrant if satisfied on information on oath given by or on behalf of the Secretary of State[1], or by a person authorised to exercise the statutory powers to obtain information and require the production of documents[2], that there are reasonable grounds for believing that there are on any premises documents whose production has been required[3] and which have not been produced in compliance with the requirement[4]. A justice of the peace may also issue a warrant if similarly satisfied (1) that there are reasonable grounds for believing that an offence has been committed for which the penalty on conviction on indictment is imprisonment for a term of not less than two years and that there are on any premises documents relating to whether the offence has been committed, (2) that the Secretary of State or the authorised person has power to require the production of the documents[5], and (3) that there are reasonable grounds for believing that if production was so required the documents would not be produced but would be removed from the premises, hidden, tampered with or destroyed[6]. A warrant under this provision authorises a constable, together with any other person named in it and other constables (a) to enter the premises specified in the information, using such force as is reasonably necessary for the purpose; (b) to search the premises and take possession[7] of any documents appearing to be such documents as are mentioned above[8] or to take, in relation to any such documents, any other steps which may appear to be necessary for preserving them or preventing interference with them; (c) to take copies of any such documents; and (d) to require any person named in the warrant to provide an explanation of them or to state where they may be found[9].

1 As to the Secretary of State see para 15 note 5 ante.

2 Ie under the Insurance Companies Act 1982 s 44 (as amended): see para 854 ante. 'Document' includes information recorded in any form: s 44A(8) (added by the Companies Act 1989 s 77(1), (3)).

3 Ie under the Insurance Companies Act 1982 s 44(2)–(4) (as amended): see para 854 ante.

4 Ibid s 44A(1) (as added: see note 2 supra). A warrant under s 44A (as so added) continues in force until the end of the period of one month beginning with the day on which it is issued: s 44A(5) (as so added).

5 Ie under ibid s 44(2)–(4) (as amended): see para 854 ante.

6 Ibid s 44A(2) (as added: see note 2 supra). If the justice of the peace is satisfied on information on oath that there are reasonable grounds for believing that there are also on the premises other documents relevant to the investigation, the warrant must also authorise the actions set out in heads (a)–(d) in the text to be taken in relation to such documents: s 44A(4) (as so added).

7 Any documents of which possession is so taken may be retained for a period of three months or, if within that period proceedings to which the documents are relevant are commenced against any

person for any criminal offence, until the conclusion of those proceedings: ibid s 44A(6) (as added: see note 2 supra).

8 Ie in ibid s 44A(1) or (2) (as added: see note 2 supra).

9 Ibid s 44A(3) (as added: see note 2 supra). Intentional obstruction of the exercise of any rights conferred by a warrant, or failure without reasonable excuse to comply with any requirement imposed in accordance with s 44A(3)(d) (as so added) (see head (d) in the text) is an offence: s 71(2A) (added by the Companies Act 1989 s 77(5)); see para 866 post. Restrictions are imposed on the disclosure of information obtained under the Insurance Companies Act 1982 s 44A (as so added): see s 47A (added by the Companies Consolidation (Consequential Provisions) Act 1985 s 25; amended by the Financial Services Act 1986 s 182, Sch 13 para 6; and the Companies Act 1989 s 77(4)); and para 854 note 6 ante.

(5) INSOLVENCY AND WINDING UP

856. Reduction of contracts. In the case of an insurance company[1] which has been proved to be unable to pay its debts, the court[2], if it thinks fit, may reduce the amount of the contracts of the company on such terms and subject to such conditions as it thinks just, in place of making a winding-up order[3].

1 For the meaning of 'insurance company' see para 15 note 3 ante.

2 'Court' means the High Court of Justice in England or, in the case of an insurance company registered or having its head office in Scotland, the Court of Session: Insurance Companies Act 1982 s 96(1).

3 Ibid s 58. The court has no jurisdiction to order a reduction of amounts which have accrued due at the date of the presentation of the petition: *Re Capital Annuities Ltd* [1978] 3 All ER 704, [1979] 1 WLR 170.

857. Financial resources: margin of solvency: form and situation of assets. If an insurance company[1] has its head office in the United Kingdom[2] and its business in the United Kingdom is restricted to reinsurance, it must maintain a margin of solvency[3] of a prescribed amount[4]. If an insurance company does not have its head office in a member state of the European Community, it must maintain a margin of solvency and a United Kingdom margin of solvency[5] of a prescribed amount[6]. The above provision does not apply to an insurance company if its business in the United Kingdom is restricted to reinsurance or if, in the case of a company carrying on business in the United Kingdom and other member states, the Secretary of State and the supervisory authorities in those member states agree[7]. However, an insurance company which has made a deposit in the United Kingdom[8] must maintain a margin of solvency and a Community margin of solvency[9] of a prescribed amount[10].

An insurance company which fails to comply with any of the above provisions must: (1) at the request of the Secretary of State submit to him a plan for the restoration of a sound financial position; (2) propose modifications to the plan, or the plan as previously modified, if the Secretary of State considers it inadequate; (3) give effect to any plan accepted by the Secretary of State as adequate[11].

If the margin of solvency, United Kingdom margin of solvency or Community margin of solvency[12] of an insurance company falls below a prescribed amount[13], the company must at the request of the Secretary of State submit to him a short term financial scheme[14]. An insurance company which has submitted a scheme to the Secretary of State must propose modifications to the scheme, or the scheme as previously modified, if the Secretary of State considers it inadequate, and must give effect to any scheme accepted by him as adequate[15].

An insurance company[16] which has its head office in a member state other than the United Kingdom or which has made a deposit in such a member state[17] must secure that the value of the assets of the business carried on by it in the United Kingdom does not fall below the amount of the liabilities of that business, that value and amount being determined in accordance with any acceptable valuation regulations[18].

Regulations have been made regarding the extent to which an insurance company must hold its assets (a) in a currency appropriate to its liabilities, and (b) in specific places[19].

Subject to certain modifications[20], provisions relating to margins of solvency, failure to maintain a minimum margin and the form and situation of assets[21] apply to members of Lloyd's taken together as they apply to an insurance company[22] which has its head office in the United Kingdom[23].

1 Ie an insurance company to which the Insurance Companies Act 1982 Pt II (ss 15–71) (as amended) applies: see para 803 ante.
2 For the meaning of 'United Kingdom' see para 2 note 10 ante.
3 The margin of solvency of an insurance company is the excess of the value of its assets over the amount of its liabilities, that value and amount being determined in accordance with any applicable valuation regulations: Insurance Companies Act 1982 s 32(5)(a). As to valuation regulations see para 863 post. The applicable valuation regulations are the Insurance Companies Regulations 1981, SI 1981/1654, regs 10–13 (amended by SI 1985/1419).
4 Insurance Companies Act 1982 s 32(1). As to the determination of margins of solvency see the Insurance Companies Regulations 1981 regs 3–8, Schs 1, 2 (amended by SI 1985/1419; SI 1987/2130; and SI 1990/1181).
5 The United Kingdom margin of solvency of an insurance company is its margin of solvency computed by reference to the assets and liabilities of the business carried on by the company in the United Kingdom: Insurance Companies Act 1982 s 32(5)(b).
6 Ibid s 32(2). As to the determination of margins of solvency see note 3 supra.
7 Ie in accordance with ibid s 9(2) (see para 33 ante): s 32(3). As to the Secretary of State see para 15 note 5 ante.
8 Ie under ibid s 9(1)(c), (2)(b): see para 33 ante.
9 The Community margin of solvency of an insurance company is its margin of solvency computed by reference to the assets and liabilities of the business carried on by the company in member states, taken together: ibid s 32(5)(c).
10 Ibid s 32(3). As to the determination of margins of solvency see note 3 supra. In the case of an insurance company which carries on both long term and general business, the provisions of s 32(1)–(3) have effect as if (1) the requirements to maintain a margin of solvency, (2) where the company carries on both kinds of business in the United Kingdom, the requirement to maintain a United Kingdom margin of solvency, and (3) where the company carries on both kinds of business in member states (taken together), the requirement to maintain a Community margin of solvency, were requirements to maintain separate margins in respect of the two kinds of business, and accordingly as if the references in s 32(5) to assets and liabilities were references to assets and liabilities relating to the kind of business in question: s 32(6). As to long term business and general business see para 18 ante.
11 Ibid s 32(4). As to the application of s 32 to Lloyd's underwriters see s 84(1); and text and notes 20–23 infra.
12 Ie under ibid s 32(1)–(3): see text and notes 1–10 supra.
13 Ie that prescribed by the Insurance Companies Regulations 1981 reg 9, Sch 3 (amended by SI 1985/1419; SI 1987/2130; and SI 1990/1181).
14 Insurance Companies Act 1982 s 33(1). Where a company is required by s 32(6) to maintain separate margins in respect of long term and general business, s 33(1) has effect as if any reference to the margin of solvency, the United Kingdom margin of solvency or the Community margin of solvency, of the company were a reference to the margin in respect of either of the two kinds of business: s 33(3).
15 Ibid s 33(2). As to the application of s 33 to Lloyd's underwriters see s 84(1); and text and notes 20–23 infra.
16 Ie one to which ibid Pt II applies: see para 803 ante.

17 In accordance with ibid s 9(2): see para 33 ante.
18 Ibid s 34(1). In the case of a company which carries on in the United Kingdom both long term and general business, s 34(1) has effect separately in relation to the assets and liabilities of the two kinds of business: s 34(2). As to valuation regulations see note 3 supra.
19 Insurance Companies Act 1982 s 35; Insurance Companies Regulations 1981 regs 25–28 (amended by SI 1985/1419; SI 1990/1333; and SI 1992/2890). As to the application of the Insurance Companies Act 1982 s 35 to Lloyd's underwriters see s 84(1); and text and notes 20–23 infra.
20 Insurance (Lloyd's) Regulations 1983, SI 1983/224.
21 Insurance Companies Act 1982 ss 32, 33, 35.
22 Ie an insurance company to which ibid Pt II applies: see para 803 ante.
23 Ibid s 84(1). The powers conferred on the Secretary of State by ss 38–41, 44 (as amended), 45 (see paras 847, 850, 852–854 ante) are exercisable in relation to the members of Lloyd's if there is a breach of an obligation imposed by s 84(1): s 84(2). See also para 22 ante.

858. Winding up of insurance companies under the Companies Act 1985.

The court[1] may order the winding up of an insurance company[2] in accordance with the Insolvency Act 1986 and the Companies Act 1985[3]. The provisions of the Companies Act 1985 apply accordingly, subject to the following modifications: (1) the company may be ordered to be wound up on the petition of ten or more policyholders[4] owning policies of an aggregate value of not less than £10,000[5]; and (2) such a petition must not be presented except by leave of the court, and leave must not be granted until a prima facie case has been established to the court's satisfaction and until security for costs for such amount as the court may think reasonable has been given[6].

1 For the meaning of 'the court' see para 856 note 2 ante.
2 Ie an insurance company to which the Insurance Companies Act 1982 Pt II (ss 15–71) (as amended) applies: see para 803 ante.
3 Ibid s 53 (amended by the Insolvency Act 1986 s 439(2), Sch 14). As to winding up see generally COMPANIES vol 7(2) (Reissue) para 1429 et seq.
4 For the meaning of 'policyholder' see para 806 note 21 ante.
5 Insurance Companies Act 1982 s 53.
6 Ibid s 53. Where the petition is presented by a person other than the Secretary of State, a copy of it must be served on him and he is entitled to be heard on the petition: s 54(5). Rules may be made under the Insolvency Act 1986 s 411 (see COMPANIES vol 7(2) (Reissue) para 2038), for determining the amount of the liabilities of an insurance company to policyholders for the purpose of proof in a winding up and generally for carrying into effect the provisions of the Insurance Companies Act 1982 Pt II with respect to the winding up of insurance companies: s 59(1) (amended by the Insolvency Act 1985 s 235(1), Sch 8 para 37(1), (4); and the Insolvency Act 1986 Sch 14). In particular, the rules may make provision for the identification and application of assets, and the identification and determination of the amount of liabilities, for the purposes of the Insurance Companies Act 1982 s 55(4) (see para 861 post): s 59(2). As to the rules see the Insurance Companies (Winding-Up) Rules 1985, SI 1985/95 (as amended); and para 862 post.

859. Winding up on petition of Secretary of State.

The Secretary of State[1] may present a petition for the winding up[2] of an insurance company[3] on the ground that the company (1) is unable to pay its debts[4], (2) has failed to satisfy an obligation to which it is subject by virtue of the Insurance Companies Act 1982[5], (3) has failed to satisfy an obligation to which it is or was subject by virtue of any provision of the law of another member state of the European Community giving effect to the general or long term insurance directive[6], or (4) has failed to keep or produce proper accounting records[7] and the Secretary of State is unable to ascertain its financial position[8].

In such proceedings evidence that the company was insolvent (a) at the close of the period to which the accounts and balance sheet of the company last deposited[9] or any statement of the company last deposited[10] relate[11], or (b) at any date or time specified in a requirement[12], is evidence that the company continues to be unable to pay its debts unless the contrary is proved[13].

If it appears to the Secretary of State that it is expedient in the public interest that the company should be wound up, he may, unless the company is already being wound up by the court, present a petition for it to be so wound up if the court thinks it just and equitable for it to be so wound up[14].

1 As to the Secretary of State see para 15 note 5 ante.
2 Ie in accordance with the Insolvency Act 1986 Pt IV (ss 73–219) (as amended) or Pt V (ss 220–229) (as amended) (see COMPANIES vol 7(2) (Reissue) para 1449 et seq): Insurance Companies Act 1982 s 54(1) (amended by the Insolvency Act 1986 s 439(2), Sch 14).
3 Ie an insurance company to which the Insurance Companies Act 1982 Pt II (ss 15–71) (as amended) applies: see para 803 ante. The company must be one that may be wound up by the court under the Insolvency Act 1986 (see COMPANIES vol 7(2) (Reissue) para 1435): Insurance Companies Act 1982 s 54(1).
4 Ie within the meaning of the Insolvency Act 1986 s 123 or ss 222–224 (see COMPANIES vol 7(2) (Reissue) paras 1445, 2375): Insurance Companies Act 1982 s 54(1)(a) (as amended: see note 2 supra).
5 Or was subject by virtue of any enactment repealed by the Insurance Companies Act 1982 or by the Insurance Companies Act 1974: Insurance Companies Act 1982 s 54(1)(b).
6 Ibid s 54(1)(bb) (added by the Insurance Companies (Amendment) Regulations 1990, SI 1990/1333, reg 8(3); amended by the Insurance Companies (Amendment) Regulations 1993, SI 1993/174, reg 2). As to the general and long term insurance directives see para 22 note 12 ante.
7 Ie in accordance with its obligations under the Companies Act 1985 ss 221, 222: Insurance Companies Act 1982 s 54(1)(c) (amended by the Companies Consolidation (Consequential Provisions) Act 1985 s 30, Sch 2).
8 Insurance Companies Act 1982 s 54(1)(c).
9 Ie under ibid s 22 (see para 843 ante): s 54(3)(a)(i).
10 Ie under ibid s 25 (see para 841 ante): s 54(3)(a)(ii).
11 Ibid s 54(3)(a).
12 Ie a requirement under ibid s 42 or s 44 (as amended) (see paras 824, 854 ante): s 54(3)(b).
13 Ibid s 54(3).
14 Ibid s 54(4) (amended by the Insolvency Act 1986 Sch 14).

860. Subsidiary companies. Where the insurance business or any part of the insurance business of a subsidiary insurance company has been transferred to the principal insurance company[1] under an arrangement under which the subsidiary company[2] or its creditors has or have claims against the principal company[3], then, if the principal company is being wound up by the court, the court must order the subsidiary company to be wound up in conjunction with the principal company[4]. By the same or any subsequent order the court may appoint the same person to be liquidator for the two companies, and make provision for such other matters as may seem to it necessary, with a view to the companies being wound up as if they were one company[5].

Unless otherwise ordered by the court, the commencement of the winding up of the principal company is the commencement of the winding up of the subsidiary company[6].

In adjusting the rights and liabilities of the members of the several companies between themselves, the court must have regard to the constitution of the companies, and to the arrangements entered into between the companies, in the same manner as it has regard to the rights and liabilities of different classes of contributories in the case of the winding up of a single company, or as near to it as circumstances admit[7].

Where any company alleged to be subsidiary is not in process of being wound up at the same time as the principal company to which it is subsidiary, the court must not direct the subsidiary company to be wound up unless, after hearing all objections, if any, that may be urged by or on behalf of the company against its being wound up, it is of opinion that the company is subsidiary to the principal company and that the winding up of the company in conjunction with the principal company is just and equitable[8].

An application may be made in relation to the winding up of a subsidiary company in conjunction with a principal company by any creditor of, or person interested in, the principal or subsidiary company[9]. Where a company stands in the relation of a principal company to one company and in the relation of a subsidiary company to some other company, or where there are several companies standing in the relation of subsidiary companies to one principal company, the court may deal with any number of such companies together or in separate groups, as it thinks most expedient, on the principles mentioned above[10].

1 Ie an insurance company to which the Insurance Companies Act 1982 Pt II (ss 15–71) (as amended) applies: see para 803 ante.
2 Ie the company transferring the business: ibid s 57(1).
3 Ie the company to which the business is transferred: ibid s 57(1).
4 Ibid s 57(1) (amended by the Insolvency Act 1985 s 235(3), Sch 10 Pt II).
5 Insurance Companies Act 1982 s 57(1).
6 Ibid s 57(2).
7 Ibid s 57(3). See COMPANIES vol 7(2) (Reissue) para 1670 et seq.
8 Ibid s 57(4).
9 Ibid s 57(5).
10 Ibid s 57(6).

861. Winding up where company has long term business. No insurance company[1] which is an unincorporated body and carries on long term business[2] may be the subject of bankruptcy proceedings[3]. No such insurance company which carries on long term business may be wound up voluntarily[4].

In the winding up of an insurance company carrying on long term business: (1) the assets representing the fund or funds maintained by the company in respect of its long term business are available only for meeting the liabilities of the company attributable to that business[5]; and (2) the other assets of the company are available only for meeting the liabilities of the company attributable to its other business[6]. However, where the value of the assets mentioned in either head exceeds the amount of the liabilities there mentioned, the restriction does not apply to so much of the assets as represents the excess[7]. In relation to assets falling within either head, the creditors for the purpose of the control of the liquidator[8] are only those who are creditors in respect of liabilities falling within that head[9].

Where, under the provisions relating to defalcations by company officers[10], the court orders any money or property to be repaid or restored to a company or any sum to be contributed to its assets, then, if and so far as the wrongful act which is the reason for the making of the order related to assets representing a fund or funds maintained by the company in respect of its long term business, the court must include in the order a direction that the money, property or contribution must be treated as assets of that fund or those funds[11].

Unless the court[12] otherwise orders, the liquidator must carry on the company's long term business with a view to its being transferred as a going concern to another insurance company, whether an existing company or a company formed for that purpose[13]. In carrying on that business the liquidator may agree to the variation of any contracts of insurance in existence when the winding-up order is made, but must not effect any new contracts of insurance[14].

If the liquidator is satisfied that the creditors' interests in respect of liabilities of the company attributable to its long term business require the appointment of a special manager of that business, he may apply to the court, and on such application the court may appoint a special manager of that business to act during such time as it may direct, with such powers of a receiver or manager as it may entrust to him[15].

If it thinks fit and subject to such conditions, if any, as it may determine, the court may reduce the amount of the contracts made by the company in the course of carrying on its long term business[16].

On the application of the liquidator, a special manager or the Secretary of State, the court may appoint an independent actuary to investigate the company's long term business and to report to the liquidator, the special manager or the Secretary of State, as the case may be, on the desirability or otherwise of that business being continued and on any reduction in the contracts made in the course of carrying on that business that may be necessary for its successful continuation[17].

  1 Ie an insurance company to which the Insurance Companies Act 1982 Pt II (ss 15–71) (as amended) applies: see para 803 ante.
  2 For the meaning of 'long term business' see para 18 ante.
  3 Insurance Companies Act 1982 s 55(1).
  4 Ibid s 55(2).
  5 Ibid s 55(3)(a).
  6 Ibid s 55(3)(b). Section 29(1) (see para 819 ante) does not apply to a winding up and s 55(3) is subject to s 55(4) (see text to note 7 infra) and rules made under s 59(2) (see para 858 note 6 ante): s 55(3).
  7 Ibid s 55(4).
  8 Ie for the purposes of the Insolvency Act 1986 s 168(2) (see COMPANIES vol 7(2) (Reissue) para 1569): Insurance Companies Act 1982 s 55(5) (amended by the Insolvency Act 1986 s 439(2), Sch 14).
  9 Insurance Companies Act 1982 s 55(5). Any general meetings of creditors summoned for the purposes of the Insolvency Act 1986 s 168 must accordingly be separate general meetings of creditors in respect of liabilities falling within each head: Insurance Companies Act 1982 s 55(5).
 10 Ie the Insolvency Act 1986 s 212 (see COMPANIES vol 7(2) (Reissue) para 1686 et seq): Insurance Companies Act 1982 s 55(6) (amended by the Insolvency Act 1986 Sch 14).
 11 Insurance Companies Act 1982 s 55(6).
 12 Ie the court having jurisdiction to wind up the company: ibid s 56(8): see COMPANIES vol 7(2) (Reissue) para 1435 et seq.
 13 Ibid s 56(1), (2). Without the sanction of the court under the Insolvency Act 1986 s 167, Sch 4 (see COMPANIES vol 7(2) (Reissue) para 1575), the liquidator may apply in the name and on behalf of the company for an order sanctioning a transfer scheme under the Insurance Companies Act 1982 s 49 (as amended) (see para 825 ante): s 56(7) (amended by the Insolvency Act 1985 s 235(1), Sch 8 para 37(1), (3)(b); and the Insolvency Act 1986 Sch 14).
 14 Insurance Companies Act 1982 s 56(2).
 15 Ibid s 56(3). The Insolvency Act 1986 s 177(5) (which requires a special manager to give security and provides for his remuneration (see COMPANIES vol 7(2) (Reissue) para 1499)) applies to a special manager appointed under the Insurance Companies Act 1982 s 56(3): s 56(4) (amended by the Insolvency Act 1986 Sch 14).
 16 Insurance Companies Act 1982 s 56(5).
 17 Ibid s 56(6). As to the Secretary of State see para 15 note 5 ante.

862. Winding-up rules for insurance companies. Special rules[1] now apply to proceedings for the winding up of insurance companies. They supplement the existing principal winding-up rules and general regulations for companies[2], but prevail in the event of conflict[3].

Assets and liabilities respectively attributable to long term business[4] and to other business are treated as if they were the assets and liabilities of separate companies[5].

Except in relation to amounts which have fallen due before the date of the winding-up order, the holder of a general business policy[6] is to be admitted as a creditor without proof for an amount equal to the value[7] of the policy[8].

In relation to long term business where no stop order[9] has been made, a policyholder making a claim under a policy which has fallen due for payment before the winding-up order is admitted as a creditor without proof for such amount as appears from the company records to be due in respect of that claim[10]. In all other respects he is admitted as a creditor without proof for an amount equal to the value[11] of the policy[12].

Where a stop order has been made, a policyholder is admitted, in relation to a claim which fell due after the date of the winding-up order and before the date of the stop order, as a creditor without proof for such amount as appears due from the records of the company and of the liquidator[13]. In all other respects he is admitted as a creditor without proof for an amount equal to the value[14] of his policy[15].

Where there are liabilities or assets in respect of which it is not clear whether they are attributable to the company's long term business, the liquidator must determine whether, and to what extent, they are so attributable[16].

Before determining the value of a policy[17], before identifying long term liabilities and assets[18], and before determining the amount, if any, of the excess of the long term business assets[19], the liquidator must obtain and consider advice from an actuary[20].

Except at the direction of the court, no distribution may be made out of and no transfer to another insurance company may be made of (1) any part of the excess of the long term business assets which has been transferred to the other business, and (2) any part of the excess of the other business assets which has been transferred to the long term business[21].

Where no stop order[22] has been made, the liquidator may pay into a local bank account[23] any money which forms part of the assets representing the fund or funds maintained by the company in respect of its long term business[24]. In the absence of a stop order, special duties are imposed on the liquidator in respect of the maintenance of records[25] and in respect of accounts and audit[26], and he has power to do all that may be necessary to carry on the long term business of the company[27].

He may fix different days for creditors to prove their debts in relation to the long term business and to the other business[28]. He may accept late payments of premiums[29] and allow compensation for policies lapsed in consequence of failure to pay any premium[30]. He must give notice of the value of each general business policy[31] to persons appearing to have an interest in that policy[32]. If in relation to long term business he summons a separate general meeting of creditors[33] before a stop order is made, he must notify the persons appearing to be entitled to a payment under or to an interest[34] in a long term policy[35], of the amount[36] of the payment or of the value[37] of the policy[38]. There are corresponding provisions as to notice where a stop order has been made[39].

At any time before the making of a stop order the court may permit payment of a dividend in respect only of debts which fell due for payment before the date of the winding-up order or, in the case of claims under long term policies, which have fallen due for payment on or after that date[40].

Provisions have been made relating to remuneration of the liquidator when carrying on long term business[41], and to the apportionment of costs payable out of the company's assets[42].

1 Ie the Insurance Companies (Winding-Up) Rules 1985, SI 1985/95 (amended by SI 1986/2002; and SI 1991/1997), made under the Insurance Companies Act 1982 s 59 (as amended).
2 Ie the Insolvency Rules 1986, SI 1986/1925 (as amended), and the Insolvency Regulations 1986, SI 1986/1994 (as amended): Insurance Companies (Winding-Up) Rules 1985 r 2(1) (amended by SI 1986/2002).
3 Ibid r 3(2) (amended by SI 1986/2002). As to the appointment of a liquidator see r 4 (substituted by SI 1986/2002).
4 For the meaning of 'long term business' see para 18 ante.
5 Insurance Companies (Winding-Up) Rules 1985 r 5 (amended by SI 1986/2002).
6 Ie a policy the effecting of which by the company constitutes the carrying on of general business: ibid r 2(1). Cf 'long term policy', defined in note 35 infra.
7 That value is ascertained in accordance with ibid r 6, Sch 1.
8 Ibid r 6.
9 Ie a court order under the Insurance Companies Act 1982 s 56(2) (see para 861 ante) requiring the liquidator to stop carrying on the company's long term business: Insurance Companies (Winding-Up) Rules 1985 r 2(1). For the form of notice of a stop order see r 28, Sch 6 (amended by SI 1986/2002).
10 Ibid r 7(1), (2).
11 Where no stop order has been made, the value of a policy of any class is determined in the manner applicable to policies of that class provided by ibid Schs 2–4: r 7(3).
12 Ibid r 7(3). For provision relating to persons entitled to a free paid-up policy see r 7(4).
13 Ibid r 8(1), (2).
14 Where a stop order has been made, the value of a policy of any class is determined in the manner applicable to policies of that class provided by ibid Sch 5: r 8(3).
15 Ibid r 8(3). For provision relating to persons entitled to a free paid-up policy see rr 7(4), 8(4).
16 Ibid rr 9, 10.
17 Ie in accordance with ibid Schs 1–5.
18 Ie in accordance with ibid rr 9, 10.
19 In determining that amount, there must be included amongst the liabilities attributable to the long term business an amount determined by the liquidator in respect of liabilities and expenses likely to be incurred in connection with the transfer of the company's long term business as a going concern to another insurance company being liabilities not included in the valuation of the long term policies made under ibid r 7: r 11.
20 Ibid r 12(1). He must also do so before determining the terms on which he will accept payment of overdue premiums and the amount and nature of any compensation for policies which have lapsed owing to failure to pay premiums: rr 12(1), 22.
21 Ibid r 13(1). Before giving a direction, the court may require the liquidator to advertise the proposed distribution or transfer: r 13(2).
22 See note 9 supra.
23 Ie a local bank account which the liquidator is authorised to open by the Secretary of State: Insurance Companies (Winding-Up) Rules 1985 r 14(2). As to the Secretary of State see para 15 note 5 ante.
24 Ibid r 14(1), (2). The Secretary of State may also require all or some such assets to be held by a trustee approved by him: r 15.
25 Ibid r 16 (amended by SI 1986/2002).
26 Ibid r 18 (amended by SI 1986/2002; and SI 1991/1997).
27 Ibid r 17 (amended by SI 1986/2002). However, the Secretary of State may give him directions relating to investments: r 17(2)(a), (b). There is also provision as to security by the liquidator and the special manager: r 20 (amended by SI 1986/2002).
28 Ibid r 21(1), (2). In submitting a proof of any debt a creditor may, but need not, claim the whole or part of such debt as attributable to the long term business or to the other business: r 21(3).
29 Ibid r 22(1).
30 Ibid r 22(2).
31 For the meaning of 'general business policy' see note 6 supra.
32 Insurance Companies (Winding-Up) Rules 1985 r 23(1).
33 See ibid r 25 (amended by SI 1986/2002) for rules governing such meetings.
34 'Interest' includes entitlement to a free paid-up policy: ibid r 23(5).
35 'Long term policy' means a policy the effecting of which by the company constitutes the carrying on of long term business: r 2(1).
36 Ie the amount as determined under ibid r 7(2) (see notes 10–12 supra): r 23(2).
37 Ie the value as determined under ibid r 7(3) (see notes 10–12 supra): r 23(2).
38 Ibid r 23(2) (amended by SI 1986/2002).

39 Ibid r 23(3). However, the amount of the payment or the value of the policy is then determined under r 8(2) or (3) (see text and notes 13–15 supra).
40 Ibid r 24 (amended by SI 1986/2002).
41 Ibid r 26 (substituted by SI 1986/2002).
42 Ibid r 27 (amended by SI 1986/2002).

863. Power to make valuation regulations. Regulations may be made with respect to the determination of the value of assets and the amount of liabilities in any case in which the value or amount is required by any provision of the Insurance Companies Act 1982 to be determined in accordance with valuation regulations[1]. Regulations may provide that for specified purposes assets or liabilities of any specified class or description must be left out of account or must be taken into account only to a specified extent[2]. The regulations may make different provision in relation to different cases or circumstances and for the purposes of different enactments[3].

1 Insurance Companies Act 1982 s 90(1). Such regulations are known as 'valuation regulations': s 96(1). See the Insurance Companies Regulations 1981, SI 1981/1654, regs 10–13 (amended by SI 1985/1419), Pt V (regs 37–49) (amended by SI 1985/1419; SI 1988/673; and SI 1992/445), Schs 7, 8 (valuation); Pt VI (regs 50–64) (amended by SI 1983/224; and SI 1985/1419), Sch 9 (amended by SI 1990/1333) (determination of liabilities); and the Insurance (Lloyd's) Regulations 1983, SI 1983/224. These regulations were made or have effect as if made under the Insurance Companies Act 1982 s 90. As to the making of regulations see para 864 post.
2 Ibid s 90(2). See the Insurance Companies Regulations 1981 reg 49, Sch 8.
3 Insurance Companies Act 1982 s 90(3). See the Insurance Companies Regulations 1981 reg 38.

(6) ADMINISTRATION AND OFFENCES

864. Administration in general. The Secretary of State[1] must cause a general annual report of matters within the Insurance Companies Act 1982 to be laid before Parliament[2]. He may make regulations under that Act for any purpose for which regulations are authorised or required to be made under it[3].

The Secretary of State has power to bring civil proceedings on behalf of an insurance company[4] to which Part II of the Act[5] applies[6].

1 As to the Secretary of State see para 15 note 5 ante.
2 Insurance Companies Act 1982 s 98.
3 Ibid s 97(1). Regulations may make different provision for cases of different descriptions: s 97(2). Any power conferred by the Act to make regulations is exercisable by statutory instrument: s 97(3). Any statutory instrument containing regulations, except regulations under s 21A (as added) (see para 838 ante), is subject to annulment in pursuance of a resolution of either House of Parliament: s 97(4) (amended by the Financial Services Act 1986 s 135(2)).
   At the date at which this volume states the law, the following regulations had been made under the Insurance Companies Act 1982 s 97: the Insurance (Lloyd's) Regulations 1983, SI 1983/224; the Insurance Companies (Accounts and Statements) Regulations 1983, SI 1983/1811 (amended by SI 1987/2130; SI 1988/672; SI 1989/1952; SI 1990/1181; SI 1990/1333; SI 1991/2736; SI 1991/2736; SI 1992/2890; SI 1993/946; and SI 1993/3127); the Insurance Companies (Legal Expenses Insurance) (Application for Authorisation) Regulations 1990, SI 1990/1160; the Insurance Companies (Credit Insurance) Regulations 1990, SI 1990/1181; and the Insurance (Fees) Regulations 1994, SI 1994/643.
4 For the meaning of 'insurance company' see para 15 note 3 ante.
5 Ie the Insurance Companies Act 1982 ss 15–71 (as amended): see para 803 ante.
6 Ie under the Companies Act 1985 s 438(1) (amended by the Companies Act 1989 s 58) (see COMPANIES vol 7(2) (Reissue) para 1226): Insurance Companies Act 1982 s 48(1) (amended by the Companies Consolidation (Consequential Provisions) Act 1985 s 30, Sch 2). Where under a judgment given in proceedings so brought a sum is recovered in respect of a loss of assets representing a fund or funds

maintained by the company in respect of its long term business, the court must direct that the sum is to be treated as assets of that fund or those funds: Insurance Companies Act 1982 s 48(3) (as so amended). For the meaning of 'long term business' see para 18 ante.

865. Service of notices. Any notice required to be sent to any policyholder[1] may be addressed and sent to the person to whom notices respecting that policy are usually sent, and any notice so addressed and sent is deemed to be notice to the holder of the policy[2]. Any notice required[3] to be served by the Secretary of State[4] may be served by post and a letter containing that notice is deemed to be properly addressed if it is addressed to that person at his last known residence or last known place of business in the United Kingdom[5].

1 For the meaning of 'policyholder' see para 806 note 21 ante.
2 Insurance Companies Act 1982 s 70(1). Where any person claiming to be interested in a policy has given to the company notice in writing of his interest, any notice required to be sent to policyholders must also be sent to that person at the address specified by him in his notice: s 70(2).
3 Ie under ibid s 46 (see para 849 ante), s 60 (see para 832 ante) or s 61 (see para 833 ante).
4 As to the Secretary of State see para 15 note 5 ante.
5 Insurance Companies Act 1982 s 70(3). For the meaning of 'United Kingdom' see para 2 note 10 ante. For a similar provision in relation to a notice to be served under s 12 see s 12(7); and para 34 ante.

866. Offences. Any person who:
  (1) makes default in complying with the statutory provisions as to the assets and liabilities attributable to long term business[1] or as to the duty to notify changes of director, controller or manager[2]; or
  (2) in purported compliance with a requirement imposed[3] in connection with the Secretary of State's power to obtain information, furnishes information which he knows to be false in a material particular or recklessly furnishes information which is false in a material particular[4]; or
  (3) causes or permits to be included in certain documents[5] a statement which he knows to be false in a material particular or recklessly causes or permits to be so included any statement which is false in a material particular[6];
is guilty of an offence[7]. Any person guilty of such an offence is liable, on conviction on indictment, to imprisonment for a term not exceeding two years or to a fine, or to both[8], or, on summary conviction, to a fine not exceeding £1,000 or, if it is greater, the prescribed sum[9].

Any insurance company[10] which makes default in complying with, or with a requirement imposed under, any provision of Part II of the Insurance Companies Act 1982[11], being a default for which no penalty is provided by the above provisions[12], is guilty of an offence[13], as is any other person who makes default in complying with, or with a requirement imposed under, the provisions of that Act relating to statements of undesirable transactions[14], declarations of dividends[15], restrictions on transactions with connected persons[16], investments[17], maintenance and custody of assets[18], limitation of premium income[19], the Secretary of State's power to obtain information[20] and to protect policyholders[21], the production[22] and deposit[23] of copies of certain transfer documents, the approval[24] of persons becoming controllers of insurance companies[25], and the duty to notify change of control[26]. Any company or person guilty of such an offence is liable, on summary conviction, to a fine not exceeding level 5 on the standard scale[27].

Where a person continues to make default in complying with (a) the statutory provisions as to deposit with the Secretary of State of accounts[28], periodic statements of business[29] or documents in connection with actuarial investigation[30], or (b) a requirement imposed under the Secretary of State's power to obtain information[31] or to accelerate the deposit of documents[32], after being convicted of that default he is guilty of a further offence and liable on summary conviction to a fine not exceeding £40 for each day on which the default so continues[33].

A person who intentionally obstructs the exercise of any rights conferred by a warrant[34] authorising the entry and search of premises or fails without reasonable excuse to comply with any requirements imposed in connection with the production of documents[35] is guilty of an offence and liable, on conviction on indictment, to a fine and, on summary conviction, to a fine not exceeding the statutory maximum[36].

A person who publishes or discloses any information or document relating to the business or other affairs of any other person without the consent of the person from whom it was obtained[37] and, if different, the person to whom it relates, is guilty of an offence under the Companies Act 1985[38] and liable accordingly[39].

1 Ie the Insurance Companies Act 1982 ss 28–30: see paras 819–820, 839 ante.
2 Ie ibid s 62(1): see para 834 ante. As to a defence available in such a case see s 71(5); and para 834 note 3 ante.
3 Ie imposed under ibid s 44 (as amended): see para 854 ante.
4 Ibid s 71(1)(b). As to the Secretary of State see para 15 note 5 ante.
5 Ie (1) any document copies of which are, by ibid s 22 (see para 843 ante), required to be deposited with the Secretary of State; (2) any notice, statement or certificate served or furnished under or by virtue of s 19(2) (see para 822 ante) or s 26(1) (see para 842 ante); (3) any document deposited with the Secretary of State under s 25(4) (see para 841 ante) or s 42(4) (see para 824 ante); (4) any statement sent out under s 49(3)(b) (see para 826 head (2) ante) or made available under s 51(2)(c) (see para 828 head (3) ante): s 71(1)(c)(i)–(iv).
6 Ibid s 71(1)(c).
7 Ibid s 71(1).
8 Ibid s 71(2)(a).
9 Ibid s 71(2)(b) (amended by the Fines and Penalties (Northern Ireland) Order 1984, SI 1984/703). As to the prescribed sum see para 19 note 5 ante. At the date at which this volume states the law, the prescribed sum is greater than £1,000.
10 For the meaning of 'insurance company' see para 15 note 3 ante.
11 Ie the Insurance Companies Act 1982 ss 15–71 (as amended).
12 Ie the provisions mentioned in text and notes 1–6 supra.
13 Insurance Companies Act 1982 s 71(3)(a).
14 Ie ibid s 26: see para 842 ante.
15 Ie ibid s 29(7): see para 819 ante.
16 Ie ibid s 31 (as amended): see para 821 ante.
17 Ie ibid s 38: see para 850 ante.
18 Ie ibid ss 39, 40: see para 853 ante.
19 Ie ibid s 41: see para 852 ante.
20 Ie ibid s 44 (as amended): see para 854 ante.
21 Ie ibid s 45: see para 847 ante.
22 Ie ibid s 49(4): see para 826 ante.
23 Ie ibid s 50(4): see para 827 ante.
24 Ie ibid s 61(1): see para 833 ante. As to a defence available in such a case see s 71(5); and para 833 note 7 ante.
25 Ibid s 71(3)(b).
26 Ie under s 63A (as added): see para 834 ante.
27 Insurance Companies Act 1982 s 71(3) (amended by the Insurance Companies (Amendment) Regulations 1992, SI 1992/2890, reg 6). As to the standard scale see para 212 note 5 ante.
28 Ie the Insurance Companies Act 1982 s 22(1), (2) (see para 843 ante) or s 24 (see INDUSTRIAL AND PROVIDENT SOCIETIES vol 24 (Reissue) para 13 note 2).
29 Ie ibid s 25(4): see para 841 ante.
30 Ie ibid s 42(4): see para 824 ante.
31 Ie ibid s 44(1): see para 854 ante.

32 Ie ibid s 43: see paras 841 note 7, 843 note 6 ante.
33 Ibid s 71(4).
34 Ie issued under ibid s 44A (as added): see para 855 ante.
35 In accordance with ibid s 44A(3)(d) (as added): see para 855 ante.
36 Ibid s 71(2A) (added by the Companies Act 1989 s 77(1), (5)). As to the statutory maximum (ie the prescribed sum) see para 19 note 5 ante.
37 Ie under the Insurance Companies Act 1982 s 44(2)–(4) or s 44A (as added), in contamination of s 47A (as added): see paras 854–855 ante).
38 Ie under the Companies Act 1985 s 449 (as amended).
39 Insurance Companies Act 1982 s 71(4A) (added by the Companies Consolidation (Consequential Provisions) Act 1985 s 30, Sch 2).

867. Criminal liability of directors. Where an offence under the Insurance Companies Act 1982 committed by a body corporate[1] is proved to have been committed with the consent or connivance of, or to be attributable to any neglect on the part of, any director[2], chief executive[3], manager[4], secretary or other similar officer of the body corporate or any person who was purporting to act in any such capacity, he, as well as the body corporate, is guilty and liable to be proceeded against and punished accordingly[5].

1 'Body corporate' does not include a corporation sole or a Scottish firm but includes a body incorporated outside the United Kingdom: Insurance Companies Act 1982 s 96(1). For the meaning of 'United Kingdom' see para 2 note 10 ante.
2 'Director' includes any person occupying the position of director by whatever name called (ibid s 96(1)), and for this purpose a person is deemed to be a director of a body corporate if he is a person in accordance with whose directions or instructions the directors of the body corporate or any of them act (s 91(2)).
3 For the meaning of 'chief executive' see para 31 note 7 ante.
4 For the meaning of 'manager' see para 31 note 8 ante.
5 Insurance Companies Act 1982 s 91(1).

868. Criminal proceedings. Proceedings in respect of an offence under the Insurance Companies Act 1982 may only be instituted by or with the consent of the Secretary of State[1], the Industrial Assurance Commissioner[2] or the Director of Public Prosecutions[3].

Proceedings for an offence alleged to have been committed under the Act by an unincorporated body must be brought in the name of that body and not in the name of any of its members[4]. For this purpose, any rules of court relating to the service of documents have effect as if that body were a corporation[5]. The general procedure on the charge of an offence against a corporation[6] is applicable to such an unincorporated body[7].

Summary proceedings for any offence under the Act may be taken against a body corporate at any of its places of business and against any other person at any place where he is for the time being[8]. An information relating to an offence under the Act which is triable by a magistrates' court may be so tried if it is laid at any time within 3 years after the commission of the offence and within 12 months after the date on which evidence sufficient, in the opinion of the Director of Public Prosecutions, the Secretary of State or the Industrial Assurance Commissioner, as the case may be, to justify the proceedings comes to his knowledge[9].

1 As to the Secretary of State see para 15 note 5 ante.
2 As to the Industrial Assurance Commissioner see the Industrial Assurance Act 1923 s 2; and INDUSTRIAL AND PROVIDENT SOCIETIES vol 24 (Reissue) para 10.

3 Insurance Companies Act 1982 s 93.
4 Ibid s 92(1). A fine imposed on an unincorporated body on its conviction of an offence under the Act must be paid out of the funds of that body: s 92(2).
5 Ibid s 92(1).
6 Ie under the Criminal Justice Act 1925 s 33 (as amended) and the Magistrates' Courts Act 1980 s 46, Sch 3 (as amended): see CRIMINAL LAW vol 11(2) (Reissue) para 874.
7 Insurance Companies Act 1982 s 92(3).
8 Ibid s 94(1). This is without prejudice to any jurisdiction exercisable apart from this provision: s 94(1).
9 Ibid s 94(2). This is notwithstanding anything in the Magistrates' Courts Act 1980 s 127 (limitation of time for proceedings: see MAGISTRATES vol 29 para 291): Insurance Companies Act 1982 s 94(2). A certificate of the Director of Public Prosecutions, the Secretary of State or the Industrial Assurance Commissioner, as the case may be, as to the date on which the evidence came to his knowledge is conclusive evidence: s 94(7).

13. REGISTRATION OF INSURANCE BROKERS

(1) INSURANCE BROKERS REGISTRATION COUNCIL

869. Establishment of council. The Insurance Brokers Registration Council ('the council') is established by the Insurance Brokers (Registration) Act 1977[1]. It is a body corporate with perpetual succession and a common seal, and has the general function of carrying out the powers and duties conferred on it by that Act[2].

1 Insurance Brokers (Registration) Act 1977 s 1(1). The Act came into force on dates appointed by order by the Secretary of State under s 30(3), and was completely in force on 1 December 1981: Insurance Brokers (Registration) Act 1977 (Commencement No 1) Order 1977, SI 1977/1782; Insurance Brokers (Registration) Act 1977 (Commencement No 2) Order 1978, SI 1978/1393; Insurance Brokers (Registration) Act 1977 (Commencement No 3) Order 1980, SI 1980/1824.
2 Insurance Brokers (Registration) Act 1977 s 1(1).

870. Constitution, general powers and duties. The Insurance Brokers Registration Council consists of:
(1) 12 members chosen to represent registered insurance brokers[1], of whom one is chairman of the council[2]; and
(2) five persons nominated by the Secretary of State[3] of whom:
    (a) one is a barrister, advocate or solicitor;
    (b) another is a member of a recognised body of accountants; and
    (c) a third is a member appearing to the Secretary of State to represent the interests of persons who are or may become policyholders of insurance companies[4].
The persons chosen to represent registered insurance brokers are to be elected by registered insurance brokers in accordance with a scheme made by the council and approved by the Secretary of State[5]. The term of office of council members is, within certain limitations, that fixed by the scheme[6].

In nominating or electing members to the council, due regard must be had to the desirability of guaranteeing that the council includes members representative of all parts of the United Kingdom[7].

The council has power to do any act which in its opinion is calculated to facilitate the proper discharge of its duties[8] and, in particular, may:

  (i)   appoint a registrar and other officers and servants[9], and pay them remuneration[10], pensions or gratuities, or provide and maintain superannuation schemes[11];

  (ii) pay attendance fees and travelling and subsistence allowances to council members[12]; and

  (iii) borrow money[13].

The council must co-operate, by the sharing of information and otherwise, with the Secretary of State and any other authority, body or person having responsibility for the supervision or regulation of investment business or other financial services[14].

1 For the meaning of 'insurance broker' see note 4 infra.
2 Insurance Brokers (Registration) Act 1977 s 1(2), Schedule para 1(a).
3 As to the Secretary of State see para 15 note 5 ante.
4 Insurance Brokers (Registration) Act 1977 Schedule para 1(b). 'Insurance company' means a person or body of persons (whether incorporated or not) carrying on insurance business; 'insurance business' means insurance business other than industrial assurance business, and 'insurance broker' is to be construed accordingly: Insurance Brokers (Registration) Act 1977 s 29(1) (definition amended by the Insurance Companies Act 1981 s 36(1), Sch 4 Pt II para 26).
5 Insurance Brokers (Registration) Act 1977 Schedule para 2(2)(a), (b). The Secretary of State may approve a scheme either as submitted or subject to such modifications as he thinks fit, but he must notify the council of proposed modifications and consider the council's observations on them: Schedule para 2(3). A scheme may be varied or revoked by a subsequent scheme duly made and approved: Schedule para 2(2)(c). See the Insurance Brokers Registration Council Election Scheme Approval Order 1980, SI 1980/62, the Schedule to which contains the scheme currently approved for these purposes. The Secretary of State, after consulting the council, may by order so amend the provisions of the Schedule as to vary the number of members and the manner in which they are chosen or appointed: Insurance Brokers (Registration) Act 1977 Schedule para 10. See further para 873 note 12 post.
6 Ibid Schedule para 4; as to the scheme see note 5 supra. A member may at any time, by notice in writing, resign his office: Schedule para 5. A person ceasing to be a member is eligible for reappointment: Schedule para 7. As to the filling of vacancies see Schedule para 6.
7 Ibid Schedule para 2(5). For the meaning of 'United Kingdom' see para 2 note 10 ante.
8 Ibid Schedule para 8(1). The powers of the council and its committees may be exercised notwithstanding any vacancy or defective appointment: Schedule para 8(3). The council may make standing orders for regulating its proceedings and those of its committees: see Schedule para 9.
9 Ibid Schedule para 8(2)(a).
10 Ibid Schedule para 8(2)(c).
11 See ibid Schedule para 8(2)(d).
12 Ibid Schedule para 8(2)(b).
13 Ibid Schedule para 8(2)(e).
14 Financial Services Act 1986 s 138(5).

871. General power to appoint committees. The Insurance Brokers Registration Council[1] may set up a committee for any purpose[2] and may delegate to such a committee, with or without restrictions or conditions, as it thinks fit, any functions exercisable by it[3] except:

  (1) the power to make rules under the Insurance Brokers (Registration) Act 1977[4];

  (2) any functions expressly conferred by the Act on any committee set up under the Act[5]; and

  (3) subject to any express provision for delegation in the rules, any functions expressly conferred on the council by rules under the Act[6].

The number of members of such a committee and their term of office must be fixed by the council[7]. A committee may include members who are not members of the council, but at least two-thirds of the members of every such committee must be members of the council[8].

1 As to that council see paras 869–870 ante.
2 Ie any purpose other than a purpose for which the council is required to set up a committee under the Insurance Brokers (Registration) Act 1977: s 21(1).
3 Ibid s 21(1). 'Functions' includes powers and duties: s 29(1).
4 Ibid s 21(1)(a).
5 Ibid s 21(1)(b). See eg s 13 (Investigating Committee); s 14 (Disciplinary Committee); and paras 885, 886 et seq post respectively.
6 Ibid s 21(1)(c).
7 Ibid s 21(2). Every member of such a committee who at the time of his appointment was a member of the council must, upon ceasing to be a member of the council, also cease to be a member of the committee: s 21(4). For these purposes a member of the council is not deemed to have ceased by reason of retirement to be a member if he has again been nominated or elected a member not later than the day of his retirement: s 21(4) proviso.
8 Ibid s 21(3).

872. Accounts. The Insurance Brokers Registration Council[1] must keep proper accounts of all sums received or paid by it and proper records in relation to those accounts[2]. The council must appoint an auditor to the council who is a person eligible[3] for appointment as a company auditor under the Companies Act 1989[4]. The council must cause its accounts to be audited annually by the auditors, and as soon as is practicable after the accounts for any period have been audited, the council must cause them to be published and a copy of them sent to the Secretary of State[5], together with a copy of any report of the auditors[6].

1 As to that council see paras 869–870 ante.
2 Insurance Brokers (Registration) Act 1977 s 25(1).
3 Ie under the Companies Act 1989 s 25: see further COMPANIES.
4 Insurance Brokers (Registration) Act 1977 s 25(2) (substituted by the Companies Act 1989 (Eligibility for Appointment as Company Auditor) (Consequential Amendments) Regulations 1991, SI 1991/1997).
5 As to the Secretary of State see para 15 note 5 ante.
6 Insurance Brokers (Registration) Act 1977 s 25(3).

873. Approval of council's rules; orders. Rules made by the Insurance Brokers Registration Council[1] with respect to registration procedure[2], practising requirements[3], professional indemnity[4], the constitution of the Investigating Committee[5] or the constitution[6] and procedure[7] of the Disciplinary Committee, do not come into operation until approved by order of the Secretary of State[8]. The code of conduct to be drawn up by the council[9] and any revision of the code also require such prior approval of the Secretary of State[10].

After consulting the council, the Secretary of State may, by order, vary or revoke any rules made with respect to registration procedure, practising requirements or professional indemnity, or revise the code of conduct[11].

The power to make orders under the Insurance Brokers (Registration) Act 1977 is exercisable by statutory instrument, and any such order may be varied or revoked by a subsequent order[12].

1 As to the Insurance Brokers Registration Council see paras 869–870 ante.

2 Ie rules made under the Insurance Brokers (Registration) Act 1977 s 8: see para 877 post.
3 Ie rules made under ibid s 11 (as amended): see para 883 post.
4 Ie rules made under ibid s 12 (as amended): see para 884 post.
5 Ie rules made under ibid s 13: see para 885 post.
6 Ie rules made under ibid s 14: see para 886 post.
7 Ie rules made under ibid s 19 (as amended): see para 887 post.
8 Ibid s 27(1). The Secretary of State may approve rules under s 19 either as submitted to him or subject to such modifications as he thinks fit; but where he proposes to approve any such rules subject to modifications he must notify the modifications to the council and consider any observations of the council on them: s 27(2). As to the Secretary of State see para 15 note 5 ante.
9 Ie the statement under ibid s 10: see para 882 post.
10 Ibid s 27(1).
11 Ibid s 27(3).
12 Ibid s 28(1). In general, any statutory instrument by which this power is exercised, except any order under s 3(4) (see para 875 post), or s 27(3), or any order under Schedule para 2 (see para 870 note 5 ante), approving a scheme subject to modifications, or an order under Schedule para 10, may not be made unless a draft of the order has been approved by resolution of each House of Parliament: s 28(3). An order of the excepted kinds is subject to annulment in pursuance of a resolution of either House of Parliament: s 28(2).

(2) REGISTRATION AND TRAINING OF INSURANCE BROKERS

(i) Registration

874. Insurance brokers register. The Insurance Brokers Registration Council[1] is required to establish and maintain a register of insurance brokers[2] ('the register') containing the names, addresses and qualifications, and such other particulars as may be prescribed[3], of all persons who are entitled under the statutory provisions to be registered therein and apply in the prescribed manner to be so registered[4].

1 As to that council see paras 869–870 ante.
2 For the meaning of 'insurance broker' see para 870 note 4 ante.
3 'Prescribed' means prescribed by rules under the Insurance Brokers (Registration) Act 1977: s 29(1). As to the prescribed particulars see the Insurance Brokers Registration Council (Registration and Enrolment) Rules 1978 r 4; those rules are scheduled to the Insurance Brokers Registration Council (Registration and Enrolment) Rules Approval Order 1978, SI 1978/1395. As to such rules generally see paras 873 ante, 877 post.
4 Insurance Brokers (Registration) Act 1977 s 2. As to the prescribed manner of application see the Insurance Brokers Registration Council (Registration and Enrolment) Rules 1978 rr 6, 7 (amended by rules approved by SI 1991/2566).

875. Qualifications for registration. Subject to certain conditions[1], a person is entitled to be registered in the insurance brokers register[2] if he satisfies the Insurance Brokers Registration Council[3]:

(1) that he holds a qualification approved[4] by the council, being a qualification granted to him after receiving instruction from an institution so approved[5]; or

(2) that he holds a qualification recognised by the council for this purpose, being a qualification granted outside the United Kingdom[6]; or

(3) that he has carried on business[7] as an insurance broker[8], or as a whole-time agent acting for two or more insurance companies[9] in relation to insurance business[10], for a period of not less than five years[11]; or

(4) that he holds a qualification recognised by the council for this purpose and has carried on business as mentioned in head (3) above for a period of not less than three years[12]; or

(5) that he has been employed by a person carrying on business as mentioned in head (3) above, or by an insurance company, for a period of not less than five years[13]; or

(6) that he holds a qualification recognised by the council for this purpose and has been employed by a person carrying on business as mentioned in head (3) above, or by an insurance company, for a period of not less than three years[14]; or

(7) that he has knowledge and practical experience of insurance business which is comparable to that of a person who has carried on business as an insurance broker for a period of five years[15]; or

(8) that he holds a qualification recognised by the council for this purpose and has knowledge and practical experience of insurance business which is comparable to that of a person who has carried on business as an insurance broker for a period of three years[16].

A person is not entitled to be registered in the register by virtue of these provisions unless he also satisfies the council:

(a) as to his character and suitability to be a registered insurance broker[17]; and

(b) in a case falling within heads (1), (2), (5) or (6) above, that he has had adequate practical experience in the work of an insurance broker[18]; and

(c) if he is carrying on business as an insurance broker at the time when the application is made, that he is complying with the requirements of rules made by the council[19] to ensure that registered insurance brokers are solvent[20].

After consulting the council, the Secretary of State[21] may by order provide that any of the requirements set out above are to be omitted or to have effect subject to such amendments as may be specified in the order[22].

Except in certain cases[23], a person is entitled to be registered in the register if he satisfies the council that he or a partnership of which he is a member is accepted as a Lloyd's broker by the Committee of Lloyd's[24].

1 Ie subject to the Insurance Brokers (Registration) Act 1977 s 3(2) (see text and notes 17–20 infra) and s 16 (applications to restore erased names: see para 890 post).
2 As to the register see para 874 ante.
3 As to the Insurance Brokers Registration Council see paras 869–870 ante.
4 As to the approval of qualifications by the council see para 880 post.
5 Insurance Brokers (Registration) Act 1977 s 3(1)(a).
6 Ibid s 3(1)(b). For the meaning of 'United Kingdom' see para 2 note 10 ante.
7 Ie he must have carried on business to an extent which provided him with adequate practical experience in the work of an insurance broker: *Pickles v Insurance Brokers Registration Council* [1984] 1 All ER 1073, [1984] 1 WLR 748, DC.
8 For the meaning of 'insurance broker' see para 870 note 4 ante.
9 For the meaning of 'insurance company' see para 870 note 4 ante.
10 For the meaning of 'insurance business' see para 870 note 4 ante.
11 Insurance Brokers (Registration) Act 1977 s 3(1)(c).
12 Ibid s 3(1)(d).
13 Ibid s 3(1)(e).
14 Ibid s 3(1)(f).
15 Ibid s 3(1)(g).
16 Ibid s 3(1)(h).
17 Ibid s 3(2)(a). An authorised person under the Financial Services Act 1986 Pt I (ss 1–128C) (as amended) is deemed to satisfy this requirement: see para 877 text and notes 13–15 post.

18 Insurance Brokers (Registration) Act 1977 s 3(2)(b).
19 Ie made under ibid s 11(1): see para 883 text and notes 1–10 post.
20 Ibid s 3(2)(c).
21 As to the Secretary of State see para 15 note 5 ante.
22 Insurance Brokers (Registration) Act 1977 s 3(4).
23 Ie applications under ibid s 16 for the restoration of erased names to the register: see para 890 post.
24 Ibid s 3(3). As to Lloyd's generally see para 21 ante.

876. List of bodies corporate. The Insurance Brokers Registration Council[1] must establish and maintain a list of bodies corporate carrying on business as insurance brokers[2], containing the names, principal places of business and such other particulars as may be prescribed[3] of all bodies corporate which are entitled to be enrolled in the list and apply in the prescribed manner to be so enrolled[4].

Subject to certain conditions[5], a body corporate is entitled to be enrolled in the list if it satisfies the council:

(1) that a majority of its directors are registered insurance brokers[6]; or
(2) in the case of a body corporate having only one director, that he is a registered insurance broker[7]; or
(3) in the case of a body corporate having only two directors, that one of them is a registered insurance broker and that the business is carried on under his management[8].

A body corporate is not entitled to be enrolled in the list unless it also satisfies the council that it is complying with the requirements of rules made by the council[9] to ensure that registered insurance brokers are solvent[10].

Except in certain cases[11], a body corporate is entitled to be enrolled in the list if it satisfies the council that it is accepted as a Lloyd's broker by the Committee of Lloyd's[12].

1 As to that council see paras 869–870 ante.
2 For the meaning of 'insurance broker' see para 870 note 4 ante.
3 For the meaning of 'prescribed' see para 874 note 3 ante. As to the prescribed particulars see the Insurance Brokers Registration Council (Registration and Enrolment) Rules 1978 r 5: those rules are scheduled to the Insurance Brokers Registration Council (Registration and Enrolment) Rules Approval Order 1978, SI 1978/1395. As to such rules generally see paras 873 ante, 877 post.
4 Insurance Brokers (Registration) Act 1977 s 4(1). As to the prescribed manner of application see the Insurance Brokers Registration Council (Registration and Enrolment) Rules 1978 r 8 (amended by rules approved by SI 1991/2566).
5 Ie subject to the Insurance Brokers (Registration) Act 1977 s 4(3) (see text and note 10 infra) and s 16 (restoration of erased names to the register: see para 890 post).
6 Ibid s 4(2)(a). 'Registered insurance broker' means a person who is registered in the insurance brokers register (see paras 874–875 ante): s 29(1).
7 Ibid s 4(2)(b).
8 Ibid s 4(2)(c).
9 Ie made under ibid s 11(1): see para 883 post.
10 Ibid s 4(3).
11 Ie applications under ibid s 16 for the restoration of erased names to the register: see para 890 post.
12 Ibid s 4(4). As to Lloyd's generally see para 21 ante.

877. Registration and enrolment procedure and fees. The register of insurance brokers and the list of bodies corporate must be kept by the registrar of the Insurance Brokers Registration Council[1]. The council may make rules[2] with respect to the form and keeping of the register and list and the making of entries and alterations in them[3]. In particular, the rules may:

(1) regulate the making of applications for registration and enrolment, and provide for evidence to be produced in support[4];
(2) provide for notification of changes in required particulars[5];
(3) prescribe fees for the entry or restoration of names in the register, or the retention of names in it[6];
(4) provide for the entry of qualifications of persons registered and the removal of qualifications, and prescribe a fee in respect of such entries[7];
(5) authorise the registrar to refuse to enter, restore or retain the name of a person or body until the prescribed fee has been paid[8];
(6) authorise the registrar to erase the entry of a person or body who or which fails to supply information required to ensure the correctness of the particulars[9]; and
(7) prescribe anything required or authorised to be prescribed by the provisions of the Act relating to the register or list[10].

Rules made under the power described above may also require an applicant for registration to state whether he is an authorised person or an exempted person under Part I of the Financial Services Act 1986[11], and if so to give particulars of the authorisation or exemption[12]. A person meets the requirement to satisfy the council of his character and suitability for registration[13] if he is an authorised person or a member of a partnership or unincorporated association which is an authorised person[14].

1 Insurance Brokers (Registration) Act 1977 s 8(1). The registrar is to be appointed by the council: s 8(1). As to the council see paras 869–870 ante. As to the register and the list see paras 874, 876 ante.
2 These rules must be approved by the Secretary of State: see para 873 ante.
3 Insurance Brokers (Registration) Act 1977 s 8(2). The rules made for this purpose and the particular purposes described in the text and notes 4–10 infra are the Insurance Brokers Registration Council (Registration and Enrolment) Rules 1978. Those rules are scheduled to the Insurance Brokers Registration Council (Registration and Enrolment) Rules Approval Order 1978, SI 1978/1395, and have been amended by rules scheduled to SI 1979/490 and SI 1991/2566.
4 Insurance Brokers (Registration) Act 1977 s 8(2)(a).
5 Ibid s 8(2)(b). See also paras 874, 876 ante.
6 Ibid s 8(2)(c), (d). Rules prescribing fees may provide for different fees in different classes of case, and for the making of arrangements for the collection of such fees with prescribed bodies: s 8(4).
7 Ibid s 8(2)(e).
8 Ibid s 8(2)(f). Rules which provide for the erasure of a name for failure to pay a fee must also provide for its restoration on subsequent application in the prescribed form and payment of an additional fee: s 8(3).
9 Ibid s 8(2)(g).
10 Ibid s 8(2)(h).
11 The Financial Services Act 1986 Pt I comprises ss 1–128C (as amended): see generally MONEY. As to authorised and exempted persons see ss 7–46 (as amended).
12 Ibid s 138(1).
13 Ie the requirement of the Insurance Brokers (Registration) Act 1977 s 3(2)(a): see para 875 text and note 17 ante.
14 Financial Services Act 1986 s 138(1).

878. Publication of register and list. The Insurance Brokers Registration Council[1] must cause the insurance brokers register[2] and list of bodies corporate[3] to be printed and published as often as it thinks fit[4]. Where the register or list is not published in any year the council must cause any alterations in the entries in the register or list which have been made since the last publication to be printed and published within that year[5].

A copy of the register or list purporting to be printed and published by the council, as altered by any alterations purporting to be printed and published by the council, is evidence in all proceedings that the individuals specified in the register are registered in it or, as the case may be, that the bodies corporate specified in the list are enrolled in the list[6]. The absence of the name of any individual or body corporate from any such copy of the register or list is evidence, until the contrary is shown, that he is not registered or, as the case may be, that it is not enrolled[7].

1 As to the Insurance Brokers Registration Council see paras 869–870 ante.
2 As to the register see para 874 ante.
3 As to the list see para 876 ante.
4 Insurance Brokers (Registration) Act 1977 s 9(1).
5 Ibid s 9(2).
6 Ibid s 9(3).
7 Ibid s 9(3). In the case of an individual or body corporate whose name does not appear in any copy of the register or list as altered, a certified copy, under the registrar's hand, of the entry relating to that individual or body in the register or list is evidence of the entry: s 9(4).

879. Appeals. Before refusing an application for registration[1] or enrolment[2], the Insurance Brokers Registration Council[3] must give the applicant an opportunity of appearing before and being heard by a committee of the council[4].

Where the council refuses an application, the council must, if so required by the applicant within seven days from notification of the decision, serve on the applicant a statement of the reasons for the refusal[5]. Within 28 days from

(1) notification of the decision, or

(2) if a statement of reasons has been required, service of the statement,

a person or body corporate whose application is refused may appeal against the refusal to the court[6]. The council may appear as respondent on any such appeal, and for the purpose of enabling directions to be given as to the costs of any such appeal the council is deemed to be a party, whether it appears on the hearing of the appeal or not[7]. On the hearing of any such appeal the court may make such order as it thinks fit, and such order is final[8].

1 Ie registration under the Insurance Brokers (Registration) Act 1977 s 3: see para 875 ante.
2 Ie enrolment under ibid s 4: see para 876 ante.
3 As to that council see paras 869–870 ante.
4 Insurance Brokers (Registration) Act 1977 s 5(1).
5 Ibid s 5(2). Any notice or other document authorised or required to be given under the Insurance Brokers (Registration) Act 1977 may, without prejudice to any other method of service but subject to any provision to the contrary in rules under the Act, be served by post; and for the purpose of the application of what is now the Interpretation Act 1978 s 7, Sch 2 para 3 (which relate to service by post: see STATUTES vol 44 para 854), the proper address of a person or body corporate to whose registration or enrolment such a document relates is the address in the register or list: Insurance Brokers (Registration) Act 1977 s 26.
6 Ibid s 5(3). 'The court' means in England and Wales the High Court: s 29(1).
7 Ibid s 5(4).
8 Ibid s 5(5).

(ii) Training

880. Approval of educational institutions and qualifications. The Insurance Brokers Registration Council[1] may approve any institution where the instruction given to persons being educated as insurance brokers[2] appears to the council to be such as to secure to them adequate knowledge and skill for the practice of their profession; such an institution is referred to as an 'approved educational institution'[3]. The council may also approve any qualification which appears to it to be granted to candidates who reach such a standard of proficiency at a qualifying examination as to secure to them adequate knowledge and skill for the practice of their profession; such a qualification is known as an 'approved qualification'[4].

Where the council has refused to approve an institution or qualification as suitable for any purpose, the Secretary of State[5], on representations being made to him within one month of the refusal, may, if he thinks fit, after considering the representations and after consulting the council, order the council to approve the institution or qualification as suitable for that purpose[6].

1 As to that council see paras 869–870 ante.
2 For the meaning of 'insurance broker' see para 870 note 4 ante.
3 Insurance Brokers (Registration) Act 1977 s 6(1).
4 Ibid s 6(2). The council must from time to time publish a list of approved educational institutions and approved qualifications: s 6(4).
5 As to the Secretary of State see para 15 note 5 ante.
6 Insurance Brokers (Registration) Act 1977 s 6(3).

881. Supervision of educational institutions and qualifying examinations.

It is the duty of the Insurance Brokers Registration Council[1] to keep itself informed of the nature of the instruction given by any approved educational institution[2] to persons being educated as insurance brokers[3] and of the examinations on the results of which approved qualifications[4] are granted[5]. For this purpose the council may appoint persons to visit approved educational institutions and to attend at the examinations held by the bodies which grant approved qualifications[6]. It is the duty of these visitors to report to the council as to the sufficiency of the instruction given by the institutions visited by them, or of the examinations attended by them, and as to any other related matters which may be specified by the council either generally or in any particular case, but no visitor may interfere with the giving of any instruction or the holding of any examination[7].

Where it appears to the council, as a result of a visitor's report or otherwise, that the instruction given by any approved educational institution to persons being educated as insurance brokers or the examinations taken by such persons are not such as to secure that they possess adequate knowledge and skill for the practice of their profession, and that for this reason the approval of the institution or qualification should be withdrawn, the council must give notice in writing to the institution or body of its opinion, sending with it a copy of any report on which its opinion is based[8]. On receipt of the notice the institution or body may, within a specified period (not being less than one month), make to the council observations on the notice and any report sent with it or objections to the notice and report[9]. As soon as may be after the expiration of the specified period, the council must determine whether or not to withdraw its approval of the institution or qualification, as the case may be, taking into account any observations or objections duly made[10]. The council must give notice in writing of any decision to withdraw approval of an institution or qualification to the institution or body concerned; the decision does not take effect until the expiration of one month from the date of the giving of the notice or, if during that time the institution or body makes representations with respect to the decision to the Secretary of State[11], until the representations are finally dealt with[12]. If any such representations are duly made, the

Secretary of State may, if he thinks fit after considering the representations and after consulting the council, order the council to annul the withdrawal of approval[13].

1 As to that council see paras 869–870 ante.
2 As to the approval of educational institutions see para 880 ante.
3 For the meaning of 'insurance broker' see para 870 note 4 ante.
4 As to the approval of qualifications see para 880 ante.
5 Insurance Brokers (Registration) Act 1977 s 7(1).
6 Ibid s 7(2). The council may pay to its visitors such fees and travelling and subsistence allowances as it may determine: s 7(9).
7 Ibid s 7(3).
8 Ibid s 7(4). As to the service of notices and other documents see para 879 note 5 ante.
9 Ibid s 7(5).
10 Ibid s 7(6).
11 As to the Secretary of State see para 15 note 5 ante.
12 Insurance Brokers (Registration) Act 1977 s 7(7).
13 Ibid s 7(8).

(3) CONDUCT AND DISCIPLINE

(i) Regulation of Conduct

882. Code of conduct. The Insurance Brokers Registration Council[1] must draw up, and may from time to time revise, a statement of the acts and omissions which, if done or made by registered insurance brokers[2] or enrolled bodies corporate[3], or by either of them in particular circumstances, constitute, in the council's opinion, unprofessional conduct[4]. In drawing up any statement the council must take proper account of any provisions applicable to, and powers exercisable in relation to, registered insurance brokers or enrolled bodies corporate under the Financial Services Act 1986[5].

The statement is to serve as a guide to registered insurance brokers and enrolled bodies corporate and persons concerned with their conduct, but the mention or lack of mention in it of a particular act or omission is not to be taken as conclusive of any question of professional conduct[6].

1 As to that council see paras 869–870 ante.
2 For the meaning of 'registered insurance broker' see para 876 note 6 ante.
3 As to the enrolment of bodies corporate see para 876 ante.
4 Insurance Brokers (Registration) Act 1977 s 10(1). See the Insurance Brokers Registration Council (Code of Conduct) Approval Order 1978, SI 1978/1394, the Schedule to which contains the code of conduct drawn up by the council under this power.
5 Financial Services Act 1986 s 138(2). The provisions applicable and the powers exercisable are set out in s 48 (conduct of insurance business) and s 64 et seq (powers of intervention).
6 Insurance Brokers (Registration) Act 1977 s 10(2).

883. Rules for carrying on business. The Insurance Brokers Registration Council[1] must make rules[2] requiring registered insurance brokers[3] who are carrying on business as insurance brokers[4] and enrolled bodies corporate[5]:
(1) to ensure that their businesses have working capital of not less than such amount as may be prescribed[6];
(2) to ensure that the value of the assets of their businesses exceeds the amount of the liabilities of their businesses by not less than such amount as may be prescribed[7];

(3) to ensure that the number of insurance companies[8] with which they place insurance business[9], and the amount of insurance business which they place with each insurance company, is such as to prevent their businesses from becoming unduly dependent on any particular insurance company[10];

(4) to open and keep bank accounts for money received by them from persons with whom they do business[11];

(5) to hold money so received in such manner as may be prescribed[12];

(6) to keep such accounting records showing and explaining the transactions of their businesses as may be prescribed[13]; and

(7) to prepare and submit to the council at such intervals as may be prescribed balance sheets and profit and loss accounts containing such information as may be prescribed for the purpose of giving a true and fair view of the state of their businesses[14].

Without prejudice to the generality of the provisions of heads (1) to (7) above, the rules may empower the council:

(a) to require practising insurance brokers and enrolled bodies corporate to deliver at such intervals as may be prescribed reports given by qualified accountants[15] and containing such information as may be prescribed for the purpose of ascertaining whether or not the rules have been complied with[16];

(b) to require practising insurance brokers and enrolled bodies corporate to deliver at such intervals as may be prescribed statements made by them and containing such information as may be prescribed for the purpose of ascertaining whether or not the rules are being complied with[17]; and

(c) to take such other steps as it considers necessary or expedient for the purpose of ascertaining whether or not the rules are being complied with[18].

Further, in making the rules the council must take proper account of any provisions applicable to, and powers exercisable in relation to, registered insurance brokers or enrolled bodies corporate under the Financial Services Act 1986[19].

1 As to that council see paras 869–870 ante.
2 The rules may make different provision for different circumstances and may specify circumstances in which persons are exempt from any of their requirements: Insurance Brokers (Registration) Act 1977 s 11(7). As to the making of rules see s 27; and para 873 ante. As to the rules made in pursuance of this duty see note 6 infra.
3 For the meaning of 'registered insurance broker' see para 876 note 6 ante.
4 Such brokers are referred to as 'practising insurance brokers': Insurance Brokers (Registration) Act 1977 s 11(1). For the meaning of 'insurance broker' see para 870 note 4 ante.
5 As to the enrolment of bodies corporate see para 876 ante.
6 Ie prescribed by rules made under the Insurance Brokers (Registration) Act 1977: ss 11(1)(a), 29(1). See the Insurance Brokers Registration Council (Accounts and Business Requirements) Rules 1979, approved by and scheduled to the Insurance Brokers Registration Council (Accounts and Business Requirements) Rules Approval Order 1979, SI 1979/489 (amended by rules scheduled to SI 1981/1630).
7 Insurance Brokers (Registration) Act 1977 s 11(1)(b); and see note 6 supra.
8 For the meaning of 'insurance company' see para 870 note 4 ante.
9 For the meaning of 'insurance business' see para 870 note 4 ante.
10 Insurance Brokers (Registration) Act 1977 s 11(1)(c).
11 Ibid s 11(2)(a).
12 Ibid s 11(2)(b); and see note 6 supra.
13 Ibid s 11(2)(c); and see note 6 supra.
14 Ibid s 11(2)(d); and see note 6 supra.
15 An accountant is qualified to give reports for these purposes if he is eligible for appointment as a company auditor under the Companies Act 1989 s 25 (or corresponding Northern Ireland legislation): Insurance Brokers (Registration) Act 1977 s 11(4) (amended by the Companies Consolidation (Consequential Provisions) Act 1985 s 30, Sch 2; and the Companies Act 1989 (Eligibility

for Appointment as Company Auditor) (Consequential Amendments) Regulations 1991, SI 1991/1997). An accountant is not qualified to report under the Insurance Brokers (Registration) Act 1977 s 11 in relation to a practising insurance broker (see text and note 4 supra) if he is an employee or partner of, or an employee of a partner of, the broker, and in relation to an enrolled body corporate an accountant is not so qualified if he is ineligible by virtue of the Companies Act 1989 s 27 (see further COMPANIES): Insurance Brokers (Registration) Act 1977 s 11(5) (amended by the Companies Act 1989 (Eligibility for Appointment as Company Auditor) (Consequential Amendments) Regulations 1991).

16 Insurance Brokers (Registration) Act 1977 s 11(3)(a); and see note 6 supra.
17 Ibid s 11(3)(b); and see note 6 supra.
18 Ibid s 11(3)(c).
19 Financial Services Act 1986 s 138(2). The provisions applicable and the powers exercisable are set out in s 48 (conduct of insurance business) and s 64 et seq (powers of intervention).

884. Compensation fund; professional indemnity. The Insurance Brokers Registration Council[1] may make rules[2] for indemnifying practising insurance brokers[3] and former practising insurance brokers[4], and enrolled[5] bodies corporate and former enrolled bodies corporate[6], against losses arising from claims in respect of any description of civil liability incurred by them, or by their employees or former employees, in connection with their businesses[7].

The council may also make rules for the making of grants or other payments for the purpose of relieving or mitigating losses suffered by persons in consequence of:

(1) negligence, fraud or other dishonesty by practising insurance brokers or enrolled bodies corporate or their employees in connection with their businesses; or

(2) failure by practising insurance brokers or enrolled bodies corporate to account for money received by them in connection with their businesses[8].

For the purpose of providing such indemnity and enabling such grants or other payments to be made, the rules may:

(a) authorise or require the council to establish and maintain a fund or funds[9];

(b) authorise or require the council to take out and maintain insurance with authorised insurers[10]; and

(c) require practising insurance brokers or enrolled bodies corporate, or any specified description of them, to take out and maintain insurance with authorised insurers[11].

Without prejudice to the generality of heads (a) to (c) above, the rules may:

(i) specify the terms and conditions on which indemnity or a grant or other payment is to be available, and any circumstances in which the right to it is to be excluded or modified[12];

(ii) provide for the management, administration and protection of any fund maintained under head (a) above and require practising insurance brokers or enrolled bodies corporate or any description of them to make payments to any such fund[13];

(iii) require practising insurance brokers or enrolled bodies corporate or any description of them to make payments by way of premium on any insurance policy maintained by the council under head (b) above[14];

(iv) prescribe the conditions which an insurance policy must satisfy for the purposes of head (c) above[15];

(v) authorise the council to determine the amount of any payments required by the rules, subject to such limits, or in accordance with such provisions, as may be prescribed[16];

Para 884

(vi) specify circumstances in which, where a registered insurance broker or an enrolled body corporate for whom indemnity is provided has failed to comply with the rules, the council or insurers may take proceedings against him or it in respect of sums paid by way of indemnity in connection with a matter in relation to which there has been a failure to comply with the rules[17];

(vii) specify circumstances in which, where a grant or other payment is made in consequence of the act or omission of a practising insurance broker or enrolled body corporate, the council or insurers may take proceedings against him or it in respect of the sum so paid[18];

(viii) make different provision for different circumstances, and specify circumstances in which practising insurance brokers or enrolled bodies corporate are exempt from any of the rules[19];

(ix) empower the council to take such steps as it considers necessary or expedient to ascertain whether or not the rules are being complied with[20]; and

(x) contain incidental, procedural or supplementary provisions[21].

Further, in making the rules the council must take proper account of any provisions applicable to, and powers exercisable in relation to, registered insurance brokers or enrolled bodies corporate under the Financial Services Act 1986[22].

1 As to that council see paras 869–870 ante.
2 As to rules made under the Insurance Brokers (Registration) Act 1977 see s 27; and para 873 ante. The rules made under this power are the Insurance Brokers Registration Council (Indemnity Insurance and Grants Scheme) Rules 1987, approved and scheduled to the Insurance Brokers Registration Council (Indemnity Insurance and Grants Scheme) Rules Approval Order 1987, SI 1987/1496 (amended by rules approved by SI 1990/2461, and by virtue of SI 1991/2684).
3 For the meaning of 'practising insurance broker' see para 883 text and notes 3–4 ante.
4 Insurance Brokers (Registration) Act 1977 s 12(1)(a).
5 As to the enrolment of bodies corporate see para 876 ante.
6 Insurance Brokers (Registration) Act 1977 s 12(1)(b).
7 Ibid s 12(1) (amended by the Financial Services Act 1986 s 138(3)).
8 Insurance Brokers (Registration) Act 1977 s 12(2) (as amended: see note 7 supra).
9 Ibid s 12(3)(a).
10 Ibid s 12(3)(b).
11 Ibid s 12(3)(c).
12 Ibid s 12(4)(a).
13 Ibid s 12(4)(b).
14 Ibid s 12(4)(c).
15 Ibid s 12(4)(d).
16 Ie prescribed by rules made under the Act: ibid ss 12(4)(e), 29(1). See note 2 supra.
17 Ibid s 12(4)(f).
18 Ibid s 12(4)(g).
19 Ibid s 12(4)(h).
20 Ibid s 12(4)(i).
21 Ibid s 12(4)(j).
22 Financial Services Act 1986 s 138(2). The provisions applicable and the powers exercisable are set out in s 48 (conduct of insurance business) and s 64 et seq (powers of intervention).

(ii) Disciplinary Proceedings

885. Preliminary investigation. A committee, known as the Investigating Committee, is established by the Insurance Brokers Registration Council[1] for the preliminary investigation of cases (known as disciplinary cases) where either:

(1) it is alleged that a registered insurance broker[2] or enrolled body corporate[3] is liable to have his or its name erased[4] from the register or list[5]; or

(2) a complaint is made to the council by or on behalf of a member of the public about a registered insurance broker or an enrolled body corporate or an employee of either of them[6].

A disciplinary case must be referred to the Investigating Committee, which must carry out a preliminary investigation of it and, unless satisfied that there is insufficient evidence to support a finding that the insurance broker or body corporate is liable to have his or its name erased from the register or list, must refer the case, with the results of its investigation, to the Disciplinary Committee[7].

1 As to that council see paras 869–870 ante.
2 For the meaning of 'registered insurance broker' see para 876 note 6 ante.
3 As to the enrolment of bodies corporate see para 876 ante.
4 Ie under the Insurance Brokers (Registration) Act 1977 s 15: see para 889 post.
5 Ibid s 13(1)(a).
6 Ibid s 13(1)(b). The council must make rules as to the constitution of the Investigating Committee: s 13(3). As to the making of rules see s 27; and para 873 ante. The rules made under this provision are the Insurance Brokers Registration Council (Constitution of the Investigating Committee) Rules 1978, approved by and scheduled to the Insurance Brokers Registration Council (Constitution of the Investigating Committee) Rules Approval Order 1978, SI 1978/1456.
7 Insurance Brokers Registration Act 1977 s 13(2). As to the Disciplinary Committee see s 14; and para 886 post.

886. Establishment of Disciplinary Committee. A committee, known as the Disciplinary Committee, is established by the Insurance Brokers Registration Council[1] for the consideration and determination of disciplinary cases referred to it by the Investigating Committee[2] and of any other cases of which it has cognisance[3]. The council must make rules as to the constitution of the committee, the times and places of its meetings, its quorum and the mode of summoning its members[4]. Such rules must secure that a person, other than the chairman of the council, who has acted in relation to any disciplinary case as a member of the Investigating Committee does not act in relation to that case as a member of the Disciplinary Committee[5].

1 As to that council see paras 869–870 ante.
2 As to the Investigating Committee, referrals by that committee, and disciplinary cases, see the Insurance Brokers (Registration) Act 1977 s 13; and para 885 ante.
3 Ibid s 14(1).
4 Ibid s 14(2). As to the making of rules see s 27; and para 873 ante. The rules made under this provision are the Insurance Brokers Registration Council (Constitution of the Disciplinary Committee) Rules 1978, approved by and scheduled to the Insurance Brokers Registration Council (Constitution of the Disciplinary Committee) Rules Approval Order 1978, SI 1978/1457.
5 Insurance Brokers (Registration) Act 1977 s 14(3).

887. Procedure of the Disciplinary Committee. For the purpose of any proceedings[1] before the Disciplinary Committee[2], the committee may administer oaths, and any party to the proceedings may sue out writs of subpoena ad testificandum and duces tecum[3], but no person may be compelled under any such writ to produce any document which he could not be compelled to produce on the trial of an action[4].

After consulting such organisations representing the interests of insurance brokers[5] and bodies corporate carrying on business as insurance brokers as appear to it requisite to be consulted[6], the Insurance Brokers Registration Council[7] must make rules as to the procedure to be followed and the rules of evidence to be observed in proceedings before the committee[8], particularly for:

(1) securing that notice that the proceedings are to be brought is to be given, at such time and in such manner as may be specified in the rules, to the individual or body corporate alleged to be liable to have his or its name erased from the register or list[9];

(2) securing that, if he so requires, any party to the proceedings is entitled to be heard by the committee[10];

(3) enabling any party to the proceedings to be represented by counsel or solicitor or (if the rules so provide and the party so elects) by a person of such other description as may be specified in the rules[11];

(4) requiring proceedings before the committee to be held in public except in so far as may be provided by the rules[12];

(5) in cases where it is alleged that a registered insurance broker[13] or enrolled body corporate[14] has been guilty of unprofessional conduct, requiring that where the committee judges that the allegation has not been proved it must record a finding that he or it is not guilty of such conduct in respect of the matters to which the allegation relates[15]; and

(6) in cases where it is alleged that a registered insurance broker or enrolled body corporate is liable to have his or its name erased from the register or list, requiring that where the committee judges that the allegation has not been proved it must record a finding that he or it is not guilty of the matters alleged[16].

1 'Proceedings' means proceedings under the Insurance Brokers (Registration) Act 1977 whether relating to disciplinary cases or otherwise: s 19(6). For the meaning of 'disciplinary cases' see para 885 text to notes 1–6 ante.
2 As to that committee see para 886 ante.
3 As to writs of subpoena see EVIDENCE vol 17 paras 243–253.
4 Insurance Brokers (Registration) Act 1977 s 19(1). As to the documents to be produced on the trial of an action see DISCOVERY vol 13 para 56 et seq.
   The Supreme Court Act 1981 s 36 (as amended) or the Attendance of Witnesses Act 1854 (as amended) (which provide a special procedure for the issue of such writs so as to be in force throughout the United Kingdom) (see EVIDENCE vol 17 para 248) apply in relation to any proceedings before the Disciplinary Committee as they apply in relation to causes or matters in the High Court or actions or suits pending in the High Court of Justice in Northern Ireland: Insurance Brokers (Registration) Act 1977 s 19(2) (amended by the Supreme Court Act 1981 s 152(1), Sch 5).
5 For the meaning of 'insurance broker' see para 870 note 4 ante.
6 Insurance Brokers (Registration) Act 1977 s 19(5).
7 As to that council see paras 869–870 ante.
8 Insurance Brokers (Registration) Act 1977 s 19(4). As to rules see s 27; and para 873 ante. The rules made under this provision are the Insurance Brokers Registration Council (Procedure of the Disciplinary Committee) Rules 1978, approved by and scheduled to the Insurance Brokers Registration Council (Procedure of the Disciplinary Committee) Rules Approval Order 1978, SI 1978/1458.
9 Ie under the Insurance Brokers Registration Act 1977 s 15 (see para 889 post): s 19(4)(a).
10 Ibid s 19(4)(b).
11 Ibid s 19(4)(c).
12 Ibid s 19(4)(d).
13 For the meaning of 'registered insurance broker' see para 876 note 6 ante.
14 As to the enrolment of bodies corporate see para 876 ante.
15 Insurance Brokers (Registration) Act 1977 s 19(4)(e). As to the statement of what constitutes unprofessional conduct see para 882 ante.
16 Ibid s 19(4)(f). As to the grounds for erasure from the register or list see paras 889, 891 post.

888. Assessors to the Disciplinary Committee. In all proceedings before the Disciplinary Committee[1] there must be an assessor[2] to advise the committee on questions of law arising from the proceedings before it[3].

The power of appointing assessors is exercisable by the Insurance Brokers Registration Council[4], but if no assessor so appointed is available to act at any particular proceedings the committee may appoint one[5].

The Lord Chancellor may make rules[6] as to the functions of assessors, which may, in particular, contain:

(1) such provisions as appear to the Lord Chancellor expedient for securing:

    (a) that where an assessor advises the committee on any question of law as to evidence, procedure or any other matters specified in the rules, he must do so in the presence of every party, or person representing a party, to the proceedings who appears or, if the advice is tendered after the committee has begun to deliberate as to its findings, that every such party or person is informed what advice the assessor has tendered[7]; and

    (b) that every such party or person is to be informed if in any case the committee does not accept the assessor's advice on any such question[8]; and

(2) such incidental and supplementary provisions as appear to him expedient[9].

1 As to that committee see para 886 ante.
2 The assessor must be a person who has a ten year general qualification within the meaning of the Courts and Legal Services Act 1990 s 71 (or an advocate or solicitor in Scotland of at least ten years' standing, or a member of the Bar of Northern Ireland or solicitor of the Supreme Court of Northern Ireland of at least ten years' standing): Insurance Brokers (Registration) Act 1977 s 20(1)(a)–(c) (substituted by the Courts and Legal Services Act 1990 s 71(2), Sch 10 para 41).
3 Insurance Brokers (Registration) Act 1977 s 20(1).
4 As to that council see paras 869–870 ante.
5 Insurance Brokers (Registration) Act 1977 s 20(2). An assessor may be appointed either generally or for any particular proceedings or class of proceedings, and must hold and vacate office in accordance with the terms of the instrument under which he is appointed: s 20(4). Any remuneration paid by the council to persons appointed to act as assessors is at such rates as it may determine: s 20(5).
6 The power to make rules is exercisable by statutory instrument: ibid s 20(6). As to the making of statutory instruments see generally the Statutory Instruments Act 1946; and STATUTES. The rules made under this provision are the Insurance Brokers Registration Council (Disciplinary Committee) Legal Assessor Rules 1978, SI 1978/1503.
7 Insurance Brokers (Registration) Act 1977 s 20(3)(a).
8 Ibid s 20(3)(b).
9 Ibid s 20(3).

889. Erasure from register or list for misconduct etc. If a registered insurance broker[1] or enrolled body corporate[2] is (1) convicted by any court in the United Kingdom of any criminal offence[3], or (2) judged by the Disciplinary Committee[4] to have been guilty of unprofessional conduct[5], the committee may, if it thinks fit, direct that the name of the insurance broker or body corporate be erased from the register or list[6]. If it appears to the committee that a registered insurance broker or an enrolled body corporate has contravened or failed to comply with any rules relating to carrying on business[7] or to professional indemnity[8], and that the contravention or failure is such as to render him or it unfit to have his or its name on the register or list, the committee may, if it thinks fit, direct that the name of the insurance broker or body corporate be erased from the register or list[9].

The committee may, if it thinks fit, direct that the name of a registered insurance broker or enrolled body corporate be erased from the register or list if it appears to the committee that any responsible person[10] has concluded that the broker or a related person[11] has contravened or failed to comply with:

(a) any provision of the Financial Services Act 1986 or any rule or regulation made thereunder to which he or it was subject at the time of the contravention or failure; or

(b) any rule of any recognised self-regulating organisation[12] or recognised professional body[13] to which he or it was subject at that time[14].

Where:

(i) the name of a director of an enrolled body corporate is erased from the register[15], or

(ii) a director of any such body corporate is convicted of an offence under the Insurance Brokers (Registration) Act 1977[16], or

(iii) the name of a registered insurance broker employed by any such body corporate is erased from the register and the act or omission constituting the ground on which it was erased was instigated or connived at by a director of the body corporate, or, if the act or omission was a continuing act or omission, a director had or reasonably ought to have had knowledge of its continuance[17],

the committee may, if it thinks fit, direct the name of the body corporate to be erased from the list[18].

If the committee is of opinion as respects an enrolled body corporate that the conditions for enrolment[19] are no longer satisfied, it may, if it thinks fit, direct that the name of the body corporate be erased from the list[20].

1 For the meaning of 'registered insurance broker' see para 876 note 6 ante.

2 As to the enrolment of bodies corporate see para 876 ante.

3 Ie not being an offence which, owing to its trivial nature or the circumstances under which it was committed, does not render him or it unfit to have his or its name on the register or list: Insurance Brokers (Registration) Act 1977 s 15(1)(a). As to the register see para 874 ante; as to the list see para 876 ante.

4 As to that committee see para 886 ante.

5 Insurance Brokers (Registration) Act 1977 s 15(1)(b). As to the statement of what constitutes unprofessional conduct see para 882 ante.

6 Ibid s 15(1). When the committee directs that the name of an individual or body corporate be erased from the register or list, the registrar must serve on that individual or body a notification of the direction and a statement of the committee's reasons for it: s 15(6). As to the registrar see para 877 ante.

7 Ie rules made under ibid s 11 (as amended) (see para 883 ante): s 15(2).

8 Ie rules made under ibid s 12 (as amended) (see para 884 ante): s 15(2).

9 Ibid s 15(2); and see note 6 supra.

10 'Responsible person' means a person responsible under the Financial Services Act 1986 or under the rules of any recognised self-regulating organisation (see note 12 infra) or recognised professional body (see note 13 infra) for determining whether any contravention of any provision of that Act or rules or regulations made thereunder, or of the rules of that organisation or body, has occurred: Insurance Brokers (Registration) Act 1977 s 15(2B)(a) (added by the Financial Services Act 1986 s 138(4)).

11 'Related person' means a partnership or unincorporated association of which the broker in question is, or was at the time of the failure or contravention in question, a member, or a body corporate of which he is, or was at that time, a director: Insurance Brokers (Registration) Act 1977 s 15(2B)(b) (as added: see note 10 supra).

12 'Recognised self-regulating organisation' means a body declared by order of the Secretary of State for the time being in force to be a recognised self-regulating organisation for the purposes of the Financial Services Act 1986: s 207(1). As to the Secretary of State see para 15 note 5 ante.

13 'Recognised professional body' means a body declared by order of the Secretary of State for the time being in force to be a recognised professional body for the purposes of the Financial Services Act 1986: s 207(1).

14 Insurance Brokers (Registration) Act 1977 s 15(2A) (as added: see note 10 supra).
15 Ie under ibid s 15(1) (see the text to notes 1–6 supra): s 15(3)(a).
16 Ie under ibid s 24 (see para 894 post): s 15(3)(b).
17 Ibid s 15(3)(c).
18 Ibid s 15(3). The committee may not, however, take a case into consideration during any period within which proceedings by way of appeal may be brought which may result in s 15(3) being rendered inapplicable in that case or while any such proceedings are pending: s 15(3) proviso. As to appeals see para 892 post.
19 Ie the conditions in ibid s 4 (see para 876 ante): s 15(4).
20 Ibid s 15(4). Where a registered insurance broker dies while he is a director of an enrolled body corporate, he is deemed for this purpose to have continued to be a director of that body until the expiration of six months beginning with the date of his death or until a director is appointed in his place, whichever first occurs: s 15(5).

890. Restoration of erased names. Where the name of an individual or body corporate has been erased from the register or list[1], it may not again be entered in the register or list unless the Disciplinary Committee[2] on application made to it in that behalf otherwise directs[3]. Such an application may not be made to the committee within ten months of the date of erasure nor within ten months of a previous application[4].

1 Ie in pursuance of a direction under the Insurance Brokers (Registration) Act 1977 s 15 (as amended) (see para 889 ante): s 16(1).
2 As to that committee see para 886 ante.
3 Insurance Brokers (Registration) Act 1977 s 16(1).
4 Ibid s 16(2).

891. Erasure from register or list for fraud etc. If it is proved to the satisfaction of the Disciplinary Committee[1] that any entry in the register or list[2] has been fraudulently or incorrectly made, the committee may, if it thinks fit, direct that the entry be erased from the register or list[3].

An individual may be registered or a body corporate enrolled under the Insurance Brokers (Registration) Act 1977 notwithstanding that his or its name has been erased under the provision described above, but if it was erased on the ground of fraud, that individual or body corporate may not be registered or enrolled except on an application in that behalf to the committee; on any such application the committee may, if it thinks fit, direct that the individual or body corporate is not to be registered or enrolled, or is not to be registered or enrolled until the expiration of a period specified in the direction[4].

Where the committee directs that the name of an individual or body corporate be erased under the provision described above, the registrar must serve on the individual or body a notification of the direction and a statement of the committee's reasons for it[5].

1 As to that committee see para 886 ante.
2 As to the register see para 874 ante; as to the list see para 876 ante.
3 Insurance Brokers (Registration) Act 1977 s 17(1).
4 Ibid s 17(2).
5 Ibid s 17(3). As to the service of documents see para 879 note 5 ante.

892. Appeals. At any time within 28 days from the service of a notification that the Disciplinary Committee[1] has directed that the name of an individual or a body corporate be erased from the register or list[2], that individual or body corporate may appeal to the High Court[3].

Where no such appeal is brought or where one is brought but withdrawn or struck out for want of prosecution, the direction appealed against takes effect on the expiration of the time for appealing or, as the case may be, on the withdrawal or striking out of the appeal[4]. Subject to that, where an appeal is brought, the direction takes effect if and when the appeal is dismissed and not otherwise[5].

The Insurance Brokers Registration Council[6] may appear as respondent on any such appeal, and for the purpose of enabling directions to be given as to the costs of the appeal it is deemed to be a party to it, whether it appears on the hearing of the appeal or not[7].

1 As to that committee see para 886 ante.
2 Ie under the Insurance Brokers (Registration) Act 1977 s 15 (as amended) (see para 889 ante) or s 17 (see para 891 ante): s 18(1).
3 Ibid ss 18(1), 29(1).
4 Ibid s 18(3).
5 Ibid s 18(4).
6 As to that council see paras 869–870 ante.
7 Insurance Brokers (Registration) Act 1977 s 18(2).

(iii) Offences

893. Pretending to be registered. Any individual or body corporate wilfully:
  (1) taking or using any style, title or description which consists of or includes the expression 'insurance broker'[1] when he is not registered in the register[2], or it is not enrolled in the list[3]; or
  (2) taking or using any name, title, addition or description falsely implying, or otherwise pretending, that he is registered in the register[4], or it is enrolled in the list[5];
is liable on summary conviction to a fine not exceeding the prescribed sum, or on conviction on indictment to a fine[6].

Where a practising insurance broker[7] dies or becomes bankrupt, then, during the period of three months beginning with his death or bankruptcy, or such longer period as the Insurance Brokers Registration Council[8] may in any particular case allow, the above provisions do not operate to prevent his personal representatives, his surviving spouse or any of his children or trustees on behalf of his surviving spouse or any of his children, or, as the case may be, his trustee in bankruptcy, from taking or using in relation to his business, but in conjunction with the name in which he carried it on, any title which he was entitled to take or use immediately before his death or bankruptcy[9].

1 For this purpose 'insurance broker' includes the related expressions 'assurance broker' 'reinsurance broker' and 'reassurance broker': Insurance Brokers (Registration) Act 1977 s 22(3).
2 Ibid s 22(1)(a). As to the register see para 874 ante.
3 Ibid s 22(2)(a). As to the list see para 876 ante.
4 Ibid s 22(1)(b).
5 Ibid s 22(2)(b).
6 Ibid s 22(1), (2) (both amended by virtue of the Magistrates' Courts Act 1980 s 32(2)). As to the prescribed sum see para 19 note 5 ante.
7 For the meaning of 'practising insurance broker' see para 883 text and notes 3–4 ante.
8 As to that council see paras 869–870 ante.
9 Insurance Brokers (Registration) Act 1977 s 23(1), (2).

894. Offences by bodies corporate. Where an offence under the Insurance Brokers (Registration) Act 1977[1] which has been committed by a body corporate is proved to have been committed with the consent or connivance of, or to be attributable to any neglect on the part of, any director, manager, secretary or other similar officer of the body corporate, or any person purporting to act in any such capacity, he as well as the body corporate is guilty of that offence and is liable to be proceeded against and punished accordingly[2].

1 As to offences under the Insurance Brokers (Registration) Act 1977 see para 893 ante.
2 Ibid s 24.

14. PROTECTION OF POLICYHOLDERS

(1) POLICYHOLDERS' PROTECTION GENERALLY

895. The Policyholders Protection Act 1975. The Policyholders Protection Act 1975 protects policyholders[1] from the consequences of authorised insurance companies[2] failing to meet their liabilities, and finances that protection by levies on the insurance industry[3].

1 'Policyholder' has the same meaning as in the Insurance Companies Act 1982 (see s 96(1); and para 806 note 21 ante): Policyholders Protection Act 1975 s 32(2)(a) (amended by the Insurance Companies Act 1982 s 99(2), Sch 5 para 16(a); and, as from a day to be appointed, by the Friendly Societies Act 1992 s 97, Sch 17 para 18(1), (3)). As to the scope of the term see *Scher v Policyholder Protection Board* [1993] 3 All ER 384, [1993] 2 WLR 479, CA; [1993] 3 All ER 384, [1993] 3 WLR 357, HL; *Scher v Policyholders Protection Board (No 2)* [1993] 4 All ER 840, [1993] 3 WLR 1030, HL; varied sub nom *Scher v Policyholders Protection Board (Nos 1 and 2)* [1994] 2 All ER 37n, HL. As from a day to be appointed by order made by the Treasury under the Friendly Societies Act 1992 s 126(2), the Policyholders Protection Act 1975 will also apply to friendly societies; thereafter, in the application of the Act to friendly societies, a reference to a policyholder is to be construed as a reference to a person who has entered into a contract of insurance with that society: s 32(2B) (added, as from a day to be appointed, by the Friendly Societies Act 1992 Sch 17 para 18(4)). 'Friendly society' has the same meaning as in the Friendly Societies Act 1992: Policyholders Protection Act 1975 s 32(1) (amended, as from a day to be appointed, by the Friendly Societies Act 1992 Sch 17 para 18(2)). See generally FRIENDLY SOCIETIES.
2 'Authorised insurance company' means an insurance company authorised under the Insurance Companies Act 1982 s 3 or s 4 to carry on insurance business of any class in the United Kingdom: Policyholders Protection Act 1975 ss 3(2), 32(1) (amended by the Insurance Companies Act 1980 s 4(1), (3), Sch 3 para 9, Sch 5; the Insurance Companies Act 1981 s 36(1), Sch 4 Pt II para 25(2); and the Insurance Companies Act 1982 Sch 5 para 16(a)). For the meaning of 'United Kingdom' see para 2 note 10 ante.
3 As to levies on the insurance industry see paras 902–903 post.

896. The Policyholders Protection Board. The Policyholders Protection Board is a body corporate[1] consisting of five persons appointed by the Secretary of State, together with any persons appointed by him to be alternate members in respect of any member in his absence[2]. Any appointment made by the Secretary of State must be for a term not exceeding two years, and the term of appointment of an alternate member must not exceed the term or the remainder of the term of the member in respect of whom he is appointed[3]. The Secretary of State must appoint one of the members of the board to be the chairman[4]. Members and alternate members (including the chairman) hold and vacate office in accordance with the terms of their appointments[5], and may resign office by giving the Secretary of State written notice signed by the member, alternate member or chairman, as the case may be, stating that he resigns his office[6]. If the Secretary of State is satisfied that a member or an alternate member is incapacitated by physical or mental illness, or is otherwise unfit to discharge his functions, he may by written notice remove him from office, and the office then becomes vacant[7]. Where, before the end of the term for which he was appointed, a member dies or vacates office, the alternate member in respect of that member may act as member in his place until a person is appointed to fill his office as member[8]; and the Secretary of State may vary the terms of appointment of the alternate member on appointing a person to fill the office vacated by the member in question[9]. The board must pay to each member or alternate member such remuneration and travelling, subsistence or other allowances as it may determine[10].

The functions of the board are (1) to take specified measures for the purpose of indemnifying or otherwise assisting or protecting policyholders and others prejudiced by the inability of insurance companies carrying on business in the United Kingdom to meet their liabilities under policies issued or securities given by them[11]; (2) to finance its expenditure by levies on insurance companies and others engaged in the insurance industry in the United Kingdom[12]; and (3) otherwise to do anything requisite for carrying out the provisions of the Policyholders Protection Act 1975[13]. The board may borrow sums for performing its functions[14], but these sums must not exceed £10m[15]. The Secretary of State may give the board guidance with respect to the performance of its functions, and the board must perform its functions in such a manner as it considers is in accordance with that guidance[16].

The board's functions are exercisable in relation to policyholders and others only in cases where the insurance companies in question are authorised insurance companies[17], and a policyholder is eligible for assistance or protection only in respect of a policy which was a United Kingdom policy at the relevant time[18].

Where it appears to the board that (a) a person is insured under a contract of insurance with an authorised insurance company which is not evidenced by any policy[19], and (b) if a policy evidencing the contract had been issued that person would have been eligible as a policyholder for the assistance or protection of the board[20], the board may take such measures for that person's assistance or protection as it would in its view have been required or authorised to take under the relevant provision[21] if such a policy had been issued and that person had been a policyholder[22].

The board may do anything incidental or conducive to the proper performance of its functions[23]. The measures open to the board under any provision of the Policyholders Protection Act 1975 which authorises or requires it to take any measures appearing to it to be appropriate for any purpose include, in particular, (i) making payments to any person on such terms (including terms requiring repayment in whole or in part) and conditions as the board thinks fit[24]; (ii) giving guarantees or indemnities to or in favour of any person[25]; and (iii) making any other arrangement or agreement with or for the benefit of any person[26]. The board may authorise any member or alternate member or any other person who is either an employee or agent of the board to perform on its behalf such of its functions as are specified in the authorisation[27].

A member or an alternate member of the board who is in any way directly or indirectly interested, whether as a member or policyholder of an insurance company or in any other manner, in any matter falling to be considered by the board must disclose the nature of his interest at a board meeting, and may not take part in any deliberation or decision with respect to that matter[28]. The duty to declare an interest does not apply where the only connection of the company in question with the matter under consideration arises from the fact that it has agreed or may agree to take a transfer of the business of a company in liquidation or financial difficulties[29].

The fixing of the board's common seal must be authenticated by the chairman or some other person authorised to act for that purpose[30]; and a document purporting to be duly executed under the board's seal must be received in evidence and, unless the contrary is proved, be deemed to be so executed[31].

Subject to the above, the board may regulate its own procedure[32].

1 Policyholders Protection Act 1975 s 1(1).
2 Ibid s 1(5), Sch 1 para 1(1), (3). At least three of the persons appointed must be directors, chief executives or managers of authorised insurance companies (defined in para 895 note 2 ante) (Sch 1 para 1(2)(a)); and at least one must be a person appearing to the Secretary of State to be qualified to represent the interests of policyholders (defined in para 895 note 1 ante) of such companies (Sch 1 para 1(2)(b)). A person appointed as an alternate member in respect of a person who is a director, chief executive or manager of an authorised insurance company must also be such a person; and a person so appointed in respect of a person appearing to the Secretary of State to be qualified to represent the interests of policyholders must also be so qualified: Sch 1 para 1(4). The Secretary of State must consult persons appearing to him to be representative of authorised insurance companies before appointing a person who is a director, chief executive or manager of such a company to be a member or alternate member of the board: Sch 1 para 1(5). The validity of any proceedings of the board is not affected by any defect in the appointment of a member or of an alternate member: Sch 1 para 10. As to the Secretary of State see para 15 note 5 ante.
3 Ibid Sch 1 para 2(1). The Secretary of State may reappoint a person as a member or alternate member of the board on his ceasing to hold office in either capacity or at any later time: Sch 1 para 2(2).
4 Ibid Sch 1 para 3(1). If the chairman ceases to be a member, he must cease to be the chairman: Sch 1 para 3(2).
5 Ibid Sch 1 para 4(1).
6 Ibid Sch 1 para 4(2).
7 Ibid Sch 1 para 4(3). The validity of any proceedings of the board is not affected by any vacancy among the members: Sch 1 para 10.
8 Ibid Sch 1 para 4(4)(a).
9 Ibid Sch 1 para 4(4)(b). Where a person ceases to be a member or an alternate member of the board and it appears to the Secretary of State that that person should receive compensation, he may require the board to pay to that person a sum of such amount as, with the consent of the Treasury, he may determine: Sch 1 para 6; Transfer of Functions (Minister for the Civil Service and Treasury) Order 1981, SI 1981/1670.
10 Policyholders Protection Act 1975 Sch 1 para 5(1). Any such determination is subject to the Secretary of State's approval, but he must not give his approval without the consent of the Treasury: Sch 1 para 5(2); Transfer of Functions (Minister for the Civil Service and Treasury) Order 1981.
11 Policyholders Protection Act 1975 s 1(2)(a). As to the measures to be taken see ss 6–16 (as amended); and paras 897–900 post. As from a day to be appointed (see para 895 note 1 ante), the board will also have the function of taking specified measures to indemnify or otherwise assist or protect persons in relation to friendly societies: see ss 1(2)(aa), 3A, 4(3), 5A, 8A, 11(3A), 11A (added, as from a day to be appointed, by the Friendly Societies Act 1992 s 97, Sch 17 paras 1–10). See FRIENDLY SOCIETIES.
12 Policyholders Protection Act 1975 s 1(2)(b). As to the levies see ss 19–21, Schs 2, 3 (as amended); and paras 902–903 post. As from a day to be appointed, levies may be imposed on friendly societies: s 1(2)(b) (amended, as from a day to be appointed, by the Friendly Societies Act 1992 Sch 17 para 1). See the Policyholders Protection Act 1975 ss 19(11), 21(10), Sch 3 paras 4A, 4B(2) (added, as from a day to be appointed, by the Friendly Societies Act 1992 Sch 17 paras 14, 15, 19).
13 Policyholders Protection Act 1975 s 1(2). As to the Policyholders Protection Act 1975 generally see para 895 ante.
14 Ibid s 1(3).
15 Ibid s 1(4).

16 Ibid s 2(1). Guidance may only be given if a draft of the document containing it has been approved by a resolution of each House of Parliament: s 2(2).

17 Ibid s 3(1).

18 Ibid s 4(1). A policy is a 'United Kingdom policy' at any time when the performance by the insurer of any of his obligations under the contract evidenced by the policy would constitute the carrying on by the insurer of insurance business of any class in the United Kingdom: s 4(2). An insurance policy is a United Kingdom policy for the purposes of s 4 if, had any of the obligations under the contract evidenced by the policy been performed at the relevant time, such performance would have formed part of an insurance business which the insurer was authorised to carry on in the United Kingdom, whether or not such obligation or obligations would have been performed in the United Kingdom: see *Scher v Policyholders Protection Board* [1993] 3 All ER 384 at 416, [1993] 3 WLR 357 at 368, HL, per Lord Goff of Chieveley. For the meaning of 'United Kingdom' see para 2 note 10 ante. As to the classes of insurance business in respect of which insurance companies may be authorised see para 18 ante.

19 Policyholders Protection Act 1975 s 23(1)(a).

20 Ibid s 23(1)(b).

21 'The relevant provision' means any provision of ibid ss 6–16 (as amended) (see paras 897–900 post): s 23(1)(b). Any expenditure of the board under s 23 is treated for the purposes of s 18 (see para 902 note 2 post) as expenditure under the relevant provision: s 23(2).

22 Ibid s 23(1).

23 Ibid Sch 1 para 7(2). As to the board's power of investment see para 904 post.

24 Ibid Sch 1 para 7(3)(a).

25 Ibid Sch 1 para 7(3)(b).

26 Ibid Sch 1 para 7(3)(c).

27 Ibid Sch 1 para 11.

28 Ibid Sch 1 para 9(1). The disclosure must be recorded in the minutes of the meeting: Sch 1 para 9(1). A notice given by a member or alternate member at a board meeting that he is a member or a policyholder of a specified insurance company and is to be regarded as interested in any matter affecting that company which falls to be considered by the board after the date of the notice, is a sufficient disclosure of his interest in any such matter: Sch 1 para 9(3). The member need not attend in person at a meeting in order to make disclosure if he takes reasonable steps to secure that disclosure is made by a notice which is taken into consideration and read at the meeting: Sch 1 para 9(4).

29 Ie within the meaning of ibid s 16 (as amended) (see para 900 post): Sch 1 para 9(2).

30 Ibid Sch 1 para 12. As to the execution of deeds see DEEDS vol 12 para 1325 et seq.

31 Ibid Sch 1 para 13.

32 Ibid Sch 1 para 8. As to the board's duty to prepare accounts see para 904 post, and as to its duty to prepare a report on the performance of its functions see para 901 post.

(2) POWERS AND DUTIES OF THE POLICYHOLDERS PROTECTION BOARD

897. Board's duties in cases of companies in liquidation. Where, in the case of any authorised insurance company[1], either (1) a resolution has been passed after 29 October 1974 for the voluntary winding up of the company[2] otherwise than merely for the purpose of reconstruction or amalgamation[3], or (2) an order has been made for the winding up of the company by the court on a petition presented after that date[4], the functions described below are exercisable by the Policyholders Protection Board[5].

The board must secure that the full amount of any liability of the company towards any policyholder[6] or security holder under the terms of any specified compulsory policy or security[7] arising in respect of a liability of the policyholder subject to compulsory insurance is paid as soon as reasonably practicable after the beginning of the liquidation[8]. Where the company's liability is towards a private policyholder[9] and is in respect of a liability not subject to compulsory insurance, the board must secure payment of 90 per cent of the amount[10]. It must secure that the full amount of any liability of the company in respect of a sum payable to a

person entitled to the benefit of a judgment under the Road Traffic Act 1988[11] is
paid as soon as reasonably practicable after the beginning of the liquidation[12]. It
must also secure that 90 per cent of any liability of the company towards a private
policyholder under the terms of a general policy[13], other than a compulsory
policy[14], which was a United Kingdom policy at the beginning of the liquidation is
paid[15]. The board is not required by virtue of the above provisions to secure any
sum by reference to any liability of the company in liquidation which is duplicated
by the liability of any other authorised insurance company which is not a company
in liquidation[16].

The board must secure that 90 per cent of any liability of a company in liquidation towards any policyholder under the terms of a long term policy[17] which was
a United Kingdom policy at the beginning of the liquidation is paid to the
policyholder as soon as reasonably practicable after the beginning of the liquidation[18]. The board must also secure continuity of insurance for every such
policyholder[19] by arranging either a transfer of the company's long term business,
or of any part of it, to another authorised insurance company[20] or the issue by
another authorised insurance company of substitute policies[21]. The board's duty to
secure continuity of such insurance extends only to securing that the policyholder
will receive 90 per cent of any future benefit[22] under his policy, subject to and in
accordance with terms corresponding, so far as appears reasonable to the board, to
the terms which would have applied under the policy[23]. During any period when it
is seeking to make arrangements for securing continuity of insurance, the board
must secure that 90 per cent of any future benefit which would have fallen due
during that period is paid as soon as reasonably practicable after the time when the
benefit in question would have fallen due under the policy (but subject to and in
accordance with any other terms which would have applied under the policy)[24];
where any sum has been paid under this provision, arrangements subsequently
made by the board are not required to cover any future benefit by reference to
which such sum was paid[25]. Where it is not reasonably practicable to secure
continuity of insurance the board must pay the policyholder 90 per cent of the value
attributed to his policy in the winding up[26].

By regulations made by statutory instrument[27], the Secretary of State may
(a) require the board, in a case where it appears to the board that it is not reasonably
practicable to secure continuity of insurance[28], to pay the policyholder at his option
a sum equal to 90 per cent of the value of the future benefits under the policy or of
such of those benefits as may be specified by the regulations, determined in such
manner as the regulations may provide[29]; (b) make such provision as appears to
him to be appropriate with respect to the time within which the board is to perform
any of its functions with regard to securing the continuity of insurance[30].

Where it appears to the board that the benefits provided for under any long term
policy which was a United Kingdom policy are or may be excessive in any respect,
having regard to the premiums paid or payable and to any other terms of the
policy, the board must refer the policy to an independent actuary[31]. Where such an
actuary reports in writing to the board stating that in his view the benefit or benefits
provided for under a policy referred to him are excessive[32] and recommending
that, for the purposes of the board's functions with regard to long term policies[33],
any liability of the company or any future benefit under the policy should be treated
as reduced or disregarded[34], the board may determine in the light of that recommendation that the liability or benefit in question be treated as reduced or
disregarded in exercising its duties under the above provisions with regard to that

policy[35]. Where a claim has been admitted in a company's winding up, in respect of any policy which is the subject of such an actuary's report[36], and that report indicates, or the actuary makes a further report indicating, what value would in his view have been attributed to the policy in the winding up if any future benefit under the policy had been treated as reduced or disregarded in accordance with the recommendation in his report in determining the claim in respect of the policy in the winding up[37], the board may determine in the light of the value so indicated that the value attributed to the policy in the winding up is to be treated as so reduced for the purpose of calculating the sum payable by the board in circumstances where it is not reasonably practicable to secure the continuity of the insurance[38].

1 For the meaning of 'authorised insurance company' see para 895 note 2 ante.
2 Ie under the Insolvency Act 1986 (see COMPANIES vol 7(2) (Reissue) para 1935 et seq): Policyholders Protection Act 1975 s 5(1)(a) (amended by the Insolvency Act 1986 s 439(2), Sch 14).
3 Policyholders Protection Act 1975 s 5(1)(a).
4 Ibid s 5(1)(b). As to winding up by the court see COMPANIES vol 7(2) (Reissue) para 1435 et seq.
5 Ibid s 5(1). The company is referred to as 'a company in liquidation': s 5(4).
6 For the meaning of 'policyholder' see para 895 note 1 ante.
7 Ie any policy which satisfies the requirements of (1) the Riding Establishments Act 1964 s 1(4A)(d) (added by the Riding Establishments Act 1970 s 2(1)(ii)) (see ANIMALS vol 2 (Reissue) para 393 note 8) (Policyholders Protection Act 1975 s 6(1)(a)), (2) the Employers' Liability (Compulsory Insurance) Act 1969 s 1 (as amended) (see EMPLOYMENT vol 16 (Reissue) para 36) (Policyholders Protection Act 1975 s 6(1)(b)), or (3) the Road Traffic Act 1988 Pt VI (ss 143–162) (as amended) (see para 729 et seq ante) (Policyholders Protection Act 1975 s 6(1)(c) (amended by the Road Traffic (Consequential Provisions) Act 1988 s 4, Sch 3 para 14(1)); and any policy evidencing a contract of insurance effected for the purposes of the Nuclear Installations Act 1965 s 1 (as amended) (Policyholders Protection Act 1975 s 6(1)); and any specific in respect of third party risks given by an authorised insurance company which satisfies the requirements of the Road Traffic Act 1988 Pt VI (Policyholders Protection Act 1975 s 6(2) (amended by the Road Traffic (Consequential Provisions) Act 1988 Sch 3 para 14(1)). A liability of a company in liquidation towards a policyholder arising otherwise than under the terms of the policy must be treated as a liability under the terms of the policy if the company's liability arises from any failure on its part to perform an obligation under the policy to provide any services or facilities on the occurrence of any event to which the risk under the policy relates: Policyholders Protection Act 1975 s 32(4).
8 Ibid s 6(4). 'The beginning of the liquidation' means (1) in relation to a case where a resolution has been passed for voluntary winding up, otherwise than merely for the purpose of reconstruction or amalgamation, the passing of the resolution (s 5(5)(a)); and (2) in relation to a case where an order has been made for winding up by the court, the making of the order (s 5(5)(b)). Section 6(4) does not apply by reference to any liability of a company in liquidation under the terms of a policy which satisfies the requirements of the provisions referred to in note 7 supra, arising otherwise than in respect of a liability of the policyholder which is subject to compulsory insurance: s 6(5). 'A liability subject to compulsory insurance' means any liability required under any of the provisions referred to in note 7 supra to be covered by insurance or (as the case may be) by insurance or by some other provision for securing its discharge: s 6(3). These provisions are subject to s 9 (see text and note 16 infra), ss 13, 14 (see para 898 post): s 6(4).
9 'Private policyholder' means a policyholder who is either an individual (ibid s 6(7)(a)) or a partnership or other incorporated body of persons all of whom are individuals (s 6(7)(b)). The following principles have been declared as to who may be a private policyholder within s 6(7): (1) a professional corporation is not an individual and cannot be a private policyholder; (2) no partnership, one or more of whose partners is a professional corporation, can be a private policyholder, nor can any individual in his capacity as a partner in such a partnership; (3) being in partnership with a professional corporation does not disqualify an individual from being a private policyholder if he contracts with the insurance company in a capacity other than that of partner: *Scher v Policyholders Protection Board* [1993] 3 All ER 384 at 397–398, [1993] 2 WLR 479 at 495, CA, per Lord Donaldson of Lymington MR; varied sub nom *Scher v Policyholders Protection Board (No 2)* [1993] 3 All ER 384, [1993] 3 WLR 1030, HL, and sub nom *Scher v Policyholders Protection Board (Nos 1 and 2)* [1994] 2 All ER 37n, HL.
10 Policyholders Protection Act 1975 s 6(6). These provisions are subject to ss 9 (as amended), 13, 14: s 6(6). The board is not under any duty unless (1) in the case of any policy, it was a United Kingdom

policy (defined in para 896 note 18 ante) at the beginning of the liquidation (s 6(8)(a)); or (2) in the case of any security in respect of third party risks, it would have been a United Kingdom policy at the beginning of the liquidation, if it had been an insurance policy and the contract governing the security had been a contract of insurance (s 6(8)(b)). References in ss 7–33 (as amended) to policies which were United Kingdom policies at any time and to policyholders in respect of such policies are construed as including references to (a) securities in respect of third party risks which satisfy the requirements of the Road Traffic Act 1988 Pt VI, which would have been United Kingdom policies at the time in question if they had been insurance policies and the contracts governing them had been contracts of insurance; or (b) security holders in respect of such securities: Policyholders Protection Act 1975 s 6(9).

11 Ie the Road Traffic Act 1988 s 151 (see paras 748–753 ante): Policyholders Protection Act 1975 s 7(a) (amended by the Road Traffic (Consequential Provisions) Act 1988 Sch 3 para 14(2)).

12 Policyholders Protection Act 1975 s 7. This provision is subject to ss 9 (as amended), 13, 14: s 7.

13 Ibid s 8(1) (amended, as from a day to be appointed, by the Friendly Societies Act 1992 s 97, Sch 17 para 6). 'General policy' means any policy evidencing a contract the effecting of which constituted the carrying on of general business of any class, other than insurance of aircraft, ships, goods in transit, aircraft liability or liability of ships, not being a contract of reinsurance: Policyholders Protection Act 1975 s 8(4) (amended by the Insurance Companies Act 1981 s 36(2), Sch 4 Pt II; and, as from a day to be appointed, by the Friendly Societies Act 1992 Sch 17 para 6). As to the classes of insurance business in respect of which insurance companies may be authorised see para 18 ante.

14 Ie a policy to which the Policyholders Protection Act 1975 s 6 (as amended) (see text and notes 7–10 supra) applies: s 8(1).

15 Ibid s 8(2). This provision is subject to ss 9 (as amended), 13, 14: s 8(2). As to the operation of s 8(2) see *Scher v Policyholders Protection Board* [1993] 3 All ER 384, [1993] 2 WLR 479, CA; [1993] 3 All ER 384, [1993] 3 WLR 357, HL; *Scher v Policyholders Protection Board (No 2)* [1993] 4 All ER 840, [1993] 3 WLR 1030, HL; *Scher v Policyholders Protection Board (Nos 1 and 2)* [1994] 2 All ER 37n, HL.

16 Policyholders Protection Act 1975 s 9(1). A liability of a company is duplicated by the liability of another company in so far as that other company is also under a liability, under the terms of any general policy which was a United Kingdom policy at the beginning of the first-mentioned company's liquidation, to make any payment to or on behalf of the policyholder in respect of the matter to which the first-mentioned company's liability relates: s 9(2). A liability of a company in respect of a sum payable under the Road Traffic Act 1988 s 151 to a person entitled to the benefit of a judgment is duplicated by the liability of another company in so far as that other company is also liable under that provision to pay any sum to that person in respect of that judgment: Policyholders Protection Act 1975 s 9(3) (amended by the Road Traffic (Consequential Provisions) Act 1988 Sch 3 para 14(3)).

17 'Long term policy' means a policy evidencing a contract the effecting of which constituted the carrying on of long term business, not being a contract of insurance: Policyholders Protection Act 1975 s 10(1) (amended by the Insurance Companies Act 1981 s 36(2), Sch 5 Pt I; and, as from a day to be appointed, by the Friendly Societies Act 1992 Sch 17 para 8). As to restrictions on and withdrawal from long term insurance business see paras 815–816 ante. For the meaning of 'long term business' see the Policyholders Protection Act 1975 s 32(2)(a) (amended by the Insurance Companies Act 1982 s 99(2), Sch 5 para 16(a)), applying the definition given in para 23 note 5 ante.

18 Policyholders Protection Act 1975 s 10(2). This provision is subject to ss 13, 14: s 10(2). As to the limitation on the board's duty to secure payments see para 898 post.

19 Ibid s 11(3). This duty is subject to the policyholder's compliance with any conditions imposed by the board with respect to the payment of sums which would have fallen due by way of premiums: s 11(11).

20 Ibid s 11(5)(a).

21 Ibid s 11(5)(b).

22 Ibid s 11(4). 'Future benefit', in relation to any long term policy of a company in liquidation, means any benefit provided for under the policy which has not fallen due to be paid by the company before the beginning of the liquidation (s 11(1)), but excluding any bonus provided for under the policy unless it was declared before the beginning of the liquidation (s 11(2)).

23 Ibid s 11(4). Where a policy contains terms relating to matters other than future benefits under the policy, this duty extends also to securing that the policy after any transfer of business or any substitute policy contains terms relating to those matters which correspond, so far as appears reasonable to the board in the circumstances, to the terms of the original policy: s 11(6).

24 Ibid s 11(7). The board's duty is subject to compliance by the policyholder with any conditions imposed by the board with respect to the payment of sums which would have fallen due by way of premiums: s 11(11).

25 Ibid s 11(8).
26 Ibid s 11(9). This provision is subject to s 11(10) (see text to notes 27–30 infra) and ss 13, 14 (see para 898 post): s 11(9). Payment is to be made as soon as reasonably practicable after any claim in respect of the policy in the winding up is admitted: s 11(9). Any sum secured by the board under s 11(7) (see text to note 24 supra) is treated as reducing any sum payable by virtue of s 11(9): s 14(6).
27 Any statutory instrument so made is subject to annulment in pursuance of a resolution of either House of Parliament: ibid s 31(1). At the date at which this volume states the law, no such regulations had been made. The power to make regulations includes power to make different provision for different circumstances, but is only exercisable after consultation with the board: s 31(2). As to the Secretary of State see para 15 note 5 ante.
28 Ie in a case to which ibid s 11(9) (see text and note 26 supra) applies: s 11(10)(a).
29 Ibid s 11(10)(a).
30 Ibid s 11(10)(b).
31 Ibid s 12(1). For the meaning of 'actuary' see s 32(2)(a) (as amended: see note 17 supra), applying the definition given in para 21 note 8 ante.
32 Ibid s 12(2)(a).
33 Ie the provisions of ibid ss 10, 11 (as amended) (see text and notes 17–30 supra): s 12(2)(b).
34 Ibid s 12(2)(b). 'Future benefit' has the same meaning as in s 11 (see note 22 supra): s 12(6).
35 Ibid s 12(3).
36 Ie under ibid s 12(2) (see text to notes 32–34 supra): s 12(4)(a).
37 Ibid s 12(4)(b).
38 Ibid s 12(5).

898. Board's duties generally. Where it appears to the Policyholders Protection Board[1] that sums due under a policy of a company in liquidation[2] could have been paid to a person other than the policyholder[3] or are subject to a charge, trust or other agreement binding on the policyholder[4], the board may secure the payment of any sum payable to the policyholder, or pay any sum so payable, to that other person or, as the case may be, to the person appearing to the board to be entitled under the trust, charge or agreement instead of to the policyholder[5]. Any sum paid to a person other than the policyholder is to be treated as a payment to the policyholder and may be made on such conditions as the board thinks fit[6]. The board may secure the payment of any sum payable to the policyholder or person entitled to the benefit of a judgment by itself making payments[7] or by securing by appropriate measures that such payments are made by any other person[8]. The board may postpone making any payment or taking any measure until its funds are adequate to meet the expenditure[9].

The board may require a policyholder or person entitled to the benefit of a judgment to assign his rights to the board[10]. The Secretary of State may by regulations[11] provide for the transfer to and vesting in the board of certain rights in such circumstances as may be specified in the regulations[12].

Any payment made by a person other than the board referable to any liability of a company in liquidation in respect of a compulsory insurance policy, third party risks against an insurance company or a general policy other than a compulsory policy[13] is treated as reducing the sum otherwise payable[14].

Where it appears to the board, in respect of a long term policy[15] of a company in liquidation, that:

(1) any other person has made a payment to the policyholder or to any other person which is referable to any liability of the company under the policy which was outstanding at the beginning of the liquidation[16], or which was made by reference to any valuation of a long term policy of a company in liquidation or of any of the benefits provided under any such policy[17], or by

reference to any future benefits under a long term policy of a company in liquidation[18]; or

(2) any other person has taken measures for assisting or protecting the policyholder (whether measures of the same description to those open to the board or otherwise) which ought to be taken into account for the purpose of excluding or modifying any of its duties towards the policyholder[19],

the board is not required to take any measures for assisting the policyholder where it appears to the board to be inappropriate to do so in view of any such payment or other measures of assistance as are mentioned above[20]. Alternatively the board may treat any sum payable to the policyholder or any sum to be secured for him as reduced to any extent which appears to it to be appropriate in the circumstances[21]. Where it appears to the board that, independently of any measures it may take, any other person (other than the liquidator) may make any such payment or take any such measure as is mentioned above, the board may postpone taking any such measures[22].

1 As to the board see para 896 ante.
2 For the meaning of 'a company in liquidation' see para 897 text and notes 1–5 ante.
3 Policyholders Protection Act 1975 s 13(1)(a). For the meaning of 'policyholder' see para 895 note 1 ante.
4 Ibid s 13(1)(b).
5 Ibid s 13(1). As to the board's duty to secure payment of any sum due to a policyholder under a policy of a company in liquidation see para 897 ante.
6 Ibid s 13(1).
7 Ibid s 13(2)(a).
8 Ibid s 13(2)(b).
9 See ibid s 13(3).
10 The board may impose conditions with respect to the total or partial assignment of (1) the policyholder's rights under or in respect of the policy (ibid s 13(4)(a)); (2) any rights in respect of any payments by way of premium made by the policyholder to the liquidator (s 13(4)(b)); (3) any rights he may have against any other person in respect of any event giving rise to any liability of the company under the policy (s 13(4)(c)); (4) as regards a person entitled to the benefit of a judgment under the Road Traffic Act 1988 s 151 (see paras 748–753 ante), any rights he may have against any other persons in respect of any event giving rise to the liability of the company in liquidation (Policyholders Protection Act 1975 s 13(5)). The board may make any arrangement which appears to it to be appropriate with respect to the manner of application of any sums received by it in consequence of the assignment of any of those rights: s 13(6).
11 As to the making of regulations see para 897 note 27 ante.
12 Policyholders Protection Act 1975 s 13(7). The regulations may provide for the transfer to or vesting in the board of (1) any such rights of a policyholder to whom the board has given assistance by any of the measures provided for by ss 6–11 (as amended) (see para 897 ante) as are mentioned in note 10 heads (1)–(3) supra (s 13(7)(a)); (2) any such rights of a person for whom the board has secured any payment in accordance with s 7 (as amended) (see para 897 text to notes 11–12 ante) as are mentioned in note 10 head (4) supra (s 13(7)(b)); and (3) any rights which a person to whom any payment has been made by virtue of s 13(1) (see text to notes 1–6 supra) may have against the policyholder in respect of the policy or any sums falling due under it or against any other persons in respect of any event giving rise to any liability of the policyholder by virtue of which the payment in question was made (s 13(7)(c)). Regulations may also provide for the manner of application by the board of any sums received by it by virtue of any rights vested in it by the regulations: s 13(7). At the date at which this volume states the law, no such regulations had been made.
13 Ie those mentioned in ibid s 6, s 7 or s 8 (as amended) (see para 897 text and notes 6–15 ante): s 14(1).
14 Ibid s 14(1). A payment is referable to a liability of a company in liquidation for the purposes of s 14 if it has the effect of reducing or discharging or is otherwise made by reference to that liability or any liability of the policyholder or any other person from which that liability arises: s 14(8).
15 For the meaning of 'long term policy' see para 897 note 17 ante.
16 For the meaning of 'the beginning of the liquidation' see para 897 note 8 ante.
17 Policyholders Protection Act 1975 s 14(2)(a), (3)(a).

18 Ibid s 14(2)(a), (3)(b). 'Future benefit' has the same meaning as in s 11 (see para 897 note 22 ante): s 14(9).
19 Ibid s 14(2)(b). As to the board's duties in relation to the holders of long term policies of a company in liquidation and the measures open to it for assisting or protecting such policyholders see ss 10 (as amended), 11; and para 897 text to notes 17–30 ante.
20 Ibid s 14(4).
21 Ibid s 14(5). As to sums payable to the policyholder see ss 10 (as amended), 11(7), (9), (10); and para 897 text and notes 17–18, 24, 26–30 ante.
22 Ibid s 14(7).

899. Board's powers to assist policyholders of companies in liquidation. A policyholder[1] in respect of a general policy[2] or a long term policy[3] of a company in liquidation[4] or provisional liquidation[5] which was a United Kingdom policy[6] at the beginning of the liquidation[7] or when the provisional liquidator was appointed is eligible for assistance[8]. The Policyholders Protection Board[9] may make payments to or on behalf of such policyholders on such terms (including any terms requiring repayment, in whole or in part) as it thinks fit[10], or secure that payments are made by the liquidator or provisional liquidator by giving him an indemnity covering any such payments or any class or description of such payments[11].

Where it appears to the Secretary of State that any circumstances have occurred in relation to an overseas company[12] which are the equivalent, under the law relating to companies in force in the country in which it is established, of the company being in liquidation[13], provisional liquidation[14] or financial difficulties[15], he may refer the company's case to the board in terms indicating whether it is to be treated as a company in liquidation for the purposes of the Policyholders Protection Act 1975 or solely as a company in provisional liquidation or financial difficulties[16]. The board's functions are exercisable in relation to a company whose case has been referred to it in accordance with the terms of the reference, and the provisions of the Act may be modified by notice by the Secretary of State to the board in connection with the reference[17].

1 For the meaning of 'policyholder' see para 895 note 1 ante.
2 For the meaning of 'general policy' see para 897 note 13 ante.
3 For the meaning of 'long term policy' see para 897 note 17 ante.
4 For the meaning of 'company in liquidation' see para 897 text and notes 1–5 ante.
5 An authorised insurance company (defined in para 895 note 2 ante), not being in liquidation, is in provisional liquidation if a provisional liquidator has been appointed under the Insolvency Act 1986 s 135 (see COMPANIES vol 7(2) (Reissue) para 1490 et seq), if the petition for winding up which led to his appointment was presented after 29 October 1974: Policyholders Protection Act 1975 s 15(1) (amended by the Companies Consolidation (Consequential Provisions) Act 1985 s 30, Sch 2; and by the Insolvency Act 1986 s 439(2), Sch 14).
6 For the meaning of 'United Kingdom policy' see para 896 note 18 ante.
7 Policyholders Protection Act 1975 s 15(2)(a). For the meaning of 'the beginning of the liquidation' see para 897 note 8 ante.
8 Ibid s 15(2)(b).
9 As to the Policyholders Protection Board see para 896 ante.
10 Policyholders Protection Act 1975 s 15(3)(a).
11 Ibid s 15(3)(b). The board may give the company an undertaking to make good any shortfall of assets resulting from interim payments: *Policyholders Protection Board v Official Receiver* [1976] 2 All ER 58, [1976] 1 WLR 447.
12 'Overseas company' means an authorised insurance company established in a country outside the United Kingdom: Policyholders Protection Act 1975 s 26(1). For the meaning of 'United Kingdom' see para 2 note 10 ante. As to the Secretary of State see para 15 note 5 ante.
13 Ie for the purposes of ibid s 5(1) (as amended) (see para 897 text to notes 1–5 ante): s 26(2).
14 Ie under ibid s 15(1) (as amended) (see note 5 supra): s 26(2).
15 Ie under ibid s 16(1) (as amended) (see para 900 note 2 post): s 26(2).

16 Ibid s 26(2).
17 Ibid s 26(3). The modifications notified by the Secretary of State must only be such as appear to him to be necessary having regard to any differences between the law in force in the United Kingdom and the law for the time being in force in the country in which the overseas company in question is established: s 26(4).

900. Board's powers to assist policyholders of companies in financial difficulties. For the purpose of safeguarding policyholders[1] of a company in financial difficulties[2] who are eligible for protection[3] against loss arising from the financial difficulties, the Policyholders Protection Board[4] may take measures for (1) transferring the insurance business of the company in financial difficulties to another authorised insurance company[5]; or (2) giving assistance to the company in financial difficulties to enable it to continue to carry on insurance business[6]. However, the board may not take any of those measures where persons who were members of the company at the relevant time[7], or had any responsibility for or may have profited from the company's financial difficulties, would benefit to any material extent[8] or where measures to be taken in the event of liquidation would cost less than the measures in question[9].

The board may also not take any of those measures for safeguarding policyholders in respect of long term policies, other than specified measures, where to take those measures would cost more than the specified measures[10]. The specified measures are any measures open to the board under the above provisions which involve conditions requiring the reduction of the company's liabilities under relevant long term policies and of benefits and premiums which have not fallen due to 90 per cent of the amount otherwise payable[11]. Where it appears to the board that the benefits provided for under a long term United Kingdom policy of a company in financial difficulties are or may be excessive, it must refer the policy to an independent actuary[12]. If an actuary makes a report in writing to the board stating that in his view the benefits are excessive[13] and recommending that, for the purposes of any measures to be taken by the board for safeguarding policyholders, any such benefit should be treated as reduced or disregarded[14], the board may determine that any benefit to which the recommendation relates is to be treated as reduced or disregarded for those purposes[15]. Where the board determines that a benefit is to be disregarded, the conditions it imposes for safeguarding policyholders must include conditions requiring the cancellation of that benefit or of any liability representing it[16]; and where the board determines that the benefit is to be reduced, the conditions will be imposed as if the amount of that benefit or of any liability representing that benefit, as reduced, were the amount which would otherwise have been payable in accordance with the terms of the policy[17].

1 For the meaning of 'policyholder' see para 895 note 1 ante.
2 'Company in financial difficulties' means an authorised insurance company (defined in para 895 note 2 ante) not being a company in liquidation (defined in para 897 text and notes 1–5 ante) if: (1) it is a company in provisional liquidation as provided for in the Policyholders Protection Act 1975 s 15 (as amended) (see para 899 ante) (s 16(1)(a)); (2) it has been proved, in proceedings on a winding-up petition under the Insolvency Act 1986 (see COMPANIES vol 7(2) (Reissue) para 1458 et seq) presented after 29 October 1974, to be unable to pay its debts (Policyholders Protection Act 1975 s 16(1)(b) (amended by the Insolvency Act 1986 s 439(2), Sch 14)); or (3) an application has been made to the court under the Companies Act 1985 s 425 (as amended) (see COMPANIES vol 7(2) (Reissue) para 2135 et seq) after 29 October 1974, for the sanctioning of a compromise or arrangement proposed between the company and its creditors or any class of them (whether or not any of its members are also parties to it) and the terms of the compromise or arrangement provide for reducing the liabilities or benefits provided for under any of the company's policies (Policyholders Protection Act 1975

s 16(1)(c) (amended by the Companies Consolidation (Consequential Provisions) Act 1985 s 30, Sch 2)); Policyholders Protection Act 1975 s 17(8).

3 A policyholder is eligible for protection if he is a policyholder in respect of a general policy or a long term policy which was a United Kingdom policy at the relevant time: ibid s 16(9). For the meaning of 'general policy' see para 897 note 13 ante; for the meaning of 'long term policy' see para 897 note 17 ante; and for the meaning of 'United Kingdom policy' see para 896 note 18 ante.

4 As to the Policyholders Protection Board see para 896 ante.

5 Policyholders Protection Act 1975 s 16(2), (3). This provision is subject to s 17 (see text and notes 10–17 infra): s 16(2), (3). For the meaning of 'authorised insurance company' see para 895 note 2 ante.

6 Ibid s 16(4). This provision is subject to s 17 (see text and notes 10–17 infra): s 16(4). The board may make the giving of such assistance conditional on the reduction of any liabilities or benefits provided for under any policies of the company to any extent appearing to it to be appropriate: s 16(5).

7 'The relevant time' means: (1) in the case of a company in provisional liquidation, the time when the provisional liquidator was appointed (ibid s 16(1)(a), (6)(a)); (2) where a company has been proved, in any proceedings on a winding-up petition, to be unable to pay its debts, the time when the petition was presented (s 16(1)(b), (6)(b)); and (3) where an application has been made to the court for the sanctioning of a compromise or arrangement, the time when the application was made (s 16(1)(c), (6)(c) (as amended: see note 2 supra)).

8 Ibid s 16(6). For these purposes the board must disregard any benefit which may accrue to such persons who are policyholders of the company in financial difficulties in their capacity as such: s 16(7).

9 Ibid s 16(8).

10 Ibid s 17(1).

11 Ibid s 17(2). A long term policy is a 'relevant long term policy' if it is included in any transfer secured or facilitated by the board under s 16(3) (see text and note 1–5 supra), or in any business continued by virtue of any assistance given by the board under s 16(4) (see text and note 6 supra): s 17(2). A bonus provided for under the policy is not included in the benefits to be reduced unless it was declared before the time when any such reduction is to take effect: s 17(3). From a day to be appointed, s 17 will apply to friendly societies in financial difficulties: s 17(8) (amended, as from a day to be appointed, by the Friendly Societies Act 1992 s 97, Sch 17 para 12).

12 Policyholders Protection Act 1975 s 17(4). For the meaning of 'actuary' see para 897 note 31 ante.

13 Ibid s 17(5)(a).

14 Ibid s 17(5)(b).

15 Ibid s 17(5).

16 Ibid s 17(6).

17 Ibid s 17(7).

901. Parliamentary reports and statements. Where, in the case of a company which is in liquidation[1] or in financial difficulties[2], the Policyholders Protection Board has exercised any of its powers with regard to making interim payments or taking measures safeguarding policyholders by arranging a transfer of the company's business or giving assistance to enable it to carry on business[3], the Secretary of State must lay before Parliament, before the end of the specified period[4], a statement with respect to the exercise of his powers under the Insurance Companies Act 1982[5] in relation to that company during the year ending immediately before the beginning of the liquidation[6] or, in the case of a company in financial difficulties, the relevant time[7]. The Secretary of State need not include in any statement any information which might in his view prejudice any criminal proceedings which have been or may be instituted against any person[8].

In each financial year[9] the board must prepare, in such manner as the Secretary of State may direct, a report on the performance of its functions during that period or during that year[10] and must publish it at such time and in such manner as the Secretary of State may direct[11].

1 See the Policyholders Protection Act 1975 ss 5(4), 28(1)(a); and para 897 text and notes 1–5 ante.
2 Ie within the meaning of ibid s 16 (as amended) (see para 900 note 2 ante): s 28(1)(b).
3 Ie under ibid ss 15, 16 (see paras 899–900 ante): s 28(1)(b). As to the board see para 896 ante.

4 The specified period is (1) in the case of a company in liquidation, the period of six months beginning with the beginning of the liquidation (ibid s 28(2)(a)); or (2) in the case of a company in financial difficulties, the period of six months beginning with the date on which the Secretary of State receives written notification from the board that it has exercised any of its powers under s 15 or s 16 (as amended) (s 28(2)(b)). As to the Secretary of State see para 15 note 5 ante.

5 As to the Secretary of State's power under the Insurance Companies Act 1982 see paras 846–854 ante.

6 For the meaning of 'the begining of the liquidation' see para 897 note 8 ante. Where the Secretary of State is required to make a statement under the Policyholders Protection Act 1975 s 28(1)(b) in relation to any company s 28(1)(a) will not also apply in the case of that company in the event of the company going into liquidation: s 28(3) (amended by the Insurance Companies Act 1982 s 99(2), Sch 5 para 16(b)).

7 Policyholders Protection Act 1975 s 28(1) (as amended: see note 6 supra). For the meaning of 'the relevant time' see ss 16(6) (as amended), 28(1) (as amended); and para 900 note 7 ante.

8 Ibid s 28(4).

9 Ibid s 1(5), Sch 1 para 14(1)(b), (4). 'Financial year' means a period of 12 months ending with 31 March in any year: s 32(1).

10 Ibid Sch 1 para 14(4).

11 Ibid Sch 1 para 14(5).

(3) LEVIES

902. Levies on intermediaries. Where the Policyholders Protection Board[1] has incurred or proposes to incur any long term business expenditure[2] in relation to a company in liquidation[3] or financial difficulties[4], and it appears to it that the company has accountable intermediaries[5], the board must impose a levy on the intermediaries[6].

A person acts as an intermediary for a company in relation to a long term contract if, otherwise than as an employee of the company, he invites any other person to take any step with a view to entering into a long term contract with the company[7], if he introduces any other person to the company with a view to his entering into such a contract[8], or if he takes any other action with a view to securing that any other person will enter into such a contract with the company[9].

A person is an accountable intermediary if he has acted as an intermediary for the company in relation to any relevant long term contract of the company[10], and his income from the contract in respect of his services in relation to any such contracts for either or each of the two years ending immediately before the specified time[11] exceeded his exempt income level for the year in question[12]. The exempt income level is, where no other person is linked with the intermidiary, £5,000[13], and in any other case, the proportion of £5,000 which the intermediary's income from the company in respect of relevant services bears to the total of the group's income from the company in respect of such services for that year[14].

The following persons are persons linked with an intermediary, whether the intermediary is a company[15] or a person other than a company:

(1) any partner of the intermediary and any partnership of which the intermediary is a member[16];

(2) any company of which the intermediary is a director[17]; and

(3) any director of any company which is linked with the intermediary[18].

Where the intermediary is a company the following are also linked with the intermediary:

(a) any person other than a company who has a controlling interest in the intermediary and any company other than the intermediary in which any such person also has a controlling interest[19];

(b) any company of which the intermediary is a subsidiary and any other subsidiary of any such company[20]; and

(c) any director of the intermediary[21].

Where the intermediary is a person other than a company the following are also linked with the intermediary:

(i) any company in which the intermediary has a controlling interest[22];

(ii) any company of which a company linked with the intermediary by virtue of the intermediary being a director or having a controlling interest[23] is a subsidiary and any other subsidiary of any such company[24];

(iii) any subsidiary of any company linked with the intermediary by virtue of the intermediary being a director or having a controlling interest[25]; and

(iv) where the intermediary is a partnership, each of its members[26].

By written notice the board may require any person who appears to it to be an intermediary of a company to give any information which appears to it to be necessary in order to determine what, if any, persons would be linked with that person under the above provisions if that person were an intermediary of that company[27]. Within one month of the date of the notice the person to whom it was sent must send a statement to the board giving any information required by the notice which he is able to give[28] or informing the board that he is unable to give any of the required information[29]. It is an offence to cause or permit to be included in any such statement any information known to be false in a material particular or recklessly to cause or permit the inclusion of any information which is false in a material particular[30]. It is also an offence to default in complying with a notice sent by the board[31].

The income of an accountable intermediary liable to levy is one half of any amount by which his income from the company in respect of relevant services for the later of the two years mentioned above[32] exceeded his exempt income level for that year[33] and one-quarter of any amount by which his income from the company for the earlier of the two years exceeded his exempt income level for that year[34]. The rate of levy in respect of any company is, where the long term business expenditure incurred by the board in relation to that company is less than the total amount of income liable to levy[35], a percentage equal to the percentage of that amount which that expenditure represents[36]; and in any other case, 100 per cent[37]. On imposing a levy the board must send notice of the levy to every person who appears to the board to be an accountable intermediary of that company[38] indicating:

(A) the name of the company in respect of which the levy is being imposed[39];

(B) the period covered, in the case of that company, by each of the two years mentioned above[40]; and

(C) in the board's view, the amount of the income of the intermediary in question which is liable to levy[41];

and must specify the rate of levy[42]. An intermediary to whom such a notice is sent must pay to the board within one month of the date of the notice the percentage specified in the notice of any income of the intermediary which is income liable to levy[43].

If the proceeds of any levy exceed the long term business expenditure incurred by the board, the board must distribute that excess among the accountable intermediaries who have made any payments to it under the levy in proportion to the sums those intermediaries have respectively paid[44].

No levy may be imposed in respect of any company after the end of the period of two years beginning with the beginning of the liquidation if the company is a company in liquidation[45], or after the end of the period of two years beginning with the relevant time if the company is a company in financial difficulties[46].

1   As to the Policyholders Protection Board see para 896 ante.
2   'Long term business expenditure' means any expenditure of the board under the Policyholders Protection Act 1975 s 10 (as amended) or s 11 (see para 897 text and notes 17–30 ante) (s 18(2)(a)); and any expenditure attributed to long term business expenditure under s 18(3) (s 18(2)(b)). The board may attribute any expenditure under s 15 or s 16 (as amended) (see paras 899–900 ante), expenditure in repaying or servicing any loans, and expenditure on administrative expenses in performing its functions under the Act, to general business or long term business expenditure, or partly to one and partly to the other, in such manner as appears reasonable in the circumstances: s 18(3). 'General business expenditure' means any expenditure of the board under s 6, s 7 or s 8 (as amended) (see para 897 ante), or, as from a day to be appointed, s 8A (as prospectively added) (s 18(1)(a) (amended, as from a day to be appointed, by the Friendly Societies Act 1992 s 97, Sch 17 para 13)), and any expenditure attributed by the board under s 18(3) to general business expenditure (Policyholders Protection Act 1975 s 18(1)(b)).
3   For the meaning of 'a company in liquidation' see para 897 text and notes 1–5 ante.
4   Ie within the meaning of the Policyholders Protection Act 1975 s 16 (as amended) (see para 900 note 2 ante): s 19(1)(a).
5   Ibid s 19(1)(b). 'An intermediary of a company' means a person who has acted as an intermediary for the company in relation to any relevant long term contract of the company: s 19(7). 'Long term contract' means a contract the effecting of which by a company constitutes the carrying on of long term business in the United Kingdom, not being a contract of reinsurance; and a long term contract is a 'relevant long term contract' if it was effected within the two years ending immediately before a specified time: s 19(9) (amended by the Insurance Companies Act 1981 s 36(2), Sch 5 Pt I). As to the specified time see note 11 infra. As to persons who act as intermediaries see text and notes 7–9 infra.
6   Policyholders Protection Act 1975 s 19(1).
7   Ibid s 19(8)(a).
8   Ibid s 19(8)(b).
9   Ibid s 19(8)(c).
10   Ibid s 19(2)(a). Section 19(2) is subject to s 19(3) (see note 12 infra), s 19(6) (see text to note 44 infra) and s 20 (as amended) (see text and notes 13–26 infra): s 19(2).
11   The specified time is the beginning of the liquidation in the case of a company in liquidation and the time when the provisional liquidator was appointed, the winding-up petition was presented or the application for a sanction or compromise was made in the case of a company in financial difficulties: ibid s 19(2), applying s 16(6) (as amended) (see para 900 ante).
12   Ibid s 19(2)(b). Such services are known as 'relevant services': s 19(2)(b). An individual is not an accountable intermediary if the services were performed in pursuance of a contract of exclusive agency: s 19(3).
13   Ibid s 20(1)(a).
14   Ibid s 20(1)(b). Where the income of the intermediary and each person linked with him did not exceed £1,000, no account must be taken of that income: s 20(2). 'The group' means the intermediary together with the person or (where there are more than one) all the persons linked with the intermediary: s 20(1). As to the persons who are linked with the intermediary see text and notes 15–26 infra.
15   'Company' includes any body corporate: Policyholders Protection Act 1975 s 20(8) (substituted by the Companies Consolidation (Consequential Provisions) Act 1985 s 30, Sch 2).
16   Policyholders Protection Act 1975 s 20(3)(a).
17   Ibid s 20(3)(b).
18   Ibid s 20(3)(c).
19   Ibid s 20(4)(a). A person other than a company must be treated as having a controlling interest in a company for the purposes of s 20(4)(a), (5)(a), if that company would be a subsidiary of the person in question if that person were a company: s 20(6). In determining whether a company would be a subsidiary of any person other than a company, any shares held or power exercisable by either of two spouses or by both spouses jointly are to be treated as held or exercisable by each spouse: s 20(7).
20   Ibid s 20(4)(b).
21   Ibid s 20(4)(c).
22   Ibid s 20(5)(a); and see note 19 supra.

23 Ie by virtue of ibid s 20(3)(b) or s 20(5)(a): s 20(5)(b).
24 Ibid s 20(5)(b).
25 Ibid s 20(5)(c).
26 Ibid s 20(5)(d).
27 Ibid s 19(10), Sch 2 para 3(1). The notice may be sent by post, and a letter containing such a notice is deemed to be properly addressed if it is addressed to the person to whom it is sent at his last known place of business in the United Kingdom: Sch 2 para 7.
28 Ibid Sch 2 para 3(2)(a).
29 Ibid Sch 2 para 3(2)(b).
30 Ibid Sch 2 para 4(1). A person guilty of such an offence is liable on conviction on indictment to imprisonment for a term not exceeding two years or to a fine, or to both (Sch 2 para 4(1)(a)), or, on summary conviction, to a fine not exceeding the prescribed sum (Sch 2 para 4(1)(b) (amended by virtue of the Magistrates' Courts Act 1980 s 32(2)). As to the prescribed sum see para 19 note 5 ante.
31 Policyholders Protection Act 1975 Sch 2 para 4(2). A person guilty of such an offence is liable, on summary conviction, to a fine not exceeding level 5 on the standard scale: Sch 2 para 4(2) (amended by virtue of the Criminal Justice Act 1982 ss 38, 46). As to the standard scale see para 212 note 5 ante.
32 Ie mentioned in the Policyholders Protection Act 1975 s 19(2) (see notes 10–12 supra): s 19(4)(a). Section 19(4) is subject to s 19(5) (see note 34 infra) and s 20 (as amended) (see text and notes 13–26 supra): s 19(4).
33 Ibid s 19(4)(a). See also note 34 infra.
34 Ibid s 19(4)(b). An intermediary's income liable to levy for either of the years mentioned or, where he had liable income for each year, the aggregate for both years, is referred to as income of the intermediary which is income liable to levy: s 19(4). A person's income from a company in respect of relevant services (see note 12 supra) for any year is the total amount of the sums paid or allowed to him by the company in respect of relevant services which were recorded as debits in the company's accounts during that year, but no account may be taken of any sums recorded in a company's accounts at any time before 1 January 1976: s 19(5).
35 'The total amount of income liable to levy' means, in relation to any company, the total amount of the income of all the persons who appear to the board to be accountable intermediaries of that company which appears to the board to be income liable to levy: ibid Sch 2 para 2(3).
36 Ibid Sch 2 para 2(1)(a). Where a levy is imposed before the exact amount of the board's long term business expenditure in respect of a company is ascertained, Sch 2 para 2(1)(a) applies as if the board's estimate of that expenditure were the expenditure actually incurred: Sch 2 para 2(2).
37 Ibid Sch 2 para 2(1)(b).
38 Ibid Sch 2 para 5(1).
39 Ibid Sch 2 para 5(2)(a).
40 Ie the two years mentioned in text to notes 10–12 supra: ibid Sch 2 para 5(2)(b).
41 Ibid Sch 2 para 5(2)(c).
42 Ibid Sch 2 para 5(2).
43 Ibid Sch 2 para 6(1). Any sum due to the board is recoverable in any court of competent jurisdiction: Sch 2 para 6(2).
44 Ibid s 19(6).
45 Ibid Sch 2 para 1(a). For the meaning of 'the beginning of the liquidation' see para 897 note 8 ante.
46 Ibid Sch 2 para 1(b). For the meaning of 'the relevant time' see para 900 note 7 ante; and for the meaning of 'company in financial difficulties' see para 900 note 2 ante.

903. Levies on authorised insurance companies. The Policyholders Protection Board[1] may, for the purpose of financing general business expenditure, from time to time impose a levy on authorised insurance companies[2] carrying on general business in the United Kingdom[3]. It may also from time to time impose a levy on authorised insurance companies carrying on long term business in the United Kingdom for the purpose of financing long term business expenditure[4].

The amount each insurance company may be required to pay under general business levies imposed in any financial year[5] is calculated by reference to the company's net premium income[6] for the year ending last before the beginning of that financial year in respect of general policies which were United Kingdom policies at the relevant time[7].

The amount each insurance company may be required to pay under long term business levies imposed in any financial year is calculated by reference to the company's net premium income for the year ending last before the beginning of that financial year in respect of long term policies effected after 31 December 1974 which were United Kingdom policies at the relevant time[8].

Levies may be imposed by the board at such times and at such rates in relation to income of authorised insurance companies liable to the general or long term business levy as the board may determine[9]. It may not impose a levy for the purpose of financing expenditure of any description unless that expenditure has already been incurred by it[10], or it appears to the board that it will be incurred within 12 months of the imposition of the levy[11].

On imposing a levy the board must send notice of the rate of levy to every authorised insurance company which may in the board's opinion have had income liable to the levy for the year ending last before the financial year in which the levy is imposed[12]. The notice must indicate (1) whether the levy is a general or a long term business levy[13], (2) what description of income is income liable to the levy in question[14], and (3) the purpose for which the levy is being imposed[15]; and it must specify the rate of levy as a percentage of the income liable to the levy[16]. An insurance company to which a notice is sent must pay to the board within one month of the date of the notice the specified percentage of any of its income for the year ending last before the financial year in which the levy is imposed which is income liable to the levy[17].

The Secretary of State[18] may by notice in writing require an authorised insurance company to send him a statement of any of its income for the year preceding that in which the notice is received which is income liable to the general business levy and to the long term business levy[19]. It is an offence to cause or permit to be included in such a statement any information known to be false in a material particular or recklessly to cause or permit to be so included any information which is false in a material particular[20]. An insurance company which defaults in sending such a statement is guilty of an offence[21].

1 As to the Policyholders Protection Board see para 896 ante.
2 For the meaning of 'authorised insurance company' see para 895 note 2 ante.
3 Policyholders Protection Act 1975 s 21(1). This provision is subject to s 21(2)–(9) and Sch 3 (as amended) (see infra). For the meaning of 'general business expenditure' see para 902 note 2 ante. Such a levy is known as a 'general business levy': s 21(1).
4 Ibid s 21(2). This provision is subject to s 21(3)–(9) and Sch 3 (as amended) (see infra). For the meaning of 'long term business expenditure' see para 902 note 2 ante. Such a levy is known as a 'long term business levy': s 21(2). The proceeds of general business levies may be applied by the board only on general business expenditure, and the proceeds of long term business levies may be applied only on long term business expenditure: s 21(8).
5 For the meaning of 'financial year' see para 901 note 9 ante.
6 'Net premium income' means the gross amounts recorded in the company's accounts during that year as paid or due to the company by way of premiums under policies of any description which were United Kingdom policies at the time when the amounts in question were so recorded, less any amounts deductible for that year in respect of policies of that description in accordance with the Policyholders Protection Act 1975 s 21(6) or (7) (see infra): s 21(5). In calculating a company's net premium income for any year in respect of policies of any description, any rebates or refunds recorded in the company's accounts during that year as allowed or given in respect of any amounts so recorded during that or any previous year as paid or due to the company by way of premiums under policies of that description which were United Kingdom policies at the time when the rebates or refunds were so recorded are deductible: s 21(6). For the meaning of 'United Kingdom policy' see para 896 note 18 ante. In calculating a company's net premium income for any year in respect of general policies, any sums recorded in the company's accounts during that year as paid by or due

from the company by way of premiums for reinsuring its liabilities towards policyholders under general policies which were United Kingdom policies at the time when the sums in question were so recorded are deductible: s 21(7).

7 Ibid s 21(3). Such income is referred to as income of the company for the year in question which is income liable to the general business levy: s 21(3). The amount required to be paid under general business levies imposed by the board in any financial year must not exceed 1% of any income of the company for the year ending last before the beginning of that financial year which is income liable to the general business levy: s 21(9), Sch 3 para 2(1).

8 Ibid s 21(4). Such income is referred to as income of the company for the year in question which is income liable to the long term business levy: s 21(4). The amount required to be paid under long term business levies imposed by the board in any financial year must not exceed 1% of any income of the company for the year ending last before the beginning of that financial year which is income liable to the long term business levy: Sch 3 para 2(2).

9 Ibid Sch 3 para 6(1). As to the limitation of the amount which may be required see notes 7–8 supra.

10 Ibid Sch 3 para 3(a).

11 Ibid Sch 3 para 3(b).

12 Ibid Sch 3 para 6(2). The notice may be sent by post, and a letter containing such a notice is deemed to be properly addressed if it is addressed to the insurance company at its last known place of business in the United Kingdom: Sch 3 para 8 (added by the Companies Act 1989 s 210(1), (5)). For the meaning of 'United Kingdom' see para 2 note 10 ante.

13 Policyholders Protection Act 1975 Sch 3 para 6(3)(a).

14 Ibid Sch 3 para 6(3)(b).

15 Ibid Sch 3 para 6(3)(c).

16 Ibid Sch 3 para 6(3).

17 Ibid Sch 3 para 7(1). Any sum due to the board may be recovered in any court of competent jurisdiction: Sch 3 para 7(2).

18 As to the Secretary of State see para 15 note 5 ante.

19 Policyholders Protection Act 1975 Sch 3 para 4(1), (2) (substituted by the Companies Act 1989 s 210 (2)). The company must send the required statement to the Secretary of State within three months of receiving it: Policyholders Protection Act 1975 Sch 3 para 4(2) (as so substituted). Where the company is required to send a statement in respect of income of both descriptions, it must send a separate statement in respect of income of each description: Sch 3 para 4(3) (as so substituted).

20 Ibid Sch 3 para 5(1). A person guilty of such an offence is liable on conviction on indictment to imprisonment for a term not exceeding two years or to a fine, or to both (Sch 3 para 5(1)(a)), and, on summary conviction, to a fine not exceeding the prescribed sum (Sch 3 para 5(1)(b) (amended by virtue of the Magistrates' Courts Act 1980 s 32(2))). As to the prescribed sum see para 19 note 5 ante.

21 Policyholders Protection Act 1975 Sch 3 para 5(2). The company is liable, on summary conviction, to a fine not exceeding level 5 on the standard scale: Sch 3 para 5(2) (amended by virtue of the Criminal Justice Act 1982 ss 38, 46). As to the standard scale see para 212 note 5 ante. The Insurance Companies Act 1982 ss 37(2)(b)(i), 54(1)(b) (see paras 867–876 ante) have effect in relation to an insurance company's obligation to send statements of premium income to the Secretary of State as they have effect in relation to obligations imposed on an insurance company under that Act: Policyholders Protection Act 1975 Sch 3 para 5(3) (amended by the Insurance Companies Act 1982 s 99(2), Sch 5 para 16(e); and the Companies Act 1989 s 210(3)). The Insurance Companies Act 1982 ss 91–94 (see paras 867–868 ante) apply in relation to an offence committed or alleged to have been committed under the Policyholders Protection Act 1975 Sch 3 para 5: Sch 3 para 5(4) (amended by the Insurance Companies Act 1982 Sch 5 para 16(f)).

(4) APPLICATION OF FUNDS

904. Application of general receipts and surplus funds. Any sums received by the Policyholders Protection Board[1] from time to time in the course of or in connection with the exercise of any of its functions under the Policyholders Protection Act 1975[2] may be applied by the board (1) in so far as they are received in repayment or otherwise by virtue of any general business expenditure[3] incurred by the board, on expenditure of that description only[4]; and (2) in so far as they are received in repayment or otherwise by virtue of any long term business expenditure[5] incurred by the board, on expenditure of that description only[6].

The board may invest any funds held by it which appear to it to be surplus to its requirements for the time being[7]. If at any time the Secretary of State, after consultation with the board, considers that the funds for the time being held by it exceed what is reasonably required for the purpose of exercising its functions under the Act, he may by order made by statutory instrument require it to distribute any of those funds appearing to him to be surplus to its requirements among authorised insurance companies carrying on business in the United Kingdom, in such manner and subject to such conditions as may be prescribed by the order[8]. Any order so made may make different provision for different circumstances and may be varied or revoked by a subsequent order[9].

The board must keep proper accounts and proper records in relation to the accounts[10], and prepare in respect of each financial year[11] a statement of accounts, in such form as the Secretary of State may direct, showing the state of its affairs, income and expenditure[12]. The statement must be audited by auditors appointed by the board[13], and the board must publish the statement at such time and in such manner as the Secretary of State may direct[14].

1 As to the Policyholders Protection Board see para 896 ante.
2 Ie otherwise than by virtue of a levy imposed under the Policyholders Protection Act 1975 s 19 (as amended) or s 21 (see paras 902–903 ante): s 24.
3 For the meaning of 'general business expenditure' see para 902 note 2 ante.
4 Policyholders Protection Act 1975 s 24(a). The board's power to apply funds under this condition is subject to any arrangement made by it under s 13(6) (see para 898 note 10 ante), and to any regulations made by the Secretary of State under s 13(7) (see para 898 text and notes 11–12 ante): s 24.
5 For the meaning of 'long term business expenditure' see para 902 note 2 ante.
6 Policyholders Protection Act 1975 s 24(b).
7 Ibid s 1(5), Sch 1 para 7(1). The board may invest in any investment for the time being falling within the Trustee Investments Act 1961 s 1, Sch 1 Pts I–III (as amended) (see TRUSTS vol 48 para 858 et seq) (Policyholders Protection Act 1975 Sch 1 para 7(1)(a)); or in any investment approved for the purpose by the Secretary of State (Sch 1 para 7(1)(b)).
8 Ibid s 25(1). Any statutory instrument containing an order made under this section is subject to annulment in pursuance of a resolution of either House of Parliament: s 25(3). At the date at which this volume states the law, no such order had been made. For the meaning of 'United Kingdom' see para 2 note 10 ante. For the meaning of 'authorised insurance company' see para 895 note 2 ante. As from a day to be appointed, surplus funds may be distributed to qualifying friendly societies carrying on such business: s 25(1) (amended, as from a day to be appointed, by the Friendly Societies Act 1992 s 97, Sch 17 para 16). See FRIENDLY SOCIETIES.
9 Policyholders Protection Act 1975 s 25(2).
10 Ibid Sch 1 para 14(1)(a).
11 For the meaning of 'financial year' see para 901 note 9 ante.
12 Policyholders Protection Act 1975 Sch 1 para 14(1)(b).
13 Ibid Sch 1 para 14(2). A person is not qualified to be appointed as auditor by the board unless he is eligible for appointment as a company auditor under the Companies Act 1989 s 25: Policyholders Protection Act 1975 Sch 1 para 14(3) (amended by the Companies Act 1989 (Eligibility for Appointment as Company Auditor) (Consequential Amendments) Regulations 1991, SI 1991/1997, reg 2, Schedule para 27).
14 Policyholders Protection Act 1975 Sch 1 para 14(5).

APPENDICES

APPENDIX 1. FORMS OF MARINE INSURANCE POLICY

(i) Statutory Form of Marine Insurance Policy

905. Form of policy. The Marine Insurance Act 1906 contains a standard form of marine insurance policy[1], which is set out below.

FORM OF POLICY

BE IT KNOWN THAT   [2] as well in their own name as for and in the name and names of all and every other person or persons to whom the same doth, may or shall appertain, in part or in all doth make assurance and cause themselves and them, and every of them, to be insured lost or not lost[3], at and from[4]   [5] Upon any kind of goods[6] and merchandises, and also upon the body, tackle, apparel, ordnance, munition, artillery, boat and other furniture, of and in the good ship[7] or vessel called the   [8] whereof is master under God, for this present voyage   [9], or whosoever else shall go for master in the said ship, or by whatsoever other name or names the said ship, or the master thereof, is or shall be named or called; beginning the adventure upon the said goods and merchandises from the loading thereof[10] aboard the said ship,   upon the said ship, etc   and so shall continue and endure, during her abode there, upon the said ship, etc. And further, until the said ship, with all her ordnance, tackle, apparel, etc., and goods and merchandises whatsoever shall be arrived at   upon the said ship, etc, until she hath moored at anchor twenty-four hours in good safety[11]; and upon the goods and merchandises, until the same be there discharged and safely landed[12]. And it shall be lawful for the said ship, etc, in this voyage, to proceed and sail to and touch and stay[13] at any ports or places whatsoever   without prejudice to this insurance. The said ship, etc, goods and merchandises, etc, for so much as concerns the assured by agreement between the assured and assurers in this policy, are and shall be valued at   [14].

Touching the adventures and perils which we the assurers are contented to bear and do take upon us in this voyage[15]; they are of the seas[16], men of war, fire, enemies, pirates[17], rovers, thieves[18], jettisons, letters of mart and countermart, surprisals, takings at sea, arrests, restraints and detainments of all kings, princes and people[19], of what nation, condition or quality soever, barratry[20] of the master and mariners, and of all other perils[21], losses and misfortunes, that have or shall come to the hurt, detriment or damage of the said goods and merchandises, and ship, etc, or any part thereof. And in case of any loss or misfortune it shall be lawful to the assured, their factors, servants and assigns, to sue, labour and travel for, in and about the defence, safeguards, and recovery of the said goods and merchandises, and ship, etc or any part thereof, without prejudice to this insurance; to the charges whereof we, the assurers, will contribute each one according to the rate and quantity of his sum herein assured. And it is especially declared and agreed that no acts of the insurer or insured in recovering, saving or preserving the property insured shall be considered as a waiver, or acceptance of abandonment. And it is agreed by us, the insurers, that this writing or policy of assurance shall be of as much force and effect as the surest writing or policy of assurance heretofore made in Lombard Street, or in the Royal Exchange, or elsewhere in London. And so we, the assurers, are contented, and do hereby promise and bind ourselves, each one for his own part, our heirs, executors and goods to the assured, their executors, administrators and assigns, for the true performance of the premises, confessing ourselves paid the consideration due unto us for this assurance by the assured, at and after the rate of   [22].

IN WITNESS whereof we, the assurers, have subscribed our names and sums assured in London.

N.B. Corn, fish, salt, fruit, flour and seed are warranted free from average, unless general[23], or the ship be stranded[24] — sugar, tobacco, hemp, flax, hides and skins are warranted free from average, under five pounds per cent, and all other goods, also the ship and freight[25], are warranted free from average, under three pounds per cent unless general, or the ship be stranded.

1 See the Marine Insurance Act 1906 s 30(1), Sch 1. This form of policy is the former Lloyd's policy, and has been largely superseded (see para 906 post). The rules of construction also contained in that Schedule and in the notes infra are applicable to this form and to policies in the like form: s 30(2).
2 The name normally given here is that of the insurance broker.
3 For the meaning of 'lost or not lost' see the Marine Insurance Act 1906 Sch 1 r 1; and para 191 ante.
4 As to the insurance of subject matter 'from' a particular place see ibid Sch 1 r 2; and para 131 ante. As to the insurance of a ship 'at and from' a particular place see Sch 1 r 3(a)–(d); and paras 131, 137–138 ante.
5 A description of the voyage insured is given here.
6 For the meaning of 'goods' see the Marine Insurance Act 1906 Sch 1 r 17; and para 114 ante.
7 As to the meaning of 'ship' see ibid Sch 1 r 15; and para 113 ante.
8 The ship's name is given here.
9 The master's name is given here, although in practice it is often omitted.
10 As to the meaning of 'from the loading thereof' see the Marine Insurance Act 1906 Sch 1 r 4; and para 125 ante.
11 As to the meaning of 'moored in good safety' see para 135 ante.
12 As to the meaning of 'discharged and safely landed' see the Marine Insurance Act 1906 Sch 1 r 5; and paras 127, 129 ante.
13 As to the 'touch and stay' clause see ibid Sch 1 r 6; and para 144 ante.
14 The value of the subject matter for the purpose of the policy is given here.
15 As to the clause enumerating the perils insured against see para 149 ante.
16 As to the meaning of 'perils of the seas' see the Marine Insurance Act 1906 Sch 1 r 7; and para 151 ante.
17 As to the meaning of 'pirates' see ibid Sch 1 r 8; and para 159 ante.
18 As to the meaning of 'thieves see ibid Sch 1 r 9; and para 159 ante.
19 As to the meaning of 'arrests, etc, of kings, princes and people' see ibid Sch 1 r 10; and para 158 ante.
20 As to the meaning of 'barratry' see ibid Sch 1 r 11; and para 161 ante.
21 The term 'all other perils' includes only perils similar in kind to the perils specifically mentioned in the policy: ibid Sch 1 r 12.
22 The rate of premium is given here.
23 The term 'average unless general' means a partial loss of the subject matter insured other than a general average loss, and does not include particular charges: Marine Insurance Act 1906 Sch 1 r 13; and see para 244 et seq ante.
24 Where the ship has stranded the insurer is liable for the excepted losses, although the loss is not attributable to the stranding, provided that when the stranding takes place the risk has attached, and if the policy is on goods that the damaged goods are on board: ibid Sch 1 r 14.
25 As to the meaning of 'freight' see ibid Sch 1 r 16; and para 115 ante.

(ii) Modern Form of Lloyd's Marine Insurance Policy

906. Lloyd's Marine Policy. The following form is the modern standard form of marine insurance policy issued by Lloyd's[1].

We, The Underwriters, hereby agree, in consideration of the payment to us by or on behalf of the Assured of the premium specified in the Schedule, to insure against loss damage liability or expense in the proportions and manner hereinafter provided. Each Underwriting Member of a Syndicate whose definitive number and proportion is set out in the following Table shall be liable only for his own share of his respective Syndicate's proportion.

This insurance shall be subject to the exclusive jurisdiction of the English Courts, except as may be expressly provided herein to the contrary.

In Witness whereof the General Manager of Lloyd's Policy Signing Office has subscribed his Name on behalf of each of Us.

LLOYD'S POLICY SIGNING OFFICE
General Manager

SCHEDULE
POLICY NUMBER

NAME OF ASSURED

VESSEL

VOYAGE OR PERIOD OF INSURANCE

SUBJECT–MATTER INSURED

AGREED VALUE
(if any)

AMOUNT INSURED HEREUNDER

PREMIUM

CLAUSES, ENDORSEMENTS, SPECIAL CONDITIONS AND WARRANTIES

THE ATTACHED CLAUSES AND ENDORSEMENTS[2] FORM PART OF THIS POLICY

Definitive numbers of the Syndicates and proportions

The List of Underwriting members of Lloyd's mentioned in the above Table shows their respective Syndicates and Shares therein and is deemed to be incorporated in and to form part of this Policy. It is available for inspection at Lloyd's Policy Signing Office by the Assured or his or their representatives and a true copy of the material parts of it certified by the General Manager of Lloyd's Policy Signing Office will be furnished to the Assured on application.

1 This precedent is reproduced with the kind permission of Lloyd's of London.
　 This form of policy largely supersedes the Lloyd's form contained in the Schedule to the Marine Insurance Act 1906: see para 905 ante. As to Lloyd's policies generally see para 21 ante.
2 For the Institute Clauses commonly attached to a marine policy see Ivamy's Marine Insurance (4th Edn) 516 et seq.

APPENDIX 2. YORK-ANTWERP RULES 1974

907. The York-Antwerp Rules 1974. The following are the rules drafted in 1974 at the Hamburg Conference of the Comité Maritime International, and amended in 1990.

RULES OF INTERPRETATION. In the adjustment of general average the following lettered and numbered rules shall apply to the exclusion of any Law and Practice inconsistent therewith[1].

Except as provided by the numbered Rules, general average shall be adjusted according to the lettered Rules[2].

RULE A. There is a general average act when, and only when, any extraordinary sacrifice or expenditure is intentionally[3] and reasonably made or incurred for the common safety for the purpose of preserving from peril[4] the property involved in a common maritime adventure[5].

RULE B. General average sacrifices and expenses shall be borne by the different contributing interests on the basis hereinafter provided.

RULE C. Only such losses, damages or expenses which are the direct consequence of the general average act shall be allowed as general average[6].

Loss or damage sustained by the ship or cargo through delay, whether on the voyage or subsequently, such as demurrage, and any indirect loss whatsoever, such as loss of market, shall not be admitted as general average.

RULE D. Rights to contribution in general average shall not be affected, though the event which gave rise to the sacrifice or expenditure may have been due to the fault of one of the parties to the adventure, but this shall not prejudice any remedies or defences which may be open against or to that party in respect of such fault[7].

RULE E. The onus of proof is upon the party claiming in general average to show that the loss or expense claimed is properly allowable as general average.

RULE F. Any extra expense incurred in place of another expense which would have been allowable as general average shall be deemed to be general average and so allowed without regard to the saving, if any, to other interests, but only up to the amount of the general average expense avoided.

RULE G. General average shall be adjusted as regards both loss and contribution upon the basis of values at the time and place when and where the adventure ends.

This rule shall not affect the determination of the place at which the average statement is to be made up.

RULE I. JETTISON OF CARGO
No jettison of cargo shall be made good as general average unless such cargo is carried in accordance with the recognised custom of the trade.

RULE II. DAMAGE BY JETTISON AND SACRIFICE FOR THE COMMON SAFETY
Damage done to a ship and cargo, or either of them, by or in consequence of a

sacrifice made for the common safety, and by water which goes down a ship's hatches opened or other opening made for the purpose of making a jettison for the common safety, shall be made good as general average.

RULE III. EXTINGUISHING FIRE ON SHIPBOARD

Damage done to a ship and cargo, or either of them, by water or otherwise, including damage by beaching or scuttling a burning ship, in extinguishing a fire on board the ship, shall be made good as general average; except that no compensation shall be made for damage by smoke or heat however caused.

RULE IV. CUTTING AWAY WRECK

Loss or damage sustained by cutting away wreck or parts of the ship which have been previously carried away or are effectively lost by accident shall not be made good as general average.

RULE V. VOLUNTARY STRANDING

When a ship is intentionally run on shore for the common safety, whether or not she might have been driven on shore, the consequent loss or damage shall be allowed in general average.

RULE VI. SALVAGE[8]

(a) Expenditure incurred by the parties to the adventure in the nature of salvage, whether under contract or otherwise, shall be allowed in general average provided that the salvage operations were carried out for the purpose of preserving from peril the property involved in the common maritime adventure.

Expenditure allowed in general average shall include any salvage remuneration in which the skill and efforts of the salvors in preventing or minimising damage to the environment such as is referred to in Art 13 paragraph 1(b) of the International Convention on Salvage, 1989 have been taken into account.

(b) Special compensation payable to a salvor by the shipowner under Art 14 of the said Convention to the extent specified in paragraph 4 of that Article or under any other provision similar in substance shall not be allowed in general average.

RULE VII. DAMAGE TO MACHINERY AND BOILERS

Damage caused to any machinery and boilers of a ship which is ashore and in a position of peril, in endeavouring to refloat, shall be allowed in general average when shown to have arisen from an actual intention to float the ship for the common safety at the risk of such damage; but where a ship is afloat no loss or damage caused by working the propelling machinery and boilers shall in any circumstances be made good as general average.

RULE VIII. EXPENSES LIGHTENING A SHIP WHEN ASHORE, AND CONSEQUENT DAMAGE

When a ship is ashore and cargo and ship's fuel and stores or any of them are discharged as a general average act, the extra cost of lightening, lighter hire and reshipping if incurred and the loss or damage sustained thereby, shall be admitted as general average.

RULE IX. SHIP'S MATERIALS AND STORES BURNT FOR FUEL

Ship's materials and stores, or any of them, necessarily burnt for fuel for the common safety at a time of peril, shall be admitted as general average, when and only when an ample supply of fuel had been provided; but the estimated quantity of fuel that would have been consumed, calculated at the price current at the ship's last port of departure at the date of her leaving, shall be credited to the general average.

RULE X. EXPENSES AT PORT OF REFUGE ETC.

(a) When a ship shall have entered a port or place of refuge or shall have returned to her port or place of loading in consequence of accident, sacrifice or other extraordinary circumstances, which render that necessary for the common safety, the expenses of entering such port or place shall be admitted as general average; and when she shall have sailed thence with her original cargo, or a part of it, the corresponding expenses of leaving such port or place consequent upon such entry or return shall likewise be admitted as general average.

When a ship is at any port or place of refuge and is necessarily removed to another port or place because repairs cannot be carried out in the first port or place, the provisions of this Rule shall be applied to the second port or place as if it were a port or place of refuge and the cost of such removal including temporary repairs and towage shall be admitted as general average. The provisions of Rule XI shall be applied to the prolongation of the voyage occasioned by such removal.

(b) The cost of handling on board or discharging cargo, fuel or stores whether at a port or place of loading, call or refuge, shall be admitted as general average, when the handling or discharge was necessary for the common safety or to enable damage to the ship caused by sacrifice or accident to be repaired if the repairs were necessary for the safe prosecution of the voyage, except in cases where the damage to the ship is discovered at a port or place of loading or call without any accident or other extraordinary circumstance connected with such damage having taken place during the voyage.

The cost of handling on board or discharging cargo, fuel or stores shall not be admissible as general average when incurred solely for the purpose of restowage due to shifting during the voyage, unless such restowage is necessary for the common safety.

(c) Whenever the cost of handling or discharging cargo, fuel or stores is admissible as general average, the costs of storage, including insurance if reasonably incurred, reloading and stowing of such cargo, fuel or stores shall likewise be admitted as general average.

But when the ship is condemned or does not proceed on her original voyage storage expenses shall be admitted as general average only up to the date of the ship's condemnation or of the abandonment of the voyage or up to the date of completion of discharge of cargo if the condemnation or abandonment takes place before that date.

RULE XI. WAGES AND MAINTENANCE OF CREW AND OTHER EXPENSES
BEARING UP FOR AND IN A PORT OF REFUGE ETC.

(a) Wages and maintenance of master, officers and crew reasonably incurred and fuel and stores consumed during the prolongation of the voyage occasioned by a ship entering a port or place of refuge or returning to her port or place of loading shall be admitted as general average when the expenses of entering such port or place are allowable in general average in accordance with Rule X(a).

(b) When a ship shall have entered or been detained in any port or place in consequence of accident, sacrifice or other extraordinary circumstances which render that necessary for the common safety, or to enable damage to the ship caused by sacrifice or accident to be repaired, if the repairs were necessary for the safe prosecution of the voyage, the wages and maintenance of the master, officers, and crew reasonably incurred during the extra period of detention in such port or place until the ship shall or should have been made ready to proceed upon her voyage, shall be admitted in general average.

Provided that when damage to the ship is discovered at a port or place of loading or call without any accident or other extraordinary circumstance connected with such damage having taken place during the voyage, then the wages and maintenance of master, officers and crew and fuel and stores consumed during the extra detention for repairs to damage so discovered shall not be admissible as general average, even if the repairs are necessary for the safe prosecution of the voyage.

When the ship is condemned or does not proceed on her original voyage, wages and maintenance of the master, officers and crew and fuel and stores consumed shall be admitted as general average only up to the date of the ship's condemnation or of the abandonment of the voyage or up to the date of completion of discharge of cargo if the condemnation or abandonment takes place before that date.

Fuel and stores consumed during the extra period of detention shall be admitted as general average, except such fuel and stores as are consumed in effecting repairs not allowable in general average.

Port charges incurred during the extra period of detention shall likewise be admitted as general average except such charges as are incurred solely by reason of repairs not allowable in general average.

(c) For the purpose of this and the other Rules wages shall include all payments made to or for the benefit of the master, officers and crew, whether such payments be imposed by law upon the shipowners or be made under the terms or articles of employment.

(d) When overtime is paid to the master, officers or crew for maintenance of the ship or repairs, the cost of which is not allowable in general average, such overtime shall be allowed in general average only up to the saving in expense which would have been incurred and admitted as general average, had such overtime not been incurred.

RULE XII. DAMAGE TO CARGO IN DISCHARGING ETC.

Damage to or loss of cargo, fuel or stores caused in the act of handling, discharging, storing, reloading and stowing shall be made good as general average, when and only when the cost of those measures respectively is admitted as general average.

RULE XIII. DEDUCTIONS FROM COST OF REPAIRS

Repairs to be allowed in general average shall not be subject to deductions in respect of 'new for old' where old material or parts are replaced by new unless the ship is over 15 years old in which case there shall be a deduction of one third. The deductions shall be regulated by the age of the ship from the 31st December of the year of completion of construction to the date of the general average act, except for insulation, life and similar boats, communications and navigational apparatus and equipment, machinery and boilers for which the deductions shall be regulated by the age of the particular parts to which they apply.

The deductions shall be made only from the cost of the new material or parts when finished and ready to be installed in the ship.

No deduction shall be made in respect of provisions, stores, anchors and chain cables.

Drydock and slipway dues and costs of shifting the ship shall be allowed in full.

The costs of cleaning, painting or coating of bottom shall not be allowed in general average unless the bottom has been painted or coated within the 12 months preceding the date of the general average act in which case one half of such costs shall be allowed.

RULE XIV. TEMPORARY REPAIRS

Where temporary repairs are effected to a ship at a port of loading, call or refuge, for the common safety, or of damage caused by general average sacrifice, the cost of such repairs shall be admitted as general average.

Where temporary repairs of accidental damage are effected in order to enable the adventure to be completed, the cost of such repairs shall be admitted as general average without regard to the saving, if any, to other interests, but only up to the saving in expense which would have been incurred and allowed in general average if such repairs had not been effected there.

No deductions 'new for old' shall be made from the cost of temporary repairs allowable as general average.

RULE XV. LOSS OF FREIGHT

Loss of freight arising from damage to or loss of cargo shall be made good as general average, either when caused by a general average act, or when the damage to or loss of cargo is so made good.

Deduction shall be made from the amount of gross freight lost, of the charges which the owner thereof would have incurred to earn such freight, but has, in consequence of the sacrifice, not incurred.

RULE XVI. AMOUNT TO BE MADE GOOD FOR CARGO LOST OR DAMAGED BY SACRIFICE

The amount to be made good as general average for damage to or loss of cargo sacrificed shall be the loss which has been sustained thereby based on the value at the time of discharge, ascertained from the commercial invoice rendered to the receiver or if there is no such invoice from the shipped value. The value at the time of discharge shall include the cost of insurance and freight except in so far as such freight is at the risk of interests other than the cargo.

When cargo so damaged is sold and the amount of the damage has not been otherwise agreed, the loss to be made good in general average shall be the difference between the net proceeds of sale and the net sound value as computed in the first paragraph of this rule.

RULE XVII. CONTRIBUTORY VALUES

The contribution to a general average shall be made upon the actual net value of the property at the termination of the adventure except that the value of cargo shall be the value at the time of discharge, ascertained from the commercial invoice rendered to the receiver or if there is no such invoice from the shipped value. The value of the cargo shall include the cost of insurance and freight unless and in so far as such freight is at the risk of interests other than the cargo, deducting therefrom any loss or damage suffered by the cargo prior to or at the time of discharge. The value of the ship shall be assessed without taking into account the beneficial or detrimental effect of any demise or time charterparty to which the ship may be committed.

To these values shall be added the amount made good as general average for property sacrificed, if not already included, deduction being made from the freight and passage money at risk of such charges and crew's wages as would not have been incurred in earning the freight had the ship and cargo been totally lost at the date of the general average act and have not been allowed as general average; deduction being also made from the value of the property of all extra charges incurred in respect thereof subsequently to the general average act, except such charges as are allowed in general average.

Where cargo is sold short of destination, however, it shall contribute upon the actual net proceeds of sale, with the addition of any amount made good as general average.

Passenger's luggage and personal effects not shipped under bill of lading shall not contribute in general average.

RULE XVIII. DAMAGE TO SHIP
The amount to be allowed as general average for damage or loss to the ship, her machinery and/or gear caused by a general average act shall be as follows:

(a) When repaired or replaced,

The actual reasonable cost of repairing or replacing such damage or loss subject to deduction in accordance with Rule XIII;

(b) When not repaired or replaced,

The reasonable depreciation arising from such damage or loss, but not exceeding the estimated cost of repairs. But where the ship is an actual total loss or when the cost of repairs of the damage would exceed the value of the ship when repaired, the amount to be allowed as general average shall be the difference between the estimated sound value of the ship after deducting therefrom the estimated cost of repairing damage which is not general average and the value of the ship in her damaged state which may be measured by the net proceeds of sale, if any.

RULE XIX. UNDECLARED OR WRONGFULLY DECLARED CARGO
Damage or loss caused to goods loaded without the knowledge of the shipowner or his agent or to goods wilfully misdescribed at time of shipment shall not be allowed as general average but such goods shall remain liable to contribute, if saved.

Damage or loss caused to goods which have been wrongfully declared on shipment at a value which is lower than their real value shall be contributed for at the declared value, but such goods shall contribute upon their actual value.

RULE XX. PROVISION OF FUNDS
A commission of two per cent of general average disbursements, other than the wages and maintenance of master, officers and crew and fuel and stores not replaced during the voyage, shall be allowed in general average, but when the funds are not provided by any of the contributing interests, the necessary cost of obtaining the funds required by means of a bottomry bond or otherwise, or the loss sustained by owners of goods sold for the purpose, shall be allowed in general average.

The cost of insuring money advanced to pay for general average disbursements shall also be allowed in general average.

RULE XXI. INTEREST ON LOSSES MADE GOOD IN GENERAL AVERAGE

Interest shall be allowed on expenditure, sacrifices and allowances charged to general average at the rate of seven per cent per annum, until the date of the general average statement, due allowance being made for any interim reimbursement from the contributory interests or from the general average deposit fund.

RULE XXII. TREATMENT OF CASH DEPOSITS

Where cash deposits have been collected in respect of cargo's liability for general average, salvage or special charges, such deposits shall be paid without any delay into a special account in the joint names of a representative nominated on behalf of the shipowner and a representative nominated on behalf of the depositors in a bank to be approved by both. The sum so deposited together with accrued interest, if any, shall be held as security for payment to the parties entitled thereto of the general average, salvage or special charges payable by cargo in respect to which the deposits have been collected. Payments on account of refund of deposits may be made if certified to in writing by the average adjuster. Such deposits and payments or refunds shall be without prejudice to the ultimate liability of the parties.

1 For a comparison of the York-Antwerp Rules 1877, 1890, 1924, 1950 and 1974, and for the French text of the 1974 Rules, see Lowndes and Rudolf's General Average and the York-Antwerp Rules (11th Edn). The rules are not a complete code and may require to be supplemented by the provisions of the general law applicable to the contract: *Goulandris Bros Ltd v B Goldman & Sons Ltd* [1958] 1 QB 74 at 92, [1957] 3 All ER 100 at 106. As to their incorporation in marine insurance policies see para 53 ante.
2 The Rule of Interpretation was added to negative the effect in practice of the decision in *Vlassopoulos v British and Foreign Marine Insurance Co Ltd* [1929] 1 KB 187, where it was held that the lettered and numbered rules in the York-Antwerp Rules 1924 had to be read as a whole, the lettered rules enunciating general principles and the numbered rules dealing with specific cases, and consequently the numbered rules had no application to cases clearly outside the lettered rules.
3 Expenditure incurred in consequence of the master's obedience to lawful orders of the Admiralty does not amount to a general average act: *Athel Line Ltd v Liverpool and London War Risks Insurance Association Ltd* [1944] KB 87, [1944] 1 All ER 46.
4 'Peril' means the same thing as danger; it does not mean immediate peril or danger: *Vlassopoulos v British and Foreign Marine Insurance Co Ltd* [1929] 1 KB 187 at 200.
5 The definition of 'general average act' in this rule closely conforms with the definition in the Marine Insurance Act 1906 s 66(2): see para 244 ante. As to general average see para 244 et seq ante; and SHIPPING.
6 Cf the Marine Insurance Act 1906 s 66(1); and para 244 ante.
7 Apart from the York-Antwerp Rules, general average contribution is not recoverable by a party to the adventure whose actionable fault has given rise to the general average act: *Schloss v Herot* (1863) 14 CBNS 59; *Louis Drefus & Co Ltd v Tempus Shipping Co* [1931] AC 726, HL. It seems that rule D does not alter this position. The first part of the rule refers to the rights to contribution in general average as they will be set out in the average adjustment, and these are properly and naturally called 'rights', because normally the holder of such rights is entitled to receive payment. The second part of the rule provides that the first part is not to prejudice remedies for faults.
8 This rule was substituted in 1990 following the Convention mentioned in head (a) in the text.

APPENDIX 3. INSTITUTE THREE-FOURTHS COLLISION LIABILITY CLAUSE

908–1000. Standard form of clause. The following is the standard form of clause drafted by the Institute of London Underwriters and known generally as the Institute three-fourths collision liability clause[1].

8.1 The Underwriters agree to indemnify the Assured for three-fourths of any sum or sums paid by the Assured to any other person or persons by reason of the Assured becoming legally liable by way of damages for

8.1.1 loss of or damage to any other vessel or property on any other vessel

8.1.2 delay to or loss of use of any other such vessel or property thereon

8.1.3 general average of, salvage of, or salvage under contract of, any other such vessel or property thereon,

where such payment by the Assured is in consequence of the Vessel hereby insured coming into collision with any other vessel.

8.2 The indemnity provided by this Clause 8 shall be in addition to the indemnity provided by the other terms and conditions of this insurance and shall be subject to the following provisions:

8.2.1 Where the insured Vessel is in collision with another vessel and both vessels are to blame then, unless the liability of one or both vessels becomes limited by law, the indemnity under this Clause 8 shall be calculated on the principle of cross-liabilities[2] as if the respective Owners had been compelled to pay to each other such proportion of each other's damages as may have been properly allowed in ascertaining the balance or sum payable by or to the Assured in consequence of the collision.

8.2.2 In no case shall the Underwriters' total liability under Clauses 8.1 and 8.2 exceed their proportionate part of three-fourths of the insured value of the Vessel hereby insured in respect of any one collision.

8.3 The Underwriters will also pay three-fourths of the legal costs incurred by the Assured or which the Assured may be compelled to pay in contesting liability or taking proceedings to limit liability, with the prior written consent of the Underwriters.

EXCLUSIONS

8.4 Provided always that this Clause 8 shall in no case extend to any sum which the Assured shall pay for or in respect of

8.4.1 removal or disposal of obstructions, wrecks, cargoes or any other thing whatsoever

8.4.2 any real or personal property or thingwhatsoever except other vessels or property on other vessels

8.4.3 the cargo or other property on, or the engagements of, the insured Vessel

8.4.4 loss of life, personal injury or illness

8.4.5 pollution or contamination of any real or personal property ot hing whatsoever (except other vessels with which the insured Vessel is in collision or property on such other vessels).

1 Institute Time Clauses (Hulls) cl 8; see also the Institute Voyage Clauses (Hulls) cl 6. This clause may also be known as the 'running down clause'.

This clause is reproduced by kind permission of Witherby & Co Ltd, 32 Aylesbury Street Street, London ECIR OET, from whom copies are obtainable.

2 The proviso as to cross-liabilities was inserted to meet the decisions in *London SS Owners' Insurance Co v Grampian SS Co* (1890) 24 QBD 663, CA, and *The Khedive* (1882) 7 App Cas 795, HL. In *The Khedive* supra, which was decided when the rule of English law was that where both vessels were to blame the aggregate damage had to be divided equally between the two shipowners, it was held that in such a case the only liability was that of the shipowner who had suffered the least pecuniary damage to pay to the other shipowner half the excess of the latter's damages over his own. In *London SS Owners' Insurance Co v Grampian SS Co* supra, it was held that it followed from the decision in

The Khedive supra, that under the form of collision clause then in use (which was to the same effect as the present clause except that it did not contain any provision for settlement on the basis of cross-liabilities) a shipowner could only recover from his insurers half the excess, if any, of the other shipowner's damage over his own, since this was the only sum which he was 'liable to pay', and consequently that the shipowner whose damage was least could not recover any sum under this clause. In *Young v Merchants' Marine Insurance Co Ltd* [1932] 2 KB 705, CA, a vessel was insured under a policy containing a running down clause which provided for settlement on the principle of cross-liabilities. She was reinsured against total loss only, and the reinsurance policy contained no running down clause. The insured vessel was sunk as the result of a collision. The original insurers settled with their assured on the principle of cross-liabilities, according to which the assured were treated as having been paid a sum by way of damages by the owners of the other vessel. The reinsurers claimed to be subrogated to this sum, but the court, affirming the decision of MacKinnon J, disallowed this claim on the ground that this payment was purely notional, and that as under the Admiralty rule the original assured had no legal right to any payment from the owners of the other vessel, there was no right to which the reinsurers could be subrogated. As to whether, under a somewhat different clause, the underwriters were liable for damages paid by the assured for loss of life, see *Taylor v Dewar* (1864) 5 B & S 58, dissenting from *Coey v Smith* (1860) 22 Dunl 955, Ct of Sess. The underwriter remains liable under such a clause even if the collision occurred during a warlike operation, and the policy contains an f c and s clause: *Adelaide SS Co Ltd v A-G* [1926] AC 172, HL.

INTERNATIONAL LAW

See CONFLICT OF LAWS; FOREIGN RELATIONS LAW

INTERPLEADER

1. THE NATURE OF INTERPLEADER

(1) MEANING OF INTERPLEADER

1001. Meaning of 'interpleader'. Where a person, for example a sheriff who has levied under a writ of execution, is in possession of property or its proceeds of sale and he is, or expects to be, sued in respect thereof by two or more persons making adverse claims thereto, he may apply to the court for an order requiring the claimants to litigate their differences and to abide by the court's final order in respect thereof[1]. He is thereafter safeguarded by being able to act in respect of the property or its proceeds of sale consistently with, or as may be directed by, the court's final order. In these circumstances he is said to apply to the court for relief by way of interpleader[2].

1 See RSC Ord 17 r 1. For a consideration of the nature of interpleader see *De La Rue v Hernu, Peron and Stockwell Ltd* [1936] 2 KB 164, [1936] 2 All ER 411, CA. For the distinction between interpleader by a sheriff and by a stakeholder see paras 1004–1005 post.
2 See RSC Ord 17 r 1(1). The interpleader summons is a proceeding the object of which is to extricate the defendant from the embarrassment of being sued, or being likely to be sued, by more than one party in respect of the same subject matter: *Eastern Holdings Establishment of Vaduz v Singer and Friedlander Ltd* [1967] 2 All ER 1192 at 1195, [1967] 1 WLR 1017 at 1021 per Buckley J.

(2) JURISDICTION

1002. Jurisdiction to grant relief. In former times, interpleader relief was given to a limited extent by the courts of common law but more widely in equity[1]. Before 1873 interpleader proceedings were brought either in the Courts of Chancery by a bill of interpleader, or in the common law courts under the Interpleader Act 1831[2]. The sheriff had rights to summon a jury to decide to whom goods belonged[3]. The High Court jurisdiction to grant relief by way of interpleader is now governed by a code of procedure[4] contained in the Rules of the Supreme Court[5], and the statutory provisions have been repealed[6]. Interpleader relief is available in all divisions of the High Court[7], and in the county court[8].

1 See EQUITY vol 16 (Reissue) paras 730–732.
2 As to the effect of 1 & 2 Will 4 c 58 (Interpleader etc) (1831) (repealed) see *De La Rue v Hernu, Peron and Stockwell Ltd* [1936] 2 KB 164 at 172, [1936] 2 All ER 411 at 417, CA.
3 Juries Act 1825 s 52 (repealed): see Mather on Sheriff and Execution Law (3rd Edn) 498 et seq.
4 Ie RSC Ord 17.
5 See *Reading v London School Board* (1886) 16 QBD 686 at 690; *Ex p Mersey Docks and Harbour Board* [1899] 1 QB 546 at 551, CA; *Fredericks and Pelhams Timber Buildings v Wilkins (Read, Claimant)* [1971] 3 All ER 545, [1971] 1 WLR 1197, CA.
6 For the repeal of 1 & 2 Will 4 c 58 (Interpleader etc) (1831) see the Civil Procedure Acts Repeal Act 1879 s 2, Schedule Pt I (repealed); the Statute Law Revision and Civil Procedure Act 1883 s 3, Schedule (repealed). For the repeal of the Common Law Procedure Act 1860 ss 12–18 see the Statute Law Revision and Civil Procedure Act 1883 s 3, Schedule (repealed); Rules of the Supreme Court (No 1) 1929, SR & O 1929/424, r 12 (spent). The statutory relief available under the Law of Property Act 1925 s 136(1), permitting interpleader by a debtor where an assignment of the debt is alleged and disputed (see para 1004 post) would be within the scope of RSC Ord 17, without this special statutory provision.
7 The court may transfer the summons to a more convenient forum, eg from the Master of the Crown Office for the Court of Appeal, following execution under an order for costs, to a master of the Queen's Bench Division. Interpleader relief may be granted in insolvency proceedings: see *Re Morris, ex p Streeter* (1881) 19 ChD 216, CA. The application is by motion to the registrar: Insolvency

Rules 1986, SI 1986/1925, r 7.3. Certain local courts formerly had jurisdiction in interpleader proceedings, but are now either abolished or merged into the High Court: see the Courts Act 1971 ss 41, 43, 56(4), Sch 11 Pt II.
8 See the County Courts Act 1984 s 101; and CCR Ord 33 rr 1, 6. As to interpleader in county court proceedings see para 1071 et seq post.

2. INTERPLEADER IN THE HIGH COURT

(1) RELIEF IN THE HIGH COURT

1003. General. If an application is made in an existing High Court action, the summons issues out of the division in which the action is proceeding, with the title and number of that action, to which is added the new parties, namely the applicant and claimant.

Relief in the High Court is available in two classes of case, known traditionally as stakeholder's and sheriff's interpleader.

An interpleader issue arising in an existing action is technically a 'proceeding' in that action, and not itself an 'action'[1]. It is, however, sufficiently distinct from the original action to be regarded for some purposes, for example a solicitor's retainer, as a separate litigation[2]. If the application for relief by way of interpleader is not made in an existing action the applicant may take out an originating summons[3], and the court may order an issue to be tried[4], in which case that issue will fall within the meaning of 'action'[5].

1 *Hamlyn v Betteley* (1880) 6 QBD 63, CA; *Collis v Lewis* (1887) 20 QBD 202, DC; *McNair & Co v Audenshaw Paint and Colour Co Ltd* [1891] 2 QB 502, CA; *De La Rue v Hernu, Peron and Stockwell Ltd* [1936] 2 KB 164, [1936] 2 All ER 411, CA.
2 *James v Ricknell* (1887) 20 QBD 164.
3 RSC Ord 17 r 3(1). The originating summons must be in expedited form (ie RSC App A Form 10): RSC Ord 17 r 3(3). For forms of summons see Queen's Bench Masters' Practice Forms PF25, PF26, and 22 Court Forms (2nd Edn) (1991 Issue) 409, 425–426, Forms 5, 27.
4 RSC Ord 17 r 5(1)(b).
5 Supreme Court Act 1981 s 151(1); *Re Fawsitt, Galland v Burton* (1885) 30 ChD 231, CA.

1004. Stakeholder's interpleader. In a stakeholder's interpleader, relief is available where the applicant is under a liability in respect of a debt, or in respect of any money, goods or chattels, and he is, or expects to be, sued for or in respect of that debt or money, or those goods or chattels, by two or more persons making adverse claims thereto[1]. Those applicants are traditionally referred to as stakeholders, and the ensuing proceedings as stakeholder's interpleader[2]. By statute, stakeholder's interpleader is available also to a debtor, trustee, or other person liable in respect of a debt or chose in action which has been the subject of a legal assignment when he has had notice either that the assignment is disputed by the assignor or any person claiming under him, or of other opposing or conflicting claims to the debt or chose in action[3]. In such a case the applicant may either call upon the claimants to interplead, or pay the debt or chose in action into court[4].

As the assignment must have been a legal assignment in order to give rise to the right to interplead, the applicant must have had written notice of the assignment before he applies to interplead[5]. Application for this relief is made under the rules relating to stakeholder's interpleader. Stakeholder's interpleader relief is available to the Crown[6].

1 RSC Ord 17 r 1(1)(a); see further paras 1007–1009 post. A sheriff who, after executing a judgment against a debtor obtained by the assignor of the debt, receives notice of the assignee's claim, is not entitled to relief under this head: cf *Plant v Collins* [1913] 1 KB 242 at 246–267, CA.

2 See *Matthew v Northern Assurance Co* (1878) 9 ChD 80 at 84–85 per Sir George Jessel MR.

3 See the Law of Property Act 1925 s 136(1) proviso. However, such relief is also available under the general provisions of RSC Ord 17. The debtor, trustee or other person must have been given express written notice of the assignment: Law of Property Act 1925 s 136(1).

4 Ibid s 136(1) proviso.

5 *Re New Hamburg and Brazilian Rly Co* [1875] WN 239.

6 See the Crown Proceedings Act 1947 s 16; and CROWN PROCEEDINGS vol 11 (Supp) para 9.

1005. Sheriff's interpleader. In a sheriff's interpleader, relief is available to a sheriff[1] where a claim is made by any person, other than the person against whom the process is issued, to any money, goods, or chattels taken, or intended to be taken, by a sheriff in execution under any process or to the proceeds or value of any such goods or chattels[2].

1 References in RSC Ord 17 to a sheriff are to be construed as including references to any other officer charged with the execution of process by or under the authority of the High Court: RSC Ord 17 r 1(2). As to persons other than a sheriff being protected see *Levasseur v Mason and Barry* [1891] 2 QB 73, CA (receiver of judgment debtor's property appointed by the court). The rule would also allow an application for relief by a sequestrator appointed by the court.

2 RSC Ord 17 r 1(1)(b).

1006. Discretionary nature of relief. Interpleader relief is discretionary and cannot be claimed as of right[1]. Provided, however, that the applicant fulfils the necessary conditions[2], and both claimants have substantive claims, the court's jurisdiction is limited only by terms of the relevant rule of court[3], and the court leans strongly in favour of granting the application if possible. Where the sheriff is the applicant the court may make a specific order barring future actions being brought against him in respect of the seizure for which he applied for relief[4]. Relief will be granted if the conditions relating to jurisdiction and procedure are fulfilled wherever the court is satisfied that it is proper to do so[5].

Relief may be granted even though the claimant may claim under an equitable title[6] or even though the applicant may be estopped, as for instance by bailment or agency, from denying a claimant's title, and even where the relief which can be given is not complete[7]. Where there is a question of estoppel the order directing the issue between the claimants should be so framed as not to shut out either claimant from asserting any claim which he may have against the applicant on the estoppel, but should leave it open to him to assert that claim if defeated by the other claimant on the issue[8].

Relief may also be granted even though the applicant admits liability as to part of the claim only[9], and though the claims made against him are not co-extensive[10]; but relief will be refused where the applicant is or may be liable to both claimants[11].

1 *Cave v Capel* [1954] 1 QB 367, [1954] 1 All ER 428, CA; *Gerhard v Montagu & Co (Low & Co, Claimants)* (1889) 61 LT 564; see *Re Baker, Nichols v Baker* (1890) 44 ChD 262, CA; *Julius v Lord Bishop of Oxford* (1880) 5 App Cas 214 at 235, HL, per Lord Selborne; *R v His Honour Judge Turner and Hodgson* [1897] 1 QB 445, DC; cf *Belcher v Smith* (1832) 9 Bing 82.

2 See para 1017 post.

3 RSC Ord 17 r 1; cf *Sun Insurance Office v Galinsky* [1914] 2 KB 545 at 552, CA, per Vaughan Williams LJ.

4 RSC Ord 17 r 8; see Queen's Bench Masters' Practice Forms PF28, PF29 (Interpleader Orders Nos 1, 1A), and 22 Court Forms (2nd Edn) (1991 Issue) 418, 421, Forms 16, 17, 21; *Hooke v Ind, Coope & Co*

(1877) 36 LT 467. In *Neumann v Bakeaway Ltd (Ghotli, Claimant)* [1983] 2 All ER 935, [1983] 1 WLR
1016n, CA, relief was granted where the sheriff had seized and sold goods admitted to be the
claimant's property.
5 *Gerhard v Montagu & Co (Low & Co, Claimants)* (1889) 61 LT 564; *Ex p Mersey Docks and Harbour
Board* [1899] 1 QB 546 at 551, CA.
6 *Duncan v Cashin* (1875) LR 10 CP 554; *Engelbach v Nixon* (1875) LR 10 CP 645; *Jenkinson v Brandley
Mining Co* (1887) 19 QBD 568; *Jennings v Mather* [1901] 1 KB 108 at 115; affd [1902] 1 KB 1, CA;
Usher v Martin (1889) 24 QBD 272. Earlier decisions to the contrary before the Supreme Court of
Judicature Act 1873 (repealed) are no longer of authority.
7 *Robinson v Jenkins* (1890) 24 QBD 275, CA; *Rogers, Sons & Co v Lambert & Co* [1891] 1 QB 318 at 326,
CA, per Lindley LJ; *Attenborough v London and St Katharine's Dock Co* (1878) 3 CPD 450 at 457, 459,
CA; *Ex p Mersey Docks and Harbour Board* [1899] 1 QB 546 at 551, CA, per A L Smith LJ, and at 555
per Collins LJ; see also AGENCY vol 1(2) (Reissue) para 132; BAILMENT vol 2 (Reissue) para 1883.
8 *Ex p Mersey Docks and Harbour Board* [1899] 1 QB 546, CA.
9 *Reading v London School Board* (1886) 16 QBD 686 at 689.
10 *Attenborough v London and St Katharine's Dock Co* (1878) 3 CPD 450 at 459, CA, per Brett LJ, cited
with approval in *Ex p Mersey Docks and Harbour Board* [1899] 1 QB 546 at 552–553, CA, per A L
Smith LJ. Earlier decisions to the contrary are no longer of authority.
11 *Greatorex v Shackle* [1895] 2 QB 249; *Victor Söhne v British and African Steam Navigation Co Ltd* [1888]
WN 84, DC; *Sablicich v Russell* (1866) LR 2 Eq 441; *Crawford v Fisher* (1842) 1 Hare 436 at 441; cf also
Farr v Ward (1837) 2 M & W 844; *Cochrane v O' Brien* (1845) 2 Jo & Lat 380 at 388.

1007. Subject matter of stakeholder's interpleader. The subject matter of a
stakeholder's interpleader is a debt, money, goods or chattels, or a debt or chose in
action which has been the subject of a legal assignment[1].

A debt for which the plaintiff has already obtained judgment against the applicant cannot be made the subject matter of an application for relief[2].

An insurance company's statutory obligation to lay out money payable under a
fire insurance policy upon a house in rebuilding it if so requested by a person
interested, unless the party claiming the money gives security as to its application[3],
is not a liability for a debt or money and, if a lessor claims the fulfilment of the
obligation and the lessee claims payment of the insurance money to him, there are
not adverse claims to a debt or money so as to entitle the company to interplead[4].

It has been held that 'money'[5] does not include a contested claim to the reward
advertised for the apprehension of a criminal[6].

The word 'chattels' in this connection is one of the widest words known to the
law in its relation to personal property[7], and includes deeds and other papers[8], and
choses in action, for instance the shares in a joint stock company[9]. Where either of
the claims is substantially one for unliquidated damages the case is outside the scope
of interpleader, but, where the main subject of dispute is specified goods or money,
the existence of a claim for damages will not in itself bar the applicant from
obtaining the relief sought[10].

An applicant may not ordinarily interplead in respect of a debt which has been
made the subject of a garnishee order absolute[11], even though a claim is made to the
debt by an adverse claimant. He is bound to comply with the garnishee order
absolute and is protected by it[12].

1 RSC Ord 17 r 1(1)(a); Law of Property Act 1925 s 136(1); and see para 1004 ante.
2 See the cases cited in para 1024 note 16 post.
3 See the Fires Prevention (Metropolis) Act 1774 s 83; and INSURANCE paras 607–608 ante.
4 *Sun Insurance Office v Galinsky* [1914] 2 KB 545 at 555–556, CA, per Buckley LJ, and at 557–559 per
Kennedy LJ. In this case it appears that the lessee had not in fact put forward any genuine claim: see at
552 per Vaughan Williams LJ, and at 558 per Kennedy LJ.

5 Ie 'money' in RSC Ord 17 r 1(1)(a).
6 *Callis v Lee* (1835) 1 Hodg 204; *Grant v Fry* (1835) 4 Dowl 135; *Gay v Pittman* (1838) 5 Scott 795.
   These were decisions under 1 & 2 Will 4 c 58 (Interpleader etc) (1831) (repealed): see para 1002 ante.
7 *Robinson v Jenkins* (1890) 24 QBD 275, CA, per Fry LJ.
8 *Smith v Wheeler* (1835) 1 Gale 163; *Walker v Ker* (1843) 12 LJEx 204; *Roberts v Bell* (1857) 7 E & B 323.
9 *Robinson v Jenkins* (1890) 24 QBD 275, CA.
10 *Walter v Nicholson* (1838) 6 Dowl 517; *Wright v Freeman* (1879) 48 LJQB 276; affd 40 LT 358, CA;
   Ingham v Walker (1887) 31 Sol Jo 271 per Pollock B (explaining *Attenborough v London and St*
   Katharine's Dock Co (1878) 3 CPD 450, CA); affd (1887) 3 TLR 448, CA.
11 As to effect of garnishee order absolute see EXECUTION vol 17 para 541.
12 *Randall v Lithgow* (1884) 12 QBD 525, DC. See, however, *Richter v Laxton* (1878) 48 LJQB 184,
   where an issue was ordered in special circumstances, and *Nelson v Barter* (1864) 10 Jur NS 832; affd
   (1864) 33 LJCh 705. As to the determination of questions before order absolute where the garnishee
   disputes liability or where there are adverse claims see EXECUTION vol 17 para 537.

1008. Possession of subject matter. Where the claim is for a specific article or
fund, any applicant for relief, other than a sheriff,[1] must be in possession of the
subject matter in dispute between the claimants, for he has to satisfy the court that
he is willing to pay or transfer it into court or to dispose of it as the court may
direct[2]. Where he has parted with possession he may be denied relief even though
he undertakes to pay over the value to the party found entitled[3]. So also he may
disentitle himself to relief if, after receiving notice of adverse claims to goods, he
sells them and disposes of a portion of the proceeds in accordance with the direction
of one of the parties[4].

1 As to the meaning of 'sheriff' see para 1005 note 1 ante.
2 *Meux v Bell* (1833) 6 Sim 175; RSC Ord 17 r 3(4)(c). See para 1020 post.
3 *Burnett v Anderson* (1816) 1 Mer 405.
4 *Poland v Coall* (1873) IR 7 CL 108.

1009. Reality of the claims. To entitle a stakeholder to relief it is essential that he
is, or genuinely expects to be, sued by two or more persons[1]. It is therefore
normally too late to apply for relief after judgment[2]. It is not necessary that he be
actually sued[3], but there must be some real foundation for the expectation. A mere
anticipation, without any intimation having been received, is not enough[4]. Where,
therefore, the applicant knows that the rival claims are about to be settled by
litigation between the claimants he cannot obtain relief by interpleader[5]. So also
where the allegation that an action is threatened is known to be groundless,
interpleader proceedings, if begun, may be dismissed with costs[6].

The claims should be at least two in number and should be adverse[7]. The conflict
between the claimants must be real in the sense that each claim, if proved, would
give a good cause of action against the applicant, so that where the applicant is not
under any obligation to one of the claimants[8], or where he can, without incurring
any liability, pay the subject matter of the claim to one of the claimants[9], he is not
entitled to relief. A mere pretext of a conflicting claim is not sufficient, and the
court must be satisfied that there is a question to be tried[10]. The claims must be
adverse in the sense of being claims to the whole or part of the same money or
goods or thing. They may arise out of the same transaction and still be so different
as to prevent relief being granted[11].

It is of the essence of interpleader that the applicant is liable to one or other only
of the claimants in respect of the same subject matter[12]. Where, therefore, the
applicant is or may be liable to both, as when two auctioneers claim agents'
commission on the sale of the same house, interpleader is not available[13].

1 RSC Ord 17 r 1(1)(a).
2 See para 1024 post.
3 RSC Ord 17 r 1(1)(a); *Morgan v Marsack* (1816) 2 Mer 107.
4 *Harrison v Payne* (1836) 2 Hodg 107; *Sharpe v Redman* (1837) Will Woll & Dav 375; *Watson v Park Royal (Caterers) Ltd* [1961] 2 All ER 346, [1961] 1 WLR 727.
5 *Diplock v Hammond* (1854) 2 Sm & G 141; on appeal 5 De G M & G 320.
6 *Re Hook, Cook v Earl of Rosslyn* (1861) 3 Giff 175.
7 RSC Ord 17 r 1(1)(a).
8 *East India Co v Edwards* (1811) 18 Ves 376; *Wright v Ward* (1827) 4 Russ 215; *Glynn v Locke* (1842) 3 Dr & War 11.
9 *Myers v United Guarantee and Life Assurance Co, United Guarantee and Life Assurance Co v Cleland* (1855) 7 De G M & G 112 at 127 per Turner LJ; see *Re Hook, Cook v Earl of Rosslyn* (1861) 3 Giff 175; *Desborough v Harris* (1855) 5 De G M & G 439 at 455 (mortgagor and mortgagee).
10 *Cochrane v O' Brien* (1845) 2 Jo & Lat 380 at 389; and see *Sun Insurance Office v Galinsky* [1914] 2 KB 545, CA (cited in para 1007 note 4 ante), where in the circumstances it was doubtful whether there was any genuine adverse claim.
11 *Greatorex v Shackle* [1895] 2 QB 249.
12 *Crawford v Fisher* (1842) 1 Hare 436.
13 *Greatorex v Shackle* [1895] 2 QB 249; *Victor Söhne v British and African Steam Navigation Co Ltd* [1888] WN 84, DC; *Sablicich v Russell* (1866) LR 2 Eq 441; *Farr v Ward* (1837) 2 M & W 844, DC; *Cochrane v O' Brien* (1845) 2 Jo & Lat 380. This principle, however, is subject to the court's power to grant relief even though the claims are not co-extensive, and even though the applicant denies liability in part to either claimant: see para 1006 ante.

1010. Wagering contracts. A stakeholder of money deposited by parties to a wagering contract will not normally be granted relief by way of interpleader, at least where a defence under the Gaming Acts[1] is open to him, or where, by ordering an issue, the court would in effect be driven into the position where it would have to decide the event of a wager[2]. This principle does not seem, however, to have been acted on consistently[3]. It may well be that the true rule is that, where both of the claimants are the parties to the wagering contract, and the real object of the interpleader is to obtain the court's decision as to which is entitled to the stakes deposited, the court must refuse relief, but not where the claimants are not both parties to the wager, and the illegality of the transaction is set up against a party who is not party to it[4]. Thus, the Court of Appeal has at least acquiesced in relief given in a court of first instance where the only question at issue was between a bankrupt and his own trustee in bankruptcy, and where the bankrupt was endeavouring to set up against the trustee the illegality of the title by which he had himself become entitled to the money in question[5].

1 See BETTING vol 4(1) (Reissue) para 18.
2 *Shoolbred v Roberts* [1900] 2 QB 497 at 500–501, CA, per Vaughan Williams LJ, and at 503 per Romer LJ; *Applegarth v Colley* (1842) 2 Dowl NS 223.
3 *Dowson v Macfarlane* (1899) 81 LT 67 appears to be an authority to some extent at least to the contrary of the proposition in the text. It is submitted, however, that it is at least doubtful whether this case would now be followed; cf also *Hill v William Hill (Park Lane) Ltd* [1949] AC 530, [1949] 2 All ER 452, HL.
4 See *Shoolbred v Roberts* [1900] 2 QB 497 at 503, CA, per Romer LJ.
5 *Shoolbred v Roberts* [1900] 2 QB 497, CA.

1011. Examples of relief in stakeholder's interpleader. Relief has been given to the obligor of a bond when sued by executors of a will, when a claim was also made by trustees for a legatee under the will[1]; to executors of a debtor when the whole debt due was claimed by one party, another claiming a part of it, and a third claiming in respect of a lien for costs[2]; to a tenant for life where conflicting claims were made as to a charge on his interest[3]; to acceptors of a bill of exchange sued by the holder after notice from a third person not to pay on the ground of fraud[4], and where actions have been brought against an acceptor by two persons claiming to be lawful owners of a bill[5], or where the proceeds of sale of a ship in the form of a bill of exchange in the hands of a third person were claimed adversely by two claimants[6]; to a carrier of goods faced with conflicting demands for delivery[7]; to warehousemen or wharfingers sued by the holder of a warrant for delivery of goods, after notice by the consignor not to deliver on the ground of fraud or other grounds[8]; to a debtor, sued by the assignee of a debt after notice of an adverse claim from the assignor's[9] trustee in bankruptcy; to brokers where goods or the proceeds of their sale were claimed adversely[10]; to a purchaser of goods, sued by assignees of the seller, a factor for sale, who became bankrupt subsequently to the sale, where a claim was made by the consignor of the goods to the factor[11]; to a bank after receipt of notice by a person alleging himself to be the husband of a depositor, not to repay the money to her, and of notice by the depositor that she disputed the marriage and had instituted criminal proceedings[12], and where the deposit was made by a married woman representing herself to be a widow, and claims were made by her husband and a transferee[13]; to an insurance company where the policy money was claimed by two or more claimants[14]; to stockbrokers, who were transferees for sale of shares claimed by a person other than the transferor[15]; and to a chief constable of police, in possession of a stolen car, to which a purchaser in good faith had done substantial works of repair at a cost which that purchaser claimed should be paid by the true owner as a condition of the car's return[16].

1 *Wright v Ward* (1827) 4 Russ 215.
2 *Jones v Thomas* (1854) 2 Sm & G 186.
3 *Vyvyan v Vyvyan* (1861) 30 Beav 65 at 71.
4 *Gerhard v Montagu & Co (Low & Co, Claimants)* (1889) 61 LT 564.
5 *Regan v Serle* (1840) 9 Dowl 193.
6 *Gibbs v Gibbs* (1858) 6 WR 415.
7 *Wilson v Anderton* (1830) 1 B & Ad 450; and cf CARRIERS vol 5(1) (Reissue) paras 455 text and note 7, 496 text and note 8.
8 *Attenborough v London and St Katharine's Dock Co* (1878) 3 CPD 450, CA. See also *Mason v Hamilton* (1831) 5 Sim 19; *Crawshay v Thornton* (1837) 2 My & Cr 1; *Ex p Mersey Docks and Harbour Board* [1899] 1 QB 546; *De Rothschild Frères v Morrison, Kekewich & Co, Banque de Paris et des Pays Bas v Morrison, Kekewich & Co, Banque de France v Morrison, Kekewich & Co* (1890) 24 QBD 750, CA.
9 *Re Hilton, ex p March* (1892) 67 LT 594.
10 *Suart v Welch* (1839) 4 My & Cr 305; see *Braik v Douglas* (1828) 4 My & Cr 320n.
11 *Johnson v Shaw* (1842) 4 Man & G 916.
12 *Crellin v Leyland* (1842) 6 Jur 733. As to the rights formerly enjoyed by a husband over his wife's property see HUSBAND AND WIFE vol 22 paras 1012–1013.
13 *Costello v Martin* (1867) 15 WR 548.
14 *Fenn v Edmonds* (1846) 5 Hare 314; *Prudential Assurance Co v Thomas* (1867) 3 Ch App 74; *Re Haycock's Policy* (1876) 1 ChD 611 at 616; cf *Desborough v Harris* (1855) 5 De G M & G 439. As to conflicting claims under the Fires Prevention (Metropolis) Act 1774 see *Sun Insurance Office v Galinsky* [1914] 2 KB 545, CA (cited in para 1007 note 4 ante). It has been held that a bill of interpleader in equity by the captain of a ship would not lie where suits had been instituted in the Court of Admiralty on the ground, inter alia, that the proceedings were not against the captain, but against the ship: *Sablicich v Russell* (1866) LR 2 Eq 441; but see, to the contrary, *Lowe v Richardson* (1818) 3 Madd 277. As to interpleader by insurers see further INSURANCE para 502 text and notes 5–6 ante.
15 *Robinson v Jenkins* (1890) 24 QBD 275, CA.
16 *Greenwood v Bennett* [1973] QB 195, [1972] 3 All ER 586, CA.

1012. Subject matter of sheriff's interpleader. Relief by way of sheriff's interpleader is available to sheriffs or other officers[1] charged with the execution of process by or under the authority of the High Court[2]. The claim for relief may be made in two sets of circumstances: (1) when the sheriff is met with a claim which is disputed by the execution creditor to money, goods or chattels taken or intended to be taken in execution under any process of the court, or to the proceeds or value of any such goods or chattels[3]; and (2) when the claim is admitted and the sheriff has withdrawn, and the sheriff requires an order restraining the bringing of an action against him in respect of his action in seizing under the writ of execution[4].

As an intended seizure is enough, actual seizure is unnecessary[5], and may be undesirable where there is nothing to identify the goods directed to be seized with ownership or possession by the judgment debtor[6], but the fact that the goods are not in the possession of the judgment debtor but are in the possession of his trustee or even of the claimant himself need not deprive the sheriff of his right to relief[7]. 'Proceeds or value of any such goods'[8] includes money paid to the sheriff under protest by the claimant himself[9], and this indicates a convenient procedure to release the goods seized from the sheriff's custody and to allow the claimant to deal in the goods[10].

1 As to the meaning of 'sheriff' see para 1005 note 1 ante.
2 See RSC Ord 17 r 1(1)(b), (2).
3 See RSC Ord 17 r 2(1), (3)(a). The sheriff must allow seven days for the execution creditor to consider the claim: RSC Ord 17 r 2(2); see para 1014 post.
4 See RSC Ord 17 r 2(4); and para 1014 post.
5 *Day v Carr* (1852) 7 Exch 883; *Lea v Rossi* (1855) 11 Exch 13; see RSC Ord 17 r 1(1)(b).
6 See para 1016 post.
7 *Allen v Gibbon* (1833) 2 Dowl 292; *Aylwin v Evans* (1882) 52 LJCh 105.
8 Ie in RSC Ord 17 rr 1(1)(b), 2(1).
9 *Smith v Critchfield* (1885) 14 QBD 873, CA.
10 See Queen's Bench Masters' Practice Form PF32 (Interpleader Order No 4), and 22 Court Forms (2nd Edn) (1991 Issue) 421, Form 22.

1013. Nature of claims in sheriff's interpleader. As in stakeholder's interpleader, the claim made by the third party must be a real one and the applicant sheriff must be or expect to be sued[1]. The claim must be one to the goods as such or their proceeds or value as representing the goods[2].

Interpleader proceedings do not lie on a claim by a third party to be the person rightfully entitled to payment of the debt in respect of which execution has been issued[3], nor on a claim by a judgment debtor to set off another judgment debt due to him from a creditor[4], nor to dispute a landlord's claim for rent made under the statutory provisions which prohibit the removal of goods from leasehold property until certain arrears of rent have been paid by an execution creditor[5].

Provided the claim has been duly made[6], a sheriff will normally be entitled to relief even though the claim is obviously bad. If he has already exercised his discretion in the matter he will not be granted relief[7]. If a sheriff is in any way indemnified he is also not entitled to relief and can refuse to accept an offer of indemnity made by the execution creditor[8]. Questions of priority of time between different execution creditors are not claims which entitle a sheriff to interplead[9], but relief may be available where, in addition to the questions of priority, there is a claim against both execution creditors[10]. If, on execution being levied against a partner, a claim is made that the property seized is partnership property and the execution creditor disputes the partnership or denies that the goods seized are partnership property, the dispute is a proper subject for interpleader proceedings[11].

If a seizure is made and a claim is made that the goods are owned by the debtor jointly with others or as tenants in common, the sheriff can sell and the question of the distribution of the proceeds if in dispute can be the subject of interpleader proceedings[12].

The claim by a debenture holder can be a subject for interpleader proceedings if, for example, the validity of the receiver's appointment is disputed, but where the charge over the company's assets has been crystallised by the valid appointment of a receiver before the completion of an execution by seizure and sale the rights of the debenture holders will have priority over those of the execution creditor[13].

1 Cf RSC Ord 17 r 1(1)(a); and para 1009 ante.
2 RSC Ord 17 r 1(1)(b).
3 See *Plant v Collins* [1913] 1 KB 242, CA.
4 *Smith v Saunders* (1877) 37 LT 359.
5 See the Landlord and Tenant Act 1709 s 1; and DISTRESS vol 13 paras 320–321. That section does not apply to a county court execution, but on receiving a landlord's claim the bailiff levying the execution must in addition distrain for the rent claimed: see the County Courts Act 1984 s 102 (as amended); and COUNTY COURTS vol 10 paras 486–487.
6 As to the making of claims see para 1014 post.
7 *Crump v Day* (1847) 4 CB 760.
8 *Ostler v Bower* (1836) 4 Dowl 605; and cf *Levy v Champneys* (1834) 2 Dowl 454, and *Harrison v Forster* (1836) 4 Dowl 558.
9 *Salmon v James* (1832) 1 Dowl 369; *Day v Waldock, Lawrence v Waldock* (1833) 1 Dowl 523; and see *Bowyer v Pritchard* (1822) 11 Price 103; *Blennerhassett v Scanlan* (1826) 2 Mol 539. In *Vyner v Buchanan-Michaelson* (13 February 1976, unreported), QBD, the interpleader issue as to ownership was extended to include a decision on priorities between different execution creditors already respondents to the issue.
10 *Slowman v Back* (1832) 3 B & Ad 103.
11 See the Partnership Act 1890 s 23 (as amended); *Peake v Carter* [1916] 1 KB 652 at 655, CA, per Swinfen Eady LJ; and PARTNERSHIP.
12 *Farrar v Beswick* (1836) 1 M & W 682; *Mayhew v Herrick* (1849) 7 CB 229.
13 *Re Standard Manufacturing Co* [1891] 1 Ch 627, CA; *Re Opera Ltd* [1891] 3 Ch 260, CA; and see *Taunton v Sheriff of Warwickshire* [1895] 2 Ch 319, CA; *Evans v Rival Granite Quarries Ltd* [1910] 2 KB 979, CA; *Robinson v Burnell's Vienna Bakery Co Ltd* [1904] 2 KB 624; *Heaton and Dugard Ltd v Cutting Bros Ltd* [1925] 1 KB 655, DC.

1014. Claim and admission in sheriff's interpleader. The sheriff's right to interplead is founded on the existence of one or more claims to the subject matter of the seizure or intended seizure, not being claims which the execution creditor admits. In order to entitle the sheriff to interplead, any person making a claim to or in respect of any money, goods or chattels taken or intended to be taken in execution under the process of the court, or to the proceeds or value of any such goods or chattels, must give notice of this claim[1] to the sheriff[2] charged with the execution of the process and must include in his notice a statement of his address, which will be his address for service[3]. On receipt of the claim the sheriff must forthwith give notice of it to the execution creditor[4] who must, within seven days after receiving the notice give notice to the sheriff informing him whether he admits or disputes the claim[5]. Where the sheriff receives a notice from an execution creditor disputing a claim, or the execution creditor fails, within seven days, to give the required notice, and the claim is not withdrawn, the sheriff may apply to the court[6] for relief[7]. On the other hand, a sheriff who receives a notice from an execution creditor admitting a claim must withdraw from possession of the money, goods or chattels claimed and may apply to the court for an order restraining the bringing of an action against him for or in respect of his having taken possession of that money or those goods or chattels[8].

1 RSC Ord 17 r 2(1). Whilst the rule does not specifically require the claim to be in writing (as did the former RSC (1883) Ord LVII r 16(1) (revoked)), this is implied; an oral claim is not sufficient but must be fully investigated by the sheriff, as if he sells without making reasonable inquiry he will not be able to claim the protection of the Supreme Court Act 1981 s 138B (added by the Statute Law (Repeals) Act 1989, which repeals the Bankruptcy and Deeds of Arrangement Act 1913 s 15) (see BANKRUPTCY AND INSOLVENCY vol 3(2) (Reissue) para 852). See *Observer Ltd v Gordon (Cranfield and ors, Claimants)* [1983] 2 All ER 945, [1983] 1 WLR 1008.
    The claim should give a description and full details of the goods and chattels claimed, as costs are frequently awarded on the basis of whether it was reasonable for the execution creditor to have been suspicious of the claim because it was vague or insufficient: see *Powell v Lock* (1835) 3 Ad & El 315. The claim need not necessarily be signed: see *J R P Plastics Ltd v Gordon Rossall Plastics Ltd (Hexa Pen Co Ltd, Claimants)* [1950] 1 All ER 241, DC.
    For a form of claim see 22 Court Forms (2nd Edn) (1991 Issue) 407, Form 1.
2 As to the meaning of 'sheriff' see para 1005 note 1 ante.
3 RSC Ord 17 r 2(1).
4 RSC Ord 17 r 2(2). For a form of notice see Queen's Bench Masters' Practice Form PF23, and 22 Court Forms (2nd Edn) (1991 Issue) 407–408, Form 2. Any clear written notice, however, enclosing a copy of the claim, will suffice. The giving of this notice is a condition precedent to the sheriff's right to claim interpleader relief: *Dalton v Furness* (1866) 35 Beav 461.
5 RSC Ord 17 r 2(2). For a form of notice admitting or disputing the claim see Queen's Bench Masters' Practice Form PF24, and 22 Court Forms (2nd Edn) (1991 Issue) 408, Form 3. Sheriff's officers usually combine in this notice a form for return by the execution creditor to indicate whether the claim is admitted or disputed. As to the execution creditor's liability for fees and expenses where he admits the claim see para 1060 post.
6 'The court' means the High Court or any one or more judges of it, whether sitting in court or in chambers, or any master, the Admiralty Registrar, a district judge of the Family Division or a district judge: RSC Ord 1 r 4(2).
7 RSC Ord 17 r 2(3).
8 RSC Ord 17 r 2(4). As to whether the sheriff is entitled to an order protecting him from future actions see *Cave v Capel* [1954] 1 QB 367 at 369–370, [1954] 1 All ER 428 at 430, CA, per Somervell LJ, where the claimant was in a caravan which was then towed to a barn by the sheriff's officers. See also *Neumann v Bakeaway Ltd (Ghotli, Claimant)* [1983] 2 All ER 935 at 942, [1983] 1 WLR 1016n at 1023, CA, per Geoffrey Lane LJ: it is the quality of the sheriff's admitted wrong which is relevant.

1015. Exercise of sheriff's right to apply for relief. The sheriff should exercise his right to apply for relief within a reasonable time of the expiry of the seven days within which the execution creditor is required to admit or dispute the claim[1]. There is no necessity for the sheriff to wait until proceedings are taken against him[2], and a claimant should first allow the sheriff to interplead before himself bringing proceedings against a sheriff[3].

The sheriff's application for protection where an execution creditor admits a claim and the sheriff has to withdraw from possession of money, goods or chattels claimed[4] is to be regarded as an application for relief under the rules relating to interpleader[5]. If the sheriff fails to withdraw after receiving a notice of admission from the execution creditor, the court will not permit him to claim relief in order to obtain protection from an action by the claimant[6], and even where the sheriff does withdraw the court will not grant him protection where it is apparent that the claimant has a real grievance[7]. In the absence of an admission by the execution creditor the sheriff withdraws in the face of a claim only at his peril, whether he withdraws without seizure[8], or seizes and then withdraws[9], or delivers up the goods or some of them[10], or pays over the proceeds to a claimant or the execution creditor[11]. In all the above cases he may be refused relief even if he offers to bring the amount into court[12].

If the sheriff relinquishes possession the goods are no longer in the custody of the law and may be distrained for rent[13], but whilst the ownership of the goods is in issue before the court pending determination by the court any removal of those goods out of the sheriff's custody by a claimant is a contempt of court[14].

1 See para 1014 text and note 5 ante.
2 *Green v Brown* (1835) 3 Dowl 337.
3 *Hilliard v Hanson* (1882) 21 ChD 69, CA. The court may show its disapprobation of a hasty claimant by not awarding him costs in any action he may begin: *Hilliard v Hanson* supra at 72 per Sir George Jessel MR.
4 See para 1014 text to note 8 ante.
5 *Cave v Capel* [1954] 1 QB 367 at 370, [1954] 1 All ER 428 at 430, CA, per Somervell LJ; RSC Ord 17 r 8.
6 *Sodeau v Shorey* (1896) 74 LT 240, CA.
7 *Cave v Capel* [1954] 1 QB 367, [1954] 1 All ER 428, CA.
8 *Holton v Guntrip* (1837) 6 Dowl 130.
9 *Crump v Day* (1847) 4 CB 760.
10 *Braine v Hunt* (1834) 2 Dowl 391.
11 *Anderson v Calloway* (1832) 1 Dowl 636; *Scott v Lewis* (1835) 4 Dowl 259.
12 *Inland v Bushell* (1836) 5 Dowl 147.
13 *Cropper v Warner* (1883) Cab & El 152; and see DISTRESS vol 13 para 324.
14 See CONTEMPT OF COURT vol 9 para 35.

1016. Wrongdoing by the sheriff or his under-sheriff. The court may refuse a sheriff relief where the difficulty arises from his own wrongdoing[1]. Thus relief will not be given where he has seized goods which he knew were not those of the execution debtor[2] or which were in the custody of a receiver appointed by the court[3]. The circumstances in which an order will be made directing that no action be brought against a sheriff who has acted in good faith but mistakenly are considered subsequently[4].

An under-sheriff who is a solicitor cannot act as such on behalf of a claimant as against an execution creditor, but the fact that he has directed a claim to be made on behalf of a claimant for whom he had previously acted as solicitor is not sufficient, in the absence of collusion or dishonest conduct, or anything to prejudice the execution creditor, to prevent relief being given[5]. The case is otherwise where there is a clear degree of culpability on the under-sheriff's part. A sheriff must not 'play on the same side' as one of the parties to the proceedings[6]. Where, for instance, the under-sheriff postpones execution of the process entrusted to him in order that other creditors for whom he formerly acted as solicitor may take bankruptcy proceedings or gives information to other creditors for whom he has acted which may have the effect of defeating or delaying the execution creditor's rights, the sheriff may be disentitled to relief[7]. A sheriff has also been refused relief where the under-sheriff or his partner was himself the execution creditor[8].

1 See the dictum of Kindersley V-C in *Tufton v Harding* (1859) 29 LJCh 225; and *Winter v Bartholomew* (1856) 11 Exch 704 at 708 per Alderson B, and at 710 per Platt B.
2 *Tufton v Harding* (1859) 29 LJCh 225; *Lewis v Jones* (1836) 2 M & W 203. If the sheriff considers he should not seize goods despite the execution creditor's instruction because he has grounds for believing the goods do not belong to the judgment debtor, he should obtain a claim from the claimant and issue a summons on goods intended to be seized.
3 *Russell v East Anglian Rly Co* (1850) 3 Mac & G 104.
4 See para 1031 post.
5 *Holt v Frost* (1858) 3 H & N 821. Formerly a stricter practice prevailed, but each case would now be dealt with on its own facts.
6 *Fredericks and Pelhams Timber Buildings v Wilkins (Read, Claimant)* [1971] 3 All ER 545 at 551, [1971] 1 WLR 1197 at 1204, CA, per Sachs LJ.

7 *Dudden v Long* (1834) 3 Dowl 139; *Cox v Balne* (1845) 14 LJQB 95; and see further para 1019 post.
8 *Ostler v Bower* (1836) 4 Dowl 605. Relief has also been refused to a sheriff to the extent of any loss sustained by an execution creditor because the sheriff had not appointed a London deputy: *Brackenbury v Laurie* (1834) 3 Dowl 180.

1017. Conditions of relief. There are three conditions precedent to interpleader relief, and evidence of them must normally support an application[1]. These conditions are that the applicant:

(1) claims no interest in the subject matter in dispute other than for charges or costs[2];
(2) does not collude with any of the claimants to that subject matter[3]; and
(3) is willing to pay or transfer that subject matter into court or to dispose of it as the court may direct[4].

A stakeholder will file an affidavit, ordinarily to be deposed to by himself personally[5], in support of his application dealing with these and any other matters; a sheriff[6] will only provide that evidence if directed by the court to do so[7], otherwise he may not obtain his costs of so doing. An affidavit on behalf of a corporation or company should be deposed to by the appropriate officer[8]. A partnership has been allowed to rely on an affidavit sworn by two only out of four partners[9].

A sheriff interpleads on the footing that he is neutral as between the parties and acting as though an officer of the court, and his claim to costs depends on his conforming to that principle[10].

1 RSC Ord 17 r 3(4). See, however, RSC Ord 17 r 3(5) (text and note 7 infra). For examples of supporting affidavits see 22 Court Forms (2nd Edn) (1991 Issue) 426–427, Forms 28–29.
2 RSC Ord 17 r 3(4)(a). See para 1018 post.
3 RSC Ord 17 r 3(4)(b). See para 1019 post.
4 RSC Ord 17 r 3(4)(c). See para 1020 post.
5 *Powell v Lock* (1835) 3 Ad & El 315. If the applicant personally cannot make the affidavit, for example because he is abroad, the reason for this must be explained fully in the affidavit that is filed.
6 As to the meaning of 'sheriff' see para 1005 note 1 ante.
7 RSC Ord 17 r 3(5). If an affidavit is required this may be sworn by the under-sheriff. The circumstances surrounding the seizure may be of use to the judge or master on the hearing of the summons.
8 A railway company was permitted in exceptional circumstances to rely on an affidavit by its solicitor instead of its secretary: *Great Southern and Western Rly Co v Corry* (1867) 15 WR 650. Where the applicant is the officer of a company specially authorised by Act of Parliament to bring proceedings in his own name, his affidavit should depose of an absence of interest or collusion both in himself and, to the best of his knowledge and belief, in the company: *Bignold v Audland* (1840) 11 Sim 23.
9 *Glover v Reynolds* (1867) 16 LT 84.
10 *Fredericks and Pelhams Timber Buildings v Wilkins (Read, Claimant)* [1971] 3 All ER 545 at 551, [1971] 1 WLR 1197 at 1204, CA.

1018. Absence of personal interest. It is unlikely that a sheriff, his under-sheriff or his officers will have any personal interest in the subject matter in dispute other than for charges or costs[1], but any such interest must be disclosed to the court on the return of the summons[2]. A stakeholder may have an interest so as to bar himself from obtaining relief even though he does not lay claim to any specific part of the subject matter if he has a financial stake in the result of the proceedings[3]. A mere affinity for one side rather than the other is of course insufficient to debar an applicant for relief[4]. The fact that the applicant has a lien over the goods in question for storage, or a claim to commission on the proceeds of sale, does not disentitle him to relief[5].

1 See RSC Ord 17 r 3(4)(a); and para 1017 ante.
2 A sheriff cannot levy in his own county for his own judgment debt; the writ must be directed to the coroner: see Mather on Sheriff and Execution Law (3rd Edn) 55.
3 *Murietta v South American etc Co Ltd* (1893) 62 LJQB 396 at 397–398.
4 See *Murietta v South American etc Co Ltd* (1893) 62 LJQB 396 at 397–398.
5 See *Cotter v Bank of England* (1833) 2 Dowl 728; *Harwood v Betham* (1832) 1 LJEx 180; *Attenborough v London and St Katharine's Dock Co* (1878) 3 CPD 450, CA; *Best v Hayes* (1863) 1 H & C 718, overruling *Mitchell v Hayne* (1824) 2 Sim & St 63; *Yates v Farebrother* (1819) 4 Madd 239. There are no modern reported cases where personal interest has been alleged against the applicant.

1019. Absence of collusion. The second condition precedent to the granting of interpleader relief is that the applicant does not collude with any of the claimants to the subject matter[1]. It is difficult to draw a clear line between interest and collusion, and the modern interpretation is that there must be no identification of interest between the applicant and the claimant. Collusion does not here necessarily entail anything morally wrong; it means that the applicant must not 'play on the same side' as one of the claimants[2]. In executing a writ the sheriff is acting as an officer charged with the carrying out of the court's orders; he is in effect in the same position as an officer of the court, and should act as such[3]. The court is entitled to expect a high standard of conduct.

1 See RSC Ord 17 r 3(4)(b); and para 1017 ante.
2 *Murietta v South American etc Co Ltd* (1893) 62 LJQB 396; *Fredericks and Pelhams Timber Buildings v Wilkins (Read, Claimant)* [1971] 3 All ER 545 at 551, [1971] 1 WLR 1197 at 1204, CA.
3 *Fredericks and Pelhams Timber Buildings v Wilkins (Read, Claimant)* [1971] 3 All ER 545 at 551, [1971] 1 WLR 1197 at 1204, CA.

1020. Willingness to bring subject matter into court. The third condition for the granting of interpleader relief is that the applicant must be willing and able to pay or transfer the subject matter of the dispute into court, or to dispose of it as the court may direct[1]. Where goods are the subject matter, the court may order them to be sold[2]. A sheriff is never directed to bring the goods into court, but he may be ordered to move them to a place of safety[3].

Where the subject matter is money or the proceeds of the sale of goods either seized and sold[4], or ordered to be sold[5], or where the claimant is prepared or ordered to pay the value of the goods to the sheriff and secure their release[6], the court may give directions as to the trial of the issue, ordering either that the money be paid into court or that it be held by the sheriff pending further order, and releasing the applicant from any further part in the proceedings with an order that no action be brought against him[7].

It is generally necessary that a stakeholder applicant should be able to bring the whole amount into court, and it is no excuse that, before the adverse claim was made, the applicant paid a part of the sum claimed to the claimant[8].

1 See RSC Ord 17 r 3(4)(c); and para 1017 ante. Where the subject matter of the dispute is a chose in action, its disposition is equivalent to payment in the case of money or transfer in the case of goods: *Robinson v Jenkins* (1890) 24 QBD 275 at 279, CA, per Fry LJ.
2 See paras 1032–1038 post.
3 This sanction is frequently applied where the claimant refuses to sign a 'walking possession agreement' which acknowledges the seizure by the sheriff and gives undertakings as to retention of the seized property in consideration of the sheriff not leaving an officer in possession. For such an agreement see the Sheriffs' Fees (Amendment) Order 1956, SI 1956/502, Schedule.
4 Ie the execution of a writ of fieri facias.

5 See paras 1032–1038 post.
6 See para 1048 post.
7 See para 1046 post.
8 *Allen v Gilby* (1834) 3 Dowl 143.

1021. Respondents to the application. Any person who alleges facts which, if true, would establish a cause of action against the applicant in respect of the subject matter of the application for relief, and who has asserted that claim by notice if the claim is against a sheriff[1], may be recognised as a claimant. The Crown may be made a party to interpleader proceedings[2].

There have been interpleader proceedings in respect of claims by minors[3], beneficiaries even though the trustees were not joined[4], administrators, executors or trustees of a settlement[5], a person claiming a lien on the subject matter in dispute[6], an agent who had leased goods to the execution debtor[7], a liquidator of a foreign company[8], the debtor's trustee in bankruptcy[9], a trustee under a deed of assignment for the benefit of creditors[10], debenture holders where the property seized was the company's property[11], a receiver appointed by the court[12], and an equitable mortgagee[13]. The execution debtor may be a claimant where he claims as executor or trustee for some other person, and not in his own right[14].

If it is desired to add a company in liquidation as a respondent to an interpleader summons or issue, the leave of the Companies Court must first be obtained[15].

1 See para 1014 ante.
2 Crown Proceedings Act 1947 s 16: see CROWN PROCEEDINGS vol 11 (Supp) para 9.
3 *Claridge v Collins* (1839) 7 Dowl 698. The sheriff may well be unaware that the claimant is a minor until after the summons is issued and served.
4 *Schroeder v Hanrott* (1873) 28 LT 704.
5 *Bradley v James* (1876) 10 ILT 180; *Fenwick v Laycock* (1841) 2 QB 108; *Burke v Routledge* (1851) 3 Ir Jur 148; and see EXECUTORS vol 17 para 1558.
6 *Ford v Baynton* (1832) 1 Dowl 357; *Rogers v Kennay* (1846) 9 QB 592; *Jones v Turnbull* (1837) 2 M & W 601.
7 *Green v Stevens* (1857) 2 H & N 146.
8 *Levasseur v Mason and Barry* [1891] 2 QB 73, CA.
9 *Jones v Turnbull* (1837) 2 M & W 601; *Bradley v James* (1876) 10 ILT 180; *Bird v Mathews* (1882) 46 LT 512, CA; *Dibb v Brooke & Sons* [1894] 2 QB 338.
10 *Adnitt v Hands* (1887) 57 LT 370.
11 *Davey & Co v Williamson & Sons* [1898] 2 QB 194.
12 *Purkiss v Holland* (1887) 31 Sol Jo 702, CA.
13 *Usher v Martin* (1889) 24 QBD 272.
14 *Fenwick v Laycock* (1841) 2 QB 108.
15 *Eastern Holdings Establishment of Vaduz v Singer and Friedlander Ltd* [1967] 2 All ER 1192, [1967] 1 WLR 1017.

1022. Respondents outside the jurisdiction. Service out of the jurisdiction may be allowed by the court[1] of any summons, order or notice in any interpleader proceedings[2]. The application for leave should be made by affidavit exhibiting the notice of claim[3], which will have an address for service.

1 For the meaning of 'the court' see para 1014 note 6 ante.
2 See RSC Ord 11 r 9(1), (4), (5); *Attenborough v London and St Katharine's Dock Co* (1878) 3 CPD 450 at 455, CA. For forms of affidavit by a sheriff for leave to serve an interpleader summons out of the jurisdiction, order and affidavit of service see 22 Court Forms (2nd Edn) (1991 Issue) 410–411, Forms 6–8. As to service out of the jurisdiction generally see PRACTICE AND PROCEDURE.
3 See para 1014 text and note 1 ante.

1023. More than one claimant. The fact that there are several claimants is no bar to relief being granted, the principle being that an applicant ought to be relieved from the vexation attending the bringing of various suits against him[1]. Nor is it an objection that all the claimants do not claim precisely the same amount[2]. The court has power to substitute one claimant for another[3] or to add a claimant[4]. Where different claimants claim different goods, or the same goods for different reasons, there may be more than one issue directed to be tried between the appropriate parties within the one trial.

1 See eg *Angell v Hadden* (1808) 15 Ves 244; *Farebrother v Beale* (1849) 3 De G & Sm 637.
2 *Hoggart v Cutts* (1841) Cr & Ph 197; *Carr (Kerr) v Edwards* (1839) 8 Dowl 29 at 31; and see para 1006 ante.
3 Eg a liquidator for a provisional liquidator: see *Ibbotson v Chandler* (1841) 9 Dowl 250 (assignees in bankruptcy substituted for provisional assignee).
4 *Bird v Mathews* (1882) 46 LT 512, CA (trustee in bankruptcy); *Kirk v Clark* (1835) 4 Dowl 363; *Walker v Ker* (1843) 12 LJEx 204.

(2) APPLICATION FOR INTERPLEADER RELIEF

1024. Mode of application. An application for relief by way of interpleader must be made by originating summons[1] calling on the claimants to appear and state the nature and particulars of their claims and either to maintain or relinquish them, unless the application is made in a pending action, in which case it must be made by the summons in the action[2], which may be taken out at any time after the issue of the writ[3].

Where the applicant is a sheriff who has withdrawn from possession of money, goods or chattels taken in execution and who is applying for relief[4], the summons must be served on any person who made a claim[5] to or in respect of that money or those goods or chattels, and that person may attend the hearing of the application[6]. A sheriff's application is made by summons in the action in which the process has been directed to him[7]. Where the action in question is proceeding in the Royal Courts of Justice, the sheriff's application may be made to a master (or, in the Family Division, a district judge or, in the Admiralty Court, the Admiralty Registrar[8]) or, if the execution to which the application relates has been or is to be levied in the district of a district registry, either to a master or to the district judge of that registry[9]. Where the action is proceeding in a district registry, the sheriff's application may be made either to the district judge of that registry, or, if execution has been or is to be levied in the district of some other district registry or outside the district of any district registry, either (1) to that district judge, or (2) to the district judge of that other registry or to a master, as the case may be[10]. The first consideration is the convenience of the majority of the parties[11].

The application must be made as quickly as possible, or the applicant may be refused relief or may not obtain all his costs[12]. The matter is urgent because in most cases the goods seized remain, throughout the application, under the control of the court, and in sheriff's interpleaders the goods are in the custody of the law awaiting the court's determination as to the person to whom the goods can be released[13]. A claimant may therefore be prevented from trading or dealing in goods which may subsequently be found to be his own. Delay may also increase the costs by storage charges or sheriff's possession fees[14].

The issue of a sheriff's interpleader summons in relation to an execution under a writ of execution extends the validity of that writ until the expiry of 12 months from the conclusion of the interpleader proceedings[15].

It is normally too late for an applicant to apply after judgment in an action, even if this were signed in default[16].

Where the applicant, knowing of the adverse claims, allowed himself to be sued by one of the parties and advised the joinder in the action of the other claimant instead of resorting to interpleader proceedings, it was held that he had forfeited the usual privilege allowed to an applicant in interpleader of being awarded his costs, and that he must pay the costs of the successful claimant[17].

A summons in a stakeholder's interpleader application must be supported by an affidavit[18], but in a sheriff's interpleader an affidavit should not be filed on behalf of the sheriff unless directed by the court[19].

1 RSC Ord 17 r 3(1). The originating summons must be in expedited form (ie RSC App A Form 10): Ord 17 r 3(3). For a form of interpleader originating summons by a stakeholder see Queen's Bench Masters' Practice Form PF25, and 22 Court Forms (2nd Edn) (1991 Issue) 425–426, Form 27.
2 RSC Ord 17 r 3(1). Because interpleader proceedings by a sheriff can only arise in the course of execution, it follows that such proceedings always arise in a pending action. For a form of summons by a sheriff for an order restraining the bringing of an action against him see 22 Court Forms (2nd Edn) (1991 Issue) 408–409, Form 4; and for a form of interpleader summons by a sheriff see Queen's Bench Masters' Practice Form PF26, and 22 Court Forms (2nd Edn) (1991 Issue) 409, Form 5.
3 The owner of goods seized may not obtain his costs if he sues the sheriff without giving him time to interplead, or waiting until the interpleader is decided: *Hilliard v Hanson* (1882) 21 ChD 69, CA.
4 Ie for relief under RSC Ord 17 r 2(4): see para 1014 text to note 8 ante.
5 Ie under RSC Ord 17 r 2(1): see para 1014 ante.
6 RSC Ord 17 r 3(2).
7 A sheriff can only take action on delivery to him of a writ of execution, which will have issued out of a division of the High Court. Summonses are issued as follows:
    (1) in the Queen's Bench Division, to a master of that division, by rota, or to a district judge, and the application is made in the form of an originating summons provided in Queen's Bench Masters' Practice Form PF26 (see also 22 Court Forms (2nd Edn) (1991 Issue) 409, Form 5);
    (2) in the Commercial Court, to the judge of that court or, if after judgment, to a master of the Queen's Bench Division;
    (3) in the Admiralty Court, to the Admiralty Registrar;
    (4) in the Chancery Division, to the assigned master of that division;
    (5) in insolvency proceedings, to a registrar in bankruptcy of the High Court or a district registrar (see the Insolvency Rules 1986, SI 1986/1925, rr 7.3, 13.2);
    (6) in the Companies Court, to the registrar of that court;
    (7) in the Family Division, to a district judge of that division, the district judge of the day;
    (8) in the Court of Appeal, to the Master of the Crown Office, who may transfer the matter to a master of the Queen's Bench Division.
8 RSC Ord 17 r 4.
9 RSC Ord 17 r 4(a).
10 RSC Ord 17 r 4(b).
11 The most convenient court in which to issue the summons will be that nearest to where the goods are seized, which will be local to the sheriff and his officers and to the claimant.
12 *Cook v Allen* (1833) 1 Cr & M 542; *Beale v Overton* (1837) 2 M & W 534; *Devereaux v John* (1833) 1 Dowl 548; *Mutton v Young* (1847) 4 CB 371; *Ridgway v Fisher* (1835) 3 Dowl 567. The courts recognise the urgency of these applications and have made arrangements for special appointments when the return date in the ordinary list would cause undue delay.
13 On this point generally see *Lloyds and Scottish Finance Ltd v Modern Cars and Caravans (Kingston) Ltd* [1966] 1 QB 764, [1964] 2 All ER 732, where the judgment debtor sold a caravan which the sheriff had seized.
14 See the Order dated 8 July 1920 (Writs of Fieri Facias, sheriffs' or sheriffs' officers fees order), SR & O 1920/1250, Schedule Fee 4 (substituted by SI 1956/502; amended by SI 1971/808): £3 per man per day for close possession; 25p per day for walking possession). As to walking possession agreements see para 1020 note 3 ante.

15 RSC Ord 46 r 8(6). Thus the provision for the sheriff's representative to inform the court at the first hearing of the interpleader summons of the date of expiry of the writ of fieri facias as provided in *Practice Direction (Interpleader Proceedings)* [1982] 1 All ER 319, [1982] 1 WLR 2, is no longer relevant.

16 *H Stevenson & Son Ltd v Brownell* [1912] 2 Ch 344, CA; *Cornish v Tanner* (1827) 1 Y & J 333; *Larabrie v Brown* (1857) 1 De G & J 204; and cf *Plant v Collins* [1913] 1 KB 242, CA, cited in para 1074 note 3 post; but see *Hamilton v Marks* (1852) 5 De G & Sm 638, where a defendant obtained relief by bill after judgment in an action at law, the effect of which was merely to ascertain the quantum of demand.

17 *Crickmore v Freeston* (1870) 40 LJCh 137.

18 See RSC Ord 17 r 3(4); and para 1017 ante. For form of affidavit see 2 Court Forms (2nd Edn) (1991 Issue) 427–428, Form 30.

19 See RSC Ord 17 r 3(5); and para 1017 ante.

1025. Service of summons. An originating summons initiating interpleader proceedings[1] must be served not less than 14 clear days before the day fixed for the hearing of the summons[2] and must generally be served personally on each of the claimants[3]. Where the application is by summons in an action, the summons must be served not less than 14 clear days before the day specified in the summons for the hearing[4]. Service of a summons upon a party to the action may be effected by leaving it at or posting it to his address for service or, where appropriate, by using a document exchange[5]; and service upon the claimant may be effected by post to his proper address[6], which will be the address for service if the applicant is a sheriff to whom the claimant has given notice of his claim[7]. Service of any summons, order or notice out of the jurisdiction may be allowed in respect of interpleader proceedings[8].

1 See para 1024 ante.
2 RSC Ord 17 r 3(6). This rule allows the claimant 14 days to serve an affidavit specifying any money and describing any goods and chattels claimed and setting out the grounds upon which such claim is based.
3 See RSC Ord 10 r 1(1).
4 See note 2 supra.
5 RSC Ord 65 r 5(1)(a)–(c), (2A). Where the party acts by a solicitor, the address for service will be the solicitor's business address, or service may be effected by FAX: see RSC Ord 6 r 5(1)(ca), (2)(a), (2B), RSC Ord 12 r 3 (2)(b).
6 Ie as defined in RSC Ord 6 r 5(2). Where the claimant acts by a solicitor, the proper address will be the solicitor's business address: RSC Ord 65 r 5(2)(a).
7 Notice of a claim must include the claimant's address for service: see RSC Ord 17 r 2(1); and para 1014 ante.
8 See RSC Ord 11 r 9; and para 1022 ante.

1026. Affidavit of claims. A summons for interpleader relief calls upon the claimants to appear and state the nature and particulars of their respective claims. In both stakeholder's and sheriff's interpleaders the claimant should swear and file an affidavit[1] setting out in detail what he claims and the grounds upon which his claim is based with such precision as to enable the opposing claimant or the execution creditor to decide whether to oppose it and so that the court may make an appropriate order[2]. The affidavit should exhibit or contain a list of the goods claimed, or otherwise describe them, so that the parties know exactly what is being claimed.

The final order as to costs may be affected by the degree of clarity and the amount of information supplied in the claimant's affidavit, upon which the execution creditor will have decided whether or not to ask the court to direct summary disposal or the trial of an issue[3]. A claimant does not fail because the case he proves differs from that contained in his particulars, at least if the matter can be dealt with by costs, amendment or adjournment[4].

No affidavit is required from the execution creditor as to the particulars of his claim[5], although there will often be an affidavit in reply to that sworn by the claimant.

1 RSC Ord 17 r 3(6), (7). Service of the affidavit must be made within 14 days of the service of the summons. For forms of affidavit see 22 Court Forms (2nd Edn) (1991 Issue) 412–415, 427–428, Forms 9–11, 29–31.
2 *Powell v Lock* (1835) 3 Ad & El 315; *Webster v Delafield* (1849) 7 CB 187.
3 As to modes of determination see paras 1040, 1046 post. The claimant may well succeed as to part only, and the order for costs may take account of this in the usual exercise of the court's discretion as to costs: see RSC Ord 17 r 8.
4 *Peake v Carter* [1916] 1 KB 652, CA.
5 *Angus v Wootton* (1838) 3 M & W 310.

1027. Sheriff's inventory of goods seized. It is for the claimant in a sheriff's interpleader to inform the court what goods he is claiming[1]. Where the claimant has not provided an affidavit the summons may be adjourned, and an order made for an affidavit to be filed. Failure to comply with such an order may result in the claimant's claim being barred[2]. The claimant may not call on the sheriff to deliver particulars of the goods seized so as to enable him to prepare his claim[3], but the master or district judge may order the sheriff to assist the court by producing an inventory of the goods he has seized, and it is for the master or district judge on the return of the summons to consider ordering the sheriff to provide the parties with such an inventory in advance of the hearing. Whilst the sheriff is not normally required to provide the claimant with the inventory, where all the goods seized are claimed the sheriff should not provide an inventory to one side only[4]. For the sheriff to prepare an inventory is a step in the execution allowing him to charge a prescribed fee based on a percentage of the value of the goods seized[5].

The issue of the interpleader summons does not of itself stay further proceedings in respect of the goods claimed: the summons asks for such a stay[6]. The court has power to grant a stay of proceedings[7], and the sheriff cannot safely advance the execution while a claim[3] remains undetermined.

1 See para 1026 ante.
2 Ie under RSC Ord 17 r 5(3) (see para 1029 post): see eg *Teltscher Bros Ltd v Rao Catering Co Ltd* (1976) 120 Sol Jo 354, CA.
3 *Bauly v Krook* (1891) 65 LT 377.
4 The provision of a sheriff's inventory was considered in detail in the judgment of Sachs LJ in *Fredericks and Pelhams Timber Buildings v Wilkins (Read, Claimant)* [1971] 3 All ER 545 at 546–551, [1971] 1 WLR 1197 at 1199–1205, CA. Expense may be saved if a claimant formulates a clear itemised claim so that the court may order the sheriff to check that the claimant has included all the goods seized. If any items are omitted by the claimant, the claim may be barred as to those items.
5 See the Order dated 8 July 1920 (Writs of Fieri Facias, sheriffs' or sheriffs' officers fees order), SR & O 1920/1250, Schedule Fee 8(2)(b) (substituted by SI 1962/2417; amended by SI 1971/808): the charge may be 5% of the value of the goods where the work done includes the preparation of a detailed inventory of the goods seized.
6 See Queen's Bench Masters' Practice Form PF26, and 22 Court Forms (2nd Edn) (1991 Issue) 409, Form 5.
7 RSC Ord 17 r 7.
8 Ie which satisfies RSC Ord 17 r 2(1): see para 1014 ante.

(3) ORDER ON THE APPLICATION

1028. General. If the claimant[1], having been duly served with a summons for interpleader relief, does not appear on the hearing of the summons or, having appeared, fails or refuses to comply with an order made in the proceedings, such as an order to make and serve an affidavit supporting his claim[2], the court[3] may by order declare him for ever barred from prosecuting his claim against the applicant[4].

If the claimant appears on the hearing of the summons the court may make any of several orders as to the mode of determining the application; for example, it may order that any claimant be made a defendant in any action pending with respect to the subject matter in dispute instead of or as well as the applicant for interpleader relief[5], or that an issue between the claimants be stated and tried[6]. It may also order that any action in which the applicant is defendant be stayed[7], may make one order in several causes[8], and may order the sale of goods taken in execution[9]. It may make provision for the safe keeping or payment into or deposit in court of the subject matter; and has general power to make such order as to costs or any other matter as it thinks just[10].

Where the claimant appears and it is considered that there is a dispute, the dispute must not be determined out of hand[11], but directions must be given for its determination[12]. An adjournment for oral evidence is not necessary if the facts appear clearly from the documents before the master[13].

1 In RSC Ord 17 rr 5, 6, 'the claimants' means the persons by whom adverse claims to the subject matter in dispute are made: see RSC Ord 17 r 5(1).
2 See para 1026 ante.
3 For the meaning of 'the court' see para 1014 note 6 ante.
4 See RSC Ord 17 r 5(3); and para 1029 post.
5 See RSC Ord 17 r 5(1)(a); and para 1045 post.
6 See RSC Ord 17 r 5(1)(b); and para 1046 post. In appropriate circumstances the court also has power under RSC Ord 17 r 5(2) summarily to determine the question at issue in a sheriff's interpleader: see para 1040 post.
7 See RSC Ord 17 r 7; and para 1031 post.
8 See para 1030 post.
9 See para 1032 post.
10 RSC Ord 17 r 8.
11 *P B J Davis Manufacturing Co Ltd v Fahn (Fahn, Claimant)* [1967] 2 All ER 1274 at 1276, [1967] 1 WLR 1059 at 1061, CA, per Lord Denning MR; but cf *Commonwealth Bank v Banco de Bilbao* (1971) 115 Sol Jo 426, CA.
12 This power arises under RSC Ord 17 r 8.
13 *Ropperelmann v Emmerson (Shield Factors Ltd, Claimants)* (13 May 1970, unreported), CA.

1029. Failure of parties to appear. Where a claimant who has been duly served with an interpleader summons[1] does not appear on the hearing of the summons, or, having appeared, fails or refuses to comply with an order made in the proceedings, the court[2] may make an order declaring the claimant, and all persons claiming under him, for ever barred from prosecuting his claim against the applicant for interpleader relief and all persons claiming under him[3]. Such an order does not, however, affect the rights of the claimants as between themselves[4].

An order under this rule cannot be made against a claimant who actually appears and makes out some sort of claim, however nebulous[5]; likewise such an order should not be made in a claimant's favour without giving the execution creditor a chance to test the claimant's evidence by cross-examination, and there should be discovery of documents in order to test whether the claim is good[6].

If the execution creditor does not appear, and there is no reasonable explanation, it will be ordered that the sheriff withdraw, that no action be brought against him, that the execution creditor pay the sheriff's costs and charges and that the claimant's costs be taxed or agreed[7]. If neither execution creditor nor claimant attends there is authority for an order that the sheriff sell so much of the goods as will provide for his costs and charges and then withdraw and that no action be brought against him by the execution creditor or claimant[8], but the more usual order will be for the sheriff to withdraw as when the execution creditor only fails to attend.

If in a stakeholder's interpleader the claimant does not appear, his claim against the applicant may be barred and he may be ordered to pay the costs[9]. Where the applicant is a defendant in an action in respect of the subject matter of the summons and the plaintiff does not appear, the action may be stayed, and the plaintiff ordered to pay the costs[10]. If neither the plaintiff nor the claimant appears, the action may be stayed and the court may make such order as it thinks just with regard to the subject matter, out of which the applicant may be allowed his costs[11].

1 There must be an affidavit of service before an order will be made: *Phillips v Spry* (1832) 1 LJEx 115. As to service of the summons see para 1025 ante.
2 For the meaning of 'the court' see para 1014 note 6 ante.
3 RSC Ord 17 r 5(3). No order is to be made against the Crown under this rule except upon an application by summons served not less than seven days before the return day: see RSC Ord 77 r 11; Crown Proceedings Act 1947 s 35(2)(c).
4 RSC Ord 17 r 5(3).
5 *J R P Plastics Ltd v Gordon Rossall Plastics Ltd (Hexa Pen Co Ltd, Claimants)* [1950] 1 All ER 241, DC.
6 *P B J Davis Manufacturing Co Ltd v Fahn (Fahn, Claimant)* [1967] 2 All ER 1274, [1967] 1 WLR 1059, CA.
7 *Doble v Cummins* (1837) 7 Ad & El 580; *Malone v Ross* [1900] 2 IR 586 at 589, CA. For the order (Interpleader Order No 1A) see Queen's Bench Masters' Practice Form PF29, and 22 Court Forms (2nd Edn) (1991 Issue) 421, Form 21.
8 *Eveleigh v Salsbury* (1836) 5 Dowl 369.
9 See RSC Ord 17 r 8.
10 See RSC Ord 17 rr 7, 8; and para 1031 post.
11 See RSC Ord 17 r 8.

1030. One order in several causes or matters. Where the court[1] considers it necessary or expedient to make an order in any interpleader proceedings in several causes or matters pending in several divisions of the High Court, or before different judges of the same division, the court may make such an order[2]. The order must be entitled in all those causes or matters and is binding on all the parties to them[3].

1 For the meaning of 'the court' see para 1014 note 6 ante.
2 RSC Ord 17 r 9. Where there are several writs of fieri facias (see EXECUTION vol 17 para 462 et seq) with a sheriff for execution and the value of the goods seized justifies it, he may have to issue several interpleader summonses. This rule conveniently allows the hearings to be brought before the same judge or master.
3 RSC Ord 17 r 9.

1031. Stay of proceedings. Where a defendant to an action applies for relief by way of interpleader in the action, the court[1] may by order stay all further proceedings in that action[2]. Where an interpleader summons has been issued, an action by a claimant in respect of the subject matter against the applicant is premature and irregular[3]. Such a claimant should await the result of the interpleader summons, and if he proceeds after notice of the summons he does so at his own risk as regards costs.

The court has power to stay an action by a claimant against a sheriff, not only for damages caused by seizure of the goods, but also for trespass, but only if no substantial injury has been done[4]. Accordingly, where the applicant is a sheriff and the court either makes an order barring the claimant or ordering the sheriff to withdraw, the court usually directs that no action is to be brought against the sheriff[5]; but the sheriff will be directed to be protected only where he has made an honest mistake in executing the process of the court and where, but for the mistake, everything that he has done would have been justified by the writ[6]. In deciding whether there has been a substantial grievance the court will look at all the relevant facts surrounding the execution including the value of goods and also the claimant's conduct. The fact that the sheriff has sold the successful claimant's goods is not of itself a substantial grievance where the claimant does not prove that the prices obtained at public auction were unreasonable and where his own claim to the goods has been delayed[7]. Where substantial grievance has been caused, even though the seizure was in good faith, and particularly where there has been misconduct[8], an action against the sheriff ought not to be barred[9]. It is the quality of the sheriff's admitted wrong which is relevant.

Where the sheriff has sold goods found to be the property of the claimant, the court should make an order directing that no action is to be brought against the sheriff unless it can be shown that the claimant had a fairly arguable case that the sheriff had no defence to the claimant's prima facie claim for conversion either at common law or by statute[10].

The court also has power to restrain an action against the execution creditor[11]. Where, however, an action has been begun before an order has been made upon the interpleader summons, and the execution creditor's solicitor has given an undertaking to appear, and an order is subsequently made for the sheriff to withdraw and no action to be brought, the court may not set aside the writ and undertaking but may only stay the proceedings[12].

Where the words of the order are 'no action', they will normally be construed as directing that no action is to be brought against the sheriff[13].

An execution creditor may not be sued for a mistake on the sheriff's part where he has not done anything to authorise the sheriff's act, and his becoming a party to an issue is not such a ratification of the sheriff's act as to make him liable as the sheriff's principal[14].

Where the execution creditor abandons the seizure and an order to bar an action against the sheriff has been refused, the sheriff may still show, if he can, that the goods really belonged to the judgment debtor[15].

1 For the meaning of 'the court' see para 1014 note 6 ante.
2 RSC Ord 17 r 7.
3 *Hilliard v Hanson* (1882) 21 ChD 69, CA; cf *Aylwin v Evans* (1882) 52 LJCh 105.
4 *Winter v Bartholomew* (1856) 11 Exch 704 (not following *Hillier v Laurie* (1846) 3 CB 334); *Smith v Critchfield* (1885) 14 QBD 873, CA; and see *Cave v Capel* [1954] 1 QB 367, [1954] 1 All ER 428, CA.
5 For the orders (Interpleader Orders Nos 1, 1A) see Queen's Bench Masters' Practice Forms PF28, PF29, and 22 Court Forms (2nd Edn) (1991 Issue) 418, 421, Forms 16, 21.
6 *Cave v Capel* [1954] 1 QB 367 at 371–372, [1954] 1 All ER 428 at 430–431, CA, per Somervell LJ; *Smith v Critchfield* (1885) 14 QBD 873 at 878, CA, per Sir Baliol Brett MR; and see *Salberg v Morris* (1887) 4 TLR 47, DC; and EXECUTION vol 17 para 459.

7 *Neumann v Bakeaway Ltd (Ghotli, Claimant)* [1983] 2 All ER 935, [1983] 1 WLR 1016n, CA, where the only part of the master's order appealed against was that ordering that no action be brought against the sheriff.

8 *Winter v Bartholomew* (1856) 11 Exch 704 at 708 per Alderson B, and at 718 per Platt B; and see para 1016 ante.

9 *Cave v Capel* [1954] 1 QB 367, [1954] 1 All ER 428, CA; *De Coppett v Barnett* (1901) 17 TLR 273, CA; *London, Chatham and Dover Rly Co v Cable* (1899) 80 LT 119, DC. As to what constitutes a substantial grievance see *Neumann v Bakeaway Ltd (Ghotli, Claimant)* [1983] 2 All ER 935, [1983] 1 WLR 1016n, CA.

10 *Observer Ltd v Gordon (Cranfield and ors, Claimants)* [1983] 2 All ER 945, [1983] 1 WLR 1008, where the sheriff sold pianos seized in the debtor's work rooms. The Supreme Court Act 1981 s 138B, (added by the Statute Law (Repeals) Act 1989 s1(2), Sch 2 Pt I para 4) provides that where any goods in the possession of an execution debtor at the time of seizure by a sheriff or other officer charged with the enforcement of a writ of execution issued from the High Court are sold by the sheriff or other officer without any claims having been made to them, the purchaser of the goods so sold will acquire a good title to those goods, and no person will be entitled to recover against the sheriff or other officer, or anyone lawfully acting under his authority, for any sale of the goods or for paying over the proceeds prior to the receipt of a claim to the goods, unless it is proved that the person from whom recovery is sought had notice, or might by making reasonable inquiry have ascertained, that the goods were not the property of the execution debtor: Supreme Court Act 1981 s 138B(1) (as so added). This provision does not affect the right of any lawful claimant (ie any person who proves that at the time of sale he had a title to any of the goods so seized and sold) to any remedy to which he may be entitled against any person other than the sheriff or other officer: s 138B(2) (as so added). It is, however, subject to the provisions of the Insolvency Act 1986 ss 183, 184 (as amended), 346: Supreme Court Act 1981 s 138B(3) (as so added). See paras 1035–1036 post; BANKRUPTCY AND INSOLVENCY vol 3(2) (Reissue) paras 663–670; COMPANIES vol 7(2) (Reissue) para 1878 et seq.

11 *Carpenter v Pearce* (1858) 27 LJEx 143.

12 *Hooke v Ind, Coope & Co* (1877) 36 LT 467.

13 *Hooke v Ind, Coope & Co* (1877) 36 LT 467; and cf para 1029 text and note 7 ante.

14 *Woollen v Wright* (1862) 1 H & C 554; following *Wilson v Tumman* (1843) 6 Man & G 236; *Whitmore v Greene* (1844) 13 M & W 104. See also *Smith v Keal* (1882) 9 QBD 340, CA; *Clissold v Cratchley* [1910] 2 KB 244, CA; and EXECUTION vol 17 para 429.

15 *Baynton v Harvey* (1835) 3 Dowl 344.

1032. Power to order sale. Where an application for relief by way of interpleader is made by a sheriff[1] who has taken possession of any goods or chattels in execution under any process, and a claimant alleges that he is entitled, under a bill of sale or otherwise, to the goods or chattels by way of security for a debt, the court[2] may and, unless the claimant pays into court the value of the goods claimed or gives security, ordinarily will[3], order those goods or chattels or any part of them to be sold and may direct that the proceeds of the sale be applied in such manner and on such terms as may be just and as may be specified in the order[4]. The court's power to order a sale is not, however, confined to that conferred by this provision[5]. In or for the purpose of any interpleader proceedings the court may make such order as it thinks just as to any matter[6], and it has a discretionary power to order sale which may be exercised whenever it appears just and reasonable[7].

1 As to the meaning of 'sheriff' see para 1005 note 1 ante.

2 For the meaning of 'the court' see para 1014 note 6 ante.

3 *Paquin Ltd v Robinson* (1901) 85 LT 5 at 6, CA, per Sir A L Smith MR. Where, however, it would appear unjust to order a sale, and security is not given, the court may vary the usual practice: see *Victor v Cropper* (1886) 3 TLR 110, CA.

4 RSC Ord 17 r 6. For the order (Interpleader Order No 4) see Queen's Bench Masters' Practice Form PF32, and 22 Court Forms (2nd Edn) (1991 Issue) 421, Form 22.

5 Ie RSC Ord 17 r 6.

6 RSC Ord 17 r 8. The court's power is to be construed as widely as possible: *BP Benzin und Petroleum AG v European-American Banking Corpn* [1978] 1 Lloyd's Rep 364, CA (mortgagees entitled to deduct expenses of running ships from charter hire when mortgagors fell into debt).

7 *Paquin Ltd v Robinson* (1901) 85 LT 5, CA. In *Twist v East African Airways Corpn* (May 1977, unreported), an order was made for the sheriff to sell a Boeing 707 airliner claimed by the receiver for the debenture holder, and when, thereafter, and before the sale was completed, the defendant company was wound up, an order was made in the Companies Court for the sale to proceed under the terms of the previous order, the sheriff to hold the proceeds of sale under the terms of the previous order pending the determination of the interpleader issue and further order.

1033. Exercise of power to order sale where goods held as security. The court may exercise the power to order sale[1] where the claimant claims under an absolute bill of sale[2] or may refrain from doing so and order the appointment of a receiver and manager where a sale might do great injury[3]. The power can conveniently be used to allow a sale to pay off a warehouseman or other person claiming a lien or right to possession of the goods against the execution debtor[4].

A sale will as a rule be ordered where the security is ample and the holder of a bill of sale asserts his rights so as to defeat the execution creditor[5].

Where the security is insufficient and a sale would provide no surplus, the proper course is to order the sheriff to withdraw[6]. Where it is doubtful whether the security would prove sufficient to pay off the holder of the bill of sale the court ought not to order a sale unless the execution creditor will guarantee the holder against costs[7].

The power to direct the application of the proceeds of the sale in such a manner and on such terms as may be just[8] enables the court to limit the payment of interest to the holder of the bill of sale out of the proceeds up to the time of payment only, and so to interfere with the contract for payment of interest for the whole time covered by the bill[9].

1 Ie under RSC Ord 17 r 6: see para 1032 ante.
2 *Paquin Ltd v Robinson* (1901) 85 LT 5, CA.
3 *Howell v Dawson* (1884) 13 QBD 67, where the court ordered the appointment of a receiver and manager at the claimant's expense, but ordered that if the claimant succeeded on this issue that expense should be paid by the execution creditor.
4 For the order (Interpleader Order No 7A) see Queen's Bench Masters' Practice Form PF36 (where other prior claims are directed to be paid in the first place out of the proceeds of sale), and 22 Court Forms (2nd Edn) (1991 Issue) 420, Form 20.
5 *Pearce v Watkins* (1861) 2 F & F 377. The statutory predecessor of RSC Ord 17 r 6 was expressly passed to deal with a situation such as this: see Day on Common Law Procedure Acts (4th Edn) 361, cited by Sir Nathaniel Lindley MR in *Stern v Tegner* [1898] 1 QB 37 at 41, CA.
6 *Pearce v Watkins* (1861) 2 F & F 377; *Stern v Tegner* [1898] 1 QB 37, CA.
7 *Stern v Tegner* [1898] 1 QB 37, CA, where the court ordered the sheriff to withdraw, as the execution creditor refused to give a guarantee against loss.
8 Ie the power under RSC Ord 17 r 6: see para 1032 ante.
9 *Forster v Clowser* [1897] 2 QB 362, CA; *West v Diprose* [1900] 1 Ch 337 at 340.

1034. Exercise of power to order sale generally. A sale may be ordered for the purpose of saving costs and sheriff's charges[1], or where the claimant refuses to acknowledge the seizure by the sheriff by signing a walking possession agreement[2]. If the goods are perishable or there is clear evidence that some of the goods originally seized have been removed from the sheriff's custody, and the security of the rest is in doubt, a sale may be ordered[3].

1 See the Supreme Court Practice 1993 para 17/5/8. See also para 1032 note 7 ante: the airport charge for parking the Boeing 707 airliner was £345.60 per day.
2 As to such agreements see para 1020 note 3 ante.
3 The courts now frequently make orders for the sale of goods where the safety of the goods is in jeopardy and the facts of the case warrant such an order.

1035. Effect of bankruptcy on sale. Where an order has been made[1] directing the sheriff to sell, and a claim is made by the official receiver or the judgment debtor's trustees in bankruptcy, the sheriff must comply with the provisions of bankruptcy law which, subject to the court's power to set aside the rights of the official receiver or trustee in bankruptcy in favour of the creditor, prevent a creditor retaining the benefit of an execution unless completed before the date of the receiving order[2] and which lay down the duties of the sheriff if he receives notice of bankruptcy proceedings[3]. Thus, subject to the court's power to set aside the rights of the official receiver or trustee in bankruptcy in favour of the execution creditor[4], where notice of a receiving order has been served on the sheriff before the sale or the completion of the execution[5] by the receipt or the recovery of the full amount of the levy, the sheriff must hand over the goods if unsold or their proceeds to the official receiver or trustee[6], subject to a first charge upon them for his costs of the execution[7]. If the official receiver asks for delivery of the goods the operation of the rule empowering the court or judge to order a sale in interpleader proceedings[8] is probably suspended[9], but if he concurs in asking for a sale there is jurisdiction to make an order to that effect, but a sale ought not to be ordered without a guarantee from the execution creditor against loss arising from an insufficiency of the proceeds to meet what is due under the bill. If no guarantee is forthcoming the sheriff ought to be ordered to withdraw[10].

1 Ie under RSC Ord 17 r 6: see para 1032 ante.
2 See the Insolvency Act 1986 s 346; and BANKRUPTCY AND INSOLVENCY vol 3(2) (Reissue) para 664. All notices must be served on the sheriff at the offices of the under-sheriff, not on the sheriff's officers: *Hellyer v Sheriff of Yorkshire* [1975] Ch 16, [1974] 2 All ER 712, CA. See also the Insolvency Rules 1986, SI 1986/1925, r 12.19.
3 See text and notes 4–7 infra.
4 Insolvency Act 1986 s 346(6).
5 For the meaning of 'completion of the execution' see the Insolvency Act 1986 s 346(5); and BANKRUPTCY AND INSOLVENCY vol 3(2) (Reissue) para 668.
6 *Heathcote v Livesley* (1887) 19 QBD 285; *Re Harrison, ex p Sheriff of Essex* [1893] 2 QB 111.
7 See the Insolvency Act 1986 s 346(2)(b). As to the sheriff's duty in the case of a judgment debt exceeding the prescribed sum to retain the balance of the proceeds of sale, after deducting the costs, for 14 days and to pay it to the Official Receiver or trustee if within that time the debtor has been adjudged bankrupt, see the Insolvency Act 1986 s 346(2); and BANKRUPTCY AND INSOLVENCY vol 3(2) (Reissue) para 664. The sheriff's costs of interpleader proceedings are not costs of the execution: see para 1061 post.
8 Ie RSC Ord 17 r 6: see para 1032 ante.
9 *Stern v Tegner* [1898] 1 QB 37 at 41, CA, per Lindley LJ.
10 *Stern v Tegner* [1898] 1 QB 37, CA.

1036. Effect of bankruptcy on money paid to avoid a sale. Where money is paid to the sheriff or the sheriff's officer to avoid a sale it becomes vested in the execution creditor. The sheriff holds the payment to the order of the execution creditor and retains it for 14 days[1]. If within the 14 day period the debtor is adjudicated bankrupt, or, being a company, is compulsorily wound up by the court, and proper notice is served on the sheriff[2], the execution creditor's title is divested in favour of the trustee in bankruptcy or liquidator[3].

1 *Re Walkden Sheet Metal Co Ltd* [1960] Ch 170, [1959] 3 All ER 333; and see the Insolvency Act 1986 s 346(3)(b) and para 1035 ante.
2 As to notice see *Hellyer v Sheriff of Yorkshire* [1975] Ch 16, [1974] 2 All ER 712, CA.
3 See *Marley Tile Co Ltd v Burrows* [1978] QB 241, [1978] 1 All ER 567, CA (interpleader proceedings on claims between execution creditor and trustee in bankruptcy).

1037. Disposal of proceeds of sale. If in an interlocutory order for sale no direction is made as to the application of the proceeds in the sheriff's hands after the sale, he is not bound to pay it over but may retain the amount until he obtains the final order to relieve him of his responsibility, and until then an action will not lie by the successful party to the issue against the sheriff for money had and received to his use[1].

1 *Discount Banking Co of England and Wales v Lambarde* [1893] 2 QB 329, CA. The usual order directing a sale is either that the sheriff pay the net proceeds into court or that he retain the proceeds pending further order.

1038. Damages. Neither the sheriff nor the execution creditor is liable to a claimant for damages sustained by him in consequence of a sale properly conducted under an interpleader order[1].

1 *Abbot v Richards* (1846) 15 M & W 194 (sheriff); *Walker v Olding* (1862) 1 H & C 621 (execution creditor); *Martin v Tritton and Jameson* (1884) Cab & El 226, CA, where the order directing a sale was subsequently rescinded, and it was held that the sheriff was not liable, although the rescinding order did not, like the original order, contain a clause restraining an action.

(4) DISPUTES BETWEEN CLAIMANTS

1039. Available methods of trial. If the claimants appear and it is considered that there is a dispute between them, however nebulous, to try[1], the court should first consider giving directions as to (1) whether a sufficiently detailed affidavit has been supplied by the claimant[2]; (2) whether the court should direct the sheriff to provide an inventory[3]; and (3) the discovery of documents[4].

The order will then continue to provide how the dispute is to be determined. The alternatives include:

(a) dismissal of the application[5];
(b) a summary determination on the merits of the claim[6];
(c) a reference of the matter to the judge[7];
(d) remission of the proceedings to the county court[8];
(e) a reference of the dispute to arbitration[9];
(f) a reference of the matter to an official referee[10];
(g) the substitution or addition of the claimant as defendant to proceedings already begun[11];
(h) an order that an issue be stated and tried[12].

1 Cf *J R P Plastics Ltd v Gordon Rossall Plastics Ltd (Hexa Pen Co Ltd, Claimants)* [1950] 1 All ER 241, DC; *Re Sheriff of Oxfordshire* (1837) 6 Dowl 136.
2 Cf *J R P Plastics Ltd v Gordon Rossall Plastics Ltd (Hexa Pen Co Ltd, Claimants)* [1950] 1 All ER 241, DC. As to such affidavits see para 1026 ante.
3 *Fredericks and Pelhams Timber Buildings v Wilkins (Read, Claimant)* [1971] 3 All ER 545, [1971] 1 WLR 1197, CA. As to such inventories see para 1027 ante.
4 See RSC Ord 17 r 10; and para 1053 post. In a sheriff's interpleader the only discovery which will be necessary is discovery by the claimant. It will be unusual for the execution creditor to have any documents relevant to the claimant's claim to ownership of the chattels seized.
5 The application will be dismissed if the conditions of RSC Ord 17 r 1 (see paras 1004–1005 ante) or r 3(4) (see para 1017 ante) have not been satisfied.
6 See RSC Ord 17 r 5(2); and para 1040 post.
7 For the power to refer a matter to a judge see RSC Ord 32 r 12 (Queen's Bench and Family Divisions), and RSC Ord 32 r 14(3) (applying RSC Ord 32 r 12 to the Chancery Division).

8 See para 1042 post.
9 See para 1043 post.
10 See para 1044 post.
11 See para 1045 post.
12 See para 1046 et seq post.

1040. Summary determination in chambers. Where the applicant on a summons for interpleader relief is a sheriff[1], or, in a stakeholder's interpleader[2], where all the claimants or any of them so request[3], or where the question at issue between the claimants is a question of law and the facts are not in dispute[4], the court[5] may summarily determine the question at issue between the claimants and make an order accordingly on such terms as may be just[6].

Where the claimant's affidavit[7] raises on the face of it a serious claim to chattels of a considerable overall value and the prospect of difficult points of law, summary determination should not be ordered even if the claimants have consented[8].

However, the great value of sums of money claimed is not of itself necessarily sufficient to preclude summary determination[9].

1 RSC Ord 17 r 5(2)(a). As to the meaning of 'sheriff' see para 1005 note 1 ante.
2 As to stakeholder's interpleader see para 1004 ante.
3 RSC Ord 17 r 5(2)(b). For the meaning of 'the claimants' see para 1028 note 1 ante.
4 RSC Ord 17 r 5(2)(c).
5 For the meaning of 'the court' see para 1014 note 6 ante.
6 RSC Ord 17 r 5(2).
7 As to claimants' affidavits see para 1026 ante.
8 *Fredericks and Pelhams Timber Buildings v Wilkins (Read, Claimant)* [1971] 3 All ER 545, [1971] 1 WLR 1197, CA.
9 *Commonwealth Bank v Banco de Bilbao* (1971) 115 Sol Jo 426, CA.

1041. Practice on summary determination. Summary determination is a procedure adopted in straightforward cases, particularly where expedition is desirable and the claimant's affidavit sufficiently defines the dispute. It avoids the necessity for an issue to be stated and tried. It is not a procedure which permits the master to deal with matters out of hand[1]. Thus where the master decides that the case is appropriate for summary disposal the practice is that, having given directions as to any preliminary matters[2], he will adjourn the summons for hearing with oral evidence before a master. The order need not be drawn up until after the matter is disposed of, unless there is a failure to carry out any of the directions given[3]. If a sheriff is the applicant, he will have the carriage of the proceedings, and will apply for the hearing date and notify the parties. When the matter has been heard and determined, the master indorses his decision on the summons, and his order is drawn up[4]. This will dispose of the whole matter; that is, the dispute between the claimants, the application for relief, and all questions of costs.

1 *P B J Davis Manufacturing Co Ltd v Fahn (Fahn, Claimant)* [1967] 2 All ER 1274, [1967] 1 WLR 1059, CA.
2 See para 1039 ante.
3 Masters' Practice Direction 18; and see the Supreme Court Practice 1993 vol 2 para 737.
4 For the form of order (Interpleader Order No 6) see Queen's Bench Masters' Practice Form PF34, and 22 Court Forms (2nd Edn) (1991 Issue) 417, Form 14.

1042. Transfer to the county court. Where the High Court[1] is satisfied that any proceedings before it are required by any specified provision[2] to be in a county court, it must either order the transfer of the proceedings to a county court[3], or, if the court is satisfied that the person bringing the proceedings knew, or ought to have known, of that requirement, order that they be struck out[4]. Subject to any such provision, the High Court may order the transfer of any proceedings before it to a county court[5]. An order may be made either on the motion of the High Court itself or on the application of any party to the proceedings[6].

Proceedings must be transferred to such county court as the High Court considers appropriate, having taken into account the convenience of the parties and that of any other persons likely to be affected and the state of business in the courts concerned[7]. In deciding whether to make such an order the court will have regard to any saving of costs, the convenience of the parties, and the particular facts of the case. Transfer must be of the interpleader proceedings as a whole, not merely of an issue for trial[8].

The power applies to proceedings by way of interpleader to which the Crown is a party[9].

1 The general principles as to transfer of proceedings from High Court to county court apply to interpleader proceedings following the repeal of the County Courts Act 1984 s 44 by the Courts and Legal Services Act 1990 s 125(7), Sch 20.
2 Ie made under ibid s 1, or by or under any other enactment: County Courts Act 1984 s 40(8) (substituted by the Courts and Legal Services Act 1990 s 2(1)).
3 County Courts Act 1984 s 40(1)(a) (as substituted: see note 2 supra).
4 Ibid s 40(1)(b) (as substituted: see note 2 supra).
5 Ibid s 40(2) (as substituted: see note 2 supra). Such transfer does not affect any right of appeal from the order directing the transfer: s 40(5) (as so substituted). As to the procedure see para 1088 post.
6 Ibid s 40(3) (as substituted: see note 2 supra).
7 Ibid s 40(4) (as substituted: see note 2 supra).
8 *Vizard v Gill, Vizard v Maule* (1893) 95 LT Jo 255. For forms of order (Interpleader Orders Nos 8, 8A) see Queen's Bench Masters' Practice Forms PF37, PF38, and 22 Court Forms (2nd Edn) (1991 Issue) 423–424, Forms 24–25. As to the procedure after transfer see COUNTY COURTS vol 10 paras 95, 104, 375.
9 Crown Proceedings Act 1947 s 20(2) (amended by the Supreme Court Act 1981 ss 152(4), 153(4), (5), Sch 7).

1043. Reference to arbitration. Where interpleader relief is granted and it appears to the High Court[1] that the claims in question are matters to which an arbitration agreement to which the claimants are parties applies, the High Court may direct the issue between the claimants to be determined in accordance with the agreement[2]. The court's jurisdiction is discretionary, but the discretion should be exercised in the same way as the discretion[3] to order a stay of court proceedings[4].

1 The jurisdiction may be exercised by a judge in chambers, a Queen's Bench master or the Admiralty Registrar (RSC Ord 73 r 3(1)), or by a district judge (RSC Ord 32 r 23).
2 Arbitration Act 1950 s 5. For a form of order see 6 Court Forms (2nd Edn) (1989 Issue) 122, Form 42.
3 Ie under the Arbitration Act 1950 s 4 (as amended): see ARBITRATION vol 2 (Reissue) para 622.
4 *Re Phoenix Timber Co Ltd's Application* [1958] 2 QB 1, [1958] 1 All ER 815, CA, where the fact that the dispute was eminently suitable to be tried by the court was not a sufficient ground for refusing to direct the issue to be determined in accordance with the agreement.

1044. Reference to official referee. If the court[1] considers that any cause or matter in the Chancery Division or Queen's Bench Division may more appropriately be dealt with as official referees' business, the court may of its own motion, but subject to any right to a trial with a jury, order that the cause or matter, or any

question or issue of fact arising, be tried by an official referee[2].An official referee
may of his own motion or on the application of any party, order a cause or matter
which is proceeding as official referees' business to be transferred to the Chancery
Division or Queen's Bench Division if he considers that it may more appropriately
be tried by a master or judge[3].

1 For the meaning of 'the court' see para 1014 note 6 ante.
2 RSC Ord 36 r 3(2); and see the Supreme Court Practice 1993 para 36/1–9/1; and para 1053 post. In
  Fredericks and Pelhams Timber Buildings v Wilkins (Read, Claimant) [1971] 3 All ER 545, [1971] 1 WLR
  1197, CA, the court directed a retrial of the issue before an official referee in view of the quantity and
  different types of chattels seized and their value (horses, farm equipment, tack and furniture).
3 RSC Ord 36 r 3(3).

1045. Substitution or addition of claimant as defendant. If the claimants[1]
appear on the hearing of an interpleader summons, the court[2] may order that any
claimant be made a defendant in any action pending with respect to the subject
matter in dispute in substitution for or in addition to the applicant for interpleader
relief[3]. If a claimant is made defendant in lieu of the applicant he may set up any
defence open to him against the plaintiff, whether or not it would have been open
to the original defendant[4].

1 For the meaning of 'the claimants' see para 1028 note 1 ante.
2 For the meaning of 'the court' see para 1014 note 6 ante.
3 RSC Ord 17 r 5(1)(a). For the form of order (Interpleader Order No 2) see Queen's Bench Masters'
  Practice Form PF30, and 22 Court Forms (2nd Edn) (1991 Issue) 428–429, Form 32.
4 *Gerhard v Montagu & Co (Low & Co, Claimants)* (1889) 61 LT 564.

1046. Issue. Where the claimants[1] appear on the hearing of an interpleader summons and the matter is not dealt with in one of the foregoing ways[2], the court[3] may
order that an issue between the claimants be stated and tried, and may direct which
of the claimants is to be plaintiff and which defendant[4].

The issue may be stated in the order, such as 'whether at the time of seizure by the
sheriff the goods etc were the property of the claimant (plaintiff in the issue) as
against the execution creditor (defendant in the issue)'; or directions may be given
for the plaintiff in the issue to serve points of claim, with points of defence to be
served by the defendant in the issue, and for a reply as may be appropriate. The
summons may be adjourned for the trial of an issue without specifying the issue in
the order directing trial, or directing pleadings[5].

The Rules of the Supreme Court applicable to discovery, inspection and
interrogatories and to modes of trial apply to such an issue[6]. If any allegation of
fraud is intended to be raised, this should be formulated in good time before the
hearing[7].

The court may try to provide for a convenient way of disposal of the subject
matter of the dispute pending the trial of the issue by sale or otherwise, but if this is
not possible the sheriff will have to remain in possession of the goods pending the
final order. If the position of the applicant[8] can be finally dealt with on the order
directing an issue to be stated, for example by ordering him to deliver up the goods
to a party to await the outcome of the issue, or to place them in store with provision
made for storage fees[9], or to withdraw from possession either unconditionally or
after a party has given security for the goods, the order will also provide for the
applicant's costs and include an order that no claim be brought against him. In these

circumstances the applicant will not have to take any further part in the proceedings. If, as is frequently the case, the applicant's position cannot be fully provided for by the order directing the issue, the applicant will remain as a party before the court, if not a party to the dispute in the issue itself, and will have to appear before the court at the trial to secure a final order protecting his position and providing for costs[10].

1 For the meaning of 'the claimants' see para 1028 note 1 ante.
2 Ie by summary decision in chambers, remission to the county court, reference to arbitration or to an official referee, or the substitution or addition of the claimant as defendant: see paras 1040–1045 ante.
3 For the meaning of 'the court' see para 1014 note 6 ante.
4 RSC Ord 17 r 5(1)(b). As to parties to the issue see para 1047 post.
5 For the position where the order does not state the issue see para 1050 post.
6 RSC Ord 17 rr 8, 10: see para 1053 post.
7 *Fredericks and Pelhams Timber Buildings v Wilkins (Read, Claimant)* [1971] 3 All ER 545 at 549, [1971] 1 WLR 1197 at 1202, CA, per Sachs LJ.
8 As to who may apply see paras 1004–1005 ante.
9 In *Vyner v Buchanan-Michaelson* (13 February 1976, unreported), QBD, Nield J ordered the claimant to pay the sheriff the storage charges as they accrued on a monthly basis pending trial of the issue where goods of substantial value had been moved by the sheriff to a place of safety under an order of the master.
10 For forms of order for trial of an issue (Interpleader Order No 3) see Queen's Bench Masters' Practice Form PF31, and 22 Court Forms (2nd Edn) (1991 Issue) 415–416, 429–430, Forms 12, 33.

1047. Parties to the issue. The question who is to be plaintiff and who defendant in the issue is one for the discretion of the court[1], but usually the order directing the issue appoints as plaintiff the party on whom the burden of proof is considered to lie at the outset.

In a sheriff's interpleader this will ordinarily be the claimant, since the judgment debtor is usually in possession at the moment of seizure[2]. Where, however, it can be established that the claimant was in possession at the moment of seizure, and not the judgment debtor, the position is reversed, and it is the execution creditor who should be plaintiff, and the claimant who should be defendant, in the issue[3]. If it is not clear before the trial of the issue who was in possession at the moment of seizure, the claimant should normally be nominated as plaintiff.

Apart from the general rule enunciated above, it is less easy to be precise in cases of stakeholder's interpleader, since the exact circumstances vary more considerably in cases of this class. Where the applicant is a defendant to proceedings already begun, then in the absence of any special considerations the plaintiff in the action is normally made plaintiff in the issue, but the decision will depend on the particular facts and the position may be reversed[4].

Where a claim was made to stolen property in the hands of the police, and an issue was directed between the claimant and a convicted person, the claimant was made plaintiff, and that person defendant in the ensuing issue[5]. Where one of the claimants who would normally have been made plaintiff was an alien enemy, it was stated that, if it were desired to dispose of the claim before the cessation of hostilities, it would be desirable to make him defendant in the issue[6].

A party aggrieved by an order nominating him as plaintiff or defendant has the same right of appeal as any other party to a discretionary interlocutory order, and his grievance is not normally a ground for an application for a new trial once the issue is disposed of[7].

There is power to add new parties both before and after the issue has been drawn up[8], and to substitute a new claimant as plaintiff to the issue where the party originally made plaintiff refuses to proceed with the trial[9].

1 *Haddow v Morton (Trout, Claimant)* [1894] 1 QB 565, CA, a case decided under what is now the County Courts Act 1984 s 100: see para 1077 post.
2 *Yorke v Smith* (1851) 21 LJQB 53; *Bentley v Hook* (1834) 2 Dowl 339; and cf also *Chase v Goble* (1841) 2 Man & G 930; *Richards v Jenkins* (1887) 18 QBD 451, CA.
3 See *Gerhard v Montagu & Co (Low & Co, Claimants)* (1889) 61 LT 564.
4 Cf *Rhodes v Dawson* (1886) 16 QBD 548, CA.
5 *Gordon v Metropolitan Police Comr* (1935) 79 Sol Jo 921, CA.
6 *Geiringer v Swiss Bank Corpn* [1940] 1 All ER 406.
7 *Edwards v Matthews* (1847) 16 LJEx 291.
8 *Bird v Mathews* (1882) 46 LT 512, CA.
9 *Lydal v Biddle* (1836) 5 Dowl 244.

1048. Security by claimant in sheriff's interpleader. Where the applicant in a sheriff's interpleader is a sheriff in possession, the claimant may be ordered either to pay into court a sum of money equal to the value of the goods or to give security to the master's satisfaction for the payment of that amount in accordance with the orders of the court[1], and also, if he desires the sheriff to withdraw, to pay to the sheriff the possession money from the date of the order until payment into court or security is given.

Where the claimant is a receiver appointed by the court he may be directed to hold the goods and keep them subject to the further order of the court[2].

Where an issue has been directed between a claimant and the execution creditor and the claimant has paid into court the value of the goods, that sum takes the place of the goods for the purposes of the dispute, so that if the successful execution creditor takes the money out of court he cannot later seize the goods again if the sum is not sufficient to satisfy the judgment[3]. But if, subsequently to the payment in, another execution is levied at the instance of a different execution creditor, and the claimant makes another claim to the goods and the sheriff again interpleads, the claimant must pay into court another sum to abide the event of the trial of the issue between him and the second execution creditor[4].

1 Each case will be considered on its merits. If the judgment debtor and claimant are associated companies, or members of the same family, or business associates, the court will be more ready to order a sale or security for costs and sheriff's charges than where there is no obvious connection between the judgment debtor and claimant and where there is no prima facie reason to doubt the validity of the claim.
2 *Purkiss v Holland* (1887) 31 Sol Jo 702, CA.
3 *Haddow v Morton (Trout, Claimant)* [1894] 1 QB 565, CA, a case decided under what is now the County Courts Act 1984 s 100: see para 1075 post.
4 *Kotchie v Golden Sovereigns Ltd* [1898] 2 QB 164, CA.

1049. Security for costs of issue. As between the parties to an issue the ordinary rules relating to security for costs apply[1], but for the purpose of ascertaining whether a party is liable to give security for costs the court will be guided by the substantial position of the parties and not by their nominal position under the order[2]. Therefore, the defendant to the issue may be ordered to give security, provided he is substantially the plaintiff[3], or, at least, as much so as the nominal plaintiff[4], and the nominal plaintiff may escape the obligation on the ground that he is substantially the defendant, or, at least, as much so as the nominal defendant[5].

Indeed the court has ordered each of two parties to an issue to give security on the ground that substantially each was making a claim and each, therefore, should be treated as a plaintiff[6].

The matter is one purely for the court's discretion[7]. In a case where the security ordered was not given and the claimant six months afterwards applied for judgment in his favour, an order was made for security to be given within a fortnight, otherwise the claimant was to be at liberty to obtain his judgment[8].

1 *Tudor Furnishers Ltd v Montague & Co and Finer Production Co Ltd* [1950] Ch 113, [1950] 1 All ER 65; see also *Maatschappij voor Fondsenbezit v Shell Transport and Trading Co* [1923] 2 KB 166, CA. The latter case was not a case of interpleader, but the authorities relating to interpleader were fully considered and applied by analogy. See further *Rhodes v Dawson* (1886) 16 QBD 548 at 553, CA, per Lindley LJ; *Belmonte v Aynard* (1879) 4 CPD 221, on appeal 4 CPD 352, CA. In *Benazech v Bessett* (1845) 1 CB 313 the plaintiff in the action and issue was ordered to give security as he was a foreigner residing out of the jurisdiction. In *Webster v Delafield* (1849) 7 CB 187 the claimant was ordered to give security for a similar reason. In *Frost v Heywood* (1843) 2 Dowl NS 801 a bankrupt plaintiff was ordered to give security, but in *Ridgway v Jones* (1860) 29 LJQB 97 insolvency was held an insufficient reason in itself for ordering security. In *Deller v Prickett* (1850) 15 QB 1081, where the claimant was substituted as defendant, security was ordered as her solvency was doubtful. As to security for costs generally see PRACTICE AND PROCEDURE.
2 *Tudor Furnishers Ltd v Montague & Co and Finer Production Co Ltd* [1950] Ch 113, [1950] 1 All ER 65; *Rhodes v Dawson* (1886) 16 QBD 548, CA; *Tomlinson v Land and Finance Corpn Ltd* (1884) 14 QBD 539, CA; *Maatschappij voor Fondsenbezit v Shell Transport and Trading Co* [1923] 2 KB 166, CA.
3 *Williams v Crosling* (1847) 3 CB 957, where the defendant to the issue residing out of the jurisdiction was ordered to give security because he was the real plaintiff; *Tomlinson v Land and Finance Corpn Ltd* (1884) 14 QBD 539, CA, where the defendant, a limited company, was ordered to give security on a similar ground.
4 See *Tudor Furnishers Ltd v Montague & Co and Finer Production Co Ltd* [1950] Ch 113, [1950] 1 All ER 65; *Tomlinson v Land and Finance Corpn Ltd* (1884) 14 QBD 539, CA, where it was held that both parties might be said to be plaintiffs and that security might be ordered from either. See also *Rhodes v Dawson* (1886) 16 QBD 548 at 553, CA, per Lindley LJ; and *Re Cie Générale d'Eaux Minérales et de Bains de Mer* [1891] 3 Ch 451 at 458, where it was held that mutual security could be ordered where both parties were out of the jurisdiction.
5 *Belmonte v Aynard* (1879) 4 CPD 221, where a plaintiff out of the jurisdiction was not ordered to give security as substantially he was defendant. See also *Rhodes v Dawson* (1886) 16 QBD 548 at 553, CA, per Lindley LJ ('It may be that in some cases each party is as much a plaintiff as the other'); and see *Tomlinson v Land and Finance Corpn Ltd* (1884) 14 QBD 539, CA, where it was held that the execution creditor and claimant were really both plaintiffs.
6 *Tudor Furnishers Ltd v Montague & Co and Finer Production Co Ltd* [1950] Ch 113, [1950] 1 All ER 65, where the plaintiff was ordered to give security conditionally on the payment into court of a like sum by the defendant; *Re Cie Générale d'Eaux Minérales et de Bains de Mer* [1891] 3 Ch 451.
7 *Workmeister v Healy* (1876) IR 10 CL 450, where the plaintiff to the issue applied that the defendant should give security as he resided out of the jurisdiction, but the plaintiff also resided out of the jurisdiction, and the application was refused. Cf *Tudor Furnishers Ltd v Montague & Co and Finer Production Co Ltd* [1950] Ch 113, [1950] 1 All ER 65; *Re Cie Générale d'Eaux Minérales et de Bains de Mer* [1891] 3 Ch 451 at 458, where mutual security was ordered. In *Ridgway v Jones* (1860) 29 LJQB 97, the court refused an application by a plaintiff to the issue for security by either the defendant to the issue, who was insolvent, or the defendant to the original action (applicant in the interpleader proceedings) on the grounds (1) that insolvency was an insufficient reason in itself; (2) that the defendant to the action ought not to be put in a worse position merely because the claimant was insolvent.
8 *Melin v Dumont* (1869) 20 LT 366; *Tassie v Kennedy* (1848) 5 Dow & L 587. In *Kelly v Brown* (1836) 5 Dowl 264, the court refused to add, to an order for security, leave to sign judgment if security was not given within the specified time.

1050. Form of the issue generally. Where the order directing the trial of an issue does not set out in terms the issue to be tried, or does not direct that the matter be dealt with by exchange of pleadings, a formal issue may be directed to be agreed between the parties, and, failing such agreement, referred back to the tribunal making the order[1]. The form of issue will be prepared in the first place by the plaintiff in the issue and then submitted to the defendant in the issue. This procedure is rare[2].

The issue should be drawn so as to permit the whole question between the parties to be disposed of without giving either party an opportunity of setting up rights outside the object of the issue[3]. It is prudent to frame the issue so as to determine the question of possession as well as ownership as between the parties and to frame it in such a way as to make it plain that the issue is limited to questions arising 'as against the defendant' or 'as between the parties'. That a claimant can only prove part of his claim does not decide the whole issue against him[4]. A claimant cannot raise an issue affirming that the title has passed to a person not a party to the proceedings[5].

1   The title of an order directing the trial of an issue will be the same as that of the summons, followed by 'In the Matter of an issue ordered to be tried . . '. This is followed by the name of the parties to the issue, setting out the plaintiff in the issue and the defendant in the issue. For an example of an issue see 22 Court Forms (2nd Edn) (1991 Issue) 430, Form 34.

2   The Sheriff of Greater London has issued over 7,000 interpleader summonses since 1965, and in no case has the court ordered an issue to be formulated in this manner. As to the parties to the issue see para 1047 ante.

3   *Peake v Carter* [1916] 1 KB 652, CA.

4   *Plummer v Price* (1878) 39 LT 657, CA. However, the claimant may not get an order for all his costs.

5   *De Borbon v Westminster Bank Ltd (Banco de Vizcaya, Claimants)* (1933) 49 TLR 414.

1051. Form of the issue in sheriff's interpleader. In a sheriff's interpleader where the goods seized were in the judgment debtor's possession at the time of the seizure, the form of the issue as a general rule is whether the goods or money or part thereof were the property of the claimant (plaintiff to the issue) as against the execution creditor (defendant to the issue) at the time of the execution of the process, not simply whether the goods or money are the property of the claimant or of the execution debtor[1].

Where at the time of seizure the goods were in the claimant's possession, the form of the issue may be reversed[2].

1   *Belcher v Patten* (1848) 6 CB 608; *Gadsden v Barrow* (1854) 9 Exch 514; *Lott v Melville* (1841) 9 Dowl 882; *Green v Stevens* (1857) 2 H & N 146; *Schroeder v Hanrott* (1873) 28 LT 704; *Richards v Jenkins* (1886) 17 QBD 544; on appeal (1887) 18 QBD 451 at 455, CA, per Lord Esher MR; *Discount Banking Co of England and Wales v Lambarde* [1893] 2 QB 329 at 332, CA, per Bowen LJ; *Shingler v Holt* (1861) 7 H & N 65. This form of issue was probably adopted for the express purpose of enabling any person lawfully entitled to possession to sustain his claim: see *Green v Stevens* supra at 147 per Pollock CB; and *Schroeder v Hanrott* supra per Bovill CJ. 'The meaning must be that the question is to be asked with relation to the moment before the sheriff seizes. The issue is whether the goods are then the goods of the claimant as against the execution creditor so as to prevent the execution creditor's having a right to require the sheriff to seize them': *Richards v Jenkins* (1887) 18 QBD 451 at 455, CA, per Lord Esher MR. In *Edwards v Matthews* (1847) 16 LJEx 291 the form seems to have been whether the goods were the property of the claimant (plaintiff) or the execution creditor (defendant). In *Morewood v Wilkes* (1833) 6 C & P 144 the issue was merely whether the goods at the time of the seizure were the property of the claimant, and the jury was directed that the question was whether all the goods seized were the property of the claimant, for if not all were his, it must find for the defendants. In *Green v Rogers* (1845) 2 Car & Kir 148 the proper issue was held to be whether the goods were the goods of the claimant (plaintiff), not whether they were the goods of the claimant or the execution creditor, and it was held that it was not in issue whether the goods were those of the execution debtor or not.

2   As to the parties to the issue see para 1047 ante.

1052. Form of the issue in special cases. The form of issue necessarily varies according to the particular circumstances. Where, after the seizure, a receiving order has been made against the execution debtor, and the trustee in bankruptcy is the claimant, the form may be 'whether the money now in the hands of the sheriff is the property of the said claimant as against the execution creditor'[1]. So also where an execution creditor had obtained the appointment of a receiver in an action against a foreign company and the money in the hands of the receiver was claimed by liquidators appointed by a foreign tribunal, an issue was directed as to whether the liquidators or the judgment creditor were entitled to the money in the receiver's hands[2].

1 *Dibb v Brooke & Sons* [1894] 2 QB 338; see *Parker v Booth* (1831) 1 Moo & S 156; *Northcote v Beauchamp* (1831) 1 Moo & S 158, where the form of the issue seems to have been whether the assignees in bankruptcy or the execution creditor were entitled to the money in the sheriff's hands. See also *Marley Tile Co Ltd v Burrows* [1978] QB 241, [1978] 1 All ER 567, CA; and para 1036 text and note 3 ante.
2 *Levasseur v Mason and Barry* [1891] 2 QB 73, CA.

1053. Discovery and mode of trial. The Rules of the Supreme Court relating to discovery, inspection and interrogatories[1] and to the mode of trial[2] apply respectively, with the necessary modifications, in relation to an interpleader issue as they apply in relation to any other cause or matter[3] and to the trial of such an issue as they apply to the trial of an action[4].

Interlocutory applications relating to the interpleader issue are made to the tribunal which directed the issue, as are any applications for postponement[5]. In a proper case the court may enforce its orders or protect its proceedings or the property in issue by committal for contempt[6]. Where a claimant does not appear on the hearing or, having appeared, fails or refuses to comply with an order made in the proceedings, the court may make an order declaring him, and all persons claiming under him, for ever barred from prosecuting his claim against the applicant[7].

The court which tries the issue may give such judgment or make such order as finally to dispose of all questions arising in the interpleader proceedings[8].

1 Ie RSC Ords 24, 26: see DISCOVERY.
2 Ie RSC Ord 35: see PRACTICE AND PROCEDURE.
3 RSC Ord 17 r 10.
4 RSC Ord 17 r 11(1). There is no right to jury trial for an interpleader issue, except where a charge of fraud is made against a party to the action: Supreme Court Act 1981 s 69. For practical purposes jury trial is now obsolete in such proceedings.
5 *Hargrave v Hargrave* (1847) 4 CB 648; *Kebel v Philpot* (1839) 9 Sim 614.
6 *Collins v Cliff* (1863) 8 LT 466; *Angell v Baddeley* (1877) 3 ExD 49 at 53, CA, per Brett LJ; *Cooper v Asprey* (1863) 32 LJQB 209. See also CONTEMPT OF COURT vol 9 para 35; EXECUTION vol 17 para 401 et seq.
7 See RSC Ord 17 r 5(3); and para 1029 ante.
8 RSC Ord 17 r 11(2).

1054. Evidence. The ordinary rules relating to evidence, burden of proof, presumptions and estoppels, both at trial and after it by way of res judicata, apply to interpleader issues as to other proceedings in the High Court[1]. Thus a party is not permitted to give evidence of a fact inconsistent with a state of affairs assumed by the form of the issue, such as the validity of prior bankruptcy proceedings[2] or the legality of a bond assumed in the issue[3], and the ordinary rules as to hearsay will be enforced[4]. Similarly a party who fails to raise a ground of defence or claim open to him in an interpleader issue is precluded as between the parties and their privies from doing so in any subsequent proceedings[5].

1 *Emmott v Marchant* (1878) 3 QBD 555; *Yorke v Smith* (1851) 21 LJQB 53 (unstamped document); *Gugen v Sampson* (1866) 4 F & F 974; *Pooley v Goodwin* (1835) 5 Nev & M KB 466 at 472; and cf *Linnit v Chaffers* (1843) 4 QB 762; *Hornidge v Cooper* (1858) 27 LJEx 314. See generally ESTOPPEL vol 16 (Reissue) para 974 et seq; EVIDENCE vol 17 para 1 et seq.
2 *Linnit v Chaffers* (1843) 4 QB 762 at 766 per Lord Denman CJ.
3 *Blackmore v Yates* (1867) LR 2 Exch 225.
4 *Coole v Braham* (1848) 3 Exch 183. See generally EVIDENCE vol 17 para 53 et seq.
5 *Re Hilton, ex p March* (1892) 67 LT 594; *Williams v Richardson* (1877) 36 LT 505. See further ESTOPPEL vol 16 (Reissue) paras 980, 1008.

1055. Jus tertii. A particular application of the rules of evidence concerns the right to set up jus tertii[1]. A claimant who is bound to establish a better title than his adversary must do so, and may not in general set up jus tertii[2]. Moreover, he must usually show that he would have been in a position to sue the sheriff or stakeholder had he resisted the claim instead of seeking interpleader relief[3]. Conversely, his adversary may, in general, rely on jus tertii[4]. Thus, in a sheriff's interpleader, if the judgment debtor was in possession at the moment of seizure, the claimant may not rely on jus tertii[5], while the execution creditor may[6]; but if the claimant was in possession at the time of seizure, the position is reversed and only the claimant may rely on jus tertii[7]. There is no difference of principle in these matters between sheriff's and stakeholder's interpleader. Thus, a claimant in a stakeholder's interpleader who was plaintiff in the issue was not allowed to raise jus tertii against the defendant in the issue who was plaintiff in the action[8]. It is sufficient that the party on whom the burden lies should establish a good possessory title as against his adversary without proving that he is absolute owner[9]. An equitable title may be sufficient, even if in the course of establishing it may be necessary to establish jus tertii, as where a second mortgagee has to establish the prior incumbrancer's position in order to prove that the equity of redemption has passed to him prior to the seizure[10]. A lien may be sufficient provided it is good against the opposing party[11], and so may the equitable rights of debenture holders[12].

1 Ie the right or title of a third person. As to the rules of evidence see para 1054 ante.
2 *Carne v Brice* (1840) 7 M & W 183, as explained in *Richards v Jenkins* (1886) 17 QBD 544 at 547 per Wills J; *Green v Rogers* (1845) 2 Car & Kir 148.
3 *Gadsden v Barrow* (1854) 9 Exch 514 at 515 per Parke B, followed by Wills J in *Richards v Jenkins* (1886) 17 QBD 544 at 548; affd (1887) 18 QBD 451, CA. For further illustrations of the principle see *Chase v Goble* (1841) 2 Man & G 930; *Belcher v Patten* (1848) 6 CB 608; *Edwards v English* (1857) 7 E & B 564, as explained in *Richards v Jenkins* supra; *Green v Stevens* (1857) 2 H & N 146; *Daniel v Rogers* [1918] 2 KB 228, CA.
4 *Richards v Jenkins* (1886) 17 QBD 544 at 551; affd (1887) 18 QBD 451, CA.
5 See the cases cited in note 2 supra.
6 See the case cited in note 4 supra.
7 *Daniel v Rogers* [1918] 2 KB 228, CA.
8 *Peake v Carter* [1916] 1 KB 652, CA, distinguishing on the facts *Flude Ltd v Goldberg* [1916] 1 KB 662n.
9 *De Borbon v Westminster Bank Ltd (Banco de Vizcaya, Claimants)* (1933) 49 TLR 414, CA.
10 *Usher v Martin* (1889) 24 QBD 272.
11 *Jennings v Mather* [1901] 1 KB 108; affd [1902] 1 KB 1, CA.
12 *Davey & Co v Williamson & Sons* [1898] 2 QB 194.

(5) COSTS

1056. General. In and for the purposes of any interpleader proceedings the court[1] may make such order as to costs or any other matter[2] as it thinks just[3]. It is the position of the applicant, who is ordinarily allowed his costs, which is unusual. As between claimants, or execution creditor and claimants, the rule which ordinarily obtains in actions, that the successful party gets his costs, is followed[4].

1 For the meaning of 'the court' see para 1014 note 6 ante.
2 The expression 'or any other matter' includes charges within the meaning of RSC Ord 17 r 3(4)(a) see para 1017 ante. Thus, an unsuccessful claimant may be ordered to pay a wharfinger's charges accruing after the summons: *De Rothschild Frères v Morrison, Kekewich & Co* (1890) 24 QBD 750, CA. As to payment of such charges out of the subject matter in dispute see para 1057 post.
3 RSC Ord 17 r 8. This power is subject to RSC Ord 17 rr 1–7: RSC Ord 17 r 8. For an order for costs on the admission of one claim and the withdrawal of another see 22 Court Forms (2nd Edn) (1991 Issue) 425, Form 26.
4 See RSC Ord 62 r 3; *Re Rogers, ex p Sheriff of Sussex* [1911] 1 KB 104 at 110.

1057. Stakeholder's costs. The ordinary rule as to a stakeholder's charges is that where he has acted properly[1] he is allowed his costs out of the fund or subject matter in dispute and the claimant who is in the wrong has to indemnify to that extent the claimant who is entitled to the fund[2].

In addition to his costs the stakeholder is allowed any charges to which he may be entitled, for example as warehouseman or auctioneer, out of the fund or other subject matter of the dispute, both costs and charges being allowed as a first charge on the fund[3].

Where, however, the applicant has unnecessarily caused any portion of the costs, he may be disallowed that portion and may be ordered to pay the costs occasioned by his misconduct[4]. Where an order directing an issue has been wrongly made, the fact that the order allowed the applicant to deduct his costs does not make the matter res judicata, but the successful party can claim the whole amount net[5].

On the hearing of an interpleader summons taken out by the defendant in an action in the Queen's Bench Division the master has power to order that the plaintiff in the action must pay the applicant's costs in the action, apart from his costs in the interpleader proceedings[6].

Where, instead of interpleading, the stakeholder litigates with both parties separately, he may have to pay costs as against one of the parties instead of being allowed his costs out of the fund[7].

1 For cases as to costs where the stakeholder's conduct was questioned see *Crawford v Fisher* (1842) 1 Hare 436 at 444; *Scottish Union Insurance Co v Steele* (1864) 9 LT 677; *Symes v Magnay* (1855) 20 Beav 47; *Elder Dempster Lines v Ishag, The Lycaon* [1983] 2 Lloyd's Rep 548.
2 *Cotter v Bank of England* (1833) 2 Dowl 728; *Duear v Mackintosh* (1833) 2 Dowl 730; *Symes v Magnay* (1855) 20 Beav 47; *Laing v Zeden* (1874) 9 Ch App 736; *Searle v Matthews* (1883) 19 QBD 77n; *Reading v London School Board* (1886) 16 QBD 686; *Goodman v Blake* (1887) 19 QBD 77.
3 *Attenborough v London and St Katharine's Dock Co* (1878) 3 CPD 450 at 466, CA; cf *Harwood v Betham* (1832) 1 LJEx 180; and see also para 1056 note 2 ante, and supra.
4 *Searle v Matthews* (1883) 19 QBD 77n.
5 *Allnutt v Mills* (1925) 42 TLR 68.

6 The master's power derives from his extensive jurisdiction under RSC Ord 32 r 11. Under a corresponding earlier rule (RSC (1883) Ord LIV r 12 (revoked)), as originally framed, the master could only award the costs of or relating to proceedings before a master, so he could not award the costs of the action as distinct from those of interpleader proceedings before him: *Hansen v Maddox* (1883) 12 QBD 100, DC.
7 *Laing v Zeden* (1874) 9 Ch App 736.

1058. Sheriff's costs generally. In the absence of misconduct, the sheriff is entitled out of the fund to all his costs, charges and expenses reasonably incurred from the commencement of the interpleader proceedings to their final determination[1]. A sheriff is in effect in the same position as an officer of the court, and should interplead on the footing that he is neutral in the dispute between the parties; his claim to costs depends on his conforming to this precept[2]. The execution creditor is primarily responsible for the sheriff's costs and charges of the interpleader proceedings, for it was he who put the sheriff into motion by delivering the writ of execution which the sheriff was obliged to accept, and he therefore, in a sense, made it necessary for the sheriff to interplead. So, even where the execution creditor has been successful as against the claimant, the execution creditor must still pay the sheriff's costs and charges of the interpleader proceedings[3]; but, in that event, the execution creditor will have a remedy over against the unsuccessful claimant for those costs and charges[4]. Where the sheriff has acted improperly in commencing or continuing the proceedings he may be disallowed his own costs[5], and even ordered to pay the other parties their costs occasioned by his misconduct[6]. However, the sheriff cannot be ordered to pay the costs of determining the claim[7]. The sheriff may not be allowed the costs of any unnecessary steps taken in the proceedings, and must not burden the fund more than his own protection requires[8].

1 *Searle v Matthews* (1883) 19 QBD 77n, superseding earlier decisions where the sheriff was refused costs because he was considered to be extremely well off in being protected against an action at so cheap a rate. As to sheriff's costs and charges generally see EXECUTION vol 17 paras 445–450; SHERIFFS; and the Supreme Court Practice 1993 para 17/8/1.
2 *Fredericks and Pelhams Timber Buildings v Wilkins (Read, Claimant)* [1971] 3 All ER 545 at 551, [1971] 1 WLR 1197 at 1204, CA, per Sachs LJ.
3 *Smith v Darlow* (1884) 26 ChD 605, CA; *Stern v Tegner* [1898] 1 QB 37, CA; *Todd v M'Keevir* [1895] 2 IR 400, CA; *Re Rogers, ex p Sheriff of Sussex* [1911] 1 KB 104 at 110; revsd on another point [1911] 1 KB 641, CA.
4 For a form of order (Interpleader Order No 1) see Queen's Bench Masters' Practice Form PF28, and 22 Court Forms (2nd Edn) (1991 Issue) 418, Form 16.
5 *C v D* (1883) 28 Sol Jo 102. See also *Glasier v Cooke* (1835) 5 Nev & M KB 680; *Prosser v Mallinson* (1884) 28 Sol Jo 411; affd 28 Sol Jo 616, CA.
6 *Ford v Dilly* (1833) 5 B & Ad 885; *Bishop v Hinxman* (1833) 2 Dowl 166, where the execution creditor's claim was clearly bad in law; *Dalton v Furness* (1866) 35 Beav 461 (failure to give notice of claim to execution creditor); *Re Sheriff of Oxfordshire* (1837) 6 Dowl 136 (claim made by holder of bill of sale dated after the levy). It seems, however, that a sheriff would not now normally be ordered to pay the costs of interpleader proceedings merely on the ground that prima facie the execution creditor's title was bad as against the claimant or the claimant's claim was bad in law, if the sheriff had followed the procedure set out in RSC Ord 17 rr 2, 3 (see paras 1014–1015, 1024 ante), and the claim had not been admitted or withdrawn.
7 *Temple v Temple* (1894) 63 LJQB 556.
8 *Crawford v Fisher* (1842) 1 Hare 436 at 444.

1059. Sheriff's charges. The sheriff's charges will include possession money per day from the date the claim is received to the date of the final adjudication. This will be disallowed in respect of such time as he has remained in possession improperly[1] or, where irregular procedure by the sheriff has led to possession money being incurred in excess of what is necessary, to the extent of the excess[2]. If, however, the sheriff remains in possession in obedience to a court order made in the interpleader proceedings, he will be allowed his costs of so acting, even if in the end it transpires that the seizure was wrongful[3].

The charges will also include the proper fee in respect of storage, the preparation of an inventory, and for any other acts the sheriff has properly carried out.

1 *Underden v Burgess* (1835) 4 Dowl 104; cf *Scales v Sargeson* (1835) 4 Dowl 231.
2 *Clark v Chetwode* (1836) 4 Dowl 635. The reasonableness of the sheriff's charges can be dealt with on taxation: see *Long v Bray, ex p Wright* (1862) 10 WR 841. If there is likely to be any dispute as to the sheriff's charges, the better practice is to ask that those charges be dealt with specifically in the final court order.
3 *Bland v Delano* (1838) 6 Dowl 293.

1060. Sheriff's costs where execution creditor admits claim. Where, on receipt of notice of a claim to goods or chattels taken in execution, the execution creditor admits the claim and notifies the sheriff within seven days, he is only liable to the sheriff for any fees and expenses incurred by the sheriff before the sheriff receives the notice admitting the claim[1]. Where, after the issue and before the return day of an interpleader summons, the execution creditor admits or the claimant withdraws the claim, the court may make all orders as to costs or any other matter as it thinks just[2].

1 RSC Ord 17 r 2(2).
2 RSC Ord 17 r 8.

1061. Sheriff's costs where bankruptcy supervenes. Where, after interpleader proceedings have been commenced, the sheriff is served with notice of a receiving order against the debtor before sale or completion of the execution, he is bound, subject to the court's power to set aside the official receiver's rights, to deliver the goods or the proceeds to the official receiver[1] and is not entitled as against him or the trustee in bankruptcy to costs for the time he remains in possession after service of the notice. He is only entitled to his costs up to the time of service[2]. The costs of the execution up to that time are made a first charge upon the goods or money[3], but poundage on goods handed over to the trustee or official receiver is not included in them[4]. Where there has been some delay during the interpleader proceedings by which possession money has been increased, but for which the sheriff is not responsible, he is entitled to withhold his possession money for the whole time[5]. He is not so entitled if his remaining in possession was, in the circumstances, improper[6]. The sheriff is not entitled to his costs of the interpleader proceedings[7], nor is he entitled to deduct the costs of the execution creditor or of the claimant[8], since these costs are not costs of the execution[9].

1 As to the effect of bankruptcy on sale see para 1035 ante.
2 *Re Harrison, ex p Sheriff of Essex* [1893] 2 QB 111; and see EXECUTION vol 17 para 448 note 8.
3 Insolvency Act 1986 ss 184(2), 346(2).
4 *Re Thomas, ex p Sheriff of Middlesex* [1899] 1 QB 460, CA; see further EXECUTION vol 17 para 446.
5 *Re Levy, ex p Sheriff of Essex* (1890) 63 LT 291; *Re Beeston, ex p Board of Trade* [1899] 1 QB 626, CA, approving *Re Hurley* (1893) 10 Morr 120. See also *Re Fenton, ex p Lithgow* (1878) 10 ChD 169; *Re English and Ayling, ex p Murray & Co* [1903] 1 KB 680.

6 *Re Finch, ex p Sheriff of Essex* (1891) 65 LT 466.

7 See *Re Rogers* [1911] 1 KB 641, CA, revsg [1911] 1 KB 104 on this point.

8 *Re Rogers, ex p Sheriff of Sussex* [1911] 1 KB 104 at 112 per Phillimore J, undisturbed on this point on appeal [1911] 1 KB 641, CA. In this case the taxing master in bankruptcy was held entitled to tax the sheriff's bill of costs and disallow the costs of the execution creditor and claimant, although they had been allowed by a taxing master acting under the order of a King's Bench master made on the interpleader proceedings: *Re Rogers, ex p Sheriff of Sussex* supra at 111–112 per Phillimore J.

9 Ie within the meaning of the Insolvency Act 1986 ss 184(2), 346(2): see text to note 3 supra.

1062. Sheriff's costs of appeal. Where a sheriff has an interest in the order appealed from he is entitled to appear at the hearing of an appeal from the judgment on an interpleader issue[1]. He has such an interest where for example it is sought to vary an order in favour of the sheriff for his costs[2] or vary an order that no action be brought against him; or where the claim has been barred and he has completed the execution by sale of the goods; or where the claim has been allowed and he has withdrawn from possession of the goods.

Similar orders dealing with a sheriff's costs on appeal are made as on the issue itself. Thus where the claimant is unsuccessful in an appeal the Court of Appeal will order the execution creditor to pay the sheriff's costs with a remedy over against the unsuccessful claimant appellant[3]. Where the sheriff has withdrawn on appeal the court may order the sheriff back into possession, his possession being deemed to have continued in the interval since the master's order, and he being protected from liability in respect of any dealings with the goods in the meantime[4].

1 *Marley Tile Co Ltd v Burrows* [1978] QB 241, [1978] 1 All ER 567, CA.

2 *Trickett & Co v Girdlestone* (1897) 103 LT Jo 81.

3 *Re Morris, ex p Streeter* (1881) 19 ChD 216, CA; and see *Marley Tile Co Ltd v Burrows* [1978] QB 241, [1978] 1 All ER 567, CA, where the successful appellant (the execution creditor) was ordered to pay the sheriff's costs of appeal and in the court below with a remedy over against the respondent (the claimant) personally.

4 *P B J Davis Manufacturing Co Ltd v Fahn (Fahn, Claimant)* [1967] 2 All ER 1274, [1967] 1 WLR 1059, CA.

1063. Costs of parties other than the applicant. The ordinary rule that the party who fails to appear, or abandons, or is unsuccessful, pays the costs of the successful party applies in interpleader matters as in actions[1], and he must also as a rule pay the applicant's costs and charges[2]. The question is, however, always one for the discretion of the court[3], and, as on the trial of an action, the successful party may in a proper case be deprived of his costs[4].

The costs of the successful party include the costs of an application to take the money out of court[5], or to obtain the subject matter of the dispute from the stakeholder[6], where such an application is necessary.

The successful claimant is either entitled to recover as costs from the execution creditor any sheriff's charges[7] which he has had to pay, or is entitled to the repayment to him by the execution creditor of the amount deducted by the sheriff from the proceeds of sale of the goods for his charges[8].

There is no power to set off against costs payable to a successful party in the original action costs payable by that party to the unsuccessful party as a result of interpleader proceedings in the action[9].

1 *Bowen v Bramidge* (1833) 2 Dowl 213 (costs of third trial of issue); *Perkins v Burton (or Benton)* (1833) 2 Dowl 108 (non-appearance of claimant); *Dabbs v Humphries* (1835) 3 Dowl 377; *Wills v Hopkins*

(1835) 3 Dowl 346; *Hyland v Lennox* (1891) 28 LR Ir 286 (abandonment); *Jones v Regan* (1841) 9 Dowl 580; *Melville v Smark* (1841) 3 Man & G 57.

2 As to the applicant's costs and charges see paras 1057–1058 ante. See also *Kimberley v Hickman* (1846) 1 New Pract Cas 468, where, the claimant having neglected to proceed to trial as directed by the order, on an application by the execution creditor that he should proceed to trial at the next assizes and pay the costs occasioned by his default, together with the costs of the application, it was held that the claimant must pay the costs occasioned by his default, but that the costs of the application ought to be costs in the cause.

3 RSC Ord 17 r 8. For general directions as to costs see the Supreme Court Practice 1993 paras 62/A4/135–142 (under heading Sheriff's costs and interpleaders).

4 See RSC Ord 62 r 10 and the Supreme Court Act 1981 s 51(1) (substituted by the Courts and Legal Services Act 1990 s 4(1)); *Field v Rivington* (1889) 5 TLR 642, CA; see also *Swaine v Spencer* (1841) 9 Dowl 347. As to the circumstances in which the court's discretion may be exercised so as to deprive a successful party of his costs see eg *Donald Campbell & Co Ltd v Pollak* [1927] AC 732 at 811–812, HL; and PRACTICE AND PROCEDURE. For the position where the claimant is only partly successful see para 1065 post.

5 *Cusel v Pariente* (1844) 7 Man & G 527; *Meredith v Rogers* (1839) 7 Dowl 596.

6 *Barnes v Bank of England* (1838) 7 Dowl 319.

7 As to these charges see para 1059 ante.

8 *Blaker v Seager* (1897) 76 LT 392.

9 *Barker & Co v Hemming* (1880) 5 QBD 609, CA.

1064. Costs against the claimant. The claimant may only be made liable for costs and charges subsequent to the date of his notice of claim[1]. Where the order directs a sale by the sheriff unless the claimant gives security within a stated time and the security is not given until the last moment, or not at all, the claimant, although ultimately successful on the issue, must pay the sheriff's charges between the date of the order and his giving security, or the sale, as the case may be, since it is for his benefit that the goods were kept, but he may be entitled to have those costs included in the costs given him against the execution creditor[2].

1 *Gaskell v Sefton* (1845) 14 M & W 802; *Goodman v Blake* (1887) 19 QBD 77.

2 *Malone v Ross* [1900] 2 IR 586, CA.

1065. Costs where the claimant succeeds in part. Where the claimant succeeds in substance as against an execution creditor, even though it happens that he is not entitled to all the goods claimed, he is, as a rule, entitled to the costs of the issue[1]; and where the claimant succeeds as to part, and the execution creditor as to the other part, the costs may be divided and ordered to be taxed on that principle without reference to consideration as to which party was plaintiff and which defendant[2]. So also on a stakeholder's interpleader, if each of the claimants succeeds in part, each party may have to pay his own costs[3].

1 *Plummer v Price* (1878) 39 LT 657, CA.

2 *Lewis v Holding* (1841) 9 Dowl 652; *Dixon v Yates* (1833) 5 B & Ad 313; *Clifton v Davis* (1856) 6 E & B 392, where the claimant succeeded as to five-sixths and the execution creditor as to the remaining sixth; overruling *Staley v Bedwell* (1839) 10 Ad & El 145; *Cummins v Kavanagh* (1890) 25 ILT 24.

3 *Carr (Kerr) v Edwards* (1839) 8 Dowl 29, where the plaintiff to an issue claimed £183, part of a sum of £492 17s 6d in the hands of a stakeholder (the defendant to the issue) claiming the whole amount, and a verdict was found for the plaintiff for £50.

1066. Costs where order for issue is discharged. Where the order for an issue reserved the question of costs, and subsequently the defendant to the issue obtained an order that the order for the issue be discharged unless the plaintiff to the issue took certain steps within a stated time, and, on the plaintiff's failure to take the steps, obtained a further order for the payment of his costs, it was held that the order for costs was rightly made, as, notwithstanding the terms of the order of discharge, there was still jurisdiction under the first order[1].

1 *Wicks v Wood* (1878) 26 WR 680.

(6) APPEALS

1067. Appeal from master or district judge. An appeal from an order[1] made by a Queen's Bench master or an order of a Chancery Division master, the Admiralty Registrar, a district judge of the Family Division or a district judge in interpleader proceedings lies to a judge in chambers[2].

An appeal lies to the Court of Appeal from any judgment, order or decision of a master on the hearing or determination of any cause, matter, question or issue ordered[3] with the consent of the parties, to be tried before or referred to him instead of an official referee[4].

Notice of appeal in an interlocutory or final matter from a master, the Admiralty Registrar, or a district judge of the Family Division, must be issued within five days[5] or, in the case of an appeal from a district judge, seven days[6], after the making of the order appealed against[7]. Notice of appeal from a final order on trial of an issue must be served not later than four weeks after the date on which the order of the court below was sealed or otherwise perfected[8].

1 Ie an interlocutory order (which includes all matters of an interim nature, such as an order for the discovery of documents, or for the sale of goods pending the trial of the dispute) or a final order. See discussion as to the procedure on an appeal from a summary determination by the master in *Observer Ltd v Gordon (Cranfield and ors, Claimants)* [1983] 2 All ER 945 at 949, [1983] 1 WLR 1008 at 1012 per Glidewell J; and see generally PRACTICE AND PROCEDURE.
2 RSC Ord 58 r 1(1), 3(1). Appeal lies as of right. Except so far as the court may otherwise direct, an appeal does not operate as a stay of the proceedings in which the appeal is brought: RSC Ord 58 r 1(4).
3 Ie under RSC Ord 36 r 11: see RSC Ord 36 rr 3, 8; and para 1044 ante.
4 RSC Ord 58 r 2(a).
5 RSC Ord 58 r 1(3).
6 RSC Ord 58 r 3(2).
7 RSC Ord 58 r 1(2), (3).
8 RSC Ord 59 rr 3(5), 4(1). For the discretion to extend time limits see Ord 3 r 5; Ord 59 r 15. For time limits, the computation, extension, and abridgment of time see the Supreme Court Practice 1993 paras 59/4/2–59/4/6.

1068. Appeal from judge on summary determination and on trial of an issue. Any judgment, order or decision of a judge given or made summarily, determining any question at issue between claimants in interpleader proceedings, whether the summary determination is by virtue of either the consent of all or the request of any of the claimants[1], or the fact that the only question at issue is one of law[2], is final and conclusive against the claimants and all persons claiming under them, unless leave to appeal to the Court of Appeal is given by the judge or the Court of Appeal[3].

1 See RSC Ord 17 r 5 (2)(b); and para 1040 ante.

2 See RSC Ord 17 r 5 (2)(c); and para 1040 ante.
3 RSC Ord 58 r 7. This rule extends to those cases where the reason for summary determination is that the applicant is a sheriff: see RSC Ord 17 r 5(2)(a).

1069. Appeal from order as to costs only. An appeal from an order of the court[1] relating only to costs which by law are left to the court's discretion[2] lies with the leave of the court making the order or of the Court of Appeal[3].

1 'The court' includes a master or district registrar when he is exercising the powers which a High Court judge can exercise in chambers: *Purcell v F C Trigell Ltd* [1971] 1 QB 358, [1970] 3 All ER 671, CA.
2 For the court's discretion as to costs see the Supreme Court Act 1981 s 51(1) (substituted by the Courts and Legal Services Act 1990 s 4(1)).
3 Supreme Court Act 1981 s 18(1A) (added by the Courts and Legal Services Act 1990 s 7(1), (3)); RSC Ord 59 r 1B(1)(b), (3). See *Hartmont v Foster* (1881) 8 QBD 82, CA.

1070. Evidence on hearing of appeal. The appeal from a summary determination by a master[1] is to be dealt with like any other appeal from a master to a High Court judge and it comes before the judge de novo[2].

Although a sheriff has a statutory duty to sell seized goods by auction[3], the auction price is not conclusive proof of the value of the goods[4].

1 See para 1068 ante.
2 *Observer Ltd v Gordon (Cranfield and ors, Claimants)* [1983] 2 All ER 945 at 949, [1983] 1 WLR 1008 at 1012 per Glidewell J.
3 Supreme Court Act 1981 s 138A (added by the Statute Law (Repeals) Act 1989 s 1(2), Sch 2 Pt I para 4).
4 *Neumann v Bakeaway Ltd (Ghotli, Claimant)* [1983] 2 All ER 935, [1983] 1 WLR 1016n, CA.

3. INTERPLEADER IN THE COUNTY COURT

(1) GENERAL

1071. Jurisdiction. The jurisdiction of county courts to grant relief by way of interpleader is governed entirely by statute and by the County Court Rules. County courts have jurisdiction in the following two classes of case:

(1) where a person makes a claim to or in respect of any goods seized under a warrant of execution, or in respect of the proceeds or value of the goods ('interpleader under execution'[1]); the district judge[2] may, as well before as after any action is brought against him, issue a summons calling before the court the party at whose instance the process was issued and the party making the claim[3].

(2) where a person ('the applicant') is under a liability in respect of any debt, money or goods and he is, or expects to be, sued[4] for, or in respect of the debt, money or goods, by two or more persons ('the claimants') making adverse claims ('interpleader otherwise than under execution')[5].

A person claiming under head (2) may do so by virtue of the statutory provisions relating to interpleader where a chose in action has been the subject of a legal assignment and its amount or value does not exceed the county court limit[6], or otherwise[7]. To entitle the applicant to relief the claims must be adverse and conflicting in the sense that they are claims to the same thing and that the applicant is not liable to both claimants[8]. It is essential that where the application arises out of an assignment, the applicant should have due notice of it in writing[9].

The procedure in a case where an application in the High Court originated by way of sheriff's interpleader is governed by special provisions which are set out elsewhere in this work[10].

1 CCR Ord 33 r 1(1); and see generally COUNTY COURTS vol 10. As to the form of summons see CCR Ord 33 r 4(1); CC Form N88 (interpleader summons to claimant claiming goods or rent under an execution) and CC Form N88(1) (interpleader summons to claimant).
2 The Courts and Legal Services Act 1990 s 74 provided that the office of county court registrar should become the office of district judge.
3 County Courts Act 1984 s 101(1).
4 Relief will not be granted unless there appears to be some real foundation for the expectation of a rival claim: *Watson v Park Royal (Caterers) Ltd* [1961] 2 All ER 346, [1961] 1 WLR 727.
5 CCR Ord 33 r 6(1). As to the form of summons see CCR Ord 33 r 8(c); CC Form N89. As to costs see para 1089 post. A district judge who, after executing a judgment obtained by the assignor of a debt, receives notice of the assignee's claim is not entitled to apply under this head: see para 1074 note 3 post.
6 See the Law of Property Act 1925 s 136 (1) proviso; and para 1004 ante. The county court has jurisdiction under this provision where the amount or value of the debt or thing in action does not exceed the county court limit: Law of Property Act 1925 ss 136(3), 205(1)(iiiA) (added by the County Courts Act 1984 s 148(1), Sch 2 Pt II paras 4, 9). The jurisdiction limit is £30,000; High Court and County Courts Jurisdiction Order 1991, SI 1991/724, art 2(5).
7 See para 1083 post. The High Court and County Courts Jurisdiction Order 1991 abolished the former limit.
8 *Greatorex v Shackle* [1895] 2 QB 249; and see para 1006 ante.
9 Law of Property Act 1925 s 136(1).
10 See CCR Ord 16 r 7; and COUNTY COURTS vol 10 para 375.

1072. Crown proceedings. The Crown may obtain relief by way of interpleader proceedings, and may be made a party to such proceedings in the same manner as a subject, and may be made a party notwithstanding that the application for such relief is made by a sheriff or other like officer[1].

1 Crown Proceedings Act 1947 s 16. All county court rules relating to interpleader proceedings have effect subject to the provisions of that Act: see s 15.

1073. Claims to damages. In two classes of case a county court has jurisdiction to adjudicate upon a claim to damages in the course of interpleader proceedings:
(1) on a district judge's application for interpleader relief, the judge must adjudicate on any claim to damages arising or capable of arising out of the execution of the warrant by the district judge[1];
(2) in transferred proceedings[2], where the High Court application originated by way of sheriff's interpleader, the county court has jurisdiction, subject to any directions to the contrary in the order of the High Court, to adjudicate on any claim for damages against an execution creditor[3].

1 County Courts Act 1984 s 101(3); Courts and Legal Services Act 1990 s 74; CCR Ord 33 r 5.
2 See paras 1042, 1071 ante.
3 CCR Ord 16 r 7(4).

(2) PROCEDURE ON DISTRICT JUDGE'S APPLICATION

1074. The claim. In order to found an application relating to interpleader by a district judge, a claim must have been made to or in respect of goods seized in execution or their proceeds or value[1]. The claim must be in respect of the goods or chattels as such or the proceeds as representing them[2]. If, after assigning his debt, a creditor recovers judgment against the debtor, and in execution of the judgment the district judge takes and sells the debtor's goods, the district judge, on receiving notice of the assignee's claim, may not seek interpleader relief, since the assignee's claim is a claim to be paid the debt and not a claim to the goods taken in execution or to their proceeds as such[3].

The claim must be in writing and must be delivered to the bailiff holding the warrant of execution or filed in the office of the county court for the district in which the goods were seized[4]. On receipt of the claim the district judge must send notice of it to the execution creditor[5] and, except where the claim is to the proceeds or value of the goods, a further notice to the claimant requiring him to make a deposit or give security[6].

Within four days of receiving the notice the execution creditor must give notice to the district judge informing him whether he admits the claim, or requesting the district judge to withdraw from possession[7]. If within the four day period, the execution creditor gives notice to the district judge, the execution creditor will only be liable to the district judge for any possession fees or expenses incurred before the receipt by the district judge of his notice[8]. Where the execution creditor gives such a notice admitting the claim or requesting the district judge to withdraw, the district judge must withdraw from possession and may apply to the judge for an order restraining the bringing of an action against the district judge for or in respect of his having taken possession of the goods or money[9]. On the hearing of the application the judge may make such order as may be just[10].

1 County Courts Act 1984 s 101(1); Courts and Legal Services Act 1990 s 74; CCR Ord 33 r 1.
2 *Plant v Collins* [1913] 1 KB 242, CA.
3 *Plant v Collins* [1913] 1 KB 242, CA. In such a case the district judge is also disentitled to claim relief by way of interpleader otherwise than by execution under CCR Ord 33 r 6(1), (2) (see para 1071 ante), since he is not a person under liability for any debt, money or goods within the meaning of that rule (*Plant v Collins* supra at 246–247); nor can he claim relief under the statutory provisions relating to interpleader in the case of a legal assignment of a chose in action (*Plant v Collins* supra at 246; and see para 1004 text and note 3 ante). For the principle that the claim must relate to the goods or their proceeds as such, cf para 1013 ante. As to a claim by a landlord for rent see para 1013 text and note 5 ante.
4 CCR Ord 33 r 1(1). For a form of claim see CCR Ord 33 r 1 and note 'Claim to goods', and 22 Court Forms (2nd Edn) (1991 Issue) 432, Form 36.
5 CCR Ord 33 r 1(2)(a). For the practice form of notice to the execution creditor see CC Form N358, and 22 Court Forms (2nd Edn) (1991 Issue) 432–433, Form 37.
6 CCR Ord 33 r 1(2)(b). For the practice form of notice to the claimant see CC Form N359, and 22 Court Forms (2nd Edn) (1991 Issue) 433–434, Form 38.
7 CCR Ord 33 r 2(1). For a form of notice see 22 Court Forms (2nd Edn) (1991 Issue) 432–433, Form 37 (a form of notice is appended to the notice to the execution creditor of the claim to the goods seized in execution).
8 CCR Ord 33 r 2(2). The judge, on the application of the district judge, has power to order the execution creditor to pay any possession fees or expenses incurred before the execution creditor has

given notice admitting the claim or requesting the district judge to withdraw from possession: County Courts Act 1984 s 128(4); CC Fees Order 1982 art 3(3).

No possession fees are now prescribed by CCR Ord 33 r 2, but if these fees become payable, it has been held that the district judge might be entitled to such fees even if the goods of which he was in purported possession were actually in the possession of the sheriff: *A W Ltd v Cooper and Hall Ltd* [1925] 2 KB 816. It was also held that an appeal would lie from an order of the judge directing payment of the district judge's fees.

9 CCR Ord 33 r 3. As the rule gives protection in relation to any action in respect of the seizure, it is not limited to an action brought by the claimant. Protection is only likely to be granted where the claimant has suffered no real grievance and his claim is only for nominal damages. The court is unlikely to protect the district judge where there is substantial grievance: see *Cave v Capel* [1954] 1 QB 367, [1954] 1 All ER 428, CA; and para 1014 ante.

It is the quality of the district judge's act which is relevant, such as selling the goods at a gross undervalue: *Neumann v Bakeaway Ltd* [1983] 2 All ER 935, [1983] 1 WLR 1016n, CA. The test is whether the claimant can show that it is fairly arguable that his claim against the district judge overrides the district judge's defences under the County Courts Act 1984 s 98 (as amended), or at common law: see *Observer Ltd v Gordon (Cranfield and ors, Claimants)* [1983] 2 All ER 945, [1983] 1 WLR 1008.

10 CCR Ord 33 r 3. See also note 9 supra.

1075. Security by claimant on claim. On receipt of the prescribed notice from the district judge[1] the claimant may deposit with the bailiff[2] either (1) the amount of the value of the goods claimed[3], or (2) the sum which the bailiff is allowed to charge as costs for keeping possession of the goods until the judge's decision can be obtained on the claim[4]; or may give the bailiff in the prescribed manner security for the value of the goods claimed[5]. For this purpose the amount of the value of the goods claimed is in case of dispute[6] to be fixed by appraisement[7], and where that amount is deposited it must be paid by the bailiff into court to abide the judge's decision upon the claim[8]. In default of the claimant's complying with these provisions the bailiff must sell the goods as if no claim had been made and must pay into court the proceeds of the sale to abide the judge's decision[9], but notwithstanding this provision the goods must not be sold if the district judge decides that in all the circumstances the judge's decision on the claim ought to be awaited[10].

Where the real owner claims the goods but makes no deposit and does not give security and the bailiff thereupon sells under this provision, the sale conveys a good title to the goods even though the judgment debtor is not the true owner[11]. It is not, however, clear whether the purchaser obtains a good title to the goods where the claimant is not the real owner and the real owner makes no claim until after the sale[12], or whether, where the claimant is not the real owner, the bailiff is liable to the real owner for conversion in respect of the sale[13].

1 See para 1074 text and note 6 ante. As to the district judge see para 1071 note 2 ante.
2 'Bailiff' includes a district judge unless the context otherwise requires: County Courts Act 1984 s 147; Courts and Legal Services Act 1990 s 74.
3 County Courts Act 1984 s 100(1)(a)(i). As to the effect of a deposit of the amount of the judgment debt and not the value of the goods see para 1076 post.
4 Ibid s 100(1)(a)(ii). For the fees see the CC Fees Order 1982 Fee 5(i) (as amended); COUNTY COURTS vol 10 para 6.
5 County Courts Act 1984 s 100(1)(b). For a form of notice to the claimant to make a deposit or give security see 22 Court Forms (2nd Edn) (1991 Issue) 433–434, Form 38.
6 'Dispute' for this purpose means a dispute between the claimant and the execution creditor: *Miller & Co v Solomon* [1906] 2 KB 91.
7 As to appraisement see the County Courts Act 1984 ss 94–96; and COUNTY COURTS vol 10 para 490.
8 Ibid s 100(2).
9 Ibid s 100(3).
10 Ibid s 100(4).

11 *Goodlock v Cousins* [1897] 1 QB 558, CA.
12 See *Goodlock v Cousins* [1897] 1 QB 558 at 561–562, CA, per Chitty LJ; and see also *Crane & Sons v Ormerod* [1903] 2 KB 37 at 39–40, CA, where the effect of what is now the County Courts Act 1984 s 100 was considered, although the sale in question was not under the enactment. The provisions of the County Courts Act 1984 s 98 (as amended) (which validate the titles of purchasers and protect district judges and other officers from actions in cases where goods are sold without notice of a claim, and which overrule the actual decision in *Crane & Sons v Ormerod* supra) will not, it seems, apply if a claim has been made, even though it was not made by the true owner.
13 See *Cramer v Matthews* (1881) 7 QBD 425 at 433; *Jelks v Hayward* [1905] 2 KB 460 (which was not a decision under what is now the County Courts Act 1984 s 100(3), and is overruled by s 98: see note 12 supra). Where, after the goods have been sold under s 100(3), a district judge is faced with a claim by the true owner, he may claim relief by way of interpleader against the true owner (cf *Cramer v Matthews* supra, *Jelks v Hayward* supra), and it seems that he will be entitled to such relief at least so far as it relates to the sale as distinct from the original seizure. As to the court's power to determine claims for damages see paras 1073 ante, 1086 post. As to the staying of actions see para 1080 text and notes 8–9 post.

1076. Deposit of amount of judgment debt but less than value of goods. It is not quite clear what the position is where the claimant deposits[1] the amount of the judgment debt and costs where these are less than the value of the goods. Where a claimant, whose title under a bill of sale was admitted, deposited the amount of the judgment debt and costs, and not the value of the goods, and the high bailiff[2] withdrew from possession without consulting the execution creditor, it was held that the high bailiff ought not to have withdrawn, and that, on the application of the execution creditor, the court had power to order the high bailiff to retake possession and to order a sale of the goods[3] if there was evidence that the proceeds of such a sale might realise sufficient to discharge the bill of sale and leave a surplus towards the judgment debt and costs[4].

In another case, however, where a claimant deposited more than sufficient to cover the judgment debt and costs, although less than the value of the goods, and the execution creditor admitted the claimant's title before the return day of the summons, it was held that the bailiff was not entitled to possession fees after the date of the deposit since, having taken the amount deposited, which he had no right to do except on the assumption that it represented the amount of the value of the goods, he ought to have withdrawn from possession and could not afterwards be heard to say that it did not represent the value[5].

1 As to deposit by the claimant see para 1075 ante.
2 Reference to a high bailiff must now be construed as a reference to a district judge: County Courts Act 1984 s 148(2), Sch 3 para 7; Courts and Legal Services Act 1990 s 74.
3 Ie under the power set out in para 1079 post.
4 *Miller & Co v Solomon* [1906] 2 KB 91.
5 *Newsum Sons & Co Ltd v James* [1909] 2 KB 384. It is somewhat difficult to reconcile this case with *Miller & Co v Solomon* [1906] 2 KB 91 on the question of principle as to how much should be deposited as security. The cases largely depend upon their special facts.

1077. Effect of deposit on second execution. Where an amount equal to the value of the goods is paid into court[1], and the district judge[2] thereupon withdraws from possession, the goods may be seized again by another execution creditor. In such a case the remedy of the original execution creditor is against the money in court and not against the goods[3]. Where the amount deposited as the value of the goods is less than the amount of the judgment debt, and the amount in court is paid out to the execution creditor on the claimant's failing to establish his claim, the execution creditor is not entitled to the amount deposited as value of the goods a second time by the same claimant on a second execution upon the same judgment being levied by the execution creditor, since he has elected to accept the money deposited in the first instance in lieu of the goods[4].

1 See para 1075 ante.
2 As to the district judge see para 1071 note 2 ante.
3 *Wells v Hughes* [1907] 2 KB 845, CA.
4 *Haddow v Morton (Trout, Claimant)* [1894] 1 QB 565, CA, where taking money out of court was held to be an election to accept it in lieu of the goods, and the execution creditor was therefore estopped from afterwards denying that as against himself the goods belonged to the claimants: see ESTOPPEL vol 16 (Reissue) paras 958 note 5, 1009 note 3. The question as to what the result would have been if the judgment creditor had seized the goods the second time on another judgment was left open. Cf *Kotchie v Golden Sovereigns Ltd* [1898] 2 QB 164, CA.

1078. Security for execution creditor's costs. Where it appears that the claimant does not reside in England and Wales, the execution creditor may apply to the court, on not less than two clear days' notice in writing[1], for an order directing the claimant to give security for costs[2] and, where such an order is made and is not obeyed, the court may make an order barring the claim[3]. Where by or under any Act or rule any person is required or authorised to give security for costs in relation to county court proceedings then, subject to any express provision, the security must be given in such manner and at such time, and on such terms, if any, as the court may direct[4].

1 CCR Ord 13 r 1(2).
2 CCR Ord 13 r 8(1).
3 CCR Ord 33 r 11(1).
4 CCR Ord 50 r 9.

1079. Sale by order of the court. In addition to the bailiff's power of sale already noted[1], where a claimant alleges that he is entitled to the goods under a bill of sale or otherwise by way of security for a debt, the judge may order[2] the goods or any part of them to be sold, and may direct the proceeds of sale to be applied in such manner as may be just[3].

A district judge cannot be compelled to interplead so as to give the execution creditor the right to invoke this power, even where the value of the goods exceeds the sum secured by it[4]; but the judge may exercise the jurisdiction, notwithstanding that the district judge has withdrawn, if satisfied that the execution creditor has not had an opportunity of disputing the value of the goods as against the claimant[5].

1 See para 1075 ante.
2 For the form of order see 22 Court Forms (2nd Edn) (1991 Issue) 436–437, Form 42.
3 RSC Ord 17 r 6, as applied by the County Courts Act 1984 s 76.
4 *Scarlett v Hanson* (1883) 12 QBD 213. As to the district judge see para 1071 note 2 ante.
5 *Miller & Co v Solomon* [1906] 2 KB 91.

1080. Interpleader summons by district judge. Where the execution creditor gives notice disputing a claim[1], or where he fails within the four day period to give notice to the district judge admitting the title of the claimant, or requesting the district judge to withdraw from possession[2], the district judge, unless the claimant has withdrawn his claim, must issue an interpleader summons to the execution creditor and the claimant[3]. On the issue of the interpleader summons, the district judge must enter the proceedings in the record of the court, fix a day for the hearing by the judge and prepare sufficient copies for service[4]. The summons must be served in the same way as a fixed date summons[5] and, notwithstanding the rules relating to the extension or abridgment of time[6], service must be effected not less than 14 days before the return day[7].

Upon the issue of the summons any action brought in any county court, or other court, in respect of the claim or of any damage arising out of the execution of the warrant must be stayed[8]. The stay is limited to the persons who would be parties to the interpleader summons[9].

1 Ie under CCR Ord 33 r 2(1): see para 1074 ante.
2 Ie under CCR Ord 33 r 2(1): see para 1074 ante. As to the district judge see para 1071 note 2 ante.
3 CCR Ord 33 r 4(1). For forms see CC Forms N88 (interpleader summons to execution creditor) and N88(1) (interpleader summons to claimant claiming goods or rent under an execution), and 22 Court Forms (2nd Edn) (1991 Issue) 434–435, Forms 39–40.
4 CCR Ord 33 r 4(2).
5 CCR Ord 33 r 4(3). As to service of a fixed date summons see CCR Ord 7 r 10; and COUNTY COURTS vol 10 para 185.
6 Ie CCR Ord 13 r 4.
7 CCR Ord 33 r 4(4).
8 County Courts Act 1984 s 101(2).
9 Thus in *Hills v Renny* (1880) 5 ExD 313, CA, it was held that the provision did not apply to proceedings against purchasers who had bought under a sale by the bailiff which had occurred before the action. It was not argued in this case that there was a discretionary power to order a stay under the inherent jurisdiction of the court. As to the protection of purchasers of goods taken in execution see the County Courts Act 1984 s 98(1); and cf *Curtis v Maloney* [1951] 1 KB 736, [1950] 2 All ER 982, CA; *Dyal Singh v Kenyon Insurance Ltd* [1954] AC 287, [1954] 1 All ER 847, PC.

1081. Particulars of the claim. The claim should state the grounds of the claim or, in the case of a claim for rent, particulars stating (1) the amount of rent claimed to be in arrear, (2) the period in respect of which the rent is due[1] and, in every case, the claimant's full name and address[2]. If damages are claimed, the amount and the grounds of the claim must also be stated[3].

Particulars which merely state that the goods claimed are the property of the claimant without giving the grounds of the claim are insufficient[4], but particulars giving the date of and parties to an assignment under which the claim is made are a sufficient compliance with the rule[5]. The goods claimed need not be specifically set out[6] and slight errors in the particulars will not invalidate their sufficiency[7]. Where the particulars are insufficient or not delivered in time the judge should either amend them or order a new summons to be issued as he is bound to adjudicate upon the claim on the merits[8]. Where he erroneously decides that the particulars are insufficient and orders the claimant to pay the costs, the High Court may order him to adjudicate upon the claim but has no jurisdiction to reverse the order as to costs[9].

On receipt of the claim, the district judge must send notice of the claim to the execution creditor[10] and, except where the claim is to the proceeds or value of the goods, send to the claimant a notice requiring him to make a deposit or give security[11].

1 CCR Ord 33 r 1(1)(a); County Courts Act 1984 s 102(2)(a), (b).
2 CCR Ord 33 r 1(1)(b). See also para 1074 ante.
3 CCR Ord 33 r 5(a).
4 *R v Chilton* (1850) 15 QB 220. See also *Richardson v Wright* (1875) LR 10 Exch 367, where the court was equally divided.

5 *R v Richards* (1851) 20 LJQB 351.
6 *Heslop v McGeorge* (1851) 18 LTOS 109; *R v Stapylton* (1851) 2 LM & P 603.
7 See *Hardy v Walker, ex p M'Fee* (1853) 9 Exch 261, where the address given was 'Elizabeth Street' instead of 'Elizabeth Terrace'.
8 *Beswick v Baffey* (1854) 9 Exch 315.
9 *R v Richards* (1851) 2 LM & P 263; *Churchward v Coleman* (1866) LR 2 QB; but see *Whitehead v Proctor* (1858) 3 H & N 532. The High Court may also prohibit the judge from proceeding on the original complaint: *Hardy v Walker, ex p M'Fee* (1853) 9 Exch 261.
10 CCR Ord 33 r 1(2)(a). As to the district judge see para 1071 note 2 ante.
11 Ie security in accordance with the County Courts Act 1984 s 100: CCR Ord 33 r 1(2)(b). See para 1075 ante.

1082. Claim for damages. Where, in interpleader proceedings, the claimant claims damages from the district judge or from the execution creditor, or the execution creditor wishes to make a claim against the district judge for damages arising or capable of arising out of the execution, (1) the party claiming damages must, within eight days after service of the summons on him, give notice of his claim to the district judge and to any other party against whom the claim is made, stating the amount and the grounds of the claim; and (2) the party from whom damages are claimed may pay money into court in satisfaction of the claim as if the interpleader proceedings were an action brought by the person making the claim[1].

A party entitled to damages which could have been made the subject of a claim in interpleader proceedings under these provisions cannot claim damages by a subsequent action brought after the interpleader proceedings have been determined[2].

Where goods are sold by the district judge or any officer charged with the enforcement of a warrant or other process of execution issued from a county court, which goods at the time of seizure were in the possession of the judgment debtor, without any claims being made to them, then damages will not be recoverable against the district judge or any person acting under his authority, unless it can be proved that notice had been given, or that it might by making reasonable inquiry have been ascertained, that the goods were not the property of the execution debtor[3]. The right of any claimant, who may prove that at the time of the sale he had a title to any goods so seized and sold, to any remedy to which he may be entitled against any person other than the district judge or other authorised officer, is not affected[4].

A sale by public auction is not conclusive evidence of an allegation by the claimant that the goods have been sold at a gross undervalue[5].

1 CCR Ord 33 r 5. As to the district judge see para 1071 note 2 ante. For a form of notice of claim by an execution creditor for damages against a district judge see 22 Court Forms (2nd Edn) (1991 Issue) 435–436, Form 41.
2 *West v Automatic Salesman Ltd* [1937] 2 KB 398, [1937] 2 All ER 706, CA; *Death v Harrison* (1870) LR 6 Exch 15. *Salbstein v Isaacs & Son* [1916] 1 KB 1 was decided under the rules relating to remitted proceedings materially different from those in force now.
3 County Courts Act 1984 s 98(1).
4 Ibid s 98(2).
5 *Observer Ltd v Gordon (Cranfield and ors, Claimants)* [1983] 2 All ER 945, [1983] 1 WLR 1008.

(3) PROCEDURE ON APPLICATION FOR AN INTERPLEADER OTHERWISE THAN UNDER EXECUTION

1083. Applicant's affidavit. Where the applicant for interpleader relief is a stakeholder[1] he must file in the court office[2] an affidavit[3] showing that he claims no interest in the subject matter in dispute other than for charges or costs[4], that he does not collude with any of the claimants[5], and that he is willing to pay or transfer the subject matter into court or dispose of it as the court may direct[6].

Where the applicant seeks relief in a pending action[7], the affidavit and copies must be filed within 14 days after service on him of the summons in the action[8].

Where a claim is made on behalf of a minor or a mental patient the claim must be in the name of the minor or patient by his next friend[9].

1 The distinction between different applications for interpleader relief is set out in RSC Ord 17 r 1, where it is stated that interpleaders may be divided into two types. The first is where a sheriff seizes or intends to seize goods by way of execution and such goods are claimed by a person other than the judgment debtor; this is analogous to the application for interpleader relief in the county court under an execution. The second type comprises all other interpleader proceedings, which are generally known as stakeholder's interpleaders. See para 1001 ante.
2 Application is made to the court in which the action is pending or, if no action is pending, to the court in which the applicant might be sued: CCR Ord 33 r 6(2).
3 CCR Ord 33 r 6(3). For a form of affidavit see CC Form N360 and 22 Court Forms (2nd Edn) (1991 Issue) 439, Form 45. The applicant must also file with his affidavit as many copies of the affidavit as there are claimants: CCR Ord 33 r 6(3).
4 CCR Ord 33 r 6(3)(a).
5 CCR Ord 33 r 6(3)(b).
6 CCR Ord 33 r 6(3)(c).
7 CCR Ord 33 r 7.
8 CCR Ord 33 r 7(a). For a form of affidavit see 22 Court Forms (2nd Edn) (1991 Issue) 442, Form 50.
9 CCR Ord 10 r 1(1). As to the appointment of a next friend see COUNTY COURTS vol 10 para 162. As to minors and patients see respectively CHILDREN; MENTAL HEALTH. Before the claimant's particulars are filed (see para 1085 post), the next friend must deliver at the court office an undertaking as to costs: CCR Ord 10 r 2(b). For the form of undertaking see CC Form N235; and COUNTY COURTS vol 10 para 4; 13 Court Forms (2nd Edn) (1992 Issue) 438, Form 10.

1084. Interpleader summons by applicant. On the filing of the applicant's affidavit[1], the procedure to be adopted depends on whether or not the applicant is a defendant in proceedings already commenced.

Where the applicant is a defendant in a pending action, (1) the affidavit and required copies must be filed within 14 days after the service of the summons[2]; (2) the return day of the application must be a day fixed for the pre-trial review of the action, including the interpleader proceedings and, if a day has already been fixed for the pre-trial review or hearing of the action, the proper officer[3] must, if necessary, postpone it[4]; (3) the claimant, the applicant, and the plaintiff in the action must be given notice of the application, prepared by the proper officer together with sufficient copies for service[5]; (4) the notice to the claimant must be served on him together with a copy of the applicant's affidavit and the summons and particulars of claim in the action, not less than 21 days before the return day in the same manner as a fixed date summons[6]; (5) the notices to the applicant and the plaintiff must be sent by the proper officer, and the notice to the plaintiff must be accompanied by a copy of the applicant's affidavit[7].

These provisions apply with the necessary modifications to an application for relief by the respondent to a matter[8].

Where the applicant is not a defendant in a pending action, the proper officer (a) must enter the proceedings in the records of the court[9]; (b) fix a day for a pre-trial review, or if the court so directs, a day for the hearing of the proceedings, and prepare and issue an interpleader summons, together with sufficient copies for service[10]; (c) send or deliver a plaint note to the applicant[11]; (d) serve the summons, together with a copy of the applicant's affidavit, on each of the claimants not less than one day before the return day in the same manner as a fixed date summons[12].

Before or after the court officer proceeds, the district judge may direct the applicant to bring the subject matter of the proceedings into court, or to dispose of it in such manner as the district judge thinks fit, to abide by the order of the court[13].

1 See para 1083 ante.
2 CCR Ord 33 r 7(a). See para 1083 ante.
3 'Proper officer' means the district judge or, in relation to any act of a formal or administrative character which is not by statute the responsibility of the district judge, and in CCR Ord 9 r 3, Ord 22 rr 7A, 10, Ord 25 r 8 and Ord 27 rr 7, 7A, 8(1B), 19(3C), 20, the chief clerk or any other officer of the court acting on his behalf in accordance with directions given by the Lord Chancellor: CCR Ord 1 r 3. As to the district judge see para 1071 note 2 ante.
4 CCR Ord 33 r 7(b).
5 CCR Ord 33 r 7(c). For a form of notice see CC Form N361, and 22 Court Forms (2nd Edn) (1991 Issue) 442–443, Form 51.
6 CCR Ord 33 r 7(d). As to the manner of service of a fixed date summons see CCR Ord 7 r 10; and COUNTY COURTS vol 10 para 185.
7 CCR Ord 33 r 7(e).
8 CCR Ord 33 r 12.
9 CCR Ord 33 r 8(a).
10 CCR Ord 33 r 8(b). For a form of interpleader summons see CC Form N89, and 22 Court Forms (2nd Edn) (1991 Issue) 439–440, Form 46.
11 CCR Ord 33 r 8(d).
12 CCR Ord 33 r 8(c). See note 6 supra.
13 CCR Ord 33 r 9.

1085. Reply by the claimant. A claimant must within 14 days after service on him of the notice (if an action is pending)[1], or the summons (where no action is pending)[2], file either (1) a notice that he makes no claim to the subject matter[3], or (2) particulars stating the grounds of his claim to the subject matter[4], together with sufficient copies for service.

The proper officer[5] must send a copy of any notice or particulars of claim to the other parties[6].

The court may hear the proceedings even if no notice or particulars of claim have been filed[7].

1 See para 1084 text and notes 2–7 ante; and CCR Ord 33 r 7.
2 See para 1084 text and notes 9–12 ante; and CCR Ord 33 r 8.
3 CCR Ord 33 r 10(1)(a). For a form of notice (if an action is pending) see 22 Court Forms (2nd Edn) (1991 Issue) 443, Form 52 and for a form of notice (where no action is pending) see 22 Court Forms (2nd Edn) (1991 Issue) 440, Form 47.
4 CCR Ord 33 r 10 (1)(b). For a form of particulars (if an action is pending) see 22 Court Forms (2nd Edn) (1991 Issue) 443, Form 53, and for a form of particulars (where no action is pending) see 22 Court Forms (2nd Edn) (1991 Issue) 440–441, Form 48.
5 For the meaning of 'proper officer' see para 1084 note 3 ante.

6 CCR Ord 33 r 10(2).
7 CCR Ord 33 r 10(3).

(4) HEARING OF INTERPLEADER SUMMONS

1086. Adjudication of claim on district judge's application. On the hearing of the summons, the judge must adjudicate upon the claim and must also adjudicate between the parties or between either of them and the district judge[1] upon any claim to damages arising or capable of arising out of the execution of the warrant by the district judge. The judge makes such order in respect of any such claim and the costs of the proceedings as he thinks fit[2].

Damages ought to be awarded against the district judge where the claimant can prove substantial loss or injury[3], although if a claim for damages is not made during the proceedings it cannot be made afterwards[4].

1 As to the district judge see para 1071 note 2 ante.
2 County Courts Act 1984 s 101(3). For the form of order where the claimant's claim is not established see 22 Court Forms (2nd Edn) (1991 Issue) 437–438, Form 43, and for a form of order where the claimant's claim is established see 22 Court Forms (2nd Edn) (1991 Issue) 438, Form 44.
3 See eg *London, Chatham and Dover Rly Co v Cable* (1899) 80 LT 119, DC, where two gas stoves of the value of £18 18s (£18.90) exempt from execution were seized and sold for £1 14s (£1.70); *Jelks v Hayward* [1905] 2 KB 460, where furniture let out on hire was seized and sold by the high bailiff, who was held liable for damages for conversion. See also *De Coppett v Barnett* (1901) 17 TLR 273, CA, and cf *Cave v Capel* [1954] 1 QB 367, [1954] 1 All ER 428, CA; and para 1031 ante.
4 *West v Automatic Salesman Ltd* [1937] 2 KB 398, [1937] 2 All ER 706, CA.

1087. Adjudication of claims in an application for interpleader relief otherwise than under execution. When the application for interpleader proceeds either in[1], or otherwise than in[2], a pending action, where the claimant does not appear at the pre-trial review or at the hearing of the interpleader proceedings, or fails or refuses to comply with an order made in the proceedings, the court may make an order barring his claim[3].

If the applicant is a defendant in a pending action[4], and the plaintiff fails to appear at the pre-trial review or the hearing of the interpleader proceedings, the action, including the interpleader proceedings, may be struck out[5].

In any other case, where a day is fixed for the hearing of the interpleader proceedings, the court must hear and determine the proceedings and give judgment finally determining the rights and claims of the parties[6].

Where the court makes an order barring the claim of a claimant, the order must declare the claimant, and all persons claiming under him, for ever barred from prosecuting his claim against the applicant and all persons claiming under him[7]. Such an order will not affect the rights of the claimants as between themselves except where a claimant has filed a notice[8] that he makes no claim[9].

1 See CCR Ord 33 r 7; and para 1084 text and notes 2–7 ante.
2 See CCR Ord 33 r 8; and para 1084 text and notes 9–12 ante.
3 CCR Ord 33 r 11(1).
4 See CCR Ord 33 r 7(a); and para 1084 ante.
5 CCR Ord 33 r 11(2).
6 CCR Ord 33 r 11(3). For a form of order (if an action is pending) see 22 Court Forms (2nd Edn) (1991 Issue) 443–444, Form 54, and for a form of order (where no action is pending) see 22 Court Forms (2nd Edn) (1991 Issue) 441, Form 49.

7 CCR Ord 33 r 11(4).
8 Ie under CCR Ord 33 r 10(1)(a): see para 1085 text and note 3 ante.
9 CCR Ord 33 r 11(4).

1088. Adjudication of claim in proceedings transferred from the High Court. Where interpleader proceedings are ordered to be transferred from the High Court to the county court under an execution[1], a special procedure applies[2].

Notice of the hearing or pre-trial review of the proceedings must be given by the proper officer[3] to the sheriff, as well as to every other party to the proceedings[4]. Within eight days of receipt of that notice, the claimant must file in triplicate particulars of any goods alleged to be his property and the grounds of his claim[5]. The proper officer must send a copy of the claimant's particulars to the execution creditor and to the sheriff. The judge may hear the proceedings or the district judge may proceed with the pre-trial review, if he thinks fit, notwithstanding that the claimant's particulars have not been filed[6].

On any day fixed for the pre-trial review of the proceedings, or for the hearing of any application by the sheriff or other party for directions, the court may order the sheriff (1) to postpone the sale of the goods seized, or (2) to remain in possession of such goods until the hearing of the proceedings, or (3) to hand over possession of such goods to the district judge[7]. Where a direction is given under head (3), the district judge will be allowed his reasonable charges for keeping possession of the goods, not exceeding those charges which might be allowed to the sheriff, and, if the district judge is directed to sell the goods, such charges for the sale as would be allowed under an execution issued by the county court[8].

No order made in the interpleader proceedings transferred from the High Court will prejudice or affect the rights of the sheriff to any proper charges and the judge may make such order with respect to those charges as may be just[9].

The order made at the hearing of the proceedings will direct how any money in the hands of the sheriff is to be disposed of[10].

Subject to any directions in the order of the High Court, damages may be claimed against the execution creditor in the same manner as in interpleader proceedings commenced in a county court[11].

1 Ie under the County Courts Act 1984 s 40 (as substituted): see para 1042 ante.
2 Ie CCR Ord 16 r 6 is subject to r 7: CCR Ord 16 r 7(1). See generally COUNTY COURTS vol 10 para 374 et seq.
3 For the meaning of 'proper officer' see para 1084 note 3 ante.
4 CCR Ord 16 r 7(2). For a form giving notice of the hearing see 22 Court Forms (2nd Edn) (1991 Issue) 444–445, Form 55, and for a form giving notice of a pre-trial review see 22 Court Forms (2nd Edn) (1991 Issue) 445, Form 56.
5 CCR Ord 16 r 7(3). For a form of particulars to be given by a claimant see 22 Court Forms (2nd Edn) (1991 Issue) 445, Form 57.
6 CCR Ord 16 r 7(3).
7 CCR Ord 16 r 7(5)(a)–(c).
8 CCR Ord 16 r 7(5).
9 CCR Ord 16 r 7(6). The charges referred to in this note and in text to note 8 supra are ultimately to be borne in such manner as the judge directs: CCR Ord 16 r 7(7).
10 CCR Ord 16 r 7(8); cf *Discount Banking Co of England and Wales v Lambarde* [1893] 2 QB 329, CA. As to the costs of the proceedings see para 1089 post.
11 CCR Ord 16 r 7(4): see para 1073 ante.

1089. Costs. In general costs in interpleader proceedings in a county court are in the discretion of the judge[1], and the judge may award costs on such scale as he thinks fit[2]. Subject to any order of the High Court, the costs of the interpleader proceedings transferred from the High Court, both before and after the transfer to the county court, are in the discretion of the judge in the lower court[3]. There is no power to order the sheriff to pay the costs of the interpleader proceedings which have been transferred from the High Court to the county court[4].

1 CCR Ord 38 r 1(2). As to costs in county courts generally see COUNTY COURTS vol 10 para 602 et seq.
2 CCR Ord 38 r 4(7).
3 County Courts Act 1984 s 45(1) (amended by the Courts and Legal Services Act 1990 s 125(7), Sch 20): see COUNTY COURTS vol 10 para 633. No order may prejudice or affect the right of a sheriff who has interpleaded to proper charges, and the judge may make such order with respect to them as may be just: CCR Ord 16 r 7(6). See COUNTY COURTS vol 10 para 375.
4 *Temple v Temple* (1894) 63 LJQB 556. If such an order has been made, the sheriff's proper course is not to appeal against it, but to apply for an order of prohibition: *Temple v Temple* supra. As to prohibition see ADMINISTRATIVE LAW vol 1(1) (Reissue) para 109 et seq.

(5) APPEALS

1090. Appeals. Subject to certain provisions, if any party to interpleader proceedings in a county court is dissatisfied with the determination of the judge, he may appeal from it to the Court of Appeal in such manner and subject to such conditions as may be provided by the rules of the Supreme Court[1].

1 County Courts Act 1984 s 77(1). The rules may make provision for appeals from the exercise by a district judge, assistant district judge, or deputy district judge of any power given to him by virtue of any enactment to be to a judge of a county court: s 77(1A) (added by the Courts and Legal Services Act 1990 s 125(2), Sch 17 para 15). Appeals to the Court of Appeal are regulated by RSC Ord 59. See also COUNTY COURTS.

INTERPRETATION OF INSTRUMENTS

See DEEDS AND OTHER INSTRUMENTS; EVIDENCE; STATUTES; WILLS

INTERROGATORIES

See DISCOVERY, INSPECTION AND INTERROGATORIES

INTESTACY

See EXECUTORS AND ADMINISTRATORS

INDEX

Insurance

References are to paragraph numbers; superior figures refer to notes

References are to paragraph numbers; superior figures refer to notes

References are to paragraph numbers; superior figures refer to notes

References are to paragraph numbers; superior figures refer to notes

References are to paragraph numbers; superior figures refer to notes

References are to paragraph numbers; superior figures refer to notes

References are to paragraph numbers; superior figures refer to notes

References are to paragraph numbers; superior figures refer to notes

References are to paragraph numbers; superior figures refer to notes

life assurance—*continued*
  beneficiary's name, insertion of, 543
  bonus, 552
  change of circumstances, effect on continuing insurance, 471
  children, in favour of, 558
  common law position as to insurable interest, 535
  conflicting claims, payment where, 502
  contingency insurance, basis of, 469
  continuing insurance, 469–471
  cover notes not issued, 388
  creditors' pecuniary interest, 540
  criminal act of assured, death due to, 530
  date for valuing interest, 544
  days of grace, 477
  death—
    criminal act of assured, by, 530
    excepted perils, due to, 531
    stipulated contingency, as, 529
    suicide, 530, 531
    wilful act of third party, 529n[3]
  deferred policies for children, 565
  disclosure—
    honest misrepresentations, 359
    material facts. *See* material facts *infra*
    persons referred to for information, 533
  early surrender or conversion of policies, taxation, 16n[8]
  endowment. *See* endowment insurance
  excepted perils, death due to, 531
  foreign currency, payment in, 555
  gaming and wagering, 535, 536
  indemnity, exception from principle of, 4
  industrial assurance, 528
  insurable interest—
    application of statutory provisions, 537
    commencement of risk, at, 2
    common law position, 535
    creditors' pecuniary interest, 540
    date for valuing, 544
    insurances not covered by 1774 Act, 538
    insurances subject to 1774 Act, 537
    name of person interested, 543
    payment to persons without, 542
    pecuniary interest requirement, 539
    relatives' pecuniary interest, 541
    statutory provisions, effect of, 536
  interest on amount payable, 554
  legislation, 14
  lien on policy, 560
  limit on sum recoverable, 536
  material facts—
    age and health, 533
    habits and history of assured, 533
    life insured that of third party, 533n[1]
    medical examination, 534
    persons referred to for information, 533
    principles generally, 532
  medical examination, 534
  misstatements by proposer, 359
  name of person interested to be inserted in policy, 543
  payment into court—
    exercise of right, 562
    statutory right, 561
  pecuniary interest—
    creditors', 540
    insurable interest, 539
    relatives', 541

life assurance—*continued*
  person entitled to payment—
    insurance on life of assured, 556
    lien on policy, 560
    life of third party, insurance on, 559
    spouse or children, 558
    third party's position, 557
    trustees, appointment of, 558
  personal representative, payment of policy money to, 556
  persons without interest, payment to, 542
  premium—
    lien acquired by payment of, 560
    tax relief, 527n[8,9]
  relatives' pecuniary interest, 541
  self-destruction, death due to, 531
  share of profits, 552
  spouse, in favour of, 558
  statutory provisions, effect on insurable interest, 536
  subject matter, 425n[2], 525
  subrogation right not applicable, 505
  suicide, no return of premium, 450
  surrender value, 553
  third party, policy money payable to, 557
  trustee in bankruptcy, payment to, 556
  unnamed persons, for benefit of, 536
  wilful act, death due to, 529, 530
life policy—
  meaning, 548n[1]
  absolute assignment, 550
  assignment—
    assignability at common law, 545
    condition against, 551
    equitable. *See* equitable assignment *infra*
    statutory rights—
      absolute assignment, 550
      assignee's right of action, 548
      conditions, 549
      writing, in, 549
  condition against assignment, 551
  deferred policy for child, 565
  equitable assignment—
    assignability, 545
    effect, 547
    form of, 546
  lien on, 560
  name of person interested, insertion of, 543
  specified period, for, 526
  transfer subject to equities, 547
  See also life assurance
lightning, marine insurance cover, 163
livestock insurance—
  scope of, 656
  slaughter, position where, 657
Lloyd's—
  accounts and audit, 23
  annual statement by Committee, 23
  certificate of auditor or actuary as to value of assets, 23n[8]
  default powers of Secretary of State, 22
  history of, 21
  Insurance Companies Act 1982, application of, 22
  margin of solvency, 22
  Marine Policy Form, 906
  registration of brokers, 875
  requirements for exemption from 1982 Act, 22, 23
  several liability of underwriters, 21
  shipping intelligence, 21

marine insurance—*continued*
  enemy alien, insurance by or on behalf of, 78
  evidence, rules of, 340
  excluded losses—
    damage to machinery not caused by maritime perils, 167
    delay, 167, 169
    exclusion clauses, 167
    inherent vice or nature of subject matter, 172
    Institute Clauses, 167
    leakage or breakage of goods, 171
    proximate cause of loss, determination of, 176
    rats or vermin, 167
    scuttling, 174
    stranding, 168
    wilful misconduct, 167
  'f c and s clause', 175n[4]
  fire, scope of cover, 153
  foundering at sea, 151n[10,11]
  fraud—
    effect on policy, 215
    over-valuation as, 223
    payment of loss after settlement induced by, 323
    return of premium, 334
  freight—
    meaning, 36n[5]
    act or election of insured, loss by, 183
    advance freight, 116, 195
    chartered—
      commencement of insurable interest, 194
      commencement of risk, 138
      commencement of risk under voyage policy, 137, 138
    constructive total loss, 301
    foreign adjustment clause, 253
    insurable interest, 193
    insurable value, 256
    insurer's liability where total loss of vessel etc, 291
    partial loss, measure of indemnity, 278
    passage money, exclusion, 115
    specific insurance of, 115
    subject matter of insurance, 36
    total loss of, 290
    York-Antwerp Rules, 907
  frustration clause, 182
  full protection policy, 166
  gambling on losses, offence and penalty, 212
  gaming or wagering contracts, 211, 212
  general average—
    average: meaning, 244n[1]
    conditions imposed by maritime law, 249
    consequential losses, 248
    contribution—
      insurer's liability, 250
      maritime law, conditions imposed by, 249
      right to, 244
    expenditure—
      meaning, 245
      extraordinary, necessity for, 247
      insurer's liability, 250
    foreign adjustment—
      meaning, 252
      binding on assured and insurer, 254
      foreign adjustment clause, 253
      Institute Clauses, 253n[1,2]
    general average act: meaning, 244
    insurer's liability—
      expenditure, sacrifice and contribution, 250

marine insurance—*continued*
  general average—*continued*
    insurer's liability—*continued*
      ship and cargo in same ownership, 251
    loss—
      meaning, 244
      consequential, 248
      general and particular losses distinguished, 246
      peril not covered by policy, 252n[5]
    measure of indemnity, 280
    place of adjustment, 252
    sacrifice must be extraordinary, 247
    salvage charges distinguished, 258
    ship and cargo of same owner, insurer's liability, 251
    York-Antwerp Rules, 250n[1], 907
  good faith, 216
  goods—
    meaning, 114
    actual total loss by destruction or damage, 285
    constructive total loss, 300, 301
    insurable value, 256
    sold at port of distress, measure of indemnity, 269
    total loss of part, 286
    voyage policies. *See under* marine policy (voyage policy)
  hulls, foreign adjustment clause, 253
  hypothecation of cargo, loss by, 180
  illegal—
    acts becoming illegal by declaration of war, 156n[3,6]
    acts illegal under UK law, 81
    agent's liability, 105
    enemy aliens, insurances by or on behalf of, 78
    foreign law, adventure contravening, 79
    neutral adventures, 80
    part voyage, 82
    premium irrecoverable, 96
    principles generally, 77
    recoverability of payments for losses, 96
    return of premium, 334
    warranty of legality, 76, 83
  Inchmaree clause, 163n[1]
  indemnity—
    insurable interest of persons entitled to, 203
    measure of. *See* measure of indemnity *infra*
  inherent vice—
    exclusion of insurer's liability, 172
    insurance against loss due to, 173
  inland navigation, 37n[6]
  Institute three-fourths collision liability clause, 908
  insurable interest—
    meaning, 35, 185
    advance freight, 195
    assignment of policy, 214
    bottomry, 201
    buyer, 196
    captors, 200
    chartered freight, 194
    consignee, 199
    contingent interest, 189
    defeasible interest, 188
    freight, 193
    interest in possession, 186
    master's and crew's wages, 201
    mortgagor and mortgagee, 197
    partial interest, 187
    parting with, without assignment etc of policy, 214
    persons entitled to indemnity, 203
    ppi policies, 211, 212
    prize agent, 200
    profits, in, 190

marine insurance—*continued*
  insurable interest—*continued*
    reinsurance, 204
    respondentia, 201
    seller, 196
    shareholders, 202
    ship, 192
    time of, 191
    transfer of, 214
    trustee, 198
    wagering policies, 211, 212
  insurable value—
    meaning, 256
    freight, 256
    goods, 256
    insurable interest, need for, 256
    relevance of, 255
    rules for measuring, 256
    under-insurance, effect of, 264
  insurance agent. *See* agent *supra*
  insurance broker. *See* broker *supra*
  insurance companies, 24
  insurer—
    acceptance of notice of abandonment, 307, 308
    apportionment of salvage on abandonment, 312
    election to avoid policy, 242
    evidence as to materiality, 230
    foreign adjustment binding on, 254
    general average liability, 250, 251
    information waived by, 226
    Lloyd's List, knowledge of matters in, 229
    measure of indemnity. *See* measure of indemnity *infra*
    measure of liability. *See* measure of loss *infra*
    non-acceptance of notice of abandonment, effect, 308
    proportional liability, 264
    return of premium. *See* return of premium *infra*
    salvage, recovery of, 324
    subrogation. *See* subrogation *infra*
  interdiction of trade, insurer's liability, 181
  interest: meaning, 112n[3]
  jettison—
    meaning, 160
    insured peril, 160
  land risks, protection against, 37
  latent defects, 163
  leakage or breakage of goods, insurer not liable, 171
  legality, warranty of. *See* illegal *supra*; marine policy (warranty)
  legislation, 11–13
  lightning, 163
  Lloyd's, 21
  loss—
    consequent on general average act, 248
    constructive total. *See* constructive total loss *supra*
    general average. *See* general average *supra*
    liability of insurer. *See* perils insured against *infra*
    losses for which insurer not liable. *See* excluded losses *supra*
    measure of. *See* measure of loss *infra*
    particular and general average losses distinguished, 246
    proximate cause. *See* proximate cause of loss *infra*
    recovery of payments for, 96
    set-off against premium, 91
    settlement of—
      meaning, 322
      broker, by, 95
      duty of agent, 106

marine insurance—*continued*
  loss—*continued*
    settlement of—*continued*
      fraud, misrepresentation etc, 323
      mistake, 323
      nature of, 322
      payment of loss after, 323
      procedure, 322
      recovery of salvage by insurer, 324
      successive, measure of indemnity, 277
    total. *See* total loss *infra*
  marine adventure—
    meaning, 36
    foreign law, contravening, 79
    neutral, validity of insurance, 80
  Marine and Aviation (War Risks) Fund, 800, 801
  marine losses: meaning, 35
  maritime perils: meaning, 36
  measure of indemnity—
    meaning, 265
    apportionment of valuation, 270
    cases where no statutory provision, 281
    docking for repairs, expenses of, 275
    double insurance, 265
    general average, 280
    goods sold at port of distress, 269
    liability formula, 265n[6]
    nature of repairs, 276
    one-third new for old deduction, 273
    part cargo—
      damage to, 268
      total loss, 267
    partial loss—
      freight, of, 278
      ship, of, 271
    proportional liability, 265
    removal expenses, 274
    salvage charges, 280
    ship sold unrepaired, 272
    successive losses, 277
    third party liability, 279
    total loss—
      part cargo, of, 267
      subject matter, of, 266
    under-insurance, effect of, 264
  measure of loss—
    indemnity. *See* measure of indemnity *supra*
    insurable value, rules for measuring, 256
    particular average, 257
    particular average warranties, 263
    particular charges—
      meaning, 257
      particular average warranties, 263
      salvage charges distinguished, 257
      suing and labouring clause, covered by, 260
    suing and labouring clause, 259–262
  misdescription, effect, 221n[1]
  misrepresentation—
    absence of fraud, 233
    answer to inquiry, in, 237
    avoidance for, 232
    breach of warranty distinguished, 232
    construction, 240
    decided cases on a materiality, effect of, 241
    expectation or belief, 234
    fact or belief, 233
    information received by assured, as to, 236
    material representations, 233
    negotiation of contract, during, 232
    non-disclosure, and, 238

References are to paragraph numbers; superior figures refer to notes

References are to paragraph numbers; superior figures refer to notes

References are to paragraph numbers; superior figures refer to notes

References are to paragraph numbers; superior figures refer to notes

References are to paragraph numbers; superior figures refer to notes

marine policy—*continued*
  warranty—*continued*
    express—*continued*
      sentence of prize court, effect of, 63
      time policies effected by mutual assurance associ-
        ations, 57
     implied—
      meaning, 54
      cargoworthiness, 72
      express warranty does not exclude, 54
      legality. *See* legality *below*; marine insurance
        (illegal)
      proof of ship's neutrality, as to, 61
      seaworthiness. *See* seaworthiness
     legality, of—
      meaning, 76
      waiver exclusion, 83
     mutual insurance association rule as, 345
     nationality, as to, 57n³
     nature of, 54
     non-compliance—
      effect of, 55
      excuse of, 56
     particular average, 263
     proximate cause of loss excluded by, 176
master of ship—
  insurable interest, 201
  justifiable sale following constructive total loss, 289
  negligence, insurance against, 163
  notice of abandonment and capacity of, 309
  shares in vessel, held by, 163n⁸
medical examination—
  life assurance purposes, for, 534
  sickness insurance, for, 590
military and usurped power, fire policy exception, 599
misconduct of insurance broker, effect, 889
misrepresentation—
  insurer, to. *See under* insurance
  marine insurance, as to. *See under* marine insurance
  motor insurance, as to, 751
motor insurance—
  meaning, 18n²³
  agricultural purposes, effect of stipulation as to use for,
    719
  authorised insurer—
    meaning, 731
    membership of Motor Insurers' Bureau, 731
    obligations. *See under* compulsory *infra*
    security, deposit of, 756
  business use by assured, 719
  certificate of—
    insurers' duty to issue, 739
    prescribed form, 739n³
    production to police, 729n⁹
    return or replacement, 739n³
    surrender, 755
    time for issue, 739n³
  company director, whether employee, 735
  composite nature of, 706
  compulsory—
    authorised insurers, 731
    certificate, duty to issue, 739
    cover note, 732
    EC states, requirements, 733
    emergency treatment, 733n⁸
    employees, exclusion of, 735
    evidence of, production to police, 729n⁹
    excepted liabilities, 734
    excepted vehicles, 729
    indemnity of assured, insurer's duty, 738

motor insurance—*continued*
  compulsory—*continued*
    information, assured's duty to give claimant, 754
    insurers' obligations—
      hospital treatment, payment for, 741
      indemnity, 738
      issue of certificate, 739
      records, 740
    insurers' rights—
      assured, against, 753
      misrepresentation and non-disclosure, as to, 751
    international motor insurance cards, 730
    liabilities required to be covered, 733
    motor vehicle: meaning, 729n⁶
    nature of insurance required, 732
    notice of insurers' declaration proceedings, 752
    passengers, 737
    penalty for contravention, 729n⁹
    permitted driver's statutory rights, 721
    persons requiring, 729
    road: meaning, 729n⁷
    statutory alternatives, 756, 757
    statutory requirements, 729
    subrogation rights. *See* third party rights *infra*
    surrender of certificate, 755
    third party rights. *See* third party rights *infra*
    to use: meaning, 729n³
    trailers, 733, 734
    valid policies, persons able to issue, 731
  consequential loss. *See* consequential loss insurance
  cover note—
    agent's authority to issue, 385
    principles affecting, 385
  damage to vehicle, 725
  disclosure—
    moral hazard, 353
    physical hazard, 352
  driver—
    permitted driver. *See* permitted driver clause *infra*
    stipulations as to, 716
  driving of other cars by assured, 723
  EC insurer providing insurance in UK, 806
  emergency treatment—
    meaning, 733n⁸
    compulsory insurance, 733n⁸
  employee—
    compulsory insurance, 735, 736
    permitted driver clause, and, 722
  excess clauses, 727
  fire and theft, 724
  forms of policy, 706n¹
  fraud, loss caused by, 728
  garaging, condition as to, 715
  green card, 730
  heads of insurance, 707
  hospital treatment, insurers' duty to pay for, 741
  indemnity as basis of contract, 708
  insolvency of assured and third party rights, 747
  international insurance cards, 730
  knock-for-knock agreements, 726
  legal liability, 709
  liabilities to be covered by compulsory insurance, 733
  limitation of area of use, 715
  loss, insurance against, 728
  maintenance of vehicle, stipulations as to, 714
  misrepresentation and non-disclosure—
    insurers' rights where, 751
    notice to third party of insurers' proceedings, 752
  Motor Insurers' Bureau. *See* Motor Insurers' Bureau

References are to paragraph numbers; superior figures refer to notes

References are to paragraph numbers; superior figures refer to notes

Interpleader

References are to paragraph numbers; superior figures refer to notes

References are to paragraph numbers; superior figures refer to notes

References are to paragraph numbers; superior figures refer to notes

Words and Phrases

References are to paragraph numbers; superior figures refer to notes